LOGARITHMIC AND PROBABILITY SCALES

Guides for laying off a logarithmic or probability scale along either axis of a graph. Unless your graph paper is semitransparent, fold it horizontally or vertically and mark the appropriate divisions along the folded edge. For the use of the probability scale see pages 204--206 of the text. A log scale can be continued, as shown in the two-cycle guide. Since equal ratios give equal distances on a log scale, the space between 10 and 20 can be subdivided the same as that between 5 and 10, so you can obtain marks for 12, 14, 16 and 18.

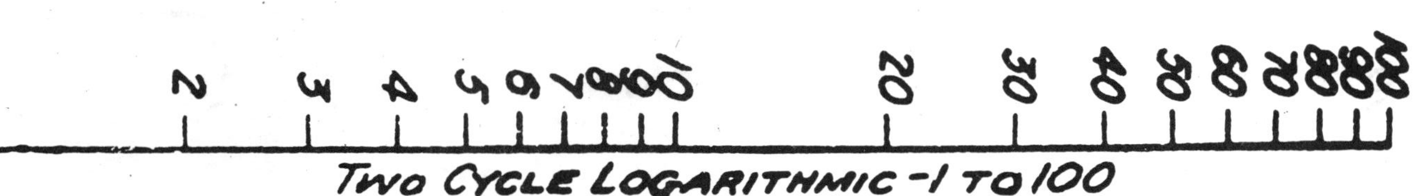

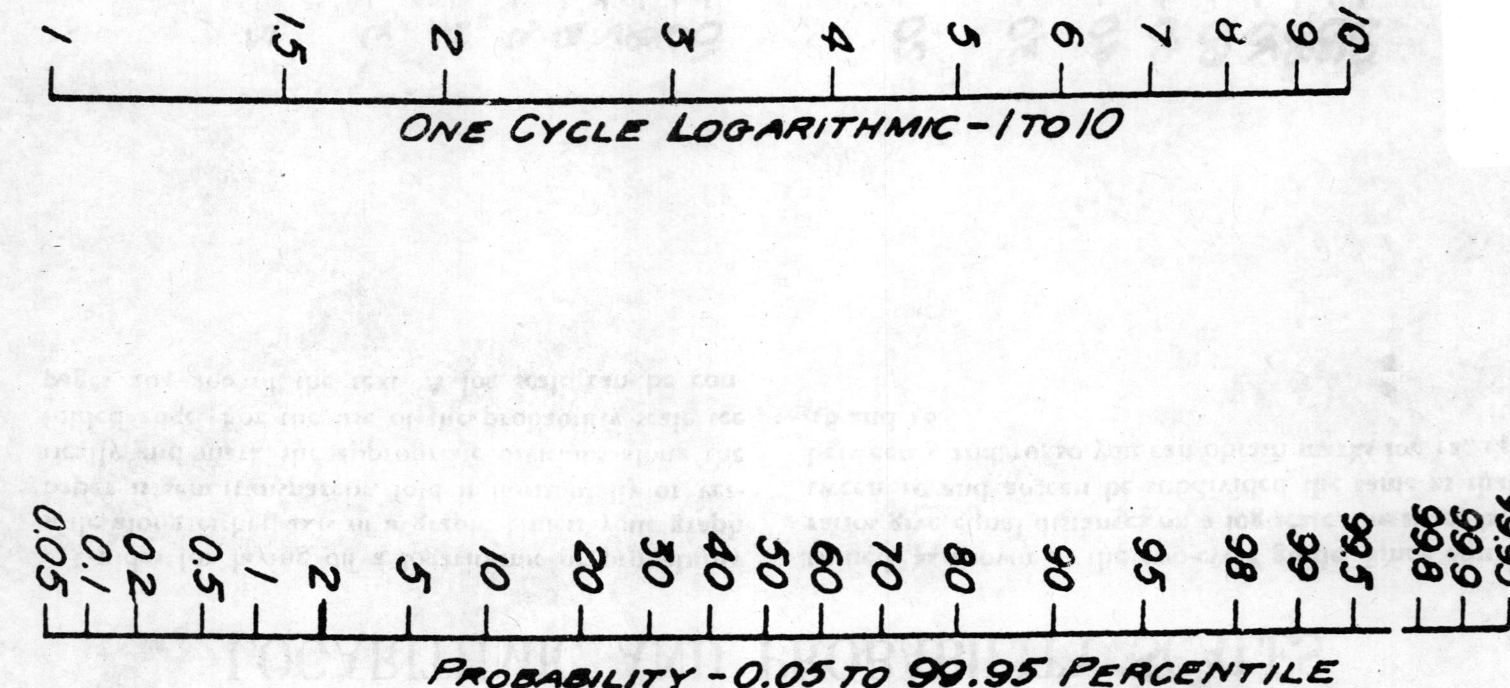

1
1.5
2
3
4
5
6
7
8
9
10
ONE CYCLE LOGARITHMIC - 1 TO 10
0.05
0.1
0.2
0.5
1
2
5
10
20
30
40
50
60
70
80
90
95
98
99
99.5
99.8
99.9
99.95
PROBABILITY - 0.05 TO 99.95 PERCENTILE

Experimental Psychology

Revised Edition

Robert S Woodworth
Columbia University

Harold Schlosberg
Brown University

Oxford & IBH Publishing Co. Pvt. Ltd.
New Delhi
(*A Unit of* **CBS Publishers & Distributors** Pvt Ltd)

CBS Publishers & Distributors Pvt Ltd

New Delhi • Bengaluru • Chennai • Kochi • Kolkata • Lucknow • Mumbai
Hyderabad • Jharkhand • Nagpur • Patna • Pune • Uttarakhand

Experimental Psychology
Revised Edition

ISBN-13: 978-81-204-1708-3
ISBN-10: 81-204-1708-9

Reprint: 2017, 2019, 2022, **2025**

OXFORD & IBH
New Delhi
(A Unit of CBS Publishers & Distributors Pvt Ltd)

Published by **Satish Kumar Jain** and produced by **Varun Jain** for

CBS Publishers & Distributors Pvt Ltd
4819/XI Prahlad Street, 24 Ansari Road, Daryaganj, New Delhi 110 002, India.
Ph: 011-23266838, 23289259 Website: www.cbspd.com
e-mail: delhi@cbspd.com

Corporate Office: 204 FIE, Industrial Area, Patparganj, Delhi 110 092
Ph: 011-4934 4934 Fax: 011-4934 4935
e-mail: publishing@cbspd.com; publicity@cbspd.com

Branches

- **Bengaluru:** Seema House 2975, 17th Cross, KR Road, Banasankari 2nd Stage, Bengaluru 560 070, Karnataka, India
  Ph: +91-80-26771678/79 Fax: +91-80-26771680 e-mail: bangalore@cbspd.com
- **Chennai:** 18/8B, Subbarayan Street, Shenoy Nagar, Chennai 600 030, Tamil Nadu, India
  Ph: +91-44-42032115, 26681266 e-mail: chennai@cbspd.com
- **Kochi:** 42/1325, 1326, Power House Road, Opp KSEB, Power House, Ernakulum Kochi 682 018, Kerala, India
  Ph: +91-484-4059061-65,67 Fax: +91-484-4059065 e-mail: kochi@cbspd.com
- **Kolkata:** 147, Hind Ceramics Compound, 1st Floor, Nilgunj Road, Belghoria, Kolkata-700056, West Bengal, India
  Ph: +033-25633055, 033-25633056 e-mail: kolkata@cbspd.com
- **Lucknow:** Basement, Khushnuma Complex, 7 Meerabai Marg (Behind Jawahar Bhawan), Lucknow-226001, UP, India
  Ph: +0522-4000032 e-mail: tiwari.lucknow@cbspd.com
- **Mumbai:** PWD Shed, Gala no 25/26, Ramchandra Bhatt Marg, Next to JJ Hospital Gate no. 2, Opp. Union Bank of India, Noorbaug, Mumbai-400009, Maharashtra, India
  Ph: 022-66661880/89 e-mail: mumbai@cbspd.com

Representatives

- Hyderabad 0-9885175004
- Patna 0-9334159340
- Jharkhand 0-9811541605
- Pune 0-9664372571
- Nagpur 0-8692091830
- Uttarakhand 0-9716462459

Printed at Chaman Enterprises, Daryaganj, New Delhi, India

From the Preface to the First Edition

THE SMALL BEGINNINGS of this volume go back to 1910 or earlier, when I worked up the then available literature on practice and memory into a few chapters of readings for a college course in experimental psychology. This material was mimeographed and from year to year chapters were added on imagery, association, reaction time, space perception, judgment and thinking. In 1920 my colleague, Professor Poffenberger, collaborated in pulling together, rounding out and organizing this rather scattered material, and a mimeographed "Textbook of Experimental Psychology" was issued under our joint authorship for the use of our students, graduate and undergraduate. At about that time I determined to go ahead to full publication, but much work remained to be done. Difficult questions of experimental method and of interpretation were attacked from time to time. Meanwhile the experimental literature was increasing by leaps and bounds, so that while I was making progress I was continually falling farther behind. In 1930 I set to work with grim determination. Finally, early in the present year, when the accumulated manuscript had grown to a rather alarming bulk, my long-suffering publishers granted me still a few months time for a final critical revision.

R.S.W.

Columbia University
July 22, 1938

Preface to the Revised Edition

A BOOK OF THIS TYPE, concerned with an active field of research, should be revised at least once a decade, but the early postwar years were scarcely ideal for such a task. There had been a sharp drop in the number of published studies, since a very large share of the active experimentalists were engaged in some sort of military work while the rest of them were overloaded with teaching and administrative duties at the universities. Immediately after the war, however, the output of research publication started to rise very rapidly and it has been climbing steadily ever since. The time was ripe for a revision which was undertaken by the present authors in 1949. We hoped then to have the revision completed in two or three years, but we found that the amount of necessary new writing was much greater than we had anticipated.

Just how different is this new edition from the old one? We believe that it is similar in style, viewpoint, and general level of difficulty. It is somewhat longer; although it has nearly the same number of pages, the new format gives about 20 percent more reading matter and cuts per page. The new bibliography lists 40 percent more titles than the old one—about 2,480 as against 1,770 in the old edition—and over 50 percent of the articles and books now cited were not used in the old edition. A distribution of these titles, decade by decade, shows how the coverage has shifted in favor of the newer work. In order to make room for the newer studies without unduly enlarging the book, we have pruned away much older material which is still of historical interest. In several chapters we have referred back to the first edition for fuller treatment of the early history of a problem. This older edition is available also in French translation.

We have adopted what seems a more logical order of the chapters, though the order is relatively unimportant, for there are many cross-references in the text, and the chapters may be used in any order. We have broken up some of the old chapters, using their material in other connections. Most of the material on Feeling and on Experimental Esthetics has been dropped, since there seems to be little recent work in these fields. Emotion, on the contrary, has been treated extensively in a triad of chapters organized so as to bring some order into this chaotic field. A few new chapters have been worked out: one on the construction of psychological scales, one on Discrimination Learning, and one on Motivation treated in connection with learning. The whole section on

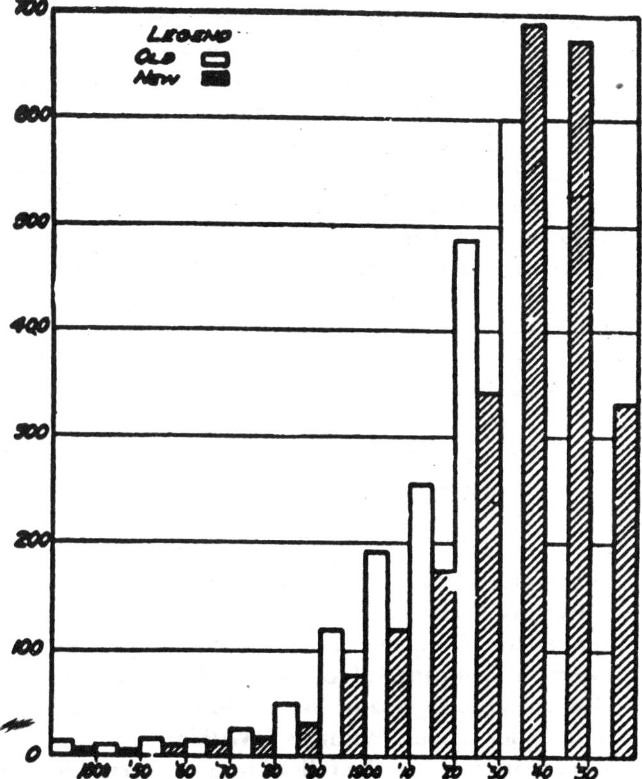

learning has been reorganized, with more use of the abundant animal experiments which are aimed at fundamental problems.

In two particular ways we have made the chapters more useful to the student. We have taken more care to make the experimental methods clear and practical in the laboratory. And we have made the chapters and subchapters more pointed by tying the data to pertinent theories.

As to a general pervasive theory or systematic viewpoint, we have tried to maintain an eclectic approach throughout the book. If our approach must be given a more systematic label, we suppose it should be called "functional," with a definite preference for objective data but no taboo against material obtained through introspection if it helps the psychologist to understand what the organism is doing in relation to the environment. Similarly, we have used mathematical analysis where it appears helpful, but without regarding it as the key to every problem or to all genuinely scientific theory. Some knowledge of elementary statistics is presupposed throughout and especially in the chapters on Psychophysics where a definite effort has been made to integrate the traditional methods with modern statistical practices.

Besides these improvements in the text there is a major change in the bibliography which has been made more informative by the inclusion of the titles of books and articles, instead of the bare references. It has been set up so as to serve also as an author index. In the work of indexing and bibliography we have had the expert collaboration of Mrs. Enrica Tunnell, the well-known Psychology Librarian at Columbia University. Without her aid in these and other phases of the revision, the book might well have been delayed another year or two!

Our publishers generously permitted us to increase the number of cuts considerably. For the preparation of these drawings we are greatly indebted to Frank H. Lee, Professor of Graphics at Columbia University. Many associates and students have made contributions, either direct or indirect, to the preparation and revision of this book. We are especially grateful to colleagues who read chapters for which neither of the coauthors felt specially competent, but we hesitate to name these friendly people lest they be blamed for our shortcomings. We assume joint responsibility for all the contents of this revised book, since whichever one of us prepared the first rough draft of a chapter, the other one exercised complete freedom in revising or rewriting it. Each of us has had a hand in every chapter.

For many of our illustrations we are indebted to the following book publishers: Appleton-Century-Crofts; Carnegie Institute of Washington; Clark University Press; Columbia University Press; Farrar & Rinehart; Houghton Mifflin Company; Liveright Publishing Corporation; Longmans, Green & Company; McGraw-Hill Book Company; Murray Hill Books; Ronald Press Company; W. B. Saunders; D. Van Nostrand Company; John Wiley & Sons; Williams & Wilkins.

We also are indebted to the following publishers of journals, proceedings and monographs: American Psychological Association; American Journal of Psychology; The Journal Press; National Academy of Sciences; American Philosophical Society; American Association for the Advancement of Science; National Society for the Study of Education; Society for Experimental Biology and Medicine; Acoustical Society of America; Optical Society of America; University of California; University of Chicago; Johns Hopkins Press; Johns Hopkins Hospital; Teachers College of Columbia University; Archives of Psychology; American Journal of Physiology; Quarterly Journal of Experimental Psychology; Année psychologique; Psychologische Forschung; Zeitschrift für Psychologie.

New York, N.Y. R.S.W.
Providence, R.Is. H.S.
March 1, 1954

CONTENTS

CHAPTER PAGE

1

INTRODUCTION

Why an "experimental" psychology? When it first began to make its appearance about a hundred years ago, experimental psychology came as a challenge to the older mental philosophy which was indeed aspiring to become a natural science with practical applications to human living but which was in great need of facts—many facts, well-attested facts, and facts relevant to its theories and hoped-for applications. The experimental method had shown itself to be extraordinarily fruitful in several other branches of science as a means of obtaining the important facts, and a few forward-looking scientists of that time felt that this method should be given a trial in psychology. But these innovators were themselves exposed to a serious challenge. Could they contribute anything of real importance, or was their experimental psychology doomed to be and remain a very small affair? A few scattered experiments of a psychological nature had been made by physicists and astronomers, and the physiologists in their study of the sense organs had amassed much factual material of at least marginal psychological interest. But the mind of man, so it seemed to many philosophers and to many physical scientists, would be forever inaccessible to experimental controls.

As regards the scope of experimental psychology, a few decades of intensive work by able pioneers showed that it was by no means narrow. Memory, training, conditioning were attacked, and the whole field of human and animal learning was found to be accessible by experimental methods. Thinking, invention, and problem solution yielded important results. Something could be done with emotion, motivation, and even willing. Almost any form of human activity could be surveyed in a preliminary way with good prospects of finding an opportunity for some incisive experiments. Today we are inclined to claim for experimental psychology a scope as wide as that of psychology itself, while admitting that we do not yet know exactly how to subject some of the biggest problems to a rigorous experiment. The present-day challenge to the experimentalist comes from within the active group of clinical, counseling, educational, and industrial psychologists, especially from those who are concerned with the problems of personality development and maladjustment. Can it be shown that the experimental method is applicable in these important fields and that psychologists trained in the laboratory will be the leaders there, especially in the research necessary for further progress? The outlook is certainly hopeful, and this book would be expanded beyond measure if it tried to cover all the experimental work that is being undertaken in these fields.

For a similar reason this book must leave aside the study of individual differences by test methods, inaugurated by experimentalists at about the turn of the century, with its modern statistical magic for correlation, analysis of variance, and factor analysis. The experimentalist needs some degree of competence in these methods, if only for checking on the reliability of his own results. The same psychologists, from the early days on, have contributed to both lines of study, and the contacts between them are close and should remain so. But the same book can scarcely do justice to both lines of attack.

The experimenter's requirements. An experimenter tries to *control the conditions* under which an event occurs. If he succeeds in doing so, he has certain advantages over an observer who simply watches the course of events without exercising any control.

1. The experimenter can make the event occur when he wishes. So he can be fully *prepared* for accurate observation.

2. He can *repeat* his observation under the same conditions for verification; and he can describe his conditions and enable other experimenters to duplicate them and make an independent check on his results.

3. He can *vary the conditions* systematically and note the variation in results. If he follows the old standard "rule of one variable," he holds all the conditions constant except for one factor which he makes his "experimental variable" and regards as responsible for the observed variation in his results.

As to this rule of one variable, it does not forbid the simultaneous variation of two or even more factors, provided the experiment is so designed that the experimenter can tease out of the data the effect of each single variable, as well as their possible interaction (Fisher, 1949). Experimental designs permitting the controlled variation of two or more factors are being found very useful by psychologists. For some relatively simple examples see Underwood's book (1949, pp. 144–148, 323–337).

Some terms and symbols. In a psychological experiment one obvious requirement is an organism to serve as subject by responding to stimuli. If we designate the stimulus (or stimulus complex, or stimulating situation) by the letter S, and the subject's response by the letter R, we can best designate the subject or organism by the letter *O*. We shall use the italicized letter *O* in this way.[1] The letter *E* stands for the experimenter. A psychological experiment, then, can be symbolized by S—*O*—R, which means that *E* (understood) applies a certain stimulus (or situation) to *O*'s receptors and observes *O*'s response. This formula suggests a class of experiments in which *E*'s aim is to discover what goes on in the organism between the stimulus and

[1] More common today is the use of the letter *S* to stand for the subject. In this book, since S will be often used for the stimulus, we shall find it less confusing to use *O* for the subject. This *O* has a long history. It was originally read "observer," because the early experiments were largely in the field of sensation and perception where the subject's task was to observe the stimulus and report what he saw, heard, etc. But the same word and symbol were carried over to reaction time experiments which called for a motor response and not for observation on the subject's part. Such was Titchener's usage in his very influential *Experimental psychology* (1901, 1905). Because of his strong emphasis on introspection, however, the word "observer" and the symbol *O* came to suggest introspective experiments and to seem inappropriate elsewhere. At the present time the word "subject" is almost universal; but *O* is a better symbol.

the motor response. A good example is Pavlov's observation of the inhibitory state in a dog between the conditioned stimulus and the delayed conditioned response. Physiological recording instruments often reveal something of what is going on in the organism during emotion, and introspection can show something of the process of problem solution.

In another class of experiments, more common and perhaps more successful on the whole, *E* does not attempt to observe directly what goes on in *O*, but hopes to find out indirectly by varying the conditions and noting the resulting variation in response. Let us ask what kinds of conditions *E* is able to vary and make his experimental variables. Since *O* certainly responds differently to different stimuli, there must be stimulus variables, S-factors, affecting the response. Just as certainly, the subject responds differently to the same identical stimulus according to his own state and intentions at the moment. There are *O* variables, *O*-factors, affecting the response. At a certain moment the organism makes a response. The response depends on the stimuli acting at that moment and on factors present in the organism at that moment. This general statement can be put into the form of an equation,

$$R = f(S, O)$$

which reads that the response is a function of S-factors and *O*-factors. Or, it can read that R-variables depend on S-variables and *O*-variables. In any particular experiment some particular S-factor or *O*-factor is selected as the experimental variable, and some particular R-variable is observed.

As to the control of these variables, we readily admit that stimuli can be controlled so far as they come from the environment, for *E* can manage the immediate environment consisting of the experimental room and the apparatus. But how can he control the *O*-variables? At first thought it seems impossible. Yet consider the example of hunger, a much-used variable in animal experiments. It can be controlled by regulating the feeding schedule. What *E* directly controls is "hours since last feeding" prior to the actual test or "trial" when a stimulus is applied and the response observed. Time since feeding is thus an antecedent variable, an A-variable, and the experimenter may find it more helpful and "operational" to speak of A- rather than *O*-variables, and to give our equation this modified form:

$$R = f(S, A)$$

Of course the A-variables have no effect on the response except as they affect *O*'s state during the test. The *O*-variables are the real factors in the response. However, they may be hypothetical, based on some hypothesis as to what goes on in the organism, and the A-variables are used to test the hypothesis. For example, expectancy or anticipation of what is coming might be a factor in the response to a given stimulus. To test this hypothesis, *E* figures out some way of building up in *O* expectancy strong or weak, correct or false; he devises an A-variable to manipulate the supposed *O*-factor of expectancy.

A preliminary survey of the variables utilized in psychological experimentation will serve to bring out some points of general interest.

Stimulus variables. Elementary stimuli differ in "modality," being visual, auditory, olfactory, etc., according to the sense which they stimulate. In every modality, stimuli vary in intensity and duration. Stimuli of light and sound vary also in the dimension of wavelength or frequency, corresponding to color and pitch

Odor stimuli differ chemically one from another, and so do taste stimuli. Area or extent is a variable in the cases of light and skin stimuli. Already we glimpse a rich field of S-variables inviting exploration by psychologists interested in sensation, perception, esthetics, and reaction time. This field was in fact one of the earliest to be partially explored by the experimentalist.

Not only elementary stimuli but also stimulus combinations or complexes are covered by the S in our formula. Spatial perception of the distance, direction, size, and shape of an object depends on the subject's ability to utilize a combination of stimuli; therefore, the investigator of this important ability must be expert in manipulating such combinations of stimuli.

In experiments on learning and problem solving no complete record is usually made of the actual stimuli received by the subject's receptors. What you find instead is a statement of the objective situation confronting the subject—a maze, for example, of specified form and size and under specified illumination. The stimuli received by an animal traversing the maze could scarcely be specified since they change from moment to moment as the animal moves. Objects, not stimuli, are recorded in this case. Similarly, little attempt is made to describe the animal's motor responses or muscular contractions. Instead, you find a report of the external result of the animal's movements, such as entering a certain blind alley or passing it by. It is customary to report external objects and results in such experiments, rather than the actual stimuli and responses; and no harm is done if we recognize that two of the main problems of psychology are being by-passed, the problem of how external objects are perceived and the problem of how muscular activity is directed toward external results.

O-variables and A-variables. A valuable analysis of what we are calling O-factors was offered by Clark Hull (1943, 1951). His ambitious project called for the identification of all these factors, the quantification of each factor by experiments with an appropriate A-factor, and the discovery of how the several factors combine into the momentary readiness for a particular response. Some of Hull's O-factors are the following:

1. Habit strength, the strength of association between a certain S and a certain R, based on previous learning which is an A-variable or combination of A-variables. Hull uses the symbol, $_SH_R$, for habit strength.

2. Drive, such as hunger, already discussed.

3. Incentive, the reward or punishment expected.

4. Inhibition, a factor or combination of factors tending to diminish the momentary readiness for a response. Obvious examples, not specially emphasized by Hull, are fatigue, satiation, distraction, fear, and caution.

5. Oscillation, an uncontrollable variation in O's readiness to act, dependent probably on a multitude of small internal causes, but not beyond measurement and prediction since an individual usually varies only within limits.

6. Individual differences and differences due to age, health and organic state.

We may add the O-factor of goal-set, akin to drive but worthy of separate consideration. In a typical human experiment *E* gives *O* certain "instructions," assigning the task to be performed; and one stroke of luck that has helped along the advance of experimental psychology from the very beginning is the human subject's willingness to cooperate by following instructions and performing the task quite eagerly. Verbal instructions are not necessary when, as in animal experiments, the situation is so arranged as to guarantee that a certain goal will be striven for by the subject.

Response variables. As already mentioned, experimenters do not usually attempt to describe the actual muscular response; they content themselves with noting the result achieved, which can vary in several ways:

1. Accuracy, as shown for example by a count of hits and misses on a target. In many experiments on perception *O*'s task is to observe and report the stimulus as accurately as possible, and his errors are measured or counted. Any measure of accuracy is almost inevitably a measure of errors.

2. Speed or quickness, illustrated by the reaction time of a single response or by the total time consumed in a complex performance. When the task is composed of many similar units, such as columns of numbers to be added, the test is conducted according to either of two plans:

Time limit: How much is done in the same time allowed?

Amount limit: How long does it take to do the assigned amount?

These are both speed tests, speed being equal to the ground covered divided by the time taken to cover the ground.

3. Difficulty level, a type of measurement often adopted in intelligence testing so as to avoid overemphasis on speed. It can be used as a response measure when the experimenter is provided with a scale of tasks graded in difficulty. The question then is: How far up the scale can the subject succeed? In athletics we have the clear example of the pole vault. The bar is raised until the athlete fails, and a measure of his performance is thus obtained. The same logic is employed in the Binet intelligence tests which consist of test items of graded difficulty, and we shall meet other examples in the experiments on memory span and span of attention. Often the difficulty scale for measuring a particular kind of performance has to be constructed by a laborious process of preliminary experimentation.

4. Probability or frequency, when a particular response occurs sometimes but not on every trial. A stimulus just at the "threshold" will be noticed about 50 per cent of the time. A partially learned response will perhaps be made in 6 out of 10 trials, so that its probability is 60 percent at that stage of learning. If there are two or more competing responses to the same stimulus or situation, the probability of each competitor can be determined in a series of trials.

5. Strength or energy of response, sometimes a useful R-variable, though the relation of muscular output to excellence of performance is far from simple. We cannot say that the stronger the muscular response, the better, for often intelligent training gets rid of a lot of superfluous muscular effort. The less energy consumed in attaining a certain result, the greater the efficiency. The student of learning is concerned with the "strength" of an S—R connection, $_{s}H_{R}$, which is very different from muscular strength.

Holding a factor constant. A large share of the experimenter's preliminary planning and labor is directed toward avoiding irrelevant causes of variability. He plans to hold all factors constant except those he wishes to investigate. If his interest lies in a stimulus variable, he must neutralize such *O*-variables as drive and habit strength. Suppose, in an experiment on dart throwing, *E* wishes to find out how the score changes with increased distance of the target. This experiment is going to extend through many trials so as to obtain a reliable average score for each distance. If he starts an inexperienced *O* at the shortest distance and increases the distance step by step, *O* is becoming more and more skillful and will do better at the greater distances than he could have done at first. This practice effect threatens to spoil the experiment by obscuring the effect of distance. There are several ways of avoiding this source of error: (1) give the subject ample practice before testing the effect of distance; (2) repeat the distances in balanced order so that in the end the practice effect is equalized; (3) use separate groups of subjects, matched groups, for the different distances.

Matched groups may seem by all odds the best method, but the matching is never perfect (unless we have identical twins at our disposal), and there are advantages in comparing the same individuals in the different experimental conditions. When, as in many cases, there are just two conditions to be compared, A and B, the balanced order is known as the "ABBA order."

In the above example we held the amount of practice constant, but in learning experiments this is one of the most important A-variables to vary. In that case we would keep stimulus and task variables constant; we would probably use the same target and the same throwing distance throughout the learning period. The progressive increase in accuracy as a function of practice would give us a *learning curve*. This curve might be plotted from average scores for each day of practice, or it might be based on *tests*, interpolated every so often during training.

The experimenter would like, of course, to reach a conclusion of some generality, but often he feels in duty bound to confess that he is not sure of it except under the specific conditions of his experiment. He would like to "extrapolate" from the laboratory setup to the conditions of daily life, but he is not sure that his *O*s are a fair sample of the population in respect to the function he has been testing—some form of learning, it may be, or of perception, or of motivation—nor is he sure that the particular task he has used is a fair sample of the function. He does right to qualify his conclusion, but in the long run the fraternity of experimental psychologists must accept the responsibility of showing how much generality their findings can claim. Brunswik (1947) has made this point convincingly.

Qualitative and quantitative experiments. All the emphasis that we have been placing on "variables" may leave the impression that every worth-while experiment must be quantitative in nature. There are important variables which are qualitative rather than quantitative. One obvious qualitative difference is that of "modality." The role of the different senses in revealing the environment is an important psychological problem. Antecedent training can differ in kind as well as in amount: training with "reinforcement" differs in its effects from training without reinforcement; training with "understanding" differs from routine drill. Responses, too, differ in kind as well as in amount: an animal will approach one object and avoid another; a human subject will report that he likes one odor and dislikes another.

The general tendency of experimentalists today is to give all the preference to quantitative work and therefore to choose lines of work that lend themselves to quantification. Some psychologists deprecate this tendency as premature in a relatively young science like psychology; they feel that it puts blinders on the research worker and conceals from him many fundamental scientific problems. How could chemistry ever have become quantitative without first being interested in the various kinds of elements and compounds? A qualitative survey is often necessary to show up the important problems and suggest hypotheses for more exact testing.

2

REACTION TIME

One of the most available response variables for experimental psychology is speed. The reason is obvious: every act takes time, and time can be measured. We can measure the time occupied in doing a certain amount of work, or we can set a time limit and measure the amount of work done in the given time. In either case we measure the speed of work. Speed is a useful measure in two ways: as an index of achievement, for the more completely you have mastered a task the more rapidly you can perform it; and also as an index of the complexity of the inner process by which a result is accomplished, for the more complicated the process, the longer time it will take. For such reasons as these the timing of responses plays an important role in psychological experimentation. Reaction Time is about the simplest case of timing.

Reaction time is not exactly what might be supposed from the term. It is not the time occupied by the execution of a response. It is the time required to get the overt response *started*. The reaction time is the S—R time interval. The response cannot come out of the organism quite as soon as the stimulus goes in. The stimulus starts a process going, but the process remains hidden or "latent" inside the organism till it reaches the muscles and produces an observable effect on the environment. The sense organ must be aroused to activity, the nerves must conduct to the brain and from the brain to the muscles, and the muscles must contract and move some external object. All these steps in the process take some time, but the most time is consumed in the brain. Work must be done in the brain. Even in the simplest possible reaction the nerve impulses coming in from the sense organ have to accumulate and build up enough excitation to arouse the motor areas of the brain and set up a discharge toward the muscles. And when the response has to be nicely adjusted to the stimulus, work is done and time is consumed in registering the exact character of the stimulus and organizing the motor response. The reaction time, also called the response *latency*, includes sense organ time, brain time, nerve time, and muscle time. It is subject to several causes of variation and is distinctly a response variable.

The reaction time experiment. A person's reaction time (RT) to light is to be measured. He is seated at a table in a dimly lighted room and sees before him a screen with a hole in it through which a light can be flashed. He is shown this light so that he knows the stimulus to be used. On the table is an electric switch or key. His instructions are to place his finger on the key when he gets a "Ready" signal and to press the key instantly when the light flashes. Behind the scenes, in the experimenter's bailiwick, there is some accurate apparatus which measures the S—R interval. The RT on the first trial may be half a second, but it diminishes within a few trials to the region of 1/5 to 1/4 sec, i. e., to 200–250 ms (where 1 ms = 1 millisecond = 1/1000 second). Further practice does not decrease the RT much below 200 ms when the stimulus is a light; when it is a sound or touch, the RT is about 150 ms after some practice, and as little as 100–120 ms in some individuals after much practice. This seems to be the minimum latency for any voluntary or learned motor response, though some true reflexes, especially the knee jerk and the eye wink, are much quicker, with a latency of about 40 ms.

The experiment just described deals with the "simple reaction," which is "simple" in presenting a uniform stimulus and requiring a uniform response. There are no alternatives to complicate *O*'s task. He knows in advance what S will come and what R he will make. In another type of RT experiment there are alternatives. There are different stimuli calling for different responses. The stimulus light may vary from red to green in irregular order; there are two response keys, one for each hand; and the instructions are to react to red with the right hand, but to green with the left hand. This "disjunctive" or "choice" reaction has a longer latency than the simple reaction, the disjunctive RT measuring about 100 ms longer than the simple RT. The associative reaction, to be considered in the next chapter, is still slower, and the RT can be prolonged indefinitely by further complications of the subject's task.

Procedure. The RT must be measured with considerable accuracy in order to serve as a response variable in a quantitative experiment. Besides the apparatus requirements soon to be considered, there are two problems of procedure which may cause trouble, as they have often done in the past history of RT work.

1. Premature reactions and other false reactions must be avoided. Since *O* is eager to respond as quickly as possible, his hand may "get away from him" once in a while and make a "response" before the stimulus! He is especially prone to do so when the stimulus follows the Ready signal at a perfectly uniform interval; accordingly, it is standard practice to vary this interval slightly from trial to trial. It might seem that a few premature reactions would do no great harm—merely a few wasted trials—but when there are obvious premature reactions, other suspiciously quick reactions are probably premature too. It is impossible to weed out the false reactions, and the only safe course is to discard such data altogether. To guard against premature reactions *E* can introduce "catch tests." Suppose his procedure is to give a series of 20 trials and then allow a brief rest. In each series of 20 stimuli he inserts one or two blanks, giving the Ready signal without any stimulus following. If *O* is caught, he is informed that the whole series of 20 trials has to be thrown out as valueless. So he learns to keep his eagerness within bounds. Special catch tests are not needed with the disjunctive reaction, for if *O* becomes too eager, he will sometimes respond with the wrong hand, or even with both hands, making it necessary for *E* to warn him and discard the series.

2. There must be as many alternative responses as there are alternative stimuli to be distinguished, and each response must be assigned to its particular stimu-

lus. Consider whether the following procedure would make a good experiment. The light is either red or green, but there is only one reaction key, which *O* is instructed to press as soon as he sees whether red or green is shown, but not sooner. He is not to make a simple reaction to the flash of light, but must hold back until he knows which color is shown. It looks like a feasible experiment, but when it has been tried, the results have been irregular and worthless. There is nothing in the procedure to prevent *O* from sliding into the simple reaction or from unduly prolonging his RT in order to be very sure he is not premature. This so-called cognitive reaction was tried out and given up in favor of the disjunctive reaction which provides two responses, one for each color, so preventing *O* from falling into the simple reaction, while leaving him free to respond as quickly as he can without making errors.

Historical sketch.[1] The reaction time experiment is just about a hundred years old. It was invented in 1850 by the famous physiologist Helmholtz, who broke ground for experimental psychology in several ways. He had succeeded in measuring the speed of conduction in a frog's motor nerve (by stimulating the nerve close to its muscle, and again far from the muscle, and finding the latency of the muscular response to be a little longer when the nerve impulse had to traverse the greater length of nerve), and he wished to extend the investigation to human sensory nerves. With a weak electric shock he stimulated a person's skin far from the brain, and again near the brain, instructing his subject in each case to make the same hand reaction as soon as he felt the shock. Though he was able in this way to obtain a rough estimate of the rate of nerve conduction, he found the method unsatisfactory because the time occupied by nerve conduction is very short, while the whole RT is comparatively long and quite variable.

The astronomers had become much concerned over the "personal equation" —the human factor in accurate timing observations—and one of them, Hirsch of Switzerland (1861–1865), utilized the new Hipp chronoscope for measuring what he called the "physiological time" of the eye, ear, and sense of touch. He obtained values for the simple RT which have remained fairly standard ever since.

The next step was taken by the Dutch physiologist, Donders, who in 1868 attempted to measure the physiological time of mental processes such as discrimination and choice. This he hoped to do by requiring these processes to intervene between the stimulus and the response. In short, he invented the disjunctive RT experiment, found that this RT was about 100 ms longer than the simple RT, and regarded this difference as the time required for the mental processes mentioned.

The Austrian physiologist, Exner, made an important contribution in 1873 by pointing out the importance of preparatory set. He introduced the term, "reaction time."

When Wundt in 1879 opened his pioneer psychological laboratory at the University of Leipzig, it seemed to him that Donders had pointed the way to a very promising avenue of experimental research, the timing of mental operations. A long line of Wundt's students made studies of simple and complex reaction times, the results being sometimes important in themselves but not very suc-

[1] Condensed from the much fuller account in the first edition of this book, Holt, 1938, pp. 298–310.

cessful in obtaining definite times for such processes as attention, perception, association, and choice.

Two of Wundt's early pupils later set up laboratories that were largely devoted to RT investigations. Cattell, after working extensively in this field at Leipzig (1886 a, b), continued it at Pennsylvania and Columbia; at the latter university over a period of years he directed students in RT studies which had a different slant from those of Donders and Wundt, a more objective slant. Külpe at Würzburg, early in the century, developed an introspective attack on simple and complex reactions, and his students demonstrated the selective influence of the preparatory set. Another laboratory which has made a series of significant contributions to reaction time is that of Piéron in the Sorbonne at the University of Paris (Piéron being a pupil, however, not of Wundt but of Binet). Many other psychologists have made important contributions and have found a variety of scientific and applied uses for the RT technique.

REACTION TIME APPARATUS

Without attempting to work out the details of an actual laboratory setup we can at least notice the instrumental problems and get some idea of their solution. The time to be measured extends from the beginning of the stimulus to the beginning of the response. These two instants must be made to register themselves on an instrument or a record which shows the elapsed time. For rough timing of a reaction lasting several seconds, a stop watch reading to the fifth of a second may give a fine enough measure and we may depend upon *E* to register the instants of S and R by his own manipulation of the stop watch. For a RT of less than a second, certainly, a finer measure and some means of automatic registration are necessary.

If we ask how fine a measurement is required, our best answer is found in the scatter of the RT. When a sufficient number of RTs have been timed, we shall want to assemble them in a distribution table containing 10–20 step intervals. When the RT ranges from 100 to 200 ms, the step interval should not be greater than 10 ms and the instrument should accordingly read to 1/100 sec. A practiced *O* in the simple reaction may show a much smaller scatter and the reading should be correspondingly fine. A unit of 1/500 sec is probably fine enough for any RT work; some of the best instruments when in good running order measure to the single millisecond.

Graphic and "scopic" registration. The chronographic method registers S and R by marks upon a steadily moving surface —a kymograph drum or photographic film—and the RT is found by measuring the distance between these marks and taking account of the speed of the moving surface. Unless the speed is known to be

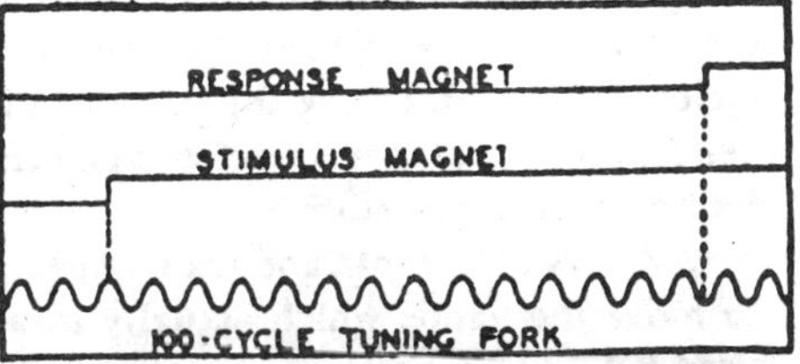

FIG. 2-1. Diagram of a chronographic record of reaction time. Three writing points are synchronized so as to write simultaneously in the same vertical line on a horizontal moving drum. One writing point inscribes the vibrations of a tuning fork and so provides a "time line"; the other two are moved by electromagnets in circuit with *E*'s stimulus key and *O*'s response key. The RT here measures 135 ms. For an actual chronographic record (photographic) see page 552.

constant, the time is simultaneously inscribed on the same surface by the vibrations, say, of a 100-cycle tuning fork, and the count of vibrations between the S and R marks gives the RT. The regularity of the tuning fork (at a constant temperature) makes this method a good check on the accuracy of other methods. But the counting of the vibrations is laborious. In the scopic method S and R are automatically registered upon a dial or other scale by a pointer which moves at a known speed, and the time is read off from the scale. The main problems are to secure uniform speed of movement and to impress the instants of S and R upon the mechanism.

The chronoscope. The early work in reaction time was made possible by the invention of the Hipp chronoscope, which was capable of measuring RT in units of 1 ms (called 1 sigma in the older literature), with an error considerably below 1 percent. It consisted of two basic parts:

1. A rapidly moving clockwork mechanism, which was started and allowed to reach normal speed well before the stimulus was given, and stopped after the response. A weight furnished the power to operate the clockwork; the speed was controlled by a reed which vibrated 1,000 cycles per second, taking the place of the pendulum or balance wheel escapement found in ordinary clocks.

2. A very light tooth and train of gears, to move the hands which actually measured RT. The tooth was thrown against the drive gear at the moment of stimulation and back to the brake gear on the response. The distance the hands moved between the moments of stimulation and response was the RT. The starting and stopping of the clutch was accomplished by a pair of electromagnets, each opposed by a spring. A number of elaborate precautions were adopted to keep magnets and springs in balance, and it was customary to check the chronoscope every 50 reactions or so. (Titchener, 1905.)

Perhaps the next advance was the Dunlap, or Johns Hopkins, chronoscope (Dunlap, 1917, 1918), which is shown in Figure 2-2. This used a synchronous motor—the grandfather of those which

FIG. 2-2. (From C. H. Stoelting Company, Chicago.) Chronoscope and accessories. The experimenter sits on the near side, *O* on the far side of the table. A, bulb used for certain responses; B, voice keys for *E* and *O*; C, visual stimuli; D, tactual stimulator; E, Dunlap chronoscope; F, sound stimulus; G, tuning fork for regulating chronoscope; H, *E*'s stimulus keys.

drive our electric clocks today. As in the Hipp, there was a clutch to start and stop the hands, but Dunlap dispensed with the troublesome springs and used an armature between two balanced electromagnets to operate a friction clutch. This eliminated variations due to relative strength of springs and electric currents. But the chronoscope was still cumbersome, and attempts to improve it have seriously impaired its original accuracy.

The modern electric clock has a compact synchronous motor, whose speed is maintained by the extremely high constancy (better than .1 percent) of the impulses in regulated lighting and power circuits. These developments have made

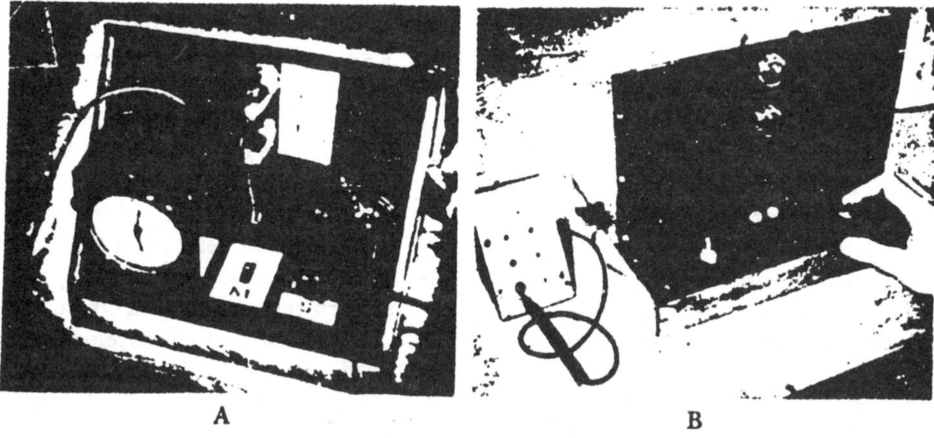

A B

FIG. 2-3. (Schlosberg, 1947.) The reaction timer.

A. Viewed from *E*'s side. The earphones, for auditory stimulus, are hung over the top right hand corner. L_1 and L_2 are lights, corresponding to points 1 and 2 on the selector switch (S). M, the master or stimulus switch, is a silent mercury toggle switch. To the left is the Precision Timer.

B. Viewed from *O*'s side. The right hand toggle switch has just been thrown to the "off" position by *O*, in a simple reaction. For a discrimination reaction both hands and both toggle switches would be used. A steadiness plate and stylus, shown on the left, can be plugged into the pin jacks just below the lights, the plate making a 45° angle with both base and panel.

possible a compact and durable chronoscope, called the "Springfield Timer" (more accurately, The Standard Electric Time Co. Precision Timer, Model S-1). One of these timers, together with accessory apparatus, is shown in Figure 2-3, A. The motor is a slightly heavier version of that in a good electric clock, and the clutch mechanism is of the combination spring-electromagnet type. It reads in .01 sec and is accurate to approximately one unit.

There are a number of other chronoscopes for various special purposes. Impulse counters (Dunlap, 1936) advance a needle one unit for each half-cycle of the alternating current in power circuits, but they are quite noisy. The only silent chronoscopes seem to be based on some measure of the amount of electrical charge that is allowed to accumulate at a constant rate during the reaction.

Helmholtz used a galvanometer for this purpose. One of the most flexible of these chronoscopes was designed by Jasper and Andrews (1936). It depends on the charge which accumulates on a condenser, which in turn controls a meter through a vacuum tube. By throwing a switch to different positions, one can vary the rate at which the charge accumulates, and thus the range of times for which the instrument is to be used. Dorcus and Hamburger (1938) among others, have described chronoscopes of this general type.

Errors in chronoscopes. All of these instruments are subject to error, and they should be checked frequently against a known duration, such as the fall of a weight between two contacts. Like most measuring devices, they are subject to two types of constant errors:

1. Terminal errors, the result of lag in starting or overshoot in stopping. These errors are absolute, or independent of the length of the interval measured.

They may be compared to failure to line up an object with the marks on a yardstick when measuring length. Most chronoscopes are liable to this type of error.

2. Running errors, the result of faulty speed of the running mechanism. These are relative and may be expressed as percentages of the interval measured. They are comparable to those introduced by a yardstick which has shrunk. This type of error is negligible in synchronous motors, as those used in Springfield Timers, unless the device is obviously not working properly.

These two types of errors may neutralize each other at some particular duration; therefore, it is well to check chronoscopes at two or three durations, as 100 ms, 200 ms, and 300 ms. By plotting the readings obtained against the intervals and drawing a line through their means, one can determine the running error by the slope of the line and the terminal error by the point at which the line cuts the ordinate. It is usually easier to apply a correction to data than it is to get rid of the errors by adjusting the chronoscope.

In addition to the constant errors, chronoscopes show some variability on successive readings. These errors will appear as spread on the graph suggested in the previous paragraph. They can be minimized by maintaining the chronoscope in optimal condition, but they set an ultimate limit on the accuracy of all chronoscopes since they cannot be eliminated by a correction applied to the data. In a properly designed instrument, this limit is of the order of one scale unit (Schlosberg, 1937a).

Stimulus and reaction keys. Given adequate time-measuring apparatus, *E*'s next problem is to devise arrangements for making or breaking a circuit simultaneously with the S and with the R. The reagent's key is usually a simple affair, though it may need careful designing to fit some of the more complicated circuits. The old standard is a simple telegraph key, which is held closed by *O* from the fore-signal to the reception of the stimulus and then released by quickly raising the hand. If the reacting movement is a downward pressure on the key, the indicated time will be longer when the force required to depress the key against its spring is greater. This element of variability is eliminated by using the upward movement for the reaction. The circuit can be arranged so that the upward movement either breaks or makes the current through the chronoscope magnet, as needed.

Telegraph keys offer some shock hazard when used with the 110 v. circuits that are widely employed today. They have the further disadvantage that *E* sometimes gets careless and does not hold his key down until *O* reacts, thus giving false readings. A standard mercury wall switch can be arranged to avoid both these difficulties, and to be silent as well. For the response, a small toggle switch is convenient. It probably adds little to the RT, if it is located so that *O* can brace his thumb against a rest and snap the switch by a pinching movement of the forefinger. (See Fig. 2-3B, p. 13.)

For disjunctive and especially for associative reactions a speech key is very desirable, and the problem here is by no means simple. Lip keys, jaw keys, chin keys and voice keys have all been used, but the difficulty with all of them is that the articulatory movements and sound vibrations differ from one spoken word to another, and the time lost in the activation of the key varies accordingly

Probably the voice key, well managed, gives the best service—unless it be a microphone or an oscillograph with photographic registration (Dunlap, 1921).

Stimulus keys or stimulators must be adapted to the sense stimulated and should not give any stimulus besides the one intended. If a visual stimulator makes a noise, the response, in case of a simple reaction, will probably be made to the noise rather than to the light, since response to sound is quicker than to light. A neon lamp lights up and also goes out with no significant latency of its own and so affords a good stimulus for the simple reaction to light. Furthermore, it does not make clicks or humming sounds as do some incandescent bulbs (Wendt, 1938). It is a more difficult problem to get rid of the noises made by chronoscopes and control equipment. The best solution is to isolate *O* in a separate room, or to mask the sounds by a noisy electric fan, or by a buzz in the earphones.

For the ear, the "sound hammer" or a telegraph sounder furnishes a convenient noise though not usually of known intensity. To obtain a tonal stimulus free from initial noise is not so easy. Jenkins (1926) used a thermionic receiver inserted into the external auditory meatus and operated by an alternating current. Modern developments in telephone and radio engineering provide facilities for this sort of psychological work. These developments are too technical to be treated in a general text; they may be found in the current literature.

A tactual stimulus key delivers a quick pressure on the skin at the same instant that it makes or breaks a circuit. For better control of the intensity, a small weight carried by a lever is made to fall through a known arc before striking the skin (Cattell & Dolley, 1896). Stimuli for the senses of taste, smell, pain and temperature ought to be free from incidental stimulation of the sense of touch—an almost impossible requirement.

The simplest chronoscope. Most chronoscopes are precision instruments, and therefore fairly expensive. But Piéron (1928) suggested a scheme for measuring RT that costs essentially nothing, and has the advantages of portability, silence, and accuracy. For visual RT, *E* holds a yard or meter stick pressed upright against a wall with his thumb. The zero end should be at the bottom, lined up with a mark on the wall at about eye level. *O* holds his thumb poised near the bottom of the stick, ready to arrest its fall by pushing it against the wall. *E* says "Ready," and suddenly removes his thumb, letting the stick fall freely. As soon as *O* sees *E*'s thumb move, he stops the fall of the stick. By reference to the index mark on the wall, *E* can read how far the stick has fallen, and convert this distance into time by the formula: $T = \sqrt{\frac{2S}{G}}$, where T is time in seconds, S is distance of fall in either centimeters or feet, and G is the acceleration due to gravity (980 cm/sec, or 32 ft/sec). Of course, it is much more sensible to construct a time scale on paper and attach it to the stick, or to draw the scale directly on the stick in place of the original inches or centimeters. The scale should be in units of .01 sec; the spacing can be calculated from a converted form of the equation; $S = \frac{1}{2}GT^2$. A few rough values are given below.

RT (sec)	.10	.15	.20	.25
Fall (cm)	4.9	11.0	19.6	30.6
" (in)	1.9	4.3	7.7	12.0

RT (sec)	.30	.35	.40	.45
Fall (cm)	44.1	60.0	78.4	99.2
" (in)	17.3	23.5	30.7	39.0

Note that the spacing between .10 and .20 sec is big enough to permit easy reading of typical RTs to well beyond .01 sec.

For auditory RT, *E* holds the stick by pressing on it with a clicker ("cricket"). For tactual RT *O* rests his left forefinger lightly on *E*'s thumb as it holds the stick. Complex RT would involve some trick release movement by *E*.

REACTION TIME DEPENDS ON THE STIMULUS

In the introductory chapter a general scheme or formula was offered as a guide for psychological experimentation. The response to be observed at any moment, we said, depends on the external situation affecting the organism and on factors present in the organism at that moment. The external factors we called stimulus variables, S-variables; and the internal factors we called *O*-variables. The ways in which the response can vary we called R-variables. In a reaction time experiment the response variable is the RT. Our formula thus takes this form:

$$RT = f(S, O)$$

The S-variables are controlled by the experimenter, being either held constant or varied systematically. The *O*-variables are not controllable by *E* at the moment, but some of them can be controlled indirectly by *E*'s antecedent operations, such as time since last feeding in the typical *O*-variable of hunger. The antecedent operations by which *E* controls *O*'s present state we called A-variables. The job of the RT experimenters, accordingly, is to give concrete meaning to the formula,

$$RT = f(S, A)$$

Experimenters as a matter of fact have usually been less interested in filling in this blank scheme than in testing particular hypotheses, such as that the RT will be lengthened by distraction or shortened by strong motivation. Even so, their results can be fitted into the scheme.

Our task will now be to consider the factors that affect the length of the reaction time, and we shall begin with the S-variables.

Reaction time depends on the sense organ stimulated. This topic could also be phrased, RT in relation to the *modality* of the stimulus. From the time of Hirsch (1861–1864) to the present it has almost universally been found that response to light has a longer latency than that to sound or to a touch on the skin. Typical values for practiced adult subjects are:

Reaction time to	*Milliseconds*
Light	180
Sound	140
Touch	140

As to touch, the RT differs with the spot stimulated, the more sensitive spots and those nearer the brain tending to give the quicker responses. Sometimes an electric shock applied to the hand or face gives a RT 10–20 ms shorter than the RT to sound, but this result is not universal. As we shall soon see, the RT depends on the intensity as well as the modality of the stimulus so that it is quite possible, by selecting a weak sound and a strong light, to obtain quicker response to the light than to the sound.

The RT to light differs with the part of the retina which receives the light. The farther out from the fovea, the longer the RT. Quickness of response runs parallel with acuity of vision (tested by ability to recognize letters and other small figures). Acuity decreases from the fovea out, and the RT increases. Along the horizontal meridian, acuity at the same distance from the fovea is somewhat better on the (more important) nasal half of the retina, and the RT is shorter, as shown in Figure 2-4.

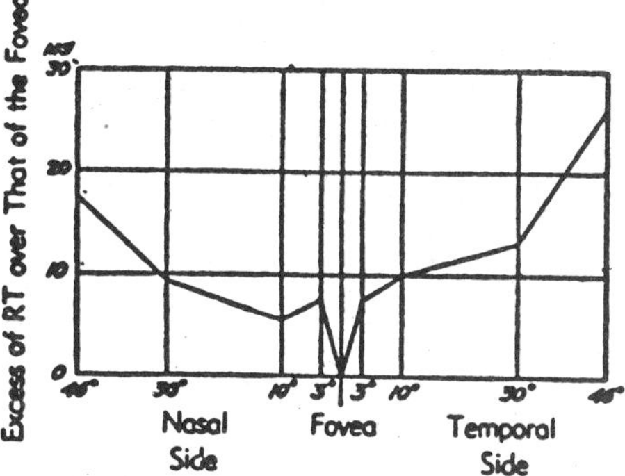

FIG. 2-4. (Data from Poffenberger, 1912.) Reaction time to stimuli applied along the horizontal meridian of the retina. The level of the base line represents the RT to foveal stimulation, and the curve shows, for example, that at 10° from the fovea on the temporal side (of the retina —reverse for external field of view) the RT is 10 ms longer than at the fovea. Data were from two practiced *Os*; each eye was tested separately, a total of 400 RTs for each point.

Sight, hearing, and touch (proper) stand in a class by themselves as far as the reaction time is concerned because they can be stimulated separately. It is almost impossible to apply sudden stimuli of warmth, cold, pain, smell, or taste without incidentally stimulating also some touch receptors. And the touch receptors receive their mechanical stimuli before the thermal or chemical stimuli can penetrate to their receptors. The subject gets a touch sensation a fraction of a second before the temperature, smell, or taste sensation, but he is instructed not to react to touch but to wait until he gets the other sensation. To hold back for a fraction of a second and still react "as quickly as possible" is a difficult task for the subject and the RTs so obtained are scarcely simple RTs like those of sight, hearing, and touch.

Taste stimuli in solution have been applied to the tip of the tongue by a little brush mounted on a suitable circuit key. The results obtained from one very competent subject were as follows (Kiesow, 1903):

Stimulus	*RT (in ms)*
Salt, sodium chloride, saturated	308
Sweet, cane sugar, nearly saturated	446
Sour, citric or phosphoric acid, dilute	536
Bitter, quinine bisulphate, saturated	1082

A stronger acid solution would probably have given somewhat quicker responses, and the slow response to bitter is explained by the relative insensitivity of the tip of the tongue to bitter stimuli.

Smell stimuli were applied by a device which blew a puff of odorous vapor into the nose and at the same time closed the chronoscope circuit (Moldenhauer, 1883). The unavoidable noise of the puff and sensations of touch and coolness from the nostrils were distracting and produced false reactions until the subjects became so well practiced that they were "fully certain they were reacting only to the odor." As a check a series of simple RTs to the noise and to the touch were obtained. The results from two subjects were as follows:

Stimulus	*RT of subject A (in ms)*	*RT of subject B (in ms)*
Noise	164	185
Touch	187	214
Odor	210	390

A relatively slow reaction to smell is indicated, but doubt remains whether true simple RTs were obtained.

Warmth or cold applied to the surface of the skin takes a little time to penetrate to the receptors and longer to reach the warmth than the cold receptors, apparently, since the latency of the warmth sensation is longer than that of the cold sensation. The long "reaction times," 300 to 1600 ms, to these stimuli are largely penetration times (see p. 280).

Pain stimuli applied to the skin usually yield a double sensation, touch followed by pain. Therefore, here as in the cases of taste, smell, and temperature, it is difficult to obtain true simple reaction times to pain stimuli. Luckily, mild superficial pain is sometimes obtained without any touch sensation, when a sharp point is applied very lightly to the skin. Eichler (1930) employed for this purpose the technique of von Frey (p. 274): a slender bristle, tipped with a thorn from a thistle plant, is applied to the skin, and the chronoscope is automatically started at the moment of application. The weak pressure gives the double touch-pain sensation on most trials, but sometimes only the pain is felt. The subject makes a simple reaction to every stimulus—this is essential—but immediately afterward reports whether he got the double sensation or pain only. The RTs are then sorted into the two classes. Four subjects consistently gave much longer RTs when only pain was felt. On the average:

When touch followed by pain was felt, the RT was 268 ms.

When pain only was felt, the RT was 888 ms.

The slow response to touch is accounted for by the extreme weakness of the stimuli, but those stimuli which happened to give only pain were no weaker and yet gave much slower responses.

Rotation of a blindfolded subject can be used as a stimulus to the semicircular canals. The chair must turn without jarring, and the acceleration must be quite moderate in order to avoid kinesthetic stimulation. With such a setup Baxter & Travis (1938) found the RT extremely variable, with a median of nearly 500 ms when the movement started from rest. Theirs was not strictly a simple reaction since *O* was instructed to respond with the right or left hand according to the direction of the rotation; an easy discrimination was required. Perhaps 400 ms would be a fair guess for the simple RT to rotation. A good share of this time may be needed for building up an adequate physical pressure on the receptors (see p. 520).

Why should the response to pain be so very slow, why should the response to light be slower than to sound, and in general why should the RT differ from one modality to another? There are several possible factors. The long RT to pain may be due to slow nerve conduction in the slender sensory nerve fibers that serve this sense—or due to the long train of sensory nerve impulses that must be summated before the pain sensation emerges. The slow reaction to warmth, cold, and taste must be due, in part anyway, to the time the stimulus takes to penetrate to the receptors. By contrast, sound entering the ear or pressure applied to the skin can reach the appropriate receptors with practically no loss of time. Light of course reaches the retina with no loss of time, but the rods and cones are not excited by the light directly and the intervening photochemical process takes an appreciable time.

By the study of amplified action currents (or variations of electric potential in an active receptor, nerve, nerve center, or muscle) it is possible to break down the total RT into its successive parts. Apply a sound to the ear of a cat: activity begins in the auditory nerve with a latency of 1–2 ms, showing that almost no time is lost in the receptors. Follow the auditory pathway up through the brain stem: the activity appears just a bit later as you go up, but it reaches the cerebral cortex in 8–9 ms from the moment when the sound reached the ear. We can infer that very little of the auditory RT is consumed in the ear or on the way to the cortex (Kemp, Coppée & Robinson, 1937). When a light is thrown into the eye, activity reaches the visual cortex in 20–40 ms, but when the retina is bypassed by direct electrical stimulation of the optic nerve, the cortical latency is as little as 2–5 ms (according to results on the rabbit by Bartley, 1934, and on the cat by Marshall, Talbot & Ades, 1943). Compared with the ear, the eye takes a long time to get its message started along the nerve to the brain. Thus, we can account for most and perhaps all of the difference between the visual and auditory RT.

On the outgoing side, nerve conduction from the brain to the finger muscles will take not over 10–15 ms, but more than that may be consumed in the muscles themselves and in the mechanical process of getting the reaction key into motion; for the muscle currents have shown a RT 30–40 ms shorter than the reaction key (Vörckel, 1922). (The lag of a heavy member, like the leg, would be considerably greater.) If we subtract from the total auditory RT of 140 ms the times indicated for the sensory and motor nerve paths and for the muscles and finger movement, we have left a central RT of 70–90 ms. At least half of the auditory RT is required for brain processes.

Reaction time depends on the strength of the stimulus. The word "strength" here includes physical intensity and similar factors such as the size of a visual stimulus and the summation of two or more stimuli. The main fact has often been observed: the RT is long when the stimulus is very weak and becomes shorter as the stimulus increases to medium and high intensities. Given adequate data we should be able to make more definite statements. Does the RT keep on shortening as long as the intensity increases, or reach a minimum at some moderate intensity? Does its decrease follow a straight line or a curve? In short it should be possible to give the schematic formula, $RT = f(I)$, the form of a definite equation or at least a definite graph. For this purpose a wide range of stimulus intensities is needed, extending from near the stimulus threshold up to stimuli about as intense as can be safely applied to the sense organs. (Right at the stimulus threshold, defined as that intensity which is perceived 50 percent of the time, valid *average* values for the RT can obviously not be obtained.)

Sound intensities. It is more feasible to cover a wide range of intensities in the auditory than in other modalities. In the Sorbonne laboratory Chocholle (1945) used tones ranging from the barely audible up to very high intensity. Two exceptionally well-trained subjects agreed closely in their results. Near the stimulus threshold their RT was about 400 ms, and with high intensities it was 110 ms, which seemed to be about the limit. Tones of low, medium, and high pitch were used in the different series. As a fair sample of the results, we give the average RT of the two subjects to a 1,000-cycle tone, the intensities [1] being stated in log units above threshold:

log I	*RT*	*log I*	*RT*	*log I*	*RT*
0	402	1	193	6	124
.2	316	2	161	7	118
.4	281	3	148	8	112
.6	249	4	139	9	111
.8	218	5	130	10	110

[1] We are using *power* as our measure of intensity; see p. 325.

A word about the unit of measurement. It is customary and convenient to express intensity in logarithmic units, "log units." To increase the intensity by one log unit is to multiply it by 10. To increase it by 2 log units is to multiply it by $10^2 = 100$; to increase it by 3 log units is to multiply it by 10^3 or 1,000; and so on. This way of measuring intensity is convenient since it enables us to compress an enormous range of intensities into a compact graph, and it is psychologically correct because of the approximate truth of Weber's law which states that we perceive ratios rather than arithmetical differences of intensity (p. 194). In the case of sound intensities log units are called bels and 1/10 of a log unit is a decibel. To increase the intensity by one decibel is to multiply the energy by 1.259 which is the tenth root of 10.

Zero in the logarithmic scale of intensity does not mean zero intensity; it means that particular intensity which is assigned the value of 1 (since $\log 1 = 0$), all other intensities being taken as multiples of this one. Usually, though not necessarily, the threshold intensity, or at least the lowest intensity used in an experiment, is taken as 1 in the numerical scale and so as 0 in the logarithmic scale. In the table just given, the log I (intensity) of 0 means near-threshold intensity, the log I of 1 means 10 times threshold intensity, the log I of 6 means 1,000,000 times threshold, and so on. It can be seen that a wide range of intensities was covered in this experiment.

What can we learn from the table or from the graph of the same data in Figure 2-5, besides the elementary fact that the RT grows shorter as the stimulus intensity increases? Each time the intensity increases by 1 log unit, the RT shows a decrement, but these decrements become smaller and smaller. From a practical standpoint we can infer that, in any situation demanding quick response to very weak stimuli, a small increase in their strength will be a great help; but if the stimuli are already of good strength, there will be little advantage in making them stronger. The data points form a curve which flattens out as if the RT were approaching a limit, and the limit for these practiced subjects seems to be nearly reached at the stimulus intensity of 10 log units (100 decibels above threshold). Their RT limit cannot be far below 110 ms.

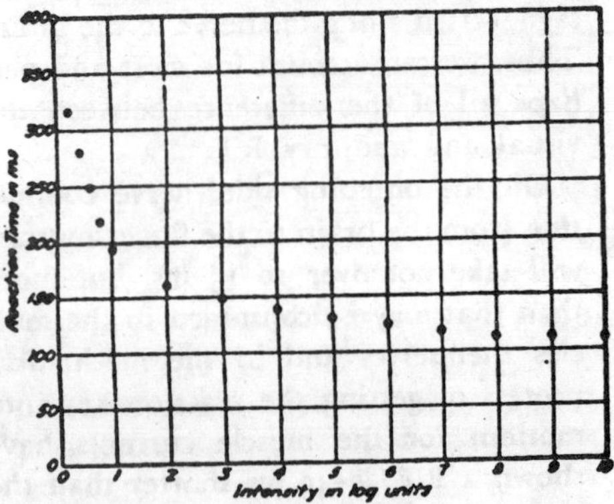

FIG. 2-5. (Data from Chocholle, 1945.) Reaction time plotted against stimulus intensity. The stimulus was a tone of 1,000 cycles per second. The RTs of two subjects are averaged.

Irreducible minimum and reducible margin. Some minimum RT (greater than zero) is to be expected. Receptor stimulation, neural conduction to and from the centers, and muscular contraction are processes that take time; they account for about 60 ms of the minimum (p. 19). The intervening brain process must also consume some time even though we cannot yet measure it directly. There is the further complication that these mechanisms do not always function at their maximum effi ciency; the RT varies somewhat from trial to trial in a "random" fashion (p. 37) so that the Mean RT approaches a limit which is longer than the absolute minimum. If we combine all these factors, we end with a rather elastic limiting value which can only be discovered experimentally. Following Piéron (1919), we may regard any RT as composed of this limiting value or "irreducible minimum," plus a remainder which he calls a "reducible margin." The reducible margin is large when the stimuli are weak and is reduced by increasing their intensity.

It is certain that the irreducible minimum will be different from experiment to experiment—short for sound, longer for a visual stimulus, still longer for pain, and longer for a choice reaction than for the simple reaction. The meaning of the "limit" will be clearer if we recall the basic nature of a quantitative experiment: we hold some factors constant, vary our experimental variable systematically and note the resulting changes in the dependent variable. In Chocholle's experiment practice, attitude, modality of stimulus and many other factors were held constant; these determined the irreducible minimum. He then noted how RT (the dependent variable) changed as a function of stimulus intensity (the independent or experimental variable). The RT varied through a certain range which was the reducible margin for this particular experimental variable. Thus the reducible margin depends on the experimental variable, but the irreducible minimum depends on the factors that are held constant.

Consider another experiment. Let us hold the stimulus constant at a medium intensity and measure the RT after different amounts of practice. We shall find that practice decreases the RT (p. 35), and our practice curve will approach a limit or irreducible minimum. This limit will not be the same as Chocholle's, since the constant factors are different. Practically this same method of analysis is found useful in the study of other learning curves (p. 664).

Fitting an equation to the data. With data as regular as those plotted in Figure 2-5 a mathematical description should be possible in the form of a definite equation to take the place of our schematic $RT = f(I)$. At least an "empirical equation" could be worked out to fit the data closely. This equation would contain some "parameters" so chosen as to make it fit the curve, though not chosen for any theoretical significance. Empirical equations may have definite practical value. Chocholle tried equations of several types and found one that fitted the whole range of data quite closely.

In contrast to the empirical equation, a "rational" or "theoretical" equation embodies some theory, some hypothesis which we can test by seeing how closely the equation can be made to fit the data. The general nature of the parameters is dictated by the theory, and their exact values must be determined to fit the data. One element of theory is the irreducible minimum or limit, and if we select 105 ms as a likely limit in this instance, we have one parameter fixed. Subtracting the irreducible minimum we have the reducible margin, $RT - 105$, to work on. It starts with a high value which we shall call A when $\log I = 0$, and diminishes by smaller and smaller steps as I increases by log units. This A is a second parameter, and a third is suggested by the diminishing decrements of $RT - 105$. Such diminishing decrements (or sometimes increments) are well

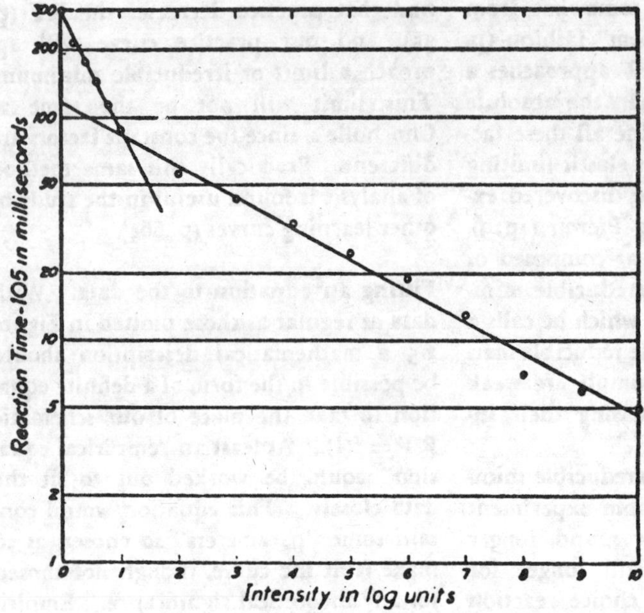

Fig. 2·6. Plot of the Chocholle data on semilog paper. The first step was to choose a value for the limit or "irreducible minimum" approached by the RT as I increased; and 105 ms was chosen as a fair estimate. The I values were laid off on the arithmetical axis, and the corresponding values of RT — 105 ms were plotted in logarithmic ordinates. Then the attempt was made, by aid of a thread, to run a straight line near and between the data points, leaving about half of them on each side, so as to follow the general trend of the data. It became clear that no single straight line could fit the whole range of data points; but the range was easily divided into two parts, with one straight line fitting the low-intensity part and another the remainder of the range.

With the straight lines drawn in, the parameters A and q are readily found. To find A, read the ordinate of the line where $I = 0$. For the short steep line we get $A = 285$ ms, and for the main line $A = 117$ ms. To find q for the short line, read the ordinate where $I = 1$; and we get 88 ms, which $= A \times q = 285\,q$; whence $q = {}^{88}/_{285} = .309$. For the main line, we can read the ordinate where $I = 10$; and we get 4.6 ms, which $= A \times q^{10} = 117\,q^{10}$; whence $q^{10} = {}^{4.6}/_{117}$; and by aid of a table of logarithms we obtain $q = .724$.

The values thus obtained for A and q are substituted in the general equation, $RT - 105 = A \times q^{I}$, to give the specific equations stated on Figure 2·7.

known in certain physical and chemical processes and in curves of growth and learning. In some processes the decrement is always a certain fraction of the amount remaining. Let us apply this conception to our problem. Let us regard the reducible margin as a quantity of delay in the RT process, resulting from a mass of delay factors. The delay can be overcome by increased stimulus intensity, and each added unit of intensity overcomes some fraction of the delay. Now here is a definite hypothesis: increase the intensity by equal steps, and each step will overcome *the same percent of the remaining delay*. For example, an increase of 1 log unit in intensity might always diminish the reducible margin by 20 percent; if the margin were 100 ms at a certain stimulus intensity, this margin would be reduced to 80 ms by increasing the intensity 1 log unit; adding a second log unit would decrease the 80 ms by 20 percent, leaving a margin of 64 ms; a third log unit would cut out 20 percent of this 64 ms; and so on. In general, the hypothesis says that each additional log unit of intensity cuts down the reducible margin by a fraction which we may call p, leaving a fraction $1-p$ or q, and we will take q as a third parameter for our equation. According to our assumptions we have the following series of values.

I	$RT - 105$
0	A
1	Aq
2	Aq^2
3	Aq^3
.	.
.	.

Since the exponent of q is always the same as the value of I in log units, we can use I to represent the exponent, and so obtain our desired equation,

$$RT - 105 = A \times q^I$$

Now we have to determine the values of A and q to fit our table of data. Such an exponential equation is best handled in the equivalent logarithmic form,

$$\log (RT - 105) = \log A + I \log q$$

which is the equation of a straight line. The computations can be made graphically, as shown in Figure 2-6.

If a straight line can be drawn (on semilog paper as in Figure 2-6) to fit the run of the data points, the data are thus shown to be consistent with the hypothesis on which the theoretical equation

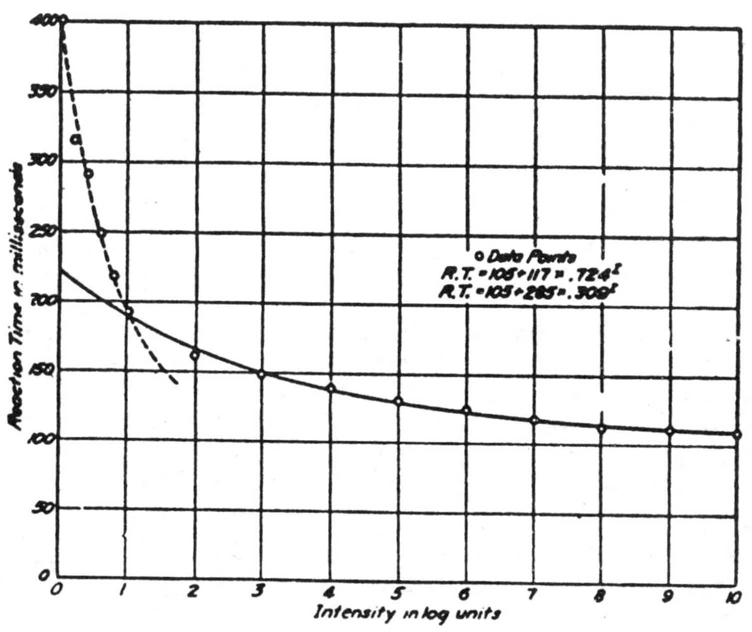

FIG. 2-7. The same as Figure 2-5, with the two theoretical curves added. The curves are equivalent to the two straight lines of Figure 2-6, and are constructed as follows: Read the ordinates of the straight line at a sufficient number of points; since these are the theoretical values of RT—105 ms, add 105 ms to each; plot the sums as ordinates in the arithmetical scale. For an example, when I = 6 units, the ordinate of the straight line is 17 ms, to which must be added 105 ms to obtain the ordinate of the curve at I = 6.

The closeness of fit can be judged by inspection, or shown more exactly by a comparison of the observed and calculated values of RT at the several values of I.

Our equations can be obtained in another way by use of the calculus. The hypothesis is that the rate of decrease of RT — 105 is always proportional to the existing size of RT — 105. Thus we have the differential equation,

$$\frac{d(RT - 105)}{dI} = b(RT - 105)$$

or

$$\frac{d(RT - 105)}{RT - 105} = b\,dI$$

a familiar form of differential equation which can be integrated into the logarithmic form,

$$\log (RT - 105) = BI + C$$

which is the same as our logarithmic equation above, with $B = \log q$, and $C = \log A$.

was based. In the present instance we have to admit that no single straight line will fit the whole range of data points. The drop of RT from I = 0 to I = 1 is much too steep to agree with the general trend. But it is possible to draw *two* straight lines, one fitting the weak intensity series and the other the range from 1 to 10 log units. In order to maintain our hypothesis, we have to split it by positing two kinds of delay factors, one kind operative at very weak intensities and overcome by a small increase of intensity, the other operative at medium and high intensities and only gradually overcome by increased intensity. A delay factor operative only at low intensities could very well be the subject's need to listen so closely for the weak stimulus as to be unready for the motor response. In a word, the steep drop from near the stimulus threshold could be the result of the overcoming of *sensory* delay factors, and the slow decline through the medium and high intensities would then be due to the overcoming of *motor* delay factors. So interpreted our analysis falls in with the distinction between sensory and motor types of reaction, soon to be considered (p. 32). It should be said that Chocholle's data for reaction to tones of 2,000 cycles and other frequencies follow curves similar to the one we have analyzed.

Light intensity. Light varies in intensity perhaps as widely as sound, but no very wide range has been used in reaction time experiments. In Wundt's laboratory at Leipzig, back in 1886, Cattell and Berger, both highly trained subjects, provided a series of reliable data over a range of 1 to 1,000, i.e., of 3 log units. They used a light of moderate intensity in a dark room as their maximum and lowered the intensity by placing smoked glasses between the light and the subject's eye. Their weakest stimulus was probably well above threshold intensity. Hull (1949) fitted to their data an equation of the type which we have used to embody the hypothesis of proportionally diminishing decrements, and the equation fits the data very closely (Fig. 2-8).

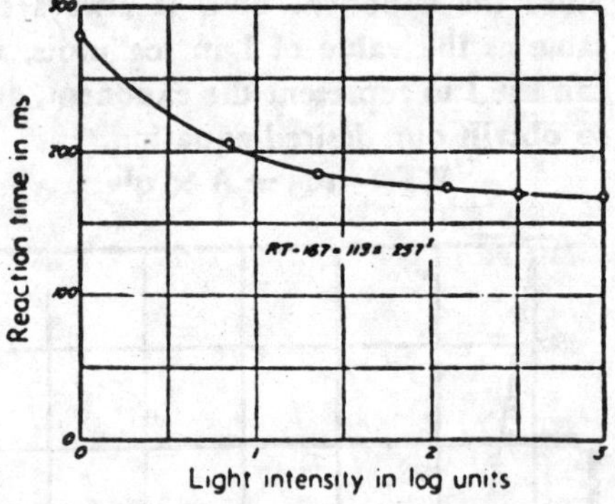

Fig. 2-8. (Berger, 1886; Cattell, 1886c; Hull, 1949.) Reaction times to light of different intensities. The data are as follows (average of two subjects):

Relative intensity	1	7	23	123	315	1000
I in log units	0	.85	1.36	2.09	2.50	3.00
Reaction time	280	205	184	174	170	169

Hull's equation, expressed in our terms and with I in log units, is as follows:

$$RT - 167 = 113 \times .257^{I}$$

which reads that the limit approached is 167 ms. and the reducible margin therefore RT − 167, and that adding a log unit always reduces the margin to .257 of its just previous amount.

In stating the strength of a visual stimulus we really should state its area and duration as well as its intensity, since these three factors substitute for each other to a certain extent (see Vision, p. 374). If we start with a very small spot of light and increase its area, we increase its apparent intensity within narrow limits. If we start with a very brief light and increase its duration, we increase its apparent intensity within narrow limits. These are the spatial and temporal summation effects (pp. 373–376). In reaction time experiments Froeberg (1907) obtained similar effects: daylight reflected from a square of white paper at reading distance being the stimulus. The effects were slight but reliable when practiced *Os* were given a large number of trials. Thus:

Area effect

Side of square in mm	3	6	12	24	48
Reaction time in ms	195	188	184	182	179

Duration effect

Duration of light in ms	3	6	12	24	48
Reaction time in ms	191	189	187	184	182

Further increase of duration does not further decrease the RT (G. R. Wells, 1913). With auditory stimuli (tones) of 100 ms and longer durations, RT seems to *increase* slightly as the stimulus duration increases (Gregg & Brogden, 1950). Why this should be sc is not clear.

More powerful than the area or duration of a visual stimulus is the state of the eye with respect to *light or dark adaptation* (p. 369). Increasing the sensitivity of the eye should have the same effect as increasing the intensity of the stimulus, and the eye is thousands of times more sensitive after a long stay in the dark than it is after even a few minutes exposure to bright light. We should expect, therefore, that a light of a certain constant intensity would not only appear much brighter after dark than after light adaptation but would also get a quicker motor response. This effect was clearly demonstrated in an experiment of Hovland (1936a). His constant stimulus was a circular patch, 20 millimeters in diameter (4/5 of an inch), 12 inches in front of the subject's eyes, illuminated by a flash of 250 foot-candles. This stimulus was seen against the background of a wall which was either completely dark or else illuminated by light of 200, 150, 100, or 50 foot-candles; and the subject's eyes were always preadapted to the illumination of the wall. That is, every time before the stimulus was given, he had been looking at the wall long enough to be adapted to its illumination. After the subjects had been thoroughly practiced in this situation, their average RT was as follows (five subjects, 100 reactions from each under each condition):

Adaptation level in foot-candles	200	150	100	50	0
Reaction time in ms	154	146	144	140	131

We can regard the series of adaptation levels as equivalent to an intensity series (though we cannot compute the exact intensity equivalents of the adaptation levels). The notably short RT after dark adaptation can thus be an index of the RT to be expected with a visual stimulus of very high intensity.

Summation of stimuli. A combination of simultaneous stimuli may give a quicker response than any one of these stimuli alone. As just suggested, the effect of increased area or duration of a visual stimulus can be due to summation, and even the effect of increased intensity may belong here, since a more intense stimulus arouses a larger number of receptor cells in the sense organ and also generates more nerve impulses per second from each cell (Adrian, 1932). An interesting example of summation is given by Poffenberger (1912). The RT is shorter with binocular than with monocular stimulation by the same light, and the difference was reliable for each of the three subjects:

Subject	*Monocular (in ms)*	*Binocular (in ms)*
F	201	185
P	175	160
A	191	178

This effect on the RT is rather surprising in view of the fact that the apparent brightness of a light is scarcely different with monocular and binocular stimulation. A similar effect in hearing was noted by Bliss (1893) when the same sound was admitted to both ears or confined to a single ear: RT to monotic stimuation, 147 ms; to diotic, 133 ms. Here, however, the result is not surprising since the subjective intensity (loudness) of a sound is greater when both ears receive the sound.

If two stimuli, a light and a sound, are applied simultaneously, it is futile to instruct the subject to react to the light, for he cannot do so consistently if he makes a truly simple reaction. He will react to the sound and so give a quicker response than he can to light. The only question is whether he can react more quickly to the sound when there is a simultaneous stimulus of light, and the answer is "No," as was found by Dunlap and Wells (1910) and also by Todd (1912). In Todd's experiment three stimuli were applied singly and in combination, with results as shown below.

Stimulus	*Reaction time of subjects*			
	M	***P***	***T***	***Av***
Light	168	176	186	176
Electric shock	141	135	152	143
Sound	135	132	160	142
Light and shock	139	137	151	142
Light and sound	133	135	159	142
Sound and shock	125	122	145	131
Light, sound, and shock	120	124	138	127

Light does not hasten the response to sound or to electric shock, but sound and shock give a quicker reaction when combined than when given singly.

Reaction to the cessation of a stimulus or to changes in its intensity. Is it possible to make a typical quick reaction to the cessation of a stimulus? From ordinary experience no special difficulty would be expected, but if the reaction is supposed to be elicited by energy applied to a sense organ, how can the cessation of the energy be an effective stimulus? Several experimenters have obtained the RT to the cessation of a light and found it no longer if not a little shorter than the RT to the onset of the same light. Woodrow (1915), using either light or sound as the stimulus, found his five subjects to give the *same* RT to onset and cessation, as illustrated by the average results from one of the subjects:

	Onset (in ms)	*Cessation (in ms)*
Sound intensity		
Medium	119	121
Weak	184	183
Threshold	779	745
Light intensity		
Strong	162	167
Weak	205	203

A quick reaction to the *cessation* of a stimulus energy would seem to be a contradiction of the S—R view. The apparent contradiction results from an inadequate definition of the stimulus. Strictly speaking, a stimulus must often be defined as a *change* in the energies falling on a receptor. In the case of visual stimulation this is particularly clear; the eye rapidly comes into balance (adapts) to a steady light falling on the retina. One can even record electrical "responses" of the retina of a nonmammalian eye on the termination of a steady beam of light (see Vision). There are no comparable "off effects" in the ear; to account for the response to termination of a sound, we must assume that some region higher in the nervous system acts like the retina, in that it quickly comes into balance as long as the incoming energies are steady but responds when a sudden change throws it out of balance. This problem is not limited to RT experiments, for in later chapters we shall note many examples of responses tripped off by changes or other relationships among stimuli.

Woodrow found the RT to be just about the same to the onset or cessation of a given stimulus, but shorter for the more intense stimuli. His inference is about the same as we have just stated. He considers the brain as a system of energies in adjustment so that either onset or cessation of a stimulus disturbs this adjustment and so sets free the motor impulse. Either onset or cessation, we might say, acts simply as a jolt which releases the prepared motor response. The cessation of a stronger stimulus would be a bigger jolt.

On the whole, however, recent evidence favors *quicker* reaction to the cessation of a light than to its onset. Jenkins (1926) found this to be true of his five subjects, who gave on the average a RT of 230 ms to the onset of a light but of only 200 ms to its cessation. A spot of light in a dark room came on and went out at intervals of about 4 sec. and *O* reacted to each onset and each cessation. A possible explanation, suggested by Jenkins, is that the eyes lost their fixation during the dark intervals and so obtained poorer reception of onset than of cessation.

This possible source of error can be avoided, as in an experiment of Steinman (1944), by having the subject react not to complete cessation or onset of a light, but to changes in its intensity. For the stimulus she used an increase or decrease in the illumination of a ground-glass disk, an inch in diameter, located two feet in front of the subject in the middle of a well-lighted screen. When the disk was illuminated (from behind), the subject prepared to react as soon as he saw the disk increase or decrease in brightness. When the brightness increased from 4.5 foot-candles to 5.5, the six well-practiced subjects gave an average RT of 205 ms; but when the reverse change from 5.5 to 4.5 foot-candles occurred, their RT was only 188 ms. The greater the amount of change, the quicker the response, but the RT to decrease was consistently smaller than to an equal increase (Fig. 2-9).

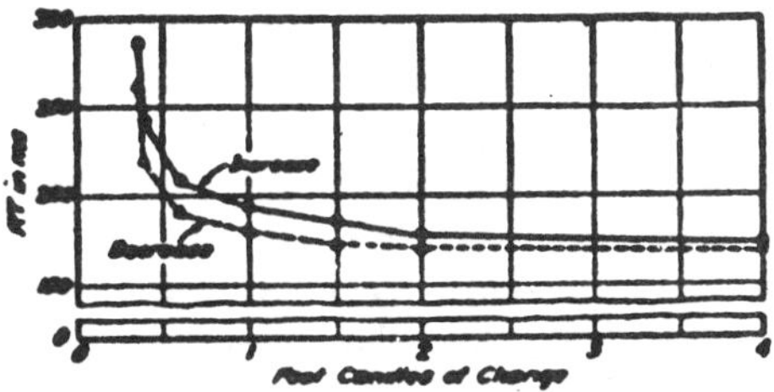

FIG. 2-9. (Steinman, 1944.) Simple reaction time to sudden increase or decrease in the intensity of light, in relation to the amount of change. The changes are upward from 4.5 foot-candles, downward to 4.5 foot-candles. The data plotted are from one subject whose results were typical.

This extra quickness of response to a decrement may be peculiar to the sense of sight because it was not found by Chocholle (1943) for up and down changes in the intensity of a sound. From recorded electric potentials in the optic nerve, there is some reason to believe that the retinal "off effect" is stronger than the "on effect." In this connection Steinman refers to Hartline (1938) and Bartley (1939).

REACTION TIME DEPENDS ON THE ORGANISM

Now that we have considered the principal stimulus factors affecting reaction time, we shall take up the *O*-variables.

i.e., the factors present in the organism when the stimulus arrives. These are due to A-variables, antecedent experimental variables, so far as they are controlled by the experimenter's preliminary operations. One A-variable has already been noticed. The subject's state of light or dark adaptation is controlled by preliminary exposure to light or dark. As a state of the organism existing at the moment when a visual stimulus is given, it is a clear example of an O-variable; being controlled by the preliminary exposure to light or dark, it can be made an A-variable.

The experimenter's instructions to the subject amount to an A-variable and a very important one, since without them the subject would have no motive for making a quick hand movement to a perfectly innocuous visual or auditory stimulus.

Reaction quickened by extra motivation. Since the subject in a reaction time experiment is motivated by the desire to react as quickly as possible, it might seem that any additional motivation would be superfluous. Johanson (1922) thought it worth while, nevertheless, to try out the effect of reward and punishment. One incentive consisted simply in telling the subject his RT after each trial so that he would know how well or poorly he was doing and thus receive reward or punishment of a mild sort. A more severe punishment was provided by an electric circuit wired through the subject's key in such a way that his finger automatically got a shock whenever he was slower than a certain allowed time, which was progressively decreased as the RT became shorter with practice. The "reward" here was an avoidance of the shock. The three conditions—no extra incentive, knowledge of results, and shock—were rotated so as to cancel out the practice effect. Figure 2-10 presents the results in the form of distribution curves, and we see that even practiced subjects, "doing their best" all the time, speed up considerably under the spur of extra motivation. Their preparatory set, we may say, is intensified.

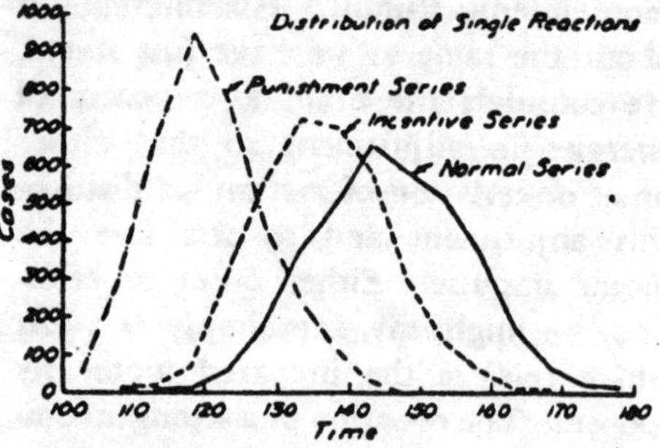

FIG. 2-10. (Johanson, 1922.) Change in the distribution of reaction time under the influence of incentives. Auditory stimulus. In the "incentive series" *O* was informed of his last RT; in the "punishment series" he received a shock in the finger when the reaction was at all slow. Each curve shows the distribution of 3,600 single reactions obtained from three *O*s whose times were nearly the same.

Preparatory set as a factor in reaction time. It is characteristic of the "simple" RT experiment that the subject knows in advance just what stimulus is coming and just what response he is to make. Even in the disjunctive and associative reactions he knows the general character of the coming stimulus and response. It is almost a matter of course that the quickness of the reaction will depend on the adequacy of the preparation. The preparation is in part voluntary and controlled by *E*'s instructions, but in part, as we shall see, it is involuntary and responsive to the exigencies of the situation as they impress themselves on the individual subject.

Without any preparation a sudden

stimulus might catch *O*'s attention, be recognized or perceived, and so lead to the selection of an appropriate movement. Some of the early students of RT assumed that these processes of attention, cognition, and choice took place in the laboratory reaction and that the simple RT gave a measure of the total time required for this series of processes. Such was Wundt's view. Others with a great deal of experience in RT work, such as Exner and Cattell, reached quite a different conception. It seemed to them that the response in a RT experiment closely resembled a reflex, and was in effect a temporary "prepared reflex."

Introspective studies by Ach (1905) and Watt (1905) in Külpe's laboratory favored this last view. When *O* was asked immediately after each response to report his experience, he found very little experience to report as occurring in the S—R interval, though he could tell much more about the preparatory period just preceding the stimulus and following the Ready signal. He was aware of preparing to respond to the coming stimulus and of making different preparations for different kinds of response. As these investigators suggested, it is useful to distinguish three consecutive periods: the foreperiod, from the Ready signal to the stimulus; the main period or RT, from the stimulus to the beginning of the overt motor response; and the afterperiod, from the beginning to the end of the overt response. If we represent the passage of time by a line extending from left to right, and mark on it P for the Ready signal, S for the stimulus, and R for the beginning of the response, we have a convenient blank diagram to be filled in by knowledge of the processes occurring:

. . . . P . . . . S . . . . . . R . . . .
foreperiod RT afterperiod

2 *

Varying the length of the foreperiod. How shall the subject's readiness to respond be controlled and varied? Presumably it will partially depend upon the duration of the foreperiod. If the foreperiod is too short, the subject will not have time to get ready, but if it is too long, his readiness may fade away. A foreperiod of about 2 sec, slightly varied from trial to trial in order to prevent *O* from attempting to synchronize his response with the stimulus, has been generally adopted as about right. Individuals certainly differ, some preferring a shorter and some a longer foreperiod. The foreperiod allowed in starting a foot race is best reduced to 1.5 sec, according to some experiments (Kobayashi & Matsui, 1938).

Telford (1931) tried out a half-second foreperiod. The auditory stimuli came in a continued series at intervals of ½, 1, 2 and 4 sec, the intervals being mixed in chance order with no ready signal except the preceding stimulus. On making each reaction *O* knew that another stimulus would arrive shortly. The average result for 29 untrained *O*s was as follows:

Interval between stimuli (= *foreperiod*)	½	1	2	4 sec
Mean RT	335	241	245	276 ms
SD	64	43	51	56 ms

In spite of the wide variation shown by SD, the RT at 1 or 2 sec was reliably shorter than at either ½ sec or 4 sec. The one-second interval was as good as any.

Woodrow (1914) extended the foreperiod to 20–24 sec, using auditory stimuli on three well-trained *O*s. It made a difference whether the foreperiod remained the same for a series of trials or varied irregularly and without warning. When it remained the same for a series of trials, so that *O* could adjust himself to its length, the optimal length was 2–4 sec. When it varied irregularly, there was no clear optimum and the reaction was slow throughout—about as slow as with the longest foreperiods in the regular procedure. Maximum readiness in these three subjects was not reached in much under 2 seconds and was not maintained much longer than 2 additional seconds.

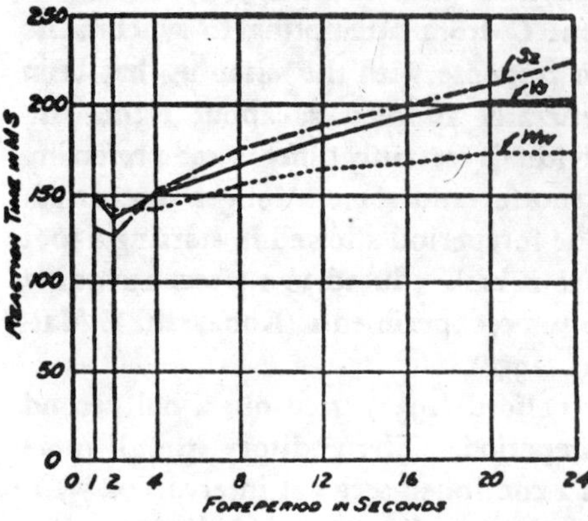

FIG. 2-11. (Woodrow, 1914.) Reaction time to sound, according to foreperiod length which was the same, however, for a series of trials. The curve for each subject is given separately.

Muscular tension during the foreperiod. General muscular tension is natural in an expectant person, and even so distant a muscle as the large quadriceps of the thigh is apt to thicken and harden during the foreperiod of a hand reaction, with relaxation following the response. This result can be obtained by mechanical registration (Freeman, 1931, 1934).

More adequate records of muscular tension can be obtained from the electric currents or potentials which occur whenever the muscle is even slightly active. These potentials can be tapped by an electrode applied to the skin over a muscle; they are amplified and photographed. This technique was used by Davis (1940), who found that the forearm muscles which execute the hand movement become tense during the foreperiod. He demonstrated certain significant parallels between these foreperiod tensions and the properties of preparatory set inferred from RT results. Thus:

a. The muscle tension begins about 200–400 ms after the Ready signal and tends to increase up to the moment of the reaction.

b. The higher the tension at the end of the foreperiod, the quicker the reaction.

c. The tension is greatest when the foreperiod is regular and of the most favorable length for short RT.

Davis concludes that the preliminary muscular tension is the actual response movement in an incipient stage. It is at least a definitely preparatory activity, and it could fairly be regarded as a conditioned response of the Pavlovian type (p. 565).

Katzell (1948) used a similar technique for recording the tension in several muscles: masseters, right and left arm biceps, hand flexors, thigh, and calf. On each trial the subject was instructed to react with a certain hand or foot movement. Muscle tension occurred in other muscles besides those executing the movement, and the participating muscles were largely the same in the foreperiod and in the reaction. The muscular pattern was the same but of course was comparatively weak during the foreperiod, being held in check so that premature reactions were avoided. The muscular preparation was thus quite specific.

Muscle tension as an alertness indicator. In certain practical situations it would be very valuable to have some gadget that would warn a person whenever he became drowsy or low in alertness. There are monotonous jobs that lull the performer into an inattentive state with resulting lapses that may have serious consequences. Travis & Kennedy (1947, 1949) thought it possible that electrical potentials from muscles could be made to do the necessary monitoring job. They pasted small electrodes to the skin of the forehead, one above each eye, to pick up the electrical activity from the brow muscles. After suitable amplification these potentials were fed into a device that turned on a warning signal when the muscle tension fell below a certain level. The obvious question is "How well do these brow potentials mirror the level of practical alertness?" These investigators ran a number of tests to answer this question. In one paper (Kennedy & Travis, 1948) they had the subject perform a continuous tracking task, moving his control stick to keep an indicator on a moving target, much as a driver turns the steering wheel to keep the car centered in his own lane. They set the alertness indicator to flash a warning red light when the muscle tension fell below a certain level. The subject had to react to the light by lifting his foot from a pedal. By changing the tension level which turned on the red light they measured RT at various tensions. The results are shown in Figure 2-12. When the brow muscle tension fell to a low level, there were many very slow foot reactions and even some failures to respond, such as would land a sleepy truck driver in the ditch. The tracking scores also showed the same tendency to tail off to very poor values when the muscle tension was low. Other visual tasks showed more or less of the same tendency. It remains to be seen whether muscle tension in the brows would serve also in nonvisual tasks as an alertness indicator. (See Emotion III, pp. 173–179.)

Sensory and motor preparation. One who is ready to respond quickly to a certain stimulus by making a certain movement is necessarily prepared (a) to

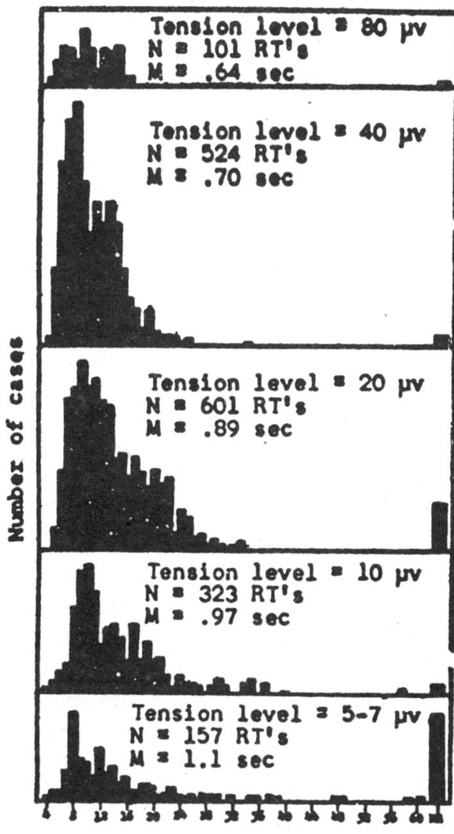

FIG. 2-12. (Kennedy & Travis, 1948.) Frequency distributions of reaction time at five levels of muscle tension. The levels are indicated in microvolts of muscle tension. NR at the right gives the count of failures to react.

receive that particular stimulus, (b) to make that particular movement, and (c) to make that movement on reception of that stimulus. There is sensory preparation, motor preparation, and what we may call a preparatory gearing of stimulus to response. The subject in a reaction time experiment ordinarily prepares about equally for the stimulus and for the response—a balanced preparation, we may say.

In Wundt's laboratory, quite early in the history of reaction time work, Ludwig Lange (1888) found it possible to train his subjects to unbalanced forms of preparation, either sensory or motor. They could concentrate their attention either on the stimulus to be received or on the response to be made. Sensory preparation gave slower reactions than motor preparation, about 100 ms slower in Lange's subjects, and the natural or balanced preparation gave an intermediate RT. Among later investigators, some have found no difference at all, but the results on the whole favor a real difference of variable amount, usually much less than Lange's 100 ms. It is not so important as was once believed to instruct the subject to adopt the sensory or the motor set, for he is not likely to follow such instructions consistently unless the experimental conditions favor one or the other type of preparation.

Some conditions do favor the motor set, other conditions the sensory set. The motor set is favored by strong emphasis on the quickest possible response, but if the subject becomes too eager, he will give some premature reactions; if he is then trapped by a catch test and warned, he will revert to a more balanced set. Long-continued practice favors the motor set, provided the stimulus is sufficiently strong and distinct. If the stimulus is so weak as to require careful listening or looking, the set is sensory and the RT is long (p. 24). The same applies for smell, taste, and pain stimuli which must be carefully distinguished from the accompanying touch stimuli (p. 17). Finally, the disjunctive reaction calls for a sensory set because different stimuli have to be distinguished in order to insure the appropriate responses.

The disjunctive reaction. When different responses to different stimuli are required, the task is an Either-Or affair—hence the name, "disjunctive reaction." Other common names are "discriminative reaction" and "choice reaction." There are two main types of disjunctive reaction, known since the time of Donders (1868) as the b-reaction and the c-reaction (the a-reaction being the ordinary simple reaction).

An example of the b-reaction: react to red with the right hand, to blue with the left hand.

An example of the c-reaction: react to red, but do not react to blue.

The disjunctive reaction takes more time than the simple RT, from 20 to 200 ms longer, with the b-reaction running a little slower than the c-reaction. In the b-reaction two motor responses are held in readiness, but neither of them can be allowed to reach "hair trigger" readiness if false reactions are to be avoided. In the c-reaction, too, motor readiness must be held down because the positive stimulus occurs in only part of the trials and must not be confused with the negative stimulus.

The disjunctive RT increases with the number of alternatives. The chief evidence for this statement is an old experiment of Merkel (1885), who used as stimuli the Arabic numerals 1 to 5, assigned in due order to the fingers of the right hand, and the Roman numerals I to V similarly assigned to the left hand. In any single series of trials two, three, or any number of these stimuli were used. The following table gives the average RT for nine subjects omitting one because, as pointed out by Wirth (1927) in an important critical review of reaction time work, this subject's exceptionally short times are invalidated by many false reactions.

Number of alternatives	*Reaction time*
1 (simple reaction)	187
2	316
3	364
4	434
5	487
6	532
7	570
8	603
9	619
10	622

The more alike the stimuli, the longer the disjunctive RT. Naturally, it takes more time to distinguish two stimuli that are very similar than two which differ greatly. Yet one would hardly predict that more time would be necessary for distinguishing red and yellow than for distinguishing red and green. One would expect the difference to be perceived "instantly" in either case. The question was put to an experimental test by Henmon (1906). The subject had two keys, one for each hand; he was shown two colors, one on the right and one on the left; he reacted with the hand on the same side as a designated color. When red and another color were shown, he reacted always to the red, with the right hand when red was on the right, with the left hand when it was on the left. This is a convenient form of the b-reaction. The following table gives the results from one of the subjects.

Stimuli to be distinguished	*Average reaction time (in ms)*	*P. E. of average (in ms)*
White and black	197	1.1
Red and green	203	1.2
Red and yellow	217	0.7
Red and orange	246	0.7
Red and (orange + 25% red)	252	0.8
Red and (orange + 50% red)	260	0.8
Red and (orange + 75% red)	271	0.8
Lines 10 and 13 mm long	296	0.9
" 10 " 12.5 "	298	0.8
" 10 " 12 "	305	0.8
" 10 " 11.5 "	313	0.9
" 10 " 11 "	324	1.0
" 10 " 10.5 "	345	1.0
Tones differing by 16 cycles	290	1.3
" " " 12 "	299	1.3
" " " 8 "	311	1.3
" " " 4 "	334	1.4

These stimulus differences, even the smallest of them, are well above the difference threshold, and few if any errors would be made in an experiment on perception of the differences. And yet the smaller differences require more time to see and use in governing a motor response. Besides Henmon's evidence for this important conclusion, we have similar findings from von Kries & Auerbach (1877) on the time required to distinguish directions of sound, and from Lemmon (1927) on the time required to distinguish a larger from a smaller number of lights (Fig. 2-13). This last experiment is quite similar to some usually classed under Span of Apprehension (p. 96); recent research has shown that RT is a valuable tool in this field, too.

Even in the field of esthetics a similar result has been found. Two colors were exposed side by side, and the subject reacted with the hand on the same side as the preferred color. The greater the difference in esthetic value of the two colors for the persons tested, the quicker was their choice reaction (Dashiell, 1937; Shipley *et al.*, 1945, 1946).

The false reactions. Reactions to the wrong stimulus are frequent when the two stimuli are hard to distinguish, as we see from the results cited in Figure 2-13. This in spite of the fact that the reaction is slowed down in the effort to avoid errors.

False reactions in the c-reaction were

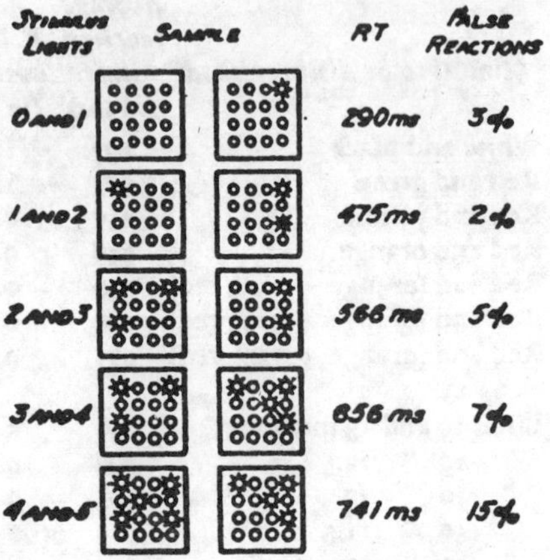

Stimulus Lights	Sample	RT	False Reactions
0 and 1		290 ms	3%
1 and 2		475 ms	2%
2 and 3		566 ms	5%
3 and 4		656 ms	7%
4 and 5		741 ms	15%

FIG. 2-13. (Lemmon, 1927.) Two square frames stood side by side, each containing 16 small light bulbs, in front of the subject. His task was to press a key beneath the frame that had the larger number of bulbs lighted on a given trial. Averages obtained from 113 college students, each making 40 reactions to each combination of stimuli, showed that the easiest discrimination, that between 0 and 1 lighted bulbs, took 290 ms, and that the RT became longer as the discrimination became harder. The errors increased in a similar fashion.

studied by E. J. Gibson (1939). Touch stimuli were applied to the subject's back by means of electrically driven vibrators. The four vibrators were placed four inches apart in a vertical line down the middle of the back. The subject was first familiarized with the feel of each vibrator. Then either the top or the bottom vibrator was designated as the positive stimulus, with instructions to respond to that one and not to any other. In the first 50 trials only the positive stimulus was given, and the subjects (18 college students) worked up to a fairly quick reaction. From that point on the negative stimuli were interspersed, about one negative to every four positive, but in random arrangement. False reactions now occurred, and the response was slowed down, from 170 to 233 ms on the average. The false reactions themselves were not slow; on the contrary they were quicker than the correct reactions. These false reactions, like the premature reactions in the simple RT experiment, doubtless occur at moments when the subject's motor readiness is too great and gets out of control. The false reactions were the more frequent, the nearer the negative vibrator was to the positive one; thus, the nearest one elicited a response 25 percent of the time, the next nearest 14 percent, the farthest only 9 percent of the time. This result is in line with those cited from the b-reaction experiments.

Parallels in other fields. There are interesting parallels between the standard disjunctive RT experiments and those usually classified under "conditioning" or "learning." For example, the c-reaction experiment of Gibson was almost a duplicate of one performed earlier by Bass and Hull (1934) except that they used the conditioned galvanic skin reaction instead of the manual reaction. Both experiments were planned to investigate the generalization gradient which has received much attention in learning theory and goes back to Pavlov's experiments with dogs (see p. 579). The generalization gradient of the conditioning experiment is the same as the similarity gradient of the c-reaction.

The parallel between the b-reaction and the discrimination box experiment comes out clearly in the report of Schlosberg & Solomon (1943). Their rats had been thoroughly trained in a black-white discrimination; with a black door and a white door to choose from they always choose the white one (and found food inside). Now a light gray door was occasionally substituted for the white one and was always chosen by the animals, the same with a medium and even with a dark gray substitute. Stimulus generalization was perfect, we might think, and yet a gradient appeared in the reaction times or "latencies" which were about as follows:

Doors to choose from	*Latency (in sec)*
White and black	4
Light gray and black	6
Medium gray and black	10
Dark gray and black	15

The slower reactions were preceded by obvious hesitation. The fact that these latencies were so much longer than human disjunctive reaction times does not tell us anything about the relative quickness of rats and men, for the conditions were very different. But the gradient has the same character.

Practice as a factor in reaction time. The simple reaction is so simple a task that we might expect a person to reach his maximum speed (his "irreducible minimum" RT) almost at once, or after a few tentative trials. Actually the average subject continues to improve for several hundred trials spaced out over several days, though the amount of improvement is certainly not large after the first 50 or 100 trials. Improvement of about 10 percent after the first day has been noted by different experimenters. Disjunctive reactions, especially the more complicated ones, have shown up to 30–40 percent improvement after the first day of practice. The same type of rational equation can be fitted to the practice curve here as previously (p. 22) to the intensity series. We can imagine, much as before, that each day's work overcomes a constant percent of the "delay factors" still remaining, and from that assumption we can derive the general form of the equation. The apparent limit or irreducible minimum must be understood in a relative sense, as holding for the given experimental conditions, for we have already seen that additional incentives may produce a further reduction of the RT even in well-practiced subjects (p. 28).

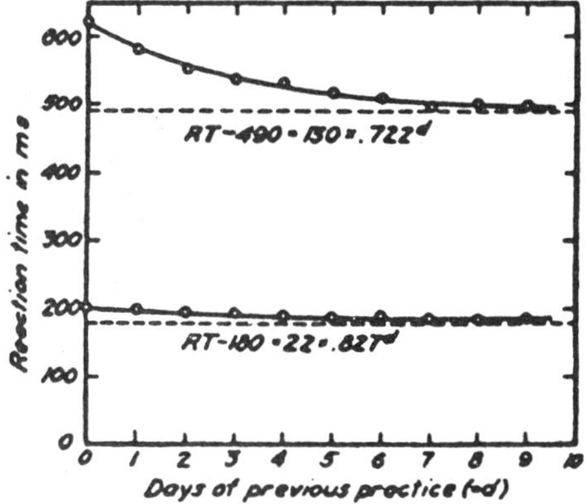

FIG. 2-14. (From G. Blank, 1934.) Practice curves in simple and disjunctive reaction time to visual stimuli. Lower curve for the simple RT to the lighting up of a small electric bulb. Upper curve for a disjunctive RT with five alternatives: there were five reaction keys numbered from 1 to 5; on any trial 1, 2, 3, 4 or 5 bulbs were lighted, and *O* responded by pressing the appropriate key. With 30 subjects, and 60 reactions per day from each subject, each data point gives the average of 1,800 reactions. The curves were calculated by the method previously explained under Figures 2-6 and 2-7 with the limit assumed to be 180 ms for the simple reaction, and 490 ms for the disjunctive, under the experimental conditions. Similar "growth functions" can be fitted to many other practice curves (pp. 534, 665).

Age as a factor in reaction time. Throughout the developmental period up to about 25 years of age the RT decreases, at first rapidly and then more slowly, following the same type of "growth function" as the practice curve (Fig. 2-15). The young child, with his

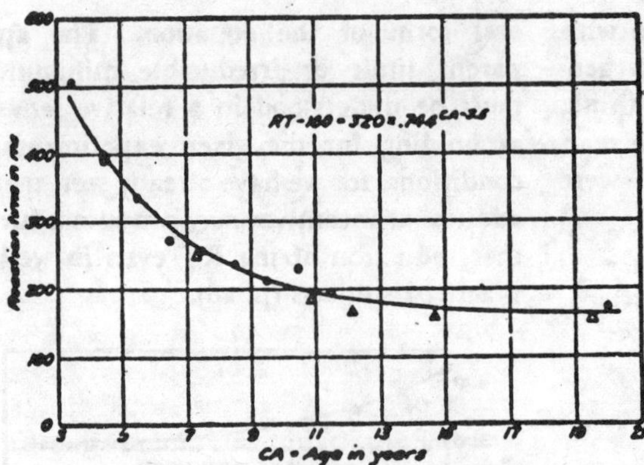

FIG. 2-15. (Data from Goodenough, 1935; Jones, 1937.) Reaction time during the developmental period. Simple reaction to an auditory stimulus. The two authors cited used very similar apparatus and procedure, with 20 reactions from each subject after about two preliminary trials. The triangles represent the Jones data, the circles the Goodenough data. The limit toward which the RT was verging was assumed to be 160 ms for a group average under the experimental conditions. Several other experimenters have obtained similar curves over shorter periods, for simple and disjunctive RT (Gilbert, 1894; Claparede, 1925; Philip, 1934; Goldfarb, 1941).

short nerve paths and general liveliness, might be expected to show a very short RT, especially since the reaction demanded is so "simple." As a matter of fact it is almost impossible to secure a good series of simple reactions from a child under three years of age. The young child's response is too diffuse and irregular to qualify as the highly integrated, though restricted act which we call the simple reaction (Luria, 1932; Goodenough, 1935). The more extreme delay factors of emotional excitement and general muscular tension are mostly outgrown by the age of seven or eight, but there is still some progress to be made before the adult level is reached.

When the adult level is reached it is maintained without much change up to the age of sixty, after which the RT begins to lengthen slowly (Fig. 2-16). This effect of old age is less marked in the RT than in many other tests of motor speed and agility, and it varies greatly from one individual to another, probably because some people age faster than others (Miles, 1942). One curious fact is that, age for age, boys and men have shorter RT than their female counterparts (Goodenough, 1935; Bellis, 1932–1933). Of some importance in the interpretation of these age curves is the fact that a similar curve is shown by the response time of rats to an electric shock. The latency of the response, 59 ms right after birth, decreased to 28 ms in the first three months and maintained this level till about two years of age, but in the next year increased again to 56 ms. The old-age effect could apparently not be attributed to endocrine factors and was more probably the result of changes in the nervous system (Brody, 1941).

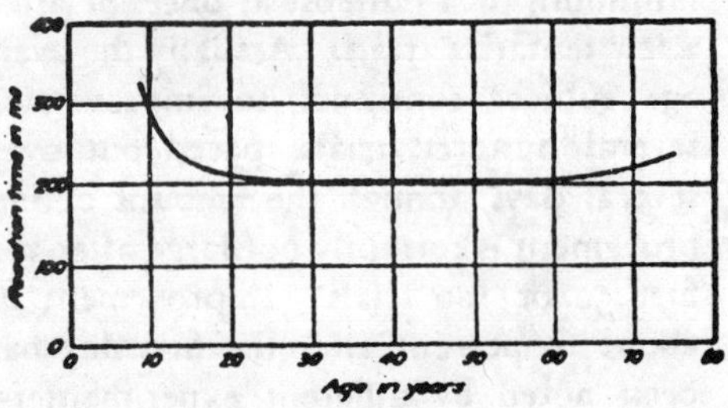

FIG. 2-16. (Data from Miles, 1942.) Reaction time through the life span. Simple reaction to sound. A similar curve was shown by the data of Bellis (1932–1933).

The factor of variability. Even holding all the experimental factors constant—modality and intensity of the stimulus, length of foreperiod, instructions to the subject and his age and previous practice—you still cannot predict what an individual's RT is going to be at a given time. There are *O*-variables which *E* cannot control. In the first place, individuals differ in RT as well as in all other respects. The distribution of means of unpracticed individuals in the simple RT appears from Figure 2-17 to be fairly symmetrical and "normal."

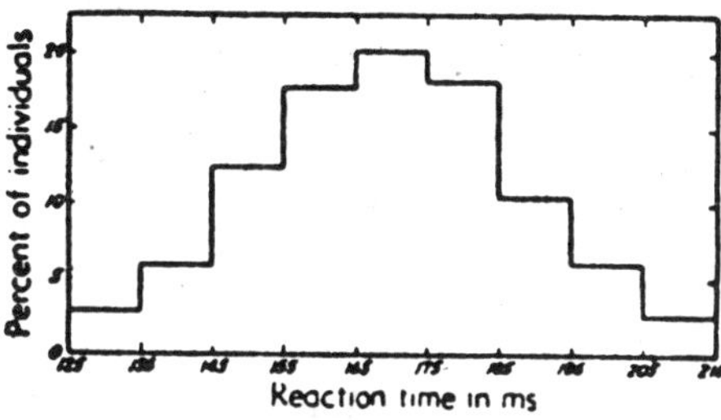

FIG. 2-17. (Data from Fessard, 1926.) Group distribution of simple RT to sound. The group consisted of 1,000 men, applicants in Paris for jobs as machinists. Each man gave 30 reactions, and the averages are plotted. Neither tail of the distribution curve is quite complete as a few extreme cases (3.5 percent of the total number) have been omitted from the graph.

With practice some improve more than others, and their positions in the distribution shift considerably, the correlation between the first few trials and the levels reached after 500 trials being practically zero (Blank, 1934). But even after prolonged practice individuals differ.

Would it be possible to predict an individual's RT from an examination of his physique? According to Smith & Boyarsky (1943) some prediction is possible. With 50 male college students as subjects, they obtained a height-weight index for each man (by dividing the height by the cube root of the weight) and measured his simple RT to a loud sound after a little practice. The men who were heavy for their height gave on the whole a slower response than those who were light for their height—145 as against 136 ms—but the correlation of only .28 is too low for any close prediction. These authors relate their finding to Sheldon's conception (1940) of endomorphic, mesomorphic, and ectomorphic factors in body build.

Perhaps no one has seriously attempted to use a person's general behavior as a basis for predicting his reaction time. The behavior of manic-depressive patients would lead you to expect a very long RT in the depressed state and a short one in the manic state, but tests have shown about the same rather long RT in both states (Wells & Kelley, 1922). The withdrawn attitude of schizophrenics might lead you to expect a slow reaction from them, and tests show that their RT is actually very long, averaging over half a second (Rodnick & Shakow, 1940).

Trial-by-trial variability. Not only do individuals differ; the same individual varies in his RT from day to day and even from moment to moment. This "behavioral oscillation," as Hull has named it (1942), is an over-all characteristic of the organism, not to be explained by any *single* factor. At the psychological level certain variable factors can be discerned. The subject's attention may wander; a fleeting emotion may disturb his adjustment; his sense organs may vary in sensitivity; his set may shift more or less to the sensory or motor side; his muscles may oscillate in their readiness for action (Tiffin & Westhafer, 1940).

Changes in body temperature, such as occur within a narrow range from hour to hour during the day, have been found to have an effect on the reaction time (Kleitman, Titelbaum & Feiveson, 1938). One well-practiced subject whose temperature and RT were measured many times at different hours had upward changes in body temperature accompanied by downward changes in RT in 95 out of 116 cases. When the body temperature was 97.5° F., the simple auditory RT averaged 137 ms: and when the body temperature was 98.9° F., the RT averaged 124 ms. There were similar changes in the simple visual RT, and larger changes in a disjunctive c-reaction (reacting to green and not to red), which was 290 ms at the lower temperature and 233 ms at the higher. The amount of change corresponds pretty well to what would be expected from the temperature coefficient of chemical processes, and suggests that the cerebral process in a reaction depends closely upon chemical activity.

A similar finding is that of van Biervliet (1894)—a quicker reaction when the individual's pulse rate is high than when it is low, though this was not true of all individuals. Strenuous muscular exercise, if not carried to the point of fatigue, might well decrease the RT, but Elbel (1940) could find very little of this effect when the exercise was mere exercise (push-ups and stool-stepping). He did, however, get the effect when the exercise consisted of sports such as boxing or basketball. He suggests, therefore, that the emotional stimulation of the competitive games, rather than mere muscular exercise, tends to speed up the reaction. Münnich (1940) tried out the effect of body position. He strapped the subject firmly to a chair. He then rotated the chair forward, backward, right or left into a horizontal position, and into an upside-down position, and took simple RT to sound in each position. The subjects found some of these positions awkward and uncomfortable, but their RT was very little affected. They seemed to compensate by extra effort for the unfavorable positions.

Anoxia resulting from actual or simulated ascent into rarefied air tends to lengthen the RT somewhat, though individuals acclimated to the high Andes make some physiological adjustment to the low oxygen and give as short RT as comparable individuals living near sea level (McFarland, 1937; Hahn, 1942). A more psychological compensation is shown by subjects tested during a rapid ascent, who overcome by extra effort the handicap of incipient anoxia, though this compensation fails them when the dearth of oxygen becomes extreme.

Drug effects are slight for ordinary doses. Caffein, which hastens a distinctively motor performance such as tapping, has little effect on RT (Schilling, 1921), though large doses hasten the disjunctive reaction (Hollingworth, 1912). With alcohol in moderate doses Kraepelin (1883) got a diphasic effect, a quicker reaction for a short time followed by slower reactions. With larger doses only the retardation phase appeared. When the degree of intoxication is measured by the alcohol content in the blood, the simple RT is found to be lengthened by 10 percent when the alcohol reaches .35 percent, and by 24 percent when the alcohol reaches the relatively high figure of 1.4 percent by volume of the blood (Straub, 1938).

No single one of these known physiological factors explains the moment-to-moment oscillation of the RT such as appears in a session of half an hour or even of a few minutes. The variability of a practiced subject at a single session, as measured by the SD of his reaction times, runs to about 10–13 percent of his Mean RT under the most favorable conditions (Chocholle, 1945; Steinman, 1944). When the stimulus is very weak, the SD may be much larger, and the distribution may be made quite skew by a scattering of very slow reactions. The SD and skewness are likely to be increased when the experiment extends over two days (Fig. 2-18) because the subject is improving and leaving behind for the most part his less efficient modes of response.

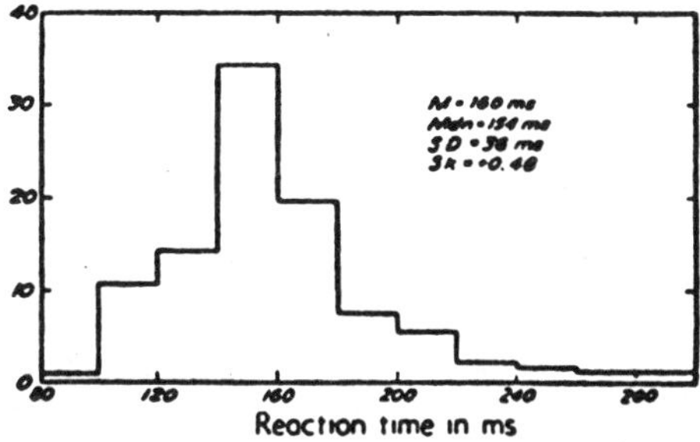

FIG. 2-18. (Data from Jenkins, 1926.) Distribution of one subject's simple RT to the cessation of a light. The 400 reactions were made on two days by a subject with some previous experience in RT work. M = Arithmetical Mean, Mdn = Median, SD = Standard Deviation of the distribution, Sk (a measure of Skewness) = 3(M − Mdn)/SD.

The form of an RT distribution. But even in homogeneous data we must expect the distribution of reaction times to be skewed. This would seem to follow from the analyses which we made earlier in the chapter, for the closer the reaction time approaches the minimum, the harder it is to shorten it further. The same sort of thing crops up over and over again when we deal with time as a measure of psychological processes; relative, rather than absolute, increments seem necessary to give constant effects. The easiest way to get relative units is to convert the time scores to logarithms (or use graph paper with a logarithmic ordinate, which has the same effect). This method will be illustrated in the chapter on Association; it is sufficient to point out here that the use of a logarithmic time scale will often correct the skewness of a distribution like that of Figure 2-18. Further, it often turns out that variability remains constant from session to session, or condition to condition, on such a scale. This results from the fact that the SD is apt to be a constant percentage of the Mean, and such relations show up as unit distances when the data are converted into logarithms.

Ideally, one should subtract the irreducible minimum from each RT before converting the remaining reducible margin to logs. This additional refinement is not always necessary to obtain fairly normal distributions. But it must be remembered that most statistical techniques are based on the assumption of a normal distribution of data. In this chapter we have been forced to base our analyses on Means from distributions which *may* be skewed; the tendency to publish Medians as well as Means is a relatively recent one. A Median has the advantage that it is always a specific (and typical) value; as such it can be converted to any desired type of scale, as a logarithmic one. On the other hand, the Mean is based on an assumed linearity of the scale originally used and is *not* convertible; the log of the Mean is not the same as the Mean of log scores, for example.

CORRELATIONS AND USES OF REACTION TIME

When we find two kinds of performance positively correlated, we know they must have something in common. The correlation method can thus add to our knowledge of the factors in reaction time. To go thoroughly into correlational analysis lies beyond the scope of this book. As between the various reaction times, substantial positive correlations have been found, varying in size in the different investigations

As between the simple RT to light, sound and touch, correlations ranging from + .43 to + .85 have been reported (Sisk, 1926; Lanier, 1934; Forbes, 1945). As between the simple and the disjunctive RT, the correlations have run a little lower, + .30 to + .70 (Lemmon, 1927; Lanier, 1934; Seashore *et al.*, 1941). On the whole, that is to say, an individual who reacts quickly to one stimulus reacts quickly to another. We may be tempted to conclude that the common factor is the finger movement which can be the same for all the stimuli. Let us then vary the movement while holding the stimulus constant, as was done by Seashore & Seashore (1941) with 50 college men as subjects. The subjects reacted to a sound, 50 times with each hand and each foot, and then 50 times more in a second round, all in a single session with some short rests interspersed. The average RT came out as follows:

Right hand	147 ms
Left hand	144
Right foot	174
Left foot	179

The two hands do not differ significantly, nor the two feet, but the feet are slower than the hands. The correlation between the hands was + .92; between the feet, + .93; between hand and foot somewhat lower, + .81. A biting movement also was tried; it gave fully as quick a reaction as the hands and correlated about + .85 with hand or foot. These correlations are high enough to demonstrate a good degree of individual consistency throughout the range of ordinary RT tests: the individual is a factor, as has been shown also by the method of factorial design (Baxter, 1942). There is a trait of reaction time quickness present in different degrees in different individuals. But we must not broaden this RT trait into a general speed trait, for the ordinary RT shows only very low correlations with many speed tests.

Aimed reactions. In the usual RT experiment the response movement has no other duty to perform except that of starting promptly. If the movement is required to follow a circular path, the RT becomes longer, and its correlation with the usual RT is much lowered (Pacaud, 1942). If the movement is aimed at a target, the RT is lengthened. In one experiment of this sort the aim was to reach just to a line located horizontally a certain distance to the right or left of the starting point. This line was in plain sight so that the subject could take aim in the foreperiod. The signal to move was the sound of a buzzer, but the average RT of 12 college men was 250 ms, definitely longer than the usual simple RT to an auditory stimulus (Brown & Slater-Hammel, 1949).

The experiment just described is a simplified version of "target tracking." When a gunner on a moving ship or plane is trying to keep his sights trained on a target, the target will be displaced from time to time and he will make a quick shift of his aim. His RT will be "disjunctive" since he does not know in advance the direction and extent of the displacement. A similar situation can be set up in the laboratory, one simple method being illustrated in Figure 2-19.

The RT in this experiment when all the displacements were in the same direction averaged about 250 ms; in other experiments when rightward and leftward displacements were interspersed, the RT was longer (Taylor & Birmingham, 1948). The primary shifting movement lasts less time than the RT—a fact of some importance as showing that this primary movement is a unit and *not* composed of two distinct reactions, a start toward the target and a braking reaction when the target is almost reached. If the braking response were separate, it would have its own RT, and there is not time enough for this RT during the movement. In this task the subject does not start out deliberately toward the target and stop

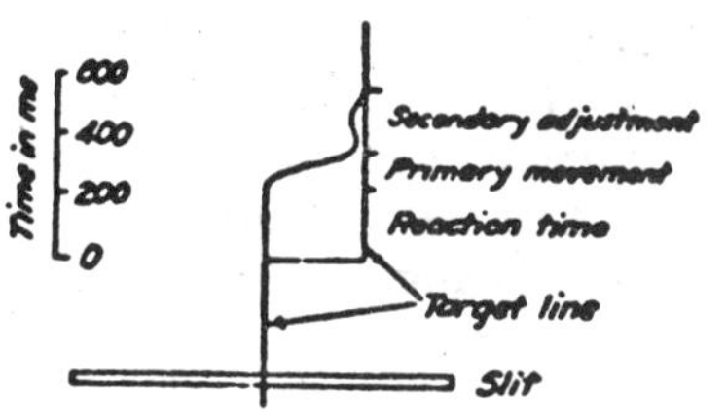

FIG. 2-19. (After Searle & Taylor, 1948.) Reaction time in target tracking. The target is a short stretch of line visible through a slit that extends at right angles to the line. The line is printed on a sheet of paper which is moved at a uniform speed (say 3 in per sec) at right angles to the slit and toward the subject who holds a pencil point on the exposed bit of the line. This target remains stationary as long as the line remains straight, but at a certain point the line jogs an inch to the right (for example), so displacing the target. The subject quickly moves his pencil point along the paper to the new position of the target, tracing his movement and RT on the paper. In the figure the solid line is the target line, the dotted line is the trace of the subject's response movement, and the time line at the left shows the speed at which the paper moves.

when he sees the target close at hand, but he throws into action an integrated motor pattern which will about reach the target. As he approaches the target and sees that he is going to miss, he throws in a corrective adjustment. The record shows that this correction must have been initiated while the primary movement was still in progress.

Serial reactions. Many variations of the tracking experiment are possible. The target may shift back and forth at irregular time intervals. When it shifts to the right and immediately back to the left, the first RT is about normal, but the second is much prolonged as if the organism were unable to take on the second target until the first movement was at least started on its way (Vince, 1948a). Again, let the subject be instructed to respond to a single auditory stimulus by pressing a key and immediately releasing it, the time being measured from the stimulus to the start of the pressing movement (the RT) and also from that point to the start of the release movement ("Ponzo's recovery time"): the RT and the recovery time are about equal, but the correlation between them is practically zero (Lahy, 1939).

These results suggest that the time required for a rapid series of responses to a series of stimuli will not depend wholly on RT. As a matter of fact, the correlation between the simple RT and such serial performances as tapping, cancelation, and color naming is not far from zero so that RT is evidently not a satisfactory index of an individual's speed of continued work. The speed of continuous work is often subject to large fluctuations which will be considered in the chapter on Attention (p. 81).

Applications. There are both scientific and practical applications. The RT method can be utilized in several parts of psychology. Short latency is an indication of strong response tendency or of freedom from conflicting tendencies. We have already noticed how RT can be used in the study of motivation, distraction, and discrimination. In psychophysics and other studies of perception it is often useful to time the responses (Cartwright, 1941a; Saltzman & Garner, 1948). Many problems in learning and memory can be attacked by this method, as well as by the more common measurement of the percent of correct responses; for learning continues even after all the responses are correct, the response latency still becoming shorter (Sackman, 1949).

Practical applications of the RT method are quite varied. The automobilist who must put on the brakes quickly takes an average of 450 ms, half of it being RT proper and the other half occupied with the foot movement across from the accelerator to the brake pedal. Braking time varies with the individual and with the conditions (Moede, 1933; DeSilva, 1938). The airplane pilot in landing has to focus his eyes alternately on the landing strip and on his instrument panel; the RT of this ocular adjustment varies with the individual about a mean of 200 ms (Travis, 1948). There are applications to athletics, as in the start of a race or of a football play (Miles, 1931b). In everyday life serial reaction is more common than the simple and disjunctive reactions of the laboratory, yet these occur whenever any sort of emergency, major or minor, calls for prompt response.

3

ASSOCIATION

In the preceding chapter it was shown that the reaction time method can be applied to a wide range of psychological processes. If the method is extended to include the use of words as both stimuli and responses, it becomes one form of the association experiment. This experiment may be traced back to the British School of Association Psychologists, who were the first group to attempt a serious approach to the psychology of learning.

HISTORICAL BACKGROUND

Even in the works of the ancient Greek philosophers some attention was paid to the sequence of ideas in a train of thought. Aristotle in particular pointed out that one idea would be followed by another which was similar or contrasting, or which had been present together with it in one's past experience. These three—Similarity, Contrast, and Contiguity in space or time—came later to be regarded as the primary "Laws of Association." As Warren shows in his *History of the association psychology* (1921), it was not until the eighteenth and nineteenth centuries that the subject was fully exploited. During these two centuries a long line of British philosophers conceived of association as the basic mechanism of the mind. As empiricists, they attempted to explain all mental life in terms of past experience. Their theories varied in many details, but the general picture that emerged can be outlined rather briefly. The source of all knowledge is Sensation produced by the impact of the outside world. The sensations, and their weaker copies, Images or Ideas, are hooked together by the automatic process of Association. The associationists attempted to work out the necessary details so as to explain even the most complex processes of thinking. It must be emphasized that all this was "armchair psychology," based on careful scrutiny by each philosopher of his own experience, and not verified by any laboratory experiments. Nevertheless, these able men developed a surprisingly consistent and detailed system which has had a profound effect on our present psychology.

Without devoting much space in a book entitled "Experimental Psychology" to a system erected without the aid of controlled observation, we should notice that the Association Psychology developed certain principles that were later found applicable in the modern learning experiments. Perhaps these principles were stated most clearly by Thomas Brown (1820). Instead of the term *association*, which was first introduced by John Locke (1700), Brown used *sugges-*

tion, but the laws are the same, whatever the name employed. Brown wished to avoid the pseudophysiological implications that *association* held for his contemporaries; like some modern psychologists he wanted a psychology which should be independent of physiology.

Brown maintained that there were three primary laws, which were Aristotle's *similarity, contrast*, and *nearness in time and space*. In addition he formulated several secondary laws. The first three of these—(1) *duration*, (2) *liveliness* (often called vividness), and (3) *frequency*—obviously refer to the previous experiences in which ideas have become associated by contiguity. They are thus laws of learning, whereas (4) *recency* is a law of forgetting. (5) *Freedom from competing associations* is a law that has often been neglected, but we shall see in later chapters that the existence of alternative possible responses must be considered in every learning experiment. The other laws or factors—(6) *constitutional differences between individuals*, (7) *emotional variations in the same individual* from time to time, (8) *temporary states* of health, etc., and (9) *prior habits of life and thought*—have quite a modern ring and would lend themselves to experimental investigation.

First experiments. It is strange, or so it seems to us today, that the associationists failed to see that experimental work would be useful for testing and developing their system. The nineteenth century was well advanced before any experiments were undertaken along the line of association and memory. It remained for Francis Galton (1879–1880) to begin experimenting. He prepared 75 stimulus words (mostly nouns), wrote each on a separate slip of paper and laid them away for several days. He then took one slip at a time and laid it "under a book, but not wholly covered by it, so that when I leant forward I could see one of the words, being previously quite ignorant of what the word would be." He started a stop watch at the instant when the word caught his eye and stopped it when the word had suggested two different ideas. He immediately reviewed these two ideas and sought in memory for their origins and the connection of each with the stimulus word. He went through his list of stimulus words four times at intervals of about a month, and on assembling his data found that he had revived 505 ideas in a total of 660 sec, or at the rate of one recall per 1.3 sec. These 505 recalled ideas were, however, not all different, since 57 had come up twice, 36 three times, and 29 four times in the four presentations of the stimulus words. Those which recurred several times dated largely from his boyhood and youth, while those that came up only once were apt to date from adult life and sometimes from quite recent events. He was able to classify the revived "ideas" as follows:

	Percent
Visual and other images of past scenes or events	32.5
"Histrionic representations," acting out an event or an attitude such as that of "abasement"	22.5
Purely verbal: names, phrases, quotations	45.

Galton found this experiment laborious but illuminating. "It would be very instructive to print the actual records at length, made by many experimenters . . . but it would be too absurd to print one's own singly. They lay bare the foundations of a man's thoughts with a curious distinctness, and exhibit his mental anatomy with more vividness and truth than he would probably care to publish to the world."

Galton was a scientist with strong quantitative leanings, and it will be noted that in this study he introduced three ways of treating association data quantitatively: (1) the associative reaction time, (2) the frequency of repetition of the same associative response, and (3) a classification of the responses with a count of the number falling in each class. These measures have been much used by later experimenters.

Galton's lead was promptly followed in Wundt's pioneer psychological laboratory, established at Leipzig in 1879. There Trautscholdt in 1883 introduced the technical improvement of providing an experimenter to announce the stimulus words and take the time; and Cattell (1886a, b; 1887) designed a voice key so as to obtain a chronoscope reading of the reaction time, the subject's response being spoken into the voice key. Cattell and Bryant (1889) simplified the setup by using a *list* of stimulus words, exposed visually, with time for the whole series of say ten responses measured by a stop watch. Galton's study was concerned with "free association"; Trautscholdt and Cattell extended the experiment to include various forms of "controlled association." In free association *O* is free to give any response suggested by the stimulus word, while in controlled association he is restricted to some specified type of response, such as the opposite of the stimulus word.

It is clear that these experiments are concerned with previously formed associations, not with the formation of new associations. Such experiments, including many that will be reviewed later in the chapter, have furnished considerable information on the operation of associations in memory and thinking, but they have done very little to advance our knowledge of the actual process of the formation of linkages between words or other items. There are two very good reasons for this failure.

Limitations of the association experiment. In the first place, the associations have been established somehow in *O*'s past experience, and the present experiment does not show how they were formed. When *O* responds to the stimulus word "Table" by saying "Chair," common sense would tell us that he has often seen chairs and tables together, and we can rephrase this statement in technical terms like contiguity and frequency. But we can go no further from the experimental data. From the standpoint of anyone who wishes to understand the process of learning, we are starting at the wrong end when we use the association experiment. A much better lead for the purpose was provided by the memory experiment of Ebbinghaus (1885). He had *O* learn *new material* and then attempt to recall it. In the memory experiment, and in other experiments directly concerned with learning, *E* can deliberately vary such conditions as contiguity, frequency, recency, etc., and trace their effects on the actual formation of associations. In later chapters we shall see that the memory and learning experiments have furnished a lot of valuable information on the relative importance of the factors or "laws" that were discerned by the association psychologists.

A second limitation of the association experiment is its predominantly verbal character. The stimuli are usually words, though they can be objects or pictures, and *O*'s responses are quite certain to be words. Now presumably the primary association between chair and table was between the objects, not between these words. Each object having also been associated with its name, the actual process now, in the experiment, may very well be: Name A–Object A–Object B–Name B. In other cases an association has been directly established between two words, as in the example, "Black–Board," a purely verbal association. The experimental data do not distinguish verbal from meaningful associations. The old standard expression, "association of ideas," referred primarily to the familiar cases where thinking of one thing immediately makes you think of another. Unfortunately, ideas do not lend themselves to precise experimental control and measurement—reaction time measurement, for example. When we get away from ideas to definite stimuli and motor responses, we have some chance of designing experiments that are instructive within the unavoidable limitations.

Association experiments are usually designed to yield quantitative results. This modern tendency (really as old as Galton's time) is brought out by Robinson in his book, *Association theory today* (1932), and also by Hilgard in his *Theories of learning* (1948). The "laws of association" attempt to identify the factors that make one association stronger and more usable than another. Such a factor as similarity is evidently a matter of more or less, a quantitative matter, and the same is true of frequency and recency and even of contiguity itself, usually regarded as the most fundamental of all the laws. It must be left to experiment to work out the exact relationships between similarity, frequency, and recency, on the one hand, and the effective strength of associations, on the other.

METHODS USED IN THE ASSOCIATION EXPERIMENT

Before we examine the various experiments in detail, it will be well to outline the basic methods employed. There is free versus controlled association, and there is also discrete versus continuous association. Combining these two dimensions we have a fourfold classification.

Discrete free association. *O* is instructed to respond with the first word that occurs to him as soon as *E* presents a stimulus word. *E* may present the stimulus word either orally or visually; *O* responds orally, and E records the response word in writing. *E* also measures the associative reaction time, either with a stop watch or, better, with a chronoscope. The chronoscope may be started and stopped by the aid of ingenious voice or lip keys. This refinement does not always increase the accuracy of measurement, for the voice key may not be tripped off until the accented syllable of the response word is reached, and the lip key may be actuated by *O*'s preliminary opening of his mouth. Further, some *O*s cannot avoid saying "Uh–Red," for example, so stopping the chronoscope before the true response word is spoken. Perhaps the most reliable procedure is to leave the timing wholly in *E*'s hands. Provide him with a single snap switch or key, and let him practice closing the key just as he speaks the stimulus word and opening it again as soon as *O* starts to speak the response word. To be sure, the measured time thus includes *O*'s associative RT plus *E*'s simple RT, but this last is relatively short and constant and can be eliminated by subtraction if necessary (Schlosberg & Heineman, 1950).

Discrete controlled association. This method differs from the first one only in the instructions given to *O*. He is told to respond in some specific way, as by giving the opposite of the stimulus word, or by naming a part of the object indicated by the stimulus word. This task is assigned in advance, so that *O* is prepared to make the assigned kind of response to any stimulus word that may come.

Although it is convenient to distinguish between free and controlled association, the difference is only one of degree. There is some control in the "free" situation, for *O* responds by single words instead of by sentences as he would in free conversation, and usually he takes care to give polite words that will not betray his private affairs. Koffka (1912) found it almost impossible to get his subjects to take a really passive attitude, free from any kind of set or involuntary control. And there is often some freedom in the "controlled" situation, for the assigned task may not restrict *O* to a single correct response to each stimulus word. An "opposites" test is highly restricted, but a 'whole-part" test much less so. The degree of restriction can be made an experimental variable so as to discover the effects of control on the speed of response.

Continuous free association. Here *E* presents a stimulus word, and *O* responds with a series of single words, usually as rapidly as possible. *O* is asked not to make an inventory of objects in the room or to use any such scheme, but to let each word that he speaks suggest the next in order. An example would be "Dog–cat–horse–buggy–wheel–tire–rubber–eraser–etc." There is always the question whether each word is solely determined by the next preceding word; both "dog" and "cat" may have contributed to the response "horse," but the latter word was probably responsible for "buggy."

A chain of 5 or 10 words may be timed with a stop watch, or the chain may be allowed to continue for a certain length of time, while *E* counts the responses. Sometimes *O* has been asked to write his responses, but writing slows the process badly; even speech may lag behind the speed of association. The difficulty has sometimes been avoided by having *O* make a tally mark or press a key every time he thinks of a word; this method gives the *speed* of association but not the *content* (except that *O* can usually recall the words immediately afterward). Bousfield and Sedgewick (1944) used a key which plots its own cumulative curve showing the speed throughout the series of responses, as shown later in this chapter (p. 59). Modern electronic recording devices offer interesting possibilities (Verzeano and Finesinger, 1949).

Continuous controlled association. The method is similar to continuous free association, except that *O* is instructed to limit his associations in some fashion. Often the control is combined with the stimulus word, as, "Name words associated with—*skating*." The stop watch should be started on the stimulus word, *skating*.

As far as timing is concerned, these continuous methods are the same as the "list method" mentioned on p. 45, the difference being that in the continuous methods *O* goes on and on from a single stimulus word, while in the list method he has a series of stimulus words before him and responds to each word separately in rapid succession. The list method thus belongs under the head of discrete association.

CONCEPTUAL FRAMEWORK

The results of the numerous association experiments would be just so many unrelated bits of information without the aid of appropriate concepts to organize them into a system. Since we have to do with certain responses to certain stimuli, we can use the same general formula that served us very well in reaction time: RT = f(S, *O*). The simple RT depended, as we saw, upon S-variables such as intensity and upon *O*-variables such as preparatory set. The associative reaction depends upon the stimulus, of course, and we have just seen that it also depends upon preparatory set or control. This control factor is governed largely by the instructions and so is made to differ in free and controlled association and from one task to another in different forms of controlled association. Thus it is entitled to rank as an experimental variable. Another *O*-variable, which is surely important, consists of the previously formed associations, direct and indirect, between any stimulus word and the possible response words. There are several other *O*-variables such as the last four listed by Thomas Brown (p. 44), but in most experiments these are supposed to be held constant. If we let Asn stand for the factor of associations previously formed, and P for the factor of preparatory set, our problem is the working out of the schematic formula,

$$RT = f(S, Asn, P, \ldots)$$

In Clark Hull's more general schematic formula (1943, 1951) which attempts to include all the factors that determine a learned response, the letter H (for habit strength) corresponds to our Asn, and the letter D (for drive) corresponds in a way to our set factor P. The drives Hull has in mind are such as hunger, thirst, sex, and escape from pain. These strong primitive drives may be of interest in certain practical applications of the association experiment (see pp. 66–70), but in the laboratory motivation is usually much less "primitive" since it depends on the instructions and on the subject's willingness to cooperate by getting set to respond quickly, or to name objects, or give the opposite of every stimulus word.

In an association experiment S and P are experimental variables, as we have seen; but how about Asn? The H in a learning experiment is more or less under the control of the experimenter, who can vary the frequency, recency, etc., of the subject's opportunities to form an association previous to the recall test. But in an association experiment previous learning is not controlled so that Asn is not an experimental variable. It is not controlled by the experimenter. But he may be able to *infer* the strength of associations from the results of the experiment. If a certain stimulus elicits a certain response quickly and frequently, the association between them must be strong. From the R-variables of frequency and speed an inference can be drawn regarding associative strength, but only if the factor of preparatory set is held constant. Thus, if we wish to know whether the association, "New–Old," is stronger than the association, "Wise–Foolish," we may include both stimulus words in an opposites test, or both in a free association test, but not one word in one and the other word in the other kind of test; we must keep the P factor the same.

Indicators of associative strength. In a typical instance of discrete free association, *E* gives a stimulus word and notes the response that *O* makes, and also his reaction time. From this and other comparable instances *E* draws certain inferences regarding the strength of the associative connection between the two words. On what indicators can such an inference be based?

The associative reaction time. It is assumed that the quicker the reaction, the stronger is the associative connection. This assumption has a sort of "face validity," which simply means that it is reasonable. It is also supported by the fact that in learning a new pair of associates the RT diminishes as the learning progresses. There is a complication, however. Any stimulus word is capable of eliciting a number of different response words, though *O* usually makes only a single response. There must be some internal process of "inhibition" or "interference" which enables one response to block all others. And the interference may well be reciprocal; that is, the unsuccessful competing response words would tend to block and retard the word which finally occurs. Therefore, we may say, the associative RT indicates "net" or relative, rather than absolute associative strength. There is one further source of delay: the connection from the stimulus word to the response may not be direct but may involve intermediate words that do not get spoken. These complications, however, do not destroy the value of the RT as an indicator of associative strength.

Response frequency, commonness, communality. A second indicator is the frequency with which a particular response is made to a certain stimulus. (This is a different "freqnency" from the one that appears in the laws of association.) Let the stimulus word be "Cat," and the response "Dog" in 8 out of 10 trials, but "Mouse" on the other two. Inference: in this *O*, the former association is the stronger. Unfortunately the 10 trials would have to be spaced out over several weeks or months to prevent *O* from simply remembering his previous response. In this predicament *E* has recourse to a device often employed in psychological experiments. He tests 10 or more persons with the same stimulus word and treats the group as a unit. If 8 out of 10 *O*s give the "Cat–Dog" response, the indication is that that association is strong for the group as a whole. This method is valid only if the group is composed of fairly comparable individuals in respect to age and previous opportunity to form the associations in question.

To summarize, the process of responding with one word to another is not as simple as it seems at first glance. Fortunately it can be outlined rather briefly: The stimulus word, through past experience, has become associated with many different response words and is capable of eliciting any of them. When the stimulus word is presented, the potential responses compete among themselves, and the strongest connection wins and governs the overt response. The frequency and speed with which a response wins out vary directly with the response's own strength, and inversely with the strength of its competitors. But the set for a specific kind of response can exercise a decisive influence. In the remainder of the chapter we shall see how this picture is filled in by the many researches that have used the association method.

The *experimental results* fall rather

definitely under four main heads which we shall take up in this order: frequency or commonness of different responses; classification of associations; associative reaction time; practical applications such as clinical and detective.

FREQUENCY OR COMMONNESS OF DIFFERENT RESPONSES TO THE SAME STIMULUS WORD

As soon as the free association experiment was tried extensively (Cattell & Bryant, 1889), it became clear that any familiar stimulus word elicited the same response from many individuals, though not from all, and that the relative frequency of different responses to the same word was a matter of interest and called for explanation. The study of Thumb & Marbe (1901) in Germany was an early landmark. They used as stimulus words nouns of family relationship (as *father, cousin*), adjectives having familiar opposites, pronouns, verbs, adverbs (such as *here* and *now*), and the number words 1–10. These were all arranged in mixed order and presented orally for oral response. When eight *O*s had been examined, it was found that nearly every stimulus word had its favorite response. To *father* (in German) the most frequent response was *mother;* to *yesterday* the most frequent was *today*. To each of the first nine numbers the common response was the next larger number; to the adjectives used the most common was the adjective of opposite meaning. Using this same list of words in a class experiment, *E* could make a hit by predicting (after the response words had been written down by the individual students but before they were reported) the most common response to each stimulus word. For such prediction to succeed the groups tested must be fair samples of the same population. Esper (1918) demonstrated that the same experiment would succeed in America as well as Germany.

The Kent-Rosanoff frequency tables. In the hope of providing a basis for the use of free association in discovering individual peculiarities, especially of an abnormal sort, Kent & Rosanoff (1910) selected a list of 100 familiar English nouns and adjectives, though a few could be taken as verbs, and gave them orally to each of 1,000 normal subjects, mostly adult men and women of varying education and occupation. The subject was seated with his back to the experimenter and requested to respond to each stimulus word by one word only, "the first word that occurs to you other than the stimulus word." If *O* responded with a phrase or by repeating the stimulus word or some grammatical variant of it, that stimulus word was given again at the end of the list. Assembling the results from the thousand *O*s, the authors prepared a table of all the responses to each stimulus word, with the frequency of each response. The responses to one stimulus word, needle, are shown in the following table.

There is a similar table for each stimulus word. Three ways have been used for obtaining the individual's score.

1. Simply count the number of "individual reactions," defined as reactions having a frequency of zero in the tables. Some variants of form or meaning should be counted as equivalent to those actually found in the table, and rules are provided for scoring these doubtful cases. Normal persons with only common-school education have given an average of 5.2 individual reactions for the list of

Stimulus word: NEEDLE

Frequency in 1,000 subjects	*Response word*
160	thread
158	pin(s)
152	sharp
135	sew(s)
107	sewing
53	steel
40	point
26	instrument
17	eye
15	thimble
12	useful
11	prick(s)
9	pointed
7	cotton
6	work
5	implement
5	tool
4	cloth
4	darning
4	knitting
4	sharpness
3	article
3	fine
3	metal
2 each	books, button(s), clothes, coat, dressmaker, hurt, hypodermic, industry, pricking, small, sting, thick, thin,
1 each	blood, broken, camel, crocheting, cut, diligence, embroidery, handy, help, hole, home, housewife, labor, long, magnetic, material, mending, nail, ornament, patching, pincushion, shiny, slippers, stitching, surgeon, tailor, use, using, weapon, wire, woman
1,000	

100 stimulus words, while college-educated subjects, perhaps because of their larger vocabulary, have averaged somewhat more, 9.3 individual reactions. But some dementia precox patients, whose responses appear incoherent and unrelated to the respective stimulus words, give 25–50 percent of individual reactions.

2. Count the number of high frequency responses given by the individual. This is nearly the reverse of the preceding.

3. The most comprehensive measure would seem to be the median frequency value of the individual's responses. This measure shows with how large a fraction of the population the individual's free associations tend to agree on the whole. If this median value is high, the individual runs to common responses, if low, he runs to unusual responses (which may be extra high grade, eccentric, or incoherent).

Other association frequency tables. There are good reasons for repeating the Kent-Rosanoff experiment with the same stimulus words, but with other groups or "populations." The individual can be fairly compared only with his own population—a college freshman with a frequency table derived from college freshmen. Schellenberg (1930) collected a set of norms from 929 entering students at the University of Minnesota, which may be found in Tinker & Baker (1938, pp. 213–214) in abridged form. Woodrow & Lowell (1916) prepared frequency tables of the responses of 1,000 Minneapolis school children, aged 9–12 to 100 stimulus words, 90 of which were taken from the Kent-Rosanoff list. The children were tested in groups and wrote their responses to the orally presented stimuli. O'Connor (1928) used the Kent-Rosanoff stimulus words and obtained oral responses from 1,000 adult men, mostly in industry. So there are four large samples to compare: children, men and women representing the general adult population (in 1910), men in industry, and college freshmen. When the four frequency tables are compared, some striking differences come to light. For example, children very seldom give opposites while adults do so very frequently. As these group differences have to do with the classification of associative responses, we shall consider them under that head (p. 54). And the value of frequency of response as an indicator of associative strength will be taken up along with that other indicator, reaction time.

CLASSIFICATION OF ASSOCIATIONS

If you examine the responses given to a stimulus word, such as those listed on p. 51, almost all of them seem sensible enough. Many of them could be attributed to association by similarity or by contrast, and perhaps all of them to association by contiguity. More definite relations can be seen, the response being coordinate with the stimulus word in the example, *needle–pin;* supraordinate in *needle–instrument;* subordinate in *needle–darning;* and there are whole-part, object-quality, and several other relations. Since the early days of the association experiment, responses have been grouped, sometimes into as many as fifteen classes, sometimes into as few as five, according to the use to be made of the classification. The hoped-for use was often clinical; an individual's intellectual and emotional peculiarities might be revealed by the nature of his free associations. Some individuals give a great many responses of an emotional or at least evaluating sort, such as *needle–hurt;* and this tendency may have clinical significance. Some *O*s seem impelled to define the stimulus words or at least show that they know them, as if in a vocabulary test.

Meaning relations of stimulus and response. In the first edition of this book (see p. 352 for a relatively full treatment of the different systems of classification), the following four classes were suggested as about all that would be needed for most experiments:

1. Definition, including synonyms and supraordinates.
2. Completion and predication.
3. Coordinates and contrasts.
4. Valuations and personal associations.

Class 1 might be called the "arriving" response, Class 2 the "staying-by" response, and Class 3 the "jumping-away" response; these three being matter-of-fact in distinction from the more emotional and personal responses of Class 4. Examples from the responses to *needle:*

Class 1: *instrument, implement, tool, article,* and perhaps *sewing.*
Class 2: *sharp, steel, point, eye, work.*
Class 3: *thread, pin, thimble, cotton, cloth.*
Class 4: *hurt, pricking, sting, blood.* and perhaps *useful.*

The distinction between Classes 2 and 3 was suggested by Murphy (1923) who noted the difference between "carrying out an idea" and "adding a new idea."

Some objection might be raised to Class 3 as a combination of both similars and contrasts. But opposites are really coordinates; *up* and *down* are vertical directions; *past* and *future* are times; *wise* and *foolish* are intellectual levels. If stimulus words like *man* and *hand* are included in an opposites test, coordinate responses such as *woman* and *foot* are given without objection. But the best reason for placing opposites and coordinates in the same class is that the two sorts behave alike. An individual who gives very few opposites in a free association test is likely to give very few coordinates. The correlation between the number of opposites and the number of coordinates has ranged from +.42 to +.90 in various samples (Conrad & Harris, 1931; Crosland, 1929; Kelley, 1913; Murphy, 1921; O'Connor, 1934).

One important question regarding any such classificatory scheme is whether it can be used consistently. We have no evidence on this question as referring to the four classes just suggested. A somewhat similar scheme which seems to be very satisfactory for use with college students has been devised and tested out by Karwoski & Berthold (1945) and Karwoski & Schachter (1948). They report that 90 percent of the responses of a group of college students can be classified, and that two competent judges will disagree in only about 20 percent of the responses. This may strike the reader as rather unsatisfactory, but there is serious reason to doubt that *any* classification would yield better agreement, without the aid of extensive explanations from each *O* as to just why he made each response. This classification is quoted here from the 1948 paper just mentioned.

1. General Identification

a. Essential similarity. Ex. large-big, say-speak, story-tale. The sense of the response word is the same as the stimulus word.

b. Functional identification. Ex. chicken-egg, lawyer-case, girl-dress. The sense of the response word is different from the stimulus word, but they are related functionally in terms of an essential operation.

c. General identification. Ex. cabbage-vegetable, dark-color, kill-destroy. The response makes a generalization about the stimulus word. The meaning of the stimulus word is always included in the meaning of the response word, but the meaning of the response word always contains other meanings than the stimulus word.

2. Specific Identification

Ex. ocean-Pacific, friend-Tom, round-sphere. The response word is one of several words that fall within the class of words defined by the stimulus word.

3. Contingent Relation

Ex. breakfast-table, lake-boat, hill-ski. These are words that do not necessarily imply or include each other, but are commonly related in experience as characterizing the same object or act.

4. Essential Contrast or Opposition

Ex. black-white, up-down, love-hate. The sense of the stimulus word is directly opposed to the sense of the response word.

This scheme and the other one presented cannot be fitted together completely, but 1 *a* and *c* would be definitions, and 4 would be contrasts. Apparently there is no place for coordinates, but in accordance with the previous argument they might well be put with the contrasts.

A scale of superficiality of response. In many situations—especially clinical ones—it is useful to know whether *O* is making quick, superficial associations, or is letting himself become emotionally involved in the situation. For such purposes, as well as for the analysis of certain theoretical problems, it is necessary to use a scale of superficiality of responses, that cuts across the classifications given above.

1. Most meaningful: the stimulus word calls up a particular experience.
2. The stimulus word calls up a particular object, though not a particular experience of it.
3. The stimulus word calls up a meaningful associate without any help from speech habit or purely verbal association.
4. The stimulus word calls up a familiar verbal associate, as in phrase completion or word compounding.
5. Mere clang association: the most superficial response.

Ziehen (1898, 1900) by retesting the same boys at intervals from ages 9 to 14, found that the type of response tended to become more superficial with increasing age. Recall of particular experiences decreased from 24 percent of all responses to 11 percent, and responses involving the recall of particular objects (including steps 1 and 2) decreased from 82 percent to 14 percent.

Jung (1919) finds that some educated adults tend to superficial responses, especially of step 4. They conceive the experiment "entirely as a verbal one; they endeavor by maintaining a ready speech-excitation to affix the first word that comes up, without entering more closely into the meaning of the stimulus word." Less educated *Os* are more inclined to say something meaningful about the object named in the stimulus word, regarding it as a question or challenge to show their knowledge. Jung found that the distraction of making pencil marks in time with a metronome, at 60 strokes per minute, tended to make the responses more superficial. The responses become more superficial also in fatigue (Aschaffenburg, 1897), under the influence of alcohol (Kraepelin, 1892; Smith, 1922), and with practice in the free association experiment (Wells, 1911a; Wreschner, 1907–1909).

Group differences in associations. Returning now to the Kent-Rosanoff list (pp. 50–52), we ask first whether the *most frequent responses* are the same with the different groups, and we find many striking and curious shifts, a few of them being shown in the list at the bottom of the page.

Very few children give the opposite of *dark* or *soft*, while more than half of the "men in industry" do so. (Why the men in industry should show the adult type of response more decisively than the men and women can only be guessed in the absence of definite information on the make-up of the two samples.) A similar shift appears in the *coordinate* responses: table–chair, man–woman, and mountain–hill. The children tend to "stay by" the thing mentioned; they tell something about that thing, complete or enlarge upon the idea conveyed by the stimulus word; whereas the adults jump to a related, parallel idea. This difference is typical, though naturally not holding of every individual or of every response of any individual.

To show that the shift to opposites is

Stimulus	*Response*	*1,000 Children*	*1,000 Men and women*	*1,000 Men in industry*
TABLE	eat	358	63	40
	chair	24	274	333
DARK	night	421	221	162
	light	38	427	626
MAN	work	168	17	8
	woman	8	394	561
DEEP	hole	257	32	20
	shallow	6	180	296
SOFT	pillow	138	53	42
	hard	27	365	548
MOUNTAIN	high	390	246	171
	hill	91	184	364

characteristic of the adults, we examine the 20 adjectives contained in the whole list which have familiar opposites, and we find the average frequency of response by naming an opposite to be:

For the children	43
For the men and women	298
For the men in industry	473

To show the shift to coordinates, we may examine first the responses to the six color names included in the list: black, white, red, yellow, green, blue.

Response	*1,000 Children*	*1,000 Men and women*	*1,000 Men in industry*
some colored object	530	348	243
the word "color"	232	218	208
another color	33	291	414

Such a response as "red-blue" was very uncommon in the children, but common in the adults. The table at the bottom of the page contains other examples of the shift to coordinates.

The great frequency of coordinate and contrast responses in adults is not to be interpreted as indicative of a strong tendency to think in these terms. The experiment as usually carried out is distinctly an experiment with words. When, instead of color names, actual bits of color were shown to college students (Dorcus, 1932) with instructions to write the first word thought of other than the name of the color itself, the response words were mostly names of colored objects, and very few coordinate colors were named. We are not to suppose that seeing a color commonly leads the adult to think of another color, but only that one color *name* tends to suggest another color name when the task is to give word responses. More in general, the frequency of opposites and coordinates in the responses of adults need not mean that "association by contrast" or by coordination is specially characteristic of adult thinking; for, again, the experiment is bound up with the use of words.

The tendency of the children as a group to "stay by" the stimulus word (and its meaning), and the adult tendency to "jump away" to an opposite or coordinate, probably belong under the head of drive or set, not under the head of associative strength.

Comparison of two college groups. The group differences already considered cannot be attributed entirely to the composition of the groups, for two college groups

Stimulus	*Response*	*1,000 Children*	*1,000 Men and women*	*1,000 Men in industry*
HAND	foot	0	239	321
BOY	girl	33	319	509
SOLDIER	sailor	0	58	102
DOCTOR	lawyer	1	36	161
LION	tiger	13	102	237
SHEEP	lamb	108	187	241
SALT	pepper	29	142	213
CHEESE	butter	49	136	194
WINDOW	door	2	57	107
STREET	road	60	91	124
CITY	town	110	258	452
MOON	sun	14	120	194

may show differences if tested under somewhat different conditions. The table below lists the first 10 monosyllabic stimulus words in the Kent-Rosanoff list, the most frequent response to each, the frequency (in percent) of this response in the Kent-Rosanoff adult sample, the frequency in the Schellenberg Frequency Tables (from 925 University of Minnesota freshmen), and finally the frequency obtained from 200 men and women students in an elementary laboratory class at Brown University (unpublished data of H.S.)

The frequencies obtained from the Minnesota students are much like those in the original Kent-Rosanoff tables. The Brown students, however, show a much higher frequency of the most common responses (with one exception, *house-home*). The reason for the difference between the two college groups is probably to be found in the conditions of the experiment. The Minnesota students wrote their responses, with relatively little pressure to respond quickly. On the other hand, the Brown students responded orally to their partners who were obviously recording the reaction time as well as the response word. They were likely to get set for quick and relatively superficial reactions which ran to opposites and coordinates. It was more probably the drive factor than the factor of associative strength that made the groups differ.

ASSOCIATIVE REACTION TIME

Two indicators of associative strength were recognized in our earlier discussion (p. 49). So far we have discussed one of these indicators, frequency or commonness of response to a stimulus word, and we have noticed rather its limitations than its value. We shall have more to say on the positive side very shortly. Meanwhile we turn to the other and more obvious indicator, the reaction time. The most comprehensive study of associative reaction times is still Cattell's pioneer study of controlled associations (1887). Later studies, less comprehensive, have confirmed these early findings. Cattell used two highly trained *Os*. Since the associative reactions were spoken and timed by aid of lip and voice keys, we need the simple oral RT as a base line. We have the following average from Cattell's two *Os* (1886a):

Simple oral RT to light 175 ms

Controlled association times. Several types of associative reaction will now be presented in the order of increasing RT. In considering this scale the reader should remember that the time between stimu-

Stimulus	*Response*	*Frequency, in percent of all responses* Kent-Rosanoff	Minnesota	Brown
DARK	light	42.7	49.5	76.5
MAN	woman	39.4	39.5	78.0
DEEP	shallow	18.0	25.0	37.7
SOFT	hard	36.5	33.5	61.6
HOUSE	home	10.3	28.5	11.0
BLACK	white	33.9	45.0	80.9
HAND	foot	20.4	15.0	42.7
SHORT	long	27.9	33.5	37.7
FRUIT	apple	25.9	28.0	37.7
SMOOTH	rough	27.7	31.0	38.2

lus and associative response depends on several factors: the *strength* of the association, the *directness* of the association, and possible *interference from competing associations.* The drive factor is presumably held constant since *O* in each case was set for a specific kind of response.

Reading reaction times. The reading response to a printed letter, word, or numeral is perfectly direct in an experienced reader, and free from competing associations. When his eyes light on *cat,* he seems actually to see the word (rather than a complex little symbol of the word), and no other response is likely except to read the word. In the experiment *O* was shown letters, words, and numbers, and he responded by reading them aloud. Cattell obtained the following average RTs from his two trained subjects:

Reading single letters	409 ms
" short words	388
" long words	431
" one-place numbers	360
" two-place numbers	396
" three-place numbers	443

The RT, though measured from the exposure of the stimulus to the *beginning* of the oral response, was longer for the longer words and numbers because, probably, more time was needed to perceive them. But we notice that a short familiar word was read as quickly as a single letter—an important result in the psychology of reading (see p. 101).

Naming colors and objects. Here *O* was shown a color or the picture of a familiar object and responded by giving its name. The average RT was as follows:

Naming a color (10 colors used)	547 ms
Naming an object (26 pictures used)	511 ms

Why should it take longer to name colors or objects than to read their names? The objects, and especially the colors, are if anything easier to see than the words (Lund, 1927), and the motor process of speaking the name is the same in both cases. The difference must lie in the intervening associative process. The association between a seen word and the saying of the word is free from competition, as already argued; whereas the ordinary response to a color or object is likely to be something else than naming it.

Other-word associations, restricted and partially restricted. The instructions call for response to each stimulus word by saying some other word. In free association (to be considered shortly) any other word is correct, but in controlled association the response word must have a certain relation to the stimulus word. The restriction may be complete so that only one response word can be correct, or it may be only partial, allowing for more than a single correct response. In an addition test the response is completely restricted, in an opposites test almost completely, in a verb-object test much less so. The most remarkable fact about controlled association experiments is that correct responses to suitable stimulus words are given quickly and with few false responses. The subject becomes set for the assigned task, and this preparatory set operates very efficiently, facilitating certain associations and inhibiting other associations which may be equally strong (Watt, 1905; May, 1917).

Cattell's (1887) average times from his two trained subjects were as shown on page 58,[1] the completely restricted responses being marked by the letter R:

[1] Cattell's published tables give "recall times," times required for calling up the required word. They were computed by subtracting from the total associative RT the naming RT for words, which averaged 409 ms for the two *Os.* We have added this 409 ms to the published figures in order to make all our RT data directly comparable.

R	Addition of two one-place numbers	690 ms
R	Multiplication of two one-place numbers	870
	Country—city (as England—London)	780
R	City—country	810
R	Month—season (as July—summer)	770
	Season—month	910
R	Month—following month (as May—June)	780
R	Month preceding month (as May—April)	1210
R	Famous man—occupation (as Raphael—painter)	820
R	Author—language (as Homer—Greek)	790
	Language—author	1000
	Author—book (as Homer—Iliad)	1330
	Whole—part (as house—door)	920
	Noun—adjective (as rock—hard)	790
	Verb—object (as aim—gun)	920
	Verb—subject (as swim—fish)	1050
	Genus—species	1040

These other-word reactions are distinctly slower than Cattell's reading and naming reactions; and the partially restricted responses tend to be slower than the wholly restricted. (The country-city associations could almost be regarded as wholly restricted since, with the countries named, there was usually some one city standing out as the only likely response.)

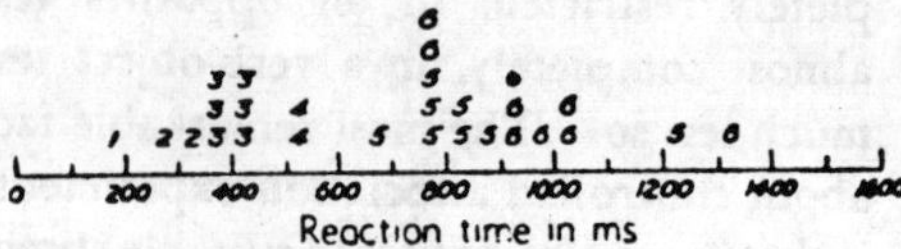

FIG. 3-1. Distribution of RT averages for the several classes of reactions, from Cattell's data:

1 = simple speech reaction to light
2 = disjunctive reactions
3 = reading reactions
4 = naming reactions
5 = other-word reactions, restricted
6 = other-word reactions, partially restricted

Of course not all restricted responses are quick and easy: multiplication is slower than addition, and the preceding month is harder to get than the following month. These differences may be due to previous habit. In general, there is little justification for assigning any definite RT for any particular class of associative responses, because different examples of the same class will vary enormously. The stimuli used in the experiments were selected to be familiar and easy. That on the whole the restricted responses were quicker than the partially restricted appears in Figure 3-1.

Timing of continuous association. Using a method which was mentioned on page 47, Bousfield & Sedgewick (1944) recorded the speed of continuous association. One record is reproduced in Figure 3-2. Association was partially restricted; the subject was asked to name objects of a certain class, such as birds, cities in the United States, or college classmates. The cumulative record shown rises rapidly at first but gradually flattens out as the subject used up his supply of available responses. The *slope* of the curve shows the rate of responding; the steeper it is, the smaller the interval between responses. The curves obtained could be fairly well rationalized by two probable assumptions (plus some mathematics): (1) each person has a certain limited stock of the required responses, a limit which he approaches without ever completely reaching it; and (2) in each successive minute he uses the same fraction of the stock not already used. These are essentially the same assumptions made in other applications of the growth function, as in reaction time (p. 22) and learning (p. 664).

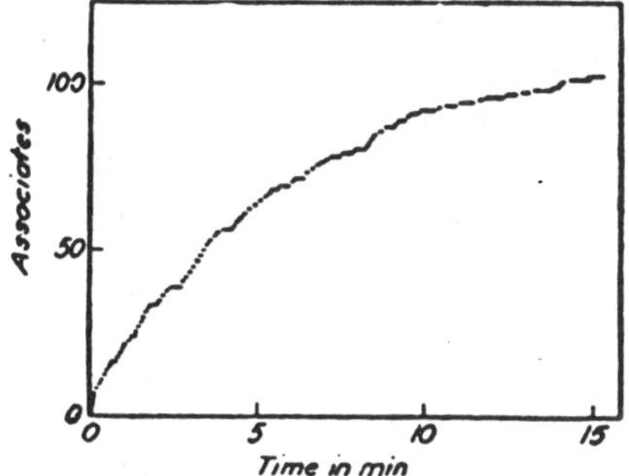

FIG. 3-2. (Bousfield & Sedgewick, 1944.) The distribution in time of continuous controlled associations. The subject was instructed to name United States cities as rapidly as possible. *E* pressed a key every time the subject named a city. The key raised the writing point on a kymograph one notch for each response. The faster the sequence of responses, the more rapid the rise of the record. An equation was fitted to the curve on the assumption that the rate was always proportional to the remaining stock. The curve fitting was done by a different method than we used on page 21. The limit could not be determined directly but had to be computed along with the rate of gain.

The curves obtained in this experiment often show little spurts when the subject hits upon a cluster of interrelated items, like the cities in a certain state, and there is often a rapid start. If we agree that the strong associations emerge first, it follows that the strong ones are also quick ones, with a short reaction time. Bousfield & Barclay (1950) have clinched this point by showing that the more common the response, the earlier it tends to appear in the series.

Free association time. Many experimenters have taken the time for free other-word responses, using either the stop watch or the chronoscope, and have (usually, not always) obtained skew distributions, with occasional responses delayed for 3–10 seconds. The median has usually been over one second but under two. Here are some of the averages from fair numbers of individuals:

Aschaffenburg (1895): 1150 ms

Jung (1919): 1800 ms; men, 1600 ms; women, 2000 ms

Wreschner (1907): 1600 ms

Cason & Cason (1925): 1520 ms with the distribution of individual averages showing an SD = 400 ms

Murphy (1917): 1276 ms, going down to 1033 ms on repetition of the stimulus list

Menzerath (1908) and also Wells (1911a) repeated the test on a series of days, and found the average to go down from 1750 to 1200–1300 ms. This result is rather remarkable since new stimulus words were used on each succeeding day. The practice effect did not consist in strengthening particular stimulus-response connections. With practice the very long RTs became few, though the minimum remained at about 1200 ms throughout, as Wells found. The gain in average speed was probably due to better adaptation to the experiment, greater freedom from inner obstruction, and the adoption of more facile and "superficial" types of response. On repeating the original list of stimulus words at the close of the long experiment, Wells noted such changes in response as are shown at the top of page 60.

The later responses given in this list are "superficial" in being phrase completions, word compoundings, or familiar pairs. Such responses are facilitated by speech habit. With practice *O* tends to be satisfied with such responses and so to cut down his average time, though he continues to give some responses of a less verbal sort.

Stimulus word	*Response before practice*	*Time (in sec)*	*Response after practice*	*Time (in sec)*
BANK	building	2.6	England	1.8
AXLE	hub	2.2	grease	1.2
SPREAD	distance	3.4	bed	1.4
SISTER	Anna	5.0	brother	1.4
SUFFER	weak	2.2	pain	0.8

All the cited RT averages are from adults. Children are slower in free association, one investigator (Anderson, 1917) giving the following results:

Age	*No. of subjects*	*Average of indiv. Medians (in ms)*	*Fastest indiv. Median (in ms)*	*Slowest indiv. Median (in ms)*
8 years	15	2600	1600	5000
10	26	2300	1400	5000
12	22	1700	1000	3000
14	18	1570	1000	3000
Adult	10	1500	1000	2200

McGehee (1937, 1938) found no significant age differences from 7 to 10 years, but girls were slower than boys (Median RT of 2.59 and 1.94 secs respectively). There were no corresponding differences in frequency of most common responses.

The free association time differs somewhat with the part of speech of the stimulus word, as indicated in the accompanying summary table, which may also serve to show the usual run of these RTs.

The free association time differs somewhat with the type of response—egocentric, predicate, contrast—but the main fact is that the more verbal responses are quicker than the more meaningful and personal.

Is the reaction quicker in free or controlled association? An a priori argument could be put up for either alternative. The "first word suggested" ought to be quicker than a response subject to restrictions. Such was Wreschner's conclusion from his data (1907), but he used many difficult stimulus words in his tests of controlled association. You can delay the restricted response to any length by

	Average (in ms)					
Stimulus word	*1*	*2*	*3*	*4*	*5*	*6*
Noun, abstract	979	1480	1950	1310	185–	
Noun, concrete	779	1330	1670	1175	1426	1640
Adjective		1450	1700	1140	1353	1550
Verb	910	1440	1900	1237	1526	1675

Sources: 1. Cattell and Bryant (1889), mouth key, single reactions, av. for 2 *Os*
2. The same, lists of 10 stimulus words, timed for list, av. per word for 2 *Os*
3. Jung (1919), single reactions timed with stop watch, av. for 26 adult *Os*
4. Wreschner (1907), voice key, single reactions, av. for 17 educated adults, each responding to 150–200 stimuli from each part of speech
5. Crane (1915), single reactions, lip key, av. for 30 college students, responding to 10–50 stimuli of each class
6. Menzerath (1908), voice key, av. for 8 educated adults, about 50 stimulus words of each class

giving a difficult task (as the opposite of *rash* or *lonely*). But since the set for opposites is certainly effective in securing opposites, and therefore in facilitating the correct as against incorrect responses, it might very well hasten the correct response by eliminating competition and interference. May (1917) found practically no difference in reaction time as between free and controlled association. But the crucial question evidently is whether *the same response to the same stimulus* is quicker in free or controlled association. Take the stimulus word *dark* which usually elicits its opposite in free association; will it elicit this response more quickly when *O* is set for opposites? We now have direct evidence that it will. Baker & Elliott (1948) selected 10 stimulus words which they knew from preliminary tests would give opposite responses from most of their *O*s (college students). The RT to each word was then measured by aid of a throat microphone. Each *O* first got half of the stimulus words for free association, and then the other half for response by the opposites, the words being rotated so that each was used equally often in each condition. The stimulus word *east*, for example, elicited the response *west* with a Mean RT of 839 ms in free association, but of only 717 in controlled association—a reliable difference. This was the largest difference, but some difference in the same direction came out for each of the 10 opposites. The same result was true with part-whole associations.

Relation of free association time to response frequency. At first thought there should be no relation of any significance between the individual's RT in giving a certain response and the number of other people who give the same response; but Thumb & Marbe (1901) found as a matter of fact that the more frequent responses were quicker. They spoke of this relation as a "law" and it has been called Marbe's law. It has been confirmed by several other investigators, whose data are embodied in an adjacent figure (p. 62). Cason & Cason (1925) checked the result by correlating the RT of the response with the frequency value of that response as given by Kent and Rosanoff. The correlation was worked out for the 100 responses of each individual separately, and was found negative in each of the 28 individuals examined, ranging from —.11 to —.59 with a general average of about —.33. The negative sign means that the greater the frequency value of a response, the shorter was its RT.

Mathematical relationship between frequency and association time. When it comes to precise formulation of the relationship between these two measures of strength of association, the earlier data are inadequate because no account was taken of the very skew distributions to be expected in such work. The experimenters reported only the Mean reaction times. From a statistical standpoint it is not correct to compare Means from two different distributions, unless both distributions are alike. Reaction time data are usually skewed so that a few long times make the Mean higher than the Mode or Median. To obtain adequate data Schlosberg and Heineman (1950) collected associative reaction times and response words from 204 members of an elementary laboratory class in psychology. The reactions were taken individually, and timed with a 0.01 sec precision timer, actuated by *E*. To eliminate the delay introduced by long stimulus words, they treated only the monosyllabic words of the Kent-Rosanoff list.

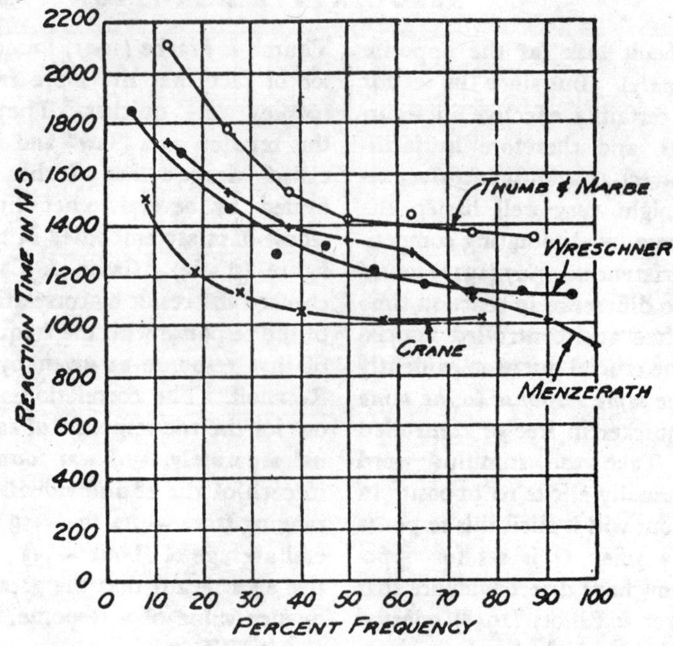

FIG. 3-3. Relation of reaction time in free association to the frequency of the response in four samples of the population. Data from: Thumb & Marbe (1901) with 8 O's and 140 stimulus words; Wreschner (1907) with 20 O's and 750 stimulus words; Crane (1915) with 30 O's and 145 stimulus words; Menzerath (1908) with 8 O's and 215 stimulus words. Altogether over 20,000 reactions are summarized in this figure. Menzerath secured 100-percent frequencies by use of especially familiar speech combinations as "einmal—zweimal," "rechts—links," "Tick—tack," "Bim—bam," and for this reason his RT curve does not flatten out at the highest frequencies.

Their first concern was with the distribution of reaction times. Figure 3-4A shows the distribution of the 1,000 reaction times obtained from the first 40 Os. It is plotted as a cumulative curve, with percentiles on the ordinate, and reaction time on the base line. If the distribution were normal, the curve would be a symmetrical ogive. However, it is clearly pulled out on the upper end.

In Figure 3-4B the same data are plotted against a logarithmic base line. The resulting curve looks fairly symmetrical. But for a better test of the normality of the distributions it is well to use a plot that shows a normal distribution as a straight line, for one can judge the straightness of a line more accurately than the symmetry of an ogive. There is a type of graph paper (probability paper) which conforms to the normal distribution by having the percentiles crowded near the center, and spread out at the edges. Figures 3-4C and 3-4D were plotted on this paper. Figure 3-4C has an arithmetic base line like that of Figure 3-4A; the fact that the plot does not yield a straight line shows that the distribution of raw reaction times was badly skewed. But when we combine a logarithmic base line with the probability ordinate, as shown in Figure 3-4D, we begin to get something like a straight line. This test indicates that the logarithm of reaction time is fairly normally distributed and may legitimately be used for comparisons from distribution to distribution. Similar tests

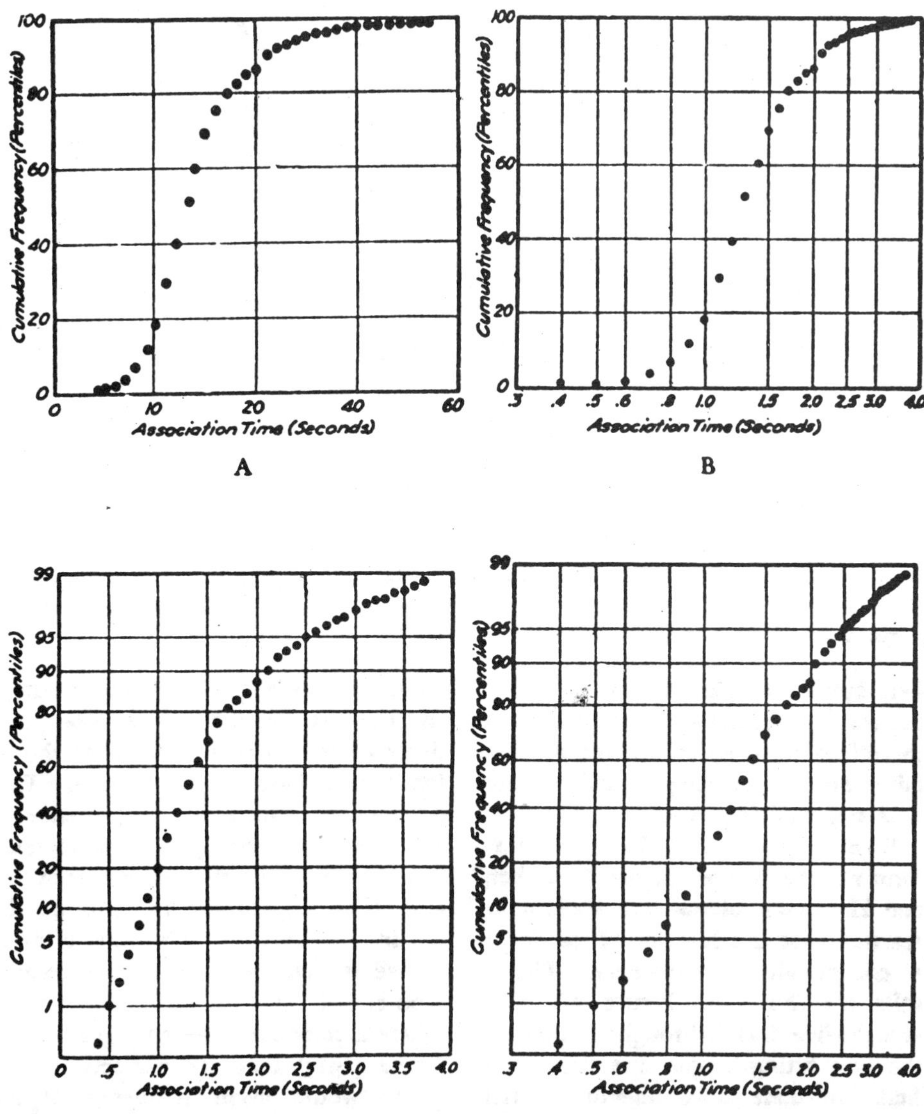

FIG. 3-4. (Schlosberg & Heineman, 1950—unpublished data.) Cumulative distributions of the same 1,000 associative reaction times in all four graphs. In A and B the percentages are plotted against a linear ordinate; the base line in A is linear, but that in B is logarithmic. In C and D the ordinate is spaced off in units that will straighten out a normal curve ("probit" paper); the base line is linear in C and logarithmic in D. Notice that the plotted points in D yield an approximation to a straight line, indicating that the logarithms of association times approach a normal distribution.

Something further on the use of "probit" paper for testing the normality of a distribution will be found in our later study of the psychophysical methods. The testing can also be done by aid of a table for the conversion of percent frequencies or p values into SD scores or z values (p. 206).

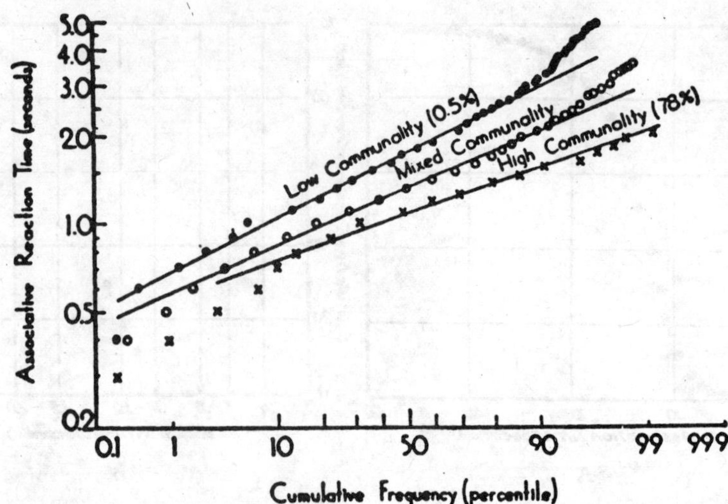

FIG. 3-5. (Schlosberg & Heineman, 1950.) The distribution of associative reaction times for three degrees of communality. The ordinate is logarithmic, and the abscissa is spaced to yield a straight line for a cumulative plotting of a normally distributed variable. The hollow circles represent 1,000 reactions of mixed communality. The solid dots are based on 630 unique responses and the crosses on 312 responses with a communality of 78 percent.

were applied to distributions of various degrees of communality, as well as to the mixed distribution shown; all were fairly normal, as long as log reaction time was used (Fig. 3–5).

Having shown that the logarithmic form was the best one to use, Schlosberg and Heineman plotted the Median log reaction time as a function of the degree of communality or frequency. The results are shown in Figure 3-6. The straight line drawn through the points is the best fitting simple one they could find, but there is considerable scatter. The correlation between log reaction time and communality is — .80, which is surprisingly high, and indicates that the two variables are very closely related. The formula in Figure 3-6 is a mathematical statement of this relationship.

The analysis just presented considers speed and commonness of association as indicators of the same factor in response, namely *associative strength*. If both are measures of associative strength, they should be positively related to each other, and the fact that they prove to be positively correlated with each other shows that they do have a common basis. The stronger an association, the oftener it will operate and the faster it will operate. In accordance with the limitations of the association experiment (p. 45), we do not inquire here into the *causes* of associative strength, such as frequency and recency of relevant past experience. There is some merit in the suggestion of Crane (1915) that commonness in the group would mean frequency of individual experience. The high communality of *east–west* in the group proves that the individual child would be frequently exposed to this combination and so would probably form a strong association between these two words and between these two points of the compass. But the important point from our present point of view is that the same two response variables that are so much used in animal experiments as indicators of

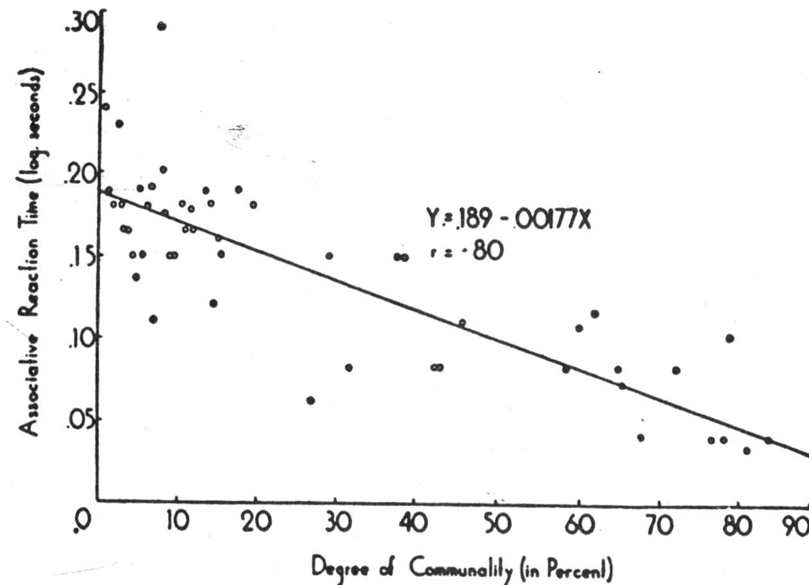

FIG. 3-6. (Schlosberg & Heineman, 1950.) The relationship between associative reaction time and degree of communality. Each point represents the Median log reaction time of all responses which occurred with a given degree of communality. In the equation, Y is in log seconds and X is in percent.

the progress of learning—that is, quickness and frequency of a response—are valid indicators also of the strength of associations used in the verbal behavior of human beings.

Introspective analysis of factors in associative reaction time. During the time that the stimulus-released energies are building up enough excitation in the brain to cross the threshold of motor response, many complicated events are happening. Introspective reports may afford some indications of these complicated events. The following factors have been introspectively reported.

Directness is a factor. When introspections are taken in a free association experiment (Aschaffenburg, 1895; Ziehen, 1898; Cordes, 1901; Mayer & Orth, 1901; Menzerath, 1908) *O* may report that the response word was reached by an indirect process, since he first thought of some object, situation, or "sphere of thought," out of which the response word emerged. Large differences in the single RTs are thus accounted for; and we have seen reasons for believing that the reading reaction is essentially more direct than the naming reaction, while any other-word reaction is still more indirect. Another fact accounted for by "directness" is the quick reaction that occurs when stimulus and response words are linked by speech habit.

Interference is an important factor. Sometimes *O* reports that two or more responses struggled for utterance one getting in the other's way. It is probable that such interferences often impede the naming reactions and contribute to their slowness as compared with plain reading. It is also probable that restricted association eliminates interferences which impede the free or the partially restricted response. In wholly restricted association the set facilitates one particular response, but where more lati tude is allowed two or more responses may compete.

Sometimes interference occurs in the form of distraction; the stimulus word may remind *O* of some interesting experience on which he dwells for a moment to the neglect of his task of responding. Sometimes a pleasant or unpleasant emotion delays the response. Sometimes *O* reports a short period of blankness in which nothing seems to occur and no progress is made toward a response; these blank periods probably indicate some kind of interference. Quick free association depends on freedom from such interferences and on a set for the more superficial or at least impersonal responses.

DETECTIVE AND DIAGNOSTIC APPLICATIONS OF THE FREE ASSOCIATION EXPERIMENT

The free association test has been used as a means of identifying a criminal from among other suspects and as a means of discovering the emotional complex supposed to underlie a neurosis. No attempt will be made here to impart the special skill required for success in these efforts, but some facts of psychological interest may be gleaned from a brief account.

Detecting guilty knowledge. A theft has been committed. Stimulus words are selected which should remind the offender of the scene and circumstances of the crime. If 20 significant words can be found, they are mingled with 80 harmless words, and the list of 100 stimulus words is presented orally, *O* being instructed to respond to each with the first other word suggested. The list is run off rapidly so that any emotional disturbance aroused by one word may carry over and affect the following responses. The response words and their RTs are recorded, *O* is carefully watched for signs of emotion, and sometimes a psychogalvanic or blood pressure record is taken (pp. 185–191). The theory is that the significant words should elicit responses directly revealing guilty knowledge or, if such responses are suppressed, should give long RT and signs of emotion.

Introduced by Wertheimer (1905) this detective experiment has been tried many times in the laboratory with made-up "crimes," and sometimes in the examination of suspects in an actual case. Some psychologists found it untrustworthy (Crane, 1915), while others got excellent results (Crosland, 1929).

Need of control subjects. The association test is apparently undependable when applied to a single person in the attempt to answer the question of his guilt; but it is more reliable when a number of persons are tested to discover which one of them is guilty. The need for comparison between the results of a number of subjects can be seen in the case of one of the main indicators—excessive RT to the significant stimulus words. A bit from the middle of a list used in a case of dormitory theft (Crosland, 1929), with the responses and RTs of the person who later confessed, follows:

Stimulus word	*Response*	*RT*
BREAD	butter	2.6
FLAG	American	2.1
HIP POCKET	pants	5.2
LIGHT	dark	2.3
GERMAN	English	2.1
MILK	butter	2.1
COTTAGE	cheese	2.1
LAUGH	cry	3.0
CAT	dog	1.9
DESK DRAWER	desk	4.5
OCEAN	rain	2.3

This subject's RT to the two significant words is suspiciously long. But we have to expect that the response to such rather special stimuli will be longer than to the general run of ordinary words. We find that the average RT of seven other *Os* who were put through this same list was 2.5 sec for *hip pocket* and 1.7 sec for *desk drawer*, longer in the first case but not in the second than their average RT for the nonsignificant stimuli. The guilty person's average RT to the 20 significant words in the entire list was nearly double his average RT to the nonsignificant words; whereas the other seven *Os* showed comparatively little difference in RT to the significant and the nonsignificant. Other indicators besides the RT were taken into account, and combined into a single statistical measure of probability of guilt. Properly used the method is laborious; at best it cannot detect every guilty person; and occasionally it may pick the wrong culprit, one, for example, who somehow knows the circumstances of the crime though not himself guilty. But it has succeeded in a good number of cases in leading to confession.

Classroom detection. As a classroom or laboratory experiment, the detection of guilty knowledge always arouses interest. A vast amount of instructor's thought has been devoted to thinking up "crimes" that will arouse enough emotion to give changes in the speed or content of associations to significant words, without overstepping legal and moral limits. But perhaps the most serious objection to these experiments is that the detection of such knowledge is more of an art than a science, for *E* must use judgment in deciding which of several indices is most significant when they are in conflict. When *E* is successful in catching the criminal, the class thinks that the method is infallible, but when he fails, they go to the opposite extreme. This difficulty can be avoided to some extent by simplifying the experiment so that it can be repeated on several "suspects" and the results treated in a statistical fashion. The most practical way to do this is to have each subject read one of five short stories, such as those written by O. Henry. *E* then gives each subject a list of 100 stimulus words, 20 of which are related to each story, and tries to find which story he read. There is one trap that *E* may fall into when treating the reaction times. A stimulus word that is particularly relevant to one story, such as the unusual name of a character, will often give a very slow reaction time in those who have not read that story, for the simple reason that they have no associations with it. Hence, it is wise to segregate such words in the statistical treatment, since a long reaction time will indicate innocence rather than suppressed knowledge.

Detecting complexes. This use of the free association test was introduced by Jung & Riklin (1904; see Jung, 1919). A "complex" here is a system of desires, emotions, and memories, containing an element of strain, failure, dissatisfaction, or sense of guilt. It is often a love affair, sometimes a business difficulty, or a family trouble. Complexes are said to be "repressed" and "unconscious" when not readily called to mind; other complexes are perfectly conscious, and yet *O* is reticent regarding them and may not recognize their connection with any neurotic trouble. The psychotherapist in his search for the troublemaker sometimes derives useful clues from the association test.

The discovery of a complex is a kindred problem to the detection of a criminal. There is, however, one important difference. The detective knows the crime but not the culprit; the psychotherapist knows the culprit but not the "crime." The psychotherapist does not know in advance what stimulus words will suit the individual case, but he can set traps for the complexes commonly encountered in clinical practice, arising from the sex life and its frustrations, from discontent with one's personal appearance or abilities, from disappointed ambition, from economic stress. Stimulus words calculated to tap such complexes are therefore included in the list, along with a padding of presumably neutral words. *O* takes a relaxed sitting or reclining position in a quiet (sometimes a partially darkened) room, and the examiner instructs him, as in other uses of free association, to respond to each stimulus word by saying the first other word suggested. As soon as the list of 100 stimulus words has been completed, it is gone through again with instructions to try and recall the response made to each stimulus word on the first round.

The evidence that a complex has been touched by any particular stimulus word is furnished by peculiarities in the response, called "complex indicators" (Jung, 1919), such as the following:

Long RT or complete failure to react.

Repetition of the stimulus word before reacting or as the sole reaction.

Misunderstanding of the stimulus word.

Response having no obvious relation to the stimulus word, far-fetched, extremely personal, or merely a clang association.

Signs of excitement or embarrassment, laughing or smiling, stammering, interjections, whispered or shouted response.

Failures to recall the original response to a word when that word is given in the reproduction test. If the stirring of a complex has disturbed the easy flow of association on the first trial, the response may be difficult to recall.

The psychogalvanic reaction may be taken along with the association test, and is likely to show large deflections when an emotion is stirred (p. 186).

Experimental checking of the validity of indicators. There are two ways of obtaining some estimate of the trustworthiness of a complex indicator. Follow up the indicated complex and see if it is genuine in the individual subject. Or, check one indicator against another. The first method corresponds to a test for "validity," the second for "reliability."

The follow-up is constantly used by the psychotherapist. He finally reaches the complex, but often by so tortuous a route that one is not clear at the end whether the complex finally brought to light created the disturbance which served as a complex indicator. An immediate follow-up with cooperative, normal subjects makes a better check on the validity of the complex indicator; where this has been tried (Dooley, 1916) the results have shown that complexes, not perhaps unconscious ones, were actually tapped by certain stimulus words in the experiment, and that delayed reaction, failure to react or failure to recall a response—as well as direct emotional expressions—were the result of stirring up a complex. But not always. No one of the indicators is absolutely dependable.

Long RT is sometimes the effect of temporary interferences or distractions which have nothing to do with any complex (Grossart, 1921; Wells, 1911a, 1927).

Failure to reproduce some of the original response words is certainly to be expected; a perfect recall score would be almost a miracle of memory.

Signs of embarrassment or excitement sometimes are due to tapping some *recent* experience. Amusement may be aroused by the examiner himself or by the whole procedure, especially in the early part of the list before the subject has settled down to the task (Hubbard, 1924).

Checking one indicator against another was a means adopted by Jung (1919, p. 396) to convince those who doubted in particular that failure to recall a response word was any sign of a complex. He showed that failure to recall went along with other indicators to quite an extent.

This method of attack was further developed by Hull & Lugoff (1921). They used Jung's list of 100 stimulus words on 50 men and 50 women believed to be a fair sample of the normal middle-class population. Taking each single reaction of any subject as a unit, they noted whether it showed one or more complex indicators. They then asked whether the coincidence of one indicator with another, or with all the others taken together, was greater than could be expected by chance; and if so, how much greater, the answer to this question being a "coefficient of association." By this statistical procedure they reached a positive result on the whole, as indicated by the following coefficients of association between each indicator and the rest taken together:

Repetition of the stimulus word	+.59
Misunderstanding of the stimulus word	+.47
Long RT	+.41
Defective reproduction of response word	+.26

Each of these four indicators seems to have a certain reliability as revealing the same kind of disturbance as the others —call it a complex or by some broader term. The first two, which seem the better, are however infrequent. "Repeated use of the same response word," previously regarded as a good indicator, was frequent enough but showed no agreement at all with the others. Regarded as reliability coefficients, the figures just given inspire no great confidence in the test, to be sure; and further studies (Hubbard, 1924) show that irrelevant factors come into play. The mere position of a stimulus word in the series of 100 is a factor; for when the words were arranged in different orders for different *O*s, on the whole the long RTs came toward the middle of the list, while the failures to reproduce and the "laughing and smiling" came disproportionately from the early part of the list, and thus meant more when they occurred late in the list. The grammatical form of the stimulus word also made a difference, since the nouns gave fewer complex indicators than the adjectives and these than the verbs. The subject may be surprised when a new kind of stimulus word appears, as "to sin" or "to part" or "caring for" after a string of single word stimuli; and may give complex indicators because of mere surprise.

The most complex-arousing words differ somewhat from one investigation to another (Conklin, 1927; Hull & Lugoff, 1921; Wells, 1927), but on the whole they tend to suggest these sides of life:

Love and marriage
Friendship
Quarrels and anger, injustice
Ridicule, contempt, pity
Danger
Expense, money
Death

The association test as a projective technique. The decade starting in 1940 saw an extremely rapid growth in the use of "projective techniques." Tests such as the Rorschach and the Thematic Apperception test bear some resemblance to free association. An inkblot is shown, or a rather indefinite picture, and *O* is asked to respond verbally in a free fashion. Since neither the stimulus nor the instructions exert much control or restriction, the direction and content of *O*'s responses must be determined mostly by his own past experience and present complexes. In this way the projective techniques are much like Jung's diagnostic form of the Free Association Test. The new interest in projective techniques has spread to the association method, which in the 1930–1940 period was showing signs of dropping out of clinical practice. A few of these recent developments will be mentioned here; the reader with a clinical interest is referred to Hunt (1944) or to Rapaport, Gill & Schafer (1946).

Multiple Choice forms of the Association Test. To avoid the subjective element in scoring and classifying free associations, several attempts have been made to put the test into objective form. Terman & Miles (1936) in their battery of tests for masculinity *versus* femininity included an association test, each stimulus word being followed by four possible response words with instructions to select the one which "went best" with the stimulus word. Maller (1936) used a similar form with two options, one of which was considered normal and the other abnormal. After reweighting the items of this test, Malamud (1946) found that it correctly identified 87 percent of 100 abnormal individuals and 77 percent of normal ones. Crown (1947) cut the test from 200 to 50 items without any apparent loss of validity or reliability, and found that a cut-off score of eight or more "abnormal" responses identified 81 percent of 200 neurotics while erroneously picking up 27 percent of a supposedly normal group. (Of course, the line separating normal from neurotic is not as sharp as the distinction seems to imply.) Crown favors the use of the test as part of a battery for "screening" normal from abnormal persons.

These forced-option tests seem far removed from the original free association method and lose a good share of the information contained in free responses. It would be very desirable to have a reliable scoring system for the free associations—such a classification as already quoted (p. 53) from Karwoski & Berthold (1945), who found it to give as reliable results as several versions of the multiple choice type.

Homographs and homophones as stimulus words. Words spelled or pronounced alike though having very different meanings may tune up the free association test for the purpose of distinguishing people of different backgrounds and interests. Goodenough (1942, 1946) has developed such a test for masculinity *versus* femininity. For example, the visually presented stimulus word *bow* usually calls out something like *hair ribbon* from girls but not from boys whose responses are more apt to be related to archery. Foley & MacMillan (1943) gave oral stimuli, including words having both legal and medical as well as everyday meanings, such as *complaint*, *expiration*, and *cell* (*sell*). They gave this test to 218 students in law, medicine, or liberal arts. It was found that the professional groups gave responses that were consistent with their special fields. The writers were interested in the theoretical rather than in the practical bearing of their results, which demonstrate the effect of particular past experiences on present associative responses. Ever since the days of the associationists, this effect has been tacitly assumed by most workers in the field, but very seldom has the assumption been subjected to an experimental check in the studies of association. For the most part we must turn for such investigations to our later chapters on learning and memory.

4 ATTENTION

The chapters on Reaction Time and Association have been concerned with experiments calling in each case for response to a single stimulus. But it is obvious that we are usually immersed in a sea of potential stimuli, each of which is capable of eliciting one or more responses. Yet we behave in a consistent and integrated fashion; irrelevant or conflicting stimuli do not generally elicit responses that would interfere with the present course of action. This selective factor has long been designated by the term *Attention*.

Many everyday observations and informal experiments have to do with this topic. They could and probably should be put into more definite shape so that the critical experimentalist could cite the results without having to say simply, "It is well known." But, the following facts can be regarded as well known.

We can attend to stimuli and external objects and events, to our own actions, or to ideas.

We can attend to a complex visible object as a whole, or we can attend to a small part of the object or to some one property of the object such as color or shape. Similarly, in the auditory sphere, we can attend to a complex sound as a whole or to some one note in a musical chord or to some property such as loudness or pitch or the direction from which the sound seems to come.

While attending to a visible object, we tend strongly to look straight at it and focus and converge the eyes for clear vision. But it is possible to attend to an object without looking toward it.

While attending to the sound coming from an object, from a speaker for example, we tend to face and look toward the source of sound. But there are other alternatives: we may close the eyes to shut out visual distraction; or we may stare fixedly at some object without noticing what we see.

Often but not always we can infer what a person is attending to from his motor adjustment for seeing, hearing, smelling, tasting, or touching. With animals we can make the same inferences and perhaps even more confidently. In animals we can regard "attending" as simply an inclusive name for these motor adjustments; but a man may look fixedly at one object while attending to something else, usually something that is not present at the moment. A cat poised at the entrance of a mousehole, or a dog waiting for a ball to be thrown, makes a good picture of the motor readiness typical of attention.

In spite of the practical reality of attending, the status of attention in systematic psychology has been uncertain and dubious for a long time. Early psychologists thought of it as a faculty or power, akin to the Will, a power that was stronger in some individuals than in others and that might lie dormant and need to be aroused by strong motives. Not very different has been the view of many functional psychologists and of educators and psychiatrists. Any such view was strongly opposed by the associationists who wished to recognize as forces only sensory stimulation and association. The Gestalt psychologists also have regarded any force of attention as extraneous to the field forces which in their view are the dynamic factors in human activity. The behaviorists have rejected attention as a mere traditional mentalistic concept.

Titchener, who held that the task of psychology was to study conscious experience, objected to the functional approach and preferred to investigate what he called "attensity," an attribute of sensory experience comparable to hue or loudness. By attensity he meant what is often called clearness, vividness, prominence, or insistence—not to be confused with the clearness of a distinct view of an object, for a vague shape in indirect vision has high attensity if (because we are attending to it) it stands out above all else in our consciousness at the moment.

PROBLEMS

In the midst of all these theoretical doubts and uncertainties research has continued on certain problems that stem from the everyday facts of attention and inattention; and some distinctive psychological experiments have been invented in the effort to solve these problems. A general formula for these experiments may be written.

$$R = f(O, S_1, S_2, S_3, \ldots)$$

in which R stands for some selective response such as looking at one of several simultaneously present objects, designated by the stimulus letters, these objects differing in some respect such as color or location. The formula states that the response depends on the stimuli and on *O*-variables (such as the individual's previous training and present state). One important *O*-variable is the task, if any, which *O* is set to perform. On this basis several problems can be distinguished.

1. *Determiners of attention.* We may speak of free and controlled attention, analogous to free and controlled association. In free attention there is no assigned task and the question is simply which of the stimuli will "catch the attention" and elicit the selective response.

2. *Shifting and fluctuation of attention.* The stimulus or stimuli remaining constant for some time, the response is likely to fluctuate in strength or to shift from one stimulus to another. The formula for this problem would have to bring in the time factor, as in

$$R = f(O, t, S_1, S_2, S_3, \ldots)$$

3. *Distraction.* Here we have to do with controlled attention, since the subject is engaged on a certain task calling (we may say) for the response R_1 to the stimulus S_1, while irrelevant stimuli, S_2, S_3, ... , tend to distract him from the task. The formula for this case might be written,

$$R_1 = f(O_1, S_1; S_2, S_3, \ldots)$$

where O_1 is the set for performing the task S_1–R_1, and the other stimuli are the distractors.

4. *Divided attention—doing two things at once.* The subject attempts to perform two tasks simultaneously. The double task-set may be represented by O_1O_2, and the formula written thus,

$$R_1R_2 = f(O_1O_2, S_1, S_2)$$

and the question is whether R_1R_2 occurs at all and if so how efficiently.

5. *Span of attention* or *span of apprehension.* Here the subject's task is to make a single comprehensive response to a collection of stimuli. Usually the task is simply to perceive and report the number of stimuli. The formula might be

$$R_n = (O_n, S_n)$$

where O_n is the set for perceiving the number and R_n is the response to the number S_n.

DETERMINERS OF ATTENTION

What makes us notice one object rather than another when both are present to the senses? What factors operate to give the advantage to one stimulus rather than another? This is obviously a question for the experimental psychologist, and it is an important question in certain fields of applied psychology. How to catch and hold attention is a very practical problem for the advertiser in any medium, for the safety engineer concerned with warning signals or road signs, for the museum director, for the headline writer and make-up editor of a newspaper, for the teacher, and in fact for anyone whose offering has to compete for the attention of an audience. The advertisers and advertising counselors were the first to be convinced of the value of psychological experimentation, and much of the work on determiners of attention has been concerned directly with advertising problems.

The experimenter has to consider first what factors are worth trying out. Just as in reaction time, there are S-factors and O-factors that may be more or less important. Size, intensity, color, motion, etc., are S-variables, sometimes called external determiners. Familiarity, emotional appeal, and the individual's permanent or temporary interests are clearly O-variables, internal determiners. How shall we classify novelty? It would seem to be an external determiner, and yet it obviously depends on O's previous experience. At any rate, it is often an effective attention-getter. When a list of probable factors has been selected, the experimenter's problems are (a) how to present the alternative stimuli, and (b) what R-variables to employ as indicators of selective attention. These two problems are closely interrelated as can be seen from the following typical experiments.

Immediate verbal report. As an informal introduction to this type of experiment, fixate (look at) a certain object and notice what *other* object stands out most clearly, "bidding for attention." Dallenbach (1923a and b) exposed two bright spots simultaneously on opposite sides of the fixation point, calling for a report as to which spot stood out with more clearness or attensity. His results showed an advantage for the brighter spot or, if the spots were equal in brightness and all other respects, for the spot that was situated above or to the left of the fixation point.

Quite a different use was made of immediate verbal report in a road test of traffic signs. The driver called out the signs as he spotted them in driving rapidly over an unfamiliar road, the experimenter being in the car to record the driver's reports. When several names of towns were shown on the same post, the uppermost one was spotted first (Forbes, 1939).

Memory tests. (1) *Recall.* The subject thumbs through a magazine, or through a dummy magazine made up to bring out certain factors, and afterward is asked to recall all the advertisements he noticed. As he will undoubtedly not recall all that momentarily caught his attention, the reports of many subjects must be pooled to furnish an estimate of the attention value of the various items. (2) *Recognition.* After the subject has read or thumbed through a magazine he is shown advertisements taken from that magazine, mixed with similar items, and asked to indicate those he noticed in the magazine. Many items that would not be recalled will nevertheless be recognized. These memory tests for attention value have been used extensively for many years.

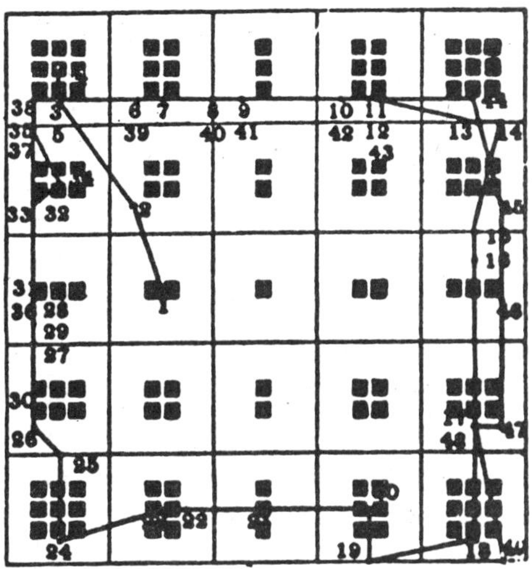

Fig. 4-1. (Brandt, 1940.) The succession of fixation points of a subject examining a page of pictures.

Eye movements and fixations. Let two objects be suitably placed in a show window and exposed to the passers-by while *E* from behind a one-way screen watches their eyes. He can tell pretty well which object first catches their attention and which one holds them longest. A similar setup can be arranged in the laboratory. The subjects should be ignorant of the purpose of the experiment so that they will freely look where they will, with several attention-getting factors balanced in the experimental design (Nixon, 1924, 1926).

Greater precision in locating and timing the eye fixations has been achieved by use of special cameras. It is possible to project the developed film back onto the original layout and plot the points on which the eyes were directly focused in examining a group of pictures or a page of advertisements. Figure 4-1 gives an example of the plots so obtained. Here as in the case of reading, the eye movement records reveal important behavioral details that never get into a verbal report (Hackman & Guilford, 1936; Brandt, 1937, 1945; Karslake, 1940. For fuller discussion of eye movements see pp. 102–103, 504–510.

Results on determiners of attention. The different methods applied to advertising problems have given fairly concordant results, which we shall not cite in detail, referring instead to the texts on applied psychology (as Burtt, 1948, pp. 688–731). A few of the most definite findings will be mentioned.

S-factors. Quantitative results are important in this work because of the expense of employing such attention-getters as large size, preferred position, or color. For example, to double the size of an advertisement doubles the cost of insertion, and the question is whether it doubles the attention value. The answer, according to both the eye-movement and memory methods, is that doubling the size increases the attention value by 40–60 percent, and not by 100 percent (Brandt, 1945; Rudolph, 1947).

One curious fact, already mentioned, is the effect of position. The upper half of a page gets more attention than the lower half, and the left half more than the right half, so that the upper left-hand quarter may be three times as favorable as the lower right-hand quarter. If we wish to test some other factor such as size or color, we have to balance out the effect of position. For example, if we wish to compare the attention value of colored pictures or advertisements with those in black and white, we have to place the colored items equally in the preferred and nonpreferred positions.

Color has usually been found to have some value as a means of attracting attention, and the same can be said for "isolation," the use of blank space framing a picture or reading matter. All these S-factors have relative rather than absolute value. The effect of color is lost if all the advertisements are colored, and it is even possible that a black and white item will stand out through novelty if a magazine is mostly made up in color. A full-page advertisement in a pocket magazine may be as attention-getting as a full-page ad in a newspaper.

O-factors. Aside from familiarity and present set, which, of course, vary from person to person and from day to day, there are more dependable interests which are strong determiners of attention. Advertisement writers try to appeal to curiosity, sex interest, desire for security, success, prestige, amusement, interest in babies, children, and people generally; and the psychologist has used his methods for measuring the relative attention value of these appeals.

SHIFTS AND FLUCTUATIONS

Given a field of stimuli, the first response is governed by the balance of external and internal determiners of attention, such as have just been considered. Now let the stimuli remain unchanged; we might expect attention to remain fixed and no change of response to occur. What happens in most cases is quite different. Attention shifts, the response quickly changes. Since the external determiners remain constant, we infer that some internal factor or factors must change. There are several varieties of shifting and fluctuation, and several types of experiment have been invented for recording and if possible explaining the phenomena. The basic method is to hold the stimulus field constant for a time and record the changes of the response.

Ordinary shifting of attention. The shifting we shall consider first is "ordinary" in comparison with the peculiar oscillations to be considered later. Suppose you are looking at a fairly complex picture—a landscape or group of people. You will look at various parts of the picture one after another, perhaps coming back time and again to some specially interesting object. What is the rate of this shifting? You can obtain a rough estimate by timing yourself for a certain number of objects spotted, and may find about one item per second to be an easy, unhurried rate. Count 20 objects one by one and you may get a rate or 2 or 2.5 or even 3 per second.

Though simple counting is a fairly rapid process, it is not so rapid as the free movement of the eyes about a picture. When the eye movements are photographed by a suitable camera, the fixations are found to vary in duration between a minimum of about 100 ms and an indefinite maximum of a second or two, usually. The distribution is skew, as determined for one large sample of adults, with a Mode of about 230 ms, a Median of about 240 ms, and a Mean of about 310 ms. We may accept the modal value of 230 ms per fixation, or 4 fixations per second, as a fair estimate of the rate of ordinary shifting of attention about the field of view (Buswell, 1935).

In silent reading, which is one of the most rapid processes that occur in human beings, the eye fixations run a little shorter than in viewing a picture, with a Mode of about 210 ms in good readers and as little as 170 ms in some exceptionally rapid readers (see p. 508). The rate of eye shifting, then, can be as great as 5 per second, though it is not quite safe to regard the fixations here as units of attention, since the reader's attention is fixed on the meaning rather than on the printed words.

If we ask, not how quickly attention can move, but how long it can remain fixed, we can obtain an estimate from an experiment of Billings (1914). He placed a picture before the subject with instructions to attend to one particular object and to press a telegraph key when attention wandered from that point. By electrical connections a record was made on a moving drum, along with a time line. The time before the first shift averaged 2 seconds, but varied from a minimum of $\frac{1}{10}$ of a second to a maximum of about 5 seconds. Of course, it is possible to attend to a complex object much longer than 5 seconds, but only by shifting from one part to another part of the object.

Oscillation in the appearance of ambiguous figures. An ambiguous drawing can be seen as representing either of two different objects. Familiar examples are the outline cube, staircase, and similar figures of reversible perspective (p. 410). Under continued scrutiny the ambiguous figure seems to change its shape or position repeatedly. The oscillation can be controlled to some extent if you fix your eyes steadily on a corner that you wish to have protrude toward you, and shift your fixation to another corner when you wish the appearance to change; but this control is far from complete, for sometimes you move your eyes without getting any reversal of appearance, and sometimes you hold your eyes steady and still see the figure change. The rate of oscillation is variable, usually slow at first and more and more rapid during continued observation. Average rates reported for samples of young adults range from 15 to 20 per minute (Hollingworth, 1939; Tussing, 1941).

In an extensive experiment (Glen, 1940) ten young adults of normal vision were first given some practice in observing the shifting appearance of the reversible cube and recording the shifts by pressing a key. The subjects varied all the way from one who reported only 3.7 spontaneous reversals per minute to one who reported 47.5. The Median for the group was about 15 per minute. This Median rate was doubled when the subjects tried for quick changes, and reduced to half (i.e., to one shift per 8 seconds) when they tried to prevent the oscillation. They reported using the eye-fixation control, and the photographic record of eye movements which was part of the experiment showed indeed an increase of eye movements when the subjects hastened the oscillation and the opposite when they slowed it. On the whole, also, the subjects who made more eye movements saw more reversals, though the correlation was far from high. The part played by eye movements was certainly not simple, for the eye movements were much more numerous than the reported shifts, and they tended to cluster around the moment of reversal, following as well as preceding the reversal.

Similar oscillations can be had from *dot figures* (p. 409) which appear to shift their grouping during continued scrutiny. The rate of oscillation is quite variable, sometimes as fast as 20–30 per minute, sometimes as slow as 5–10 per minute.

Retinal vivalry (p. 399) is the most spectacular of all these varieties of oscillation. The rate here depends on stimulus factors such as intensity; 12 shifts per minute may be taken as a representative value.

All these "peculiar" oscillations—rivalry, dot figures, ambiguous perspective —are very different from what we called the "ordinary" shifting of attention. They are much slower in rate, usually from 5 to 30 shifts per minute, as against 4 per second (240 per minute) in the movement of the eyes about a picture or scene. This ordinary shifting has a positive function in behavior. While you are looking at one object, you glimpse another in indirect vision and shift the eyes toward it. Here there is a goal or incentive—to obtain a clear view of an object—but there is nothing like a goal or incentive in rivalry or ambiguous figures unless it is the artificial goal of a subject who is trying to speed up the rate of oscillation. The absence of any positive incentive to shift may account for the relative slowness of the shifting of ambiguous figures and rivalry.

A factor that may account for the shifting of ambiguous figures and rivalry is the probable development of fatigue, adaptation, or satiation. An ambiguous figure is a stimulus complex capable of eliciting either of two perceptual responses, one of which has the initial advantage and persists until enough fatigue or satiation has accumulated to switch the advantage to the alternative response. This alternative response now undergoes fatigue or satiation until the advantage returns to the first response and so on as long as the stimulus continues. This fatigue or satiation factor probably plays some part also in the ordinary shifts of attention. For why do the eyes rest longer on some parts of a picture than on others? They probably rest longer on the more interesting objects and shift from an object as soon as the momentary interest in it has become exhausted. On this theory two factors operate in the ordinary shifting, attraction toward an object glimpsed in indirect vision and partial satiation for the object now fixated, while only the satiation factor operates in the case of ambiguous figures and rivalry.

Sensory fluctuation. In 1875 the aurist Urbantschitsch, while engaged in testing a subject's hearing, noticed that a watch held at such a distance from the ear as to be barely audible did not remain audible all the time but "went out" and "came back" repeatedly. Similar oscillations of faint visual and tactile sensations were quickly reported and the phenomenon was named "fluctuation of attention." The "attention wave" consists of a positive phase (when the stimulus is perceived) and a negative phase.

Instead of the watch an audiometer can be used for better control of faint auditory stimuli. A visual stimulus is barely perceptible either when it is very small in area (as a black point on a white surface viewed from a distance) or when it differs very little in brightness from its background (as can be conveniently accomplished by aid of the color wheel, Fig. 4-2). For faint cutaneous stimuli weak electric currents have been used, or light corks resting on the skin.

The rate of fluctuation varies considerably. A general average is about 8–10

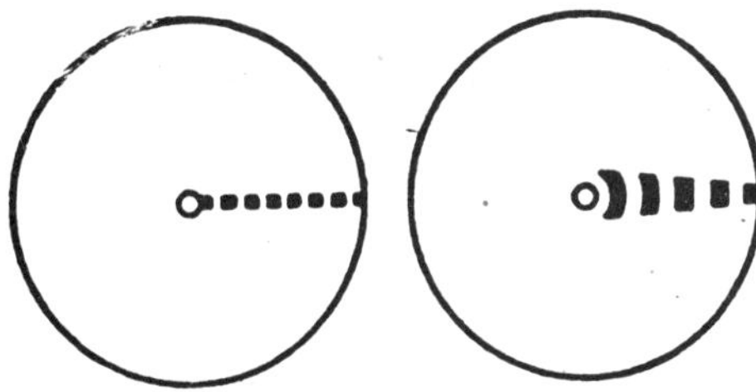

FIG. 4·2. Masson disks for color wheel.

seconds per complete wave, with individual averages ranging from 3 to 6 seconds (Slaughter, 1901; Taylor, 1901). The rate is far from constant even for the same individual, as can be seen in the following continuous series of wave lengths obtained by Marbe (1893) from a subject watching a small black spot on a white ground. Time in seconds:

17, 4, 14, 3, 9, 8, 6, 11, 13, 9, 8, 13, 6, 7

The positive and negative phases vary irregularly, as seen in the following continuous series from Eckener (1893):

Positive phase	2.4		4.0		4.0		2.9		3.7		8.1	
Negative phase		6.8		0.6		4.1		5.2		4.3		11.5

An experiment of Wiersma (1901) revealed one bit of regularity. He held a watch sometimes so far from the ear that it could scarcely ever be heard; sometimes so near that it was heard most of the time; and at intermediate distances. Each test lasted 300 sec, and the table below shows the total time during which the watch was heard.

Relative intensity of the stimulus	*Time audible (in sec)*	
	Subject H.	*Subject W.*
1	102	126
1.2	164	213
1.5	190	221
1.8	226	245
2.3	257	283
3	284	299

The duration of the positive phases increased with the strength of the stimulus. Similar results were obtained with visual stimuli.

In very general terms, these fluctuations are explained by supposing that the whole receptive apparatus must be functioning perfectly to perceive a weak stimulus. Any momentary lapse in efficiency interrupts the sensation. The locus of the fluctuations may be the sense organ or the brain or both. One possible factor has been exploited by one investigator, and another by another.

Muscular unsteadiness. For the ear to have maximum receptivity for the ticking of a watch, the tympanic membrane needs perhaps (see p. 326) to be held at exactly the right tension by the little muscles of the middle ear; if these muscles should relax, the sound would fail to register. But the importance of this factor was promptly discounted when Urbantschitsch (1875) found typical auditory fluctuations in persons whose tympanic membranes had been removed. Similarly, while unsteady action of the ciliary muscle that controls the lens of the eye could produce visual fluctuations, the importance of this factor was disproved by the finding (Pace, 1902; Slaughter, 1901; Ferree, 1906) that the fluctuations still occur when the ciliary muscle is paralyzed by atropin, and even in patients whose lenses have been removed.

Sensory adaptation. Adaptation or sensory "fatigue," a partial or complete disappearance of sensation when the stimulus remains perfectly constant, is characteristic of the tactile and visual senses (pp. 286, 367). When a tactile stimulus is adequately controlled and kept perfectly steady, the sensation fades out and does not return (Freiberg

1937a). In less precise work slight movements of the subject bring the stimulus to bear on fresh receptors and thus renew the sensation. So fluctuations are produced.

Visual fluctuations may perhaps be produced in a similar way. A steadily fixated pattern of light and shade fades out. Partial fading out is indicated by the negative afterimage which appears when the stimulus pattern is replaced by a plain gray field. Using this indicator Pace (1902) found that retinal adaptation occurred during the positive phase, with recovery during the negative phase. This conception of visual fluctuations was confirmed by the elaborate experiments of Ferree (1906, 1913) which revealed a thoroughgoing parallelism of the conditions favorable to fluctuation and to adaptation.

Eye movements. Retinal adaptation cannot possibly be the complete explanation of visual fluctuations. It explains the disappearance but not the reappearance of the sensation. How can the retina recover from its adaptation? The answer is that stimulation must change, and there is one sure way of changing the retinal stimulation even while the external stimuli remain unchanged—simply move the eyes. As soon as they shift their fixation point, the stimulus pattern falls on fresh parts of the retina which are not adapted to that particular pattern of light and shade. Retinal adaptation to produce disappearance, plus eye movements to produce reappearance, would furnish an adequate explanation of visual fluctuation. But do eye movements actually occur as demanded by this theory? Some evidence that they do is afforded by Guilford's experiment (1927) in which fluctuations and eye movements were recorded simultaneously. The eye movements were photographed and the subject's finger movements signaling each disappearance and reappearance of the stimulus pattern were recorded on the same film. The result was not so clear as might be hoped, since the eye movements were not confined to any one phase of the fluctuation, but they were most frequent just before reappearance. That is, relatively steady fixation during the positive phase tended toward adaptation, and more eye movement during the negative phase tended toward recovery.

By "retinal adaptation" is meant adaptation of the receptors, the rods and cones, the most peripheral level of the visual apparatus. There might be adaptation (or satiation) at higher levels also, as in the visual area of the cerebral cortex. One of Guilford's experiments was designed to check on this possibility. The apparatus was so constructed that when the stimulus pattern became invisible and the subject pressed his key, one of three things could happen:

1. The stimulus remained unchanged until some eye movement occurred. Result: the stimulus pattern reappeared after 10–12 sec, the usual duration of this subject's negative phase.

2. The stimulus was instantly moved to another position on the retina, so bringing into play fresh rods and cones and also fresh cortex. Result: the pattern reappeared in about 1 sec.

3. The stimulus was instantly transferred to the corresponding part of the other retina, so bringing into play fresh rods and cones but not fresh cortex because of the well-known fact that corresponding points of both retinas are connected to the same cortical point. Result: the pattern reappeared in 3 sec.

Comparison of these periods of invisibility—10 sec when both retina and cortex remain fatigued, 1 sec when both are fresh, 3 sec when retina is fresh but cortex fatigued—indicates that the invisibility is partly a cortical affair, resulting from something in the nature of cortical fatigue, adaptation, or satiation.

Another factor to be considered is the border contrast between lighter and darker portions of the stimulus pattern. This contrast effect is a valuable aid in pattern vision, and it is believed to occur not in the rods and cones but in the retinal synapses where the necessary interaction of different parts of the pattern can occur. Fry and Robertson (1935) furnished several convincing lines of evidence for the importance of this factor in comparison with receptor adaptation and eye movements which they regarded as of minor importance. For one thing, blurring of the borders in the stimulus pattern by the action of a lens increased the duration of the negative phase. The sharper the focus the longer the pattern was visible. Further, different borders in a complex pattern did not all appear and disappear simultaneously as they probably would if disappearance were due to receptor adaptation and reappearance due to eye movement.

All this incisive experimentation on visual fluctuation has little bearing on the auditory fluctuations which originated the whole line of investigation. Their genuineness is reaffirmed by careful experiments with modern sound-producing apparatus. No appeal can be made to adaptation of the auditory receptors which apparently does not occur, and muscular movements and contrast effects seem not to play any part. Subjective noises (tinnitus) make accurate observation difficult and may be an important factor in producing auditory fluctuations (Freiberg, 1937b).

Possible circulatory factor. The arterial blood pressure is normally subject to a slight fluctuation known as the Traube-Hering wave, which can be seen in a plethysmographic tracing from the arm. Its period, while somewhat variable, agrees on the average with that of the still more variable "attention wave," and this agreement suggested that the fluctuations of attention might depend on oscillations of blood pressure affecting the efficiency of the brain. Early experimenters (Bonser, 1903), recording the two waves simultaneously, found some correspondence, phase for phase. Later critical examination revealed so many exceptions as rather to spoil the rule. Griffitts & Gordon (1924) tallied the appearances and disappearances of a faint visual stimulus and found them to occur almost impartially at the different phases of the Traube-Hering wave. However, there was a slight (and statistically reliable) preponderance of disappearances at the Traube-Hering crest, and of reappearances during the rise of the wave. Such a distribution does not make sense, physiologically, but the data are consistent with a view that changes in cerebral circulation are somehow factors in the fluctuations which we have been considering.

Fluctuations of efficiency in continuous work. Approaching the problem of oscillations from quite a different angle, students of work and fatigue have taken note of continual fluctuations of speed and accuracy such as occur in a series of reaction times or of hits at a target. These are minor fluctuations for the most part, but there are also momentary lapses scattered through the performance of uniform tasks, showing as extra long reaction times or as hits that are wide of the mark. The subject himself is sometimes conscious of being blocked and unable to function properly for a brief moment. These periods of hesitation appear very clearly in the color naming test (Woodworth & Wells, 1911, p. 52).

In another early experiment (Sterzinger, 1924) the task was more difficult and there were numerous lapses from perfect performance. The subject had before him a long series of letters and letter groups, such as:

abc fg h lnm nob ra b edif glo r ua wa amn o lo gm no e l
bb ban ac ha ho u es ab c d n erah fgh abc pm n ofm n o opp el i
u k xp pfab cam nob s fgh sgli b emno fan nix bw a bc abc
sal t ra o eo n u s e fgh ra bg fl abc cid ah a abc csa ab c

Three tasks, first learned separately, were then to be carried along together:

1. Cancel every letter that stands alone and between two vowels.

2. Cancel every letter that is identical with the one just before it.

3. Cancel every group of two letters that immediately follows another group of two.

The subject chose his own speed but was not allowed to retrace his steps. There were many errors of omission, and they seemed to Sterzinger to show some periodicity. The successful responses seemed to occur in consecutive "runs" more than would be expected by chance. Some subjects tended to miss one in every three, others one in every four, as if they had a habit of relaxing after just so many attentive acts.

These momentary lapses or blocks were extensively studied by Bills (1931, 1935a, 1935b, 1937). His experiments called for a long, rapid series of very easy responses, such as alternately adding and subtracting 3 to and from a list of numbers, or writing *abababab* and so on. The response was vocal in some experiments and manual in others, and the blocks occurred in either form of response. A block was defined objectively as an interval between two successive responses that was at least twice as long as the individual's average interval during the same work period. It was, then, an extra long reaction time.

There is no doubt of the reality of such blocks. The work proceeds at a fairly uniform rate for several or many responses, but then one or two much delayed responses intervene before the usual speed is resumed. There is a question whether these lapses come at anything like regular intervals. The rhythm, if any, is certainly not a simple one—with a block after every 12 responses, for example—but there may be a compound rhythm consisting of a slower wave with a faster wave superposed. Bills at least made some headway in this type of analysis. More important, perhaps, is his hypothesis that the blocks are involuntary rest periods which delay the onset of fatigue. If so, brief pauses introduced by the experimenter should take the place of the blocks. In one experiment (1935b) color stimuli for naming were presented by serial exposure apparatus at the rapid rate of 2 per second, but blanks were introduced giving the subject a 1.5-second rest four times a minute; and with this arrangement there were almost no blocks in 5 minutes of work.

Another inference (Bills, 1937) is that blocking will be increased by a low oxygen content of the inspired air. Brain activity demands a steady supply of oxygen, rapid brain work crowds the supply, and a momentary lack of oxygen will cause a block—such is the reasoning. Experiments showed that blocks were actually increased when the oxygen content of the inspired air was 60 percent of normal or less, and that the "fatigue effect," a progressive increase of blocks as the work proceeds, was much more pronounced when the oxygen content was low.

In a follow-up of these experiments by Weaver (1942) the subject had before him a screen with a small round window showing one of four colors, and he had at hand a reaction key for each color. When the window showed red, he pressed the red key which instantly changed the color and called for another response; and so on for 1,000 stimuli. The apparatus registered the responses on a tape running at constant speed and also caught all the errors which had to be corrected before the color would change. On the tape *E* could afterward measure every successive reaction time. The median RT of 100 college students was 800 ms, the same practically for both sexes. There were three or four errors on the average per 100 stimuli, these false reactions resulting from excessive haste. The very long reaction times (blocks) were less frequent than in the Bills experiments, averaging 17 in the series of 1,000 responses, with a wide range of individual differences, the extremes being 85 blocks for two or three subjects, as against no blocks at all for two or three. There was little fatigue effect but a large practice effect in a second day's work. The blocks seemed to be due to interference between the different responses.

Tests of attention. There are a large number of relatively simple tasks that have been used as possible tests of attention: letter cancelation in pied type, addition, following directions, etc. We need not concern ourselves with their practical applications, but there are two developments that may turn out to have theoretical significance. The first of these is a method of analysis of work curves on tasks of continuous addition and others of this type. Philpott (1932) showed that the efficiency of such work yielded regular cycles if plotted on a logarithmic base line. That is, the spurts or moments of maximum output occurred at geometrically increasing intervals, such as 45, 90, 180, and 360 seconds from the beginning of the work. The method has given good results in two additional experiments (Entwhistle, 1937; Warburton, 1943). The significance of the various cycles is not yet clear.

A second line of quantitative analysis is illustrated by the work of Wittenborn (1943). He administered a large number of relatively simple tests and treated the results by the method of factor analysis. Two of his tests seemed to be almost pure measures of the ability to do sustained mental work. A long series of letter pairs was presented orally, and the subject's task was to make different marks on a tally sheet if a pair was vowel-consonant, consonant-vowel, or vowel-vowel. The other test was roughly similar but used numbers. Factor analysis showed that these two tests were heavily loaded with a new factor that was not related to the previously recognized factors of rote memory, perception, or visual space. One is inclined to conclude that if there is anything that should be called "Attention," this factor is it! Or, better, this is what the man in the street means by the term. But it must be obvious to the reader that *this factor—or any other single factor—is not responsible for all the things that have been called shifts or fluctuations of attention.*

DISTRACTION

You are engaged in some task that calls for close attention, but extraneous stimuli break in and tend to distract you, i.e., to attract attention to themselves and away from your chosen task. You may stop your work and notice the extraneous stimuli, or you may try to keep on with your work. What happens then? Does your work suffer, and if so, how much? A natural supposition is that the work must suffer more or less, if the external stimulus is intense or has any of the characteristics of a strong determiner of attention. But there are other possibilities: (1) additional energy may be thrown into the work; (2) the extraneous stimulus may be taken care of by some automatic response that does not require attention.

Experiments on distraction, of which there have been many, follow a pattern symbolized by the formula already given,

$$R_1 = f(O_1, S_1; S_2, S_3, \ldots)$$

where O_1 stands for the subject engaged in a certain task, S_1 stands for the stimuli pertaining to the task, R_1 stands for the appropriate responses to these stimuli, and $S_2, S_3, \ldots$ are the irrelevant stimuli, the distractors. The main question has to do with the R_1 responses, as to how much they lose in speed or accuracy. This is the practical question, but one of equal theoretical interest asks what responses are made to the distractors, for it would seem that they must get some response.

A distractor must not interfere directly with the ongoing performance. If the task calls for comparing two tones, extraneous sounds would be more than distractors since they would mask the tones. Visual distractors would be used in such a case. When the task demands use of the eyes, auditory distractors are usually employed.

With young adults, easily put on their mettle, the result of such an experiment is usually that the distractor does not distract, except perhaps for a short time while they are becoming adjusted to the situation. A convincing experiment of this sort is that of Hovey (1928). A class of college sophomores was divided into two matched groups on the basis of their scores in one Form of the Army Alpha test. Six weeks later the control group took another Form of Army Alpha under normal conditions, while the experimental group took it under conditions of auditory and visual distraction. The distraction was planned to be severe. Seven electric bells of different tones sounded intermittently from different parts of the room; besides, there were four efficient buzzers, two organ pipes, three whistles, a circular metal saw that was struck from time to time, and a phonograph playing lively music. A spotlight in the rear of the hall flashed continually here and there though not into the subjects' eyes, and *E*'s accomplices entered noisily and queerly garbed, carrying strange pieces of apparatus. The conditions were disagreeable and fatiguing for the experimental group, but their test scores were scarcely affected. They did almost, not quite, as well as their mates in the control group. On the average the two groups, which had been equal in the first test, made the following scores in the second test:

Control group, working under normal conditions	137.6
Experimental group, working under distraction	133.9
Apparent loss through distraction	3.7

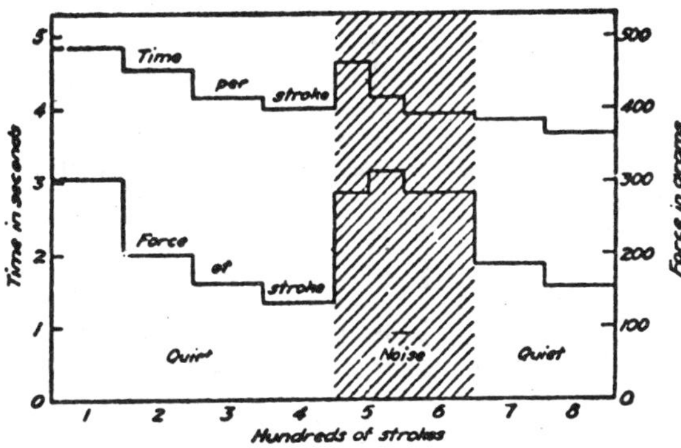

FIG. 4-3. (Data from Morgan, 1916.) Speed and force of movement in a serial reaction test. Median values for six subjects. Each subject made 800 reactions without intermission. The room was quiet for the first 400 reactions, then noisy for 200, and finally quiet for 200.

In a similar experiment (Kendon R. Smith, 1951) the distractor was a loud (100 db) noise occurring in bursts lasting 10-50 sec, with intervening short periods of silence, and the tasks were number checking, name checking, and the paper form board test. The distracted group worked somewhat faster and less accurately than the control group, but these differences were too slight to be of any practical importance.

How distraction is overcome. *Muscular effort.* It is a reasonable supposition that more energy must be thrown into the work to overcome the distraction. Morgan (1916) tested this hypothesis by recording the force of the subject's finger movements in a serial performance somewhat like typewriting. There were ten numbered reaction keys. A letter being exposed to view, the task was to translate it into a number by use of a complicated code, and then to strike the proper key. The apparatus immediately exposed another letter, and the operation continued indefinitely. The time and force of the subject's finger reactions, and also his breathing movements, were automatically recorded. He was alone in the work room, but *E* could watch his behavior through a peekhole. After he had worked for a time in quiet, bells, buzzers and phonograph records suddenly began to sound from all parts of the room. He kept on working and after a while the noise ceased and the last part of the work was done in quiet. Some of the results are shown in Figure 4-3.

We see that the time per stroke decreased gradually during the initial quiet period. This practice effect was interrupted by the onset of noise The distraction worked for a time but was pretty well overcome before the end of the noisy period, after which the practice effect continued. The force with which the subject struck the keys was high at first but went down as part of the practice effect. At the onset of noise, however, the force rose to its original level, and it remained high while the noise lasted. The breathing record (not shown here), along with *E*'s peekhole observations, revealed speech activity on the subject's part, especially during the noise. The letters and numbers were often spoken aloud. In his fairly successful effort to overcome the distraction the subject threw extra muscular energy into his work—so much is clear—though it is not clear how the surplus muscular activity operated to overcome the distraction.

A similar experiment by Ford (1929)

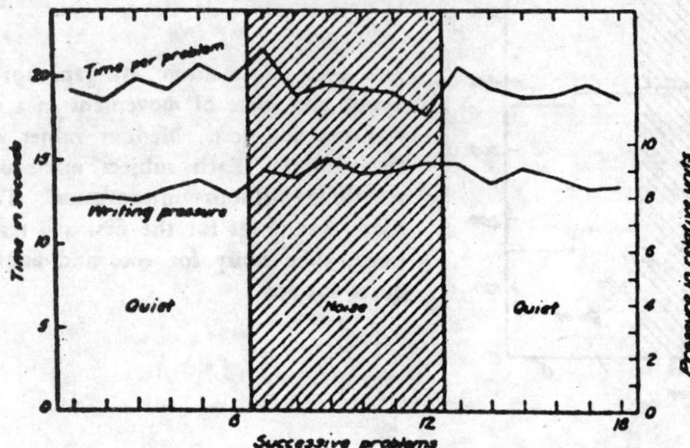

FIG. 4·4. (Data from Ford, 1929.) Median time and writing pressure per problem; 41 subjects, total of 183 series. In each series six problems were done in quiet, then six under noise distraction, and finally six in quiet, with no intermissions between problems. Each problem called for finding and adding about seven one-place numbers embedded in a line of letters, as in the sample,

Gd7Fc8NfEaW9MBcPT5FzA4NvC-Xz6MkhgP9xtb

and writing down the sum. The time per problem and the pressure exerted by the hand in writing the sum were measured.

The first problem during noise was slowed down, but not the remaining five problems during noise. On the sudden cessation of noise, the first problem again was slowed down. Having adjusted themselves to the noise, the subjects were surprised and momentarily disturbed by the onset of quiet—so many of them reported. The muscular finger pressure in writing was stronger during and after the noise than before.

No practice effect shows in the graph because the results of three series at weekly intervals are here combined. There was considerable improvement in speed from one series to the next.

gave similar results, as shown in Figure 4·4: increased muscular activity during the noisy period and successful resistance to distraction. The subjects were disturbed at the very beginning of the noise but recovered quickly. They were also surprised and momentarily disturbed by the onset of quiet after they had become adapted to the noise.

Adaptation. It is certainly natural, perhaps even instinctive, to throw additional muscular effort into your responses to the S_1 stimuli when they are interfered with by the tendency to respond to the irrelevant stimuli designated by S_2, S_3, etc. What, however, can be accomplished by the extra muscular effort, since it is not required for the work itself? We may speculate that the S_1—R_1 activity is thus made a bigger thing and more able to dominate the organism against interference. But to say that distraction is overcome by putting more energy into the work is to tell only half the story. If the work is continued day after day under similar distraction, a second adjustment takes place and output is maintained without extra effort.

A new type of experiment was suggested by the desire to know whether work under noisy conditions made a continued drain on the worker's energy. The energy expended was measured by the subject's oxygen consumption as determined by a respiration apparatus. The oxygen content of the expired air when compared with that of the inspired air showed how much oxygen was being consumed by the subject's activity. The work was adding, and the distractor was noise similar to that of a battery of typewriters. In a typical experiment there were 20 minutes per day of work in noise and 20 minutes in quiet. The oxygen consumption was higher in noise than in quiet for the first few days, but by the seventh day it was the same under both conditions. The subjects became adapted to the noise. This important result has been obtained in several experiments (Harmon, 1933; Freeman, 1939; Poffenberger, 1942, p. 134).

This second adjustment, which enables you to study serenely in a noisy room and to disregard almost any everyday distractor, evidently depends on the learning process known as "negative adapatation" (p. 559). Any novel or appealing stimulus tends to elicit responses that compete with the work in hand. Competition between the two S—R patterns builds up muscular tension, clearly visible in the wrinkled brow and rigid jaw that are usually regarded as the mark of strong voluntary attention. These surplus muscular tensions use up energy—physical energy—which can be measured by oxygen consumption. But if the motivation behind the main task is strong, learning takes place and the original distractors become background stimuli that may even help maintain the work. The importance of such background stimuli will be considered in another chapter (p. 175).

Variability in experimental results on distraction. The analysis just offered makes some sense out of the apparently conflicting results obtained by different experimenters. Fendrick (1937) found that students were really distracted by phonograph records played while they were reading; there was a consistent loss in comprehension of the reading matter, as measured by true-false tests. On the other hand, an experiment of Henderson, Crews & Barlow (1945), which required subjects to take a standard (Nelson-Denny) reading test while popular music was being played, showed no loss in the vocabulary section, though there was some loss in paragraph comprehension. Classical music had no effect whatever.

It must be remembered that these are average results, and that individuals often show opposite effects in the same experiment (Cason, 1938). These individual differences may be partly the result of past experiences with the stimuli used as distractors. But the subject's attitude also is of great importance, as demonstrated by an experiment of Baker (1937). The subject's task was oral serial addition: to start with a given number, as 23, and add 6, then 7, then 8, then 9, then 6, 7, 8, 9 and so on until stopped by *E* at the end of 30 seconds. Each day's work consisted of 20 such problems, half of them done in quiet and half during the playing of phonograph records of dance music or of twelve persons talking at once. The work continued for 10 days. Of the 40 subjects, 10 were led to expect a loss of efficiency during the noise, 10 to expect a gain, and 10 to expect a loss followed after a few days' experience by a gain, while the remaining 10, the control group, were not given any such suggestion. The three experimental groups gave results that were consistent with their expectations. The control group showed no clear-cut effect either way, though there were the individual differences to be expected from spontaneous sets and attitudes. This experiment makes it clear that the reaction to distraction is a very complicated affair, dependent largely on such *O*-variables as expectation and motivation. If noise while you are trying to work makes you angry, this internal distraction is worse than the mere noise.

DOING TWO THINGS AT ONCE

The above is a noncommittal title for a line of investigation that has often gone under the name *division of attention*. Whether there is actually a division of attention in doing two things at once is a question which we shall not try to answer at the outset. Division of attention would mean a simultaneous focusing upon two separate activities. If one is automatic and goes forward smoothly without any conscious control, no division of attention is required. If both are combined into a single integrated performance, no division of attention is required. If two activities, while carried on simultaneously in a loose sense, are kept going by a rapid shift from one to the other and back again, there is in the strict sense no division of attention. Whether or not the concept of attention can be given a perfectly scientific definition, surely a problem of great importance in psychological dynamics is posed by the fact that a person sometimes does two or more things at once.

We might better say that he always does more than one thing at once. Aside from the physiological processes of breathing, heart action, and digestion, he is standing or walking while seeing or hearing, or in some such way engaged in more than one line of activity. It is a fair question whether such simultaneous activities run along independently or are necessarily integral parts of a single total activity.

Interaction of simultaneous performances. Experiments on this problem began as early as 1887, when Paulhan tried to recite one familiar poem orally while writing another and found it possible to do so. Sometimes a word that was being recited would be written also, but on the whole such mutual interference was rather slight. Without interrupting the flow of the oral recitation, he would swiftly rehearse a line to be written and proceed to write it without any further attention. He could recite a poem while performing a very simple multiplication on paper, and neither operation was retarded. But an operation presenting any difficulty was retarded even by so automatic a simultaneous performance as the recitation of a familiar poem. Similar results were published by Binet (1890) and by Jastrow & Cairnes (1891–1892). The latter authors even found one person who could add or read more rapidly if one hand was simultaneously engaged in rapid tapping. Binet noted the difficulty of making discrete movements of the two hands unless these movements were combined as in sweeping, chopping, or producing some such unitary result.

Efficiency of a dual performance. Usually one or both of two simultaneous performances will show some impairment. So, in a free association test (p. 54) combined with a simultaneous counting performance, the associative responses tended toward the low level of rhyming and word completion (Black–Board), responses to the sound rather than to the meaning of the stimulus words (Speich, 1927).

In some occupations, as that of the telephone operator, it is necessary to do two or more things at once, or to switch rapidly back and forth between two or more performances. Vocational tests for ability to do this sort of thing have been tried, as by Sterzinger (1928). A story is read to the subject while he is adding columns of one-place numbers. He then stops adding and writes all he remembers of the story. Control tests are made with adding alone, and with the story alone, so the score in the double and single performances can be compared. One subject scored as follows:

(A)	Numbers correctly added, single task	52
(B)	" " " , double task	43 = 83 percent of A
(C)	Items of story recalled, single task	31
(D)	" " " " , double task	10 = 32 percent of C

The 83 percent and 32 percent must somehow be combined into a single index of efficiency in doing two things at once. The arithmetical mean of the two percents will not serve. For suppose the subject to be utterly unable to keep the two performances going. Let him become wholly absorbed in the story and forget to add; in this way he might score 100 percent in the story and zero in adding. The arithmetical mean would give him 50 percent, whereas he should be marked zero in *combining* the two activities, which is what we are trying to measure. This difficulty is overcome by taking the geometrical mean of the two percents instead of the arithmetical. So computed, the index for the data given above is $\sqrt{.83 \times .32} = .52$. The index for Sterzinger's 26 subjects ranged from .30 to .90, with a group average of about .60. Using similar tests on 10-year-old boys, Dambach (1929) obtained some indices of over 1.00, at least one of the tasks being better done in combination than alone.

Another occupation demanding simultaneous performance of two tasks is that of the airplane pilot. An experiment simulating some of his work required the subject to keep the pointers centered in two circular instrument dials in spite of continual disturbance. The further apart the two dials, the more difficult was the double task. The score was the percent of time both pointers were simultaneously on center; 61 percent was the best average score (Fitts & Simon, 1949). Somewhat similar experiments were noticed under the head of reaction time (p. 40).

Does muscular tension facilitate mental work? In solving a difficult problem, performing a novel act, or getting ready for any important performance, one almost inevitably engages in the additional activity of tensing the muscles (p. 174; Freeman, 1934, pp. 440–443). Is this muscular tension of any positive value? Positive results were obtained by Bills (1927) from college students. During the tense condition the subject had a dynamometer in each hand and exerted steady pressure on both of them. During the relaxed condition his hands rested easily in his lap. In both conditions he memorized, added, or read disconnected letters, trying for maximum speed. The output was greater in the tense than in the relaxed condition, the difference being statistically reliable for the experiment as a whole. Other investigators (Zartman & Cason, 1934; Block, 1936) have obtained less uniform results. Block tested the same subjects many times and found little individual consistency, since one who did best on one day while exerting a fairly strong squeeze on the dynamometers would do better on another day with only a weak squeeze or none at all. It did not seem possible to determine an optimum tension for the individuals or for the group as a whole, and it certainly was not true that the greater the muscular tension the better the mental performance. We noticed on page 87 that the subject's attitude or expectation was a factor in a distraction experiment; probably the same is true here too.

Can two attentive acts be done at the same instant? This question has not been squarely met in the experiments so far described since the possibility of rapid shifting between the tasks has not been excluded. Sensory and memory afterimages may make such a shift possible. If the stimuli are weak as well as brief, use of the afterimages will be minimized. In one experiment (Mager, 1920; Pauli, 1924) weak pressure was applied to one finger of each hand, and the subject had to say which pressure was stronger; at the same instant there was a brief visual exposure of 3-6 short lines to be counted. Either task was so easy that, when presented alone, it gave nearly 100 percent of correct responses; but, when the two tasks were presented simultaneously,

Both were correct in	12 percent of cases
One was correct in	60 percent of cases
Neither was correct in	28 percent of cases

The conclusion is that simultaneous performance of two attentive acts of cognition did not often if ever occur.

Besides the frequently reported alternation between two tasks which are being done "at once," there is sometimes the possibility of combining them into a single coordinated performance, and when this can be done, it is the most successful and agreeable way of handling the problem (Westphal, 1911; Schorn, 1928).

SPAN OF ATTENTION OR OF APPREHENSION

One of the oldest experiments in psychology, aside from some on the senses, was inspired by the philosophical question whether the mind could apprehend more than one object at a time. If the mind is a unit, how can it simultaneously perform two acts or attend to two distinct objects? But if it cannot hold two objects together, how can it compare or distinguish them? Few modern psychologists would admit any interest in this question, but they are interested in the line of experiments it suggested. In order to be put to an experimental test, the question had to take some concrete form, and operationally it became a question on the perception of number, which is a matter of psychological significance.

Early experiments. The first definitely reported experiment on the span of attention was no more than an informal demonstration; Sir William Hamilton (1859) in one of his famous lectures on "metaphysics" used to tell his students that if they threw a handful of marbles on the floor, they would "find it difficult to view at once more than six, or seven at most, without confusion; but if you group them into twos, or threes, or fives, you can comprehend as many groups as you can units because the mind considers these groups only as units."

A more serious attack on the problem was made in 1871 by Jevons, usually classed as a logician and economist rather than as a psychologist. It seemed to him "one of the very few points in psychology which can, as far as we yet see, be submitted to experiment." He placed a flat, white tray in the middle of a larger black tray and tossed a handful of black beans so that some of them landed in the white tray. He "estimated, without the least hesitation," the number in the white tray as soon as they came to rest, recorded his estimate, and then counted the actual number. In this fashion he made over a thousand trials; his results are tabulated in the following table.

Estimated Number	*Actual number* 3	4	5	6	7	8	9	10	11	12	13	14	15
3	23												
4		65											
5			102	7									
6			4	120	18								
7			1	20	113	30	2						
8					25	76	24	6	1				
9						28	76	37	11	1			
10						1	18	46	19	4			
11							2	16	26	17	7	2	
12								2	12	19	11	3	2
13										3	6	3	1
14										1	1	4	6
15											1	2	2
Totals	23	65	107	147	156	135	122	107	69	45	26	14	11
Mean estimate	3.0	4.0	5.1	6.1	7.1	8.0	8.9	9.7	10.5	11.5	12.2	13.1	13.7
SD of estimate	0.0	0.0	0.3	0.4	0.5	0.7	0.7	0.9	1.0	0.9	1.0	1.3	1.0
Percent correct	100	100	95	82	72	56	62	43	38	42	23	29	18

Jevons was surprised to find that he sometimes erred even with five beans, but he noticed especially the gradual increase of errors as the number of beans became larger. The problem, he saw, was to find a general law covering the whole series of numbers and estimates (of stimuli and responses, as we might say). For each column, i.e., for each actual number, he computed the average estimate and the scatter of estimates. The average estimate was practically correct as far as eight, but beyond that tended to underestimation. The scatter (SD) increased with the number.

It is possible to do still more with the data. For each number shown, we can find the whole range of estimates and the probability of each estimate. And we can turn about and ask, "For each estimate made what was the range of actual numbers and the probability of each?" To answer this question we sum up the horizontal rows and reduce the frequencies in each row to percents of the total for that row. So, when Jevons said, "Nine beans," the chances were 50 percent that the actual number was 9, 18 percent that it was 8, 25 percent that it was 10, 7 percent that it was 11, and less than 1 percent that it was 12. Often in a court of law or elsewhere, someone offers an estimate of a number of objects he has seen, and we want to judge what the actual number probably was and the range of probabilities. A complete table of data, like that given by Jevons, lends itself to a variety of such statistical treatments.

Computation of the span. But Jevons's successors, as well as his predecessors, have been mostly interested in measuring the "span." How large a number of beans or other uniform objects can be grasped in one glance—one momentary act of perception—and reported correctly? Jevons saw that the span must vary from moment to moment. When 8 beans were reported correctly, the span at that moment was *at least* 8, but when this number was misjudged, the span at that moment was something less than 8. The span is a kind of threshold, to be computed by the methods of psychophysics (p. 200), particularly by the

Method of Constant Stimuli, as pointed out by Fernberger in 1921. Since the span varies, we need a measure of its average (or Median) and of its scatter. For this purpose we extract from the Jevons table only the percent of correct responses for each actual number of beans, and we ask what number was correctly estimated 50 percent of the time. That will be the Median span for this individual subject.

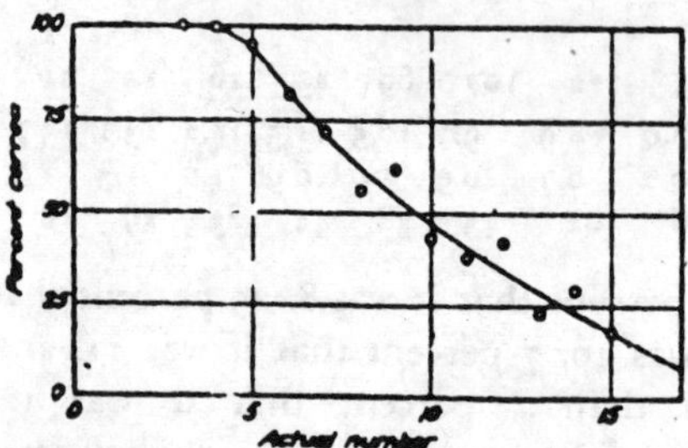

FIG. 4-5. The Jevons data handled by the graphic method (p. 204). The ringed points are the observed percents of correct estimates. The curve is drawn to fit these data points as closely as seems possible. It has the general shape of a skewed ogive. A similar graph from more regular data is shown on page 94. The 50-percent horizontal crosses the curve at a point corresponding to 9.7 beans, which was, therefore, the Median span for Jevons. Similarly, the upper and lower quartile can be located.

The pronounced skewness of this "ogive" (Fig. 4-5), with its long tail upward, suggests that two kinds of responses may be lumped together, a direct and exact perception of the smaller numbers and an estimate of numbers that are too large to be exactly perceived. This question will recur on pages 94 and 98.

The tachistoscope. For a first-class experiment better control of the stimulus variables was obviously needed. This requirement has been met by the tachistoscope, an instrument for giving "quick looks" by limiting the duration of the exposure. The simplest one is a weighted plate that drops like a window sash in its frame, with an opening in it that exposes a collection of dots, letters, or other stimulus material. It helps to add a screen in front, with a fixation point, so that the eyes are properly

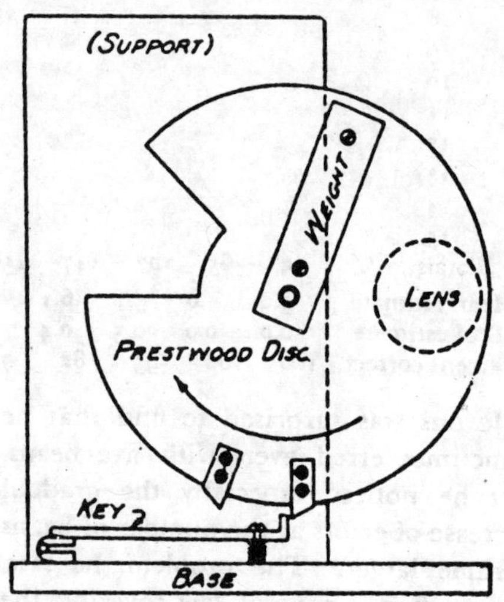

FIG. 4-6. A typical rotary disk shutter. A disk containing an open sector is a very convenient device for giving brief flashes of illumination. If the open sector crosses the light beam rapidly, the light comes on and off sharply instead of waxing and waning. The size of the opening is often variable, to change the duration of the flash. The disk may be driven by a motor, or may be weighted like the one here, so that it acts like a pendulum. Such a shutter converts an ordinary lantern slide projector and screen into a very reliable tachistoscope, suitable for individual or class-room work.

In the drawing above, the disk is "cocked" so that the weight is at 1:00 o'clock. When the key is depressed, the disk will rotate clockwise, carrying the weight almost up to 11:00 o'clock; the second stud will catch on the key and prevent a backward swing. The disk is moved forward to its original position to cock it for the next trial. The exposure material is photographed on film; the front lens of the 2 in × 2 in projector is just behind the disk, as shown by the dotted circle. The position of the open sector is such that it crosses the beam of light at the time of most rapid rotation, i.e., when the weight is at 6 o'clock. The duration of the flash is about 50 ms. With a 200-watt projector, this is adequate for a class of 50, in a dimly lighted room.

focused in advance and have no tendency to follow the falling plate. Ideally the pre-exposure field, the stimulus card, and the post-exposure field should be of the same brightness so as to minimize afterimages. A good instrument of this type is the Whipple tachistoscope (1914), which is a pendulum-actuated rotary disk, rather cumbersome to be sure, but fairly silent and designed to solve many of the technical problems.

A second type operates by cutting a beam of light but allowing it to illuminate the stimulus card for a controlled duration. Dodge (1907a, b) invented a much used instrument of this type, employing a semisilvered glass mirror which reflects the pre- and postexposure field when one lamp is on and smoothly shifts the illumination to the stimulus material (seen through the glass). But perhaps the most flexible arrangement is to put the stimulus material on film or lantern slides to be projected on a screen. A sectored disk, a pendulum, or even a photographic shutter cuts the projection beam as near its nodal point as possible so as to expose all the material simultaneously. This type of apparatus is equally suited to individual or classroom experiments. There is a growing tendency to prepare the exposure material by photographic methods; for anything except faces or scenes it is probably best to use a negative of the material so that the exposure will simply throw dots or lines of light on the uniformly dark screen.

The exposure is usually kept well below 200 ms in order to be shorter than the reaction time of the eyes in shifting from one fixation point to another (p. 502). The theory may be that with only one fixation there can be only one "act" or "stroke" of attention; at least the successive fixation characteristic of serial counting or spelling cannot occur. The exposure may perfectly well be cut down to less than a millisecond, if a corresponding increase is made in the illumination (see p. 96).

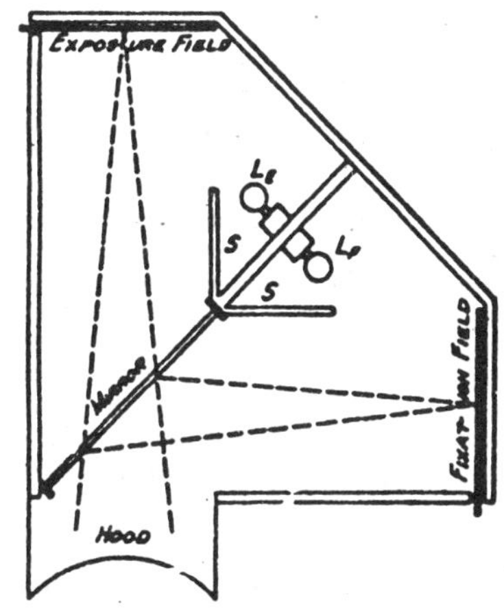

Fig. 4·7. A simplified diagram of the mirror tachistoscope. The observer looks into the hood. When one light (L_F) is lighted, he sees only the fixation field, which is reflected in the semisilvered mirror. For the exposure, L_F is turned off and L_E on at the same time, so that *O* sees only the exposure field through the mirror. At the end of the exposure the lights are reversed, returning the fixation field.

This simplified version does not solve the problems of uniform illumination, stray light, or lag of the lamps. Dodge's original model (1907a and b) introduced the light through windows in the upper right hand side of the diagram, with mirrors at L_E and L_F. The light was controlled by a sectored disk, as in Figure 4·6.

The span for number of simultaneously seen objects. With the instrumental and statistical techniques perfected the century-old question of the span of apprehension has been reopened and sufficient data have been obtained to provide an answer under certain definite conditions. The conditions need to be specified since they affect the size of the span.

When the requirement is simply that the *number* of objects shall be correctly reported—the objects being black dots scattered over a white card and exposed to clear foveal vision for 100 ms—the average span for keen adults is about 8 objects. Individual averages range from 6 to 11, and every individual varies

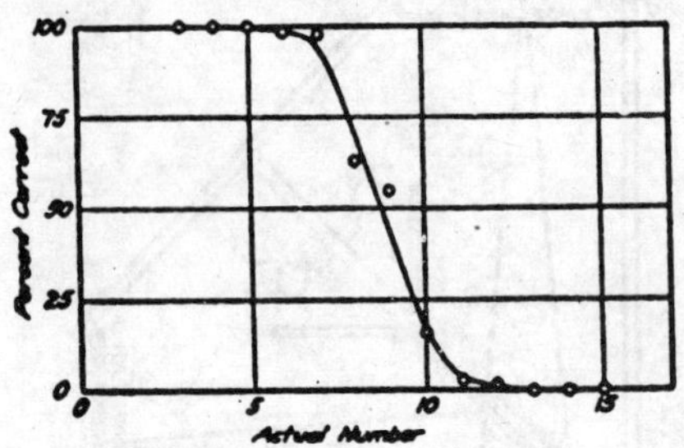

FIG. 4-8. A smoothed ogival plot of the decline of correct judgments with an increase in the number of dots exposed.

about his own average, as indicated by the SD which is large for some individuals and small for others. The table on this page shows these results, and Figure 4-8 shows the fairly regular plot from one of the subjects (subject G_3 in the table).

Different ways of ascertaining a number. The most obvious way is to *count* the beans, dots, or other items. But counting, "One, two, three, ..." is a series of steps, not a single perceptive act such as is implied by the concept of span of attention or apprehension. Not many such steps could be taken within the exposure time of 1/10 of a second. The sensation, to be sure, outlasts the stimulus if the light is fairly intense. Even so, only a few items could be accurately counted. If you get a good strong afterimage of a large collection of dots, you will bog down in counting them because you cannot fixate one after another as you do in counting real objects. Without counting you can make a quick *estimate* even of large numbers, admitting however that your estimate is only approximate. Small numbers can apparently be directly *perceived;* so two items are seen as a pair, three items as a trio, four as a quartet, and so on, the question being how far you can go in this direction and still be sure of

SPAN OF APPREHENSION FOR NUMBER OF DOTS

Data from Fernberger (1921), Oberly (1924), Glanville & Dallenbach (1929)

Dots exposed	*Subjects* G_1	F_3	F_1	O_5	G_3	O_1	O_4	O_6	O_3	O_2	F_4	F_2	F_5	G_2	*Group average*
2				100		100	100	100	100	100					
3	100			100	100	100	100	100	100	100				100	
4	100			100	100	98	100	98	100	100	100	98	90	98	
5	100			100	100	95	97	98	98	99	96	94	80	78	
6	100	99	99	97	98	86	82	90	94	94	91	87	62	49	
7	97	97	95	84	98	69	65	88	68	77	70	58	42	38	
8	84	92	80	79	63	57	63	49	59	58	22	9	34	3	
9	83	76	58	51	55	32	23	8	16	10	5	0	21	2	
10	74	63	43	34	16	20	13	3	2	0	0	0	17	4	
11	68	48	24	27	3		2	0						0	
12	58	24	16	17	2		0	0						0	
13	5				0									0	
14	8				0									0	
15	3				0									0	
Mean	11.30	10.49	9.65	9.39	8.85	8.07	7.95	7.84	7.87	7.88	7.34	6.96	6.96	6.22	8.34
SD	2.15	1.73	1.81	2.03	1.32	1.82	1.72	1.19	1.28	1.10	1.05	1.02	2.25	1.43	1.56

your numbers. And sometimes you can see a collection as falling apart into a few small *groups* as was suggested in our first quotation from Hamilton.

If the dots are objectively grouped, the number that can be perceived at once may increase enormously (Freeman, 1916). What happens can be brought out by a classroom demonstration. If a slide is exposed containing 5 groups of 5 dots each, arranged like the spots on a playing card (quincuncially) both within each group and in the grouping of the groups, most students will correctly report the 25. They are not perceiving 25 dots, but 5 groups of 5 dots each; for if a dot has been omitted from one group, it will rarely be missed.

Even if the dots are not objectively arranged in distinct groups, it is often possible for the subject to group them and so ascertain the number in a collection exceeding his ordinary span. One of Fernberger's subjects (F_2 in the table on p. 94) reported a successful perception of 10 dots, exposed for 100 ms or less, which instantly fell apart into groups of 4, 3, and 3 dots. In an experiment of Oberly (1924) the subjects reported after each exposure whether they were aware of counting, grouping, or directly perceiving the number of dots. According to these reports, as plotted in Figure 4-9, the smallest numbers were usually perceived directly, the medium numbers (5 and 6) by grouping, and the larger numbers about equally by grouping and counting.

Factors determining the size of the number span. No doubt the "span of attention" was originally supposed to be a fixed quantity. Just as with other thresholds, however, experiment showed it to vary from moment to moment about an average value. Besides this oscillation under apparently constant conditions, there are definite factors which raise or lower the average span. There is grouping, both the S-factor of objective grouping, and the subject's ability to impose grouping upon some collections of dots, which is an *O*-factor.

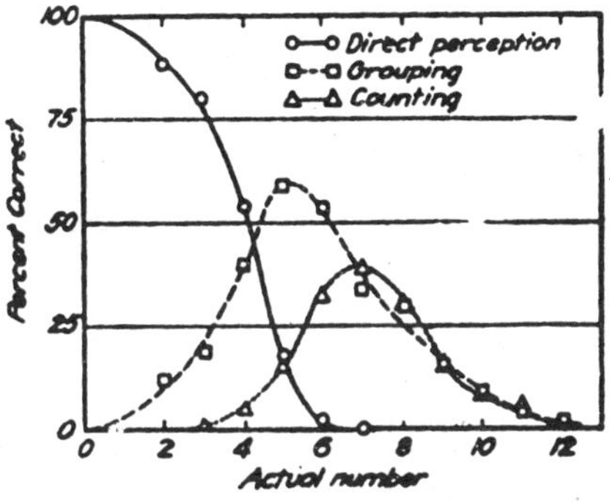

FIG. 4-9. (Data from Oberly, 1924, and Cooper, 1928.) Three methods of ascertaining the number of tachistoscopically exposed dots. Average results from 10 subjects. Direct perception did not succeed beyond 6 dots, and none of the methods had much success beyond 10 dots.

Closely related to it is the *O*-factor of previous learning. Many studies, including those already considered, have shown that the span increases with practice. The learning is of two types: generalized skill in tachistoscopic observation is built up; and specific dot collections, exposed repeatedly, become familiar and easily identified.

Stimulus factors. In span experiments the usual practice is to favor the subject by good exposure of the field of dots so that his span will not be limited by low illumination or very brief exposure. These factors were investigated by Hunter & Sigler (1940). They varied the illumination from very faint to fairly strong, and the exposure time from 4 ms up to 4 sec, and asked whether the span would not thus be made to vary from zero up to perhaps 10 dots or more.

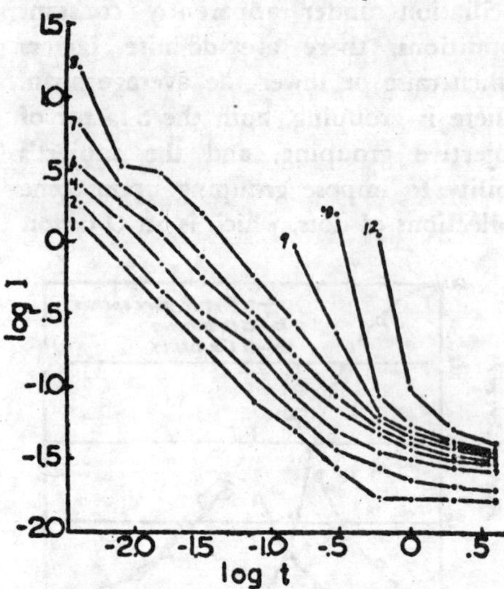

FIG. 4·10. (Hunter & Sigler, 1940.) The number span as dependent on light intensity (I) and duration of exposure (t). The sloping lines labeled 1, 2, 3, . . . 9, 10, 12 are equal-span contours. With both variables plotted in logarithms, the product I × t is constant so long as the line slopes downward at an angle of 45°. Spans of 8 dots and less were obtained with even the shortest exposures if the light was strong enough to compensate for the short exposure time, but this compensation did not work above 8 dots; more time was then necessary.

Inspection of the figure reveals another significant regularity. With any given exposure time, more light is required to see a larger number of dots. This result, confirmed by Schlosberg (1948) and by Casperson & Schlosberg (1950) is related to visual acuity which is known to improve as the light increases from faint to moderately strong (p. 385). Let the light be so faint that a single dot has a 50-50 chance of being seen at a given moment, and let the chances be the same for a second dot projected on a different retinal point. If these two probabilities are independent, the chance of seeing both dots at the same moment is 50 percent of 50 percent, i.e., 25 percent; and to reach the 50-percent threshold for two dots more light is required. This explanation has to be complicated in order to take care of binocular vision.

Such a problem demanded a large mass of data. There were two experimental variables: light intensity (I) and duration of exposure (t). For each I × combination an ogive like that in Figure 4·8 was obtained—over 60 such ogives from each of two highly trained subjects each ogive yielding a 50-percent span All these spans were brought together into a single plot (Fig. 4·10), which shows the light intensity and exposure time necessary to obtain spans of from 1 to 12 dots. To obtain a span of 6 dots, for example, you can use either a high intensity with a short exposure, or a lower intensity with a proportionately longer exposure. So far as the lines slope downward at an angle of 45°, the meaning is that the span remains constant for a constant I × t product. The effective S-factor, then, is neither I nor t separately, but the quantity of light represented by their product. This result conforms to the well-known Bunsen-Roscoe law (p. 373). We see, however that spans of 9, 10, and 12 dots could only be obtained with fairly long exposures which the subject could utilize for counting or grouping the dots.

Timing the number responses. In a typical experiment on the span of attention a number of dots are exposed to the subject's view, and he responds by saying a number word. What are the response variables which could be of service in the investigation? (1) The response can simply be scored as right or wrong, and the percent of correct responses can be used for computation of the span. (2) The response can be recorded as such and such a number word so that the distribution of number responses to each stimulus number can be worked out, as was done by Jevons (p. 91). (3) The response can be timed as in reaction time experiments.

What use could be made of the reaction times? They would show whether the response to the small numbers, below the span, was definitely quicker than the response to slightly larger numbers, just exceeding the span. According to one natural expectation it should take no longer to identify 3 dots than 2, since both lie within the span; and it should take the same time up to 6 dots, if that were the span, but definitely longer for 7 dots which would have to be counted or grouped.

The fact of the matter, as brought out by a succession of experimenters starting with Warren (1897) and Bourdon (1908), is that the RT increases gradually even within the limits of the span. For Warren's two subjects, with an exposure time of 131 ms, the RT of the spoken response crept up from 560 ms when 1 dot was exposed, step by step, to 951 ms for 5 dots and 1175 ms for 6 dots. Bourdon took the precaution of timing the mere pronunciation of the number words and found that some of them activated the voice key a little more promptly than others; but when allowance was made for this factor, it was still true that the smaller the number the quicker the response.

A modified procedure was introduced by Von Szeliski (1924) in order to secure correct responses to numbers exceeding the span. The subject was instructed to ascertain the exact number of dots, and the exposure was lengthened so as to make this possible. The times so measured are not strictly reaction times because the stimulus is not fully received at the beginning of the exposure but only after some exploration by aid of eye movements. However, the modified experiment has given some good results, and the measured time (from the beginning of the exposure to the subject's response) has increased gradually with the number of dots, up to 9 dots at least in Von Szeliski's experiment, and up to 18 dots at least in a similar experiment of Hunter (1942). In both cases there was a discontinuity in the curve at about 6-7 dots, probably indicative of a change in the subject's method of ascertaining the number. The results of Saltzman & Garner (1948) are somewhat different. The average response time of 5 subjects gave a smooth curve with no obvious discontinuity (Fig. 4-11).

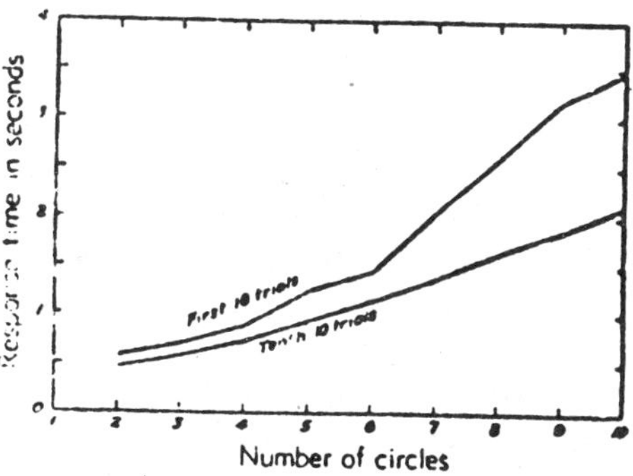

FIG. 4-11. (Saltzman & Garner, 1948.) Time required for correct identification of number of items, which were concentric circles in this case. Mean for five subjects.

They concluded that the subject's process of ascertaining the number was essentially the same from 1 to 10 at least, and that the "span" was nothing more than a convenient statistic.

As against this iconoclastic conclusion, several points should be considered. (1) Since the larger numbers are certainly counted, we must infer that even the smallest numbers are counted, if the process is the same throughout—a conclusion contrary to other good evidence (pp. 93, 95). (2) A discontinuity present in the curves of separate individuals is likely to be blurred out when the results of several individuals are pooled because one person's span will be somewhat larger than another's. (3) Another cause of blurring is that the same individual will sometimes count, and at other times directly perceive, a number lying close to his span—or, better expressed, his span varies somewhat from moment to moment. (4) The increase of reaction time from 1 to 5 or 6 dots, i.e., within the span, is quite in line with well-known facts of the disjunctive reaction (p. 33). It takes longer to distinguish red from yellow than red from green, though both discriminations are certainly direct and not accomplished by any process analogous to counting. The bigger a difference, the more quickly it is perceived; and the (relative) difference between 1 and 2 dots is greater than that between 2 and 3, and so on up the scale. In identifying 5 dots, you have to distinguish this number from 4 and 6; in identifying 2 dots, you need only make the easier discriminations between 2 dots and 1 and 3.

Number estimates. Instead of being required to ascertain the exact number of items in a collection, as in the experiments just considered, the subject may get only a brief exposure and be asked to estimate the number. *Numerousness* is the name given by Stevens (1939) to that property of a collection of items which you discriminate, without counting, when you estimate the number of items. You can employ a very rough scale of numerousness with steps like these: few, several, many; or you can use numbers with the understanding that they are only meant to be approximate. In a class experiment Taves (1941) exposed sample collections of dots, ranging from 2 to 180, with exposures of only 200 ms, and asked his subjects to estimate the numbers and to rate their own confidence in the accuracy of their estimates. Up to 6 dots the estimates were nearly all exactly correct and the confidence was practically perfect. Above 6-7 dots the subjects began to differ in their estimates and their confidence rapidly fell toward zero. In another experiment of Taves the discontinuity at about 6-8 items came out clearly. A larger and a smaller collection of dots were exposed alternately, and the subject adjusted the smaller number until it appeared to him half as numerous as the larger. When the results are plotted (Fig. 4-12), with the

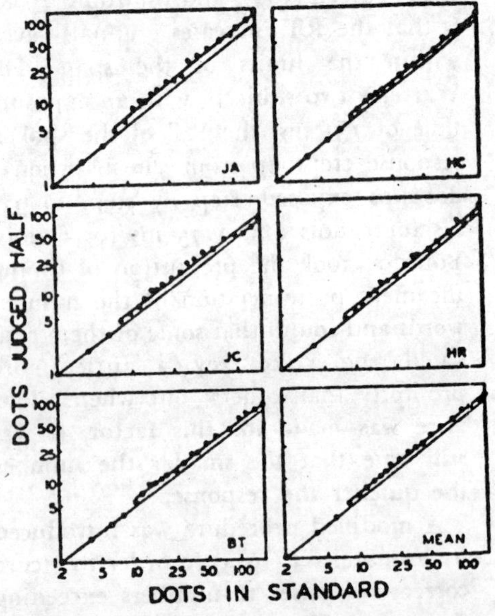

FIG. 4-12. (Taves, 1941.) Half-adjustment data for five subjects and for their Mean. Data points lying on the longer oblique line record arithmetically exact judgments, while points lying on the additional line stand for half-adjustments which are about 20 percent too large. The shift from exact to approximate is fairly abrupt.

larger number on the abscissa and the apparent half on the ordinate, the halving is seen to be arithmetically exact up to a whole number of 6-8 dots, but beyond that level the estimated halves are about 20 percent too large, half of 10 being (apparently) about 6, half of

20 about 12, half of 50 about 30, half of 100 about 58. There is a break in every function (or "curve") when the collection to be halved reaches the neighborhood of 8 dots. With these short exposures which do not allow time for counting, the subject's method shifts from exact perception of the smaller numbers to approximate estimation of the larger ones.

This line of investigation has been further developed by Reese, Volkmann and their associates at Mount Holyoke College. They have combined the reaction-time and tachistoscope techniques for the study of counting, estimating, and what they call *subitizing*. This coined word is derived from the Latin word for "sudden" and is used to designate the rapid perception of small numbers exposed very briefly. In one experiment, by Kaufman, Lord, Reese & Volkmann (1949), collections of dots sampling the range from 1 to 210 were exposed for only 200 ms. A chronoscope started as the material flashed on the screen and stopped when the subject spoke his report into a microphone. As would be expected, the reports were almost always correct up to 5 dots, beyond which errors became increasingly frequent. The reaction time curves agreed with those of Saltzman & Garner (Fig. 4-11), in that it took longer to report 5 dots than to report 1 or 2. But beyond 6 with this brief exposure, the number of dots exposed had no marked effect on the RT. The discontinuity is shown in Figure 4-13, in which the Median RT is plotted against the number of dots (the base line scale being logarithmic to avoid crowding the left-hand side of the curve). It is obvious that we are dealing with two functions, one holding up to 6 dots and then giving way rather abruptly to a different function. A similar break was found in the subject's rating of confidence in his accuracy.

If the subject is informed, after he has given his judgment, of the true number of dots in the collection, his errors quickly decrease in size. A subject who has been overestimating the larger numbers will compensate or even overcompensate for this tendency; and similarly with a subject who has been underestimating. But this training does not obliterate the distinction between subitizing and estimating nor even raise the transition point. Errors still make their appearance at the same number of dots (Minturn & Reese, 1951).

In another experiment of this series Jensen, Reese & Reese (1950) used the timing method with one important difference: the projected dot cluster remained on the screen until the subject made his report. Thus he had the opportunity to count. The result up to 6 dots was like that of the first experiment, with a discontinuity at 6 dots. But the function for the larger numbers was quite different; instead of remaining level as in Figure 4-13, it rose at an

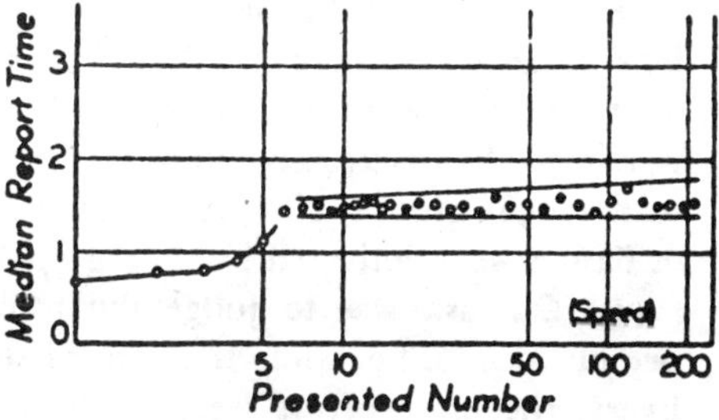

FIG. 4-13. (Kaufman, Lord, Reese & Volkmann, 1949.) Median report time as a function of number of dots, when the exposure was brief (200 ms) and instructions were to respond as quickly as possible. Group data.

accelerated rate as the number of dots increased. This difference makes sense, for you can estimate 50 dots as easily as

25, but you need longer to count the larger number and even disproportionately long since you are likely to lose your place in the count.

These experiments show that the basic formula, R = f(N), is too simple. When N is less than 6, one function is found. When N is greater than 6, one of two other functions appears according as the conditions favor estimating or counting. These distinctions hold good when the response measure is accuracy, confidence or reaction time. Here we have about as clear evidence as one could desire that there is a distinct process with an upper limit at about 6 units. It matters little whether we speak of the *limit of subitizing* or of the *span of attention;* the important fact is that there is a process whose upper limit can be determined.

Number span for successive stimuli, auditory and visual. In telegraphy a "dot" is a very brief sound or flash of light, while a "dash" is somewhat longer. Some symbols of the Morse Code consist entirely of dots: · for E, ·· for I, ··· for S, ···· for H, and ····· for 5: and a code operator must distinguish these symbols at high speed (p. 813). The span is a matter of practical concern, especially in wartime. In an extensive study of Taubman (1950) groups of 1–10 brief tones or flashes were delivered by timing apparatus; *O*'s task was to judge the number of dots. The faster the rate of delivery, the more errors were made and the lower was the span of 50-percent correctness. At any rapid rate the visual flashes run together because of the positive afterimages (p. 396). The ear recovers from stimulation much more quickly and can manage more rapid rates. The data yielded approximate spans as follows:

Flashes per second	*Span*
2	greater than 10
3	about 6
4	" 4
5	" 4
7	" 3

Tones per second	*Span*
8 or 10	greater than 10
12	about 7
14	" 5
16	" 4

The tendency to underestimate the larger numbers, especially at the more rapid rates, is shown in Figure 4-14.

Flashes of light received at a rate of 10–30 per second produce a flickering sensation (p. 380). When *O* tries to count them, he finds himself counting something quite definite, but the subjective flashes that he counts occur at a rate of not over 6–8 per second. For example, a series of 5 flashes is seen as 3 when the objective rate is 10 per second, but as only 2 flashes when the objective rate is 30 per second. That is the way the visual mechanism scores (Cheatham & White, 1952).

The span for printed words and letters. What we have so far considered is essentially the number span. The beans, dots, or other items are all alike, and the subject's task is accomplished if he reports the correct number of items. His task would presumably be more difficult, and his span smaller, if he had to report more than the mere number. This presumption was verified in a tachistoscopic experiment of Glanville & Dallenbach (1929), who exposed varied material and demanded different levels of report. The average results from their three subjects were as follows:

Span for number of dots	8.8
Span for letters to be read	6.9
Span for geometrical forms to be named	3.8
Span for report on both form and color	3.0

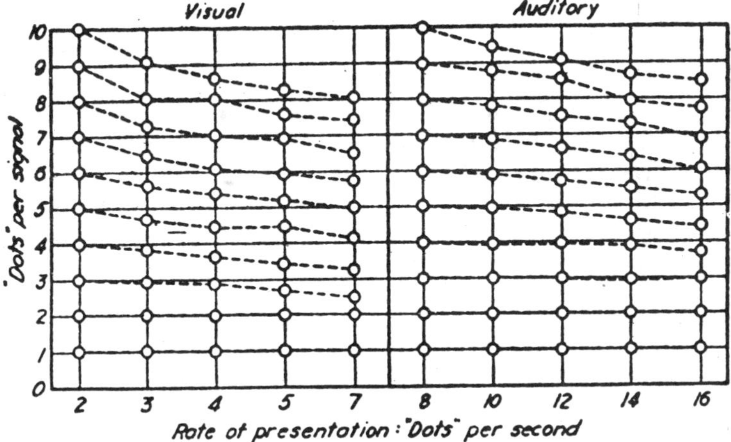

FIG. 4·14. (After Taubman, 1950.) Number estimates of "dot" series, visual or auditory. The horizontal lines show the stimulus numbers, and the circled data points show the average response numbers. The Mean estimate was computed for each of the five well-trained subjects, and the Median of these Means is shown. The larger the stimulus number, and the faster the presentation, the greater is the tendency to underestimation; and this tendency is decidedly greater for the visual dots than for the auditory ones.

The use of the tachistoscope in *experiments on reading* goes back to the pioneer work of Cattell (1885), who found that with a very brief exposure under adequate illumination:

3–4 unconnected letters could be read.
2 unconnected short words could be read.
4 connected short words could be read.

Since even the two short words, not to speak of the four-word sentence, exceeded the letter span—and since, as Cattell found in his reaction time experiments (see p. 57), a familiar short word could be read as quickly as a single letter—it was clear that the words were not read by spelling them out. What could be the reader's basis for recognizing a word? Cattell reasoned that it must be the "total word picture." His results were confirmed by Erdmann & Dodge (1898), who found the span for unconnected letters to be 4–5, while familiar words, even as long as 12–20 letters, were correctly read from a single exposure of 100 ms. They inferred that the "general shape of the word" must be the primary cue for word recognition, with a few clear letters close to the fixation point as supplementary cues. By "general word shape" they probably meant the external configuration of the printed word, while Cattell's "total word picture" covers also the internal pattern of curves and vertical strokes. As far as external outline is concerned, these two combinations are alike:

consonants
commumfs

But the internal patterns are different enough to prevent their being easily confused.

As children advance in reading ability they become familiar with many word pictures, and their span for words increases much faster than their span for unconnected letters (Fig. 4·15).

An important discovery of Erdmann & Dodge was that the visual data in reading were obtained wholly during the fixations of the eye and not during actual eye movement. The eyeball, with its quick saccadic movements from one fixation to the next (p. 506), is in effect a tachistoscope which provides the reader with a series of brief exposures. The experimenter's tachistoscope can limit the reader to a single exposure, and to a single fixation if the exposure is too short to permit the eye to shift its fixation; and thus experiment can discover how much can be read from a single fixation and what errors will be made.

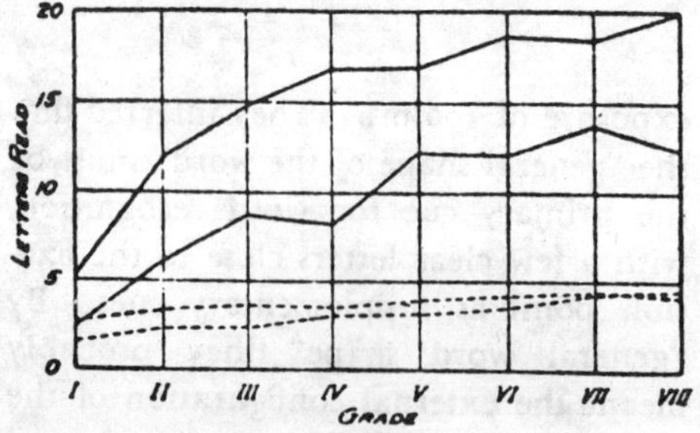

FIG. 4-15. (Hoffmann, 1927.) Increase of tachistoscope span for letters and words with advance in school grade. Each grade is divided into an upper quarter, a medium half and a lower quarter, on the basis of intelligence as judged by the teachers. The curves give the average span for the upper and the lower quarters; the middle half and the general average lie between these paired curves. Full line, span for familiar words; dotted line, span for jumbled consonants; both spans being measured in terms of one letter as unit. The span for words increases much faster and further than the span for letters.

Misprints and misreadings. Some of the best evidence on cues for word recognition has come from the errors made in attempting to read long or misprinted words. Pillsbury (1897) exposed typewritten words with one letter omitted, replaced by a false letter, or blurred by an "x" typed over it. The omission of a letter was detected in only 40 percent of the cases, the substituted false letter in 22 percent, and the blurred letter in 14 percent. Yet the mutilations made some impression on the subjects as can be judged from their comments, such as these:

Letters exposed	*Word read*	*Subject's comment*
fashxon	fashion	"Didn't see the i."
foyever	forever	"There is a hair across the r."
verbati	verbatim	"The last two letters seemed a little dim."

The reader, according to these comments, often sees details which he disregards in reading the word. Now if such details are visible when he cannot use them, correct details must also be visible in an unmutilated word and help to make up the complete word picture. Therefore, the visual impression received during a brief exposure must be much more complete and detailed than is implied by the phrase "general word shape."

This conclusion is fortified by a curious observation made by all the experimenters just mentioned. Even when a subject can report only a few of the letters shown, he firmly believes he has seen all of them clearly during the actual exposure. He forgets some before he can report them all because mere memory cannot retain so many disconnected items. Unless mistaken in this impression, then, he gets for an instant fully adequate cues for reading any familiar word. If for a fraction of a second he sees the whole word and all its parts, he has all the cues he could desire.

This possible explanation of word perception was taken seriously by Schumann (1921–1922). He urged his subjects to attend broadly to the whole row of exposed letters, and he found that the clearly seen letters were by no means restricted to the 3–6 close to the fixation point. One of his students, Wagner (1918), exposed a series of letters for 100 ms with instructions to attend to the whole series. Here are two examples:

Letter series exposed for 100 ms	*Letters reported*
L n z d w r r t s c h n f t s	L z d t s c h f t s
V a r w c z h u k z e w p o t	V a w h u z k p o t

The subject certainly read the first, the last, and some of the inside letters in each series. According to these results, the "total word picture" seen under favorable conditions is adequate for word recognition. The word is not spelled out, letter by letter, but all the letters may be clearly seen even in a very brief exposure.

Like the number span, the reading span for letters or words depends on *O*-factors and *S*-factors. Among the *O*-factors are previous acquaintance with the letters and words and previous training directed toward widening of the span. Intensive practice with the tachistoscope has been found to enlarge the span considerably (Weber, 1942; Renshaw, 1945) and may be a useful device for overcoming inefficient reading habits (Sutherland, 1946; Gates, 1947). Among the *S*-factors are the illumination and the duration of exposure—or, better, within the usual short exposures (see p. 373), the combination I $\times$ t. Here belong also the size and shape factors in the legibility of type and the brightness contrast between the letters and the paper background (Paterson & Tinker, 1929, 1947). As to the important factor considered in the next paragraph, there might be some dispute where to class it.

The role of indirect vision in reading. The farther an object is from the fixation point, the less clearly can its shape be perceived. Letters cannot be read very far out from the center of clear vision, i.e., in retinal terms, very far from the fovea. Yet the transition from good to poor form vision is gradual rather than abrupt (cf. pp. 16, 386).[1]

If you fix your eyes on the first letter in a line of print and read as far as possible into the line, you may see distinctly one long word or two or three short ones; beyond that you get vaguer impressions. The tendency to shift the fixation point to the object of interest is so strong that this informal experiment is untrustworthy unless you have someone watching your eyes. Hamilton (1907) avoided this source of error by use of the tachistoscope. He briefly exposed a whole line of print, the subject's task being to read the beginning of the line and see as much as possible of the remainder. The typical result was that the first one or two words were perceived, and something resembling the next word could be tentatively reported. For example, for "flowers" the subject guessed "follows."

For determining how far out single letters can be read, the tachistoscope can be used. A visible fixation point is present before the exposure, and a letter may then be shown either right or left of that point, the subject not knowing in advance on which side the letter will be exposed (Ruediger, 1905). Or two letters may be simultaneously exposed at equal distances to right and left, the subject being asked to report both of them (Woodrow, 1938). The results of these two experiments (Fig. 4-16) agree in showing a gradual, ogivelike, decline of correct perception as the distance from

[1] Distance from the fixation point is best expressed in angular degrees. At a reading distance (or viewing distance) of 12 in., 1 in. along the line of print = 5° of visual angle; ⅕ in. (5 mm) = 1° of visual angle; or, in general, each sideways distance of 1/60 the viewing distance = 1° of visual angle. These approximations are reasonably exact up to about 15°.

the fixation point increases. The exact values would depend on such conditions as the size of the letters used. The important fact is that slightly indirect vision is good enough to aid in reading a string of letters. In reading a newspaper a good reader will average about four fixations per line (p. 505).

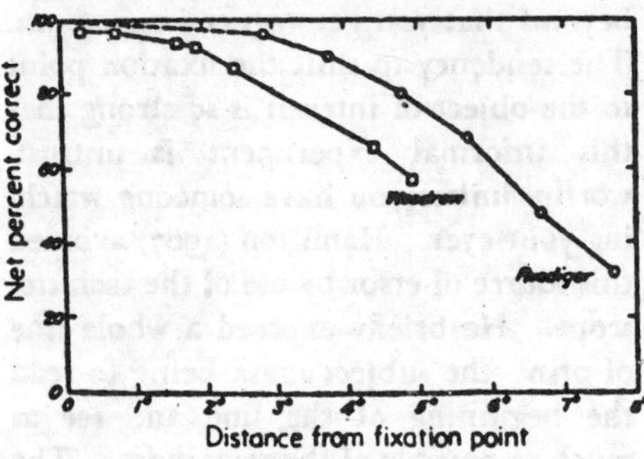

Fig. 4-16. (Data from Ruediger, 1905, and Woodrow, 1938.) Percent of letters read correctly when exposed slightly to right or left of the fixation point. Ruediger exposed either n or u and instructed the subject to guess when not sure; the "net score" for his experiment is percent right — percent wrong. Woodrow used all the letters of the alphabet, so that allowance for chance success is unimportant.

Mdsking or mutual interference of adjacent letters in indirect vision. Korte (1923) found that a group of letters, as compared with a single letter, must be brought closer to the fixation point in order to be read. Even a word, though it can be read as quickly as a single letter in central vision, is less distinct in slightly indirect vision. Some explanation is called for: if the single letters can be read, why not the word composed of these letters? There is some kind of interference. Woodrow (1938, p. 93), who in one of his experiments observed this effect with pairs of letters, suggested that "letters close together . . . cause greater confusion, or more mutual inhibition than widely separated . . . letters." For a first-hand acquaintance with this effect, fixate the central point in each of the following lines, and try to read the letters at the sides (without allowing your eyes to move!):

```
     t      .   s
    nte     .   hsx
    n t e   .   h s x
    o       .   w
    moa     .   nwi
    m o a   .   n w i
```

is it not true that the interior letter is more obscured than the end letters? The effect may be due to contrast. Brightness contrast tends to darken the letters and so make them stand out better. Where a letter has a considerable area of white next to it, this helpful contrast effect will be enhanced (p. 490). And it may well be that the contrast effect is especially necessary for distinctness in indirect vision. The "masking" would then be due to lack of contrast, though we are not ready to make this assertion strongly at the present time.

The reading span as a function of interest. The helpful influence of the context in ordinary reading is well known. A long word is easily read if it fits the context. In proofreading you must not allow yourself to become interested in the subject matter—otherwise you will overlook misprints. Akin to this *O*-factor is the factor of personal interest demonstrated in a tachistoscopic experiment of Postman, Bruner & McGinnies (1948). Their procedure was to expose a word at first for only 10 ms, which at the illumination used was insufficient for correct reading, and to lengthen the expcsure step by step till the word was correctly reported. There were six stimulus words for each of the six Spranger interests (theoretic, economic, esthetic, social, political, religious). Each subject's interest profile was determined by use of the Allport-Vernon Scale of Values (1931). The question was whether words related to a subject's dominant interests would be recognized at shorter exposures than words lying remote from his interests; and the answer was affirmative. On the average of 25 subjects, the required exposure time was 65 ms for the words of greatest interest, but 97 ms for those of least interest. In a similar study of McGinnies (1949) the list of stimulus words included some that are socially taboo, like "belly" and "bitch," along with neutral words; and the exposure time required for the "bad" words was 98 ms, on the average, as against only 53 ms for the neutral words—a reliable difference.

But is this difference in ease of recognition necessarily because of personal interests? Familiarity may be a factor, as pointed out by Solomon (1951). The greater your interest in religion, for example, the more you read in that field and the oftener you see the words current there. And words that are taboo are not often encountered in reading. Viewed in this light, the experiments merely furnish striking examples of perception as a learned response based on reduced cues. The more extensive your previous experience of an object, the more the cues can be reduced and still permit recognition. This factor undoubtedly contaminates the results mentioned, but it does not explain away some of the observed facts. The subjects were instructed to make the best guess they could after each exposure. When they misread a stimulus word that was related to their dominant interest, their guesses were in line with this interest; whereas their errors in guessing at a low-interest word, or at a "bad" word, tended to go far afield, as if they were putting up some kind of unconscious defense against the uninteresting or forbidden topic. In the second experiment mentioned the subject's psychogalvanic response (PGR or GSR, see p. 158) was measured while he was guessing at the exposed word; and PGR was stronger when the unrecognized word was objectionable than when it was neutral. Apparently the subjects, as a result perhaps of punishment in childhood for saying "bad words," were anxiously avoiding even the recognition of such words. Further research is admittedly necessary, but these pioneering experiments may open up a valuable use of one old standard method of experimental psychology in the study of personality and social psychology. However, a word of caution is in order: the effects just mentioned do not seem easy to reproduce under somewhat varied conditions.

SUMMARY

It must be obvious to the reader that the problems we have covered in this chapter will never be understood in terms of some single faculty or function called "Attention." Each of them must be analyzed in terms of the stimuli and responses involved.

To get away from any subjective factors, it might be well to consider what might be called attention in a lower animal. Consider a cat, poised at the entrance to a mousehole (*an effective determiner of attention*). This cat illustrates most of the problems we meet in the field of attention. In the first place, her eyes and ears are directed to get the maximum stimulation (*clearness, attensity?*) from the hole. Breathing is modified to sniffs, which will give maximum smell stimulation. Partly as a result of these adjustments, and probably also because of lowered thresholds or raised levels of activity of certain neural centers, any stimulus which emerges from the mousehole will be potent in determining a response. The corollary to these lowered thresholds for certain stimuli is an increase in other thresholds; the cat is not *distracted* from the job at hand by people moving around the room, or calling her name. However, she may stop looking to scratch, which might illustrate *division of attention* (or better, alternation). Periods of greater alertness are at least analogous to *fluctuations of attention*. Anything comparable to *span* is less obvious.

This example brings out an aspect of attention that we are apt to forget in studies with human *Os*, the motor aspect. The cat has a distribution of muscular tension such that she is ready to spring instantly. This shows up as a high general level of tension, as well as a particular disposition of members. Many psychologists of the behavioristic slant have emphasized the importance of these tonic sets (see Paschal, 1941, for summary). But in their emphasis on receptor and effector adjustments, they are apt to forget the central nervous system (Mowrer, 1941). The receptor and effector adjustments are integrated by complex interactions of the neural processes of summation and inhibition, occurring at various levels in the central nervous system. Ultimately the problems of attention will probably be greatly clarified when we know more about the mechanisms of neural integration. Until that time, the psychologist might keep his bearings by maintaining the functional approach suggested by the cat and the mousehole.

5

EMOTION I: EXPRESSIVE MOVEMENTS

The topic of Emotion has perhaps generated more unprofitable controversy among psychologists than any other with which they have concerned themselves. Yet it is by no means a topic which they can cast aside, for it covers a very important group of phenomena. Witness the fact that all literatures, ancient and modern, are permeated with descriptions of emotional states. In these descriptions one can find three different aspects of emotion. In the first place, an angry man *behaves* in a particular way: his actions are gross and powerful, often without due regard to the finer requirements of the situation; he may "have the strength of a demon" but be "blind with rage." In the second place, he manifests clear symptoms of internal *physiological changes* in his rapid breathing and flushed face. Finally, he has characteristic *introspective experiences* that he can report. Many of these introspective experiences have long been traced to physiological changes such as dry mouth, rapid heartbeat, and constricted breathing; examples from many literatures have been collected (Kurath, 1921; Kanner, 1931).

The method of impression. At one time or another each of these aspects has been of major interest to psychologists. The early experimentalists (ca. 1900) hoped to reach an orderly description of introspective emotional experience by using the method of impression. A stimulus was given, and the subject reported his experience. Wundt (1896) proposed a system of three dimensions of feeling—the traditional pleasant-unpleasant dimension, one which he called the excited-quiet, and the tense-relaxed dimension. An emotion was a complex conscious state or process characterized by these feelings and also including a multitude of bodily sensations. Titchener (1909), Wundt's pupil, regarded only pleasantness and unpleasantness as elementary feelings, all the rest consisting of sensations. The general view at the time was that the core of an emotion was the conscious state which aroused the bodily changes and so produced the sensations.

A revolutionary suggestion had been made by William James (1884, 1890). He regarded the emotion of fear or anger as primarily a form of instinctive behavior and only secondarily as the mass of sensory experience produced by the various bodily responses. A roughly similar theory was proposed independently by the physiologist Lange (1885). The James-Lange theory, which created quite a stir because of its reversal of the common-sense view of emotion, states that the sight of a bear in the woods causes running, rapid breathing and heartbeat, etc., and that the sensations resulting from such bodily changes fuse with the perception of the object (or situation) to produce the experience of fear. In other words, first there is the perception of danger, then the escape reactions, and last the feeling of fear. It should be noticed, however, that James as well as Wundt and Titchener considered the emotional experience as the major fact for psychology which was then defined as the descriptive science of consciousness.

The method of expression. Although neither physiological processes nor behavior were the primary concern of these early psychologists, both received some attention as indicators of feelings and emotions. Hence, the method of expression was adopted, and much effort and ingenuity went into the development of apparatus for recording the breathing, the heartbeat, and vasomotor changes. Whether the kymographic records were expressions of mental states or indicators of bodily states was of less concern to the experimentalist than to the more philosophically minded psychologists who were worried by the problem of mind-body interaction *versus* parallelism. We can follow custom and speak of emotional "expression" without implying any view on such philosophical questions or even on the James-Lange theory.

Physiological changes. The brilliant work of Cannon on the autonomic responses of smooth muscle and gland threw considerable light on the bodily changes that James and others had held to be so important to the experience of an emotion. Further work showed the importance of the hypothalamus, a small area in the diencephalon, in integrating emotional behavior. There resulted the Cannon-Bard theory of emotion (see Bard, 1934), which held that the conscious experience ensued upon an upward discharge from the hypothalamus to the cerebral cortex, rather than upon return impulses from the muscles (James-Lange). For a couple of decades the arguments between the proponents of the James-Lange and Cannon-Bard theories filled the literature; in some ways it was a fruitless debate, for the debaters were attempting to pin down the nature of the felt emotion. Gradually psychologists and physiologists became more interested in the physiological and behavioral changes and stopped worrying about the conscious experience.

An activation theory of emotion. As a result of much research and thought, the picture is beginning to clear. The name *activation theory* (Lindsley, 1951) is as good a name as any for a working theory that integrates many of the facts accumulated. We shall sketch the theory first and then fill in the details.

The term *activate* means a bit more than *to make active;* the dictionary tells us that it also means *to render capable of reacting.* This would seem to be a very good term for what the *O*-state called emotion does to us; the angry man overreacts to stimulation. Strong emotion thus represents one end of a continuum of activation. The opposite end, the condition of minimum activation, is found in the sleeping man, who does not react to stimulation. (If we wish to be accurate, we should put the state of zero activation at death, rather than sleep, for the sleeping man does react to strong stimuli. But psychologists do not usually study organisms at activation levels below that of deep sleep!)

The activation theory grew directly from work on electrical activity of the brain. It holds that the cerebral cortex is activated by discharge of the hypothalamus, a lower center. But if we generalize the term activation to apply to the whole organism, as well as to many of its key processes, we have a good integrating concept with which to tie together the many and apparently diverse facts that are covered under emotion. In this more general form the theory is not radically new. In many ways it is a form of the *energy-mobilization* theory of emotion. Cannon (1915) emphasized the energy-mobilization aspects of emotion when he showed how the body prepares for emergency action during fear and rage. Duffy (1934, 1941, 1951) has stressed energy mobilization in her stimulating papers on this topic. But perhaps we should use the more general term, activation, since energy mobilization has numerous connotations which may cause confusion.

To illustrate what we mean by the continuum of activation levels, let us start with a sleeping man, one near the zero level of activation. His cerebral cortex is relatively inactive, showing only slow bursts of electrical activity on an electroencephalograph. The muscles are relaxed and send few return impulses to the central nervous system. The sympathetic or emergency division of the autonomic nervous system is inactive. As a result of all these changes, our subject does not respond to ordinary stimuli; he is "unconscious."

Now let the alarm clock ring. It is a strong stimulus and breaks through the high threshold. Gross muscular responses occur and feed impulses back into the central nervous system. There is also autonomic discharge and some secretion of adrenin, a "stimulant." The resulting changes in smooth muscle also feed back impulses, probably through the interwoven brain-stem paths called the *reticular substance*. A very important terminus of these tracts is the hypothalamus, which amplifies these return impulses and activates the cortex. The electroencephalograph shows that the cerebral cortex is functioning at a higher level (Lindsley, 1951). In short, the individual is awake and responsive to stimulation. As he goes about his duties, the level of activation builds up, culminating in a state of alert attention, in which there is excellent discrimination among stimuli and appropriate responses.

But the level of activation is still far from its upper limit. Suppose that someone has taken a book our subject needs in his work. He becomes a bit angry, i.e., the level of muscular activity goes higher, there is more autonomic activity, and his hypothalamus feeds more impulses into the cortex. A moderate increase in activation will make him a little more energetic in finding the book, but it may well interfere with other important activities. For example, he may forget to make an important phone call. Finally, if he is blocked a few more times, he may go into a strong rage. Here the activation is very high, with resulting violent behavior. But the behavior is no longer nicely adjusted to stimuli; it is "blind" and uncoordinated. The increased feedback and chemical changes have so stimulated the hypothalamus that it largely breaks loose from cortical control. He responds almost as if he had no cerebral cortex, no previous learning about office routine or polite behavior (Darrow, 1935). It is only after the level of activation has dropped down to more normal levels that he regains his previous efficiency.

This sequence places emotion in a different light. Emotion need no longer be considered a special state that takes possession of the organism; it is merely one end of a continuum of activation. This does not mean that we should dispense with the term emotion, as Duffy and others have suggested, for it is a useful one to apply to these highly reactive states. But we must remember that there is always some degree of activation (emotion, if you prefer) in all waking states. The individual who is markedly lacking in such activation is dull and apathetic. In fact, we shall see that activation is at the heart of the problem of *drives* as well as of emotions. This comes as no surprise to anyone who has a feeling for words; the terms *emotion* and *motivation* both come from the Latin stem, *mot-*, meaning *move* (cf. Leeper, 1948; Webb, 1948).

Differentiation of emotions. Thus far we have been concerned with emotion-in-general; we have chosen anger to illustrate the energy relations in emotion. But any complete description must consider the obvious fact that many emotions exist. It may be true, as Bridges (1932) suggested, that the newborn infant shows only one pattern, *excitement,* but this primitive state soon differentiates into *delight* and *distress,* and the differentiation continues, ending with the large collection of emotions and emotionally toned attitudes of the adult. Much of this differentiation is the result of learned patterns grafted onto the basic patterns of discharge inherent in the structure of the nervous system. But there are undoubtedly a number of basic patterns. Thus, stimulation and extirpation experiments (Morgan & Stellar, 1950; Dempsey, 1951) suggest that different parts of the hypothalamus and related structures are involved in the organization of different emotions and drives. Furthermore, there are many other neural structures, both above and below the hypothalamus, that are involved in emotional behavior. The net result is that we find some organization and differentiation among emotional states; the activation is both specific to a certain organic pattern and general to the whole response mechanism. There was evidence of this specificity in our example of the man who had lost his book. He became more responsive to anything that concerned the book and less sensitive to other stimulus objects. A similar sharpening and restriction of perception and behavior occurs in states of drive, as in hunger; a hungry man responds to objects related to food and disregards other objects. We shall see that this principle may account for the fact that a thirsty rat does not learn to locate pellets of food, even though he has to push them aside to get to the water bottle (p. 642). Of course, the extreme examples of single-track behavior are found in strong emotional states. The matador is fairly safe as long as the bull makes blind charges; therefore, the preliminary phases of a bullfight are designed to enrage the bull. In short, emotion is both organizing and disorganizing. Mild emotion organizes as well as energizes coordinated behavior as it cuts down unrelated behavior. But as the level of activation increases, the behavior becomes more gross, with more and more restriction of the sensory field. In strong emotion the behavior is organized in terms of the inherent neural patterns of the lower centers, rather than the learned patterns of the cortex (cf. Leeper, 1948; Hebb, 1949; Young, 1949).

In a sense, *all* behavior is organized or patterned; when we say it is disorganized, we are evaluating it in terms of its efficiency in attaining some specific objective that confronts the organism. It is a safe bet that there is an optimum level of activation for each task; it would be low for reading a light novel, higher for working a math problem, and still higher for playing football. Below the optimum level the organism lacks energy, persistence, and concentration, but above this level his performance lacks precision; it is disorganized as far as the task is concerned.

It is clear, then, that there are two problems interwoven throughout the topic of emotion. One of these, the *organization* or *patterning* of emotions, will be our concern in this chapter. The other problem, the *level of activation,* will be postponed for the two following chapters (cf. Duffy, 1934, 1941, 1951, whose writings have had a marked influence on these chapters).

FACIAL EXPRESSION

Literature and common sense unite in suggesting the obvious place to seek patterning in emotions—the face. The musculature and skin of the face are extremely mobile. Furthermore, they are associated with important sense organs, with breathing, and with intake of food and water. Finally, any facial changes that might be associated with these vital functions are exposed to full view of others. Therefore, we might expect the facial changes to acquire value in controlling others; they might become a form of communication. There are other responses, such as voice and gesture, which might serve as social stimuli, but these have received rather less systematic study. Hence, we shall devote most of our attention to facial expression.

Problems. Biologists and psychologists who have worked in this field have studied a number of different problems, but perhaps the problems can be grouped under two major questions.

How much patterning exists in facial expressions? Here belong such problems as the number of different facial expressions that can be recognized, how consistently they can be judged, what expressions are confused, what methods are used by judges, and the objective measurement or description of the various expressions. We shall note that there is considerably less patterning or differentiation than most people would believe; thus, anger and fear are frequently confused by an observer.

Are the patterns of facial expressions inherited or acquired? This question has been tackled by comparing different cultural and national groups, different age levels, and blind *versus* normal *Os*. We shall see that there are both inherited and acquired elements in facial expressions, as in almost any other type of behavior.

Now that we have a preview of the questions and a hint of the answers, we are ready to examine a few of the more typical studies. As we go over these studies, we must remember that facial expressions are more than mere *expressions* of mental states called rage or fear; each "expression" is an integral part of the complex pattern of neural, muscular, and glandular changes that constitute the emotion.

Antecedents. The psychologist was preceded in this line of study by the anatomist, the painter, and the actor. A great anatomist, Sir Charles Bell (1806,

1844), well known for his discovery of the distinct sensory and motor roots of the spinal nerves, pointed out the value of anatomy for the painter and the special importance of knowing the facial muscles which produce the different expressions. As to the question whether these facial movements are primarily expressive or practical, he believed the latter alternative to be the better general theory. When an angry dog bares his teeth, it is a practical movement. Physiologically the facial movements, like those of speech, are connected with the general function of respiration. Yet Bell believed that certain muscles peculiar to man (better, to the primates), such as the corrugators that "knit" the brows or the triangularis that depresses the corner of the mouth, have no other function than that of expressing the finer shades of emotion.

The greatest of the early students of emotional expression was Charles Darwin, who followed up his *Origin of Species* and *Descent of Man* by a work which was a contribution to psychology as much as to the theory of evolution, his *Expression of the Emotions in Man and Animals* (1872). Disagreeing with Bell, Darwin held that every facial movement was primarily "serviceable," and that its expressive function was derived from the practical function according to one or another of his three principles of emotional expression.

1. The principle of "serviceable associated habits." Many expressive movements are remnants or vestiges of practical movements. Originally directed to the securing of practical results, these movements became automatic habits and might even be inherited. But they were modified in two respects. On the side of the stimulus, they became associated with situations which were merely analogous with the original exciting causes; and on the side of the response they were weakened and toned down till only vestiges of the original practical movements remained.

2. The principle of "antithesis." Opposite impulses tend to opposed movements. If one emotion gives a certain movement, the opposite emotion will give the opposed movement even though the latter never had any practical value.

3. The principle of the "direct action of the excited nervous system on the body"—of the overflow of nervous activity into all available motor channels. Muscular trembling is an example.

Most characteristically Darwinian is the first principle. The expression of grief in the adult is toned down from the frank crying of the infant. The vocal part of crying is a practical call for help, and the facial part was originally an adjunct to the vocal. The wide-open mouth involved the muscles which depress the corners of the mouth, and this little movement remains as a sign of grief after vocal crying has been eliminated. Similarly, firm closing of the mouth, originally adjunct to the practical movement of straining, remains as a symptom of mental effort and determination. Raising the upper lip and showing the canine teeth in anger may be a remnant of practical teeth-baring in simian combat.

Darwin's principle of antithesis can be used to explain laughter which is the opposite of sobbing in that sobbing involves spasmodically interrupted inspiration, laughter expiration.

Piderit (1859), a German anatomist who lived for many years in Chile, wrote on facial expression both before and after Darwin. Like Bell, he hoped to make anatomy useful to the painter and sculptor. In many paintings he found a lack of harmonious facial expression, which stimulated him to analyze the total expression of the face into elementary expressions of the several features in the belief that combining such elements would insure a harmonious total.

In Piderit's theory expressive movements are not mere remnants of practical movements. They have a present utility which can be discovered without going back into individual and racial history. The facial muscles, he believed, are adjuncts of the sense organs, serving to assist or impede the reception of stimuli. Just as opening or closing the eyes facilitates or impedes the reception of visual stimuli, so certain positions of the nose facilitate smelling while other positions keep out unpleasant odors. A sweet substance is savored by pressing tongue and lips against the front teeth, a bitter taste minimized by lowering the tongue away from the roof of the mouth.

In developing his theory Piderit suggested that an object thought of should give the same facial response as when present to the senses. With an unpleasant thought, the mouth behaves as if avoiding a bitter taste, the eye region as if avoiding an unpleasant sight, the nose as if avoiding a foul odor. A pleasant thought gives open eyes, a "sweet" mouth, and a sweet nose if the individual's nose is sufficiently mobile. In general, movements such as impede the reception of stimuli express unpleasant emotion. Receptive movements may express attention as well as pleasure. Wide-open eyes express attention, suddenly raised brows surprise, extremely raised brows amazement, half shut eyes indifference. Similarly, Piderit recognized the open mouth of listening or other attention, the stubborn mouth (agreement with Darwin here), and the appraising or sampling mouth, with lips protruding. Many combinations of these elements are possible.

Piderit illustrated his analyses by drawings. Simple line drawings they were, profile and front views, stripped of all accessories that could suggest emotion. Such bare outlines afford the fairest test of the reality of the proposed elementary expressions.

Judgments of facial expression. The experimental psychologist took his cue from Darwin and Piderit. Darwin himself introduced one of the typical experiments. Obtaining some photographs intended to represent several emotions, he showed them "without a word of explanation," and asked for a judgment of the emotions expressed. Among his 20 judges there was general agreement regarding some of the photographs but little agreement on others. Where the judges disagreed, Darwin concluded that the picture did not truly express the emotion, though he himself, on first examining it and being told what emotion it represented, had been fully satisfied. The experiment convinced him that suggestion was a factor in reading facial expression.

On the basis of Piderit's drawings, Boring & Titchener (1923) prepared interchangeable features which could be inserted in a profile drawing of a human face. With an assortment of brows, eyes, noses, and mouths, they built up 360 compounds and found, strangely enough, that almost every compound was accepted by some *O* as a genuine expression, even when the parts were contradictory. When *O* had entered into the spirit of the game, he saw the Piderit elements in the separate features and intelligible expressions in the built-up faces.

The question remained whether these

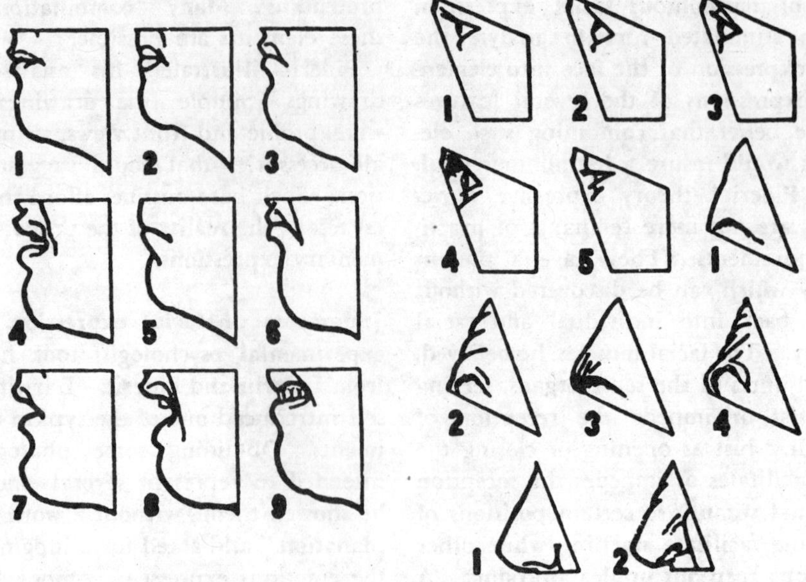

FIG. 5·1. (Boring & Titchener, 1923.) Piderit features.
Mouths: 1, normal; 2, sweet; 3, bitter; 4, very unpleasant; 5, stubborn; 6, stubborn and unpleasant; 7, attentive; 8, unpleasant and attentive; 9, snarl or sneer.
Eyes: 1, normal; 2, exalted; 3, attentive; 4, very attentive; 5, inattentive, withdrawn.
Brows: 1, normal; 2, attentive; 3, unpleasant or thoughtful state; 4, unpleasant attention.
Noses: 1, normal; 2, unpleasant attention.

compounded expressions would convey the same meanings to observers who received no guidance or suggestion from the experimenter. This question was put to the test in an experiment of Buzby

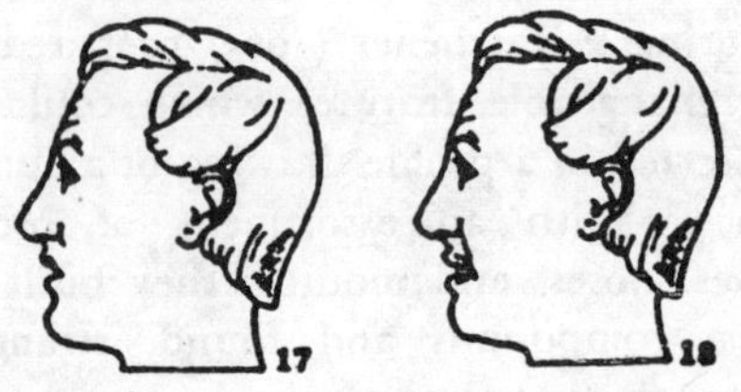

FIG. 5·2. (Boring & Titchener, 1923.) Compounds of Piderit features: 17, bewildered; 18, amazed.

(1924) and of Fernberger (1928). Some of the Piderit faces were shown to students who were supplied with a list of emotion names from which to select the most appropriate name for each facial expression. The results, as presented in the next table, show that the *O*s did not agree closely with each other or with the theoretical meanings of the expressions. If we accept the faces as correct, and regard the experiment as a test of ability to read facial expression, we conclude that these students did poorly. If we assume that in such a matter the pooled judgment of a large number of unprejudiced observers is correct, we must conclude that the faces were not very expressive of the supposed emotions. The expressions were, however, very unequal in success. The "dismayed" face seldom gave the impression of dismay, more often suggesting simple attention. The "bewildered" face usually conveyed the impression of something akin to bewilderment, if we count the 26 percent of "amazed" and the 14 percent of "quizzical." We have to reckon with some vagueness in the use of these emotion words.

Where the facial expression is susceptible of different interpretations, there is room for suggestion. Fernberger (1928) tried the effect of suggesting a "false" interpretation. To several groups, totaling 658 students, he showed these same five faces, assigning to each a "false" designation and asking the subjects to judge whether the given face expressed the designated emotion well, fairly well, poorly, or not at all His results are seen at the very bottom of this page.

The suggestion worked except when conflicting strongly with the intended expression. Probably suggestion affects our ordinary reading of a person's emo-

HOW THE PIDERIT FACES APPEARED TO 1382 STUDENTS

(Busby, 1924, and Fernberger, 1928)

The list of names at the left of the table was provided and each subject selected what seemed to him the best-fitting name for each of the five faces. The table gives the percent selecting each name, an "e" denoting less than ½ of 1 percent.

	Intended expressions of the faces shown				
Terms used	*Dismayed*	*Horrified*	*Disdainful*	*Disgusted*	*Bewildered*
Pleased	e	1	e	0	e
Displeased	3	1	4	2	e
Stubborn	2	e	9	1	e
Attentive	45	0	1	0	11
Quizzical	18	e	1	0	14
Inattentive	1	e	5	0	3
Dismayed	5	3	2	e	6
Reverential	5	0	3	e	5
Affable	2	e	e	0	2
Bewildered	8	2	1	e	32
Amazed	2	7	e	0	26
Horrified	e	57	0	e	e
Raging	e	11	e	e	0
Disapproving	4	2	14	7	1
Disdainful	2	2	34	9	e
Angry	e	2	1	e	0
Contemptuous	1	3	19	33	0
Disgusted	1	10	6	48	0
	99	101	100	100	100

EFFECT OF SUGGESTION ON THE INTERPRETATION OF FACIAL EXPRESSION

(Fernberger, 1928)

Expression intended *Response suggested*	*Dismayed* *quizzical*	*Horrified* *attentive*	*Disdainful* *displeased*	*Disgusted* *contemptuous*	*Bewildered* *reverential*
Percent selecting this response without suggestion	18	0	4	33	5
Percent accepting the suggestion *	74	10	77	95	70

* The "percent accepting the suggestion" judged the face as expressing the suggested emotion well or fairly well.

tion from his face, only that the suggestion is conveyed by the situation in which the person is placed and by his total response. "Reading the emotion from the face" amounts in large part to reading the emotion into the face. As Fernberger puts it, the results "indicate that little can be determined of an emotional state in another individual from the perception of an abstracted facial expression completely divorced from a general, total stimulus situation. If a stimulus situation is indicated, the emotional state is judged in accordance with that situation rather than in accordance with the facial expression."

Judgments of posed facial expression. The Piderit profiles are not merely "divorced from the total situation"; they are outline drawings, and photographs of actual faces might be more accurately judged. Photographs would escape from the criticism of Arnheim (1928), who prepared silhouettes with some parts identical and found that the part was changed in its appearance by being brought into different combinations. He inferred, going to be sure beyond his evidence, that Piderit's analytical way of studying facial expression was entirely beside the mark.

As a service to artists, Rudolph (1903), a painter with some anatomical knowledge, made a study of facial expression and published some hundreds of photographs of a male actor in various poses, the photographs being retouched and somewhat idealized by the author. Rudolph's own theory was that all facial expressions were based on a few primitive types, which fundamentally were movements of approach and withdrawal. His actor subject possessed a very mobile and expressive face, and the collection of photographs is a storehouse from which psychologists have drawn. Collections of female poses have been provided by Feléky (1914, 1922) and by Ruckmick (1921, 1928). Perhaps the best series of all is that of Frois-Wittmann (1930). Hulin & Katz (1935) published the best 72 of his pictures, and 24 are shown (very much reduced in size) in Figure 5-4 (p. 129).

The experimental procedure is to take facial poses intended by the actor to express certain emotions and to try them out on unprejudiced observers. Sometimes *O* is provided with a list of emotion words; sometimes he is free to use his own words.

Langfeld (1918) used 105 of the Rudolph poses and instructed his 11 *O*s to give a name descriptive of each pose. His most successful *O* gave 58 percent of "correct" names (agreeing closely with the actor's intention), and the least successful 17 percent. These low percents have led subsequent writers to say that facial expression is not read with much success; but the mere percent correct is a very inadequate measure, as we shall see.

Langfeld also tried suggestion, by presenting each picture a second time with a name purporting to be correct (but actually incorrect in half the cases), and asking whether this name was acceptable. Incorrect names were often accepted even though *O* had previously given a correct interpretation of the same poses. One *O* accepted as many as 47 percent of these false suggestions, another as few as 16 percent. On the whole, suggestion had considerable effect—a result quite in line with that obtained with the Piderit faces.

Another important result is improvement through instruction and training (F. H. Allport, 1924). A class of 12 college women were shown by lantern 14 of the best Rudolph poses, and made an average score of 49 percent correct. *E* then gave a brief but comprehensive lecture on facial expression, covering the anatomy of the facial muscles and the contribution of each part of the face to each major type of emotion: Pain-Grief, Amazement-Fear, Anger, Disgust, Pleasure, Attitudinal (including doubt, determination, etc.). After this instruction the same pictures were presented again, and the average score rose to 55 percent.

Repeating this experiment, Guilford (1929) used 96 Rudolph poses, divided into four approximately equivalent sets. The average scores made by the 15 *Os* were:

	Percent
Set 1, before instruction	27
Set 2, after study of the facial muscles	27
Set 3, after reshowing of Set 2 with correct names given, and after study of Allport's six groups and his analysis of expression	[illegible]
Set 4, with special directions to analyze	39
Set 1, repeated at end	41

The implications of this improvement through training in the judgment of facial expression are rather uncertain. Allport infers that the ability to interpret facial expression is acquired by learning, not inborn, and that the differing ability of different individuals results from their differing attention to this matter. The fact that the individuals who score high in the initial test improve little, in comparison with those whose initial score is low, may be explained, Guilford suggests, by supposing that training in analysis does not help those who take the face as a whole in reading its expression, which very likely is the best way to read faces. Incidentally, this is one of the few cases in which individual differences are decreased by training.

As to the method by which one attempts to diagnose the emotion expressed in the face, introspections were obtained by Langfeld and other experimenters. So far as the judges could tell, there are two main methods: imitate the pose and notice "how it feels"—the method of empathy; or, imagine a situation in which the pose would be appropriate. Neither is a sure method.

How accurately can facial poses be interpreted? The low percents of "correct" judgments obtained in several experiments have seemed to justify the conclusion that reading facial expression is mostly a myth, and that we depend in real life on the situation in which a person is placed and on what he says and does, rather than on his face, to reveal his emotion.

The truth lies somewhere between this extreme conclusion and the popular view, for the experiments impose a rather unfair task on *O*. In most cases, the actor poses an expression that *he* thinks represents a specific emotion, and *O* is asked to guess the emotion. Thus a double chance for disagreement exists. Then the question of synonyms arises. If *O* is allowed free choice of names for the expressions, *E* has to decide which among the following are correct judgments for *rage*—rage, anger, wrath, indignation, resentment, etc. One way to avoid this decision is to give *O* a limited list of labels to apply to the different expressions, eliminating synonyms as much as possible. One can further improve the situation by forgetting what the actor *intended* the picture to represent and by counting *O* correct if he agrees with the majority of his fellows. This leads naturally to the next step, which is to discover which pictures are confused by most *Os*. Frois-Wittmann (1930) used this method to find out the relationships among various expressions. For example, he found that *rage* was closely related to *horror* on the one hand and to *anger* and *hate* on the other. The final step is to discard names entirely. Brigham (1932) and Hulin & Katz (1935) had *O* decide which pictures belonged together. It is a little difficult to know what to do with the results of this extreme method, for *E* ends with a table showing the number of times picture No. 23, for example, is judged similar to Nos. 35, 18, 46, etc. Such a table does not tell much about the accuracy with which *O* can judge facial expressions.

A scale for judging facial expressions. The fact that some expressions are more similar than others does suggest that all errors are not equal. What is needed is a scale which will give *O* credit for "near misses." In the first edition of this text Woodworth developed such a scale. He built it up from a careful examination of the distributions of judgments of 100 *O*s on 86 poses, which had been published in detail by Feleky (1922). After some trial and error, he found the following scale to be satisfactory:

I. Love, Happiness, Mirth
II. Surprise
III. Fear, Suffering
IV. Anger, Determination
V. Disgust
VI. Contempt

The scale was satisfactory in that a pose which most *O*s judged to be Fear might seem to others to represent a neighboring step, as Surprise or Anger, but was rarely called anything as remote as Love or Disgust. With this rough scale, the correlation between pose and judgment in the original data became .92, which suggests much better accuracy in judging facial expressions than previous work had indicated. The scale worked very well on other sets of data collected on other pictures (Ruckmick, 1921; Gates, 1923). We shall return (p. 124) to this linear scale.

Another method of scoring judgments. Other evidence that a posed emotion can be fairly well recognized from a still photograph of the actor's face is given by Kanner (1931). Some of the Feleky poses were shown to groups of students totaling 409 individuals. They were not furnished any list of emotion names but were instructed (1) to give the "best term" for each pose, (2) to state the situation to which the actor was probably reacting, and (3) to guess what the actor would say along with his facial expression. With all these responses taken into account, each judge was rated on a 10-point scale, and a score of 7 points or more was counted as a success. Nearly all the judges did much better than chance, and nearly every pose gave better than a chance percent of successful responses. The poses were quite unequal in this respect, Surprise being recognized by 77 percent of the judges, Fear by 70 percent, Horror by 62 percent, Shame by 53 percent, Rage by 50 percent, Suspicion by 27 percent, Pity by 19 percent.

Children's judgments of posed facial expressions. Six pictures from Ruckmick's collection were tried on children of 3–14 years by Gates (1923). There was a gradual increase with age in the percent of approximately correct judgments. With a liberal allowance for childish vocabularies, the pose for Laughter gave 70 percent correct judgments even at ages 3–4, and an increase to 100 percent at age 10. Surprise and Contempt, on the contrary, got practically zero scores at ages 3–5. The level of 50-percent correct was attained at different ages for the different facial expressions:

Pose	*Age*
Laughter	below 3
Pain	at 5–6
Anger	at 7
Fear-horror	at 9–10
Surprise	at 11
Contempt	above 14

Children and adults differ in the relative difficulty of the several expressions. Contempt, the hardest for the children, is among the easiest for adults, and there are other discrepancies. Laughter is, however, about the easiest for both children and adults. Anger usually gives low scores and wide scatter of the judgments. Surprise is easily understood in the Feleky and Ruckmick poses, but not in the Rudolph poses. There are probably cultural differences in the conventional expression of anger; and individual actors have their specialties, some registering one emotion more successfully and some another.

Spontaneous facial expression. Granted that actors express in their faces a variety of emotions to a recognizable degree, it does not follow that the faces of everyday folk are spontaneously expressive. There is probably a strong element of convention in stage expressions, as there is a strong element of control and suppression in the facial behavior of the ordinary adult. It would be worth while to photograph the spontaneous expressions of children and adults, while undergoing emotion, and to check such photographs as the poses have been checked, by submitting them to the judgment of unprejudiced observers. The difficulty is to secure the photographs under known conditions of emotion.

Sherman (1927) took motion pictures of infants a few days old, in situations presumed to produce different emotions:

Rage	(restraint of the infant's head)
Fear	(sudden loss of support)
Pain	(needle prick)
Hunger	(feeding overdue)

Students and other observers attempting to judge these pictures were unable to distinguish the several conditions, even though they had a picture of the whole baby and a motion picture at that. Apparently, at this tender age, there is practically only one expression for all these unpleasant situations.

Schulze (1906, 1912) had better luck with older children. He placed before them pictures intended to arouse different emotions, photographed the children while they were examining the pictures, and presented the photographs to judges who endeavored to identify the picture at which the children must have been looking. The judges had some success, and the reproduced photographs certainly show characteristic differences of facial expression.

Dunlap (1927) obtained unposed facial expressions by applying to adults in the laboratory stimuli calculated to arouse laughter, startle, pain, disgust, strain, relaxation. His special interest was in the relative expressiveness of the eyes and the mouth. He took two photographs of the same person, expressing very different emotions, cut the photographs in half horizontally, and combined the upper half of one with the lower half of the other. The result was, in general, that the synthetic expression was dominated by the mouth. A face with sober eyes and laughing mouth appeared unquestionably to be laughing. The laughing mouth dominated the face, and the same was true to a considerable degree of the disgusted, startled, pained or strained mouth. Dunlap's photographs certainly indicate that unposed facial expressions differ with the subject's emotional state. Coleman (1949) did a roughly similar experiment, but he used motion pictures instead of still ones. He found that the relative effectiveness of eye and mouth region varied from expression to expression. (See also Frois-Wittmann, 1930; Hanawalt, 1942, 1944.)

Objective analysis of spontaneous facial expressions. An especially thoroughgoing attempt to bring genuine emotions into the laboratory was made by Landis (1924). In a three-hour session he introduced 16 situations intended to produce varied emotions and to build up finally a strongly excited and irritated state. He obtained the irritation but did not secure any specially agreeable states. His *Os* took the whole affair rather seriously and were probably set for endurance rather than enjoyment. They were for the most part psychologists going through unpleasant experiences in the presence of another psychologist and for his benefit. For that reason, perhaps, the facial expression did not differ markedly from one situation to another. Considerable muscular tension showed in the lines of the face and increased with the progress of the trying experience. The eyes were partly closed much of the time, and the upper lip was raised or drawn to the side. A smile was present even in situations which must have been disagreeable.

Landis made an analytical, objective study of the photographs taken during the several situations, so as to determine which muscles were active in each expression. He looked for patterns of muscular action characterizing particular emotions. The ideal positive result would be to find a certain pattern present in all the faces photographed in one situation and never present in any radically different situation. The ideal negative result would be to find all the situations, all the reported emotions, alike in their pattern of muscular contraction. The actual result lay between these ideal extremes and, in Landis's judgment, much more to the negative side. He reached the conclusion, "So far as this experiment goes, I have found no expression other than a smile, which was present in enough photographs to be considered as typical of any situation." There were expressions, or facial postures, characteristic of individuals, but not characteristic of emotions. It must be admitted, however, that the range of emotions actually aroused was rather narrow, that the *Os* were probably not expressing their emotions freely, and that the analytical data are difficult to handle by any recognized statistical procedure. A poker-faced individual can undergo a variety of experiences without revealing his emotions, and still the naive face may be very expressive. Thus, Coleman (1949) took movies of 12 *Os*, in situations roughly like those of Landis and found that the best two *Os* yielded pictures that were judged quite consistently.

As far as the ubiquitous smile is concerned, there are two possible explanations. Frois-Wittmann (1930) pointed out that situations such as cutting off the head of a live white rat (which was one Landis used) might have involved some sadistic pleasure. Perhaps a more reasonable guess is that the smile is the typical "overflow" expression for strong emotions in a social situation. Klineberg (1938, 1940) points out that the Chinese use it in anger, and there is the smile of deprecation, etc.

Candid-camera photos. The ideal unposed pictures would be those snapped in actual life situations without *O*'s knowledge. These are harder to obtain than one would anticipate. It is a safe bet that a fair proportion of the allegedly candid shots in newspapers and magazines are actually posed. But Munn (1940) took advantage of these sources and collected 14 reasonably good pictures from *Life* and *Look*. In one study he had groups of *Os* judge the expressions when the face alone was exposed. The students judged the emotions at least as well as others had judged posed photos. As a matter of fact, examination of the published table shows rather small scatter in terms of Woodworth's scale.

At a later time Munn showed the pictures again, but this time he included the whole picture, thus furnishing some knowledge of the situation in which the expression had occurred. This additional knowledge sometimes markedly improved the judgments. For example, the face of a girl engaged in a sock race was judged very consistently as Sorrow, but when the rest of the picture was included, the judgments shifted to Strain and Determination. This shift would probably involve a change of perhaps half a scale division. Another picture gave judgments spread from Surprise to Disgust, with only a slight Mode in Anger, when the face alone was shown. But when the *Os* could see that the face belonged to a man who held a strikebreaker by the coat collar, the judgments concentrated heavily on Anger and Hate. It is fairly obvious that such situational cues are very important, not only in sharpening the judgments in terms of our scale categories, but also in bringing out fine shades that are lost in scaling.

The role of the hands in expression. In addition to the situation, other factors clarify the significance of facial expressions. One of these is hand gestures. Skilled actors often depend heavily on gesture, and many cultures use them freely (cf. Critchley, 1939; Efron, 1941). An experimental test of the effectiveness of the hands alone in expressing emotion was made by Carmichael, Roberts, & Wessel (1937). They took both still and motion pictures of the hands of a skilled actor as they protruded through a screen. Groups of judges were able to recognize the emotions portrayed in the hand photos about as well as other groups of *Os* had identified facial expressions. The movies averaged no better than the still photos. There seems to have been some loss in detail in the motion pictures, which counteracted the possible gain from motion. (Cf. Dusenberry & Knowrer, 1938.)

Vocal expression of emotion. The voice may well add another clue for our judgment of emotion, although that statement is based more on common experience than on experimental evidence. When Sherman (1927, 1928) finds an observer unable to tell from the sound of the voice alone whether a baby is crying from hunger, from colic, or from restraint, the differences in question are slighter than those between the sound of a baby's crying and the sound of his cooing or laughing. Certainly we can tell by the sound whether a person is laughing or not, and there are various other tones and intonations which we believe we can recognize—until some experimenter proves the contrary—the determined tone, the sarcastic tone, the coaxing tone, and others.

The sound of the voice may differ in loudness, in pitch, in timbre, and in inflection, the last amounting to a slide in pitch. It is safe to say that "raising the voice"—which means raising its pitch or increasing its loudness, or both—occurs naturally in excited states. Apparently the baby does not have to learn to cry more loudly as he becomes more "worked up."

That a change in the timbre of the voice may go with changing emotional state is suggested by the "sweet voice" and the "harsh voice" which we believe we can distinguish and interpret. But there is a minimum of scientific evidence on this point.

Inflection was studied by Merry (1922) from transcribed phonograph records. Using records of actors and orators delivering impassioned speeches, he found an extraordinary mobility of the pitch of the voice. Far from using a monotone, these artists in vocal expression move rapidly up and down a large share of their whole voice range. E. H. Sothern, in Shylock's speech, showed a total range of over two octaves, while single inflections or glides of his voice extended a full octave and more. How much of this modulation of the voice is the spontaneous expression of emotion, and how much is histrionic convention, we do not know.

The voice is commonly said to "tremble" with excitement. A trembling would have to be either a rapid waxing and waning of loudness, or a rapid rising and falling of pitch. Both of these kinds of trembling occur not only in emotion but at all times. The pitch always wavers slightly. Even the best singers seldom maintain a constant pitch for more than half a second (Schoen, 1922).

As singing, like other forms of musical performance, attempts to give expression to emotion, the singing voice has been examined to see how the emotion is actually expressed. Quite a series of studies on the singing voice came from Seashore's laboratory at the State University of Iowa. Attention was directed especially to that peculiar ringing heard in the voices of professional singers and known as the *vibrato*. It is a sort of tremulo effect, though it should not be called tremulo, because the tremulo is regarded as objectionable, whereas the vibrato is used by the best singers. The difference between the two is only a difference in degree, a vibrato being smoother and better controlled.

The vibrato consists in a periodic rise and fall in the pitch of the sung tone, or in a periodic waxing and waning in its loudness, or in both. An artificial vibrato can be produced by machinery which does either of these things to an otherwise uniform tone. Such "synthetic" vibratos were studied by Tiffin (1931), who produced the tone by a rapid series of flashes of light falling upon a photoelectric cell which operated a loud speaker by aid of an amplifier. He obtained a pitch vibrato by periodically hastening and slowing the series of flashes, and a loudness vibrato by periodically varying the amount of light in the flashes. Thus he produced 5–8 pulsations per second in the tone, and this pulsating tone was heard as a vibrato. It apparently made no difference whether it was the vibration rate or the intensity of the tone that was made to vary; an observer could not readily distinguish these two kinds of pulsations. The tone did not seem to oscillate in pitch even when such was the objective fact; it seemed to maintain a steady pitch but to pulsate in some undefined way. A periodic variation even as small as 1–2 cycles per second, in a tone of 420 cycles, could be heard as a pulsation by the average person.

The pitch variations produced by singers are much larger than this. According to measurements by Metfessel (1928) of phonograph records of eleven great singers, the rate of the pulsations averages 7 per second. The accomplished singer, while ostensibly sustaining a tone of constant pitch, actually lets his voice range above and below that pitch, about a quarter of a tone in each direction, covering a width of half a tone in all, and does this so rapidly and evenly that the effect on the hearer is of a pulsating or ringing tone.

Both the rate and the width of the vibrato vary from singer to singer and from moment to moment. The rate varies from 5 to 10 pulsations per second in superior singers, but does not often pass the limits of 6 and 8 per second. The width varies from 0.1 to 1.35 full tones, but does not often pass the limits of .25 and .85 full tones.

According to Kwalwasser (1926), the vibrato appears in the singing of many children, but seldom in adults, without voice training. Singers with some training tend to have a vibrato with a width of a quarter of a tone, half as great as that of the stars. Untrained voices do not maintain their pitch any more closely than trained, but waver irregularly and so do not give the vibrating effect. Trained singers were unable to sing without vibrato; they did not succeed even in decreasing it to any considerable degree. When asked to exaggerate it, however, they about doubled their usual vibrato width.

The process of learning to execute the vibrato was revealed by the experiments of Wagner (1930). He found that some young boys could acquire it after preliminary training in voice production and singing. They started with rhythmical panting, and, under the guidance of a skilled vocal teacher, after a few lessons produced a pulsating tone. Adults whose vibrato, after some training, was slow, could be taught to increase its rate by keeping time with a metronome, three or four pulsations to the beat.

With all these facts before us regarding the vibrato, shall we regard it as expressive of emotion, or not? Schoen's original interest in 1922 was based upon the supposed relation between this "trembling of the voice" and the muscular trembling which is often observed in strong excitement. Rather, it appears that the vibrato is very much a matter of technique, and that it is used practically all the time by professional singers, without much regard to the particular emotion appropriate to a given song. Probably the emotion actually felt by the singer along with his vibrato is one of mastery rather than one of being "shaken."

How well can simulated vocal expressions be judged? For our purposes it is more important to note how well judges can recognize emotions portrayed by the voice. Dusenberry & Knowrer (1939) had recordings made of someone reading the letters A through K in various emotional tones. Judges were able to recognize the intended emotions about as well as they usually recognize posed facial expressions. Knowrer (194.) played the recordings backward and found that *Os* still did better than chance; the tempo of sounds seemed to be more important than the tone. Other experiments, using more complicated speech content, gave a little better recognition (Fairbanks & Pronovost, 1939; Fairbanks & Hoaglin, 1941).

A general point. In all these studies we must remember that single factors are being isolated for study. Facial expression, gesture, or vocal expression *alone* may give only fair recognition of the emotion, but in normal life all are combined, *plus* an actual situation. The sum of these components may well give pretty good recognition of emotion. There is still another factor, emphasized especially by Hebb (1946). He examined extensive objective records of the emotional behavior of chimpanzees at the Yerkes Laboratory. The objective records show very little consistency that would enable one to recognize a particular emotion in a particular chimp. But a person who has worked with one of these animals learns to make very accurate estimates of its emotional status —an important skill when experimenting with an animal as strong as a chimp! Hebb argues that one recognizes emotions in both animal and man by an intuitive process; i.e., he learns to utilize a large number of subtle cues that tell the sort of action which the particular animal is apt to do next. There can be little doubt that one can recognize a very complex pattern, even when the elements of the pattern resist adequate analysis. We shall find many examples in the chapters on Perception (pp. 293, 464). Part of the job of the psychologist is to ascertain what patterns can be recognized, but he must not stop until he has made some analysis of these patterns. Hebb's discussion should not make us discard attempts to analyze facial and other expressions of emotion. It should make us realize that facial expressions are only one part of a continuous flux of behavior occurring in an animal with a long past history.

THE PRIMARY DIMENSIONS OF FACIAL EXPRESSION

But just how is one to analyze facial expressions? We have seen a number of attempts of a somewhat qualitative nature, as the use of the Piderit models, or judgment of half of the face at a time. For an adequate analysis we should go beyond the qualitative and obtain some quantitative dimensions. The Woodworth linear scale (p. 118) is a first step in this quantification, for it enables us to say how far apart two different expressions are. But if we are going to use such a scale, the obvious thing to do is to try it as a method of *collecting* data, rather than to apply it after the data have been obtained in some form that is not easy to convert to the scale units. Otherwise we are like the man who measures a distance as "three strides and half the length of my foot" and then tries to convert it to inches.

Schlosberg (1941a) tried the scale for collecting judgments on the Frois-Wittmann pictures. He set up a row of six bins, labeled with the names of the scale divisions. There was also a seventh bin, "Scattering," into which *O* might put poses that resisted classification in one of the six steps of the scale. Each of 45 *O*s sorted the 72 poses of the Frois-Wittmann pictures three times, giving 135 judgments on each picture. The judgments were tabulated as shown in the table on page 125. (Note that here we have conserved space by listing only every fifth picture from the original table. Hence, there are 15 instead of 72 pictures.) For the present, forget the last four columns of the table.

Examine a picture near the middle of the table, as No. 1. Fifty of the judgments put it under (II) Surprise, but it spread somewhat into the neighboring categories. This is exactly what we would expect; some judges confused it with (III) Suffering, Fear, or with (IV) Determination, Anger, and a few called it (I) Love, etc. But notice that nobody made the serious error of putting it in (V) Disgust, or in (VI) Contempt. Given this distribution of judgments, one can compute the *modal category* (number italicized in table), *mean scale position*, and *average deviation* of judgments for each picture. It begins to look like a real scale!

The circularity of the scale. But now look at the first picture, No. 6. Its modal category is (I) Love, etc., and it spills over only a little into the next step, (II) Surprise. But it does show a very large number of judgments in the last step, (VI) Contempt. This means that one end of our scale, Contempt, must be next to the other end, Love, etc. We immediately think of the spectrum, where opposite ends, red and violet, are similar to each other. In vision the problem is handled by a *circular scale*, the color circle. Perhaps our scale of facial expression is circular too. Note that the spread in the last two pictures (Nos. 13 and 15) in the table is consistent with this view.

THE DESCRIPTION OF 15 OF THE 72 FROIS-WITTMANN PICTURES OF FACIAL EXPRESSION[1]

No.	I	II	III	IV	V	VI	Average	Average Deviation	AXES		Scale Position	
	Love, Mirth, Happiness	Surprise	Suffering, Fear	Determination, Anger	Disgust	Contempt			P-U	A-R	Pred.	Error
6	67	5	0	2	2	52	.55	.58	7.0	4.2	.62	.07
68	118	1	0	1	0	4	1.00	.07	7.2	4.7	.85	.15
52	80	9	4	0	2	7	1.06	.32	6.5	3.8	.32	.74
10	39	62	8	0	1	3	1.65	.58	7.0	7.0	1.75	.10
26	2	98	22	1	0	1	2.20	.85	5.0	7.0	2.50	.30
1	5	50	18	22	0	0	2.65	.81	4.4	6.1	2.97	.32
54	0	0	119	2	3	0	3.06	.12	2.3	6.0	3.67	.61
35	7	21	59	37	3	2	3.00	.69	5.6	7.6	2.28	.82
33	1	0	70	20	10	0	3.47	.71	1.8	6.1	3.70	.73
60	0	0	4	110	7	5	4.10	.25	1.3	6.8	3.58	.52
63	2	10	5	72	29	15	4.21	.74	3.2	6.4	3.38	.83
16	2	0	5	88	7	10	4.34	.53	2.6	6.9	3.37	.97
40	3	1	9	17	91	12	4.86	.50	2.4	4.6	4.15	.71
13	5	1	2	10	12	90	5.74	.53	4.8	3.6	5.35	.39
15	50	0	0	3	12	54	6.27	.61	6.2	4.3	6.47	.20

[1] The entries in the six colums after the identifying number show the number of times (out of 135) that the picture was placed in each bin of the linear scale. The seventh bin (scattering) has been omitted. The next two columns give the mean and average deviation of the scale positions, calculated on the assumption that the scale is circular. Thus, No. 6 has its mode in category I; this was taken as the assumed mean and adjusted for deviations above it (step II) and below it (steps VI, V, etc.). These data are from Schlosberg (1941a).

The next two columns give means of ratings on the axes Pleasantness-Unpleasantness and Attention-Rejection, respectively. From these are calculated the Predicted position. (See text and Fig. 5-3.) The final column, Error, is the difference between predicted and obtained mean scale positions. (Data from Schlosberg, 1952)

Do other series of poses show circularity? One may argue that Frois-Wittmann habitually mixed a little contempt in his mirth, and vice versa, and that this would account for the circularity of the scale. Hence, it is necessary to examine other series. The original Feleky (1922) data are inconclusive on this point, for her *Os* gave little spread in the pictures at the ends of the scale. But Kanner (1931), using Feleky's pictures with different *Os*, presents data in agreement with a circular scale. Two pictures with modes in Contempt showed the expected symmetrical spread to Disgust and to Mirth, etc.

M. L. Brown, in an unpublished Honors Thesis, used the sorting-bin method on 32 pictures of the Ruckmick (1921) series and found that four poses in Mirth, etc., and two in Contempt spread across the ends of the scale. She also tried 32 supposedly "candid-camera shots" from magazines (cf. Munn, 1940, and p. 121). They showed little evidence of spread across the ends of the scale. Perhaps they were selected for publication because they were relatively unambiguous.

The circular surface. The reader will recall that the color circle is actually a *circular surface,* with hue scaled around the circumference and saturation varied as we go out from the center. Thus, one can start with a saturated blue, and gradually work toward the center, through the blue-grays, to gray. If he continues along the same axis, beyond gray, he goes through the desaturated yellows to a good yellow. There also must be some other axis. Red to blue-green is a typical example. With the aid of these two axes, one can describe the whole color surface and locate any sample (although a third dimension, brightness, may be needed).

Perhaps it would be possible to arrange our facial expressions on such a surface, putting the more pronounced expressions out near the periphery and the neutral ones near the center. To do it we would need two axes. Examination of a set of Frois-Wittmann pictures, lined up on the circular scale, suggested that the major axis was Pleasantness–Unpleasantness, running from step I (Love, Happiness, Mirth) to IV (Anger, Determination). P—U is often considered the basic dimension of affectivity or emotion. The other axis was harder to find and name. It may be called Attention–Rejection. Attention is exemplified by Surprise, in which the eyes, nostrils, and sometimes the mouth are open, ready to receive stimulation. The opposite end, Rejection, is shown in Disgust and Contempt, in which the eyes, lips, and nostrils are forcibly closed, as if to shut out stimulation. Note that simple *Inattention* is an intermediate state between these two extremes. It is like gray on the color surface.

Plotting the circular surface. If these axes are adequate, we should be able to use them to determine the location of each picture on the surface. Suppose we had our judges rate the 72 Frois-Wittmann pictures on a nine-point scale, ranging from Pleasantness to Unpleasantness, and then repeat the job on a similar scale for Attention–Rejection. We could then describe each picture in terms of its mean rating on P—U and A—R. Figure 5-3 shows how the Frois-Wittmann series is distributed on the surface. Notice that the axes are used as coordinates in plotting these loci. The circular scale has been circumscribed around the surface, and the construction line shows how one can use

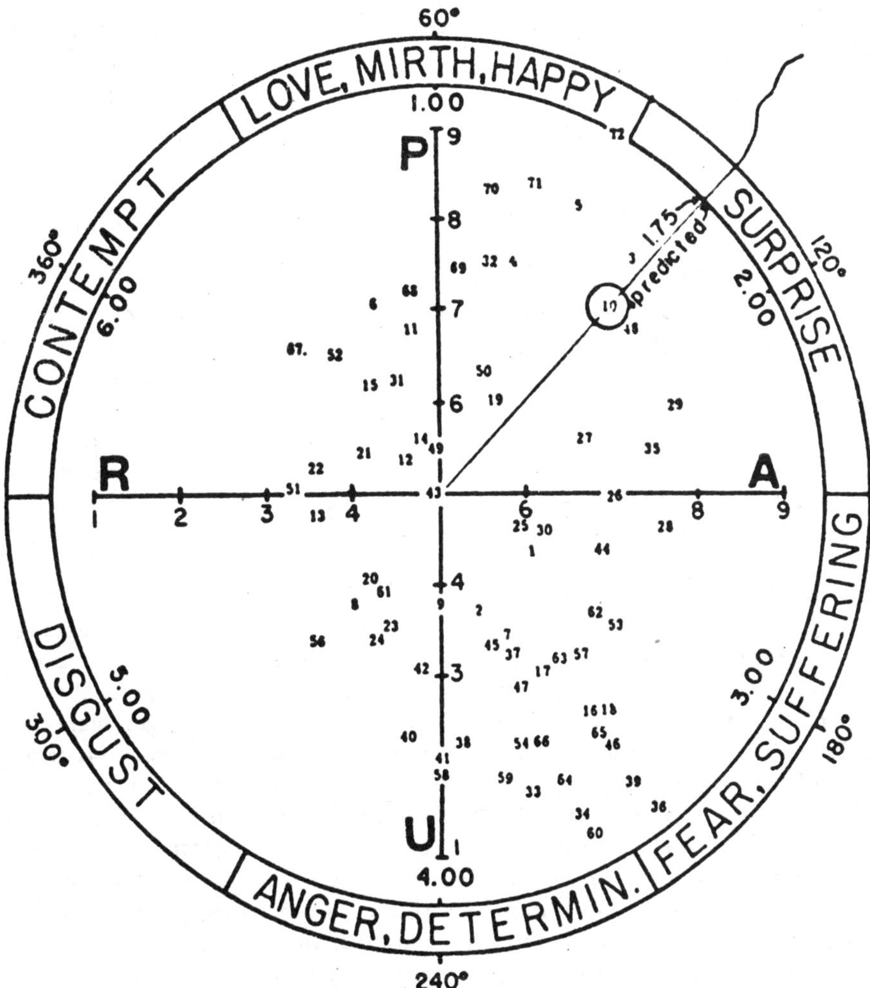

FIG. 5-3. (Schlosberg, 1952.) The location of each of the 72 Frois-Wittmann pictures on an oval surface. Picture No. 10 (encircled) serves as an example of the method used. It is plotted at axis values of P—U = 7, A—R = 7, as determined by the rating scales. A thread is then stretched from the intersection of the axes (5, 5) across the plotted point, and its position read off in degrees. Dividing by 60 yields the predicted circular scale value (1.75), which is compared with that obtained earlier by direct sorting on the scale (1.65). This picture might be called "Pleased Surprise," and both predicted and obtained values place it in the appropriate step of the Woodworth scale.

the axis plot of a given picture to predict its circular scale value. In 1952 Schlosberg obtained such ratings and compared the predicted scale values with those obtained in 1941 (p. 124) by the bin method of sorting directly on the scale. In two separate experiments the predictions correlated .94 and .92 with the earlier values. The axis values, predicted scale positions, and errors have been added at the right of the table on page 125.

To prove the point more thoroughly, the experiment was tried on the Ruckmick pictures. The correlation between predicted and obtained values was .96. Further, the error of prediction was only about a half scale step, where chance would predict three times this error. By making some logical adjustments of the scale, the mean error of prediction was cut to .33 scale steps

Predicting the circular scale positions is a convenient way to test the general validity of the surface positions, but it is probable that the surface is actually the better way to describe the series of pictures. Consider Figure 5-4 in which about a third of the Frois-Wittmann pictures are mounted in their appropriate positions. Notice how the expression often remains roughly the same in quality, but increases in strength as you run out a radius. The series from No. 43 (center) to No. 36 (lower right) is a good example. The Woodworth scale made no provision for this variation in strength; it forced the judge to treat a relatively neutral picture (e.g., No. 43) as he would a strong one. The result is that the neutral pictures are sorted into the bins almost by chance and show high mean variation in their positions (Schlosberg, 1941a; Table 1). This is one limit to the accuracy of predicting scale positions from axis positions; the scale positions themselves are almost certainly less accurate descriptions of the pictures than are their positions on the circular surface.

HEREDITY AND LEARNING IN FACIAL EXPRESSION

Thus far we have seen that there are a number of patterns that can be identified. But it takes a combination of facial expression, gesture, voice, and knowledge of the stimulus situation and of the past history of *O* before the judge can make very precise identifications. Certainly the discriminations among the many fine shades of emotion and attitude that we find in popular speech are beyond the power of most judges, even with all these cues available. Further, if we eliminate knowledge of the stimulus situation, most judges make many errors, confusing such emotions as anger and fear. Perhaps it is better to look for a few basic patterns, such as the steps on our qualitative scale. The fact that even these categories merge gradually into each other suggests still fewer basic patterns, the basic dimensions of Pleasantness–Unpleasantness and Attention–Rejection. We got this far through analysis of judgments of facial expressions.

But are these patterns basic in the sense that they are determined by fundamental neural structures or mechanisms, or are they patterns that we have learned? We grow up in a society that uses facial expressions as a means of communication. Perhaps we merely learn these patterns from imitating our associates. This problem has been a background one in many of the experiments we covered earlier in this chapter. It accounts for the attempts to study

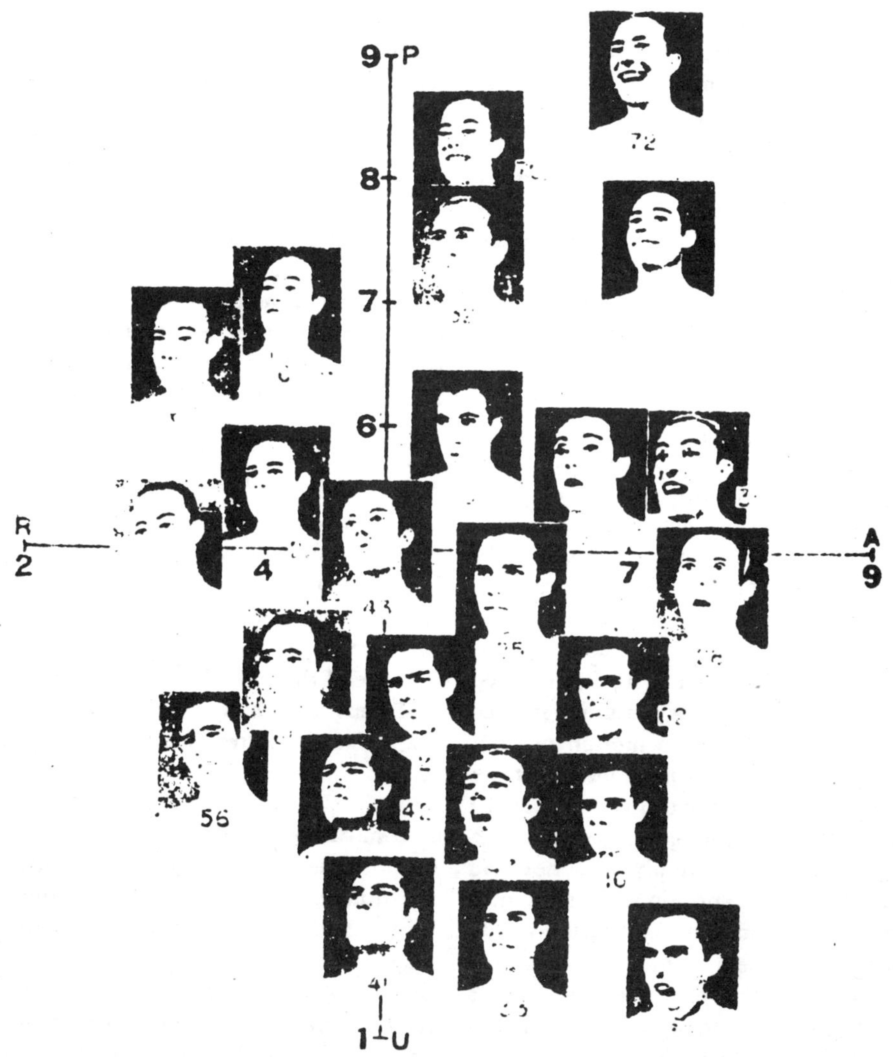

Fig. 5·4. (Schlosberg, 1952.) The location of typical pictures of the Frois-Wittmann series. This display includes those pictures which are shown around the margin of the surface in Figure 5·3 and, as many of the more centrally located ones as could be mounted. The average error of prediction for these 24 pictures is a half scale step, just as it is for the whole series of 72. The picture with the worst prediction of the whole series is No. 43 at the intersection of the axes.

spontaneous rather than posed expressions on the ground that posed expressions might be more conventional, more the result of learning (p. 119). The experiments of Schulze (1906, 1912) with children, of Dunlap (1927) with adults, and of Munn (1940) with candid-camera photos all indicated that unposed pictures were patterned in about the same way as posed ones. But one might argue that once the expression was learned, anyone would use it spontaneously as well as deliberately. The Landis (1924) studies were an attempt to break through this learned layer by using extreme stimuli. The results may be interpreted to show that at most only one or two basic patterns exist, although we have seen that there are reasons for doubting the generality of the experimental result .

Another approach to the problem is to study the development of facial expression in children. It will be recalled that the Sherman (1927) studies showed very poor patterning in motion pictures of infants' facial expressions. But we do not know whether this means that the infants were too young to have differentiated emotions or simply had not had time to learn expressions from adults. This is the familiar maturation-versus-learning problem, which is usually a tough one. But fortunately we have a pretty good way to separate the factors in the field of facial expression.

Facial expression in the blind. If facial expressions are learned, blind children should be markedly inferior to seeing children, for the blind would have no chance to imitate their associates. In 1932 Goodenough studied the expressions of a 10-year-old blind and deaf girl. She observed the girl in daily living and took some pictures of the child's typical expressions. Goodenough published a series of single shots from a motion picture sequence taken after a small doll had been dropped down the girl's neck. Startled surprise soon gave way to interested attention. During unsuccessful attempts to retrieve the doll the girl showed determination, anger, and dejection. Eventual success brought marked happiness. All of these expressions seem reasonably clear, even in the rather poor enlargements made from the film. Fear was not observed in this sequence, but it was sometimes found. Notice that the only scale divisions not mentioned in this study were disgust and contempt. We would guess that a strong odor would have elicited disgust, but that the blind girl might have failed to show the rather sophisticated expression of contempt. Thus, there seem to be basic patterns in all but one of the scale divisions, for a blind and deaf girl had no opportunity to learn facial expressions through mimicry.

A comparison of blind and seeing children. Others have made some study of the differences between large groups of blind and normal children. Dumas (1932; cf. 1948) found that blind children were very inadequate in their ability to form voluntary facial expressions, on request of *E*, but that they expressed normal emotions in a normal way. Mistschenko (1933) found that blind children were even inferior in their ability to move the facial muscles, let alone form expressions. These findings are exactly what one would expect if there were a few basic patterns, dependent on lower centers up to the hypothalamus (cf. Weinstein & Bender, 1943), which would be evoked only as a coordinated part of true emotional behavior. Blind children would have these basic patterns but would be deficient in the "voluntary" control of the face, for they have never seen their own faces, or any others, in the process of moving.

These studies offered a challenge to Landis, who had failed to find consistent patterns in normal adults under emotional stress. Hence, one of his students, Thompson (1941), decided to take motion picture records of blind and normal children at various age levels from 7 weeks to 13 years. There were 26 blind children, matched fairly well in age, institutional environment, and IQ to a control group of seeing children. Many of the motion pictures were taken during natural situations, but it was necessary to add some deliberate stimulation, such as breaking the child's balloon, to procure enough pictures. The resulting pictures were projected and analyzed for the amount of movement in key muscle groups. Three expressions were studied —laughing, smiling, and crying. There were some hints of differences between the two groups of children. For example, laughing and smiling seemed to be more vigorous in the young blind children. But the outstanding impression is one of similarity of blind to normal children in the amount of facial movement during spontaneous expression. The same generalization holds for the patterning of the expressions. Judges were asked to name the emotions portrayed by these pictures, plus a few others representing anger, sulkiness, annoyance, and sadness. The judges seem to have been at least as successful in naming the expressions of blind children as they were with seeing children. But there was a suggestion that there were some peculiarities in the expressions of the blind, for those who had worked with blind children were especially good at recognizing their emotions.

Voluntary facial expressions in the blind. This experiment gives us quite clear evidence that there are certain basic unlearned patterns of facial expression and that they show up in "real" emotional situations. But there still remains the problem as to whether blind children can deliberately form facial expressions. Another student of Landis, Fulcher (1942), tackled this problem. He used blind and seeing *O*s over an age range of about 5 to 20 years. They were photographed against a uniform background with the motion picture camera behind a screen so it would be less of a distraction. *E* stood behind the screen and told *O* to "First pretend as if you were very happy and *look* just as happy as you can!" When *E* saw that *O* had assumed the expression, he took the pictures. This was repeated for sadness, anger, and fear. Analysis of the resulting pictures shows some interesting changes with age. The youngest blind and normal children did not differ greatly in either the amount of facial movement or in the adequacy of th expressions. But the normal children improved with age in respect to both sharpness of expression and amount of movement, while age had the reverse effect, if any, on blind children. This is a familiar finding in studies of maturation. A native pattern develops to a certain level, and then it fails to develop further unless it is integrated into learned behavior. The younger children were probably not moving the facial muscles in a directly "voluntary" manner; it is more likely that they were imagining a fear situation, for example, and giving the expression as part of an actual emotion. The older seeing children could go much beyond this point as they learned the fine *nuances* of expression in their daily life. We might guess that the differences between blind and seeing children would have been much more pronounced if Fulcher had asked for more subtle expressions, such as disgust, amazement, and a host of others.

Cultural differences in facial expressions. Klineberg (1938, 1940) has emphasized the fact that there are striking differences in the significance of facial expressions from culture to culture. This may be taken as an argument for the nurture side of the heredity-environment controversy. But as one reads through his lists of descriptions of emotions from the Chinese literature, one is struck by the fact that analogues can often be found in our own culture. For example, widely opened eyes may be a strange way to express rage, but how about the American mother who "raises her eyebrows" to express displeasure when Johnnie helps himself to a second piece of cake! We have already mentioned the smile which means sorrow or regret in Eastern cultures, but remember the silly grin you often adopt when being scolded. One emerges from a study of this topic with the conviction that there *are* certain basic emotional patterns in man, but that different elements of these patterns are selected and stressed by specific cultures. This is especially true when facial expressions serve as a conventional means of communication. It is a far cry from these conventional expressions to the basic patterns found in young blind children; perhaps the surprising fact is that the basic patterns show up as well as they do in the conventional expressions of a sophisticated adult or of an actor.

6

EMOTION II: ENERGETICS

In our chapter on facial expressions we found that emotions are rather less differentiated than one would expect. Facial expressions per se, shorn of situational cues, can be described quite well in terms of two axes, Pleasantness–Unpleasantness and Attention–Rejection, although we could probably do a better job with the addition of a third dimension—Level of Activation—to cover the intensive aspects. But facial expression is only one of the many bodily changes that have been studied in an effort to understand emotion. Psychologists and physiologists have made extensive investigations of many physiological functions in the hope that they would find some patterning to correspond to the common-sense distinctions among the various emotional states. We shall devote the next two chapters to their findings, but we may as well warn the reader now that he will discover very little evidence for differentiation among emotions when he looks inside the skin. What he will find is a relatively widespread increase in the level of activation or of energy mobilization, corresponding roughly to an increase in what the layman calls "tension" or "excitement."

THE ACTIVATION MECHANISMS

An outstanding characteristic of strong emotional states, already pointed out (p. 108), is the high level of activity and reactivity. When a person is in an emotional state, his level of activation is high, in contrast to the moderate levels which characterize normal states and the very low level in sleep. Before we examine the various measures that can be used as indices of activation level, we may well examine the physiological mechanisms that interact in building up this level.

The Autonomic Nervous System. The Cannon-Bard theory of emotion (p. 109) stresses the fact that strong emotions prepare the organism for vigorous activity during an emergency The hastened breathing and circulation, the release of blood sugar from the liver and a host of other changes make more energy available to the muscles, and there are also neural changes that increase the responsiveness to stimuli. For many decades most of these changes have been attributed to the Autonomic Nervous System. This system has its higher centers in the brain, connected with those of the Central Nervous System, the hypothalamus probably being one of the most important of these regions. But the peripheral distribution of the autonomic nerves is functionally separate from the nerves of the CNS.

Of the three divisions of the autonomic, the cranial and sacral taken together are called the Parasympathetic System, while the middle or thoracicolumbar division is the Sympathetic System. The sympathetic connecting fibers from the spinal cord are medullated, like all other efferent fibers emerging from the brain and cord. They run to the sympathetic ganglia where they make synaptic connections with unmedullated postganglionic fibers which relay the nerve impulses to viscera, blood vessels, glands, hair erectors, and the pupil-dilating muscle fibers of the iris. In the sympathetic chain of ganglia, extending up and down slightly forward of the spinal column, nerve impulses spread diffusely from any one ganglion to all the others. This spreading makes the sympathetic system act as a unit; so it tends to raise the general level of activation.

The parasympathetic system is less diffuse and unitary in its action. Its ganglia are located directly on or near the organs innervated, rather than in a single chain, and its action tends to be specific. Since each autonomic organ, in general, receives both sympathetic and parasympathetic nerve fibers having opposite effects (such as constriction and dilatation of the blood vessels), the specific and localized action of the parasympathetic can modulate the function of any organ against the general sympathetic background.

Following Cannon, it is often said that the parasympathetic takes care of normal metabolic functions, while the sympathetic is an emergency system, putting the body on a warlike status, mobilizing energies for violent action. Certainly the sympathetic is functioning at a high level during the emotions of anger and fear, while "peaceful" activities like digestion are mediated by the parasympathetic. Yet we must be wary of such a dichotomous view, for the two systems interact in a complex manner (Lindsley, 1951). There is always some degree of activation or energy mobilization; a moderate amount of diffuse sympathetic discharge occurs constantly and serves as a background on which parasympathetic effects produce local variations.

There is one big advantage in remembering the comparison with war and peace: it is a rough guide to the effects of the two systems on specific organs. Most organs receive nerve fibers from both systems; organs like the digestive glands, concerned with "peaceful" activities, are stimulated by the parasympathetic and inhibited by the sympathetic. For the heart this relation is reversed, for the sympathetic accelerates the heartbeat to an emergency level, whereas the parasympathetic (vagus) tones it down to a moderate rate. This distinction holds good throughout the various functions—try predicting the effects of the two systems on the structures and functions indicated on the left side of Figure 6-1.

Notice especially the *adrenal gland*, underlined in the name column to catch your eye, and notice that it is innervated wholly by the sympathetic. Sympathetic nerve endings control their effectors by releasing a substance, *sympathin*. Part of the adrenal gland, the *adrenal medulla*, acts like a large mass of sympathetic nerve endings in that it releases large quantities of a similar compound, *adrenin*, directly into the blood stream

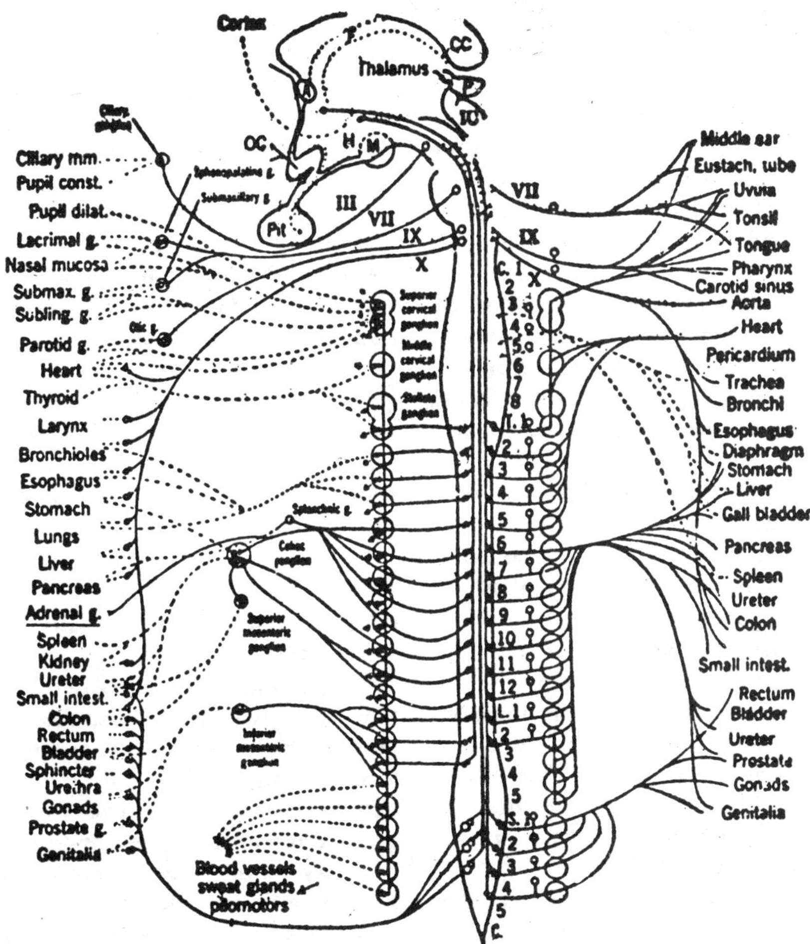

FIG. 6-1. (From Lindsley, 1951, after Mettler, 1948; Buchanan, 1948; Strong and Elwyn, 1943: with modifications.) Schematic representation of the autonomic nervous system, showing the central origin and the peripheral termination of *sympathetic* and *parasympathetic efferent pathways* on the *left* and the origin of *visceral afferent pathways* on the *right*. The larger circles represent ganglia, both those of the sympathetic chain near the spinal cord and a few others. Cell bodies of pre- and postganglionic neurons of the parasympathetic system are symbolized by very small open circles; those of the sympathetic system, by solid circles. Arrows projecting from sympathetic chain ganglia symbolize postganglionic fibers to blood vessels, sweat glands, and pilomotors. Dotted lines on left of figure represent efferent postganglionic fibers; those on right are nonautonomic fibers of the phrenic nerve. Key: A—anterior commissure; CC—corpus callosum; F—fornix; H—hypothalamus; IC—inferior colliculus; M—mammillary bodies; OC—optic chiasma; P—pineal body; Pit—pituitary or hypophysis.

through which it soon reaches all other effectors. Adrenin (or adrenalin) is said to be *sympatho-mimetic* in that it produces results like direct sympathetic stimulation—speeded breathing and heart rate, etc. Thus adrenin serves to increase and prolong the energy mobilization brought about by sympathetic discharge. Of course, there are a number of other important glands, as the pituitary, whose function is integrated with that of the autonomic, but their functions are less generalized; the relationship between adrenin and emotion is so striking that it has attracted a great deal of study (cf. Cantril & Hunt, 1932).

Feed-back mechanisms. We have described to some extent the autonomic activity, for the role of the autonomic system in emotion has been stressed in physiological and psychological research for many years. Recently another factor in the activation picture has been recognized: the sensory feed-back from intero- and proprioceptors. The extensive visceral changes brought about by autonomic activity stimulate interoceptors, whose impulses seem to feed back through the reticular substance to the hypothalamus. Similarly, the increased level of muscular tonus characteristic of emotions also feeds back a mass of impulses. The importance of these response-induced stimuli was recognized in the James-Lange theory (p. 107), but many people forgot about them when they lost interest in the introspective approach to emotion. As we learn more about the neural mechanisms, the importance of these feed-back mechanisms is being emphasized again (Lindsley, 1951). We still have a long way to go before we have the details, but the general picture is gradually becoming clear. Chemical changes in the blood stream furnish more energy to the neural centers as well as to the muscles, and at the same time these centers are subjected to an increasing barrage of return impulses from viscera and from skeletal musculature, which in turn increase the activity of the centers, leading to more muscular activity, and so on, in an ascending spiral of activity and reactivity. Fortunately, there are self-limiting mechanisms, notably parasympathetic, which check this build-up so that we do not always end in a state of violent emotion.

Thus, at any one moment the organism is in balance at some specific level of activation. There are other possible terms for this level, such as level of energy mobilization, of excitement, of tension, of alertness, of effort, etc. Many of the terms are useful for limited regions of the range, but the best term is *level of activation*, which is to be understood as the factor which is common to many of the bodily changes involved in "emotion."

General level of activation as a construct. At this point it might be well to emphasize that general level of activation or of energy mobilization is a construct. It is quite comparable to the *general level of prosperity*, as applied to a community. We have little trouble in agreeing that the level of prosperity of a given community is high or low, as the case may be, but this does not mean that all families in the community are equally prosperous. The economists can furnish indices of the general level of prosperity; some of them will be more valuable than others, and no single index will be ideal. In general, the best indices will be based on key processes in the economic life of the community, such as banking and major industries. Similarly, we do not have much trouble in deciding whether an individual is highly activated or half asleep, without meaning that all his functions are equally activated. The physiologists and psychologists have found useful indices to the general level of activation, but we must not expect to find any one index completely adequate. Again, the best indices will be based on key functions, for example, hypothalamic and sympathetic activity.

Level of activation of the organism, like level of prosperity of the community, is more than a statistical abstraction, for the general level is an important determiner of the levels of the part systems. The autonomic nervous system yields several good indices of the general level of activation, and it also acts as a key structure in determining and controlling this level. One of the best indices of its activity is the electrical conductance of the skin. We shall treat this index in this chapter and others in the next one following.

ELECTRICAL SKIN CONDUCTANCE

Perhaps the most widely used index of level of activation is the electrical *conductance* (or its reciprocal, *resistance*) of the skin, usually of the palms of the hands. There has been much heated discussion concerning this index: its physiological basis, the best apparatus and most appropriate units [1] for its measurement, and finally, whether or not its measures "emotion." We shall see that there is reasonable agreement on the first three questions and that the last question is not a good one. It can be answered in the affirmative if we substitute *activation* for *emotion*. We shall note that skin conductance ranges from a low level in sleep to a high level in strongly activated states like rage, and it is sensitive enough to detect the mild interest aroused by a new sound in a quiet room.

Before we become involved in the details of experiments we must make clear a few terms. The conductance of the skin varies constantly. We can measure the absolute level at a given time, or we can determine the rapid variations that result from stimulation. The absolute level of conductance has received less attention than it deserves. It seems to be a good measure of the general level of activation, for conductance is high when *O* is alert and low when he is relaxed. It has no special name, although it is sometimes called *basic conductance* when it is used as a reference point for the rapid changes. On the other hand, the rapid changes in conductance have been studied extensively and suffer from too many names. The oldest is *psychogalvanic reflex* (PGR), but many dislike the implications that it is psychic or a reflex, and even the galvanic part of the term is not correct from the standpoint of physics. *Galvanic skin response* (GSR) is a bit better, and *electrodermal response* (EDR) is the safest. The abbreviation GSR is popular at present; therefore, we shall use it, but include PGR occasionally in order to maintain contact with the older literature.

The reason that the GSR has received so much attention is the speed and sensitivity with which it follows stimulation. A sudden loud noise will cause a sharp increase in skin conductance in a few seconds, with nearly complete return to the old basic level in perhaps half a minute. The apparatus used to measure it is relatively simple to operate once it is built, and it does not inconvenience *O*. It is the GSR, rather than the basic level of conductance, that is usually thought to measure emotion. But from our present viewpoint, the GSR simply measures

[1] Shall we speak of skin conductance or of skin resistance? Logically it makes no difference, one being simply the reciprocal of the other, but confusion can easily arise. Conductance suits our purpose better because it varies directly with the level of activation which we wish to measure, while a rise in resistance means a fall in that level.

momentary and brief activation, a transient burst that anticipates increased demands on *O*.

Two basic phenomena. In 1888 Féré attached two electrodes on the forearm, connected in series with a weak source of current and a galvanometer. He found that the galvanometer gave quick deflections when *O* was stimulated by a tuning fork, an odor, or a colored glass before his eyes. Féré confused the phenomenon with static electricity generated by friction with dry skin, but fortunately he collaborated with d'Arsonval, the physicist for whom a familiar type of galvanometer is named. D'Arsonval (1888) straightened out things and emphasized the importance of the secretion of sweat. But we still speak of the *phenomenon of Féré* when we measure the increase of electrical skin conductance with the aid of a galvanometer and an external (or exosomatic) source of current.

In 1890 Tarchanoff found that he could get similar deflections without the aid of an external source of current. Almost any two parts of the skin, connected through a galvanometer, showed a potential difference which moved the galvanometer off center. After the galvanometer needle had come to rest, a stimulus would cause additional movement. Whether this last deflection resulted from a change of potential difference between the two skin areas, or from a change of conductance, is even now not perfectly clear. But the Tarchanoff and Féré phenomena are probably both dependent on the same basic physiological processes (Jeffress, 1928). Tarchanoff's method, using only an *endosomatic* electric potential, is still used occasionally because of its convenience; you need only a galvanometer and a pair of electrodes. But the Féré method has some advantages: it yields a measure of the absolute level of conductance as well as of the changes and seems to be a little more dependable. The great majority of recent experiments have used this method.

Experimental technique. Though the genuineness of the phenomena is easily demonstrated, good technique is required for any serious psychological use of the GSR. The next few paragraphs will consider important laboratory details.

Methods of measurement. In discussing the electrical measurements we shall find it more convenient to speak of resistance (in ohms) rather than of conductance (in mhos), largely because the instruments are calibrated in terms of resistance.

The resistance of the skin is fairly high. The value you get, of course, is dependent on the type and size of electrode, the skin region employed (as palm or forehead), and the level of activation at the moment. A moist electrode, an inch in diameter, attached to the palm will usually show resistances of from 10,000 to 100,000 ohms; a ¼-inch electrode might show over 1 million ohms. The GSR to a strong shock may lower the resistance to half its basic value, that to a verbal stimulus may be only a 5-percent decrease. From Ohm's Law (current = potential/resistance, or amperes = volts/ohms) we can compute the current forced through the skin by the potential applied (usually a volt or two). The current will lie in the range from 1 to 100 micro- (millionths) amperes. The old d'Arsonval moving-coil-and-mirror galvanometer is fully adequate for measuring such weak currents, since the changes are not too rapid (cf. p. 271 where we point out the difficulty early encountered in measuring spike potentials, which are rapid as well as small). As a matter of fact the ordinary needle type of meter, a precision version of the ammeter in your car, is available with a full-scale range of a few microamperes; it is sensitive enough to measure basic resistance level and all but the smallest GSR. With such an instrument one would employ an external source of a few volts; a higher voltage causes itching and irritation of the skin.

The simplest instrument would employ a flashlight cell (1½ volts) in series with a microammeter and two electrodes to complete the circuit. But this would not permit very accurate measurement over the wide range of resistances encountered—perhaps 10,000 to several million ohms, as extremes. This problem can be solved by using a potential divider to cut down the voltage when low resistance is found. By flipping a switch *E* can select one of several ranges of sensitivity. Meter readings are linearly related to conductance. Such a circuit is an inexpensive and convenient one for measuring basic resistance, but not very satisfactory for GSR. Suppose the basic resistance was such that the needle read 50 on a 100-point scale, and that the GSR decreased this resistance by 5 percent of itself. The GSR would show up as only 2½ scale divisions, which might well be less than the accuracy of reading the instrument.

The most popular circuit for measuring the GSR is the Wheatstone bridge (p. 145). In using it one balances out the unknown (that is, *O*'s) resistance by adjusting the calibrated resistor until the meter reads zero; he then reads off *O*'s resistance from the scale on the calibrated resistor. The GSR, a decrease in resistance (or increase in conductance), throws the meter off zero, and *E* determines the size of the GSR by rebalancing the bridge, or even by noting the deflection. This is a very sensitive arrangement.

Electronic circuits. In actual use the simple arrangement we have described is cumbersome and a bit cranky. The advent of the vacuum tube amplifier soon gave rise to a number of better circuits, which permit the use of weaker currents through the electrodes, with relatively inexpensive and rugged galvanometers on the recording end. So it is possible to record the GSR with ink-writing meters, rather than by the photographic or manual tracing that was necessary with the older mirror galvanometers.

Some of these instruments use direct current amplifiers. They have the advantage of measuring true skin resistance, but direct current amplifiers offer certain technical difficulties (Trueblood & Grings, 1950). On the other hand, the more familiar alternating current amplifiers, like that in a radio set, are easier to build and are more stable, but they measure "apparent resistance" (impedance), a combination of true ohmic resistance and capacitance (the condensor effect of cell walls). Unfortunately, the capacitance, and hence the apparent resistance, vary with the frequency of the alternating current sent through the skin (Forbes & Landis, 1935). The truth of the matter is that any one of these newer circuits is very satisfactory as long as *E* does not try to compare the absolute resistance values he obtains on different types of circuits. Agreement on a single standardized circuit has been delayed by the rapid advances in electronics; like an airplane, a circuit is obsolete by the time it is in use! (Cf. Haggard & Gerbrands, 1947; Lacey & Siegel 1948.)

Electrodes. Simple round disks of an inactive metal are often used for electrodes. Perhaps the simplest method is to solder insulated wires to two silver coins (quarters), and fasten one coin to each palm with a rubber band. One improvement is to substitute plastic wrist-watch straps for the rubber bands, with a bit of sponge rubber between metal and strap to supply uniform pressure and good contact with the skin. Still better contact can be obtained by putting a moistened disk of paper towel between skin and silver. Movement of the hand disturbs the contact; if one hand must be used in the subject's task, the electrodes may be placed on the palm and back of the other hand. This is a somewhat less sensitive method, for the GSR is strongest on the palm, and two palms are better than one palm plus some other point. The skin should be clean and free from its oil.

Although this type of electrode is widely used, it suffers from polarization. That is, the passage of current quickly deposits a thin layer of ions on one electrode, which markedly increases its resistance. For careful work it is better to use nonpolarizing electrodes, composed, for example, of silver, silver chloride, and Ringer's paste, in series. Silver disks are given a thin layer of silver chloride by connecting them to the + pole of a storage battery or dry cell, and immersing them in a glass bowl of dilute salt solution until electrolysis has given them a gray appearance. The other pole of the current source must also be in the solution to complete the circuit. (It may be attached to a scrap of silver.) Polish the contact surface of the electrodes before you put them in the solution, for fingerprints will prevent an even coating of chloride. A few minutes in the solution is sufficient, for too thick a layer of chloride is apt to scale off. Then carefully spread on a layer of paste, about one sixteenth of an inch thick, and attach the electrodes to the skin by one of the methods suggested in the previous paragraph. The paste may be made in quantities and stored in an airtight jar. It is a mixture of roughly equal parts of bentonite (white clay) and glycerin, which can be thinned to the consistency of putty by Ringer's (or physiological salt) solution. The first two ingredients can be purchased in any drug store, and any physiology lab has gallons of Ringer's solution. The exact constitution of the latter is not important; you can even substitute one level teaspoon of table salt in a pint of water. Some workers use commercial electrode jelly instead of the above paste. This practice is of doubtful value, for the electrode jelly contains irritants; it is designed to *minimize* skin resistance for electrocardiography, whereas we wish to measure *normal* skin resistance. If you must cut corners, you might better omit the chloriding than the special paste. Some workers use zinc—zinc chloride electrodes. (The zinc chloride may be in solution or a paste.)

Even with the best electrodes there is polarization, and consequent resistance changes, in the skin itself. One advantage of alternating current amplifiers (see above) is that they are relatively free from this trouble. Polarization can be minimized in direct current circuits by keeping the current low and by turning it off except during actual measurement.

A few words are in order about electrode size and placement. The smaller the electrode the better the chance of obtaining uniform contact. But the sensitivity of the apparatus sets limits, for the resistance varies inversely with the contact area. If *O* must use both hands, the soles of the feet are almost as good. One of us (H. S.) has used one-inch flat silver and paste electrodes, attached under each arch with sponge rubber and Scotch tape, and protected with slippers to keep the feet warm; measurements were taken intermittently over three hours as *O* engaged in various seated tasks. The brow is another good location for electrodes, although possibly less active than palms or soles (Conklin, 1951). Wrists and backs of the hands are relatively inactive, and the underlying tendons vary the electrode contact during hand movement. On such irregular or curved surfaces it helps to use very thin and flexible sheet silver for the electrodes.

Units of measurement. The obvious unit for measuring resistance is the *ohm*. But is a GSR of 1,000 ohms in a basic resistance level of 50,000 ohms equivalent to one of 1,000 ohms at a level of 20,000 ohms? One could make a good case for using percentage change, rather than absolute change. Another way of getting relative units is to convert all measurements into logarithms. Perhaps conductance is what we should measure. Or even conductance relative to basic conductance, or log conductance. Far too often we select our units because the dial happens to be engraved with that type of scale (usually ohms). There should be a better reason than that. Darrow (1934) found that the amount of perspiration varied with the conductance of the area (p. 142) and preferred *micromho* as a unit. (A micromho of conductance corresponds to 1,000,000 ohms of resistance.) Later (1937a) he gave reasons for using log conductance. More recently Haggard (1945, 1949) obtained a large number of paired measurements of basic resistance and GSR to verbal stimuli, and subjected them to varied statistical treatment in an effort to find which unit gave the most uniform size of GSR despite differences in basic level. Of the most common scales, log conductance proved to be best, but a more complicated transformation was still better. Lacey (1947) and Lacey & Siegel (1949) found that conductance units resulted in normal distributions of scores for both basic level and GSR, and that log changes in conductance were also acceptable for GSR. Schlosberg & Stanley (1952) examined 24 small distributions of conductances, taken at various levels. Conductance units gave fairly normal distributions, but square root of conductance was slightly better. Conductance would seem to be adequate for most purposes, but the square root conversion might be advisable whenever elaborate statistical treatment is based on the assumption of strict normality of the distribution of scores. The upshot of all this discussion is that one should convert all readings to either conductance or $\sqrt{C}$ *before* adding or averaging them, let alone subjecting them to more elaborate statistical analysis. It might be well to calibrate our dials in *mhos* instead of *ohms* in the first place (p. 138); if not, tables of reciprocals and square roots make the conversion less of a chore. It might be noted that one can go from resistance to either conductance or $\sqrt{C}$ in a single operation on a slide rule. Incidentally, such careful consideration of the proper unit of measurement is a sign of maturity in this particular field; far too few psychological measurements have been so analyzed (Stevens, 1951b).

The reader may think this question of units is unimportant, but it makes a vast difference how scores are computed. For example, consider a couple of resistances obtained before and after electric shock on each of two *O*s (from data of Lacey & Siegel, 1949). We start with the four resistances obtained, and enter them in the first column. Then we express these resistances in different units, and note how the differences between pre- and post-shock scores vary.

	Resistance (R) in ohms			*Conductance (C) in micromhos*			
	R	*percent*	*log*	*C*	*percent*	*log*	$\sqrt{C}$
Subject A							
Basic level	100,000	100	5.00	10	100	1.00	3.2
After shock	50,000	50	4.70	20	200	1.30	4.5
Difference (GSR)	50,000	50	−0.30	10	100	+0.30	1.3
Subject B							
Basic level	10,990	100	4.04	91	100	1.96	9.5
After shock	9,344	85	3.97	107	118	2.03	10.3
Difference (GSR)	1,646	15	−0.07	16	18	+0.07	0.8

How do these two *O*s compare in strength of GSR to shock? In simple resistance units A has about 30 times the response of B. In terms of both percentage and log resistance scores, A has about three times as strong a response as B. But in terms of simple conductance B has slightly the *larger* response. Percentage change in conductance gives a large superiority to A, and log conductance gives a smaller one. (Note that log R and log C, taken without regard to sign, give the same measure for GSR.) Clearly the choice of units is of the greatest importance, if this choice can make the same basic data show subject A to have anywhere from ⅝ to 30 times the response of B.

The fact that so many different units have been used in various studies makes comparison of results difficult. As we noted above, we shall talk of *conductance* wherever possible. But when Means have been computed in resistance units, it is misleading to convert the Means into conductances; simple arithmetic shows that the Mean of reciprocals is very different from the reciprocal of a Mean. Whenever we give numbers, we shall adhere to the units used in the original reports. In graphs we shall do the same but invert ordinates so that the top of the graph indicates the highest conductance.

Local determiners of skin conductance. In the first edition of this text considerable space was devoted to the evidence indicating that GSR was the result of sweat-gland activity. Since that conclusion is now generally accepted, we can be briefer on this physiological matter. (See a review of pertinent recent literature by McCleary, 1950.) The easiest theory to understand, and to discard, is the *muscular theory*. This regards GSR as a potential change under the electrodes due to muscular activity (Sidis & Nelson, 1910). Muscular contraction, either local or general, does register a good GSR. Since muscular contraction is accompanied by "muscle currents" or spike potentials (p. 177), the obtained GSR might be the summed potentials of muscles situated under the skin of the region. Both the Tarchanoff and the Féré effects could be plausibly explained on this basis. But the theory encounters a fatal objection: puncturing the skin under the electrodes—and thus eliminating skin resistance from the circuit—knocks out almost all the basic resistance as well as the GSR (Richter, 1929a). Blood, lymph, and the moist subcutaneous tissues have very little resistance compared to the horny skin. It is, therefore, in the skin that we must seek for conductance changes. The GSR found during muscular effort must result from the energy mobilization involved in effort, rather than from the actual muscle potentials (p. 177).

Now that we have the conductance changes tied down to the skin, we still have two theories as to what happens, the *circulatory theory* and the sweat *secretory theory*. Since the little blood vessels of the skin are known to dilate and contract during emotions, we might assume that the resulting changes in amount of circulating blood would change skin conductance. The critical experiment for the circulatory theory was done by Darrow (1927). He obtained simultaneous records of GSR, local volume (p. 162), blood pressure (p. 161), and secretion of sweat. There was no consistent relation between GSR and volume of the body member, suggesting that neither vasodilation nor vasoconstriction was responsible for the changes in skin conductance. On the other hand, GSR and sweat secretion *were* associated. This experiment was not an unsurmountable obstacle for a complex circulatory theory like that of McDowell (1933), but it certainly favored the secretory theory. Further studies by Darrow showed that the sweat appeared on the skin about a second after the conductance change and that the extent of change in electrical conductance correlated very well with the actual amount of sweat secreted (1934, 1936). But it is the *response* of sweating, and not the sweat itself, which causes the conductance change. This point is often overlooked by those who know that salt water is a good conductor of electricity; they assume that the sweat merely moistens the skin and gives better contact with the electrodes. If this were the answer, we would get little GSR with the preferred paste electrodes, and even simple silver disks would soon be thoroughly wet. One advantage of the paste electrode is that it minimizes slow conductance changes due to the accumulation of sweat, giving stable contacts with which to measure the fundamental changes. The exact nature of these changes is not known, but we do know that there are electrical changes in gland cells just before and during the active phase of secretion. Such changes as depolarization and increased permeability of the membranes of the sweat glands would account for both the Tarchanoff and Féré effects (Thouless, 1930).

Direct measurement of sweating. If skin conductance is so intimately bound up with sweating, perhaps it would be better to measure the sweating directly rather than bother with skin conductance. The trouble with this suggestion is that the quantities of sweat secreted are so minute that they are hard to measure. Darrow (1934) and Miles (see Wenger & Gilchrist, 1948) made such measurements with elaborate gadgets built around hygroscopic fibers that changed tension as they became moist. A more convenient method was developed by Silverman & Powell (1944). It employs the reaction between two chemicals, one dried on the skin and the other dried on filter paper. When the paper disk is pressed against the skin, the perspiration dissolves minute amounts of the chemicals and permits the chemical reaction to occur. The resulting precipitate, a stain, varies in density with the amount of perspiration. Wenger and Gilchrist compared the stain method with skin conductance, and with several other measures of autonomic activity, as blood pressure and oral temperature. They made these measurements on 251 *Os*. They found that palmar conductance gave more reliable measures than did the stain method and that it correlated better with the other autonomic variables. So skin conductance seems to be the better method, even for assessing the general level of activation; as for GSR proper, any direct measure of sweating is either too cumbersome or too slow to pick up the rapid spurts of activation that show so clearly on the galvanometer.

The neurology of skin conductance. A large mass of evidence indicates that the sweat glands are innervated by postganglionic fibers of the sympathetic nervous system (McCleary, 1950; Lindsley, 1951). Insofar as this system tends to discharge as a unit, the skin conductance at any point is a measure of sympathetic activity. As we have already noted, the sympathetic system is basic to emotion, or more specifically, to activation. Thus the skin conductance is a valuable measure of activation. But it would be a mistake to assume that the sympathetic system always functions as a unit and that all skin surfaces give identical GSR. For example, Richter (1924, 1926, 1929b, 1931) has shown that palmar and plantar (soles of feet) conductance tends to fall during sleep, while that of other areas tends to rise. We must remember that sweating is a method of getting rid of excess heat; to the extent that activation means more muscular activity, and thus more heat production, it will show up in a generalized rise in skin conductance. Apparently the palmar areas represent a rather specialized type of sweating, very intimately related to activation. (See p. 144.) In fact, Darrow (1936) suggested that the palmar GSR was an essential part of the preparation for action, quite analogous to the laborer's habit of spitting on his hands before he grasps the pick handle.

Like other autonomic functions, skin conductance is controlled by brain centers. The hypothalamus is involved (Wang & Richter, 1928), and even the cerebral cortex—notably the premotor region (Langworthy & Richter, 1930)—plays a part. Since this same premotor area is concerned also with the control of grasping, there is here some incidental support for Darrow's preparation-for-gripping theory of the GSR (1937b).

Limitations of the GSR. We have skimmed rather lightly over some complicated questions of neurophysiology, but we must mention two facts that set limitations on skin conductance as a measure of activation. In the first place, adrenin seems to inhibit the GSR (Darrow, 1936), contrary to the expected effect of this sympathomimetic substance. Hence GSR may not be an adequate measure of changes in activation level during strong emotion. Darrow suggests (1936) that blood pressure may be a better measure at high levels of activation.

The other limitation is imposed by the relation between sweating and temperature. On a very hot day even the palms participate in the general sweating, so giving high conductance even during muscular relaxation. And conductance is lowered by extreme cold. Accordingly, skin conductance will give a safe measure of activation level only when the subject has been in a normal room temperature long enough to be adjusted to it, and if the electrodes are on the palms or soles, which are not as much affected by moderate variations in room temperature (Duffy & Lacey, 1946). However, neither of these limitations is a serious restriction against the vast number of possible psychological uses of skin conductance; these uses will be our next concern.

PSYCHOLOGICAL DETERMINERS OF ELECTRICAL SKIN CONDUCTANCE

Slow changes in conductance level. If skin conductance is a measure of activation via the sympathetic nervous system, we should be able to show that conductance varies directly with alertness. Palmar conductance should be low during sleep, which is about the most unemotional state one can imagine in a living person. A number of studies have shown that palmar conductance *is* low during sleep, and that it rises rapidly on awakening (Farmer & Chambers, 1925; Richter, 1926; Freeman & Darrow, 1935). Landis & Forbes (1933) were able to confirm this only for the palms, and not always there; and Jones (1930a) on examining sole-leg resistance in eight infants under one year of age—infants in whom he had obtained good PGR—could find no change in sleep.

The reason for the somewhat equivocal results is shown by a chain of experiments started by Richter and his associates (Richter & Woodruff, 1942; Richter, Woodruff & Eaton, 1943). They designed a very simple *dermohmeter* (skin resistance meter) which consisted of a couple of 4½ v. (radio "C") batteries whose output could be varied with a potentiometer; the current ran in series through two electrodes and a microammeter (20 μa). One electrode, the "indifferent" one, consisted of a zinc-zinc sulphate cup attached to the lobe of the ear like an earring. The skin was pricked under this electrode to reduce resistance. The exploring electrode was a ½-inch disk of zinc attached to a convenient handle. The potentiometer was adjusted to give very little deflection of the ammeter needle when the exploring electrode was placed on an area of low conductance, such as the wrist in a moderately cool room. As the exploring electrode was tried at various points toward the palm, it suddenly crossed over into an area of high conductance, shown by a marked deflection of the needle. In this way they were able to plot the boundaries of high-conductance areas. At normal room temperatures such boundaries enclose the whole palm, the sole of the foot, and on the face, an irregular area including the lips, nose, and eye region. If *O* is subjected to cold, as by soaking in a cold tub, the boundaries shrink; the last high-conductance areas are the finger tips, toes, and mouth, although there is also a patch on the palm that holds out almost to the end. Conversely, with immersion in a hot bath the areas expand. On the face the high-conductance area expands to all hairless parts, even following to within half an inch of the receding hairline in bald men.

So much for the temperature changes. It is particularly interesting for our present purposes to note that the pattern in sleep is very similar to that in the cold. Infants, for example, show the high-conductance area limited to the mouth and lips during sleep, with expansion to the rest of the face on awakening. It was not possible to make very adequate parallel studies on adults, for the electrodes woke them up.

Richter and his associates were not particularly interested in variations of resistance within areas; they were looking for boundaries or contours of areas that were above a certain arbitrary level of conductance. But suppose the conductances of various points on the skin at one moment varied among themselves like the altitudes of various points on a hilly coast. If the whole pattern of conductances moved up and down under changing conditions, Richter would be measuring only the size of the areas that were "above the water line," or above his arbitrary level of

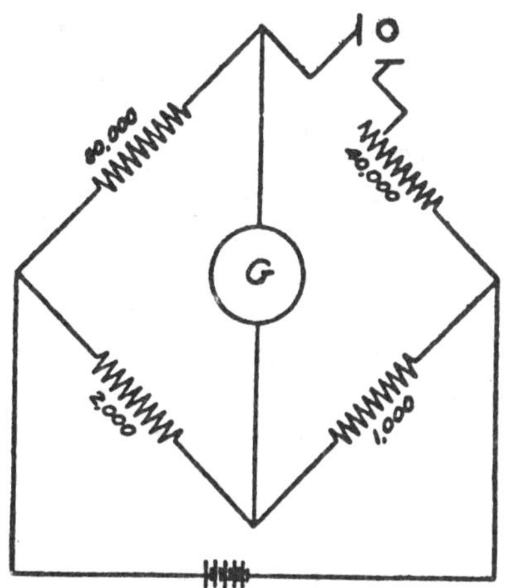

FIG. 6-2. A Wheatstone bridge for measuring resistance levels and magnitude of GSR. No current will flow through the galvanometer G when the potential is equal at the opposite corners of the square connected through the galvanometer. The remaining two corners, being in direct connection with the poles of the battery, have a certain difference in potential. As you follow along either of the two circuits between these poles, the potential difference decreases in proportion to the resistance traversed. With the resistances indicated (the 40,000 ohms being the resistance of *O* plus that of the adjustable coil), the potential is equal at the two ends of the bridge. Let *O*'s resistance decrease: the balance is disturbed and current flows through the galvanometer, causing the needle to swing. *E* may now increase the resistance in series with *O*, noting the amount added, till the needle comes back to zero. By introducing known resistances in place of *O* the amplitude of the galvanometer deflections can be calibrated and so the temporary drops in *O*'s resistance which constitute the GSR can be measured.

Most circuits in actual use complicate the simple diagram shown here to provide a galvanometer shunt, known resistances to be substituted for *O*, amplification for the current changes, etc.

The galvanometer deflections can be read, or traced by hand on a kymograph as they occur (they are slow enough to allow of such tracing), or photographed.

conductance. There is evidence that there is such a pattern of varied skin conductances and that it moves up and down in absolute level. E. Neumann (1950) in an unpublished dissertation done with Pfaffmann, reports careful measurements of such patterns under varied environmental temperatures. She attached small electrodes in a line running from the fingertip well up the forearm; a multipoint switch permitted *seriatim* measurements of resistance on a modified bridge circuit (cf. Fig. 6-2). In a cold room there were high conductances at the fingertip and palm, and lower ones further up the wrist and arm. As *O* became adapted to a room at normal temperature, *all* conductances rose, but they retained their relative values. With further increase in room temperature to a very uncomfortable level, the pattern changed; although palmar conductance still continued to rise somewhat, the forearm values showed a more marked increase.

These changes sound complicated, but they can be covered fairly well by two general principles:

1. General bodily skin conductance chiefly reflects the temperature control mechanism of the body. Hence conductance is high (sweating) when there is need for heat loss, and low when heat must be conserved. It is less dependent on the degree of activation.

2. The palms (and soles) also participate in temperature control, but chiefly at extreme temperatures. Through normal temperature ranges the palms (and soles) especially reflect the level of activation. Hence these areas are to be preferred for electrode placement.

Now to return to the question as to whether conductance is low or high during sleep (p. 144). Conductance of the palms and soles should fall as *O* relaxes in sleep, but the resistance of the rest of the body should be more dependent on the number of blankets! Failure to find low palmar conductance during sleep may result either from comparing it with that of a cool body, or from recording with one electrode on a nonpalmar, nonplantar surface.

Skin conductance during hypnosis. The superficial resemblance between hypnosis and sleep suggests that we might find low conductance in hypnotized subjects. Davis and Kantor (1935) put *O* under light hypnosis and suggested to him either that he would sleep deeply or that he was unable to move his arms or legs. Suggestion of sleep tended to lower conductance, as expected, but the more alert condition of (active) immobility tended to raise conductance. The authors conclude that "the lethargic condition of hypnosis resembles sleep in the behavior of skin resistance; the active hypnotic condition resembles the waking state."

Conductance changes during activity. Waller (1919) and Wechsler (1925) measured palmar conductance at intervals from morning to night, during waking hours only, and found it low in the morning, rising to a maximum during midday, and falling again in the evening. This corresponds rather nicely with the slight diurnal variations in body temperature (oral, a few tenths of a degree) observed by Kleitman (1950; cf. Kleitman and Ramsaroop, 1948). The highest conductance and the highest temperature would presumably be found when *O* was at his peak efficiency; Kleitman suggests that the peak may come in the morning for some people and in the afternoon for others. These diurnal variations in level of alertness or energy mobilization undoubtedly represent the build-up effect of external and internal stimulation during daily activity. It takes some time for the build-up to occur in the morning and after the peak it is cut down by fatigue. Desk workers might be expected to have a later peak than manual laborers. Habit enters in, too, for the energy level starts down toward the usual bedtime—unless excessive external stimulation interferes ("Don't go home yet, it's still too early to go to bed!")

The effects of the task. Superimposed on these slow diurnal drifts of level of energy mobilization there should be changes as *O* varies his task. It is quite simple to show such changes. Consider the course of skin conductance in a typical experiment. When *O* has been harnessed into the recording apparatus and readings are started, his palmar con-

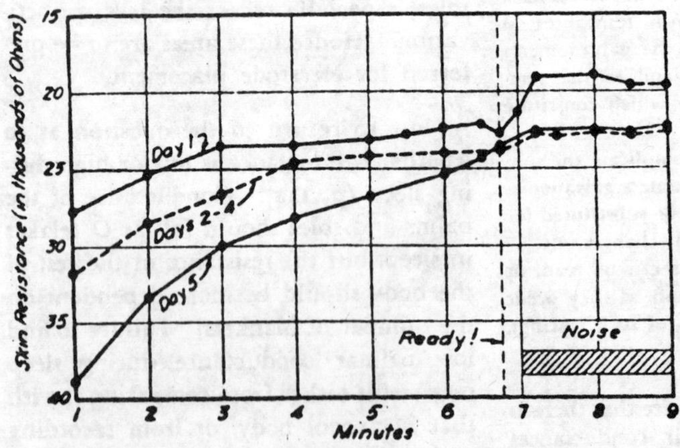

FIG. 6-3. (Data from R. C. Davis, 1934.) Change of finger-tip skin conductance during several minutes of quiet waiting followed by a Ready signal and then by a loud, rough noise. The curves give the average resistance for eight adult *O*s. Notice that a rise in the curves means a decrease of resistance and so an increase of conductance. Conductance rises gradually during the period of waiting and more rapidly after the Ready signal; it was highest during the actual noise. The fact that conductance became lower day after day shows habituation to the conditions.

ductance is usually found to be rather high, and it rises slowly while he is waiting to see what *E* will do to him; if *E* gives him electric shocks or loud noises, PGR is elicited and the conductance level is raised; when a rest period is announced the level tends downward only to go up again when announcement is made that the experiment will soon be resumed. (See an especially full record by Darrow & Heath [1932, p. 62], and see also the conductance changes plotted in Figures 6-3 and 6-4.) If the experiment is repeated day after day, *O*'s skin conductance is progressively less at the start of each session and, while rising in the course of each session, it tends to remain lower than on the first day. As *O* becomes accustomed to the situation, his sympathetic is less involved. The conductance is high during active mental work, and still higher during work under conditions of distraction (R. C. Davis, 1934).

The increase in skin conductance during a sitting cannot be attributed to any local effect of the current passed through the skin, for the change occurs even in experiments in which the current is passed only for brief periods at the beginning and end of the session when the galvanometric readings are taken (Syz & Kinder, 1928; Davis, 1934). The changes in conductance are related to apprehension, relief, intense mental work, habituation, and perhaps other psychological factors.

If the task does not call for speed or great effort nor involve any "threat to *O*'s ego," we may expect a gradual decrease of sympathetic activity during the performance and on repetition of the same task. *O* is likely to start off with some apprehension and therefore with high palmar conductance, which will decrease as he gets to know the task. When the task is repeated after a brief rest, or especially after a day's intermission, we may expect some initial recovery of activation (conductance) followed again by a decrease. This adaptation or relaxation effect appears clearly in the results of Duffy & Lacey (1946) as shown in Figure 6-5. Palmar conductance was recorded at 15-second intervals during the determination of *O*'s lower threshold for intensity of sound (weakest audible tone). Starting with an intensity well above threshold *E* lowered the intensity step by step until the threshold was reached—a procedure requiring 4–9 minutes. After a 2-minute rest the procedure was repeated.

These last findings are in sharp contrast with those shown in Figures 6-3 and 6-4, where conductance *increases* during the task. What happens clearly depends on

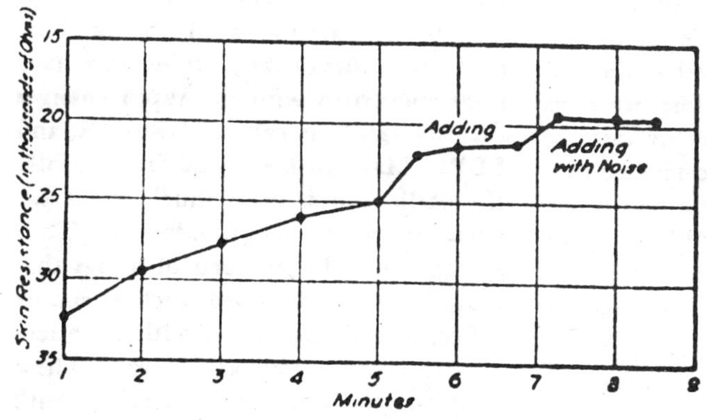

FIG. 6-4. (Data from R. C. Davis, 1934.) Increase of skin conductance: first while waiting for the work to start, then while adding at top speed, and finally while adding under distraction by a loud noise (which reduced the speed of adding by 10 per cent).

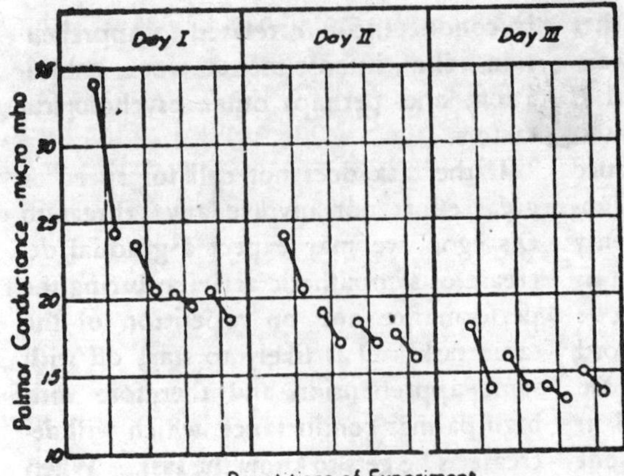

FIG. 6-5. (After Duffy & Lacey, 1946.) Decrease of palmar conductance during four daily repetitions of a stimulus-threshold experiment. The 10 women college students were given a series of short tones interspersed with blanks and had to indicate whenever they heard the sound. As the sounds decreased in intensity the task became gradually more difficult, but still palmar conductance fell from the initial 2.5 minutes to the final 1.5 minutes of each experiment. The sloping lines connect these two measurements for each separate experiment.

how *O* is reacting to the task. There will usually be a sharp rise in conductance as he is activated to start the task. If he finds it difficult, conductance will probably continue its rise, but if all goes well, he will relax somewhat with a gradual fall of conductance.

Roughly the same picture emerges from other studies, although the details may vary. For example, Stanley and Schlosberg (1953) [1] measured conductance during a 2½-hour session made up of five cycles of tests like reaction time, steadiness, and attention, with an interpolated task of long division. Each of the longer tests and the arithmetical task showed the characteristic sudden rise in conductance at the start, followed by a steady fall as *O* settled down to work. But in this experiment the session was long and strenuous. Hence there was not the gradual drop in level as the successive cycles of tests and task were repeated. Instead, there was an increase in the general level of conductance during the first half hour so that the second round of a given test showed higher conductance than had the first round. This seems to have been a warm-up effect, for the general level stayed fairly constant during the last two hours (except for the changes within a given test, and with tests of different difficulty, as we noted above). There was a slight suggestion that the general level climbed slightly toward the end of the session, perhaps indicating that *O* was exerting extra effort to overcome increasing fatigue. As a matter of fact, the conductance measurements were taken in the hope that they would detect such increased effort, a factor that has been assumed to complicate the measurements of the effects of fatigue. This particular attempt was not very successful, for the problem is a knotty one. We shall meet it again later (p. 804).

[1] The paper cited describes the experiment and gives the test scores, but the conductance measurements have yet to be published.

Rapid changes in skin conductance. As we have already indicated, the vast majority of studies of skin conductance have been concerned with the rapid changes that are variously called PGR, GSR, and EDR. Many of these studies, especially the earlier ones, leave much to be desired from a technical standpoint. They average and plot all sorts of things that should not be combined, such as simple deflections of the meter, with no attention to basic conductance level. These inadequacies sometimes interfere with interpretation of fine points, but there are many major points that survive a surprising amount of mistreatment. It is these major points that will be our concern.

GSR obtained by sensory stimuli. When difficulty is encountered in obtaining this response, the reason is usually to be sought in inadequate electrical apparatus. With a good setup the response is practically certain on the application of a strong electric shock or a pistol shot. Other dependable stimuli are: pinching or pricking the skin, striking the face, unexpectedly touching the skin, tickling. Odors and flashes of light have been used with success. Stimuli of any modality, it appears, can elicit PGR, and they need not be very intense, though the more intense stimuli are more certain to give the response. It would be going much too far to assert that *every* stimulus that reaches the organism gives this response. Stimuli arrive every instant, but "spontaneous" responses, occurring in the absence of any stimulus applied by the experimenter, appear only sporadically during a sitting.

Not all stimuli are equally effective (Fig. 6-6). Effectiveness is gauged by the percent of trials in which a given stimulus gives the response, or (if the apparatus is adequate) by the amplitude of the galvanometric deflections. Another measure which one would expect to find correlated with amplitude is the quickness of the response; but Davis (1930) finds the latency of PGR about the same for strong and weak stimuli, though the amplitude is greater with strong stimuli. The latent period was longer for visual than for auditory stimuli, being 1.7 sec for a sound and 2.1 sec for a light—a result which recalls the longer reaction time to light than to sound (p. 16) and also the everyday fact that sounds, more than flashes of light, are apt to be startling.

PGR is readily obtained from the cat, the electrodes being applied to the pads of the feet; also from young dogs and from several other animals. Pinching or pricking the skin is an effective stimulus when a cat is awake. Even under anesthesia (Wang, Pan & Lu, 1929) a dependable PGR is found in the cat's forefoot when electrical stimulation is applied directly to a large sensory nerve from the hind limb.

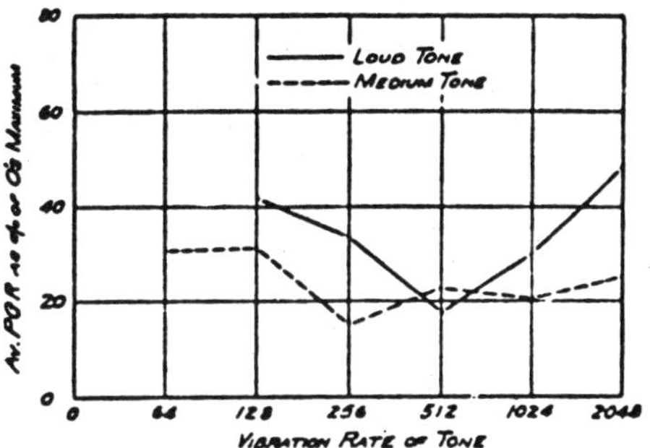

Fig. 6-6. (Data from Misbach, 1932.) Average PGR to tones of different pitch but of equal subjective loudness. Loudness equality was first worked out on one group of subjects, and the equated tones were given as stimuli to a second group. The tones were given in chance order, and each tone was turned on gradually so as to avoid startle. Both frequency and magnitude of PGR were greater for high and low tones than for those of middle pitch. The data points in this graph were obtained by multiplying frequency by average magnitude of responses obtained, each *O*'s magnitude of response being first expressed as a percent of his maximum actual response. Smoothing would evidently give a relatively flat curve for the tones of medium intensity and a steeper dip toward the center for the loud tones. (The tone of 64 cycles could not be amplified sufficiently to bring it up to the upper loudness level.)

The effect of stimulus intensity. Many experiments agree that a strong stimulus elicits a larger GSR than does a weak one, but we can go further, and examine the function which relates these two variables. Hovland and Riesen (1940) measured the amplitude of the (Tarchanoff) GSR to five tones, ranging from zero to 120 db above absolute threshold. There were 20 *Os*, arranged in groups to balance the order of testing the various intensities. Only three measurements of the response were made at each intensity, to avoid adaptation effects (see below). Their results are plotted in Figure 6-7. It will be seen

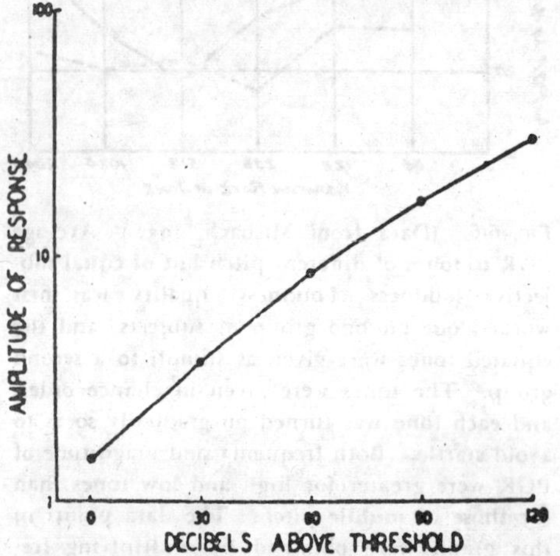

FIG. 6-7. (From Hovland & Riesen, 1940.) Amplitude of galvanic response (Tarchanoff potential method) to varying intensities of tone. Ordinate scale is millimeters of response (spread logarithmically); abscissa is decibels above threshold. The tone was 1,000 cycles.

that log GSR goes up regularly with stimulus intensity. Reference to the sone scale (p. 239) will show that subjective loudness increases in very much the same way, even to the slight bend in the curve. Perhaps GSR will turn out to be another psychophysical method!

Adaptation effects. As a psychophysical method, the GSR has at least one serious disadvantage; unless there are very long intervals between successive stimulations, the response falls off rapidly as the series progresses. Farmer & Chambers (1925) found that *Os* who were used day after day in an intensive experiment came finally to give no PGR even to strong stimuli; but a restful weekend in the country restored them to condition and PGR reappeared. Davis (1930), measuring the magnitude of PGR quite accurately, found a decrease on repetition of the stimulus (the flash of a neon light) at one-minute intervals. The average reaction for 15 *Os* was as follows:

First flash	1099	ohms decrease of resistance
Second flash	268	" " " "
Third flash	190	" " " "

Seward & Seward (1934) using 12 adults as *O*'s, applied in each daily session a series of five strong electric shocks at one-minute intervals, and recorded skin resistance and PGR, respiratory changes, and general bodily movement. They wished to discover how much adaptation and habituation occurred within the daily session and from day to day. Each day *O* gave a subjective rating of the intensity and unpleasantness of the shock, and adaptation appeared in these ratings since the shocks became less unpleasant and seemed less intense as the long experiment advanced, anxiety and apprehension decreased and the shocks were taken less as disturbances and more as localized, objective stimuli. This adaptation appeared also in the records of bodily movement, respiration and PGR. Taking the record for the first day as 100, we have for sample days throughout the experiment:

Day No.	*1*	*8*	*15*	*22*	*29*
Body movement	100	91	47	19	11
Respiration	100	84	66	26	14
PGR	100	82	81	81	75

We see that PGR decreased in amplitude from week to week, but much less than the muscular response to the shock.

Within the single sitting, also, there was progressive adaptation as seen in the following average relative values.

Shock No.	*1*	*2*	*3*	*4*	*5*
Body Movement	100	64	55	50	50
Respiration	100	77	70	64	60
PGR	100	78	71	69	69

Here again there is less adaptation in PGR than in the muscular responses to the shock.

In the association test also, PGR decreases on repetition of the same list of words (p. 59), and it tends to decrease even within the word list, especially for the more neutral words, those later in the list giving smaller deflections than similar words early in the list (Jones & Wechsler, 1928).

There are undoubtedly two phenomena involved in these experiments. One factor is habituation to the general situation, which is evinced as a decrease in the basic level of conductance (p. 148). As *O* becomes more relaxed, he is less apt to be activated by each stimulus. But there is also a second factor, habituation to the specific situation. Sears showed this effect in 1933, when he found that a shift to a radically different stimulus will restore a GSR that has been "adapted out" to a repeated stimulus. Coombs (1938) went further in working out the details of adaptation. He used six different auditory stimuli, adapting *O* to one after the other. He needed a total of 187 *O*s to counterbalance the series properly, thus making sure he was not dealing with effects peculiar to one particular stimulus. In the first place, he found that the GSR falls rapidly on the first few repetitions of a given stimulus, and then more slowly. Secondly, he found some transfer or general effect, in that adaptation to successive series, each consisting of a new stimulus, proceeds more rapidly. Finally, he showed that repetition of the stimulus at 15-second intervals gives more rapid adaptation than does a 30-second spacing. We may mention one other finding for future reference: the strength of GSR was related to *O*'s judgment of how much it startled him, but *not* very closely related to judged pleasantness or unpleasantness.

Porter (1938a) carried the research still further, by studying cross-modality adaptation effects, from a buzzer to a light. After *O* had shown complete adaptation of GSR to a series of buzzes (30-second intervals), Porter started a similar series of lights and got a new "extinction" curve—although the second curve tended to be shorter than the first, after due allowance had been made (by counterbalanced order) for the greater original effectiveness of the buzzer. Again we see that adaptation of the GSR is partially specific to the stimulus, but also shows some generalization to other sudden stimuli.

It is clear from these studies that the strength of the GSR is dependent on both intensity and novelty of the stimulus. The reader will recall that these two stimulus aspects were called *determiners of attention* in an earlier chapter (p. 74). This is more than coincidence, for GSR, attention, alertness, and activation are very closely related topics. In fact, one study has used GSR to determine the effectiveness of different advertisements; the ad which gave the greatest GSR was the one that surveys showed to be the most effective seller (Eckstrand & Gilliland, 1948). If we were making a radical revision of the traditional categories of psychological material, we might well put here much of the material that we have already presented under *attention*. But the reader must realize by this time that topics and chapters are no more than convenient groupings of related aspects of behavior—merely arbitrary categories in a filing system. Like any other filing system, the present one is not ideal, but a new one would call for just as many cross references, since psychological material is all part of a complex whole. So we had better keep the old filing system, in which people know where to find things. But we must be on the alert for cross references; some of the most brilliant advances in theory have been made by those who refused to let conventional categories blind them to new interrelationships.

Conditional stimuli for GSR. Many experimenters have observed that the sensory stimulus need not actually be applied in order to give GSR. *Warning* that a shock is soon to be applied gives a fall of resistance, either abrupt or gradual, and the threat of repeating a shock, pinch, or loud noise will sometimes give a larger response than the actual application of the stimulus. From these facts one would expect GSR to be readily conditioned and experiment shows that such is the case. A few repetitions of an innocuous click along with a strong shock established a conditioned GSR to the click, and extinction was obtained by a few quick repetitions of the click alone (Darrow & Heath, 1932, p. 62). Similar results were obtained with a faint light as the conditioned stimulus (Switzer, 1933). In fact GSR is one of the most readily conditioned responses in human adults. In infants, 3–9 months old, unconditioned GSR was obtained with weak shocks, loud sound, removal of the bottle during nursing, or sudden loss of support; but visual stimuli were ineffective until after conditioning. A few combinations of a faint glow of light with a weak shock established conditioned GSR to the glow, and once established this conditioned response was retained for seven weeks (Jones, 1928, 1930a, b).

The ease with which the conditional GSR may be established and measured has made it a handy tool for studying various aspects of conditioning (p. 552). The GSR is involuntary in the sense that *O* cannot control it on demand, but it is certainly not independent of instructions, sets and attitudes. For example, if *E* remarks "That part is finished, so I'll turn off the shock," and snaps a switch, the conditional GSR will drop out immediately in some *O*s—partly depending on whether *O* believes *E*. Best results will be obtained if the experimental situation is so complicated that *O* never knows what is happening.

An illustration of such complication of design may be taken from the experiments of Welch & Kubis (1947) and Schiff, Dougan & Welch (1949). Fifty-four nonsense syllables were presented in mixed order on a screen. One of these syllables was reinforced by a loud buzzer every second time it appeared. Under such partial reinforcement (p. 563) *O* develops a conditional GSR to the critical syllable in relatively few trials. It is interesting that the speed with which *O* reaches the criterion seems to be related to *anxiety* (in the clinical sense). All but four out of 81 normal adults took 14 or more buzzes to reach the criterion of conditioning, whereas the vast majority of patients diagnosed as having anxiety took fewer trials. Similarly, a group of children who were patients in a psychiatric ward required a mean of 18 buzzes, compared to a mean of 35 for a normal group. This difference cannot be attributed to greater general responsiveness among anxious *O*s, for the criterion of conditioning was three successive conditional GSRs that were higher than the responses to intervening noncritical syllables. This line of research looks promising for a better understanding of both conditioning and anxiety.

PGR in the free association test. Whether we think of GSR as a measure of activation or of emotion, it is clear that words which stir up the subject should call out a reaction. Peterson & Jung (1907) conceived that PGR might make a good "complex indicator" along with slow verbal reaction; and their results satisfied them that such was the case. Whately Smith (1922) spoke 100 stimulus words as stimuli for free verbal response and concluded that PGR was a very good indicator of emotion. The ten words in his list which gave the largest average PGR from 50 educated subjects, and the ten which gave the smallest average, are as follows, with numbers indicating the relative magnitudes of the galvanometer deflections:

Rank	*GSR*	*Rank*	*GSR*
1. Kiss	73	91. Carrot	18
2. Love	59	92. Bury (berry)	18
3. Marry	58	93. Hunger	18
4. Divorce	51	94. White	18
5. Name	49	95. Glass	18
6. Woman	40	96. Give	17
7. Wound	38	97. Flower	16
8. Dance	37	98. Pond	15
9. Afraid	37	99. Pencil	15
10. Proud	37	100. Swim	14

Jones & Wechsler (1928) tried most of the above words on 35 students and obtained very nearly the same order of the stimulus words as regards the magnitude of the response.

Correlation of PGR with reported emotion. So far we have been studying PGR from the stimulus side; now we turn to the question, what the total activity may be of which PGR is a part. Is the total activity an emotion, necessarily? If so, the amplitude of PGR should correspond with the intensity of the emotion. Wells & Forbes (1911) gave words as stimuli and required *O* to estimate the intensity of the emotional response to each word, using a scale of four degrees, A, B, C, F, with A indicating the greatest intensity. The average magnitude of PGR was greatest for the A cases, next for the B cases, and so on, but with many exceptions. The magnitude of PGR could not serve as an index of the reportable emotionality of the single experience. Essentially the same result was obtained by Wechsler (1925) and by Syz (1926b). The latter investigator used as stimuli words and phrases suggesting various life situations. The subjects, medical students, listened to the stimuli without making any verbal response at the time, but later, after the list of stimuli had been gone through twice, it was laid before them and they were asked to indicate which stimuli had aroused emotions. The table on page 154 gives a few of the stimuli, with the percent of *O*s who gave PGR to each stimulus and the percent who reported an emotion.

The decreased percent of galvanic responses on second hearing exemplifies the adaptation effect which has already been noticed. The discrepancies between the first and third columns are specially emphasized by the author. PGR occurred a vast number of times without any remembered and reported emotion, and on the other side a good many emotions were reported where there had been no PGR. No one hesitates to admit experiencing emotion on hearing the word "Mother," as one may on hearing "Unpaid bills." The conclusion drawn by Syz from these dis-

Stimulus word	*Percent of Os giving a PGR on 1st hearing*	*on 2nd hearing*	*Percent reporting emotion*
O's first name	84	68	36
O's last name	74	40	28
Kiss	72	40	34
Misspent youth	48	20	4
Unpaid bills	36	24	2
Cheating	28	22	10
Mother	26	12	30
Stupid	18	24	0

crepancies is the opposite of what might perhaps be expected. Instead of condemning PGR as invalid because of its frequent conflict with verbal report, he accepts PGR as the better index of emotion and condemns the verbal report as unreliable.

Syz may be correct in explaining discrepancies between reports and GSR in terms of unreported emotion, but anyone who tries the GSR-association word experiment runs into all sorts of perplexing problems. For example, a student once tried to measure GSRs of psychiatric patients, using words and names from the individual case histories as stimuli. His first patient was a schizophrenic woman; *E* mixed her husband's name with several others and presented them all a few times. Sometimes she gave large responses to his name, but at other times she gave no response. To one who is familiar with schizophrenic behavior this is not surprising; the name probably did not penetrate on every trial. This brings out the point that the size of the GSR is only a measure of the extent to which the stimulus arouses *O* (cf. McCurdy, 1950); it is part of a total reaction. In complex situations it may be as unpredictable in individual cases as is any total reaction. This variability of the GSR has undoubtedly discouraged many *Es* who tried to use it, as it discouraged the student we have just described! But by careful experimental design, with due attention to *O*'s attitudes as well as to stimulating and recording apparatus, it is possible to eliminate some of the variability; the rest must be achieved through statistical control. McCurdy, after surveying many such studies, stressed the consistently high correlations between GSR and reported strength of emotion.

Relationship of GSR to pleasantness and unpleasantness. Perhaps we would make better progress if we considered the *type* of reported emotion rather than its mere intensity. The most obvious distinction to look for is that between pleasantness and unpleasantness, and perhaps the easiest way to tackle the problem is to use pleasant and unpleasant odors. Shock & Coombs (1937) recorded GSRs of 40 boys and 40 girls to each of 16 odors. They also had the children rate the odors on a five-point scale running from very pleasant to very unpleasant. The girls gave the highest GSR to odors at both extremes of the scale, falling off to the middle (indifferent) category. The boys showed a fair GSR to stimuli judged very unpleasant, but relatively small responses to those in the other categories. The children were 12½ years of age; perhaps the boys might have been more interested in perfume a few years later!

Dysinger (1931) did a comparable experiment with words as stimuli. In the course of three sittings he presented 150 stimulus words intended to run the gamut from very pleasant ("darling," "vacation") through indifferent ("basket," "make") to very unpleasant ("suicide," "vomit"). After each stimulus word *O* reported its pleasant or unpleasant effect on him, using a five-point scale. Meanwhile a galvanometer was registering PGR. Pooling the results from the 13 *O*s (so far as comparable) we find PGR to be smallest, on the average, when the stimulus word was "indifferent," as seen from the mean PGR readings:

Effect of stimulus	
Very pleasant	129
Pleasant	98
Indifferent	79
Unpleasant	101
Very unpleasant	147

(The SD_m for these values is about 6; the unit is arbitrary.) The increased PGR with either pleasantness or unpleasantness, shown here, is particularly interesting.

Lanier (1941a, b) added another category to the judgments, *mixed* affective tone. He reasoned that this judgment would indicate "affective conflict" which would show up as high GSR, and also as increased time to make the judgment. His hypothesis was correct, as these values indicate:

Judged category	*Indifferent*	*Pleasant*	*Unpleasant*	*Mixed*
Percentage of responses falling in category	15.4	50.2	24.4	10.0
Median GSR (ohms)	166	165	177	263
Median judgment time (sec)	2.38	1.79	1.89	2.73

Lanier also showed the greater impact of the "mixed" category by immediate and delayed recognition memory tests. Words in this category showed significantly better retention.

There is one other point in the data that deserves comment. Note that "indifferent" gives about the same strength of GSR as "pleasant," an unexpected result. Perhaps the reason may be found in the long judgment time for indifferent words. This judgment seems to have been a difficult one to make, which might arouse a little extra tension.

GSR in more differentiated emotional states. The level of activation is probably relatively slight in many of these experiments with verbal stimuli, for college students are apt to respond at a rather superficial level (p. 54). Bayley (1928) and Patterson (1930) worked with more varied stimuli. Bayley's stimuli, intended mostly to arouse fear, included loud noises (whistle, pistol), holding a lighted match till it burned the fingers, electric shock received on making error in arithmetic example, preparation for taking drop of blood from finger, reading of gruesome story, oral quiz on laboratory apparatus, subsequent assurance that the quiz was not serious, piece of chocolate candy, statement that the experiment was "all over." Patterson sought to awaken surprise rather than fear by giving *O* a jar to hold which contained mercury, by showing *O* his own face in a mirror when he was expecting to see a skull, by reading a ghost story to *O* and inserting a sentence from a mathematical book, by dropping a pile of scrap tin in the midst of soft music. When the cases were sorted according to reported *intensity* of the emotion aroused, there was a fair positive correlation, ranging from .53 to .88, between this intensity and the magnitude of

PGR (Patterson). When the cases were sorted according to *kind* of emotion, the two studies agree in showing the largest average PGR for startle, medium for apprehensive expectancy, small for relief and for indifference. One *O* who was informed during the experiment of his election to an honor society reported "joy" and gave an extremely large PGR.

Another experiment combining PGR with immediate verbal report is that of Abel (1930) in which *O* was given a variety of problems to solve and was asked to report the "attitude" or "state of his functioning organism." The reports were sorted into two main classes: reports of "predicament" or sense of encountering difficulty; and reports of "ease" or smooth progress toward the solution of the problem. The frequency of PGR was determined for these two classes and was found to be:

76 percent for "predicament"
16 " " "ease"

The author's conclusion is that PGR is an index not so much of feeling or emotion as of an attitude of the organism directed toward *overcoming difficulty*. This organic attitude is often experienced as a "predicament."

As pointed out by Landis & Hunt (1935), PGR occurs in such a variety of mental states that a fallacious case can be made out for its connection with any one state by employing only stimuli suited to produce that state. These authors consequently presented varied stimuli intended to arouse fear, amusement, sex emotion, pleasantness and unpleasantness, and other states. *O* was required after each response "to give a verbal description of what happened in your consciousness during the period of stimulation." When the galvanic responses were sorted according to the mental state reported by the *O*s, the average PGR in ohms (account being taken of both frequency and magnitude of PGR) came out as follows:

Subjective state reported	*Mean PGR in ohms*
Tension	1248
Startle, surprise, fear	846
Confusion	740
Amusement	514
Expectancy	401
Inhibition, uncertainty	319
Unpleasantness	260
Effort	169
Pleasantness	105

The authors conclude that PGR, while not attached specifically to any one conscious state, is "more nearly related to startle or to tension than to anything else." (See also Bagchi & Greenwald, 1937.)

PGR during mental work. PGR is not limited to states which we ordinarily regard as emotional. The slow increase of skin conductance, as well as the brief deflections which we call PGR, occurs in adding, learning nonsense syllables, or solving problems. Prideaux (1920) points out that PGR during mental work need not result from the mere intellectual labor, since as he says, "Very often a strong affect is produced by the surprise at the question or by the embarrassment and possible annoyance that the solution of the problem may be incorrect." Wechsler (1925) makes a similar comment: *O* "feels he is being tested, that by the correctness of his answer he will make a favorable or unfavorable impression." He gave problems of the type, $7 + 3 + 6 \times 5 - 6 \ldots$, and found PGR largest at the start and finish, i.e., at the moments when the problem was attacked and when the answer was stated, rather than during the arithmetical work.

A special study of PGR in mental arithmetic was made by Sears (1933) with 24 college women as subjects. He gave: (1) easy examples to be done without any time limit or demand for speed; (2) easy examples to be done rapidly; (3) more difficult examples. When a whole list of 20 examples was easy and done at leisure, PGR showed a gradual decline. When the first 10 examples were easy and the second 10 difficult, there was an abrupt increase of PGR at the onset of the difficult examples. When all the examples were easy and the first 10 done at leisure and the last 10 with a time limit, there was a sudden increase of PGR with the beginning of effort for speed. In short, there was a gradual decrease of PGR with continuance of the same kind of work, but an abrupt increase in PGR on shifting to more speedy or difficult work, and also an abrupt decrease on shifting from more rapid or difficult to more comfortable work.

The reader will recall the marked changes in level of conductance that were evinced during repeated series of hard and easy psychophysical judgments; they seem to parallel the changes in GSR (p. 148). There is a knotty problem here; does the increased basic conductance lead to spuriously high GSRs, or does it merely indicate an increased level of reactivity? We do not really have a good answer to this question. Part of Sear's change in GSR may have resulted from failure to allow for basic level of resistance, but that is not the whole story. Staudt & Kubis (1948) found that GSRs to verbal questions were smaller when *O* was sitting or reclining in a relaxed fashion than they were when he was under muscular or attitudinal tension—conditions which would favor low and high conductance, respectively. Yet these workers had made some correction for basic level, for they used relative changes ($\Delta R/R$) rather than absolute measures of resistance changes. These results are consistent with the plausible view that a high level of activation leads to greater reactivity.

In the work of Bartlett (1927) we find illustrations of the minute analysis necessary in order to identify the precise stimulus that gives PGR during continued mental activity. In one experiment *O* counted "one, two, three . . ." as rapidly as possible, either silently or aloud. Counting aloud gave much larger deflections. But as merely talking aloud gave no deflections it was not the speech movement that aroused PGR. Careful observation showed that in counting aloud *O* stumbled in his speech, and Bartlett attributes the deflections to this stumbling, accompanied as it probably was by an "awareness of possible failure."

PGR in combination with bodily movements. One very sure way to obtain the galvanometric deflection from a subject is to ask him to draw a deep breath or to cough. PGR does not occur with ordinary quiet breathing, but it does occur regularly with deep breathing. Besides the cough, other respiratory movements in which it occurs include the sneeze, sigh, laugh, clearing the throat, and the yawn. Claparède (1931) shows that yawning is associated with stretching. Though the experiment may not have been tried, there is no doubt that PGR would accompany the stretching movement. Yawning and stretching, Claparède urges, are preparatory movements with a wakening effect. Straining is another movement accompanied by PGR. It occurs in other vigorous muscular movements (Starch, 1910b), as well as in quick or accurate movements such as those of aiming or the reaction time experiment. One may generalize from these observations that PGR accompanies energetic or attentive muscular movement and also preparation for such movement.

GSR to unrecognized stimuli. In the chapter on Attention it was pointed out that *Os* recognize words related to their dominant interests more readily than other words (p. 105). Further, McGinnies (1949) showed that *O* has higher than normal recognition thresholds (he needs more exposure time) for "naughty" words. He attributed this increased threshold to a hypothetical mechanism, *perceptual defense*. But it is hard to see how *O* can defend himself against recognizing a word before he knows what it is. Obviously we need independent evidence that such a mechanism exists. McGinnies thought he could furnish such evidence through GSR; so he recorded this response to taboo and to ordinary words, presented tachistoscopically. As predicted, there *were* strong GSRs to taboo words when *O* reported that he did not know what they were or gave incorrect readings. There is the immediate suggestion that *O* really recognized the words, gave a GSR, but hesitated to say the forbidden words in the presence of a respected *E*. (Howes & Solomon, 1950; McGinnies, 1950.)

To check on this question, Lazarus & McCleary (1951) decided to give emotional significance to nonsense syllables —an emotion that involved no social taboos. They presented ten nonsense syllables to *O*, pairing half of them with shock. After good GSRs had been conditioned to the critical syllables, all syllables were presented at about threshold duration. Under these unfavorable exposure conditions many of the syllables were not recognized, but the critical syllables gave significantly more GSR than did the neutral ones. The experimental design was neatly balanced to eliminate any unwanted variables, as amount of practice. Hence the experiment furnishes clear evidence for what the writers call *subception*, or "autonomic discrimination without awareness."

From a superficial viewpoint these results are very puzzling since they imply that *O* can show an emotional response to stimuli that he does not perceive. But the puzzle is largely a result of a residual dualistic type of thinking. It assumes that the Ego must first perceive a word and then proceed to release an emotional response. All that these experiments actually show is that stimuli can elicit relatively low-level responses even though they do not evoke correct verbal responses. This sort of thing occurs constantly in perception; we recognize faces without knowing the specific features, and we throw and catch balls when their trajectories are far too complex for a physicist to predict (cf. page 358, 359). Clearly *O* is always responding without full conscious awareness of the details.

The significance of GSR for psychology. We raised the question as to whether or not the GSR measured emotion and suggested that it was a poor question. All we have written since then confirms the judgment. Yet a vast amount of paper, not to mention much good research time, has been wasted in an attempt to answer the question. Around 1930 a symposium on GSR was held at a meeting of psychologists. After a half dozen people had argued that the GSR was not a good measure of emotion. Wechsler pointed out that the trouble was with the concept of emotion, rather than with GSR. We should stop thinking of Emotion with a capital E, as a special mental or behavioral state; this type of thinking is a heritage from the prescientific trilogy of Cognition, Volition, and Affection. Instead, we should use emotion to describe the individual who is highly energized, active, tense, or activated. For emotion in this sense, both basic level of conductance and the GSR become pretty good measures, since they reflect various degrees of activation, of readiness for action, ranging from sleep to rage. Of course, the skin conductance will show changes to sudden stimuli, or with the shift from relaxation to a challenging task. *O* is simply showing general activation as preparation for a potential increase in gross activity. The rapid change is the GSR; the conductance will return to its old level if the threat is false, or it may stay high if continued activity is appropriate. The GSR may not be measuring traditional *emotion* in these cases, but it is measuring a much more fundamental dimension of behavior.

The sensitivity and convenience of conductance measures have made them popular indices of level of activation, but there are other measures available. We shall consider them in the next chapter.

7

EMOTION III: OTHER BODILY CHANGES

The GSR has received careful attention as a convenient index of the level of activation, and it is probably the best general measure available. But if the concept of activation is a good one, we should be able to measure its level through half a dozen different processes and note how well they agree among themselves. Further, there may well be some physiological difference between different emotions; according to the poets and novelists, the face is pallid in fear but red in anger. As you go through this chapter, you will find little additional evidence for such physiological differentiation. What you will find are signs of the *strength* rather than of the *kind* of an emotional state.

CIRCULATION

The ability of the bodily cells to do their work depends on the adequacy of the system that brings them fuel and oxygen and removes their waste products. The amount of blood flowing through an organ is a critical factor, but it is obviously difficult to measure. Besides, what we want is a general index of circulatory adequacy for the whole body. Let us look at the parts of the circulatory system and see what indices are possible.

The heartbeat. The heart is a hollow muscle that squirts pulses of blood into the arteries, not unlike the rubber bulb on an atomizer. It futher resembles the rubber bulb in having check valves on the inlet (veins) and outlet (arteries) which prevent back flow. The contraction or squeezing phase is the *systole*, the relaxation phase the *diastole*. Obviously the amount of blood pumped through the system in a given time will depend on the strength and rate of the heartbeat. These and other characteristics of the heart action can be observed in several ways. You can listen to the heart sounds, either with an ear against *O*'s chest or by aid of the stethoscope. A small microphone held against the chest will drive an amplifier and loudspeaker and enable a large audience to "listen in." If the output of the microphone drives a counter or other recording device, you have a *cardiotachometer*, which will count heartbeats during a night's sleep.

There are also electrical changes in the contracting heart muscle, relatively massive action potentials which have long been recorded in the familiar *electrocardiogram* (abbreviated EKG, from the German form of the word). The modern electronic amplifiers make it possible to obtain detailed records with a convenient portable instrument. As a matter of fact, these potentials are so large that they intrude on the amplified records from other organs and become a nuisance (as in Fig. 7-7, p. 185).

A third way of recording the heart action is by means of its mechanical effect, the arterial *pulse*. Each systole starts a wave coursing through the arteries which can be felt and counted without instrumental aids or recorded in detail by use of the *sphygmograph*.

Blood pressure. The force of the heartbeat drives the blood through the arteries, large and ever smaller, through the microscopic capillaries, and on through the veins, small and ever larger, back to the heart. Because of the resistance of the small-bore arterioles (and perhaps capillaries), the heart action builds up pressure in the arteries, the amount of pressure depending on the output of the heart and on the resistance encountered. Further, in each pulse wave there is a maximum and a minimum of pressure: the minimum is called *diastolic* pressure because it corresponds to the diastole of the heart, and the maximum is the *systolic* pressure. The difference between the two is the *pulse pressure*, sometimes taken as a measure of the useful work accomplished by the heartbeat. As a rough rule pulse pressure, diastolic and systolic, vary together in the ratio 1:2:3. Typical values of SP/DP, in millimeters of mercury as the unit of pressure, would be $^{120}/_{80}$, from which the pulse pressure, 40, is found by subtraction. The systolic pressure is often the only one measured.

Blood pressure can be measured directly in animals by inserting a pressure gauge into an artery. The standard method in man is somewhat indirect. *E* wraps the arm or leg with a band or cuff which contains a large air sac, and finds how much pressure must be pumped into the sac to just counteract the blood pressure. By listening to an artery below the cuff, he finds the following three stages:

1. *External or cuff pressure below diastolic.* There is silence, for the blood flows continually through the artery.

2. *External pressure between diastolic and systolic level. E* hears a regular *thud* or *thump* since the blood gets through the blocked area only on the systolic surges.

3. *External pressure above systolic level.* Again there is silence, for no blood gets past the cuff.

The transition point between 1 and 2 is the diastolic pressure and that between 2 and 3 is the systolic. Both are read from a manometer, or pressure gauge, inserted in the air line. The modern watch-case gauges are still calibrated in the same units as the old mercury ones, millimeters of mercury. The apparatus, including gauge, cuff, and pressure bulb, is called the *sphygmomanometer*.

A skillful *E* can make several pairs of measurements per minute, accurate to a millimeter or two, but it is doubtful that there are any satisfactory ways of getting a continuous record of the blood pressure. It is possible to inflate the cuff to a level between SP and DP, and to record pressure changes in the air system of the apparatus. The records so obtained can be very useful (as in lie detection, p. 190), but they are not records of the blood pressure alone.

They represent complex interactions of blood pressure and arm volume.

Volumetric changes. Besides heart rate and blood pressure there is a third possible circulatory index of the level of activation. The distribution of blood to the various members changes from time to time and produces changes in the volume of the members. The smooth muscle in the walls of an artery, by contracting and relaxing, brings about local *vasoconstriction* and *vasodilation.* Like the other circulatory functions, these changes are under autonomic control. In an inactive state of the organism the large abdominal vessels dilate and hold a large volume of blood, but under stress they constrict and inject blood rapidly into the heart which in turn circulates it to the active muscles and brain. It is possible to detect some of these changes by use of the *plethysmograph* or volume recorder. This is a jar or cylinder of air into which the arm, for example, is inserted and sealed airtight, while a tube leads to a tambour or other device for recording the volume changes due to vasodilation and vasoconstriction in the arm. This instrument was more popular with psychologists years ago than it is now because the changes of volume result from various causes, including the external temperature. A sudden loud noise will cause vasoconstriction in the arm when *O* is very warm, but not dependably when the arm is already vasoconstricted in response to cold surroundings.

Neural control of the circulation. The heart muscle and the smooth muscle of the arteries are not completely dependent on their nerves but can continue their activities even when the nerves are severed. But the shifting needs of the organism demand a dual control of the circulation, to increase and decrease its activities. For the heart, the vagus nerve (parasympathetic) inhibits or slows down the beat, and the sympathetic speeds it up—quite according to the "peace" and "war" functioning of these two autonomic systems. The picture is more complicated for the arteries; the sympathetic will cause vasoconstriction in the digestive organs and vasodilation in the muscles, whereas the parasympathetic will have the reverse effects.

As the blood pressure rises, it stimulates "pressure gauge" receptors in the aorta and carotid sinus which act on the centers in the medulla and bring about reflex slowing of the heart and dilation of the arteries, thus moderating the blood pressure. Besides such self-regulation, the circulation, in common with the other homeostatic processes, is under the control of the hypothalamus (Morgan & Stellar, 1950; Lindsley, 1951). The circulation also reflects cortical events and in turn alters the level of cortical activity by varying the oxygen supply to the brain.

Circulatory changes in sleep. As we did in discussing the GSR, we shall start our treatment of circulatory factors and indices at the minimal level of activation in sleep. So we shall have a base line for examining the changes that occur higher up along the continuum toward the emotional states. Boas & Goldschmidt (1932) obtained continuous heart rate records from over 100 adults in various activities. A "basal heart rate" was obtained in the same conditions in which the basal metabolic rate is measured (p. 169) that is in the postabsorptive resting state while *O* is lying awake in the morning long after the last meal and before engaging in the activities of the day. This basal heart rate averaged 61 for the male subjects and 70 for the female. In ordinary indoor occupations the average male rate was 78 and the female 84, with wide individual variations. In sleeping the male average was 59 and the female 65, not much less than the basal waking rate. In some *O*s the heart rate went down to 40 during sleep, in some it rose to 170 or higher during muscular exercise. Noises during sleep, especially during the light sleep just before awaking, caused a momentary quickening of the heart. The pulse also rose when *O* turned in bed. In awakening there is sometimes a quick rise of heart rate, sometimes a gradual rise which begins before awaking and continues afterward. The heart rate curve for a full night's sleep varies with the individual, in some showing an early drop to a low level which is maintained until awaking, in others showing a progressive decline until awaking, in still others showing more oscillation with a gradual rise for the last hour before awaking. As judged from the heart rate there are different ways of sleeping and different ways of waking up.

Landis (1925) took the blood pressure of male students in going to sleep, during sleep and in awaking. In ordinary going to sleep the systolic pressure fell from 108 to 94 mm of mercury in two or three minutes; this typical result was obtained even when the subject was reclining instead of lying flat in bed. Normal quiet awaking showed a gradual rise of the blood pressure, as from 94 to 108 mm in two minutes. When *O* was awakened by an alarm clock, the rise was more rapid—for example, from 92 while asleep to 114 within 50 sec. This sudden rise was followed by a decline back to 104 in another 20 sec. The picture varied, however; sometimes the rise was more gradual even on being wakened by an alarm clock.

An experiment by Shepard (1906, 1914) was quite comprehensive since in addition to heart rate, breathing rate and hand volume he was able to record the *changes in brain volume* in two young men whose skulls had been trephined because of head injury. A portion of the skull had been removed and the scalp sewed together over the hole. The brain could be felt to pulsate as in a baby's fontanelle. A piece of cork, attached to the rubber diaphragm of a receiving tambour, was bound firmly over the opening in the skull, the tambour being connected by air transmission with a piston recorder. After some preliminary sittings the subjects became well adjusted to this instrumentation and took the experiments as a routine matter; they sometimes slept all night in the laboratory while their brain volume, arm volume and breathing were being recorded.

Shepard's setup was very complete and accurate and he obtained many records with consistent results. So, though his results differ from those obtained in earlier less complete experiments, they are probably correct. In agreement with other experimenters he found the general blood pressure low and the hand volume large during sleep. These findings indicate general vasodilation during sleep. The vasodilation showed up even in the brain, for the skin over the trephine hole bulged enough to show clearly on the record. Of course, brain volume cannot change very much in the intact skull, although brain tissue may bulge slightly through the orifices for cranial nerves and vessels. But there was obviously enough relaxation of the blood vessels to more than counteract the decreased general blood pressure, giving a net increase in brain volume wherever the skull permitted it—in this case, through the trephine hole. The vasodilation may be thought of as a way of protecting the brain from an excessive drop in blood supply as the general level of circulation slows down; the brain is very dependent on a good blood supply, much more so than are the muscles.

The picture that emerges from these and other studies (Kleitman, 1939) shows a generally low level of activation in sleep, with increased brain volume, general peripheral vasodilation, lowered blood pressure and heart rate, slow, regular and deep breathing (see below) and lowered body temperature. All of these indicators tend to reach their lowest levels after a few hours of sleep and to build up again toward the usual time for waking. But an external stimulus may raise their level briefly, even though it does not actually awaken *O*. Thus, Shepard found that such a stimulus causes a transient decrease in brain volume, sometimes preceded by a slight rise—probably depending on whether increased blood pressure comes before or just after the change in vasodilation.

Startle, surprise and sudden shifts of attention. Here we shall take note first of Shepard's results on his trephined subjects during the waking state. Stimuli then gave an increase in brain volume, not a decrease as was the case during sleep. A sudden loud noise gave a compound response: first a rise, then a small fall and finally a further rise of volume. The same startling stimulus gave a rise of hand volume followed by a fall. The net result was rise in brain volume, fall in hand volume.

These seemingly complex results are not inexplicable. We have a right to assume a constriction of the large abdominal veins in response to a startling stimulus, with consequent increase of blood poured into the heart and increased output into the arteries. The first effect in both hand and brain is an increase of volume. Vasoconstriction in the hand soon reduces the volume there, while brain vasoconstriction, we may assume, is comparatively ineffective so that the net result is increased brain volume. The whole thing is a consistent sympathetic reaction. But how then shall we explain the *fall* in brain volume on disturbance during sleep? We need only assume further that the brain vessels are so much relaxed during sleep that their constriction in response to a startling stimulus amounts to a big change, sufficient to counteract the increased heart output.

With startling stimuli, a loud whistle or a pistol shot, the heart rate takes a sudden jump and quickly returns toward normal (Berg & Beebe-Center, 1941). Blood pressure takes a similar course.

Expectancy. A. E. Nissen (1928) obtained blood pressure readings from two patients in the dentist's chair. The pressure rose sharply when the dentist came into the room; in fact, the rise at this time was more regular than when he began his operations. Even the expectation of a neutral stimulus, announced a few moments in advance, tends to raise the pulse rate, increase the volume of the brain, and decrease the volume of the hand (Shepard, 1906).

Changes during and after muscular exertion. Shock (1944) reports some interesting changes brought about by making children run up four flights of stairs.

The experiment was part of the Adolescent Growth Study at the University of California, which involved an extensive series of physiological measurements made over a period of years on the same children (see H. E. Jones, 1939, 1943). The record of a 14½-year-old boy is shown in Figure 7-1. The record shows the changes during recovery rather than during exercise, since the record starts after the boy got to the top of the stairs, but we can assume that the pre-exercise level was fairly close to that attained after a half hour of recovery. Exercise obviously raised systolic and lowered diastolic blood pressures, thus giving a double increase in pulse pressure. Pulse rate was also high during exercise. The picture is thus one of greatly increased heart activity during exercise, with rather slow recovery during rest. This slow recovery represents the body "working off its debt," repairing the deficits run up during exercise, removing waste products and rebuilding local food supplies in the tissues themselves. We shall say more about the other two curves, respiratory volume and oxygen consumption, later; they are part of the same general picture.

Mental activity. Muscular activity increases the heart rate and the flow of blood for excellent physiological reasons. Mental activity is likely to involve some muscular activity and for that reason to increase the circulation. Mental arithmetic, involving very little muscular activity, produces no noticeable increase; in fact, the heart rate may sink during the prolonged muscular inactivity of this particular experiment. In other kinds of mental work some increase in the pulse rate is found, especially if the conditions involve competition or working against time.

Excitement. From much experimental evidence it is perfectly clear that excitement speeds up the circulation. Tigerstedt (1926) measured the blood pressure of 13 students before and after an important six-hour examination, and found it very high, 165 mm on the average, beforehand; 152 mm, still high, after-

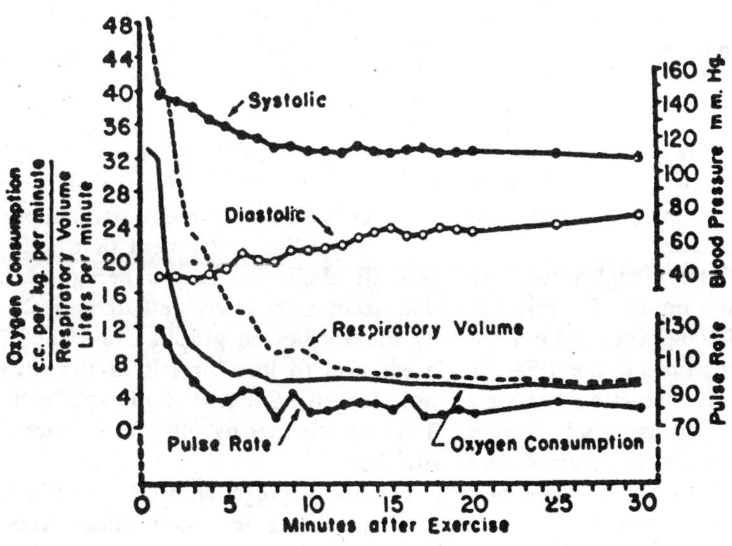

FIG. 7-1. (Shock, 1944.) Physiological displacements and their recovery after exercise. Just before the start of the base line, a 14½-year-old boy had run up four flights of steps (58½ ft). The various measures are to be referred to the appropriate ordinate scales. Some curves appear to drift slightly to the end, suggesting that they have not quite reached their basal levels.

ward. In another experiment he had a student step forward and face the class, who passed remarks while this student's blood pressure was being taken. The average from 10 students was 166 mm. These same students then reported individually to the professor for several successive days and gave average blood pressure, day by day, of 152, 140, 139, 130, 129 mm, the last reading being down near the norm for young adults. Tigerstedt concluded that the high pressure in the earlier days of this series was a hangover from the exciting conditions under which the measurement had first been made, a sort of conditioned response.

Other tests of circulation and respiration before examinations are summarized by Brown & Van Gelder (1938). These authors themselves measured a large number of students. One group of 17 college seniors, before and after the sessions of a two-day final comprehensive examination in psychology, were above their normal state by the following amounts:

	First Day		Second Day	
	Before	*After*	*Before*	*After*
Systolic B.P.	15 mm	2 mm	4 mm	0
Pulse rate	23 beats	5 beats	16 beats	4 beats
Breathing rate	3 cycles	−1 cycle	1 cycle	0

As remarked by Luria (1932) individuals differ in their anticipatory reaction to an examination, some being relatively immune to this influence.

Landis & Gullette (1925) piled one emotional situation on another through a long sitting. Though they did not obtain differential reactions to the different situations, the general reaction was high blood pressure during the whole sitting. In the effort to produce severe emotional upset, Landis (1926) induced three psychologists to undergo a two-day fast and a sleepless night, after which they were given the strongest electrical stimulation that they could stand for as long as they would endure it. There were many symptoms—inhibition of stomach contraction and of rectal contraction, gasping, nausea and gagging, marked sweating, incoordination of behavior—and along with these signs of excitement went a marked rise in the blood pressure.

That stimulation of the circulation is not confined to unpleasant excitement is shown by a record of Boas & Goldschmidt (1932) in which they demonstrated the wide range of application of their cardiotachograph by obtaining a complete record of heart rate during sex behavior of a married couple, and found sharp peaks (143–146 beats per minute) during orgasm. A milder degree of pleasurable excitement was shown by a man listening to a phonograph record of a song which was connected in his mind with a woman of whom he was very fond. On hearing this song his pulse rate increased from 64 to 121.

The problem of introducing any strong pleasurable emotion into the laboratory has been a difficult one for the psychologist. *O* needs to become so well adapted to the recording instrument that he forgets all about the record being taken. This seems to be fairly well accomplished by the cardiotachograph. The subject needs also to lose himself in the situation, forgetting that it is an experiment. This need is met by the motion picture situation.

J. C. Scott (1930) showed a 40-minute motion picture to 100 medical school sophomores, taken one at a time into the laboratory. The film contained a love scene, an episode likely to arouse anger in which the hero was badly treated, and a third episode intended to arouse fear, in which the city was destroyed by earthquake and the hero was in danger. These episodes were separated by about 10 minutes of relatively neutral film. *O* sat alone in a room watching the show, his blood pressure being recorded by means of the Tycos recording sphygmometer which although not giving a continuous record enables the experimenter to obtain the pressure at intervals without being in the immediate presence of the subject. At the close of the picture *O* gave a retrospective estimate of the degree of his emotion in viewing the different episodes. From these reports the sex emotion was most successfully aroused, and it showed a definite rise of blood pressure in nearly every one of the subjects. It must be remembered that moderate changes in blood pressure amounting to a rise or fall of 10 mm occur without obvious cause, either emotional or physiological. The subjects in this experiment had been adapted to the laboratory situation by previously coming several times and having their blood pressure taken.

A neat physiological demonstration of abdominal vasoconstriction in fright and excitement is provided by an experiment on a dog (Barcroft & Florey, 1929; Drury, Florey & Florey, 1929). By a preliminary operation a bit of the lining of the dog's intestine was grafted into the skin while still retaining its own proper nerves and blood vessels. Thus a sample of the intestinal mucous membrane was exposed to view. Whenever this dog was frightened, as by the approach of a strange person, the membrane blanched, showing vasoconstriction. The latency of this reaction was 4–5 sec, much longer than that of the external signs of fright, a fact which may be, as the authors suggest, a telling point against the James-Lange theory of emotion. Again, the dog was held by one of his friends while another called him from a distance; and the patch of mucous membrane blanched, while the external behavior indicated excitement, not fear or anger.

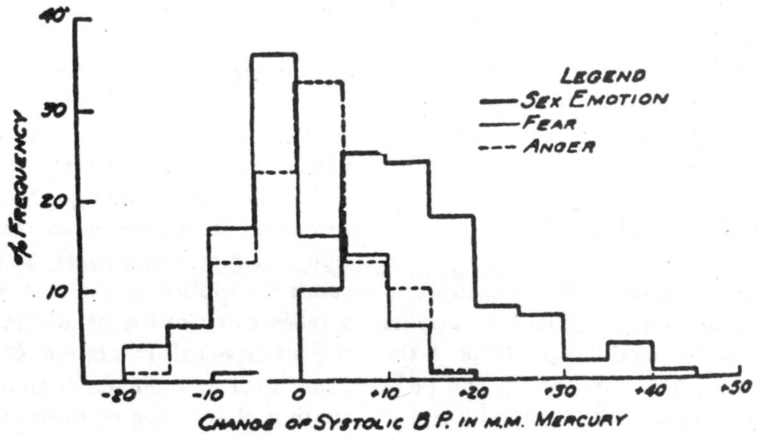

Fig. 7-2. (Data from J. C. Scott, 1930.) Systolic blood pressure during a motion picture episode which aroused a sex emotion reported as at least "moderate" by 88 of 100 subjects tested. The episodes intended to arouse fear and anger were less successful according to the introspective reports. The graph shows the distribution of responses.

Differential changes. Most of the experiments we have described have shown the relationship between circulatory changes and level of activation or "excitement." We may well ask if there are any different patterns of changes that correspond to the various emotional states. We have very little clear evidence on this point. One of the most striking among these few experiments is that of Wolf & Wolff (1942, 1943). They had a patient who had a gastric fistula, which is a direct opening into the stomach made to permit feeding after an accident had closed his throat. They employed him as a technician and had an opportunity to observe the vascular and other changes in the lining of the stomach under different emotions. In worry or fear the mucosa became pale, and both stomach motility and digestive secretion were inhibited. But states described as hostility, resentment, or anxiety gave a red lining, with an increase in stomach motility and in acid secretion. These writers stressed the fact that altered gastric function is a part of a general bodily pattern, and not the simple result of sympathetic discharge. Their results may give us a clue to the difference between anger and fear, but we are still a long way from a full understanding of the details of physiological changes in these and other emotional states.

RESPIRATION

The primary function of breathing is to ventilate the lungs. The air supplies oxygen to the blood flowing through the capillaries of the lung lining, and picks up the carbon dioxide that the blood has brought from the active tissues. Since all muscular action involves consumption of oxygen and production of carbon dioxide, and since the rate and depth of breathing adjusts nicely to bodily needs in this respect, breathing is an excellent indicator of the level of activation.

Neuromuscular mechanism of respiration. The main respiratory apparatus belongs to the skeletal system and not to the autonomic. The diaphragm, intercostal and abdominal muscles are striped muscles, controlled directly by the central nervous system. The phrenic nerve issuing from the cervical cord supplies the diaphragm and is the principal motor nerve of breathing. The chief sensory nerve is the vagus which supplies the lungs with sensory fibers. These are stimulated by the stretching of the lung tissue in inspiration and, acting on the respiratory center in the medulla or bulb, inhibit that center and check inspiration. The stimulus to inspiration seems to arise within the center by the local effect of venous blood. Excess of carbon dioxide in the blood stimulates the center to strong activity; a few deep, rapid, voluntary inspirations reduce the carbon dioxide content of the blood, lower the activity of the respiratory center and cause a temporary cessation of breathing. Chemoreceptors in the carotid sinus and aorta also play a part. They test the CO_2 content of the blood and exert some regulatory effect on breathing.

This mechanism though relatively self-contained is responsive to the stimulation of almost any sensory nerve. Cold suddenly applied to the skin will cause a reflex catch of the breath, as will also the unexpected inhalation of a sharp vapor such as ammonia or chlorine. Irritation of the nose or throat interrupts the regular breathing rhythm and gives a sneeze or cough. In swallowing the respiratory movements are inhibited. The influence of the cortex upon the bulbar center is seen in voluntary control of breathing, in the peculiar breathing of speech or singing, and in the momentary arrest of breathing which is apt to occur in attending to a faint sound or to a sudden interesting thought. In short, we have here a reflex-automatic mechanism serving a metabolic function but very responsive to all that is going on in the behavior of the organism.

Recording breathing. Since breathing is a massive response, there is little trouble in recording it. In general there are two types of methods, those that depend on the volume or other aspect of the inspired and expired air, and those that depend on changes in girth of chest and abdomen.

Volume recorders. A typical method is that used in the doctor's office. O breathes into a mouthpiece, and the air goes into a tank or *gasometer,* which measures the volume of the air forced into it by expiration. This apparatus is sometimes used to give *vital capacity,* or the maximum amount of air that can be handled in one breath, an index of physical fitness.

By a slight modification the same apparatus becomes suitable for measuring *metabolism,* one of the best indices of level of activity. The tank contains a substance which will take the carbon dioxide out of the expired air, converting it to a solid, so that it occupies essentially no space. If O inspires and expires continuously through a mouthpiece connected to such a tank, the level of the tank will gradually fall as O uses up the oxygen (cf. Fig. 7·1, p. 165). This instrument is usually employed to give *basal metabolism,* a useful measure of the rate of energy expenditure during a resting condition (cf. basal heart rate, p. 162). Some form of this apparatus is also very good for measuring the metabolic "costs" of any kind of activity. But as a measure of activation the method has two faults: (1) it is cumbersome, since it calls for a mask or mouthpiece and a bulky tank or bag, and (2) it does not reflect rapid changes, for O incurs an "oxygen debt" during a short burst of energy mobilization, and "pays it back" over a period of minutes.

There is another way in which volume of air may be recorded. Instead of putting the breath into a tank, O is put in the tank, as in the modern artificial respirators. Golla & Antonovitch (1929) used such a *body plethysmograph.* O's head protrudes through a hole in the tank, and there is a rubber seal around the neck. Thus when O breathes in, an equivalent amount of air is displaced from the tank by the chest and abdominal movement, and appropriate gauges record this displaced air. Under some circumstances this arrangement may be superior to the mouthpiece-tank method since it makes O less conscious of his breathing. He may not even know it is being recorded if he is given some plausible reason for being put in the plethysmograph, such as "This is just to measure your heat loss."

The Pneumograph. Much more convenient are the devices that measure chest movement directly. They all employ a belt or chain passing partly around the chest or abdomen. The ends of the belt are attached to an instrument that will stretch as the chest changes girth, and convert the stretch into some signal. Thus the belt may pull a contact over a series of points recording on an electric marker (Cason & Cason, 1933). Or the belt may work a resistor, like some modern automobile gasoline gauges. Much more widely used is a pneumatic recording system. The older ones used tambours or rubber cylinders reinforced with springs, but these have been largely supplanted by the accordion-pleated hose used on gas masks. This is a thin-walled rubber tube, about an inch in diameter, so constructed that it will stretch readily but not collapse. A foot or so of this hose is closed off at both ends except for a connection for a small rubber tube in one end. This tube leads to a tambour or bellows, equipped with a writing lever for smoked drum or ink writing—or for photographic recording, along with EKG or other delicate measures. The rubber hose is stretched slightly across the chest, with its ends attached to a belt passing around the back. As *O* breathes in, the hose stretches, increasing its volume, and sucking down the head of the recording tambour or bellows.

Measurements of the breathing records. Horizontal distances in the record denote time; vertical distances indicate, directly, pressure changes within the recording tambour. More or less indirectly they indicate changes in amplitude of breathing, i.e., in the volume of inspired and expired air, and changes in the position of the chest or abdomen produced by the activity of the respiratory muscles. Very careful calibration would be required before the breathing record could be made to yield any absolute measures of muscular contraction or air volume, but *changes* in amplitude can be read from the curve within the compass of a single continuous record. For example, a series of shallow breaths followed by a deep breath can be detected with certainty.

The time characteristics of the breathing curve are read off and measured with relatively high accuracy. The points at which inspiration and expiration start can usually be located, and from them we determine the duration of the respiratory cycle and of its two phases, inspiration and expiration. A pause at the end of inspiration or expiration cannot be sharply delimited and is best counted as part of the preceding phase (Fig. 7-3).

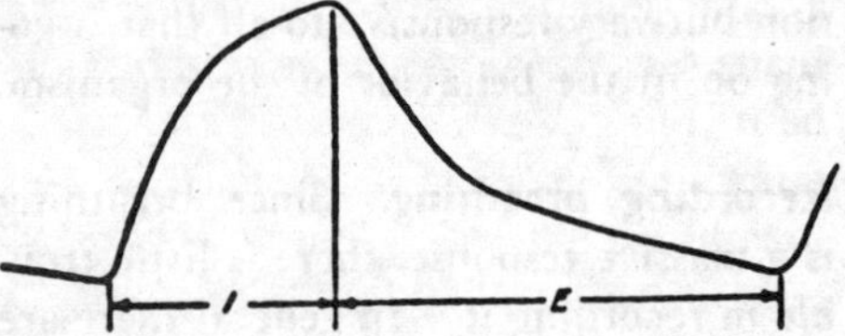

FIG. 7-3. Diagram of a single cycle in the breathing curve. I signifies inspiration; E, expiration.

Changes in rate and amplitude of breathing. Muscular exercise, as everyone knows, hastens and deepens the breathing. It is interesting to note (Cannon, 1932) that respiration and circulation increase with the beginning of the muscular activity and do not delay till oxygen dearth and excess of carbon dioxide have actually developed. There is a physiological anticipation of the needs of the muscles. Might not imagined or suggested muscular activity have the same effect and give increased respiration? Respiratory movements can be speeded up voluntarily, but the question is whether they increase involuntarily in excited "states of mind." Rehwoldt (1911) had his *O*s engender an emotion by recalling or imagining some emotional experience, such as a scene from a drama, and he found that respiration was increased when *O* reported excitement. There is agreement among experimenters that the breathing tends in excitement to be both fast and deep. This is the clearest known correlation between respiration and emotion. Pleasantness and unpleasantness show either increased or decreased breathing, usually increased, apparently because both pleasant and unpleasant stimuli are apt to be exciting.

Another clear correlation is that between momentary attention and partial or complete inhibition of breathing. Sudden stimuli will make the subject "catch his breath." If he is listening to a faint sound, arrested breathing eliminates disturbing respiratory sounds; if he is trying to read letters at a great distance, his fixation is steadier if the breathing movement is suspended (a good marksman holds his breath while squeezing the trigger); and the kinesthetic sensations from the chest may be a distraction which one avoids at a moment of intense mental application (Suter, 1912). In continued mental work, no matter how attentive, this inhibition of breathing naturally does not continue, but the breathing tends to be shallow and quickened. Skaggs (1930) compared the breathing in quiet relaxation and in several kinds of activity, and noted the following effects, along with much variation:

1. In mental multiplication, compared with the resting condition, breathing was usually quick and shallow.

2. In anxious expectancy, the rate tended to increase and the depth to remain normal.

3. After a shock or surprise, too, the rate was high and the depth about normal, and the breathing was irregular.

The results are explicable by supposing that: (1) in mental work, unaccompanied by increased muscular activity, maximum efficiency is sought by keeping the breathing as quiet as possible while maintaining the normal supply of oxygen; (2) in excitement there is an actual increase in muscular activity calling for increased respiration, or at least a physiological readiness for muscular activity.

As to irregular breathing, varying in depth or rate or both, we know one definite cause for it, namely the use of the breath for speech. Fossler (1930) finds the rate much more irregular in speech than in the resting condition. Expiration is much prolonged and varies greatly in duration from one cycle to another; inspiration is shortened and varies considerably. The reason is obvious—one wishes to talk continuously but one must stop to take breath. The vocal cords are operated by the expired air which is paid out economically and replenished by rapid inspirations whenever time can be spared from the talking.

An interesting experiment was that of Blatz (1925) who smuggled a genuine fear into the laboratory. A trick chair tilted the unsuspecting, blindfolded subject suddenly backward into a nearly horizontal position, while a pneumograph registered his breathing and an electrocardiograph the rate and force of his heartbeat. There were 21 *O*s. The heart showed definite changes. The pulse shot up from 84 to 104 beats, on the average, receded promptly to 87 only to rise again to 97 after which it gradually slowed down but remained irregular. The force of the heartbeat was increased and remained high during the afterperiod of six minutes while *O* rested in a reclining position.

O returned on another day for a repetition of the experiment. Expecting the chair to fall he showed in advance a strong rapid pulse. When the fall actually came, the cardiac changes were the same as on the first occasion—the same in kind though less in degree. The subjects did not make overt movements of saving themselves as they had on the first occasion, and they reported no fear the second time. The author draws the conclusion that a genuine emotion of fear requires the overt escape reaction as well as the internal organic changes.

As to the respiratory effects, the rate went down from 14 cycles a minute before the original fall to 11 cycles immediately after; it returned toward normal at first quickly and then gradually. It did not, as it usually does, run parallel to the rate of the heartbeat. The first effect of falling was to *lengthen the inspiration.* If the fall of the chair occurred during an inspiration, that inspiration was prolonged, and when it occurred during expiration the expiratory movement stopped abruptly and gave way to inspiration. This "catch in the breath" seems like an exaggerated form of the familiar arrest of breathing which occurs at any sudden shift of attention.

Relative duration of inspiration and expiration. This last effect and the previously mentioned long expiration during speech both suggest that some scientific use might be made of the time ratio of inspiration and expiration. This suggestion was first made by Störring (1906) and has proved to be quite fruitful. Störring introduced the *Inspiration-Expiration Ratio,* I/E, in which I = the duration of inspiration, and E = that of expiration. Some authors have omitted the pauses from the measure of I or E, others (as recommended above) have included them, counting I as extending to the beginning of the expiratory movement, and E as extending thence to the beginning of the next inspiration. It makes quite a difference which measure is used.

Statistically, the I/E ratio is not a very good measure. It is all right for single cases but not good for averaging, when the single ratios differ considerably; though the geometrical mean, or more simply the median, can be used without distortion of the results. A simpler and more intelligible measure is the I-fraction, here recommended. *The I-fraction is obtained by dividing the duration of inspiration by the duration of the whole cycle.* It shows what proportion of the time is occupied by inspiration. Since inspiration is ordinarily the active muscular phase of the cycle, the I-fraction shows how much of the time is consumed in this necessary labor of supplying air. The use of the air for metabolic purposes is of course continuous; the use for voice production is usually confined to expiration. The I-fraction during speech shows how much of the time is consumed in the necessary task of taking in the air for voice production. According to the records of 13 *Os*, obtained by Fossler (1930), the I-fraction in speech averages .163, individual averages ranging from .090 to .258. That is, we have to sacrifice on the average about one-sixth of our speaking time for supplying the necessary air. In ordinary quiet breathing the I-fraction averages about .40–.45, somewhat less than half.

Provided I and E are so measured as to comprise the whole cycle, there is a simple arithmetical relation between the I-fraction and the I/E ratio. For example, I takes 1 second and the whole cycle 3 seconds; the I-fraction = ⅓ = .33, and the I/E ratio = ½ = .50. When one of these measures increases, so does the other, but the changes in I/E are larger—exaggerated, we might say. The absolute limits of the I-fraction are 0 and 1.00, while I/E has no upper limit.

Some early results with the I/E ratio were:

1. It is low in attentive mental work, such as mental multiplication, and the greater the reported feeling of tense attention the lower the ratio (Suter, 1912). The I-fraction averaged .30 for brief periods of attentive mental work.

2. It tends to be low when *O* reports a feeling of tension (Drozyński, 1911).

3. It is high in excitement, the I-fraction being then over .60 (Rehwoldt, 1911).

4. It is very high in posed wonder, i.e., when *O* imagines a wonderful or surprising situation and expresses his feeling by face and gesture (Feleky, 1916); the I-fraction averaged .71 for six *O*s, ranging from .62 to .78. *O* tends to hold his breath in inspiration. This is the same result as obtained by Blatz (1925) after the backward drop of the chair; the I-fraction in his *O*s ranged from .50 to .80 just after the fall.

5. It is very low during laughter (Feleky, 1916), the I-fraction ranging from .18 to .28 with a general average of .23. This figure is near that quoted above for speech, and the cause of the small I-fraction is the same: the breath is drawn in rapidly in both laughter and speech and paid out bit by bit in the vocal function.

To recapitulate in tabular form, the I-fraction averages:

in speech	.16
in laughter	.23
in attentive mental work	.30
in the resting condition	.43
in excitement	.60+
in posed wonder	.71
in sudden fright	.75

In singing, which requires more "wind" than speech does and allows only scraps of time for replenishing the supply, the I-fraction goes down to very small values.

Interest in the I/E ratio or I-fraction has fallen off in recent years, partly because other measures of activation are more convenient and perhaps more satisfactory. But breathing records offer a great challenge to those who try to interpret them, for they are exceedingly sensitive to all sorts of psychological changes; the problem is to get the desired information out of the records. The I/E ratio is only one method; amplitude, form, area under the curve, and other aspects offer possible measures, but measuring records for all these variables is very time consuming.

MUSCULAR TENSION

In its common-sense meaning, the word *tension* is roughly equivalent to our phrase, *level of activation*. We have avoided this loose use of "tension," for the word has a more appropriate application to the state of sustained contraction, or *tonus*, of skeletal muscle. The muscles of our arms, legs, trunk, and neck receive a continual barrage of nerve impulses which keeps them in a state of partial contraction. The muscles are generally arranged in pairs of antagonists, as *flexor* and *extensor*. There is a very neat interaction of tension between the two members of a pair so that one relaxes as the other contracts, thus keeping the limb under control, but without waste energy. Sherrington (1906) has described this relationship as *reciprocal innervation*.

Postural tonus. But in addition to this reciprocal action, there may be a change in level of tension or tonus in both members of a pair. In sleep the level is low; we are relaxed (Jacobson, 1938). As we become more active, the level of tension in all muscles of the body builds up, and it continues to increase as we become more alert. To a certain extent this tonus is helpful in controlling movement, for there is less slack. But if the tension becomes too high, coordination is impaired. In tracing a straight line, if the arm is too relaxed, the line wavers, but if the arm muscles are too tight, there may be spasmodic jerks or tremors. If you try this experiment, you may notice that the tension is not limited to the arm, but spreads over the whole body. The jaws are tight, the brow wrinkled, the back is erect, and the neck may be rigid. Several lines of evidence show that the neck muscles are key indicators of the general level of muscular tonus. Their importance in motor coordination goes back to the postural mechanisms so ably analyzed by Magnus and his co-workers (Magnus, 1924; Dusser de Barenne, 1934). It must be remembered that (1) the head is a heavy structure, and its balance largely determines the balance of the body, and (2) the head contains most of the important distance receptors, and turns this way and that in anticipation of the gross bodily movements (cf. eye movements). These head-neck-trunk relations are important in man as well as in animals (cf. Alexander, 1932; Jones and Kennedy, 1951). All this suggests that the neck is a crucial place to study muscular tension. But tensions can be observed in many different parts of the body. They represent the foundation on which specific responses are based; the general level of muscular tension is a *preparation for action*, one aspect of general activation.

Tonic level is more than the *result* of alertness; it is one of the mechanisms *producing* alertness. As we pointed out at the beginning of the last chapter, the feedback of kinesthetic impulses from the muscles to the central nervous system, particularly to the hypothalamus, is a very important determiner of the level of activity of these centers (Kleitman, 1939, 1950). Again the neck muscles are very important, for they send back a disproportionate share of impulses. It is clear that the level of tension of the various skeletal muscles may furnish an excellent index of the level of activation, a fact anticipated by the popular use of "tension" to mean "nervousness." So let us turn to the measurement of muscular tension.

The measurement of muscular tension. There are so many different ways of measuring muscle tension that we shall not try to cover them in detail before we consider representative experiments. But we can take a quick preliminary look at the methods, if only to see how they may be classified. In the first place, we may measure local tensions, as in the arm or leg, or we may measure the general level of tension of the body as a whole. As an intermediate stage, we may take local tensions in key areas, as the neck or brow, in the hope that they will mirror general tension. Or we may be interested in the patterning of tensions, as right *versus* left arm, etc. The other major breakdown is in terms of the general method used. It may be direct, as the force of grip exerted on a pencil. Another direct method that is coming into increased use is the recording of electrical potentials from muscles; an action potential is an integral aspect of every muscular contraction, and these potentials can be recorded quite well with modern electronic amplifying systems. There are also some indirect methods: we saw that reaction time may be taken as a measure of tension (p. 30). Another indirect way is the testing of reflexes; whenever a doctor tests your knee jerk, he is measuring the general level of tension (among other things that need not concern us here). Finally, the most indirect method of all is the measurement of metabolic rate, or total oxygen (and hence fuel) consumption. Each method has its advantages and disadvantages so that choice among them will be dictated by the nature of the problem and by the equipment available at the time.

Overcoming distractions. Some of the early work on muscular tension was done by recording force of key stroke or of pencil pressure while the subject was working under distraction. Since these experiments were covered in some detail in the chapter on Attention (p. 85), they need only be mentioned here. In our present terminology these experiments showed that noise and other distractions set up an emotional state, or raised the level of activation, as was necessary if *O* was to continue his task. As in other cases of increased activation, *O* became adapted to the new situation and soon did as well as ever, despite the noise, but no longer had excess tension. Some of these studies (p. 86) used measures of metabolic rate to determine the energy expenditure. Notice that even the studies that measured local tensions of the hand and arm were often interpreted in terms of general bodily tension; presumably squeezing of the pencil went with clenched jaw, rigid back, and all the other surplus movements that are so obvious in a child who is first learning to write.

Muscular tension as a measure of effort. These early experiments suggested that muscular tension might be a good measure of effort, a variable that is very hard to control in experiments on learning and efficiency. Muscle tension might well give us a hint as to why some *O*s learn faster than others. Further, it might clarify the repeated findings that *O* often shows an *end spurt* in work curves or fails to show the expected loss in efficiency on short tests administered after a fatiguing task (Bills, 1927; Ryan, 1947; Bartley & Chute, 1947). The obvious explanation for these anomalous variations in efficiency is that *O* compensates for fatigue by exerting extra effort, by mobilizing his energies, by raising his level of activation.

A large number of studies were devoted to the level of muscular tension in the hope that it would be the key to the poorly defined subjective factor of effort. Although these experiments are not usually treated under the topic of emotion, they are clearly relevant to our present discussion. Unfortunately, the problem of effort turned out to be a more complicated one than it appeared at first and may be best presented in reverse order. First, we shall ask what we might expect to find, and then we shall examine a few typical experiments. The reader who wishes to go more deeply will find full bibliographies of the earlier work in reviews by Davis (1942) and Courts (1942). Freeman (1948a, b) presents good discussions of this topic, although his general picture is clearer than the experimental results would seem to justify.

Hypothetical picture of the changing muscular tension during a task. From casual observations we might expect something like the following picture. Let us start with a resting and relaxed *O*. When a task is presented, tension should rise to a level reflecting *O*'s estimate of its difficulty. As he gets into the task, he may find it harder or easier than he anticipated and readjust his level of tension in a corresponding fashion. If he makes a lot of errors at the start, tension should go up, but if all is smooth sailing, tension should drop slowly. If the task is one that involves learning, *O* should find it easier on successive trials and show a repetition of the original course of level of tension, but at a lower absolute level. There may be a change of pattern as well as level; the general level of bodily tension may fall more than that of the muscles directly involved in the task. This brings up our first difficulty. The results we get if we record from a region which reflects general tension, like the neck, may differ from those we obtain from the forearm in a task such as mirror tracing.

A task that involves little formal learning, like cancelation of selected digits, or long division, may still show a fall of tension as *O* becomes adjusted and relaxed in the general situation. These changes would be quite parallel to those reported for skin conductance during a psychophysical task (Duffy; cf. p. 147). But toward the end of the task session, what is loosely called fatigue might set in. For some tasks there is very little evidence that the work has clogged the system with waste products; in such tasks fatigue is better called *boredom* or *ennui*, and may be nothing more than the results of the fall in muscular tension. In other tasks, as in weight lifting on the *ergograph,* there may be an actual accumulation of metabolic wastes in the muscles involved, thus cutting down the response—although most of the impairment is still due to central factors, rather than to the muscle itself. In all these cases it is possible to overcome local inefficiency by increased effort; the general level of activation is raised and should show up in increased tension and surplus activity of muscles not involved in lifting the weight. (See pp. 578 ff.)

Variations on the basic theme. Muscular tension may vary from individual to individual and from task to task. Your "tense" individual will overestimate the difficulty of any new task, and start with a high level of muscular tension, which will fall off if he meets with success. Your relaxed and self-confident person will start with low tension which may increase as he warms up to the task. But these predicted changes may not appear in all subjects; the tense *O* may overreact to any failure, and the relaxed one may "take it easy" throughout the performance. Lumping together the results obtained from different individuals will give ambiguous or misleading conclusions. Here we observe a major source of difficulty in this field of investigation. Another is equally obvious: we cannot freely combine the results obtained with different tasks.

Efficiency as a function of level of muscular tension. These predicted changes of muscular tension are based on the assumption that efficiency increases with the level of activation. However, the curve may not show a regular increase of efficiency with increased muscular tension. There may be an *optimal* level of tension (p. 111)—optimal for a given individual at a specific phase of a certain task, with tensions above and below the optimum yielding inferior performance. This generalization is plausible, but very hard to prove (Bills & Stauffacher, 1937; Stauffacher, 1937; Courts, 1939, 1942; Block, 1936). The reason will become clear if you try to plan an experimental design for testing the generalization. You have too many variables! In the first place, you have to determine the optimal tension level for each *O* and see whether performance falls off regularly on both sides of the optimum. This program calls for a lot of tension measurements during repeated performances of the task. But in repeating the task you may get practice effects, or increased interest and confidence, or boredom, so that the task is no longer the same for the performer. It is very difficult to balance out such effects by experimental design. Hence some investigators have tried short experiments on many *O*s, divided into groups showing high, medium, or low initial tension; but the results have been equivocal. One of the clearest results was obtained from a single *O*, whose skin resistance and reaction time were recorded at 100 periods scattered through many days, at various times of day, and with *O's* subjective condition ranging between half asleep and extremely tense (Freeman, 1940). The results as plotted in Figure 7·4 show a

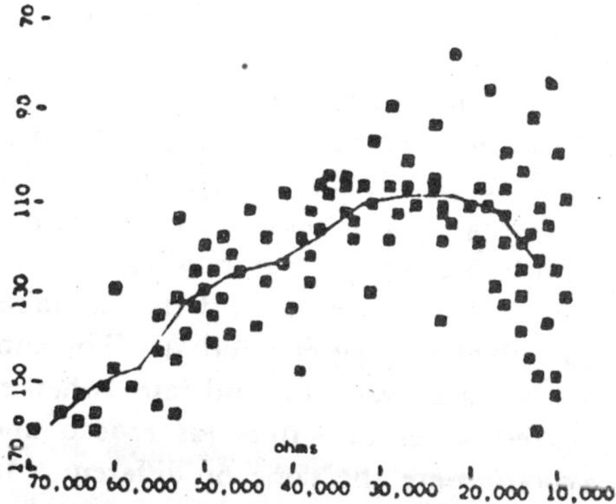

FIG. 7·4. (Freeman, 1940.) The relation between palmar skin resistance and reaction time in a single subject during various states of alertness. Each point represents the average of five auditory reaction times taken at a certain period when skin resistance was also measured.

fairly clear optimum activation level for quick reaction, though the performance was extremely variable at the highest levels. We need confirmatory studies with various tasks, different individuals, and more direct measures of muscular tension. (See also the chapter on Attention, especially p. 89.)

Electromyographic recording of local tension. Most of the studies we have mentioned were done with simple mechanical methods of recording muscle tension. In recent years a more promising method has been developed, that of amplifying and recording the electrical potentials produced during muscular contraction. These are found in both the tonic (background) contractions of posture and the phasic (rapid) contractions involved in movement. Modern amplifiers will handle the potentials picked up by simple electrodes attached to the skin surface, especially if a little electrode jelly is used. In general, the active electrodes used here are smaller than those used in GSR (p. 139), perhaps ½ inch in diameter.

Jacobson (1951) presents a brief summary of the development of these recording methods, in which he was a pioneer. The methods before 1930 were very insensitive, but about that time rapid strides were made in electronic amplification. In 1939 Jacobson rectified the currents, permitting the use of a dial reading in place of the older laborious job of counting spike potentials on many feet of record. In 1940 he improved the apparatus still further by adding a condenser which averaged the readings over a duration of ⅕ to 2 or more seconds. More recent improvements arrange the circuit to discharge every time a certain charge accumulates on the condenser; the resulting "pips" show on the record and can be counted, very much as one might measure the flow of water from a pipe by tallying the number of buckets that were filled (Stevens, 1942; Ryan, Cottrell & Bitterman, 1951). The averaged records of the potentials may be recorded with ink-writing equipment, and the pips may be added to the same record, as well as counted directly by an electrical gadget. Thus, the technical problems are mostly overcome, but it still takes a person with considerable physiological and electronic background to make sure of avoiding artifacts.

Muscular changes during thinking. A good portion of the early work was concerned with the correlation between consciousness and muscular tension. At that time many psychologists held that consciousness was more directly associated with the muscles than with the brain (cf. Langfeld, 1931; Holt, 1931). Jacobson trained his *O*s to relax completely so that tension was essentially lacking from most of the skeletal muscles. In this condition their "minds were blank." But if *O* thought of moving his arm, for example, electrical potentials showed up in his arm muscles. Similarly, tension in the region of the eyes accompanied visual images. (See Jacobson, 1932; 1938; 1951 gives additional references.) Max (1934, 1935, 1937) made somewhat similar studies, but with an interesting innovation; he recorded from the arm muscles of deaf mutes. When they thought of talking, or dreamed they were talking, there were electrical signs of tension in the muscles which moved the fingers, the deaf mutes' organs of speech! (See p. 816.)

These experiments show clearly that consciousness is intimately associated with muscular activity, but they do not prove that consciousness resides in the muscles, as some versions of the motor theory of consciousness might seem to imply. A more conservative interpretation would be that changes in muscle tension are intimately bound up in the process of activation of the corresponding neural centers; as we have constantly emphasized, the muscular tensions result from central activity, and they feed back impulses that increase this activity. Therefore, these experiments serve as additional examples of activation, but of local mechanisms, rather than of larger systems.

Electromyographic records of general muscular tension. In the present chapters our interest is in generalized activation rather than in local tension. Electrical potentials can serve as useful indices of the general tension state of the musculature, if the electrodes are properly placed. One good place is the forehead, as indicated in the chapter on Reaction Time (p. 31). Electrodes there can furnish an excellent indication of the general level of alertness (Kennedy & Travis, 1947, 1948; Travis & Kennedy, 1947, 1949).

Another recent study of general muscular tension is that of Ryan, Cottrell & Bitterman (1950, 1951). They obtained simultaneous records from a leg, an arm, the back of the neck, and the ear lobes (by silver earring electrodes). The subject's task was to indicate whether paired series of letters (as *ccooco* and *ccocco*) were the same or different. In some work periods *O* was subjected to the glare of a 100-watt bulb a little above the exposed letters. Since some *O*s reacted to the glare by slowing down their work, others by speeding it up, a constant rate of work was enforced by mechanical exposure of the test items at the rate of 3 seconds per item. Other difficulties which we have already described were encountered, especially order of conditions and individual differences, and could not be fully overcome. But the results showed that the electrical potentials (from all the regions tested) increased as a result of the glare. The experimenters concluded that muscle potentials can serve as an objective index of the amount of effort put into a visual task.

We may hope that this general method will help us to unravel the complex factors that determine efficiency in various tasks and under varied conditions. But the method is not going to do the unraveling in a hurry; it will require a lot of careful thought and experimentation, for we are dealing with the complex reaction of individual organisms, each with its own past history and present attitudes toward the assigned task. It is not surprising that muscle tension and other measures of the level of activation vary in somewhat unpredictable ways; they are all parts of the organism's reaction to the situation.

OTHER CHANGES AND INDICES

We have now covered the major bodily changes that have been used as indices of emotion, or of level of activation. There are a number of others that have been studied less extensively. We shall list a few of them, with brief comments and a reference or two for each one. Additional references will be found in Lindsley (1951).

Skin temperature. This can be measured with a thermocouple applied to the skin. It has not been widely used, but the recent experiment of Ax (1951) suggests that it has some possibilities. He found that hand and face temperature fell during strong emotion; especially anger. Fall in skin temperature is largely determined by vasoconstriction (p. 162).

Oral temperature. The traditional value of 98.6 degrees F. is only a rough mean of oral temperatures; the actual value varies over a range of a degree or so. Kleitman (1950; also Kleitman & Ramsaroop, 1948) suggested oral temperature as a measure of alertness. This seems plausible, since increased bodily activity means more heat production. But we mustn't forget that we have built-in thermostats to control body temperature; hence the proposed index is based on a partial failure of this homeostatic mechanism. Some of Kleitman's findings are promising, but the work needs to be extended. (See p. 37).

Pupillary response. The iris of the eye is under autonomic control. Pain and strong emotion cause dilation (Bender, 1933). This is a hard response to record, and the basic changes are obscured by constant small fluctuations.

Salivary secretion. Saliva is relatively easy to collect (p. 573; also Wenger & Ellington, 1943). Sympathetic discharge decreases the flow, and makes it thicker. This change was reputedly used in lie detection (p. 185) in primitive peoples: the fear involved in telling a lie dried up the suspect's salivary secretion so that he could not swallow dry rice.

Gastrointestinal activity. One of the early experiments on the emergency or energy mobilization function of strong emotion was that of Cannon (1915). He showed that the sight of a dog caused inhibition of normal digestive movements in a previously relaxed cat. This is in keeping with the idea that strong emotion inhibits normal "peacetime" activities, like digestion. In man, the changes can be observed by fluoroscopic examination after the stomach has been filled with an opaque solution of barium. Another method is to train *O* to swallow a balloon, with a tube leading to a pneumatic recording tambour. (Fig. 22-1, p. 659.)

Tremor and steadiness. Most muscles show a fine tremor, varying in frequency somewhat with the weight of the member. The extended finger has one of 10–12 oscillations per second (Travis & Hunter, 1931). The tremor can be recorded through a lever system, an optical system, or electrical means (Berrien, 1939). Another approach is to have *O* insert a stylus into a hole, with electrical record of contacts with the edge of the hole. Steadiness and tremor have been employed for a variety of purposes since the time of Whipple (1915), as for drug and fatigue effects (Tufts College, 1949). Tremor increases in amplitude during strong emotions (cf. "trembling with rage" or "the jitters"), but there may also be an increase in tremor and unsteadiness under marked relaxation. Thus steadiness seems to bear an inverted U-shaped relationship to level of activation. This is just another way of saying that control of fine movements, like many other performances, is best at some optimal level of activation, and is disorganized at either extreme of the continuum.

Eye blink. The frequency of spontaneous blinking seems to increase with emotional and other tension. It has been used as a measure of effort or fatigue during visual tasks, but is a highly controversial one (Tinker, 1947; Bitterman, 1944, 1945).

Blood chemistry. A large number of homeostatic mechanisms involve changes in the blood and other body fluids. To the extent that these mechanisms participate in emotion, any one of the changes may serve as a useful index. We described a number of these mechanisms in the previous chapter (pp. 133–136; see also Dempsey, 1951; Lindsley, 1951).

The electroencephalogram. Now we come to a technique that may eventually develop into a valuable index of emotion. Until the present time it has served chiefly as (1) a clinical and diagnostic tool and (2) a means of studying the interrelations between hypothalamus, thalamus, and cortex. Our concern is with the second point; the activation theory of emotion rests heavily on the work of the "brain-wavers." If electrodes are attached to the scalp, and led off to electronic amplifiers, it is possible to record "brain waves," electrical changes associated with brain processes. The outstanding waves have been known since Berger (1929) demonstrated the *alpha rhythm*, which consists of a regular series of fairly strong waves with a frequency of about 10 per second. They are picked up chiefly from the back of the head, but appear only if *O* is relaxed and inattentive. The alpha rhythm seems to represent the cerebrum and thalamus in an "idling" condition, for the waves drop out on stimulation, especially visual stimulation. They are replaced by small fast waves, perhaps because the brain cells get out of step with each other during activity so that their effects no longer summate into large waves. This blocking of alpha is shown clearly in Figure 7.5. In general, any stimulus that arouses attention will block the alpha rhythm; a buzzer will do so a few times,

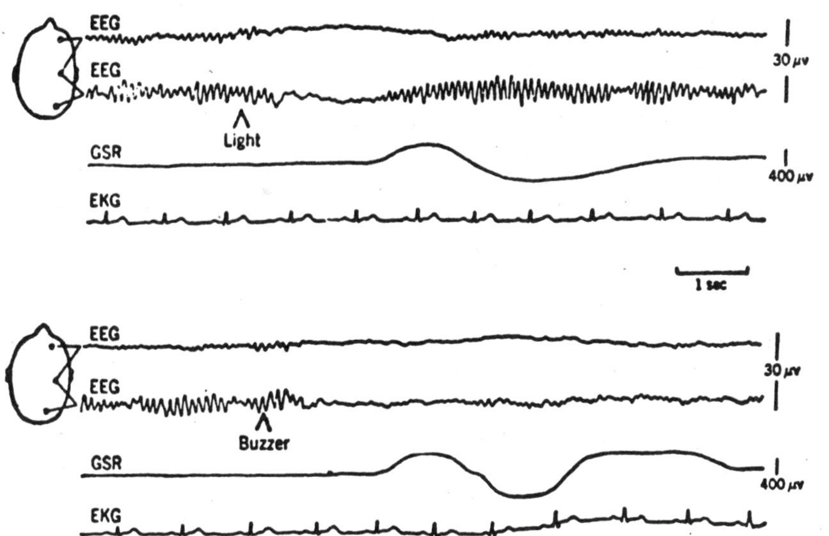

FIG. 7·5. (Lindsley, 1950, 1951.) Effect of unexpected light and sound stimuli upon the electroencephalogram (EEG), the galvanic skin response (GSR), and the electrocardiogram (EKG). The upper EEG record was led off from the front half of the cerebrum, the lower one from the rear half, including the visual area. The scales of the electrical records are shown at the right. Both the stimuli, light and buzzer, block the alpha rhythm after a latency of about .4 sec, while the latency of GSR is a second or more.

but *O* soon adapts to it. A light shows less adaptation, perhaps because the alpha comes chiefly from the occipital lobe, a visual area.

Sudden stimulation is not the only way to block the alpha rhythm; it does not appear when *O* is in an apprehensive state. During apprehension or anxiety the records look very much like the right hand half of the lower record in Figure 7·5, the part following the buzzer. Such records are called "activated"; the cerebrum is activated by upward discharge from the hypothalamus. The hypothalamus, in turn has been activated by the autonomic and feed-back discharge characteristic of an anxious person. Lindsley assumes that extremely high levels of activation bring out inhibitory discharges in the cerebrum, which would account for the partial loss of control during strong emotion. (See Darrow, 1946, for review.)

PATTERNS OF ACTIVATION

We have been treating various systems and processes separately, examining each to see how it can be used as an index of general level of activation. This is similar to what the economist does when he considers bank balances, typical salaries and earnings, etc., as possible indices of the general level of prosperity of a community. But now it is time to bring the indices together, to see how well they agree.

There have been quite a few studies in which two or more measures have been taken simultaneously. The correlations among these measures vary all the way from insignificant ones to those that approach the limits set by the reliabilities of the measures themselves. One extreme is represented by the work of Gaskill & Cox (1941), who subjected heart rate and blood pressure changes to analysis of variance and of covariance; they concluded that a plain indicator of emotion does not exist, for there was no indication of simple variables in their results. The opposite extreme is an r of .84 between respiration rate and muscular tension in the hand *O* was using for mirror drawing (Telford & Storlie, 1946). Various measures of EEG correlate around .50 with GSR (Darrow, Jost, Solomon & Mergener, (1942) and with heart rate (Hadley, 1941). Berg & Beebe-Center (1941) found small correlations between heart rate and both amount of skeletal movement and judged startle, using a pistol shot as stimulus. The correlations were limited by the low reliability (.53) of the cardiac response itself.

Sometimes it is instructive to take measurements of two functions during repeated trials on the same *O*, and see how the values are related. Hovland and Riesen (1940) used a graded series of shocks on each of eight *O*s, recording GSR and plethysmographic volume of the middle finger. The resulting eight correlations between GSR and vasoconstriction ranged from .32 to .71, with a Median at .55.

How can one account for such a range of correlations between measures that are supposed to be indices of level of activation? There are many answers. In the first place, one can question the way in which the original measures were handled. In addition to the matter of adequate instrumentation and measurement, there is the problem of selecting the proper units. We spent some time on this problem when we discussed GSR; obviously it makes a lot of difference whether we use resistance or conductance as our measure. There is also the question as to whether each measure is being used in its appropriate range; it will be recalled (p. 143) that Darrow suggested the use of GSR for low and medium levels of activation, but favored blood pressure for high levels.

Individual differences in patterning of activation. Another source of variation lies in the individual. Freeman & Pathman (1942) recorded palmar GSR to a pistol shot, while *O* rested on a mattress that recorded bodily movement. They reported that *O*s who made marked overt responses showed less prolonged GSR. Perhaps this is an example of the common belief that those who express their emotions freely are less disturbed than those who "bottle them up" and show no external changes. Wenger (1941, 1942, 1943) similarly reported evidence of two different factors, although he arrived at them in a very different way. He took measurements of a number of physiological variables on some 60 children and subjected them to factor analysis. Most of the intercorrelations among the measures could be referred to two independent factors, Nu (neural, autonomic) and Mu (muscular). By assigning appropriate weights to the scores on various tests, he was able to develop two composite scores, one for each factor, and thus to describe each *O* in terms of two numbers. Retests over a year showed few *O*s who changed their scores markedly, and what changes there were seemed to correspond to real changes in *O*'s adjustment to his social environment. The method seems very promising (cf. Wenger, 1948).

Another approach to the patterning within the general level of activation was made by Malmo & Shagass (1949). They selected 74 psychiatric patients, some of whom had histories of heart complaints, while others had recurrent headaches. All were given a "stress test," consisting of pain induced by radiant heat on the forehead. Records were made of heart, breathing, and potentials from the neck muscles. The results showed that the head-complaint group developed significantly greater potentials in the neck than did the others, even though most of them had no headache at the start of the test, while the heart-complaint group showed greater changes in heart and respiratory functions during the test. This result suggests that some *O*s respond to any stress by increased activation of the neck muscles, which are known to be related to headache (Wolff, 1948), while other *O*s respond by visceral changes. Such variation from *O* to *O* in the systems that are most affected by (or contribute to) changes in general level of activation may well explain why correlations among measures are not uniformly high.

Differentiation of emotions. Ever since psychologists started the study of bodily changes during emotion, there has been the hope that some patterns would turn up that would differentiate one emotion from another. There have been a number of hopeful leads, but they have not turned out very well; the patterns were lost in the general level of activation. It is too early to evaluate two of the more recent leads. One of them is the difference between anger and fear that Wolf & Wolff (1942, 1943) found in the patient with a gastric fistula (p. 168). Part of their success may be attributed to the fact that their *O* was a regular employee, who felt real resentment or anxiety about his relations with the boss.

In the more usual laboratory experiment it is extremely difficult to set up emotional situations that are real enough to fool the average *O*. Ax (1951) seems to have been successful. He got *O* all trussed up in apparatus to record heart stroke, blood pressure, palmar sweating, breathing, and skin temperature. Then he "accidentally" gave *O* a mild shock and promptly consulted an assistant in an excited fashion. This seemed to frighten *O* in a most satisfactory manner. Anger was induced by accusing *O* of failure to cooperate, etc. When the results were analyzed, it was found that the rise in diastolic pressure and fall in hand and face skin temperature were greater during anger than fear. Conversely, systolic pressure, heart stroke, pulse rate, and palmar sweating showed greater increases in fear than they did in anger. If further research bears out these results, we shall know why the physiological differentiation of anger and fear has eluded us for half a century. The difference will be in the relative *degree* of activation of the various systems in anger *versus* fear, rather than in the systems which are activated. To put it another way, the same changes appear in both emotions, but some changes are more pronounced in anger, and others in fear. The fact remains that both of these emotions have a characteristically high level of general activation

The startle pattern. There is one clear-cut and characteristic pattern that is easy to elicit in the laboratory. Any strong and unexpected stimulus will produce a startle response. The most effective and convenient stimulus seems to be shooting a .22-caliber blank cartridge. The physiological changes induced by such a stimulus include all those we have discussed as measures of level of activation, but they are short-lived; the heart, respiration, skin conductance, etc., return to normal in perhaps a half minute. The changes in skeletal muscle are even more fleeting; there is a generalized flexion of the whole body that is so rapid that it must be photographed by ultrafast motion pictures. Landis & Hunt (1939) have made a thorough analysis of the startle pattern.

The gross pattern is illustrated in Figure 7-6. The eye-blink is the most

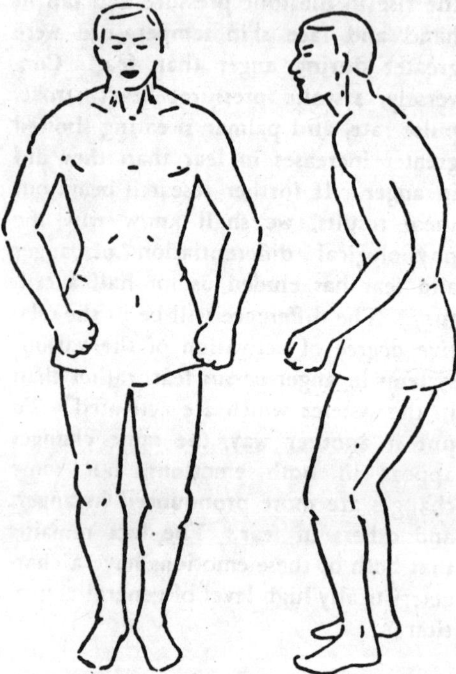

FIG. 7-6. (Landis & Hunt, 1939.) The startle pattern, elicited by a pistol shot.

stable element, and also the fastest; it has a mean latency of 40 ms. The other components follow in order, with their mean latencies: widening of mouth (69 ms), forward head movement (83 ms), neck muscles (88 ms). The wave of response follows down to the shoulders, abdomen, and reaches the knees in about 200 ms. The gross musculature returns to the prestartle position in as little as .3 sec—hence the need for cameras with speeds as high as 1,000 frames per second.

Another and more convenient way of recording the startle response is through action potentials. Jones & Kennedy (1951) attached electrodes to the neck, brow, back, abdomen, arms, and legs, and recorded 60 cases of startle. They found latencies roughly parallel to those reported by Landis & Hunt, but of course all were somewhat lower, for the action potential occurs at the start of the contraction, and a little additional time is required for the attached limb to overcome its inertia and move. One of the most interesting of the Jones & Kennedy findings was that the first response (aside from the eye blink) was most apt to appear in the neck muscles. This fact is in keeping with the importance of the neck as a key structure (p. 174). (Fig. 7-7.)

Landis & Hunt recorded the startle pattern from a large variety of *Os*, under different instructions and with different intensities of stimulation. It appeared in all the mammals they tested in a zoo. Among various psychiatric categories, only the epileptics were markedly deficient in the startle pattern--and the reason for their failure is not clear. The pattern is surprisingly resistant to extinction or adaptation, as shown by the fact that a group of experienced marksmen showed at least the eye blink, and usually the head and face components. The startle thus turns out to be a highly stable and rapid patterned response.

The later phases of startle. Davis (1948) has made a number of electromyograms during response to strong stimuli. He finds two components, a fast one and a slow one, called *a* and *b*, respectively. The *a* component is prob-

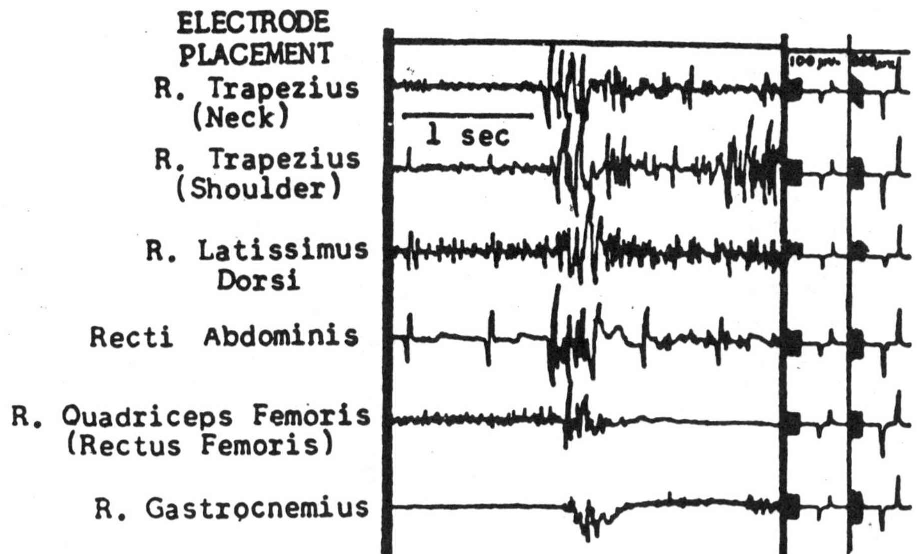

Fig. 7-7. (Jones & Kennedy, 1951.) The startle response as recorded from muscular action potentials. The arrow indicates the calibration of the record in microvolts. Two heartbeats (EKG) appear in the abdominal record and in the two records just above it.

ably the one Hunt & Landis called the startle pattern. The *b* component has a latency of about a second, which is comparable to that of the GSR. Lindsley (1951) suggests that both the *b* component and the GSR represent discharge from the hypothalamus, indicating a general activation, a preparation for action. The final response may come still later, as the cortex is activated and releases a response appropriate to the whole situation. Thus the startle pattern, a single brief episode, presents most of the features one finds in the more protracted emotional states; it shows an increased general level of activation and a pattern of response, involving very nearly all parts of the body.

LIE DETECTION

The various indices of level of activation have been widely used in lie detection. In the chapter on Association (p. 66) we described the basic method. The suspect is asked to respond to words or questions, some of which are related to the details of the crime, while others are neutral. If he is guilty, he probably has knowledge of details that are not generally known, and he should show evidences of any attempts to cover up this knowledge. In the association method, these evidences show up as (1) significant or unusual verbal responses to the critical words or (2) increased or (3) variable associative reaction times on the critical words. The association time method works fairly well, but is cumbersome and not too dependable. Hence, a number of attempts have been made to improve the method by adding various indices of emotion, the assumption being that the effort to avoid incriminating responses will show up as an increase in the level of activation. We shall devote a few pages to this topic since it brings together much that we have discussed in this and the preceding chapter.

The GSR. One of the most impressive demonstrations one can make before a lecture group is to detect deception with the aid of the GSR. The galvanometer should be so arranged that the whole class can see the deflection. A volunteer is hooked into the electrodes, and asked to select one of 10 cards, remember it, and return it to the pack. *O* is then told to try to keep *E* from finding out which card *O* saw. The cards are shown to him, one at a time, and he says "No" to each. There will be a GSR with each reply, but the biggest deflection will usually be to the card he has seen. Although it sometimes fails, the GSR is a fairly effective method of detecting even such mild deception as this demonstration involves. Ruckmick (1938) reported 83 percent success in detection of cards.

In practical lie detection the GSR appears to be less satisfactory. Summers (1939) was quite successful with it, and considered it almost infallible *in the hands of an experienced interpreter.* But others find it somewhat uncertain (Marston, 1938; Inbau, 1942). Perhaps the trouble is that GSR is too responsive to incidental stimuli, thus obscuring the changes involved in deception. A GSR unit may be attached to the Keeler polygraph (see p. 189), and is so used by some operators, but only in conjunction with other indices of level of activation, as breathing and blood pressure. Imbau mentioned one practical use; if all the indices indicate a lie on a given question, the GSR record is usually striking enough to convince the suspect that he has given himself away so that he confesses. Confession is usually the chief aim as well as the validating criterion in lie detection.

Respiratory signs of deception. Breathing would seem to offer good promise in lie detection for two reasons: (1) it is an extremely rapid and sensitive indicator of increase in activation level; and (2) it is intimately associated with the act of replying to the questions. Sharp catches, breaks, and other changes in the pattern of breathing do pick up many cases of deception (see polygraph, p. 189), but psychologists are apt to look for some quantitative index such as the I/E ratio (p. 172). Benussi (1914a) arranged an experiment as follows. The subject is placed in the situation of a witness in court. He is handed a card containing letters, numbers or both, arranged in a regular way, and he is to give either true or false testimony regarding the contents of that card, according to a secret sign placed upon it. Oral questions are put to him by the examining "lawyer" as to whether the card contains letters or numbers, how many, and in what arrangement; finally, he must read the letters in order; but if his task is to lie he must answer every question falsely, trying however to appear truthful to a "jury" sitting there before him. The jury tries to judge from the witness's general behavior whether he is lying or telling the truth, while the experimenter judges entirely by the pneumograph record.

The jurymen in Benussi's experiment did no better than chance, but Benussi from the breathing records made nearly 100 percent of correct judgments in over a hundred trials. He used entirely the I/E ratio (the I-fraction would of course have served him just as well). He compared the ratio before and after each answer, measuring 3–5 cycles immediately before O's response and 3–5 cycles immediately after it. In a sample of 10 double experiments, half with lying and half with truth-telling, the median I-fraction was as follows:

	Before answer	*After answer*
Truth told	.39	.32
Lies told	.40	.50

The difference between the breathing of the truthful and lying witness might be attributed to the harder intellectual task of the liar who must make his false statements consistent to escape detection by the jury. To check on this possibility, Benussi tried a modified experiment in which it was understood in advance between the witness and the jury whether the report on a given card was to be true or false. The intellectual task remained as before, but the emotional situation was flattened out. The result was that the I/E ratio behaved the same in this pretended lying as in truth-telling. Benussi concluded that the breathing in genuine lying was dominated by the emotional situation. Since the I-fraction is essentially the same before either true or false statements, what we have to explain is the difference *after* the testimony. The increased I-fraction after lying can be explained as the result of (suppressed) excitement. The decreased I-fraction after a true statement might mean that O immediately became attentively expectant of the next question.

Benussi found that voluntary control of breathing did not eliminate the index of lying, and he hoped the test would prove practical. Those who have repeated the experiment (Burtt, 1921; Landis & Gullette, 1925) have not obtained very satisfactory results. It is possible that the exact conditions of Benussi's experiment have not been duplicated. It would make a difference how rapidly the questions were fired at O and how promptly he was forced to reply.

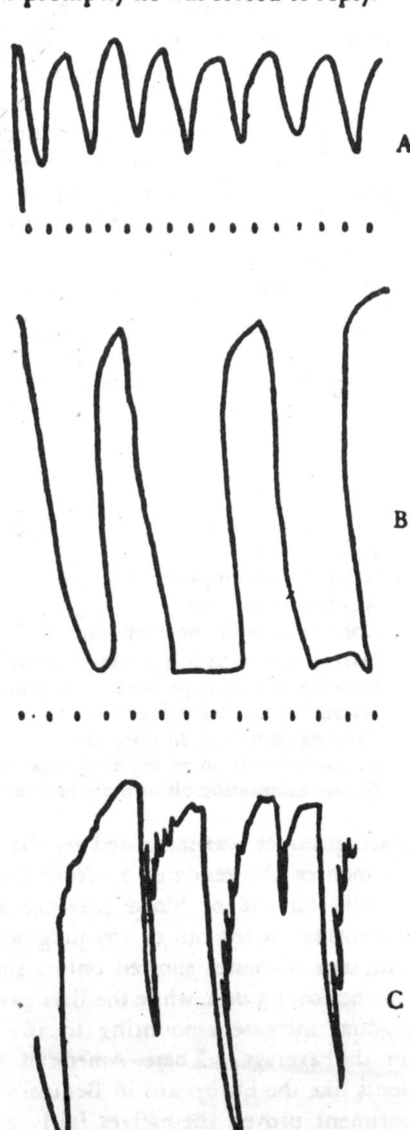

FIG. 7-8. (Feleky, 1916.) Breathing curves during posed emotions. A, normal; B, pose for "wonder"; C, laughter. The curves read from left to right. Inspiration carries the curve down, expiration up. Time in seconds. A talking curve would be somewhat like the laughing curve, though less regular.

Blood pressure in deception. Soon after Benussi had introduced his respiration test of lying, Marston (1917) performed a similar experiment with blood pressure as the indicator. Ten students served as subjects, testifying before a "jury." *O*'s friend was supposed to be accused of a crime, and *O* tried to save his friend by establishing an alibi. *O* could choose whether to follow a ready-made "true" alibi or to invent a "false" one. He was examined before the jury who rendered a verdict according to their impressions of *O*'s truth or falsity. At intervals before and during the examination *O*'s blood pressure was measured by the experimenter who rendered a verdict based entirely on rise of blood pressure and was correct in 103 out of 107 judgments. The true witnesses showed only a small rise, not over 5 mm, while the liars gave a gradual increase amounting to 16 mm on the average. These American students like the Europeans in Benussi's experiment proved themselves fairly competent liars so that the jury had only a 50–50 chance of reaching a correct verdict. The students preferred lying (under the experimental conditions) to the rather humdrum task of telling the truth. Their reported emotions included interest in deceiving the jury, a feeling of adventure, fear, and occasionally anger on being cornered by the "lawyer."

Marston attributed the blood pressure rise to this emotional state of the lying witness rather than to the intellectual activity involved. In control experiments with intense mental work—arithmetic, studying a lesson, inventing a story—his *O*s showed no large rises but usually a decline in blood pressure. In a later experiment (1923) he studied the blood pressure changes in a variety of situations, more or less exciting, and got considerable rises in most of them as shown in the table:

	Average rise for 10 Men (in mm)	Average rise for 10 Women (in mm)
Resting with eyes covered	11	19
Reading story	9	15
Reading difficult psychological book	8	14
Reading newspaper	5	19
Conversing with one of opposite sex, met for the first time	14	28
Narrating story read 2 weeks previously	7	15
Narrating exciting personal experience	9	20
Narrating own actions for last 24 hours	6	24
Cross-examination on story read	7	13
Cross-examination on exciting experience	7	16
Cross-examination on own actions for last half day	12	28

Results equally favorable for the blood pressure test of deception, at least under laboratory conditions, were obtained by Chappell (1929) in a true-or-false-alibi experiment similar to Marston's but without any jury. Chappell's truth tellers showed an average rise of 5 mm with very few going above 12 mm increase, while his liars averaged 19 mm with very few less than 12 mm. The use of 12 mm as a critical value separated the sheep from the goats in 87 percent of the individual cases.

In control experiments Chappell found: (1) a blood pressure rise in an intelligence test which worried the subjects; (2) no rise in mental arithmetic free from all worry; and (3) no rise in making false statements where there was no test situation involved. Chappell concludes that the blood pressure rise, where it occurs, is due to excitement rather than to lying. The test can therefore be used successfully "when the deception situation gives rise to excitement and when other causes of excitement are eliminated." (See the Keeler Polygraph, below.)

The Luria technique. The Russian psychologist Luria (1932) found that involuntary finger movements were a valuable adjunct to the association word method of lie detection. He reasoned that the act of lying involved conflict between two responses, the true word and the lie. This conflict should disorganize behavior. But to obtain a good measure of this disorganization there should be some simple behavior pattern that could be disorganized. Luria set up such a pattern by instructing *O* to press a key simultaneously with the response word, and to keep the other hand on a duplicate key. The keys were actually rubber bulbs, so arranged that they would record all changes of pressure, as well as the major stroke. A signal marker was also added to permit measurement of associative reaction time—it was presumably operated by *E*, who signaled the moments of stimulation and of response. A sample record is presented in Figure 7-9; it will be more convenient for the reader if we describe it directly beneath the record rather than in the text. But here we may summarize the types of clues that show up in various records. Perhaps the most obvious clue is a premature stroke on the reaction key, indicating a word that almost slipped out. There may also be marked irregularity in key pressure during the reaction period. Tremors frequently show up. The "inactive" hand may also show irregular pressure on its key, or tremor, or even strokes like those which *O* is instructed to give only with the other hand. The Luria method is properly a clinical technique; it involves the combination and evaluation of many

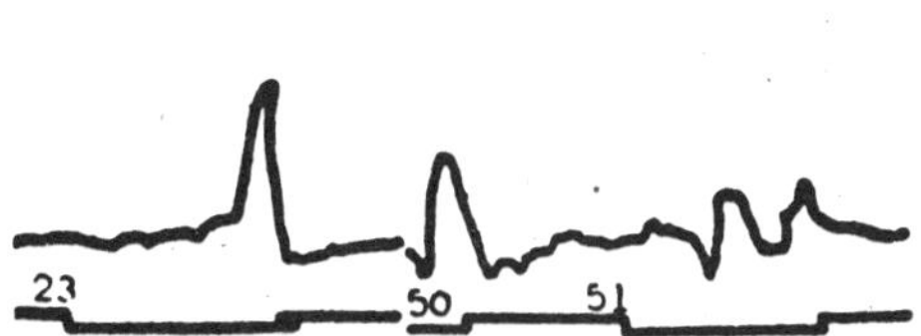

FIG. 7-9. (Luria, 1932, p. 33.) The record of left-hand (upper line) and right-hand (lower curve) strokes and key pressures as indicators of guilt. The bottom line indicates the associative reaction times, and the numbers indentify the stimulus words. The *O* was accused of strangling a woman with a strap. The first word, No 23, was Russian for *train*, but it was heard as a similar word meaning *belt*. The response was *strap*. The reaction time was a bit long (3.2 sec), and there were hints of irregularity in the right-hand pressure. The next word shown, No. 50, was *water;* the response, *lake*, followed in 1 sec, and no marked irregularities occurred in the hand records as is expected in a word not associated with the crime. But, the next word, *strap* (No. 51), caused a lot of disorganization. Tremor appeared in the record of the left hand, and the right hand began at least two partial strokes. The verbal responses were *well* and *fur coat*, taking 4 sec. Note that both response words appear unrelated to the stimulus (cf. p. 68).

separate clues to conflict so that success or failure depends largely upon the skill of the investigator who examines the records. (Cf. Morgan & Ojemann, 1942.)

Polygraphic recording. When the newspapers report the use of a "lie detector," they usually refer to the *Keeler polygraph*. In this connotation a polygraph is simply a portable ink-writing instrument that records breathing, fluctuations in blood pressure (but see p. 161 and Chappell, 1931), and associative reaction time. Some polygraphs include the GSR. Of course, the polygraph is not a "lie detector" any more than the microscope is a "germ detector"—in each case the instrument merely furnishes clues that must be interpreted by the expert. This is more than a mere quibble, for it must be emphasized that the interpretation of polygraph recordings requires specialized training and experience.

The development of the polygraph as an instrument suitable for routine investigation of deception goes back to Larson (1923; see also 1932). In 1926 Keeler (see Inbau, 1942) made some improvements; the Keeler Polygraph is the usual instrument in police work. An excellent description of the actual techniques is given by Imbau (1942).

The use of the polygraph. There are a number of different ways in which the interrogation may be set up. Perhaps the most dramatic is the peak-of-tension method, which we have illustrated with a record from Inbau (Fig. 7-10). This method is designed so that the suspect watches the critical question "creep up on him," and builds up tension; that is, he shows a steady increase in level of activation. Once the critical question is passed, he gradually relaxes. The peak may be picked up from the blood pressure curve, and it sometimes shows in breathing.

Another method is the relevant-irrelevant question method. Here the suspect is asked a series of questions, some of which are unrelated to the crime. Deception is indicated by various disturbances in the record, as suppressed breathing and an increase in blood pressure immediately after an (untruthful) answer. As a matter of fact, this method was used to pick out the suspect who later gave the peak-of-tension record shown in Figure 7-10; before he was tested, the relevant-irrelevant question method had cleared two other people who were originally under greater suspicion than was the guilty man.

The practical utility of the lie detector test. The first question is with regard to its accuracy. We should limit the question to its use in the hands of a trained operator rather than someone who has merely read an instruction man-

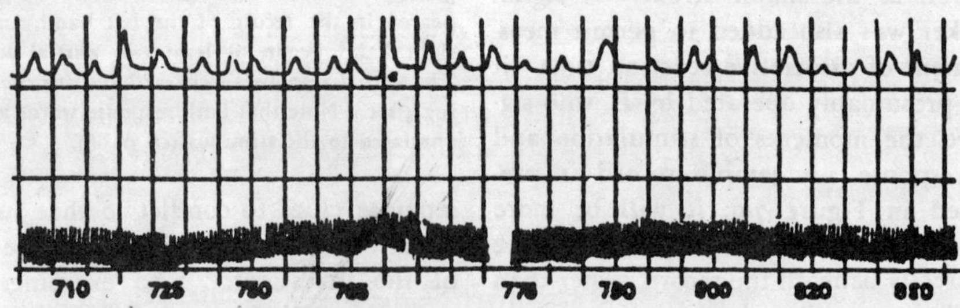

Fig. 7-10. (Inbau, 1942.) The peak-of-tension method of lie detection. A man was suspected of having stolen a roll of bills containing about $750. (The man from whom it was stolen was not certain of the exact amount.) The polygraph was attached to the suspect, and he was asked if he knew the amount that had been stolen—"Was it $710?" "Was it $725?" etc., as shown below the blood pressure (lower curve). Note that the general level of blood pressure rises up to the $765 question, and then starts to fall on higher sums. (Disregard the blank space just before $775; the pen ran dry.) The respiration record (upper line) shows an unusually deep inhalation (marked C) at the $765 question. Later it was found that the amount stolen was exactly $765! The record is abbreviated here; the whole series ran from $650 to $850

ual. The need for such training and experience is recognized by the distributor of the Keeler polygraph, who arranges for training as part of the transaction. In the hands of a competent person, Imbau estimates that 70 percent of the cases will be correctly judged innocent or guilty. Another 20 percent will show so little response, or such inconsistent ones, that a cautious investigator would not make a judgment. The remaining 10 percent represent true errors, and they are largely in favor of the suspect.

This brings up the question of what one does with the results. Perhaps it is not too important whether they are admissible as court evidence, which is a complex legal problem. A more important function of the test is to clear innocent suspects; leaving aside the human values, this saves a lot of police time that can be devoted to other aspects of a crime. The test is also useful in picking up clues, accomplices, etc., which will strengthen the case. Finally, the suspect will often confess after he has seen how the record gives him away. A symposium by Wicker, Cureton & Trovillo (1953) is devoted to the legal and other practical aspects of lie detection.

Summary. In all methods of lie detection the questions are set up so that the guilty person—and *only* the guilty person—will show an increase in level of activation ("emotion") in answering relevant questions, but *not* on control questions. Any index of level of activation may be used to measure the increase; several indices are better than one. Finally, it takes special training and experience to interpret the records; lie detection is an art, and not a laboratory science.

But lie detection is a fitting topic with which to end the chapters on emotion, for it shows that the laborious and sometimes discouraging experiments on bodily changes in emotion have turned up at least one very practical and useful technique. Lie detecting puts level of activation to work!

8

PSYCHOPHYSICS I: THE DETERMINATION OF THRESHOLDS

When Fechner, one of the chief precursors of experimental psychology, published in 1860 a voluminous treatise on "Psychophysics," he was trying to work out in a scientific manner the relations between mind and body, or between the psychical and physical worlds. Being a physicist and mathematician, he hoped to discover some definite quantitative relations between the physical stimulus and the resulting conscious sensation. First he had to devise suitable methods of experimentation and statistical treatment of the data. A large share of his book was devoted to these "psychophysical methods," as they are still called, though they have long since lost the metaphysical significance attached to them by Fechner.

We need not delve into the metaphysics or even into the long and animated debate about "sensation" and whether it can be measured. Operationally, the experiments are straightforward and fit easily into our familiar formula, R = f(S, *O*), or R = f(S, A). Here R is typically the observer's verbal report regarding S, and S is at any moment a particular stimulus. *O* is instructed in advance to make a certain kind of report regarding the stimulus. Without these instructions he would be at sea; they are obviously an important A-variable, and *O*'s set to follow them is the corresponding *O*-variable. For example, the stimulus, S, may be one of a number of tones which differ in the physical dimension of wave amplitude or in that of wavelength, and the instructions specify the dimension to be observed. But since *O* cannot observe the sound waves directly, he is instructed to report on loudness or pitch, as by saying that "This tone is louder or softer than a standard tone," or that "It is higher or lower in pitch than the standard." Loudness corresponds to wave amplitude and pitch to wavelength, but the relationships are by no means simple and linear, as we shall see in a later chapter. Loudness and pitch depend on the characteristics of the auditory apparatus in ear and brain. They are sensory dimensions. Operationally, then, "sensation" in a psychophysical experiment means some such dimension as loudness or pitch of sound, brightness or color of light.

The response, R, is not always a verbal report. The instructions may require *O* to adjust one tone to match another in pitch, or to react with his hand as soon as a tone changes its pitch. The instructions are still necessary. Pavlov, indeed, found a way to conduct psychophysical experiments on animals by the conditioning method (p. 585). In the early days of behaviorism Watson (1916) suggested that this method might well be employed in the human laboratory, for it seemed to him that such terms as "louder" or "yellower" were tainted with subjectivism. He wanted to get rid of the instructions. But the conditioning procedure would mean a frightful waste of time with human subjects who can be told what they have to do and if necessary given a little preliminary training in responding to such a dimension as pitch. And we might add that *O* seems to himself to be perfectly objective and not in the least introspective when he reports that one light is yellower than another or that one tone is higher in pitch than another. He is observing stimuli just as much as in any physical experiment. But the data are used for investigating his power of discrimination.

At the present time, no less than traditionally, the psychophysical methods are used in a variety of ways. The present chapter is devoted to various kinds of *threshold* or minimum discriminable. The following chapter will take up the *scaling* of any sensory dimension.

Thresholds. This word *threshold* and its Latin equivalent, *limen*, mean essentially what one would guess: a boundary separating the stimuli that elicit one response from the stimuli that elicit a different response. For example, let a very light weight be placed gently on *O*'s palm. If the weight is below a certain value, his report is "No, I don't feel it." But if the weight is increased trial by trial, it eventually reaches a value which gets the positive response, "Yes, now I feel it." The value of the weight has crossed the *lower threshold,* often called the *stimulus threshold* and abbreviated into RL (from the German "Reiz Limen" —psychophysics having begun as a German enterprise).

Any threshold has to be measured repeatedly and an average found because its exact location varies from moment to moment. Such random variations in sensitivity are found in every sense field, and they are easily demonstrated in hearing. Hold your watch far enough from one ear so that you can barely hear it ticking; the sound will wax and wane every few seconds (p. 78). Because of this variation, a threshold is always a statistical value; customarily the lower threshold is defined as that value of the stimulus which evokes a positive response on 50 percent of the trials.

But what happens if we proceed to increase the weight in our experiment beyond the stimulus threshold? *O* will report that it feels heavier and heavier, and we can determine a *difference threshold,* abbreviated DL for "difference limen," and also known as *just noticeable difference* (j.n.d.). This value is the answer to the question, "What is the least increase of weight that can be reported correctly in 50 percent of the trials?" Starting at the stimulus threshold, we could laboriously determine the additional weight necessary to advance one j.n.d. upward, then the further addition required for a second j.n.d., and so on until we had empirically divided the whole range of stimuli into DL units. But we should certainly hope to discover some regularity that would reduce our map to a law. We might suppose that the j.n.d. would always be the same, 1 gram for example, but this supposition does not square with the facts.

We might find that 1 gram was a sufficient addition to a 50-gram weight on the palm to be just noticeable. But starting with a 100-gram weight we should have to add 2 grams before the difference was noticed, and starting with a 200-gram weight, we should have to add 4 grams. The j.n.d. would seem to be always 2 percent of the starting weight. This proportionality was pointed out by E. H. Weber (1834) and has since been known as Weber's law. The law can be stated in several ways, perhaps most simply as follows: "A stimulus must be increased by a constant fraction of its value to be just noticeably different." This fraction is often written $\Delta I/I$, in which I stands for intensity and Delta I for the increment just sufficient to yield a report of "more intense." The fraction is variously called the Weber fraction, Weber's ratio, and Weber's constant. Weber's law can then be stated as follows: $\Delta I/I = K$.

Now comes the obvious question, "How constant is Weber's constant?" We shall see later that it is fairly constant throughout the middle range of intensity in most of the senses. It differs widely from sense to sense, being as small as .016 in brightness and as large as .33 for loudness. Thus it furnishes a very valuable index of the discriminating powers of the various senses. The smaller the Weber fraction, the keener the discrimination.

As the intensity of a stimulus keeps on increasing, the just noticeable increments also become larger and larger. This cannot go on indefinitely; every sense has its limit beyond which it yields no greater sensation. This limit is the *terminal threshold*, TL. The TL is differently defined in the different senses. For cutaneous pressure and for loudness of sound it denotes the stimulus intensity which just begins to be painful. For pitch it denotes the vibration frequency (about 20,000 cycles per second) above which no tone can be heard.

These introductory considerations can be summarized in graphic form (Fig. 8-1). Two hypothetical senses are represented, a very keen one with a Weber fraction of .01 and a fair one with a fraction of .05. Graphs A and B show two ways of plotting the data. In A the DL is plotted against the stimulus intensity; as the intensity increases, the DL increases proportionally, giving a straight oblique line rising from the RL to the TL. The two straight lines mean that Weber's law holds good throughout the ranges of both senses, and the steeper slope of one line means that its DL is larger, its discriminating power smaller. In B the same data are plotted but with the Weber fraction, $\Delta I/I$, shown on the ordinate. The two lines are still straight, but now horizontal because the Weber fractions remain constant throughout the intensity range. The difference between the two senses shows in the level, the keener one being lower because its Weber fraction is smaller.

These two senses are necessarily hypothetical since no actual sense obeys Weber's law throughout the whole stimulus range. The Weber fraction seems to be always smaller in the middle of the range than at the lower and upper extremes. Instead of the horizontal lines in B we should have a flattened U, more or less like the curve for pitch in Figure 8-14, page 222. The straight lines are a sim-

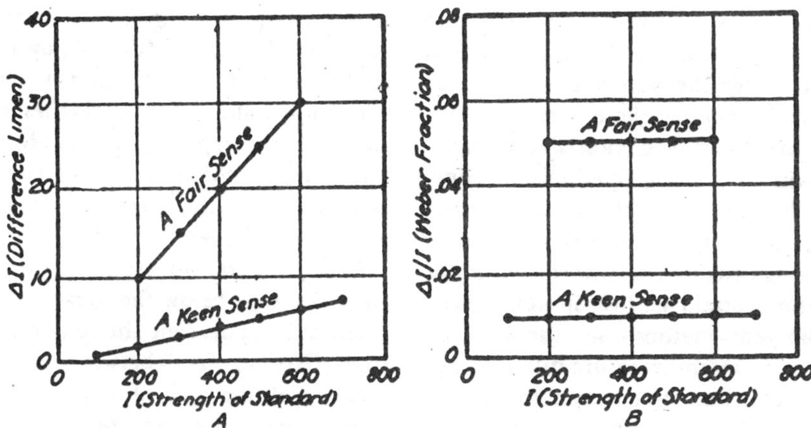

FIG. 8-1. Two ways of plotting thresholds over a range of stimulus values. Two hypothetical senses, each with an assumed RL, DL, and TL, are plotted in each figure. The base lines represent I, the strength of the standard stimulus. The ordinate in Figure A is the ΔI, or the absolute change in the Standard that is just noticeable. In Figure B the ordinate is $\Delta I/I$, Weber's fraction, or the relative change that is just noticeable. See text.

plified model with which the actual senses can be compared.

The psychophysical methods. Thresholds are of obvious importance in the study of the senses, in testing Weber's law, and in the whole field of perception. Before they can be measured, accurate experimental and statistical methods must be available. There are three basic methods which are alike in certain respects but quite different otherwise. They are alike in presenting for comparison a constant Standard stimulus (St) and a variable Comparison stimulus (Co). And they are alike in instructing *O* to make use of prescribed categories in his report. When RL is being determined, St is zero, Co is weak, and the categories amount to "Yes" and "No," as already illustrated. When DL is being measured, St is a stimulus of some strength, Co may be greater or less, or equal to St, and the prescribed categories may be "Greater," "Less," and "Equal." The basic psychophysical methods are as follows in bare outline.

1. The Method of Limits. In this, the only direct method of locating a threshold, Co is made to approach and recede from St by short steps, and the step is noted where *O*'s response shifts from one category to another.

2. The Method of Average Error. *O* adjusts Co to apparent *equality* with St. He does so repeatedly, and the average and variability of his settings measure his accuracy of discrimination.

3. The Frequency Method. Each Co is compared with St many times and the relative frequency of the different response categories is counted. Several Co values are treated in this way and the 50-percent threshold between one category and another is located by interpolation or statistical treatment.

Our aim in the following pages is to enable the student, given suitable apparatus, to conduct a valid experiment by each basic method and to handle the data statistically. The mathematics used will not require anything beyond elementary algebra and the rudiments of normal curve statistics. In order to avoid getting lost in details, the student should master the paragraphs in regular type before tackling those in smaller type which are concerned mostly with variations on the basic methods. Things would be simpler if the psychophysical experts could agree on a single method and discard the rest as historical bygones. Something would be lost, however, since the different methods set the observer different tasks and measure different performances. For that reason the thresholds found by the Method of Limits cannot be duplicated with the other methods. But so long as the same method is used throughout an investigation, Weber's law can be tested and other problems studied by any of the basic methods.

THE METHOD OF LIMITS

This direct method for threshold determinations has been called by various names: Method of Least Noticeable Stimuli or Differences, Method of Minimal Changes, Method of Serial Exploration. The last name characterizes the procedure which consists of "descending" and "ascending" series, each carried far enough to locate the momentary transition point or threshold from one response category to another.

The stimulus threshold (RL). The procedure and computations for determining the lower pitch threshold by the Method of Limits are shown in Example 1. *O* has been instructed to report "Yes" when he hears a tone and "No" when he hears no tone (disregarding incidental audible noises that may be emitted by the apparatus). The first column, read downward, records his responses in a descending series. *E* starts with a stimulus of 24 cycles per second, *O* reporting "Yes." *E* lowers the stimulus by 1 cycle per trial, and *O* continues to report "Yes" until the stimulus reaches 14 cycles when he reports "No." Thus, the threshold for this series lies between 15 and 14 cycles; it is taken as 14.5, the T value entered below this column.

Next *E* starts an ascending series at 10 cycles, well below the so-far indicated threshold. This time the response shifts from "No" to "Yes" between 15 and 16 cycles, yielding a T of 15.5 cycles. Alternate descending and ascending series are continued until *E* is satisfied with the relative uniformity of the T values. He varies the starting point of the successive series so as to prevent *O*'s falling into a routine. Near-threshold judgments are difficult, and even a conscientious *O* may fall into the habit of utilizing some incidental cue that seems to facilitate his task.

Now for the final determination of the stimulus threshold (RL). The T values can be averaged in any one of three ways, two of which are shown at the bottom of the table. (1) Below the upper line all the single values of T are added across the page and averaged; the Mean, 14.5 cycles/sec, is the RL. The SD of this distribution measures the variability of *O*'s performance. (2) Below the second line each pair of T values (one from a descending and one from the following ascending series) is averaged to give a neutral T value, and then these averages are averaged. The final RL remains the same, of course, but the SD is smaller because the variation due to the direction of the separate series is eliminated. (3) All the descending Ts may be averaged to give a descending RL, and all the ascending Ts similarly. The final neutral RL is the average of these two averages and will be the same, of course, as obtained above. But the ascending and descending RL values may be different because of certain "constant errors." The *error of habituation* is the tendency to keep on reporting "Yes" in a descending series, or "No" in an ascending series; the *error of anticipation* is just the opposite. The primary purpose of the alternate ascending and descending series is to average out either of these constant errors when it is present.

As to the reliability of the Mean RL in the present example, we can obtain the SD of the Mean by the usual formula, $SD_M = SD_{dist}/\sqrt{N-1}$, but the N, i.e., the number of Ts averaged, is so small that the reliability is low. Still, it is good enough to indicate high probability that this *O*'s lower threshold for tone was somewhere between 14 and 15 cycles per second. Looking along the horizontal lines in the table, we see that there is no chance at all that his RL was as high as 16 or as low as 13.

The difference threshold (DL). On each trial two stimuli are presented for comparison, the Standard (St) and a Comparison stimulus (Co). Three response categories are prescribed which may be symbolized by +, =, and —. Responses of "Doubtful" (?) are counted as "Equal." The rule (or convention) for locating the T points is as follows: In a descending series, consider only the first shift from plus to any not-plus, and the first shift from any not-minus to minus; and similarly in an ascending series locate the

Example 1. DETERMINATION OF STIMULUS THRESHOLD BY THE METHOD OF LIMITS

(Data from Titchener, 1905, II, p. 6)

Lower limit of audible pitch

Stimulus in cycles/sec	*Alternate descending and ascending series*									
	↓	↑	↓	↑	↓	↑	↓	↑	↓	↑
24	Y									
23	Y									
22	Y		Y							
21	Y		Y							
20	Y		Y						Y	
19	Y		Y				Y		Y	
18	Y		Y		Y		Y		Y	
17	Y		Y		Y		Y		Y	
16	Y	Y	Y		Y		Y		Y	
15	Y	N	Y	Y	Y	Y	Y		Y	Y
14	N	N	N	N	•?	N	?	Y	?	N
13		N		N		N		N		N
12		N		N		N		N		N
11		N		N		N		N		
10		N		N				N		
9				N				N		
8				N				N		
7				N				N		
(1) T =	14.5	15.5	14.5	14.5	14.5	14.5	14.5	13.5	14.5	14.5
M = 14.5; SD = .45										
(2) AvT =	15.0		14.5		14.5		14.0		14.5	
M = 14.5; SD = .32										

• ? = "Doubtful," and counts as a shift in sign from the previous [illegible]

first shift from minus to any not-minus, and the first from any not-plus to plus.

Illustrative data are given in Example 2. *E* starts with Co well above St and runs a descending series. *O* shifts from plus to equal when Co is 5. *E* continues the descending series till the first minus judgment occurs at the Co value of 3. Splitting the step intervals where the two shifts occur, we have for this series T(+) = 5.5, and T(—) = 3.5. The scoring of the last two columns shows how the rule applies to somewhat irregular series. It is best to follow the rule rigidly or else discard a very irregular series altogether.

To reduce this table to average values we find the Means for T(+) and T(—). These divide the whole range of Co stimuli into three parts: an upper part where plus judgments predominate, a lower part where minus judgments predominate, and a middle "interval of uncertainty" (IU) where neither plus nor minus has a majority vote (because of the = and ? responses). Now we take half of IU as the best estimate of DL, and we take the mid-point of IU as the best estimate of the "point of subjective equality" (PSE). This mid-point is theoretically the exact point where Co is most likely to appear equal to St, or where plus and minus judgments balance. Strangely enough, PSE is rarely identical with St. If it lies above St, there is a positive constant error (CE); if below, a negative one. In the present example PSE lies below St and CE is accordingly negative. Now we see that the Co values must extend both sides of St, so as to give a DL uncontaminated with CE. Constant errors must be balanced out when DL is being found. But constant errors themselves are interesting and will be considered at the end of this chapter.

Variations on the Method of Limits. The method is usually described for use with stimuli varied by steps. In some situations there is difficulty in adjusting the apparatus for each new step, as in an experiment on brightness when *E* has to shift filters. He may have recourse to the *Method of Serial*

Example 2. CALCULATION OF THE DIFFERENCE THRESHOLD BY THE METHOD OF LIMITS

Values of Co	Responses in alternate descending and ascending series								
	↓	↑	↓	↑	↓	↑	↓	↑	
8	+	+		+	+	+			
7	+	+	+	+	+	+	+	+	
6	+	+	+	=	=	?	+	+	
St = 5	=	?	—	+	+	+	?	?	
4	=	—	—	—	—	=	+	+	
3	—	—		—	—	—	=	=	
2	—	—				—	—	—	
1	—						—	—	
T(+) =	5.5	5.5	5.5	4.5	6.5	4.5	5.5	3.5	AvT(+) = 5.125
T(—) =	3.5	4.5	5.5	4.5	4.5	3.5	2.5	2.5	AvT(—) = 3.875

Usually T(+) and T(—) will mean the average values.

IU = Interval of Uncertainty = T(+) — T(—) = 5.125 — 3.875 = 1.25

DL = Difference Threshold = ½ Interval of Uncertainty = 0.625

$$\text{PSE} = \text{Point of Subjective Equality} = \frac{T(+) + T(-)}{2} = \frac{5.125 + 3.875}{2} = 4.5$$

CE = Constant Error = PSE — St = 4.5 — 5.0 = —.5

Groups. Instead of giving Co only once at each step before passing to the next step, he gives the same Co several times in succession (without *O*'s knowledge) and counts the step as *plus* if it yields 9 plus out of 10 trials (Stratton, 1902a) or 2 out of 3 (Thorne, 1934). By concentrating his efforts near the T(+) and T(−) values of Co he may obtain a good measure of the momentary threshold and so be able to trace a change of threshold during the progress of dark adaptation, for example.

If Co is made to increase or decrease continuously instead of stepwise, *O*'s task is to respond promptly when his judgment shifts from one category to another. There are no step intervals to be split; otherwise the computation of thresholds is not changed.

Sometimes, as in the measurement of a brightness DL in the dark-adapted state, *O* must not be exposed to a long descending series which would raise the adaptation level. This difficulty is minimized if *E* makes a rough preliminary determination of IU and then uses relatively short series extending only a little beyond the IU. This device is widely used in practical threshold determinations and is usually what writers mean when they speak of "a modified method of limits." An alternative in this situation is to use a frequency method (see p. 200).

From what has been said the Method of Limits is obviously a very flexible one. It can be used with a wide variety of stimuli and for a wide variety of purposes. It has one final merit; it is the one method that shows clearly the operations which define the concept of "threshold." That is, it shows directly where the stimulus passes the boundary separating one response category from another. It is thus the reference experiment for the concept.

THE METHOD OF AVERAGE ERROR

This is also called the Equation Method, or the Adjustment Method. In its most typical form, *O* is instructed to adjust a Co stimulus until it appears equal to a given Standard. He does so repeatedly. The treatment of results consists in computing by ordinary statistical methods:

(1) The Mean setting of Co This gives the point of subjective equality directly, and PSE — St gives the CE.

(2) The SD of the settings, from which if desired the PE of the distribution can be found by the usual formula, $PE_{dist} = .6745$ SD. Or Q may be found by the quartile method. This PE or Q corresponds, though not exactly, to the genuine DL of the Method of Limits (Guilford, 1936). The SD, if used consistently throughout an investigation, serves perfectly as a measure of discrimination or in a test of Weber's law. For the IU we use the interval between Q_1 and Q_3, or the interval between M — PE and M + PE. The reliability of the measures can be estimated in the usual statistical manner.

This general method has several advantages. One has been mentioned, the regular statistical treatment of the data. Another is that the experimental procedure appeals to *O* as natural and straightforward—though he would prefer to be informed of his errors. His interest is maintained because he himself manipulates the value of Co. Further, the method gives a direct measure of his response. As a matter of fact, this last advantage is likely to be somewhat spurious because *O* makes several trial settings, judging each one before attempting a better match. He may overshoot what seems to him at the moment the equality point and therefore make a reverse corrective movement. If he is very cautious, or if the value of his PSE varies considerably from moment to moment, he may spend inordinate time in making a single setting. He can probably learn to be satisfied for the moment with a fairly quick adjustment; or he can learn the practical "bracketing" procedure of moving steadily in one direction, taking note of his momentary T(+) and T(−), and then splitting the difference. Or it may be better for *E* to manipulate Co and change it steadily in one direction, ascending or descending; then *O* is forced to make his judgment of "Equal" before it is too late.

A careful study of this method in comparison with a frequency method was made by Kellogg (1929). Both proved to be perfectly feasible for measurement of loudness and brightness discrimination. In the Average Error experiment on loudness an electric timing device delivered the following sequence of sounds: St lasting ½ sec, pause of ½ sec, Co lasting ½ sec, rest period of 2½ sec before repetition. During the rest period *O* adjusted Co toward equality with St, and in successive rest periods he continued the adjustment until he was satisfied; but he was not allowed to make reverse adjustments. He adjusted the Co intensity by turning a small handwheel which offered no chance for associating any specific position of the wheel with a particular loudness. The St intensity was constant throughout the experiment. *E* first started Co at a higher intensity than St, and *O* adjusted downward until both tones seemed equally loud. *E* recorded the result of this first trial, and then started another trial with a weak Co which *O* adjusted upward. A block of 10 ascending and 10 descending trials was obtained in each daily session and its Mean and SD were computed, the SD taking the place of DL as a measure of discrimination. The SD tended to become smaller from day to day —a practice effect which shows the importance of giving your *O*s some preliminary practice before using their services in any serious psychophysical investigation.

Sounds for comparison are almost necessarily presented one after the other, but lights can best be shown side by side. In Kellogg's Average Error experiment on brightness discrimination *O* saw a small circle of light, divided by a vertical black line, one half being the constant St and the other half the adjustable Co. This whole field was exposed for 1 sec at a time with 2-sec intervals during which *O* adjusted Co toward equality with St, as in the loudness experiment. As before, a strong practice effect was shown by the decrease of SD from day to day.

Considerable ingenuity is sometimes required to devise apparatus enabling *O* to adjust the Co stimulus. The familiar Galton bar is a comparatively simple example: *O* adjusts the position of a marker to bisect a line. In a more complex example of this general sort (p. 419) *O* adjusts a horizontal line to apparent equality with a vertical one, and *E*'s interest is in the amount of the illusion, i.e., in the constant error.

Before we leave the Method of Average Error two points should be made clear. The outstanding characteristic of the method is *not* that *O* makes the adjustments, for *E* may actually manipulate the apparatus. The essential requirement is that *O* judges when Co and St are *equal*. The second point follows from the first: *O*'s equality settings should usually fall *within* the interval of uncertainty, and the PE or Q of their distribution should be *less* than the DL obtained by the Method of Limits. The results of the two methods are not directly comparable.

THE FREQUENCY METHODS

If a stimulus lies in the transition zone between stimuli that can always be perceived and those that can never be perceived, it obviously can be perceived some of the time though not all of the time. It can be perceived in a certain percent of the trials, and the stronger it is, the larger the percent. If it is perceived 50 percent of the time, it locates the stimulus threshold. We may wish to map the whole transition zone. We choose a convenient number of stimulus intensities— often five or seven such stimuli—distributed evenly over the range from the rarely noticed to the almost always noticed. Since we use the same stimuli throughout the experiment, the procedure is called the Method of Constant Stimuli. We repeatedly present these stimuli in random order, having *O* report each time whether or not he perceives the stimulus; hence one alternative name, the Method of Right and Wrong Cases, though this name is rather out of date. When we tabulate our results, we can find the frequency with which each stimulus was reported; from this aspect comes the most general name, the Frequency Method. By plotting these several frequencies we obtain a map of the whole transition zone, but we still have the statistical task of determining what stimulus would give 50 per cent frequency and thus be the RL.

When the DL is to be determined, the procedure is essentially the same. Since stimulus differences are presented, the Frequency Method here is sometimes called the Method of Constant Stimulus Differences, but the commonest name is Constant Stimuli.

Why do we need this additional method? The Method of Average Error is impracticable in some fields, as in the discrimination of lifted weights, because the stimulus is not readily adjusted continuously either by *O* or by *E*. The Method of Limits brings in the errors of habituation and anticipation which are avoided in a frequency method because the stimuli are given in random order. Besides, the Method of Limits discards most of *O*'s responses and uses only the one or two transition points in each ascending or descending series. A frequency method can utilize all the responses. It may demand a large number of trials, but each trial takes very little time. The experiment should be carefully planned; a preliminary tryout is usually necessary to show what series of equally spaced stimuli will adequately cover *O*'s transition zone.

Our great concern in what follows is with the treatment of frequency data. Fuller mathematical discussion of treatments can be found in Guilford (1936) and in the first edition of the present book. Here we wish merely to provide the student with relatively simple ways of handling the data and to show that they are reasonable.

The Method of Constant Stimuli for stimulus thresholds. A typical batch of data is shown in Example 3. The problem was to find out how little binocular disparity would suffice to yield a depth effect (p. 469). *E* varied the disparity

Example 3. STIMULUS THRESHOLD FOR BINOCULAR DISPARITY IN STEREOSCOPIC DEPTH

(*Courtesy of W. J. Richards*)

(*The numbers in brackets indicate the order of presentation*)

Row	*Dial units* 270	300	330	360	390
1	(7)−	(1)+	(4)−	(2)−	(5)+
2	(13)−	(8)−	(6)+	(3)+	(15)+
3	(17)−	(10)−	(9)−	(12)+	(22)+
4	(18)−	(11)−	(14)+	(21)−	(23)+
5	(24)+	(16)+	(19)+	(25)+	(28)−
.	.	.	.	.	.
.	.	.	.	.	.
.	.	.	.	.	.
19	(94)−	(97)−	(87)+	(90)−	(92)+
20	(100)−	(99)−	(98)−	(96)−	(95)+
Total +	1	3	11	13	18
Proportion, p(+)	.05	.15	.55	.65	.90

by setting a dial; the five dial settings gave equally spaced amounts of disparity; they are our "constant stimuli," and we need not go deeper into the significance of the experiment.

On his record blank *E* has provided 20 blank spaces under each stimulus; he records one judgment (+ or —, i.e. Yes or No) in each space. He may or may not follow a predetermined "random" order in working down the sheet. In this experiment the order was predetermined and indicated by small numbers written beforehand in the spaces. If this plan is not used, *E* must be careful to avoid any systematic order in giving the stimuli. He need not fill out one horizontal row before making entries in the next row below; he should sometimes repeat the same stimulus immediately, since in a chance order each stimulus will follow itself as often as it follows any other one.

When the data have been obtained, *E* counts the pluses in each column and divides by the number of trials per stimulus, here 20, to obtain p(+), the proportion or relative frequency, shown at the bottom of the column. As a check he may also count the minus judgments and compute p(—), but, since p(+) + p(—) = 1.00 for each column, he has no further use for the minus judgments. This statement is true only if *E* has refused to accept a report of "Doubtful." Such a third category of judgments complicates the problem, as we shall see when we come to the DL experiments. For the present we will assume that *E* has not recorded any ? judgment but has said, "O.K., I'll give it to you again later," and left the space blank for the moment.

E now has five equally spaced s (stimulus) values, with the probability that each will get a + response. What is the threshold? Logically RL is that stimulus value which gets the + response in 50 percent of the trials. Since no one of the stimuli used got a p of .50, *E* has somehow to figure out what stimulus value *would* have given a p of .50 if it had been tried. There are several ways of calculating this value, some of them rather complicated. Graphic methods are the most instructive and will give sufficiently accurate results if the data are carefully plotted on good-sized sheets of coordinate paper. If you want to master only one method, try the s-z plot, fitted by averaged z scores (pp. 204–206).

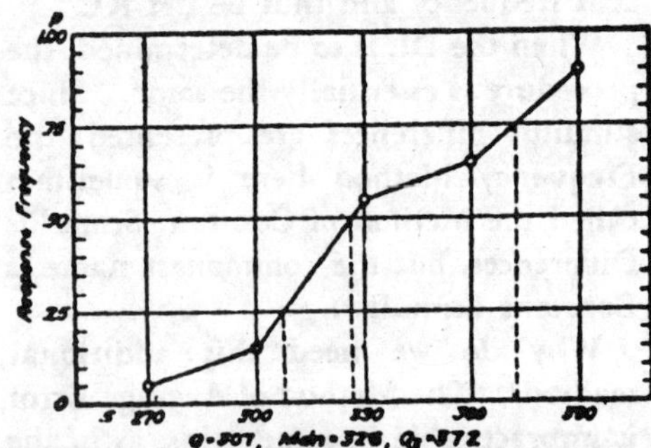

FIG. 8-2. An s-p plot and graphic linear interpolation. Dotted verticals show the location of the Median and Quartiles. The Mean of these three, i.e., $\frac{1}{3}(307 + 326 + 372) = 335$, affords an estimate of RL; and $Q = \frac{1}{2}(372 - 307) = 32.5$, a measure of the variability of *O*'s threshold. SD can be found from the levels of p = .16 and .84; here it is $\frac{1}{2}(383 - 301) = 41$.

Simple interpolation on the s-p plot. Lay off the s values on the abscissa and the p values on the ordinate. Connect the data points by straight lines. Draw horizontal lines at the 25-percent, 50-percent, and 75-percent levels, and notice where these cross the data lines. So computed, the RL or 50-percent level is reached when s is 326, approximately. (The same result can of course be obtained arithmetically, as in the computation of any Median. Here Mdn = $300 + 30(.50 - .15)/(.55 - .15) = 300 +$

30(35/40) = 326, approximately.) But there are two obvious defects in this treatment of the data. (1) The RL is computed from only two of the data points, the others being disregarded. Now the p values found for the various stimuli are subject to sampling errors; some may be a little too high and some a little too low. Such irregularities will have less effect on the computed RL if more of the data are used. One way of doing so is shown below the graph: since Mdn is normally halfway between Q_1 and Q_3, the Mean of these three is a surer bet than the Mdn alone. (2) The zigzag line joining the data points cannot possibly represent the true function. Some smooth curve would be a truer picture of the transition zone.

Values read from a freehand ogive. A straight line is an ideal "curve" if it can be made to fit the data points reasonably well. But the ogive is probably the best-fitting regular curve that can be drawn through these data. Hundreds of similar frequency experiments, some of them with a great number of trials, indicate that the ogive is the appropriate curve. Theory suggests the same. Whenever a biological function (or structure, either) varies, it tends to show an approximately *normal distribution* of values, as pictured in the familiar normal distribution curve. The ogive is simply the summated or cumulative form of this curve, as can be seen from Figure 8-3 and its legend.

The graph of Figure 8-3 is in fact a cumulative distribution of O's variable threshold values. It can be reduced by subtraction to an ordinary distribution chart (p. 207). As it stands, it is an

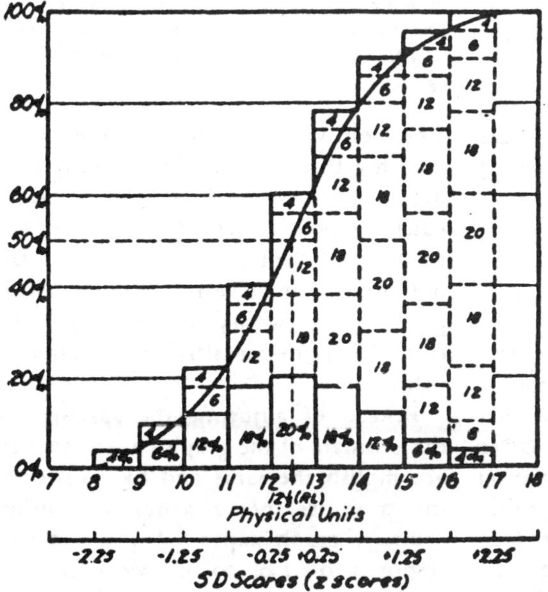

FIG. 8-3. The normal ogive: lower threshold. The solid blocks resting on the base line represent a normal distribution of hypothetical threshold values. The height of each block shows the percentage of trials on which the threshold would be *between* corresponding stimulus values, as 18 percent between 11 and 12. But a stimulus of strength 12 would be effective whenever the threshold was *below* 12, or the sum of all blocks up to this value (18 + 12 + 6 + 4 = 40). This piling up of blocks, shown in broken lines, yields the normal ogive. Since it is a cumulative plot of percentages, its height expresses the percentage of trials on which the threshold is below (or equal to) any corresponding stimulus value. The thin line drawn at 50 percent intercepts the ogive at 12.5, which is taken as the mean stimulus threshold (RL).

This distribution was constructed from a table like that on page 206. The distances are indicated below the base line; the actual stimulus values were chosen to have a mean of 12.5 and an SD of 2.0. The figure assumes a hundred or so trials; if there had been several thousand, it would be seen that the ogive merely approaches 0 percent and 100 percent, without actually reaching those limits.

ogive distorted by sampling errors. A logical plan, accordingly, is to try to fit an ogive to these five data points. The curve in Figure 8-3 affords a general pattern, and there are certain rules and checks to observe:

The curve should pass fairly close to the data points, leaving some of them above and some below (since small sampling errors are more probable than large ones, and since some errors are likely to be on the positive side and some on the negative).

The slope is steepest at and near the 50-percent level.

The curve is almost a straight line from p = .30 to .70.

The curvature is greatest at about p = .16 and .84.

The curve flattens out toward the base line at the left and toward the 100-percent line at the right. Theoretically, these two horizontal lines are "asymptotes" which are never fully reached by the ogive; practically, they are often not reached within the limits of the stimulus series used in the experiment.

The Median should be just halfway between Q_1 and Q_3 because the ogive, like the ordinary normal distribution curve, is symmetrical about its own mid-point.

By dint of some trial and error, a freehand ogive can be drawn to meet these specifications, though different people will get somewhat different curves. One such attempt is shown in Figure 8-4.

Transformation of the s-p plot into an s-z plot. A good ogive is not easy to draw, especially when we try to make it pass as near as possible to the data points. It would be more satisfactory if we could transform the ordinate so that a straight line would be the proper curve to draw. In the chapter on Association we mentioned a type of graph paper that has the ordinate spacing condensed in the middle and spread out at the top and bottom; normally distributed data will yield a straight line when plotted as cumulative percentages on this paper. If this special "Probit" paper is not available, you can convert ordinary graph paper by using the scales printed on the front flyleaf of this book. Simply plot the s values on the base line, the p values on the ordinate, and draw in the best-fitting straight line. You will still have to use judgment, for this conversion does not eliminate sampling errors.

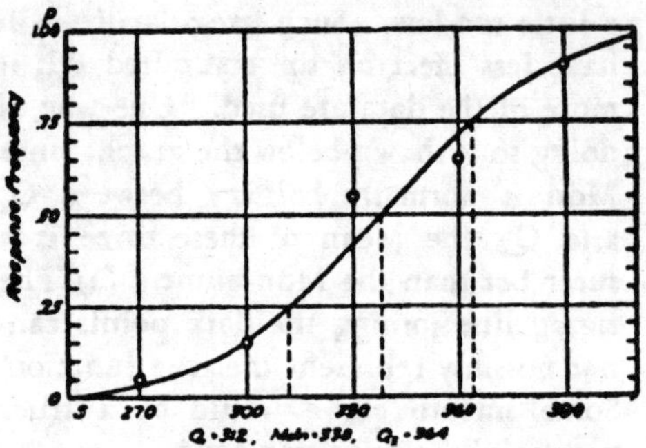

FIG. 8-4. A freehand ogive drawn to fit the s, p data points. Besides Q = 26, the SD can be obtained by noting where the ogive crosses the levels of p = .16 and .84. So we get M − SD = 301, and M + SD = 375; whence SD = 37. The fact that the Q and SD are not quite in the ideal proportion shows that the curve drawn is not a perfect ogive.

The best way to place the line is to stretch a thread across the graph, adjusting it until you are satisfied that it passes as close as possible to the various points, and then draw in the line. Do not pay undue attention to points with p values below .05 or above .95, for this plot is oversensitive to extreme p values.

Instead of adjusting the spacing on the ordinate of the graph paper, we may accomplish the same end by transforming p values into z scores, and using ordinary graph paper. A p of .50 corresponds to a z of .00, and we work both ways from this middle, using SD as the step; z is positive or negative, depending on whether p is above or below .50. Much more detailed conversion tables are available in the statistics books, but the abbreviated one (p. 206) is adequate for most psychophysical experiments. The conversion table and the probability paper give no z values for p values of 0 and 1.00 because the mathematical ogive never reaches the asymptotes.

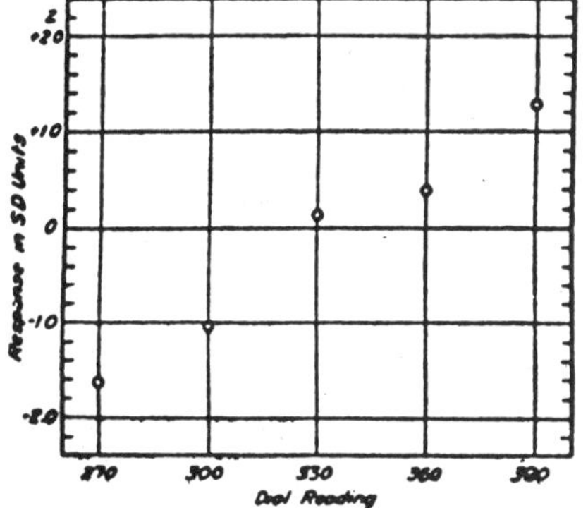

FIG. 8-5. The data points shown on an s-z plot. The horizontal lines for the Mean and for levels 1 and 2 SD above and below the Mean are drawn in. Stretch a thread across the plot so as to fit the data points as well as seems possible, and note exactly where this line crosses the horizontals for 0, +1.00 and −1.00. So the values of M and SD can be estimated rather accurately.

When the straight line has been located and drawn on the graph, the points where it crosses the horizontals for z = 0 and + or − 1, if projected on the base line, will give the indicated values of M and SD. Or, if preferred, the Q or PE of the distribution of RL values can be found by aid of horizontal lines drawn at the level of $z = \pm .67$. Some such measure of variability is desirable.

Even the straight line fitted by the eye is open to question. Another person might locate it somewhat differently. And the judgmental process by which it was obtained cannot be precisely defined so as to be perfectly reproducible. Some definite procedure for locating the line and deriving the values of M and SD would be very desirable. There are three fairly simple procedures.

1. The use of averaged z scores. All we need are two well-defined points on the line; with them the line can be drawn. Here is a defensible rule (for five data points) which establishes two points and utilizes all the data: Take the Mean (middle one) of the three lowest s values and assign to it, for its z, the Mean of the three corresponding z values; and similarly assign to the middle one of the three highest s values, for its z, the Mean of the three corresponding z values. Mark these two derived s, z points on the s-z plot, and draw a straight line through them ex-

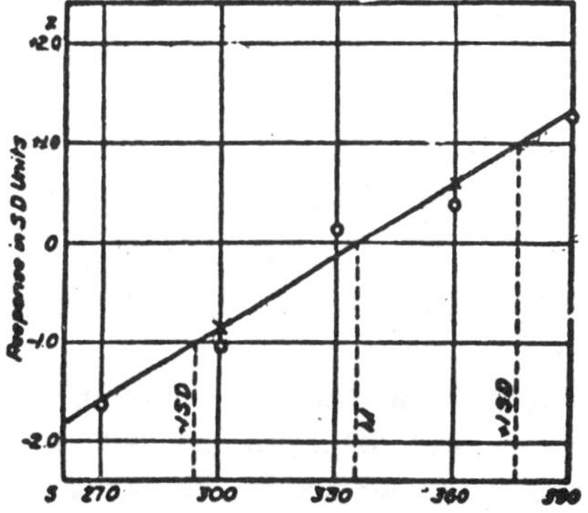

FIG. 8-6. Two-point line located by averaged z scores. The necessary computations are as follows:

s	z	
270	−1.64	Mean z for 300, −.85
300	−1.04	
330	+ .13	
360	+ .39	Mean z for 360, +.60
390	+1.28	

The points, (s = 300, z = −.85) and (s = 360, z = +.60), are located on the plot and connected by a straight line, which cuts the horizontals at points giving M = 335, SD = 335 − 294 = 41.

The same results can be obtained arithmetically, without any graph. Since 300 is .85 SD below the Mean, and 360 is .60 SD above the Mean, the distance from 300 to 360, i.e., 60 s units = .85 + .60 = 1.45 SD; whence SD = $^{60}/_{1.45}$ = 41.4. And the Mean is located .85 SD above 300, i.e. at 335.2.

TABLE FOR CONVERTING p VALUES INTO z VALUES

p	01	02	03	04	05	06	07	08	09	10
z	−2.33	−2.05	−1.88	−1.75	−1.64	−1.55	−1.48	−1.41	−1.34	−1.28
p	11	12	13	14	15	16	17	18	19	20
z	−1.23	−1.18	−1.13	−1.08	−1.04	− .99	− .95	− .92	− .88	− .84
p	21	22	23	24	25	26	27	28	29	30
z	− .81	− .77	− .74	− .71	− .67	− .64	− .61	− .58	− .55	− .52
p	31	32	33	34	35	36	37	38	39	40
z	− .50	− .47	− .44	− .41	− .39	− .36	− .33	− .31	− .28	− .25
p	41	42	43	44	45	46	47	48	49	50
z	− .23	− .20	− .18	− .15	− .13	− .10	− .08	− .05	− .03	00
p	51	52	53	54	55	56	57	58	59	60
z	+ .03	+ .05	+ .08	+ .10	+ .13	+ .15	+ .18	+ .20	+ .23	+ .25
p	61	62	63	64	65	66	67	68	69	70
z	+ .28	+ .31	+ .33	+ .36	+ .39	+ .41	+ .44	+ .47	+ .50	+ .52
p	71	72	73	74	75	76	77	78	79	80
z	+ .55	+ .58	+ .61	+ .64	+ .67	+ .71	+ .74	+ .77	+ .81	+ .84
p	81	82	83	84	85	86	87	88	89	90
z	+ .88	+ .92	+ .95	+ .99	+1.04	+1.08	+1.13	+1.18	+1.23	+1.28
p	91	92	93	94	95	96	97	98	99	99.5
z	+1.34	+1.41	+1.48	+1.55	+1.64	+1.75	+1.88	+2.05	+2.33	+2.58

tending to the limits of the graph. Obtain M and SD by noting where this straight line crosses the horizontal lines for z = 0, + 1 and −1 (Fig. 8-6).

(For any even number of s values, the rule is to take the lower and the upper half of these values, find the Mean s for each half, and assign to it the Mean of the corresponding z values. For any odd number of s values, do the same, except that the middle s and its z are used twice, once in each half.)

The averaging procedure recommended is defensible because the relation of z scores to s values is linear, SD (when found) being a certain number of s units. Hence the average of certain s scores designates the same quantity as the average of their z scores. Averaging of p scores would not be defensible because of the nonlinear relation of s and p, as seen for example in Figure 8-3.

2. *The straight line fitted by "least squares."* We have assumed that the threshold varies according to the law of probability so that its momentary values are normally distributed, except for sampling errors. On that basis we substitute normal z values for the obtained p values. The data points then lie in a straight line, except for the sampling errors. Now the most defensible way of fitting a straight line to such a series of data points is the standard statistical method of least squares. It determines a line such that the (vertical) deviations of the data points, each deviation being squared and the sum of these squares being taken, shall be a minimum. In the first edition of this book, on page 410, formulas were given for determining this best-fitting straight line; and it was also shown that the general formulas could be much simplified if the number of (equally spaced) s values used in the experiment was odd, say five or seven.

It is necessary to code the s values into what we will here call x values, with the middle s represented by $x = 0$, and the others represented by $x = -2, -1$ and $+1, +2$ (for five s values). Then the formulas become, in our present notation:

$$SD = \frac{\text{Sum}(x^2)}{\text{Sum}(xz)} \times i; \; M = s_0 - \frac{\text{Sum}(x^2)\,\text{Sum}(z)}{n\,\text{Sum}(xz)} \times i;$$

where i is the step interval, and s_0 is the value of the middle stimulus which was coded as $x = 0$. These two values are needed in decoding and getting back to the original stimulus scale. n here is the number of s values used in the experiment. If $n = 5$ or 7, as is common in Constant Stimuli, the formulas can be further simplified. When $n = 5$, Sum $(x^2) = 2^2 + 1^2 + 0^2 + 1^2 + 2^2 = 10$; and when $n = 7$, Sum $(x^2) = 28$. Substituting these constants, we have

For $n = 5$:

$$SD = \frac{10}{\text{Sum}(xz)} \times i; \; M = s_0 - \frac{2\,\text{Sum}(z)}{\text{Sum}(xz)} \times i.$$

And for $n = 7$:

$$SD = \frac{28}{\text{Sum}(xz)} \times i; \; M = s_0 - \frac{4\,\text{Sum}(z)}{\text{Sum}(xz)} \times i.$$

In our example, then, M and SD are computed as follows:

	s	x	z	xz
	270	−2	−1.64	+3.28
	300	−1	−1.04	+1.04
$S_0 =$	330	0	+ .13	0
	360	+1	+ .39	+ .39
	390	+2	+1.28	+2.56
		Sum (z) =	− .88	+7.27 = Sum (xz)

$$SD = \frac{10}{7.27} \times 30 = 41.3$$

$$M = 330 - \frac{2(-.88)}{7.27} \times 30 = 337.3$$

When M and SD have thus been determined, the best-fitting line can be drawn on the s-z plot by locating M on the middle horizontal, and M + SD on the horizontal 1 SD above the middle.

The Müller-Urban weights. A refinement of the least-squares method was introduced by Müller (1904) and perfected by Urban (1909, 1912). It aims to take account of sampling errors that may affect the exact positions of the data points in an s-z plot. Two opposed factors are considered: (1) chance errors in the p values are likely to be larger when p lies near .50 than when it lies near 0 or 1.00; (2) but an error in p makes more difference in z when p lies nearer to 0 or 1.00. The combined effect of these two opposed factors is for example that a p lying between .40 and .60 deserves three times as much weight (when converted into z) as one of .04 or .96. Formulas utilizing these weights are given by Boring (1917), by Guilford (1936), and in the first edition of the present book. The arithmetic is laborious and tricky and scarcely worth while except for extensive data, for the Mean found by use of the weights is usually very close to that found by the simpler computations.

Many results in the older literature are stated in terms of h instead of SD, h being called the "precision" and being simply related to SD, as follows:

$$SD = \frac{1}{h\sqrt{2}} = \frac{.7071}{h}$$

If we prefer PE to SD as our measure of variability, we can obtain it as usual by the formula, $PE_{dist} = .6745$ SD. From the inverse relation of h and SD we see that the smaller the scatter, the greater the precision, and the sharper the transition from the never-perceived to the always-perceived. The h is, in fact, the slope of the practically straight portion of the ogive adjacent to $p = .50$.

3. *The Spearman distribution method.* As the distribution curve is built up by summation into an ogive (Fig. 8-3), so the ogive, by subtraction, can be made over into an ordinary distribution curve. By subtraction we can find what percent of *O*'s thresholds fall within each step interval. When he gives a positive response to a certain stimulus, his momentary threshold lies somewhere below that stimulus strength. In our example, we know, therefore, that the momentary threshold lies below 330 in 55 percent of the trials, and below 300 in 15 percent; therefore, it lies in the 300–330 step interval in 55 − 15 = 40 percent. Similarly for the other step intervals, as shown in Figure 8-7.

There is some uncertainty at each tail of the distribution. We know that 5 percent of the

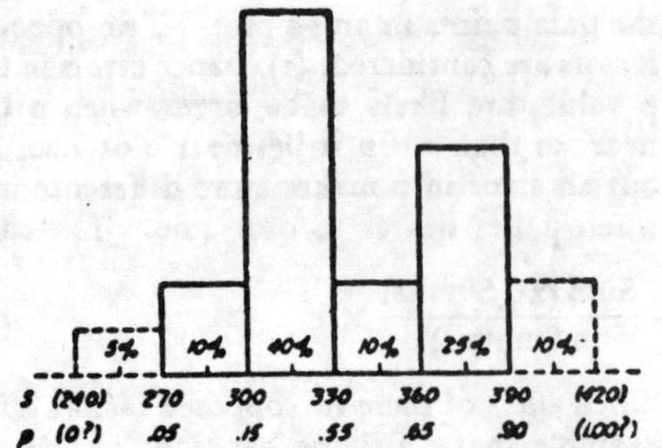

FIG. 8-7. Distribution of threshold values, obtained from the frequency data of Example 3, p. 201. The frequency for each step interval is found by subtracting the percent at the bottom of the step from the percent at the top of the same step. The bottom of the lowest interval and the top of the highest are uncertain, lying outside the range of stimuli used in the experiment.

Mid-point	*Frequency (f)*	
255	5	
285	10	
315	40	*Results:*
345	10	$M = 336$
375	25	$SD = 40.4$
305	10	
	$N = 100$	

threshold values lie below 270, but we can only assume that all of these 5 percent lie within the interval 240–270. This assumption is probable enough, but at the upper end it seems rather improbable that all of the 10 percent lying above 390 belong in the next equal interval. We see here a weakness or limitation of the method; it is fully justified only when *E* has extended his stimulus series far enough down to reach practically to the 0-percent level, and far enough up to reach practically to the 100-percent level.

But the computation itself is simple and accurate. Each frequency in percent is assigned to the middle of its step interval, as tabulated under Figure 8-7, and M and SD are computed by the usual procedure.

Spearman showed also how to obtain the same results directly from the p values by a neat "summation" process which requires less computation but is somewhat tricky. It is described in the first edition of this book, pp. 402–404. We have derived from it a simple check on the value of M. Make a column of the original p(+) values and a parallel column of p(−) values. Sum each column and use the formula given in our example below.

As to the *reliability of the computed Mean and SD*, any of the computation methods gives a value of SD_{distr} from which we can find SD_M by dividing by the square root of N. The only question is what N to adopt. When the Spearman computation is used, the answer seems clear: N is the whole number of cases. When one of the other methods utilizes all the cases in computing the Mean, we seem to be justified in using this same N. A more conservative rule has sometimes been advocated: use as N the number of trials per stimulus, which is 20 in our example. Of course, if *E* has tested a considerable number of

s	*p(+)*	*p(−)*
270	.05	.95
300	.15	.85
330	.55	.45
360	.65	.35
390	.90	.10
Av s = 330	Sum p(+) = 2.30	Sum p(−) = 2.70
i = 30		

$$M = \text{Av } s + \frac{i}{2}\,[\text{Sum } p(-) - \text{Sum } p(+)]$$
$$= 330 + 15\,[2.70 - 2.30]$$
$$= 330 + 15(+.40)$$
$$= 336$$

Os, he can find the group M and SD and use the number of *Os* as his N in estimating reliability.

Computations compared. If the various methods we have used gave very different results, we might have to conclude that no reliable threshold could be found by Constant Stimuli. Here are the results obtained:

	M or Mdn	*SD*
Linear interpolation (p. 202)	326	41
The same using Mdn, Q_1 and Q_3 (p. 203)	335	
Freehand ogive (p. 204)	338	37
Freehand straight line on s-z graph (p. 205)	(left to the reader)	
By averaged z scores (p. 205)	335	41.4
By least-squares formula (p. 207)	337	41.3
By Spearman distribution (p. 208)	336	40.4

Aside from the first value for Mdn, obtained by linear interpolation from only a part of the data, the methods are in much better agreement than we might expect from the rather irregular distribution revealed by Figure 8-2. The last three methods, the "defensible" ones, are certainly in close agreement. One is as good as another, as far as this example goes. Which will be better depends on the way the experiment is planned.

The Spearman method is preferable if the stimulus series extends practically to the limits of the transition zone so that there is no cut-tail error. There need not be many steps, but the step interval should be long enough to cover the transition zone. Otherwise the SD is sure to be too small, and the M may be displaced from its true value.

If one of the z methods is to be used, the stimulus series is best confined to the interior of the transition zone so that the p values shall all lie between say .15 and .85 (where the Müller-Urban weights are unimportant).

If an odd number of stimuli, usually five or seven, are used, the least-squares formula has a little advantage because all the data are used equally.

With an even number of stimulus values, as four or six, the method of averaged z scores is best, the lower half of the data points providing one average point, the upper half the other, and no middle point being used twice.

In any case, a graph of p scores or else of z scores should be made, to serve as a check on the arithmetical work and to show whether a normal ogive can reasonably be assumed or whether the data as they stand cannot properly be handled by normal curve statistics. The ogive may show a definite skew with a long upper tail, suggesting that the base line should be scaled in log units. If such a result is foreseen, the stimuli themselves may be spaced by equal log intervals (equal ratios). Otherwise, care must be taken to compute the correct average s for each average z. At any rate, a graph gives a good over-all view of the experimental results.

An example for practice in the various methods. Here are some hypothetical data, with the stimuli stated in seconds, for determination of a threshold:

s	30	50	70	90	110 sec
p	.04	.12	.36	.86	.94

First construct an s-p plot, fit an ogive to it as well as you can "by the eye," and read off the Mdn and Q. Then, by aid of the conversion table, construct an s-z plot, fit the best straight line you can to it, and read off M and SD. Finally, compute M and SD by the three standard methods. It will be interesting to see how closely your "eye-fitted" values agree with those computed by these methods. Here are the correct answers obtained by the standard methods:

	M	*SD*
From two average z points	73.7 sec	21.5 sec
By least-squares formula	73.0	22.6
By Spearman method	73.6	21.3

Difference thresholds as found by the Method of Constant Stimuli. The two thresholds, RL and DL, can be defined in almost the same terms. In the one case *O* is asked to discriminate between a zero stimulus (one that is not perceived at all) and a weak stimulus that is perceived. In the other case he is asked to discriminate between a fixed perceptible stimulus, the Standard, and a stimulus that is slightly stronger (or weaker) than the Standard. In either case, when the Frequency Method is used, *E* selects a small number of stimuli, usually from four to seven, and presents them many times in random order. He counts up the positive responses to each stimulus and determines the average threshold and the variability by one or another of the methods already described.

In such an experiment *O* is instructed to respond by using certain prescribed categories. When two categories are used, the results show the Mean (or Median) transition point between one category and the other. It is an intercategory threshold. When three categories are used, there are two intercategory thresholds to be determined. Sometimes the number of categories and intercategory thresholds is still larger. The mathematical procedures for determining any threshold are the same. The basic question is whether *O* can use the prescribed categories in a consistent and definable manner. Then we must carefully consider what *O* has been doing before we compare the resulting constants with DL, IU, etc., obtained by other methods.

Two categories: plus and equal. The Standard (St) may be a light of steady intensity to which *O*'s retina becomes adapted, with the Comparison stimulus (Co) a momentary brightening of the light in the center of the field. A ready signal precedes the momentary increment. If *O* perceives the increase, he says "Yes": otherwise "No." The intercategory threshold marks the value of the increment that is as apt to be perceived as not; so the mean increment (ΔI) is the DL. Presumably any "time error" is automatically eliminated by this procedure because each increment of the light comes on and goes off within a fraction of a second, so that each Co is preceded and followed by St. Mueller (1951) has used this method to determine Weber's fraction over a wide range of light intensities. The "warble technique" in auditory DL determinations is similar (p. 222).

If this method were used with lifted weights, *O* would be told that Co was sometimes equal to St and sometimes heavier and that he should use these two categories in his responses. If he sometimes reported that Co seemed lighter than St, this response would be treated as an *equal,* for the threshold that is being determined is really between plus and not-plus, as in the Method of Limits (p. 196). The time error would not be revealed unless there were a companion experiment calling for discrimination between equal and lighter; we could then combine both experiments to produce two category thresholds, yielding a DL for heavier, a DL for lighter, a PSE, and a CE. Either DL by itself would not adequately represent the difference threshold, for it would be contaminated by the CE.

Two categories: plus and minus. Instead of doing two complementary experiments, as described in the preceding paragraph, why not combine them into one? There are several ways in which this can be done, but perhaps the simplest is to use a series of Co stimuli extending both above and below St, and make *O* respond with "Greater" or "Less." Most *O*s are willing to drop the "Equal" judgment if they are told to guess when uncertain; if *O* gives an occasional "Doubtful" response, he is told that the stimulus pair will be repeated later. The method gives usable results even in an ordinary undergraduate laboratory experiment, like that reported with Figure 8-8.

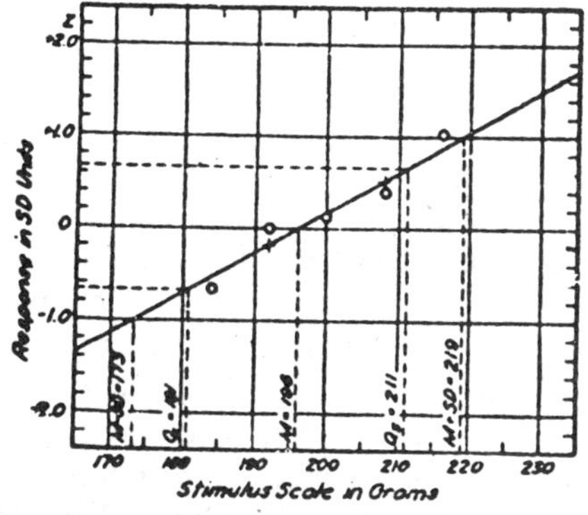

FIG. 8-8. (Data by courtesy of Carl Pfaffmann.) Results of a students' weight-lifting experiment. The weights were wide-mouth pill bottles filled with appropriate amounts of lead shot and paraffin. St was 200 grams, with five Co weights of 184, 192, 200, 208 and 216 grams. *O* was blindfolded and held his forearm on a rest with the hand in position to lift a bottle by a wrist motion. *E* arranged the weights around the edge of a turntable and moved them one at a time under *O*'s hand, first St and then Co, saying "Ready" when each weight was in position. *O*'s motion consisted in raising a weight and putting it down again promptly. After a little practice by both *E* and *O*, the work went forward at a regular rate, with 1 or 2 seconds between St and Co, and perhaps 5 seconds between pairs. Uniformity in these details promotes stable results. *E* recorded *O*'s + and − judgments on a work sheet like that on page 201 and obtained 20 judgments for each Co, with results as follows:

Co	*184*	*192*	*200*	*208*	*216*
Total +	5	10	11	13	17
Percent +	25	50	55	65	85
p	.25	.50	.55	.65	.85
z	−.67	00	+.13	+.39	+1.04

We shall make an s-z plot of the plus judgments and fit a straight line to the data points by aid of the two average z scores which are shown by crosses on the graph. Where this oblique line crosses the horizontal for $z = 0$, we have M; where it crosses the $z = \pm 1$ horizontals, we have M ± SD; and where it reaches the ±.67 levels, we have M ± PE. So we have (as nearly as we can read the graph) M = 196 grams, SD = 23 grams, and PE = 15 grams. Since M here is PSE, we have a CE of PSE − St = 196 − 200 = −4 grams.

Though these data cannot make any strong claim for regularity, the different methods of computation yield very nearly the same values for M and SD (and consequently for PE, computed from SD). These values are shown below.

Method	*M*	*SD*	*PE*
Average z scores, arithmetical computation	196.1	22.9	15.3
Least-squares formula	196.3	21.0	14.1
With Müller-Urban weights	196.3	21.6	14.5
Spearman distribution	197.6	14.8	9.9

We have included the Spearman method mostly as a warning against its use with data like these, with the lowest p value nowhere near zero and the highest nowhere near 1.00. These cut tails of the distribution may not displace M seriously, but they are bound to produce a spuriously small SD by the Spearman method because the largest deviations from the Mean are not represented. The table brings out another important point: the relatively simple methods using average z scores or the least-squares formula give practically the same results as the laborious formulas that use the Müller-Urban weights—one reason being that the p values all lie in the middle range where the weights do not differ greatly and so are unimportant.

The intercategory threshold obtained by this method is obviously that between plus and minus. Hence it is *not* DL

It is PSE, and PSE — St = CE, as before (p. 198). In a strict sense, the method does not yield a DL, but we can readily compute something quite analogous to the usual DL. The Mean, or PSE, at 50 percent, represents no discriminable difference, while 100 percent would represent a perfect discrimination; take the halfway point, 75 percent as a difference that is noted half the time, marking the DL. Thus Q1 and Q3 (Fig. 8–8) show one DL above and below PSE, and the PE may be taken as the DL. The interquartile range is comparable to the interval of uncertainty. The DL is a substitute one, and not strictly the same as that obtained by other methods, but it may be used to compare sensitivity under other conditions or in other senses so long as the same method is used for all. The same comment applies to SD, which is sometimes used as a measure of discrimination.

Three categories: plus, equal, minus. Suppose *E* in a weight-lifting experiment prescribes or allows the three categories, Heavier, Equal, and Lighter. His purpose is probably to determine two intercategory thresholds, as in the Method of Limits (p. 197). The one will separate the minus from the equal, and the other the equal from the plus category. More precisely, one will separate the minus from the not-minus, and the other the plus from the not-plus, again as in the Method of Limits. For this purpose *E* needs the middle category, and his experiment would be spoiled if *O* always responded with plus or minus.

Or *E*'s purpose might merely be to accommodate an *O* who insisted on being allowed to say "Equal" or "Doubtful" when getting no other impression. *E* would then have the task of dividing the equals somehow between the plus and minus frequencies, so as to reduce the three categories to two and then handle the data just as in the preceding two-category experiment. He might follow Fechner and divide the equals equally between plus and minus, at each separate value of the Co. Or he might follow another early suggestion and divide them in proportion to the plus and minus frequencies. (If at a certain value of Co there were 45 plus, 15 minus, and 40 equals, these 40 would be divided 3 to 1, and 30 of them assigned to plus, 10 to minus, so that the corrected percents would be 75 for plus and 25 for minus.) Neither of these schemes is psychologically sound, for if *O* is induced to guess plus or minus instead of equal, he guesses right more often than wrong, but not so often as when his judgment is more confident (Fullerton & Cattell, 1892, p. 132). If *E* wishes to use only two categories, he should induce *O* to divide his own equals, as by guessing plus or minus.

If *E* wishes to use the data for computing the two thresholds, from plus to not-plus and from minus to not-minus, his course is perfectly clear. Let him take the plus frequencies alone and determine M, SD and PE by any of the methods already described. What is this M? It is the mean transition point between plus and not-plus—what we labeled T(+) in the Method of Limits. In the same way, let him take the minus frequencies alone and determine T(—).

Now what lies between T(+) and T(—)? It is the interval of uncertainty, IU, where neither plus nor minus judgments have a clear majority. And one half of IU is the DL, as before (p. 198).

Because of some constant error, the IU is usually not centered exactly on St. Where is the PSE? (1) It is best taken as the mid-point of IU, halfway between T(+) and T(−). (2) Logically it should also be the point where plus and minus judgments are equally frequent, i.e., the point of intersection of the plus and minus curves in Figure 8-9. (3) Again logically, it should be the point where equal judgments are most frequent, i.e., in perfectly regular data, the Mean of the equals distribution. In fairly regular data these three determinations of PSE will agree pretty closely, as they do in Figure 8-9, page 214.

Instability of the IU. Whether IU shall be large or small depends on the total frequency of equal judgments. If *O* gives many of them, his IU will be large; if few, small; if none, zero! Since DL is half of IU, it is similarly dependent on the number of equal judgments. To use this DL as a measure of *O*'s keenness of discrimination can lead to ridiculous results. If *O* happens to be a very confident individual, he may plunge for the plus and minus responses and avoid "equal" as a sign of indecision or overcarefulness. So he gets a very small DL and is credited with very keen discrimination, even though his plus and minus responses may show poor discrimination. At the other extreme is the cautious person who will not give a plus or minus response unless he is perfectly sure; he gets a large DL though his discrimination may be good. Obviously such results run counter to common sense and make the whole three-category use of Constant Stimuli appear invalid.

Moreover *O*'s attitude toward the equal category is likely to change in one direction or the other in the course of a long experiment. It may change from one experimental condition to another. If discrimination becomes more difficult, *O* may drop the equal category because he feels that two categories are all he can manage. So his DL goes down, and the difficult conditions appear to favor discrimination. Such misleading results have appeared in the literature.

The IU as a measure of attitude. In the light of these facts, Fernberger (1931a) undertook to control *O*'s attitude toward the equal category by suitable instructions. He hoped in this way to vary the size of IU and of DL defined as half of IU. His experiment was one in weight lifting with a standard of 100 grams and the instructions took three diverse forms.

1. Neutral instructions such as are commonly given:
Heavier means that the second weight is heavier than the first.
Lighter means that the second weight is lighter than the first.
Equal means that the second weight is equal to the first.

2. Instructions intended to minimize the number of equal judgments:
Heavier means that the second weight is heavier than the first.
Lighter means that the second weight is lighter than the first.
Do not know means that in spite of an effort to find a difference *O* is unable to tell which weight is heavier.

3. Instructions intended to maximize the number of equal judgments:
Heavier means that the second weight of any pair is certainly heavier than the first.
Lighter means that the second weight of any pair is certainly lighter than the first.
Equal means that the second weight seems equal or uncertain.

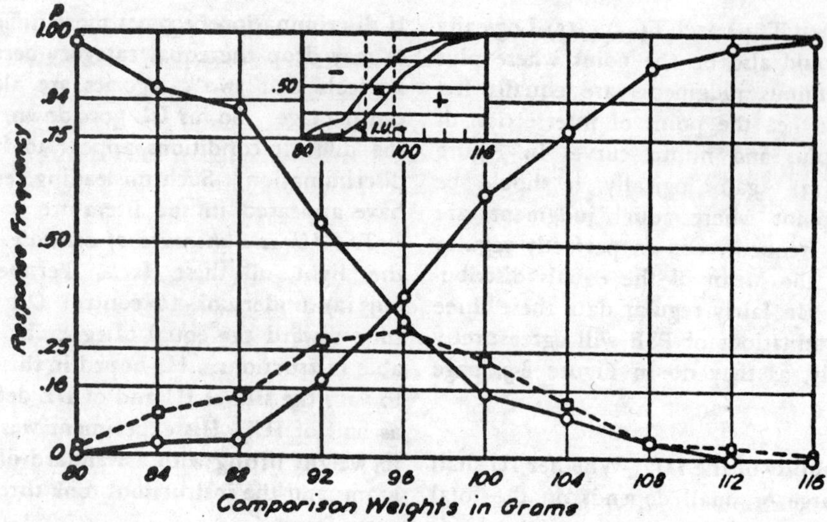

FIG. 8-9. (Data from Bressler, 1933, p. 65.) Results from a three-category weight-lifting experiment. The categories were Heavier, Equal, Lighter. St was 100. The p frequencies were as follows:

s	80	84	88	92	96	100	104	108	112	116	120
p(+)	0	.03	.04	.18	.38	.62	.77	.92	.97	.99	1.00
p(=)	.02	.10	.14	.27	.30	.23	.13	.04	.03	.01	0
p(−)	.98	.87	.82	.55	.32	.15	.10	.04	0	0	0

There were 500 trials for each of the 5 central s values, 92 to 108, with smaller frequencies tapering to 100 trials at each extreme. The curves are regular enough to give almost the same values of M, SD, etc., by all the methods we have described, including even that of simple interpolation. Here are the computed values:

	T(+)	T(−)	PSE $= \frac{T(+) + T(-)}{2}$	DL $= \frac{T(+) - T(-)}{2}$	Av SD $= \frac{SD(+) + SD(-)}{2}$
Simple interpolation	98.0	92.9	95.4	2.6	7.0
Müller-Urban	98.3	92.9	95.6	2.7	7.4
Spearman	98.4	93.3	95.8	2.5	6.8
Least-squares formula	98.4	93.7	96.0	2.4	7.6
2 Av z's	98.4	93.9	96.1	2.3	7.5
5 middle s's:					
least-squares formula	98.3	92.3	95.3	3.0	7.9
2 Av z's	98.2	91.9	95.1	3.1	8.0

PSE as determined by the intersection of the plus and minus curves is 95.5, and the same when taken as the M of the equals distribution. CE, which is PSE − St, measures about −4.5 grams, a negative time error (since Co was lifted after St). DL comes to about 2.5 grams, which is only half as much as PE_{dist} computed from the SD values and previously suggested (p. 212) as a substitute for DL. The different kinds of DL have to be kept separate!

The last two rows in the table give some indication as to whether the 5 middle values of s would serve as well as the complete series. They give nearly the same results as the whole series, though the DL and SD are somewhat too large. In selecting his Co series E might well take account of any CE that is expected, so as to center the series on PSE rather than on St. So he would obtain a better balance of p values.

The table shows the average results from four *O*s:

	Minimize equals	*Neutral*	*Maximize equals*
Interval of Uncertainty	2.12	4.34	9.80
DL	1.06	2.17	4.90
SD	6.67	6.20	7.29
PSE	94.73	95.46	95.34
CE	−5.27	−4.54	−4.66

Three important results appear in the table:

1. DL was strongly influenced by the instructions which worked as expected to decrease and increase the frequency of equal judgments. The *O*s were however affected in different degrees and not brought to a common standard. Fernberger concludes that the difference between individuals in the use of the middle category is partly temperamental, though partly controllable by instructions.

2. SD and CE were not much affected by the instructions; they were fairly stable, and apparently are not strongly influenced by instructional, attitudinal and temperamental factors.

3. DL is not closely related to SD and CE. It therefore measures something different from accuracy of judgment. It measures directly *O*'s inclination to use the middle category, and indirectly the complex of factors responsible for this inclination. It does not measure *O*'s differential sensitivity, his keenness of discrimination.

Nothing that we have just said is meant to discredit the DL, defined as half of IU, when obtained by the Method of Limits. In an ascending or descending series *O* is motivated to spot the equality point before he gets past it, but in the random order of Constant Stimuli he has no such clear incentive. The IU of Constant Stimuli is a measure of attitude rather than of discrimination. Culler (1926), among others, pointed out this difficulty and proposed taking PE of the plus curve as DL(+) and PE of the minus curve as DL(−). These two values can be combined into an average DL, which would be essentially the same "substitute DL" as we advocated for the two-category experiment (p. 212). The only difference is that two sets of calculations must be made, one for each curve. PSE will still be the average of M(+) and M(−).

Shall a middle category be allowed in Constant Stimuli? This question was hotly argued back and forth by the older

---

The inset brings out more clearly what we have been doing with three-category data. The curve for p(+) is the same as in the main figure. Instead of plotting a curve for p(=) and a third curve for p(−), we have made a curve for the sum of p(+) and p(=); it is really the p(−) curve turned upside down. The 50-percent point on the p(+) curve locates T(+), and that on the combined curve locates T(−). If we draw vertical dotted lines through these points, they include an area equivalent to that occupied by the equals. This vertical band is the IU.

When the Spearman computation is followed, the IU obtained is identical with that given by this formula,

$$\text{IU} = i \text{ Sum } p(=)$$

If you add up the p(=) values given below the figure, the sum is 1.27. Multiplying by *i* which is 4 grams, you have IU = 5.08 grams; half of this is the DL. This formula does not hold exactly when other methods of computation are used, but IU and DL always depend closely on the total frequency of equal judgments.

If *E* is interested only in IU and PSE and their derivatives DL and CE, he can find IU as just explained and PSE from the Mean of the Equals. All he needs is the p(=) data.

psychophysicists, as reviewed by Fernberger (1930). Some *Os* are said to prefer two categories while others want three. The published results (as by Kellogg, 1930) indicate that either method will yield about the same variability, as measured by the SD, or by the PE suggested as a substitute for DL. A few equals or even a good many of them will not spoil the experiment, so long as *E* disregards the traditional DL and uses variability as his measure of discrimination.

It is probably wise to explain to an inexperienced *O* that the differences to be discriminated are so small that no one can judge correctly in every trial but that he need not be afraid to make quick judgments and even to guess, since his guesses will be oftener right than wrong so long as he is giving good attention. The most convincing evidence comes from two studies by Warner Brown (1910, 1914), both made by the two-category method. In a weight-lifting experiment (Fig. 8-10) he obtained

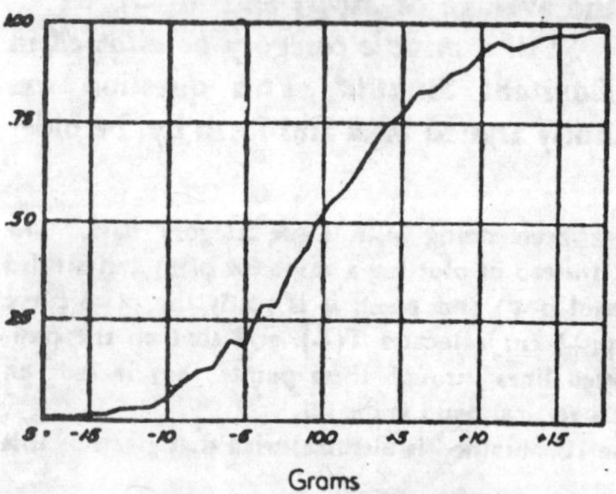

FIG. 8-10. (Data from Warner Brown, 1910.) Relative frequency of the response Heavier in a two-category weight-lifting experiment. The Standard was 100 grams and the Co ranged from −18 to +18 grams by steps of 1 gram (with two additional steps of ½ gram adjacent to the Standard). Method of Constant Stimuli, 700 trials at each value of s.

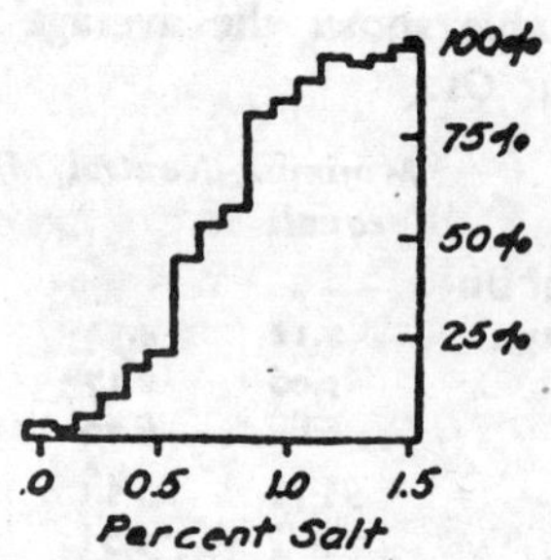

FIG. 8-11. (Brown, 1914.) An experiment on the stimulus threshold for taste. Solutions of salt were applied ranging in strength from 0 to 1.5 percent by steps of 0.1 percent. The *O* whose results are plotted made 80 trials with each concentration, judging whether the solution applied to her tongue tasted salt or not. The stronger the solution, the more frequently taste was reported, and this relation held down practically to zero concentrations, so that there was no stimulus threshold in an absolute sense but only a mean transition point between solutions giving and failing to give the taste sensation.

a smooth ogive in spite of the unusually small step interval. The curve shows only two reversals, and minor ones at that; and at the steepest part of the curve each increment of 1 gram has a clear effect in the percent of plus judgments—this in spite of the fact that DL, taken as PE, is a trifle over 4 grams. Thus the Weber fraction obtained in this experiment was about 1/25, which compares favorably with the value obtained by other experimenters. Clearly this *O* showed good discrimination with only two categories allowed. Naturally, it required many trials to obtain so smooth a curve.

Figure 8-11 gives the results of Brown's experiment on the stimulus threshold for taste, again with a small step interval and only two categories permitted. A taste experiment is a slow job because of the necessity to getting rid of the taste left over from one trial before another trial is given. Hence, there were only 80 judgments for each stimulus intensity. Nevertheless, the curve shows a steady rise with only two small reversals, one near each end, where the ogive is nearly flat and easily reversed.

No doubt the three-category procedure gives fascinating results, as pictured in the three curves of Figure 8-9. On the whole, however, one of the two-category methods deserves the preference in psychophysics; it gives all the usable results with economy of time and effort.

The Method of Single Stimuli. When serving in an experiment with Constant Stimuli, *O* compares Co with St on each trial. Ostensibly, that is all he is doing. When he has become used to the range of Co stimuli, however, each of them is likely to seem large, small, or medium in a quasi-absolute sense (Martin & Müller, 1899). If the St were discontinued, he could still go on using these categories confidently. The Method of Single Stimuli (Wever & Zener, 1928; Volkmann, 1932) takes advantage of these "absolute impressions" and saves time by omitting St altogether. A series of perhaps five stimuli is prepared and presented repeatedly in random order, and *O* is instructed to classify them under certain categories, as Heavy, Medium, and Light in the case of weights. *E* may increase the number of assigned categories by adding Very Heavy and Very Light and perhaps even more steps, or he limits the number to two by refusing to accept a judgment of Medium. The method is essentially the same as the Rating Method to be considered in the next chapter (p. 251).

The data can be treated by the same computations as are used with Constant Stimuli. Intercategory thresholds, their M and SD (or PE), are determined (Fig. 8-12). With only two categories permitted, there is one threshold to be found, as in the two-category experiment by Constant Stimuli (p. 211). With three categories, there are two thresholds: as from Heavy to Not-Heavy, and from Light to Not-Light. With four categories, A, B, C, and D, there is a threshold between A and not-A, one between D and not-D, and a middle one between A + B and C + D (Rogers, 1941). This middle threshold, then, is the stimulus value that would give 50 percent responses of A or B, and 50 percent of C or D. With any even number of categories, the middle intercategory threshold can be called the subjective mid-point of the stimulus series. With an odd number of categories, where is the subjective mid-point? It is the midpoint of the middle category. It is the same as the PSE of Constant Stimuli. When compared with the objective midpoint of the stimulus series, it shows something analogous with the CE (see p. 198). For DL the PE_{dist} will serve when only two categories have been used, and any even number of categories may be reduced to two by treating the lower half of them as minus responses and the upper half as plus. Any odd number of categories presents the problems we faced with the equal judgments in three-category Constant Stimuli.

For ordinary psychophysical purposes the question is whether Single Stimuli yield anything like the keenness of discrimination shown by the older methods. Results have shown precision comparable with that obtained by Constant Stimuli (Wever & Zener, 1928; Fernberger, 1931 b; Pfaffmann, 1935). Even keener discrimination can be obtained by a modification of Single Stimuli which calls for estimates in physical units such as grams, inches, or decibels (Bressler, 1933; Long, 1937), though the work is more strenuous for *O*. The results

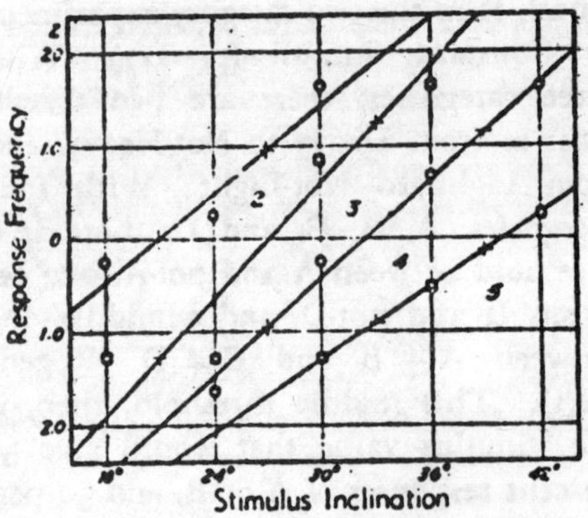

FIG. 8-12. Five-category data in an s-z plot. The threshold lines are located by the use of two average z points shown by crosses. Hypothetical data. *Instructions:* "You will be shown straight lines differing in steepness which you are to classify in five categories, category 1 being the least steep and category 5 the steepest. You will become acquainted after a few trials with the range of inclinations used in the experiment."

The sloping lines are the intercategory boundaries, and the numbered areas between the lines show where and how much each of the five categories was used by *O*. Where the sloping lines cross the middle horizontal, we have the Mean intercategory thresholds; where they cross the next horizontals above and below the middle, we have the SD values. The steeper the lines, the more precise and consistent was *O*'s use of the categories. If the stimuli had been so different from each other that *O* could always use category 1 for the smallest stimulus, category 2 for the next, and so on, his intercategory boundaries would have been vertical lines (and the SD values all zero).

The tabular matter below the figure shows how the data have been treated. For each stimulus value the 20 responses are counted by categories. These frequencies are reduced to p values. The p values are cumulated downward in each column. If these cumulated p values were plotted we should get four rough ogives. Instead, they are converted into z values by aid of the table on page 206. The s-z data points are plotted downward in each column, with the negative z's on top. When p = 0 or 1.00 we have no z values, but we do have three or four usable z's for each *row* of our table, which are treated just as in the two figures on page 205.

		18°	24°	30°	36°	42°
Responses after a few preliminary trials		2	2	3	5	5
		2	2	4	3	4
		1	2	3	5	5
		2	1	4	4	5
		1	2	3	5	5
		.	.	.	.	.
		.	.	.	.	.
		.	.	.	.	.
		.	.	.	.	.
Frequencies (by categories)	f(1)	12	8	1	0	0
	f(2)	6	10	3	1	0
	f(3)	2	1	8	4	1
	f(4)	0	1	6	9	7
	f(5)	0	0	2	6	12
p values	p(1)	.60	.40	.05	0	0
	p(2)	.30	.50	.15	.05	0
	p(3)	.10	.05	.40	.20	.05
	p(4)	0	.05	.30	.45	.35
	p(5)	0	0	.10	.30	.60
Cumulated p values	p(<2)	.60	.40	.05	0	0
	p(<3)	.90	.90	.20	.05	0
	p(<4)	1.00	.95	.60	.25	.05
	p(<5)	1.00	1.00	.90	.70	.40

Intercategory thresholds
M = 21.0; SD = 6.3
M = 27.1; SD = 4.8
M = 32.4; SD = 5.7
M = 40.1; SD = 7.8

can be treated by the Frequency Method or by the Method of Average Error—here the Average Error of Estimate.

The comparability of results from Single Stimuli and Constant Stimuli is brought out by Figure 8-13.

VARIATIONS ON CONVENTIONAL FREQUENCY METHODS

In some cases it is inconvenient to change the stimulus on every trial. Shaad and Helson (1931) found that it was perfectly satisfactory to concentrate on one value at a time, both for lifted weights and for the tactual two-point limen. They used from 10 to 25 trials before changing stimuli. This method has been used a great deal in recent years for auditory work. We can collect judgments rapidly if we present St continuously, introducing a momentary increment every three seconds or so. In such cases it is much simpler to set the apparatus so that it will give the same increment on every trial of a series. Judgments ob-

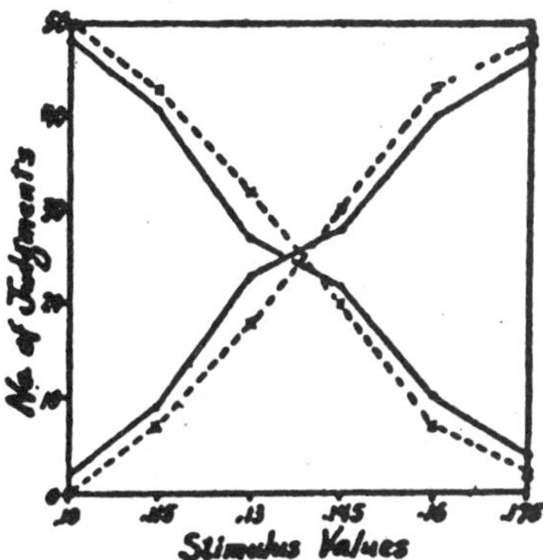

FIG. 8-13. (Pfaffmann, 1935). Psychometric functions for sodium chloride, obtained by the methods of Constant Stimuli and Single Stimuli. Six Co stimuli were used in each method. In constant stimuli, the two-category method was employed, and the two solid lines show the functions for greater and less. In Single Stimuli, *O* was required to assign a number from one to six to each stimulus, six being the strongest; the responses were reduced to two categories by combining 1, 2, & 3 vs. 4, 5, & 6, which are then plotted in broken lines. For this *O* the Method of Single Stimuli yielded the smoother curves. Computation by Urban's method showed no advantage to either method in any of three *O*s, but Single Stimuli saved a lot of time, for it involved only half as many stimuli, and minimized the adaptation effects which are troublesome in taste.

tained under these conditions are often more stable than those from randomized Co values. Even when the trials are spaced, rather than continuous, the modified method seems to be easier on both *E* and *O* (Koester, 1945; Koester & Schoenfeld, 1945). For example, if St is 1,000 cycles, it will be paired with 1,000.5 and 999.5 for about 20 trials. Then *E* will substitute another symmetrical set of Co, as 1,002.5 and 997.5, etc. This is very similar to Fechner's original "Method of Right and Wrong Cases." The same general method may be used with Single Stimuli. Koester & Schoenfeld got very good results by presenting two stimuli, say 1,001.5 and 998.5 in random order, *O* judging *high* or *low*. Ogives can be constructed from two stable points, especially if the stimulus values are chosen to yield about 25 percent and 75 percent correct judgments of *high*.

Logarithmic versus linear stimulus series. The stimulus series is usually selected so that it has equal steps, and is balanced around St. For example, in the lifted-weight experiment (p. 211), St was 200 grams, and the Co series was 184, 192, 200, 208, and 216. These are equal arithmetic steps; if Weber's law is correct, perhaps we should use equal logarithmic steps. The test would seem to be whether or not the series gives a good ogive, or straight line on a *z* score plot (cf. p. 209). Thurstone (1928b) predicted that psychophysical judgments would not be normally distributed if plotted on a linear stimulus scale. This prediction is not supported by the data illustrated in Figure 8-9, or by a replotting of Warner Brown's (p. 216) extensive data on lifted weights. But the Weber fraction for this sense is small, about 1/25 or 1/30, so a relatively short series range of weights is enough to reach the DL ±. Such a short series does not give much basis for distinguishing between logarithmic and arithmetic spacing. A better test would be in a sense field with a large DL, as taste, where the series of Co stimuli must be larger. Pfaffmann (Fig. 8-13) used a linear series of Co so it should serve as a good test of Thurstone's prediction. But the data, when located on an *s-z* plot with linear base line scale, show no indication of the predicted skew. It is possible that *O*'s experience with the linear series distorted his judgments, through some sort of *series effect* (pp. 229–233); it would be interesting to see what sort of ogives would be obtained with a logarithmic series of Co.

In certain sense fields it *is* usual to employ a logarithmic series. For example, in audition, where the DL for loudness is about 1/11, we always use a logarithmic unit, the decibel (p. 20). Visual filters are usually calibrated in terms of density, another logarithmic unit. Both yield good ogives. Perhaps the best advice is to use a logarithmic stimulus series whenever convenient, and especially where the DL is large. Then make an *s-z* plot, using the series steps on the base line, and check for any skew which would indicate the need for a transformation into another scale.

THE NATURE OF THRESHOLDS

All of the methods we have discussed thus far are based on a general view of the nature of the threshold. Let us make this view explicit. A stimulus, falling on a receptor, initiates a train of impulses which produce an effect in the brain centers. The size of this central effect will vary with the strength of the stimulus, the sensitivity of the receptor, the efficiency of the conducting paths, and the background level of activity of the center. If the central effect on a given trial is greater than a certain minimum (see below), the center will discharge, yielding a response; i.e., "I hear it." The stimulus which produces this minimum effect is the stimulus threshold *on that trial*. But the complex of factors listed above will vary randomly from trial to trial, yielding a more-or-less normal distribution of momentary Ts. The Mean of this distribution represents the most typical value of the stimulus threshold; the various psychophysical methods are simply different ways of obtaining and treating the data so as to measure the typical value and its variation.

Now turn to the difference threshold, where there are two stimuli, each producing a central excitation that varies randomly. Suppose we give 100 trials with two stimuli, St and Co, of equal objective strength. If there is no constant error, the distributions of the two excitations will be identical, with the same Means and SDs. Statistics tells us that the differences between randomly selected pairs of excitations will be normally distributed, with a Mean of 0, and an SD which is equal to $\sqrt{2}$ times the SD of either single distribution. The difference will be positive as often as negative. If we are using the Method of Constant Stimuli, with *equal* judgments prohibited, *O* will split his judgments 50-50 between greater and less.

Next consider 100 pairs on which Co is slightly stronger than St. The distribution of excitations from Co will be displaced upwards; the Mean will be higher, though the SD may stay the same. The Mean of the distribution of differences is now positive (favoring Co), and we get perhaps 60-percent judgments of greater, with 40 percent less. By trying several different values of Co, we determine the stimulus difference which is necessary to displace the Means enough to give us 75 percent greater judgments, and call that stimulus difference the DL. The absolute size of this DL depends on the size of the SD of the distribution of differences in excitation, mentioned above; in short, the DL is a measure of the variability of the particular sense field under consideration.

So far we have assumed that *O* is making a sharp cut in that he never reports the two excitations as equal. This has been forced on him by the instructions. But if we had permitted an equal category, he would have applied it whenever the two excitations differed less than a certain amount. In a way he is setting up a sort of unconscious "critical ratio," saying, in effect, that the difference is not great enough to give reliable evidence that one stimulus is really stronger than the other. The size of this critical ratio determines the interval of uncertainty, and itself depends on a complex of factors, as we saw earlier. Fundamentally, it is probably due to the fact that *O* has to have some way of allowing for changing excitation levels from constant environmental stimuli; whether the mechanism is native or learned need not concern us here. Recent evidence suggests that something like a critical ratio is also involved in the RL for some of the senses. For example, in vision and audition there is a spontaneous sense-organ discharge, a "noise level," to use a current term from communication theory. The incoming neural signal, released by the stimulus, must be significantly higher than this noise level before it is reported.

Is discrimination step-wise? This variability theory of the threshold has been accepted in one form or another since the time of the classical psychophysicists (cf. Fullerton & Cattell, 1892; Boring, 1917; Thurstone, 1927b; Guilford, 1927). It offered no theoretical problems as long as we thought that the nerve impulse worked like an ordinary current in a circuit, increasing or decreasing its intensity to reflect stimulus changes. But as we became aware that the nerve impulses are all-or-none, it seemed reasonable to expect that sensations would also vary in a step-wise fashion. For example, assume that a brief tactual stimulus is just strong enough to set up a burst of 10 impulses; gradual increase in strength of the stimulus would not increase the strength of the sensation until the stimulus was strong enough to elicit 11 impulses, whereupon *O* would feel a sudden increase in tactual sensation. It was generally assumed that these discrete steps did not show up because they were very small and were swamped out by the variability of the receptive system. But in 1930 von Békésy showed that evidence for these steps could be found in auditory thresholds, if the experiments were designed to minimize variation. Stevens, Morgan & Volkmann (1941) obtained similar results in both loudness and pitch. The theory which goes with these results is usually called the *quantum* theory of discrimination. The *quanta,* or steps, are determined by the organism in this theory, and not by the stimulus; this theory is to be contrasted with Hecht's *quantum* theory of vision, where the *quanta* are in the stimulus, in agreement with the physicists conception of light (p. 376).

It requires very special conditions, minimizing variability, to demonstrate these steps. Flynn (1943) was sometimes able to obtain evidence for them, but failed at other times. Comparable results were found by G. A. Miller & Garner (1944). Koester & Schoenfeld (1947) found that their data often departed from the predictions of the quantum theory, even though taken under favorable conditions. All of these experiments were in audition, and there has been no adequate test of the theory in other sense fields. It is interesting that we can demonstrate intensity steps in one sense field, under ideal conditions, but it is more important to realize that any step-like mechanism is usually obscured by fluctuations in *O*'s sensitivity. So even if the psychophysical ogive is just a smoothed flight of steps, in the vast majority of experiments it is smooth enough to be treated as an ogive!

THRESHOLDS AND WEBER'S LAW

The student of psychophysics is apt to get the impression that it is an example of methodology for its own sake. There seems to be more debate and discussion on the best methods to use in determining thresholds than on the results themselves. To some extent this criticism is valid. However, the impression is greatly exaggerated by two simple practical matters. In the first place, a list of all the thresholds that have been determined for the various senses, under all possible conditions, would clutter up a textbook, and would be extremely dull. Hence such tables may be relegated to handbooks (Tufts College, 1949; Stevens, 1951a). A summary table, like that below, is apt to be misleading; remember that the values listed in the table on page 223 represent Weber's ratio ($\Delta I/I$) in the optimal region for each sense field, and are only rough measures of the precision of the modality at its best.

The second reason that one usually does not find detailed results under the heading of "psychophysics" is that the results are meaningful only in relation to our other knowledge about a sense field. Hence, they are scattered around in chapters on Vision, Audition, and Depth Perception, to mention only a few. In other words, the psychophysical

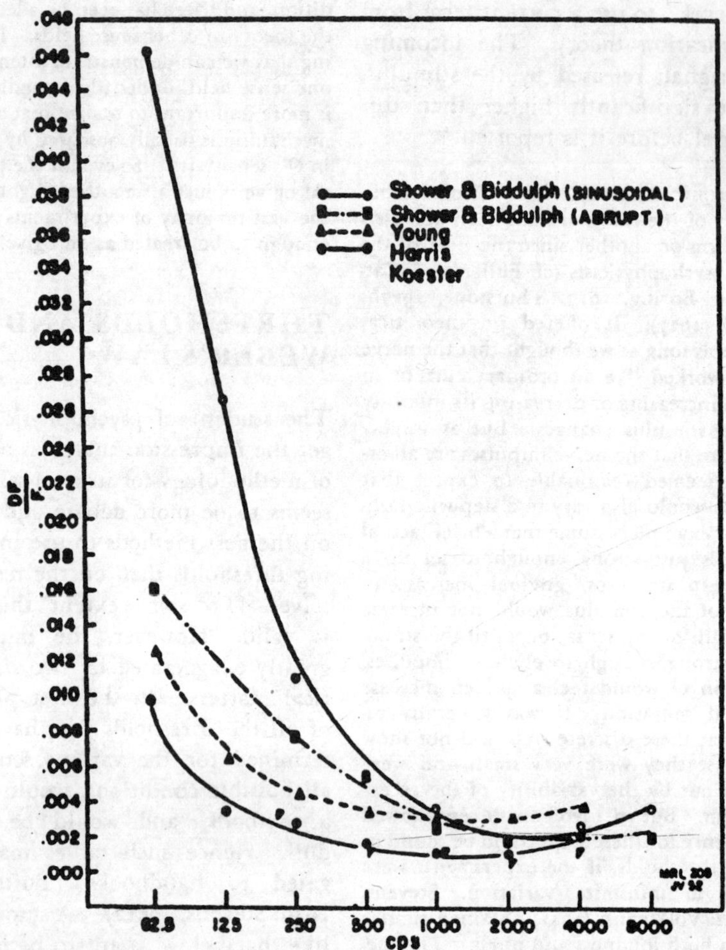

FIG. 8-14. (Harris, 1952.) Pitch discrimination (DF/F) in relation to frequency (cycles per second). The steep curve was obtained by rapidly alternating St and Co in a gradual or sinusoidal fashion, to produce a warbling tone. This curve has long been considered correct; it can be described as showing the DL to be a fixed number of cycles (about 3) up to a St of about 250 cycles, with Weber's law holding above that value.

The other curves were obtained by the more conventional Method of Constant Stimuli, with St and Co presented in discrete pairs. They indicate that Weber's fraction is constant at about .002 beyond 250 cycles, rising somewhat at the lower frequencies.

methods are the tools with which we obtain much of our knowledge of how senses work; it is a good idea to get our tools all ready so we shall have appropriate ones at hand for the various problems we meet.

Weber's law. However, there are certain questions one can ask about thresholds-in-general. The most familiar is concerned with the size of the DL at different absolute values of the stimulus. The usual answer is known as Weber's

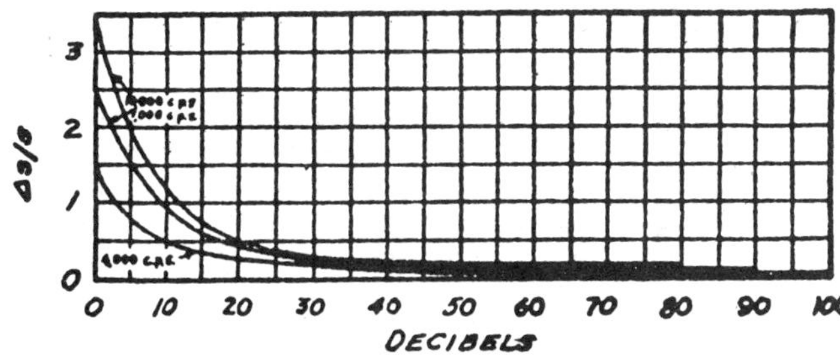

FIG. 8-15. (Adapted from Riesz, 1928.) Test of Weber's law in discrimination of intensity of sound. The sound was a pure tone produced in a special telephone receiver by the alternating current from an oscillator. Combined with this current was a second weaker current differing in vibration frequency by 3 cycles/sec and producing beats or fluctuations of intensity in the main tone, the amount of fluctuation being controlled by varying the intensity of the second current. The question for *O* was whether the tone was heard to beat. Δs was determined at various vibration rates of the main tone, and over the whole range of intensities from near the stimulus threshold to near the pain threshold. The Weber fraction was found to be lowest (the discrimination best) when the tone had a high pitch, about 2,500 cycles, three octaves and more above middle C of the musical scale. In this region the ear is most sensitive to very faint sounds, i.e., the stimulus threshold is lowest. Discrimination of pitch also is best in the region of high tones. Average of 12 *O*s. "c.p.s." = cycles per second.

law, which we discussed at the beginning of this chapter. Is it true that the DL is a constant fraction of the magnitude of the stimulus? Are just noticeable differences relative? Figures 8-14 to 8-17 show results in various sense modalities. The form of these plots is that used in Figure 8-1B, in which Weber's fraction is plotted against the magnitude of the Standard. In such a plot, Weber's law holds true wherever the curve describes a straight line, parallel to the base. In all except the first graph, the base line is in logarithmic units, to condense the range. Perhaps the best single way to summarize the results is to say that Weber's fraction is fairly constant for the middle ranges of stimulus values, but that it increases rapidly at extremes, near the RL and TL. Certainly there is little suggestion that the DL is an absolute value, independent of the magnitude of the stimulus, for in that case the curves would start at the upper left corner, fall progressively toward the base line, and never level off, much less start to climb again.

If we are looking for a universal and accurate law of judgment, Weber's law obviously is not it. Other laws have been suggested. Fullerton and Cattell (1892) proposed the square root law, that DL increased as the square root of the stimulus, rather than as the stimulus

MINIMAL WEBER FRACTIONS

(Boring, Langfeld & Weld, 1948)

*Pitch, at 2,000 cycles per sec	0.003 =	1/333
Deep pressure, at 400 grams	0.013	1/77
*Visual brightness, at 1,000 photons	0.016	1/62
*Lifted weights, at 300 grams	0.019	1/53
*Loudness, at 1,000 cps, 100 db	0.088	1/11
Smell, rubber, at 200 olfacties	0.104	1/10
Cutaneous pressure, spot, at 5 gm per mm²	0.136	1/7
Taste, saline, at 3 moles per liter	0.200	1/5

* Compare these values with Figs. 8-14 to 8-17.

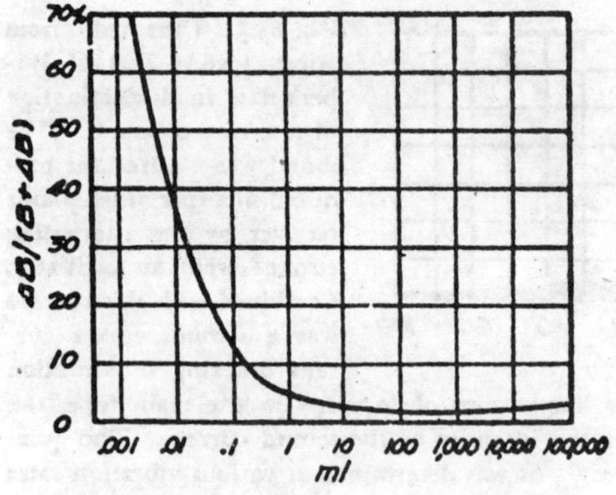

Fig. 8-16. (Data from König & Brodhun, 1888, recomputed in millilamberts by Nutting, 1908.) Weber's law in brightness. Discrimination of upper and lower halves of a small round field, tested by just noticeable difference. Data from one O.

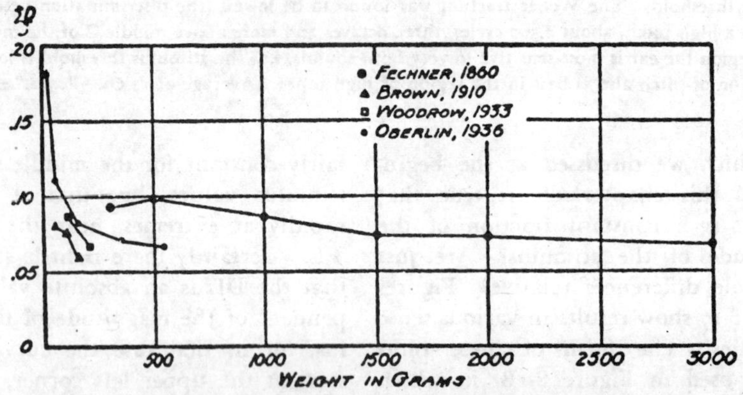

Fig. 8-17. (Data from several authors.) Weber's law in lifted weights. The weights were lifted successively with one hand. Method of Constant Stimuli. Number of Os: Fechner, 1; Brown, 1; Woodrow, 5; Oberlin, 5. The results, given by the several authors in terms of h, Q or complete distributions, are here reduced to terms of SD, and are seen to be in good agreement as to the absolute values of SD, and especially as to the course of the Weber fraction with change of S.

itself. This law does not hold any better—if as well. Woodworth (1914) suggested that a compromise between the two laws was theoretically sound, and many data do fall between the values predicted by the two laws. Finally, Guilford (1932) proposed a still more general nth power law, which may be written $\Delta S = KS^n$, which may be read "the just noticeable increment in a stimulus is equal to a constant times the nth power of the stimulus." In Weber's law, n would be 1, whereas in the square root law, n would be ½. The actual value of both K and n would be determined for a specific sense by curve fitting. Such a highly generalized law will fit most data. But it would seem to be too general a law to have much theoretical significance.

A vast amount of argument has been devoted to the question of whether or not Weber's law holds. If we stop worrying about whether or not it is a universal law of judgment, the answer is simple. It holds as a rough empirical generalization in the mid-ranges of most senses—both for intensity and for quality, although it was originally proposed for intensity alone. By and large, these mid-ranges are the working area of the senses. For example, normal conversation is well within the flat parts of the curves for pitch and loudness (Figs. 8-14, 8-15). This statement, and others like it, involve some interesting circular arguments, but it is still true that Weber's law furnishes us with a valuable description of the discriminating power of the important sensory ranges. As such, it is extremely useful.

The fact that Weber's law holds as well as it does is not surprising, if we remember the way a threshold is obtained. It is essentially a measure of the variability of the effects of a stimulus. In most biological phenomena, variability tends to be proportionate to the magnitude of the quantity involved. This is not an ultimate explanation of Weber's law. What we must do is to examine the physiological details of the S—R process in each sense field. Such examination will give an ultimate explanation, not only of Weber's law, but also of the actual shapes of the various curves shown in Figures 8-14 to 8-17. To some extent this can already be done, as we shall see in chapters on the various senses. As for the law itself, any student who has gone beyond the elementary level in any science has met many "laws" that turn out to "hold within limits" (e.g., Hooke's law). They are very useful at the predictive and descriptive level.

CONSTANT ERRORS AND SERIES EFFECTS

Psychophysics has other interests besides the testing of Weber's law. Sometimes incidentally and sometimes by special experimental design the attempt has been made to discover how judgments of magnitude are made and made so accurately. Something can be learned from introspection on *O*'s part as to his aims and criteria and any techniques he may devise for making fine distinctions and avoiding errors. But the process is usually too smooth and rapid to be examined introspectively so that the investigator is forced to depend on objective data such as the errors that are committed under different experimental conditions.

What is true of target practice is true of any performance that can be checked for accuracy; there are many errors which scatter this way and that but usually in one direction more than another. The hits on the target scatter around some point that is not the bull's-eye. If this center can be located and the scatter measured, the performance is pretty well analyzed from the standpoint of accuracy. The psychophysical methods provide this sort of analysis; they yield some measure of variability, and they locate the PSE. The distance and direction of PSE from the Standard (or bull's-eye) make up the constant error of *O*'s performance.

Constant errors are often of practical importance. In shooting at a target you wish to know whether your aim is mostly too high or too low; for if you know your CE, you can make a judicious correction. Constant errors may also be of theoretical interest as indicative of significant *S*-factors and *O*-factors in a performance. In psychophysics they throw light on the process of judgment. Thus the ascending and descending series of the Method of Limits encourage over- and undershooting, called errors of habituation and anticipation, respectively. In the other methods, especially Constant Stimuli and Single Stimuli, the most interesting examples are the Time Error (TE) and the Series Effect. A time error, or time-order effect, is likely to occur when one stimulus follows another in time, the second being compared with the first, i.e., when Co follows St. A series effect is likely to occur when several unequal stimuli have preceded the one that is now to be judged. Some care is necessary to obtain either of these effects uncontaminated with the other, though they are really quite different. In a word, TE is (usually) a tendency to overestimate the second stimulus in relation to the first, but a Series Effect is a tendency to over- or underestimate a stimulus according to its magnitude in relation to the series as a whole.

Time error. To get this effect in its pure form, let there be only two stimuli, Co following St and being objectively equal to it. If Co is judged greater than St, we have what is called a negative TE. This apparently perverse usage straightens itself out if we think in terms of PSE and of our previous formula (p. 198), CE = PSE − St. Perhaps the significance of the minus sign can be seen most clearly in the Method of Average Error, where *O* adjusts Co to apparent equality with St. If he makes Co less than St (on the average), his TE is clearly negative; his PSE is less than St and shows that the effective magnitude of St has shrunk during the St-Co time interval. In the Method of Constant Stimuli *O* never tells directly where the equality point seems to lie, but if he judges Co to be greater than St when both are objectively equal, he is saying in effect that St was less than this Co so that his PSE is evidently below St and his TE is negative.

A rough but widely applicable measure of TE is obtained from the percents of plus and minus judgments when Co is objectively equal to St. To keep the sign correct, subtract the percent of *pluses* from that of *minuses;* the difference is called D percent. If the Co stimuli are symmetrically arranged about St as a center (as with weights of 92, 96, 100, 104, and 108 grams, St being 100), D percent can be obtained from the total percents of pluses and minuses in the whole experiment. The PSE as computed by the regular method (p. 212) affords a more adequate measure.

Trace and set as factors in the time error. When Fechner (1860) discovered the negative TE in his extensive experiment on lifted weights, he offered a fading-image explanation. The St weight was lifted and set down, the kinesthetic sensation ceased; in a few seconds the Co weight was lifted and the resulting sensation compared with the kinesthetic image remaining from the first lift; this image having faded somewhat, the second weight appeared heavier. This apparently logical explanation failed to stand up in careful introspective studies of weight lifting (Schumann, 1898, 1902; Fernberger, 1919) and of comparison of sounds (Whipple, 1901, 1902; Köhler, 1923; Needham, 1934a). The supposed image was not observable in many cases. Köhler suggested that *trace* be substituted for image in the theory. He thought of the trace as an electrical process in the brain which could be "silent" or unconscious and yet able to function in place of the sensory impression that had ceased. Certainly there must be a trace of some sort whenever a previous stimulus is remembered or utilized in the judgment of a following stimulus; and this trace might very probably weaken in the St-Co time interval. So we have the *fading-trace* theory of the negative TE.

Functioning together with the trace there is an active attitude of the observer. He is not going simply to receive the Co; he is prepared to judge it in a certain respect. He is "all set" to judge it. The most concrete example of such a set is seen in the experiment with lifted weights. *O* becomes adjusted to the rather narrow range of weights used; he knows that Co and St will not differ much. Müller & Schumann (1889) proposed a possible mechanism for this performance. *O* prepares to lift Co with a muscular force just previously found adequate for lifting St. If Co comes up quickly and easily, it seems light and is judged lighter than St; if it resists and comes up slowly it seems heavy and is judged heavier than St. (This theory accounts nicely for the size-weight illusion, which makes an empty candy box seem lighter than a lead slug of the same actual weight. The large object looks heavy and is lifted with more force than the small object.) Now if *O* should lift Co more cautiously and deliberately than St, he would give a preponderance of "Heavier" judgments and so show a negative TE. In general, we may add, the apparent intensity of Co would be raised by closer attention paid to it than to St (Newhall, 1923).

Fortunately the Müller-Schumann theory can be subjected to a direct test, as was done by Payne & Davis (1940). They recorded the activity of the weight-lifting muscles by leading off and amplifying the electric potentials (action currents) from *O*'s forearm while he was judging weights. "Heavier" judgments occurred mostly when Co was lifted more strongly than St, and "Lighter" judgments when it was lifted less strongly than St. The St lift itself varied in strength, and when it was weak it left behind it a relatively weak muscular tension during the 3-second interval before the lifting of Co. The weaker the tension when *O* started to lift Co, the more resistance would be offered by Co, and so the more strongly *O* would lift Co, this lifting movement being a response to the resistance encountered, and the resistance being dependent on the initial tension (inversely) and on the weight of Co (directly). Payne & Davis concluded that the Müller-Schumann theory was tenable but might better be stated in peripheral terms than in terms of a central set. The negative TE shown by the (single) *O* in this experiment seemed to be connected with the lifting movements, for the PSE fell just about where the St and Co lifts were equal. There is some indication in the graphs that the Co lift started from a slightly lower tension level than the St lift, and rose a bit more slowly till the Co resistance was felt; if genuine, these factors would account for a negative TE.

Auditory time errors. In respect to loudness, fairly strong TEs have been found by many experimenters, as in the extensive experiment of Postman (1946). Using Constant Stimuli with pure tones in one series and noises in another, he found in both cases a *positive* TE when the time interval between St and Co was short (1 or 2 seconds) but a *negative* TE with longer intervals (4 and 6 seconds). Köhler (1923) had obtained a similar result: a positive TE at 1.5 sec. practically zero TE at 3 sec. and a negative TE at 6 and 12 sec. Köhler found, however, that the positive phase disappeared with continued repetition of the experiment; and Needham (1934b) even found the TE curve to reverse itself after several days of practice, becoming negative after a short interval and positive after a longer interval (Fig. 8-18). Neither set nor fading trace takes care of these peculiarities in any obvious way.

When the pitch of tones, not their loudness, is judged, there is no time error. Postman (1946) paralleled his just cited experiment on loudness with one on pitch, keeping the conditions and observers the same; and Koester varied the procedure in several ways, using

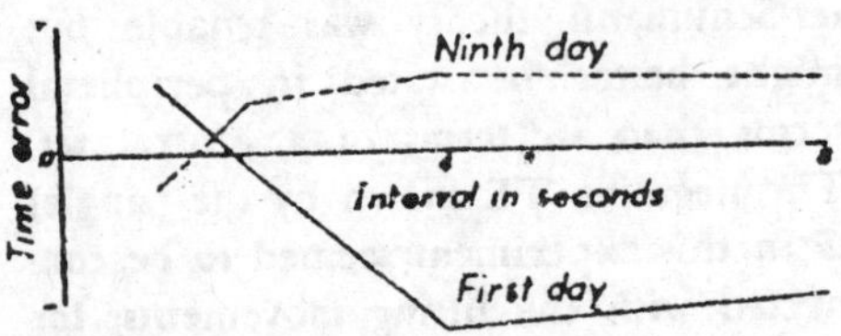

FIG. 8-18. (Data from Needham, 1934b.) The time error curve for loudness as changed by continued repetition of the experiment. Average curves for six *Os*. On the first day the TE was positive at the 1-sec interval between St and Co, negative at 2, 4, and 8 sec. By the ninth day it became negative at the shortest interval and positive at the longer ones.

both practiced and unpracticed observers. Neither of these investigators was able to demonstrate any time error, positive or negative. This result makes sense in terms of auditory theory. Tones differing in pitch probably have different loci in the cortical area for hearing, but tones differing only in loudness must have the same locus. The trace left behind in any locus might fade or weaken, but it would scarcely shift to another locus; i.e., the trace would scarcely become sharper or flatter in pitch. In general, the fading-trace TE perhaps occurs in judgments of intensity but not in judgments of sensory qualities such as pitch and hue (Stevens, 1939).

Visual time errors. Intensities of light are usually presented side by side (p. 200) with a possible space error but no chance for a time error. When two spots of light are presented successively to the same retinal area with only a short time interval, the second intensity is underestimated (Fullerton & Cattell, 1892; Lauenstein, 1933). This positive TE is easily explained by retinal adaptation; St leaves behind it some brightness adaptation (p. 369), and Co, therefore, is received by a less sensitive retina. When the successive lights are presented to different retinal areas, 20° to right and left of the fixation point, a negative TE is obtained (Kreezer, 1938). Here the successive stimuli certainly affect different cortical loci, one in the left hemisphere and one in the right—a fact which rather complicates the task of imagining a plausible cortical mechanism for successive comparisons.

Exactly how the trace can operate is a baffling problem. A residual level of excitation left behind by the first stimulus might be pushed upward or downward by the second stimulus, so producing an impression of Greater or Less. More probably, however, the second stimulus would push the level upward in all cases; otherwise the second stimulus would not be sensed at all. Evidently the trace functions in some other way, not easily imagined in our present ignorance of what goes on in the sensory cortex. We must remember also that a motor readiness for making the judgment response operates along with the sensory trace. With two categories of judgment to choose from, there are two motor responses more or less ready, and the one that is more ready has the advantage whenever the two stimuli are objectively equal (Davis, 1952; cf. Preston, 1936).

Assimilation of the Standard toward an interpolated stimulus. Usually the St-Co time interval is vacant. If *O* is comparing lifted weights, he keeps his hand quiet in the interval. If he did lift an interpolated weight, we might expect either of two effects: (1) any weight might raise the trace level and so tend toward a positive TE, or (2) a heavy weight might do this but a light weight have the opposite effect. Guilford & Park (1931) found the second alternative correct. Their St was 200 grams, with Co weights ranging from 185 to 215 grams, and they obtained a PSE of 192.5 grams, i.e., a TE of —7.5 grams. But with an interpolated weight of 100 grams, they pushed PSE down to 188.2 grams, and with an interpolated weight of 400 grams they pushed it up to 199.2 grams, so practically canceling the negative TE though without introducing a positive TE such as might have been expected. Their *Os* reported trying to *disregard* the interpolated weight, and they evidently succeeded to a large extent in keeping the trace of St uncontaminated by the interpolated weight. To a certain degree, however, the St trace was "assimilated" to or toward the interpolated stimulus.

This term, *assimilation*, was introduced by Lauenstein (1933), a pupil of Köhler. He obtained results on loudness similar to those of Guilford & Park on weights. The trace of St was attracted upward toward a loud interpolated stimulus, downward toward a soft one. He doubted that traces ever fade or sink in a passive way. An empty St—Co interval, he suggested, is a "zero stimulus" which attracts the St trace, so producing the usual negative TE. Later evidence indicates that assimilation is a genuine factor but that sinking trace is also genuine. One crucial test was made by Pratt (1933a). He produced different intensities of sound by the use of a "sound pendulum" which fell from graduated heights against a block. The St—Co interval was 4 sec. In three series he interpolated a loud, soft, or zero sound. The St fall was from 45°. PSE came out as follows:

With loud interpolated sound	48.19°
With soft interpolated sound	42.19°
With silent interval	44.14°

So the St trace was assimilated toward the loud or soft interpolated sound, but not toward the zero interpolation. Assimilation does not account for the ordinary TE with a vacant interval. Pratt concluded that fading trace was a genuine fact, even though its physiology was not clear. Time order is one thing and assimilation another thing. Assimilation belongs with the series effects which we shall now consider.

Series effects. The observer is confronted by a situation in which he is to judge one particular stimulus, the Co of the moment, against the background of a series or assemblage of other stimuli that have preceded. There are several effects which belong together in this situation.

1. *The series as a frame of reference for the judgment of the single stimulus.* In the Method of Single Stimuli no St is given but each Co as it comes is to be judged in absolute categories, such as H, M, and L (High, Medium, Low). The first few Co stimuli are judged pretty much at random, but *O* soon adjusts himself to the range of stimuli encountered and uses the categories consistently and in fair correspondence with the objective stimuli. If *E* then shifts the range of the stimuli, as by removing the lowest and adding some higher ones, *O* soon follows suit by readjusting the category values (Wever & Zener, 1928; Tresselt, 1947).

2. *Displacement of the frame.* When three categories, H, M, L, are available for judging the Single Stimuli, H and L should logically be used equally often, and PSE should be in the middle of the stimulus series. Otherwise some factor extraneous to the series must be exerting an influence on the judgments. One such factor is previous experience. A muscular chap who is accustomed to lifting heavy weights may find all the weights of the experimental series rather light and accordingly use the L category oftener than the H (Tresselt, 1948). If the sounds presented in a loudness series are all soft in comparison with the everyday range of sounds, the L category will be used more often than H (Pratt, 1933b). These effects may wear off quickly as *O* becomes adjusted to the actual series of stimuli. Another extraneous factor which is not so easily brushed aside is the fading trace. Just as the trace of the St sinks in Constant Stimuli, so, in Single Stimuli, the combined trace of the whole series of stimuli may sink and produce a negative TE to complicate the pure Series effect. The preponderance of H judgments in Single Stimuli was noted in the case of weights by Wever & Zener (1928) and by Fernberger (1931b), and in the case of moderate degrees of loudness by Pratt (1933b). But it was absent in judgments of pitch, as it should be to conform to the absence of a negative TE in this qualitative dimension (Truman & Wever, 1928).

3. *Compression of the frame.* The combined trace of the stimulus series shrinks, the component stimuli attracting each other and gravitating toward the Mean of the series. This "central tendency" was discovered by Hollingworth (1909, 1910); it was rediscovered by Ipsen (1926a) who gave it the name we have adopted, "series effect." To tease out this compression we have to go somewhat beyond the regular psychophysical methods; we have to use more than a single St. Preferably we use every stimulus in the series as a St some of the time so as to discover whether it is attracted toward the center of the whole series. If it is so attracted and *O* attempts to reproduce it, his reproduction of a low St will be too high, and his reproduction of a high St will be too low. This Hollingworth found by a suitable modification of the Method of Average Error (cf. p. 226). By a similar modification of Constant Stimuli, each member of the series is used as St and followed by an objectively equal Co; this Co will be predominantly judged less than a low St, but greater than a high St because each St has gravitated toward the middle of the series (Woodrow, 1933). Each St, we may say, is assimilated into the series, and the Co is thus contrasted with the series as a whole.

The compression effect can be most fully brought out by the Method of Single Stimuli, modified to call for estimates in physical units (p. 217). If the intensity of a series of sounds is estimated in decibels, the least intense stimuli are underestimated and the most intense overestimated (Long, 1937). As can be seen in Figure 8-19, when the series extended from 30 to 50 db, the 30-db stimulus was underestimated by 2.5 db and the 50 db was overestimated by 2 db.

The series effect can be stated in different ways. We can say that *O* builds up a scale of categories conforming fairly well to the series of stimuli. The category scale is likely to be displaced downward by fading traces of the stimuli, and it may be displaced upward by previous (or interpolated) experience with stimuli greater than those of the series. The category scale is likely to be compressed

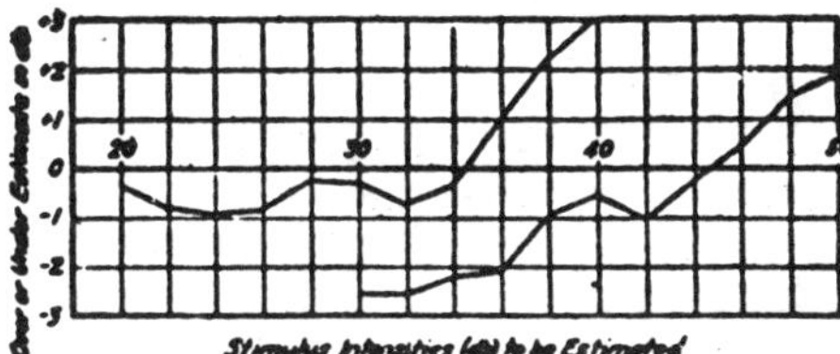

FIG. 8-19. (Modified from Long, 1937, p. 37.) The series effect in estimation of sound intensities. Each stimulus was a tone of 1000~. The upper curve shows *O*'s estimates of intensities ranging from 20 to 40 db with a Standard of 30 db sounded just before each Co stimulus. The lower curve, similarly, shows *O*'s estimates of the 30-50 series with a St of 40 db sounded before each Co. St and Co were each sounded for ½ sec and with a ½ sec interval between them. *O* estimated the intensity of each Co in decibels. At the beginning of the whole experiment *O* was familiarized with the db values of the range of stimuli to be used, and at the beginning of each session he was given "anchor" stimuli of 10, 20, 30, 40, 50, and 60 db and estimated them correctly. *O* knew that all the stimuli would lie between 10 and 60 db, and he knew that the St was 30 db in one series and 40 db in the other, but he was not informed of the exact limits of each series because such information would have restricted the range of his estimates and led to "end errors." The curves still show some end error in the estimates of 20 and 50 db; the 20-db point would be lower and the 50-db point higher, except for *O*'s tendency to avoid extreme estimates.

There were four *O*s and a total of 360 estimates averaged for each point on the curves. The SD_M is about .2 db for each point.

The chief results brought out by the curves are: (1) that the estimates in each series were internally consistent and well correlated with the stimulus intensities; (2) that the lower intensities in each series were underestimated and the higher ones overestimated; and (3) that in the overlapping range from 30 to 40 db the same stimuli received lower estimates when in the higher than when in the lower series. Each stimulus is estimated against the background of the series in which it occurs.

toward the Mean of the series, so that the higher categories are used for Co stimuli that are not high enough to deserve so high a rating, while the lower categories are used for Co stimuli that are not low enough to deserve so low a rating; i.e., the high Co stimuli are overrated and the low ones underrated.

Displacement of PSE predicted from weighted average of the stimuli. Why should PSE in so many experiments be smaller than the Arithmetical Mean of the Co stimuli? Sinking trace is only a partial explanation. It was suggested by Johnson (1944a) and by Helson (1947) that the Geometrical Mean would be a more logical average, in view of the fact that the sensory effect of stimuli is at least roughly proportional to the logarithm of the physical intensity (Fechner's law). The simplest case is that of Single Stimuli, which would call for the following formula,

$$\log GM = Av \log Co$$

where Co stands for the stimuli to be judged, and Av tells you to find the Arithmetical Mean of the logs. That is, you find the log of each Co, add these logs, divide by the number of Co, and find the antilogarithm of the quotient. When you have thus computed the Geometrical Mean of the Co, you find (in an experiment with weights anyway) that it is still too large; the actual PSE is smaller than the value predicted by the formula. Probably the difference here is the negative TE, so that PSE = GM + TE.

In many experiments *O* is confronted with other stimuli besides those of the Co series. There may be a Standard, as in Constant Stimuli, or an interpolated stimulus designed to modify the trace, or an "anchor" (Rogers, 1941) at the top or bottom or middle of the Co series. All these stimuli, Helson urges, tend to raise or lower the "adaptation level," a concept derived from work on vision (p. 367) and equivalent to the PSE, or functional mid-point of the whole series. (Adapta-

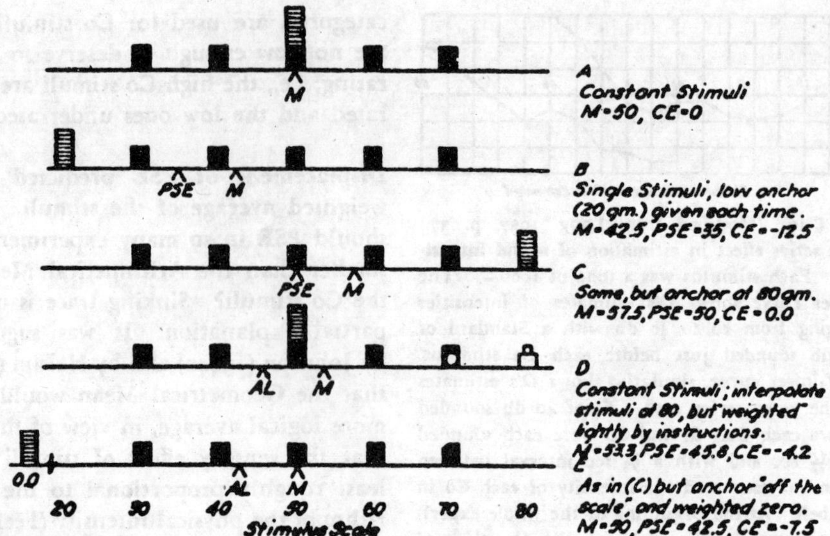

Fig. 8-20. PSE as the center of gravity of all the stimuli in an experiment. Lay a meter stick on a table and represent Co intensities of 30, 40, 50, 60, and 70 units by 3-oz weights laid at corresponding marks along the stick. If a St of 50 units is given before each Co, we must pile on five additional weights at the 50 mark, but these must be only 1-oz weights corresponding to the small weight of St in the formula. Now raise the loaded meter stick and find its center of gravity; it will balance nicely on a pencil slid under it at the 50-cm mark. It represents *O*'s state of readiness to judge the next Co; any Co applied above or below the PSE of 50 will tip the stick to its side and get a + or − judgment. So far we have disregarded the TE; to take account of it here and in the following diagrams we simply imagine all the stimuli (weights) to slip toward zero by three-fourths of the step interval of 10 cm. PSE is thus in each case .75 i to the left of M which is the weighted mean of the stimuli. (The stick itself is supposed to have no weight so that its center of gravity is determined wholly by the weights resting on it.)

The situation in Single Stimuli with a low anchoring stimulus given before each Co is shown in diagram (b). The anchor is treated the same as St in (a) with a loading of 1 oz per trial. The low anchor pulls PSE downward by a predictable amount and by combining with TE produces a large CE. But an anchor located above the Co series (c) raises PSE and may exactly cancel the TE or even do more and produce a positive CE, as in the "assimilation" experiments. The further out the anchor is from the middle of the Co series, the further it would displace PSE, according to the formula.

But interpolated stimuli that *O* is told to disregard must be given smaller weights (d). They have less assimilative effect on PSE. Finally, diagram (e) illustrates what happened in Pratt's experiment with a silent St-Co interval. This zero anchor is off the scale and has no effect on the balance. Not being regarded as any stimulus at all, it is completely disregarded. Other stimuli can probably be kept wholly out of the picture when they are obviously extraneous.

tion level is a more general term than PSE, for it can be applied to Single Stimuli, where there is no St to which Co may be "subjectively equal"; we shall meet adaptation level again, in later chapters, but for present purposes we will stick to the familiar PSE.) But to return to "anchoring" stimuli—they probably have less effect than the Co stimuli which receive the maximum of *O*'s attention. Good fit to experimental data was obtained when each Co was given 3 times as much weight as its paired St, and when TE was taken as equal to ¾ of the step interval (i) of the series. So Helson derived an empirical formula which reads, in slightly changed notation:

$$\log(\text{PSE} + 0.75\, i) = \frac{3\,\text{Av}\log\text{Co} + \log\text{St}}{4}$$

He elaborated this formula further to take account of an interpolated stimulus besides St and worked out the weight to be given this interpolated stimulus to fit certain data (Helson, 1947, pp. 6, 18).

For our purposes this approach serves to isolate some factors that are often lumped together as "the constant error." They can be illustrated by aid of a meter stick to represent the physical dimension along which the stimuli vary. We ought strictly to have a stick divided logarithmically, but the meter stick will do well enough (Fig. 8-20).[1]

[1] Problems like those described in this and the next chapter are often encountered in industry. For example, those who process foods and beverages may wish to find out whether a change in production methods yields a noticeable change in flavor, or whether the new product is preferred to the old. Many practical techniques have developed; although they were often set up independently, they resemble the standard psychophysical methods we have described. One very popular method is essentially a three-stimulus Frequency Method, called the Triangle Test; *O* tastes three samples, two of which are identical, and one slightly different, and is asked to pick out the odd one. The two substances are considered different if a group (*panel*) of *O*s does significantly better than chance. The literature is scattered in various technical journals, but a general view of the field will be found in a Symposium "Food Acceptance Methodology" to be published in 1954 under the auspices of the National Research Council and the Quartermaster Corps. Dawson & Harris (1951) presented an earlier summary (cf. p. 298).

9

PSYCHOPHYSICS II: SCALING METHODS

The preceding chapter was concerned with methods for determining the acuteness or sensitivity of our senses. It dealt with absolute and differential thresholds. Now we have the task of stepping off the whole range of each sense, of scaling it so that we can say that this sound is twice as loud as another, or that this gray is halfway between white and black. Of course, there are excellent physical scales for measuring stimuli, but we need something else; we need psychological scales for measuring sensations and perceptions. For example, suppose a radio engineer wants to design a set that sounds twice as loud as a competing brand. If he merely doubles the physical output, he will be disappointed to find that he has increased loudness by only a trifle more than a j.n.d., for Weber's fraction for loudness is about ⅓. How much *will* he have to step up the physical output to double the loudness? The methods for answering questions like this will be our concern in the present chapter. They have considerable theoretical as well as practical importance.

Before we go on to the actual methods, we must point out there are several types of scales, even for physical measurements:

1. *Ordinal scales,* which merely arrange things in order. An example from common experience is found in a race; we know that the man who took second place was slower than the winner and faster than he who took third place, but the ranks do not tell us how much difference there was between the three contestants. We shall see that statistical treatment of large masses of ranked data make it possible to develop fairly useful scales, but untreated ordinal scales are pretty primitive measuring devices.

2. *Equal-interval scales* go one step further, and let us say how much *difference* there is between two items or individuals. For example, on the ordinary thermometer there is as much difference between 60° and 70° as there is between 70° and 80°. But these scales do not have a true zero; so they do not permit absolute measurement; it is meaningless to say that 80° F. is twice as warm as 40° F.

3. *Ratio scales* have true zeros as well as equal steps. The scale of absolute temperature that is used in physics is an ex-

ample, but more familiar are inches, pounds and quarts. It is quite possible to say that an 8-inch stick is twice as long as a 4-inch one. This is the ideal type of scale.

How can we build psychological scales that will have equal units and a true zero? Perhaps we can get some hints from physical scales. Suppose you want to measure the length of some small objects but do not have a ruler handy. You can take a sheet of paper, and find the mid-point of one edge by folding it in half. You can continue to divide it into quarters, eighths, etc., to produce a scale of equal units. After you have measured your objects on this arbitrary scale, you can compare them as to relative length, just as well as if you had used a footrule. Can we do this sort of thing with sensations? We can certainly ask *O* to judge whether one sound is twice as loud, or half as loud, as another. We can also ask him to choose a series of gray cards that seem to represent equal steps of increasing brightness. This direct approach to building psychological scales seems plausible, but until recently psychologists—not to mention physicists—viewed it with doubt. It was pretty "subjective," and you could not check the size of units in different parts of the scale by direct comparison between them. On our improvised paper scale of length it was possible to measure the same object at any point on the scale, and still get the same results. You cannot do precisely that with sensations, but we shall see later in our discussion that there *are* internal checks on the equality of sensory units.

Because of these doubts, most workers resorted to indirect methods of building sensory scales. Our physical scale of temperature, given in degrees F., is an indirect scale. The unit of *temperature*, the thing scaled is defined in terms of its effect on a column of mercury in a thermometer. In other words, we scale temperature with the aid of equal units of length—the spacing of the marks on the thermometer. Perhaps we can find some comparable indirect unit for building scales of sensation. Several have been used: the DL, reaction time, and confidence of judgment. We shall describe the actual methods later; here we must point out that there is always the question whether the indirect measurement gives us a good psychological scale. At present the indirect scaling techniques are more highly developed than the direct ones, and they have given us some very useful scales. But the current tendency seems to be to accept the direct method as the ultimate check; if indirect and direct scaling methods yield different scales for the same sensory dimension, accept the direct scale as the correct one

SCALES BASED ON LIMINAL DIFFERENCES

Fechner's law. The most familiar method for scaling sensation goes back to Fechner (1860), who thought that Weber's law furnished the key to the measurement of mind. It is an indirect method, based on j.n.d. steps. Since Weber's law states that the DL is a constant fraction of the Standard stimulus, these steps must get bigger as we go up the scale of intensity. For example, consider a hypothetical sense with an RL of eight units, and a Weber's fraction of ½; the stimulus value of each new step is 1½ times the preceding one. This is shown in the first two columns appearing on page 236.

Steps	Stimulus value	Log stimulus	Increment of Log
0 (RL)	8.0	0.903	
			0.176
1	12.0	1.079	
			0.176
2	18.0	1.255	
			0.176
3	27.0	1.431	
			0.176
4	40.5	1.607	
			0.177
5	60.75	1.784	

These data are plotted in Figure 9-1. It is clear that successive steps require larger and larger increments in stimulus value. But the problem is difficult to

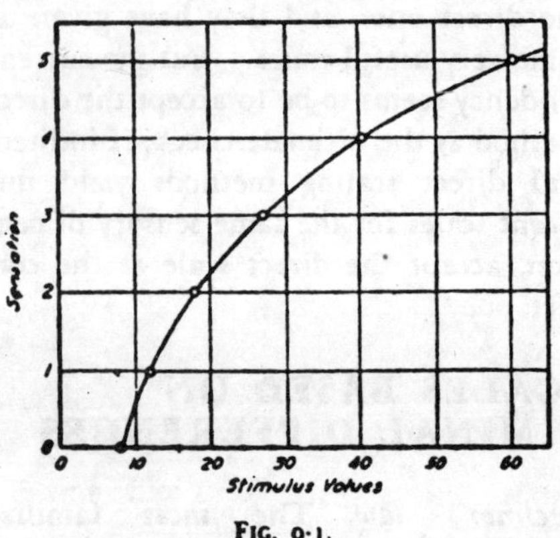

FIG. 9-1.

handle by straight arithmetic; even though we chose values for RL and Weber's fraction that would minimize decimals, the numbers started to get unwieldy by the fifth step, and we would have had to start rounding off decimals before many more. It is much more convenient to use logarithms. The corresponding log values have been entered in the third column; it will be noticed that the increments in the logs (last column) are constant. This is because we are always multiplying by a constant value ($1\frac{1}{2}$) which is accomplished by adding the log (0.176) of this value. When we plot log stimulus values on the base line, as in Figure 9-2, we get a straight line instead of a curve.

It is obvious that the logarithms are especially easy to use when we are interested only in the relative strength of a strong and a weak sensation. Without bothering to add up intermediate steps we can calculate the log stimulus value required to produce any desired level of sensation. Multiply the number of the step by the increment in log (which will be the log of one-plus-Weber's-fraction), add in the log of the RL, and we have the log of the desired stimulus. Fechner

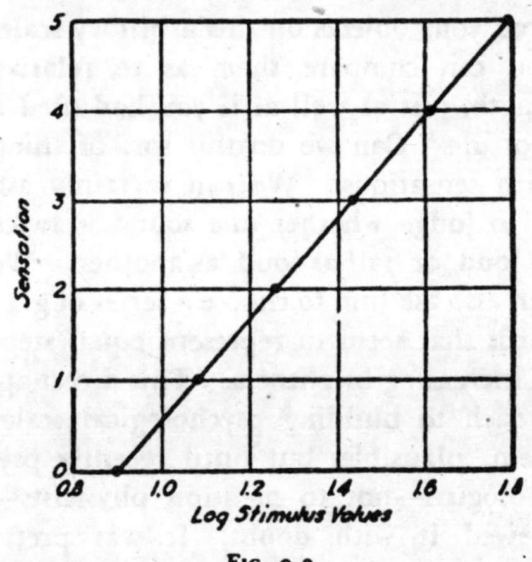

FIG. 9-2.

wrote several formulas for carrying out this operation, the most familiar of which is

$$S = K \log R$$

Remembering that R is the German abbreviation for stimulus, we read the formula: The strength of the sensation varies directly as the logarithm of the stimulus.

What Fechner did was to assume that (1) the j.n.d. was an equal increment in sensation, regardless of the absolute level at which it was taken, and (2) that a strong sensation was the sum of all the j.n.d. steps which came before it in the scale. Both of these assumptions have been questioned, and there has been a vast amount of fruitless controversy over the metaphysical question as to whether or not Fechner really measured mind with his formula. But if we forget this question, we can recognize his real contribution; he has given us a useful way of constructing sensory scales. The DL is at least a specific and defined step, regardless of the intensity level at which it is determined; a j.n.d. scale tells us how many discriminable steps separate two stimulus intensities, which is often useful. Further, we must remember that the DL is ultimately a measure of *variability* of the effectiveness of a stimulus (p. 220). Since the amount of variability in many biological and psychological processes is a constant fraction of the intensity of the process, we have many scales based on variability as the unit step; the use of standard scores (SD scores) in psychological testing is probably the most familiar example of this type of indirect scaling. So the summated j.n.d. scale has a fair claim to being an equal-step type of measurement. The steps are equally *perceptible*.

If we are going to base a scale on the DL, we can either add up the individual DL steps or we can use the more convenient logarithmic type of formula. The additive method is the more accurate if we are dealing with extremely weak or strong stimuli where Weber's law does not hold too well (p. 223), but the logarithmic treatment is satisfactory for the middle ranges in which the DL is a fairly constant fraction. Fortunately, the middle ranges are usually the more important ones.

Fechner's formula is a bit too compact for convenient use; we can specify the actual calculations better in a pair of general formulas. Let

s = any value of the stimulus;

s_0 = that particular value of the stimulus which is selected as the center or arbitrary zero, analogous to the zero of the thermometer;

r = the constant stimulus ratio by which each value of s must be multiplied in order to give the value lying one perception step higher up the scale (r = Weber fraction + 1.0). The perception step is defined in terms of the subject's responses and may be the DL, the SD or some other.

n = the number of perception steps from s_0 to s.

Then

$$s = s_0 r^n$$
$$\log s = \log s_0 + n \log r$$
$$n = \frac{1}{\log r}(\log s - \log s_0)$$

To adapt this general formula for use in any particular sense field, we need a well defined perception unit and the numerical value of r which corresponds to this unit. We must select an arbitrary value of the stimulus, s_0, analogous to the zero of the thermometer, above and below which we count our perception units. That is all we need, and the logarithmic formula is merely a convenience, involving no assumptions beyond Weber's law.

For example, to find the location in the musical scale of any assigned vibration frequency, we can take middle C of 260 cycles as our zero and the octave ($r = 2$) as our perception unit. The last equation then reduces to this: $n = 3.322 (\log s - 2.415)$. If $s = 10{,}000$ cycles, the equation gives us $n = 5.265$; i.e., the tone of 10,000 cycles is 5.265 octaves above middle C (cf. Michels & Helson, 1949).

The usefulness of Fechner's law. In the period before 1915 quite a few sensory scales were constructed (cf. Boring, 1942). But the objective psychologists of the next two decades had little interest in anything as "subjective" as a sensory scale (Boring, 1942, 1950; Murphy, 1949). But all during this period the facts subsumed by the law were utilized in practical affairs. For example, the telephone engineers found it convenient to use the *decibel* as a unit in specifying the intensity of auditory stimuli; the db is 1/10 of a log unit and corresponds very roughly to the DL. Those who worked in photography and optics were apt to use filters calibrated in *density*, again using a log scale. Munsell (p. 251) developed a three-dimensional system for specifying color, based on j.n.d. steps of hue, value, and chroma (i.e., hue, brightness, and saturation).

The sensory physiologists were also uncovering elevant facts through the use of electrical recording. In 1946 T. C. Ruch summarized the results as follows:

> Whatever its original derivation, Fechner's equation appears to express a fundamental feature of sense organ behavior. Over a certain range of intensities, the frequency of discharge is a linear function of the logarithm of the stimulus. This has been shown for the muscle spindle by Matthews, and for the *Limulus* eye by Hartline and Graham. Whether it describes the behavior of all forms of sense organs cannot be stated. (T. C. Ruch, 1946, p. 314; see also C. T. Morgan, 1942.)

The application of electrical recording techniques to audition yielded a lot of precise information about the functioning of the cochlea in animals. Here was a clear challenge; how do these results compare with those obtained by psychophysical methods on the human animal? To meet it, one could even try out "subjective" direct methods, like halving and doubling loudness, now that there were physiological data against which the findings could be checked. Let us turn to these direct methods of sensory scaling.

FRACTIONATION METHODS

The *method* of *sense-ratios*, as Boring (1942) calls this group, was used by Merkel around 1890; it involved the *doubling* of a sensory magnitude in an attempt to derive a scale. The method received relatively little attention until the 1930's, when Stevens (1936) pointed out its value for building a ratio scale for loudness. The results in this field were so impressive that the method was widely used in other dimensions. At present, many would consider it the fundamental one in constructing scales of subjective magnitude. The preferred operation is *halving*, rather than doubling, although checks have been made at setting 1/3, 3/4, ×2 and ×3 as well as 1/2. Let us start with the experiments in audition and follow the gradual extension of the method to other fields.

A scale of loudness. Stevens took his lead from Churcher (1935) who had brought together the results of several investigations to develop a loudness scale for industrial noise measurements. The methods used were as follows:

1. *O* was given a fixed tone of a certain loudness and asked to adjust another until it sounded half as loud. This was repeated at several values throughout the intensity range.

2. It happens that a tone will seem twice as loud if presented to both ears as it would if only one were stimulated (assuming both ears are equally acute). Accordingly, we find out how much stimulus energy must be fed into one ear to make the tone seem as loud as does the St delivered to both ears.

There were two minor methods of getting at "half-loudness" levels of a tone and all four methods yielded about the same values. Therefore, it was reasonable to assume that *O* could make satisfactory judgments to half of the loudness of a given tone.

Before constructing any scale we have

to define our units. For example, one *foot* is defined as the length of a standard object carefully preserved in a central location, with duplicate samples deposited in various places, such as the Bureau of Standards. Once this arbitrary unit is defined, the whole scale of length is tied down. This is true only of ratio scales, where there is a true zero point; for equal-interval scales, like temperature Fahrenheit, you need two points, as the freezing point of water (32°) and the boiling point of water (212°). Since the "sone" scale is supposed to be a ratio scale, one point should suffice. Stevens (1936) defined *one sone* as the loudness of a 1,000-cycle tone at 40 db above absolute threshold—a reference point used for other purposes in audition. To construct the scale we work step-wise; our one-sone tone was judged half as loud as one produced by about 47 db, so the loudness at this stimulus intensity is 2 sones. Similarly, we find the db equivalent of 4 sones (55 db) etc., as shown by the solid line in Figure 9-3, and carry our scale as far up as we wish. Then we work down from our reference standard to get the loudness of tones below 1 sone, but these cannot be read from the graph in Figure 9-3.

The surprising thing about the sone scale is the way it builds up at high intensity levels. The first 40 db contribute only one sone, but by the 80 db level we have reached 25 sones, and an additional 20 db gets us to a loudness of 80 sones. Compare this increasing build-up with the linear growth we would get if Fechner's law held; if sensation increased as the logarithm of the stimulus, we should obtain the straight broken line shown in Figure 9-3, for the base line is already in logarithmic units (dbs). It is clear that Fechner's law predicts a loudness scale very different from the one we obtain by halving apparent loudness. But what would we get if we corrected Fechner's law for the fact that Weber's fraction is larger at low intensities than at high? We could construct a *summated*

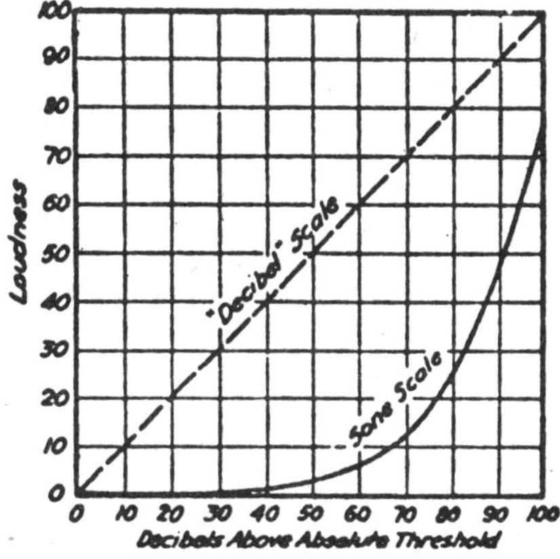

FIG. 9-3. (Redrawn from Stevens & Davis, 1938.) Loudness as a function of stimulus intensity. The solid curved line represents the increase in judged loudness (sones) as a function of stimulus strength in db. The ordinate in this figure is linear, for ease of reading values, but the more usual version uses logarithmic units to spread out the lower portions of the curve. The dashed line represents the growth of loudness as predicted by Fechner's law: since the ordinate is linear and the base line is logarithmic, the function must be a straight line. The slope of the Fechner line depends upon an arbitrary choice of unit size; for convenience we have taken the loudness change produced by one db as our unit. A summated DL curve would fall midway between the other two in position and shape.

DL curve to allow for this; Stevens (1936) showed that it is a halfway compromise between the two curves shown in the figure.

Which of these three curves is the "true" loudness scale? This may not be a good question, for our choice of scale may depend on the use to which we want to put it. Certainly the Fechner type of scale, the common db one, is useful in acoustics and telephone work. The summated DL scale tells us how many discriminable steps there are between any two points on the scale. But the sone scale has one major advantage; it agrees with the observed fact that fairly large increases in the db level of the stimulus have very little effect on loudness at low intensity ranges, whereas a few db added to high intensities make a great increase in loudness. This is just another way of saying that the sone scale has a certain amount of plausibility or "face validity" in that it is based on, and agrees with, direct judgments of relative loudness of various tones.

As a further check on the halving method, it is possible to try a different kind of fractionation. In a sense, the sone scale was constructed by halving the interval between zero stimulus and various standards. We could also try halving the interval between two tones of different loudness, as 60 and 100 db, to obtain a halfway point. The upper and lower halves of the interval could be bisected again, yielding ¼ and ¾ points. Now by bisecting the interval ¼ — ¾, we should get back to the original halfway point; actually we land a trifle too high for the indirectly determined halfway point, as shown by both Gage (1934) and by Newman, Volkmann & Stevens (1937). The discrepancy is not serious, and seems to be due to some constant error. In general, the results may be taken as confirming evidence for the sone scale. (But see Garner, 1952a, b.) This method is an old one, called the *method of equal sense distances* (p. 246).

A pitch scale. Encouraged by the success of the sone scale for loudness, Stevens, Volkmann & Newman (1937) tried the method on pitch. The scale used in music is a logarithmi ne, as indicated by the sequence of octaves: 256, 512, 1,024 . . . . cycles. These are musically equal through the middle range, though as long ago as 1883 Stumpf observed that the uppei octaves are perceptually larger than the lower ones. The question calls for an experiment. Ir the experiment, the fixed and variable stimuli alternated at 2 sec intervals. *O*'s task was to set the variable, by turning a crank, until it seemed half as high in pitch as St. This was done by five *O*s at each of 10 frequency values distributed over the range 125–12,000 cycles. There was moderate agreement among the *O*s as to the setting at each value The Geometric Means of the stimulus values judged half as loud are plotted against a log abscissa in Figure 9-4. It will be

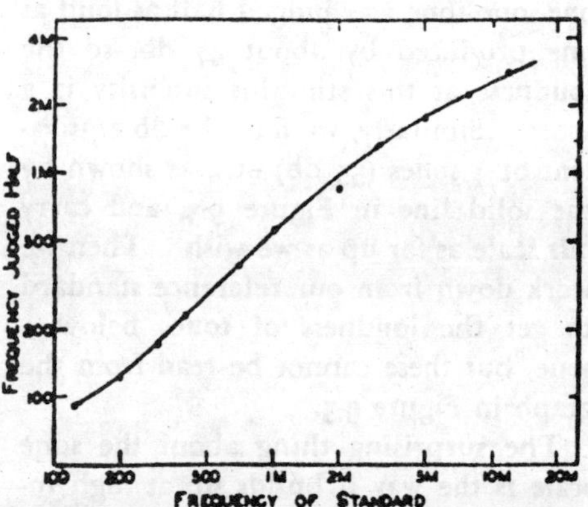

FIG. 9-4. (Stevens, Newman & Volkmann, 1937.) The ordinate value of each plotted point represents the frequency of the tone which is judged half as high as the base line value of the point. Logarithmic units are used to condense the upper end of the curve.

seen that they yield a smooth curve, which suggests that a stable function is being measured.

Now for the method of computing an equal-interval scale of psychological pitch. We shall explain a graphic method, which is more accurate than the crude method we described for sones, but a bit harder to follow. Set up the graph shown as Figure 9-5 in which frequency is on the base line, and the psychological unit ("mels") on the ordinate —both in log units, to condense the upper parts of the curve. Then assign the value of 1,000 mels to the tone of 1,000 cycles, as a reference point. The tone judged half as high would have a value of 500 mels, by definition; it had been found in the experiment to correspond to 558 cycles. Hence plot the value for 500 mels (ordinate) at 558 cycles (base line). To determine the 250-mel point read up from 558 cycles, using an enlarged version of Figure 9-4, find the frequency of the tone that would have been judged half as high, and plot that. To compute values above 1,000 mels, it is necessary to reverse the process. Find the stimulus value of the tone which, when halved, gives 1,000 mel; this value can be read by running a line over to the curve from 1 M on the ordinate, and dropping a line to the base line from the point of intersection. This will be the stimulus value for 2,000 mels, and can be used to determine 4,000 mels, etc. When the points are connected with a smoothed line, as in Figure 9-5, the final scale is graphically represented.

This curve gives us another chance to test Fechner's law. If it held, the curve should be a straight diagonal line, since equal sensory units on the ordinate are plotted against log cycles on the base line. Fechner's law does not hold in its simple form. But if correction is made for the varying size of Weber's fraction, by plotting the sum of DLs on the ordinate, one gets very good agreement with the mel scale.

There were minor errors in the original mel scale. Stevens and Volkmann (1940) made some internal checks on it, and eventually found that the trouble arose because some *O*s could not formulate a stable idea of zero pitch. Hence *E* made available to *O* a *very* low pitch, which he could sound as desired. *O* was told that the tone was essentially at

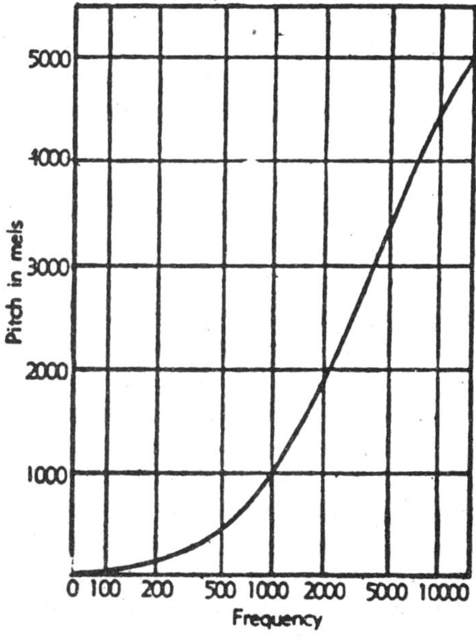

FIG. 9-5. (Stevens, Newman & Volkmann, 1937.) The pitch in mels—ordinate—of the frequencies represented on the base line. This curve is derived from Figure 9-4 by the method described in the text.

zero pitch. This seemed to clear up the trouble. In a sense this changed the method from "halving" to "bisection of an interval," but the two methods are highly similar. Perhaps the biggest difference is that halving, as usually employed, is supposed to give a true *ratio scale;* not only equal intervals, but a zero point. Perhaps the mel scale is merely an equal-interval scale, like Fahrenheit or Centigrade; in that case, its zero would be merely an arbitrary and convenient reference point. At any rate, the experiment furnishes a good example of the methods (and pitfalls) of scale construction.

Other sensory modalities. Why does the integrated DL scale agree with the "halving" scale for pitch and not for loudness? Stevens, Volkmann and Newman suggested a possible explanation. A change in pitch, according to the *place* theory of hearing, involves a change in the locus of the excitation on the basilar membrane. Hence, the DL for pitch depends on the spatial separation of stimulated areas, and these distances add up, like inches. But in the case of loudness, the DL and subjective magnitude seem to depend on different mechanisms. This raises an interesting point. Fechner had suggested that the *magnitude* of a sensation represented the sum of DL units; the extension to *qualitative* dimensions, like pitch and hue, came later (Boring 1942). Yet, in audition the rule seems to hold for the quality (pitch) and not the magnitude, (loudness). What happens in other sensory modalities?

A subjective scale of weight. Harper & Stevens (1948) used the halving method to construct a scale of perceived weight using the word *veg* to describe the unit. The integrated j.n.d. scale does not agree with the new scale; the j.n.d. is about 10 times as many vegs at 300 grams as it is at 100 grams. Is there any obvious source of distortion in the veg scale? *O* may have been committing what Titchener called the *stimulus error;* that is, halving the physical weight of the stimulus rather than the magnitude of the resulting sensation. This error should be particularly dangerous when we deal with familiar objects like weights. Not only have we had extensive experience with a formal physical scale, so that we can make rough estimates in terms of pounds, but we also know how much heavier two books "feel" compared to one, etc. This lifelong experience with physical objects that can be added and subtracted would seem likely to distort any subjective scale of weight, based directly on some physiological sensory process. If Titchener was right in claiming that the stimulus error accounted for the failure of "equal-appearing interval" scales to agree with Fechner's law, the veg scale should repre-

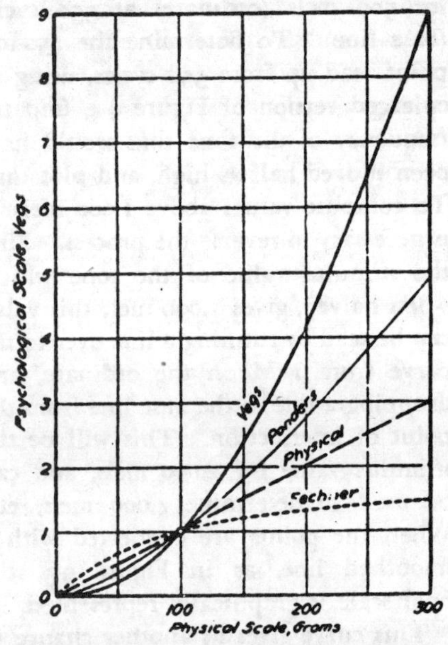

FIG. 9-6. Various scales for weight. The veg and ponder curves were constructed as was the mel scale (Fig. 9-5). Since the units differed in these two scales, the ordinates have been adjusted so that the curves meet at 100 grams. If *O* judged weight correctly in terms of grams or some other physical unit, the resulting scale would be shown by the diagonal line labeled "physical." On the other hand, if Fechner's law held, the reversed curve would be obtained. The slopes of the two latter curves have been adjusted to meet the first two curves at 100 grams. The corresponding ordinates have been omitted for simplicity. The veg scale rises to 40 vegs at 700 grams. It holds only for weights lifted by a hand-and-forearm movement.

sent a compromise between a logarithmic (Fechner) and a linear (physical) scale. That it does not is shown in Figure 9-6. The heavy curve in the cut shows how subjective magnitude in vegs (ordinate) increases as a function of the stimulus in grams (base line). For comparison, we have added a straight diagonal line to represent a subjective scale which conformed to the physical one, and a logarithmic curve to follow Fechner's law. The veg scale is clearly not a compromise between them; it even bends in the opposite direction. We have also added a fourth curve, labeled "ponders." This comes from an unpublished experiment by Taback (1940) and seems to have been obtained by a method similar to that used for vegs. Fortunately Rogers (1941) gives enough representative values to permit construction of the curve, adjusted by a constant to bring the mid values into agreement with vegs. The "ponder" scale looks like the veg scale, flattened a bit by stimulus errors. All things considered, it looks as if the Fechner type of scale differs fundamentally from one constructed by halving in the case of weights, as was true in loudness.

Taste. Lewis (1948) constructed scales of subjective magnitude for the four primary tastes (salt, sweet, sour and bitter). The methods and results were quite similar to those for loudness and weight. There were available in the literature j.n.d. scales for salt, sweet, and bitter; in each case the new scale disagreed with the old. The difference was in the usual direction in that the subjective size of the j.n.d. increased fairly regularly as the stimulus became stronger.

This work was followed up (Beebe-Center & Waddell, 1948; Beebe-Center, 1949) by cross-modality comparisons. It is possible for *O* to select a solution of sodium chloride which is as salty as one of sucrose is sweet, for example. By this method they were able to tie together scales for all four qualities. It remained to define the unit (one *gust*) as the subjective strength of a 1-percent solution of sucrose. Once the sweet

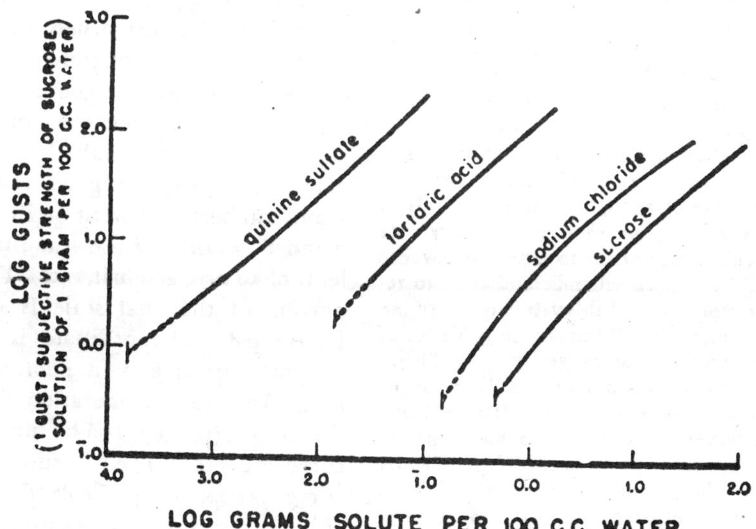

FIG. 9-7. (Beebe-Center & Waddell, 1948.) Taste scales.

scale had thus been anchored to a stimulus value, it was possible to specify all four scales in terms of stimulus concentrations. From the resulting figure (Fig. 9-7) you can tell how to make up a solution of quinine sulphate which will be as bitter as a given concentration of tartaric acid is sour! Using these scales, Beebe-Center made up a set of standards, and used them to test and describe substances like jam, coffee, and pickles. Again we see that subjective scales might have some practical value.

It is probably too early to consider the gust scales as more than approximations. In taste (and in weights, too) it is necessary to supply *O* with a limited range of Co stimuli from which he must pick the one he judges to be half as strong as St. It is perfectly possible that *O* picks his "half" stimulus as the mid-point of this series, rather than as half as strong as St. It will be recalled that Helson proposed a formula for computing this mid-point, PSE or "Adaptation Level" (p. 231). This formula, or even the simple geometric mean of the Co stimuli, agrees very well with the values Lewis gives for halving, except in the case of salt. Similarly, the geometric means of the stimuli fit the Harper and Stevens veg scale almost as well as do their own data. At first glance this would suggest that *O* doesn't halve the sensation at all; he merely picks the stimulus which corresponds to the level of adaptation induced by the stimuli given him. Actually this is not the case; MacLeod (personal communication) found that *O* would not pick a "half" stimulus if there is no Co strong enough to suit him. It is necessary to carry out some preliminary tests with a wide range of Co to determine where the "half" stimulus will fall, and then to restrict the range around this value to determine it more accurately. Thus the coincidence of the mid-point of Co range and the "half" point, which we noted above, is the result of preliminary experimentation. It is still possible, however, that the series has some influence on the "half" value. This difficulty was particularly troublesome in the difficult cross-quality judgments, as matching a sweet and a sour solution for subjective strength (Beebe-Center & Waddell)

A second source of error in the gust scale may be found in simple sensory adaptation. In Lewis' experiment *O* always tasted St first, rinsed his mouth, and then tasted one of the Co samples immediately. Thus, the Co should seem too weak against the background of remaining adaptation to the relatively stronger St. MacLeod (1952) repeated the halving experiment with sugar solutions, but allowed one minute between stimuli. This may have introduced a TE, but some controls were made to check against this new error. At any rate, MacLeod's curve is much more bent over at the upper end than is the sucrose curve in Figure 9-7.

Brilliance. So far we have found that intensive subjective scales in three different sense modalities depart consistently from Fechner's law. One qualitative scale, pitch, obeys the summated DL version. What would happen in the case of visual brilliance? This dimension may be considered an intensive one, since it is primarily related to the amount of light energy reflected from the object. But in some ways it resembles a quality. This is especially clear when we deal with colored objects, where the average person is apt to use *strong* to apply to saturation as well as brightness.

Hanes (1949a, 1949b) tried the halving method on the brightness of a patch of light. In the two studies he covered a range from 0.0001 to 500 millilamberts —a ratio of 1 to 5,000,000, compared to about 1 to 20 obtainable with papers. Hanes arbitrarily assigned 100 *bril* to 1 millilambert, and went on in the usual manner to calculate the stimulus equivalents of 50 bril, 200 bril, etc. The major portion of the final scale is shown in Figure 9-8. The ordinate is in *brils*, and the base line is in *photons*, a unit that takes into consideration the size of the pupil (p. 367). The dots on the curve are taken from a summated DL curve prepared by Troland (1929–II). In this dimension it seems to be true that subjectively equal units correspond closely to the DL at various points in the scale of intensities. In fact, one can convert from brils to DLs by multiplying by 1.61. This indicates that they both measure the same thing, just

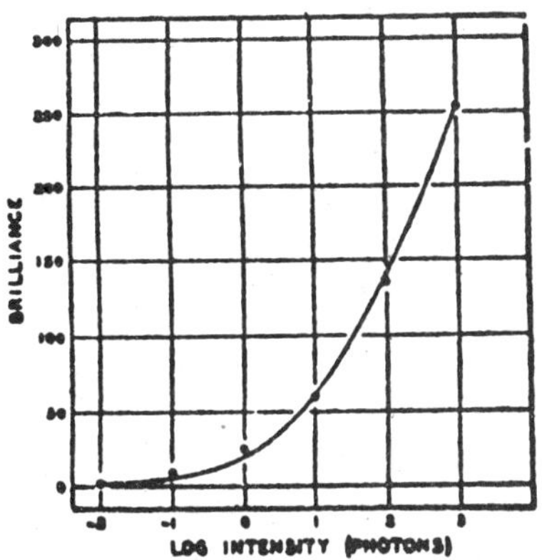

FIG. 9·8. (Hanes, 1949a.) The relation of the brilliance function (solid curve) to the integrated DLs (circles) for brilliance. The ordinate is in DLs, which must be multiplied by 1.61 to give brils. The base line is in units of retinal illumination.

as inches and centimeters are both measures of length.

Hanes made a number of internal checks on the scale, such as having *O* make estimates of ⅓ St, double St, and triple St. These estimates are harder than "half" to make, and yield more variable results, but they are not badly out of line with predictions made from the original bril scale based on halving. These internal checks are considered important if we are to claim that the subjective scale is a true ratio scale, comparable to physical ones of length and weight. The fact that they rarely work out perfectly is often taken as an argument against the validity of subjective scales, but probably simply mirrors the effect of specific factors in the experimental situation, as series effects, or the difficulty *O* has in imagining fractions like ⅓: Hanes found ¾ particularly bad. As a result, present sensory scales are somewhat crude, like the folded-paper rule we described on page 235, but they seem fundamentally sound.

Subjective scales for more complicated dimensions. Thus far we have limited our discussion to halving in traditional sensory dimensions, where we have other data, such as the DL, and physiological knowledge, with which we can compare our new scales. Now let us turn to other applications of the halving method. One of the earliest uses of the halving technique was the construction of a scale for *numerousness* of dots (Taves, 1941). We have already discussed the results, for the scale shows a break or discontinuity at about six dots, and was taken as evidence for the importance of the span of attention or apprehension. Taves used the typical halving method. He exposed slides containing from 2 to 180 dots, and asked *O* to pick a slide that contained half as many. *O* did not have time to count the dots; he just made his choice on the basis of impression. Figure 4·12 (p. 98) shows that Taves obtained a regular scale. Numerousness acts like other intensive magnitudes, in that DLs are not subjectively equal.

Reese (1943), after a careful examination of the theory underlying measurement, concluded that the equal unit scale of this type comes nearer to meeting the criteria than does any other. He then proceeded to construct scales for three quite different magnitudes; visual rate, subjective difficulty of memory span items (digits), and subjective difficulty of multiple-choice vocabulary items. He was successful in all three. In the visual-rate experiment he had *O* set the rate of a variable stimulus so that it appeared to be flashing at one half the rate of St. The results showed a break in the function, quite similar to that found by Taves, at about 5 flashes per second. Reese presented evidence that two different processes were involved; below the break *O* was judging the *duration* of each flash, and doubling it, while above the break he was judging *rate* directly, and halving it.

The extension of the halving method to dimensions like subjective difficulty of memory span or test items offered no new difficulties. However, it is interesting in that we are constructing a subjective dimension that has no physical counterpart. This points up the fact that psychological scaling is not dependent on a physical scale; all that we need is some way of identifying the items that are to be scaled. One or more of these items can then be used as reference points for the subjective scale, and all other items, old and new, arranged at appropriate points on the scale. We shall see later that the same thing is true of other scaling methods, as rating; when so used, the methods might better be called psychometric than psychophysical.

Before we go on to other methods, it might be well to evaluate the "halving" method of subjective scaling. It received a lot of attention in recent years because it was relatively new. Furthermore, it seems to be a direct way of constructing ratio scales, rather than an indirect one, which gives it a sort of "face validity" that the other methods do not have. The ultimate test of the method will come when it is compared with some more fundamental knowledge about the physiological mechanisms of the individual senses. We must keep two questions separate: (1) Is the method fundamentally sound? and (2) What errors crop up in applying it to specific subjective dimensions? Dividing a chocolate bar "by eye" is a valid method of halving it, but the two segments do not always turn out to be exactly equal.

METHOD OF EQUAL SENSE DISTANCES

There are a number of methods in which *O* tries to select or adjust a series of stimuli so that they mark off subjectively equal distances along some continuum. The first of these, *bisection*, was used by Plateau in the 1850's. He had artists paint a gray which was midway between white and black—in other words, there was as much distance, subjectively, between white and gray as between gray and black. The method was developed by Delboeuf, Müller, and Titchener (1905, II, ii; cf. Boring, 1942). The basic purpose was to test Fechner's law. If the mid-point fell at the Geometric, rather than the Arithmetic Mean, Fechner was right. Sometimes the mid-point fell at one Mean, sometimes at the other, and sometimes in between. We shall not go into the old arguments to which Titchener devoted a large section of his book (above). The method is clearly subjected to the same errors we discussed under fractionation. Indeed, the method of bisection of an interval is very similar to halving a magnitude. About the only difference is that halving may give a true zero for the scale as we have already seen (p. 235).

Sanford's experiment. Of course, there is no reason to limit experiments to bisection; one can break up a subjective distance into as many equal intervals as desired. Thus in Sanford's weight experiment (Titchener, 1905, I, p. 33) 108 envelopes, ranging between 5 and 100 gm. are sorted into five heaps, keeping approximately equal sense distances between piles. If the average of all the weights placed in each pile is plotted on a logarithmic ordinate, against linear units (subjective magnitude) on the base line, Fechner's law would predict that they should fall on a straight line. Figure 9-9 plotted from one "typical" O (Titchener, 1905, II, p. 82) is in fair agreement with Fechner's law. But

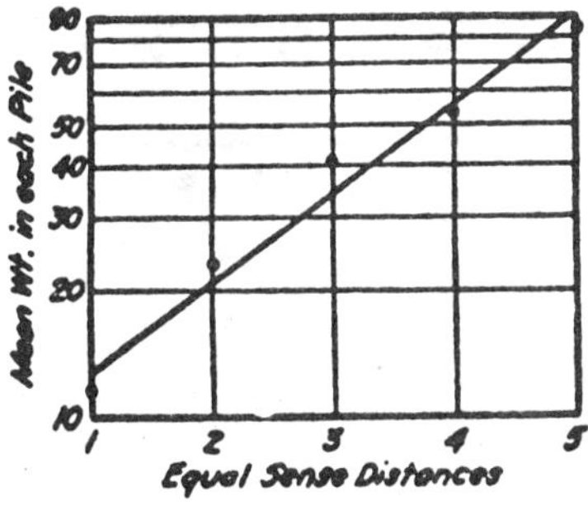

FIG. 9-9. (Data of an experiment of Sanford, reported by Titchener, 1905, ii, p. 82.) Mean weight assigned to each of five equal-sense-distances piles. The line shows where the points would fall if Fechner's law held.

there are a couple of things wrong with the experiment. In the first place, Titchener used the arithmetic mean of each pile; if you are going to end up with a log stimulus scale, you should start by averaging log stimulus values, to obtain a geometric mean. This point probably makes little actual difference in the results for the short range of weights that would fall in one pile, but one should be consistent throughout statistical treatment, and not start by averaging raw numbers, and end with a logarithmic scale.

The second difficulty is the distribution of the weights themselves. The 26 small ones differed from each other by only 0.2 gm, whereas the heaviest 25 differed in 2-gm steps. Here we encounter the old question of series effects, but this time with a vengeance. If O merely arranged the five piles to have an equal number of weights in each, the series is so constituted that the average weight for each pile would be very similar to the result actually obtained. In other words, the results are apt to be forced by the original selection of stimuli. This difficulty is not peculiar to the present method, for it plagues everyone who attempts psychological scaling. In some fields it can be minimized by letting O adjust a continuously variable stimulus until its intensity satisfies him, as in the Stevens, Volkmann & Newman (1937) experiment on halving pitch (p. 240). But you cannot readily vary weight in a continuous fashion by turning a crank. Perhaps the next best bet would be to let O take his weights, one at a time, from a very large pile, on the theory that he would not expect a small sample from a large pile to be equally distributed on his scale. But the best way to meet the difficulty is to vary the series of stimuli in a known way and see what effect this variation has on the resulting scale. We have already made some beginnings in this direction in our discussion of series effects (p. 225), which we ended with a discussion of a meter stick model. Let us return to it now.

Asymmetrical scale distortions. The meter-stick model does very well in telling us what happens to the PSE, or midpoint of the series when anchors (or extra Co stimuli, for that matter) are added to one end of the series. In other words, it suffices for judgments lumped into two categories, with only one intercategory threshold. But sometimes we want to carry several categories through our calculations, and compute N-1 intercategory thresholds (p. 212). In such cases we often find that unbalanced stimulus series distort our whole judg-

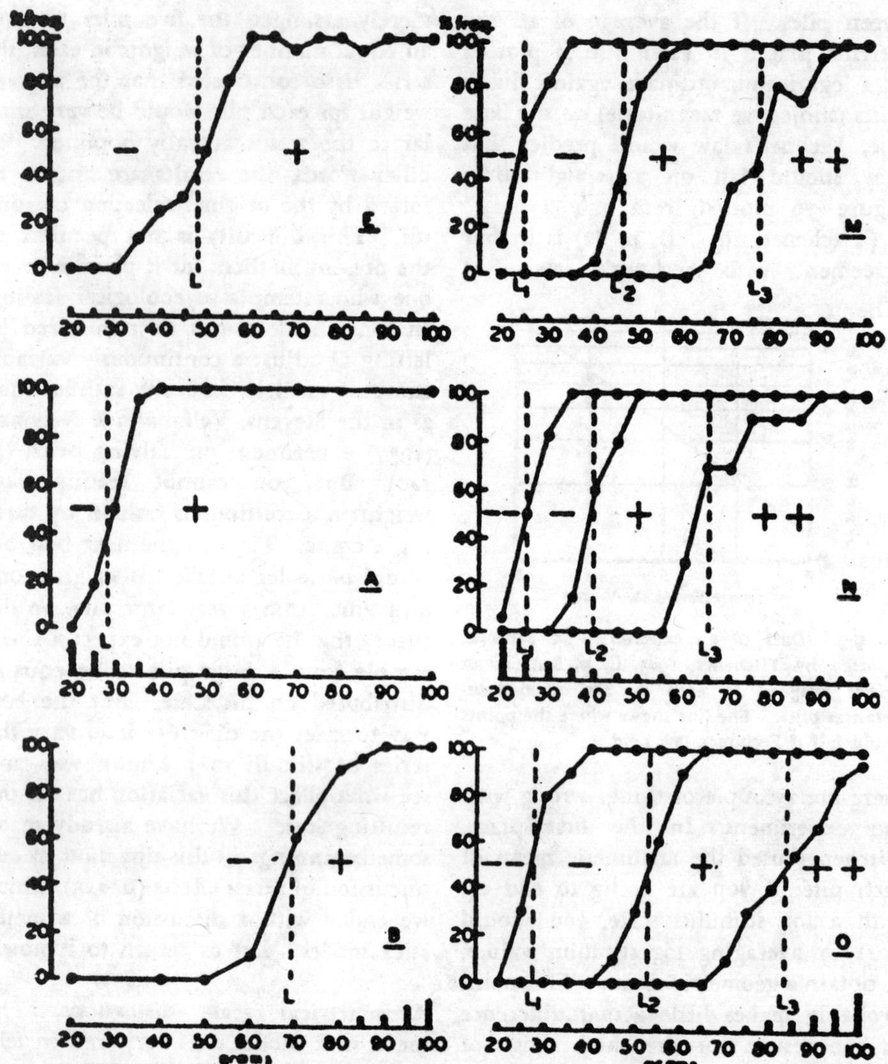

FIG. 9-10. (From D. M. Johnson, 1944a.) Psychometric functions from two- and four-category judgments. The dotted vertical lines represent limens, or transition points between categories, based on 50 percent. The upper figures were from normal series, with Co weights evenly distributed. The middle figures show the effects of loading the lower end of the series, with weights distributed as shown by dots on the base line. The bottom figures come from series loaded at the upper end.

ment scale, shrinking some categories and stretching others. These distortions are neatly illustrated by some work of D. M. Johnson (1944a). He used lifted weights, distributed as shown by the dots on the base lines below the various graphs in Figure 9-10.

The upper two curves present results from normal series; the one on the left uses two categories, while that on the right has four. The single ogive separating the two categories looks symmetrical, with the PSE shifted by a time error, as expected. The three inter-category thresholds in the right-hand figure are fairly evenly spaced. But notice what happens in the second pair of figures, where the Co stimuli are stacked up at the lower end of the series. The two-category method, on the left, shows only a shift downward of the ogive, and its PSE is appropriately displaced, as our meter stick would have predicted. However, the four-category plot shows that much more happened; all three ogives are displaced downward, with the lowest category having the greatest shrinkage. The third pair of figures shows that concentration of Co at the heavy end has just the opposite effect.

Johnson worked out a logarithmic formula to handle the shifts in an approximate fashion, and Helson's weighted Geometric Mean (p. 231) does a very good job of predicting the two-category results.

We can produce even more striking changes in the category thresholds by introducing unrealistic anchors. For example, in Rogers' (1941) experiment on judging inclination of lines, *E* asked *O* to use six categories, assigning No. 1 to the smallest slope and No. 6 to the greatest. *E* always presented an anchor before each line to be judged, telling *O* that the anchor was the slope which should be called No. 6. The inclinations of the stimuli always varied within the range between 10° and 40°. In the first series, the anchor was 40°, and perfectly regular data were obtained. But on successive series *E* moved the anchor, defining category No. 6, more and more beyond the actual range of stimuli that were to be judged. The scale of judgments seemed to stretch, following the anchor at one end, but remaining attached to the bottom of the stimulus range at the other end. Thus, with an anchor at 60°, the scale had stretched so that only four categories were used by *O* to cover the stimulus range. But the stretching was not always uniform, and sometimes the scale seemed to break loose from a very unrealistic anchor. Rogers found that different *O*s showed different breaking points; in short, he thought that the reaction to a conflicting stimulus series and anchoring stimulus might be an individual personality characteristic.

Anchoring effects with other materials. These results are not peculiar to a scale of inclination of lines. Rogers ran a parallel experiment on weights and got the same sort of phenomena. In a later study H. R. McGarvey (1943) obtained strikingly similar results with verbal materials. She used two types of items: *social prestige of occupations* in one experiment and *undesirability of forms of behavior* in a second one. When dealing with such material, one does not have any sort of physical scale for the stimulus objects, as grams or degrees. Before McGarvey could start her main experiment, she had to collect a large number of possible items, and have them scaled by a rating method: she used a graphic method, tied down by examples which the *O*s judged as extreme (see p. 252). She then picked 12 items, two at each of six equally spaced intervals, for her series stimuli, and additional ones as anchors—all based on the preliminary rating by the *O* with which they were to be used. Once the items were scaled in this fashion, they were used much as were the weights or lines in Rogers experiment. The fact that verbal materials are subject to the same anchoring effects as are simple physical objects may be taken as evidence that we are dealing with some general laws of judgment.

In an earlier experiment, Hunt & Volkmann (1937) showed that anchoring effects worked in a roughly similar fashion in judgments of pleasantness and unpleasantness of colors. In this experiment they used an imaginary anchor. *O* was instructed to think of the most pleasant color he could and assign it category *seven* (they used a seven-point scale). Hunt (1941) extended the study of anchoring effects, with both real and imagined anchors, to judgments of ivory carvings, paintings, and "crimes." Although these experiments were not as detailed as those of Rogers and McGarvey, they certainly show the generality of the phenomena. Volkmann did a number of related experiments that have appeared only in abstracts of verbal reports; they are described in greater detail by McGarvey (1943), who studied under Volkmann.

What do equal sense distance scales measure? The study of anchoring effects serves to emphasize the fact that the equal-appearing interval scale is strikingly subject to the conditions under which it is built up. This should be a warning to those who attempt to find out anything about basic sensory processes by this method. But with proper precautions the method can be made to yield good results, even in scaling a sensory dimension. This is illustrated by some results which Newhall (1950) gave in a description of a convenient device for collecting judgments. Both the device and the results are shown in Figure 9-11. In this case *O* was given a strip containing a series of 12 gray samples, ranging from white to almost black. The strip, labeled in terms of Munsell "value," is drawn at the top of the figure, for convenience. *O* is also given a sheet of graph paper and some small markers—buttons would do. He places a marker in each vertical column, and

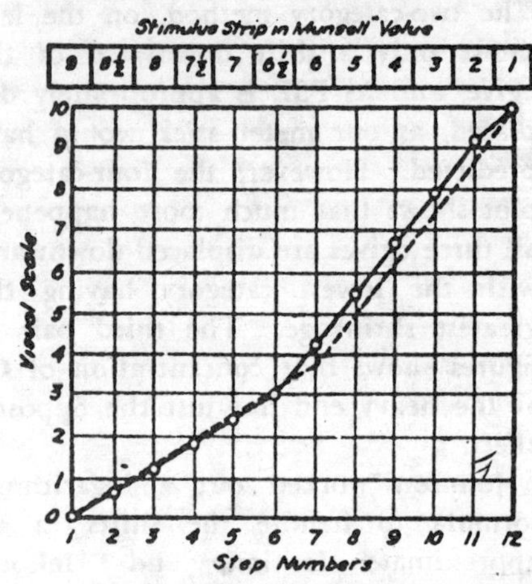

FIG. 9-11. (After Newhall, 1950.) A method of evaluating the spacing of visual scales. The strip at the top is made up of 12 gray samples of paper. A marker is assigned to each sample, and *O* arranges the markers so that the vertical distance between them is proportional to the subjective distance between samples. Each circle represents the average position of the markers set for the particular strip above, which is labeled in terms of Munsell steps of "Value" (brightness). Since the first six samples increase by full steps, and the second six by half steps, the theoretical position of the markers would conform to the broken line.

adjusts all the markers until he is satisfied that their vertical spacing corresponds to the sensory "distances" between their brightnesses. *E* then reads off on the ordinate the relative position of each marker, which gives directly the position of the stimulus on a subjective scale.

The circles in Figure 9-11 represent

the average settings of 10 *Os*, using the stimulus series shown. In this case we know a lot about the stimuli. They were chosen from the Munsell scale (Munsell, Sloan & Goodlove, 1933), in which the units represent equal steps on a summated j.n.d. scale. Further, we know that a j.n.d. scale for brightness agrees with one constructed by halving (p. 244). Hence we can plot the position at which each marker *should* be placed if Newhall's method agrees with other results. The predicted position is shown by the broken lines. Note that Newhall put the method to a severe test by using an unbalanced series, increasing by single units to a value of 6, and then by half units to 9. The resulting series effect caused only a small distortion at the point where the stimulus series shifted from whole to half unit jumps. Newhall got at least as good "fits" with two other irregular series. The results are not due to suggestion, for *O* was not told anything about the samples—he was merely asked to judge them.

This method is something like the Method of Adjustment, applied to scaling. Unlike methods that force single judgments, it permits *O* to work up and down the scale at will, making as many readjustments of the markers as he wishes before the results are tabulated. At any rate, it certainly seems to minimize series effects in judging visual brightness, and it yields results in agreement with those obtained by integrating j.n.d.'s and by the halving method (but not the logarithmic formulation of Fechner and of Michels & Helson, 1949, or the square root of reflectance scale of Fullerton & Cattell, 1892). It would be interesting to try the method on weights, where Fechner's law, integrated j.n.d.'s, and halving all yield different results; if Newhall's checkerboard method agreed with one of these other methods, it would be reasonable to assume that both methods had avoided series effects and were really doing a good job of scaling the sensory dimension.

Rating scales. Most of the studies we have discussed so far are called *psychophysical;* i.e., they are concerned with the psychological scaling of objects which can be arranged on a physical continuum. Thus we can plot the relationship between *sones* (psychological) and *decibels* (physical). The fact that we can specify our stimulus objects in physical terms is a great help in studying various types of constant errors. But we can construct psychological scales perfectly well even when there is no convenient physical continuum on which we can arrange the stimulus objects, as we noted previously (pp. 245–246; cf. McGarvey, 1943). Such scales are often called *psychometric.* Perhaps the most familiar example of this type is the rating scale.

Galton (1883) seems to have been the first to develop a scale of this type. His purpose was to quantify a strictly psychological function, the vividness of images. Major (1895) used a sort of rating scale for the determination of the affective value of colors. Since then, the rating scale has been used intermittently for various purposes in experimental psychology. But the average person is much more familiar with rating scales for the description and evaluation of personality characteristics. Very few people get through high school without being rated, and the method is widely used in industry, the armed forces, and wherever some simple numerical description of people is desired. Many of the scales are amateur affairs.

but the better ones are constructed to minimize constant errors, and are excellent measuring instruments.

The ideal rating scale is one with equal intervals. From what we know of the Method of Equal-appearing Intervals, it is clear that the rating scale must be tied down or anchored if it is to have equal units or a stable reference point. The difficulty is how to do this. One typical way is to use descriptive adjectives, thus:

Very Poor Poor Fair Good Excellent

The rater, of course, makes a check on the line above the phrase which best describes the person rated. The only trouble is that most of the checks are apt to land in the central category—unless the rater is a chronic optimist or pe imist. To spread out and stabilize the ratings, the descriptive phrases are often made more specific, even to the extent of listing typical items of behavior. Or the rater may be told to let each category represent 20 percent of the college population, for example. Still another attempt to tie down the scale uses specific individuals, known to all raters, as anchors for each category. In spite of all these devices, the rater will tend to approximate a normal distribution if he rates many individuals. One can never be sure whether this represents a "series effect" in the rater, or the fact that most traits are normally distributed; there is no external check.

Considerable attention has been devoted to CEs, as "halo" effects, and to individual differences between judges. These systematic errors can be minimized by the construction of the scale, or adjusted by using standard scores.[1] The reader who is interested in further information about rating scales should consult Guilford (1936). He will find many parallels between rating scale and single stimulus methods. In fact the chief difference is not between the two methods, but between the types of material on which they are used. Single Stimuli, the method used with stimuli that can be controlled and specified in physical terms, would seem to be the better place to study the laws of judgment. Rating scales are extremely convenient devices when dealing with the important stimulus objects and qualities that cannot be specified in this fashion.

[1] One convenient method of treating data from rating scales is to convert each judge's ratings into ranks and then treat as shown on pages 257–259.

PAIRED COMPARISON

At least two accepted methods of scaling—*relative* scaling—can be traced back to Fechner's pioneer work in experimental esthetics (1876) and to his *method of choice.* This rudimentary method is illustrated by his study of the pleasingness of rectangles. He prepared cardboard rectangles ranging in proportion from a square to a narrow oblong and spread them haphazard on a table. He asked several hundred persons, individually, to choose the most pleasing shape and also the least pleasing. Then he could use the relative frequency of choices as an index—so he argued—of the true esthetic appeal of each rectangle. The favorable choices fell mostly in the middle of the series (near the "golden section") and the unfavorable ones toward the extremes.

The two more highly developed forms of the method of choice are known as the Ranking Method and the Method of Paired Comparison. If Fechner had asked O to arrange all the rectangles in a row with the most pleasing at one end and the least pleasing at the other, this rank order would have furnished much additional information. If he had shown only two rectangles at a time and asked *O* to choose the more pleasing, and done the same with all the possible pairs, again he would have obtained much more information than by his simple method of choice. Or he could have taken a certain rectangle as the Standard, presented each of the others as a Co along with the St, and had *O* judge Co as more or less pleasing than St, after the manner of the Method of Constant Stimuli. This last suggestion has not been found very good psychologically in studies of esthetic or other values, because *O* becomes oversatiated with the recurring Standard specimen. Logically and mathematically, however, we shall see that the Method of Paired Comparison is reducible to that of Constant Stimuli, and furthermore that the Ranking Method is reducible to that of Paired Comparison.

The Method of Paired Comparison was introduced by Cohn (1894) in his study of color preferences. It is often regarded as the most adequate way of securing value judgments. *O*'s task at any one moment is simplified to the utmost because he has only two specimens before him. He compares these in a certain respect, passes to another pair, and so on till all the specimens have been judged. If every specimen is paired with every other one, the number of pairs is $n(n-1)/2$, which makes 45 pairs of 10 specimens, or 190 pairs of 20 specimens. The job can sometimes be legitimately shortened; one plan is to break up a

PAIRED COMPARISON: DATA AND TREATMENT

I. RECORD FORM

Specimens	*A*	*B*	*C*	*D*	*E*	*F*	*G*	*H*	*I*	*J*
A	.	A	A	A	A	A	A	A	A	A
B		.	B	B	E	B	G	B	B	J
C			.	D	C	C	C	C	C	C
D				.	E	D	D	D	D	J
E					.	E	E	E	E	E
F						.	F	F	I	F
G							.	G	G	G
H								.	I	J
I									.	J
J										.
C score	9	5	6	5	7	3	4	0	2	4

II. COMPUTATIONS

Specimens arranged in ascending order of C scores

	H	*I*	*F*	*J*	*G*	*D*	*B*	*C*	*E*	*A*
C score	0	2	3	4	4	5	5	6	7	9
$p = C/(n-1)$	0	.22	.33	.44	.44	.56	.56	.67	.78	1.00
z	?	−.77	−.44	−.15	−.15	+.15	+.15	+.44	+.77	?
$C' = C + 0.5$	0.5	2.5	3.5	4.5	4.5	5.5	5.5	6.5	7.5	9.5
$p' = C'/n$	.05	.25	.35	.45	.45	.55	.55	.65	.75	.95
z′	−1.64	−.67	−.39	−.13	−.13	+.13	+.13	+.39	+.67	+1.64

long series of specimens into two or more overlapping series.

In preparing his shuffled list of all the pairs to be given *E* can guard against time and space errors by placing each specimen first in some pairs and second in others. For an individual experiment he can prepare a record blank in tabular form, like the one on page 253, shown filled out. Each specimen is assigned a row and a column. If, for example, *O* prefers G to B, the letter G is written at the intersection of the G column and the B row. When all the choices have been made, *E* counts all the G entries (which will be in either the G row or the G column) and records the count at the foot of the G column. So he obtains his choice scores (C scores). With 10 specimens in the lot, each is compared with the remaining 9; to obtain the percent score or p score, accordingly, each C score is divided by 9, or in general by (n — 1). There are certain checks: the sum of the C scores must be n(n — 1)/2; and the average p score must be .50.

Treatment of Paired Comparison data. Since *O* makes a choice between the members of each pair of specimens, the experiment is a two-category one, and so far the same as a two-category experiment with Constant Stimuli. We might call the two categories "win" and "lose." Each C score tells how often the given specimen won, and the corresponding p tells in what percent of cases it won. Won against what? Against the field, we may say, the field comprising the whole lot of specimens. Specimen A scored 100 percent against the field, specimen H zero. The win-lose threshold was not fixed in location, for in 22 percent of the cases it lay below specimen I, and in another 22 percent of cases above specimen E. In this respect, again, the data are similar to those of Constant Stimuli (p. 210).

Though such data throw no light on an absolute zero of merit, they enable us to estimate the relative size of the steps or intervals between the specimens. Can we accept the steps in p or frequency as measures of steps in merit? In an experiment with Constant Stimuli, where the "specimens" can be physically measured, we know that equal steps of frequency correspond closely to equal steps of physical size along in the middle of the frequency scale, say from p = .30 to p = .70, but not out near the extremes of frequency (p. 203). We found it possible to assume a normal distribution of threshold values and convert p into z values. It is important to notice that it is the responses, not the stimuli, that are normally distributed. The distribution of weights in the weight-lifting experiment is perfectly flat (rectangular), but the distribution of the greater-less threshold is normal.

It is reasonable, accordingly, to handle Paired Comparison data on the following basis: the experiment is equivalent to one with Constant Stimuli; the given field of specimens takes the place of a single Standard; and the p values can legitimately be converted into z values by use of our table on page 206.

The introduction of z scores into the scaling of Paired Comparison data was the achievement of Thurstone (1927a, b, 1928a, 1948). His justification of the procedure was based on different reasoning from that offered here, which is due to Guilford (1928, 1936). Guilford thought it necessary, however, to add a further refinement. Each specimen, we have said, wins a certain C score against the field. But the field should be the same for all, whereas, as we have left the matter so far, each specimen competes with a different field. The field for specimen A includes all but A, the field for B includes all but B, and so on. To correct this inequality we can say that A ties with itself, B with itself, etc. Each specimen's C score is thus increased by half a point, and each specimen is compared with the whole n specimens instead of with n — 1. So we obtain the C′, p′ and z′ values shown at the bottom of the table. One advantage of this procedure is that it gets rid of the unusable p values of 0 and 1.00. How much difference it makes in a serious scaling job we shall consider in a moment.

The preferences of a single individual would be a shaky foundation for a valid scale; a good sample of individuals is required. The individual C scores for any one specimen are added and averaged, yielding the group C score for that specimen; this score is divided by n — 1 (where n is the number of specimens); and the p so obtained is converted to a z value. (Somewhat different procedures are possible. The z values may be found for each individual and averaged for the group. Or, each cell of such a table as that on page 253 may be taken as a unit and its group p and z found. The question is whether these more laborious procedures make any appreciable difference in the final scale.)

As an example of a serious scaling job based on Paired Comparison data we may take a study by Folgmann (1933) of the preferences of musicians for the music of different composers. The judges were 308 members of the Philadelphia, Boston, Minneapolis, and New York Philharmonic orchestras. The 19 composers' names appeared in pairs on a multigraphed sheet, each name being paired with every other one; and the instructions were "to underline the name of the one composer of each pair whose *music you prefer* in general, *not* taking the personality or greatness of the composer into consideration. . . . To make this experiment valid, it is absolutely necessary not to omit any pair, even if it is difficult to make a choice."

Folgmann's published tables show the percent choosing each composer when compared with every other one. Beethoven was preferred to Brahms by 67 percent of the musicians, to Tschaikovsky by 90 percent, etc., and his average p score was .872. Victor Herbert was preferred to Beethoven by 3.6 percent, to Schubert by 5 percent, etc., and his average p score was .128.

The table headed "Scaled preference of musicians for 19 composers" gives first the average p score for each composer and the equivalent z score. The rest of the table shows the results of different ways of handling the data. Evidently no absolute zero or ceiling of merit can be found from such data, since the experiment is limited to a given range of specimens and merely enables us to divide the range between the highest and lowest given specimen and locate each specimen within this range. If the top specimen is taken as 100 and the bottom specimen as zero, the location of each specimen can be adjusted to this range of 100 units, and a fair comparison made of the results obtained by different scaling procedures.

The adjustment to the 0-to-100 range proceeds as follows in the case of the "Unconverted p scale": Beethoven (p of .872) and Herbert (p of .128) are placed at 100 and 0 respectively, so that the difference, .872 — .128 is called 100. What, for example, is Schubert's position, his p being .650? Evidently he stands .650 — .128 above our zero, and his position is given by the proportion, (.650 — .128)/(.872 — .128), which locates him at 70 on the scale. The same procedure is used for all the other composers. We can similarly adjust the z scores to a range of 100, the whole z range from Herbert to Beethoven being 2.28, and Schubert standing 1.53 above Herbert. The last two columns are similarly adjusted after treatment of the p or z values as recommended by Guilford and Thurstone, respectively.

Guilford's recommendation has already been described (p. 254). Thurstone's procedure, used by Folgmann, converts the p in each cell (such as Beethoven's 67-percent preference over Brahms) into z before averaging. This procedure has the effect of giving more weight, and perhaps too much weight, to any very high or low p value. Actually there is very little ultimate difference among the three z-type scales, as can be seen from the last three columns in the table. The "Unconverted p scale" diverges from the others, spreading out the middle third and compressing the two end thirds. This effect would have been more serious if the range of p values had been greater—say from .05 to .95, instead of only from .13 to .87. The use of z scores is certainly desirable, but the "straight p-z conversion" seems as good as any.

These scales should not be misunderstood. They do not state, for example, that Beethoven was judged twice as good as Mendelssohn. They only state that Mendelssohn stood midway between Herbert and Beethoven. The numbers mark off distances along a continuum, some longer than others, and Paired Comparison data provide a measurement of these relative distances. The large gap between Grieg and MacDowell could have been occupied by worthy composers who were not included in Folgmann's list.

SCALED PREFERENCE OF MUSICIANS FOR 19 COMPOSERS

	Raw scores		Adjusted to range 0 to 100			
Composer	*p*	z	*Unconverted p scale*	*Straight p-z conversion*	*Guilford conversion*	*Thurstone conversion*
Beethoven	.872	+1.14	100	100	100	100
Brahms	.798	+ .83	90	87	87	88
Wagner	.774	+ .75	86	83	84	85
Mozart	.772	+ .75	86	83	83	86
Bach	.748	+ .67	84	79	80	79
Schubert	.650	+ .39	70	67	67	71
Haydn	.591	+ .23	62	60	60	61
Debussy	.565	+ .16	59	57	57	59
Schumann	.527	+ .07	54	53	53	54
Mendelssohn	.479	— .05	47	48	48	48
Tschaikovsky	.422	— .20	39	41	41	42
Berlioz	.399	— .26	36	39	38	39
C. Franck	.370	— .33	32	35	35	36
Chopin	.357	— .37	31	34	33	35
Verdi	.325	— .45	27	30	30	31
Stravinsky	.305	— .51	24	28	27	28
Grieg	.291	— .55	22	26	25	26
MacDowell	.129	— .13	0	0	0	1
V. Herbert	.128	—1.14	0	0	0	0

THE RANKING METHOD

Another name for this method is *Order of Merit*. Either title is almost self-explanatory; *O* arranges a number of specimens in an ordinal series along a given dimension. So a single rank order is obtained. The same specimens are ranked several or many times, usually by different *Os*, and the Mean Rank is computed for each specimen. It is a very convenient method unless the number of specimens is too large. Usually the whole lot of specimens is presented together and *O* is allowed to proceed as he wishes so long as he comes through with a single rank order. When there are many specimens, he may be asked to sort them roughly into grades before he attempts the final ranking.

The development of a full-fledged Ranking Method was the work of Cattell (1902, 1903), with refinements and various applications by several of his pupils (Sumner, 1898; Thorndike, 1904; Wells, 1907; Strong, 1911; Hollingworth, 1911a, b, 1914; the last article reviews all this early work). Meanwhile Spearman (1904) had shown how to use rank orders in the measurement of correlation—an important contribution to the method.

Cattell's chief use of the Ranking Method was for identifying the leaders in each natural science in the judgment of their colleagues. He asked 10 representative psychologists to rank the 200 people in the United States who had some claim to be considered as psychologists. The 10 judges worked separately and independently. Cattell then computed the Mean of the 10 ranks assigned to each psychologist. He published a list of the highest Mean Ranks in 1903 and revealed the names of the men in 1933. Our table (p. 258) combines 51 names and their ranks. Some of the men on the list were philosophers rather than phychologists, and some near and beyond the low end of our list were young men who had not yet won their spurs. As to the significance of such a list, we cannot do better than quote Cattell's original statement (1903):

> It should be distinctly noted that these figures give only what they profess to give, namely, the resultant opinion of ten competent judges. They show the reputation of the men among experts, but not necessarily their ability or performance. Constant errors, such as may arise from a man's being better or less known than he deserves, are not eliminated. There is, however, no other criterion of a man's work than the estimation in which it is held by those most competent to judge.

We have here nothing like a normal distribution; we have only the upper tail of such a distribution, the upper quarter of what was itself a selected group of men and women who had won degrees and teaching positions. We could not possibly use such data for constructing a scale of achievement or reputation based on an absolute zero at the bottom. We could do somewhat better by taking the top man as our reference point and asking who was half as eminent as William James. But that would be a different experiment. What can we do with the Mean Ranks as they stand?

Let us ask why the Mean Ranks are so close together near the bottom of the list. Suppose we had 10 weights, all differing very perceptibly from each other, and asked a dozen *Os* to rank them. Every *O* would rank them in the same order and the Mean Ranks would be simply 1, 2, 3 . . . . 9, 10. But suppose we tried the same experiment with 10 equal weights: each *O* would rank them in a different order and the Mean Ranks would all be nearly the same. Now let the weights differ by small amounts so that every *O* would be apt to make a few errors: the Mean Ranks would lie between the two extremes mentioned, and they would come out pretty nearly in the true order of the objective weights.

There is a useful principle here. Given a sufficient number of competent judges ranking the same specimens, the Mean Ranks will be nearly equal where the specimens are nearly equal and will differ widely where the specimens are very unequal; in short, the Mean Ranks will agree fairly well with the specimens in both order and spacing.

In the list of psychologists, accordingly, we infer that numbers 2, 3, and 4 were nearly equal in psychological merit so far as it was visible at the time; the same for the next three men, and again for the last half dozen on the list. We can also infer, as Cattell insisted, that the exact order is very uncertain where the Mean Ranks are nearly equal.

For fuller use of the Ranking Method there must be a definite number of specimens all of which are ranked by every judge. It is then possible, as shown in the first edition of this book (pp. 372–375) to measure the amount of agreement or disagreement among all the judges. We shall now show, as a contribution to scaling, how the same sort of scale can be derived from Ranking as from Paired Comparison. Ranks can be reduced to choice frequencies (C) and so to p and z values.

Close relation of the Ranking and Paired Comparison methods. If a judge

MEAN RANKS OF LEADING AMERICAN PSYCHOLOGISTS OF 1903

(Cattell, 1903, 1933)

Mean Rank	Name	Mean Rank	Name
1.0	William James	41.6	Raymond Dodge
3.7	J. McKeen Cattell	42.9	James H. Hyslop
4.0	Hugo Münsterberg	44.7	Carl E. Seashore
4.4	G. Stanley Hall	44.9	Charles A. Strong
7.5	J. Mark Baldwin	45.5	Arthur H. Pierce
7.5	Edward B. Titchener	46.4	Robert MacDougall
7.6	Josiah Royce	47.1	Max Meyer
9.2	George T. Ladd	48.0	Ernest H. Lindley
9.6	John Dewey	49.3	James H. Leuba
11.6	Joseph Jastrow	49.6	Frank Angell
12.3	Edmund C. Sanford	49.9	Walter B. Pillsbury
16.8	Mary W. Calkins	51.1	William R. Newbold
17.1	William L. Bryan	52.6	Livingston Farrand
17.9	George S. Fullerton	53.3	Herbert Nichols
18.7	George M. Stratton	54.5	Jacob G. Schurman
19.3	Edward L. Thorndike	54.5	Margaret F. Washburn
19.6	Edmund B. Delabarre	56.2	Robert S. Woodworth
21.6	Edward W. Scripture	56.3	Shepherd I. Franz
21.8	Christine Ladd-Franklin	56.5	Harry K. Wolfe
22.4	Henry Rutgers Marshall	58.6	James E. Creighton
24.5	Charles H. Judd	59.0	Harry N. Gardiner
27.0	James R. Angell	59.0	George Santayana
29.5	Lightner Witmer	59.2	Edward F. Buchner
37.5	G. T. W. Patrick	59.2	Andrew C. Armstrong
37.7	Howard C. Warren	59.6	Thaddeus L. Bolton
40.4	William T. Harris		

ranks a certain specimen No. 1, at the top, of 10 given specimens, he evidently prefers it to the other 9; if he ranks it No. 2, he prefers it to 8; and so on. So each rank (R) can be converted into a choice score (C). In general, with n specimens,

$$C = n - R$$

and since this equation holds for all the ranks assigned by the judges to the same specimen, it holds for the Mean Choice score (M_C) and the Mean Rank (M_R) of that specimen, so that

$$M_C = n - M_R$$

Having the M_C values we can convert them into p values just as we did on page 253, according to the formula,

$$p = \frac{M_C}{n - 1}$$

and from each p we can obtain the corresponding z from the table on page 206.

If we wish to use Guilford's corrected choice scores (C' on p. 253), we can proceed as in Paired Comparison and obtain the p' values, which are identical with the familiar Percentile Ranks obtained by the formula $PR = 1 - (R - .50)/n$, as given by Garrett (1953, p. 326).

RANKS REDUCED TO CHOICE SCORES

(The data are taken from Cattell's 1906 study of the 10 leading astronomers of that time; these data were used also in the first edition of this book, p. 373.)

	Specimens									
Judge	*A*	*B*	*C*	*D*	*E*	*F*	*G*	*H*	*I*	*J*
I	1	2	4	3	9	6	5	8	7	10
II	1	4	2	5	6	7	3	10	8	9
III	1	3	4	5	2	8	9	6	10	7
IV	1	3	4	5	2	6	10	8	7	9
V	1	9	2	5	6	3	4	8	10	7
VI	1	4	9	2	5	6	7	3	10	8
VII	1	3	5	10	2	6	9	7	8	4
VIII	1	3	5	7	6	4	8	10	2	9
IX	1	2	8	4	9	6	3	7	5	10
X	1	2	4	5	9	8	6	3	7	10
Sum of ranks	10	35	47	51	56	60	64	70	74	83
M_R	1.0	3.5	4.7	5.1	5.6	6.0	6.4	7.0	7.4	8.3
$M_C = n - M_R$	9.0	6.5	5.3	4.9	4.4	4.0	3.6	3.0	2.6	1.7
$p = M_C/(n - 1)$	1.00	.72	.59	.54	.49	.44	.40	.33	.29	.19
z	?	+.58	+.23	+.10	−.03	−.15	−.25	−.44	−.55	−.88
$M_C' = M_C + .5$	9.5	7.0	5.8	5.4	4.9	4.5	4.1	3.5	3.1	2.2
$p' = M_C'/n$	.95	.70	.58	.54	.49	.45	.41	.35	.31	.22
z'	+1.64	+.52	+.20	+.10	−.03	−.13	−.23	−.39	−.50	−.77

Checks: The average M_R must $= (n + 1)/2$.
The average M_C must $= (n - 1)/2$.
The average p must $= 1/2$.
The average M_C' must $= n/2$.
The average p' must $= 1/2$.

Validity of scaling by Mean Ranks and percent frequencies. Objection is sometimes raised to the Ranking Method on the ground that ranks are merely ordinal numbers and must not be used for any quantitative purposes. We admit of course that scaling by ranks is limited to the range of specimens judged and locates no absolute zero, without which the scale is not fully quantitative. We cannot say that one specimen is twice as good as another, any more than we can say that 80° F. (or C.) is twice as hot as 40°. But Mean Ranks, we can claim, are something more than ordinal numbers. When the single judge ranks the specimens, he says nothing about their spacing. Some may be close together and others far apart, but all he says is that each one has more of the specified quality than those ranked below it. Mean Ranks, however, are not the output of the single judge. They are the output of a group of judges (or sometimes of repeated, independent judgments by the same individual). Though the single judge is limited to the ordinal numbers, the group has a much finer scale at its disposal. It uses fractional Mean Ranks, some close together and some wide apart, and its Mean Ranks agree quite well with the actual spacing of the specimens when the spacing is objectively known—as in the case of weights, already mentioned.

Mean Ranks, as we have shown, can be converted into frequencies and handled as other frequencies are handled in Paired Comparison and in Constant Stimuli. Even in Constant Stimuli, the original single datum is an ordinal number. Co is judged to be greater or less than the Standard, but how much greater or less is not reported. No use could be made of the single judgment, but when each Co is compared with St 20 times, the frequencies go beyond the ordinal numbers. If one Co is judged greater than St only 60 percent of the time, while another is judged greater 90 percent of the time, the latter lies much farther above the Standard in the psychological continuum. This whole group of methods is based on a psychological principle that is not covered by the logic of number—unless that logic includes the study of variability and frequency.

To construct a complete scale of any psychological dimension by the Frequency Method is no small job. The scale should show equal steps reaching down to zero. We should begin, as Thorndike and his pupils did in scaling school skills like handwriting and English composition (Thorndike, 1910; Hillegas, 1912), by assembling a large assortment of specimens ranging from near zero (a mere scrawl in the case of handwriting) up to the best obtainable. We should not want a random sample or normal distribution, which would contain many indistinguishable specimens in the middle range. Rather we should want all degrees of goodness and poorness about equally represented. We should submit our specimens to an adequate number of competent judges. We might use the halving technique, or obtain ratings, or have the specimens compared in pairs, or have them ranked in order of merit. For weeding out superfluous and troublesome specimens we could take account of the Mean Ranks and also of the scatter of ranks assigned to each specimen by the judges. Any specimen that showed no scatter at all we should eliminate—unless we kept it as an anchor at the top or bottom of the scale—and in general we should prefer specimens showing nearly equal scatter of ranks. So we could avoid certain obstacles pointed out by Thurstone (1927a) that prevent free use of the 75-percent threshold. Our final scale might include specimens each of which was placed above the next one below by 75 percent of the judges.

THE USE OF REACTION TIME FOR SCALING

In most of the discussion up to this point, we have placed heavy reliance on frequency of response. But frequency is only one measure of response strength, as we shall see in the chapters on Conditioning and Learning; another very useful measure is Latent Time. We have also shown that one type of latent time, namely, reaction time, is regularly related to stimulus intensity in simple reactions, and to stimulus difference in discrimination reactions. Further, we saw that associative RT and communality (frequency) of response were closely related measures in the association experiment. Hence it seems likely that RT would serve as an alternative measure to frequency in psychophysical experiments.

This possibility was apparent to Cattell in 1902, when he wrote a paper entitled "The time of perception as a measure of differences in intensity" (see pp. 27, 33). There have been a dozen or so experiments since that time, but the method certainly has not been pushed to the limit. In general, the studies have used one of the following two approaches:

1. Determination of RT over a wide range of stimulus intensities, and then scaling the range in terms of RT units.
2. Determination of stimulus differences at various levels that yield equal RT, and then scaling on the assumption that these stimulus differences represent subjectively equal increments.

1. Direct scaling of sensory strength through reaction time. In Chocholle's experiment (p. 19) we saw that it was possible to write a formula that described the relationship between RT and the physical intensity of an auditory stimulus. Without repeating the formula, we can point out the assumptions on which it was based:

1. The stimulus should be described in log units (decibels).
2. RT consists of two parts: (a) an irreducible minimum, representing certain constant delays in the nervous system, and (b) a reducible margin, representing the time required for the stimulus to do its work.
3. Increasing the stimulus by one log unit will decrease RT by a constant fraction of the existing reducible margin.

It follows that if we plot log reducible margin against log stimulus, we shall get a straight line with negative slope. The results are in agreement with the predictions, if we make the additional assumption that there is a shift in attitude or set once we get above very low stimulus intensities. This looks like evidence for the truth of the assumptions, and the first assumption is essentially that Fechner's law is true! So we have at least a minor victory for the Fechner type of scale, in contrast to a sone scale.

Brightness. This sensory dimension should furnish a good test for the RT method, for we already have three scaling methods in essential agreement on results; Hanes' *bril* scale, summated j.n.d.'s, and Newhall's adjustment method (pp. 244, 250). All differ from the simple log scale of Fechner. Hull (1949) tried a log reducible-margin type of analysis on some old data of Cattell (1886) on RT as a function of brightness, and got a fairly satisfactory curve. But he went a step further. He had already determined the relationship between RT and a generalized scale of response strength, Reaction Potential, $_sE_R$ (Gladstone, Yamaguchi, Hull and Felsinger, 1947). By substituting the formula for RT in that for $_sE_R$, he could calculate $_sE_R$ as a function of stimulus intensity. Unfortunately, the resulting scale agrees with neither the bril nor the Fechner scale; brightness in brils builds up faster at high intensities than does a log scale, whereas "brightness" in $_sE_R$ units grows as a negatively accelerated function. This should not be taken as a defeat for any of the more conventional methods of scaling, for Hull used old human data, treated by a formula derived by a modified Thurstone method from latent times in a rat learning problem! Hull was a bit overenthusiastic to call it even a "first approximation."

We have described two attempts to develop a formula that would permit a direct transformation from RT to sensory scale values. Although the results were a trifle disappointing, it may well be that we need more and better experiments with this general method. But until we have them, we must content ourselves with the somewhat more extensive work with indirect scaling by means of RT.

2. Indirect scaling through RT. The basic assumption here is that equally difficult discriminations will have the same RT. The method goes back to Cattell. Henmon (1906) tried it out on length of lines, color, and pitch. He did find that equal relative differences gave fairly constant RT. Further, with fairly strong stimuli the RT tended to fall somewhat for a given relative stimulus difference, just as does Weber's fraction.

There have been several studies in which RT has been compared directly with the frequency-of-judgment ogive. One of the most extensive was carried out by D. M. Johnson in 1939. He used the two-category method in Constant Stimuli. His materials were lengths of lines, meanings of words, position of the hand, and recognition of figures, but the most extensive data were on lengths of lines. The stimulus was a heavy black horizontal line on cardboard, with a short vertical line at either end, and another vertical to divide the line into two segments. The left segment was always 50 mm, and served as St. The right segment, Co, varied from 40 to 60 in steps of 2 mm. The stimuli were presented by a modified Dodge tachistoscope (p. 93). *O*'s task was to signal which segment was longer by pressing one of two keys. RT was recorded in .01 sec. After each response, *O* expressed his confidence that it was correct by making a check on a line. A check in the middle meant complete uncertainty, one at the extreme right (left) complete certainty that the right (left) segment was longer, and intermediate points represented corresponding degrees of certainty. The results from one of the three *O*s are shown in Figure 9–12. The ogive labeled %L is the familiar psychophysical function, based on *percent longer,* and should be referred to the extreme left-hand ordinate. The ogive labeled C_M is the Mean confidence rating of the 10 judgments made at each value of Co. The ordinate (second on left) to which it is referred varies from −100 to +100, corresponding to certainty that the right or left segment, respectively, was the longer. It passes through zero (complete uncertainty) at the 50-percent point of the %L ogive, where *O* was "guessing," but extends much further in each direction. This shows that *O* was making correct judgments 100 percent of the time when the stimulus difference was still not great enough to make him absolutely certain of his judgments.

The RT curve is the one marked T_M. Notice that it reaches a peak at a Co value of 50 mm, wh h was equal to St. Incidentally, this peak shows much

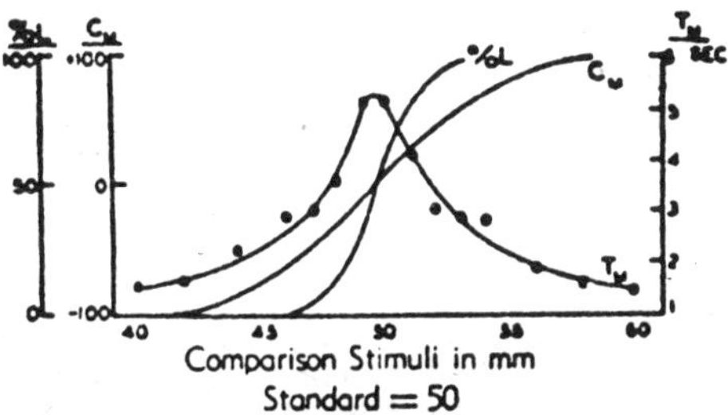

FIG. 9-12. (Johnson, 1939.) Confidence, time, and frequency functions.

less CE than does either of the other two curves. It is clear from this curve that RT falls off as a smoothly decreasing function of stimulus difference. Further, it is still falling at stimulus differences that yield 100-percent correct judgments, and even 100-percent certainty. It is this feature that makes RT promising for equating stimulus differences that are greater than the DL.

Johnson's main interest in the experiment seems to have been in the relationship between confidence and speed. He concluded that "as doubt or uncertainty increases arithmetically, judgment time increases geometrically." Both are obviously measures of the difficulty of the judgment, in many respects quite comparable to the more familiar percentage correct ogives.

Reaction time to change. The discriminative reaction experiment is closely parallel to the familiar psychophysical experiments in that both demand a discrimination between two stimuli, or between a stimulus and some reference point, as AL or PSE. This complicates the problem. But there is one version of Constant Stimuli that would permit the use of simple, rather than discriminative RT. Pitch and loudness DLs are often determined by presenting a continuous tone, which suddenly changes by one of several increments or decrements. Why not measure RT to these changes? Piéron (1937) tried out the method for brightness, and Flynn (1943) used it for pitch. The most extensive experiments are those of Steinman & Veniar (1944) and Steinman (1944). It will be recalled (p. 27) that *O* responded to a sudden change in the level of illumination of a small stimulus patch. Figure 2-9, (p. 27) shows the relationship of RT to size of change at one level of illumination; we can plot a whole family of such curves, covering a wide range of intensities, in the same way that we can plot frequency ogives at different values of St. When using frequency ogives, if we take the simple case in which we deal only with increments (p. 210), we define the increment which is noticed 50 percent of the time as the DL. We then compute Weber's fraction at each of several intensive levels by dividing DL by St. In a parallel fashion, we can use some arbitrary value of RT to define a new base line constant, which we may write DL_T. It would probably be possible to find a relatively long RT which would give a value of DL_T which was equal to the usual DL. But this would sacrifice the chief value of RT; the RT curves are still falling long after the frequency curves have reached 100 percent. Hence, it is perfectly possible to select an RT value which will correspond to quite large stimulus increments—say 10 or 20 DL. We can use these large "equally rapidly noticed" intervals for scaling, and for testing Weber's law on large stimulus differences.

The results the experiment on brightness were in substantial agreement with those obtained by the more traditional methods. Both showed that $\Delta I/I$ is fairly constant but tends to reach a minimum value at middle intensities. The method would seem to be a good one, and it offers the hope of approaching scaling by a third technique, based on neither equal-appearing intervals nor equal-variability units. All three methods agree in the case of brightness; now it would be interesting to try the equal-RT method on loudness, where the other two methods are in marked disagreement. Unfortunately, the experiment has not been done yet.

RT scaling of affective distances. One of the most challenging fields for scaling is that of likes and dislikes, where we have no appropriate way of quantifying the stimuli in physical terms. We saw that Paired Comparison has been widely used in scaling preference for colors (p. 253). How would RT work out on these materials? Dashiell (1937) and Shipley, Coffin & Hadsell (1945) have tried out the method; we shall consider the more recent experiment. The basic method was to present a pair of colors to *O*, who would express her preference by pressing one of two keys, depending on whether she preferred the right or left color. A shutter served to present the stimulus and start the timer, and the key stopped it, giving RT in .01 units. Six reactions were obtained from each of 40 *O*s on each possible pair of colors, properly randomized with respect to order and position. There were six colors, making 15 pairs.

When the RTs were tabulated, it was found that the *O*s varied markedly

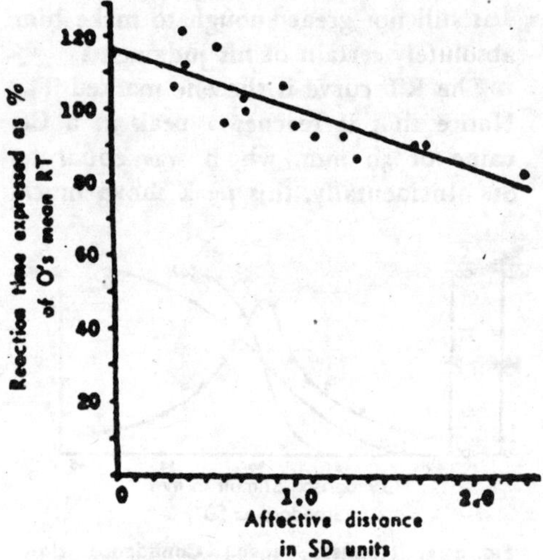

Fig. 9·13. (Shipley *et al.*, 1945.) Discriminative RT as a function of the affective distance between stimuli. See text.

among themselves in Mean RT. This variability would have swamped out the effect of color preference; it was eliminated by expressing all RTs for a given *O* as percentages of her own Mean RT. These values were then averaged for each combination of colors. In Figure 9·13 these relative RTs are plotted against affective distance in SD units. This base line was computed from the preference scores, by a variation of Thurstone's Method for Paired Comparisons (p. 254). It will be seen that the two methods of scoring preferences are in substantial agreement, as indicated by the way the dots cluster around a straight line. The two measures correlate well ($r = -.86 \pm .045$). Again we find the RT method of scaling to be promising, but still in a somewhat rough form.

SUMMARY OF SCALING METHODS

It might be well to bring the chapter to a close by summarizing the various scaling methods. There seem to be three "families" of methods, with some intermarriage.

One family of methods is based on direct judgment of subjective magnitudes. In Fractionation, *O* either chooses or adjusts one stimulus so that its subjective magnitude is ½ (or some other fraction or multiple) of another stimulus. By repeating this type of judgment at various intensive levels we can construct a scale that has some claim to being a *ratio* scale; i.e., it has a true zero and equal steps, so that it lets us say that one sensation is twice (or 10 times) as strong as another. Another direct scaling method is Equal-Sense Distances, in which *O* arranges three or more stimuli so that their subjective *distances* are equal. This method yields an equal-interval scale, but not an absolute zero point; it enables us to say that there is as much difference between A and B as between B and C, or E and F, but *not* that B is twice as strong as A. The basic weakness of these direct methods is their sensitivity to various types of constant errors.

A second family of methods is based on the principle that equal variability of judgment can be used to step off equal distances on a subjective scale. Fechner's law and summated j.n.d. scales belong here, for they are based on the DL, which is ultimately a measure of variability. These methods yield equal-interval scales, with no absolute zero, but they can be very useful. They are indirect methods, and depend on the assumption that the DL or SD units are psychologically equal throughout the scale. This is a plausible assumption.

The third family of methods is based on reaction time. We are not yet able to make the equation $RT = f(S)$ definite, but we have made some headway. Perhaps more fruitful is the method of using equal RT to specify equal steps along the stimulus continuum. The chief use of the RT method may well be in evaluating the results of the other two methods, since it depends on neither judgments of subjective magnitude nor on variability.

Rating, Paired Comparison, and Ranking do not fall neatly into one of our three categories. A simple rating scale would seem to resemble Equal Sense Distances, and thus be a direct method, but a well-developed rating scale is apt to be based on statistical treatment that employs variability as the unit. Similarly, we can start with the simple ordering of stimuli that we get directly from Paired Comparison or Ranking, and convert it into a scale whose steps have equal variability. Hence, these three methods would usually be placed in our second family.

With all these different methods of scale construction, one is tempted to ask which is the best. That may not be a good question; the method we choose will depend on the stimuli to be scaled, and on the purpose of our scaling. Often several methods may yield very similar results, especially if we equate the lengths of the two scales by multiplying one of them by a constant. Perhaps the most striking disagreement is between fractionation and j.n.d. scaling in the intensive dimensions of loudness, weight, and taste. It is too soon to say whether the two methods are measuring different processes, or that one of them is in error. But for the present, the important thing is that we have several good methods for building useful scales of subjective magnitude.

10

THE CUTANEOUS SENSES

One of the most remarkable characteristics of an animal organism is the presence of specialized receptors which are sensitive (or "tuned") to different physical and chemical agents. Some receptors are tuned to light within a certain range of wavelengths, others to sound waves within a certain range, others to certain chemical agents. This manifold sensitivity is not only remarkable; it is important for the organism in its interaction with the environment. It enables the organism to respond to objects in the environment which emit light or sound or chemical agents. Even without any ability to learn, the organism could move away from intense light or toward a food substance; and with the ability to learn comes the possibility of acquiring a vast range of adaptive responses to various objects in the environment.

Signaling. A physical or chemical agent acting on an appropriate receptor is called a *stimulus.* It may also be regarded as a *signal.* It is a stimulus, physiologically, because it arouses activity in the receptor and starts a train of activities in a sensory nerve, nerve center, motor nerve, and muscle or other effector. It is a signal, psychologically, because the motor response is adjusted to the environment that provided the stimulus. In Pavlov's conditioning experiment on a dog, the tone quickly and regularly followed by food became a signal of food and enabled the dog to make an advance salivary adjustment for the food. (We can make this statement without assuming conscious anticipation on the dog's part.)

The human subject can go the dog one better by making a verbal report of stimuli received. Two kinds of report are possible for him; he can say, "I hear a low droning sound that is becoming louder"; or he can say, "An airplane is coming this way." In one case he is reporting a stimulus without regard to its meaning or signal value, while in the other case he is reporting the object signalized for him by the stimulus. Experiments requiring the subject to report the stimulus are abundant in the study of the senses and are often called experiments on *sensation,* while experiments calling for a report of the object or objective fact indicated by a stimulus belong in the study of *perception.*

Other words often used instead of "signal" are *sign* and *cue.* We speak of "visual signs" of the distance of an object. We ask what "cues" a rat follows in finding his way through a maze, and we seek an answer by depriving him of visual cues, olfactory cues, etc. This convenient word has spread from the animal to the human laboratory so that, we speak of visual cues of distance, and of auditory cues of direction, when perhaps the word "clue" would be more in accordance with general usage (Harper & Boring, 1948).

The meaning of a signal has to be learned in most cases, often by a process akin to conditioning—not in all cases, however. Location on the skin, direction of visible objects, direction of a source of sound, and perhaps other spatial facts may be indicated by "natural" signals.

With all the vast number of environmental objects and facts to be signalized, a great variety of stimuli is evidently necessary, and the organism must be able to discriminate the stimuli, one from another. Stimuli differ in intensity, and *O*'s ability to discriminate them on that basis has been examined in the chapters on psychophysics. Stimuli also differ in kind—light, sound, etc.—and the organism is equipped with receptors sensitive to several kinds of physical and chemical agents. The study of these sense organs, of their neural connections, and of the organism's ability to discriminate between the many qualitatively and quantitatively different stimuli that affect them is the province of sensory psychology and its sister science, sense physiology.

In a psychological context, then, we can speak of an organism as receiving or sensing signals and responding according to their meaning. Among the *O*-factors covered by the formula, R = f(S, *O*), are *O*'s ability to receive the S and his ability to perceive its meaning. In a physiological context we can speak of the sense organs as sending signals to the brain by way of the sensory nerves. A sense organ receives stimuli that differ in kind, in intensity, and in location. If these differences are to be discriminated and utilized in the organism's behavior, there must be some adequate signaling system from the sense organ to the brain. What evidence, we may ask, does the brain have that one stimulus differs from another in kind, intensity, or location? This question is more difficult than it may seem, and since it is basic in the study of all the senses, a few paragraphs will be devoted here to the physiology of the matter.

SENSORY NERVE CONDUCTION

The basic function of a receptor is to signal the stimuli to the central nervous system by way of the sensory nerve supply of the particular sense organ. The unit conductor is the nerve fiber, and the unit signal is the single nerve impulse. Actual signals are composed of many impulses transmitted by several or many nerve fibers.

The nerve impulse. The nervous system has some resemblance to an extremely complicated telephone system. The connections between the outlying stations (sense organs, muscles) and the switchboards (nerve centers) are provided by cables (nerves) consisting of many slender conductors (nerve fibers). Each nerve fiber is microscopic in diameter, but some are long enough to reach from the toes to the spinal cord. The fibers are more or less completely insulated from each other.

At this point the analogy with wires must stop. The nerve fiber is a living structure, made up of protoplasm and maintained by its own cell body. Instead of conducting energy in a passive way, as a wire conducts electricity, it has its own supply of energy, stored inside the fiber along its whole length. A small portion of this energy is available at the surface of the fiber for immediate use, but most of it is held in reserve. When the surface is disturbed by a stimulus to one point, a local reaction of the fiber occurs, consuming the local supply of available energy and exciting a similar reaction in the neighboring surface area. This local disturbance, propagated continuously along the fiber, is the *nerve impulse*. An integral part of the local process is an electrical change; the active portion of the fiber surface, where the impulse is at the moment, becomes negative with respect to neighboring portions of the surface. This *action potential* can be picked up and recorded by suitable electrodes, amplifiers, and recording instruments. A good share of our present knowledge of how nerves and sense organs operate has been obtained by such recording.

The process of nerve conduction has been likened to the burning of a fuse or train of gunpowder, since both processes involve the progressive release of energy by local action. One grain of powder is ignited, sets off its neighbor which in turn ignites a third, and so on—all the powder being burned, all the available energy consumed. As a result, both processes have the fundamental characteristic of being *all or none*. That is, the strength of the propagated action depends only on the amount of available energy, and not at all on the strength of the force (stimulus) that sets off the process. It is true that not all gunpowder trains, or all nerve fibers, have the same amount of energy available; thick fuses, thick nerve fibers, transmit a larger disturbance and transmit it faster. It is further true that the available energy in any nerve fiber varies from time to time, with corresponding changes in the magnitude and speed of the impulse. But the all-or-none law still holds good since the nerve fiber either reacts with all its available energy, or else does not react at all (if the stimulus is too weak).

The speed of the nerve impulse is often said to be 100 meters per second, but this is nearly the top speed, reached only in the large fibers. Thin fibers conduct at much slower rates, down to one meter per second in cold-blooded animals.

We could find still other analogies between the gunpowder train and the nerve fiber, but there is at least one fundamental difference—the nerve fiber restores itself after each impulse. It will be recalled that only a small portion of the stored energy is momentarily available at the surface of the fiber where the local activity occurs. As soon as this portion is consumed by the single nerve impulse, it is promptly replaced from the internal reserve. But this replacement takes a little time. A second impulse cannot follow immediately; the fiber is said to be in *absolute refractory phase*. Within a millisecond or two the fiber has recovered enough to permit a very strong stimulus to initiate a very weak impulse, and during the following *relative refractory phase* there is a gradual build-up of available energy, with the stimulus threshold falling and the speed and magnitude of the impulse increasing. A large fiber is back to normal at the end of perhaps 12 ms; the whole process is slower in the thinner fibers.

Neural correlates of stimulus intensity. Now we are ready to consider how stimulus intensity can be signaled from a sense organ to the brain. The external energy of the stimulus may impinge directly upon the fine terminal branches of a sensory nerve fiber or upon a tissue of specialized receptor cells. In either case it sets up a local excitatory process, which initiates an impulse in a nerve fiber. The excitation persists, but a second impulse cannot start on its way until the fiber has recovered from the first, partially at least. A moderately intense stimulus may initiate a second impulse midway in the relative refractory period, say 5 ms after the first. This new impulse has its own refractory phase which prevents a third impulse from starting until another 5 ms has passed. So the successive impulses start up along the nerve fiber once every 5 ms, i.e., at the rate of 200 per second. A weaker stimulus will have the same effect except that the fiber must recover more fully after each impulse before the next one can start. For example, 10 ms is needed for recovery to the point where the weak stimulus can take effect so that 100 impulses per second will be transmitted by the nerve fiber. With 2 ms allowed for the absolute refractory phase, the strongest stimulus could excite 500 impulses per second. With 10 ms additional allowed for complete recovery, the weakest effective stimulus, barely above the stimulus threshold, would excite $^{1000}/_{12} = 83$ impulses per second. Still lower rates may be impressed on a nerve fiber by receptor cells which receive the stimulus and have their own relatively long refractory period. It is clear, then, that intensity gradations in the stimulus will be reflected in the frequency of the nerve impulses transmitted by the single nerve fiber.

A second neural correlate of stimulus intensity is the number of fibers excited. The stronger the stimulus, the more numerous are the affected nerve fibers. The skin, for example, is richly supplied with sensory nerve fibers. Press a pencil point gently on the wrist and you make a small depression, exciting a few sensory nerve fibers; press it harder and the depression spreads so that more fibers are brought into play. Thus stimulus intensity is signaled by the total number of impulses per second arriving at the nerve center, this number depending both on the number of fibers excited and on the impulse frequency in the single fibers.

Sensory adaptation. So far we have assumed a stable condition such that the magnitude of excitation in the receptor remains constant, and the nerve fiber maintains a constant recovery time. Such constancy rarely occurs even when the external stimulus remains unchanged. In the first place, the excitation level of receptor cells typically declines during steady stimulation; in some receptors it declines very quickly. Further, even the nerve fiber slows down its recovery to some extent; its refractory period lengthens. The net result is that the rate of impulses in the sensory nerve fibers falls off under continuous uniform stimulation. This "adaptation" is a familiar fact in several sense fields, as in sight, smell, and touch, and its physiological mechanism may not always be the same. The same word is used elsewhere in psychology with various shades of meaning (p. 559). But enough has been said here to bring out the fact that *change* is a very important aspect of stimulation. A more technical treatment of the general subject is given by Ruch (1951), and the reader who wishes to follow up the matter of sensory adaptation, and other phenomena we have barely mentioned, is referred to two monographs by a leading contributor to the subject, E. D. Adrian (1928, 1932).

Recording neural activity. The nerve impulses we have been discussing are usually recorded through their electrical aspects (Brink, 1951). As the impulse passes a given region on the nerve fiber, this active region becomes negative in relation to the adjacent inactive regions. This change is called the *spike potential,* or the *negative variation.* Roughly synonymous terms, *action current* and *action potential,* include also the series of minor electrical changes which follow the spike. The spike itself may have a duration of about one millisecond and a strength of 100 millivolts (though most of its strength is short-circuited by local tissues, so that only a few millivolts are available for recording). For a long time it was necessary to record from nerve trunks, where many fibers combined their individual contributions to give a sizable total action current. The problem then was to try to figure out what was happening in the individual fiber. But the rapid development of vacuum-tube or "radio" amplification during the 1920s freed research workers from this limitation. They could amplify the action current a millionfold and use the output of their amplifiers to drive extremely rapid recording instruments. One of these, the cathode ray oscilloscope (the screen of a television set), has essentially no inertia. Since 1930 great strides have been taken in our knowledge of sensory nerve impulses as research workers have found better ways to use their new tools. One of the remaining problems is to develop minute electrodes that can pick up the output of only one of many fibers, all closely packed in a nerve trunk. Another difficulty is that some fibers show spontaneous discharge; in the absence of external stimulation they fire sporadic impulses generated by their own metabolic processes. In such cases the effect of a stimulus is to change the rate of discharge, so that the subject's stimulus threshold is more precisely a difference threshold (p. 220). To employ terms that have crept in from communication engineering, the "signal strength" must be sufficiently above the "noise level" to be discriminated. The more we study the senses, the more we realize that the nervous system is in constant activity and that external stimuli merely modify and *control* this activity. These problems will recur under the treatment of the several senses.

Locality signals. The ability to locate an object in the environment goes beyond what we have in mind here. It belongs under the head of perception rather than sensation. We are referring to location on the skin or on the retina and to what has been called the local sign of a sensation. Two stimuli applied to the skin may be alike in quality and intensity but be distinguishable in locality. The same is true of two visual stimuli thrown upon different points of the retina and seen as in different points of the visual field. Since the retina is projected faithfully upon the primary visual area of the cortex, and the skin upon the somesthetic area, the locality-signaling system seems obvious. Each part of the skin or retina sends nerve impulses to a corresponding part of the cortex, and the local sign of the sensation depends simply on the part of the cortex that receives the impulses. There is a complication, however. It is not true that each bit of skin is served by a single sensory nerve fiber. On the contrary, each bit of skin receives fine terminal branches from more than a single fiber, while the branches of a single fiber spread over more than a single cutaneous spot. Each hair receptor, for example, is supplied by branches of two to seven sensory nerve fibers, and each fiber is distributed to several hairs. Therefore, the easy theory of "one fiber to each spot" has to be abandoned in favor of some such theory as this: each cutaneous spot is identified by the cortical location of the maximum concentration of impulses received from the skin region (Tower, 1943). It can still be true that stimulus locality is signaled by the projection of the impulses upon the cortical "map" of the receptive surface.

Quality signals. At first glance there is no problem here. If the skin receives a warm stimulus, it naturally will signal warmth to the brain, and if the retina receives a red or a blue stimulus, it will naturally signal the color to the brain. On second thought, the problem appears rather serious, since certainly the nerve fibers do not transmit the warmth or the color to the brain. They only transmit nerve impulses.

In 1826, long before much was known about nerve impulses, the great physiologist, Johannes Müller, proposed a doctrine of *specific nerve energies* (Boring, 1929, 1942). The theory was that each sensory nerve had its characteristic type of activity so that the optic nerve would signal light and color, the auditory nerve the quality of sound, the olfactory nerve that of odor, and so on. This theory is vividly expressed by the statement, "If we could cross the auditory and optic nerves, we could see thunder and hear lightning." This experiment is obviously impractical, but there are a number of satisfactory substitutes. For example, turn the eyes far to the left and gently press on the outer corner of the right lid. So you stimulate the outer edge of one retina, and you see a dark disk in the left margin of the visual field. You get a visual sensation, corresponding to the receptor stimulated, rather than to the pressure stimulus. Similarly, most receptors can be stimulated by an electric current, and the resulting sensation is reported as touch, pain, light, or sound, again according to the receptor stimulated. The facts of such *inadequate stimulation* are in agreement with Müller's theory.

But our present knowledge of nerve impulses makes a literal acceptance of Müller's conception impossible. All nerve impulses, both sensory and motor, are fundamentally the same, being waves of electrochemical activity moving along the nerve fibers. They vary in frequency and in the number of fibers thrown into activity by a stimulus, but these variations signal intensity, as we have seen. They vary in the cortical area to which they go, and it may be that retinal stimulation yields visual rather than auditory sensations because it sends nerve impulses to the occipital lobe rather than to the temporal lobe. There is some evidence for this view. A blow on the back of the head, over the occipital lobe, makes a person see a flash of light. It seems reasonable to assume that the characteristic qualities of the different senses are dependent on sensory localization in the brain. On that basis we might expect the differences between the sensations of red, blue, and green to depend on finer localization within the general visual area. But then we remember that such finer localization provides for the locality signals. We should need two sets of subcenters in the visual area, one set for the colors and the other for retinal locations. The localization theory thus becomes quite complicated though perhaps not impossible. Another possibility is that different qualities of stimuli are signaled by nerve fibers of different thickness, with their corresponding differences in amplitude and temporal pattern of the impulses. There is some evidence for this possibility in the cutaneous senses.

DELIMITATION OF THE CUTANEOUS SENSES

For over half a century psychologists have been insisting that there are more than the traditional "five senses" and that the number ought to be increased to about ten. There is the highly important muscle sense, there are the receptors of the semicircular canals in the inner ear, and there are the distinctive sensations from the stomach and other internal organs. And another reason why the number five must be discarded is that the traditional "sense of touch" can be shown to include several senses. To understand how such a conclusion has been reached we may ask what, in general, is meant by a "sense." Why do we say that Sight is one sense and Hearing another? There are several criteria which set them off as two separate senses. In the first place, they have markedly *different sense organs*, the eye and the ear. Each has its *own nerve*, and the sensory impulses in these nerves go to *different areas of the brain*. Further, each of these two senses is responsive to its *characteristic stimuli*. Finally, the sensations differ markedly in *quality*, the colors seeming to belong together and to be quite distinct from tones and noises. In view of all these differences we have no doubt that Vision and Audition are separate senses.

The same criteria are used in distinguishing Taste and Smell, but here some difficulty is encountered. The sense organs are clearly different, but the sensations are apt to blend so that one speaks of the "taste" of an orange which is really odor for the most part. The trouble is that both sense organs are stimulated by the same stimulus object. Good experimental controls are necessary to limit the chemical stimulus to a single sense organ.

From the skin we get a variety of sensory qualities, including contact and pressure, warm and cold, pain, itch, and tickle, hard and soft, rough and smooth, wet and dry. But some of these might be blends or even perceived properties of external objects. The experimental approach is to control the stimuli and apply them to small areas of the skin, in the search for little sense organs that would respond differentially to different stimuli.

Sensory spots of the skin. The skin is tested spot by spot, the question being whether different spots respond to different stimuli and yield different sensory qualities. If you stamp a grid of ink lines on the hairless surface of the wrist (Fig. 10-2, p. 277), and explore it with appropriate stimuli, you find some spots responsive to pressure, some to warmth, some to cold, and many others to the prick of a needle—the test of this "responsiveness" being your ability to identify the stimulus in each case. The original discovery of these spots affords a striking instance of independent investigators reaching the same result almost simultaneously. Three physiologists—Blix the Swede, Goldscheider the German, and Donaldson the American—conducted the experiment at practically the same time and published their results in that order, within the few years from 1883 to 1885. The full demonstration of the pain points was not achieved till the work of von Frey (1894), another German physiologist.

Von Frey's experiment aimed to make sure whether the pain sense was separate from the pressure sense. He knew of course that strong pressure was likely to give pain while light pressure gave only a sensation of contact. It was therefore probable, if there were two separate senses, that the pressure sense had the lower threshold. Accordingly he needed a graduated series of very weak stimuli. He found that straight hairs, human and other, could be used for his purpose. He used hairs an inch long or more, fastened sideways at the end of light wooden handles. He pressed the free end of the hair vertically against the skin so as barely to bend the hair. It exerted upon the skin a definite pressure. A fine hair, pressed down on one pan of a balance, can barely raise a weight of one milligram placed in the other pan; a stiff hair can raise 100 times as much. The threshold of any spot of the skin was determined by ascertaining the weakest hair that gave rise to a sensation. The diameter of each hair was measured by aid of a microscope, and the pressure exerted per square millimeter was computed. Expressed in this last measure, the threshold was as follows on different surfaces (one subject):

STIMULUS THRESHOLD FOR PRESSURE

	Grams per sq mm
Tip of tongue	2
Tip of finger	3
Back of finger	5
Front of forearm	8
Back of hand	12
Calf of leg	16
Abdomen	26
Back of forearm	33
Loin	48
Thick parts of sole	250

The threshold depends partly on the thickness of the skin and partly on the amount of nerve supply. Hairy portions of the skin are shaved before the sensitiveness of the skin itself is measured, because a hair acts as a lever conveying stimulation to the nerve ends about its base, and any pressure sufficient to bend a short hair will ordinarily give a sensation.

Von Frey selected for more minute exploration a small area, one centimeter square, on the skin of the leg. He explored it first with very weak hairs and found a few points giving a sensation of contact. Using slightly stiffer hairs he found about 15 points that responded, each one having a threshold of 33 grams per square mm, or less. Gradual increase of the stimulus above this value yielded scarcely any further sensitive points till he reached 200 grams per square mm, above which pressure numerous points gave a pricking and painful sensation. There were thus two sets of spots, one with low threshold giving sensations of contact or pressure, and the other with high threshold giving sensations of pain. The distribution of the two sets was different, as the pressure spots were clustered near the roots of the hairs, while the pain spots were scattered over the whole surface. The pressure spots lie mostly on the "windward" side of the hair, i.e., close over the hair follicle. A few others are found, not close to any hair, even on hairy surfaces; and on the hairless surfaces there are of course many pressure spots (von Frey, 1894, p. 288).

Using a very sharp needle, von Frey pressed it into pain spots and pressure spots, getting sharp pain from the former, and usually only a pressure sensation from the latter. In spots that gave both pain and pressure to the needle stimulation, both pressure receptors and pain receptors might be present.

On the front of the eyeball (cornea and conjunctiva) the sensitive spots were numerous, and their threshold low, but the sensation was always painful, diffuse and outlasting the stimulus. It appeared that these surfaces were provided with a pain sense but not with a pressure sense.

The pain threshold was found to differ greatly in different regions, but the local differences were not parallel to those of the pressure sense. Some of the thresholds for pain were as follows:

STIMULUS THRESHOLD FOR PAIN

	Grams per sq mm
Cornea	.2
Conjunctiva	2
Abdomen	15
Front of forearm	20
Back of forearm	30
Calf of leg	30
Back of hand	100
Sole	200
Finger tip	300

For temperature spots, the skin is explored with dull-pointed brass or copper rods, maintained a few degrees warmer or colder than the skin by frequent immersion in water. More constant stimulus temperatures may be obtained by a hollow metal jacket through which circulates water at the desired temperature (Fig. 10-1). A fairly elaborate arrangement is needed to keep the water at a uniform temperature. Recently there have appeared some small electrical "soldering pencils"; with the aid of a rheostat to reduce the current flow, these can be maintained at a very satisfactory temperature for warm stimulation. For cold, it is convenient to insert a brass rod through a rubber stopper into a large test tube, filled with ice and water. The longer the portion of the rod projecting into the tube, the colder the stimulating end will be. The test tube may be covered with rubber tubing, to avoid its "sweating."

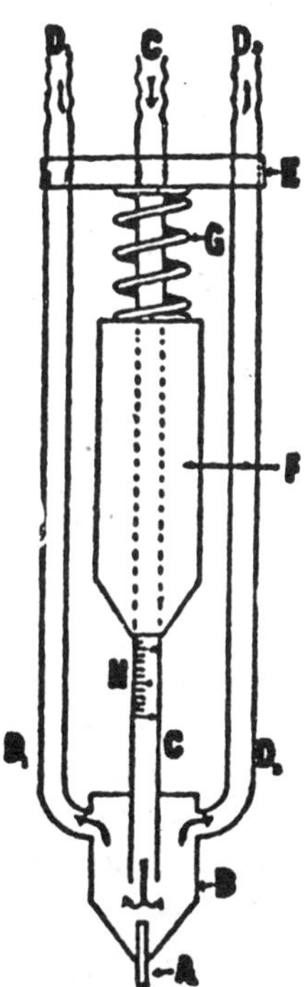

FIG. 10-1. (Dallenbach, 1927.) Improved thermal stimulator. Either cold water (8–9° C.) or warm water (42–44° C.) was forced into the chamber B through the tube C and out by D_1 and D_2. The projecting copper stimulus point, A, 1 mm in diameter, can be seen by the experimenter as he applies it to the skin, and is kept at a constant temperature by the water in B. The experimenter holds the handle F, supporting the weight of the apparatus through the spring G, and lowering it upon the skin till the handle reaches a certain mark on the scale H. Thus the pressure of A upon the skin is controlled.

Explored with a cool stimulus, the skin yields cool or cold sensations at some spots, and not at others. Explored with a warm stimulus, it yields warm sensations at certain spots and not at others. Usually more cold than warmth spots are found.

In general, the pain spots are the most numerous, next the touch or pressure spots, then the cold spots, and finally the warmth spots. The skin has been widely explored by Strughold and others and the results assembled by von Skramlik (1937) from whom a few counts are cited.

SPOTS PER SQUARE CENTIMETER

	Pain	Touch	Cold	Warmth
Forehead	184	50	8	.6
Tip of nose	44	100	13	1.0
Chest	196	29	9	.3
Volar side of forearm	203	15	6	.4
Back of hand	188	14	7	.5
Ball of thumb	60	120		

These results suggest the hypothesis that each sensory spot contains a receptor sensitive to a particular stimulus. One would expect to find warmth receptors in the warmth spots, cold receptors in the cold spots, pressure receptors in the touch spots, and pain receptors in the pain spots. Three questions are raised which can be submitted to experiment: (1) Are the spots stable in their sensitivity, so that the same spot always gives the same sensation? (2) Does the microscope reveal a characteristic end organ in each kind of spot? (3) Does each spot yield its characteristic sensation not only when excited by its "adequate" or normal stimulus, but also on the application of electric or other "general" stimuli? Affirmative answers to these three questions would demonstrate the punctate distribution of the skin senses.

Stability (or instability) of the sensory spots. The original investigators certainly leave the impression that they found stable spots which yielded the same sensation on retest. But when a student in the laboratory has mapped out a small area on the back of the hand, recording on his map each cold spot, and re-examines the same area on another day, he finds rather poor agreement. With the same stimulus he gets about the same number of cold spots, but not exactly in the same locations. Even experienced psychologists find only moderate correspondence in remapping

Another disturbing fact is that intensifying the stimulus increases the numbe of spots. Stimuli just slightly warmer or colder than the skin yield a few warmth or cold spots, while stimuli several degrees warmer or colder yield a much larger, though still a limited number (Heiser, 1932). The hypothesis of fixed spots can take care of this fact by assuming some receptors to be more sensitive than others, and by appealing to the undoubted fact that the physical effect a strong stimulus spreads over an preciable area of the skin. Increasi the pressure increases the area of sk subjected to stretch, raising the temperature of a stimulus increases the warmed area; and thus a strong stimulus will reach receptors situated some distance from the point of application to the skin.

Still we must admit that these two facts—the apparent instability of the spots and their increasing number with increasing stimulus—are more in line with an alternative hypothesis which discards the idea of punctate distribution of the skin senses and assumes only that the sensitivity of the skin varies from spot to spot, and in each spot from time to time. This alternative is at least worth keeping in mind.

The instability observed might be due to experimental errors. Dallenbach (1927) found many sources of error, some of which were very hard to avoid. Error arises from inexact mapping of the results. An exact record is necessary because two spots only a millimeter apart may give different sensations. The grid stamped on the skin for purposes of identification, though in indelible ink, rubs off in a few days unless protected by a ring of felt. Where the skin is loose, the map is sure to be inexact. The pressure of the temperature stimulator must be kept constant, and the duration of stimulation as well; and the skin itself should be at the same temperature during test and retest. A rise of one degree in its temperature makes

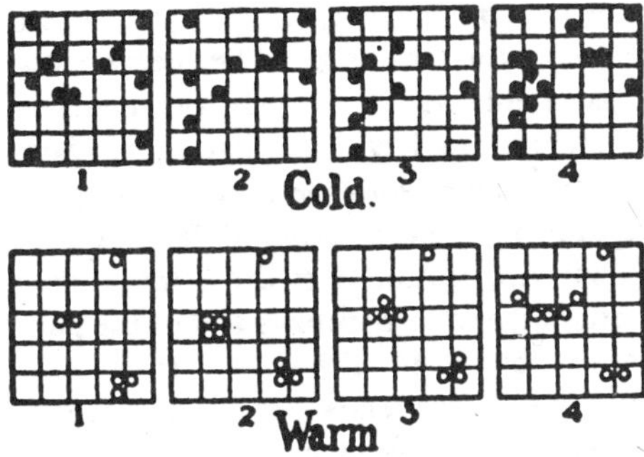

FIG. 10-2. (Dallenbach, 1927.) The same area, mapped four times for cold spots and four times for warmth spots, on four days within about a week. The area was 1 cm square on the subject's upper arm. The black dots are the cold spots, the little rings the warmth spots. Each square of the grid contains four tested points.

The four "warm" maps show perfect agreement if allowance is made for some variable spread of the warmth from the surface down into the skin to a receptor (cf. p. 280). Just three receptors can thus account for the four maps.

For the cold spots, they are too numerous to permit the above appraisal of the results, but there are four points (millimeter squares) that give the positive response every time and 78 that give the negative response every time. Even this small measure of agreement is much better than would be expected by chance, i.e., on the hypothesis that for a given stimulus intensity a certain percent of the points will give positive responses, the exact location of the responding points being a matter of chance. (Approximately 12 percent of the stimuli gave the cold sensation, and on this basis no point should give four successive positive responses—instead of four such points as observed—while only 60 instead of the observed 78 should consistently give negative responses.)

the skin less sensitive to warm stimuli, and a fall of one degree makes it less sensitive to cool stimuli. With so many causes of error and variation, perfect agreement of two maps cannot be expected. By using an improved stimulator which permitted precise control of the temperature and location of the stimulus, by securing the services of very competent *Os*, and by observing all possible precautions, Dallenbach obtained a degree of correspondence which can be seen in Figure 10-2.

While not conclusive, the evidence is rather in favor of localized receptors and punctate sensitivity. In another type of experiment no attempt is made to map all the warmth or cold spots in an area, but the specially sensitive spots are marked for later stimulation and prove to be very dependable. Pendleton (1928, p. 369) after locating 36 cold spots with great care found that only two of them ever failed to give the cold sensation

Search for the receptors of the cutaneous senses. Any theory of cutaneous sensation is incomplete until it can point out the anatomical structures which serve as pressure receptors, pain receptors, warmth receptors and cold receptors. It is incomplete until it can also show exactly how these structures are affected by their respective stimuli. Two methods have been employed in seeking for the receptors. The less direct method is to *compare the distribution* of the four senses over the skin with the distribution of different types of nerve ending. The more direct method is to *excise the spots* and see what nerve endings are present.

1. *Indirect method.* Histological examination of the skin reveals several types of nerve endings:

a. Free-branching nerve ends, the most common type of sensory nerve ending, present practically everywhere in the skin.

b. Hair receptors. The root of each hair is embedded in the mass of free nerve endings, and there is no difficulty in understanding how the hairs can serve as touch receptors, by transmitting pressure to the nerve endings around their roots. The great sensitiveness of the hairs can be understood from the leverage with which they act on these nerve endings.

c. Meissner corpuscles, found on the hairless portions of the skin. They are usually supposed to serve the pressure sense, and are even called "touch corpuscles."

d. Krause end bulbs, spherical in shape, each bulb (like the Meissner corpuscle) containing the ending of a sensory nerve fiber enclosed in a little capsule of epithelial cells.

e. Other end bulbs of cylindrical and other shapes.

f. Pacinian corpuscles, large and with well developed capsules, found in the subcutaneous tissue (and elsewhere) rather than in the skin itself.

As to distribution, the free nerve endings are everywhere, the hair receptors over the whole hairy surface, the Meissner corpuscles over the hairless areas. The end bulbs are apparently rather limited in distribution, as they are not easy to find microscopically, and have seldom been reported in histological studies of the skin.

All regions of the external skin are provided with all four senses. But this is not true of the mucous membrane of the mouth and throat, nor of the front of the eyeball, nor of some portions of the external genital organs. These regions have been explored in the hope of obtaining light on the temperature and pain receptors.

Von Frey (1895) found that the center of the cornea gave a sensation which, even when too faint to be painful, had the characteristics of pain as against touch, namely long latency and slow waxing and waning. The nerve endings there are exclusively of the free-branching variety. In that area, then, the *free nerve ends were obviously pain receptors.* The additional fact of universal distribution over the external skin both of free nerve endings and of the pain sense confirmed the correlation. But the free nerve ends may take care of other senses *besides* pain.

The outer margin of the cornea gives, in addition to pain, sensations of cold though not of warmth, and here Krause end bulbs are common. From this von Frey concluded that these *spherical end bulbs were probably the cold receptors,* though he left the question open whether such end bulbs are abundant enough in the external skin to take care of its cold sense.

Von Frey's experiments on the eyeball were repeated and improved by Strughold (1926). As a stimulator, he used a camel's-hair brush lightly covered with cotton wool, dipped into warm physiological salt solution, shaken out and then applied to the cornea or conjunctiva. He tested the outer skin of the eyelid, the conjunctiva just to the side of the cornea, the conjunctiva just below the cornea, usually covered by the lower lid, and the lower margin of the cornea, obtaining results which are tabulated below.

The skin of the lid here gives what may be called the normal or regular run of temperature sensations, with a physiological zero at

	Temperature of stimulus						
Area tested	*28–30°*	*31°*	*32–38°*	*39–46°*	*47–51°*	*52–55°*	*56–68°*
Skin of lid	cold	none	warm	warm	hot	burning-hot	burning
Conjunctiva, side	cold	none	none	none	cold	burning-cold	burning
Conjunctiva, below	none	none	none	none	none	burning	burning
Cornea, margin	cold	none	none	burning	unendurably-burning		

31° C. The side of the conjunctiva gives no temperature sensation between 31° C. and 46° C. the interpretation being that it has no warmth sense, though it gives "paradoxical cold" (see p. 282) in response to rather hot stimuli. The "burning cold" is interpreted as a combination of this paradoxical cold with the pain aroused by high temperatures.

The second area tested in the conjunctiva had no cold sense, or warmth sense either, and its only response to temperature was the burning sensation which occurred when the temperature was high enough to arouse the pain receptors.

The corneal margin shows the cold sense, no warmth sense, and a low threshold for the pain sense.

The inner corner of the eye, the caruncula lacrimalis, does give warmth and possesses also the pressure or touch sense absent from the conjunctiva and cornea. The touch and warmth sensations we get from the eye come from this inner corner and the outer skin and edge of the lids.

To summarize: the pain sense is present all over the cornea and conjunctiva, and is the only sense present in the middle of the cornea. The margin of the cornea and most of the conjunctiva have also the cold sense, but not the warmth nor the pressure sense.

The glans penis and clitoris have been tested by von Frey (1895) and by Hauer (1926), because of the presence in those areas of spherical end bulbs and of "genital corpuscles" which may be simply a large variety of the same. The pain sense is present, the pressure sense is said to be absent, the warmth sense present but not well developed, and the cold sense present and well developed. Thus the tie-up of the cold sense with the spherical end bulbs is strengthened.

In the mouth, a small area of the mucous membrane on the inside of the cheek opposite the second molar tooth has the distinction of lacking the sense of pain (Kiesow, 1894). The pain sense is the only one present in certain parts of the throat (tonsils and rear wall). Cold is more widely present in this region than warmth and pressure sensitivity. Inside the nose, all the cutaneous senses extend into the nostrils about 1 cm, and pain about 1 cm further (Schriever & Strughold, 1926). No close correlations with different forms of nerve endings have been made out for the mouth, throat, or nose.

2. *Direct method: examination of the skin or mucous membrane beneath the sensitive spots.* The conjunctiva of the eye is highly sensitive to cold, and it has numerous Krause end bulbs; moreover the distribution of the cold spots and of the end bulbs is similar as far as general topography is concerned: where the cold spots are numerous the end bulbs are also numerous. But such correlations are indirect evidence. Strughold & Karbe (1925) made a direct attack on the problem by intravital staining with methylene blue, a dye which stains nerve tissue. The procedure was to drop a little methylene blue solution into the eye, and observe the conjunctiva through a microscope until nerve fibers and receptors could be seen. A wait of 2–3 hours was necessary for the stain to take, and by the time the end bulbs became visible the dye had deprived the eye of both the cold sense and the pain sense, for the time being. Accordingly a map of the observed end bulbs was carefully made and the cold stimuli applied to their locations on the following day when the dye had disappeared and the sensitivity had returned. Almost all the spots in which end bulbs had been located gave the cold sensation. This result seems to clinch the question for the eye: its spherical end bulbs must certainly be cold receptors.

The matter cannot however be regarded as settled for the external skin. In the first place, there is no sure histological evidence of end bulbs in the skin. In the second place, several investigators, from Donaldson (1885) to Pendleton (1928) have applied the direct method, by locating cold spots, cutting them out, staining the excised bit of skin, and examining the nerve endings. All these investigators have been on the watch for end bulbs but have not seen any. One possible exception is Weddell (1941) who found two groups of endings resembling Krause end bulbs under a single excised cold spot. Walshe (1942) has critically examined the evidence and regards the claim of the Krause end bulbs to be cold receptors as fairly well established. They occur in clusters, like the Meissner corpuscles in the touch spots.

3. *Depth of the warmth and cold receptors in the skin.* If the receptors could be located as to depth, they would probably be easier to find and identify. It has long been believed that the *warmth receptors lie deeper than the cold receptors.* There are several bits of evidence in favor of this view.

First, the reaction time to warmth is longer than to cold—warmth about .18 sec., cold about .15 sec. Probably it takes longer for warmth applied to the surface of the skin to reach the warmth receptors—longer than it takes cold to penetrate to the cold receptors.

Second, the warmth spots are less sharp and punctate than the cold spots. Since the heat conduction must spread, a deep-lying receptor could be stimulated from a wider area of the surface than could a receptor lying near the surface.

Third, when the skin is cocainized by the electrosmotic method—the solution of cocaine being applied to the surface and carried in by electricity—it is known that only the superficial layers of the skin are reached by the anesthetic in the first few minutes, and deeper and deeper layers as the anesthetization continues. Schriever (1926) finds that three minutes of electrosmotic cocainization impairs the cold sense considerably, while leaving the warmth sense unaffected. After eight minutes both are gone. Pain and touch are usually the last to go (Cummings, 1938).

Fourth, data have been secured on the conduction of heat into and out of the skin, and on the concomitant temperature sensations (Bazett, McGlone & Brocklehurst, 1930). The temperatures at the surface and at various depths in the skin were measured by thermocouples connected with galvanometers, the deflections of the galvanometric needle being recorded on moving photographic paper. A cold or a warmth spot was first located on the back of the forearm. A sharp needle was then pushed horizontally through the skin under the cold or warmth spot, at a depth of about one millimeter. The needle being removed, a loop of slender wire was passed through the hole, and a thermojunction brought exactly below the spot; an X-ray photograph was taken to assist in this adjustment. Another thermocouple was placed on the surface of the skin directly over the spot. A warm or cold stimulus was then applied to the spot in question, *O* reacting as soon as he felt warmth or cold; the record on photographic paper showed the time of application of the warm or cold stimulus, the time of *O*'s reaction, and the temperature changes at the surface and at a certain depth in the skin.

The rate of conduction of heat through the outer layers of the skin was measured by noting in the records the instant when the galvanometer connected with the deep thermocouple first showed any rise or fall of temperature. The conduction of heat inward was at a rate of a little less than 1 mm per second, while the conduction outward (i.e., the penetration of cold) was somewhat slower.

The temperature at a depth of 1 mm started to rise about one second after the application of a warm stimulus. It continued to rise during the application of a brief stimulus and even for a few seconds after the withdrawal of the external stimulus (Fig. 10-3).

O signaled the sensation of warmth or cold with a variable reaction time, a second or more. A constant allowance of .15 sec was made for the true reaction time, the remainder was taken as the time required for heat or cold applied to the surface to reach the receptors, and their depth was computed from the speed of conduction. Though the several experiments gave somewhat different results, the most probable depth indicated for the cold receptors was only .15 mm, ± .1 mm, and that for the warmth receptors .6 mm ± .2 mm. These depths would locate the cold receptor in the papillae or in the Malpighian layer, and the warmth receptors in the dermis.

The authors found that the vascular condition of the skin had much to do with the rate of penetration of heat or cold, and suggested that constriction of the capillaries may be an important factor in the stimulation of the cold receptors.

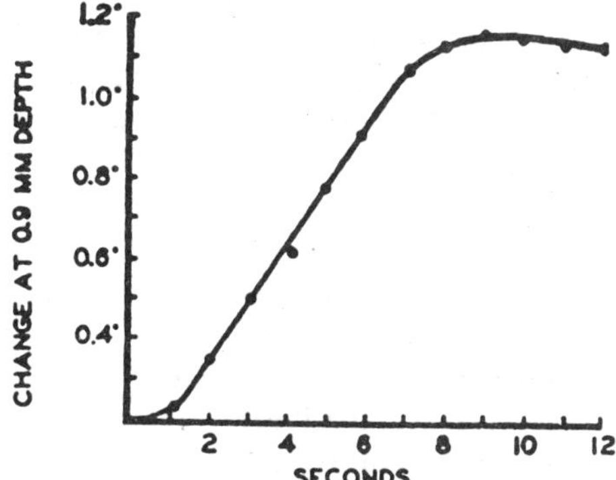

FIG. 10-3. (Data from Bazett, McClone & Brocklehurst, 1930.) Change of temperature at a depth of .9 mm from the surface of the skin, when a temperature 7.5° above that of the skin surface was applied for 5.4 sec. The inner temperature was scarcely affected at all for the first second; it then rose steadily at a rate of .18° per sec for 7 sec before tapering off and starting to fall. A warmth spot was present in the warmed area, and a sensation of warmth was signaled with a latency of 1.17 sec.

Another method of dissociating the skin senses. When a skin region is regaining its sensitivity during the regeneration of a severed nerve, there are some irregularities which suggested to Henry Head, an eminent English neurologist, that the recovery process deserved closer examination than was possible in clinical cases. In 1903 he had a cutaneous nerve in his forearm cut by a surgeon and carefully explored the corresponding skin area during the following months. At first there was only *deep sensitivity,* due to subcutaneous receptors and nerves; the area responded to even a few grams of pressure and gave dull pain when the pressure was increased. The first stage in cutaneous recovery was the appearance of what Head called *protopathic sensitivity,* a primitive affair which gave intense and unpleasant sensations to strong stimuli, but none to moderate ones. Eventually what he called *epicritic sensitivity* was superimposed on the cruder sort, bringing the skin back to normal. Head believed that his results contradicted the von Frey spot theory (Head, 1920).

Naturally this novel theory provoked a lot of controversy and stimulated others to cut nerves in their own arms (Trotter & Davies, 1909; Boring, 1916, 1923, 1942; Lanier, Carney & Wilson, 1935). In general the later studies found a less sharp break between the stages of recovery than had Head. There is undoubtedly an irregular recovery of the different sensations, but it can probably be explained by a gradual return of innervation, spreading inward from the edges of the anesthetic area. A number of different lines of evidence show that a given spot of skin may be innervated by several different nerve fibers (Bishop, 1946), and the combined action of these fibers may account for some of the complications that follow nerve section (Boring, 1923).

These complications can be eliminated by using temporary blocks on the cutaneous nerves. This can be done by injecting a local anesthetic around the nerve (Bishop, 1944), cutting off the blood supply (Lewis, 1942), or by applying pressure to the nerve (Raffel, 1936). (An accidental pressure block is probably largely responsible when "your leg goes to sleep" after it has been crossed over the other knee.) These temporary blocks have more rapid action on one skin sense than on another. The local anesthetic knocks them out in the order, touch, pain, warmth, and cold, and they return in inverse order. Other methods yield a different sequence, but all suggest separate mechanisms for the four senses. Some progress has even been made in assigning them to specific types of fibers in the cutaneous nerves. The large nerve fibers seem to "carry" touch, while slightly smaller ones are involved in warmth and cold. Pain may utilize two types of fibers: medium, and small unmedullated ones, perhaps corresponding to pricking and dull pain, respectively (Bishop, 1946).

Nonadequate stimulation of the sensitive spots of the skin. The "adequate" stimulus of any receptor is that agent to which the receptor is specially sensitive. Light is the adequate stimulus for the retina. The adequate stimulus for the pressure sense is a bending or stretching of the skin, for the temperature senses, roughly, warmth and cold, while for the pain sense it is strong pressure, penetration of the skin, strong heat, biting chemicals, etc. The pain stimulus seems to be anything that injures the skin or comes to the point of injuring it. The pain sense, in other words, has a high threshold and is not specially adapted to any particular kind of external stimulus. In accordance with the principle of specificity (p. 272), we must get a sensation of cold whenever a cold receptor is aroused by any stimulus whatever, and the same with the other receptors.

Von Frey (1894) found that interrupted electric currents gave a piercing sensation at the pain spots and a whirring or hammering sensation at the pressure spots. The pressure spots registered the vibratory character of the stimulus up to as many as 100 pulses per second, and this was true whether the pulses were electrical or mechanical, the latter sort being given by a vibrating tuning fork. The pain spots, on the contrary, gave a continuous sensation even when the pulses were as slow as 5 per second.

Kiesow (1895) applied mechanical and electrical stimuli to temperature spots. He first located and marked for identification the most sensitive warmth and cold spots he could find. A blunt-pointed stick of soft wood, applied to a sensitive cold spot gave a brief cold sensation; applied to a warmth spot it gave a longer-lasting warmth sensation. These results could not be got every time, but at best in about 50 percent of the trials. With electric stimuli his percentage of successes was nearer 75.

Electrical stimulation has one decided advantage over other types; its intensity and duration can be adequately controlled. Perhaps there might be some characteristic differences among the four skin senses in thresholds for electrical stimulation, which would suggest functional differentiation of the corresponding receptors. The intensive threshold (the minimum current that will stimulate) is not too promising, for it varies with the skin resistance. But how about the minimum duration necessary for stimulation? Such a time measure is the *chronaxie*. It is the duration required for stimulation by a current whose intensity is twice the threshold in value. Chronaxies have been determined for pressure, pain, warmth, and cold by several investigators (Neff & Dallenbach, 1936; Jones, 1940; Jones & Jones, 1941). They increase in the order given, which is very similar to the sequence in which these senses drop out under anesthetic blocking of the nerve.

Paradoxical cold and synthetic heat. One of the most interesting phenomena is the paradoxical sensation of cold which results from a warm stimulus. This discovery again goes back to von Frey (1895). Having located and marked a number of cold spots, he went over them with a hot stimulus, and some of them responded by a sensation of cold. Rather a high temperature was needed to arouse the cold spots, 45° C. in most areas, whereas 33° C. is usually high enough to give a gentle sensation of warmth.

Paradoxical cold cannot be obtained by applying a *broad* hot stimulus, because, obviously, the warmth receptors thus stimulated mask the cold. Thunberg (1901) found, however, that paradoxical cold could be got by areal stimulation of well *warmed* skin. He applied a temperature of 45° C. for two minutes to the front of the forearm, and immediately followed with a stimulus at 48° C., which gave a pure cold sensation at first, with some warmth creeping in later. This apparently strange result is explained by the adaptation of the warmth receptors to the 45° C. and their consequent weak response to the 48° C. The feeble response of the warmth receptors permitted the cold receptors in the area to deliver their sensation unmasked.

Paradoxical warmth has been reported a number of times, but is very difficult to obtain.

Paradoxical cold is our evidence for asserting that a moderately hot stimulus applied to an area arouses both the warmth and the cold receptors in that area. It was suggested by Alrutz (1908) that this simultaneous arousal of warmth and cold receptors gave the sensation of *heat*. A still higher temperature would also arouse the pain receptors. Alrutz gives the following scale of sensations above the physiological zero:

At physiological zero	no temperature sensation
At warmth threshold	barely warm
A little higher	definitely warm
At paradoxical cold threshold	heat resembling warmth
A little higher	heat resembling cold
At pain threshold	burning heat
A little higher	pure pain

The threshold temperatures for heat and burning heat differ somewhat with different individuals, and probably with the temperature of the environment. Lowenstein & Dallenbach (1930) determined these thresholds in 100 individuals, at a room temperature of 20–25° C., and found the heat threshold to range from 40–46°, with an average at 42–43°, and the burning heat threshold to range from 43–51°, with an average at about 46–47°.

The clearest demonstration of hot sensation resulting from the simultaneous stimulation of neighboring warmth and cold receptors is the *synthetic heat* experiment, in which no genuine heat is applied, but warmth spots are subjected to moderate warmth, and cold spots to cold. Several experimenters have succeeded with this experiment. An effective procedure is the application to the front of the forearm of a "temperature grill" built of small copper tubing. The tubes are parallel, a few millimeters apart, and alternate tubes are warmed and cooled by warm and cold water circulating through them. *O* is kept in ignorance of the nature of the stimulation (Burnett & Dallenbach, 1927).

The first sensation is usually cold, followed by heat which often disappears after a few seconds and gives way to cold again. Warmth also is often experienced at some time during a 10–15 sec stimulus.

Synthetic *burning* heat has been obtained by the simultaneous application of cold, warmth (not heat) and weak electric shocks (Ferrall & Dallenbach, 1930).

In spite of all this impressive evidence for paradoxical cold and synthetic heat, the case is not yet closed. Jenkins (1938b) found that only two out of four *Os* reported paradoxical cold or warmth, giving only 27 such reports out of 9,000 stimulations. In further studies (1938c) he found that few untrained *O*s got "synthetic heat" from warmth plus cold or from warmth plus cold plus shock, and there was other evidence against the Alrutz theory. Apparently the experimental results are very dependent on conditions of stimulation, including the attitude of *O*. This variability can readily be demonstrated in a simple fashion. Attach a dozen thin brass rods to each of two backing strips, so that they resemble two combs, with the teeth spaced enough so that they can be intermeshed. Now soak one in cold water, and the other in warm (not hot) water. Remove them, whip off the surplus water, and intermesh the rods so they are alternately warm and cold. Have *O* quickly place his wrist across them, as the line is drawn, thus:

WCWCWCWCW

Some *O*s will pull the arm away, as if burned, some will merely report "Heat," and others, "Warmth plus cold."

There may be a relatively simple solution to the controversy over synthetic heat. Let us assume that a hot object actually stimulates warmth, cold, and pain receptors. We have seen that the reaction time to cold is the shortest of the three. Hence if we touch a hot object, cold will flash up first, followed by warmth, and then pain. If we are set for heat, we withdraw our hand as soon as cold plus a little warmth comes through, and report "heat." But if we continue to hold the skin in contact with the grid, we soon discriminate the regular patterning of the alternate rods, which is quite different from the hit-or-miss pattern of warmth and paradoxical cold that results from a hot surface or liquid.

The concentration theory of cutaneous cold. In a further series of studies, Jenkins (1940, 1941) has obtained evidence that may call for some modification of the spot theory of the temperature senses. He used a technique of seriatim mapping; this involves repeated stimulation of each of perhaps 50 points, with 24 or more stimulations per point distributed over several sessions. Each stimulation yielded a report of 3 (strong cold) down through 2 and 1 (weak cold) to 0 (neutral). Thus, each skin point could be given a composite score, representing its sensitivity. According to the spot theory, points directly over a cold receptor should be very sensitive; neighboring points which affect this receptor by spread should be less sensitive. This was generally found to be true. But it should follow that simultaneous stimulation of the sensitive point and its less sensitive neighbor would summate the effect, yielding higher scores than would either point alone. Jenkins found that such stimulation of two points yielded a score that was consistently *lower* than the more sensitive one. Jenkins thinks that his results demand a very large number of receptors in a given area, rather than a few spots. The intensity resulting from stimulation of a given area depends on the average concentration of active spots beneath the area.

There are certainly not enough encapsulated endings to satisfy Jenkins' theory. Hence, he assumes that the more numerous free nerve endings are temperature receptors. As a matter of fact, they may also serve touch and pain. Perhaps we have placed too much emphasis on the more striking end bulbs. But if the free nerve endings subserve all four of the skin senses, they must be differentiated in some way that we have not yet detected. There is plenty of evidence for four relatively separate and functionally distinct sensory systems in the skin, subserving warmth, cold, touch, and pain. (Cf. Jenkins, 1951.)

Radiant heat. Most of the work on temperature has been done with stimulus objects in actual contact with the skin. Somewhat different results are obtained with radiant heat (Hardy & Oppel, 1937). In the first place, if the stimulus area is much less than a square inch, no temperature is reported until the pain threshold is reached; this area is about 700 times as large as the tip of a contact stimulator (1 mm). Further, there is marked summation from two areas so that the threshold for radiant energy applied to both hands is lower than that for either hand alone. This finding is also in marked contrast to the lack of summation reported by Jenkins (1940) for contact stimulators. Jenkins (1951) suggests that these differences may mean that there are different mechanisms for radiant and contact stimulation. But it is more reasonable to attribute the differences to the tactual component of the contact stimulation. The precisely-localized pressure stimulation may "tie down" the vaguer warmth when a contact stimulator is used; lacking the stabilizing tactual component, the radiant temperature may be harder to recognize.

Pain. Over-strong stimulation of any sort will elicit pain from almost any part of the body. Hence it was long believed that pain was a special quality that resulted when any receptor was overstimulated (cf. Dallenbach, 1939). But certain lines of evidence, such as the fact that specific neural lesions will eliminate pain without disturbing touch, and vice versa, pointed to a separate pain sense. The discovery of pain spots in the skin gave strong support to this view. The receptors for pain are undoubtedly free nerve endings, which branch widely throughout the skin and other sensitive tissues. Stretching these endings results in pain (Geldard, 1950). The resulting impulses travel in specific nerve bundles; the surgeon sometimes severs these nerves to remove persistent pain. There are even reports of people who have a congenital lack of pain, and often cut or burn themselves without knowing it (Boyd & Nie, 1949).

Pain is undoubtedly a separate sense. It is quite possible that it should be considered multiple rather than single. The pain we have dealt with in this chapter, that aroused by stimulation of a pain spot, may be called pricking pain, and it is not particularly unpleasant. With stronger stimulation, applied over a wider area, the quality changes to dull or aching pain. The same shift occurs when an exposed cutaneous nerve is subjected to increasing intensities of electrical stimulation (Pattle & Weddell, 1948). The pain from an aching muscle or distended bladder may be still different. We cannot say whether these are separate qualities within a single sense, or different senses. The problem is further complicated by the common confusion between pain and the reaction to it. This is readily observed when mild electric shocks are delivered to the skin; a "nervous" person will often jerk his hand away as soon as the shock is perceptible as a faint intermittent tactual sensation, not unlike that yielded by touching a vibrating tuning fork. Whether we call this a conditioned reflex or an hallucination is not important at the moment. It is certain that these reactions lead to endless confusion when we try to study the pain sense in a quantitative fashion. These problems are becoming increasingly important in modern medicine. A great deal of research has been devoted to pain in recent years. Much of it has been done with the Hardy-Wolff-Goodell apparatus, which throws a spot of radiant heat on the blackened surface of the forehead and is reported to give highly stable thresholds (see Wolff & Wolf, 1949). It would take us too far afield to cover the extensive literature on this confusing blend of sensation and reaction to it. A review by Edwards listed 101 papers (1950a).

ADAPTATION OF THE SKIN SENSES

All these senses show the phenomenon of "negative adaptation": under continuous, unchanging application of a stimulus they cease after a time to give their characteristic sensations. From ordinary experience we might imagine the *pain sense* to be nonadaptable, but under ordinary conditions the stimulus is more or less intermittent and the sense is afforded intervals for recovery. A sharp needle applied to the forearm with the small pressure of 2.5–25 grams gives cutaneous pain without complication from deep pressure; and the pain fades out in a time which varies in general between 10 and 100 sec. The process of fading may be complicated by momentary recurrence of a pain which has once vanished. A typical case gives the following sequence of reports: "(1) sharp intense pain, (2) sharp pain, (3) pain, (4) dull pain, (5) weak pain, (6) pressure, (7) weak pressure, (8) tickle, (9) nothing." On removal of the stimulus, after-sensations of itching, pricking, heat, etc., are often quite strong (Wells & Hoisington, 1931; Burns & Dallenbach, 1933). When several needles are simultaneously applied to an area 15 mm in diameter on the forearm, adaptation may require as long as 5 minutes but it is eventually complete in practically all cases (Stone & Dallenbach, 1936).

Pressure sense adaptation. "Touch proper" is extremely subject to adaptation. Pull on a glove and then hold the hand perfectly still. The strong initial sensation of pressure fades rapidly till the glove is scarcely felt unless the

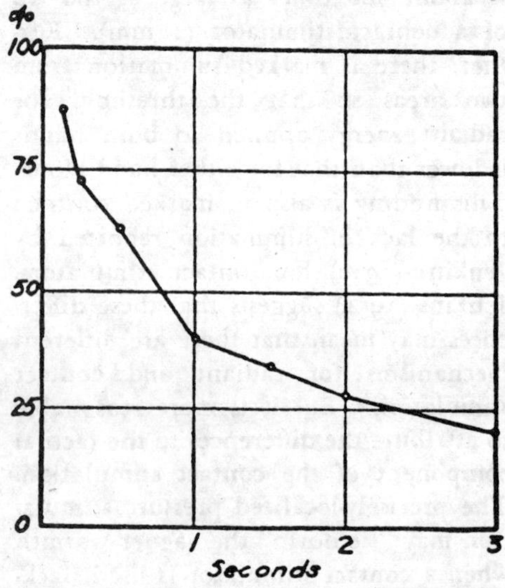

FIG. 10-4. (After von Frey & Goldman, 1915.) Rapid fading of pressure sensation during steady stimulation. Two neighboring areas on the forearm were stimulated, one with a steady pressure lasting 4 sec, the other with a momentary pressure thrown in at some time during the application of the steady pressure to the other area. In a series of trials the momentary pressure was adjusted till judged equal in intensity to the steady pressure at the same moment. The momentary stimulus provided a yardstick to measure the declining sensation of the steady stimulus. The ordinate shows the momentary pressure judged equal to the steady pressure, in percent of the initial matching value. After a 3-sec application the steady pressure has declined to about 20 percent of its initial matching value.

stimulus becomes intermittent because of pulsating arteries.

Experimentally, the adaptation to steady pressure follows a course which is indicated, for the first few seconds, in Figure 10-4. A simpler experiment answers the question, how long a steady pressure can be felt at all. A weight is gently lowered upon the skin and allowed to rest there till *O* signals that it is no longer felt. A paper disk is first laid on the area to be stimulated so as to avoid temperature sensations. Adaptation time is found to be quite variable, differing apparently with the individual, with the weight applied and with the region of skin stimulated. The averages from eight *O*s are shown in the table.

ADAPTATION TIME FOR STEADY PRESSURE

(In seconds)
(Zigler, 1932)

Applied weight (milligrams)	*Region stimulated*			
	Back of hand	*Fore-arm*	*Fore-head*	*Cheek*
50	2.42	2.31	5.07	5.71
100	3.82	3.28	6.22	6.37
500	6.01	4.86	9.96	11.63
1000	6.71	5.60	10.43	13.51
2000	9.52	7.76	16.03	19.36

Though the adaptation time of 2 seconds to the lightest pressures seems very short, there is reason to believe that the receptors, or some of them, adapt almost instantly to a perfectly steady stimulus. They may respond positively only to *changes* of pressure reaching the fine endings of the sensory nerve fibers. The longer adaptation times may represent gradual mechanical adjustments of the skin which bring in fresh receptors or cause the stimulation of some receptors to be intermittent (Adrian, 1932; Cattell & Hoagland, 1931).

As a matter of fact, there is some clear-cut evidence on this point. Nafe & Wagoner (1941) arranged an elaborate lever system which gave a greatly enlarged record of the rate at which a light weight sank into the skin. The weight sank rapidly at first, and gradually slowed up until it reached equilibrium with the tension of the skin. When the rate of sinking approached zero, *O* reported that he no longer felt the weight. If part of the weight was suddenly removed, the remaining portion slowly rose, again yielding a tactual sensation until it reached a new equilibrium. Hence, it is well established that cutaneous pressure is a "dead-beat" sense, responding only while the skin is changing shape. But deep pressure, arising from subcutaneous receptors, especially those in muscles, shows very little adaptation. You can usually feel the pressure of the chair, even though you have been sitting motionless for some time. If the receptors in the muscles did not have this characteristic resistance to adaptation, we could not maintain a bodily posture.

The rapid adaptation of cutaneous pressure is one of the reasons why active touch is superior to passive touch. Fine differences in texture can be recognized if they are moved over the finger, or vice versa. But one can barely tell coarse sandpaper from fine by merely resting the finger on it, and if there are any immediate differences, they fade almost immediately. In short, most everyday "tactual sensations" are actually *perceptual* blends of a temporal sequence of cutaneous pressures and temperatures, tied in with muscle sensations.

Temperature sense adaptation. Ordinarily, in a comfortable room, there is little sensation of either warmth or cold from any portion of the skin, though different portions are at different temperatures. This fact indicates some adaptation of the temperature senses. Exposed parts of the skin usually have a surface temperature of 30–32° C., which is 86–90° F., several degrees below the internal body temperature. The exposed parts are adapted to their own temperature, which is the "physiological zero" of the subjective temperature scale.

The physiological zero is not fixed; it varies from one part of the skin to another, and in the same part from time to time according to the surface temperature. If 32° C. is the surface temperature of the hand, water at that temperature will feel neither warm nor cool to the hand. Transfer the hand to water at 35° and you find it definitely warm at first, but after a few minutes of steady immersion it becomes neutral. If the hand is then transferred back to water at 32°, the latter feels cool instead of neutral. The physiological zero has been raised, and it can similarly be lowered by holding the hand in water a few degrees below the usual surface temperature of the hand.

The same temperature may seem simultaneously warm to one hand and cold to the other, as in the classical adaptation experiment of Weber (1846). Three bowls of water are provided, at 20°, 30°, and 40° C. Hold one hand in the warm water and the other in the cold water for a minute or two, and then transfer both to the medium water.

Weber's experiments led him to a theory of the adequate stimuli for the temperature senses. The warmth sensation he held to result from a rise in temperature of the skin, the cold sensation from a fall of temperature. With a stationary temperature of the receptors, there would be no sensation, no matter what the temperature.

An opposed theory was formulated by Hering (1877). He held that when the skin was adapted to any temperature, a higher temperature constituted a warmth stimulus, and a lower temperature a cold sense stimulus.

A large share of the numerous experiments devoted to the temperature sense had these two theories in view, but no generally accepted decision has been reached—except, perhaps, that neither theory comes very close to the real physical character of the stimulus as it reaches the receptors. We may as well accept that decision and utilize the experimental data for the light they throw on important questions of fact, such as: (1) What are the limits of temperature within which the warmth and cold senses are capable of adaptation? (2) How rapidly do they become adapted? (3) Do the two temperature senses keep pace with each other in becoming adapted to a given temperature? Does the physiological zero move in adaptation? (4) Is the physiological zero really a zone of some width, and does the width change with the adaptation temperature? (5) Is the whole scale of temperature sensations moved bodily up or down in adaptation to a high or low temperature?

Limits of adaptation. The facts are complex. If the hand is held in water that is only a few degrees above or below the usual skin temperature, the sensations of warmth or cold diminish and cease in a few minutes. If the hand is held in water much above 45° C. (113° F.), the burning heat soon becomes unendurable, and apparently the pain sense does not become adapted to this high temperature until the surface of the skin is cooked. If the hand is held in water as low as 10° C. (50° F.), the sensation of cold persists for a long time and perhaps never does disappear. These facts by themselves indicate that there are limits to the possible range of adaptation, though the exact limits may be difficult to establish.

An introspective account of the process of becoming adapted to a cold stimulus (about 20° C.) is given by Abbott (1914):

> There was scarcely any noticeable change in the sensation for a longer or shorter time, depending on the individual, and then the temperature sensation faded with remarkable quickness. . . . But this first disappearance was not permanent. The sensation returned and there was likely to be a fluctuation . . . for some little time before adaptation was complete and permanent. Each time the sensation returned it was a little fainter and lasted a shorter time.

All of Abbott's subjects reported complete disappearance of the temperature sensation, after a longer or shorter exposure to any temperature within the range of 17.5 to 40° C.

Somewhat similar results were obtained by Gertz (1921), who found that adaptation proceeded intermittently when the hand was held in cold water, the cold sensation disappearing, reappearing with less intensity and finally disappearing altogether. Adaptation to warm water proceeded more smoothly. But when the cold water was below 18° C., there was, according to Gertz, never a complete loss of cold sensation. A deep sensation of cold, compounded with deep pressure—in short, a numb feeling—persisted even when the skin itself had ceased to deliver the sensation of cold. It was not altogether easy to decide whether the cold came from the skin or from deeper in the hand, and for this reason it was difficult to locate the exact lower limit of cutaneous adaptation. Gertz was inclined to place the lower limit at about 16° C., certainly not lower than 12° C. He placed the upper limit at 41–42° C. We shall have occasion shortly to return to his findings.

Rate of adaptation. The further an applied temperature is from normal skin temperature, the longer time is needed for the skin to become adapted to it. Holm (1903) and Gertz (1921) applied a "temperator" (an instrument for warming or cooling a skin area) and kept the temperature constant till the skin ceased to feel it as warm or cold. The following table shows the time required for the sensation to disappear.

Applied temperature	*Duration of warmth or cold sensation* (*Holm*)	(*Gertz*)
45°C	152 sec.	
40°	126	162 sec.
30°	31	
25°	47	52
20°	72	102
15°	112	126
10°	165	
5°	210	

The main result here is the progressive increase of adaptation time as the applied temperature lies further away from the initial surface temperature of the skin (here 31–32°). Holm's results seem peculiar, or exceptional, in that he reports complete adaptation to temperatures as high as 45° C. and as low as 5° C. But his main result, just noted, is probably correct even if adaptation was not really complete.

In another interesting experiment, Gertz managed to change the applied temperature so slowly that no warmth or cold was ever felt. This result was accomplished when a change of 10°, up or down, occupied 35–45 minutes, in the making. A change of 0.2° C. per minute was about the threshold.

We are not to infer from the results so far cited that adaptation proceeds at a uniform rate from the time the hand is plunged into warm or cold water up to the time when that water ceases to feel warm or cold. The adaptation curve is not a straight line. To determine the nature of the curve a different sort of experiment is necessary, such as is described under Figure 10-5.

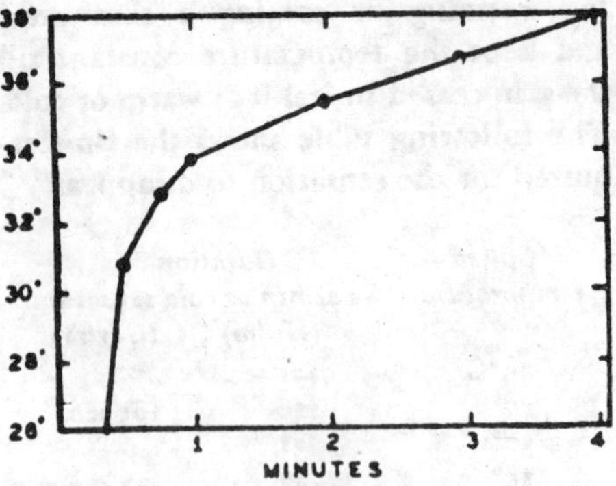

FIG. 10-5. (Data from Hahn, 1930.) The progress of temperature adaptation. Both hands were first adapted to 38° C. by being held for 5 min in water at that temperature. Then the left hand was transferred to water at 26° to become adapted to that new temperature, while the right hand remained in the 38° water. After ½ min, a series of tests showed that the 26° felt just as cold to the partially adapted left hand as a test bowl at 31° felt to the other hand which had preserved its 38° adaptation. The abscissa denotes time from the beginning of immersion in the 26° water; the ordinate shows the temperature of the test bowl which seems the same to the right hand as 26° seems to the partially adapted left hand. At the end of 4 min, 26° feels to the left hand the same as 38° seems to the right; both feel neutral and adaptation is complete. The upward trend of the curve shows the approximation toward complete adaptation. The curve resembles a growth curve (p. 23). A curve of similar shape was obtained by Hahn for the process of adaptation between any initial and any final temperature, except that adaptation to extreme temperatures never reached completion.

Simultaneous adaptation of the warmth and cold senses—shifting of the physiological zero. Recognizing two temperature senses we must inquire whether adaptation to cold means only an adaptation of the cold sense, or whether the warmth sense also becomes adapted to the low temperature. Adaptation of the cold sense to cold means that the threshold for cold has been pushed down the scale. Adaptation of the warmth sense to cold would mean that the threshold for warmth also has been pushed down the scale. Thus if 20° C. no longer feels cold (or cool), then the cold sense is adapted to 20° C. If a temperature of 21° or 22° now feels warm, then the warmth sense also is adapted to 20°. One sense might conceivably become adapted alone. In that case, adaptation to 20° C. would mean that temperatures between 20° and 32° were neither cold nor warm to the skin; the neutral zone would be expanded to cover all the temperatures down to the adaptation temperature.

The fact of the matter is that, in cold adaptation, temperatures above the adaptation temperature feel warm, and in warm adaptation temperatures below the adaptation temperature feel cool Thunberg (1901) reports that when the skin has been exposed for some time to 11° C., a temperature of 12° gives a distinctly warm sensation, and that when it has been adapted to 39°, temperatures a little below that give a cold sensation. At these adapting temperatures the neutral point may fall a degree short of that of the adapting bath. The failure becomes more pronounced at extreme temperatures; Gertz (1921) found that application of 45° adapts the warmth sense to 41° and the cold sense to about 39°.

Width of the neutral zone. Gertz' results bring out the fact that there is really a neutral *zone,* rather than a point. This is to be expected from what we know of psychophysics. We may treat the warmth and cold senses as separate ones, and determine the absolute threshold (RL) in each direction from the indifference point. Or we may consider the adapting temperature as the Standard, and use the Method of Constant Stimuli to determine a difference threshold (DL) above and below it. This is the method used by Culler (1926a). The fingers of both hands were used alike. They were first adapted to a given temperature by immersion in a jar of water at that temperature for 3–5 minutes. They were then transferred in succession to two test jars, remaining in each for 2 sec, and then were replaced in the adaptation jar for 12 sec before making a similar test. *O*'s task was to say which of the two test jars was warmer. One of them was always at the adaptation temperature, and the other a fraction of a degree higher or lower (or sometimes the same). The computation gave the warmth and cold thresholds above and below the given adaptation temperature.

A sample of the results for a single adaptation temperature is the following:

If we are willing to take as our measure of the neutral zone the difference between the 50-percent thresholds for warmth and cold, we have the very small figure of .087°, less than 1/10° C. We saw earlier (p. 214) that the interval of uncertainty was of doubtful value, so perhaps we should examine other measures. One SD either side of the point of subjective equality (PSE) would give double the estimated width of the neutral zone (.079 + .094 = .173). Or splitting the equal judgments between the other two categories, and interpolating for the quartiles, gives an interquartile range of roughly .20°. All of these estimates are considerably smaller than those obtained by Gertz; the psychophysical method seems to force *O* to make the best discrimination possible

Adaptation temperature	*Width of neutral zone*	*Median SD*
44 C.	.166	.241
40	.156	.163
36	.117	.096
32	.079	.076
28	.071	.077
24	.081	.099
20	.112	.131
16	.143	.128

Culler's results at several adaptation temperatures are given above. Note that the SD is roughly the same as the width of the neutral zone, and that both

Adaptation temperature = 24.00°C. Each comparison temperature was compared with this.

Comparison temps.	*24.20°C.*	*24.15°C.*	*24.10°C.*	*24.05°C.*	*24.00°C.*	*23.95°C.*	*23.90°C.*	*23.85°C.*
Percent of judgments								
warmer	100	75	58	31	18	10	00	00
equal	00	19	32	35	37	28	15	8
colder	00	6	10	34	45	62	85	92

Computation of these data, by the Summation Method gives—

warmth threshold at	24.079,	SD = .079
cold threshold	23.992,	SD = .094
difference	0.087 degrees	

reach minimum values at an adapting temperature of 30° (86° F.), which is in the neighborhood of normal skin temperature for the hand.

Distortion of the sensation scale in adaptation to high or low temperatures. So far, we have seen that the physiological zero moves up or down in adaptation, and also that the neutral zone widens when the adaptation temperature lies far from the normal temperature of the skin. This last fact leads us to expect some loss of sensitivity to differences of temperature. Will a temperature 5° above (or below) the physiological zero always feel equally warm (or cold), no matter how much the physiological zero has been displaced by adaptation? Very elaborate experiments would be required to answer this question, but the data at hand (see Fig. 10-6) indicate a loss of sensitivity such that, for example, 8° of warmth (or cold) to the adapted hand feels only as warm (or cold) as 5° to the normal hand.

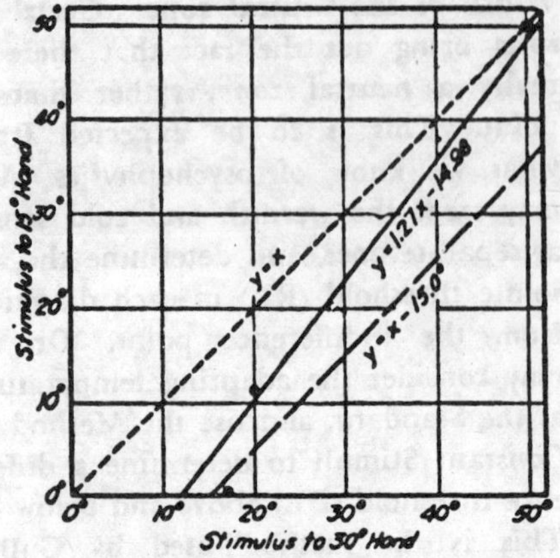

FIG. 10-6. (Data from Hummel, 1926.) Equivalent stimulus temperatures for differently adapted hands. The Y hand was adapted to 15° C., the X hand to 30° C. The adaptation was scarcely complete since the hands (forefingers) were immersed only 1 minute before each test. They were taken from the adaptation jars, rapidly dried on a towel and at once placed in two test jars, and O judged which of the test jars was warmer. In a series of such tests an equation was worked out between the two hands, differently adapted as they were. Each round dot in the graph records one such equation, the ordinate showing the temperature applied to the cold-adapted hand, the abscissa the subjectively equivalent temperature applied to the normal hand. The broken line, $y = x$, shows where the data points would have fallen if both hands had got the same sensation from the same test stimuli. The other broken line, $y = x - 15$, indicates where the points would have fallen if adaptation had been fully effective. The full line is the regression line of y on x, the best-fitting straight line to the data. The slope of this line shows that, on the average, a difference of 1.27° in the temperatures applied to the cold hand counted for only as much as a difference of 1.00° applied to the normal hand. Adaptation seems then to have done two things: shifted the physiological zero down a certain number of degrees, and diminished the sensitivity of the cold-adapted hand. Several other experiments have reached results consistent with this conclusion, though the evidence is still far from adequate.

Adaptation in limited areas. Most of the studies on temperature adaptation have been made with large areas. When smaller areas are used, of the order of magnitude of a few sensitive spots, somewhat different results are obtained. A single warm or cold spot can be knocked out rather quickly by intermittent stimulation (Levine & Dallenbach, 1936). As the size of the stimulator is increased, so is the time required for adaptation—but the increase is related to the perimeter rather than to the area. Thus adaptation time is longer for a square or ring than for a disk of the same contact area (Jenkins, 1938a). The problem becomes even more complicated when the area to be stimulated is surrounded by a ring-shaped constant temperature field, which adapts the surrounding skin to some specific temperature (Jenkins, 1937).

These results will eventually have to be integrated into some theory of the temperature senses, but nobody has developed a satisfactory one up to the present. One attempt at such a theory was made by Nafe (Nafe, 1934; Nafe & Wagoner, 1936). It emphasizes the vascular effects of temperature stimulation. The skin is richly supplied with small blood vessels, and these undoubtedly constrict and dilate as the temperature of the skin is changed. These changes are probably of importance, but it seems unlikely that they represent the sole mechanism of the temperature senses, as Nafe supposes (cf Jenkins, 1939, 1951). Perhaps we shall end with some combination of the spot theory, the concentration theory of Jenkins, and the vascular theory.

Adaptation to radiant heat (pain). Although the adaptation experiments are hard to fit into a theory of warmth and cold, the picture on pain is beginning to make sense. Using the radiant heat method (p. 286), Hardy, Goodell & Wolff (1951) found that the lower the initial temperature of the skin, the more heat had to be added to get pain. From their data they calculated that pain results when the skin temperature reaches about 45° C. (113° F). This is the temperature at which tissue damage starts. Thus the pain threshold for radiant heat is a fairly fixed temperature; unlike thresholds for warm and cold, it does not change with adaptation. Once again we have evidence that pain is a separate sense, evoked by stimuli which can cause tissue damage.

CUTANEOUS PERCEPTION

Up to the present we have been chiefly concerned with the analysis of the simple elements which go to make up the complex wholes that we call objects; in short, sensations rather than perceptions. Warmth, cold, pressure and pain are direct effects of cutaneous stimuli, and there are usually added components from deep or subcutaneous pressure and the various receptors involved in movement. It is only in the laboratory that one tries to isolate these components, by careful control of the stimulus and by special training. The naïve *O* usually commits the *stimulus error.* Titchener (1909, p. 267) suggested a better name, the *object error.* The error consists in attending to and reporting the object or the objective fact rather than the stimulus or the simple sensation.

The two-point threshold. The tendency to commit the object error is nicely illustrated in the two-point threshold. With a pair of "touch compasses" two points at graduated distances are simultaneously applied to the skin; as a check only one point is applied. In a perception experiment, *O*'s task is to distinguish between two points and one. In an experiment on sensation, his attention is directed to the exact impression derived from each application of the stimulus, and he reports whether the impression is compact, elongated, dumb-bell-shaped, or clearly double (Boring, 1921). *O* would be committing the object error in this last experiment if he attempted to decide whether two points or one were being applied. But are not the two points and the one point the stimuli? No, for a stimulus must be defined in relation to the receptors—light is not a stimulus except as it strikes the retina. The tactual stimulus consists in deformation of the skin and stretch applied to the receptors. In describing the sensation *O* gets as close as possible to the stimulus.

The two-point threshold is smallest on the tip of the tongue (1 mm) and largest in some parts of the back, thigh, and upper arm where it is given as 68 mm. It shows a large practice effect (p. 738).

A long-known fact which may appear strange is that the two-point threshold exceeds the error of localization in the same region. On the volar surface of the forearm, near the wrist, where the two-point threshold is about 14 mm, the error of localization is about 4 mm. In determining the localization error, *E* touches a point on the skin and *O*, blindfolded, tries to touch the same point with a stylus. Or, to make conditions more like those in the determination of the two-point threshold, *E* touches two points successively and *O* judges "Same place" or "Different place." By this method the localization error measures about ¼ of the two-point threshold. Zigler (1935) who obtained this result explains it as follows: when a blunt point is applied to the skin, stimulation is not limited to a point, since the surrounding skin is somewhat stretched. The receptors must be stimulated in decreasing amount from the directly touched point as a center. Localization is probably determined by the center of strongest stimulation, while the whole stretched area is effective in giving a broad impression and obscuring the presence of two points. (See also Boring, 1930.) For other methods of studying localization and for results on constant errors of localization, see Cole, 1929; Hulin, 1935; Grannis & Walker, 1936. For values of the two-point threshold see Ladd & Woodworth, 1911; von Skramlik, 1937. The history of the two-point threshold and of errors of localization shows some very interesting controversies. They were discussed in some detail by Boring in 1942. In recent years these fields have been quite inactive, but at one time they seemed to offer one key to the basic mechanisms of the skin senses.

Perception of rough and smooth. One of the most extensive attempts to break down a relatively simple perception into its sensory components was made by Katz (1925). From a large assortment of papers he selected a scale of 14, extending from glazed paper at one end, through writing paper, drawing paper, blotting paper, and wrapping paper to a very rough cloth paper. Over two sheets of paper to be compared, was laid a sheet of cardboard having windows 4 × 6 inches through which the papers were felt with the fingers, the eyes being closed. With very few errors, *O* distinguished all the papers with respect to roughness and smoothness. Asked to describe the papers, he characterized most of them with fair success.

O's spontaneous procedure in examining the papers was to move the finger balls from side to side along the surface. When he was required to eliminate this movement and to place his fingers on the paper and take them off immediately, he was unable to perceive roughness and smoothness, though this type of exploration revealed hardness and softness. It appeared that friction between the skin and the paper somehow furnished the cues of rough and smooth. In order to determine whether active movement was necessary, the papers were mounted on a turntable and moved under *O*'s motionless fingers, with the result that he was still able to distinguish the papers though perhaps not quite so well as with active finger movement. Explored with a wooden rod held like a pen the papers were distinguished fairly well. A thin coating of collodion on the fingers hampered the perception very little, but a coating of liquid glue made all the papers feel equally smooth.

Is the up-and-down bouncing movement impressed on the finger by the unevenness of the rough surface sufficient in extent to constitute a stimulus? Katz found that a lightly etched piece of glass felt rough though the up-and-down of the surface amounted to only .001 mm, too little to constitute a mere spatial stimulus, but enough, by friction, to produce irregular vibrations in the skin. These vibrations are even audible and make it necessary to plug the ears with cotton in order to limit perception to tactual cues.

Perception of vibration by the skin. For a handy demonstration of cutaneous vibratory sensation, simply hum a note while partially closing the nostrils. Damp a tuning fork or piano string with the finger and you feel the vibration. Set a tuning fork in vibration and apply its shank or foot to the skin and the vibration will be felt for a longer time. For testing the cutaneous perception of vibration, the most adequate apparatus uses vibrators driven by radio oscillators, with control of both frequency and amplitude of vibration and with liberal possibilities of amplification (Knudsen, 1928; Roberts, 1932; Geldard & Gilmer, 1934; Hugony, 1935). Further strides were made when Geldard (1940) added the use of a slightly mistuned stroboscopic light and a binocular microscope. If the stimulus is set at 100 ~, and the light at 101 ~, *E* can actually measure the movement of the skin as it appears to vibrate up and down once per second. With such equipment, several problems in perception can be attacked.

1. *The range of perceptible frequencies, and the amplitude threshold at each frequency.* At low frequencies, such as 10 per second, pulsation is sensed rather than vibration; and there is probably no exact point of transition to the vibratory sensation. Of more interest is the question of an upper limit, but the results indicate no upper limit, provided the amplitude of the high frequencies is sufficiently great. *O* lays his finger gently on the vibrator and reports when it is activated. By varying the amplitude, using the psychophysical Method of Limits (p. 196) *E* determines the stimulus threshold for each frequency. In the region of 200–300 cycles per second amplitudes as small as .001 mm can be sensed as vibration, this being the region of greatest sensitivity. Positive reports have been obtained with frequencies as high as 12,000 cycles per sec when the amplitude was sufficient (Knudsen, 1928; Goodfellow, 1933; Setzepfand, 1935; Geldard & Weitz, 1948).

2. *Perceptible frequency differences.* Can the skin duplicate in any degree the ability of the ear to distinguish small differences in frequency (p. 222)? There is a qualitative difference in the sensation obtained from low and from high frequencies applied to the skin, and smaller differences, as between 200 and 225 cycles per second, can be correctly judged after some practice. After intensive training, 400 and 420 cycles can be distinguished, but the interrelations of frequency, amplitude and energy leave it possible that something besides frequency furnishes the differential cues (Knudsen, 1928; Roberts, 1932).

3. *"Hearing" speech through the skin.* Amplified speech vibrations can be felt by the fingers, and different words and phrases differ enough to be distinguished after specific practice. Though the in-

tensity pattern, rather than the frequency pattern, probably furnishes the cues, these tactual vibrations are of some value to the deaf in lip-reading practice and in learning to manage their own voices (Gault, 1927, 1936).

4. *Is there a separate vibratory sense?* A number of different lines of evidence have led some writers to posit a separate vibratory sense, either cutaneous or subcutaneous. But after reviewing all the evidence, Geldard (1940) showed very convincingly that vibration is nothing but a temporal-spatial pattern of the normal pressure sense. The extremely rapid adaptation of which the pressure sense is capable makes it a "dead-beat" sense; that is, it responds only during the actual application of the single thrusts of a vibrating body. To this extent it is similar to the ear, which will send bursts of impulses up the auditory nerve in faithful synchronism with the stimulus up to several thousand vibrations per second (p. 329). Indeed, we shall see that some of the evidence Wever (1949) uses in support of the "volley theory" of hearing comes from studies of the vibratory sensitivity of the skin. The skin is so elastic that vibrations applied to one point must spread widely; in fact, Geldard's observations with the stroboscope, and those of Weitz (1939) with a phonograph pickup, show that this spread does occur. Hence large skin areas, and many pressure receptors, are available for the rotation of activity demanded by a volley theory. No one fiber need fire at a rate beyond a hundred times per second; as long as there are hundreds of fibers, several will be set off by each vibration of the stimulus, permitting the total nerve to follow up to 12,000 ~. The pressure sense is well equipped to handle perception of vibration, and there is no need to look for other receptors. It does leave the integration of these impulses to the brain, but we shall find that other facts of perception make more serious demands on the brain than this one! The more we study the sense organs, the more we seem compelled to emphasize the role of the higher centers. This necessity will become progressively noticeable as we continue to the more complicated senses in the following chapters.

11

THE CHEMICAL SENSES

The word *stimulus* makes us think of a physical energy, such as pressure, air vibrations, or radiant energy. However, there are a number of stimuli which can best be specified in chemical terms. Common salt, vinegar, benzene, and hydrogen sulphide are examples; and the corresponding sensory mechanisms are grouped under the heading, *chemical senses*. Besides *taste* and *smell*, there is some reason for recognizing a more primitive *common chemical sense* (Parker, 1922). Most organisms that live in water, from paramecium to frog, will respond when certain chemicals are applied to almost any body surface. Thus, they avoid harmful substances and find food and mates. In terrestrial animals this common chemical sense is largely limited to moist surfaces, notably the membranes of mouth, nose, and eyes. Stimulation of these surfaces by irritating substances usually evokes protective reflexes, as watering of the eyes or gross avoidance movements. Mild stimulation by the same agents may add zest to food; many spices, as pepper, seem to "bring out" the taste of bland foods.

Taste and smell are much more highly developed senses. Each has its own specialized receptors and yields characteristic qualities. But careful observation an' experimentation are required to separate true taste from smell, and bo. from common chemical sensitivity. The trouble is that the receptors for all three senses are located in the intercommunicating cavities of the mouth and nose. A mouthful of orange soda-pop, for example, will simultaneously stimulate all of the following components:

Taste—sour, sweet.
Temperature—cold.
Common chemical sense—a mild sting or tingle, as in all carbonated beverages.
Touch and kinesthesis—a rather complex pattern of pressures due to the physical characteristics of the liquid.
Smell—a complex, but characteristic quality, which can be described as fruity or fragrant.

Analyses of this sort are not particularly easy to make, for all the elements blend into the whole which we call the "taste" of orange soda. But it is obvious that the temperature and touch components are the same ones we have considered in the chapter on the skin senses. The smell can be recognized by sniffing the glass before we taste the liquid. Or it may be eliminated by plugging the nostrils with cotton—although there is still danger that swallowing will set up eddy currents in the air at the back of the throat, thus bringing the odorous particles into the nose by the back door, as it were. The surest way to plug the nostrils is to get a bad head cold; foods then lose their "flavor" because they cannot penetrate to the olfactory epithelium (see p. 304). Of course, we can isolate the common chemical sense by using simple carbonated water as the stimulus, or get rid of it by letting the orange soda stand until it is "flat." If we plug the nostrils, and take a mouthful of flat, luke-warm orange soda, all that remains is the true taste—sour plus sweet.

If we had chosen other examples, the task of analysis would have been even more difficult. This is particularly true with odors. There is little question that common chemical sensitivity, and even taste, enter into many things we loosely call odors. One suspects that the sweet smell of chloroform, for example, may involve actual stimulation of appropriate receptors in the mouth; certainly the acrid and sharp components of an "odor" like ammonia are due to stimulation of the free nerve endings of the chemical sense, rather than to the olfactory cells.

Before turning to taste and smell, let us finish our discussion of the common chemical sense. Its receptors are free nerve endings in the mouth and nose, served by the trigeminal nerve. It is thus distinct from either taste or smell, and presumably from touch. Although some writers think it is also distinct from pain, their evidence is not completely convincing (Pfaffmann, 1951). Since naked nerve fibers can be stimulated by noxious chemicals, as well as by cutting, the branching nerve endings in the mucous membranes may well be similarly stimulated. Further, the quality of the sensation is identical with pain. There is no apparent reason to consider the common chemical sense, at least in the oral and nasal cavities, as anything other than pain. If anyone is disturbed by the idea that sprinkling a little pepper on his food adds flavor by bringing in pain, he must remember that pain is a sensation, and is not necessarily unpleasant (cf. p. 285). A mild tingling of the mouth cavity may stimulate flow of saliva; at least the sting will lend character to an otherwise dull cream soup!

Generations of students have spent laboratory periods in experiments designed to bring out the varied components that make up the characteristic flavor of typical foods and beverages. The experiment is instructive if it does no more than show that one cannot tell ground coffee from cracker crumbs if the nose is plugged. Some of the more careful *Os* will be able to analyze tactual and kinesthetic clues that enable them to judge texture, crispness, softness, etc. But a complete description of the flavor and smell of various substances is not the task for science; it is a job for those responsible for the quality of commercial products. A large store of practical information is available on some of these topics (Moncrieff, 1944), but it is hard to separate fact from tradition. The field is a promising one for the application of psychophysical methods, with an emphasis on control of random variables. There is an increasing use of "panels" of subjects for the description and evaluation of food products. (Cf. Pfaffmann & Schlosberg, 1953; and see p. 233.)

TASTE

The tongue, if one examines it closely, is seen to be covered with small elevations, the *papillae* (Fig. 11-1). Most numerous are the filiform papillae, which seem to have about the same function as the nonskid tread on tires. The three remaining types serve the sense of taste. The mushroom-shaped fungiform papil-

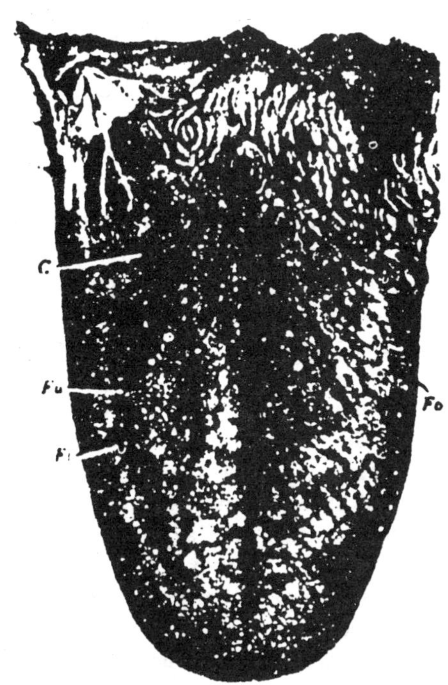

FIG. 11-1. The tongue, showing papillae. Taste buds are located in circumvallate (C), fungiform (Fu) and foliate (Fo), but not in filiform (Fi) papillae. (From Wenzl, reproduced from Warren & Carmichael, 1930.)

lae are scattered over the tongue, the leaf-like foliate papillae are at the sides, and the large circumvallate papillae are arranged in a chevron near the base. Each gustatory papilla contains one or more taste buds, which also are found elsewhere in the mouth, especially during childhood. In a typical taste bud there are several spindle-shaped receptor cells, each with a hairlike end projecting through the pore of the bud into the mouth cavity. These hair cells are the receptors for taste; they connect with nerve fibers which run to the brain stem by the VIIth and IXth cranial nerves but are united in their further course to the somesthetic cortex.

Taste qualities. For a long time there has been general agreement on just four primary taste qualities: salt, sour, sweet, bitter. Alkaline, which some workers would add (Hahn, Kuckulies & Taeger, 1938), is probably a combination of several tastes, even including touch or pain (Kloehn & Brogden, 1948). If there are four primary tastes, we might hope to find some taste buds that yield one and no others. Prepare four strong appropriate solutions. Common table salt, NaCl, is excellent for the salt stimulus, and vinegar or any dilute acid will serve for sour. Sugar will give us sweet, and we can use quinine or quassia for bitter. With the aid of a fine brush, place drops of these solutions on selected areas of the tongue. We must wipe off the tongue after each trial and rinse the mouth frequently. Bitter should be left until last, for it tends to linger.

The results from this experiment are not as conclusive as might be desired, but they do show some specificity. A few of the fungiform papillae respond only to sweet, others only to acid, and still others to salt, but none of them seem specialized for bitter. Most of these papillae respond to several solutions, but we must remember that each papilla may have several buds, each of which contains several hair cells. If we consider areas of the tongue, rather than individual papillae, we find that different parts of the tongue are differentially sensitive. Bitter is most effective at the back, near the circumvallate papillae and along the back portions of the edges. Sweet is just the opposite, stimulating the tip and front edges. Sour reaches its maximum effectiveness about the middle of the edges, and salt is best sensed in the forward part of the tongue. The central part of the top surface of the tongue is quite insensitive (Fig. 11-2).

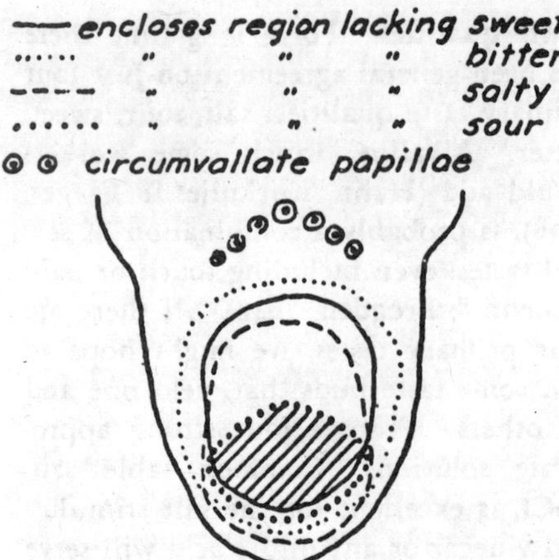

FIG. 11-2. (After Henning, 1927.) Diagram of upper surface of the tongue, with lines enclosing the regions *not* yielding the four tastes.

Gustatory nerve impulses. If there are four types of receptor cells, each of which responds to one of the four primary tastes, it is reasonable to assume that the specificity is maintained in the cranial nerves that carry the resulting impulses to the brain. Thus we might hope to find that one nerve fiber was active only in response to salt, another to acid, etc. Pfaffmann (1941) recorded impulses from various isolated fibers of the cat's gustatory nerves. Certain fibers responded only when the tongue was washed with mild acid. Other single fibers responded to both acid and salt, and a third group could be stimulated by both acid and bitter. No response was obtained from sweet in this study, but this was almost certainly due to technical recording difficulties. A decade later Pfaffmann (personal communication) was able to pick up "sweet" impulses in the cat, rabbit, and rat. Andersson, Landgren, Olsson & Zotterman (1950) reported them in the dog. We must remember that it is difficult to pick up impulses from single fibers, and to separate these impulses from the background "noise" that one gets in high-gain amplification of neural potentials. The brain seems to do the job rather better. Not only does it respond appropriately to the "sour" fibers, but it must "decode" the mixed signals; if the acid-salt fibers fire without the acid ones, the stimulus must be salty by a process of elimination.

Electrical stimulation, though holding some promise for future analytic experiments, so far has yielded no pure taste qualities except sour; the sour may result from hydrogen ions liberated by electrolysis of a little saliva, rather than from direct stimulation (v. Skramlik, 1926). Some years ago, Weinberg & Allen (1925) reported that intermittent electrical stimulation gave an intermittent taste, rather like a flickering light (p. 380). Further, they found four different fusion frequencies, presumably corresponding to the four primary tastes. But other workers have been unable to verify these results (Jones & Jones, 1952). In general, electrical stimulation of the tongue yields sensations that are very difficult to describe; therefore, we had better adhere to chemical stimulation for the present.

Differential stimuli for the four tastes. Though it is easy to select substances that will give the four tastes, the discovery of the actual gustatory *stimuli* is quite a different task. Naming a substance that will give a certain taste is like naming a flower that looks red and another that looks blue. Our real aim here is like that in the study of vision when we ask what wavelengths of light are the stimuli for red and blue, and when we go on to ask what changes these wavelengths produce in the photochemical substances of the retina. Our gustatory (and olfactory) chemistry, we must admit, is a baffling subject and not far advanced at most points. We can make a start by assembling substances that give a certain taste, and trying to discover what they have in common

Sour. The stimulus here is fairly clear. All the dilute acids that yield a fairly pure sour taste have one characteristic in common: when they are in solution, their molecules *dissociate* into two parts, the hydrogen cation (H ion) and an anion. Thus hydrochloric acid breaks down into H^+ and Cl^-. The H ion seems to be the stimulus for sour.

Salt. Sodium chloride is apparently the only substance which gives a purely salt taste. There are many others which give salty plus sweet, bitter or possibly tactual-pain components. The typical salty substances are compounds of one of these cations—sodium, calcium, lithium, potassium—with one of the following anions—chlorine, bromine, iodine, SO_4, NO_3, CO_3. Both anion and cation seem to be important in generating the salty taste. (Perhaps the only one of these salty substances that has been widely used to substitute for NaCl as a table salt is lithium chloride; in large quantities it seems to cause illness—Hanlon *et al.*, 1949.)

Sweet. Unfortunately we cannot tie down the chemical property of a substance that makes it sweet. Sucrose (cane or beet sugar) is a carbohydrate, and so are glucose, which is less sweet, and starch, which is not sweet at all. The alcohols are sweet, but so is saccharine, decidedly, though very different in chemical composition; and so again is the poisonous salt, "sugar of lead," which is anything but a sugar except in taste.

Bitter. We are no better off here. The most typical bitter substances are the vegetable alkaloids, such as quinine, but some metallic salts also are bitter. There are even some substances, as phenyl-thio-carbamide, which are extremely bitter to some people and almost tasteless to others (Blakeslee & Salmon, 1935; Rikimaru, 1937; Cohen & Ogdon, 1949). Bitter and sweet substances are in some cases very similar in chemical composition

There is some reason to believe, then, that the sweet and bitter mechanisms are rather closely related, as distinguished from sour and salt which respond to the simple electrolytes. There might even be a single bitter-sweet mechanism which if tipped one way would yield the sweet, in the other way the bitter. Here is a challenging problem for the investigator, but he must be broadly equipped!

Stimulus thresholds. The minimum concentration at which a given substance can be tasted depends on a number of factors, such as the area to which the solution is applied, the temperature of the solution, and the psychophysical method employed. The solution may be described in one of several ways. Most obvious is percent concentration. This is usually computed by dividing the amount of the substance by the amount of the solvent; 2 gms of NaCl in 100 cc of water would be a 2-percent solution. Where greater accuracy is desired, the divisor may be the total amount of solution; that is, 2/102 in the above case. The result is often expressed as *parts per thousand* (p.p.m.) rather than percent.

A more useful method, especially if we are to compare different substances, is *molar concentration.* A solution has a strength of *one mole* if the molecular weight of the substance, in grams, is added to 1,000 cc of water. Thus equal molar solutions of any substances contain the same number of molecules. A *normal solution* is like a molar one, except that it is corrected for the number of valences in either ion. Molar concentration is probably the best way to compare the effectiveness of two substances if we are interested in the chemistry of excitation.

A rough idea of the absolute thresholds for common stimuli is of some value, if only to show the relative sensitivity of the four primary tastes. The following data give two values for sweet, since sugar and saccharin are so different.

Substance	*Taste*	*Percent concentration*	*Molar concentration*
Sucrose	sweet	0.7	.02
Sodium chloride	salt	.2	.035
Hydrochloric acid	sour	.007	.002
Crystallose (saccharin)	sweet	.0005	.00002
Quinine sulphate	bitter	.00003	.0000004

Methods of stimulation. There are three methods of applying the stimuli. The simplest may be called the sip method; *E* hands *O* a small glass of a specified solution, lets him taste it, and then report. This method yields the lowest thresholds, since large areas of the tongue are involved. Care must be taken to clear the mouth between trials by spitting out the solution and rinsing. Further, it is necessary to train *O* to sip and spit in a standardized manner to insure uniform trials. At least a half minute is advisable between trials, to avoid adaptation effects (MacLeod, 1952).

In studying single areas, the drop method may be used. A brush, pipette, or syringe places a fixed amount of solution where it is desired. Still better is the *gustometer*, used by Hahn & Günther (1932). This is essentially a U-tube, laid on the tongue. A hole opening downward at the bend of the U is placed over the desired portion of the tongue so that the stimulating solution washes over the area as it comes in one arm and goes out the other. Alternative supply tubes make it possible to shift rapidly from one solution to another. For example, water at a constant temperature may suddenly be displaced by salt solution at the same temperature, thus eliminating temperature and touch clues that come in with the drop or sip method. Or, a strong adapting solution may be instantly replaced by a weaker test solution so as to determine whether the latter can still be tasted.

Difference thresholds, scales, equations. The difference threshold varies markedly with the substance, the concentration, and the method used. Some of the pioneer studies on the Method of Single Stimuli were done on taste, and have been reviewed in Chapter 8 (p. 217). Since the exact values are so dependent on specific conditions, it seems pointless to list them here; suffice it to say that $\Delta I/I$ is about 1/5 in the mid-ranges for most substances. As in most senses, $\Delta I/I$ holds reasonably constant in the mid-ranges of intensities; how badly it breaks down at the extremes is not settled (Holway & Hurvich, 1937; Saidullah, 1927; Kopera, 1931; Bujas, 1937).

It will be recalled from Chapter 9, page 243, that Beebe-Center and his co-workers built a scale of equal-appearing intervals in strength of taste and christened the unit a *gust*. It was possible to make cross-quality comparisons and adjust a salt solution to taste as salty as a sugar solution was sweet, both expressed as so many gusts. With this scale, Beebe-Center (1949) examined a lot of common foods and beverages. One of the results was that bitter and sour at fairly high scale values were accepted as pleasant in ale and pickles. Once again, as in the case of mildly painful spices, we find that sensations which are considered unpleasant in isolation are valued when they become part of the blend which constitutes a familiar flavor.

Even without the use of such a scale it is of course possible to judge that one solution is sweeter than another and to work out an equation of sweetness between two kinds of sugar. A sample of such work is given in Figure 11-3.

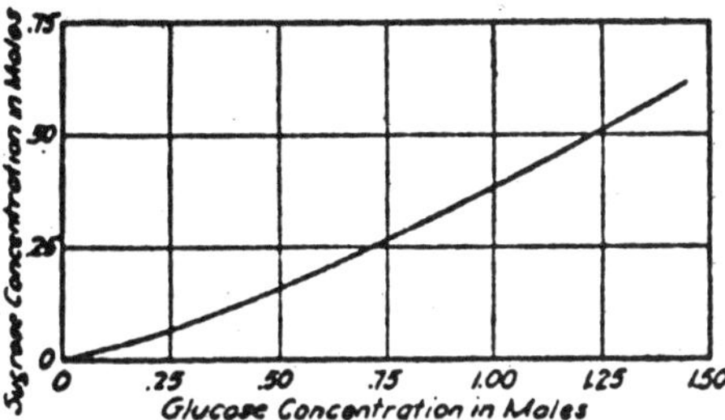

FIG. 11-3. (After Cameron, 1947.) Equally sweet solutions of sucrose and glucose. At each point on the curve the glucose concentration given by the abscissa is judged equally sweet with the sucrose concentration given by the ordinate. The fact that the abscissa is always greater than the ordinate shows that glucose is always less sweet than the same concentration of sucrose.

Such results in terms of solutions of different sugars (and other substances) judged equally sweet would be sufficient if doubling a concentration doubled the sweetness. But we know from the experiments on psychological scaling that this is not true. Now that we have the gust scale, based on actual judgments of a solution which *tastes* half as sweet as another, an interesting problem arises. Suppose we construct a scale for sweetness of cane sugar, sucrose, by the halving technique (p. 240), and call the units "sucs." Then construct a similar, but independent one on another sugar, glucose, calling the units "glucs." Now suppose we find that a 10-suc sucrose solution is judged to be as sweet as an 8-gluc glucose one. Would a solution of 5 sucs match one of 4 glucs? Would 2½ sucs equal 2 glucs? MacLeod (1952) who did this experiment found that the predicted matches worked out pretty well. If further work continues to give such matches, we shall be justified in using this type of scaling more widely in describing tastes.

Adaptation. One of the most striking facts about taste is the rapid rate at which it adapts. A drink which tastes sweet or sour at the first sip often seems almost neutral by the end of the glass. Contrast is equally marked; a pickle would taste very sour after an ice cream dessert. A number of careful studies have been made on these changes. A particularly neat, but elaborate, series of experiments was carried out by Hahn (1934). Using the gustometer, he passed a given concentration of sodium chloride over a small area of the tongue for 1–30 seconds, and then immediately substituted a test concentration. In a series of such trials the stimulus threshold was determined. It rose rapidly and then more slowly as the adaptation period was prolonged. The results for three adapting concentrations are shown in Figure 11-4. In this subject there was complete adaptation to even the 15-percent solution within 30 seconds. To obtain the recovery curves, the adapting solution was replaced by plain water for a certain time and then followed by a test solution.

Adaptation to a sugar solution was almost equally rapid. It would be a mistake, however, to generalize from this experiment to everyday experience. Substances are rarely applied steadily to the same small area of the tongue; usually you move them around, varying the area and intensity of stimulation from second to second, and so preventing rapid adaptation. But if we are to understand how the receptors work, we must use controlled stimulation.

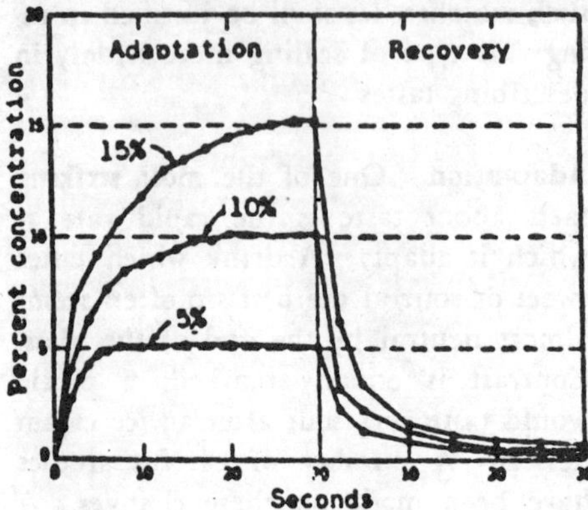

FIG. 11-4. (Hahn, 1934, reproduced from Pfaffman, 1951.) Taste adaptation and recovery. The adapting solution was sodium chloride in concentrations of 5 percent, 10 percent, and 15 percent, and stimulus thresholds were determined by use of weaker solutions of the same salt. The ordinate of each point shows the threshold after adaptation for the duration shown on the base line. The recovery curves all start after 30 sec of adaptation; complete recovery was not reached within the 30 sec allowed. There were individual differences.

Adaptation was most marked to salt, next to sweet, and considerably less to sour and bitter. The difference was not so much in speed of adaptation as in the completeness that could be attained, or in the maximum attainable shift of the threshold. The resting or unadapted threshold was raised in the following proportions:

Salt	300 times	Bitter	2–3 times
Sugar	6–20 times	Acid	1.6 times

SMELL

Receptors and stimuli. The receptors for smell are found in two small patches of yellowish *olfactory epithelium*, which lie at the extreme top of the two nasal passages. They are out of the main pathway which the air takes in breathing and are further protected by ridges which deflect the air, moisten it, and remove dust. The epithelium itself is covered by mucus. As a result of this sheltered position, the odor-laden air reaches the receptors only in the form of eddy currents. Sniffing accentuates these eddies. As we noted above, odors may also reach the receptors from food held in the mouth, passing up into the nose by the back door. The inaccessibility of the olfactory epithelium is one of the most serious handicaps in research on olfaction.

The actual receptor cells are imbedded in the epithelium, with hairlike tips projecting into the mucus. The cells are numerous; there are 50,000,000 in each patch in the rabbit (Allison & Warwick, 1949). The axons of these cells go directly through the thin and perforated cribriform plate, which separates the top of the nasal cavity from the brain cavity. They then join the club-shaped olfactory bulb from which connecting fibers lead back to other parts of the brain. The arrangement is duplicated on each side; corresponding to the two nostrils, there are two patches of epithelium, separated by the septum, and two olfactory bulbs.

Olfactory stimuli are obviously airborne, for they must reach the locus of the receptors. If not a gas, an odorous substance must at least be volatile. However, the volatility need not be marked, for the sense of smell is incredibly sensitive. Ethyl mercaptan can be detected at a concentration of only 4×10^{-8} mg per liter of air. But even at this high dilution, there are several million molecules per sniff. If these were adsorbed, side by side on the receptor surface, they would give a reasonably complete film. Perhaps this is what happens. (Moncrieff, 1944.)

Ordinary objects, like flowers, cheese, and rubber are not simple odorous substances; the odor is due to certain volatile constituents rather than to the object as a whole. Even the essential oils which give flowers their characteristic odors are often mixtures of several compounds. Many of these compounds have been produced synthetically and are used to make imitation flavors and perfumes. But the imitations often differ from the original, apparently because of the minute quantities of additional compounds that exist in the natural essence. The experimenter's difficulties in studying olfaction are great enough without adding to them by using complicated mixtures; it is more sensible to use pure compounds for basic research. The purer the compound, the better, for a small amount of impurity may change the odor markedly.

Classification of smell qualities. Ordinary experience leaves us with an unorganized manifold of odors and with no start toward a scientific system. In taste we have the common names, sweet, sour, bitter and salt, which are found to be adequate for scientific classification. In color we have a similar set of common names, and we find it easy also to arrange the hues in a circular series. In hearing, the names high and low picture the one-dimensional character of the pitch series. But in smell common experience and language give us no clues toward a system. We speak of agreeable and disagreeable odors, but the agreeable have various odor qualities and the disagreeable likewise. We speak of "sweet" smells, and "sweet" here does not mean simply agreeable, since the odor of camphor is certainly not "sweet" though it is agreeable; but whether olfactory sweetness is simply gustatory or points to some true olfactory quality is not clear. We speak of "sharp" or "pungent" odors, but here we are confusing the olfactory with the other nasal senses. We also speak of "spicy" and of "putrid" odors, and here we are approaching a classification of true smell qualities.

The poverty of our odor vocabulary is keenly felt on consulting the dictionary to discover what may be the odor of some chemical substance such as thiophene or geraniol or citral or ethyl acetate. If there were some system or scheme by reference to which the chemist or the botanist could designate the quality of an odor, it would be a great aid in communication, if nothing more.

The first scientist to make a serious effort at filling this need was the Swedish botanist Linnaeus (1756). He distinguished seven classes of odors, namely:

Aromatic — as carnation
Fragrant — as lily
Ambrosial — as musk
Alliaceous — as garlic
Hircine — as valerian
Repulsive — as certain bugs
Nauseous — as carrion

The Linnaean classification did service for over a century. Zwaardemaker (1895, 1925) sought to perfect it by subdividing some of the classes and by adding two new classes, the etherial and the empyreumatic, so as to do justice to the modern products of organic chemistry. Zwaardemaker's 1925 classification had nine classes and many subclasses.

Henning (1915–16, 1924) made a radical revision of Zwaardemaker's arrangement, ending up with the following six classes: fragrant, etherial (fruity), resinous, spicy, putrid, and empyreumatic (burned).

Henning claims for his classification (1) that it is more than a mere classification, being in fact a system, and (2) that it is based on a more comprehensive experimental study of odor qualities than had been attempted by any of his predecessors. He claims to have made the first really psychological investigation of the odor manifold.

The manipulation of stimuli. A systematic attempt at classification, such as Henning's, involves more than random sniffing of odors found in a kitchen pantry. One must have a large series of odorous substances arranged so that they can be compared with each other. But unless these substances are handled with care, they will soon fill the room with a blend of many odors. Usually a small amount of each substance is put in its own small bottle. The bottles should be about an ounce in size, which gives room for a few drops or particles of the substance with plenty of air to take up the odor. The mouth of the bottle should be wide enough to permit a sniff. Tight stoppers are essential, and should be kept on the bottles between sniffs. The modern plastic-capped pill bottle is probably superior to the older ground-glass stoppers that were once standard equipment. The bottles should be filled in the supply room, and carefully wiped off with alcohol, hot water, or hydrogen peroxide before they are brought into the experimental room. The experimental table should be large enough to permit wide spacing of the bottles, and should have a porcelain or metal top that will stand scouring and hot water. It is especially important to have the room well ventilated.

For rough qualitative work one often uses an assortment of odorous substances. Some will be solids, as iodine crystals, camphor, tar, and cheese. The druggist can furnish a wide variety of "essential oils," such as oil of wintergreen, of juniper, of cloves, of lemon, etc. These are dispensed in a bland, odorless oil and are better for our purpose than the "extracts" or "essences," which contain an odorous alcohol. Certain volatile liquids, as ether, acetone, and alcohol, and some freshly prepared spices will complete the collection. Many of these are complex substances; it would be better to use pure chemicals for careful research.

The odor prism. Henning prepared 415 different odors in this fashion. His general method was to let *O* sniff an unidentified substance and report what it smelled like. Trials were spaced by several minutes, to avoid confusion and mixing of odors. At first the *O*s gave highly variable and vague reports, but after considerable practice they were able to identify the odor, assign it to a class (as "cooking spice") and point out its resemblance to other odors. Even errors of identification were significant, for confusion should arise only between two similar odors.

Observers differ markedly in their ability to make such judgments. Henning

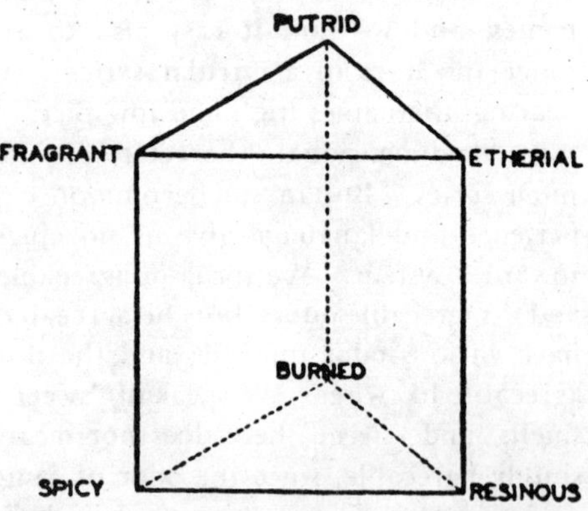

FIG. 11-5. (Henning, 1915–16, 1924.) The smell prism. The English names, suggested by Macdonald (1922), have the advantage of providing six different initial letters to serve as convenient symbols of the salient odors.

finally selected six good *Os* and put his chief reliance on them. They seem to have agreed very well among themselves, but it is at least possible in any experiment on such difficult material that the agreement was indirectly forced by the instructions and training.

Although the details of the experiment are not clear, Henning ended up with a prism that was supposed to represent the similarities and differences among odors (Fig. 11-5). The significance of this prism may be clarified by starting with the front (FERS) face (Fig. 11-6). The four corners, according to Henning, do not represent elementary odors. They are turning points in a qualitative continuum. That is, starting along the bottom at *sassafras*, and working left, *nutmeg, pepper*, and *cinnamon* seem to become more Spicy. But you seem to turn a corner with *cassia*, and its neighbors, *cloves, bay*, and *thyme*, are becoming distinctly Fragrant. Since there seem to be four such corners, we end with a square face.

Certain odors do not seem to belong along the edge. Thus *arbor vitae* has some resemblance to all four of the classes; so it goes in the middle of the face. Other odors do not belong on the front face at all. By adding two new classes, Putrid and Burned, we make the figure tridimensional, with three faces. Tobacco smoke would belong on the FPBS face, varying in distance from the Fragrant, Spicy, Putrid, and Burned corners with the blend of tobacco. Fish scales are said to be on the ERBP face, between Putrid and Resinous.

Unlike the color solid (p. 387) the smell prism is hollow. Every pure odor

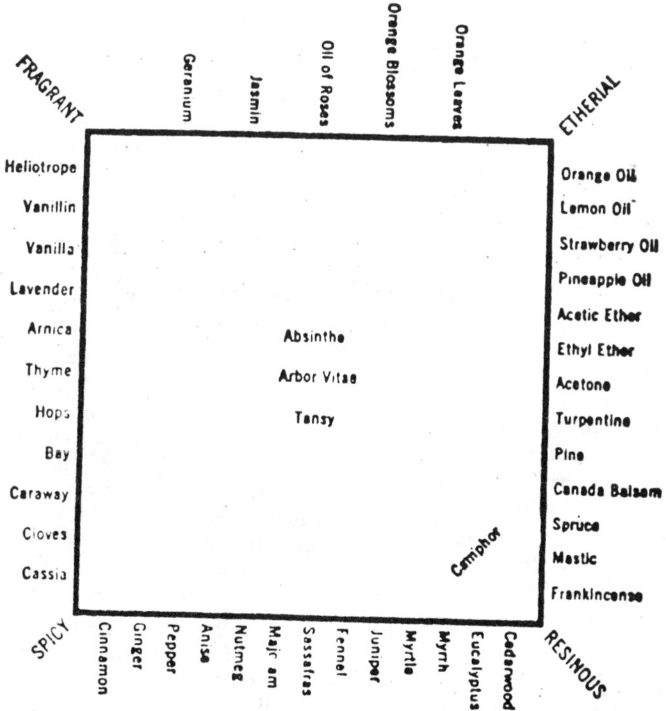

FIG. 11-6. The FERS odor square, a part of Henning's smell prism.

should be located on an edge or face, and only mixed odors inside. Further, every pure odor is simple, according to Henning. *Sassafras* is located between *cinnamon* and *cedarwood;* this indicates that it resembles both of the other odors, but it cannot be produced by their mixture. This peculiar appearance of uniqueness among odors that resemble each other has impressed laymen and scientist alike. There is a comparable phenomenon in pitch, where the note D is part of an orderly series B, C, D, E, F, etc., but cannot be produced by mixing its neighbors. This suggests that there may be many different types of receptor cells in the olfactory epithelium, each "tuned" to a different stimulus (cf. the place theory of hearing, p. 327).

Checks on the validity of the odor prism. Henning's prism promised to bring order into a chaotic field. Hence it was immediately subjected to experimental test in other laboratories. The results have not confirmed the figure in detail. It obviously needs a lot of revision, but it seems to be the best description we have to date. Some of the experiments will be summarized below; the problem is found to be complicated by mixed substances, nonolfactory sensations, and observer differences.

Macdonald (1922) and Findley (1924) went to work in a systematic way to test out the resemblances of various odors to the six salient odors of the smell prism. The stimuli used for the salients were as follows:

	Macdonald	*Findley*
Fragrant	Oil of jasmine	Oil of jasmine
Etherial	Citral	Oil of lemon
Resinous	Eucalyptol	Turpentine
Spicy	Anethol	Cinnamon
Putrid	Thiophenol	Hydrogen sulphide
Burned	Pyridine	Oil of tar

Besides these standards there was an assortment of odor stimuli to be compared with the standards. One standard was first presented (held under *O*'s nose in a wide mouthed bottle), then the odor to be judged (the comparison odor), and finally a second standard; and *O* decided whether the comparison odor was more like the first or the second standard. The judgment was supposed to be based wholly on the odor quality, without regard to intensity or to accompanying nasal sensations of cold or pricking. Each comparison odor was thus compared with every possible pair of standards, two or three times in the course of the experiment.

The most striking result of this type of experiment, apart from the great variability of the judgments, was that nearly every comparison odor was at one time or another said to resemble every one of the standards. So pinene, a chemical unit present in turpentine and oil of juniper, obviously a good representative of the Resinous class, was sometimes said to be more like the F, E, S, P and B standards. We should have to assign it a position inside the prism, which is supposed to be empty, except for mixed odors. By the same criterion, every odor tested belonged inside, so that the whole theory of the prism seemed to break down.

Henning's reply to this criticism (1924, p. 424) was that the prism showed the relations of odor *sensations*, not of odor stimuli, and that the same stimulus gives different sensations at different times. This rejoinder does not meet a difficulty pointed out by Macdonald (1922), who conducted a second experiment, using only the four standards located at the corners of the FERS square, and asking *O* to assign a place in this square, or along its sides, to each of 11 stimuli which belonged in this general region and had no marked resemblance to P or B. *O* found this task quite difficult, though possible with some stimuli. The main difficulty was that a given odor usually seemed to belong inside the square and yet did not resemble all the corners of the square. For example, nutmeg and geraniol seemed intermediate between E and S, requiring a place along the diagonal ES, and yet they did not resemble R nor always F; whereas the middle of the diagonal ES is also the middle of the diagonal FR and an odor intermediate between E and S must at the same time be intermediate between F and R, according to the logic of the prism. There were other odors that resembled F, E and S, and so belonged inside the square, and yet did not resemble R. The mere geometry of the prism unfits it for expressing some of the factual resemblances.

Another difficulty is that F, E and S resemble one another much more than they do R so that the face FERS is not properly a square but a kite-shaped figure. Also it appears that P and B resemble each other closely. Thus the regular prism is far from an adequate representation of the actual relations between odor sensations.

Herrmann (1926), on asking his *Os* to describe a large number of odors by reference to Henning's six salient odors, encountered vigorous objection. They found it unnatural to describe the odors in this particular way, and they did not accept Henning's six as any more outstanding than several other odors—mint and camphor, for example. Herrmann concluded that true corners did not exist and suspected that everyday associations were responsible for the supposed outstanding character of Henning's six fundamentals.

Hazzard (1930) found well-practiced *Os* able to locate many odors on the smell prism, while certain odors (cinnamon oil, tar, apiol) had no place. They also gave a free description of the odor experience, couched largely in terms of "texture, volume, brightness, extent and temporal course." They could locate the odors along no fewer than ten scales or dimensions: loose—tight, light—heavy, smooth—rough, soft—hard, thin—thick, sharp—dull, bright—dull, lively—inert, surfacy—deep, small—large. Spicy odors were sharp, bright and lively, while Putrid odors were dull and inert; Fragrant odors were soft, loose and light in texture, while Burned odors were the reverse. These "textures" suggest possible cutaneous components in the total nasal sensation.

Sensations accompanying smell. The interior of the nose, as has been said, is provided with the cutaneous senses of touch, pain, warmth and cold, and the throat which receives the inspired air from the nose is provided with taste buds. With these facts in view it is not surprising that inhaled substances may "smell" sweet, sour, prickly, warm or cold.

The sharp, pungent or biting "smell" of ammonia surely arises from stimulation of the pain receptors in the nose, and the cool or fresh "smell" of menthol from the cold receptors. The sweet "smell" of chloroform doubtless arises from the taste receptors in the throat and probably the sour "smell" of vinegar comes from the same source.

Henning found that untrained *Os* did not distinguish odor proper from the other sensations obtained in smelling. He mentions in this connection the prickly sensation of oil of mustard, the sweet of jasmine, the cold of garlic, the warm of heliotrope, and the soft, heavy, or sticky pressure sensations of certain perfumes. Training in odor analysis makes it possible to isolate the odor quality partially but not wholly.

These smell-accompanying sensations have been studied with special care by von Skramlik (1925). Out of a collection of 200 odorous chemical substances, tried out on several *Os*, all but 50–60 gave recognizable sensations besides odor. Over 50 of them were sharp or prickly, about 30 were cold, about 30 sweet, a few were warm and a few sour.

Von Skramlik's chief question was whether pure odors could be localized as coming from the right or the left nostril in monorhinic stimulation. His procedure was to hold two bottles simultaneously under the two nostrils, one bottle containing an odorous substance and the other distilled water. Keeping his eyes closed, *O* refrained from breathing while the bottles were being placed in position, and then drew a long breath which he expired through the mouth. He reported in which nostril the odor was localized. The result of the experiment was very curious. Some stimuli could be localized easily, while others could not be localized at all. Those that could be localized were such as give other sensations besides smell, and those that could not be localized were pure odors. (There were some minor exceptions and doubtful cases, in which it was impossible to be sure whether or not the odor was entirely pure.) It appeared that the olfactory centers made no distinction between right and left, whereas the taste and trigeminal apparatus made that distinction.

Among the pure smells were representatives of five of Henning's six classes; thus:

Fragrant: geraniol (roses), terpineol (lily of the valley);
Etherial: limonene (lemon);
Resinous: pinene (turpentine), cadinene (juniper);
Spicy eugenol (cloves), anethol (anise);
Putrid indol and skatol (fecal odors).

As examples of the several classes of impure smells the following may be cited:

Smell plus sweet: chloroform, bromoform, iodoform, ethyl chloride, nitrobenzol.

Smell plus sour: acetic, propionic, butyric and valerianic acids.

Smell plus cold: camphor, menthol, phenol, eucalyptol, safrol (sassafras).

Smell plus warm: ethyl alcohol, propyl alcohol, amyl alcohol.

Smell plus pain (prick): chlorine, bromine, iodine, ammonia, SO_2, xylol, toluol, formic and acetic acids, acetone, pyridine, nicotine, thiophene.

The presence of smell-accompanying sensations makes it imperative that the classification of odor qualities should be revised or at least re-examined experimentally with the object of factoring out the nonolfactory components. Certain classes might coalesce if the nonolfactory components were eliminated. It might even be that the whole FERS face would coalesce into a single class, if pungency (pain sense), freshness (cold sense) and sweetness (taste) could be factored out. The outcome might be a simplification of the system of odor qualities, or it might be the recognition of fundamental odors which fail to be "outstanding" when blended with nonolfactory components (Komuro, 1921; Ohma, 1921).

A matching technique for the description of odors. Instead of relying on one's memory in attempting to describe a present odor, it would be more satisfactory to have a system of standards for direct comparison. Crocker & Henderson (1927) developed such a technique based on four components: (1) fragrant, (2) acid, (3) burnt, and (4) caprylic (goaty). Each component might depend on its own type of receptor, though this assumption is perhaps unnecessary. At any rate, most odors will contain all the components but in varying degrees, and any given odor can be assigned its strength in each component, and thus located in the system. A set of eight standard degrees is provided for each component, graded by equal logarithmic steps of concentration. Any given odor is to be matched on the eight-point scale for each component. Thus the smell of a rose might be 6423, the outstanding component being fragrant, with a strength of 6, but some acid being present, less caprylic, and a trace of burnt. Even without much practice, an observer can use the system with fair consistency (Boring, 1928; Crocker, 1945). Such a system is found to be of value in practical situations, and no fewer than 500 substances used in the perfume industry have been assigned standard ratings (Crocker & Dillon, 1948).

A question can be raised as to the adequacy of the scaling. College students were given the eight standards of each scale to be arranged in order of intensity (Ross & Harriman, 1949). The average ranks assigned by these 15 observers corresponded fairly well with the standard ranks except in the fragrant scale which showed large discrepancies. The scale steps, however, were far from equal, and the individual rank orders varied greatly. The halving technique (p. 240) might provide a better set of scales.

Leaving aside the question of the commercial value of the Crocker-Henderson scheme, we must ask whether it contributes to our basic understanding of the sense of smell. Here the answer seems to be negative. There is no evidence at all that there are only four primary qualities, or four types of receptors. In fact, all the evidence we have examined and shall cover later suggests many more than four.

Interaction of odors. One of the major difficulties in building any systematic classification of olfactory qualities is the way the stimuli interact. Two or more stimuli presented simultaneously may have any one of a half dozen results; it sometimes makes a difference whether both stimuli are presented to one or both nostrils (monorhinic, dirhinic) or one substance to each nostril (dichorhinic stimulation). The reader will recall that the two nostrils are separate receptors, each leading to its own olfactory nerve (p. 304).

1. The commonest result is a blend or fusion of the odors of the two stimuli. The blend is a unitary impression, though resembling the odors of the components. Thus violet combined with H_2S may give a blend resembling both components. The more the components resemble each other in odor, the more likely they are to blend and the more difficult it is to attend separately to one or the other component (Henning, 1924).

2. When the component stimuli are such as to give very dissimilar odors, the usual result is a successive smelling of the two odors (Henning), though fusion is not impossible.

3. With dichorhinic stimulation, this successive smelling of the two odors has some analogy with rivalry, though it is not so clean-cut as binocular rivalry and according to von Skramlik (1925) is nothing more than ordinary shifting of attention and should not be labeled rivalry.

4. The two odors may be smelt simultaneously and yet separately. They may appear as a pattern, analogous to a chord of musical tones, or they may be smelt as two distinct and unrelated odors. This high degree of separateness can only be obtained with dichorhinic stimulation, according to Henning, while von Skramlik finds that the same result can be obtained with monorhinic or dirhinic stimulation. He asserts indeed that all the impressions obtained with one form of stimulation can be obtained with the others as well.

5. One odor may mask the other altogether, as happens especially when one odor is much the stronger.

6. Neutralization or "compensation." In this case the combination of stimuli gives no odor whatever. There is a violent controversy over this asserted neutralization. Zwaardemaker (1895, 1925) finds that by carefully selecting the stimuli and carefully graduating their strength he can obtain complete neutralization. Titchener (1916) confirms Zwaardemaker's finding, while admitting that complete absence of odor lasts only for an instant at a time. Henning (1924) denies the phenomenon altogether and reports that he has never been able to obtain it under any conditions; but he does not make it clear that he has put the matter to a thorough and patient test. If certain odor stimuli were related in the same way as complementary color stimuli, this relationship would be very important in olfactory theory, but thus far we have little light or leading from this source.

Considering the complex interactions that happen when we start with two separate stimuli, how can we ever be sure that even a single substance does not yield an odor that is actually an interaction of several different physiological components? This question makes the isolation of any "primary" qualities very difficult.

OLFACTORY THRESHOLDS

As an attempt to isolate the primary odors, the study of similarities and differences has not been very successful. Perhaps we could make more progress by examining changes in sensitivity to various odors, such changes as can be induced by adaptation to some one strong odor. Then there are the cases of partial anosmia, either permanent or temporary, which may shed light on the relationship of different odors. If a certain group of odors drops out together in adaptation or anosmia, the indication is that they depend on a single receptive mechanism.

Another possible lead is afforded by selective adaptation, or the qualitative change in the odor of a substance that is continuously presented to the receptors. Nitrobenzol smells like bitter almonds at first and gradually shifts to a tarry odor; and there are other striking examples. The theory, of course, is that the substance has a compound odor, with one component adapting out before the other. In order to make good research use of these shifts of odor sensation, quantification of the stimuli is a laboratory desideratum. Few of the many techniques proposed from time to time meet all the requirements.

The dilution technique. From a physical standpoint, the ideal way of describing the strength of the stimulus would be in terms of vapor pressure, or in terms of the amount of the odorous substance present in a unit volume of the air which passes over the olfactory epithelium. But the quantities involved are far too small to measure directly. One obvious way to get around this difficulty is to release a small amount of a volatile substance in a room, and allow enough time for it to become completely mixed with the air. Knowing the amount released, and the size of the room, we can compute the concentration. This is the way the threshold for mercaptan was determined (p. 304). Another method involves successive dilution of the material; a known quantity is released in one jar and allowed to diffuse, and then a portion of the contents is transferred to another jar, etc. (Pfaffmann, 1951).

Odorless environments. Smoking or chewing gum during or even an hour or so before starting an experiment will raise thresholds. Background odors are undoubtedly important sources of error. One way to get rid of them is the *camera inodorata*, a large glass box into which *O* can insert his head (Komuro, 1921). It is necessary for *O* to shave his head and coat his face with vaseline to eliminate his own odor. More practical is the *olfactorium* described by Foster, Scofield, & Dallenbach (1949). It is a room and antechamber constructed of glass and stainless steel so that it can be cleansed thoroughly by steam—the only practical way to eliminate all odors. The observer wears a plastic parka, which can be baked. Air is forced into the room after it has passed through appropriate filters, heaters, and washers, at controlled temperature and humidity. The stimuli may be delivered by adding known quantities to the air stream—the principle of the *flow-meter odorimeter.* An ideal environment like this will undoubtedly give much lower thresholds than have been obtained by other methods; we do not know yet what other results it will yield.

Stimulus thresholds. In addition to the background level of adaptation, many other factors affect the threshold, as temperature, diluent, and method. But if thresholds are determined for a number of different substances by one method, their relative effectiveness can be found. Typical values for a few substances are given below. They were obtained by Allison & Katz (1919), using the flow-meter odorimeter; many additional substances were reported in the original paper, and repeated in Pfaffmann (1951).

Substance	*Mg per liter of air*	*Substance*	*Mg per liter of air*
Ethyl ether	5.83	Methyl salicylate	.100
Carbon tetrachloride	4.53	Valeric acid	.029
Chloroform	3.30	Butyric acid	.009
Ethyl acetate	.69	Propyl mercaptan	.006
Ethyl mercaptan	.046	Artificial musk	.00004

The first four are fragrant or etherial. Valeric and butyric acid and the mercaptans are foul; they are sometimes added as alarm signals to otherwise odorless gases. Methyl salicylate is oil of wintergreen. Musk is hard to classify; it is widely used as a base for perfumes.

The olfactometer. The various dilution methods are best if one wishes an absolute value of stimulus strength. But for many purposes a rather crude relative measure is adequate. The most convenient apparatus for this purpose is Zwaardemaker's olfactometer (Fig. 11-7). It consists of two glass tubes, one of which slides on the other like a sleeve. The inner tube is about ⅜ by 5 inches, and ends in a bent tip which fits conveniently into the entrance of the nostril. The sleeve may be lined with the odorous solid, or with an absorbent material that will hold an odorous liquid. If the sleeve is pushed in as far as it will go, the inner tube projects from the other end of the sleeve, and takes in air free from the odorous substance. But if the sleeve is pulled out a bit, as in the figure, the incoming air passes over a fixed area of the odorous material before it enters the inner tube, and thence to the nostril. The more of the sleeve that is exposed, the stronger the odor. Calibrating marks are usually scratched on the inner tube, giving directly the number of linear centimeters of exposed area. For convenience, and to block O's vision, the inner tube passes through a screen just before the bend. The single form of the apparatus is rarely used; there are usually has protecting caps at both ends, to prevent escape of the odor. Two such units may be used

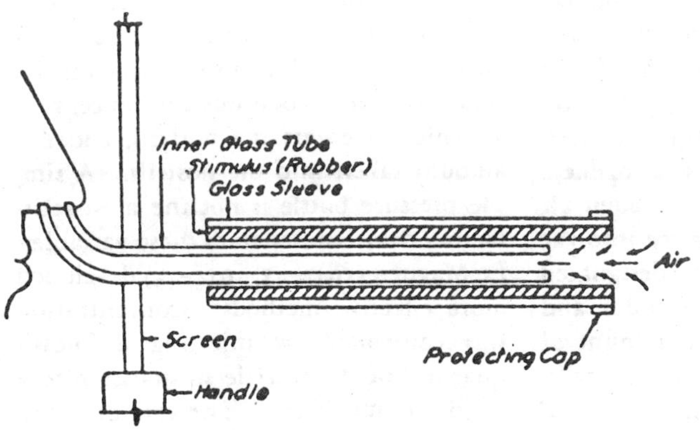

FIG. 11-7. A schematic cross section of the Zwaardemaker olfactometer, set up to give a relatively weak rubber odor. Some calibrating marks inscribed on the inner tube make it possible to read how large an area of the stimulus substance is exposed to the incoming air. Here the left end of the sleeve is 3 cm from the end of the scale, indicating that 3 cm of the stimulus substance are exposed to the incoming air at the other end. The sleeve usu-

ally two tubes, one for each nostril. There may also be connecting units so that two odors may be introduced to one nostril, etc.

Since substances differ so markedly in their stimulating value, a relative unit is often employed to equalize them. The usual unit is the *olfactie*, which is the amount of the material that must be exposed to give a barely perceptible odor. By multiplying this area (or the linear reading, in centimeters, since it is a uniform tube) by 2, 3, or 4, etc., we can get 2, 3, or 4 olfacties of stimulus. The unit is especially valuable for describing adaptation (p. 316). It is also stable enough to study threshold changes from day to day, if the odorous substances are carefully standardized.

The blast injection method. The basic objection to all the methods we have described is that *O* determines the amount of air he inhales and the way he inhales it. A sudden deep sniff will bring more of the stimulus up to the remote olfactory epithelium than will regular breathing. In an attempt to avoid this source of variability, Elsberg & Levy (1935–36) developed the blast injection technique (Fig. 11-8). A tightly stoppered bottle is equipped with an inlet and an outlet tube. With both tubes closed, the air in the bottle becomes saturated with vapor from the odorous liquid in the bottom of the bottle. A known amount of air is injected into the bottle to build up pressure. Then the outlet tube is opened, permitting a small jet of odor-laden air to escape through the nosepiece into the nostril. The threshold is designated MIO, or minimum identifiable odor, and is expressed in terms of the amount of odorous vapor released into the nostrils. The device seems to yield stable thresholds, and is useful for clinical purposes. But when one actually tries to identify the stimulus variables involved, the physics of the situation turn out to be complicated. For one thing, the pressure seems to be more important than the volume (Jerome, 1942). The volatility of the substance is very important (Elsberg, Brewer & Levy, 1935–36); this simply means that some substances will put out more molecules under given pressures than will others, and it really tells us little about the basic process of stimulation. For ultimate analysis, one of the dilution methods seems to be preferable, at least until the physical variables of the blast technique are worked out more thoroughly (cf. Wenzel, 1949).

FIG. 11-8. Elsberg's blast injection device. The bottle contains odorous fluid or solid. The pressure in the bottle is raised by introduction of a specific volume of air by the use of the hypodermic syringe on the left. On the release of the pinch clamp on the outlet tube, odorous vapor is forced into the nostrils.

Le Magnen's methods. There would seem to be three primary variables involved in the blast injection method: concentration of odorous substance, rate at which it enters the nostrils, and the amount taken into the nostrils. A simple pressure bottle is not the most satisfactory device to separate these variables. Le Magnen (1942–43, 1944–45) developed more effective methods. Concentration was controlled by injecting a known quantity of the volatile substance into a fixed volume of air. The rate of inhaling was controlled by training *O* to breathe in at a specified rate, monitored by either a visual gauge or the pitch of a small siren in the nosepiece. Pressure was kept constant by a floating piston on the reservoir, which fell as air was removed by breathing. With this type of apparatus he was able to show that the threshold was independent of the total amount inhaled; a long breath was no more effective than a short one, as long as rate of inhaling was constant. The effect of rate on threshold concentration was somewhat complex. As long as the rate was within the normal breathing range, doubling the rate halved the threshold concentration. So far, the significant thing was the number of molecules per unit time that entered the nostril. But when *O* inhaled sharply, at a rate that corresponds to a sniff, the sensitivity showed a sudden increase. The obvious explanation is that the eddy currents set up by rapid inspiration carried a larger proportion of the odor to the olfactory epithelium. Once *O* was in the sniff range, an additional doubling of rate again halved the threshold concentration. In short, the significant determiner of olfactory stimulation is the number of molecules of the odorous substance reaching the olfactory epithelium per unit time.

Difference thresholds. Zwaardemaker's olfactometer and Elsberg's blast injection bottle are convenient devices for determining the DL, since they permit rapid changes of stimulus strength. Most of the early work on DL in olfaction was done with the olfactometer. In 1898 Gamble determined the DL for 17 solids and 13 solutions, using the Method of Just Noticeable Differences (p. 196). Weber fractions ($\Delta I/I$) varied from about ⅙ to ½. In spite of great variability from substance to substance, Gamble concluded that Weber's law held for smell and suggested that the fraction was between ⅓ and ½.

Hermanides (see Wenzel, 1949) found fractions from .25 to .62 for nine substances; they seem to have been constant at two different intensities. On the other hand, Zigler & Holway (1935) report marked deviations from constancy. They used the Method of Single Stimuli (p. 217) with six basic intensities: 10, 50, 100, 200, 300, and 400 olfacties (of india-rubber). The fraction decreased from about 1.0 in the weakest range, to .17 at 400 olfacties. This would seem to be the most extensive of the studies with the olfactometer, even though it was done on only one substance.

With the Zwaardemaker olfactometer one is not sure that the concentration of the odorous molecules goes up linearly with the area exposed. As the incoming air passes over the exposed surface, it becomes increasingly saturated with vapor, and it may pick up fewer molecules from the tenth centimeter than from the first one. This would tend to inflate the apparent DL at higher intensities; the fact that DL falls with increasing intensity indicates that the error cannot be large.

In an effort to get better quantitative measures of the stimulus, Wenzel (1949) used a variation of the blast injection technique. Somewhat elaborate apparatus made it possible to control duration, pressure, and temperature of the blast. The independent variable was pressure; with duration and temperature constant, she could then calculate thresholds in terms of the number of molecules delivered to the nostril. She made an intensive study of one concentration of phenyl ethyl alcohol, using Single Stimuli, and obtained a Weber fraction of .15–.18, indicative of rather keen discrimination.

But in a control experiment on one subject she put no odorous substance in the tank and merely had him estimate the blast pressure. The psychometric function obtained for pressure essentially duplicated that for odor. Quite possibly, then, the *Os* had all along been discriminating air pressure rather than olfactory intensity. They believed themselves to be judging odor strength, and may have been doing so, but the olfactory sense is notorious for its tendency to "borrow" from other senses. The Wenzel study shows the need for control experiments in this difficult field.

Olfactory adaptation. Now that we have some acquaintance with the quantitative methods available for measuring olfactory sensitivity, and with the stimulus thresholds and difference thresholds obtained, we are ready to examine the changes in sensitivity that are referable to changes in the receptive system. Aside from the intrinsic interest of these *O*-factors, there is always the hope that they will shed some light on the basic nature of olfactory stimulation.

The most familiar of these changes in sensitivity is adaptation, shown by the increase in stimulus threshold which results from continued exposure to an odor. In one of the earliest quantitative studies of this change, made by Zwaardemaker in 1895, two basic factors in adaptation were demonstrated, exposure time and the strength of the adapting odor. Exposure to a rubber odor of moderate strength doubled the stimulus threshold for this odor in 15 seconds and quadrupled it in 45 seconds; but exposure to a stronger rubber odor raised the threshold still faster. A third factor was the kind of odor, for adaptation to rubber was less rapid than to benzoin (which has a somewhat resinous smell).

Cross-adaptation (or co-adaptation). The specific-receptor theory, which has dominated much of the thinking on olfactory qualities, makes possible certain predictions regarding the spread of adaptation from one odor to related odors. According to this theory, certain odors are similar because they exert strong stimulation on a single type of receptor cell, which we may designate as A; and the differences among these similar odors are due to relatively weak stimulation of other types of cells, which we shall designate by small letters, b, c, d, etc. If this theory were true, continued exposure to one odor, say that which stimulated Ab, would adapt or fatigue these cells so that they would not respond. Then a similar odor which stimulated Ac would show partial adaptation because of the lack of the A-response. The most careful study of this matter was made by Ohma (1922). He worked with the broad group of aromatic odors. During fairly complete adaptation to camphor, the stimulus threshold was considerably raised for eucalyptol and for eugenol (cloves) but not for benzaldehyde (bitter almonds), and adaptation to this last did not much raise the threshold for the first three. He concluded that he had distinguished two physiological odor factors, and by the same method he discerned a third (citrus) within the general aromatic class. His analysis was thus somewhat different from that shown by the FERS face of Henning's prism.

Perhaps further careful work with the cross-adaptation technique will solve some of the difficult problems of odor classification. Unfortunately, it is a laborious procedure and subject to certain pitfalls. There have been signs of a renewed interest in the technique. Le Magnen (1948a) has been studying cross-adaptation effects in a number of substances that have similar odors Both benzaldehyde and benzonitrile, for example, smell like bitter almonds. A 10-minute period of adaptation to benzonitrile raises the threshold of benzaldehyde and makes it smell like safrol (sassafras). When the safrol component is also adapted out, there is an additional residual which smells like indol (jasmine, orange blossoms). This suggests that three or more types of receptors were stimulated by benzaldehyde; that type shared with benzonitrile, that shared with safrol, and the residual type, corresponding to indol. Of course, there is no reason to assume that any one of these types is pure; benzonitrile, for example, may itself involve several types. Le Magnen believes that a variety of receptors is stimulated by any one odor. It is obviously going to be difficult to identify an ideally small number of olfactory elements.

Anosmia. In contrast to adaptation, an anosmia is a relatively lasting loss of smell. One type results from obstructed transport of odorous vapors to the olfactory epithelium, as by a head cold. Such general losses are less instructive than the partial anosmias, losses of sensitivity for particular kinds of odor. Some losses are due to continued exposure of the receptors to odorous agents such as tobacco smoke. A heavy smoker who "swears off" is often amazed at the new world of odors he encounters in a few days.

Variations of sensitivity may come as a result of infections or of chemical changes in the blood stream. The popular belief that pregnancy causes heightened smell sensitivity—*hyperosmia*—is not borne out by actual measurement (Hansen & Glass, 1936), but, of course, there may be an unusual *aversion* to strong odors. Tests do indicate an increase in sensitivity just before and during menstruation (Elsberg, Brewer & Levy, 1935), but the change is not necessarily because of hormone action on the receptors; brain tumors can produce partial anosmia (Elsberg, 1937), and functional changes in the centers may very well modify the responsiveness to smell.

Sensitivity to the odor of musk is subject to curious variations which may prove instructive. The natural substance comes from the musk glands of a small deer, the glands being confined to the male. There are several synthetic forms much used in perfumes; they all have a similar odor, but some *O*s are anosmic to one and not to others (Guillot, 1848a, b). In a series of studies aimed at an explanation of these variations, Le Magnen (1948b) finds that the vast majority of men, boys, and young girls are insensitive to musk, relatively at least, while most women report that it has a strong odor. Further, the sensitivity in women varies greatly from phase to phase of the menstrual cycle. The threshold reaches a low value at the time of ovulation; it may go down to $\frac{1}{1000}$ of its normal value. Le Magnen regards these changes as due to changes in blood hormones and thinks that the olfactory receptors are sensitized to the musk odor by some hormone. Such sensitization is not limited to musk or to hormone action. Penicillin injections render people very sensitive to the odor of this substance. Results of this sort suggest that the mechanism of olfactory stimulation will turn out to be related to the complex cellular reactions that occur in allergy and immunity; certain cells may become sensitized to specific olfactory substances.

Other partial anosmias probably occur sporadically in the population. To get hold of such cases Patterson & Lauder (1948) distributed small bottles of the foul-smelling mercaptan to school children who used them for testing parents and friends. Out of some 4,000 persons tested, 17 were unable to smell the standard solution; and these individuals were then tested with stronger solutions of mercaptan and with odors representing the other five corners of the Henning prism. These workers were interested in heredity and found some evidence of a hereditary factor in the partial anosmia; but the method of securing cases also might be worth using by students of olfaction. Partial anosmia and selective adaptation are promising leads, but the follow-up quantitative work is laborious, suggestive of a long pull ahead rather than any sudden insight into the mechanism of the olfactory sense.

STIMULI, AND THE NATURE OF THE RECEPTIVE PROCESS

Up to the present, we have said very little of the stimulus dimensions that might be related to odor qualities. The reason for this delay is simple; there are thousands of odorous substances, and they vary in a great number of ways. The case is quite different in vision and audition; in these two senses there is one simple dimension, frequency (or wavelength) of vibration, which is primarily related to the qualitative dimensions of pitch and hue, respectively. But the stimuli for smell are so complicated that it seemed better to examine them after we had become more familiar with the sense as a whole.

We have already said a few things about what may be called *transport factors;* some of the stimulus substance must reach the vicinity of the olfactory epithelium. It may be in the form of a pure gas, as hydrogen sulphide, in which case there is no particular problem. If the substance starts out as a volatile liquid, it evaporates molecules into the air, which then act as a gas. Finally, the substance may be distributed in the air in the form of larger particles, as smoke or fine dust, and reach the membranes in this solid form. One of the major variables that determine sensitivity to a given odor is the efficiency of this transport factor. Methods of stimulation must ultimately control this factor so that the stimulus can be stated in vapor pressure, or concentration of substance at the membrane. There are some difficulties inherent in the small amount of the substances involved, but they are merely technical physical difficulties.

Given the substance at the olfactory epithelium, our troubles begin. It is very difficult to see why some substances are odorous, and others not.

Chemical composition. A first step toward a knowledge of the smell stimulus is afforded by the work of the chemists in isolating the essential ingredients of odorous substances and determining their composition and molecular structure. Instead of speaking of vanilla as an odorous substance, we can speak of vanillin, $C_8H_8O_3$, the chemical compound occurring in vanilla and chiefly responsible for its odor; instead of speaking of violets, we can speak of ionone, $C_{13}H_{20}O$; instead of speaking of roses, we can speak of their chief odorous constituent, geraniol, $C_{10}H_{18}O$; and instead of speaking of onions, we can speak of $C_6H_{12}S_2$. These chemical substances can be extracted from their respective flowers, fruits, etc., or in many cases can be prepared chemically from quite other sources such as coal tar. Von Skramlik (1925) gives the chemical formulas for about 200 odorous substances. Moncrieff (1946) gives more.

Of all the chemical *elements*, about 90 in number, only about 16 seem to play any role in the production of odors (Haycraft, 1889). These 16, according to their chemical families, are:

a. Hydrogen
b. Carbon, silicon
c. Nitrogen, phosphorus, arsenic, antimony, bismuth
d. Oxygen, sulphur, selenium, tellurium
e. The halogens: fluorine, chlorine, bromine, iodine

Only the halogens (and ozone O_3) are odorous as elements. The great majority of odorous substances are compounds of carbon, containing also hydrogen, oxygen, nitrogen—one or more of these three.

Within each of the families, similar compounds have similar odors. In the halogen family, for example, the elements themselves have somewhat similar odors; and homologous compounds, chloroform ($CHCl_3$), bromoform ($CHBr_3$) and iodoform (CHI_3), also have similar odors. From chlorine through bromine to iodine the atomic weight and other atomic properties change progressively; and to this chemical series corresponds an odor series. The odor of bromine is "heavier" than that of chlorine, and the odor of iodine is heavier still. Similarly, the odor of bromoform is intermediate between those of chloroform and iodoform.

There are many series of homologous organic compounds which show a gradation in odor quality and also in odorous power, the latter being measured inversely by the value of the stimulus threshold. The "lower" members of a series, with small or light molecules, have little odor, the intermediate members have more odor, while the still higher members are nonvolatile and have no odor. One such series consists of the fatty acids:

Serial No.	*Name of acid*	*Formula*	*Threshold in .001 mg per liter*	*Quality of odor*
1	formic	CH_2O_2	25.	pungent
2	acetic	$C_2H_4O_2$	5.	sour
3	propionic	$C_3H_6O_2$	.05	sour
4	butyric	$C_4H_8O_2$	.001	rancid
5	valeric	$C_5H_{10}O_2$	.01	rancid
6	caproic	$C_6H_{12}O_2$	.04	rancid—aromatic

The threshold values are from Passy (1893), the odor qualities are those reported by Zwaardemaker (1922).

The threshold is lowered steadily with the increase in the size of the molecule up to and including butyric acid, beyond which point it remains fairly steady up to about No. 14 of the series, myristic acid, $C_{14}H_{28}O_2$, which is odorless, as are the still higher acids.[1]

[1] The formulas are more adequately written by separating out the carboxyl group,—COOH, characteristic of the fatty acids, and writing formic acid as HCOOH, acetic acid as CH_3COOH, propionic acid as CH_3CH_2COOH, butyric acid as $CH_3CH_2CH_2COOH$, and so on, thus indicating the open chain character of these molecules, especially of the larger (longer) ones.

Molecular structure. So far we have found some regularity, but there are many perplexing facts. Though similar chemical substances give similar odors, the converse is not true, for quite dissimilar chemical substances may also give similar odors. There is no one element that we can hold responsible for all odors of a given class; nor is there any one sort of chemical compound, nor any one atom-group, that we can hold responsible. It appears that we must take account of the molecular structure, as Passy (1892) urged on the ground of the different odors or different odorous power found in isomers (such as butyl alcohol and isobutyl alcohol), the molecules of which contain the same atoms but differently arranged.

Henning (1924) held that the odor of a substance depended on three factors: (1) the core of the molecule, such as the benzol ring, (2) the atom-groups attached to this core, and (3) the mode or place of attachment. He believed he could make out a fair case for the following relationships between molecular structure and type of odor:

Fragrant: two atom groups attached to adjacent members of an open chain or benzol ring (an ortho-substitution in the latter case):

Spicy: benzol ring with parasubstitution:

Resinous: benzol ring with cross link (or open chain with extra side-link):

or

Etherial: Forked atom group attached to ring or to open chain:

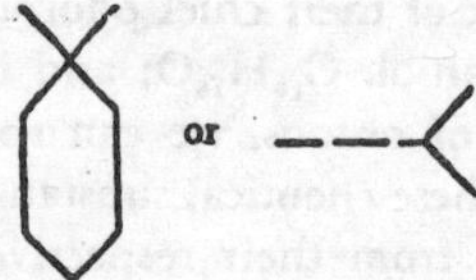

Burned: Heterocyclic ring including an N member:

Putrid: Here other elements usually are present, S, Se, Te, As, Sb, Bi, P; but instead of any of these N plays the decisive role in the fecal odors, indol and skatol.

Henning admitted that these rules had exceptions and were only first approximations. Zwaardemaker (1922) regarded them as interesting though speculative. Macdonald (1922) gave a clear statement of Henning's chemical theory and pointed out certain difficulties.

Ultraviolet absorption spectrum. Even if these or similar rules were established, we still should not know the stimulus, but should want to know how these atom groups and molecular structures act upon the olfactory receptors. They might act by vibrations of some kind (Haycraft, 1889; Zwaardemaker, 1922): vibrations of the atoms or atom groups, or vibrations of the electrons. An electronic oscillation would betray itself, in spectroscopic examination, by an absorption band of the odorous gas; and Heyninx (1919), after assembling the known facts on absorption bands of odorous substances, was well pleased with the result as evidence for the vibration theory of the smell stimulus.

The vibrations in question are in the ultraviolet region, with wavelengths of 360 mμ down to 200; and within this region he maps out a complete odor spectrum, with bromine near one end, wavelength = 330; and with the following classes in order:

Putrid, e.g., CS_2 at 320;
Rancid, e.g., butyric acid at 280;
Burned, e.g., phenol at 270, xylol at 265, naphthalin at 260;
Spicy, e.g., caraway at 255, cinnamon at 240;

Fragrant and etherial and resinous, scarcely separated, e.g., geraniol at 220, acetone at 210, camphor at 210.

When the odorous gas is drawn into the nose and comes in contact with the olfactory receptors, then, according to this theory, the electronic vibrations characteristic of the substance excite the receptors and excite them differently according to the vibration rate. It would be premature to take this theory as anything better than a suggestive hypothesis. Like all the other rules that have been suggested it appears to have many exceptions.

The infrared theory. Recently attention has been directed to the infrared absorption lines in the spectra of odorous substances (Beck & Miles, 1947). The cells of the human body, because of their temperature, emit wavelengths of 4–20 microns, and most odorous substances absorb selected waves within this range. The olfactory cells tend to radiate such waves, but their radiation is ordinarily blanketed by the air in the narrow chamber or cleft containing the olfactory epithelium. Now let this chamber be filled with an odorous gas which absorbs some of the heat rays, so permitting freer radiation. The olfactory cells thus lose heat, and this incipient cooling, according to the theory, stimulates them and sets up impulses running along their axons into the brain. We can think of different olfactory cells, because of their sizes and shapes, as being tuned to different wavelengths and so getting stimulation from different odorous substances. In its simplest form the theory misses the fact that certain optical isomers have the same absorption spectrum but different odors (Young, Fletcher & Wright, 1948), but Beck (1950) has introduced additional stimulus characteristics, as solubility in the receptor cell surface, which may account for the odor differences. It is too early to evaluate this theory. No doubt molecular structure is responsible for odor and also for the absorption spectrum, but the causal relationship may not be exactly as supposed by the theory (Pfaffman, 1951).

Olfactory nerve impulses. In regard to some of the senses a great deal can be learned by "tapping the wires" and recording the electrical potentials in the sensory nerve during stimulation of the receptors. This operation is not so easy in smell, since the sensory fibers pass directly from the receptors through a thin layer of bone into the olfactory bulb of the brain. Still some success was achieved by Adrian (1942, 1948). He inserted needle electrodes into the olfactory bulb of anesthetized animals and picked up impulses one or more synapses removed from the receptors. He found the hedgehog the most convenient animal for this work, but obtained records also from rabbits and cats. Some fibers seemed to respond to the pressure of incoming air, for they fired chiefly during inspiration. Other fibers, however, fired when an odorous substance was brought near the nose. They were apparently not specific for particular odors; the same fiber responded to many odors, though with some differences in latency and rate of firing. The animals showed maximal sensitivity to the odors that were most important in their natural lives. Therefore, the rabbits gave the strongest response to grassy odors, the cats to meaty odors. The results are consistent with the multireceptor view suggested by so many other studies, but Adrian himself prefers a pattern theory. He points to the millions of cells in the olfactory epithelium and suggests that this sense may very well be as complex as vision or audition. We humans are apt to regard it as simple and relatively unimportant, even though we make good use of olfactory signals of objects and objective conditions. In some animals it is of great importance and provides much complex information, approaching the other distance senses in this respect. We may have been trying to put operations in the receptors that actually involve elaborate central mechanisms. Perhaps the odor of a violet is as much a patterned perception as the sight of one. The numerous odors which we recognize so easily are perhaps analogous, not to the notes of the musical scale but to the characteristic sounds (timbre) of different instruments or to the vowels and consonants which are complex patterns, physically, but easily recognized as we hear them spoken.

SUMMARY

Food in the mouth or vapor in the nostrils may stimulate several senses, including pressure and temperature which are not chemical senses. The primitive "general chemical sense" turned out to be a simple affair. Its receptors are free nerve endings, and it is similar in other ways to the pain sense found elsewhere in the body. Its stimulus may be any chemical that irritates the free nerve endings.

Taste proved to be more highly organized. It has specialized receptors. There seem to be four primary taste qualities: sour, salt, sweet, and bitter. We know the stimulus for sour and find single nerve fibers that respond only to this stimulus. Presumably there is a specific type of receptor for this stimulus. Salt is a bit more complicated, but not too badly. Our knowledge of bitter and sweet is still in an unsatisfactory state.

Regarding smell we know a vast array of facts, but unfortunately they do not lend themselves to systematization. Perhaps the trouble is that our control, and even our knowledge, of the important stimulus dimensions is very inadequate. We are beginning to secure good physical control of the stimulus, and the rapid advance of organic chemistry and biochemistry should work to our advantage. We have some promising leads, notably the changes in sensitivity to similar odors, as produced by adaptation, by changes in body chemistry and by partial anosmias. But the sense of smell is apparently more complicated than we are apt to assume. Coordinated research will be required to solve its problems.

12

AUDITION

Those modern auditory "miracles"—the telephone, phonograph, radio—no longer arouse the dumbfounded amazement that they did when they were first presented to the public; and if anyone is genuinely curious as to how they can reproduce the complex sounds of speech and music, the scientific and engineering basis of their invention is a matter of record and open to intelligent study. How much more amazing is a little gadget that has been in constant use for untold generations—that pea-sized structure, the inner ear, which can pick up sounds out of the air, analyze their complexities, and enable us to respond to the subtleties of pitch, loudness, and timbre. Just how the inner ear accomplishes these results is not a matter of record but a scientific problem. It has been a fascinating problem for several centuries. The oldest of the reasonable theories was first fully stated by Helmholtz in 1863, but hints of his *resonance theory* go back another 250 years (Boring, 1942; Békésy & Rosenblith, 1948; Wever, 1949). The early thinkers had very few facts on which to build their theories, but the last century has provided a vast store of facts.

Lines of investigation. 1. *Psychophysical.* The experimenter controls the physical stimulus and measures the organism's ability to discriminate different sounds. Such experiments fit our formula, $R = f(S, O)$, with R standing for some sort of discriminant response. Range of hearing, thresholds, the interaction of stimuli, intelligibility of speech, and similar problems have received careful attention. These endeavors have often been motivated by practical needs. Telephone engineers seeking to improve communication equipment have found it necessary to investigate the capacities and limitations of the human auditory sense. The armed forces have faced the problem of transmitting clear messages over the din of modern warfare. But these practical aims are not the only motives; anyone who works on Audition may become intrigued with the question of *how* the ear works and find himself doing research that is aimed at auditory theory.

2. *Anatomical.* The auditory portion of the inner ear, the cochlea—so named from its resemblance to a snail shell—is not an easy structure to describe. It occupies a space of only 5 by 9 mm. It is extremely complicated, buried in bone, and with important fine details of jellylike consistency. Sections of the ear must be "fixed" or hardened, and the bone softened, before they are cut for microscopic study. In spite of these technical difficulties, a fair knowledge of

the cochlear anatomy has been achieved. Early auditory theories were based largely on anatomy.

3. *Electrophysiological.* As we noted earlier (p. 271), modern electronic amplifying and recording equipment has opened up whole new avenues of research. One can now observe the electrical changes resulting from stimulation of the cochlea, and even trace the resulting nerve impulses well up into the nervous system. The first really successful attempt of this sort was made in 1930 by psychologists who hoped to settle the argument between the two major theories, "resonance" and "telephone." Twenty years of research with this method in as many different laboratories have shed a great deal of light on the question, how the ear works, but without providing unequivocal support for either theory.

These three methods may be combined with each other and with auxiliary ones in an integrated attack on the problem of how the ear works. Research by all methods continues at an increasing rate. A large proportion of the findings can be united under a comprehensive theory which combines certain aspects of the two theories we have mentioned—as has been done by Wever (1949). This combined theory may not be the "final truth," and it certainly is not simple, but can at least serve to integrate the diverse facts in this complicated field.

The elementary facts of hearing, such as can be reviewed in a beginner's textbook of psychology, need not be repeated here. One should be acquainted with the physical stimulus: the simple sine wave with its dimensions of amplitude (intensity) and frequency; the upper partial vibrations, harmonic in the case of tones, inharmonic in the case of noises; the analysis of complex waves into a harmonic series of simple waves; resonance; and the transmission of sound waves through the air. There are corresponding psychological facts: to physical intensity corresponds the sensory dimension of loudness; to vibration frequency corresponds pitch; to the composition of a complex wave corresponds the timbre of a musical instrument and the vowel quality of speech; and the ear (or brain) has some power of analysis, as shown by the human ability to dissect a chord and to hear out some of the overtones in the timbre of an instrument.

Physical notation. We need convenient ways of designating the frequency and intensity of the auditory stimulus. Frequency, or vibration rate, is measured in cycles per second. A cycle, formerly called a double vibration, is like the double swing of a pendulum, from the central position to one side, through the central position to the other side, and back again as far as the central position. A frequency, as 1,000 cycles per second, is often written 1,000 cps, or as 1,000 ~, where the ~ is a miniature picture of a wave. The musical scale is also used for designating frequency, "middle C" standing for 256 ~ (though the musicians tune their instruments a little higher, making their middle C about 260 ~). Go up an octave and you double the frequency; go down an octave and you halve it. The lowest audible tone is about 20 ~, the highest about 20,000 ~.

As for intensity, it can be measured in absolute units of energy or of pressure. But a relative measure, somewhat like the octave, has been found very convenient. The octave is a ratio of 2 to 1 in frequency, while the *bel* is a ratio of 10 to 1 in energy. This unit was introduced by telephone engineers and named after the inventor of the telephone. The *decibel* (*db*) is $\frac{1}{10}$ of a bel and is a convenient-sized unit for psychological purposes. An energy ratio of 10:1 is 1 bel or 10 db; an energy ratio of 100:1 is 2 bels or 20 db. Since log 10 = 1, log 100 = 2, etc., the bel is a simple log unit and easy to handle by aid of a table of logarithms. To use the decibel scale, you start with the energy ratio of two stimuli, find its log to get bels, and multiply by 10 to get decibels. (If one stimulus has 3 times the energy of the other, you find log 3 = .4771, and multiplying by 10 you get 4.771 db as the difference, the ratio, of the two stimuli.) If, as often, your measuring instrument gives you pressure units, such as volts, instead of energy units, you have to square the pressure ratio to get the energy ratio; or you simply find the log of your pressure ratio and multiply by 20 to obtain the energy difference in decibels. (If your stronger stimulus has 15 times the voltage of the weaker, you find log 15 = 1.1761, and multiplying by 20 you have an energy difference of 23.522 db.)

To speak of a stimulus as having an energy of 40 db is like saying that a town is located at 40 miles. You would ask, "Forty miles from where?" And you should ask, "Forty decibels above (or below) what zero point or reference level?" You might find your subject's stimulus threshold and compute decibels up from that zero point. Or you might use a conventional zero point. The reference level adopted as standard in acoustics and audition is .0002 dynes per square centimeter, which in terms of energy is 10^{-16} watts per square centimeter. This is roughly the average human stimulus threshold for a tone of 1,000 ~, and so it is a convenient zero point in psychological research (Sivian & White, 1933). Figure 12-1 gives some idea of the intensity of familiar sources of sound, as measured from this zero point.

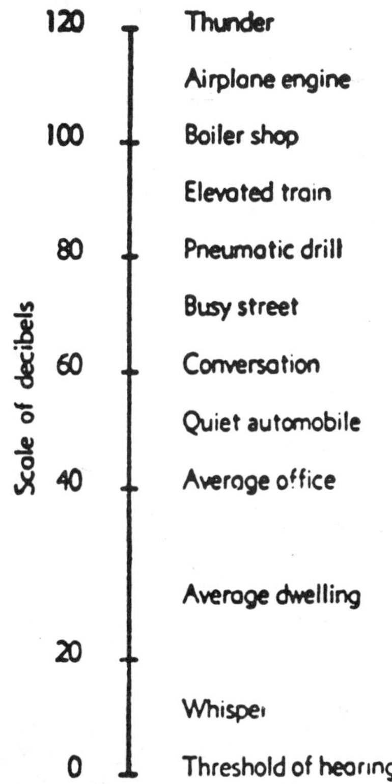

FIG. 12-1. (Stevens & Davis, 1938.) Energy levels measured in db above a reference level of .0002 dynes per square centimeter.

The few elementary psychological facts already stated will serve as a background for the theory to which further facts will be pinned. First we must bring in the necessary anatomical facts.

THE COCHLEA AND AUDITORY NERVE

In Figure 12-2 we have a highly schematized diagram of the ear. Sound waves

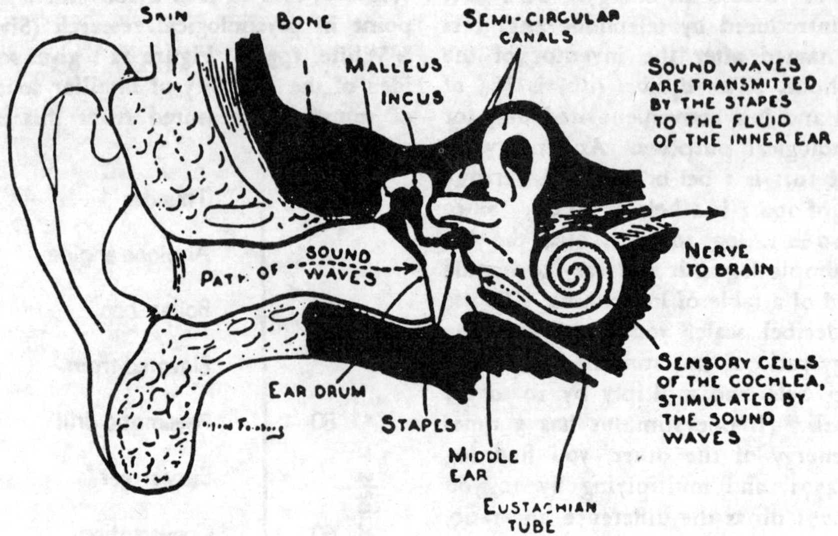

FIG. 12-2. (Davis, 1947.) Schematic diagram of the ear. For explanation, see text.

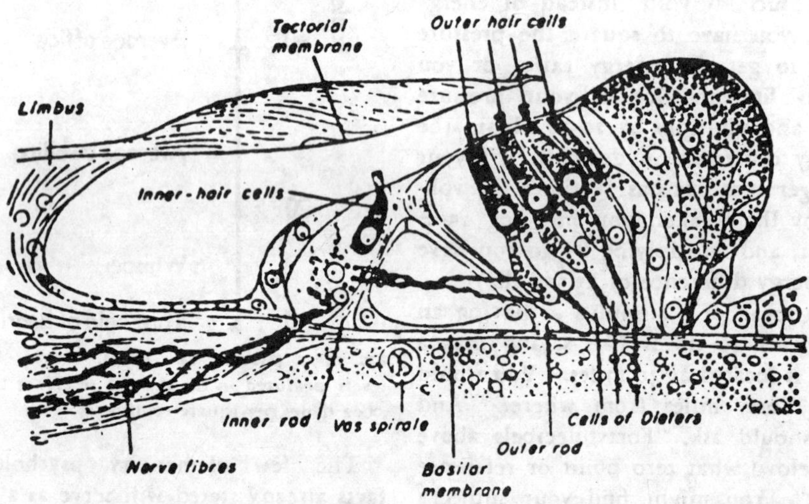

FIG. 12-3. (Lickley, 1919.) The organ of Corti in the human ear. The outer hair cells are probably more sensitive receptors than are the inner ones.

come in through the external auditory canal and set the tympanic membrane (eardrum) into vibration. The vibratory movement is transmitted across the middle ear by the three bones (ossicles) shown in solid black, known respectively as the hammer (malleus), anvil (incus), and stirrup (stapes). The footplate of the stirrup makes contact through the oval window with the fluid of the inner ear. The function of the drum and bones is to collect the vibrations from a light-weight medium, the outside air, and give them enough thrust to set the relatively heavy inner-ear liquid into vibration.

The inner ear consists of membranous tubes, filled with liquid, and buried in bone. Only the lower half, the snail-like cochlea, is concerned with hearing. The cochlea is a curled-up tube, or rather two half tubes, for the basilar membrane divides it longitudinally, making it look like a rounded B in cross section. This membrane supports the sensory cells. A thin roof over these cells creates an inner tube, the cochlear duct. As an arrow shows, the pressure waves from the stapes travel up one of these half tubes (the ascending canal, or scala vestibuli), and at its extreme end (the helicotrema), where the basilar membrane is absent, the pressure waves can pass through and start down the other half tube (the descending canal, or scala tympani), finally escaping into the air of the middle ear at the round window, marked by a second arrow. It would take only a fraction of a millisecond for a pressure wave to traverse the whole distance from the oval window to the helicotrema and back to the round window.

Resting on the basilar membrane is the organ of Corti, shown in cross section in Figure 12-3. Thousands of such cross sections would be needed to cover the whole length of the organ The receptors or hair cells are synaptically connected to the fibers of the auditory nerve. The sensitive hairs are perhaps imbedded in the gelatinous tectorial membrane; it is hard for the histologist to be sure on this point because the very delicate structures are disturbed when the tissue is prepared for microscopic examination. At any rate, it is generally assumed that the vibrations of the fluid in the ascending canal pass directly through the basilar membrane into the descending canal, so exerting vibratory pressure on the hair cells. Thus stimulated, the hair cells excite impulses in the attached nerve fibers. Exactly how this complicated mechanism works is a matter of theory; for the present we shall content ourselves with the oversimplified description just given.

AUDITORY THEORIES

How can the organ of Corti respond differently to the different audible frequencies, ranging from 20 ~ to 20,000 ~, and send different signals to the brain, enabling *O* to distinguish these different tones? This is the main question which an auditory theory attempts to answer, and it must also account for *O*'s ability to distinguish different intensities of sound.

The resonance theory. Often called the Helmholtz theory, after the man who first gave it an adequate formulation (1863, 1870), this theory is *one form of place theory* since it maintains that pitch is determined by the part of the organ of Corti that is stimulated by a given frequency. You could use a harp as a large-scale model for it. Let someone sing a steady note near the harp; the string that is tuned to that pitch will be set into resonance or sympathetic vibration, much as a pendulum can be set swinging by a series of gentle pushes, properly timed. Your model would also require electric connections from each separate string of the harp to an annunciator (the brain) so that any vibrating string could send in its signal. In the Helmholtz theory the resonant elements are the transverse fibers of the basilar membrane, while the hair cells and connected nerve fibers are the signaling mechanism which informs the brain what part of the basilar membrane is vibrating, and hence the pitch of the tone. The intensity of the tone, in accordance with the all-or-none law (p. 269), must be signaled by the number of nerve impulses sent in per second. Increase the intensity, and you presumably get more impulses in the single nerve fiber as well as more fibers taking part in the signal. So, you have a correlate for loudness.

The basilar membrane is widest near the helicotrema and narrowest near the oval window. The longest transverse fibers are presumably tuned to the lowest frequencies, as in the harp, and the shortest fibers to the highest frequencies. Accordingly, the resonance theory assigned the low tones to the region near the helicotrema, the high tones to the region near the oval window, and the intermediate tones to the intervening regions. This assignment has received some experimental support, as we shall see.

On the whole, however, the simple and attractive resonance theory is no longer tenable. Neither the anatomical details nor the physiological effects of stimulation permit us to assume that the transverse fibers of the basilar membrane are sharply tuned: they are interwoven with other fibers and damped by the overlying cell masses and by the surrounding liquid. One important suggestion (Gray, 1900) was that considerable lengths of the membrane must be thrown into vibration, with a maximum at a certain point and the signal to the brain issuing from that point. It seems best today to get away from the oversimplification implicit in the idea of resonance and to speak instead of a place theory. Different regions of the organ of Corti are probably most stimulated by different frequencies (Békésy, 1950) so that some version of the place theory is still widely accepted (Fletcher, 1953). The most thoroughgoing nonresonance place theory is probably that of Meyer (1950).

The telephone theory. This theory, associated with the name of the physicist Rutherford (1886), is a *frequency* theory; it supposes the frequency of the external sound to be impressed on the receptors and transmitted by them to the nerve fibers and by the nerve fibers to the brain. An incoming wave generates a single impulse in each connected nerve fiber. Loudness is correlated with the number of receptors and nerve fibers stimulated—the stronger the vibrations the farther they travel up the ascending canal and the more hair cells they stimulate. This theory gets into trouble with the high frequencies, for it assumes that the auditory nerve fibers can transmit impulses corresponding to the highest audible frequencies, 20,000 ~ in man, and considerably more in rats (Gould & Morgan, 1942) and in bats (Galambos & Griffin, 1942). But no mammalian nerve fiber can transmit more than 1,000 impulses per second, as far as known; the absolute refractory period (p. 270) sets a limit. And the auditory neurones seem to be no exception, for when Galambos & Davis (1943, 1944, 1948) recorded the impulses in single auditory neurones, they found a maximum rate of 400 per second, quickly declining to 150–200, even in response to strong high-pitched tones.

The volley principle. Wever & Bray in their pioneer studies (1930a, b, c, d) set out to test the rival theories by picking up nerve impulses from the anesthetized cat's auditory nerve. They amplified the nerve potentials and fed them into a telephone receiver. Listening to the nerve, they heard the same tone as was applied to the cat's ear, and the nerve followed the stimulus frequency up to 4,100 ~. Later experiments showed that Wever & Bray were picking up cochlear potentials (p. 330) in addition to neural ones, but no doubt remains that the nerve potentials themselves persist up to frequencies of several thousand cycles per second, keeping pace with the stimulus vibrations. How could the nerve as a whole carry these high frequencies if its component fibers could only carry relatively low frequencies?

Imagine a company of soldiers equipped with slow-loading rifles. Some of the men load more quickly than others. If the captain allows time for all to load before giving the command to fire, he will get a full company volley. If he gives the command to "fire when ready," he will get no volleys, but the rifles will be popping continuously and irregularly. Suppose he tells his men to fire only at his command, and gives his commands at short intervals. At the first command, say a quarter of the men are ready, fire, and start to reload; at the second command another quarter fire; at the third command still another quarter; at the fourth command the slowest loaders are ready and fire; and at the fifth command the first quarter is ready again. So the captain secures "volleys" at a rapid rate—more rapid than any individual soldier could manage. His system might break down into miscellaneous firing if he tried to increase the frequency of the volleys unduly.

In the auditory nerve fibers the reloading period is of course the relative refractory period (p. 269) when the fiber is recovering from a discharge. Even though not fully recovered, it will fire during this period if the stimulus is strong enough. Increasing the intensity of the auditory stimulus, therefore, will increase the number of fibers firing in each volley, but the number of volleys per second will remain the same, each volley being the response to a single wave of the stimulus. So volley frequency is the signal of pitch, while the number of fibers per volley is the signal of loudness.

This volley principle is pretty well established by a mass of interrelated experimental evidence and is essentially only a description of what happens in the auditory nerve (as in a cutaneous sensory nerve, p. 296). It shows how the nerve can carry well-synchronized impulses up to perhaps 4,000 ~, far beyond the power of any single fiber. But it breaks down far below 20,000 ~, the upper limit of audible frequencies, missing it by as much as two octaves (Wever, 1949) or even three (Stevens & Davis, 1936, 1938). So even the volley principle does not enable a frequency theory to handle the highest pitches.

The volley theory. Named by Wever (1949) because it depends definitely on the volley principle, the volley theory could be described as a place-volley theory, or a place-frequency theory, since it makes use also of the place principle, the principle that different regions of the organ of Corti are responsive to different frequencies of sound. The volley principle breaks down at high frequencies, as just stated, and the place principle breaks down at low frequencies, which seem to stimulate, not small parts, but extensive regions of the organ of Corti. The comprehensive theory supposes, accordingly, that high frequencies are signaled to the brain by the place or part of the organ that is set into vibration, that low frequencies are signaled by volley frequencies in the nerve, and that a combination of both kinds of signals takes care of the intermediate frequencies. Wever thinks it most likely that place is of some importance down to 400 ~ and that volley frequency plays a role up to about 5,000 ~. Accordingly, both factors operate in complementary fashion in the medium stretch from 400 to 5,000 ~ (Fig. 12-4, p. 332).

Wever (1949) is able to make good use of the volley theory for knitting together a large variety of known facts in audition. His hope is that the protagonists of the older theories may see in it at least a step toward a generally acceptable theory, and there is some evidence that opinion is moving in that direction. Psychologists who emphasize the place principle are admitting that volley frequency *may* be a pitch signal at low frequencies (Newman, 1948, 1950) so that the major area of dispute lies in the middle frequencies.

Cochlear potentials as an index of receptor activity. The nerve fiber potentials led off from the auditory nerve during stimulation of the ear by sound are sure to be contaminated by stronger potentials spreading through the tissues from the cochlea (unless special measures are adopted to exclude them). This contamination was demonstrated by Saul & Davis (1932). A nuisance in experiments on the nerve, these cochlear potentials are of positive value in the study of the end-organ. They are best picked up by an electrode placed on the round window. They differ in several respects from the nerve potentials. They have no stimulus threshold, but can be produced by even the weakest sounds within the audible frequency range of the particular organism. They can be elicited shortly after the death of the animal, and more and more weakly for an hour and more—while the nerve impulses drop out as soon as the animal is dead. We obtain the following picture of the cochlear reception of sound: when a wave in passing through the organ of Corti compresses the hair cells, it generates electric potentials; these act on the nerve ends and (if strong enough) arouse impulses in the nerve fibers. (Cf. Stevens & Davis, 1938; Wever, 1949.)

THE DIMENSIONS OF HEARING

We turn now to psychophysical experiments. We have the fundamental sensory dimensions of pitch and loudness to be explored in relation to the stimulus dimensions of frequency and intensity. We are concerned first of all with stimulus thresholds and difference thresholds. Not all frequencies of sound are audible; we wish to determine the range of audible frequencies from the upper to the lower limit. Not all intensities are audible; we wish to determine the least audible intensity at each frequency of vibration—for the intensity threshold differs greatly with different frequencies.

The range of hearing—stimulus thresholds. Our first task is to find the limits of audible frequency and intensity. For this purpose we use as pure tones as possible, free from overtones and transient noises; otherwise we should not know which frequency was arousing a response. This ideal stimulus was formerly approached, but only approached, by tuning forks and high-pitched whistles. Modern electronic oscillators, feeding through amplifiers into earphones or loudspeakers, do a much better job. These newer instruments give the experimenter excellent control of the stimulus and enable him to vary its two dimensions in precisely determined steps. A typical procedure is to hold frequency constant while varying intensity until the stimulus threshold is determined and to do the same for other frequencies which sample the range from the lowest to the highest audible tone. For our purposes, earphones are better than a loudspeaker, and even so the room should be relatively soundproof so as to avoid the masking effects of extraneous noises. Our measure of stimulus intensity is the pressure produced at the eardrum from an earphone.

Figure 12·4 gives the results of a standard series of experiments. It shows the range of stimulus frequencies and intensities which produce tonal sensations, and it covers the whole range of tonal sensations in the dimensions of pitch and loudness. A striking fact is the incredibly low intensity to which the ear responds in the most sensitive part of its range, from 1,000 to 4,000 ~. Greater sensitivity in this region would do no good, for the slight internal sounds of breathing and circulation would be a constant disturbance. Consider the frequency of 1,000 ~: it is audible at the minute pressure of .001 dynes per square centimeter; as the pressure is increased, the tone becomes louder and louder, but not unbearable until the pressure reaches about 1,000 dynes per square centimeter. This upper limit is indicated by the top of the shaded area and is sometimes called the *threshold of feeling*. Thus, the ear responds effectively through a millionfold range of pressures. In terms of energy the figure is even more impressive, since energy varies as the square of pressure. So the loudest tone the ear can handle with reasonable safety corresponds to a million times the energy of the weakest one it can hear—an energy range of 120 db, as shown by the scale at the right.

With a minimum intensity threshold at say 2,000 ~, the curve rises on both sides in accelerated fashion. The ear loses its sensitivity quite rapidly below 200 ~ and above 10,000 ~. At the upper end it reaches a frequency limit at about 20,000 ~ or a little higher (in young people and with some individual variation).

The lower frequency limit is not so easily determined. At the high intensities required, subjective overtones (p. 343) are generated by distortion of the waves in the ear itself. Something is heard but not the low tone that should correspond to the stimulus frequency. Wever & Bray (1937) solved the problem by using a "pistonphone," a miniature pump with strokes adjustable in frequency. The resulting air compressions are conducted to the ear through a tube. As the frequency falls below 100 ~, the tone begins to sound rough. Near 30 ~ it grades into intermittence. In the neighborhood of 15 ~ pitch drops out, and we may take this (rather than the convenient round number of 20 ~) as the very lowest frequency for tonal sensation.

The "threshold of feeling" is simply the approximate level of safe intensity. Above this level itches, pains, or other annoying sensations are felt. They probably arise from the outer and middle ear rather than from the cochlea; they tend to protect the cochlea from overload by making *O* get up and leave the sound field. This limit is practically important in the design of hearing aids for deaf people (p. 346). Its absolute level has varied somewhat from one experiment to another, depending presumably on the tolerance of the individuals tested.

The lower intensive threshold is comparatively stable. You can do a fair job of calibrating an oscillator-amplifier-earphone setup by testing ten undergraduates with it, aver ging their thresholds, and comparing your result with the curve of Figure 12-4. In this way you convert relative measurements, like "15 db below 1 volt" on your instrument, to absolute ones. The validity of this simple method is based on the fact that most people under 25 years of age have normal and fairly equal hearing. If one of your subjects has a hearing loss, his results will stand out from the others and should be discarded —this being one of the relatively few cases in which it is legitimate to discard

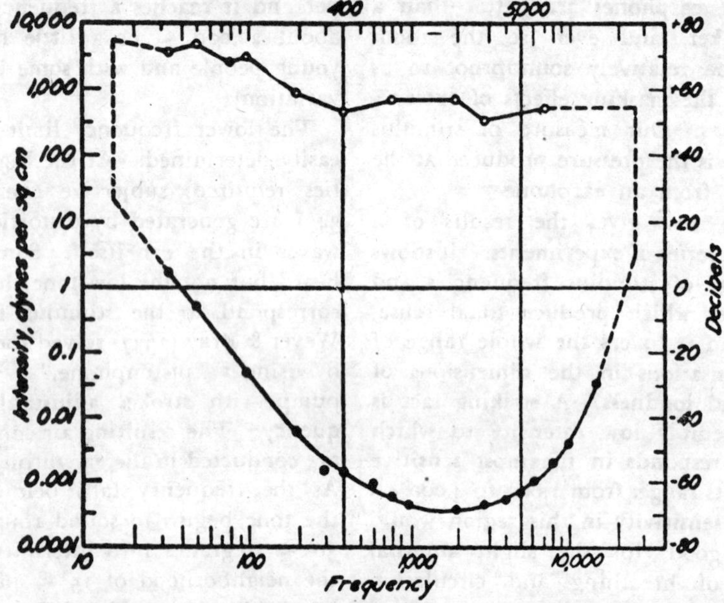

FIG. 12-4. (After Wegel, 1932; Wever, 1949. Reproduced by permission of John Wiley & Sons, Inc.) The two-dimensional range of hearing. The upper boundary shows the stimulus intensities which are high enough to produce sensations of pain or pressure in the ear region, a warning that the limit of safe intensities is about reached. The lower curve shows the much smaller intensities which arouse a minimum sensation of tone at each frequency. The intensity scale at the left is in absolute units of pressure; that at the right is in relative units of energy, measured up and down from a central value. Data from 10 individuals of normal hearing.

In relation to the volley theory (p. 329), the middle area covers the frequency range in which both place and volley frequency are important for hearing, while the outer areas show where place alone (at the right) and volley frequency alone (at the left) provide the signals of pitch. The volley principle alone cannot account for the sensitivity (threshold) curve. But by computing the probable effects of mechanical resonance of the basilar membrane as a whole and of its different regions (dependent on their location and the load of cells and fluid which they carry), and the probable effects of number and excitability of hair cells and nerve fibers, Wever has deduced a theoretical sensitivity curve which fits the empirical curve with surprising exactness data because they disagree with the general trend.

Auditory discrimination. As a registering instrument the ear has the demonstrated merit of being sensitive to a wide range of sound vibrations—a wide range of both frequencies and intensities. But how acute is its differential sensitivity, its power to respond differently to different frequencies or intensities? This is obviously a routine question for the psychophysicist, and it does have important bearings on auditory theory and on the practical utility of hearing in the organism's behavior. Experimenters over many decades have employed a variety of psychophysical methods and of stimulators. Recent studies have taken advantage of the pure tones and fine gradations made available by electronic equipment, and a novel psychophysical method has emerged, the "warble" technique. Instead of discrete standard and comparison stimuli separated by a short interval of time, there is a continuous tone which oscillates in frequency or intensity (as the case may be) several times a second. The observer's task is to report whether or not he hears the warble, and the experimenter's task is to determine the least difference in frequency or intensity that elicits the report of warbling. This very rapid method may yield difference thresholds which are somewhat smaller than those obtained by the more conventional methods—no disadvantage so long as all the thresholds compared are determined by the same method.

The DL for pitch. When engaged in checking on Weber's law (p. 222), we assembled the older results in Figure 8-14, which showed that the Weber fraction, $\Delta F/F$, was small and fairly constant through the middle frequencies, say from 400 to 4,000 ~, but increased greatly toward each end of the range. The excellent data obtained by Shower & Biddulph (1931), using the warble technique, give the same picture, except that the upswing starts at about 8,000 instead of 4,000 ~. Since we are now concerned with hearing rather than Weber's law, we may discard the Weber fraction and simply ask how the just noticeable difference in pitch changes (if it does change) as you go up the pitch scale. We see in Figure 12-5 that this DL holds steady up to 2,000 ~ and then climbs

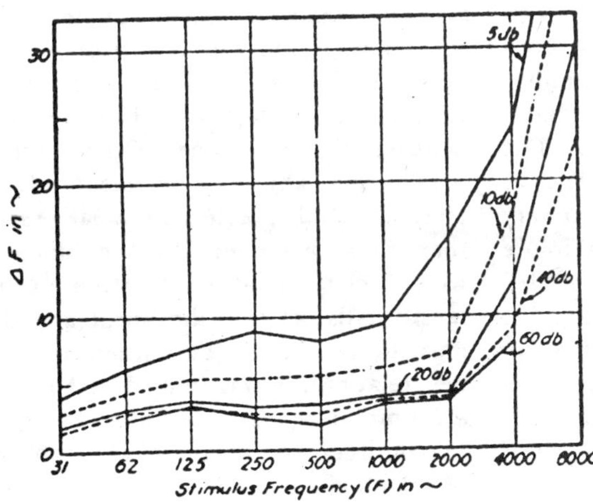

FIG. 12-5. (Data from Shower & Biddulph, 1931.) The absolute size of the DL for pitch as a function of stimulus frequency and intensity. Average results from five young men. At the lower intensities (5 and 10 db) the DL is relatively large. Except for the 5-db intensity, the curves are almost level from 31 to 2,000~, a range of 6 octaves. (The piano extends a couple of semitones lower and a whole octave higher.) Above 2,000 the DL increases enormously.

rapidly. We see another thing: the DL for pitch depends on stimulus intensity as well as frequency; the louder the tone, the smaller the DL.

If we desire to utilize exact values of the pitch DL in a theory of hearing,

Frequency	31	62	125	250	500	1,000	2,000	4,000	8,000	~
10-db level	7.4	5.5	4.2	3.4	2.8	2.4	2.0	2.3	3.2	db
40-db level	1.8	1.3	1.0	.7	.6	.6	.6	.7	.9	db

we are disturbed by this last fact because we hardly know which intensity level to work with. Another difficulty lies in individual differences, some persons being much keener than others in pitch discrimination, and practice has a strong effect. If we counted up successive DLs from the lowest to the highest audible tone, our count would be 10 times as large with pitch-keen *O*s listening to loud tones as with pitch-dull *O*s listening to weak tones. Still the quantitative facts of pitch discrimination ought to be of some use in auditory theory, since the remarkable capacity of the cochlea to signal pitch to the brain is a basic fact to be explained. Ingenious efforts have been made to fit the quantitative data to the place theory (Stevens, Davis & Lurie, 1935) or to the combined volley-and-place theory (Wever, 1949).

The DL for loudness. We have seen that the DL for pitch varies with both frequency and intensity of the stimulus. The same is true of the DL for loudness, as shown in Figure 8-15, page 223. The Weber fraction is about 1/8 (or less) at high intensities but much larger at very low intensities. Close to the absolute threshold a stimulus must be doubled (or more) in order to be noticeably louder. The same figure shows that intensity discrimination is keener with tones of 4,000 than with tones of either 1,000 or 10,000 ~; below 500 ~ it is much less keen, as shown below by some of the same author's results (Riesz, 1928), arranged to answer the question: What is the smallest intensity difference in db that will make a tone warble? The answer is given for two intensity levels and for a range of frequencies:

All in all, the ear shows the greatest efficiency at what we ordinarily consider very high frequencies, centering around 2,000 ~, which is about an octave above the "high C" of the soprano.

Loudness as a function of stimulus intensity and frequency. This matter was discussed under Psychophysics (p. 238) and has been treated at length by Stevens & Davis (1938) and by Wever (1949). We might expect loudness to increase in proportion to the intensity of the stimulus, but this is very far from being the case. Remembering Fechner's law, we might expect loudness to be proportional to the logarithm of the stimulus intensity, but this supposition also proved to be far from the truth. If Fechner's law held for loudness, any increase of 1 db (a relative unit) should give the same increment of loudness regardless of the initial intensity. Actually an increase of 1 db in a strong tone sounds much greater than the same increase in a weak tone. On the other hand, equal absolute increments of intensity sound greater in weak tones than in strong ones. So the function which relates loudness to stimulus intensity falls between the linear and the logarithmic curve. This intensity-loudness relationship was studied by Fletcher & Munson (1933) and by Churcher (1935) in connection with practical problems of telephonic communication and noise abatement. The results have a theoretical bearing, too, since they are not what we might expect from the electrophysiological facts of cochlear activity. The cochlear potentials increase linearly with stimulus intensity; the cochlear output is directly proportional to the stimulus input as long as the input is not excessive; or, we may say, the cochlea is a high-fidelity microphone. But the cochlear output has to excite the nerve fibers, and the peculiar loudness function may reflect a complex process of increasing both the firing rate of individual nerve fibers and the number of fibers participating in a volley.

Interaction of intensity and frequency. Loudness is not dependent on stimulus intensity alone. It is somewhat dependent on frequency. An observer can match two tones for loudness even though they differ in pitch. In an important experiment of Fletcher & Munson (1933) a standard of 1,000 ~ at a constant intensity of 40 db above threshold was sounded alternately with a comparison tone of 100 ~ which *O* could adjust in intensity until both tones were equally loud for him. He gave the 100 ~ tone 25 db more intensity than the 1,000 ~ tone to make them equally loud. By many such matches a family of equal-loudness contours was worked out. At low-loudness levels the contour resembles the threshold curve of Figure 12-4, p. 332, which can be called a minimum-loudness contour; but the higher the loudness the more the contour flattens out. Thus, low-level loudness shows a marked frequency effect which is absent from high-level loudness. A boy who wants to make as much noise as possible can do it equally well with a drum or a whistle.

Loudness, then, depends to a considerable degree on the frequency of the sound vibrations; and pitch, it is found, depends to a slight degree on stimulus intensity. As the vibrations of a large tuning fork die away, the tone seems to rise a little in pitch. This effect has been known for over a hundred years. Stevens (1935) found the reverse effect at high frequencies. He presented alternately two tones of slightly different frequency and required *O* to adjust the intensity of one tone until both were equal in pitch. In the middle range of frequencies, 1,000 to 3,000 ~, intensity had no effect on pitch; at low frequencies increased intensity tended to lower the pitch; at high frequencies, to raise it. These effects have been confirmed by Morgan, Garner & Galambos (1951) but with the qualification that the shifts in pitch are very slight on the average and differ greatly in amount with the individual. Binaural stimulation has similar slight effects on pitch: a strong tone is delivered alternately to both ears and to one ear, and the monaural stimulus is varied in frequency until it matches the binaural stimulus in pitch (Thurlow, 1943a). These effects of intensity on pitch are not clearly predictable by either the place or the volley theory, and the binaural effect points to the nerve centers rather than to the cochlea as the probable source of the whole phenomenon.

Duration. Another stimulus variable that might have some effect on loudness and pitch is duration. With a stimulus of constant intensity, the sensation increases in loudness for perhaps 200 or 300 ms (Munson, 1947); up to this limit you can balance time against intensity and get the same loudness if you keep the product, $I \times T$, constant (as in visual brightness, p. 373). Yet even a short exposure to a tone raises the threshold for that tone momentarily.

Sound a tone for 300 ms at moderate intensity, and after a silent period of only 80 ms sound the same tone for 30 ms at low intensity, *O* reporting whether he hears it the second time. The more intense the first or "fatiguing" tone, the higher the threshold immediately afterward. If you prolong the silent period, you find recovery practically complete in less than half a second (Harris, Rawnsley & Kelsey, 1951; Rawnsley & Harris, 1952). These duration effects are not shown by the cochlear potentials but may occur in the process of nerve fiber stimulation.

Duration affects pitch in a different way. If a tone is extremely brief, no definite pitch is heard. It takes only a few cycles to establish pitch at low frequencies, but as many as 150 cycles are needed at a frequency of 8,000 ~. In terms of duration, however, there is not so much difference, the time required being about 30 ms for a tone of 100 ~, 10 ms for one of 1,000, and 20 ms for one of 8,000 (Turnbull, 1944; Wever, 1949).

The fundamental S—R correlates. All these complicated interactions of frequency, intensity, and duration should not be allowed to obscure the fundamental correlations. Loudness is primarily determined by stimulus intensity, even though the ear is much more sensitive to some frequencies than to others. Pitch is even more closely tied to stimulus frequency, with intensity having some minor effects. The auditory mechanism is an amazingly efficient analyzer of both frequency and intensity in the important middle ranges, even though less faithful at the extremes.

Other possible dimensions of pure tones. As a stimulus a pure tone has only the dimensions of frequency and intensity (along with duration), and it arouses a sensation having the corresponding dimensions of pitch and loudness. Can the sensation have any other dimensions? We cannot rule out such a possibility a priori, for the ear and nerve centers might introduce other variables. Several other psychological dimensions have been suggested: volume, brightness, density, tonality, and vocality (vowel quality). These possible dimensions were a challenge to many eminent psychologists, as shown by Boring (1942). The basic question is whether a suggested dimension is a fundamental way in which simple tonal sensations can vary or merely another name for pitch or loudness. Take volume, for example. This term is often used as a synonym for loudness, as on your radio set, but in psychology it means voluminousness or size. A loud tone seems large, a weak tone small. But it is also true that a low-pitched tone seems large and a high-pitched one small. To test the claims of this dimension *E* can vary one of the stimulus dimensions and require *O* to say which of two tones is more voluminous, the question being whether *O* can make such judgments with reasonable consistency and whether the DLs so obtained will be any different from those obtained in pitch or loudness discrimination.

Rich (1916, 1919) used the approach just suggested, varying the stimulus in frequency, and his results are shown in Figure 12·6. His *O*s judged volume with reasonable consistency, and their DLs were much larger than for pitch. Rich concluded that volume was a genuine dimension. From similar experiments he concluded that brightness was identical with pitch and that vocality had a dubious claim to recognition.

To differentiate volume from loudness a parallel experiment was needed,

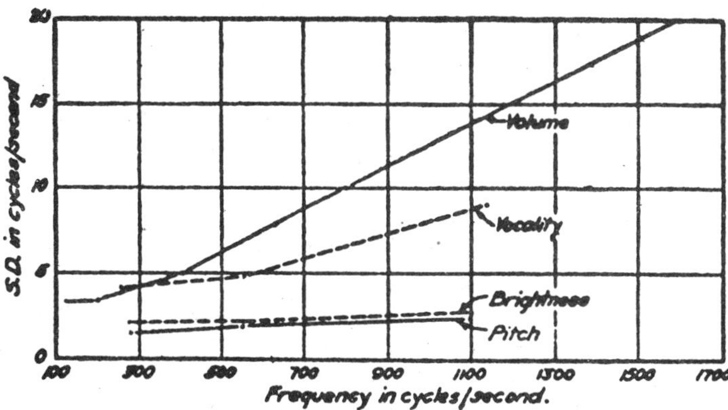

FIG. 12-6. (Data from Rich, 1919.) Values of SD obtained in discrimination of pure tones, when the stimulus was varied in frequency, and the tones were compared, in different series, as to their pitch, brightness, vocality and volume. The question is whether the run of the SD values in the different series is sufficiently different to justify admitting separate dimensions of tonal sensation. The data on volume are really too scanty to give a reliable curve.

For plotting these curves we have used Rich's data on "precision" or "h," transmuted into SD values (p. 207). Rich's DL values show about the same relations.

with intensity as the stimulus variable. This experiment also gave positive results (Halverson, 1924; Dimmick, 1933), so that the status of volume was quite well established.

Another approach to the problem was adopted by Stevens (1934 a, b, c). It was the balancing method as employed for loudness contours (p. 335). Frequency and intensity were balanced against each other. The output of a loudspeaker driven by an oscillator was varied in frequency so that two pure tones of different pitch were presented in rapid alternation, 40 single stimuli per minute. The even-numbered tones were higher in pitch than the odd-numbered, and so less voluminous, but *O* could increase their volume by increasing their intensity by aid of a rheostat. Or, the even-numbered tones were lower in pitch, and so more voluminous, and *O* could reduce their volume by decreasing their intensity. By this means an equal-volume contour was worked out, as shown in Figure 12-7. It was possible for *O* to make these equations with some confidence and regularity. He could at-

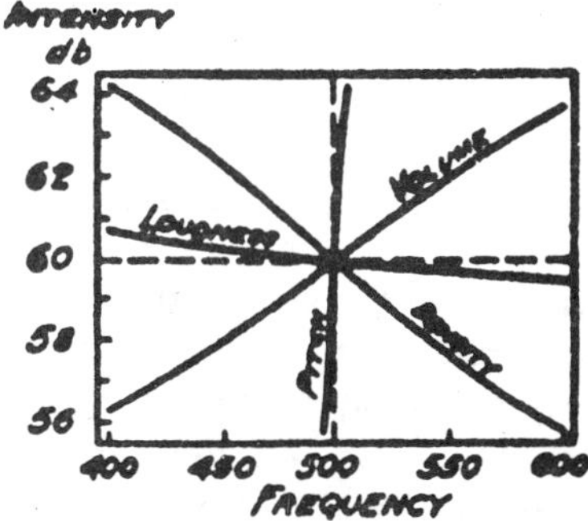

FIG. 12-7. (Stevens, 1934b.) Volume, loudness, density, and pitch equations between tones of differing frequency, the frequency difference being compensated by a difference in stimulus intensity. The rectangular framework represents the physical dimensions, intensity and frequency, while the curves are lines of equal volume, density, etc. The volume line reads that, on the average of several *Os*, the following stimuli gave equally voluminous tones:

400 ~ at 56 db
450 " " 58 "
500 " " 60 "
550 " " 62 ", nearly
600 " " 63.5 db, approx.

The other lines are read in a similar way: thus a tone of about 508 ~ at 64 db was regarded as having the same pitch as the standard tone of 500 ~ at 60 db.

test equality of volume in spite of inequality in both pitch and loudness. Volume had the earmarks of a separate dimension. By the same method "density" contours were worked out. A very high tone was unhesitatingly reported to be more dense than a low-pitched one and a loud tone more dense than a soft one. Density had a good case. Brightness seemed to be identical with density (Boring & Stevens, 1936).

The equal-volume contours have been confirmed and extended by Thomas (1949) using the same general method as Stevens but a wider range of frequencies and intensities. His *O*s were able to match the volume of these three: 200 ~ at 22 db, 1,000 ~ at 62 db, and 4,000 ~ at 100 db. The inter- and intra-individual variation was surprisingly small for so difficult a task. This finding emphasizes the stability of volume as a dimension.

We seem to be justified by the experimental results in adding volume and density to the dimensions of pure tonal sensations. They may depend on some physiological process in the ear or auditory nerve centers, but it is equally likely that they are learned perceptual responses, acquired by association. All our lives we have felt the deep tones of our own voices swell diffusely and voluminously in our chests, while the higher tones are connected with constriction of the throat. As Boring has said (1942), the ultimate basis of volume is still a matter of speculation.

Tonality. This dimension of pure tones refers to the similarity of a note and its octave. Middle C and the C next above it sound much alike—more alike than middle C and the G next above it, even though the C and G are more alike in pitch. One obvious explanation comes from the overtone structure: the fundamental and all overtones of middle C are duplicated in the next higher C with its overtones and their difference tones. Thus, in a physical sense ordinary musical tones separated by an octave are very similar. But pure tones, though lacking overtones, still show tonality. And tonality cannot be simply something we have learned, for Blackwell & Schlosberg (1943) found that rats in a conditioned avoidance situation confused the octaves—presumably without previous musical experience! It is possible that subjective overtones (p. 343) are involved, but we have no sure explanation of tonality.

Vocality. The question for us right here is whether a simple tone of a certain frequency sounds like the vowel *oh*, and a tone of another frequency like the vowel *ah*, and so on. There is no doubt that complex tones produced by the human vocal organs do have vowel sounds, and the question regarding simple tones will be better understood in connection with the analysis of these complex tones (p. 340).

COMBINATIONS OF SIMPLE TONES

A pure tone or simple sine wave—like the fall of a body in a vacuum—is something of basic scientific importance but not often encountered in ordinary life. Sounds that reach the ear are practically always complex; yet many of them become familiar and indicative of objects in the environment. We recognize a musical instrument by its timbre, the wind and the rain by the noises they make, and spoken words by their patterns of complex speech sounds.

Timbre. A violin, a flute, and a trumpet somehow produce different sounds even though they play the same note with the same loudness. How can these sounds differ? The waves emitted by the instruments, and by practically all sources of sound, are compounded of simple waves of different frequencies, called *partials*, or fundamental and overtones. The upper partials are harmonic with the fundamental in the case of musical tones, and the frequencies of harmonic partials are in the ratios of 1: 2: 3: 4. . . . A note of 100 ~ sung by a bass voice or played on any instrument, in the air consists of a complex wave containing the frequencies 100, 200, 300, 400, 500, and many more. It seemed possible to Helmholtz (1862) that these partials might vary in relative intensity from one instrument to another and thus produce the various timbres. He put his hypothesis to the test by aid of resonators, which were hollow spheres of different sizes, responsive to different frequencies. Each resonator had a wide mouth to admit air vibrations and a small orifice to be inserted into *O*'s ear. A resonator "sings" when the frequency to which it is tuned is present in the complex wave reaching it from any source. By this means Helmholtz found certain partials strong in the tone of one instrument, other partials strong in another instrument. After practice *O* is able to "hear out" the overtones without the aid of resonators. Timbre thus depends on the overtone structure, the intensity pattern of the partials. This result is amply confirmed by the use of modern electric harmonic analyzers.

There has been little straight psychophysical work on timbre, and the reason is not hard to see. Since a given fundamental may be combined with 10 or 20 overtones, each of them capable of variation in intensity, it would be an endless job to work over the effects systematically. A more practical experiment, with modern equipment, is to filter out one or more partials altogether and find out whether the difference can be detected. There is the interesting "case of the missing fundamental." Fletcher (1929, 1934) had 10 generators with frequencies of 100, 200, 300, . . . 1,000 ~, feeding together into a telephone receiver or a loudspeaker. The combination gave a full, rich timbre with a pitch of 100. Filtering out the fundamental made no appreciable difference in the pitch or timbre. The usual explanation calls attention to the difference tone of 100 ~ generated in the ear by the upper partials: $300 - 200 = 100$, $400 - 300 = 100$, and so on. Jeffress (1940) found that this experiment was less successful with any organ pipe as the source of the complex tone. When the fundamental was filtered out, the pitch seemed to many *O*s to be an octave higher. Fletcher found that removal of an upper partial from the complex described made a slight difference in timbre.

Noise. Though noise has a bad name as something which ought to be "abated," actually many noises are important and distinctive signals. A noise differs from a tone in having no clearly marked pitch. A medley of tones has the effect of a noise. In a musical tone, all the partials are multiples of the fundamental frequency, as in the example given of 100, 200, 300 ~ , . . . In a noise there is no such simple relationship of the component frequencies. The vibration is said to be *aperiodic;* it cannot be analyzed into regular sine waves. A *pure noise* can be produced by amplifying the random emission of electrons in a vacuum tube; the resulting random vibrations of the loudspeaker produce a sort of continued "Shh" sound, sometimes described as "white noise" because, like white light, it combines a whole range of frequencies. But most noises are not pure in this sense, for they contain some outstanding tonal elements. If you pound the desk with your fist, the auditory energy is concentrated in the low frequencies and has a very different sound from the complex of high frequencies which result from jingling keys. Kettle drums and xylophones produce sounds that are somewhere between tones and pure noises.

Vowel sounds. We meet the same question here as in the case of timbre: How can these sounds differ when they are alike in frequency and intensity? The vocal apparatus is really a musical instrument, adjustable not only for intensity and frequency but also for something akin to timbre. Tones are produced by the vocal cords and pass out through the throat and mouth. Helmholtz (1862) suggested that the throat-and-mouth cavity serves as an adjustable resonator which strengthens various partials present in the voice tone—different partials according to the size and shape of the cavity. When the mouth is constricted for saying "bit," the cavity resonates to the relatively high frequencies around 2,500 ~, no matter whether the fundamental of the tone is bass at 100 ~, soprano at 500 ~, or an unvoiced whisper which is a faint noise consisting mostly of high frequencies. The larger but almost closed cavity when the mouth is shaped for "true" resounds to the much lower frequencies around 325 ~.

Hermann (1890) proposed a theory that is slightly different. The mouth in any given position is tuned to a certain frequency and (he thought) contributes a mouth tone of this specific frequency to the complex voice tone—instead of reinforcing certain partials of the voice tone. This specific mouth tone he called a *formant*. There has been much debate between the adherents of the two theories, but the physics of resonance favors Helmholtz. The term *formant* is currently used without regard to theory.

There are two ways of testing these theories experimentally, or of finding out the composition of vowel sounds without regard to the theories. One is to have the vowels pronounced and to record and analyze the vibrations so produced. The other is to present a known combination of frequencies and ask the listener to report what vowel, if any, he hears.

Analysis of spoken vowels. The vibrations produced by a human speaker are recorded and subjected to harmonic analysis (Miller, 1922; Fletcher, 1929; Steinberg, 1934; Black, 1937); or the frequency bands in a vowel are made visible by the sound spectrograph (Steinberg & French, 1946; Potter, Kopp & Green, 1947). The records show slightly different frequencies for the same vowel pronounced by different persons, as might be expected from variations in its sound. For every difference in pronunciation there is a difference in the throat-and-mouth cavity and so in the frequency band that is reinforced. Yet the various experiments do at least agree in placing the vowels in a certain order, with approximate frequency bands as follows:

u	(as in true)	about	325 cycles/sec
oo	(as in book)	"	420
o	(as in go)	"	500
aw	(as in jaw)	"	730
a	(as in father)	"	1000
a	(as in bat)	"	1800
e	(as in ten)	"	2000
i	(as in tin)	"	2200
i	(as in machine)	"	2500–3000
m, n, ng		"	250
s		"	5000–9000

More recent analysis divides the lower bands into two formants and adds a third higher one (Dunn, 1950). The point to be stressed is that two or three frequency bands, rather than a single frequency, make up the characteristic of each vowel. Even an isolated vowel, carefully intoned, is a complex and somewhat variable affair. When it is part of a spoken word or sentence, it is still more complex and variable, as we can see from the visual record of the vibrations in Figure 12-8. To read this form

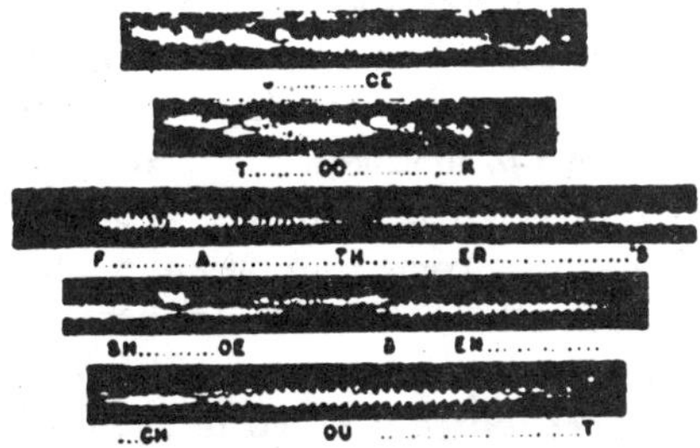

FIG. 12-8. (Licklider, Bindra & Pollack, 1948.) Oscillograms to show the form of speech waves for a standard sentence, "Joe took father's shoe bench out." This particular sentence has a large range of vowel and consonantal sounds.

When the electrical oscillations, before being fed into a telephone receiver or loudspeaker, are "clipped," so that the top and bottom of the waves are removed and only the central portions left intact, the stimulus is reduced to a series of "square waves." The frequencies are preserved, and also the time pattern of the words and sentence. With sufficient amplification the physical effect is to strengthen the upper frequencies at the expense of the lower frequencies of the speaker's voice. To a listener it is queer-sounding speech, but intelligible and less disturbed by strong noise than normal speech.

of written language would be an arduous task and require much training. But the ear provides the auditory data, and the brain recognizes the sound patterns instantly. No doubt this auditory perception required much training in early childhood.

Do pure tones have vowel quality? If the vowel *o* as in go has a strong frequency band in the region of 500 ~, a pure tone of this frequency ought to have the *o* quality. Köhler (1909) set up this hypothesis, at first very doubtfully. Finding that his subjects after a little practice thought they detected vowels in certain pure tones, he avoided suggestion by the following psychophysical procedure. He altered the frequency step by step in ascending and descending series, asking the subjects to report when the *o* quality came out most clearly; and the same for other vowels in their respective frequency bands. His four subjects agreed closely on the pure tones that gave the several vowel sounds, and these tones were approximately in the frequency bands found prominent in spoken vowels.

Rich (1919), whose results on vocality are included in Figure 12-6, page 337, found it difficult to train his subjects and to avoid the possibility of suggestion. He was inclined to reject vocality as a dimension of pure tones. Even Köhler's subjects complained that the vowels heard in pure tones were somewhat thin as compared with spoken vowels. Full vowel quality is perhaps present only in complex tones.

Realistic synthetic vowels have often been produced by appropriate combinations of a few pure tones corresponding to the formants. Tuning forks or organ pipes were formerly used for this purpose, but electric oscillators are the most convenient.

Elimination of frequencies. If certain frequency bands are present in the sound of a vowel or consonant, filtering out these bands would make the speech sound difficult or impossible to recognize. Eliminating the high frequencies has a surprisingly large effect. Without the frequencies over 1,000 ~, only a few words can be recognized, but with only the frequencies over 1,000 ~ present, almost all words can be recognized (French & Steinberg, 1947). High-frequency elimination kills most of the consonants—and if you pronounce a sentence without the consonants, you will admit that its intelligibility must be pretty low. Frequencies above 7,000 ~, however, are unimportant in speech though quite important for recognition of some noises. If we divide the speech spectrum at 1,900 ~, the upper and lower parts are equally important for intelligibility; about 70 percent of test words or syllables are correctly perceived with either the upper or the lower part transmitted to the listener's ears. Other factors in intelligibility—the intensity and pitch of the speaker's voice, his rate of talking, interfering noise, and the training of both speaker and listener—are covered in the review of Licklider & Miller (1951). Communication under difficult conditions is a serious military problem, and much of the effort of the Harvard Psycho-Acoustic Laboratory during the last war was devoted to the question, what you could do to speech without impairing its intelligibility. The standard method was to present lists of words under various unfavorable conditions and determine the percent that a listener could perceive correctly (Egan, 1948). Telephone engineers have long been concerned with this type of communications problem and have made notable contributions to what we may regard as the psychology of speech perception.

AURAL INADEQUACIES

Though the cochlea is a remarkably faithful receptor or microphone, it does introduce into auditory sensation certain peculiar phenomena which are "subjective" though by no means imaginary. They are definitely sensory phenomena, originating in the ear itself. Difference tones are the best example, but we may first notice the simpler example of beats, which are indeed not entirely subjective since they result from interference between the physical waves entering the ear.

Beats. Let there be two separate sources giving out simple tones; and let one remain at 256 cycles while the other is raised gradually in frequency. When one source is giving out 256 vibrations per second and the other 257, the listener hears only a single tone but this wavers in loudness. It waxes as the two sources come into like phase and wanes as they come into opposite phases with each other. The listener hears one waxing-waning unit per second. When the higher source is raised to 258 cycles, there are two of these units per second. Their number is always equal to the difference in the vibration frequency of the two sources. Up to about 8 per second they can be counted by an attentive listener. As the number increases the gentle waxing and waning give way to a beating which is not only heard but also felt in the region of the ear drum. The beats become rattling and unpleasant as the upper source is raised to 284 cycles per second; there are then $284 - 256 = 28$ beats per second, far too many to be counted. Beyond this point the beats become less prominent but the whole tonal effect is quite rough.

The intertone. When the two beating primary tones differ in vibration rate by only a few cycles per second, only a single tone is heard, intermediate in pitch between the two primaries. As the difference increases, say at 256–272, this intertone becomes fainter and fainter and the primaries become separately audible.

Difference tones. When two pure tones are sounding, say at frequencies of 400 and 500 ~, a careful listener can hear also a third tone, much lower in pitch. In fact, he can match it with a separate tone of 100 ~ in this case, and in general with a tone of a frequency equal to the difference between the two primaries. But this is only the "first difference tone."

If we let l = the frequency of the lower primary tone; h = the frequency of the upper primary tone; D_1, D_2, . . . = the frequencies of the first, second, . . . difference tones; we have

$$\begin{aligned} D_1 &= h - l \\ D_2 &= 2l - h \\ D_3 &= 3l - 2h \\ D_4 &= 4l - 3h \end{aligned} \quad \left.\begin{matrix} \\ \\ \\ \end{matrix}\right\} \text{Reverse sign of difference when it is negative}$$

Difference tones are most audible: (1) when they are not too low, and therefore when the primaries are fairly high, as from 500 to 2,000 cycles; (2) when the primaries are of good intensity; (3) when the primaries are of equal intensity. The last two conditions are best met by oscillator tones.

A difference tone can be reinforced or annulled by introducing an extra physical tone of the same pitch, and adjusting the *phase* of this extra tone. At a certain phase position the reinforced difference tone reaches its maximum loudness, while at another phase position, half a wave length from the first, the difference tone is obliterated or reaches minimum loudness. By this interference method the phase of the difference tone and its intensity can be determined. Having these determinate physical characteristics, the difference tone is undoubtedly a physical vibration generated in the ear (Lewis & Larsen, 1937).

Beating difference tones. Let two sources emit the frequencies 400 and 600; they are tuned to a "perfect fifth" with each other. The first difference tone has a frequency of 600 — 400 = 200, one octave below the lower of the two primaries. The second difference tone is 2 × 400 — 600 = 200, the same as the first. Now mistune the fifth, raising it to 601 cycles: the first difference tone is 601 — 400 = 201, and the second difference tone is 2 × 400 — 601 = 199. The two difference tones are now two cycles out of step with each other and give two beats per second. In general, when two primaries are tuned to a perfect musical interval, as an octave, a fifth, a fourth, a major third, etc., the difference tones coincide, drop out, or are harmonic with each other and with the primaries; but if the primaries are not tuned to any perfect interval (simple ratio of frequencies), the difference tones beat with each other and make the tonal complex inharmonious.

Summation tones. There is also a whole family of tones whose frequencies are the sum of the components; that is, the formulas are $h + l$, $2l + h$, etc. Except that they are weaker and higher than the corresponding difference tones, they are very similar. Summation and difference tones are often grouped together under the name *combination tones.*

Subjective overtones or aural harmonics. Suppose a simple sine wave is applied to the ear, will it remain simple after passing through the middle and inner ear, or will the physical properties of the ear add overtones? A delicate test for aural harmonics makes use of an "exploring tone" of adjustable frequency, thrown in while a steady tone is sounding. Both are pure tones, simple sine waves. Let the question be whether a pure tone of 400 cycles generates a subjective overtone of 800. If present, this overtone must beat with the exploring tone in the neighborhood of 800, but the beats will disappear when the exploring tone is tuned exactly to 800. The results of this experiment were definitely positive. When the primary tone was 400 cycles, subjective overtones were located at 800, 1,200, 1,600 and 2,000 cycles (Fletcher, 1929).

However, this experiment alone does not prove the existence of subjective overtones, since the results can be explained in terms of difference tones. When the primary is 400 cycles and the exploring tone 798 cycles, the first difference tone will be 398, the third difference tone 396, and the two will beat. If we assume several orders of difference tones, we can explain the observed beats without assuming subjective overtones. But we can just as well follow Helmholtz (1862) and assume subjective overtones, and then reduce all difference tones to the first order. The second difference tone, 2l — h, is evidently the first difference tone between h and 2l, the latter being the first overtone of l. All the difference tones are of the first order if only there are real subjective overtones. To make sure of them we must appeal to close observation by the hearing subject, or we must find a way of observing the vibrations in the inner ear.

The cochlear microphonic effect (p. 330) furnishes the desired tool. Potentials picked up from the round window of the cochlea, and suitably amplified, show an amazing array of frequencies when only two sine waves are fed into the ear. All of the subjective overtones can be analyzed out of the complex potentials, and so can difference and summation tones (Stevens & Newman, 1936b; Wever & Bray, 1938).

Masking of tones. It is familiar knowledge that one sound may be difficult to hear in the presence of another sound. The older scientific results indicated that a low tone could mask or conceal a higher tone but that the reverse was not possible. More recent results (Fletcher, 1929) show masking in both directions, up and down, the maximum effect being exerted upon tones just above or just below the masking tone in frequency. The stimulus threshold for the masked tone is raised by the presence of the masking tone, and the rise in threshold furnishes a measure of masking. A tone of 800 cycles masks a tone of 400 only slightly. The amount of masking increases as the masked tone rises from 400 to 800 where the maximum effect is produced. Above that frequency the amount of masking falls off. In the immediate neighborhood of the masking tone, beats are heard between the two tones and these beats

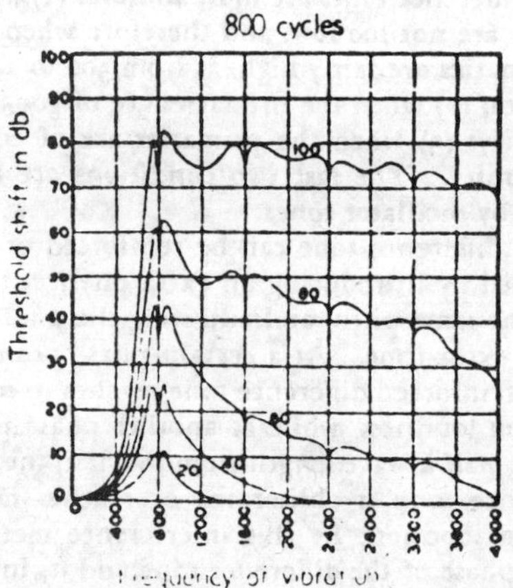

FIG. 12-9. (Fletcher, 1929; courtesy of D. Van Nostrand Company, Inc.) The masking effect. The masking tone here is a pure tone of 800 cycles; the masked tone has in any single test a constant frequency and is raised in intensity till it can just be detected by the listener. The curve shows the results obtained with a given tones of various frequencies when subjected to the masking effect of the 800-cycle tone. Each curves show the stimulus threshold for masked intensity of the masking tone, in db

betray the presence of the masked tone and lower its stimulus threshold, as shown by the little sharp dip at the frequency of the masking tone and its overtones.

Implications for auditory theory. You could not predict these phenomena from either the place or the frequency-volley theory. You would need more knowledge of the physics of a structure like the cochlea subjected to vibrations of different frequencies and intensities. In a broad way the place theory regards the ear as an analyzer, while the frequency theory regards it as a transmitter. As an analyzer, the ear would pick out the component frequencies in a complex incoming wave and signal the results of this analysis to the brain. As a transmitter, the ear would simply impress the incoming frequencies on the nerve and leave it to the brain to do the necessary analysis. The volley theory admits both possibilities.

As to beats, there would be none if the basilar membrane were sharply tuned to each discriminable frequency; the ear would simply signal the two incoming frequencies to the brain. But by admitting a little spread of response along the basilar membrane, the place theory can take care of beats. The small area between the points responsive to 256 and 276 ~, for example, will be driven by both frequencies; as they come into and out of phase with each other 20 times a second, this intermediate area will wax and wane in its vibration and yield 20 beats per second. The volley theory simply points to the actual waxing and waning of the compound vibrations reaching the ear and suggests that the cochlea excites a larger or smaller nerve fiber volley according to the amplitude of the momentary vibration.

Combination tones and aural harmonics are the result of distortion of the incoming waves somewhere in the ear. If the eardrum and ossicles could not follow an intense sine wave perfectly, the cochlea would receive a distorted wave and analyze it into its partials, just as it analyzes a complex tone coming from the external air. According to this Helmholtz explanation, you would not get these effects in the absence of the drum and ossicles. But Wever, Bray & Lawrence (1940a, b) found all the aural harmonics and combination tones in the cochlear response of an animal whose drum, hammer, and anvil had been removed. This result shows that a large part of the distortion must occur inside the cochlea, presumably in the movements of the hair cells themselves. Whether the place theory can handle this situation is not clear at the moment. For a full account of the function of the middle ear, with evidence that subjective overtones and difference tones arise not there but in the cochlea, see Wever & Lawrence (1954).

Since tones that are near together in pitch tend to "mask" each other, the effect could be due somehow to interaction between neighboring parts of the organ of Corti, and the spread of masking could even be utilized in mapping the frequencies along the length of the basilar membrane (Wegel & Lane, 1924). But, as shown in Figure 12-9, the spread of masking is actually too wide to be acceptable to a strict place theory. Galambos & Davis (1944), recording nerve impulses from single neurones in the cochlear nucleus, the first nerve cell station as the auditory nerve enters the medulla, discovered a novel inhibitory effect which may have a bearing on the problem of masking. When a neurone was responding to one frequency applied to the ear, the addition of another frequency sometimes inhibited the response. This result presumably reveals the presence of inhibitory interaction among the auditory nerve units, analogous to what happens in vision (p. 375).

Aside from the masking effect which can be a practical nuisance, these "aural inadequacies" do not often hamper adequate behavioral use of auditory data. Difference tones and summation tones, like visual afterimages, are habitually disregarded, most people finding it more difficult to observe than to overlook them.

DEAFNESS

Until we have made some acquaintance with the psychology of hearing, we are apt to think of deafness as an all-or-none affair as far as the frequencies are concerned. Of course, there are cases of complete deafness resulting sometimes from failures in prenatal development. Much more frequent is partial deafness or impairment of hearing which shows up as an increase in the stimulus threshold for some or all frequencies. The most accurate and revealing hearing tests are made with electronic equipment. There are now a number of commercial *audiometers* available.

Audiometry. A typical audiometer is built around an oscillator which will produce eight frequencies, ranging by octaves from 128 to 16,384 ~, each frequency being available at the setting of a dial. There is an attenuator which will vary the intensity over a range of 100 or 120 db. An earphone converts the electrical waves into air vibrations. A signal light and push button enable *O* to indicate silently when he hears the tone. There may also be included a bone-conduction phone, as well as a buzzer for use in masking tests. The whole outfit is assembled in a convenient case.

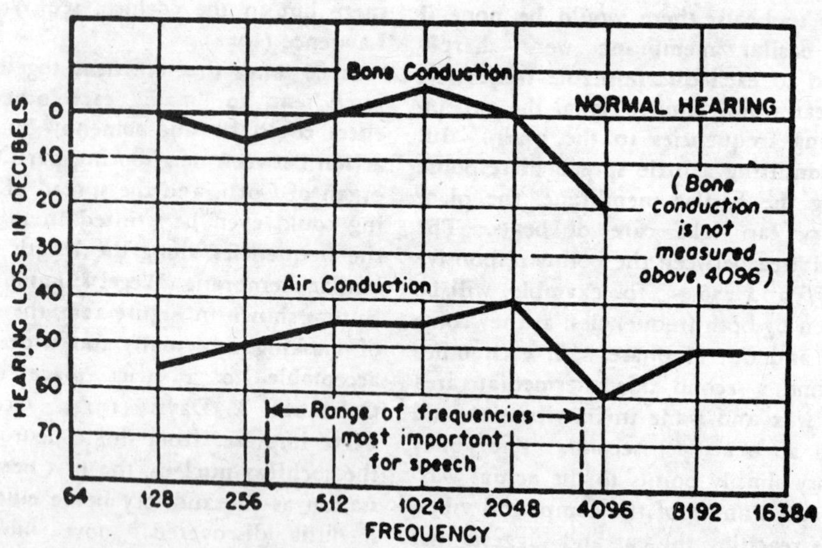

FIG. 12-10. (Davis, 1947, by permission of Murray Hill Books, Inc.) Audiogram of an ear, indicating marked conduction deafness. There may also be some "nerve deafness" in this case, indicated by the failure of the air conduction curve to climb toward normal at the upper frequencies.

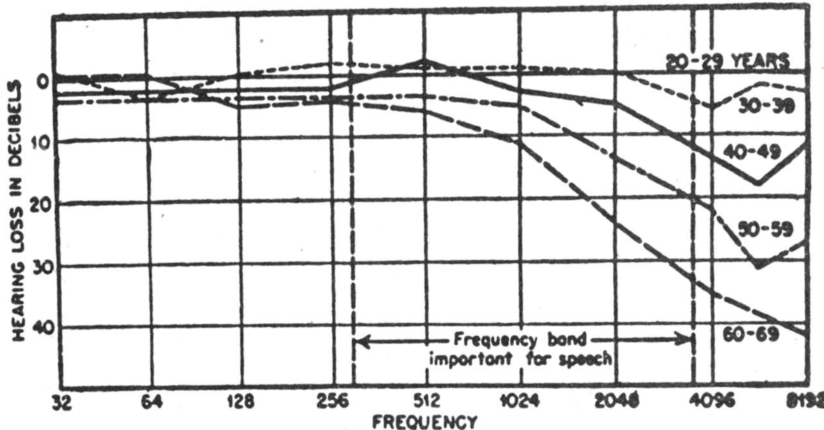

FIG. 12-11. (Davis, 1947, by permission of Murray Hill Books, Inc. Data from Bunch, 1929.) Average audiograms for different age groups, showing loss of the high frequencies. Individuals differ greatly in this respect.

In the laboratory it is instructive to assemble your own oscillator-attenuator-earphone setup, calibrate it as explained on page 332, and compare an individual's thresholds with the standards shown in Figure 12-4. On such a figure any loss of hearing is shown by a rise above the standard threshold for a given frequency. This procedure would be cumbersome in the clinic. The commercial audiometer reads directly in hearing losses. Normal thresholds are assigned the value of zero db and plotted along a horizontal line near the top of the blank audiogram (Fig. 12-10). The ordinate reads in db of *hearing loss*, measured down from the normal line.

Types of deafness. Impairment of the middle-ear conduction mechanism is one cause of deafness. The drum may be thickened by old scar tissue, or the ossicles may be "gummed up" by permanent or temporary deposits. This condition often gives an audiogram that is low at the left and nearer normal at the right; that is, the hearing loss is greatest at the low frequencies which demand relatively large movements of the drum and ossicles. This type of deafness can be detected by the bone conduction phone, which is applied to the skull so as to transmit vibrations through the skull to the fluids of the cochlea, without any dependence on the middle ear. There is a separate set of norms for this kind of stimulation. If a subject shows loss by the earphone test, but no loss by the skull test, he has middle-ear conduction deafness, which may be largely compensated for by a hearing aid with a bone-conduction receiver.

More interesting from the standpoint of the rival auditory theories is another type of hearing loss known as inner-ear deafness or "nerve deafness." It is characterized by loss at high frequencies. All of us may expect to develop a progressive loss of this type as we grow older (Fig. 12-11). It is not entirely due to a failure of neural elements, for there is likely to be a degeneration of the hair cells near the base of the organ of Corti. Just why the inner ear should age in this particular way is not clear.

So-called nerve deafness may take another form, in which the loss is confined to a certain range of frequencies. There is a "tonal gap." If the audiogram shows a large area of loss with a small area spared, there is a "tonal island." These gaps and islands seem to offer another chance to map the basilar membrane.

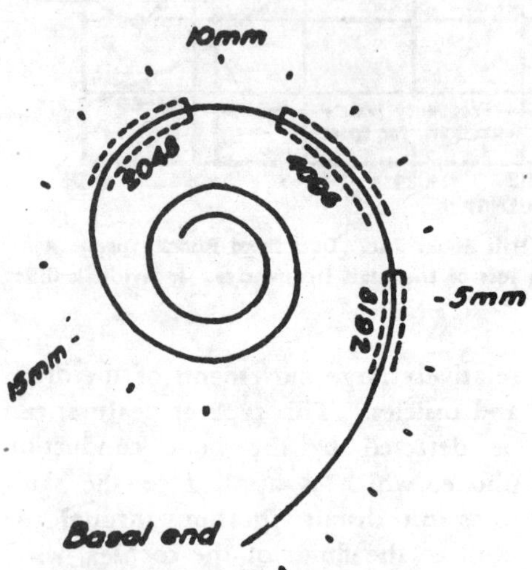

FIG. 12-12. (Crowe, Guild & Polvogt, 1934.) Cochlear localization of high tones, based on pathological data. If the nerve fibers and receptors at the basal end of the cochlea are atrophied for a distance of 10 mm, the tones above 2,048 ~ are lost or impaired. When 4,096 ~ can be heard, the atrophy does not extend so far from the basal end.

If we could correlate the losses shown by audiograms with histological changes in particular parts of the cochlea, we might identify the places corresponding to certain frequencies or frequency bands. The difficulty is in securing the necessary post-mortem examination of the cochleas of patients with pre-mortem audiograms. The most extensive series of such cases has been collected by Crowe, Guild & Polvogt (1934). Their map of the cochlea is shown in Figure 12-12. It is only half a map, and for a very good reason. Low-tone deafness of cochlear origin is rare, and the few available cases fail to show the clear-cut picture of deterioration toward the apex that the place theory would predict.

Stimulation deafness. If you cannot *find* cases of low-tone cochlear deafness in man, why not produce such cases in animals? It has long been known that continued exposure to intense noises will cause impairment of hearing. Such deafness, termed "boiler-maker's deafness," has become a serious problem in modern warfare—though damage can be minimized by the use of earplugs, called "ear wardens." The animal experiment may include some or all of the following steps:

1. Obtain the normal audiogram of the animal by establishing a conditioned breathing or withdrawal response, based on shock as the unconditional stimulus (p. 545).
2. Expose the animal to a very loud tone, continued for a number of days. Different frequencies will be used with different groups of animals.
3. Recondition the animals to overcome any extinction that may have occurred, and obtain a new audiogram.
4. Obtain a "cochleogram" from the round window of the response to various frequencies.
5. Sacrifice the animal and make a histological examination to determine the locus of cochlear damage.

The experiment seems simple; in practice it is very laborious and time-consuming. Nevertheless, several studies of the sort were made around 1930 (Upton, 1929b; Finch & Culler, 1934a; Horton, 1934, 1935; Kemp, 1935, 1936). The results were not clean-cut; the deafness resulting from stimulation by a certain frequency was by no means confined to that frequency, but was general and widespread. The intense vibration sometimes loosens most of the organ of Corti from the basilar membrane (Stevens, Davis & Lurie, 1935). A hammer blow to the animal's skull is an effective means of damaging the organ of Corti (Shuknecht, 1950; Shuknecht, Neff & Perlman, 1951). The resulting hearing losses and cochlear lesions are similar to those found in human nerve deafness (Fig. 12-10). Another operation consists of severing a part of the auditory nerve in an animal (Neff, 1947; Wever & Neff, 1947). The results again are consistent with Figure 12-12 in showing fairly precise localization of high tones near the basal end, with no sign of precise localization for the low tones. The half map of Figure 12-12 represents all that we are justified in asserting at the present time regarding the localization of frequencies along the basilar membrane. The volley principle may be necessary to account for the signaling of low frequencies to the brain.

In the interests of simplicity the breakdown of a straight "place" theory may seem unfortunate. The experimentalist would like to have as much of the total auditory function as possible performed by the cochlea where he can get at it. He sees no way of discovering how the brain translates frequency into pitch, discriminates tones, analyzes chords, or hears overtones out of a complex tone. But the brain centers are certainly capable of handling very complex patterns of sensory stimuli, as was clear in relation to the perception of speech (p. 341). The additional responsibility thrown on the brain by the volley theory will scarcely be the straw that breaks the camel's back.

AUDITORY SPACE PERCEPTION

Physically, the ear is classed as a distance receptor because its stimuli come from some distance; behaviorally, hearing is a distance sense because auditory data enable the organism to respond appropriately to distant objects. An animal will turn the head, eyes, and ears toward the source of sound, and a man can point toward it or indicate its direction verbally. Response to the distance of a sounding object, though less accurate and regular than to its direction, is often good enough for practical purposes.

We have here a problem for the psychologist: he wishes to discover the *cues* of this behavior. The distance of an object is often indicated by the loudness of its sound as heard; if the sound grows louder or softer, the object is perceived to be approaching or receding, though this cue can be deceptive. As to the direction of the sounding object, the psychologist's problem is difficult, and the anatomy of the ear offers no solution. The sound waves, from whatever direction they come, must traverse the external auditory meatus, the ossicles, and some of the curved cochlear passage, before reaching the receptors. What can remain of the original direction of the sound? One would almost declare that the direction of sound cannot possibly be heard, except perhaps in familiar surroundings and with familiar sources of sound.

The sound cage or sound perimeter. The early experimenters wished to make sure that the direction of sound could be perceived under standard conditions. They blindfolded *O*, provided a chin rest to insure a fixed head position, placed him in a padded room or out of doors to minimize echoes, and surrounded him with possible sources of sound at a uniform distance. Sometimes his head was at the center of a circle or skeleton sphere of stiff wire to enable *E* to deliver the sound from known positions. One or more telephone receivers could be arranged to emit the sound from any point on the cage. The early work was summarized by Pierce (1901).

The results were perfectly clear on one point: right and left are practically never confused with each other or with sounds coming from anywhere in the median plane of the head projected into space. Allow the subject a leeway of 2–3° on each side of the median plane, and he almost never makes a mistake in judging right, left, or middle. He can judge how far (at what angle) the source of sound diverges from the median plane, though his accuracy decreases as the source moves away from the median plane to a position near either ear.

Another result was equally clear: while right-left discrimination is good, up-down and front-back discriminations are poor. Sounds coming from above are often heard as if coming from below, and vice versa; and similarly with sounds coming from in front and behind—unless the head itself is turned.

The excellence of the right-left discrimination suggested that binaural (two-eared) hearing was important. Plugging one ear did in fact impair localization very considerably. Individuals completely deaf in one ear gave a history of poor localization immediately after their loss, followed by some improvement, but they were still subnormal and liable to right-left confusion such as was almost wholly absent from normal binaural hearing (Starch, 1908).

Similar experiments gave similar results with animals, and dogs and cats were, if anything, superior to human beings in detecting the direction of a source of sound (Engelmann, 1928).

From the results of the sound cage experiments it is clear that the cues of direction depend on the possession of two ears. Strong confirmation of this conclusion is afforded by the *pseudophone* experiment (Young, 1928; Willey, Inglis & Pearce, 1937): by means of tubes passing over the head, each ear gets the sound that normally goes to the other; and the sound appears to be coming from the right when the source is on the left!

Possible binaural cues of direction. The main difference between the two ears is that they are not in the same place. Accordingly, the problem is to discover differences in stimulation that result from this difference in place. Geometry and physics show that there are certain differences, and the experimenter has the task of ascertaining which of these stimulus differences actually serve as cues of direction.

The geometry of the matter is fairly simple. When the source of sound lies anywhere in the median plane of the head, extended out into space, the path of the sound waves to one ear is the same in length and curvature as the path to the other ear (aside from slight asymmetries of the head which have little effect). But from any source outside the median plane the paths to the two ears differ in length and curvature, as illustrated in Figures 12·13 and 12·14.

The extra distance which the sound has to traverse to reach the farther ear is an important datum. It is called

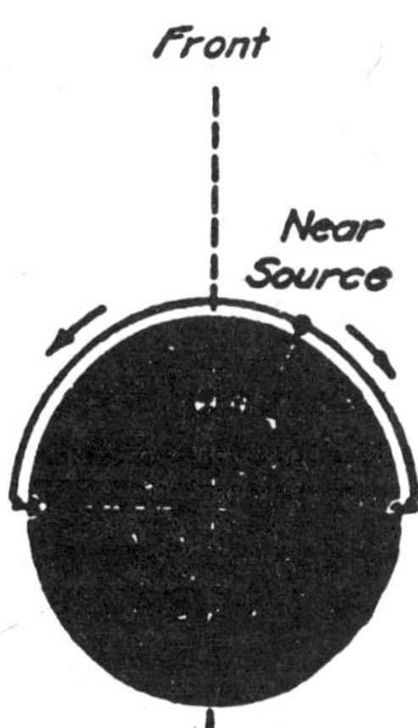

FIG. 12-13. Binaural distance difference when the source of sound is close to the head. To reach the nearer ear the sound travels $90° - \theta$; to reach the farther ear, $90° + \theta$; so the difference is 2θ. If θ is 30°, the difference comes to 60°, or ⅓ of the semicircumference from ear to ear, i.e., ⅓ of 27.5 cm, or 9.17 cm.

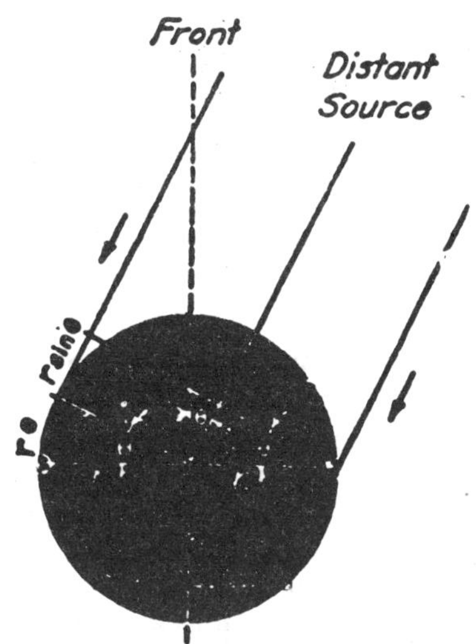

FIG. 12-14. Binaural distance difference when the source of sound is more than a few feet away so that the waves pass in practically parallel lines to the two ears. The construction lines show the geometry of the formula, $D_s = r(\theta + \sin\theta)$.

Here r is the head radius which = 8.75 cm, since the semicircumference is 27.5 cm. The value of sin θ is found in a trigonometric table. For example, sin 30° = .50. The angle θ must be expressed in "radians" for use in this formula. A radian is the length of the radius when laid off on the circumference. (The semicircumference = 3.1416 radians, and also = 180°, whence 1 radian = 57.3°.) Thus 30° = .52 radians. Substituting these values in the formula we have in our example, $D_s = 8.75(.52 + .50) = 8.93$ cm.

the "binaural distance difference" and denoted by the symbol D_s. If the source is close to one ear, the sound waves must traverse about 11 inches (27.5 cm) around the head to reach the other ear. This is the maximum possible distance difference.

Sound from any source approaches the center of the head at a certain angle with the median plane. Let θ stand for this "direction angle." If the head is erect and the source at the level of the ears, θ is the angle between the source and straight forward. It is, for example, 30° to the right. The binaural distance difference can be computed with fair accuracy on the assumption that the head is a perfect sphere, as illustrated by Figures 12-13 and 12-14. The following formulas give the binaural distance difference for any direction:

(1) for a source close to the head,
D_s in cm $= 8.75 \times 2\theta$

(2) for a distant source
D_s in cm $= 8.75(\theta + \sin\theta)$

This geometrical reasoning is not restricted to the horizontal plane through the ears. For suppose the source to be above the ear level, and imagine the figure (either figure) to be rotated on the binaural axis so as to take in the source and the paths of the waves to the two ears. The figure will remain the same, if the head is a sphere; and, given the same direction angle with the median plane, the binaural distance difference will be the same. There are an indefinite number of points in space—in front, above, behind, below—that have the same direction angle and therefore the same binaural distance difference. How much information, then, can *O* possibly derive from hearing with two ears? Only that the source is to his right or left, and how far to right or left in terms of direction angle. Binaural data do not enable him to distinguish sources that have the same direction angle. He is likely to confuse sounds from in front, above, behind, below. To each direction angle corresponds a whole conical surface in space—a "cone of confusion" —which is everywhere the same as far as binaural hearing is concerned.

What possible cues of the direction of sound are to be found in these geometrical facts? The fact that a sound has to go farther to one of the ears means that that ear gets the sound a little later; there will be a binaural time difference. The fact that the sound waves have to bend around some of the head to reach the farther ear means that that ear gets less intense stimulation; there will be a binaural intensity difference.

Binaural time difference. Sound travels through the air at a speed of about 1,130 feet per second. This is the same as 344 meters per second, or 34.4 centimeters per millisecond. For each cm of binaural distance difference, then, there is a time difference of $1/34.4 = .029$ ms. So the distance difference can be reduced to a time difference, D_t:

(1) for a source close to the head,
D_t in ms $= .254 \times 2\,\theta$, since
$8.75 \times .029 = .254$

(2) for a distant source,
D_t in ms $= .254(\theta + \sin\theta)$

These formulas give the maximum and minimum time difference for any direction of sound, as detailed in the table on page 353.

There is no time difference between up and down nor between front and back, but there is always some time difference between right and left. The question is whether so small a time difference can be an effective cue of the direction of sound. Even the largest difference is less than a millisecond, and the fine discrimination possible (3° to the right or left of the median plane) would require the use of a difference of only 3/100 of a millisecond.

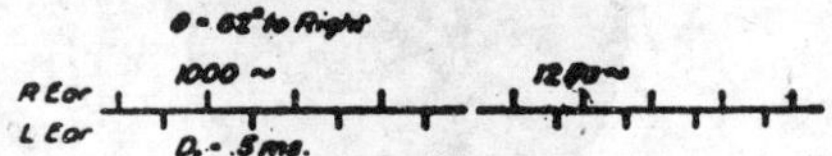

FIG. 12-15. **Breakdown of the binaural time cue with high-frequency tones. Let the source lie 62° to the right, so that D_t, according to our table, is ½ ms. This time difference will be the same for all vibration frequencies. When the frequency is 1,000 ~, so that the interval between crests is 1 ms, each crest strikes the farther ear ½ ms after it strikes the nearer ear, but also ½ ms *before* the following crest strikes the nearer ear. Since the auditory mechanism has no way of identifying the individual waves, it cannot tell (we may say) whether the sound is coming from the right or from the left. And if the frequency is increased to 1,250 ~, crests will strike the farther ear .300 ms before the nearer ear, as if the sound were 35° to the left. So, confusion and false impressions would be expected on the basis of binaural time difference.**

The binaural time difference is a physical fact that holds good for a click or the abrupt onset of any sound. But what about a continuous tone? Except for its onset it would seem to act on both ears simultaneously, and yet it may be correctly heard as coming from a certain direction. The answer is that a "continuous" tone consists of waves. Each wave reaches the nearer ear first, and the time difference which we have computed holds good for each successive wave crest. This cue of direction breaks down at high frequencies of the continuous tone, as illustrated in Figure 12-15.

Binaural intensity difference (ratio).

BINAURAL TIME DIFFERENCE ACCORDING TO DIRECTION (AND DISTANCE) OF SOURCE OF SOUND

Direction angle	Time difference in milliseconds: Source close to head	Source distant
0°	0	0
1°	.009	.009
2°	.018	.018
3°	.027	.027
4°	.036	.036
5°	.044	.044
10°	.089	.088
15°	.133	.132
20°	.178	.176
25°	.222	.218
30°	.266	.260
35°	.311	.301
40°	.355	.341
45°	.400	.379
50°	.444	.416
55°	.488	.452
60°	.533	.486
65°	.577	.518
70°	.622	.549
75°	.666	.578
80°	.710	.605
85°	.755	.630
90°	.799	.653

When the source lies behind the aural axis, reckon its direction angle from the rear; so for $\theta = 100°$, use $180° - 100° = 80°$.

It may seem that we have been hunting for obscure cues of direction when a very good one is perfectly obvious. Must not the stimulus be more intense at the nearer ear? The farther from its source, the weaker the sound. The difference would be appreciable when the source is close to the head, but we hear the direction of distant sounds also, and if you figure how much less intensity would result from adding 10 inches to 1,000 feet of distance, you will admit that this factor can be of only minor importance.

The "sound shadow" effect is a more likely binaural cue. The waves that reach the farther ear have bent around some of the head (Fig. 12-14), while those that reach the nearer ear are free from this cause of weakening. Hence, the stimulus is more intense at the nearer ear. If the source is anywhere in the median plane—directly ahead, above, or behind—the ears will be stimulated equally. Equal intensity of the sound in both ears would thus indicate a source lying somewhere in the median plane, and greater intensity in one ear would indicate a source somewhere on that side. If the source moved farther to the right, the waves to the left ear would have to bend more and lose more force, and thus the amount of binaural intensity difference would indicate the direction angle. The same "cones of confusion" would apply to the intensity difference as to the time difference.

So far everything looks favorable to the intensity cue. But there is a further physical factor to be brought into the picture. Only high-frequency sounds, with short waves, cast any appreciable shadows. The long waves bend around the head with little loss. The situation is similar to the way ripples on the water are stopped by a rock, while long swells bend smoothly around it. At an auditory frequency of 100 ~, the wave length is $^{1130}/_{100} = 11.3$ feet, which is certainly long enough to bend smoothly around the head. The shorter the waves (the higher the frequency) the larger the binaural intensity difference. With a source 15° from the median plane, the intensity ratio is as follows, according to threshold determinations by Sivian & White (1933):

Tone		Intensity ratio
300 ~	<	1 db (1.26 to 1)
1,100 ~	=	4 db (2.51 to 1)
4,200 ~	=	5 db (3.16 to 1)
10,000 ~	=	6 db (4 to 1)
15,000 ~	=	10 db (10 to 1)

These data suggest that the intensity cue will be of little value for pure tones below 3,000 ~. However, if we deal with complex sounds, there will be a timbre difference, due to the loss of high overtones in the sound shadow.

Experimental methods for testing the possible binaural cues. In ordinary hearing the several binaural differences operate together. A sound from the left reaches the left ear sooner than the right ear, with greater intensity, and with richer overtones. With all the cues working together you cannot tell which one is effective as a sound locator. The experimentalist seeks to control these factors so as to present a time difference with equal intensities at both ears, or an intensity difference with no time difference.

It should be noted that the experimenter is thus applying *inconsistent cues.* If the two ears get equal intensity with a time difference, the intensity cue indicates a source in the median plane while the time cue suggests a source at one side. The question is, then, which cue the listener will follow.

The technical word, *dichotic* (from the Greek word for ear with a prefix meaning apart, separate) conveys in a nutshell the nature of a whole class of experiments designed to sort out the different cues of direction. Each ear receives separate stimulation by way of a tube or telephone circuit.

The tube apparatus used in dichotic experiments usually resembles a binaural stethoscope, with the subject at the hearing end. Tubes inserted in his ears, or held very close to them, unite into a single tube which opens close to the source of sound. A time difference is introduced by making one tube longer than the other; an intensity difference by partial closure of one of the tubes. This style of apparatus was much used in the older investigations, and it still has some advantages, not the least of which is the fact that the student readily understands what he is doing to the sound waves.

The telephonic dichotic apparatus uses earphones, each having a separate circuit with amplifiers or attenuators to control intensity, and with adjustable condensers to produce a binaural time difference. The source for both ears is an oscillator producing tones of known frequencies, the frequency always being the same for both ears. The composition of the sound wave, its overtone structure, can be controlled to some extent by sound filters and other means. Clicks at any desired time difference can be produced in the earphones by an adjustable contact apparatus which interrupts the circuits through the two telephones. The two earphones must be carefully selected to secure clicks of the same quality which will fuse and be heard as a single click when presented simultaneously to the two ears. (The first edition of this book gives many older references on apparatus.)

Results with clicks. When Klemm (1919, 1920) began experimenting with dichotic clicks, he assumed naturally enough that a binaural time difference of a few ms would be as small as could have any effect on perception, but he found that, while absolutely simultaneous clicks were localized in the median plane, a time difference as small as 1 ms was confidently localized to one side; a single (fused) click was heard to come from the side of the ear that got the stimulus first. With an improved contact apparatus, Klemm delivered clicks at still smaller intervals. He was surprised to find that a difference of only a few *hundredths* of a millisecond was sufficient to give a definite lateral localization of the click. He suspected some experimental error, but the apparatus proved to be physically accurate and the psychological data, though showing individual differences, were reasonably consistent.

Other investigators, repeating this experiment with some modifications, have found the minimal effective binaural time difference to vary with individuals between .03 and .3 ms. As the time difference increases, *O* reports that the sound is moving around to the side; at a difference of .65 ms it is close to the ear where it stays if the time difference keeps on increasing, up to about 2.5 ms, when the single click breaks up into two, one heard on each side (Wittmann, 1925; Banister, 1926b; Trimble, 1928; Wallach, Newman & Rosenzweig, 1949).

Most people, including many of the older experimenters, were inclined to regard the intensity difference as the really important cue. Von Hornbostel & Wertheimer (1920) were perhaps the first to come out emphatically in favor of the time difference. They based this conclusion on *balancing* experiments of this sort: with the right ear getting the click first (say by .1 ms) and intensity equal in both ears, the sound was localized on the right. Then the intensity was made to favor the left side, but the sound was still localized on the right until the intensity difference became very large. So a small time difference prevailed over a large opposing intensity difference.

Before discarding the intensity cue altogether, we should try the reverse experiment. Klemm (1920) began with a time difference of zero and an intensity difference (ratio) of 3 to 1. The sound was localized on the side of the greater intensity. A time difference was now introduced such that the ear which got the lower intensity got it first. The time difference necessary to compensate for the intensity difference was about .6 ms, a relatively large amount. Wittmann (1925), on repeating these two balancing experiments, confirmed both results, and reached the conclusion that both time difference and intensity difference are potent factors in the localization of short sounds.

The geometry and physics of the binaural time difference enable us to make very definite predictions which are nicely confirmed by the dichotic click experiments. Our table on page 353 shows that a time difference of .65 ms should indicate a source directly opposite one ear, and this is where the dichotically presented click is localized by *O* when the time difference is of this size. The table shows that a time difference of .03 ms should indicate a source about 3° from the median plane, and the sound-cage experiments showed that 3° is about the smallest divergence from the median plane that can be perceived. Probably it is impossible to make such definite predictions from the physics of the binaural intensity difference, partly because this difference depends both on the direction angle and on the wave-length of the sound.

Results with continuous tones. Once the apparatus is available for delivering a tone separately to the two ears and for controlling time and intensity differences, interesting phenomena can be readily obtained. If both differences are zero, the tone is heard as coming from the median plane, usually from straight in front. If the time difference is zero, the tone is localized toward the side of the greater intensity, and vice versa. With the intensities kept equal and an increasing time difference, the tone seems to move around to the side. But the time difference, as explained on page 352, cannot exceed half a cycle. With low frequencies, therefore, the time difference can be increased enough to bring the sound opposite one ear before it shifts across to the other side, but with high frequencies the maximum time difference is only enough to bring the sound out 60°, 45°, or less. And the time difference cue breaks down altogether at a frequency of about 1,500 ~ on the average (Hughes, 1940).

Two sounds, differently localized, are sometimes heard in these experiments. When the time difference has been increased to half a cycle, so that the ear which has been leading no longer has the advantage, two tones are sometimes heard, one at each ear. Or, if time difference favors one side but intensity difference the other, two tones may be heard, one on each side (Banister, 1926a). Or again, if time difference is zero, but intensity much greater in the left ear, two sounds may be heard, one in front and one on the left (Halverson, 1922a, b). In all these cases the stimulation corresponds to what would be received in the open air from two differently located sources of sound.

These results with continuous tones are consistent with those obtained with clicks. Time difference is the dominant cue where it has a fair chance. But its role is somewhat limited in the case of continuous tones. The *onset* of a sound from one side has a clear time difference, but this difference becomes confused as the waves follow at high frequency.

Binaural phase difference. In the case of a continuous tone, the binaural time difference can be stated also as a phase difference. At a frequency of 1,000 ~, each complete cycle lasts 1 ms, and a time difference of .50 ms is thus ½ a cycle, a phase difference of 180°. If the frequency is only 500 ~, however, the same time difference is ¼ a cycle, a phase difference of 90°. Phase difference alone would be no cue of direction, depending as it does both on direction and on the frequency of the tone. Yet phase difference was formerly regarded an important cue, perhaps because one convenient way of producing a time difference was to retard the phase of the tone conducted to one ear. A good experiment was required to demonstrate the irrelevance of mere phase difference. Shaxby & Gage (1932) used the balancing or "centering" method. *O* adjusts the factors until the sound seems to him to come from the median plane (usually from straight in front). In effect, he faces directly toward the apparent source of sound—the most accurate way of locating the source. Centering has been used with "sound locators," in determining the direction of an airplane or submarine. In the Shaxby & Gage experiment an intensity difference threw the tone off center, and *O* could bring it back to center by manipulating the phase. The larger the intensity difference, the larger must be the compensating phase (time) difference. The result of prime importance was that the time difference necessary to compensate for a given intensity difference was approximately the same at different frequencies, whereas the necessary phase difference varied with the frequency of the tone.

For example, to balance an intensity difference of 6 db, the following adjustments were necessary, expressed in phase and time differences:

	Frequency		
	500	*800*	*1200*
Phase difference as fraction of complete cycle	.005	.009	.012
Time difference in ms	010	.011	.010

And to balance an intensity difference of 14 db, the following were found necessary:

	Frequency		
	500	*800*	*1200*
Phase difference	.011	.019	.025
Time difference	.023	.024	.021

According to these results, there is a definite relationship between the time and intensity factors in centering, but no approach to any definite balance of phase against intensity. What counts as a localization factor is not phase but binaural time difference.

Open-air localization of tones. The dichotic experiments smell strongly of the laboratory, and there may be some lingering doubt whether the same factors and limitations hold good of our ordinary hearing. In the case of continuous pure tones, will it hold good that time and not intensity is the important cue at low frequencies, but the reverse at high frequencies? If so, certain predictions can be made, as pointed out by Stevens & Newman (1934, 1936a). In the open air both low and high tones should be accurately localized, but not tones of medium frequency, from 1,500 to 3,000 or 4,000 cycles. In this medium range localization should be inaccurate because neither time difference nor intensity difference would be of much use. These experimenters seated *O* on a high stool on the roof of a building where sound reflection was avoided. They attached a loud speaker at the end of a 12-foot arm which could be moved noiselessly to any angle at the level of *O*'s ears. Fairly pure frequencies from 60 to 10,000 ~ were fed into the speaker without clicks at the onset and cessation of the sound. The tones were sounded from front, side, rear, and intermediate positions. *O*'s task was to designate the position of the source after each stimulation. Right-left reversals practically never occurred. Front-back reversals were frequent but were not counted as errors so long as the direction angle was correctly reported.

The main prediction was verified, as can be seen in Figure 12-16. Two other

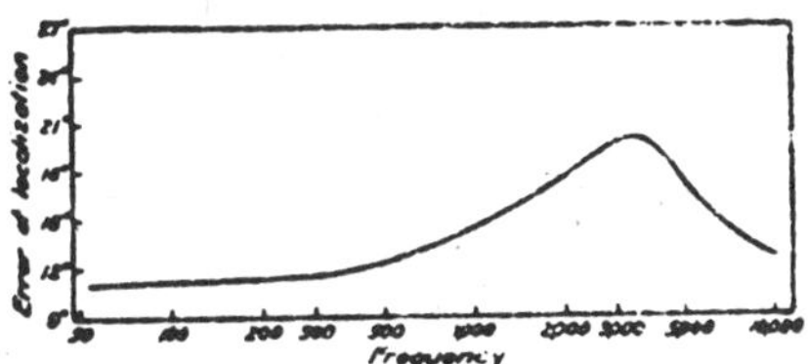

FIG. 12-16. (Stevens & Newman, 1934.) Open-air localization of (nearly) pure tones. The abscissa gives a logarithmic scale of frequencies, and the ordinate shows the average error in degrees of the judgments of direction by two *O*s.

findings are of theoretical importance. (1) Front-back reversals, though common at low frequencies of the tone, were almost absent at high frequencies. Now the outer ear is so constructed that it should cast a sound shadow, making sounds from the rear weaker than the same sounds from the front; but, as we have seen, such shadows are cast only at high frequencies. Even at the best this front-back intensity difference is not so direct as a binaural difference; it is a difference between *successive* presentations of a sound from front and back, and depends on *O*'s previous experience with the sound source in both positions. (2) The errors of localization were smallest near the median plane and largest out near 90°, opposite the ear. This result had been obtained in the early sound cage experiments (Pierce, 1901; Starch 1908), and it has a good theoretical ex planation since binaural time difference and intensity difference both change slowly as the source is moved forward and back in the 90° region. We might have expected, before looking into the geometry and physics of the matter, that sound would be located most accurately at the side of the head, and least accurately at the front and rear—just the opposite of the facts.

One further point deserves consideration in connection with the Stevens & Newman experiment and Figure 12-16. If both time difference and intensity difference break down in the middle frequency range, why does not the error curve rise much higher? Why are right-left reversals mostly absent in this range? And why, as these investigators and many others have found, are clicks localized more accurately than continuous tones? The sudden onset of the click is highly favorable to binaural time difference; and though the onset of the tone in this experiment was kept free from any click, the tone did have an onset, and the onset would have a binaural time difference which could serve as a cue of right or left at least. All in all, it seems that binaural time difference is the most universal and precise cue of sound direction in everyday life.

We are not to suppose that the observer *notices* the time difference and *infers* the direction of sound. The small fractions of a millisecond that prove to be cues of direction are imperceptible as time intervals. We have to think in physiological terms. We can imagine a neural mechanism controlling the muscular movements which turn the head and eyes toward a source of sound. If nerve impulses should arrive from one ear only, the neural mechanism would turn the head toward that side. When the impulses arrive first from one ear, the initial response toward that side maintains its advantage unless offset by considerable counterpressure from the other ear. This *precedence effect* (of which we saw some evidence in the balancing experiments, p. 355) has been clearly demonstrated by Wallach, Newman & Rosenzweig (1949). No additional neural mechanism need be assumed to take care of binaural intensity difference, for the more intense stimulus, by summation of impulses, would force its way through the synapses with less delay and so become in effect a time difference (Girden, 1940).

In all the experiments we have considered *O* is supposed to keep his head stationary, a restriction that does not apply to everyday hearing and localizing of sounds. When zero binaural differences indicate a sound anywhere in the median plane, a person can turn his head and produce binaural differences which will indicate the location of the source more definitely. By turning his head to right or left (on its vertical axis) he can distinguish front and back, and by tilting his head to one side or the other (on a horizontal front-back axis) he can distinguish up and down. In the same ways he can distinguish parts of any "cone of confusion." Synthetic experiments duplicating the binaural changes normally produced by head movements (Wallach, 1938, 1940) have shown that these binaural changes are actually utilized in the localization of sounds.

When you *see* the source of sound, the visual cue ordinarily confirms the binaural cues of direction. In a laboratory setup the visual cue can be made to conflict with a binaural time difference. Visually the source is straight ahead; aurally it may be 10–20° to the left before you trust your ears (Witkin, Wapner & Leventhal, 1952).

Auditory cues of distance. The loudness of a sound is certainly of some value as an indication of the distance of the source, in spite of the facts that a weak sound may come from a source near at hand and a loud sound from the distance. This cue would seem to depend on familiarity of the sound. The timbre of the sound, as received by the ears, may afford a more general cue of distance, since the high frequencies in a complex sound are likely to be lost in transmission. A sound rich in high frequencies suggests a source near at hand (v. Hornbostel, 1923).

Echoes. A contrast between the senses of sight and hearing is worthy of notice. The light which we utilize in perceiving objects is mostly reflected rather than received directly from a source of light, and what we "see" is usually an object that reflects the light rather than the sun or a lamp. What we "hear" is usually the source rather than any object that may be reflecting the sound. This distinction is not so sharp as we are apt to suppose, however, for usually some reflected sound is combined with the waves received directly from the source. The sound so modified reveals the acoustic character of the surroundings. When your car runs under a bridge, or your train through a tunnel, you *hear* the bridge or tunnel. Human beings are noisy creatures, with their voices, footsteps, horns, drums, saws, hammers, guns and vehicles, and the sounds they make are reflected back to them after more or less of a delay according to the distance of the reflecting surfaces. In a room the sound comes back in a few milliseconds and merges with the original sound. Outdoors the interval may be several seconds, and you distinguish a second sound, an echo. How far away is the object that sends back the echo? You could compute its distance by aid of a stop watch and a knowledge of the speed of sound transmission through the air. Even without any such exact knowledge and timing you obtain a rough impression of the distance of the reflecting object. You virtually hear that object and localize it in distance and direction. You also hear the clear intervening space without which there would be no distant echo. These auditory cues of the environment are of special value in the dark, in a fog, on the water, and under other conditions unfavorable to the visual sense.

That nocturnal flying mammal, the bat, is remarkably successful in avoiding obstacles. If his ears are plugged, he bumps into things. Sound records show that he emits high-pitched cries during flight, and if he is gagged to prevent the emission of these cries, he no longer avoids the obstacles. These cries have a wave frequency in the region of 50,000 per second; each cry lasts about 20 ms, and they are emitted at the rapid rate of 30–50 per second. Such interrupted high-frequency sounds are well reflected from even small objects and evidently enable the bat to localize the objects in both direction and distance. The bat thus employs a kind of auditory radar (Griffin & Galambos, 1941; Galambos & Griffin, 1942; Galambos, 1943; Griffin, 1944, 1950).

How blind people avoid obstacles. In finding their way around a town, as many blind persons do successfully, they are able to detect the direction and distance of walls, open doors, and other objects. If you ask them what cues they follow, they may offer the old theory of "facial vision." They somehow feel the presence of an object before them and are inclined to think that the object sends out waves of some kind and that their faces are sensitized to those waves. Others believe the cues to be auditory. Many other theories that have been offered are reviewed by Hayes (1935, 1941). A determined effort to identify the cues was made by Dallenbach and his associates (Supa, Cotzin & Dallenbach, 1944; Worchel & Dallenbach, 1947). Their procedure was to place an upright slab of masonite at a variable location in a long hall and to start the subject at a variable distance from this obstacle with instructions to walk toward it till he could detect its presence and then to advance further till he came as close as possible without colliding with the obstacle. Two blindfolded normal subjects were able after some practice to perceive the obstacle at a distance of 3–4 feet and to advance to within a foot of it with very few bumps. Two blind subjects did better than this, one of them much better. As a check against guessing, blank trials were interspersed, but none of the subjects claimed to perceive the obstacle when it was not before them. When the subjects had to walk in stocking feet on a strip of carpet, their performance was impaired and they tried to make as much noise as possible with their feet. When the hypothetical pressure waves against the face were eliminated by a heavy felt veil surrounding the head but not touching the skin—and slightly interfering with hearing—the ability was slightly impaired but still definitely present. But when the ears were well plugged, the ability was lost altogether. Exposure of the face to the "pressure waves" did not help if the ears were shut off. The experiments so far disproved the importance of facial cues and proved the importance of aural cues, but there was still a possibility, favored by some previous theories, that pressure waves against the skin of the external ear and ear drum provided the essential cues. Therefore, the investigators secured the services of several persons who, though both blind and deaf, were able to make their way around with fair confidence and success. But these subjects failed completely in the laboratory tests so that the final conclusion was that the "obstacle sense of the blind" depended on auditory cues.

As a rough summary of this extensive series of experiments, we may use the percent of trials under each condition which resulted in collisions with the obstacle:

	Percent
Blind subjects without either veils or ear plugs	5
Blind subjects with veils	7
Blind subjects with ear plugs	100
Blind-deaf subjects	68

The apparent superiority of the blind-deaf to the others when temporarily deprived of hearing was due to the fact that the blind-deaf often stopped 3, 6, or even 12 feet from the obstacle, signifying that they could go no closer without colliding. These subjects were able to get usable cues from irregularities in the floor and to locate a wall in relation to a well-explored floor, but they certainly made no use of facial or aural cues. No doubt air currents and temperature stimuli on the cheeks can indicate objects in less uniform surroundings. Deaf persons when blindfolded have the same inability as the deaf-blind to perceive an obstacle and avoid colliding with it (Worchel & Berry, 1952). College students when blindfolded learned rather quickly to detect an obstacle in the path, and some of them even had a measure of success when also wearing ear plugs, the test being conducted outdoors on the campus where a variety of subtle cues were occasionally available (Ammons,

Worchel & Dallenbach, 1953). But the most dependable and definite cues, in the absence of vision, are sounds produced by *O* himself, as in walking on a floor or sidewalk, and reflected back to him from an obstacle. Only the high-frequency tones or components, of 10,000 ~ and up, play any important part in this sort of auditory radar (Cotzin & Dallenbach, 1950).

Quantitative tests of the ability of blind persons to avoid obstacles and perceive objects at some distance were devised by Jerome & Proshansky (1950). They equipped a long alley, 9 feet wide, with upright slabs of various widths, located irregularly. *O*'s task was to pass between these obstacles without touching them. On any one trial, six of them were physically present and six others were represented only by marks on the floor. These phantom obstacles furnished no cues to a blind subject, and the question was whether he could avoid the real obstacles any better than the phantoms. The answer was "No" when his ears were plugged, but "Yes" when his ears were free. Auditory cues were thus of definite value in the avoidance test. In the test for the ability to perceive objects at a distance, *O*'s task was to decide whether or not a slab was present at a distance from his observation point, a real slab being present on only half of the trials. If he reported perceiving a slab on 90 percent of the trials when one was present, but also on 20 percent of the trials when none was present, his net score was 90 — 20 = 70 percent. The net scores decreased as the distance increased, as shown by the medians of four blind subjects:

Distance of object	3	4	5	6	7	8	9 ft
Median net score	94	87	87	85	72	50	42 %

Because of the large individual differences in these abilities, such tests can be of service in the vocational guidance of blinded soldiers.

13

VISION

Because of its rich and obvious contributions to both behavior and experience, Vision has received as much attention from physiologists and psychologists as have all the other senses put together. Some of the studies have been made at the descriptive or "phenomenological" level, which is concerned with the reports of how objects appear, what they look like (cf. Gibson, 1950a, b). This approach is often very useful, for it deals with everyday objects, and it can readily be phrased in terms that the layman can understand. But on analysis the perception of objects proves to be a very complicated process, involving many different sensory elements, as well as the effects of past learning. Many workers prefer to study simpler or more generalized processes, such as perception of form or space. Even these processes are too complicated to satisfy other researchers; they want to get down to the simplest sensory elements. Their problems are concerned with what happens when a patch of light falls on the eye. Research at all levels is important in giving us a full account of vision—no single level is enough. But since we must start somewhere, we shall devote this chapter to the simpler sensory processes and work up to the more complicated perceptual ones in later chapters.

THE VISUAL STIMULUS

Although elementary textbooks (Munn, 1946, 1951; Boring, Langfeld & Weld, 1939, 1948) give fairly complete decriptions of the basic facts of vision, it might be well to include here a brief description of the stimulus, receptors, and basic qualities. The stimulus is radiant energy, which originates at a primary source, as the sun or a light bulb. The energy sometimes comes directly to the eye, but more commonly it reaches the eye after reflection from some object. Fortunately, the energy travels in reasonably straight lines, permitting it to form a retinal image which resembles the surface from which it is reflected.

Now consider one of the rays. Modern physics is apt to treat it as a stream of particles or *quanta*, and this conception of radiant energy has some advantages for treating certain problems in vision, as we shall see later. But for most of our purposes the wave conception of classical physics is more convenient. Newton, in 1704, reported that a prism breaks up a band of white light into a spectrum of colors, ranging from red to violet. That is, the prism spreads out the mixed waves that comprise the white beam into a sheath of waves, each element of which is homogeneous with respect to wavelength. These wavelengths have been measured with much precision; the ones that correspond to the visual spectrum run from about 380 *millimicrons* (mμ, or thousandths of a millionth of a meter) at the violet end to 720 at the red end. Since we shall refer to some typical values from time to time, Figure 13-1 has been prepared to show the wavelengths which correspond to the more important hues.

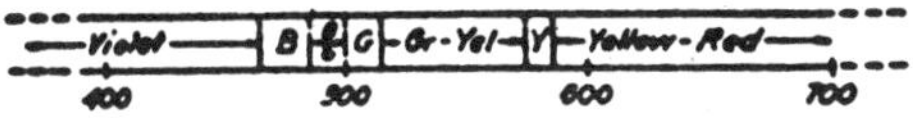

Fig. 13-1. (Ladd-Franklin, 1929, p. 34; Hurvich & Jameson, 1951.) Wavelengths corresponding to the principal hues of the spectrum. Since the shift is gradual from one hue to its neighbor, the delimitation of an orange area, for example, is arbitrary. But there are three hues that are surprisingly stable for any given observer; he can repeatedly and consistently set blue, green, or yellow within a few wavelengths of his mean setting. These three are called *pure* or *primal* colors. The pure red is off the end of the spectrum but is obtained by mixture of spectral red with some shorter wavelengths, as is also the case with purple.

The spectral limits are often given as 380 and 720 mμ, but these values are arbitrary, for the spectrum "peters out" at each end, as suggested by the broken lines in the figure.

In technical writing it is advisable to describe the stimulus in physical terms, as "Radiant energy at 580 mμ;" rather than in psychological ones, as "Yellow light." The distinction is more than a terminological one, for the physical specification is the more precise. Even the normal observer will apply a word like *red* to a fairly wide range of the spectrum, and a color-blind *O* will apply it quite differently. But where accurate specification of the stimulus is not necessary, the familiar color names are satisfactory, and are certainly more meaningful to the average reader. Hence, we shall use them when the occasion permits, and not bother to use circumlocutions to maintain terminological purity.

Homogeneous light. There is another matter that is related to this point. In everyday light we rarely encounter homogeneous light, and even in the laboratory we usually deal with fairly broad bands, including quite a range of wavelengths. Most primary sources emit light of all wavelengths throughout the visible spectrum; if the light appears yellowish or bluish, rather than white, it is because the emission spectrum is loaded at one or the other end. If one wishes a relatively restricted band of wavelengths for work in color vision, he can break up white light with a prism, and use the portion of the spectrum he wishes. This is a cumbersome method for most purposes; a filter is handier. This is merely a transparent sheet of glass or plastic that absorbs some wavelengths and passes others. The band that gets through is often fairly wide; its average value determines the color. For example, red cellophane transmits some energy in the *yellow* and in the *blue* regions, as well as in the red. Since the yellow balances out the blue, the resulting light looks almost as red as does that from a narrow-band or monochromatic red filter, but it acts differently in dark adaptation (p. 367), and ruins photographic negatives. Recently some very good monochromatic filters have been prepared; they should be used where very accurate control of wavelength is important.

The third method of getting color is through the use of colored surfaces. Certain pigments have the property of absorbing some bands and reflecting others. When white light falls on such a surface, of course we see only the wavelengths that are reflected to the eye. The reflected bands are usually wider than in the case of filters, but the eye averages them in the same way. If the band is very wide, including a substantial part of the spectrum, the colors look *desaturated.* The end point in desaturation comes when the incident light is reflected fairly evenly throughout the spectrum; the surface is then white, gray, or black, depending on the total amount reflected and on certain other phenomena that will be discussed later (contrast, adaptation, constancy).

We can summarize our points so far by comparing vision with hearing. The basic qualitative dimension is *hue,* corresponding to *pitch.* The physical correlate of hue is *wavelength,* as it is for pitch (although the reciprocal, *frequency* is used more frequently in audition). *Saturation* is a more complex dimension, related to homogeneity or purity of wavelength; it is comparable to *timbre,* or better, freedom from noise, in audition. Besides these qualitative dimensions there is an intensive one in both senses, related to the energy level of stimulation. This is *brightness* in vision, corresponding to *loudness* in hearing. Let us turn to a more careful consideration of the intensive dimension.

Measurement of intensity. The energy level of radiation is dependent on *amplitude* of the waves, but this is not a practical unit of measurement. The overall energy of a light beam may be determined by physical instruments, but it is more common to use psychophysical methods. The power of a primary source to stimulate the eye is often given in *candlepower;* i.e., it is compared with the old "standard" tallow candle. There are several ways of making the comparison, but perhaps the simplest one is that shown in Figure 13-2. Today we use a carefully calibrated electric bulb instead of a candle, but the principle is the same.

For many purposes we are less interested in the light thrown out by a source than we are in the amount of light which falls on a unit area of the surface that is to be seen. This may be expressed in *foot-candles.* The level of illumination of a surface held facing a standard candle one foot away is one foot-candle. Since

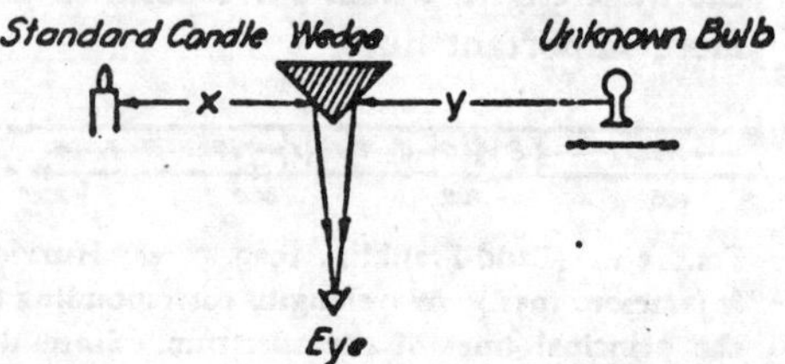

FIG. 13-2. A simple method for measuring the power of a light source. The "unknown" source is moved further from the wedge until both faces appear equally bright. Since the intensity of the Standard is taken as unity, we can calculate the intensity of the Unknown through the inverse square law, $1/X^2 = U/Y^2$. Conversely, we may get the match by adjusting the distance, X, of the Standard.

illumination falls off as the square of the distance from the source, the level would be $\frac{1}{4}$ foot-candle at 2 ft, $\frac{1}{9}$ at 3 ft, etc. Your desk probably has an illumination level between 2 and 20 foot-candles, as you can readily determine with the aid of the handy little photoelectric light meters that are used by photographers. At one time there was an effort to use a unit in the metric system, the meter-candle, but it did not take hold in this country. A *meter-candle* is the level of illumination of a surface one meter from a standard candle.

Not all the light that falls on a surface is reflected from it. White paper will absorb perhaps 20 percent, and reflect only 80 percent, while black may reflect as little as 3 percent of the incident light. It is only the reflected light that falls on the eye. Hence, an additional unit is needed to describe the *brightness* of a surface. The present United States standard unit is the *foot-lambert*, sometimes called the *apparent foot-candle;* it is the brightness of a perfectly reflecting surface at one foot from a standard candle. Thus a surface that reflected 50 percent of the incident light would have a brilliance of 3 foot-lamberts if it were illuminated at a level of 6 foot-candles. (In the technical literature you will often find another unit, the *millilambert,* which is about 1.06 foot-lamberts. The millilambert was derived from the metric system, and is equal to 10 apparent meter-candles.)

The actual measurement is usually made with the aid of an instrument (as the Macbeth illuminometer) which permits matching of two parts of a divided field, one of which is the unknown surface, and the other a variable field whose brightness can be calculated or read from a scale on the instrument.

Just to stamp in these terms, take an example that brings them all together. Start with a source that has a brightness of 40 candlepower. By the inverse square law it will illuminate a screen two feet away at a level of 10 foot-candles $[40 \times (\frac{1}{2})^2]$. If the screen has a reflectance of 30 percent, the brightness of the screen will be 3 foot-lamberts.

In using these measurements, one must always remember that they are made with the aid of the human eye. We shall see later that the eye is very much more sensitive to radiations in some regions, as yellow, than in others, as red or blue, so that an equal-energy spectrum looks brightest in the middle. This means that our measurements will hold for absolute energies only if we use the same colors for both the Standard and the Comparison stimuli. Furthermore, *heterochromatic* (between different colors) matching is difficult. But since our chief interest is in the effect of radiant energy on the eye, it is often useful to equate two different wavelengths in terms of this effect, rather than in terms of physical energy. (See Judd, 1951, for a detailed discussion of the visual stimulus and its correlates.)

The eye. There is no need to go into the elementary anatomical facts of the eye, for they are well covered in many introductory texts (Munn, 1951; Boring, Langfeld & Weld, 1948). The reader will recall that the eye is similar to a camera in many respects (cf. Wald, 1950). The main feature that concerns us in the present chapter is the *retina,* roughly corresponding to the film in a camera. The image is focused on this network or mosaic of receptive cells, the *rods* and *cones,* and thus signaled up the optic nerve to the brain. Many of the characteristics of vision are related to the nature, arrangement, and connections of these cells, as we shall see in the next section. The reader who wishes further details of the anatomy of the retina should consult Polyak (1941). Pirenne (1948) has an excellent discussion of this topic. For a good popular treatment, see Wald (1950).

ROD AND CONE VISION

The brilliance, hue, and saturation of a color sensation depend not only on the stimulus but also, to a marked degree, upon the receiving apparatus and on its condition. The receptor apparatus is "duplex" according to a theory which is now so well established as to count almost as a statement of fact (von Kries, 1929). It is an anatomical fact that the retina contains two types of receptor cells, the rods and the cones, and all the evidence goes to show that they differ in functional characteristics. The rods become adapted to very faint light, far surpassing the cones in this respect. But the rods are exclusively a light-dark sense; they do not respond to differences of wavelength by sensations of different hues. And the rods do not contribute much to the accurate perception of form. Some of the evidence for these statements will be presented.

Anatomical differences between the rods and the cones. Though these two types of receptors are very similar, they do show significant differences.

1. The rods are smaller and appear less highly developed than the cones.

2. There are no rods but only closely packed cones in the fovea. The rod-free area is usually not over 2° in horizontal diameter, and a little less vertically. A one-cent coin (18 mm in diameter), held at arm's length, just about fills this area. Rods begin to appear outside the fovea and become more numerous toward the periphery, in proportion to the cones, though there are a few cones even in the extreme periphery.

3. With respect to nerve supply, the cones are the better off. Several adjacent rods feed into one ganglion cell and so into a single optic nerve fiber. Each cone, at least in the fovea, has its own separate path back to the interbrain.

4. "Visual purple" is present in the rods but not in the cones. This substance is rapidly bleached on exposure to bright light and gradually restored in dim light or darkness. It must have something to do with dark adaptation—a suspicion which is fortified by the fact that the responsiveness of the dark-adapted eye to different wavelengths of light corresponds closely with the degree of absorption of the several wavelengths by visual purple (Hecht, 1934).

5. Nocturnal animals possess mostly rods and few cones. This was the fact which first (Schultze, 1866) suggested that the rods were receptors for dim light.

Pathological evidence for the duplicity theory. Certain patients suffer from "night blindness"; they cannot become adequately dark-adapted. Sometimes this is due to a lack of vitamin A in the diet (p. 371) and sometimes to degeneration of the pigment layer at the back of the retina (Duke-Elder, 1939). But in either case the resulting lack of visual purple in the rods prevents dark adaptation. There is also a condition of "day blindness" in which vision is painful and inefficient in strong light, and the individual is totally color-blind—just as if the cones were undeveloped and unfunctional. The fovea should therefore be completely blind—a prediction which has been verified in a majority of the cases examined. These individuals must direct their eyes a little to the side in order to see an object, and they commonly show some nystagmus or unsteadiness of fixation (Ladd-Franklin, 1929).

Experimental evidence for the duplicity theory. If it is the rods that respond to very faint light, such light should not elicit any response from the fovea which would be night-blind in all persons. In order to test this prediction, the eye is dark-adapted and a faint light is thrown on the fovea alone. Very exact fixation is required; otherwise the light will fall outside the fovea and reach some rods. Instead of a single fixation point, a ring of weakly luminous points is used. If the ring has a diameter of 3° and is fixated as a whole, the center of the ring will correspond to the fovea. The test light is given in the center of the ring. By such experiments the foveal threshold, during dark adaptation, is found to be very much higher than that of the parafoveal region (von Kries, 1897b). You can see a faint star—or a ship at night—better by looking a little to one side. This was an important bit of information for those who needed to see things at night during the war.

A very weak spectrum has no visible color but only a gradation of brightness. Its maximum brightness lies at a wavelength of 500 mμ instead of at 560 as is the case in a bright spectrum. The brightness curve of the spectrum is the same for the normal dark-adapted eye, with dim illumination, as it is for the totally color-blind eye under any illumination. (See Fig. 13-3.) The rod apparatus is evidently tuned to a shorter wavelength than the cones.

A related fact has long been known under the name of the Purkinje phenomenon. If a red paper and a green or blue paper are matched for brightness under good illumination and are then taken into much dimmer light, the green or blue appears the brighter. In good light the cones, in dim light the rods, contribute most of the sensation. Consequently, the reds are relatively bright in strong light and the greens and blues in dim light. The greens and blues in dim light are not only relatively bright but also whitish because of the colorless contribution of the rods. The Purkinje phenomenon is said to fail when the stimulus is confined strictly to the rod-free region, and also in cases of night blindness (von Kries & Nagel, 1900; Kohlrausch, 1931).

The response of the dark-adapted eye to weak light is called "scotopic" vision (literally, darkness vision); it is almost pure rod vision. "Photopic" vision is the response to stronger light, dominated by the cones. To exclude all rod vision you may confine the stimulus to the fovea, and to exclude all cone vision you must work below the threshold of dark-adapted cones. As indicated by the curves of Figure 13-3, you can be quite sure of excluding most rod vision if you confine the stimulus to the extreme red.

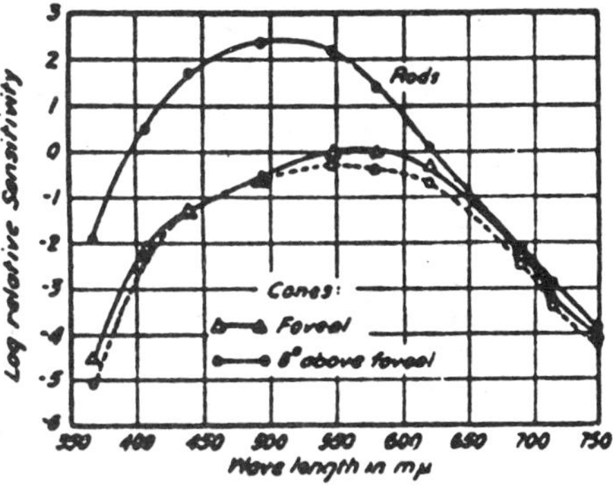

FIG. 13-3. (From Judd, 1951; after Wald, 1945.) The sensitivity of the eye to various wavelengths. The three curves represent sensitivity of rods, peripheral cones, and foveal cones, respectively. Sensitivity is defined as 1/threshold, with the foveal threshold at a wavelength of 555 mμ taken as unity. The left-hand ordinate gives sensitivity in logarithmic units. Note that the rods are considerably more sensitive than the cones to short wavelengths, toward the violet end of the spectrum.

LIGHT AND DARK ADAPTATION

The visual apparatus has ways of compensating for the intensity of light. The most obvious change is in the size of the pupil, but by far the greater portion of the adjustment occurs in the retina. Some data on the extent and speed of the pupillary adjustments are given in Figures 13-4 and 13-5. These are average values; individual differences are great, age levels differ, and there is

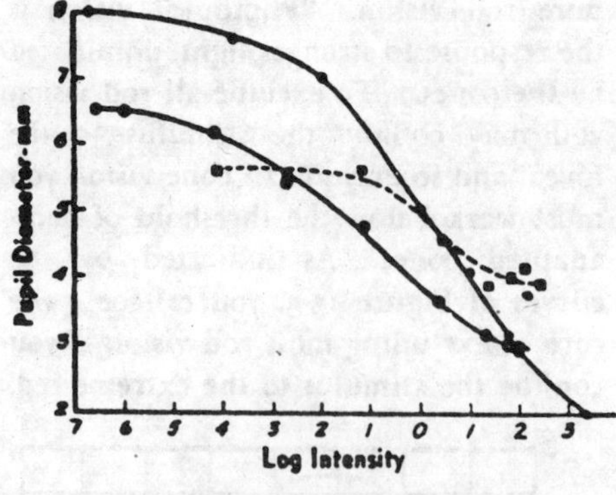

FIG. 13-4. (Wagman & Nathanson, 1942) Diameter of the pupil as a function of illumination. The hollow circles represent data from the human eye, after Reeves. Solid circles and squares represent human and rabbit eyes, respectively. All points are averages of six to ten eyes, thus eliminating the variability that would have given quite irregular curves. Note that these curves represent pupil size after adaptation is complete; the rate at which this end state is approached is shown in Figure 13-5.

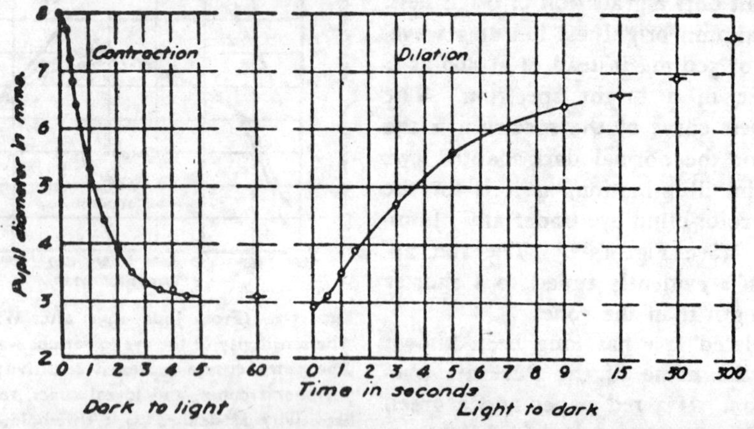

FIG. 13-5. (Data from Reeves, 1918a.) Progress of pupillary contraction and dilation. Average results from six *O*s. The contraction curve was obtained by first keeping *O* in the dark long enough to obtain practically complete dilation and then exposing the eye to a brightness of 100 ml, and photographing it at short intervals during this exposure. The dilation curve had to be built up from several experiments in each of which, starting from practically complete adjustment of the pupil to the bright light of 100 ml, *O* was kept in the dark for a certain number of seconds and his eye then photographed by aid of a flash of light. The pupillary response to light is a much quicker process than that to darkness.

considerable variation in the same individual from day to day. Even the greatest range shown in these figures is a fourfold one; square it, since the area of the pupil is what determines the amount of light admitted, and we get a range of 16. This is certainly inadequate to compensate for the corresponding change in level of illumination, which covered 10 log units, or 10,000,000,000-fold.

Adaptation of the retina goes much further in the way of compensation. Everyone is familiar with the effects of retinal adaptation: after "getting used" to either a dim or a bright illumination, one sees objects much more distinctly than at first. That the retina rather than the cortex becomes light-adapted and dark-adapted is indicated by the bleaching of the visual purple in the light and its reappearance in prolonged exposure to the dark. Another relevant fact is that one eye can be light-adapted and the other simultaneously dark-adapted.

The progress of adaptation to light or dark is traced by determining the stimulus threshold, the lowest intensity of light which can be perceived at a given time. The rod-free fovea requires separate study, since the rods go much further than the cones in adaptation to dim light. In an experiment of Piper (1903) the test field was a 4-inch square of milk glass, illuminated from behind and placed one foot from *O*'s eyes. The apparatus was set up in a dark room, but *O* was first sent out of doors for a quarter of an hour in order that the experiment might start with light-adapted eyes. When he returned, a first determination of his threshold was made, the illumination of the milk glass being altered till he just barely saw it. He then remained in the dark room, and his threshold was measured at intervals till it reached a fairly stable level, as it usually did in 40–60 minutes. At this level it was only $\frac{1}{8500}$ of the threshold first determined after entering the dark; and this first threshold was certainly too low, because dark adaptation had advanced to some extent during the minute or two consumed in measuring the threshold. A quicker method of determining the threshold (Blanchard, cited by Kohlrausch, 1931) is to have *O* look at a large field of known brightness for a certain time, for adaptation, and then to darken the field completely except for a small central portion—the question being whether *O* can see this central portion. By varying its brightness the stimulus threshold is determined. This method gave results indicating fully a million times the sensitivity in extreme dark as in extreme light adaptation. Since the test field in the experiments so far described was large enough to extend beyond the rod-free region, the results apply to the rods rather than the cones.

Adaptation of the cones is studied by confining the test field to the fovea. Hecht (1921) used for a test field a small red cross illuminated from the rear. It subtended a visual angle of 2.5°, which is not quite small enough to restrict the field to the rod-free region, but the additional precaution of using red light (a Wratten filter transmitted only the red end of the spectrum) was doubtless effective since the rods are relatively insensitive to that light. An initial state of light adaptation was secured by directing the eyes for 5 minutes upon a bright surface. This surface was then darkened, and *O* had simply to raise his head and look into the apparatus for the red cross, and to signal when it became visible. A very quick first determination was thus secured; *O* remained in the dark and was retested at intervals. The results indicated a rapid but limited dark adaptation of the cones. It was nearly complete in 3 minutes, but the sensitivity was only 100–200 times that in light adaptation. Cook (1934a) found about the same amount of change which was almost complete in 8 minutes though it continued for 10 minutes longer. Hecht's results are shown in Figure 13-6.

Instead of determining the stimulus threshold, Wright (1934) obtained a brightness equation between two monocular fields lying side by side in the combined binocular field of view. One eye was kept in a state of dark adaptation while the other was exposed to a bright surface. A match was then made between two test fields, one exposed to each eye. The light-adapted eye required a much brighter test field than the dark-adapted eye in order to obtain an equation. But as the light-adapted eye recovered from its light adaptation (or became dark-adapted) by being kept in the dark, less objective difference was needed in order to obtain the equation. The course of dark adaptation was so nearly linear for the first few minutes that the initial sensitivity could be estimated by extrapolation. This initial sensitivity was thus determined after

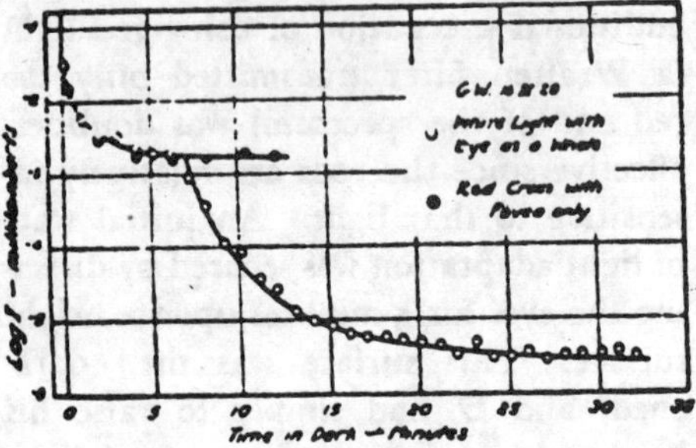

FIG. 13-6. (Hecht, 1921; 1934.) Visual sensitivity as a function of length of dark adaptation. The shallow curve, with solid circles, shows the development of dark adaptation of the foveal area and is a cone curve. The deeper curve, with hollow circles, was obtained with white light over the whole retina and represents the sensitivity of rods. The break in the curve at 7 minutes shows when the slower adaptation of the rods overtakes the more rapid but more limited adaptation of the cones.

different durations of exposure to light, and by this means Wright obtained indirectly what is very difficult to obtain directly, a curve of *light adaptation*. The progress of foveal light adaptation, according to this evidence, is extremely rapid and is nearly complete at the end of one minute's exposure to the light.

Adaptation with red goggles. During World War II a very interesting application of the implications of the duplicity theory was made by Miles (1943). Reference to Figure 13-3 will show that red light (beyond 620 mμ) is a reasonably effective stimulus for cones. If a man wears special red goggles that transmit only this band, he can read with his cones, while the rods are relatively unstimulated by the room light and are adapting. This procedure avoids tedious waiting in the dark for half an hour before night duty; he needs only 5 minutes of real darkness to complete the very last portion of the curve, which he cannot achieve with red goggles. Of course, he must take his goggles off before he tries to see in the dark, for they screen out the short wavelengths which most effectively stimulate the dark-adapted rods. If he has to go into a lighted area, he can put the goggles back on, and save most of his dark adaptation. The same principle favors the use of red lights on instrument dials and in chart rooms; one can see reasonably well with such light, without sacrificing dark adaptation. The only difficulty comes from colored lines on charts, or numbers on dials; red lines are indistinguishable from white background, and blue looks black. Hecht & Yun Hsia (1945) have made extensive studies of adaptation with various filters and illuminants.

THE ROLE OF VISUAL PURPLE (RHODOPSIN)

Thus far we have largely limited our discussion to human vision. In some cases we could have presented animal experiments that yielded the same results. For example, R. H. Brown (1937) set up a conditioned breathing response to light in a rabbit and found both scotopic and photopic visibility curves, in agreement with his other finding that the rabbit has color vision. There seems to be no reason for describing animal experiments where the data from man are satisfactory, but there are certain experiments in which only animals can be used. This is particularly true when we wish to study the actual events in the retina.

One important series of experiments is concerned with the role of visual purple (p. 366). It has long been known that this chemical is found in the rods of dark-adapted eyes, and in much smaller quantities in light-adapted ones. When a large amount of this substance has been extracted from the eye of a frog, it can be studied in a test tube. It was in this fashion that the absorption spectrum of visual purple was found to be essentially the same as the scotopic visibility curve of the eye (Hecht, Shlaer, & Pirenne, 1942). Further, the amount of visual purple bleached is proportional to the amount of light which it absorbs. The obvious conclusion is that the breakdown or bleaching of visual purple is the first stage in the stimulation process. But the reaction is reversible, for the breakdown product can be reconstituted into visual purple. This has been demonstrated in the eye (Peskin, 1942) and even in the test tube (Hecht, Chase, Shlaer & Haig, 1936). The details of the intermediate steps between breakdown of visual purple and excitation of impulses in the optic nerve are too complicated to discuss here, especially since several alternative formulations are available (Hecht, 1934; Bartley, 1941, 1951; Wald, 1942, 1950.) But it is reasonably clear that (1) the amount of visual purple broken down by light determines the strength of the visual response, and (2) the sensitivity of the rods in light and dark adaptation is determined by the amount of visual purple available. There is probably a comparable substance in the cones, but it is present in such small quantities that it is hard to study (Bliss, 1946).

Night blindness. One especially practical bit of information has come from these and related studies. It has been known since antiquity that some people are night-blind; they do not dark-adapt well. When the facts about the chemistry of visual stimulation were worked out, it seemed likely that vitamin A was part of the cycle—in fact, the precursor from which visual purple was built up. Perhaps some night blindness was due to lack of this vitamin. Hecht & Mandelbaum (1938) showed that 35 days of a vitamin-A deficient diet could raise the minimum level of dark adaptation by about two log units. This means a hundredfold loss in sensitivity! Soon all the night-fighting pilots in England were munching carrots, which are rich in this vitamin. Most of the carrots were probably wasted, for there is no evidence that a surplus of the vitamin gives better vision than does a bare minimum, and the normal diet presumably gave the pilots an adequate supply. Not all night blindness is due to vitamin-A deficiency, for there may be other defects in the rod mechanism.

The electroretinogram. The data on which Hecht and the other workers erected their formulations came from animals ranging from the clam to man. The clam (Mya) has a very clear-cut response to light, siphon retraction. Furthermore, it responds more rapidly the stronger the stimulus. Hence Hecht (1934) was able to study the development of light and dark adaptation by recording the progressive changes in reaction time, and even to determine the temperature coefficients of the reactions —a valuable clue to their nature.

Much of the visual purple used in test tubes has come from the frog. Hence, it is highly desirable to know if this animal has an eye that works like ours. Anatomical studies show similarity, even to the presence of both rods and cones. Correspondingly, Riggs (1937) showed that the frog's dark-adaptation curve (Fig. 13-7) has a break, suggestive of that between human cone and rod curves (Fig. 13-6).

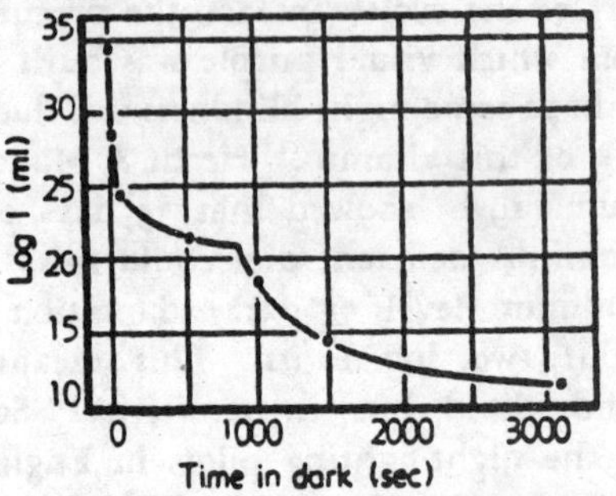

FIG. 13-7. (Riggs, 1937.) The dark-adaptation curve of the frog, as measured by the intensity required to evoke a standard height of the retinal potential in the frog. Note the similarity to human dark-adaptation curves.

But how did Riggs know whether or not the frog saw a given dim light at a specific level of adaptation? He could have used some gross behavioral response, learned or unlearned, but instead, he tested the eye directly. Like all sensitive tissues, the retina shows an electrical change or potential on stimulation; the change, which can be recorded, is called the *electroretinogram*. This wave of electrical activity has several phases, and its wave form depends on such factors as color, intensity, and duration of the light which arouses it (Fig. 13-8). We shall not go into detailed description of the wave form or the components into which it may be analyzed (Granit, 1935), but we shall simply point out that the most prominent feature is the large B wave. It was this wave that Riggs used as an index of response to plot the dark-adaptation curve of Figure 13-7; he arbitrarily selected a given height of B wave as the threshold response and found how much light was necessary to reach this value at the various stages of dark adaptation.

The electroretinogram has been studied in animals for half a century. The early insensitive recording devices made it necessary to pick it up directly from the retina, but modern electronic amplifiers make it unnecessary to enter the eye with electrodes. All that is needed is a thin moist wick on the cornea, and another contact grounded somewhere else on the animal. This method was used by Hartline, Graham (cf. 1934b for summary), Granit, and others.

Human retinal potentials. The electroretinogram may tell us a lot about how the retina works, but how is it related to vision? The animal experiments do not tell us whether or not the light is actually seen. The best way to answer the question would be to put a human *O* in a psychophysical set-up, getting simultaneous reports and electroretinograms on the same stimulus flashes. Riggs, Berry & Wayner (1949) succeeded in doing this difficult job. The secret of their success rested on the use of an electrode imbedded in a contact lens (Riggs, 1941). The thin glass or plastic shell of this lens clings to the eyeball for a period of hours and permits normal vision; at the same time it holds the electrode in electrical contact with the cornea, through natural secretions which fill the hollow between contact lens and eye. A fine wire leads off to appropriate amplifiers, and the electrical changes are recorded photographically. Figure 13-8 is a tracing of a human electroretinogram obtained in this fashion. The results showed that the visibility curve of the human eye, as determined by the B wave, is very similar to the scotopic curve obtained simultaneously by verbal report.

A number of lines indicate that most of the response arises from scotopic mechanisms. The height of the response increases progressively with the dark adaptation of the retinal rods (Adrian, 1945; Johnson, 1949; Riggs & Johnson, 1949). Night-blind individuals do not show the normal increase in response because their rod receptors are not capable of recovering their sensitivity in the darkness.

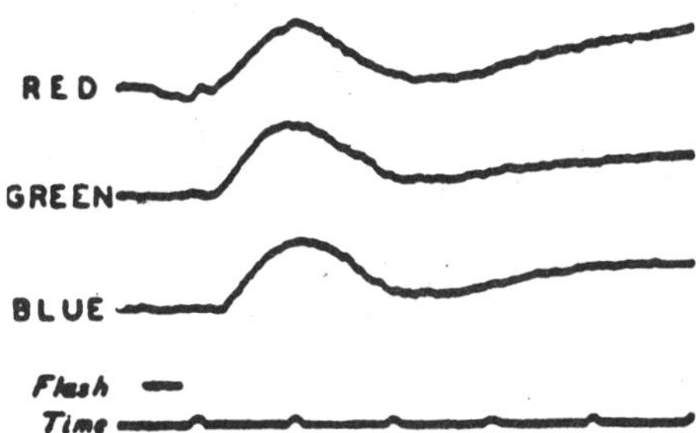

FIG. 13-8. (Riggs & Johnson, 1949.) The human electroretinogram. Electrical responses to three separate flashes, each of a different color, have been assembled in one figure. The flash lasted .04 sec, as may be seen by comparison with the 1/10-sec time line beneath it. Note that all three curves have the same predominant B wave but that the red curve shows a marked preliminary dip.

The human electroretinogram shows some specific changes with wavelength, as may be seen from Figure 13-8. The most striking difference is in the small dip just before the principal (B) wave to red light. This initial deflection, attributed by Adrian (1945, 1946) to the photopic mechanisms of the eye, is present to a lesser extent in response to other colors. In protanope observers, who are nearly blind to red light, the initial deflection is missing from the electroretinogram (Armington, 1952). In short, although small preliminary deflections are probably photopic in origin, the major part of the electroretinogram reflects primarily the scotopic mechanisms, especially in the dark-adapted eye.

TEMPORAL AND SPATIAL FACTORS

Duration of stimulus. Until now we have avoided any mention of the *duration* of stimulation, but the time during which a stimulus persists may be quite as important as its intensity. The photographer must lengthen his exposure if the light is weak. He thus recognizes what is known as the Bunsen-Roscoe law, $I \times T = C$; or, the intensity (I) of a light multiplied by its duration (T) determines its effect. This law is the keystone of all photochemical processes, from the effect of light on the growth of wheat seedlings to the breakdown of visual purple in the eye. It is the *quantity* ($I \times T$) of light that determines its effectiveness. Thus, an electric spark that lasts a millionth of a second looks as bright as a light $1/10{,}000$ as intense that lasts for $1/100$ second.

A little reflection on what we know about the chemical processes in the retina warns us against extending the law to cover indefinitely long durations. Remember that the breakdown of visual purple is reversible and that this chemical is restored by a recovery process. It takes from 50 to 200 ms in the human eye for the back-reaction to get going; this period is called the *critical duration* (Graham & Margaria, 1935) or *retinal action time* (Pirenne, 1948). As long as the duration is kept below this value, the simple product of intensity and duration determines the effectiveness of the stimulus, but when the duration is larger than the critical duration, intensity is the only determiner of the effectiveness.

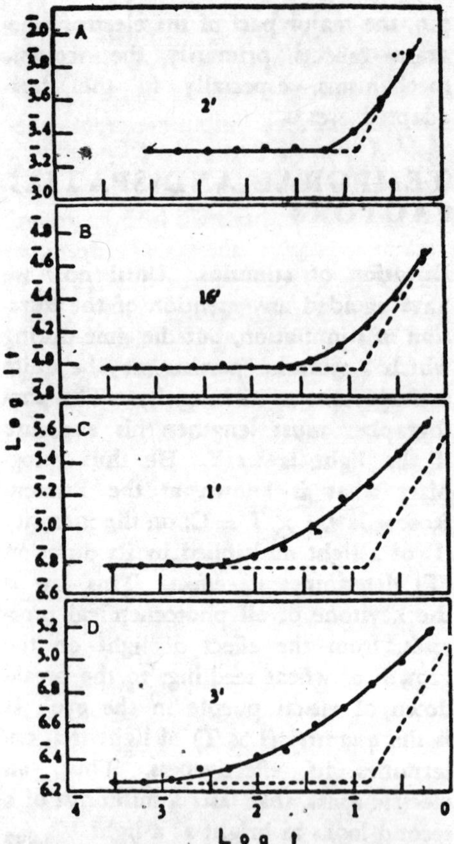

FIG. 13-9. (Graham & Margaria, 1935.) Intensity-time curves for the four areas indicated. The ordinate shows the *amount* of light—intensity × duration—which is just visible if it lasts for the *duration* shown on the base line. Both axes are logarithmic, to condense the graph. In the smallest area (top graph) the Bunsen-Roscoe law holds up to about $\log T = -1.0$ ($T = .1$ sec); so far the data points run parallel to the base line, showing $I \times T$ to remain constant. But for exposures longer than the *critical duration* the curve climbs at a slope of unity; this means that T is no longer a factor in determining the threshold, and the formula becomes $I = C$. Note that the graphs for successively larger retinal areas show less sharp breaks at the critical duration. This is because interaction among the more numerous retinal elements in the larger areas obscures the simple relationship. The broken lines show where the points would be expected to fall if it were not for spatial interaction.

This is shown rather clearly in Figure 13-9, for stimulus threshold determinations. The same general facts hold whenever we are dealing with the effects of intensity of visual stimulation, as in brightness discrimination, visual acuity, or even recording retinal potentials. In fact, the results obtained from optic nerve discharges in the compound eye of the horseshoe crab look very similar to those plotted in Figure 13-9—the chief difference is that the break is sharper (Hartline, 1934). The implications of these facts for practical research are fairly obvious. If you are interested in stable thresholds, either use an exposure of a half second or more, or carefully controlled durations below 1/25 second, to keep away from the uncertain region where the curve bends sharply. The short exposures have the advantage that they avoid eye movements, which would complicate things by shifting the stimulus to new retinal points.

Spatial summation. If a surface is of uniform objective brightness, a small bit of it appears less bright than a larger bit. Increasing the visible area of the surface from a mere point to the small size of half a degree of visual angle increases the apparent brightness, but further increase has little effect. Evidently more light enters the eye from a broader than from a narrower surface of the same brightness. Perfect summation would require the same quantity of light to be barely perceptible whether it came from a broader or narrower area; area and brightness would be interchangeable factors in perceptibility. Denote brightness by the letter I and area by A, and let K be a constant; then perfect spatial summation would be expressed by the statement: for constant perceptibility,

$$I \times A = K$$

an equation which is sometimes called Ricco's law, and the validity of which is disputed.

An experiment of Pieron (1929) was designed to measure spatial summation within the confines of the fovea. To confine a stimulus to the fovea is not easy because of wavering fixation, especially in dim light. Piéron used instead of a single fixation point a little square consisting of four red points, and found it comparatively easy to maintain fixation in the blank center of this square. Within the square he presented from time to time a circular spot of faint light; and for each size of the spot he determined the brightness threshold. It decreased as the diameter of the spot increased, up to over 1° which is about the diameter of the fovea. But summation was not perfect, for the I value did not go down as fast as the A value went up. If we write, instead of Ricco's law, the more general expression,

$$I \times A^m = K$$

we have in the exponent, m, a measure or indicator of the degree of summation. If $m = 0$, the area makes no difference, there is zero summation. If $m = 1$, summation is perfect, as already said. Piéron's data gave $m \doteq 0.3$ which would indicate quite imperfect summation in the fovea. Other experiments showed a higher degree of summation outside the fovea, and the value of m increased toward the periphery of the retina. Also, the further from the fovea the stimulated area, the broader it could be and still show some summation.

These functional results probably depend on the anatomical fact that in the peripheral zone of the retina several receptor cells connect with a single ganglion cell and optic nerve fiber. The further from the fovea, the more convergence of neural impulses from the receptors.

Summation occurs between *separated* spots, so that the threshold is lower when two spots receive the same intensity simultaneously than when only one of the spots gets the stimulus. The spots cannot be far apart, however—not more than 10′ apart in the fovea, and not more than 2° at some distance from the fovea. Here again we see more summation in the periphery than in the fovea (Beitel, 1934).

The two-spot experiment suggests that summation over a long distance will be small. In a larger stimulus patch there are more elements summating, but they summate less perfectly because they lie farther apart. When the stimulus patches are varied over a wide range of size, these two opposing factors interact in such a way as to make even Piéron's formula inadequate, since the exponent m cannot be taken as a constant (Graham, Brown & Mote, 1939; Graham & Bartlett, 1939, 1940).

Spatial summation must impair acuity unless it is offset by the reverse type of interaction. Graham & Granit (1931) were able to detect an inhibitory or subtractive influence exerted by the brighter of two neighboring spots upon the dimmer one. While the dim spot increased the apparent brightness of the adjacent bright spot, the latter seemed to diminish the apparent brightness of the former. For fuller discussion of this interesting type of interaction see Graham (1934b).

It will be seen that interaction effects are quite complicated. Simple summation is particularly important at threshold values of illumination, but inhibition, and also the presence of stray light, become quite important at higher levels of illumination (Fry & Bartley, 1935; Bartley, 1935).

Interaction in the fovea. The relative freedom of the fovea from cross-connecting fibers would lead us to expect that interaction would be at a minimum in this area. There is considerable experimental proof that this is true (see Graham, 1934b). Separate foveal points are surprisingly independent of each other. We shall mention one experiment to illustrate this point. In the chapter on Attention (p. 96) we described the Hunter-Sigler (1940) experiment, which showed that it takes more light to see two dots than one, and still more light as the number of dots is increased. This looks like mutual inhibition, even though all dots were well within the fovea. But it might also be a simple statistical matter (Schlosberg, 1948). Remember that the threshold is always defined in terms of a certain probability. A single dot might be reported on 25 percent of the trials at one intensity level, 50 percent at another, and 75 percent at a still higher level of illumination. Hunter & Sigler defined their threshold as 50-percent correct reports on the number of dots exposed. But suppose the perception of each dot on a multidot plate was an independent event. Take an intensity that will let us see any single dot on 50 percent of the trials. We should expect .5 correct reports on a one-dot plate, but only .25 ($.5^2$) on a two-dot plate. The problem is the same as tossing coins; if the probability is .5 that a single coin will land head up, it is $.5^2$ that two coins will both land heads, and $.5^n$ that n coins will all land heads up. Returning to the dots, we must start with enough light to give a higher P value for each dot if we want .50 correct on two dots. The actual figure would be $\sqrt{.5}$, or about .7. To give 50 percent correct on n dots, we would need enough light to give $\sqrt[n]{.5}$ on any single dot. So it is easy to see why it takes more light to get 50-percent correct reports as the number of dots increases, without recourse to interaction effects.

To check this formulation, Casperson & Schlosberg (1950) ran an intensive study of two *O*s at one level of illumination. The results were in very good agreement with the prediction that the probability of correct reports of from two to seven dots varied as the nth power of the probability for one dot, with the intensity of illumination remaining constant. This may be taken as reasonable evidence that the small foveal areas corresponding to the separate dots showed little interaction. It further suggests that they varied independently in sensitivity, rather than as a result of some common factor like pupillary size or level of attention. But recently we have come to realize that the source of variability which creates the psychophysical ogive may not be entirely an *O*-factor; the quantum theory of the threshold blames the variability on the essential nature of the stimulus. Let us turn to this theory.

The quantum theory of the visual threshold. We now know that the total *quantity* of light (I $\times$ T $\times$ A) is the significant thing in determining thresholds, so long as we keep time of exposure short and area small. The actual quantity needed for the dark-adapted eye turns out to be very small, of the order of 5×10^{-10} ergs. Pirenne makes this vivid by pointing out that the mechanical energy of a pea falling one inch, if converted into luminous energy, would be sufficient to give a faint impression of light to every man that ever lived (1948, p. 78).

Earlier we pointed out that modern physicists often think of light as made up of *quanta*, or particles, which cannot be subdivided. These quanta are very small units of energy. Hecht and his collaborators (see below) calculated that the minimum effective flash described in the last paragraph consists of 54–148 quanta. About half of them get lost through reflection or absorption by the cornea, lens, and liquids that fill the eye, and not all of the remaining 26–70 hit the sensitive tips of rods or cones. It can be shown in several ways that perhaps 80 percent pass between the elements, and are absorbed by the black pigment at the outer surface of the retina. So we are left with perhaps 5–14 of our original quanta as the actual threshold stimulus. Now spatial summation seems to be complete over an area that includes 500 rods. With approximately 10 quanta spread over 500 rods, it is unlikely that more than one quantum will hit a single rod. So it seems that a single quantum is enough to initiate the minimum photochemical event in one rod—but not enough to make us report a flash. Apparently 5–14 rods must summate their effect to cross the response threshold. The fact that they are anatomically connected to permit spatial summation is one thing that makes rod vision so sensitive. As a matter of fact, it is hard to see how the retina could possibly be much more sensitive than it is. If one quantum, tripping off one rod, were enough to make us see a flash, we would have a rather chaotic visual field, for sensitive elements often fire spontaneously (p. 271). The requirement that several rods summate to produce a sensation is just another example of the need for a "signal strength" above "noise level" before the signal can be observed.

It is still too early to see all the implications of this brilliant analysis, but some of them are pointed out by Hecht, Shlaer & Pirenne (1942) as well as in the less technical accounts by Hecht (1944) and Pirenne (1948). We may mention one of these implications, without going into great detail. In our discussion of Psychophysics (p. 219) we saw that the threshold was a statistical concept. That is, we define the lower threshold as that intensity which will call out a response in a certain percentage of trials, as 60 percent or 75 percent. Stronger stimuli call out the response with a higher frequency, and weaker ones less frequently. The typical psychometric function is an ogive. The so-called frequency-of-seeing curves are of this type. It has generally been assumed that the random variations which produce these curves are within *O*. But if quanta are discrete particles, and hits on individual rods are merely chance events, it is possible that the variability is in the stimulus, and not in *O*. By making this assumption, the authors cited above were able to predict some very interesting things about the detailed form of the psychometric functions under specific conditions. Of course, it is not time to scrap the concept of variations in the sensitivity of *O* as a factor in psychophysical experiments, but it is consoling to blame *some* of the variability on the essential nature of the stimulus.

BRIGHTNESS

Difference thresholds. Most of the experiments we have considered up to this point have been concerned with the intensitive RL, or lower threshold, which is a valuable tool for working out basic visual processes. Once these have been established, they can be extended to the other phenomena. An excellent illustration of this point is furnished by research on the DL for brightness. How large must a brightness difference be made before it is detected? Does Weber's law ($\Delta I/I = K$) hold? We have already seen that Weber's fraction is very high at low stimulus intensities, and falls to a fairly flat minimum for the upper half of the (logarithmic) stimulus range (Fig. 8-16, p. 224). These data were taken by König & Brodhun in 1888. Let us examine some recent experiments to see how the data are obtained, and what they mean.

Perhaps the most obvious way to set up the experiment is to show *O* a small circular field, split into two semicircles by a thin line down the middle. Appropriate light sources, lenses, and filters can be arranged to illuminate the two half fields independently. The task is to report which half field is brighter. Now comes the problem of how the actual observations are to be made. If both half fields are lighted simultaneously, and *O* is allowed to look back and forth to compare them, there will be all sorts of complications with adaptation and afterimages. Perhaps it

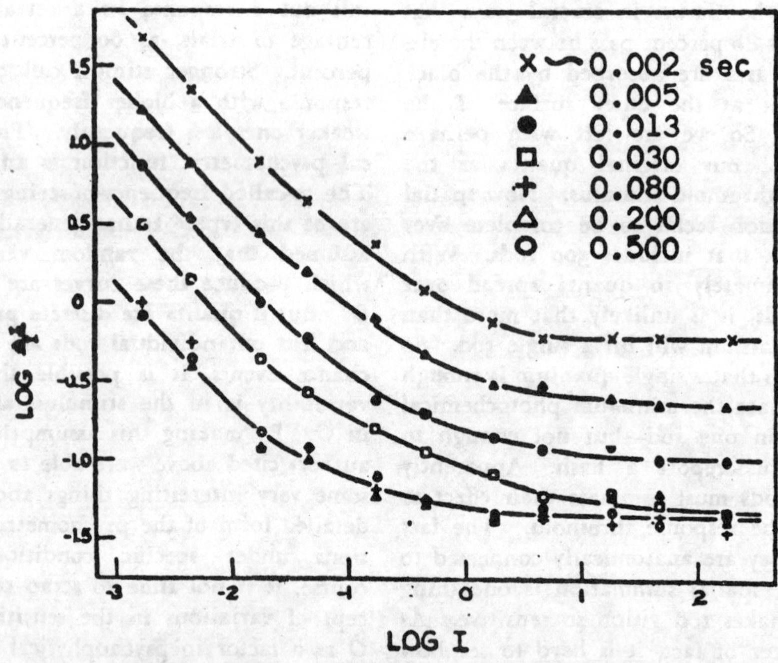

FIG. 13-10. (Graham & Kemp, 1938.) The relation between Weber's fraction ($\Delta I/I$) and the intensity (I) of the Standard. Each curve represents data obtained at the indicated duration of flash. Note that the three largest time values all give the same curve; they are beyond the critical duration. The curves look less steep than that of Figure 8-16, because the ordinate is plotted in logarithmic units here.

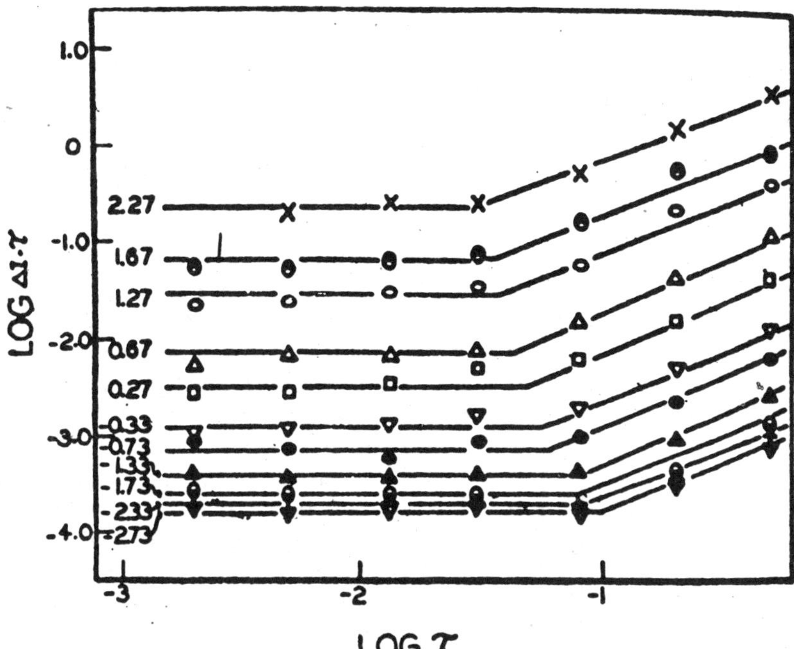

FIG. 13-11. (Graham & Kemp, 1938.) I × T difference thresholds and different adaptation levels.

would be better to flash them on for only a brief period, say 1 second, while O maintains fixation on the center of the field. But then there is the problem of the pre-exposure field; if it was dark, O is partially dark-adapted. Of course, E can decide to keep the pre-exposure field at one specific intensity, regardless of the level of the actual stimuli. This is what Kellogg (1929) did, as we mentioned on p. 200.

Another option was taken by Graham & Kemp (1938). They illuminated both half fields at the (same) desired intensity, and permitted O to fixate at their center. When O was ready, he released a shutter which added an additional flash to one half field, and he then reported whether he saw it or not. Intensity and duration of the incremental flash could be varied from trial to trial. They were thus able to determine difference thresholds and plot a curve that was very similar to that obtained by König & Brodhun. As a matter of fact, Graham & Kemp obtained a whole family of ΔI/I *vs.* I curves, one for each duration. (Fig. 13-10.)

If we plot these data in a different way, a very interesting thing occurs. Consider the intensity level of the two half fields (before the flash is added to one) as an adapting intensity. This is reasonable, for O has been fixating the circle for some time before the flash is added. We should get a family of I × T *vs.* T curves, roughly similar to those of Graham & Margaria (Fig. 13-9, p. 374), with each curve representing a different level of adaptation. It will be seen from Figure 13-11 that this is exactly what we get, even including sharp breaks at the critical duration. This line of reasoning suggests that the DL is very closely related to the RL; in either case stimulation depends on the breakdown of a certain amount of the receptive substance within a critical duration. The amount (I × T) of light required to do the job depends on the level of adaptation, and hence on the amount of available photosensitive substance. Essentially the same results emerged when Graham & Bartlett (1940) examined the effect of size of the stimulus area on the difference threshold for brightness. Large areas yielded smaller Weber fractions (ΔI/I) than did small ones, showing that spatial summation within areas is important for DL as it is for RL (p. 374).

Scaling brightness. Experiments such as these may seem far removed from the question of brightness as a dimension. In our discussion of the construction of psychological scales (p. 244) we found that it was possible to arrange a series of grays, reaching from white to black, so that each step would appear to be equal to every other one. Furthermore, such a scale of brils turns out to be in substantial agreement with a scale constructed by summating j.n.d. units, in

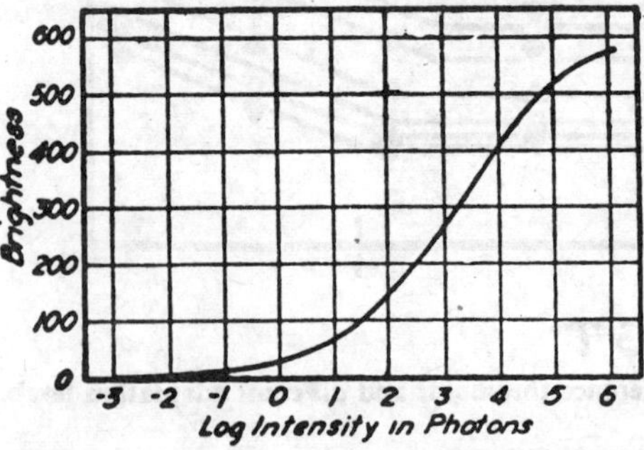

Fig. 13-12. (Troland, 1930.) Brightness (= Brilliance) as a function of log stimulus intensity. The base-line unit is the photon, which takes into account both intensity and the size of the pupil, thus representing retinal illumination. The ordinate shows how many j.n.d. steps a given intensity is above the stimulus threshold.

the spirit, if not the letter, of Fechner's law. A summated j.n.d. curve is presented in Figure 13-12. An interesting fact to note now is that both the bril and the summated j.n.d. scales are very similar to the *value* scale of the Munsell system of color classification, which has been used as a practical device for several decades (see Adams, 1922). It is surprising that the carefully controlled experiments with small spots of light yield results that apply to a series of gray papers, especially when we realize that the papers are viewed on various backgrounds ("surrounds"), under varied illumination, and with all the complications introduced by a moving eye (p. 250).

Intermittent light. Flicker and fusion. If the eye were a perfect light-registering instrument, it would give an intermittent sensation whenever the stimulus was intermittent. There would be no "retinal lag." The retinal response would start up instantly with full force at the beginning of each flash of light and stop instantly with the end of each flash. This is too much to expect of any instrument consisting of biological structures, and as a matter of fact we find a lag both at the beginning and at the end of the stimulus. This lag is more an advantage than a disadvantage in perceiving *objects* under intermittent illumination. A modern electric bulb driven by alternating current would show all objects as flickering if the eye had perfect resolving power in time.

A regularly intermittent light can be regarded as consisting of cycles, each cycle composed of a dark phase and a light phase. Frequency is measured in cycles per second. At low frequency *O* perceives a series of flashes of light; as the frequency is gradually increased the impression changes successively to coarse flicker, fine flicker, and perfectly steady light. The frequency at which all flicker disappears is called the *fusion frequency*. The higher the fusion frequency, the more efficient is the operation of the light-registering mechanism, the better its resolving power in time.

Fusion frequency depends on several stimulus variables: on the intensity of the positive phase and the difference between the two phases; on the time proportion of the two phases; on the area of the flickering field; on the part of the retina stimulated.

Let the negative phase have zero intensity, then fusion frequency increases with the intensity of the positive phase. The increase follows a logarithmic curve expressed by the equation:

$$n = a \log I + b$$

in which n is the fusion frequency in cycles per second, I is the intensity of the positive phase, and a and b are parameters which remain constant under constant conditions of the experiment, though varying slightly from time to time and from *O* to *O*. This equation is called the Ferry-Porter law. It is the same in form as the Weber-Fechner law (p. 236), and the correspondence indicates that fusion frequency can be used as a measure of apparent intensity.

Fusion frequency is as low as 5 cycles per second at very low intensities, and as high as 50 or 55 cycles per second at high intensities. In motion picture projection the retina receives intermittent stimulation since a dark phase intervenes between each two successive frames. The normal projection rate is about 20 frames per second; at high screen brightness there might be annoying flicker. But modern projectors interrupt the beam once between frames and twice during each frame, giving about 60 flashes per second.

According to the above equation, n is a linear function of log I, and the plot of the fusion frequency against log I should therefore be a straight line. This law breaks down not only at very high intensities, where the receptors are overloaded, but also at low intensities when the rods are doing most of the work—or rather at those fairly low intensities at which the contribution to brightness is shifting from the rods to the cones. If the cone function is emphasized, either by using red light or by confining the stimulus to the fovea, the Ferry-Porter law holds very well over a wide range of intensities (Hecht, 1934, pp. 741–743).

Fusion frequency increases with the *area* of the flickering field as well as with its intensity (Granit & Harper, 1930) and the same logarithmic relation holds good:

$$n = c \log A + d$$

where A = area, and c and d are parameters. The fact that a larger area gives higher fusion frequency is further proof of spatial summation and shows that spatial summation assists the resolving power in time.

Fusion frequency differs in different parts of the retina. It is usually said to be higher in peripheral than in central vision. Bring a color wheel just to fusion frequency in direct vision and then turn the eyes somewhat to the side: you find the flicker to reappear in indirect vision. In this experiment quite a broad area of the retina is exposed to the intermittent stimulus. When the stimulus is restricted to a very small area, the opposite result is obtained (Granit & Harper, 1930): fusion frequency is highest in the fovea. The cones, accordingly, have a higher fusion frequency than the rods, and the usual result first cited is due to greater spatial summation in the periphery.

Spatial summation can be well demonstrated by the flicker method (Granit, 1930). Four small spots are made to flash synchronously, and the fusion frequency is determined when all four are used and when only one flashes. The fusion frequency is higher for the four than for the single spot. The difference is greatest when the four spots are close together and when the periphery of the retina is stimulated. If we query how spatial summation can raise the fusion frequency, the answer is that it has the effect of intensifying the positive phase of the intermittent stimulus.

The relative duration of the light and dark phases of the cycle has an effect on fusion frequency, though the relation is rather complex. The longer the light phase the higher its effective intensity rises through temporal summation; but the longer the dark phase, the more complete the recovery and the more nearly zero is the dark phase (Cobb, 1934).

When the two phases of the intermittent light differ not in intensity but in wavelength, flicker is much less in evidence. Rotate a color wheel with red and green sectors of about the same brightness, and you get some flicker at low speeds, but any flicker remaining at higher frequencies is due wholly to brightness difference. This principle is used in flicker photometry: you alternate a colored and a white light and adjust the intensity of the white to give minimum flicker; the two will then have equal effective intensity. The equations so obtained do not agree perfectly with those given by direct impression of the relative brightness of two colors (Tufts, 1907).

Once the fusion frequency is reached, further increase of frequency—for example, further increase in the speed of a rotating color wheel—produces no change in sensation. The sensation is the same as would be produced by the same flux of light spread uniformly throughout the cycle—the well-established Talbot-Plateau law. For example, let a color wheel contain ¼ white and ¾ black, and suppose for the moment that the black has zero brightness. Suppose also that the white, under the given illumination, has a brightness of 100 millilamberts. Then the effective brightness of the fused surface is ¼ of 100 = 25 ml. If the "black" sector really reflects enough light to have a brightness of 4 ml, it will contribute during rotation ¾ of 4 ml = 3 ml to the effective brightness of the mixture, which will therefore be 25 + 3 = 28 ml. This principle is constantly assumed and utilized in color mixing.

The higher the frequency at which an individual can see flicker, the greater the fidelity and efficiency of his sensory visual mechanism. This efficiency declines in age, as shown by the relatively low fusion frequency in age groups of 55 and over—an average result with individual exceptions (Misiak, 1947, 1951). From the more practical standpoint of visual perception, however, fusion is sometimes an advantage and flicker a nuisance, as in motion pictures and television. Fusion is one factor in apparent visual movement (p. 512).

We have said enough to show that critical fusion frequency (c.f.f.) is a much more complicated phenomenon than we might suspect. It is a simple experiment to set up and carry out, and it sets an easy task for *O*. Unfortunately, it is difficult to integrate the findings into a general theory of vision. But even though we do not fully understand its significance, c.f.f. is a very useful research tool, for it is intimately bound up with many visual phenomena (Graham, 1934b; Bartley, 1951). We now have a practically complete annotated bibliography of the very numerous investigations of this subject (Landis, 1953).

VISUAL ACUITY

When you "have your eyes tested" you take a practical test of visual acuity. You stand 20 feet from a standard chart which contains rows of letters of various sizes. If you can read the row that is normal for 20 feet, you have 20/20 vision.

But if you need a bigger row, as that which is normal for 40 feet, you have $^{20}/_{40}$ vision, etc. This test is good enough to tell whether or not your eye has optical defects that can be corrected by glasses, but it is inadequate for the study of the ultimate resolving power of the retina. Different letters present tasks of different difficulty, depending on their shape. This variability can be eliminated by using a broken ring (Landolt C) in place of the letters, and rotating it between trials. Or the rows of the chart may be made up of many such rings, each with the gap in a different place. Thus *O* always has the same task, the discrimination of the position of the same gap. It would be meaningless to give the size of the gap in inches or millimeters, for the size of a just perceptible gap would vary with the distance from the eye. Both geometry and experiment indicate that the kind of unit we want is an angular one; it is the angle subtended at the eye by the size of the gap, or of any object. This is called the *visual angle*. It may be converted directly into retinal distance, if we know the size of the eye—to be more specific, the distance from the nodal point, near the rear of the lens, to the retina. Visual angle is an inverted measure; the bigger the angle, the worse the acuity. Hence, it is conventional to express acuity as the reciprocal of the visual angle, measured in minutes of arc. A nickel (diameter, 20.6 mm) subtends about one minute at 233 ft (71 m), and corresponds to a visual acuity of 1.0. This is a reasonable value under good conditions; if the light were poorer, you might have to halve the viewing distance to detect the gap, thus doubling the angle. The resulting visual acuity would be ½, the reciprocal of the doubled angle.

Laboratory methods for measuring acuity. There are many other methods of measuring acuity. Many of them stem from the classic work of Helmholtz (1856–66), who hoped to use them to determine the resolving power of the retina. Remember that the retina is a mosaic of receptor cells; the acuity of the eye should bear some relation to the fineness of spacing of these elements. Many of the problems will be clearer if you think of them in terms of the halftone reproductions of photos in newspapers. Even with the naked eye, it is possible to see that such photos are made up of a pattern of dots. But in some of the better magazines, a much finer pattern of dots is used, often visible only with a hand lens; such reproductions permit a large amount of fine detail. It is essentially this type of reproduction that the eye was supposed to perform. Hence, one should be able to match the fineness of the retinal mosaic with the fineness of detail that can be discriminated by the eye.

The first method one might try is the *minimum visible*. How small a dot can be detected? But a bright dot, against a dark ground, will tell us nothing about the spacing of retinal elements, for we could see the dot as long as it stimulated a single receptor. Thus a star, in terms of its actual visual angle, is too small to measure, even with a telescope. Its apparent size, or *magnitude*, depends on its brightness, for its light may spread to several retinal elements, thus seeming to be considerably larger than a point.

The other version of the minimum visible is a black dot on a white ground. The reasoning here is that the black dot has to cover a receptor cell, leaving an unstimulated element in a sea of stimulated ones. The trouble here is that even the best eye is far from a perfect instrument. Light is scattered by the various media of the eye, and it is reflected around inside the eye. A more serious blur is produced by diffraction, a physical phenomenon based on interference among light waves. Finally, the eye undergoes constant small tremor, or physiological nystagmus (p. 498), which jiggles the image over the retina.

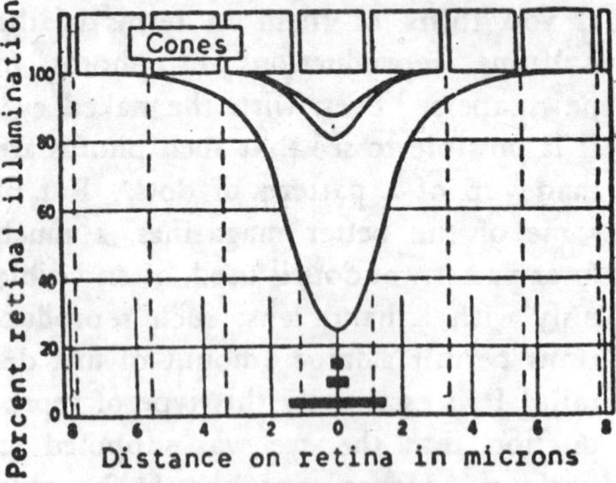

FIG. 13-13. (Hecht & Mintz, 1939.) The pattern of retinal illumination produced by three widths of wires against a white field. The diameter of each wire is shown by the solid lines at the base of the figure. The hollow squares at the top indicate the spacing of cones in the retinal mosaic. Notice how light spreads from the neighboring to the shadowed areas. If we take the level of illumination of the background as 100 percent, the thinnest visible black wire cuts the illumination of one row of cones by only 5 percent. Thicker wires give denser and wider images, effecting more than one row of cones.

Hence, our "unstimulated point" is actually a fuzzy disk, somewhat larger than a single cone. If the black dot is to be seen, at least one receptor element must be discriminably less stimulated than its neighbors. This discrimination will depend on the brightness difference threshold, as well as on the size and brightness of the dot and of the surrounding field.

Some idea of the amount of spreading of the image that results from simple physical factors may be gained from Figure 13-13, which shows the distribution of light produced on the retina by three black wires of different diameter. Note that even the widest wire, well above the minimum visible one, results in only a 75-percent decrease in illumination of one cone. The thinnest wire that can be seen subtends only 0.5 seconds of arc (Hecht & Mintz, 1939), which is about one sixtieth the diameter of a single cone (Polyak, 1941). One can think of this line as being represented by an occasional cone that is slightly less stimulated than its neighbors, just as a thin line may be suggested by a sparse row of small dots (to return to our newspaper picture analogy).

Another general method for measuring acuity is the *minimum separable.* It asks how far apart two points must be separated before they are seen as two, rather than one. Logically, this discrimination would demand that there be at least one unstimulated cone between two stimulated ones, lest we see one large dot. To avoid some of the spreading light, we may substitute two black dots for two white ones. Of course, either of these minimum separable measurements may be made with parallel lines substituted for the dots. Or one may use a whole block of alternate black and white lines, an *acuity grating; O* must report whether the lines run in a vertical, horizontal, or diagonal direction. Results come out about as they do for black-dot minimum visible; the lines must be separated by about 30 seconds, although the actual value depends on brightness of illumination (Graham & Cook, 1937—see p. 386). A much more sensitive method is used for *vernier acuity,* in which *O* must judge whether two halves of a line are continuous or offset, thus:

—————— ——————

Acuity as a function of illumination. Perhaps the most interesting results on visual acuity are shown in Figure 13-14, which is based on some data obtained by König in 1897. Notice that acuity in-

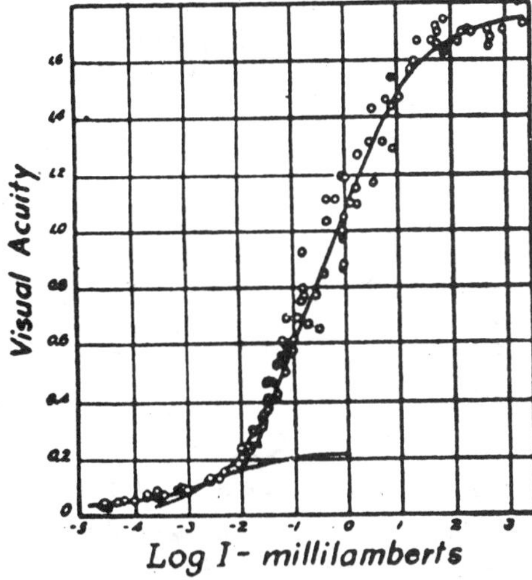

FIG. 13-14. (Hecht, 1934.) Visual acuity as a function of brightness. The circles represent König's 1897 data, replotted by Hecht in millilamberts. The two solid curves represent probability ogives fitted to the rod and cone portions of the data.

creases markedly as a function of illumination. The low values of acuity under dim illumination, in the lower left of the figure, are obviously due to the fact that only the rods function at this level. But why should the curve climb steadily as it does? If we stick to the classical mosaic type of explanation, it looks as if the retina were getting more receptor cells (finer mosaic) as the light increased. As a matter of fact, this was Hecht's (1934) explanation. He assumed that the individual receptors varied markedly in sensitivity. Under dim light, only a scattered few of the very sensitive elements came into activity. As the illumination increased, it crossed the lower threshold of more and more elements, bringing them into play. This theory would even explain the fact that the curve of acuity resembles the normal probability ogive (p. 203); he assumed that the sensitivity of the population of rods and cones was normally distributed so that as the light increased, it brought more and more of them into action, yielding the summated or ogival form of the curve.

A second theory is also based on probability, but here the probability is of chance hits by quanta of light. The more intense the illumination, the more quanta there are, and the more receptive elements will be active, which means a finer functional mosaic (Pirenne, 1945, 1948). And there is still another factor involved. It will be recalled that spread of light breaks down sharp contours between light and dark areas, bringing in the question of differential intensive thresholds between neighboring areas (p. 384). It is also a well-established fact that Weber's fraction, $\Delta I/I$, decreases markedly as illumination increases (p. 224). Thus *O* is better able to discriminate the slight differences in brightness of neighboring retinal areas as illumination increases. The fraction $\Delta I/I$ in the brightness discrimination experiment is about 1 or 2 percent at high levels of illumination; Hecht & Mintz calculated that a $\Delta I/I$ of 5 percent would be necessary to explain their acuity for a minimum visible thin wire, so that correspondence is very good. (See Bartley, 1951; Senders, 1948.)

All these factors may play a part in determining visual acuity. The problem is to determine the relative importance of each factor. With no final answer yet in sight, there is an increasing tendency to stress the relationship between acuity and brightness discrimination. This relationship helps us to understand the reappearance of two old friends in the acuity data. One of them is the rod-cone break that is clear in Figure 13-14. The construction lines suggest that the whole curve is the sum of two separate ones, rods and cones, as we have seen in so many other curves. The other old friend in the Bunsen-Roscoe law. Graham & Cook (1937) did an I × T *vs.* T study using a different degree of acuity as the parameter for each of several curves, which are practically identical with those of Figure 13-11 (p. 379). These results show that any specific level of acuity will be maintained by a constant I × T product up to the critical duration, beyond which I is the only factor.

Still another "old friend" is adaptation. If a test field of very low intensity is presented while the retina is adapted to a high intensity, visual acuity will be zero, since nothing can be seen. The effective brightness of a surface depends on the momentary adaptation level as well as on the physical illumination (pp. 367–370). In an experiment of Craik (1939) the eye was first adapted to a plain field under a certain illumination; a test field was then instantly presented and *O* reported whether he saw the two parallel black lines or only one line. In general the acuity was best when the eye was adapted approximately to the level of the test field. As you might expect, however, a dark-adapted eye could not do so well with a dim as with a well-illuminated test field—a matter of cone vision *versus* rod vision. A similar factor is the brightness of the field around or near the test object; the blinding effect of glare is well known—too well known in night driving.

Foveal and peripheral visual acuity. There are several good reasons why visual acuity is so much better in the fovea than it is in the outer portions of the visual field (Fig. 13-15). In the first place, the cones are slender and closely packed in the fovea. Further, the foveal

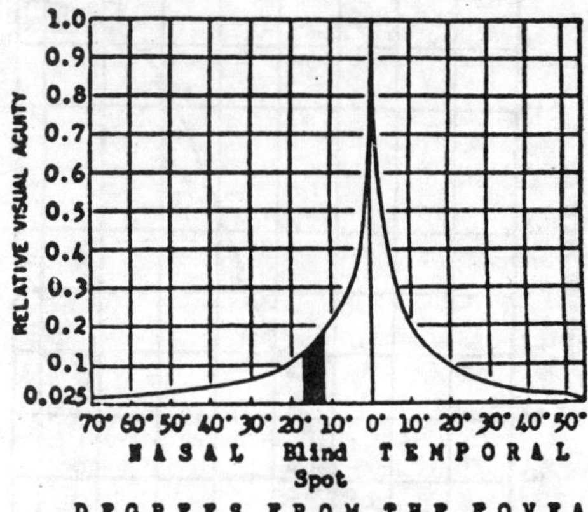

FIG. 13-15. (From Chapanis, 1949c, after Wertheim, 1894.) Visual acuity at different retinal positions. Note that the ordinate is in terms of relative visual acuity, rather than in absolute units, so that all values are expressed as percentages of foveal acuity. The region where the optic nerve leaves the eye has no receptors, and is shown by the black area labeled "blind spot."

cones have direct lines to the higher centers, whereas the peripheral receptor cells are tied together in groups so that a single nerve fiber has a large receptive field. The central nervous system cannot discriminate one point from another within this receptive field, since they all set up impulses in the same nerve fiber. Finally, the actual image at the rod-and-cone layer is sharper in the fovea than in the periphery. The center of an optical system always works best, and the peripheral image is still further blurred by the neural layers that cover the rods and cones everywhere but the fovea. There are some nice problems involved in calculating the specific contribution of each of these factors to the acuity curve of Figure 13-15, but a mere enumeration of the factors makes it clear why we do not see well out of the corner of our eye.

Since acuity is very important in practical problems, there has been much research on the influence of such stimulus factors as size and form of letters and numerals, color of illumination, brightness of surrounding field, as well as *O*-factors like fatigue and oxygen deficiency. Many of these and other practical aspects of vision are treated in some detail by Chapanis (1949c) in the first chapter of *Human factors in undersea warfare*.

We have come a long way from the simple classical theory which accepted visual acuity as a measure of the fineness of the retinal mosaic. We now know that visual acuity represents a dynamic interaction of many factors, ranging from purely physical spread of light, through interaction at retinal and higher levels, and finally involving the higher neural processes that are characteristic of perception.

COLOR VISION

Now that we have the facts of intensity and brightness cleared up, we can tackle the knotty problem of color vision. The human species, in common with day-flying birds and some higher mammals, has the ability to make discriminations on the basis of wavelength as well as intensity of light. Putting it in terms of $R = f(S, O)$, we say that man can respond with words like red, green, or blue as a function of different wavelengths of the stimulus. By variation of the stimulus, one can study the systematic changes in response words evoked; the results may be represented schematically in a three-dimensional spindle (Fig. 13-16) on which all colors may be represented.

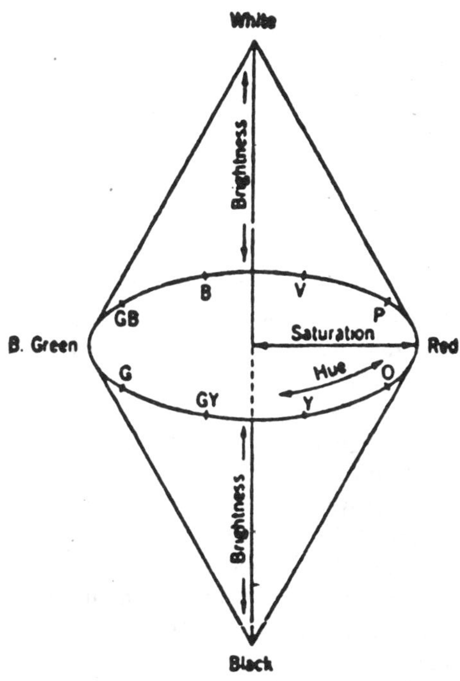

Fig. 13-16. (Munn, 1951.) A schematic representation of the relationships or dimensions of color. See text.

The first of these dimensions, *hue*, is the familiar one found in the spectral series (red, orange, yellow, green, blue, violet). It is represented in the figure by the horizontal circle, for the spectrum seems to bend back on itself, with red resembling violet (a nonspectral hue, purple, has been added to complete the circle). This circle must be considered as the perimeter of a circular surface, with gray at the center, to permit us to represent desaturated colors, like bluish gray, or brown; the radial dimension is *saturation*. But we know that colors may also vary in a third dimension, *brightness;* this has been added as a vertical dimension, running from black to white. There results the spindle or double cone shown in Figure 13-16; it tapers at the black and white ends to show that very light or dark colors are desaturated.

Even the schematic diagram in Figure 13-16 is very useful in understanding the facts of color vision, for it represents many different relationships and laws quite well. It can be made to give more accurate predictions by certain changes. Thus, the circle may be tipped, with yellow higher than blue, to represent the fact that a well-saturated yellow is very much brighter than a well-saturated blue. Further, the circle may be made eccentric and irregular, since some hues are relatively unsaturated at best. Perhaps the most accurate of these figures has been designed by Munsell (1915), who has developed a system of color nomenclature that goes with it. In his figure the spindle is transformed into quite a complicated shape.

Other ways of representing colors have been based on the laws of color mixture (see below). They represent the fact that three primaries, as red, green and blue, can be mixed to give almost any color. But some of the colors produced by such mixtures are quite unsaturated; a line run from blue to green in Figure 13-16 would pass well in from the edge of the circle, indicating a grayish blue-green mixture, instead of a saturated hue. In order to describe the whole color circle in terms of three primaries, one must use imaginary "supersaturated" red, green, and blue, serving as corners of a triangle that is large enough to include the whole color circle. This general method is widely used in specifying colors for practical purposes. Figure 13-20 (p. 394) is an early version of this triangle (see Judd, 1951).

Theories of color vision. Before we undertake the detailed and numerous experiments that have been done in this field, let us try to imagine what kind of a mechanism we need to discriminate wavelength. We get an excellent suggestion from the experiments on visibility curves (p. 367). Figure 13-3 is replotted with linear coordinates as Figure 13-17,

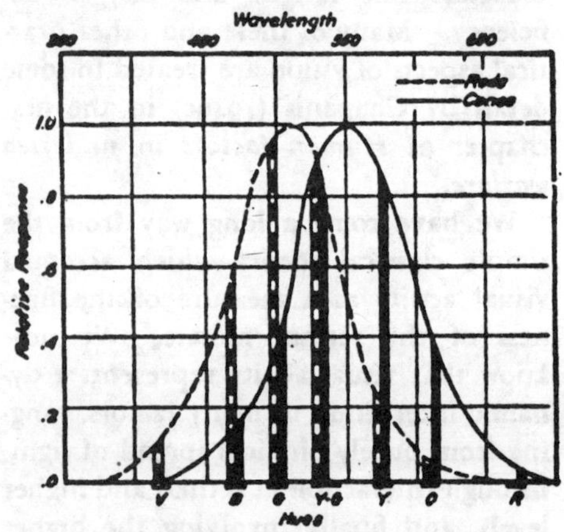

Fig. 13-17. How a two-element visual system would discriminate certain colors. It is assumed that the two types of elements have different sensitivity curves, like the rods and cones of Figure 13-3. The extent to which each process would be stimulated by various hues is shown by the vertical bars; solid bars for "cones," and broken ones for "rods." Note that yellow-green stimulates them equally, just as would white light.

with a few construction lines added to simplify matters. Suppose a hypothetical animal had only one type of rods and one type of cones, each with a characteristic sensitivity curve as shown. Such an animal might do a fair job at discriminating colors. Reds and violets would be separated easily, for one would stimulate only cones, and the other only rods. Oranges and yellows would be characterized by relatively greater stimulation of the cones, and blue would be largely effective on rods. But consider yellow-green) which would stimulate rods and cones equally; this could not be discriminated from white light, which would also stimulate the two types of receptors equally. In other words, the animal would be green-blind. Furthermore, if this hypothetical animal could arrange colors on the color circle of Figure 13-16, he would be satisfied with a straight line stretching from red to violet, which would be very different hues to him. It is clear a third type of receptor is necessary to give normal color vision. It should have its peak in the yellow-green region.

At this point we had better drop our hypothetical animal, lest we seriously suppose that the rods are involved in color vision. But we can keep our idea of several types of receptors, each with its own sensitivity curve. Let them all be cones. The fact that we usually obtain only one sensitivity curve for cones is no objection. As a matter of fact, very careful measurements of the cone sensitivity curve show well-defined humps, suggesting that the familiar curve is simply a smoothed summation of three separate curves (Hsia & Graham, 1951). Analysis of such complex curves into their components is not too safe a task; we must depend on many converging lines of evidence for a theory of color vision. One promising line comes from Granit (1945, 1947) who has been able to pick up electrical potentials from the neural layers that cover the retina. He uses microelectrodes, in an effort to pick up impulses from a single neural unit. Once he has a unit isolated, he can plot a sensitivity curve for it by recording the response to different wavelengths. Working on a number of different species, he finds evidence for as many as four different sensitivity curves, with peaks in the regions of red, green, blue and yellow. If further research with this difficult method substantiates his results, we may end with a four-component theory, instead of the more usual one with three components. This is not a serious objection, for some of the indirect evidence has favored a four-color theory, although three primaries are enough to explain many of the phenomena of color vision. As we examine the evidence, we shall note that the three-component theory proposed by Young and developed by Helmholtz (1856–1866), is probably dominant today. The four-component theory was proposed by Hering (1874), and an interesting combination of both theories was devised by Ladd-Franklin (1929). (See Judd, 1951; Bartley, 1951.)

Color mixing. The dependence of hue on wavelength, as already stated, is very definite. Aside from certain effects of intensity and of peripheral vision, each wavelength gives a specific hue. But the converse of this proposition is not true. Each hue is not bound to a specific wavelength. The same yellow hue which we get from a homogeneous ray of wavelength 580 mμ can be obtained from a mixture of 570 and 590, and from an indefinite number of mixtures centering about 580. Any hue can be obtained from suitably balanced mixtures of wavelengths, and in fact most of the colors we see are produced by mixed lights, since homogeneous rays seldom reach the eye.

The sensation obtained from a mixed light is apt to be less saturated than that from a homogeneous light, but as far as hue is concerned the effect is unitary in both cases. The effect is altogether different from that obtained in the auditory sphere by mixing two wavelengths (or frequencies). Sound *do* and *mi* at once and you do not hear *re;* but superpose red and yellow and you get, not a red-yellow chord, but an intervening hue, orange. Color mixture is not a mixture of sensations, but a mixture of stimuli which gives a unitary sensation. Yellow, though surely a unitary hue, can be obtained by mixing red and green lights, and white can be obtained by mixing yellow and blue.

Mixing pigments. The painter will rebel against the last statement, as he knows from abundant experience that mixing yellow and blue pigments gives green and not white. Yet it is easy to demonstrate that yellow and blue lights thrown together on a screen or directly into the eye, in proper proportions, produce a colorless white and that in other proportions they give either yellow or blue and never green. There is an important physical difference between mixing lights and mixing pigments. Mixing lights is addition, mixing pigments is a double subtraction. The color of a pigment is the light remaining after the pigment has absorbed certain wavelengths. A yellow pigment absorbs certain rays, a blue pigment certain other rays, and the mixture of the two pigments absorbs both sets of rays. Let us take two color filters, one letting the yellow rays pass through, the other the blue rays. If these filters were strictly monochromatic, the yellow one would absorb all the rays except yellow, and the blue one all except blue, and no light whatever could pass through both. If the filters, like most pigments, were not monochromatic, their combination might well transmit a mixture of rays which would be so balanced as to give the sensation of green.

Ways of mixing color stimuli. Mixing pigments will not serve when we wish to *add* one light to another of different wavelength. We may extract two rays from the spectrum and superpose them on a dead white screen or throw them directly upon the same part of the retina. We must be able to regulate the intensity of the two rays, as by use of gray filters or other means.

A good set of color filters of known transmission can be substituted for the parts of the spectrum without loss of precision in most experiments and with great increase of convenience for the experimenter.

For demonstrations, and for some qualitative work, the familiar color wheel is adequate. Two or more interlaced disks of different colors will blend, when rotated above the critical flicker frequency (p. 380), and produce a smooth mixture. The characteristics of the mixture will be intermediate with relation to the colors and brightnesses of the papers that make it up, each color contributing according to the proportion of its disk that is exposed. Perhaps the major difficulty with this method is that the colored papers from which the disks are made are far from homogeneous in their reflectance (p. 363). They transmit broad bands so that the mixtures are quite unsaturated. Thus, the average red and green yield a yellow, as one would predict, but it is such a grayish yellow that most *O*s call it brown or tan. But if one is quite familiar with the relations described by the color spindle, and makes allowance for the low saturation of the papers, he will find that the color wheel obeys the usual laws of color mixture. One apparent exception is that brightnesses of the components add in mixture with lights, whereas the brightness of the color wheel mixture is intermediate between the components. This apparent exception disappears when we realize that the component disks on a wheel are only partially exposed. Thus a blue and yellow, each half exposed, add *half* the brightness of each to yield a mixture that is equal to half the sum of their total brightnesses.

Most quantitative work is done with transmitted light, mixed on a white surface. By such methods it is possible to work out *color equations*. The sensory effect of the mixture is matched with that of the Standard, which may be a homogeneous light, or itself a mixture. Though the interest often lies in hue, the brightness or saturation must also be matched, for it is almost impossible to be sure of an exact equation of hue unless these other characteristics are also equated. The equation should state that the mixture is indistinguishable from the Standard. To secure a perfect match between yellow and a red-green mixture, we must be prepared to reduce the intensity of the yellow and also to lower its saturation by the admixture of white.

Results in color mixing. By mixing red and yellow in different proportions we obtain all the orange hues intermediate between our red and yellow. By mixing red and grass green we get all the hues of orange, yellow and yellowish green. It might seem that we had found a rule, to the effect that mixing any two colors of the spectrum gave the intermediate colors. But when we push the matter a little further by mixing red and a bluish green, we get no intermediate hues. If red predominates in this particular mixture we get only unsaturated shades of red; if the bluish green predominates we get unsaturated shades of that same green; and if the red and the bluish green are rightly balanced we get white or gray. Red and this particular bluish green are said to be complementary. If we advance still further and mix red and blue, in different proportions, we obtain all the hues of purple and violet. In the spectrum, these hues are not intermediate between red and blue, but in the color circle they are intermediate "around the back way."

Experimenting with other pairs of colors we obtain similar results. When two colors differ comparatively little in wavelength, their mixture gives the intermediate hues; when they differ just enough they are complementary; and when they differ by more than this amount they give the purples. The color that two components will give always lies on a line connecting the two components in the color spindle (Fig. 13-16). Its precise position on the line will be determined by the relative proportions of the components. Thus the color spindle summarizes the facts of color mixture in a convenient way.

A systematic search for complementaries shows that individuals differ somewhat (Fig. 13-18). Some of the values are given below:

PAIRS OF COMPLEMENTARY COLORS

(Wavelengths)

Red	660 mμ	*and*	Blue-green	497 mμ
Orange	610	*and*	Green-blue	492
Yellow	585	*and*	Blue	485
Yellow-green	570	*and*	Violet	430

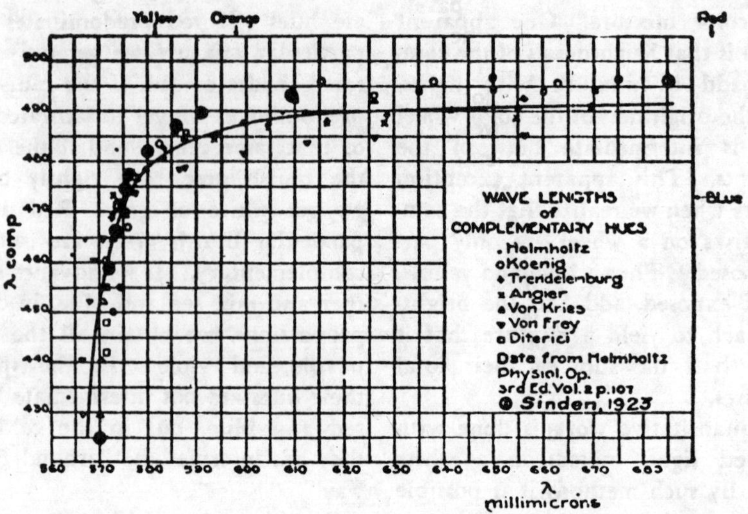

FIG. 13-18. (Priest, 1920, with added data from Sinden, 1923.) Wavelengths of complementary colors. On the abscissa is given the longer, on the ordinate the shorter, of two complementary wavelengths. Thus for a red of 655 mμ the complementary as determined by different observers ranges from 485 to 493; and for a greenish blue of 495 it has ranged from 585 over to 655, i.e. from yellow to red. The most probable paired values as computed by Priest fall on the curve, but the later measurements by Sinden call for lifting the upper arm of the curve somewhat. λ = wavelength.

We notice that the strict greens, lying between yellow-green at 570 and blue-green at 497, have no complementary wavelength. To obtain a colorless mixture with green we have to use *two* other wavelengths, one long and one short. Green is complementary to purple which is a mixture of red and blue.

Obtaining all the hues by mixture of three wavelengths. It is of importance for the theory of the color sense, and for the practice of color printing and color photography, to know how few colors will by various mixtures yield all the hues of the color circle and also white, gray or hueless sensation. From experiments with two colors, already described, we infer that two colors are not enough. We must use at least three, and no two of them can be complementary. For if we selected a pair of complementaries, as yellow and blue, what color should we take for the third? If we took red, mixing it with yellow would give orange, and mixing it with blue would give purple and violet, but we could not get green; and if we chose green instead of red, we could get only the yellow-green-blue series, and not red, purple, or violet. Two complementaries and one other component will give us only half of the color circle. But if we choose red, blue, and a yellowish or straight green of wavelength between 497 and 570, we can obtain all the hues from mixture of these three. The wavelengths need not be exactly specified; some latitude is permitted. Each component is complementary to a mixture of the other two, and therefore some mixture of all three will give white.

The color mixture triangle. Having properly chosen three component wavelengths, we combine them in various proportions to match all the hues in the color circle. Each match shows the proportions of red and green required to match some orange or yellow hue, or the proportions of green and blue re-

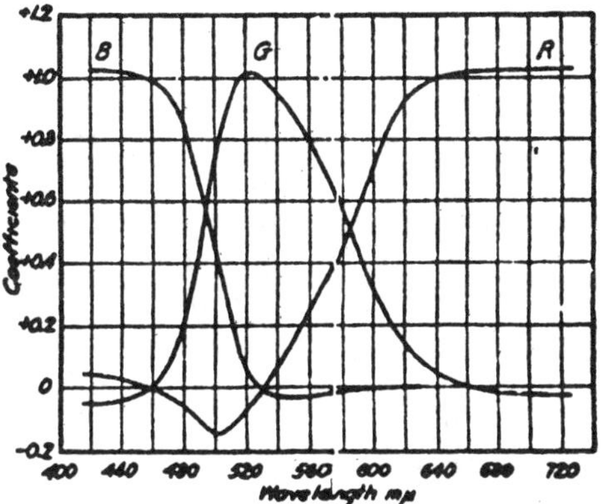

FIG. 13-19. (From Troland, 1930, p. 160; data from Wright.) Proportions of red (650), green (530) and blue (460) required to match each hue of the spectrum. Average results from ten subjects. The ordinate scale of "coefficients" was obtained by determining the amounts of the three components necessary to give white and regarding these amounts as the units for the three respective components. The figure reads that if the three components mixed in the proportion, R: G: B = 1: 1: 1, give white, then, for example, the wavelength of 600 is matched by mixing the same three components in the proportion, 0.74: 0.28: 0, approximately. When one of the component lines goes below zero, the meaning is that the spectral color in question was more saturated than the mixture and had to be whitened by adding to it a little of the complementary color. Thus the hue of wavelength 500 was matched by a mixture of B and G, but some R had to be added to the spectral color to reduce its saturation.

The chromatic power of blue is large in comparison with its low brightness, and if these curves were transformed to read in brightness units the blue curve would shrink almost out of sight.

quired to match a blue-green, or the proportions of red and blue required to match a purple or violet. We also determine the proportions of red, green and blue required to match white. If we had no white and no differences of saturation on our hands we could represent all our results by a triangle with the three components at the corners and the various hues located along the sides at distances indicating the mixtures found necessary. (The distance of yellow from the red and green corners would be inversely proportional to the amounts of red and green required to match the yellow.) To take account of saturations also we locate white inside the triangle, as in the color circle. Much more color knowledge can be incorporated in the triangle, as illustrated in Figure 13-20, and as explained by Troland (1930).

Color blindness. In total color blindness, which apparently is pure rod vision, all wavelengths and all mixtures differ only in brightness and there are no differences of hue. In order to match all parts of the spectrum, only *one* component is necessary and this one may have any wavelength within *O*'s visible spectrum. Totally color-blind individuals are very rare. Relatively common in males is red-green blindness, betrayed by confusion of green with brown, and of pink with pale blue. In the color mixing experiment the red-green blind *O* needs only *two components*, one from the red half of the spectrum and one from the blue half. With these two, mixed in different proportions, he can match every hue and saturation. In color mixing, the red-green blind eye is dichromatic, as the normal eye is trichromatic.

The Young-Helmholtz theory of color vision, i.e., of cone vision, starts from the fact that three components are sufficient to yield all the colors including white. It assumes separate receptors for three primary color responses, red, green, and blue or violet. It supposes dichromatic vision to lack one of these three primary

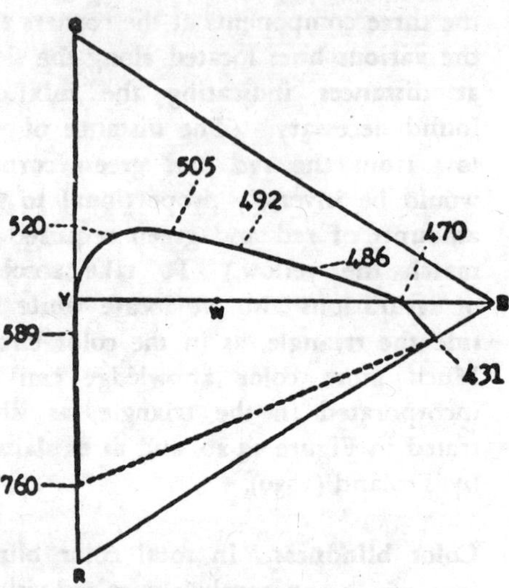

FIG. 13·20. (After König & Dieterici, 1892.) The color mixture triangle modified to show the mixtures of an ideally saturated green and blue and of a slightly purplish red. The colors of the spectrum are arranged in order on the heavy solid line, and the purples along the heavy dotted line. Inside the heavy line are located colors less saturated, and outside are colors more saturated than those of the spectrum. A line drawn from any point on the spectrum to the point W (white) contains tints all of which have the same hue. Continuing this same line through W we have the tints of the complementary color.

Every point in the triangle stands for a color of a certain hue and saturation, brightness being disregarded. The straight line connecting any two points contains all the colors obtained by mixing those two particular colors in all proportions. Take two points on the spectrum line, as the sodium yellow, 589, and blue-green, 492; draw a straight line between them, take the middle point of this line, representing equal amounts of the two mixed colors, and draw a line from W through this point to the spectrum line to discover the hue of the mixture. (See p. 395.)

responses, usually the red or the green. Red-green blindness should therefore have two forms, red-blindness and green-blindness. This expectation is realized in color mixing experiments, especially in matching spectral yellow with a red-green mixture, since some color-blind individuals, called *protanopes*, require an undue amount of red—i.e., are relatively insensitive to the red rays—while others, the *deuteranopes*, are relatively insensitive to green. The brightness curve of the spectrum (Fig. 13·17) is about the same for normals and deuteranopes, while for the protanopes the red is less bright than normal. Some individuals possessing trichromatic vision agree with the protanopes in finding the red end of the spectrum lacking in brilliance, and there are all gradations between normal and protanope in this respect (Tufts, 1907; Kohlrausch, 1931). Probably the protanope combines two defects of color vision, one consisting in low sensitivity to red and the other consisting in the reduction of trichromatic to dichromatic vision. This interpretation of protanopia makes it possible to do justice to a fact which is inconsistent with the Young-Helmholtz theory—the fact that dichromatic vision, so far as direct testimony goes, is yellow-blue vision. A few individuals have been tested who proved to be red-green blind in one eye only and able, therefore, to make a direct comparison of the color sensations of the dichromatic and the trichromatic eye. In dichromatic vision, according to their reports, the red-orange-yellow-green half of the spectrum is reduced neither to shades of red nor to shades of green—as the Young-Helmholtz theory demands—but to shades of yellow. This description of dichromatism is confirmed by the normal eye in indirect vision. A red or green stimulus, on being displaced gradually from the fovea toward the periphery, loses its red or green hue and merges into a dull yellow before finally becoming colorless near the extreme periphery. At a certain distance from the fovea yellow and blue retain their hues, while both red and grass green appear a dull yellow.

Figure 13-20 is a modified form of the color circle, explained on page 387. It illustrates several possible ways in which normal vision could be reduced to dichromatism. If the eye were green-blind, it would give sensations lying along the R-B line only; if it were red-blind, along the G-B line only; and if it were blue-blind, along the R-G line only. The color equations obtained from protanopes and deuteranopes correspond to those required by the diagram for red-blindness and green-blindness respectively. Anything corresponding to blue-blindness is excessively rare. Thus, the triangle affords a picture of the Young-Helmholtz theory of color vision. But another form of dichromatism conforms better with the facts of peripheral color vision and with the testimony of individuals color-blind in one eye only. According to this evidence, the reduced color series extends not from red to blue, nor from green to blue, but from yellow to blue. The Ladd-Franklin theory does justice to these facts by regarding dichromatism as always yellow-blue vision and as due not to the absence of either the red or the green receptor mechanism but to the coalescence of these two systems into a yellow-receiving system (or to the non-differentiation of the red and green out of the more primitive yellow). On this theory the triangle is reduced to the line Y-B in dichromatic vision.

Detection of color blindness. Testing for red-green blindness is more difficult than one might think. People who have been color-blind all their lives have learned the socially approved color names for many objects. They know that grass is green, though without understanding "why people should call that particular shade of yellow by a special name." The problem is further complicated by the existence of people who are color-weak, as noted above. They are called *anomalous trichromats* and subclassified as *protanomalous*, etc., according to the color that is weak. At present the best tests for color-deficient individuals are the *pseudo-isochromatic charts* such as those devised by Ishahara (1920). An example is given by Munn (1946). Each chart presents an irregular mosaic of dots differing in brightness and also in certain colors that are confused by a particular type of deficiency. Some of the dots, for example, make up a figure 3 in mixed shades of red which stands out clearly to a normal *O*, but not to the color-deficient *O* who will see instead a figure 7 composed of red and green dots all of the same brightness. Color dominates the configuration for one *O*, but brightness for the other. With specific practice a color-deficient person can learn to "pass" one set of charts, but he will still fail in a new set (Chapanis, 1949a, b).

Color zones of the retina. One of the most striking facts of normal color vision is that everyone is completely color-blind in the periphery of the retina. A patch of any color looks gray when seen in the margin of the visual field. This is not surprising, for peripheral vision is rod vision. As the patch is brought further in toward the center, it reaches a place where it appears blue or yellow, depending on which of the two is dominant. Thus an orange patch looks yellow, as long as it is in this intermediate "blue-yellow" zone. Only when the patch reaches the inner zone does it appear in normal hue: this inner zone adds the two missing hue and is therefore called the "red-green" zone. The two members of a pair do not give exactly the same boundaries, but perhaps that is because the boundaries vary somewhat with the size and brightness of the test patch.

This pairing of blue with yellow, and of red with green is consistent with the Hering theory of color vision, which has long been the chief competitor of the Helmholtz theory. Hering held that there were three basic substances in the retina, each of which could change in two directions. Anabolism (building up) of the three substances resulted in black, blue, and green respectively, while catabolism (breaking down) gave white, yellow, or red, depending on which substance was involved. The theory fits in rather well with the color zones, and with some other phenomena, but the idea of stimulus-produced anabolism no longer meets with much favor.

Ladd-Franklin's theory also fits the facts of color zones well. The outer color-blind area has only the primitive and undifferentiated light sense of the rods. In the intermediate zone the primitive photosensitive substance has split into two, a "yellow" and a "blue" one. In the inner zone the "yellow" substance again splits into two, one of which is red-sensitive, and the other green-sensitive. In color mixture the red and green substances combine in their action to give the same result as their yellow prototype. This theory combines some of the advantages of both three-color and four-color theories, permitting us to eat our cake and have it, too. It probably deserves more attention than it has received, for it has been somewhat overshadowed by the greater prestige of the Young-Helmholtz theory. Perhaps work like that of Granit (p. 389) wil lend it some support. But at present no simple theory of color vision seems adequate to handle all the facts.

Without delving further into this interesting field here, we shall refer to several books devoted to color vision, notably Parsons (1924), Ladd-Franklin (1929), and, more recently, Wilmer (1946), Wright (1947) and Evans (1948).

Afterimages. If *O* fixates a patch of color for perhaps 30 seconds, he brings about changes in his retina that persist for some time. The original color will last for a brief time after the stimulus is removed, for there is some lag in the retina. This is the first of the positive afterimages, called positive because it is similar in hue and brightness to the original. Usually it gives way very promptly to the negative afterimage, which is opposite in brightness and complementary in hue to the original. It wells up in a few seconds, and subsides over a somewhat longer period. Blinking or change of illumination may bring it back, or may set up another positive afterimage. Prolonged exposure to a strong light will bring on a whole train of afterimages, including a surprising number of hues (Berry, 1927). This experiment is dangerous, for it may cause damage to the fovea.

Perhaps the simplest explanation of the negative afterimage follows the Helmholtz theory. It holds that the three receptive elements or processes are fatigued or adapted in the exact proportion that they are stimulated by the original patch. When this stimulation is discontinued and white light is substituted, these three processes respond only to the extent that they are *not* fatigued, which means that we shall see the complement of the original color. The explanation is probably too simple, and the experimental facts are more complicated than we have indicated above. We shall refer to the first edition of this text for fuller discussion, since afterimages have been mostly neglected by recent psychological theory and investigation. The same back-reference and comment apply to the topic of *simultaneous contrast.*

Simultaneous contrast. The negative afterimage is sometimes called *successive contrast;* there is also a simultaneous variety. This no longer receives as much attention as it once did, either. If you place a square of gray paper on a red surface, the square will take on a strong tinge of the complementary hue—in this case bluish-green. The contrast is most marked around the edges of the square. Part of this is due to small eye movements, which make the negative afterimage of the red background overlap the gray square. But that is not the whole story. There are a good many factors involved in this seemingly simple experiment; so perhaps we had better leave it until we have more background (see p. 449).

BINOCULAR VISION

The fact that human beings have two eyes, directed forward and with overlapping fields of view, is of special importance in perceiving the three-dimensional characteristics of things in the world and will loom large in our later chapter on visual space. Apart from space perception, the interrelations of the two eyes raise a number of dynamic problems indicated by the phrases, binocular rivalry, fusion, summation.

Binocular vision is not merely the normal condition, it is practically unescapable. Closing one eye does not put that eye out of commission; it simply gives it a dark field to combine or compete with the bright field of the open eye. We can secure monocular vision of an object, monocular reception of a particular stimulus, but we cannot secure completely monocular vision. If you close the right eye, your field of view includes the objects visible to the left eye, around to the nose, and beyond that, on the right, a dark field around to the normal limit of the right eye's field.

Corresponding points of the two retinas. With both eyes open and directed upon the same small object, that object is seen single in spite of the two optical images, one on each fovea. The foveas are said to be corresponding points (better, spots) because of this single vision. Any point on one retina corresponds to a point on the other if light striking the two seems to come from the same object or at least from the same direction. Though corresponding points are thus defined primarily in functional terms, experiment shows them to correspond geometrically as well since they are nearly identical in their distance and direction from their respective foveas. (See Carr, 1935, for further elucidation.) When the light from an object falls on noncorresponding parts of the two retinas, the object is seen double, or can be seen double after practice. Ordinarily, we scarcely notice the double images which are constantly present in the binocular field.

When, as often happens, the light from an object is screened from one eye by some intervening object, we do not ordinarily notice any difference between the monocular and binocular views, nor can we tell which eye is seeing the object; but perhaps we could tell with practice. In an experiment by Thelin & Altman (1929) a small circle of light, 11 feet distant in a dark room, was screened by shutters from one eye. *O* judged which eye was stimulated and was informed of his errors. In the course of 400 trials, nearly every *O* showed improvement, except indeed for those accustomed to monocular work with the microscope, who were practically perfect from the start of the experiment.

In a type of experiment which might be called *dichopic* (by analogy with the dichotic and dichorhinic experiments in hearing and smell) discrepant stimulation is applied to corresponding parts of the two retinas. What response will the brain make to such a conflict of cues? It might disregard one retina and respond only to the other, or it might respond to the combination in several ways: by fusion of the monocular fields, by seeing one through the other, or, where possible, by getting a depth effect.

To effect dichopic stimulation, the simplest procedure is simply to close one eye; the result for most of the time is complete unawareness of the dark monocular field. A small mirror held close to one eye at a suitable angle gives a reflected field overlying the directly seen field of the other eye. The stereoscope (p. 467) is a very convenient means of presenting radically different colors or figures to corresponding areas of the two eyes.

Binocular Summation. First let us consider a simple situation. Pirenne (1943) arranged a small patch of light so that it would fall on corresponding areas near the periphery of both eyes. Thresholds could be taken binocularly, or monocularly with either eye. He obtained the three curves shown in Figure 13-21. The binocular threshold was lower than that of either eye. This looks like summation, but it can be

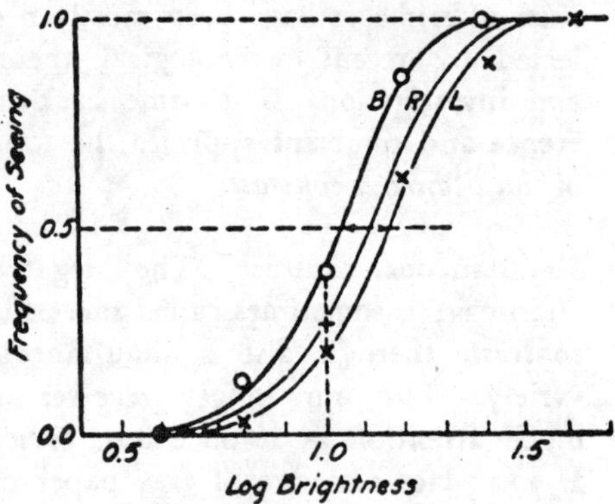

FIG. 13-21. (Pirenne, 1943.) Binocular and monocular sensitivity curves of corresponding areas in the peripheral retinas. The binocular curve was computed from the monocular ones from the formula $q_B = q_L \times q_R$, where q is the probability of not seeing $(1 - p)$.

shown to be a simple statistical matter (cf. p. 376). Erect a line at some log brightness value, as 1.0. It shows a frequency of seeing the patch as 20 percent for the left eye and 26 percent for the right eye. Therefore the probabilities that it will *not* be seen by right and left eye are .80 and .74, respectively. Now let us assume that the two eyes are completely independent, and merely "report" to higher centers. We can determine the probability that neither eye will see the flash by multiplying together the individual probabilities of not seeing it; $.80 \times .74 = .59$. That leaves a combined probability of seeing (right, left, or both eyes) of .41, which is almost identical with the actual binocular probability of .38 as obtained in the experiment. Similar calculations can be made at other points on the curve; as a matter of fact, Pirenne calculated the binocular curve from the two monocular ones and found that it gave a good fit for the binocular data. This means that the eyes acted independently as if they belonged to two different *Os*, at least in this experiment.

Unfortunately, it does not always work out this way. Even with simple flashes some *Os* seem to give binocular data that are identical with those of the better eye (Graham, 1930). If there is a marked difference in the sensitivity of the two eyes, the poorer one will contribute little to the probability of binocular seeing. This can be shown by substituting disparate values, as 10 percent and 90 percent, for the figures (20 percent and 26 percent) we used in our previous example.

Although the Pirenne type of analysis is a promising one, it does not tell the entire story. The two eyes do not always summate; on the contrary, in normal seeing the two fields are combined in a complex way, as we saw at the beginning of this section. For example, there is some evidence that the dominant eye suppresses the nondominant eye when the visual field has five dots, rather than only one (Casperson & Schlosberg, 1950). When we get to the level of perception of everyday objects, we have to describe the interaction of the two eyes at a grosser level; we shall cover some of the major phenomena in the following sections.

Binocular rivalry. Radically different colors or figures presented simultaneously to corresponding areas of the two eyes are not usually combined. At first only one is seen, the other being entirely invisible, but sooner or later a shift occurs, what was invisible coming into view and what was visible disappearing. The reverse shift follows and the alternation becomes more rapid as the double exposure continues.

Using a prism stereoscope, Breese (1899, 1909) presented a red square to one eye and a green square to the corresponding area of the other eye. To increase the discrepancy he ruled parallel oblique lines on each square but in different directions on the two squares. By use of electric keys and markers, *O* recorded on a kymograph the time during which each field was seen.

Since the two colors were seen alternately, we can speak of a whole cycle as consisting of two phases, a right-eye phase and a left-eye phase, or a red and a green phase. The kymograph record provided an answer to two main questions, concerning the duration of the cycle and concerning the relative duration of the two phases; i.e., concerning the *rate* of rivalry and concerning conditions of *prevalence* or advantage.

Rate of alternation. When parallel changes were made in the two monocular stimulus fields, the following factors were found to change the rate:

1. Light intensity. With low illumination the cycle duration averaged 8.5 sec; with increased illumination this decreased to as little as 2.5 sec. The intense field gave the rapid alternation.

2. Area of field. The larger the field the more rapid the alternation.

3. Distinctness of lines. When the stereoscope slide was moved out of focus, blurring the lines, the alternation was slower.

4. Central vision gave more rapid alternation than peripheral vision. Increasing the distance of the stimulus fields from the fovea increased the cycle duration, which averaged:

In central vision	4.9 sec
3.6° to right or left	9.1
3.6° up or down	11.1
7.2° to right or left	10.8
7.2° up or down	11.8

Evidently conditions which make for efficient vision favor rapid alternation (cf. flicker, pp. 381, 382).

Prevalence. In this part of Breese's experiment the two eyes were treated differently in some respect, and the question was, which stimulus field would be seen a larger fraction of the time—which phase of the cycle would be longer. The following factors were effective.

1. Light intensity. The brighter stimulus field was visible 60 percent of the time when the intensity ratio was 4 to 1. When the intensity difference is very great—as when both eyes are closed, one being also covered by the hand while a bright light is brought close to the other—the dark field is invisible most of the time.

2. Presence of figures. A field containing lines prevails over a plain field as much as 70 percent of the time. A single letter written on one field remains visible almost the whole time, even while the rest of its field is invisible; around the letter a halo of its own background is usually seen.

3. Movement. When both fields contain figures and the figure on one is made to move, it remains in sight more than half the time.

4. Attention. As between two absolutely plain fields, voluntary effort has no effect, but if there is anything to examine in either field, that field can be held more than half the time. When both fields offer a multitude of details, attention to either one will hold it for most of the time.

As to the cause of rivalry, one ready suggestion would attribute it to eye movements; but Peckham (1936) could find no better than chance coincidence of eye movements and rivalry changes. Any adequate explanation would have to cover three points: (a) why response is made to only one at a time of the stimulus fields, (b) why the stronger, clearer or more interesting field has the advantage, and (c) why the advantage shifts. Fatigue of the momentarily active response mechanism seems a likely explanation of the third point. The first point is quite in line with the selective response to conflicting stimuli, as observed in reflex action (Sherrington, 1906). As to the second point, evidently selection depends not only on stimulus characteristics but also on the available responses (cf. pp. 76–81).

Binocular fusion. Rivalry amounts to a cortical response to one or the other of the competing fields, and to only one at a time. Binocular fusion amounts to a unitary cortical response to the combination of the two fields. Under what conditions does fusion occur? We have no adequate answer. It occurs, or so we believe, when the two fields are almost alike in color, brightness, and pattern. Even here rivalry can be observed under experimental conditions (stereoscope) and may be more common than we suppose. When the fields differ very much, rivalry is the rule and fusion the exception. But we may get combination of two fields that are physically quite different if their significance is mutually consistent. With a stereoscope it is possible to combine one field containing an arrow with the other containing a bow, if both objects are appropriately placed in their respective fields. Here the bow and arrow are not presented to corresponding areas of the two retinas and are not in direct competition. Each figure is competing with a plain background in the other eye and prevails over that background. Rivalry occurs between corresponding areas of the two retinas, not between the entire retinas.

Binocular color mixture. If a red glass is held before one eye and a green glass before the other—or if by aid of a stereoscope or just by suitable convergence of the eyes red and green are presented in corresponding areas of the two fields—the usual result is rivalry; but some *Os* get fusion which in this case gives a yellow mixture of the red and the green. Many competent observers have found it impossible to obtain this fusion, while others have secured it without difficulty.

In a stereoscope experiment of Johannsen (1930) approximately monochromatic colors were presented by use of Wratten filters. With four *Os* there was never any fusion of the following pairs, one color to each eye: yellow and blue, red and blue, red and blue-green; while fusion occurred practically always with yellow and yellow-green, with blue and blue-green, and with yellow-green and blue-green, i.e., with colors lying close together in the spectrum. Fusion was favored by equal intensities of the two colors, and also by low intensity.

Hecht, however (1928), had good success in obtaining binocular mixture of quite diverse colors of high intensity, by use of the following setup. *O* faces a square of white cardboard, 1 meter in front of him, from which projects a 250-watt bulb. The bulb strongly illuminates the cardboard and almost forces *O*'s eyes to converge on the glowing filament. He looks at the lamp through a black-inside box which carries a red Wratten filter before one eye, and a green one before the other eye. He thus gets a red square before one eye, a green one before the other eye, the two squares partially overlapping in the binocular field. Fusion instantly occurs in the overlapping part, in most *Os*, who report seeing red and green at the sides and yellow in the middle. If the filters are yellow and blue, they report white in the middle.

This experiment is important for color theory. If a red in one eye and a green in the other yield yellow, the obvious locus of the mixing is in one of the neural centers, rather than in the retina. Hence, there is no need for a "yellow" process in the eye, and we can get along with the Helmholtz three-color theory. Of course, the argument hinges on whether or not there was any yellow in the original red and green. Hecht's filters both passed a bit of yellow light which might have stimulated a "yellow" process in both eyes, leaving the brain only the job of getting rid of red and green by cancellation. Prentice (1948) repeated the experiment with narrow-band ("interference") red and green filters, and got the same result, a good binocular yellow. But Hurvich and Jameson (1951) pointed out that even Prentice's filters were both a bit toward the yellow, rather than at optimal red and green, respectively. When these workers picked out what they judged to be good red and green, and mixed them binocularly, they got white, rather than yellow.

In short, the binocular color mixture experiments have so far failed to prove or disprove either a three- or four-color theory. But they do show that some color mixing takes place in the brain, rather than in the retina. This result is in line with the current trend to push analysis and synthesis back from the receptor to higher centers (p. 349). There may be three, four, or more color-sensitive processes in the retina, each of which sends "signals" to the brain, where they are integrated into the appropriate response.

Much remains to be said about vision, but it belongs under the head of perception rather than with the sensory problems considered in the present chapter.

14

THE PERCEPTION OF FORM

Up to this point we have had little to say about spatial relations in the visual field, of distances, directions, sizes, and shapes. In ordinary observation these characteristics of an object appear to be just as directly *seen* as its color and brightness. Yet they are not so directly related to the mass of variegated stimuli received by the retina. Something more than reception of the stimuli must occur before certain parts of the mass separate out from the rest and appear as a definite shape such as a straight line, an angle, a square, or a circle. So it is customary to speak of Perception rather than sensation of shape. Perception is not meant to describe a known process. It identifies a result achieved by the organism, not the process of reaching the result. Those stock questions—(1) whether the elements of a figure get together and build up the whole, or whether the whole figure emerges and organizes the available elements; and (2) whether the perception of form is a native ability or acquired by learning—are perhaps not well framed for the experimenter's purposes. At least, there is little experimental evidence on these broad questions. What we shall find instead, as we survey several types of experiments, consists of detailed studies in the dynamics of form perception, attempts to isolate specific factors contributory to the perceptual process. The forms used in these experiments are mostly two-dimensional and presented in a frontal-parallel plane as is most convenient for accurate observation. Depth effects will come to light in Chapter 16.

FIGURE AND GROUND

In his stimulating book, *The organization of behavior,* Hebb (1949) makes the point that the *primitive unity* of a figure is its simplest aspect. By this he means that a bounded area, the figure, will be seen as a unit, standing out from the background, even before the figure is recognized as a particular figure—i.e., before it has *identity.* Senden (1932) reported that patients who had congenital cataracts removed, thus seeing for the first time when they were adults, saw figures from the start long before they could discriminate between different figures, as a triangle and a square. Hebb finds further evidence for the distinction between primitive unity and identity in the studies on figural discrimination in the rat (pp. 591 ff.).

The distinction that Hebb draws is very close to one that was first brought out clearly by Rubin (1915, 1921), though of course figure and ground are familiar concepts in the graphic arts.

Rubin found it possible to see any well-marked part of a visual field as the figure, leaving the rest as the ground. If the total field consists of a black portion and a white portion meeting in a contour, either the black or the white portion can be seen as figure, the other being the ground. If either the black or the white portion is entirely enclosed by the other the enclosed portion is more easily seen as the figure, but with practice the enclosing portion can be so seen. If the contour separating the two portions is approximately vertical without enclosing either part of the field, figure and ground are easily reversed. When the reversal occurs, the change of appearance is surprising because the shape of the two parts of the field is very different—which is rather curious since these shapes depend on the common contour separating the two parts (Figs. 14-1, 14-2).

The phenomenal differences between figure and ground are classified by Rubin as follows: (1) the figure has form, while the ground is relatively formless, or if the ground has form it

FIG. 14-1. (Rubin, 1921.) Type of field presented with instructions calling sometimes for taking the enclosed portion as figure, and sometimes for taking the enclosing portion as figure.

is due to some other figuration upon it and not to the contour separating it from the figure; (2) the ground seems to extend continuously behind the figure and not to be interrupted by the figure; (3) thus the figure has some of the character of a *thing*, whereas the ground appears like unformed *material;* (4) the figure tends to appear in front, the ground behind; (5) the figure is more impressive, better remembered, and more apt to suggest meaning.

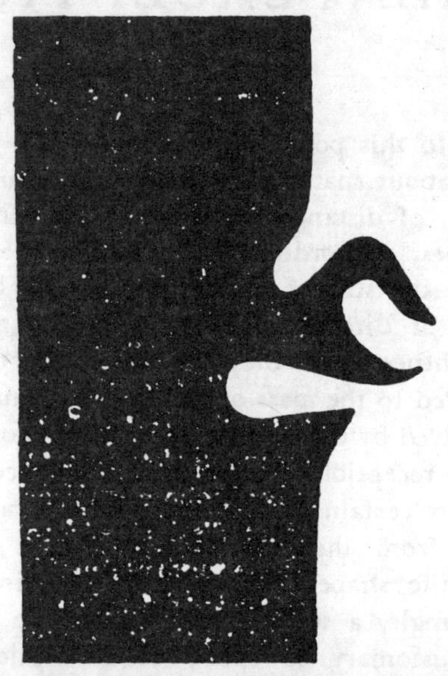

FIG. 14-2. (Rubin, 1921.) Figure and ground. Here the two fields have about an equal chance of being the figure, though the white field, being the same in color as the page, is more likely to be seen as ground.

We might suspect that the distinction of figure and ground was simply the old distinction between the field of attention and the field of inattention. This criticism would imply that it is impossible to attend to the ground. Granted that the figure is more apt to attract attention, it is possible to attend to the ground as ground. If we define attention in terms of clearness, we cannot say that the ground is simply less clear than the figure, for ground often has the positive property of seeming to extend behind the figure.

Rubin's experiments led to two important discoveries which may be called

(1) figural persistence and (2) nonrecognition of the field when reversal of figure and ground has occurred.

Figural persistence. Rubin prepared nonsense figures by cutting irregular portions out of cards and placing the cards before a lantern with green glass interposed so that on the screen there appeared an irregular green area surrounded by black. With a 4-second exposure for each single figure, he presented a series of 9 figures, four times over, with instructions to see the enclosed green area as the figure, the black

Fig. 14·3. Reversible contour.

as ground. This was followed by a series of 9 similar figures with instructions to see the enclosing black area as the figure. The experimenter now shuffled these 18 figures with 9 new ones and presented them in mixed order, after an interval of 30–45 minutes, with instructions to remain passive as regards which part should be seen as figure, but to report in each case whether the figure was the enclosed or the enclosing portion and whether the field was recognized as one previously shown.

The results revealed a moderate tendency to see the same figure on the second exposure as in the original experience. As the subject had divided the field the first time into figure and ground, so he was likely to do the second time, even when remaining passive; 64 percent of the figures were seen in the same way as before, 33½ percent were seen with reversed figure and ground, and 2½ percent were seen in both ways. There was thus a tendency to carry over the same figure-ground organization of a given field from one exposure to another.

Nonrecognition of reversed fields. Rubin's experiment on recognition of fields with reversed figure and ground was conducted in the same general manner as just described. First *O* examined 9 fields under instructions to see the enclosed figure and 9 under instructions to see the enclosing figure. Then these 18 were shuffled with 9 new fields of similar general character and presented in a recognition test with instructions to *look for the enclosed figure,* to report whether he could see it and whether he recognized it. In a parallel experiment the learning task was as before, but the recognition test called for noting the *enclosing* figure. The question was whether the fields seen the second time with reversed figure and ground would be recognized. The answer in general was negative. Combining the results from the two experiments, with two *O*s and a total of 324 fields used, we obtain the following percents recognized:

Figure and ground remaining the same	49
Figure and ground reversed	9
New fields (false recognitions)	6

The percent of reversed fields recognized is scarcely larger than would occur by chance, as indicated by the false recognitions of new figures.

This experiment proves that a field is not recognized if its division into figure and ground is reversed. What is recognized, then, is not the stimulus aggregate but the perceptual response which we call a figure. Reference may be made to pages 723 and 775 for other experiments on recognition of figures and to page 773 for the more difficult task of reproducing figures from memory.

The learning of figures. Atkinson & Ammons (1952) presented a Rorschach inkblot to *O* and asked him to press a key as soon as he saw a prescribed figure—say a cat's face. *E* recorded the latency of the recognition response—the time between the opening of the shutter and *O*'s pressure on the key. After the first trial he was required to examine a magazine advertisement for a few moments (so as to break up his set for the seen figure). He was given a second trial on the same inkblot, looking again for the cat's face, then another advertisement to examine, and so on for 10 trials. The latencies of his successive recognition responses yielded the typical learning curve shown as a solid line in Figure 14-4.

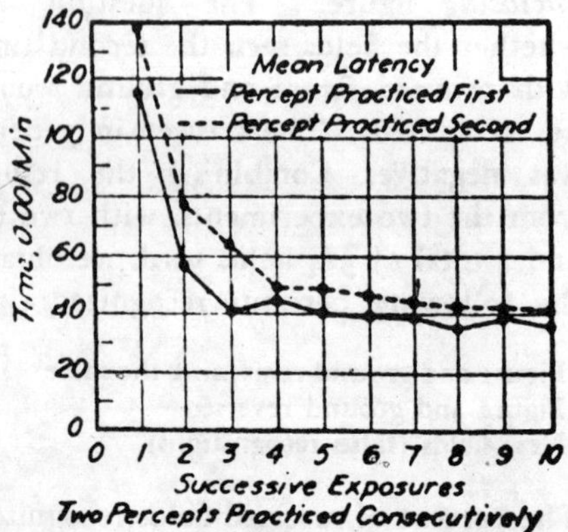

FIG. 14-4. (Atkinson & Ammons, 1952.) Learning curves for the recognition of a prescribed figure in a Rorschach inkblot. The ordinate shows the average recognition time on successive trials. The solid line represents the learning of the first percept, while the broken line shows the acquisition of a new percept of the same inkblot by the same 24 college students.

Atkinson & Ammons went on to demonstrate another typical phenomenon of memory experiments—the interference effect. After a rest *O* had 10 additional trials with the same inkblot, but he was required to find a second figure, such as a motorcycle. The learning curve for this second percept is shown as a broken line in Figure 14-4. The second learning curve is consistently higher than the first; *O* took longer to find the second figure in the same inkblot because of interference from the first figure learned. The difference was not due to the fact that the cat's face was easier to find than the motorcycle, for the experiment was counterbalanced among the 24 *O*s so as to eliminate such effects. The experiment links the Rubin type of perceptual experiment with the more contemporary interest in learning.

Development of a figure-ground experience. The experiments we have just discussed were done under conditions of intensity and duration that permitted an adequate perception to develop. What would happen under less favorable conditions? The extreme case would be a completely homogeneous field. Such a field may be obtained by closing the eyes, or by a combination of screens (Engel, 1930; Metzger, 1930). If time is allowed for residual afterimages to drop out, such a field gives no figure-ground differentiation, unless the level of illumination is high enough to show the texture of the screen. Loss of figure-ground differentiation can also be produced in another way (Pikler, 1928; Galli, 1934). Let the figure be a square of gray paper against a ground of figured wallpaper. With good illumination *O* sees the figure surrounded by the ground. With lower illumination the figure loses its sharpness of outline and only its central part remains definitely perceived. As the illumination is further decreased, the ground overspreads the figure, intermittently at first, and then completely at the lowest illumination. Essentially the same results were obtained by Helson & Fehrer (1932) with self-lighted figures small enough to be within the fovea. They found that light could be perceived before the figure was bright enough to be seen as a definite figure. This is, of course, a reasonable expectation from what we know of the effect of illumination on visual acuity.

Wever (1927) made a very careful study of figure-ground perception with brief tachistoscopic exposures and postexposure fields designed to blot out afterimages. Under the conditions of illumination he used, the shortest exposures gave no figure and ground, but a bare homogeneous appearance. With slightly longer exposures *O* reported smudges or blotches (the actual figure was black on white). When the smudge began to take on a vague shape, *O* was willing to call it figure on ground. This step, or the one just before it, would seem to correspond to Hebb's *primitive unity* (p. 403). With further increases of exposure duration, contour appeared, and the figure stood out clearly differentiated from the ground. All this might happen in exposures as short as 14 ms. When the exposure was increased to several seconds, the figure took on the appearance of some object, as a bird or a helmet, and this appearance was fairly stable, in contrast with the fluctuations of figure and ground. On the whole, the figure-ground experience was decidedly complex.

With a similar tachistoscopic setup and bright postexposure field to extinguish the positive afterimage, Ehrenstein (1930) studied some other determiners of the figure-ground experience. His measure of effectiveness was the exposure time necessary for perception of figure. High illumination, good contrast, meaningful figures, and symmetrical figures gave quick figure-ground differentiation. Ehrenstein denies that figure must always appear in front of ground. For example, in looking through a window screen at an object, the screen is seen as ground, but in front of the figure. The point is that the broad expanses of the field are apt to be seen as ground, while the projecting points are apt to appear as figure. Similarly, the fixated area is apt to be figure, although it is possible to see figure in the periphery (p. 103).

Nonvisual figure and ground. Both figure and ground are characteristically visual phenomena; yet analogies are not wanting in the other modalities. Vernon (1934–1935) shows how the figure-ground conception can be applied in hearing. There is usually a background of relatively uniform sound; standing out from this ground is some shrill or otherwise sharply delimited sound analogous to a figure. In music we should think of the melody as the figure and of the chords and other accompaniment as the ground. Vernon analyzes the characteristics of figure in music as follows: figure is apt to be higher in pitch and louder than the ground and is apt to have a different timbre because played by a different instrument. The figure has more movement and a different rhythm, its crescendos and diminuendos are different from those of the ground. To make the musical figure distinct it is started either before or after the ground; the accompaniment may begin first, and when the hearer is used to that, the melody appears; or the melody may be announced first in isolation and later interwoven with the accompaniment. The figure often contains notes discordant with the accompaniment which are not experienced as discordant but as belonging to the figure.

In the field of bodily movement one can easily think of any phasic movement as figure and of the supporting posture as ground (p. 174).

PERCEPTUAL UNITS

Now we come to the question of how figure is constituted. Are there any laws that tell us why some elements of a visual field form into figure, while other units become part of the ground? Wertheimer (1923) studied this problem by presenting various patterns of dots, and observing which dots grouped themselves into figures most readily. As one might expect, past experience was an important determiner of such grouping, as *O* saw the dots form familiar figures. But there were also some laws that seemed to be intrinsic to the organizing process in that they were not clearly dependent on past experience. In the list that follows, we shall start with the principles that seem to depend most clearly on the objective arrangement of the elements, and work toward those which are

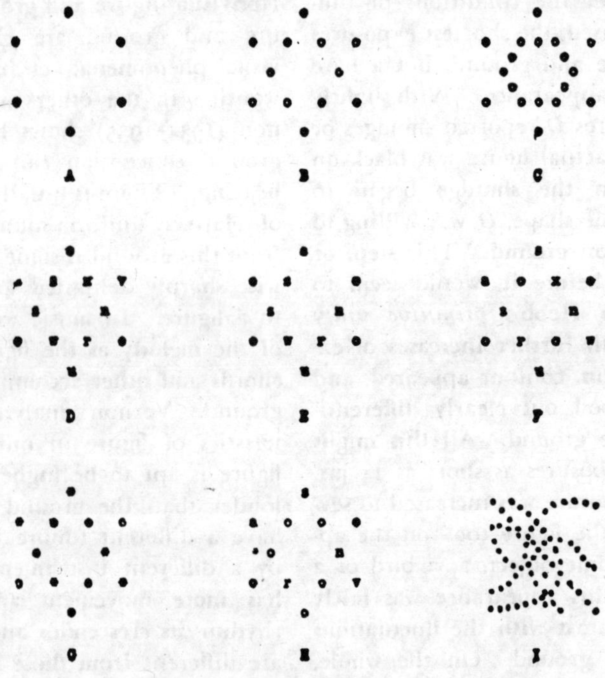

FIG. 14·5. Dot figures illustrating the factors of nearness, sameness, continuation and good figure. The hexagon so clearly visible in A is somewhat obscured in B by the additional dots, but reappears in C as a leftover group when the addition of still more dots in close proximity to each other brings out the interior hexagon. In D, E and F the sameness of certain items favors grouping them, and the leftovers readily fall into a complementary group, when they make a regular figure, or when, as in G, they are similar; whereas in H, where the leftover items are dissimilar and irregularly arranged, they do not get together readily. I shows the factor of homogeneous continuation, in that the dots are readily seen as lying along straight lines or fairly definite curves.

more dependent on the *O*-variables of experience:

1. *Nearness or proximity in the field of view.* Dots relatively close together are readily seen as a group.

2. *Sameness or similarity.* Dots of the same color are readily seen as a group in distinction from dots of another color, which may form another group. The likeness may be one of shape instead of color.

3. *"Common fate."* Dots which move simultaneously in the same direction are readily seen as a group. They possess a sort of similarity in their sameness of motion.

4. *Good continuation or good figure.* The group follows a uniform direction in some respect. The closed line has the advantage over an open one. Another important case is symmetry or balance of the total figure.

5. *Conformity with the individual's momentary set or Einstellung.* Wertheimer distinguished subjective and objective *Einstellung.* Subjectively the observer can set himself for a certain grouping and so resist the factors of proximity and similarity. By objective *Einstellung*, Wertheimer means essentially the same thing as perseveration. Let dots be arranged in a straight line with alternately smaller and wider spaces between them—*O* pairs them according to proximity. Let the spaces be gradually equalized—*O* adheres to the original grouping.

6. *Past experience or custom,* illustrated by a series of words printed without spaces, which can nevertheless be separated and read. Wertheimer urges that this factor must not be too readily invoked. To prove the reality of the experience factor in any concrete case, one must show that the more direct perceptual factors do not account for the grouping obtained.

The first three of these factors refer to objective characteristics of the field of dots. The last two factors are subjective or organismic, dependent on the observer and on conditions present in him. The fourth factor, good continuation or good figure, occupies a middle ground, since some conditions of "goodness," as closure and symmetry, are described in objective terms, while others depend on the observer and on what he finds easy or pleasing.

It is difficult by any form of experiment to obtain exact information on what *O* really sees. Verbal description is inadequate, and if *O* is asked to draw, he cannot reproduce all he sees (Rupp, 1923). However clear the total figure may appear, it requires some analysis, some noting of relations, before it can be copied (p. 715).

Attempts to unify the principles of grouping. Musatti (1931) combined these principles into one comprehensive law of homogeneity. Homogeneity with

FIG. 14-6. (Schumann, 1904.) A dot figure readily shows a variety of grouping

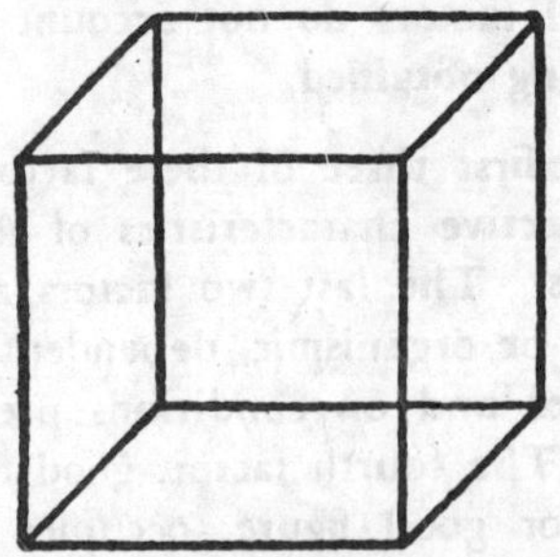

FIG. 14-7. The Necker cube.

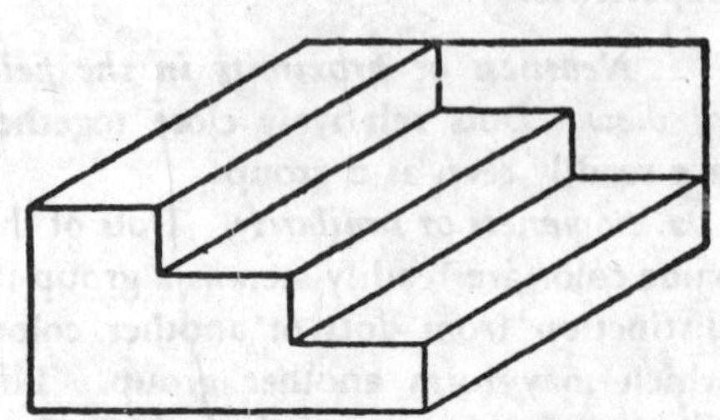

FIG. 14-8. The Schröder staircase.

respect to place is proximity; with respect to quality, similarity; with respect to movement or change, common fate; with respect to direction, good continuation. As to the factors of set and past experience, we may think of homogeneity between what is presented now and what has been prepared for in the immediate or more remote past.

If we think of perception as a reactive process, all the principles have to do with ease of response, and the question becomes, why it is specially easy to make a unitary response to dots which lie near together or are similar or homogeneous in some respect. From the response conception we can deduce one or two further factors. The reaction must not only be easy but it must be satisfactorily reinforced or do its job; accordingly, a grouping which leaves out some of the dots will be at a disadvantage as compared with a grouping which includes them all—a factor of *inclusiveness*.

We can also deduce that where the factors favoring two or more groupings are about equally balanced, the perception will be unstable and tend to *shift* from one response to another, as, indeed, we know to be the fact (p. 77).

Figures seen in three dimensions. Many ambiguous figures are two-dimensional, as Figure 14-3; Rubin worked with several others. It is also possible to make figures that will shift into three dimensions. The Necker cube and the Schröder staircase are the best known. Geometrically, a line drawing can be the projection upon a plane of any one of many different three-dimensional objects, but only rather simple or familiar three-dimensional objects are actually seen in the drawings. It is also true, geometrically, that the same three-dimensional object, seen from different angles, presents many different plane projections. As shown by Kopfermann (1930), some of these projections are readily seen in three dimensions, others much more readily in two dimensions. According to this author, it depends upon how "good" the figure is in two dimensions. If it is compact and symmetrical, there is little urge toward the three-dimensional appearance. Figure 14-9 shows several projections of a cube; those that are unsymmetrical are seen as cubes; the regular hexagon most readily appears as a two-dimensional figure, but with continued examination a three-dimensional appearance comes out. Similarly with the tetrahedron; some of its projections, unsymmetrical as plane figures, are seen in three dimensions, whereas others are regular as plane figures and scarcely suggest a three-dimensional appearance.

However we must grant a proneness to see in three dimensions even against the dictates of good figure. The per-

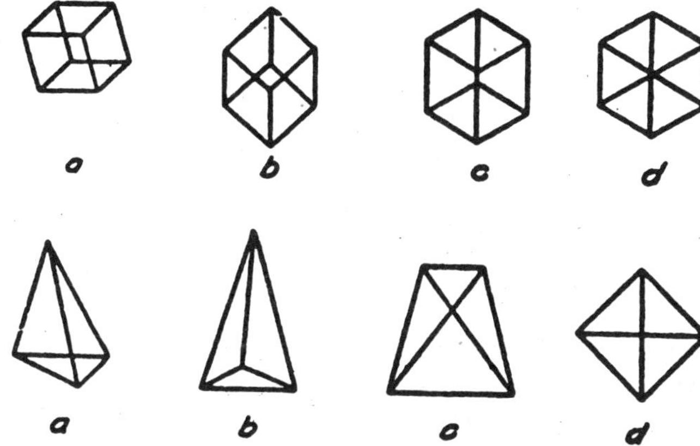

FIG. 14-9. (Kopfermann, 1930.) Plane projections of cube and tetrahedron.

fectly regular star in Figure 14-10 will nevertheless give way, if steadily viewed, to a three-dimensional appearance which is less symmetrical but more exciting.

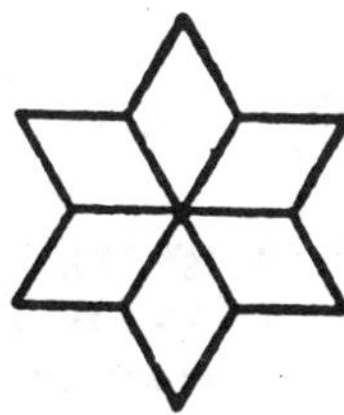

FIG. 14-10. This figure though perfectly regular as a flat figure is readily seen in three dimensions.

The fact that we tend to see regular and familiar figures whenever possible suggests that the laws of figural perception are not limited to surface forms. Hebb (1949) suggests a possible neural mechanism that would take care of perception of forms, whether they were limited to surfaces or extended to three dimensions.

CONTOUR

Implicit in our discussion of reversible figures is the obvious fact that one of the most effective ways of setting a portion of the visual field off from the ground is to draw a line around it—to outline it. Such an outline is a special case of *contour*, perhaps especially effective because of our experience with drawing. But the contour need not be sharp; if the contour is vague and broad as when one part of the field shades off gradually into another, the shape of either part is indefinite. Rubin (1915, 1921) called contour formative of shape, "shape producing." When the field is divided by a contour into figure and ground, the contour shapes the figure only, the ground appearing shapeless. A curved contour tends to exert its effect upon the enclosed space, that is, upon the concave side of the contour. It exerts its forming influence inward rather than outward.

But though contour gives shape to a figure, we cannot say that the shape *is* the contour or that *O* experiences the contour directly. Some analysis is necessary before he sees the contour. Even in copying a figure with a pencil attention is directed rather to the shape of the figure to be copied than to the exact run of the contour. Rubin reports an interesting demonstration of this fact. Draw on a sheet of paper a wavy line, then draw another line below it so as to mark off a stripe or ribbon of uniform width. When the upper and lower contours of the stripe are examined carefully, they are found to be very different. They have to be different in the case of curved contours in order to make the stripe seem equally broad. It is clear that O in outlining the stripe attends to its width rather than to the exact run of the contour.

Shape not identical with contour. When two parts of the field are separated by a contour, the two parts may appear very different in shape, though they have the same contour. Jigsaw puzzle fans know that the piece need not look like the hole it fits! In an experiment of Galli & Hochheimer (1934) a rectangular

FIG. 14-11. (Galli & Hochheimer, 1934.) Forms and contour.

piece of black cardboard was cut in two along a curved but somewhat irregular line, and the two parts were mounted on white cards so that the same contour was presented twice, once with the black part at the left and again with the black at the right. These black-white fields were presented tachistoscopically with the curved contour approximately vertical. After each brief exposure *O* reproduced the contour as well as possible with pencil. That the contour looked different according as it ran with the right or left side figure was clear from his different drawings and also from the fact that he very seldom recognized the same contour in the two types of presentation.

When you attend to the shape of the figure you are apt to look rather fixedly at some part, but when you are directing your attention to the contour you take it as a path to be followed. You *follow the contour* in more or less detail, but exactly what this "following" is cannot easily be determined. *O* reports that he feels his eyes moving around the contour (Rubin) but his eyes do not do so with any regularity as we know from the photography of eye movements (p. 501). Rubin found it possible to follow a contour while maintaining the eyes in a fixed position, or even to follow the contour of an afterimage.

What produces contour? Mach pointed out as long ago as 1865 (see Mach, 1914, p. 217) that contour is not simply a change of color or brightness at some portion of the field of view, for a steady brightness gradient gives no contour at any point. Contour is a sudden change; mathematically it is a change of change, that is to say, it is the second differential of brightness and not the first: $\left(\frac{d^2i}{ds^2}, \text{ not } \frac{di}{ds}\right)$. A contour is a relatively *abrupt change of gradient* in either brightness or color. It belongs in the same class of phenomena as marginal contrast. Contrast enhances contour, and makes the outlines of objects more distinct than they are in the retinal image itself.

Not only peripheral factors like contrast but also central factors enhance and complete contour. This fact is brought out especially well by figures (such as Fig. 14-12) in which a contour is subjectively completed across an objectively homogeneous portion of the field. The extended contour is often called a "tied image"; at least, it is a central addition to the retinal image. In dot figures, contours change with the grouping of the dots—a proof of central origin. Also the contours change with the meaning conveyed by the figure (Zigler, 1920).

In a penetrating analysis of contour

Fig. 14-12. (Schumann, 1904.) Subjective contour. Note the appearance of a vertical white stripe bounded by straight lines at the right and left where it is separated from the semicircular figures.

formation, Werner (1935) exposed two figures successively and very briefly to the same retinal area, a black square, and a white square of the same size surrounded by a black frame. If the black square was followed, after a vacant (gray) interval of 150 ms, by the framed white square, curiously enough the black square was not seen at all. When the sequence was reversed, both squares were seen. The same results occurred when black and white were interchanged in each figure, with a dark gray background. The framed square obliterated the plain square, which did not have time to establish itself before being wiped out by the opposed gradient of the framed square; but when the framed square came first, its double contour was too strong to be obliterated. By use of this obliteration method Werner found the corners especially strong. It would also appear from his results that parallel contours of opposed gradient reinforce each other in proportion to their nearness.

Fry & Bartley (1935) used the threshold method in studying contours. They determined the minimum difference of illumination or brightness necessary to make a visible contour under different field conditions. They obtained results consistent with the hypothesis that a contour exerts an inhibitory influence upon a neighboring parallel contour and a reinforcing influence upon one which it approaches at right angles. It would seem, however, that it should make some difference whether the gradients of the two parallel contours are in the same or opposite directions. At the present writing this subject of contour formation seems still to be in its beginnings. At any rate, as we saw in the chapter on Vision (p. 376), interaction effects are of greatest importance.

Fig. 14-13. (Werner, 1935.) Experiment on the development of contour. The square *a* is of the same size as the interior white space in the frame *b*. Expose them in cyclical sequence to the same part of the retina, with blank (uniform gray) time intervals, longer after *b* than after *a*, so that a cycle runs:

a	20 ms
blank	150
b	20
blank	300

Then *b* only is seen, or at the most the only trace of *a* is a graying of the interior square field. But if *a* and *b* change places, so that *b* comes first, *b* is not obliterated by *a*, but both are seen. The prevalence of *b* over *a* can be observed also in binocular combination of the two figures (as by crossing the eyes, p. 468). Therefore, it cannot be due to purely retinal processes.

MASKING OF FIGURES

Though puzzle pictures may seem below the dignity of scientific investigation, they are no more unpromising than dot figures and nonsense figures. By what means can a picture be concealed? Still better, by what means can a simple figure be concealed? We find ourselves facing a fundamental problem in the perception of form. If we knew the factors in form perception, we could so con trol them as to conceal one form in another.

Since shape depends so largely upon contour, one way of concealing a figure is to remove portions of the contour. The observer is forced to reconstruct the figure by supplying the missing contour, as is possible within limits. To reconstruct most of the contour, to go as far as Michelangelo who saw the statue in a block of marble, is to go beyond mere perception.

Foley (1935) demonstrated the difficulty of supplying missing contour by requiring *O* to find small figures within a total figure. He first tested the hypothesis that a part is more easily isolated from a meaningless than from a *meaningful* figure. The results seemed to confirm this hypothesis until the greater *compactness* of the meaningful total figures was pointed out. A second experiment compared three conditions: (A) a meaningful whole; (B) an equally compact meaningless whole; (C) a less compact, broken-up pattern of the same masses. The results showed no difference between the meaningful and equally compact meaningless totals, but a considerable advantage for the broken-up figure, the parts of which were more easily isolated. Then it was noticed that the less compact figure presented the *contour* of the parts more completely. When the three sorts of total figure were equalized in this respect by drawing fine lines across them without destroying their total shapes, the total shape was found to be of no consequence. Since *O* was all intent on finding parts, the shape of the whole made no difference to him while visible contour of the parts made a great difference (Fig. 14-14).

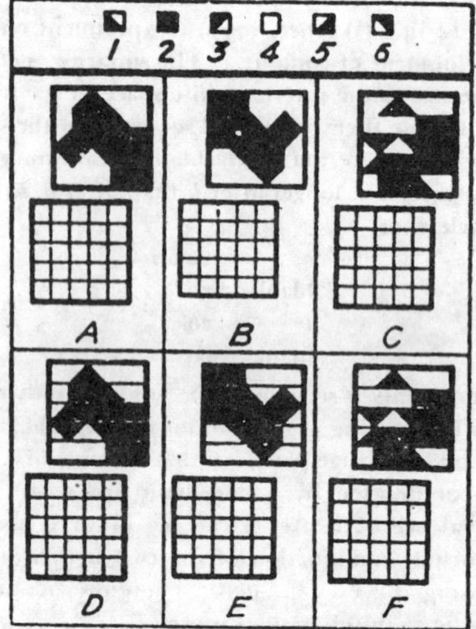

Fig. 14-14. (Foley, 1935.) Portions of a substitution test. The blank squares are to be filled in with numbers identifying the corresponding parts of the "pictures," according to the key at the top. Picture A suggests an object; B, though equally compact, does not suggest an object; C was made by transposing some of the horizontal rows of A; D, E and F are the same as A, B and C, except that fine horizontal lines equate the three in respect to the visible contour of the separate squares. The whole test contained many sets of figures made up in the same way. The small figures were equally difficult to find in A and B, and easier in C; but the addition of the fine horizontal lines made D, E and F all equally easy.

In this last experiment, *O* devoted considerable time to each total figure. In very brief exposures, the regularity or irregularity of the total figure is a factor of some importance; a part is found more quickly in an irregular figure. An irregular total figure gives a first impression of an uninteresting mass and leaves attention free to search for the designated part, while a pleasing total figure delays the search for the part (Seifert, 1917).

Gottschaldt (1926, 1929), guided in part by Wertheimer's laws of configuration (p. 408), became very skillful in concealing figures. His purpose was somewhat different. He wished to check the common belief that a familiar figure is easily seen and that past experience is an important factor in form perception. He believed his results to prove the contrary, but this conclusion is disputed (Moore, 1930; Braly, 1933). He did not show whether a familiar figure was as easily concealed as an unfamiliar one. But he succeeded in concealing familiar figures, and also good figures, by devices which we will consider presently (Fig. 14·15).

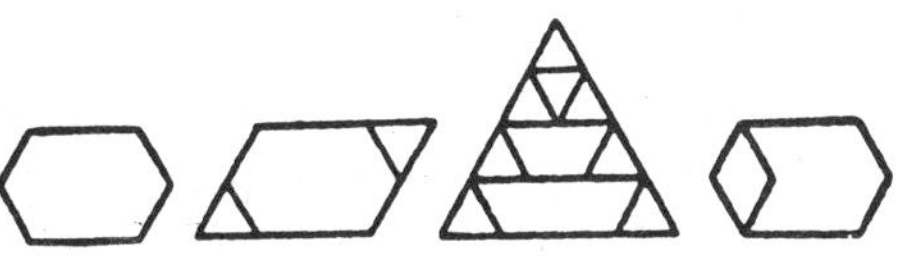

FIG. 14·15. (Gottschaldt, 1926, 1929.) A figure hidden in more complex figures. The hidden figure (hexagon) is both familiar and "good."

Galli & Zama (1931) conducted a similar experiment to study the masking of figures. Their object was to hamper the process of seeing a figure and in that way to bring that process out into the open. They drew on paper a geometrical figure, as a square or circle, and on the same paper superimposed another figure masking the first to a greater or less degree. The combined figure was presented to *O* without time limit, and he was instructed to find the masked figure which was present and to describe the process. His introspection indicated a process somewhat as follows: certain lines suggest some familiar figure which is taken as a blank schema with missing parts to be found. These parts are found, and the masked figure is then seen more or less clearly (Fig. 14·16).

How to conceal figures. The main information we can derive from both of these experiments pertains to ways and means of concealing a figure. The rules of the game call for complete presentation of the concealed figure. At least, all its lines must be there so that it can be traced out completely in the inclusive figure. A large share of the concealed figure can still be omitted from the total figure. We can actually *omit much of the contour* of a figure while playing the game and presenting all the lines.

A freely projecting corner is a strong part of the contour of a figure; remove this part by prolonging the lines beyond the corner so that it no longer projects. A flat end is an important part of a contour; remove it by placing other lines out beyond it. Embed part of the contour in a series of parallel or radiating lines, and so make it impossible to pick out this part of the contour except in direct vision (whereas the figure has to be seen partly in indirect vision). Apart from contour, interior clear space is a prominent character of some figures;

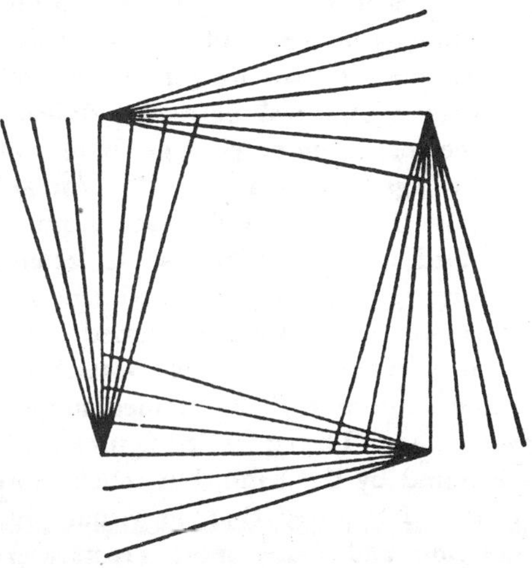

FIG. 14·16. (Galli & Zama, 1931.) Concealed square. The task is to *see* the square.

remove this character by drawing lines across this space. If the original figure gives an impression of three dimensions, remove this impression by added lines which give the total a two-dimensional appearance; or vice versa. If the original figure is symmetrical, add lines to skew the total figure to one side.

So there are many characteristics of a figure which can be subtracted by the addition of new parts. The observer's job in finding the thus-concealed figure is to prune away the additions and so recreate for himself what the "artist" has destroyed. The artist can conceal from the observer even the best and most symmetrical figure—which certainly does not disprove the advantage of such figures in ordinary perception. Similarly, the ability of the artist to conceal even the most familiar figures does not disprove the importance of experience in ordinary perception.

Witkin (1950a) found an additional means of concealing figures. He applied different colors to the inclusive figure in such a way as to favor the wrong combinations. He found large individual differences in the time required to find the masked figures, and men were definitely quicker than women, while children found the task extremely difficult.

The *tactile-motor perception of concealed figures* was studied by Yamane (1935). The figures were made of points stamped in paper (like Braille letters), arranged in a circle, square, triangle and hexagon. They were concealed somewhat after the method of Gottschaldt. Blind subjects and blindfolded subjects were used. The concealed figures could be found by the hand, but much more time was required than in visual presentation and many more errors were made. A complex figure which can be grasped visually in a few seconds may take a blind person as long as 10 minutes. Collective apprehension of the whole figure is difficult while the separate apprehension of small portions is relatively easy. The "span" (p. 90) is broad in vision and narrow in tactile-motor perception. That this difference of span is important was proved by artificially limiting the visual span: the presented figure was seen through a hole, one cm in diameter, which *O* could move around so as to see the figure part by part. The results were similar to those obtained with tactile-motor examination.

PROPORTION AS A CHARACTERISTIC OF SHAPE

Our everyday use of such words as *square, oblong, slender* is pretty good evidence that some characteristic of a shape is easily perceived, a characteristic which on analysis comes down to a ratio between length and breadth. Bühler (1913) asked whether proportion is directly perceived, and sought an answer from psychophysical determinations. For a rough preliminary experiment he drew on paper two series of rectangles, one series with a base of 20 mm and an altitude ranging from 7.5 to 12.5 mm, the other series twice as large. When a pair of rectangles, one of the larger size and one of the smaller, was presented for comparison, *O* had little difficulty in deciding which was more slender.

For more exact work, rectangles were outlined in fine lines scratched through black shellac on glass, and were exposed by projection in a dark room. Standard rectangle, 340 × 255 mm. Comparison rectangles, base of 600 mm and heights ranging from 535 to 650 mm by steps of 5 mm. The Variable was exposed after the Standard, farther to the right and a little below. Exposure times: ¾ sec for Standard, interval of 2 sec, ¾ sec for the Variable. *O* judged the Variable in relation to the Standard as slenderer, stouter (plumper), or of the same shape.

The main point was to discover whether shapes were as accurately perceived as lengths. If rectangles were compared in shape by an indirect process involving estimation of four lengths, the length and width of each rectangle, the shapes could not possibly be as accurately judged as the single lines, because of the combination of errors. In a parallel experiment under the same conditions in every respect, except that not rectangles but merely the lengths of two vertical lines were compared, two *O*s were less accurate than in the comparison of rectangles. Their results are shown below:

	DL		*SD*	
Subject	*Lines*	*Rectangles*	*Lines*	*Rectangles*
Kü	.012	.009	.031	.021
Ak	.018	.013	.038	.032

These decimal fractions give the DL and the SD divided by the Standard. The relative DL is smaller for the rectangles than for the vertical lines, and the relative SD is also smaller.[1] The advantage of the rectangles over the separate lines is not great, and perhaps the safest conclusion would be simply that proportion is perceived *at least as well* as length.

The introspective reports indicated that two rectangles differing considerably in shape were compared so directly that no process was observable. When they were nearly of the same shape, care was necessary and *O* was aware of examining the separate dimensions, but without any attempt to compute their ratio, as this procedure when attempted was found to be useless. Bühler tried a number of variations of the experiment. Horizontal lines of different length were exposed one after the other at intervals of 2 seconds. The first was divided by a mark into parts having the ratio of 3 to 4. The second was divided in some ratio not far from that, and *O* judged whether the two lines were divided in the same proportion. This proved to be a difficult task at first but after some practice the judgment was about as accurate as with the rectangles. (Cf. Lenk [1926] and Schneider [1932].)

[1] The senior author has computed the SD from Bühler's tables (1913, pp. 142, 149), as a check on the conclusions drawn from the DL which here as always are somewhat at the mercy of *O*'s attitude toward "equal" judgments (p. 214).

THE GEOMETRICAL ILLUSIONS

Errors in apparent length, area, direction, or curvature occur in the perception of patterns of lines. Such illusions are "normal." A few of them, like the vertical-horizontal illusion, may be due to the structure of the eye or to the position of the lines in the field of view. But the majority depend on the *pattern* of lines. In a general way they are errors in the perception of parts of a figure and are incidental to the perceived form of the whole figure.

These illusions are often divided into: (1) contrast illusions, (2) confluxion or assimilation illusions. If a short person standing between two tall persons looks shorter than he objectively is, that is a contrast illusion, but if he should look taller than he actually is, that would be an instance of confluxion or assimilation.

Like other errors these illusions are more than mere curiosities, for they afford clues to the process of perception. They have long attracted the interest of psychologists and many figures have been devised which give illusory effects. Instead of attempting a full account we will first state the principal theories that have been suggested to explain them, and give a selection of illusory figures on which the reader can try out these theories. Finally we shall report a few experiments of a more analytical character.[2]

The principal theories deserving consideration are as follows:

1. *The eye-movement theory,* in its simplest form, assumes that the impression of length is obtained by moving the eye along a line from one end to the other. If vertical movements of the eye are more strenuous than horizontal, a given vertical distance calls for more effort than the same horizontal distance and therefore seems longer. Again, if the outward lines in one part of the Müller-Lyer figure cause the eye movement to exceed the length of the included line, whereas in the other part of the figure the inward pointing lines cause the eye to move a smaller distance, the first line will seem longer than the second. A less direct form of the eye-movement theory admits that actual eye movements do not occur in all cases, but assumes that a tendency to such movement is sufficient to give the impression of length.

It is also possible to use the eye movement theory in reverse, if the illusion works the other way. If the lines in a figure draw the eyes beyond the end of the figure, *O* sees that he has gone too far, and may interpret the figure to be shorter than it is. Thus an eye-movement theory can "explain" any results that are obtained! A comparable objection may be raised to the empathy theory (below).

2. *The perspective theory,* starting from the undoubted fact that a line drawing readily suggests objects in three dimensions, infers that the apparent length of the lines is affected by the perspective read into the figure. For example, a short vertical line in a drawing may represent a relatively long horizontal line extending away from the observer. The horizontal-vertical illusion

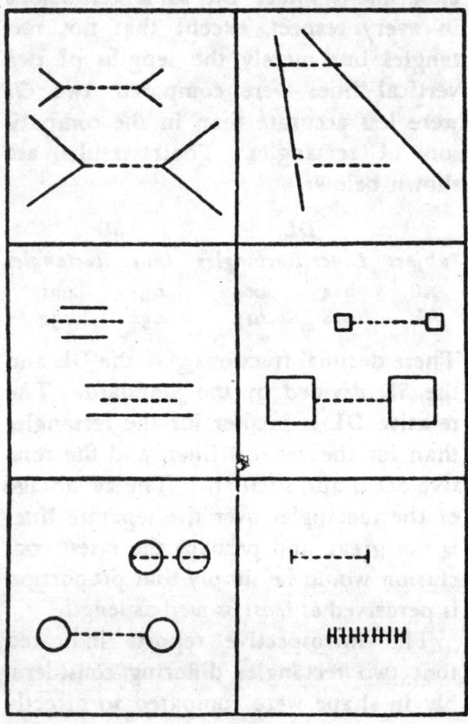

FIG. 14-17. Several illusion figures. Compare the dotted lines. A crucial test of any theory is the ability it confers not so much to explain facts already known as to predict the results that will occur under certain untried conditions. It would be interesting to see whether the reader can predict what illusion will occur in each case. The Müller-Lyer illusion is the upper left one.

can be explained by supposing the vertical to represent such a foreshortened horizontal line. In the Müller-Lyer figure the obliques readily suggest perspective and if this suggestion is followed one of the horizontal lines appears farther away and therefore objectively longer than the other.

3. *The empathy theory* of Theodor

[2] A more complete account of such illusions can be found in Sanford (1898), Ladd & Woodworth (1911) or Ebbinghaus (1911). Some excellent demonstrations appear in Luckiesh (1922).

Lipps (1897) is the theory by which he sought to explain the esthetic effects of architecture. He held that even in looking at relatively simple figures the observer's emotional and reactive nature is stimulated. A vertical line, resisting gravity, suggests effort and thus appears longer than an equal horizontal. One part of the Müller-Lyer figure suggests expansion and the other limitation and thus the first line appears the longer.

4. *The confusion theory.* To judge the lines and angles of a figure requires analysis which is difficult because the observer is engrossed in the appearance of the figure as a whole. One of the Müller-Lyer segments taken as a whole is really longer than the other. If *O* cannot rid himself of this impression and narrow his attention down to a particular line, he carries over the total impression to the lines which he imagines himself to be judging.

5. *The pregnance or good-figure theory.* The metaphorical use of "pregnance" here is somewhat novel in English, though not far from that used in the expression a "pregnant sentence," meaning a sentence containing a wealth of meaning. Among the German psychologists a "pregnant" figure is one which expresses some characteristic fully. "Goodness" of figure means in part the same thing. When the observer sees a figure as having some characteristic, his tendency is to see this characteristic as fully expressed as the conditions allow, according to the theory. A near-circle is seen as a true circle or as a better circle than it is. If one of the Müller-Lyer figures is seen as consisting of two things standing apart, the apartness will be exaggerated by the observer. If the other figure is seen as a single compact object, the compactness will be exaggerated.

Some of the more incisive experiments which have been done with geometrical illusions are the following.

1. **Measurement of an illusion under varying conditions.** The method used may be either that of adjustment (p. 199) or of Constant Stimuli. By the former method *O* is given an adjustable figure and is asked, for example in the case of a Müller-Lyer figure, to make one of the horizontal lines apparently equal to the other. The error is measured and the test is repeated a number of times to permit computation of the constant error and variability. This method was used by Heymans (1896, 1897) by Thiéry (1895), by Judd and his coworkers (1899, 1902, 1905), and by many subsequent writers. By the method of Constant Stimuli one of the two Müller-Lyer figures is kept of constant length and used as a Standard, while the other figure is the Variable, presented in a "full series" of differing lengths; *O* judges on each presentation whether the Variable is equal to the Standard, longer or shorter. This method was used by Ipsen (1926a) in an elaborate study of the Sander parallelogram illusion (Fig. 14-18).

The advantages of a quantitative study of these illusions are: (1) that it brings out slighter illusions than can be demonstrated without measurement; (2) that it gives definite facts to be explained by any theory; and (3) that it can be extended to other parts of the figure besides the part which is most obviously subject to illusion. We have mentioned one notable example in the 1947 experiment of Finger & Spelt (p. 200), in which they showed that the usual inverted T form of the vertical-horizontal illusion is contaminated by the effects of the bisected cross-bar. Hence the illusion is markedly smaller if set up in the form of an L instead of a T.

Some of the results of quantitative study may be briefly cited.

Heymans (1896) made a thorough study of the Müller-Lyer figure and its variants. He found the average strength of the illusion to be 25 percent under optimum conditions: i.e., when the obliques were 1/4 as long as the horizontal segments and made only a small angle with the horizontal. The amount of the illusion was proportional to the cosine of the angle between the obliques and the horizontal, being zero when this angle was 90° and increasing to its maximum when the angle was almost zero.

Judd (1899) found that the illusory effects were not confined by any means to the main lines of the Müller-Lyer figure. All parts within and adjacent to the figure were affected; all the space relations in the immediate neighborhood were distorted by the arrangement of the figure.

Ipsen (1926a) on measuring the illusion in the Sander figure found it to exceed even that in the Müller-Lyer, which is the typical strong illusion. The greatest error affects the diagonals of the two parallelograms into which the whole

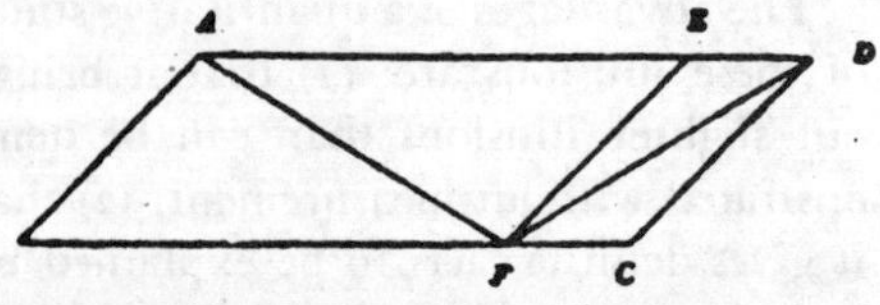

FIG. 14·18. (Sander, 1926.) The Sander parallelogram AF = FD.

parallelogram is divided; but the base lines of the smaller parallelograms are also affected, and so are the areas and angles (Fig. 14·18).

2. Recording eye movements during examination of illusory figures. These experiments were undertaken as a check on the eye-movement theory. Judd (1905) used a motion picture camera (p. 495) to photograph the eye movements during the examination of several illusory figures both before and after practice. From the eye-movement theory in its simple form one would expect that a line that was underestimated would be examined with a short easy movement. But the photographs gave no support to this hypothesis. The eyes made more fixations on the underestimated line with the inward directed obliques; they seemed to labor over it more than over the more open line with outward directed obliques. No clean-cut explanation of the illusion could be deduced from the eye movements. Yet the eye movements were not unrelated to the figure nor to the illusion. Where the figure appears crowded, the fixations of the eye were more frequent; where the figure is more open, they were fewer. The guess may be hazarded that the eye movements were dependent upon the appearance of the figure, instead of the appearance being dependent on the eye movements.

This guess is confirmed by the eye movements during the examination of a reversible figure (p. 410). It had often been held that the fixation point determined the appearance, since it is possible to reverse the figure (though not instantly) by shifting the fixation point. The point fixated tends to appear near the observer. Zimmer (1913) had his subjects examine the cube figure while the experimenter watched *O*'s eyes through a laboratory telescope. Whenever *O* experienced an involuntary inversion of the cube, he pressed a telegraph key; and whenever *E* observed a movement of *O*'s eyes, he pressed another key. The kymographic record showed that the eye movements occurred about a second *after* the inversion rather than before. The relation of cause and effect is probably that *O* fixates the part of the figure which seems nearest to him, rather than that any part seems nearest which he happens to fixate.

Sisson (1935), on photographing the eye movements during examination of the reversible staircase figure, obtained a somewhat less regular result: 33 percent of the eye movements were followed by recorded inversions and 46 percent of the inversions were followed by eye movements. These are the average percents when a rather generous time allowance is made. But if we assume that a change of fixation point must *instantly* cause a reversal of the appearance, "there remain only 5.7 percent of the total 332 movements that are followed by reversals within a time interval which might indicate causal relationship." Sisson like Zimmer concludes that in all probability the shifting appearance is due to central factors and that the eye movements depend upon the shifting appearance rather than vice versa.

3. Experimentally controlled attitudes of observation. In order to bring out central factors in the illusions, Benussi (1904) instructed *O* in one case to observe with a whole-perceiving attitude, in another case with a part-isolating attitude. The Müller-Lyer illusion was greater in the whole-perceiving attitude than in the part-isolating. Objective conditions increased or diminished the illusion, according as they made the isolation of the required lines easy or difficult.

A sample of the results is shown in the accompanying table. Conspicuousness of the main lines breaks up the total form and weakens the illusion. But the totalizing attitude, after being practiced, overcame even unfavorable objective conditions.

Benussi later (1912) combined this attitude experiment with a stroboscopic presentation of the Müller-Lyer figure. A series of figures was shown in rapid succession so that the figure appeared to be in motion (see p. 512), as can be understood from the diagram in Figure 14-13. The illusion here is a shift of the point of intersection toward the inner side of the angle. If *O* attends strictly to the lines and regards the crossing point only as a pivot, this point does not move, but if attention is directed to the changing shape of the total figure, then the mid-point seems to glide along the vertical line, upward when the side lines move up and downward when they move down.

It is safe to conclude with Benussi (1914b) and most other investigators that the typical geometrical illusions are incidental to the perception of form. They are errors in the apparent size and direction of parts of a figure resulting from the total impression of the figure.

ATTITUDE AND OBJECTIVE CONDITIONS FAVORING TOTAL AND PART-ISOLATING PERCEPTION

(Benussi, 1904)

Main lines of Müller-Lyer	*white*	*white*	*dark gray*
Oblique lines	*white*	*dark gray*	*white*
Background	*black*	*black*	*black*
Average illusion under			
whole-perceiving attitude	4.95	2.20	7.66
part-isolating attitude	1.02	−.50	3.20

Each figure in the table is the average of 20–30 measurements, all on a single *O*, but confirmed by results from other *O*s.

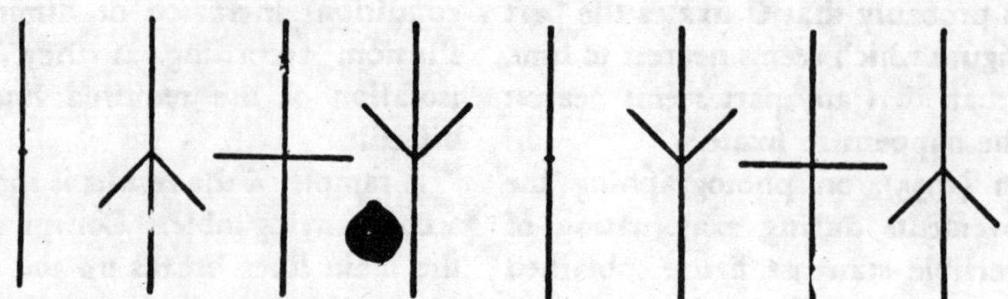

FIG. 14-19. (Benussi, 1912.) Successive positions of the Müller-Lyer element, shown in rapid succession, and giving an appearance of up and down movement of the point of intersection along with the apparent movement of the side lines.

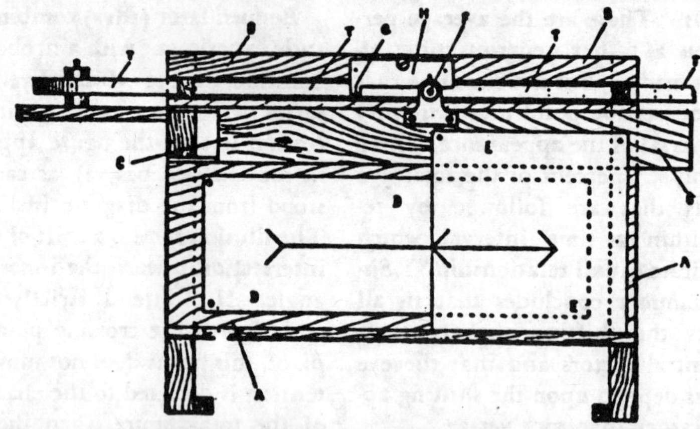

FIG. 14-20. (Judd, 1905.) Apparatus for measuring and recording the amount of the Müller-Lyer illusion. AABB is a fixed wooden frame, to which is attached the card DD containing one part of the Müller-Lyer figure. CC is a sliding board, adjustable by the subject, and to it is attached a card containing the remainder of the figure. *O* adjusts the sliding part till the two main lines appear equal. He then records his setting by pressure on the rod F, which makes a pinhole in the ticker tape TT and at the same time makes a double pinhole (like this :) in the tape under G. As G is attached to the fixed frame, whereas F is attached to the sliding board, the distance along the tape between the double and the single pinholes indicates the setting and so the amount of the illusion.

We are not to suppose that these illusions occur only in the special figures of the laboratory; they occur in innumerable patterns and designs.

4. The practice experiment in illusions. Heymans (1896) and others had noticed that continued experience with one certain figure diminished the amount of the illusion. Judd (1902, 1905) made a systematic study of this practice effect. *O* was not informed of his errors but simply examined the figure time after time, each time setting the apparatus to a subjective equation. The illusion gradually diminished to near zero (Fig. 14-21), and this was true of all three of the illusions tried, the Müller-Lyer, Poggendorff, and Zöllner. This practice effect held good, however, only for the original position of the figure. If it were reversed right and left, the illusion returned in full strength, and in some *O*s was exaggerated, but in others was overcome by a relatively small amount of further practice. The illusion was revived even in the original figure by standing off and looking at it casually

FIG. 14-21. (Judd, 1905.) Decrease of the Müller-Lyer illusion through repetition. The subject used the apparatus shown in Fig. 14-20, making in all 600 settings, 25 per day. At the outset the line included between the outward obliques was made on the average 17 percent shorter than the line included between the inward obliques; at the end of practice this error had decreased to about 2 percent.

as a whole. Eye-movement photographs showed that *O* was by no means passively receptive in viewing the figure. He explored it rather minutely, especially the part with the inward-slanting lines. This minute examination of the figure diminished toward the end of the practice.

Lewis (1908) and Seashore *et al.* (1908) made similar experiments, confirming and extending the results under different conditions of practice, but no perfectly convincing explanation appeared at the time. The natural explanation in terms of learning has to meet certain objections. (1) How can there be learning without knowledge of results? (2) Why did the results of learning disappear, partially at least, when the figure was reversed end for end? (3) Why did learning sometimes overshoot the equality point and end up with a negative illusion? In reply to these objections something can be said. (1) The subject soon sees that his task of equating the main lines is difficult because of the complexity of the whole figure; he examines the figure in detail and gradually attacks it in a different way, probably more analytically. (2) After long practice his procedure becomes habituated to the right-and-left arrangement of the figure and breaks down temporarily when the sides are reversed. (3) He always varies somewhat from trial to trial, and when his average error has been reduced to zero, it is sure to be negative on some trials. Besides, he may overdo his analytical attitude toward the figure. But a much more challenging explanation has now been offered by Köhler and his associates, based on the figural aftereffects which we shall now consider for the remainder of the chapter

FIGURAL AFTER-EFFECTS

Some curious phenomena that cropped up incidentally in the course of other visual investigations were reported by Gibson in 1933 and are proving to have considerable theoretical significance. He presented a slightly curved line in a vertical position for *O* to inspect steadily for 5–10 minutes. By the end of the inspection period the line appeared less curved than at first, and when a straight vertical line was then shown, it appeared to be curved in the opposite direction. These effects—both the adaptation and the negative aftereffect, as Gibson called them—could be demonstrated just as well with the curve replaced by a line bent in the middle. The effects could be measured by aid of a flexible rod which *O* adjusted to appear straight. The loss of curvature in the inspected curved line was equal to the gain of curvature in the straight line shown just after the inspection period. The aftereffect, strong at first, faded out gradually. This experiment was successfully repeared by Bales & Follansbee (1935); in fact, it is one of the most dependable experiments for an elementary laboratory class.

Gibson explored a number of variables in the situation. He obtained similar results with a horizontal or oblique curve, but the aftereffect was limited to lines having the same general direction as the inspection curve. It was limited also to the particular retinal region that was stimulated by the inspection line. It was evidently a cerebral rather than a purely retinal effect, for when one eye was closed during the inspection and then tested alone, the aftereffect was present, in half strength at least. The same effects were found in the kinesthetic field if the hand followed a curved edge repeatedly and then shifted to a straight edge. Again, a line tilted slightly from the vertical lost its tilt during prolonged visual inspection, after which a true vertical appeared to tilt in the opposite direction (Vernon, 1934; Gibson & Radner, 1937; Gibson, 1937a). Gibson offered no physiological theory to account for these effects, though he did point out their analogy with the adaptation that is so common in sensory and perceptual processes (1937b). We may refer to our previous discussions of adaptation level (p. 231) and of the shifting zero in temperature sensation (p. 287).

The electrical theory of figural aftereffects. The theoretical significance of Gibson's results was not evident at first. But Köhler (1938, 1940) saw that they might furnish a way to get at the dynamic cortical fields which he considered to be the basis of form perception. In 1944 he and Wallach reported an extensive study of these effects and of many others, all of which they were finally able to reduce to one general law. A typical experiment is illustrated in Figure 14-22.

Köhler & Wallach found that any line or figure could serve as the inspection figure (I-figure) especially if the eyes were held fixed on or near it, and that prolonged inspection would induce aftereffects on any test figure (T-figure) substituted for the I-figure and presented close to the same retinal area. The T-figure is *displaced away* from the previous retinal location of the I-figure. It is as if an area (not of the retina, probably, but of the visual cortex), after being subjected to continued uniform stimulation, repelled the T-figure; and as if the repellent force were greatest rather close to the location of the I-figure. The dis-

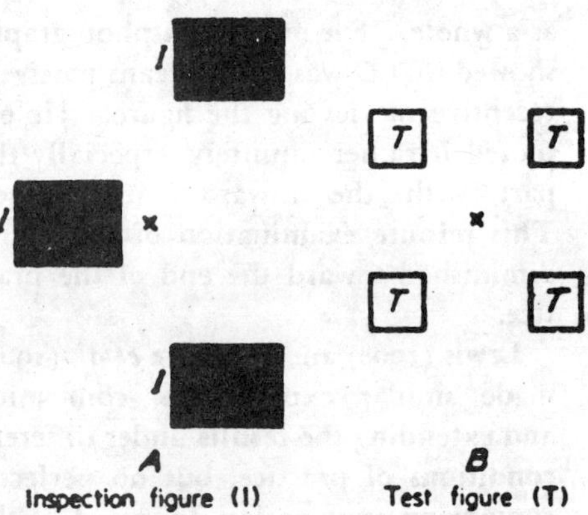

FIG. 14-22. (Köhler & Wallach, 1944.) Demonstration of displacement effects. With the page about 18 inches from the eye, fixate the x in the inspection figure for 40 seconds, and then look at the x in the test figure. Without moving the eye from this spot, notice the apparent distance between the test squares. The area exposed to the left-hand black oblong will now fall between the two left-hand test squares, repelling them so that they look further apart. The right-hand black oblongs will straddle the right-hand test squares, pushing them closer together. Thus there is a double effect. If it does not work the first time, fixate the inspection figure again and try it. It may help to cover the T-figure while looking at I-figure, and vice versa.

placements are likely to distort the T-figure. All these "figural aftereffects" are brought under the general law of displacement.

The *satiation theory* offered by these authors may be roughly sketched. In the stimulus field, and so on the retina and on the cortical projection of the retina, let there be a boundary between black and white areas. The electric potential will be higher on one side of the boundary than on the other, and an equalizing current will spread through the immediately adjacent tissue and fluid. This current produces a condition of electrotonus in the tissue; it polarizes cell walls and so decreases the electrical conductivity of the tissue. So the area adjacent to the location of the I-figure becomes resistant or satiated, and the currents generated by the T-figure will be forced into the less satiated region farther away from the I-figure location. Moreover, as figural aftereffects often last for weeks and months, we must assume that the affected tissue may undergo a relatively permanent change amounting to increased polarizability.

Since the original report on figural aftereffects there have been many variations of the experiment. Fox (1951) presented experimental evidence for the genuineness of both satiation and adaptation as factors in figural aftereffects. Hammer (1949) studied the time relations, measuring the displacement after different inspection periods and after different recovery periods. She found a slight displacement even after only 5 seconds of inspection, with a maximum reached after about 60 seconds; in the recovery period, displacement was maximal at first and reached zero in about 90 seconds. Surprisingly enough, the same displacement shows up in visual depth (Köhler & Emery, 1947; Fernberger, 1948). Figure 14-23 shows a typical experiment. But this depth effect offers some difficulty for the theory. The satiation is conceived as an electrical change on a surface, the occipital surface of the cerebral cortex. There is a fair though somewhat distorted "map" of the retina on the cortex. Thus the two-dimensional forms of the visual world have corresponding cortical representation. But there is no known spatial representation of the third dimension, depth, in the cortex. Hence it is hard to apply the satiation concept to figural aftereffects in depth.

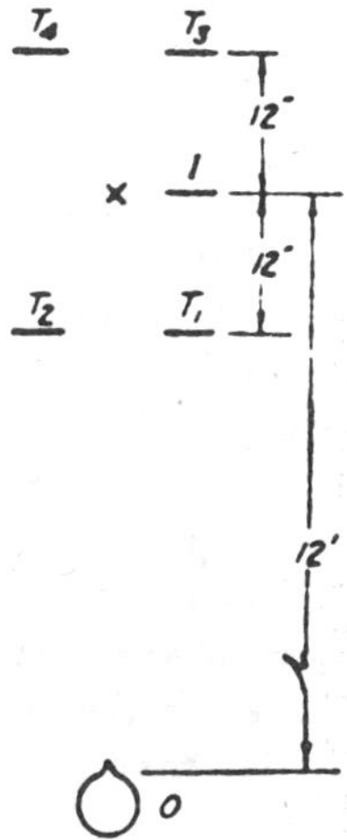

Fig. 14-23. (After Köhler & Emery, 1947.) Diagram, drawn from above, of setup for demonstration of displacements in the third dimension. O sits 12 feet away from the fixation point, x. All the figures, I, T_1, T_2, T_3, T_4, are identical white squares; the background behind T_1 and I, is black. During the inspection period only I is present. This square is then removed and the pair of squares, T_1 and T_2, is quickly presented in a plane 12 inches in front of the fixation point. The result is that T_1 is repelled by the previously stimulated area and seems nearer to O than T_2, which lies aside from the stimulated area. But when the test squares presented are T_3 and T_4, lying beyond the fixation point, T_3 is repelled in the reverse direction and appears farther from O than T_4.

The Müller-Lyer illusion. Köhler & Fishback (1950) offer evidence for satiation as the cause of the reduction of this illusion with continued repetition, i.e., of the "practice effect" reported by Judd and other early investigators (p. 422). Satiation, it should be noticed, is not offered as an explanation of the illusion itself, but as a cause of its reduction and final destruction. Consider any one of the three angles or V's that somehow produce the illusion. Satiation would build up more rapidly within the V than in front of its point, and the V would be pushed forward. The space between the points of two V's would thus be decreased, while the space between the open sides of two V's would be increased. The illusion was reduced rapidly in some *O*s, much more rapidly than in Judd's curve (Fig. 14-21). To make certain that the reduction was not due to practice in *comparing* the two parts of the Müller-Lyer figure, the experimenters exposed only one part of the figure at a time (except for a few test trials). This procedure seemed to destroy the illusion about as fast as when many comparisons were made; accordingly, it must be the steady inspection and not the comparison that destroys the illusion. Other variations of the experiment confirmed the authors in their conclusion that the illusion is destroyed by satiation and the resulting change in actual sensation, and not by practice and learning. At least, not by learning in the usual sense—but there were some resemblances between satiation effects and commonly observed effects of learning. For one thing, figural aftereffects last for months if they are firmly established. Again, satiation seems to progress faster under distributed practice (p. 786). These resemblances suggest the possibility that memory traces may consist fundamentally of satiation patterns (Köhler & Fishback, 1950).

Criticisms of the satiation theory. Much more in the way of quantitative data will be required before the theory can be properly evaluated. For example, the Müller-Lyer figure, at the viewing distances employed, subtended only a visual angle of 3° in the Köhler-Fishback experiment, as against 26° in the Judd experiment. More satiation would be necessary to destroy the illusion in the larger figure. That may be the reason why the illusion was destroyed more slowly in Judd's *O*s than in some of Köhler's; but are we sure that satiation could ever spread far enough to cover the larger figure—or that, the smaller the figure, the more quickly the illusion would be destroyed?

Other objections have been raised by K. R. Smith (1948) and Hebb (1949). The most serious attack is that of Lashley, Chow & Semmers (1951), who begin by saying that Köhler's electrical field theory "deserves a place of honor among the most original and systematic theories that scientific ingenuity has produced," but proceed to marshall cogent evidence against it. For one thing, the anatomical arrangements of the cortex are not at all what the theory demands; the division of the visual area between the right and left hemispheres, each with many fissures, would make the currents spread in strange directions. For another thing, once the sensory pattern gets out of the afferent neurones into the electric field, how does it get back into the efferent neurones and produce the appropriate pattern of motor response? Finally, Lashley *et al.* devised an experimental check on the theory. They placed sheets of gold foil on the occipital surface in one monkey and inserted gold pins through the cortex of another, so as to short-circuit the currents and so destroy any definite configurations. But in the postoperative tests the monkeys showed no impairment of pattern vision.

Some rebuttal of these charges is to be expected from the protagonists of the satiation theory. Also, it is quite possible that someone will work out a rival theory in more acceptable neural terms. Meanwhile, much remains to be done in the laboratory toward extending and quantifying the facts. At one time it was thought that the geometrical illusions would lay bare the nature of form perception. This hope has not been realized, but perhaps further study of the new class of illusions —figural aftereffects—will help us on our way.

15

PERCEPTION OF COLOR

From the practical standpoint of any individual who uses his eyes to "see the environment," the retinal image ought to reveal the objects out in front of him in their proper qualities and relations. Carefully considered, however, the retinal image is seriously defective as a direct representation of the environment. There are no objects in the image, but only juxtaposed patches of color. The image, like any other picture, is in two dimensions, the environment in three. The image of an object changes in size and shape as the observer views it from different distances and angles, while the object itself is unchanging. In color, too, the image changes with the illumination, while the object retains its own color. In spite of these inadequacies, the retinal image must somehow provide good indications of objective distance, size, shape, and color, for the observer sees them readily and often quite accurately. So arises the general problem of visual perception. The psychologist wishes to ferret out the visual indications of distance, size and the rest and to discover how they are utilized in perception and behavior. A direct attack on the problem, by asking *O* what indications ("cues") he uses, would be futile since *O* reports that he sees the size and distance of an object directly without needing any cues. The experimenter has to attack the problem, as usual, by varying the conditions, the *S*- and *O*-factors, sometimes eliminating or exaggerating a certain cue, and taking note of the resulting variations in *O*'s reports or practical responses.

PROBLEMS IN COLOR PERCEPTION

It is a fact of common observation that coal looks black even in sunlight, and chalk white even in shadow. Yet under these conditions the eye receives much stronger light from the coal than from the chalk. The retinal image of the coal is much the brighter, but the observer's impressions seem to conform to the objects rather than to the stimuli. He sees no paradox here, for if coal is really black, it certainly ought to look black in a good light. Not a bad answer, perhaps, but one that poses a problem for the psychologist.

Early theories. Interest in the problem dates from those early giants of physiological optics, Helmholtz and Hering. Helmholtz said (1866, p. 408):

> Colors are mainly important for us as properties of objects and as means of identifying objects. In visual observation we constantly aim to reach a judgment on the object colors

and to eliminate differences of illumination. So, we clearly distinguish between a white sheet of paper in a weak illumination and a gray sheet in strong illumination. We have abundant opportunity to examine the same object colors in full sunlight, in the blue light from the clear sky, the weak white light of the clouded sky, and the reddish yellow light of the sinking sun or of candlelight—not to mention the colored reflections from surrounding objects. Seeing the same object under these different illuminations, we learn to get a correct idea of the object colors in spite of differences of illumination. We learn to judge how such an object would look in white light, and since our interest lies entirely in the constant object color, we become unconscious of the sensations on which our judgment rests.

Intellectual judgment based on unconscious sensations seemed to Hering (1874, 1876, 1879) an unrealistic account of the process of color perception. He believed that physiology should have more to say on the matter. He pointed to the peripheral factors that compensate for changes of illumination: contraction and dilation of the pupil, retinal adaptation, and contrast. He admitted that these peripheral factors were not wholly sufficient and accordingly suggested also a cerebral factor. The sensory effect of any stimulus, he said, depends not only on the retina but also on the receiving center of the brain, the "sensorium," and the brain structure may be modified by use in looking at objects. With a modified sensorium we get a modified sensation from the same stimulus, and our impression is thus an actual sensation and not an intellectual judgment. Later (1907, reprinted 1920) Hering elaborated this conception of "memory color":

> The color in which we have oftenest seen an external thing impresses itself indelibly on our memory and becomes a fixed characteristic of the memory image. What the layman calls the real color of a thing is a color which has become firmly attached to the thing in his memory; I might call it the memory color of the thing. All the things which are known to us from past experience, or which we believe to be known to us in respect color, are seen through the spectacles of the memory colors.

This "approximate color constancy of seen objects," Hering urged, was one of the most remarkable and important facts in the whole realm of physiological optics.

Regarding the problem as equally appropriate for psychology, Katz (1911) introduced it into the psychological laboratory and showed that neither memory color nor Hering's peripheral factors provided an adequate explanation of the perception of object colors. At first inclined toward the Helmholtz two-stage process, he spoke of a cerebral "transformation" of color from its stimulus value to its object value. After Gelb's (1929) important critique Katz in his second edition (1930) discarded transformation while still retaining the Helmholtzian concept of "allowance for the illumination."

Many psychologists have worked on the problem, and the catchword, "color constancy," along with "size constancy" and "shape constancy," has become familiar psychological jargon though not always understood. For a more comprehensive term, Thouless (1931) suggested "phenomenal regression to the real object," which might better read "toward the real object." The regression or shift is from the stimulus color, size, or shape *toward* the object color, size, or shape, but the apparent or "phenomenal" color, size, or shape usually lies between these two "poles" (Brunswik, 1929, 1933, 1934; reviewed by Ansbacher, 1937). The coal looks black in any light but not quite so black under a very bright as under a relatively dim light.

A painter wishing to reproduce a scene will try to catch the stimulus colors, sizes, and shapes that meet his eyes—a difficult task—but the ordinary observer is interested in the objects in the environment before him. Before we examine the experiments on perception of object color, we should ask what object color means; and, since illumination is evidently an important factor, we should ask whether we can credit the observer with any ability to perceive or register the illumination so as to allow for it in perceiving the color of the illuminated object.

What are "object colors"? An important distinction between surface color and other color was made by Katz (1911, 1930), who was trying to discover how the color patches of the retinal image appear to the naive observer. Most of the patches appear to be surfaces of objects, and their color appears to be present in these surfaces. Even the sky, as it ordinarily appears, is a surface some distance away and its color seems to inhere in that distant surface. But the sky does not necessarily appear like a surface; it can appear as a blue expanse at no definite distance—as when viewed from an open field or mountain top—and its blue color can then be called expanse color. Small patches of such expanse color can be seen if you look through a tube at the sky or at any perfectly uniform surface. Roll a paper tube small enough so that only one uniform color is visible. The surface vanishes and a mere expanse of color is seen through the tube. A hole in a card will do as well as the tube. This simple piece of apparatus, much used in experiments on object color, is called the hole screen or reduction screen.

Expanse color is known by other names, the most appropriate being perhaps *aperture color*. The aperture may be the hole in the screen or the slit or circular opening in an optical instrument which emits light directly into the eye. It appears self-luminous, whereas a surface color appears to be illuminated and not self-luminous. Aperture color ranges from dim to bright, from zero to an unlimited brightness. Surface color varies in what is best called *lightness;* in the achromatic series it can also be called whiteness, ranging from black through the shades of gray to the definite upper limit of pure white. Both surface color and aperture color can vary in hue.

Whiteness vs. *reflectance under uniform illumination.* Since the early days of psychophysics, scaling of the black-white continuum by the bisection method has been undertaken from scientific and more recently from practical interests. Apparent whiteness is a definite function of physical reflectance, but by no means a linear function. A 50–50 color-wheel mixture of white and black gives a light gray, not a medium gray. When the complete black-white range is divided into 10 equal steps of apparent whiteness, the reflectances come out approximately as follows (Newhall, Nickerson & Judd, 1943):

Whiteness	*Reflectance*	*Whiteness*	*Reflectance*
0	0	6	.29
1	.01	7	.42
2	.03	8	.58
3	.06	9	.77
4	.12	9.5	.88
5	.19	10	1.00

Surface color is a certain physical property of substances, the property of absorbing some of the incident light and reflecting the remainder. A perfectly black surface would absorb all the light that strikes it and reflect none; a perfectly white surface would absorb none and reflect all; while a gray reflects some proportion of the incident light. The *reflectance* of a gray is measured by the ratio of the reflected to the incident light. A certain mixture of white lead and lamp black will reflect 25 percent of the light; its reflectance is therefore 25 percent. It reflects more light when it receives more, but always 25 percent of what it receives. If you identify a gray as the same under brighter and dimmer illuminations, you are perceiving this physical property of reflectance.

The reflectance of white or of any neutral gray is nonselective. Selective reflectance gives surface colors of the chromatic series—red, yellow, green, blue, purple. A red surface absorbs predominantly the short waves and reflects the long ones; a green surface reflects predominantly the waves of medium length; a blue surface reflects predominantly the short waves. In yellowish artificial light, these statements are still true, so that the light reflected from a red surface, for instance, is redder than the yellowish illumination. If *O* is able to identify a red surface under various illuminations, it is because he sees this surface as redder than the general illumination of the field of view. He sees the particular color in relation to its surroundings, taking the surroundings as his cue of illumination.

White—to repeat—is not any specific degree of brightness; it is bright or dim according to the illumination. But under any given illumination no surface color can be brighter than the best available white. If a surface emits more light than it receives from the illumination, it is luminous and so appears. Black also has a unique standing among the surface colors. Absolute black would reflect no light under any illumination, but absolutely black surfaces do not exist. A good black paper will have a reflectance as low as 3 percent, while good whites run around 80 percent. The lightest gray in sight may be taken for white and the darkest gray for black.

In the achromatic or white-gray-black series, if we let M = illumination, S = the reflected light which enters the eye (the stimulus brightness), and A = the reflectance (sometimes called *albedo*) we have as the physical measure of reflectance:

$$A = S/M$$

As data for perceiving the surface color, the observer therefore needs S, which he certainly gets, and some indication of M, good enough to account for his relative success in perceiving A. Reserving till later the question, how he utilizes the data and "solves" the equation, let us look first into his chances of obtaining adequate cues of illumination.

Registering the illumination. We say "registering" so as not to imply in all cases an explicit perception of the illumination. In many cases we certainly do perceive illumination. We notice the change when the light is turned on or off, when the sun goes behind a cloud, when we pass from a dark to a light room. Looking out of the window in the morning for a weather observation, we know instantly from the light on the ground, trees or buildings whether the sun is shining and about how brightly it is shining. Even with closed eyes we notice changes in the light falling on the lids.

Since the eye in early stages of its evolution has no lens or cornea and cannot furnish a picture of objects, it is easy to believe with Bühler (1922) that response to general illumination is more primitive than perception of objects and that the initial response to each new field of view may be a registering of the general illumination.

Hering (1907) raised a logical difficulty: we must know the object color in order to utilize the reflected light as an index of illumination, while we must know the illumination in order to use the reflected light as an index of object color. We seem to be involved in a circle. The answer is:

1. In any normal field of view, more than one object is simultaneously visible, and the illumination falling on a particular object can be gathered from the stimuli received from the surrounding objects (Kardos, 1929).

2. The field of indirect vision yields little in the way of object color but affords a total impression of the illumination.

But it is not enough to register the general illumination, since different parts of the visible environment are often differently lighted. Can we perceive *regions of different illuminations?* Nothing is more certain. High lights and deep shadows, the flecks of sunlight under the trees, the shadow of a house or of a person—examples could be multiplied indefinitely.

A shadow is betrayed by the *penumbra* or half shadow along its edges, and the same is true of an area of extra illumination. We do not always notice the penumbra, but we utilize it in perceiving the shadow (Wundt, 1911). A famous experiment of Hering (1907) demonstrates the importance of the penumbra in the perception of a shadow.

It is the *ringed shadow experiment.* Place some small object so as to cast a shadow on a sheet of white paper; the shaded part is seen as white paper lying in shadow. Now outline the shadow with a heavy black line so as to conceal the penumbra: the appearance of a shadow is gone, and the shaded portion appears like gray paper. The reverse experiment can be made by screening the light from the paper except for one spot of light coming through a hole in the screen. Outline that spot in black and it appears like a whiter paper or even a luminous surface.

What is objectively a *shadow can be perceived in three ways,* according to conditions; we have mentioned two ways, perception of a shadow and perception of a dark surface color. The third is the perception of the *shape* of an object or, more generally, the perception of spatial relations and especially of the third dimension. When a white towel is hanging from a nail or a crumpled white handkerchief is lying on the table, some parts catching the light more strongly than others, the whole appears white, and the numerous shadows serve as indications of the folds and creases into which the cloth has fallen. The roughness of a wall or the coarse texture of a fabric (its microstructure) is revealed to the eye by numerous little shadows not separately observed but seen as unevenness of surface. A rounded surface shades off from high light to deep shadow, but the gradation is not easily seen as mere shading; a novice attempting to reproduce the object in water color or charcoal scarcely knows how to start, though he sees the shape of the object clearly enough, depending for this perception on that very shading which he has such difficulty in analyzing and reproducing. Many other instances could be given in which shadows are not seen as shadows but are utilized in perceiving spatial relations.

Conversely, if the spatial relations are clear from other cues, they will provide cues of illumination. If the three-dimensional form of a box is clearly revealed, its darker side is seen as shaded rather than painted black.

Lights and shadows stand out most clearly on a physically uniform surface such as a wall, a floor, or a lawn. When different parts of a uniform wall are differently illuminated, the illumination differences are easily perceived because of the spatial and material continuity of the wall. Let two duplicate objects hang on the wall under different illuminations. If one of them reflects twice as much light as the adjacent wall, so does the other. Since the wall is visibly uniform, the two objects should and do appear equal in reflectance. Any fairly uniform environment provides a base line for the registration of illumination and object colors.

Summing up this nonexperimental evidence we conclude that the general momentary level of illumination is registered, roughly at least, and that differences of illumination within a landscape or other visible environment can be clear and impressive.

OBJECT-COLOR PERCEPTION UNDER NORMAL CONDITIONS OF ILLUMINATION

As an introductory experiment we cite a study by Burzlaff (1931). He prepared a series of 48 gray papers which ranged by nearly equal steps from the best white to the best black obtainable. He determined the relative reflectance of each gray by matching it with a white-black color-wheel mixture, both gray and color wheel being under the same illumination for this calibration. Each gray was then designated as containing a certain percent of white. There were two pieces of each gray, 6 cm square, and one set of the 48 grays was mounted in regular order upon a large medium-gray cardboard, 60 × 80 cm, while the other set was mounted in irregular order on a similar cardboard. The irregular set was placed near a window where it was illuminated by diffuse daylight, and the regular set was placed back in the room, so far from the window that the illumination was only $\frac{1}{20}$ that of the irregular set.

O stood near the window, with his back to it, and saw both charts against the same background, the dark rear wall of the room. A certain piece of gray paper on the near chart being designated as the Standard, *E* pointed to the grays on the far chart, asking *O* to compare each of them with the Standard and tell whether it was the same, lighter or darker. This procedure was gone through six times with several Standards and the points of subjective equality were computed according to the Method of Constant Stimuli (p. 212).

The result in a word, was that *O* equated approximately the same grays, the one on the near, well-lighted chart and the other on the dimly lighted chart. He matched a given gray on one chart with almost the same gray on the other, in spite of the difference of illumination.

Burzlaff's main question was whether young children had ability to perceive surface colors. The table on page 434 gives the results for each age group and for five grays. It shows the average dim-light match for each bright-light Standard.

	Standards				
	75%	51%	25%	11%	5.6%
5 adults	81	53	25	12	6.0
4 seven-year-olds	80	53	24	12	5.8
5 six-year-olds	78	55	25	12	5.7
6 five-year-olds	79	54	25	11	5.7
5 four-year-olds	77	54	24	11	5.7

The table reads that adults matched a light gray (75 percent white) seen in good light by a somewhat lighter gray (81 percent white) seen under relatively weak illumination; and so on.

There is little sign of any age difference in these results. The four-year-olds match the grays as well as the older children or adults. Until one thinks over the situation, one sees nothing remarkable in such results and is inclined to ask why any person, child, or adult, should not see the same gray paper as the same, in good light or dim. Considering that the light reflected from any particular gray into the eye was only 1/20 as much in the dim as in the bright illumination, one begins to see a problem. The stimulus is diminished to 1/20, yet the object color seems the same, or nearly the same. The diminution of the stimulus has *some* effect, for the errors are mostly in one direction: it takes a somewhat lighter shade in the dim light to match a given shade in a bright light. The actual match is a *compromise* between an object-match and a stimulus-match, but is much closer, in this experiment, to the object-match.

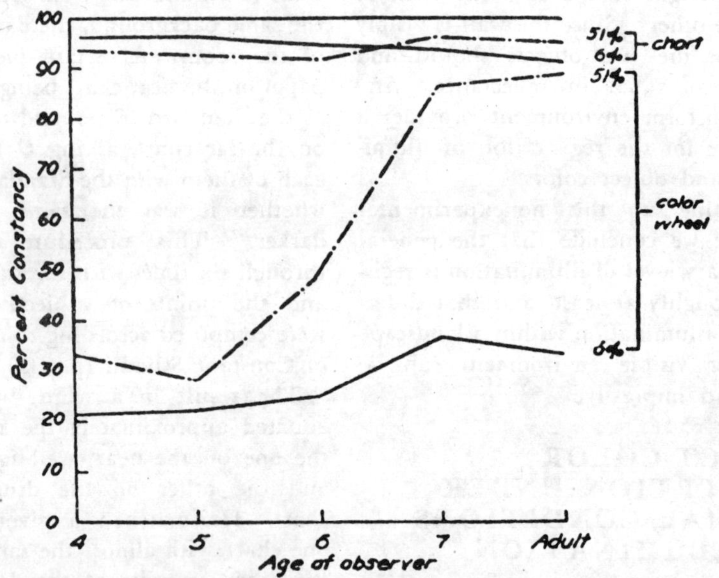

FIG. 15-1. (Data from Burzlaff, 1931.) Object color perception as dependent on age. Matches were made, by observers of different ages, between a well-lighted and a dimly lighted gray. Had the matches been according to stimulus brightness they would all have fallen on the base line, and had they been in strict accordance with object whiteness (reflectance) they would all have fallen on the upper horizontal (100-percent) line. They actually fell between these extremes, on the intervening lines. In the experiment with charts they approximated closely to reflectance matches, and changed little with age; but in the color-wheel experiment they were rather near to stimulus matches at ages 4 and 5 and approached object color matches with increasing age, this being truer of the light gray (51 percent white) than of the dark gray (6 percent white).

Matching color-wheel grays in different illuminations. The same author performed another experiment not so favorable for perception of surface color. Two color wheels, one placed near the window and the other back in the room where the illumination was only 1/20 as bright, were seen against the same dark background. A certain black-white mixture was rotated on one color wheel, and a similar mixture on the other wheel was adjusted until the two appeared equal to an observer standing near the window. Some of the results are presented in Figure 15-1 together with comparable results from the previous experiment in which gray papers on charts were matched. The diagram brings out three important results:

1. The actual match always (except for scattering individual exceptions) lies between what is demanded by the object color and what is demanded by the stimulus received from the object. It is a compromise between these two ideal values.

2. The actual match approaches much more closely to object color in the experiment with charts of gray papers than in the color-wheel experiment.

3. The experiment with charts of grays shows no change with age, but the color-wheel experiment shows a development with age toward accurate perception of object color.

Why was it more difficult to perceive the object color of a rotating color-wheel mixture than that of a plain gray paper on a chart containing various shades of gray? The rotation of a color wheel washes out the grain of the paper and so increases the difficulty of separating the surface color and illumination. Burzlaff lays less stress on this factor than on the simultaneous presence of many grays on the charts. He believes that "articulation" of the diversified field is important. Other authors have said "organization" of the field. These suggestions are rather vague, and it is more to the point to notice that each chart presented a whole scale of grays ranging from black to white so that the black and white served to *anchor* the two sets of samples (p. 249). Further, the charts themselves, the immediate backgrounds of the samples, were of the same medium-gray cardboard. Thus the *brightness ratio* of each sample to its background was the same on both charts, and each sample should appear to have the same reflectance provided the two backgrounds appeared identical (as in the case of the wall, p. 433).

Age curves similar to those of Burzlaff with the color wheels were obtained by Brunswik (1929) with squares of gray paper. However, he exposed only two isolated squares at a time, at different distances from the source of light. Up to 9–11 years of age, there was improvement in approximation toward the object-color level (Fig. 15-2).

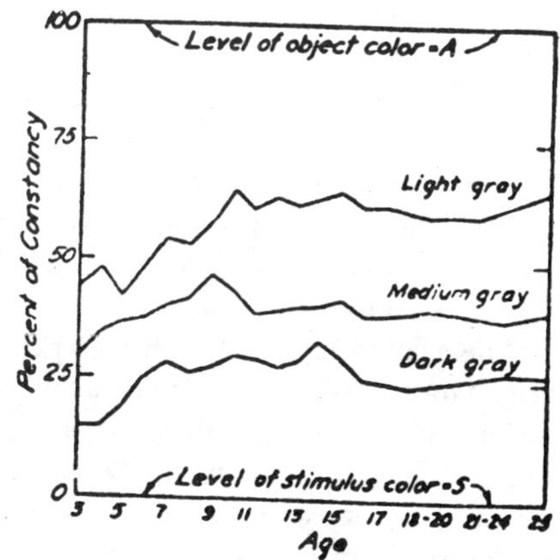

FIG. 15-2. (Data from Brunswik, 1929.) Age curves in matching grays under different illuminations. Each gray was five times as bright under one illumination as under the other.

Measurement of "constancy." Brunswik (1929) introduced a convenient way of stating the approximation of a perception toward object size, color, etc. When *O* attempts to match two grays seen under different illuminations, his response usually lies somewhere between two extremes, one conforming to stimulus brightness, the other to reflectance. If he responds strictly according to stimulus intensity, he shows zero tendency toward a reflectance match (or whiteness constancy); if he responds strictly according to reflectance, he shows 100-percent whiteness constancy. His actual match can be given a percent value according to its position in this continuum.

The best way to avoid confusion in this matter is by aid of a diagram. Locate three points on a line:

S(stimulus, percent reflectance for a stimulus match),
A(albedo, percent reflectance of the object to be matched),
R(response, percent reflectance of the subject's matching sample).

S	R	A
8 percent	24 percent	40 percent

Then the degree of constancy, as expressed by the formula,

$$\text{Brunswik ratio} = (R - S)/(A - S)$$

is the distance between stimulus and response, compared to the distance between stimulus and object. We have entered values below the line from a typical example.

The gray to be matched has 40-percent reflectance. We put it under an illumination of 10 foot-candles, to serve as our Standard. We have *O* select a match from a series of grays standing under an illumination of 50 foot-candles, five times the other illumination. For a stimulus match (zero constancy) *O* would choose a gray of 8-percent reflectance, 1/5 of our Standard. Enter 8 percent under S. For an object match (100-percent constancy) *O* would need a gray of the Standard reflectance; therefore enter 40 percent under A. Assume that *O* actually selects a sample with 24-percent reflectance; therefore enter 24 percent under R. Our formula becomes:

$$(24 - 8)/(40 - 8) = 16/32 = 50\text{-percent constancy.}$$

Partly because apparent brightness is more nearly proportional to the *logarithm* of the physical brightness, and partly for other reasons, a modified ratio was proposed by Thouless (1931) and sometimes, though not always, seems to give fairer results. The logs of A, S, and R are used. So we have the

$$\text{Thouless ratio} = (\log R - \log S)/(\log A - \log S)$$

which gives 68-percent constancy in our example.

Perhaps a better formula could be derived from the equal-step whiteness scale (p. 430). Look up the scale equivalents of the three reflectances and work out the ratio from these whiteness values. From our abridged table (p. 430) we obtain rough whiteness values as follows:

	Reflectance (percent)	*Whiteness (scale value)*
For S	8	3.3
" R	24	5.5
" A	40	6.8

$$\text{Whiteness ratio} = (5.5 - 3.3)/(6.8 - 3.3) = 63\text{-percent constancy.}$$ The justification for this whiteness ratio is that if *O* had seen the three reflectances mentioned all under the same illumination, he would have rated them in whiteness according to the standard table of equivalences. Because of the illumination

differences he chose for his match a whiteness that was 63 percent of the distance on the whiteness scale from the stimulus to the object values. For accurate work with this table, use should be made of the Munsell series of grays which have been carefully measured both in physical reflectance and in psychological whiteness.

Color constancy in animals. Since young children have shown considerable ability to perceive albedo or reflectance, we ask whether animals have any of this ability. Locke (1935) tested four rhesus monkeys and five human adults under similar conditions. The subjects saw before them a black and a white field separated by a partition. It was a black-white discrimination test (p. 582). When a monkey reached into the white field, which was sometimes on the right and sometimes on the left, he found a raisin as his reward. Once the discrimination habit was established, extra light was projected on the black field, to bring its stimulus intensity above that of the white field, but the monkey continued to choose the white field until the stimulus intensity strongly favored the black field. Brunswik ratios for the individual subjects were as follows:

Human adults: .10, .13, .13, .19, .23
Monkeys: .47, .53, .59, .65

Thus the monkeys showed decidedly more tendency than the men to persist in taking their cue from the reflectance rather than from the stimulus brightness of the two fields.

Burkamp (1923) went far down the vertebrate scale in his experiments on certain aquarium fishes. He had two problems in mind: to test the color sense, and to discover whether the fish responded to the stimulus color or to the object color. The procedure, in outline, was to train the fish to seek their food in troughs of a certain color, and then to apply tests showing (1) whether the fish were able to pick out this color from an assemblage of grays and other colors, and (2) whether they could do so even when the illumination was so changed as to alter the stimulus values.

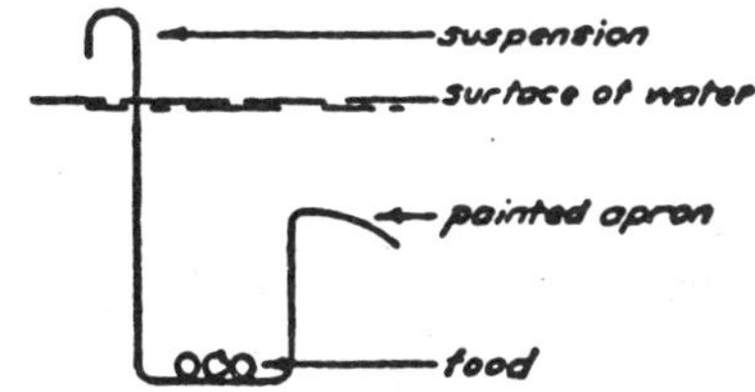

FIG. 15·3. (Burkamp, 1923.) Food trough for experiment on aquarium fish.

The troughs were made of sheet zinc and were shaped somewhat as shown in Figure 15·3. They were suspended near the top of the water so that *E* could easily see when a fish entered a trough. The "aprons" were painted various colors and shades of gray.

In the training series, which required 9–15 days, two feedings per day, the food was placed in 2 troughs of a given color hanging among 22 empty troughs of other colors. When the fish had learned to go to the troughs of the given color, they were tested with a fresh set of 24 troughs, one being the precise color for which the fish had been trained, and others of the same hue but lighter or darker in shade, of other hues, and of various grays. The result, as regards the color sense, was definitely positive, except for confusions between red and yellow.

When the illumination was altered by moving the aquarium closer to the north window, by drawing the shutters, or by passing the light through colored filters, there was very little change in the learned responses. Increasing the light did not make the fish go to the darker shades, decreasing it did not send them to the lighter shades, nor did colored illumination send them to the grays or to non-training colors. Most remarkable was the slight effect of very dim illumination: the fish picked out the object color in very dim light better than the human observer could do. Their color constancy—i.e., response to object color—was better than human. Burkamp points out that correction for illumination is even more important for a fish than for a land-living animal, since the fish is sub jected to large changes in illumination every time he moves from one depth to another in the water.

Though these results from children and animals indicate that no exalted intellectual process is necessary in correcting for illumination so as to see object colors, it would be going much too far to infer that no learning is involved. The opportunities for learning are certainly abundant from the time the young creature begins to use his eyes. As the mother moves about in sight of the baby, her face, her clothes, pass moment by moment from one illumination to another. If we assume merely that the object during these gradual and partial changes continues to appear to the baby as the same object, he is being conditioned to make all the necessary corrections. Perhaps it is relevant that Cruikshank (1941) found *size* constancy fairly well developed by six months in infants.

Various normal modifications of the illumination. In everyday life there are several different ways in which the illumination differs from one time to another and from one part of the field to another. Katz and others have tested human adults under these various conditions.

1. *The reduction screen or hole screen.* As already explained (p. 430) the hole screen allows the light reflected from a surface to reach the eye but conceals the surroundings and in particular the illumination conditions. The resulting appearance is one of expanse color, not surface color. If therefore the light from two surfaces is received through a hole screen—and if no microstructure or other little cues of illumination are visible (Sheehan, 1938)—the observer can only compare the two spots of light according to their stimulus values. The two spots seem equally bright when the stimuli are equally intense. Thus the hole screen affords a convenient means of matching two *stimuli* or determining their relative brightness and hue. When the screen is removed and the objects are viewed in the objective situation, *O* usually compares the object colors rather than the stimuli.

It should be noted, however, that *O* in most of the experiments has not been instructed to compare the object colors. He has been instructed to tell how the two surfaces appear to him, whether one looks brighter than the other, whether they seem to have the same or different colors. The point of view has been "phenomenological." *O* is supposed to maintain the naive attitude of everyday observation, which undoubtedly is the attitude of looking for object colors. Yet the instructions are somewhat ambiguous, and some *O*s adopt a more critical attitude, like that of a painter who tries to recapture the stimulus colors on his canvas. In most of the experiments *O* has not aimed definitely to capture either the stimulus colors or the object colors; and his observations have in most cases been a compromise between these two.

2. *Illumination perspective* is the term used for the gradation of illumination that depends on the distance of a surface from the source of light. Burzlaff's experiment employed this means of varying the illumination. With a point source, the illumination of a surface could be calculated, since it is inversely proportional to the square of its distance from the source; but in practice the hole screen or an illuminometer is used to establish a physical equation between the stimuli.

3. *The angle of incidence* of the light

upon the surface is an important factor. The more obliquely the light strikes the surface, the larger the area over which a given flux of light is distributed and the less dense the illumination. The arrangement of apparatus for one of Katz's experiments is shown in Figure 15-4.

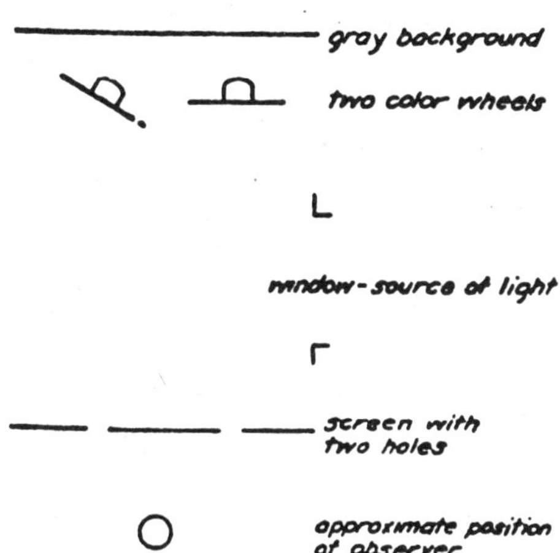

FIG. 15-4. Setup for varying angle of incidence.

The left-hand color wheel, being further from the window and also receiving the light more obliquely, was so much less brightly illuminated than the right-hand wheel that, when viewed through the hole screen, an all-white disk on the left-hand wheel was matched with 13 percent white and 87 percent black on the right-hand wheel. But with the screen removed and direct view of the whole objective situation, the all-white disk at the left was matched with 45 percent white and 55 percent black at the right. The Brunswik ratio figures out at .37, the Thouless ratio at .61, and the whiteness ratio at .52.

4. *Shadow*. One object plainly stands in the light, the other in shadow, and *O* makes an equation between them. Katz (1930) describes the setup shown in Figure 15-5. In the shadow was a 100 percent white color wheel, to be matched with an adjustable wheel on the bright side of the partition. *O*'s match through the reduction screen furnished the *S* values; and the *A* value was obviously 100. The actual matches given by two *O*s were as follows:

	First O	*Second O*
Reduction screen match	1.2% white	2.3% white
Open view match	32.2	27.1
Brunswik ratio	.31	.26
Thouless ratio	.74	.65
Whiteness ratio	.58	.50

The observers found it easy to reach a satisfactory equation when looking through the hole screen, but difficult in open view. They were apt to shift toward the stimulus equation in long-continued inspection of the field; the above equations were obtained with a view of only 3 seconds at a time.

Instead of a shadow, a spot of additional illumination may be used. For example (Katona, 1929) two gray squares are attached to the wall of the room, both being illuminated by a ceiling lamp and one of them standing in a bright circle of light projected on the wall by a lantern. The brightly illuminated gray is taken as the Standard and other grays are tried outside the bright circle till one

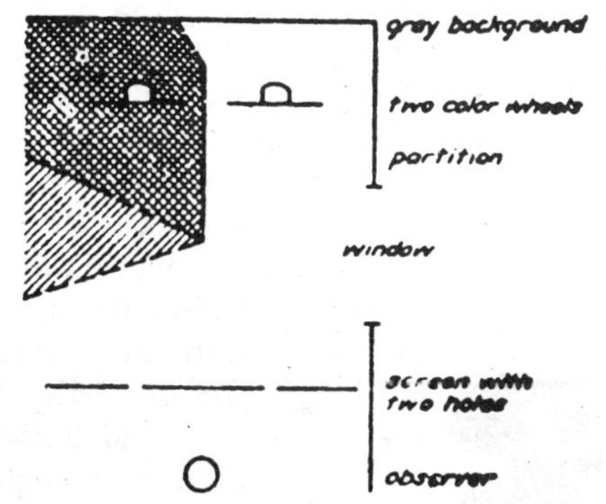

FIG. 15-5. (After Katz, 1930.) Arrangement of room for shadow experiment.

is found that appears the same as the brightly illuminated gray. Equations made with and without the use of the hole screen differ as they do in the shadow experiment; the observer makes some allowance for the extra illumination, but not enough.

5. *Looking through colored glass, smoked glass, or an episcotister.* If *O* is wearing gray glasses which absorb 9/10 of the light, allowing only 1/10 to reach his eyes, the stimulus he receives from any single surface is the same as if the illumination itself had been reduced to 1/10 by the interposition of a sheet of the same glass between the source of light and the object. If he is wearing yellow glasses, he receives the same stimulus as if the illumination had been made yellow by a filter of the same glass around the light bulb. If he holds a sheet of gray glass so as to see only a part of the field through it, he gets the same stimuli as if this part of the field were under reduced illumination. Thus the sheets of glass can be used in much the same way as a shadow or a colored spot of light in experiments on the perception of object color, and equations can be obtained between one surface seen through the glass and another viewed directly.

The episcotister (or "darkener") is a rotating disk with a sector cut out allowing light to pass a fraction of the time. With a cut-out sector of 180°, the light passes through in flashes with aggregate one half of the whole time; and if the speed of rotation is high enough to avoid flicker, the Talbot-Plateau law holds good (p. 382), and the stimulus is the same as if the illumination were reduced to one half. This statement assumes however that the episcotister disk is perfectly black or so screened as to reflect no light into the eye. In some experiments the episcotister surface is colored and gives the effect of colored light falling on the part of the field seen through the episcotister (Tudor-Hart, 1928).

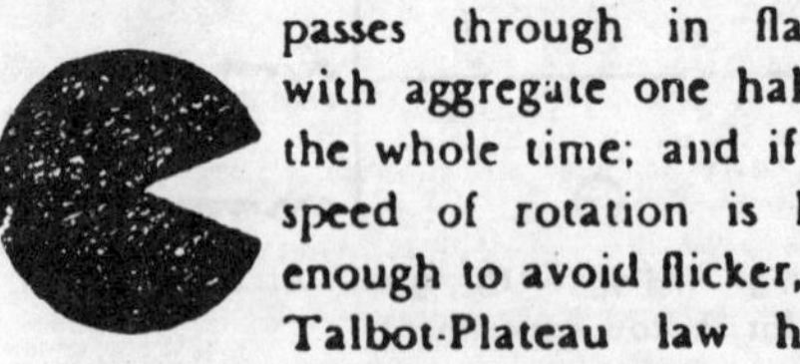

In an experiment of Katz (1930, p. 153) *O* looked alternately through two small windows in a screen. Just beyond one window was an episcotister, through which he saw a disk of white paper, standing a few feet away, its surroundings also being visible. Through the other window a color wheel was seen at the same distance, with no episcotister intervening. Black and white sectors were adjusted on this color wheel until a match was obtained with the white disk seen through the episcotister. The opening of the latter was changed from experiment to experiment, so as to reduce the "illumination" of the white disk to 1/4, 1/12, 1/36, and 1/120 of that received by the color wheel, and equations were obtained as follows:

Fraction of illumination received through episcotister	.250	.083	.028	.008
Fraction of white in matched color-wheel mixture	.330	.280	.240	.230
Brunswik ratio	.107	.215	.218	.224
Thouless ratio	.200	.489	.602	.696

The matches in the second line of the table would have tallied with the numbers in the first line, if *O* had matched according to the stimuli received, and would all have been 1.000 if he had matched white with white. He actually compromised, as shown by the ratios.

6. *Separately illuminated subfields.* *O* is shown two chambers, right and left, separated by a central partition, each chamber being lighted by its own ceiling lamp. *O* does not see the ceiling lamps but only the lower part of each chamber, with the floor and a side wall revealing

the illumination. In each chamber stands a gray disk, and the two grays, standing under different illuminations, are to be matched by *O* for whiteness. This direct and controllable setup was introduced by Hsia (1943) who found it to yield good constancy effects. He varied the illumination of one chamber quantitatively by raising or lowering its ceiling lamp, while holding the illumination of the other chamber constant. *O* could adjust the brightness reflected from the disk in this second chamber until the two disks seemed equal in whiteness. Some results are shown in Figure 15-6.

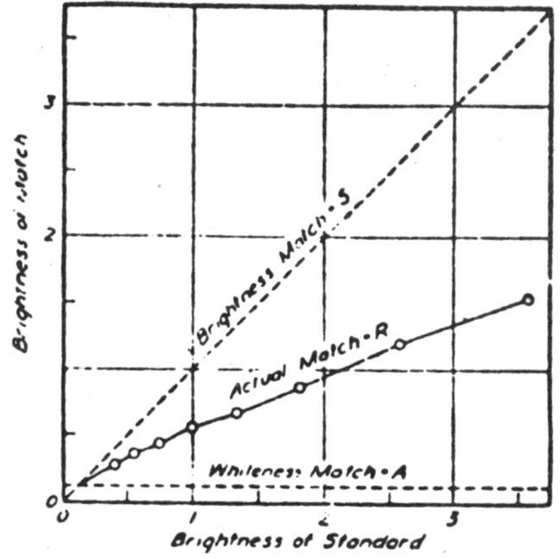

FIG. 15-6. (After Hsia, 1943.) Apparent whiteness as affected by intensity of illumination. Average for 12 adult subjects. A dark gray disk (reflectance = .12) was shown under different illuminations, its brightness in reflected foot-candles being shown by the abscissa. *O* tried to match it in whiteness by a disk standing under constant illumination but adjustable in brightness by aid of a spot light, the reflected foot-candles of the match being shown by the ordinate. The curves for the individual subjects differed considerably, but they all fell between the lines for a straight brightness match and a straight whiteness (reflectance) match.

Hsia's setup had certain other advantages. The chambers were open at the rear and both disks were seen against a distant black background. Thus direct contrast was equalized. The brightness ratio of the disks to the floor and side wall of the chambers was always different in the two chambers, and so could not be used as a simple basis for the judgment of whiteness.

DECEPTIVE INDICATIONS OF ILLUMINATION

Since the stimulus received from a surface depends both on its reflectance and on the illumination, so that successful perception of the reflectance must somehow take the illumination into account, we should be able to mislead an observer by deceptive cues of illumination and obtain utterly false reports of object color. Such experiments might bring out the important cues. Hering's ringed-shadow experiment (p. 432), in which the penumbra is concealed by a black ring, eliminates what is evidently an important cue, since *O* no longer perceives the true color of the white shaded surface. This experiment contains the germ of two strikingly deceptive setups designed by Gelb and by Kardos.

Concealed illumination. Gelb (1929) presented a wall and several objects standing in the rather dim light of a ceiling lamp, while in the foreground was a disk of black paper, receiving the bright light of a concealed lantern, which fell only on the disk. No penumbra was visible on the disk or the background (Fig. 15-7). *O* reported a *white* disk standing in the general illumination—white in the dim light instead of black in the bright light. But the instant a small bit of white paper was held just in front of the disk, in the bright light, the disk was seen to be black. When the white paper was removed, the disk snapped back into its former appearance. We might have expected *O*, once made

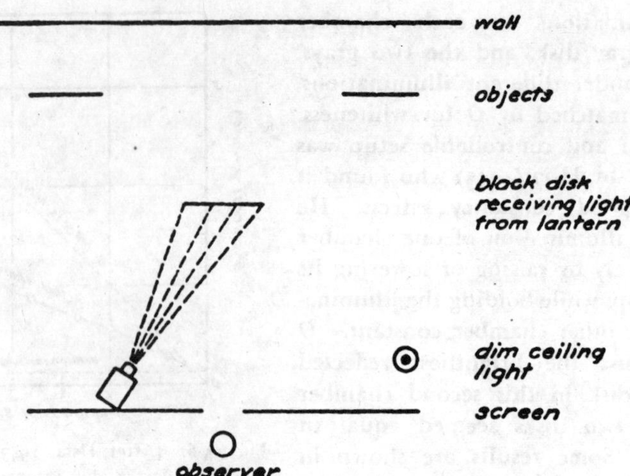

Fig. 15-7. Gelb's concealed illumination experiment. The lantern at the left is invisible to the observer, and its light is confined to the black disk. The wall and all objects in the room receive the rather dim light from the ceiling lamp.

aware of the extra illumination on the disk, to maintain this awareness after the white paper was removed. So he did no doubt, intellectually, but he needed a concrete visible indicator of extra illumination in order to *see* the illumination, or in order to see an object as receiving the illumination.

How could the bit of white paper make the extra illumination visible? There are two possible ways. It might have cast a visible shadow on the disk behind it. Or, if *E* took care to eliminate that cue, *O* still got brighter light from the white paper than could possibly have been reflected by any surface from the dim general illumination. The black could not appear white with the much brighter bit of paper so obviously in the same spot of light. This spot thus revealed itself as under special illumination. What would have been the effect of substituting a plain white disk for the black one, and having only the white in the spotlight? The white disk would send to the eye more light than could be accounted for by the visible illumination. It could only appear *luminous;* and this prediction was verified by Henneman (1935, p. 30). This last investigator found the spotlight from a concealed lantern a very satisfactory method of raising the apparent whiteness of a black-white color-wheel mixture; and it was later used by Hsia (p. 441) for raising the apparent whiteness of a plain gray paper. In a strict sense these experimenters, no less than Gelb, were deceiving the observer, since the true reflectance of the gray paper or mixture was obviously not changed by the extra illumination.

Concealed shadow. Parallel to this experiment of Gelb is one of Kardos (1934): a good light floods a field of objects, except for one disk of white paper which stands in the shadow of a concealed shadow-caster. The size and position of the shadow-caster are so regulated that the shadow covers the whole disk and nothing more. There is no penumbra or other indicator of shadow on the disk (Fig. 15-8). *O* reports a *black* disk standing in the good light. Move the shadow-caster a little to the side so that the edge of the shadow is visible on the disk, and the disk is at once seen to be white—white in shadow instead of black in good light. Return the shadow-caster to its original position, and the appearance of the disk reverts to black-in-good-light.

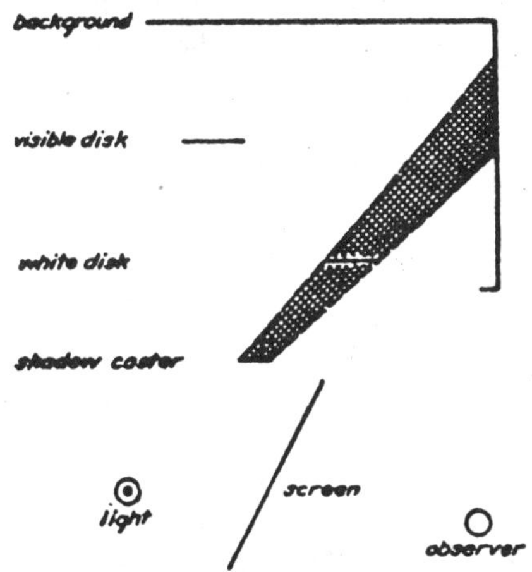

FIG. 15-8. The Kardos concealed shadow experiment. The only visible object shaded by the shadow-caster is the white disk which stands entirely in full shadow. O sees this disk as black or dark gray. Screening the shadow-caster is unnecessary, for even if O sees it he gets no suggestion that it is shading the white disk. See page 442.

MacLeod (1932) invented still another method of deceiving O regarding the illumination of an object. A shadow on the background made an object standing in front of it appear somewhat shaded. Thus the apparent reflectance of the object was raised. The larger the background shadow, the stronger was this suggestion and the lighter colored the object appeared.

Colored background. Cramer (1923) created a false impression of colored illumination by papering a corner of the room in a uniform color and illuminating it with white light from a concealed source (Fig. 15-9). The whole corner seemed to be receiving colored light, not quite so saturated as the actual color of the walls. The stimuli in this experiment were ambiguous: they could result from strongly colored walls under

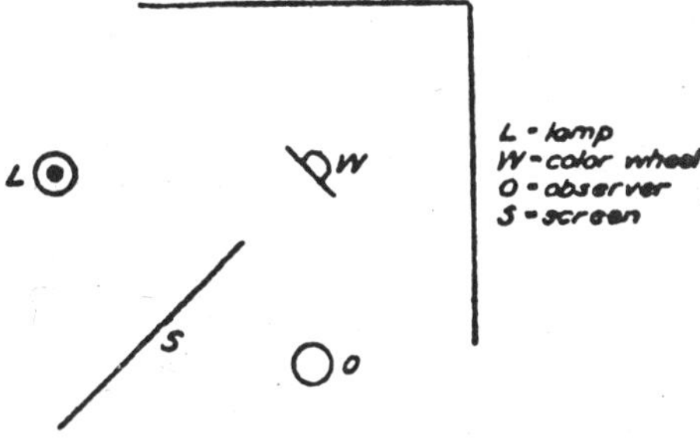

FIG. 15-9. (After Cramer, 1923.) Colored-corner experiment. The walls were papered in some color; the light was white. The color wheel contained a disk of the same paper as that on the walls, along with a disk of white, and the mixture was adjusted till it appeared white. Only a little white was required, since the disk seemed to be standing in colored light.

white light, or from white walls under strongly colored light. The phenomenal impression lay between these extremes—another instance of compromise perception.

In another experiment Cramer projected lantern pictures upon a yellow screen in a dark room. A white house, well focused, appeared in three dimensions and in its object color; it looked like a white house standing in yellow light. When poorly focused, it lost its object color along with its three-dimensional appearance and became a mere assemblage of stimulus colors. A blue square projected on a yellow screen appeared gray, as it should according to the color mixture; but the pictur of a child wearing a blue dress showed very clearly a blue dress in yellow illumination. The importance of good focus shows that indicators of the shape, size, and other spatial qualities of the object are strong supports for the perception of object color.

Still another experiment of the same author: between the prisms and the slide of a stereoscope was placed a sheet of blue glass. When the slide presented a snow-covered landscape, the observer saw the snow as white in blue illumination, and the white of the snow came out best when there were definite, outstanding objects in the foreground of the picture. Lowering the illumination deprived the picture of depth and made the snow itself appear blue.

Lack of depth. Illumination is so closely bound up with the three-dimensional structure of a scene that any way of concealing "depth" is likely to create a false impression of the illumination. The experiments just mentioned show this effect as produced by blurring and by dim light. Another way of concealing depth is to place the observer far away from a landscape or other real scene. In an experiment of Katz (1930, p. 354) a white disk was viewed through a rotating episcotister and thus in reduced "illumination" (p. 440). The disk stood only a few inches (20 cm) behind the episcotister, but when viewed from a short distance (50 cm), it was clearly seen to stand behind the episcotister and to be a light-colored disk in low illumination. When viewed from a considerable distance (7 m), it appeared to be simply a dark gray disk standing about in the plane of the episcotister. The depth was lost and with it went the appearance of reduced illumination and the white object color. The microstructure of a surface, often a good indicator of the illumination received, is invisible from far away. For this reason, too, surface color is best seen from a short distance (Katz, 1930; Henneman, 1935).

All in all, the striking results of the experiments with deceptive cues of illumination have demonstrated the importance of the penumbra, of visible surroundings of an object, of its surface microstructure and of its three-dimensional relations to other objects in the field of view.

FIELD FACTORS

The field in question is the retinal image, or the pair of retinal images, superposed in the visual cortex. Aside from some binocular disparity (p. 459) the field can be represented by a picture consisting of patches of colored light of various hues, and various degrees of saturation and brightness. This changing patchwork is very different from the seen environment with its three spatial dimensions and its objects of stable shapes, sizes, and colors, standing in certain locations and under certain illuminations. The retinal field must somehow get organized or play its part in a process of organization. There may be central organizers related to the organism's needs. There may also be more peripheral factors in organization. We know something of spatial summation and inhibition between neighboring rods and cones in the retina, and on a broader scale Wertheimer's field factors of proximity and similarity may operate at a relatively low level, even though in the brain rather than in the eye. Not limiting himself by any means to these few factors, but emphasizing stimulus gradients in the retinal image, Koffka (1935) made a valiant effort to explain spatial and color perception as a unitary process of organization.

He made good use of experimental data, but we shall not try to summarize his elaborate argument.

Field diversity. When the field is perfectly uniform over the whole extent of the retina (p. 430), what is seen is a luminous expanse and not an illuminated surface. The expanse may be white in distinction from red or blue, but not in distinction from gray. It is high, medium, or low in brightness, but not in whiteness. Some diversity is necessary for any reflectance to show itself.

In a perfectly dark room, let a round spot of light be focused on a white screen. It appears luminous, not a white surface under illumination. If a second spot of higher intensity is focused on another part of the screen, you see two luminous spots, one brighter and one dimmer—not one white and one gray. Now let the brighter spot be a ring just large enough to encircle the dimmer spot, and bring the two together in this arrangement—and an appearance of surface emerges. Some of the luminous appearance is gone, and the whole looks like a surface under a single illumination, the ring being white and the inner circle gray. If the tw lantern beams are weakened proportionally, you see the change of illumination, but the ring still looks white and the circle as gray as before. Wallach (1948) obtained these results, using two lanterns, one for the ring and one for the inner circle, with episcotisters controlling the intensities of the lantern beams. By duplicating the equipment he projected two ring-circle combinations, well separated, on the white screen in the dark room, and made a psychophysical test of his intensity-ratio theory of achromatic color constancy. A given gray reflects a constant fraction of the incident light, physically; therefore, two grays should appear equal if they stand in the same intensity ratio to white (or to what appears to be white). Specifically, in Wallach's double setup, the inner circles should be taken for equal grays if they stand in the same intensity ratio to their respective rings. In one test the Standard ring was set at the full intensity (100 percent) of the lantern, and its inner circle at 50 percent. The other ring was set at 12.5 percent and its inner circle was adjusted in intensity to match its Standard inner circle in whiteness (or grayness). The Mean of five *Os* was 6.7 percent, amazingly close to prediction. The constancy was almost perfect, and a similar result was obtained with other intensity ratios.

What was the role of the dark room in this experiment? It served to separate the two ring-circle units and prevent the brightness of one from affecting the appearance of the other. With a general illumination over the whole field the interaction would not be confined to the separate units, several intensity ratios would be present, and the constancy would be imperfect, as it usually has been found. Another possibility, not emphasized by Wallach, is that the dark background surrounding each unit played the role of black, and anchored that end of the black-white scale. With the brightest area in each unit perceived as white, both ends of the scale would be anchored and judgment of the medium gray would be stabilized.

Though Wallach stressed the importance of close spatial contiguity of two areas in order for their intensity ratio to be effective, other experimenters on field diversity have found it possible to enhance constancy by adding a visible white to push a gray down the scale or a visible black to push it up, the white or black being fairly near the gray but not in direct contact with it (Katona, 1929; Henneman, 1935; MacLeod, 1940).

Central organizers. Operating together with field factors such as intensity ratios, there must be factors pertaining to the person himself, *O*-factors, which have some influence on his way of seeing and matching colors in these experiments. Otherwise the large individual differences would be inexplicable. Under the same field conditions one *O* will give a Thouless ratio as low as .10, another as high as .80; the one matches nearly according to stimulus brightness, the other nearly according to reflectance. In everyday life we need to see object colors, but the painter needs to catch the picture colors, i.e., the stimulus colors. In the laboratory most adult subjects seem to compromise between these two divergent attitudes, some leaning more to one side and some to the other. Henneman (1935) queried whether these attitudes could be changed by a short course of instruction. Individuals who spontaneously gave a low ratio were instructed in "allowing for the illumination" so as to see the true gray of a shaded disk, and individuals whose original ratio was high were told of the painter's interest in stimulus colors. Most of the individuals were able to shift their observational attitude to some extent. The average Thouless ratios were as follows for originally low and high groups:

Original ratio	.22	.72
Ratio after instruction	.57	.47

We are not to suppose that this shift of attitude changes the apparent *brightness* of a patch of light. If you succeed in making the shifts, a patch of low brightness changes to white in shadow, or the reverse. A white object in dim light can be seen as white without looking the same as in strong light. You would probably say, as some subjects have said, "It looks like white in dim light." It lacks forcefulness or insistence (*Eindringlichkeit*), to use a descriptive term of Katz (1930). Insistence corresponds to brightness and to stimulus intensity. Katz found that the size of the pupil varied with stimulus intensity and not with the degree of whiteness as perceived. Also fusion frequency and the impression received from indirect vision tallied with stimulus intensity and not with perceived whiteness. Thus, stimulus intensity has direct effects besides serving along with other factors in the perception of object color.

If an observer is interested in perceiving an object (size, shape, color, etc.), registering its illumination is a step toward the goal of perceiving its color. Since the means precedes the end, the illumination ought logically to be registered before the object color is perceived. (In some cases, to be sure, we wish to perceive the illumination and use the known color of some familiar object as a means to the end.) In terms of the reflectance formula, $A = S/M$, the subject wants to perceive A; he has S from the interesting object, and he gets cues of M from the region surrounding the object. Once he is "set" for the illumination of a region, the stimuli from that region reveal the object colors instantly and without any process of computation.

The same formula can be applied to size constancy, with S standing for stimulus size, M for distance, and A for object size. In perceiving the size of an object we have to be set for its distance, and then we perceive its objective size instantly. We sometimes work the other way around, using stimulus size and known object size for perceiving distance (p. 480).

This little formula does not pretend to solve the more fundamental problem, how the observer transforms a set of stimulus variables into a quite different set of objective variables. He is given, for example, the brightness of a retinal patch and the brightness of its surround, but he perceives objective illumination and reflectance How he accomplishes this result is no easy problem for the psychologist. Field factors are certainly important, but the practical attitude demanded by life in an environment must be a potent organizer. Any theory of objective perception is forced to introduce "intervening variables" or hypothetical operators which are assigned the function of producing the observed response to the observed stimulus aggregate, the operation itself being unobservable at the present time. In our case, the intervening variable has been called "allowance for the illumination," or "taking the illumination into account," or "adjustment to the illumination." That the illumination is perceived is often a well-reported fact; what remains hypothetical is the supposed operation of perceived illumination in producing the perception of object color. Illumination and object color might be perceived simultaneously as results of some integral process of organization. Such would be the Gestalt type of theory.

Still other psychologists prefer to think and experiment at as physiological a level as possible and to discover how much importance for color perception can be assigned to such factors as Hering originally emphasized (p. 429), especially adaptation and contrast.

ADAPTATION

Adaptation to the intensity of light entering the eye is a clear example of adjustment to the illumination and has an undoubted effect on the apparent brightness of any surface. It will be recalled (p. 368) that the retina increases its sensitivity by a factor of a billion after half an hour in darkness. Without this adaptation a sheet of white paper would not only fail to maintain its whiteness in moonlight, but also it would become lost in a uniform undifferentiated darkness. Even the cones become adapted to a considerable range of intensities. But such long-time general adaptation does not account for the ability to compare the whiteness of objects in two subfields presented simultaneously under different illuminations. There is also some adaptation to the wavelength of light, and experiments along this line are especially welcome in view of the paucity of work on this phase of color constancy.

Think first for a moment of the familiar afterimage experiment. You fixate a red spot for half a minute, or long enough to "fatigue" or adapt a part of the retina to red. You then look at a gray surface, exposing the adapted part of the retina to white light from which, in effect, the red is subtracted, leaving a balance of blue-green. The effect is much the same as if, without the preliminary adaptation, you were shown a spot of blue-green illumination on a gray surface. If the spot appears to you as gray in blue-green light, you are perceiving the surface color and showing color constancy. But if the spot looks like a bit of blue-green surface, you are perceiving the stimulus color and showing little or no color constancy.

The interest in the afterimage experiment is in the stimulus color, but individuals differ in their response.

An experiment of Helson (1938) was much more drastic. The whole retina was exposed to a certain color for 15 minutes (though 5 minutes was later found to push color adaptation as far as it would go) and the grays to be judged were under this same illumination. *O* sat in a light-tight booth, flooded with nearly homogeneous light (all of one wavelength, p. 363). Walls and sorting table were covered with uniform paper. The illumination might be either red, green, blue, or yellow, and the paper lining the booth might be white, gray, or black, with reflectances of 80 percent, 23 percent, or 3 percent, respectively. Let us consider a session with red light and gray walls. When *O* first entered the booth, everything looked quite red, or at least flooded with red light. But after a few minutes he became adapted to the illumination. Then he was asked to judge a set of 19 samples, all nonselective reflectors (grays) ranging in equal-appearing steps from white to black. Ratings were made in terms of hue, lightness, and saturation according to the Munsell scale (p. 388), with which *O* had previously practiced in daylight. Samples with about the same reflectance as the gray walls and background were judged gray, of medium brightness. Brighter samples were judged red, and looked more saturated the higher their reflectance. Now comes the surprising thing; samples darker than the walls were seen as green or blue-green, the afterimage complement of the red illuminant; and the lower the reflectance, the more saturated the blue-green appeared. The lightness ratings of the grays were about the same throughout as in daylight.

In another session, the walls were covered with white instead of gray paper, and thus the eyes received stronger red stimulation during the adaptation period. So a higher *adaptation level*—to use Helson's term—was established. Only the two lightest grays appeared red, the next two appearing neutral and all the rest blue-green or blue. In still another session the walls were papered in black, the adaptation level was way down, and all but the darkest gray appeared red. Quite comparable results were obtained with yellow, green, or blue illuminants. In each case an adaptation level was established, with grays near that level appearing neutral, brighter grays appearing in the same hue as the illuminant, and darker grays taking on the afterimage complement of that hue.

A formula was worked out for computing the adaptation level from the stimulation received from the walls and samples (p. 233). We might expect the background white or gray to appear neutral after 15 minutes of adaptation, but it still showed some of the illuminant color. It still was above the adaptation level; complete adaptation to strong color was not obtained.

The experiment was repeated (Helson & Jeffers, 1940) with samples of various hues under (nearly) homogeneous illuminations. Practically every hue, as perceived under these conditions, was altered either toward the illuminant or toward the complementary hue.

According to these results, there is very little color constancy, very little ability to perceive the true surface color, when the illumination is confined to a single wavelength or narrow band of the spectrum. Fortunately, from a practical standpoint, we almost never have to contend with pure red, yellow, green, or blue illumination. Reddish, yellowish, greenish, or bluish light, such as is common, contains an admixture of white, and the authors cited find that even a small admixture of white light greatly improves the perception of surface colors.

Adaptation level sounds like a good physiological concept, something that might correspond to the momentary concentration of photoreceptive substances in the retina (p. 370). But when Helson (1948) attempts to apply the same concept to all the facts of constancy and contrast, to lifted weights and even to social phenomena, there is little left of physiological value.

CONTRAST

Contrast, like adaptation, is presumably a physiological and retinal process which may help to explain color constancy. We are using "contrast" to refer to a sensory response and not merely to a strong difference between stimuli (such as we have already found to play an important part, p. 435). As a sensory response, simultaneous contrast exaggerates the difference between two stimuli. Thus, a small gray square will look dark on a white background, light on a black background, blue on yellow, reddish on green, etc. It is easy to see that such effects could interfere with the correct perception of object color, but under certain conditions they might supply the necessary "correction for illumination." An object standing in shadow is ordinarily seen against a dark background; when well lighted, it is usually seen against a bright ground. Thus the background contrast tends to compensate for the difference in illumination.

Experimenters working with color constancy have usually taken pains to avoid direct contrast effects. In Hsia's setup (p. 441) two disks were seen in separate chambers and under different illuminations, but the chambers were open at the back so that both disks

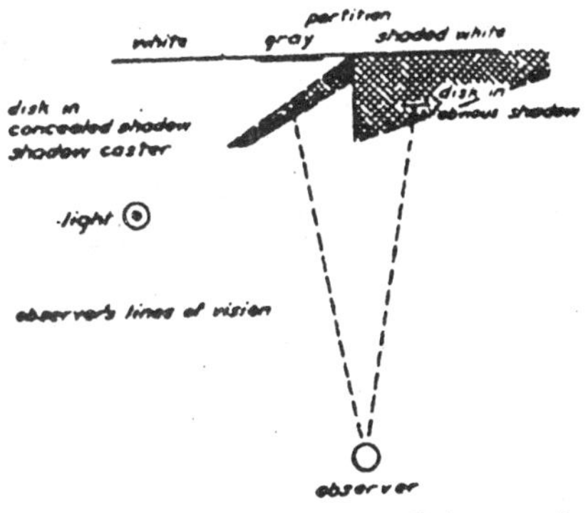

FIG. 15-10. (MacLeod, 1932.) Color constancy in the absence of direct contrast. The two disks were both white and both shaded, but the one on the right stood in visible shadow and the one on the left in concealed shadow. The immediate background of each disk was the same in physical brightness, one being gray paper, the other white in shadow. Yet the disk on the right was seen as white in shadow, the one on the left as black in good light. Nonadjacent parts of the left-hand field were white, to be sure, but the contrast effect is supposed to be slight between nonadjacent areas.

were seen against the same uniform black background. Typical whiteness matches were obtained with no aid from direct contrast. MacLeod (1932) obtained similar evidence from a modification of the concealed shadow experiment as explained under Figure 15-10. In spite of general and long-standing agreement that the constancy effects are different from the contrast effects, there are some points of similarity deserving of notice.

Peripheral and central theories of contrast. According to Hering (1874, 1876) the activity of one retinal area induces an opposed activity—a complementary chemical reaction—in the adjacent area. One difficulty was to explain the increased brightness of a gray field surrounded by black. How can black, the absence of a stimulus, have any effect on the adjacent region? The explanation is that white when present over a considerable area darkens itself by *internal contrast.* Each part of any uniform bright area induces the dark reaction in neighboring parts of the same area; a large white area is thus darkened more than a small area surrounded by black. Of many bits of evidence advanced in favor of the peripheral theory, perhaps the strongest is that of Sherrington (1897) who showed that the critical fusion frequency of a black and white disk could be raised by the contrast effect (Fig. 15-11). It is scarcely possible

Fig. 15-11. (After Sherrington, 1897.) Disk for demonstrating the influence of contrast upon flicker. The ring contains the same proportions of black and white as the rest of the disk, but they are enhanced by contrast which is effective not only in the immediate impression received but also in raising the rate at which the disk must be rotated in order to extinguish flicker. Flicker persists at a higher rate in the ring than in the rest of the disk.

that flicker could be affected by the psychological factors brought forward by Helmholtz.

Helmholtz's theory is sometimes said to attribute the contrast effect to an error of judgment, but this account of the theory is scarcely adequate. According to his view, the main factor in brightness and color contrast is the same as in many other cases of contrasted objects. A medium-sized man appears tall when standing with short men, short when standing with tall men. A loud note breaking into a soft passage seems remarkably loud, a medium speed following full speed of the automobile seems very slow. The principle, according to Helmholtz, is that clearly perceived differences are enhanced or exaggerated. Another factor in visual contrast comes into operation when the field of view is predominantly of one color: the average color of the field, Helmholtz said, is accepted for the time being as the norm and identified with white. In many cases the predominant color of the field gives the impression of illumination rather than of object color. In yellow illumination a pale yellow appears white or neutral, and a neutral gray stimulus therefore appears tinged with the complementary color. Gelb (1932) presents good evidence that contrast depends on the apparent illumination of the field rather than on adjoining object colors. Quite similar to Helmholtz's emphasis on the average color of the field is Koffka's (1932, 1935) conception of a general level, with particular bits of the field having apparent color according to their divergence from this level. These writers, however, avoid Helmholtz's intellectualistic phraseology and his reference to "illusions of judgment." They are more apt to think in terms of "organization of the field," a topic which we discussed more fully in the chapter on Perception of Form (see especially p. 408).

Even if contrast effects originate in the retina, they may still be enhanced in the visual centers, or they may be reduced by the effort to perceive the true colors of objects. When a piece of gray paper is laid openly on a sheet of colored paper, little contrast color appears. The surfaces are so distinct that the true surface colors are easily seen. If the surfaces are made less distinct by an overlying sheet of tissue paper, the contrast effect is unescapable. Another way of blurring the surfaces and so bringing out the contrast color is to hold the gray paper with its colored background just a few inches from the eye, too near for sharp focus. Conditions which facilitate clear perception of the spatial situation tend to annul contrast (Thouless, 1931). When one wishes to see the contrast colors, a contemplative rather than an object-directed attitude is favorable (Riedel, 1937).

Contrast effects in the perception of hue. When you are trying to perceive the true color of a surface, it is usually the daylight hue that you are after, though at times you are more concerned to make out how the surface will look in lamplight. Daylight or white light can be taken as the standard reference illuminant for hue perception. Yellowish or any other colored (but not homogeneous) illumination can be regarded as displacing the true surface hue toward the illuminant hue. Thus green in yellowish light looks yellow-green, and blue in reddish light looks purple. Wallach & Galloway (1946) point out that this pull of the illuminant toward its own hue is counteracted by a contrast push exerted by the surroundings under the same illumination. Thus, let a green object in gray surround receive yellow light: the object reflects yellow-green light into the eye, but the surround reflects yellow which tends to push the yellow-green away from yellow (and toward the complementary blue). If the contrast effect were equal to the primary discoloring effect, the daylight hue would remain unchanged under any illumination! Qualitatively this factor in hue constancy is certainly genuine, but quantitatively it is likely to depend on a number of variables. Wallach & Galloway showed that under certain conditions contrast could fully account for constancy in perceived hue. They set up parallel experiments on contrast and constancy of hue. They prepared two fields like Figure 15-12, making them

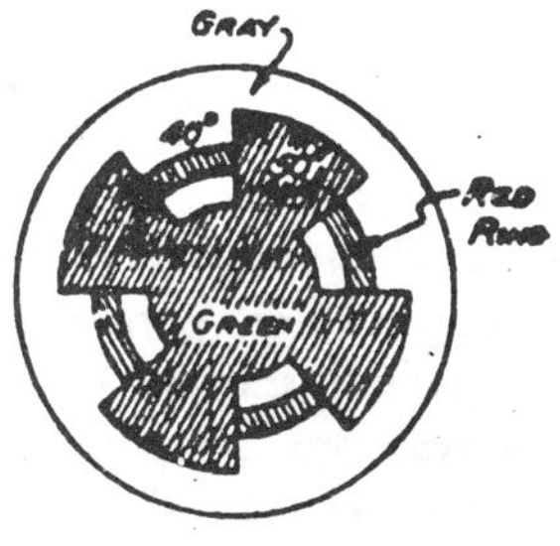

Fig. 15-12. (Wallach & Galloway, 1946.) Simultaneous contrast or color constancy? This setup is typical for simultaneous contrast when the green sectored disk is pasted over the red ring on a gray disk for the color mixer; the ring appears red, although the green and red have been carefully proportioned to give a neutral gray. The same setup is typical for color constancy when the green sectored disk is rotated separately as an episcotister; *O* reports a red ring seen through a transparent sheet of green.

differ in just one respect. In one arrangement the parts were clamped together and whirled on a color wheel—a typical setup for the contrast effect; in the other arrangement the green sectored disk was rotated an inch or two in front of the stationary red ring on gray—an episcotister setup for color constancy. In both cases the ring during rotation consisted of red and (bluish) green in such proportions as to fuse to a neutral gray. But in both cases the green background induced a contrast red in the gray ring, and this induced color was judged to be exactly the same in both. In one case the green appeared simply as a background surface color; in the other case as illumination. But the result was the same. No "taking account of the illumination" seemed necessary, since the perceived hue of the ring was predictable from the "well-known rules of contrast." Wallach would probably explain both contrast and constancy by the dynamics of field forces (Köhler & Wallach, 1944).

This ingenious experiment deserves a little further discussion from the standpoint of "perception of object color." Since *O* reported a red ring when there was a red ring present, his performance may seem to demonstrate an excellent grade of object-color perception. Actually, *O* was not shown the red ring but only a gray one composed of fused red and green sectors. (It could have been composed of white and black sectors, or of yellow and blue; the apparatus would be more difficult to construct but could be made to deliver the same effective stimuli—Heider, 1932.) To demonstrate accurate perception of object color, *O* should have reported a gray ring. If we query why he failed to report the gray ring, we find that he had to contend with subtly deceptive cues of illumination. The episcotister green "seemed to cover the ring and the rest of the field equally." Actually, the green did not cover the gray ring, for the gray was composed of balanced green and red, with no surplus green covering the gray. But from *O*'s standpoint the ring reflected gray while under green illumination, and must therefore be a red ring. So *O*'s report of a red ring conformed to the available cues, but the red color that he saw was doubtless induced by contrast with the green surround.

In an earlier experiment of Heider (1932) the contrast effect was kept down and a correct cue of the objective situation was presented. Yellow spots seen through a blue episcotister (Fig. 15·13) showed as bluish gray, the blue not be-

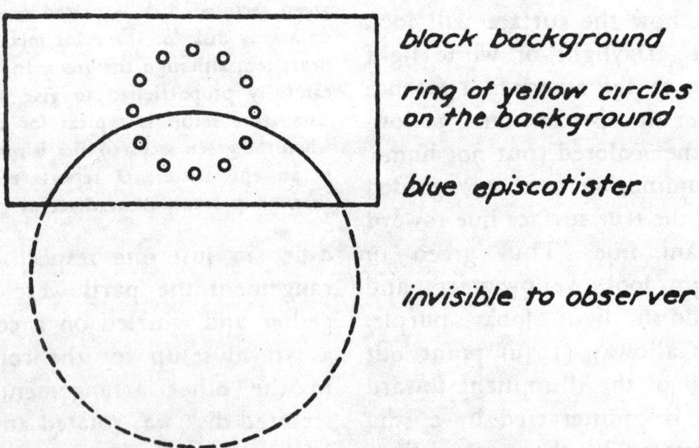

Fig. 15·13. (G. M. Heider, 1932.) Setup for study of hue perception. The blue episcotister stands well in front of the background plane. In one condition this background is concealed except for the segment seen through the episcotister; in the other condition the entire background is visible. The whole field is well lighted by ceiling lamps.

ing completely neutralized by the yellow, and the contrast effect from the dark blue background not being noticeable. But these same spots, when seen as parts of a circle of yellow spots on the wall, appeared correctly to be yellow spots seen through a blue veil.

It seems that contrast can work either for or against the perception of object colors, much depending upon how clearly the spatial structure of the situation is revealed.

Color constancy in photographs and painting. We have seen that the perception of color involves consideration of much more than a bit of physics and of retinal physiology. It is a very complicated process, involving interaction at many levels in the nervous system. Although several approaches are possible, a broad functional viewpoint seems to organize the experimental findings in an adequate fashion. By functional approach we mean asking what the *O* is doing; he is dealing with colored objects, like books, tables, and walls, rather than with patches of pure color. But to perceive object color correctly, he must make allowance for varying conditions of illumination; so we say he registers the illumination. At worst, registration of the illumination is a construct, useful in organizing the facts. But there is always the hope that we shall find a physiological mechanism that performs this function.

The functional approach gives us some hints as to why constancy is often incomplete in laboratory experiments. The simplified situation may lack many cues that tie down the perception in a normal situation. Especially important is *memory color;* a dollar bill looks green in any illumination because we know it is green, but a slip of green paper may change its appearance with deceptive illumination. Another factor is the attitude or task adopted by *O*. As we have seen, the laboratory *O* may set himself for a stimulus match, in contrast to the object-set characteristic of daily life. Several of these points are nicely illustrated in photographs (Evans, 1943; Evans & Klute, 1944). Offhand, one would think that the best photograph would be the one which represented the physical distribution of light and shade most accurately. This is far from true. For example, a white patch in the moderate shade would look quite gray in a photograph. This is not a failure of photography but a failure of perceptual constancy. But why should not constancy hold in a photograph as well as in a real view? The answer seems to be that there is an inadequate perception of light and shade in a photograph. Much of the failure is due to the lack of depth in photographs; remember Katz's demonstration that three-dimensional diversity favored constancy. Another factor is the better memory color of objects, as compared to pictures of objects.

Some of the factors are illustrated by a series of photographs taken by Evans. We shall not reproduce it; printers' ink destroys the fine gradations that are important. The scene was a room containing a man and other diversification. A patch of sunlight came through a window and fell on a bare wall. Two identical series of gray samples were fastened to the wall, one in sunlight and the other in shade. In the actual room one would have had little difficulty matching the grays correctly, despite differences in illumination. But in the photograph a middle gray in sunlight seemed to match the white sample in shadow. There was some constancy, perhaps 50 percent, even in this black and white print. A stereoscopic picture gave considerably better whiteness constancy, and a single color transparency in a viewer was still a bit better. By far the best reproduction of the visual effect was obtained by stereoscopic color photography. Clearly the more clues you give *O* as to the actual arrangement of objects in a world of light and shadow, the better will be his color constancy. Incidentally, the reader who is interested in photography might well read the references given above, for they illustrate the importance of the psychology of perception to anyone who works with photography, either old-style or colored.

And now a final word about the artist. We have to qualify a statement we made earlier in this chapter. The painter must not make an accurate reproduction of his scene, in the sense that a color photograph can be accurate. If he did, the picture would suffer from too great contrasts, due to partial failure of perceptual constancy. For example, constancy lets us see a white wall as uniformly white even when it is partially shadowed. Obviously, the painter must not paint it all white, or there would be no shadow. On the other hand, he must not darken the shadowed wall as much as a light meter tells him it actually is darkened, or it would appear too dark in the finished picture. The artist must learn to adjust his colors and shapes so that the finished picture, hung on a wall, will create the perception of something like the original scene. The actual picture will not be an accurate projection of the scene, nor will it be a copy of the perception; but you would get a more realistic impression from the painting than from a good color photograph.

16

VISUAL DEPTH PERCEPTION

Artists, philosophers, and psychologists have long been challenged by the everyday fact of three-dimensional seeing. The problem is set by the very structure of the eye, which forms an optical image on a *surface,* the retina. Such a mechanism can indicate the *direction* from which light waves come, but not, in any obvious way, the *distance* of a visible object from the eye. The difficulty is clear in Figure 16-1 which shows how several points in the visual field are projected on the retina. Light coming from different directions (A, B) falls on different retinal areas (a, b) and so can be discriminated. But, since all points lying in the same direction (A_1, A_2, A_3) are projected on the same retinal area (a), how can *O* possibly tell which point is nearest and which farthest from his eye? This is the problem of depth perception.

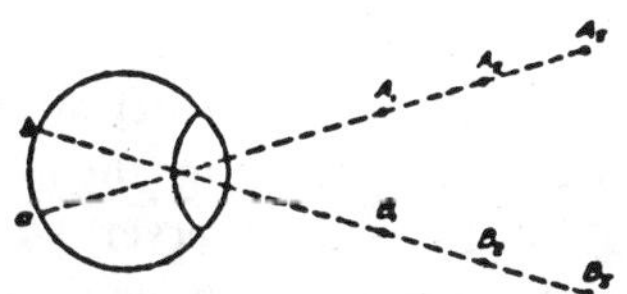

FIG. 16-1. The problem of depth perception. The images from all points on a given line, as A_1, A_2, A_3, all fall on the retinal point, a. Hence, the retinal point can indicate only the direction of an object, not its distance from the eye.

The problem can be framed in our familiar formula, $R = f(S, O)$. The R to be used is a matter of convenience. In animal experiments, which are unfortunately very scarce, we could use some motor response, such as a jump which might be accurately adjusted to the width of a gap in the path (p. 584). In a human experiment some verbal report, or an equivalent, is specified in the instructions. *O* may be asked to estimate the distance of the stimulus object in feet away from him. He may have to set two objects at equal distances from him (Method of Adjustment, p. 199); or he may have to judge which of two objects is farther away (Method of Limits, or Method of Constant Stimuli). Our problem is to discover what variables, both S- and *O*-variables, control the response. Here we encounter some complications. There are eye movements of adjustment to the distance of an object—movements of focusing and convergence—which are clearly responses and could be used as indicators of adequate or inadequate response to distance (pp. 457, 492). But they are not the R-variables used in most studies of depth perception. The contracting eye muscles feed back kinesthetic impulses into the brain, and when we are checking on the possible role of these kinesthetic impulses on depth perception, they belong under S-variables. In most experiments the eye movements are not definitely either R-variables or S-variables and have to be classed as *O*-variables or perhaps as intervening variables. There is another and very important class of *O*-variables, the effects of past experience, including both the long-term effects of learning and the short-lived effects of "set" (p. 4). One of the traditional problems in depth perception—a problem we shall not consider at any length—is the relative importance of past experience and original nature as *O*-variables.

Laboratory studies of visual depth perception are mostly concerned with the S-variables, which are signs or indicators of the distance of an object. Nowadays they are commonly called *cues* of depth or distance. How shall we discover and evaluate these cues? Why not ask the observer to tell us what cues he is using when he judges one object to be farther away than another? The trouble is that he usually cannot tell. He may even assert that he needs no cues, since he sees the distance of the object directly. He is mistaken here, as our previous analysis shows. It has been argued at times that the observer cannot possibly use a cue without being aware of the cue. The cue is a sign of distance, distance being the meaning of the sign; if *O* is not aware of the sign, how can he be aware of its meaning? The answer is that *O*'s whole interest is in the meaning, and if he gets the meaning promptly, the sign is forgotten or not even noticed apart from its meaning. At any rate, there are numerous examples of cues that are used without being noticed—such as the binaural time-difference cue of sound direction (p. 352). Sometimes, to be sure, the observer can tell what cue he is using, as when he says at sea, "That ship must be far away, for you can only see its smoke-stack peeking over the horizon." In general, we should avoid an overintellectualized view of the process of perception. Think, rather, of such a gadget as the modern antiaircraft gun director. People feed data into it by turning cranks, setting dials, etc., so providing cues or S-variables. The machine integrates these data and responds by pointing the gun and setting the fuse for the direction and distance of the target. It might be called a "depth-perception machine." The question of awareness need not concern us any more in the case of the human observer than in the case of the machine. If we can demonstrate that certain stimulus variables control the observer's response, that is the essential thing.

There is one important difference between the machine and the human observer with respect to cues of distance. Irrelevant or superfluous data are not fed into the machine as they constantly are fed into the human observer. We can approach our problem accordingly by inquiring first what possible cues of depth are present in the situation, and proceeding to work out the actual utility of these possible cues experimentally.

POSSIBLE CUES OF DEPTH

If we were going to construct an optical instrument for measuring the distance of an object from an observer, we could utilize either one of two basic principles, focusing and triangulation. Let us consider these principles as a framework into which we can later fit the diverse facts of depth perception

Focusing. In order to obtain a clear picture of an object, the camera must be focused for the distance of the object, and the same is true of the eye as shown in Figure 16-2. A camera could be arranged to measure the distance of an object. It would need both (1) a distance gauge such as is used to indicate how far forward the lens should be placed to focus for a known distance,

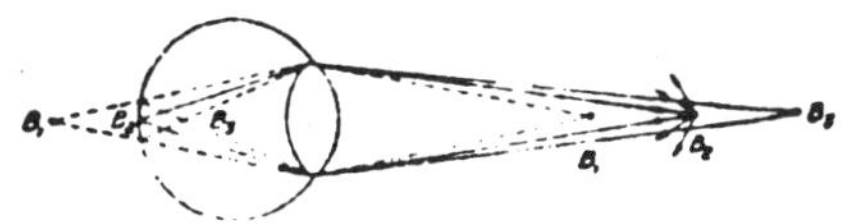

FIG. 16-2. The optics of focus. The point B_2 emits rays in all directions, as suggested by the arrows. The rays which fall on the lens are bent to converge on the retina, at the point b_2, as indicated by the solid lines. Rays from point B_1 reach the lens at a flatter angle and are brought to focus as b_1, in front of the retina. Since there is no surface to stop them at b_1, they diverge again, forming a blur circle on the retina. Rays from B_3 are brought to a (theoretical) focus behind the retina, giving a blur circle on the retina itself. All points at the distance to which the lens is *accommodated* or focused at the moment will be sharp; all others will yield blur circles.

and (2) a ground glass plate to substitute for the film while you move the lens in and out until you get a clear picture of the object. If you first get the clear picture and then read the gauge, you have a measure of the (otherwise unknown) distance of the object.

The eye focuses on an object, not by moving the lens forward and backward as in the camera, but by changing the convexity and strength of the lens. This result, called *accommodation*, is accomplished by the ciliary muscle. If the object is relatively distant (6 feet or more), the muscle is relaxed; as the object comes nearer and nearer, the muscle contracts more and more, so causing the lens to become more and more convex. Here then is a possible depth cue. First, secure a clear image of the object (by a process of trial and error); then the degree of contraction of the ciliary muscle will be signaled to the brain by kinesthetic impulses and can serve as an index of the distance of the object. If you focus on a very near object, such as the point of a pencil held a few inches from the single open eye, you may be able to detect a sensation of strain in the eye, but the conscious sensation is not necessary, according to our previous discussion. This cue might be serviceable at short distances, in the absence of anything better. But the fact that we ordinarily shift focus from one near object to another, without any "feeling around," shows that other cues get in their work first and render the kinesthetic cue rather superfluous. Whether it has any actual value can only be determined by experiments in which all other cues of distance are excluded.

Triangulation. A second source of possible cues of distance is found in the properties of a triangle. A surveyor can measure the width of a river by running a base line along the near bank and sighting from each end of this line at a point on the opposite bank. Having measured one side and the two adjacent angles of a triangle, he can compute the desired width by trigonometry. Similar data are available to the human observer in binocular vision. He faces straight toward the object and converges his eyes so as to obtain single vision by bringing the image of the object to the fovea of each eye. He then has a triangle to work with, the base line being his fixed interocular distance, and the adjacent angles being the amounts of convergence of the right and left eyes or the sum of these amounts which is the convergence angle (Fig. 16-3). We cannot expect him to know his interocular distance in inches or

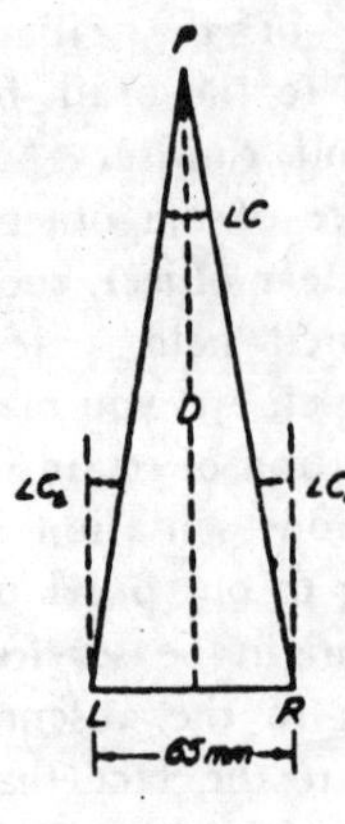

FIG. 16·3. The angle of convergence and the distance of the fixated object P is the object; L and R are the eye positions, assumed to be 65 mm apart (interpupillary distance). In converging upon P the left eye turns inward by the angle C_L, the right eye by the angle C_R, and the sum of these angles (which are equal if O is facing directly toward the object) is the total convergence and = the angle C. Given the distance D, the ∠C can be computed; or given this angle, the distance can be computed. The computation can use this formula: tan ½ ∠C = 32.5/D, 32.5 mm being ½ the interocular distance. However, it is more convenient and sufficiently accurate for most purposes to treat the interocular distance, LR, as the arc of a circle, with D in mm as the radius, so that ∠C = 65/D, when measured in radians (p. 351). A radian = approximately 57.3°, and more exactly 206,265 angular sec. So we have the following formulas:

(1) Given D in mm, to find ∠C in seconds,

$$\angle C = \frac{65}{D} \times 206{,}265 = \frac{13{,}407{,}225}{D} \text{ sec}$$

(2) Given the ∠C in sec, to find D in mm,

$$D = \frac{13{,}407{,}225}{C} \text{ mm}$$

For example, when single vision is secured by a total convergence of 10°, the distance of the object $= \frac{13{,}407{,}225}{36{,}000} = 372$ mm (about 15 in).

In experimental work, D is the primary measurement and the angle C is computed from D. Here are a few corresponding values:

D in mm	*∠C in sec*	*= approx.*	*D in mm*	*∠C in sec*	*= approx.*
100	134,072	36°	1,000	13,407	3.7°
300	44,691	12°	10,000	1,341	0.37°
600	22,345	6°	50,000	268	0.07°

millimeters, but it is a distance to which he is thoroughly habituated. Nor can we expect him to perceive the convergence angle in radians or degrees, but he might register it in terms of muscular contraction. Single vision of a distant object (say over 150 feet away) is obtained with the eyes in the parallel position, but as the object comes nearer, the internal rectus muscles contract more and more to secure proper convergence and single vision. Kinesthetic impulses from these muscles, fed back into the brain, furnish a possible cue of distance. Even if this cue is not precise enough to give the absolute distance, it might enable *O* to tell which of two points was farther away.

Double images. The kinesthetic cue of convergence, like that of accommodation, can operate only after clear single vision has been secured by the aid of some prior cue or by trial and error. A good prior cue of an optical nature is always present in binocular vision. The fundamental fact is brought out by a simple experiment. Take a straightedge such as a ruler or piece of blotting paper and hold it in front of the nose pointing forward, one flat side on the right and the other on the left. With the right eye alone you see the right side, with the left eye alone the left side. Looking with the right eye alone you see the far end to the right of the near end; and accordingly, in shifting your fixation from the near to the far end, you turn this eye to the right; to the left in shifting from the far to the near end. Looking with the left eye alone you see the far end of the left of the near end, and make the opposite shifts. Now look with both eyes, and you see both sides at once. If you fixate the near end, the far ends diverge, making a V opening away from you, with the right-eye view on the right; but if you fixate the far end, the V opens toward you, with the right-eye view on the left. In shifting fixation binocularly, each eye follows its own image, the same as if it alone were open.

In general, if a near and a far object are both straight in front and you fixate the near object, you get double images of the far object, the right-eye image being to the right of the left-eye image; but if you fixate the far object, so getting double images of the near object, the right-eye image is to the left of the left-eye image. If you get *crossed* double images of an object, that object is this side of your present fixation point and you must cross your eyes more to see it single; but if you get *uncrossed* double images of an object, that object lies beyond your present fixation point and you must converge less, look farther away, to see it single.

When the near and far points are not both straight in front or in the same line of sight, the eye movement from one fixation point to the other is compounded of a conjugate movement (p. 492) and a convergence movement. The conjugate movement is a response to direction and can be regarded as equal in both eyes, while the convergence movement is a response to depth and is essentially the same as in the simple case examined.

The significance of double images as cues of depth was pointed out very early by Hering (1861–1864) but has sometimes been overlooked by later investigators. The fact that some persons cannot observe them, perhaps because of strong dominance of one or the other eye, is no argument against their functional importance. But there is one difficulty in the way of a perfect demonstration: there is no way of eliminating them from binocular vision so as to find out how much depth perception would be left.

Binocular disparity. Double images occur when the rays from an object fall on noncorresponding areas of the two retinas. With both eyes converged upon an object, its image falls on the two foveas which are corresponding areas. Other objects may be seen single because they are at the same distance as the convergence point and so are imaged on corresponding areas. But objects nearer or farther than the convergence point are imaged on noncorresponding or "disparate" areas of the two retinas and are said to show disparity. The amount of disparity is a measurable quantity. If you hold your two forefingers straight before your nose and maintain fixation on the nearer one while moving the farther one away—or maintain fixation on the farther one while bringing the nearer one toward you—in either case disparity increases with the difference in depth. This fact is illustrated by the "Vs" of Figure 16-4.

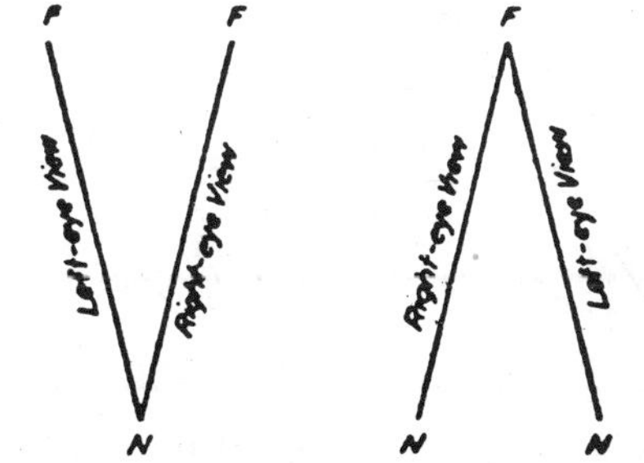

FIG. 16-4. Double images. When the near point is fixated binocularly, the far point gives uncrossed double images; when the far point is fixated, the near point gives crossed double images.

In angular measure, disparity is equal to the convergence angle of the nearer point minus the convergence angle of the farther point; i.e., it is equal to the change of convergence in shifting from either point to the other. So from the little table under Figure 16·3, we find that the disparity of a point 300 mm away is 36 — 12 = 24° when the eyes are converged on a point 100 mm away. This would be uncrossed disparity. If the fixation point is 300 mm away, the disparity of a point 100 mm away is again 24°, this being crossed disparity.

Disparity can be represented more pictorially in a projection of the retinal images upon a frontal-parallel plane through the convergence point, as illustrated in Figure 16·5. Here we are working with the tangents of the convergence angles instead of with these angles measured in degrees.

The horopter. For the sake of completeness, we should mention the horopter. This is the locus of all points in space that give nondisparate images at a given degree of convergence. For example, fixate an object at 10 feet from the head. The object fixated will appear single, since the eyes are converged to throw its image on corresponding foveal points of the two eyes. Objects nearer than or beyond the fixation point, but in essentially the same line of regard, will give double images because they stimulate noncorresponding retinal points. But now consider objects off to one side, in the periphery of the visual field. How far from the eye must they be to stimulate corresponding points and be seen as single? At first thought it would seem that all points at the same distance from the eyes, 10 feet in our example, would be seen as single, that is, that the horopter would be a

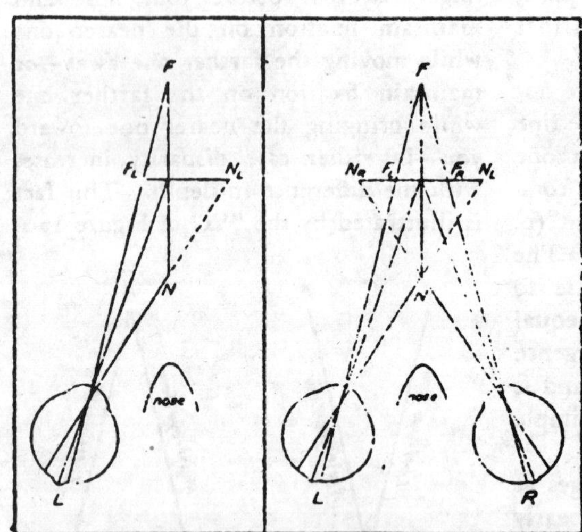

FIG. 16·5. Disparity as shown by the projection method. The straightedge NF, extending forward in the primary line of sight, is viewed with the eyes fixated on its middle point. To simplify matters we show the left eye view alone in the first frame. The fixated middle point is imaged on the fovea, the far end to the right of the fovea and the near end to the left. Projected upon the frontal-parallel plane through the fixation point, the far end falls at F_L and the near end at N_L. The right eye alone would give a similar projection, but reversed.

In the second frame the same straightedge is viewed binocularly, and the right-eye and left-eye views are combined. The double images of F are seen to be uncrossed, those of N crossed. The disparity of the F images shows as F_L F_R, and the disparity of the N images as N_R N_L.

If the straightedge were placed obliquely or to one side, the same method could be used to work out the disparities. The resulting figure would be unsymmetrical but would still show the same main fact, namely, that whenever a point in space lies beyond the plane of the fixation point, the right-eye projection of this point lies to the right of the left-eye projection, etc.

spherical surface, with a radius of 10 feet, centered at the bridge of the nose. This turns out to be quite incorrect. It can be shown by geometry that the *theoretical* shape of the horopter is a circle which passes through the point of fixation and the centers of rotation of the two eyes. But even this turns out to be wrong when put to an experimental test, for there are certain complicating factors in the eye itself. The experimental determination of the actual or *empirical* horopter is simple in theory, but tedious in practice. *O* simply maintains fixation on one rod, and adjusts another at various peripheral positions until it looks single in every case (Fig. 16-6). As can

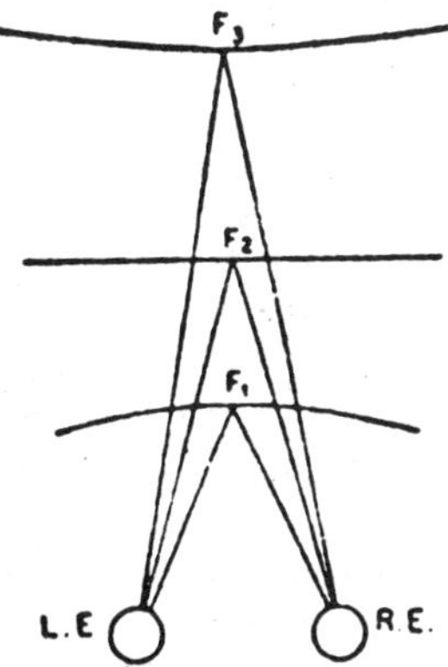

FIG. 16-6. (Ogle, 1950.) The empirical horopter. If the eyes are converged on a rod at F_1, a rod at any other point on the curve passing through F_1 will be seen as single; rods nearer to, or further from, *O* will be seen as double. The actual shape of the horopter changes with fixation distance, as shown by the curves through F_2 and F_3.

be seen, the actual shape of the horopter varies with the fixation distance.

A knowledge of the horopter is of importance in a thorough mathematical analysis of certain aspects of depth perception (Helmholtz, 1925; Ogle, 1950), but for most of us, fortunately, a nodding acquaintance with this complicated topic is sufficient.

Motion parallax. Parallax in general is the change in direction of an object resulting from a change in the observer's position. Binocular parallax is due to the slight difference in position of the two eyes. A much larger parallax results from a shift of head position by 6 inches to the right or left. By such a shift you may obtain strikingly different views of an object, but not obtaining them simultaneously you do not get the impressive stereoscopic effect of binocular vision. While moving, however, you do get an impressive view of relative motion within the visual field. As you move to the right, all the objects before you move relatively to the left, but the angular displacement of distant objects is much less than that of near objects—a pure matter of geometry.

The observer's eyes do not remain passive during a shift of head or body position. They are apt to fixate some object and maintain fixation on it by a backward pursuit movement (p. 510). If you fixate an object in the middle distance, so keeping the image of that object on the fovea while you move your head to the right, the images of all the nearer objects will move in one direction along the retina and those of all the farther objects in the opposite direction. You see the farther objects move with you and the nearer objects move backward. And the nearer any object, the more rapid is its relative backward motion; the farther it is, the greater its relative forward motion. How much use is ordinarily made of this excellent cue of depth we do not know. In the woods or any similar intricate environment, the distance comes to life as soon as you begin to move. In rapid vehicular movement even the far distance comes to life.

Size as a depth cue. If you know the real size of a visible object, you have a good indication of its distance. This cue, like those just considered, belongs under the head of triangulation. In Figure 16-7, A is the size, and D is the distance of the object, while *a* is the size of the retinal image, and *d* is the distance from the nodal point of all rays (rear of lens) to the retina. We have a pair of similar triangles, in which $a/d = A/D$. When *O* looks at an object, both *a* and *d* are given physiologically, even though he has no conscious knowledge of either of them. The size of his eyeball, being constant, can be taken as 1 and dropped from the equation, leaving $a = A/D$. The size of the retinal image obviously registers in his nervous system. If *O* knew the real size (A) of the object, he could solve the equation to get its distance (D). Since he obviously does know the sizes of many familiar objects, the probability is that he uses this knowledge constantly in judging distances. Many of the cues that the artist uses in depicting depth belong under this heading. Relative size, linear perspective, and position in the visual field all may be reduced to the same general formula.

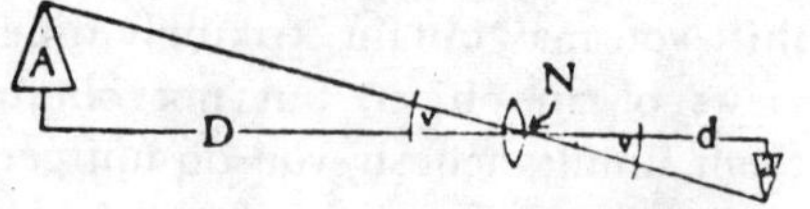

FIG. 16-7. (Schlosberg, 1950.) The geometry of visual size and depth. A and *a* represent the size of object and retinal image, respectively. D and d represent the distance from Nodal point (N) to object and retina, respectively. Since d is constant, the equation may be written $a = A/D$. The fraction A/D is the *tangent* of the visual angle (V).

For example, on a railroad track the ties are a series of objects of known (and equal) size, which subtend successively smaller retinal sizes; since A remains constant while *a* decreases, the equation demands an increase in D, and so the ties and tracks are seen in depth. There is one strictly visual factor in this group that the artist cannot use; the rate at which an object of known speed moves across the retina serves to give its distance, since the speed and rate are simply A and *a* per unit time. The same equation provides a means of finding A when D and *a* are given, as in experiments on "size constancy" and in many everyday situations.

Interposition or covering. The impossibility of seeing around a corner is certainly one of the elementary facts of visual experience and one which the little child learns very early in his career. He learns that one object may be hidden behind another, that the hidden one is farther away, and that he can often get to see the hidden object by moving to the right or left. So, by the combined principles of interposition and motion parallax, he can make the acquaintance of other depth cues. When the farther object is only partly covered by the nearer one, their common contour may show which is in front even without any movement on the observer's part or any familiarity with the two objects (Ratoosh, 1949). Also, the figure which looks more complete is likely to appear in front (Chapanis & McCleary, 1953). In certain situations, interposition is the only dependable cue of relative distance, as in the case of field artillery: if the shell burst obscures the target, the aim is "short," but if the target stands out against the burst, the shot is "over" and the range is too great. When Schriever

(1925) pitted the depth cues one against another, interposition came out the strongest. A "transit of Venus" is clear evidence that that planet is located between the earth and the sun.

Shadows. Another indication of depth and relief, much used by the painter, is the shading on a rounded or angular surface (p. 432). Also the shadow cast by one object upon another shows which object is farther away, provided the source or direction of light is clearly revealed. False shading or false indications of the source of light can give some very interesting effects such as converting positive relief into intaglio, convex into concave, and the reverse. Shell craters photographed from the air look like mounds when the picture is turned upside down; and many other examples have been found and published. A simple example (Fig. 16-8), if tried on a number of

FIG. 16-8. (After v. Fieandt, 1938.) Convexities and concavities on a plane surface, with light coming from one direction. Turn the picture over.

persons, will bring out several factors affecting the appearance: (1) the light in a picture seems usually to come from above; (2) the convex has the advantage over the concave; (3) there is some tendency to see all the figures as alike in relief. The assumption of overhead lighting seems to be just as strong in young children as in adults (v. Fieandt, 1938).

Is the tendency to assume overhead lighting the result of almost universal experience, or is there perhaps an inborn adjustment to this characteristic of the environment? Young chicks can be reared from the time of hatching in cages that receive all their light from below through the wire-mesh floor, the top and sides being covered with black cloth and even the feeding troughs being of glass. Hess (1950) raised an experimental group in this way and a control group with light from above. A realistic photograph of scattered wheat grains was prepared and mounted vertically in the test cage. In one half of the picture each grain had a shadow below it, as if from overhead lighting, but in the other half the shadows were above the grains. At 7 weeks of age, many of the chicks would peck at the pictured grains, and practically all that did peck chose first the grains conforming to the illumination in which they had been reared. Those accustomed to light from below chose the grains with shadows on top. A second experiment with samples tested after 1-6 weeks was less successful and seemed to show that adjustment to lighting from below was quite difficult—as if overhead lighting was after all more in accordance with the nature of chicks. The nature-nurture question could be raised in connection with every one of the depth cues; but experimental evidence is hard to obtain because so much spatial learning may occur in the first few months of even the human infant's life.

Aerial perspective. The distant mountains are blue in the (fairly) clear country air, and the buildings a few blocks away are gray in the smoky city. There are always some particles of water or dust in the air to produce this effect. When the other cues fail because of great distance, aerial perspective begins to play an important role.

Gradients. In a stimulating book on space perception Gibson (1950a) calls attention to the importance of surfaces such as the floor or ground over which we creep or walk or drive or fly. When psychologists speak of cues of depth, they are usually thinking of the distance of an isolated object or of the relative distance of two objects, and in their experiments they are apt to conceal the floor, ceiling, and side walls of the laboratory room because, with them in plain view, the observer would have no difficulty in seeing the distance of a specific object. Gibson argues that *O* has direct visual evidence of the floor as a flat surface extending out in front. If there is any regular marking or visible texture in the floor, this texture becomes gradually denser to the eye as the distance increases; and similar gradients of texture are seen in the road or field or water surface as we look ahead (Fig. 16-9). Such

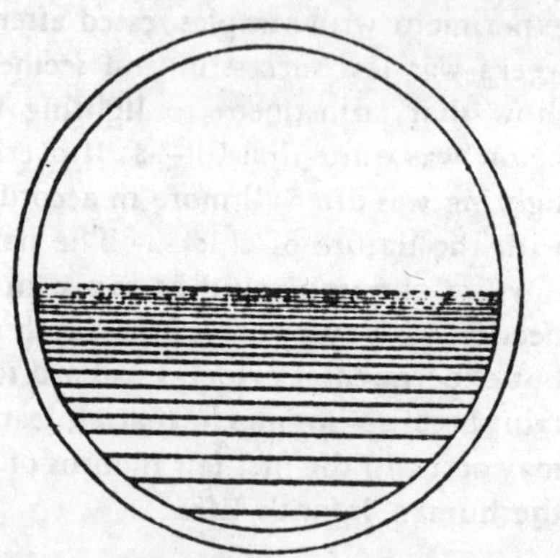

FIG. 16-9. (After Gibson, 1950a.) A texture gradient giving an impression of depth.

a texture gradient is just as truly a matter of retinal stimulation as the color or brightness of bits of the retinal image. Other gradients that contribute to the comprehensive spatial view are furnished by linear perspective and by motion parallax. These gradients in the retinal image are directly correlated with objective distance on the one hand and with *O*'s impressions of distance on the other. So an all-embracing spatial view of the immediate environment is likely to be obtained before, rather than after, a perception of the distance of particular objects. Such is Gibson's theory in bare outline.

Interaction of cues. In any actual experience several of these factors may be fed into our depth-perception machine. The outcome is not necessarily a mere sum of the effects of single factors. One strong factor, such as covering, may determine the perception, nullifying the others. Or the perception may be unstable and shifting. In general, known objects are surprisingly stable and often resist distortion by inappropriate accommodation, convergence, or retinal disparity. Hence, the attempt to isolate the effect of any single factor must be made with extreme care. Many of the discrepancies in the literature are due to a failure to consider this point, as we shall see. The difficulty has led some psychologists to become discouraged with the analytic approach (Vernon, 1937). But let us turn to the experimental attempts to evaluate the various possible cues which we have been considering.

In the *history of the subject*, the first important experimenter was the eminent painter and engineer, Leonardo da Vinci (1452–1519). Painters were having trouble in securing good depth effects. Leonardo advised the following experiment:

> Go into the country, select objects situated at distances of 100, 200 yards, etc., . . place a sheet of glass firmly in front of you, keep the eye fixed in location, and trace the outline of a tree on the glass. Now move the

glass to the side just enough to allow the tree to be seen beside its tracing, and color your drawing to duplicate the color and relief of the object. . . . Follow the same procedure in painting the second and third trees situated at the greater distances. Preserve these paintings on glass as aids and teachers in your work.

Besides taking note of practically all the depth cues that can be utilized by the painter, Leonardo made a beginning in the study of binocular effects. But it was the philosopher George Berkeley in 1709 who first pointed to the nonvisual, kinesthetic cues produced by the eye muscles in accommodation and convergence. Berkeley made no experiments to check on the actual value of these possible indicators of distance. The next important name is that of the physicist Charles Wheatstone, whose discovery of stereoscopic vision and invention of the stereoscope (1838) inaugurated the modern era of experimentation on space perception. (For much more on this history see Boring, 1942, pp. 263–311.)

THE STEREOSCOPE AND STEREOSCOPIC VISION

The fact of binocular parallax and the probable value of double images in three-dimensional seeing have been discussed. But something very important remains to be said on the binocular cues of depth. What Wheatstone pointed out in 1838 was that the two eyes get different views of a three-dimensional object located fairly near the observer. The combination and fusion of these disparate views, he conjectured, might produce the vivid depth effect of binocular vision. He set about testing this hypothesis by making appropriate drawings of the two monocular views of an object and presenting them separately but simultaneously to the two eyes, and he found that correct and realistic three-dimensional vision was so obtained.

Some ingenuity was required to secure good focus on the separate views. If small drawings or pictures are held rather close to the eyes, accommodation has to be strong while convergence is relaxed—a difficult trick for most people to learn. A pair of tubes to look through is some help. But Wheatstone invented a much better device.

The mirror stereoscope. The pictures are placed at the right and left and viewed by way of small oblique mirrors close to the eyes (Fig. 16-10). The pictures are at the same distance as the object represented and in the same direction from each eye by way of its mirror. So accommodation and convergence are correct, and the two retinal images are the same as would be received from the actual object. The observer's visual mechanism combines the two pictures and gets the same three-dimensional effect as if viewing the object.

Construction of stereograms. By the aid of construction lines like those shown in Figure 16-10, accurate monocular views can be prepared for use in a stereoscope. The construction lines are in a horizontal plane through the nodal points of the eyes, N_L and N_R. The mirrors can be omitted from the diagram, and only the nodal points of the eyes are necessary. At first it is safer to stick to objects that are uniform in horizontal cross section, like a wedge pointing toward you or a cube. Then the lines drawn from N_L to A, B, and C intersect the line ST at points that give the location of the vertical edges for the left eye, and similarly for the right-eye view. The resulting stereograms are shown in Figure 16-10,

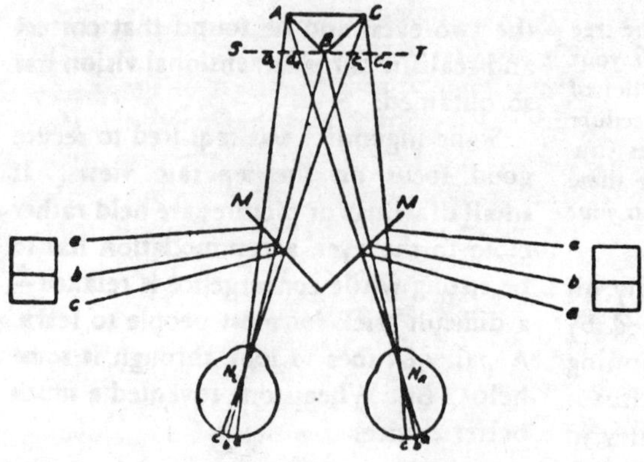

FIG. 16-10. The optics of the mirror stereoscope. The eyes are to converge and accommodate as they would in viewing the actual object, here a wedge ABC, and the two retinal images are to be the same as in viewing a projection of the wedge on the plane ST through the convergence point. With the eyes fixated on the near edge B, single foveal vision is obtained of B, but there is some (uncrossed) disparity for A and also for C. This disparity, as present in the projection plane ST, is copied in the two drawings to be placed at P_L and P_R and viewed through the mirrors, M and M. If the disparity is not too great, the double images are evidently fused, for O sees a single wedge in depth.

turned face up. With a more complicated object a separate diagram of this sort is needed for each important cross section; an upright pyramid would require two, one at the base and another at the apex. In such constructions it is necessary to stick to scale, and the scale had better be much larger than in Figure 16-10. If you assume 2½ inches as the interocular distance from N_L to N_R, you must represent the distance to the object on the same scale. You will rarely find disparities as large as those shown in Figure 16-10, which represents a rather extreme case.

This geometrical construction of stereograms is instructive but scarcely practicable with complicated objects. It is possible to look at the object with one eye at a time (without moving the head) and so obtain the two desired drawings. Still easier it is to take two photographs, moving the camera laterally between shots by the amount of the interocular distance. There are twin-lens cameras —really two cameras in one—that take excellent stereograms in a single snap of the twin shutter. Such photos are often taken at somewhat more than the normal interocular distance so as to increase the depth effect. For distant views the lateral distance may even be increased to many feet, as in successive airplane photos. If the disparity is too great, fusion of the two views will not occur: instead you get double images or binocular rivalry. This failure is frequent in stereograms prepared by students in a laboratory exercise.

It must be stressed that binocular disparity, resulting from the different locations of the two eyes, is horizontal rather than vertical. Only a small amount of vertical disparity can be tolerated, corresponding perhaps to the amount that would be introduced into a real situation by a slight cocking of the head. This requirement sometimes causes trouble with stereoscopic views taken from an airplane. The camera for such pictures must be oriented so that the movement of the airplane is lateral with respect to the desired picture, or the separate views will refuse to combine.

Reversed and increased disparity. The Wheatstone mirror stereoscope has a number of advantages in its large and open construction. For one thing, you can interchange the right-eye and left-eye cards and obtain a *pseudoscopic* or reversed depth effect. This little experiment is very instructive, because some pictures will give the effect and some not, depending on the objects represented and the various depth cues that may be present. In a line drawing, such as the wedge of Figure 16-10, reversing the direction of disparity by interchanging the right and left views converts a convexity into a concavity; the wedge becomes hollow and points away from the observer. But such reversal rarely succeeds with pictures of more concrete objects like a chest of drawers or a human face. A face inside out is scarcely a possible perception, though the reversal will work if the face is painted to look like a mask.

If large mirrors are substituted for the right and left pictures in Figure 16-10 and adjusted to be roughly parallel to the small ones, the lines of sight are directed outward toward objects in the environment. The disparity is increased, for the eyes are in effect separated by the distance between the large mirrors, perhaps a couple of feet. So the binocular depth effect is extended to faraway objects. In this form the mirror stereoscope becomes a *telestereoscope.* It increases the depth effect, making an ordinary room appear like a long corridor. Prism binoculars embody this principle in a smaller degree. By another arrangement of mirrors the lines of sight of the two eyes can be interchanged and a pseudoscopic view of objects obtained. (For a mathematical analysis see Riggs, Mueller, Graham & Mote, 1947.)

The prism stereoscope. The mirror stereoscope is too bulky for any but research and demonstration purposes. More convenient is the *prism* or *lenticular* stereoscope (Fig. 16-11) which is usually associated with the name of Brewster (1856), though Wheatstone also developed it independently. This is the gadget that was to be found in almost every home around the turn of the century. Its prisms take the place of the mirrors of Figure 16-10, deflecting the lines of sight outward just enough to center them on R and L pictures mounted

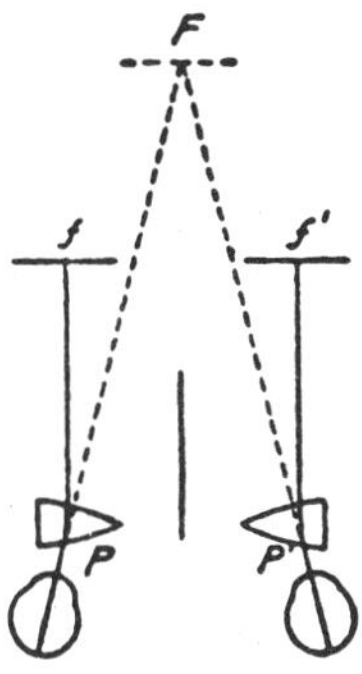

FIG. 16-11. Plan of a prism stereoscope. A cardboard slide presents the two views, f and f', the rays from which are bent by the prisms P and P' so as to reach the eyes as if from F, the point in space on which the eyes are converged.

on a card and placed straight in front of their respective eyes. A thin wooden partition or separator limits each eye to its own picture. The prism is usually ground with a slight convex lens component, so that the picture will be sharp at about 6 inches from the eye, even with accommodation completely relaxed. A large collection of carefully prepared photographic slides was available for these prism stereoscopes, and people could see the Grand Canyon, Niagara Falls, and London Bridge in surprisingly realistic fashion, all in their own parlors.

Other stereoscopes. The recent development of miniature cameras makes possible an even simpler and more compact stereoscope. The paper prints or colored transparencies are small enough to be placed directly in front of the two eyes, and with a pair of convex lenses in the eyepieces both convergence and accommodation can be relaxed as for a distant object. The colored transparencies are particularly effective since they can present all the depth cues except those requiring motion of the observer or of the field.

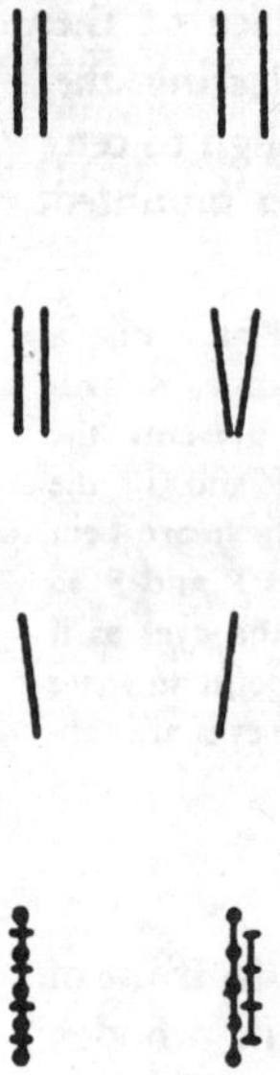

FIG. 16-12. (After Panum, 1858; Werner, 1937.) Width disparity and the elementary depth effect. If a vertical strip, such as one side of a ruler, is held directly in front with both edges equally distant, its width is the same for both eyes and there is no disparity. But if the left edge is farther away than the right, the strip is wider for the left eye, and there is width disparity. Fixate the near edge and the far edge is farther to the left for the left eye than for the right. (Cf. p. 459.) The double images of the far edge tend to come together and fuse, giving the depth effect. This principle predicts the depth effect to be obtained from a great variety of figures, a few of which are presented here.

For trial in a prism stereoscope, the R and L parts of each figure would have to be separated by the interocular distance. You may be able to combine them as they stand by the trick of "crossing the eyes." Hold a pencil point between the paired views as a fixation point and bring it slowly toward you, so bringing the paired views together. When they have come together, you may be able to remove the pencil and still hold the combined view of the lines. Since the eyes are crossed, the R eye seeing the L picture and vice versa, the depth effect is the reverse of what you would get with a stereoscope. It is a pseudoscopic effect but very clear when you get it. Play a waiting game, simply keeping the lines together and watching for the depth effect that may appear. Binocular vision is somehow able to superpose widths that are slightly unequal—to bring the double images together and obtain single vision from somewhat disparate retinal areas. The fusion must obviously take place in the lower or higher centers of the brain. A complex three-dimensional object presents many different width disparities for fusion. The fusion need not be complete in order to give some depth to the binocular view. Slight eye movements are always occurring without necessarily disturbing the three-dimensional appearance.

Some means for bringing stereoscopic vision to a group watching pictures on a screen has long been desired. The problem is how to keep the right-eye and left-eye views separate. The *Anaglyph*, or red-green stereoscope, is fairly successful. The picture is to appear in black and white, not in colors. The R and L pictures are superposed on the slide or film. The R picture is printed in green ink (better, blue-green) and viewed through a red filter, so that the figure appears black. Similarly, the L picture is printed in red and viewed through a green filter. The lighter background comes through in the filter colors which combine into white and gray by binocular color mixture. This stereoscope is perfectly satisfactory if each member of the movie audience is provided with a pair of cellophane filters conveniently mounted in cardboard spectacle frames. Of course, we cannot have technicolor pictures if we use this method.

The invention of Polaroid, a thin and inexpensive plastic film that polarizes light, has opened the way to a method that does permit both color and stereo depth. R and L pictures are projected by light polarized in two different planes, and viewed through cardboard frames with Polaroid film instead of red and green cellophane. At present (1953) several producers are promising feature pictures employing this method, and hope that it will help in the competition with television. In the early trials we may look for many impressive demonstrations of stereoscopic depth, as the producers show off the possibilities of the new medium; it remains to be seen whether a normal amount of disparity will add appreciably to the fair illusion of depth that is obtained by simple photography, plus the factor of relative motion of objects in the picture (p. 462).

The grid stereoscope. Store-window advertisements of certain products make use of the grid stereoscope. In its simplest form, narrow black vertical bars hide alternate vertical stripes of the picture from the right and left eyes, when *O* is at the correct viewing distance. These alternate stripes are cut from R and L photos of the same scene. Thus, the right eye gets its proper view only, and the left eye similarly. The more usual form of this stereoscope has a whole series of views, taken by a sliding camera, instead of just two photos. Thus, the two eyes get appropriate views at any reasonable viewing distance (Carmichael, 1951).

Depth without disparity. Even without the aid of binocular disparity a picture can give good depth if *O* can get rid of the cues that tell him it is really a flat surface. Some people can become so absorbed in the pictured scene that they forget the frame and other cues to flatness. The artist often finds it easier to eliminate such cues by examining the picture monocularly, through a tube. The little picture viewers that are becoming so popular are still more effective; in addition to cutting out the binocular cues that tell us the picture is flat, they also correct accommodation with the aid of a lens. Once freed from the restraining influence of negative cues, factors like shading, size, and covering can produce almost stereoscopic depth. (Schlosberg, 1941b.)

Instead of eliminating binocular vision, it seems to be possible to overcome the binocular flatness cues by supplying a mass of other depth cues. This is the basis of Waller's "Cinerama," demonstrated on Broadway in the fall of 1952. A very large curved screen, filling the whole stage, carries three pictures taken and projected from different angles. The net result is that the theater-goer seems to be surrounded by the picture, and gets very important peripheral gradients of movement, texture, etc. (p. 464). When stereophonic sound is added, it is reported that the depth effect is very impressive (Kaempffert, 1952).

ACCURACY OF DEPTH PERCEPTION

Several equivalent terms are in use: depth or stereoscopic acuity, stereoacuity, stereopsis. Sensitivity to slight disparity is almost incredibly keen, as can be appreciated on examination of carefully prepared stereoscope cards. For example, a standard test of stereopsis, prepared by the Keystone View Company, is a stereoscope card presenting several rows of five symbols each. The two views are duplicates, except that one figure in each row is displaced in opposite directions in the R and L views. The disparity decreases from top row to bottom, thus:

(line 1)

X M O WH   X M OW H

(line 9)

X M O W H   X M O W H

In line 1 the disparity is so great that the letter W would appear much closer to the observer than would the rest of the line. In line 9 letter M is similarly displaced, but by an amount that is barely noticeable, yet it would also stand out clearly in front of the other letters if viewed through a stereoscope. We shall give some thresholds presently, but here it might be interesting to note that sensitivity to slight disparities makes the stereoscope a very useful device for comparing two very similar objects. If a counterfeit note and a good one are compared in a stereoscope, even a minor dif ference stands out like a sore thumb. The same holds true of microphotos of two bullets which may (or may not) have been fired from the same pistol. The use of binocular disparity also reveals the relief of terrain in airplane photos. A cannon may be so neatly roofed over by artificial foliage as to escape detection in a single photo; but if two snapshots taken a hundred feet apart are combined in a stereoscope, the disparity will make the roof stand up like a mountain.

Early determinations of stereopsis. How small a difference in depth can be perceived in binocular vision; i.e., given D, a standard distance, what is the smallest additional distance, ΔD, that can be perceived? The fundamental experiment was designed by Helmholtz (1856–1866); it is the famous *three-needle experiment*, explained in Figure 16-13. From the depth threshold can be computed also the smallest amount of disparity that can function as a cue of depth. Without pushing the determination to its limit Helmholtz found that his disparity threshold was certainly less than 60 seconds of angular measure. Later determinations show that the average threshold is much smaller than even this small amount.

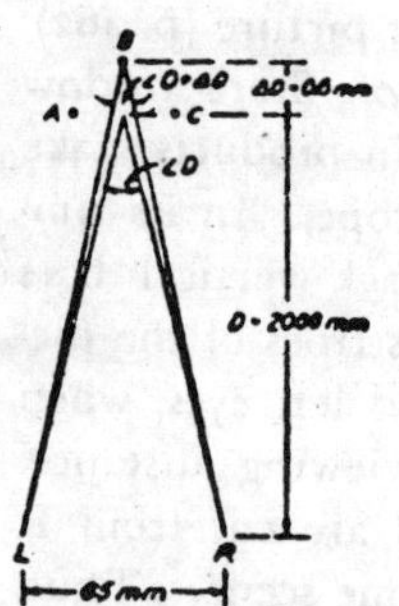

FIG. 16-13. The Helmholtz three-needle experiment. The dots A, B, C represent vertical needles, mounted on little blocks which are placed on a level table. Only the needle shafts are visible to *O* who is represented by the nodal points of his eyes, L and R. The needles are a few millimeters apart laterally. *O* must judge whether B is lined up accurately with A and C so that all three are equally far from him, or whether B is a little nearer or farther away. His average error is primarily measured in millimeters (ΔD), but such a measure cannot be compared directly with one taken with a different distance, D, from *O* to the plane of the needles A and C. A better measure is the *angle of disparity*, or angular measure of disparity, which, as explained on page 458, is the convergence angle for the nearer object minus that for the farther object. In the figure, then, the angle of disparity = the angle marked ∠D minus the angle marked ∠D + ΔD. A method for computing these angles has been explained under Figure 16-3 and will be applied here to a result of Bourdon (1902) who found one *O* successfully discriminating an offset of 0.6 mm at a distance of 2 meters (2,000 mm), as indicated on the figure. We have:

$$\angle D = \frac{13,407,225}{2000} = 6703.6 \text{ sec}$$

$$\angle D + \Delta D = \frac{13,407,225}{2000.6} = 6701.6 \text{ sec}$$

$$\text{Angle of disparity} \qquad = \qquad 2.0 \text{ sec}$$

We usually consider 1° as a pretty small angle, but in this performance an angle of only 1/1800 of a degree was perceptually utilized.

The Howard-Dolman apparatus. A rather crudely made version of the three-needle apparatus has been widely used in studies of binocular depth perception. It was devised by Howard in 1919 and taken over as a screening test to eliminate aviation candidates who might have poor depth perception. It consists of two vertical black rods, mounted on blocks and parallel tracks so that either rod can be moved toward or away from *O*. The rods are usually 1 cm thick, and about 25 cm long (2/5 in by 10 in), and are seen through an aperture which conceals the bases and tops of the rods. One rod, the Standard, is usually set at 6 m (20 ft) from *O*, and the other rod at a different distance. All *O* sees is two black rods; often his task is to adjust the Comparison stimulus (by pulling on an endless cord) until both rods look equidistant from him. In the original experiment Howard used a simple form of the Method of Constant

Stimuli, taking as the threshold the 75-percent point. Out of 106 *Os*, the best 14 had thresholds around 2 sec of arc, and the worst 24 ranged from 10 to 130 sec. This corresponds to a depth error of about 5.5 mm for the best *Os*, and 360 mm for the poorest ones. The poorest *Os* probably were not using disparity at all. A certain percentage of *Os* in any unselected population will be found to have little or no stereoscopic vision. The reason may be poor acuity in one eye, or habitual inhibition of one image. The latter often results from muscular imbalance, either slight, or in the obvious form of strabismus. The inhibition of one image may persist even after correction of the imbalance.

In a supplementary experiment with 9 observers Howard obtained comparable data on the monocular and binocular depth thresholds. The averages were: monocular, 285 mm; binocular, 14.4 mm—a ratio of 20 to 1 in favor of binocular vision. This result bears strongly on the adequacy of *size of the retinal image* as a depth cue, for this is the best cue left in monocular vision so long as *O* holds his head still. Unless his head is firmly controlled he has a strong tendency to shift it a few inches to the side, so bringing into play the additional cue of motion parallax (p. 461). Such behavior bears witness to *O's* dissatisfaction with the retinal-size cue.

The retinal image of the Comparison rod in this apparatus is of course smaller when the rod is farther away, but the large monocular threshold just mentioned indicates that this cue can play little part in the measurement of the binocular depth threshold. As a check on this question, Woodburne (1934) replaced the rods with illuminated slits, one slit being constant in position and the other variable in its distance from *O*. The variable slit was so designed that its width changed as it moved, maintaining a constant *retinal* size regardless of distance. The average threshold angle of disparity was 2.12 sec which is about the same as shown by the best *Os* on the Howard-Dolman apparatus.

Another way to attack the problem is to make the rods different in size, and see what effect this has on the judgments. Hirsch, Horowitz & Weymouth (1948) set up a Howard-Dolman apparatus with a rod two cm in diameter substituted for one of the usual rods (1 cm). This change had no marked effect on the variability of settings, but it did introduce a constant error in the expected direction; the larger rod was set further away, as partial compensation for its larger retinal size, which would make it appear nearer. The effect was small, of the order of 25 mm (at a viewing distance of 12.7 m). Note that *O* would have set the double-sized rod at *twice* the distance of the standard if he had been judging solely by retinal size: in that case the error would have been 500 times as big!

Variables that influence stereoacuity. There have been several studies on the effect of illumination, lateral distance between rods, color of rods, etc. on thresholds with the Howard-Dolman apparatus. Some of them are summarized by Graham (1951) and in the Tufts College handbook (1949). There are more recent experiments which employ a more compact type of apparatus, the variables being well controlled by rigid metallic construction, with micrometer drive for adjustment of the objects. The objects themselves are needles, fine lines on glass stereoscope slides, airplane silhouettes, etc. The head is kept in place by some sort of rest or by peepholes for observation.

During World War II a device of this type was used as a binocular *range finder* or *height finder*. The operator looked through a pair of reticles at two images of an airplane, for example. A knob varied the optical system of one eye's field so that its image could be moved laterally. Once fusion was obtained, the airplane appeared nearer or farther than the reference lines in the reticle, but additional adjustment of the knob brought it to the same apparent distance as the reticle lines. Its actual distance in space could then be read from a dial, or transmitted automatically to the computing machines at the guns. The practical importance of this device stimulated much research, both on the selection of good operators and on improvement of the design of the instrument itself.

The effect of illumination. Mueller & Lloyd (1948) set up two monocular fields on glass plates. Each field contained 3 vertical reference lines, called *fiducial lines* or a *reticle;* since these lines were equally spaced they fused binocularly and appeared all at the same distance; they corresponded to the fixed rod in the Howard-Dolman apparatus or to the two outer needles in the Helmholtz setup. The right field contained also a variable line which could be fused with a fixed line in the left field. *O* adjusted the position of the variable line until the fused "target" appeared to be at the same distance as the reference lines. Determinations were made at 10 levels of brightness, and the average thresholds for two *O*s are shown in Figure 16·14. The stereoacuity improves (the threshold becomes smaller) as brightness increases. The familiar rod cone break (p. 370) is visible in the figure, but some binocular depth acuity is shown even at scotopic levels of illumination (cf. Berry, Riggs & Duncan, 1950).

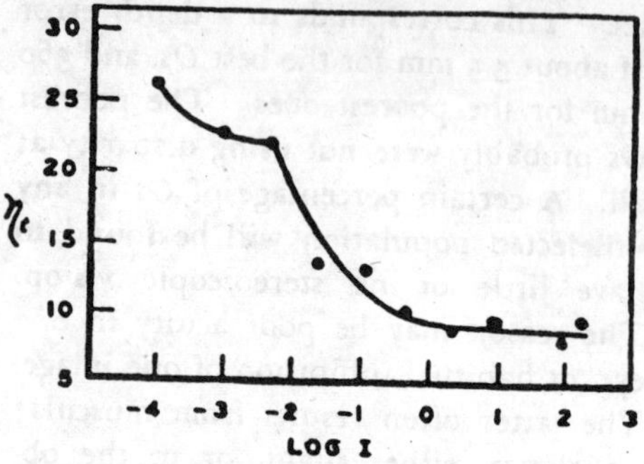

FIG. 16·14. (Mueller & Lloyd, 1948.) Stereoacuity as a function of illumination.

Lateral distance of target from reference line. A study by Graham, Riggs, Mueller & Solomon (1949) used apparatus like that of Mueller and Lloyd, though there was only one reference line in the reticle, and the target was an airplane figure instead of a mere line. Stereoacuity was at its highest when the target was close to the reference line, and fell off regularly as the lateral separation increased. The following table gives the geometric mean variation in the observer's settings, expressed in seconds of angle of disparity, for various separations of target from reference line:

Line-target separation (degrees)	1.0	2.5	4.0	5.2
Geometric Mean disparity (seconds)	23.0	40.1	51.4	61.7

These results, which are in agreement with some obtained earlier by use of the Howard-Dolman apparatus, seem quite "natural," since the relative distance of two objects ought to be best perceived when they lie nearly in the same line of sight; but no adequate theory of the effect has been worked out.

Depth and lateral acuities compared. Lateral acuity, the ordinary "visual acuity" (p. 385), refers to small differences in *direction* of two objects from the observer, while depth acuity refers to small differences in *distance* from him (Fig. 16-1). The two acuities should be

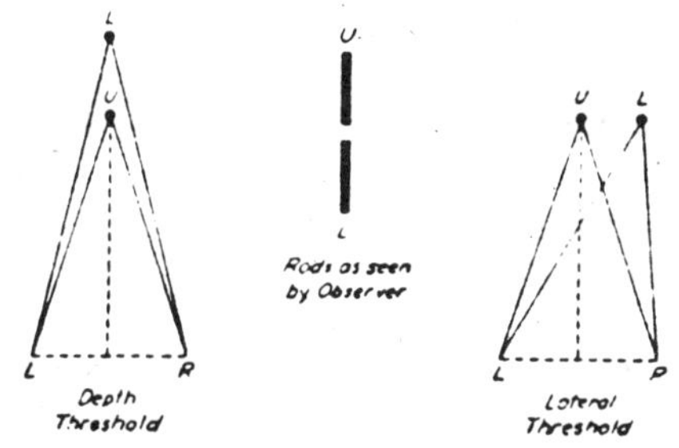

Fig. 16-15. (After Berry, 1948.) Diagram of the observer's tasks in an experiment comparing depth acuity with lateral (vernier) acuity. *O* saw the two vertical rods, U and L, as shown in the center. At the right and left are horizontal cross sections suggesting the displacement of the lower rod, to one side or the other for determination of the lateral threshold, forward or back for determination of the depth threshold.

closely related, since the important depth cue is the disparity of (fused) double images, which is a lateral disparity on the retina. To obtain strictly comparable threshold values it is necessary to measure both acuities on the same *Os* and with the same setup. A satisfactory device for accomplishing this result was employed by Berry (1948). *O* looked at two vertical rods, one just below the other, as shown in the middle of Figure 16-15. They were steel knitting needles, 2.4 mm in diameter, painted flat black, and were seen as silhouettes against a uniformly illuminated background. The viewing distance was 4.6 m (about 15 ft). The upper rod was fixed in position, but the lower one could be displaced either laterally or in depth. *O*'s task in one case was to judge whether the lower rod was *right* or *left* of the upper rod, and in the other case to judge whether it was *front* or *back*. It was thus a two category experiment by the Method of Constant Stimuli; *E* employed five different settings of the variable rod. The lateral acuity, as will be noted, was what is known as *vernier acuity*, *O*'s task being to judge whether the two rods stood in the same straight line; this is a sensitive method of determining simple visual acuity.

In this experiment the vertical separation of the upper and lower rods was varied from half a millimeter at the least to 20 mm at the most. The results for each separation are shown in Figure 16-16. The two acuities were both very good, and about equally good, when the rod separation was a millimeter or less, and the depth acuity remained about the same for the greater separations, but the lateral acuity was considerably less good when the separation was 3 mm or more. The flat curve for depth threshold may seem inconsistent with the results just previously cited from the experiment

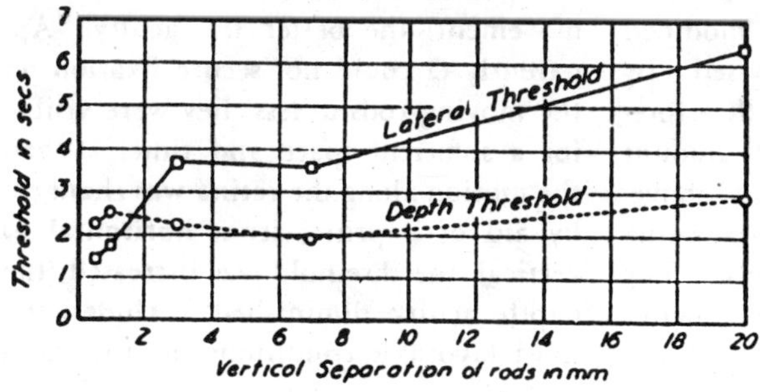

Fig. 16-16. (After Berry, 1948.) Lateral and depth thresholds as related to the vertical separation of the U and L rods of Figure 16-15. The values plotted are arithmetical means from three *Os* who agreed very closely among themselves.

with an airplane figure, but the separations in the present experiment were much smaller in angular magnitude, ranging up only to ¼ of a degree, instead of ranging from 1° up as in the airplane experiment.

The binocular depth threshold is much smaller than could be accounted for by the monocular angle between the near and far rods. The cue must be the binocular angle of disparity which is twice the monocular angle, as shown in Figure 16-15. The binocular disparity can operate only in the brain where the nerves from both eyes come together. We may recall that the brain centers were important even in simple monocular disparity (pp. 383–387). Until we know more about these higher functions, our explanations of acuity are bound to be rather speculative. One theory is offered by Werner (1938).

Berry used his setup also for presenting the rods by aid of mirrors, as the pictures are presented in the Wheatstone stereoscope (Fig. 16-10), and he found the depth acuity to be just about as good as when the rods were viewed directly. This finding justifies the use of the stereoscope in the study of depth perception.

Depth acuity with motion parallax as the cue. The probable value of motion parallax has been pointed out (p. 461), but the question remains as to how accurately depth can be perceived when only this cue is available. A modified three-needle setup was devised by Tschermak-Seysenegg (1939) with a forehead rest which allowed a small amount of side-to-side or up-and-down movement of the head, the needles being vertical or horizontal, respectively. The side-to-side head movement gave better depth perception than the up-and-down. Binocular disparity was the best cue of all when the needles were vertical, but the poorest of all when they were horizontal (p. 466). Thus vertical motion parallax can play an important role when binocular disparity fails because the salient lines in the environment are horizontal, as on a flight of stairs or a landing field. Monocular depth perception enforced by blindness or partial blindness of one eye seemed in this author's practice to depend very largely on motion parallax.

The observer's head movements cannot be accurately controlled in extent or speed. For better control the head is kept stationary while certain test objects are moved from side to side (Graham, Baker, Hecht & Lloyd, 1948; Zegers, 1948). Two vertical rods like those pictured in Figure 16-15 were mounted in a frame, the upper rod being fixed and the lower one adjustable in depth; the whole frame was then given a lateral motion in a plane perpendicular to *O*'s line of sight. So the motion of the rod images along the retina was the same as if the rods were stationary while *O* moved his head. His task was to judge which rod was nearer or to adjust the depth of the lower rod until both were at the same distance and no motion parallax remained. There were several S-variables to be considered. Low illumination was unfavorable for good depth acuity. The faster the lateral movement, the poorer the acuity; the longer the movement, the better the acuity. Apparently *O* could not secure fixation on the moving rods unless they were visible for a sufficient space and time. When the motion along the retina was changed, by aid of a prism, from horizontal to vertical, the threshold was increased (the depth acuity diminished). Under the most favorable conditions the threshold was about 30 sec—fairly good though not so good as the 2 sec recorded for binocular vision.

ACCOMMODATION AND CONVERGENCE

The reader will recall that Berkeley pointed out two possible muscular cues to depth, convergence and accommodation. These physiological processes appealed to the earlier experimenters in the field of depth perception, for they seemed like obvious and clear-cut factors for investigation. The general conception was that *O* adjusted accommodation and convergence until he had a sharp and single image of the object, and then judged its distance on the basis of sensations of muscular strain from the eye muscles. But are these possible cues actually used in visual depth perception? In order to attack the question experimentally, it is necessary to eliminate the visual cues—if possible—so as to discover what impressions of distance remain. There must be no perspective, aerial perspective, covering, movement parallax or binocular parallax to assist the observer. The difficulty of meeting this requirement will appear as we proceed.

Two sorts of experiment have been tried. The more direct attack is to present a real object in space, and the less direct to present separate pictures to the two eyes by use of a stereoscope. We shall consider the direct experiment first. It was introduced by Wundt (1862).

Wundt's thread experiment. *O* looked through a short flat tube into a room at the far end of which was a smooth illuminated wall; nothing else was visible except a single thread suspended from above and weighted so as to hang vertically through the center of the field of view. Neither the top nor the bottom of the thread was visible but only a middle portion. *O*'s task was to observe the distance of the thread, to turn his eyes aside while *E* altered that distance, and then to look again and judge whether the thread was nearer or farther than before. There were two conditions, monocular and binocular. Wundt's single *O*, when restricted to the use of one eye, was able after some practice to compare the two distances of the thread with a difference threshold of about 7 percent. With two eyes he found the task much easier and his difference threshold was reduced to 2 percent. Wundt concluded that the convergence sensations available in binocular vision yielded a much finer cue than the accommodation sensations alone which were available in monocular vision.

Wundt was assuming (1) that in monocular vision convergence did not occur, at least no accurate convergence, and (2) that the single thread visible before the bright background presented no binocular disparity or other visual cues.

After being widely accepted for thirty years, Wundt's conclusion was called in question by Hillebrand (1894), a pupil of Hering. He challenged both of Wundt's assumptions.

1. It cannot be assumed that convergence is absent in monocular viewing, for the two eyes work as a team even when one eye is closed. This can be observed if you watch the corneal bulge under the closed lid of a friend who alternately looks at a far and near fixation point with his open eye. An even more delicate check is to close one of your own eyes, monocularly fixate a near object, and then observe quickly whether

or not you have fair fusion when both eyes are opened. Repeat the experiment with distant monocular fixation. If you have normal ocular balance, the closed eye has maintained convergence on the fixated object, so there is little need for adjustment when it is opened. If there *is* a major readjustment of convergence, you will notice it; observe the way the double images of your finger drift into one as you shift binocular fixation from a far point to the finger.

Hillebrand's point was that convergence in monocular vision might be a cue for depth. There seems to be one flaw in this reasoning; with one eye closed there is no disparity to control convergence; so convergence must itself depend on the perception of depth, rather than serve as a primary cue.

2. Wundt's assumption that he had eliminated all but muscular cues neglected the possibility that *O* might fixate the background and thus get double images of the thread, varying in separation with the distance of the thread from the background. But if the background were free from detail, it is doubtful that *O* would converge on it. There was also the possibility of other non-muscular cues, such as better detail vision of irregularities on the thread as it came nearer.

Variations on the experiment. Hillebrand and others after him (see the first edition of this book) varied the experimental conditions in an effort to clear up some of the difficulties. They used straightedges, disks, and patches of light. They worked at near and far distances, with long and short exposures, and with slow and rapid shifts of the target. For example, Bourdon (1902) used a lighted box with a round window in front, *always* varying the size of the window directly with its distance from *O* so that the size of the retinal image remained constant. When *O* viewed the disk of light, binocularly, at 4 m, he judged it to be 3–10 m away. The comparable monocular experiment employed two lights, one at 20 m and the other at 1–2 m; no *O* was sure which spot was the nearer, unless he brought in monocular parallax by moving his head. But perhaps accommodation would work better at closer distances. To check this possibility, Bappert (1922) repeated Bourdon's monocular experiment at short distances, as 16½ *vs.* 25 cm. He found that *O* actually did *worse* than chance, although Bappert watched the convergence changes in *O*'s closed eye, and found them nearly always correct. Here we find a contradiction; *O* must have been making the correct convergence shifts as the result of some cue, presumably accommodation, but *O*'s verbal report was incorrect. One possible explanation sounds far-fetched, but fits in with a lot of observations we shall meet in the rest of the chapter. Remember that the retinal size of the image remained constant, despite its distance, whereas a normal object has increasing retinal size as it approaches *O*. If we assume that the perceptual process involves several levels, the explanation would go like this: The accommodation cue makes the nearer object register as nearer, at one level. But its retinal image is smaller than it should be for an object of constant size at that distance; so the object looks smaller. However, decreased retinal size is a cue to increased distance. Therefore, *O* judges the object as further away than its mate. In other words, the peculiar results are due to breaking up the normal association of various depth cues in an attempt to hold all but one of them constant.

Fifty years of experiments of this sort left us with the conclusion that accommodation is a pretty weak depth cue, even at short distances. Convergence is probably a bit more powerful, but only for near objects. But we are never quite convinced that the experimenters have solved the problems inherent in using real depth situations; perhaps we can control the various cues more effectively with the aid of the stereoscope.

Stereoscopic experiments. The mirror stereoscope makes it possible to vary convergence without changing any other cues; one merely moves the pictures laterally in their holders. The expectation would be that increasing convergence would make the pictured object seem nearer. There should also be a secondary effect; from our equation $a = A/D$ (p. 462), decrease in apparent distance with constant retinal size should make the object appear smaller. Wheatstone tried the experiment in 1852, and Judd repeated it with a different type of apparatus in 1897. Both of them found the expected secondary effect, the decrease of apparent size with increased convergence, retinal size remaining constant. But the judgments of distance were confused and equivocal. Wheatstone found no apparent decrease in object distance during the actual movement of the pictures and resulting increase in convergence, but after the shift was over, the object looked nearer. On the other hand, Judd reported that the object seemed to move nearer during the convergence change, but its apparent distance became indefinite during steady fixation with increased convergence. The differences between the two sets of results are probably due to differences in experimental conditions, such as the degree of familiarity of the object used as a target. But the fact that the secondary change, apparent size, was more stable than the supposedly primary one, apparent distance, seems to be a logical contradiction. We have already met a similar problem in Bappert's experiment (p. 476), and proposed a solution in terms of a multilevel view of perception; again we may assume that convergence and the resulting appropriate distance are registered at a low level of the perceptual sequence and serve as cues for judgments of size, although the cues themselves are not directly available through introspection. The size judgments then serve as cues for another judgment of distance, which may conflict with the lower-level cue.

The postage stamp experiment. The results just cited can be verified with very simple apparatus. Place two identical postage stamps about 3 inches apart on the table, in good alignment. Maintain fixation on a pencil point while you bring it closer and closer to the eyes, starting midway between the stamps. While maintaining this fixation, notice the two stamps coming together; if necessary, true the alignment so that they can be exactly superposed and appear as one. Notice the apparent size and distance of this one. Then relax your convergence and let the two stamps drift apart till you are fixating them normally.

This experiment is essentially the same as the old "wall paper experiment," for which any repeated figure or a typewriter keyboard will serve (Fig. 16-17). Use the pencil point as before. Adjacent or nonadjacent figures can be superposed by sufficiently increasing convergence. Notice the apparent size and distance of the combined images. With regard to size, all observers will probably agree that the greater the conver-

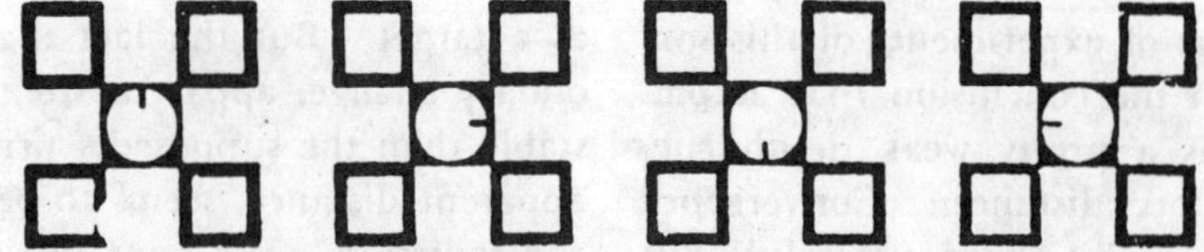

FIG. 16·17. Repeated figure for convergence experiment.

gence the smaller the combined figures appear. The apparent distance is not so definite; sometimes the combined figure appears nearer, sometimes farther than the objective distance. When the apparent distance is less than the real distance, convergence is apparently the cue; but when the figure appears farther away than it is, the apparent size is the dominant cue.

Improved research stereoscope. In order to reach a valid conclusion on the role of the supposed tactile-kinesthetic cues of distance, all visual cues must be excluded or at least equalized. Carr (1935) invented a new type of mirror stereoscope which permits accommodation, convergence, and image size to be changed independently (Fig. 16·18). With this instrument Swenson (1932) obtained fairly good agreement between estimates of distance and the "convergence distance" at which the tubes were set. It will be seen from the following results that the actual distance of the targets ("accommodation distance") had little effect on the judgments. The entries in the body of the table are judged distances as indicated by *O*'s hand. The averages are from five subjects.

Convergence distance	Actual distance of the milk glass 25 cm	30 cm	40 cm
25 cm	24.80	26.51	27.54
30 cm	28.55	29.88	31.74
40 cm	36.95	36.36	39.81

This experiment has aroused a lot of discussion. Perhaps the most obvious criticism is that the milk glass offers no good points on which the eyes can focus, thus making any control of accommodation somewhat doubtful. Grant (1942) solved this problem by using a row of small numbers, illuminated from the rear, as a target that would ensure good accommodation. He obtained changes in accommodation by inserting lenses of strength equivalent to the desired distance, thus avoiding retinal size changes that would have occurred if he had moved the numbers further away. His results showed much less accuracy than those of Swanson, but still indicated some ability to judge the distance of an object for which the eyes were focused and converged. (Cf. Ittelson & Ames, 1950.)

At best, the kinesthetic feedback from accommodation and convergence can only furnish *secondary* cues of the distance of an object, for the correct adjustments must first be achieved in response to some primary cue. Of the cues present *before* the correct ocular response, neither the blurred image of an object that is out of focus nor the double images in imperfect convergence can be eliminated in these experiments by any of *E*'s controls. They can only be eliminated by *O*'s own adjustment for the correct distance.

These experiments, as well as the fact that it has been found necessary to use lenses and prisms in a stereoscope, indicate that accommodation and convergence play some part in depth perception of near objects. The attempt

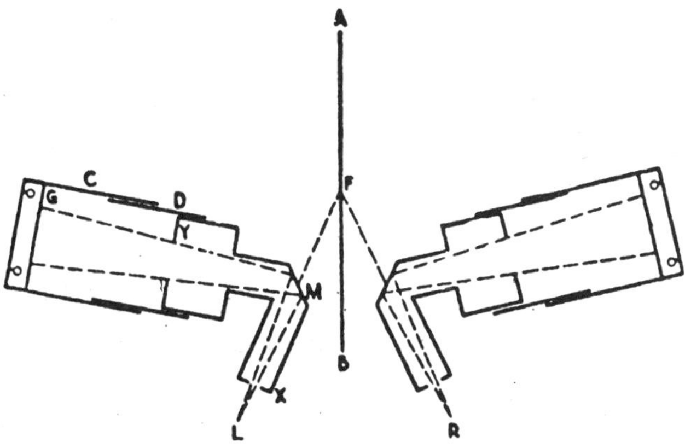

FIG. 16-18. Carr's mirror stereoscope (Carr 1935, p. 248. Published by Longmans, Green & Co.). The figure shows a horizontal section of the instrument. The eyes (more precisely, their centers of rotation) are placed at L and R, looking into the tubes. The left eye receives light reflected by the mirror M from the milk glass G which is illuminated from behind. The distance of the surface G can be changed by telescoping the farther section of the tube; G can be brought as close as 25 cm from the eye, or removed as far as 40 cm. But these changes in distance do not affect the size of the retinal image, for that is bounded by a circular hole in the screen Y, placed at a constant distance from the eye. And the changes in distance of G do not affect the brightness of the retinal image, since the area of G exposed increases as the square of its distance, while the light from the unit of area decreases as the square of the distance. If the milk glass were perfectly uniform and free from visible markings and texture, changes in its distance from the eye would make no difference in the retinal image. Close to the eye, at X, is an eye hole which was sometimes only 1/16 in in diameter, at other times 5/16 in, without noticeable effect on the judgment of distance.

The right eye is treated the same as the left in every respect. Each tube is mounted on a carriage and can be rotated about L and R as centers. With the eyes properly placed and converged, this rotation does not change the retinal images; but by means of the rotation, different degrees of convergence can be enforced on the eyes, in the sense that each eye must look straight into its tube to see its circle of light complete, and to secure single binocular vision of the circle. With any symmetrical position of the tubes, the eyes converge upon a point F somewhere in the straight line BA extending straight forward from the mid-point between *O*'s eyes. F may be called the "virtual fixation point," and its distance the "convergence distance." A metal rod, fixed in the position AB, carries a slider which *O* grasps (without seeing it) and moves forward or back to indicate the apparent distance of the seen circle of light, much as if *O* first located the position of a small object with the eyes, and then closed the eyes and brought his finger to the object. It can be done fairly accurately, and thus the hand indicates the apparent distance of an object.

to isolate and measure the importance of either of these factors runs into trouble when *E* tries to control all other factors. For example, the retinal size of the image of an object normally varies with the distance. In both the Swenson and the Grant experiments the retinal size was kept constant, despite changes in accommodation and convergence that normally accompany changes in object distance, and hence changes in retinal size. The resulting conflict in depth cues is resolved differently from *O* to *O*. Depth perception is not the mere sum of various cues; *O* acts as if he were assigning appropriate weights to each cue and comes out with a reasonable response to the whole situation. At least, the response is usually reasonable in a normal viewing situation. The trouble comes when we try to isolate single factors in the laboratory, using the traditional method of varying one factor while holding all others constant. It is possible to use this method when the independent variable is extremely powerful: for example, retinal disparity thresholds can be determined by such slight changes in object distance that image size, accommodation and convergence are not important variables. But when one tries to get thresholds for accommodation, while holding factors like object size and convergence constant, he runs into trouble. He is like the driver who tried to evaluate the effect of a new gasoline, but forgot to take off his brakes, and had blocks holding his front wheels! (Vernon, 1937; Schlosberg, 1941b.) In daily life a large number of factors, physiological and psychological, interact in a complex way. We shall now turn to a consideration of some of these more psychological factors, for they are receiving increasing experimental study.

THE RELATIONSHIP BETWEEN SIZE AND DISTANCE

In an earlier part of this chapter (p. 462) we showed that the retinal area (a) subtended by an object (A) varies inversely with its distance (D); $a = A/D$. We have had one or more opportunities to apply this formula to experiments, but now we must examine more extensive applications. The first of these is to *size constancy* (cf. Chapter 15).

Size constancy. This term is applied in two different ways. An object of known size, like a man or an auto, is always judged to be the same size, even though the retinal image may vary a thousandfold. In terms of our formula, we retain a fixed value for A, and balance the changes in a by our estimate of D—the man or auto looks further away as his retinal image gets smaller. In this sense size constancy is a depth cue. It sometimes breaks down at excessive distances, or under unusual conditions, as looking down from a tower. But even under these conditions, the size of an object is often judged accurately (Gibson, 1950a; see p. 483).

The second situation to which size constancy is applied is one in which the size of an unknown object is judged on the basis of a and D. In some ways this is the simpler case; therefore, we shall consider it first.

Judged size as a function of depth cues. Although there have been other experiments on this topic, we might well start by describing a series performed by Holway & Boring (1941). Their *O* stood at the intersection of two long corridors, stretching out like the arms of an L. In one corridor they had a Comparison stimulus, placed at a distance of 10 ft from *O*. It was a disk of light, adjustable in size. At various distances (10–120 ft) down the other arm of the L they exposed a similar disk; this Standard disk was always large enough to subtend exactly 1 degree of visual angle. The task was to set the size of the Comparison stimulus so it looked as big as the Standard.

The results are plotted in Figure 16-19. Before we consider them, we had better become familiar with the meaning of the plot. Consider the broken line that runs parallel a bit above the base. This is the locus of settings that would be made if *O* always adjusted the Comparison stimulus to subtend the same visual angle as the Standard (remember that the Standard was always maintained at 1 degree, regardless of its distance). Now consider the broken line that runs diagonally across the graph. This is the locus of settings that would be made if *O* showed complete size constancy; that is, *O* always set the Comparison at the same physical size as the Standard. By trigonometry it can be shown that an angle of 1 degree subtends about 8½ in at 40 ft, 17 in at 80 ft, etc., as the line indicates.

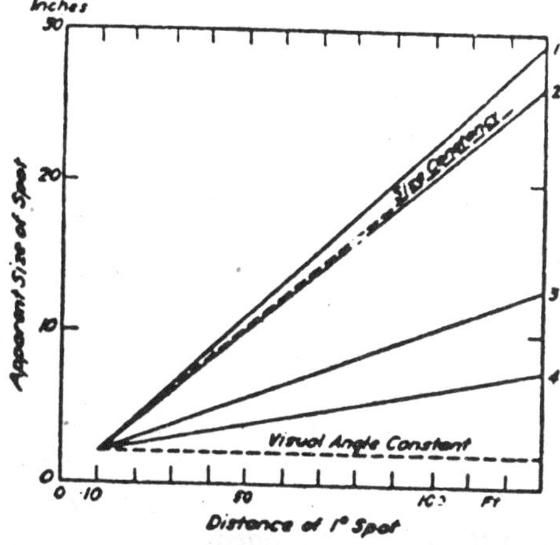

FIG. 16-19. (Holway & Boring, 1941.) Perceived size as a function of depth cues. The Standard was a disk of light, displayed at various distances from *O*. Its actual size was increased as the distance was increased to yield a constant retinal angle. *O* varied the Comparison disk until it appeared to be the same size as the Standard; the distance of the Comparison was held constant at 10 feet. There was good size constancy under conditions 1 and 2, which employed binocular and monocular vision, respectively. In 3 some depth cues were removed by use of an artificial pupil, reducing the constancy. Further reduction of cues by the use of drapes to kill reflections (4) forced *O* to make matches almost entirely in terms of visual angle.

Now for the results. When *O* was allowed normal binocular vision, he gave the results shown in line 1. He actually overshot constancy slightly; perhaps overcompensation, or a slight exaggeration of depth—remember that he was looking down a long corridor. Line 2 shows the results with monocular observation. Depth perception was still good, as shown by the fact that the settings are in agreement with the law of size constancy. But when an artificial pupil was added, eliminating accessory depth cues, the settings (line 3) fell midway between the law of size constancy and the law of visual angle. There were some remaining depth cues available from faint reflections in the doors that lined the corridor. When these were minimized by black drapes, the settings (line 4) approached still closer to those determined by visual angle. In a later experiment Lichten and Lurie (1950) reduced these depth cues still further by the use of screens that permitted *O* to see nothing but the targets. Under these conditions there remained no trace of size constancy. These two experiments show clearly that *O* can judge the size of an unknown object accurately only to the extent that he has reliable cues as to the distance of the object.

Interpretation. The results obtained under conditions (1) and (2) are what one would expect: given a and adequate clues for D, *O* solves for the unknown, A, in the equation $a = A/D$. But what happens in condition (4), when D also becomes an unknown? There are two possible ways of explaining the results. One method is to say that *O* judges entirely in terms of visual angle (a), or of the *proximal stimulus* (Koffka, 1935). This is an adequate description of the *results* obtained, but it may not do justice to the *mechanism* which produces them. There is a serious question as to whether a person can judge either the size of his retinal image, or the visual angle subtended by an area in the field. We just do not perceive free-floating objects at unspecified distances. This suggests a second explanation for the results of condition 4. If there are adequate cues for neither object size nor distance, we automatically assume consistent values for these two variables. For example, one would guess that *O* in condition 4 with a 5-inch disk at 60 ft would "see" any one of the following: 5 in at 60 ft, 2½ in at 30 ft, 10 in at 120 ft, etc. The particular one he saw would not be determined by the stimulus situation, and would be a very unstable perception. Subtle factors tie down such ambiguous perceptions; in this case it might well be that the object would be seen at the distance on which *O*'s eyes converge when at rest. At any rate, we have a reasonable explanation of the results of condition 4 (no depth cues) if we assume that *O* always perceives the object at some specific distance, and enter the perceived D in our formula, $a = A/D$.

Perceived *versus* real distance. One must always remember that judged size is dependent on perceived distance, rather than on real distance. But how do we get at perceived distance? We shall see shortly (Brunswik's experiment, p. 484) that an estimate of D in feet is not what we want, for that is a derived and secondary measure, from a psychological viewpoint. We want a subjective or psychological unit, of the sort used in *sone* and *veg* scales of loudness and weight, respectively (p. 238). Gilinsky (1951) has shown us how we can handle the problem in a neat way. On the basis of several lines of evidence she shows that *O* acts as if his horizon, his "infinite distance," were relatively close; this limit is of the order of 50–300 ft, depending on both *O* and the situation. For example, she let *O* stand at one end of an 80-ft archery range, and direct *E* as she marked off successive distances that looked like 1 ft each. The "subjective feet" actually increased in length as they got further from *O*, as shown in Figure 16-20. Such a curve can be

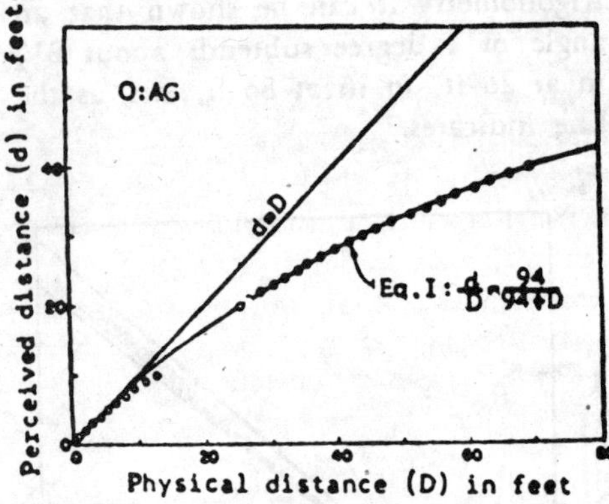

FIG. 16-20. (Gilinsky, 1951.) Perceived distance as a function of physical distance. See text.

described by the equation $d/D = L/(L + D)$, where d and D are subjective and objective distances, respectively, and L is the limit mentioned above. (Gilinsky uses A for the limit, but we have already used A for object size). In this particular experiment the limit turns out to be 94 ft. Given the equation, one can calculate the subjective distance that corresponds to any given objective distance; it is the subjective distance that would be used in our formula $a = A/D$.

Open-field experiments. Apparent (or *phenomenal*) size turns out to be a very complicated affair. We have already noted that size constancy seems to break down at great distances, in the sense that a very distant man *appears* small, even though we still estimate his height at 6 feet. The same thing shows up in railroad tracks, which appear to converge, even though we know they do not. It should be noted, however, that the apparent linear convergence is not nearly as great as it is in terms of actual retinal angle; as so often happens, apparent size falls somewhere between the law of size constancy and that of visual angle. This fascinating topic received a lot of attention during the last century, under the general name of the *alley problem* (Boring, 1942). One of the neatest experiments on this topic was done by Hillebrand in 1902. His task was to adjust an alley of suspended threads, like a double row of trees lining a road, so that they would appear to be parallel (Fig. 16-21). It is clear that

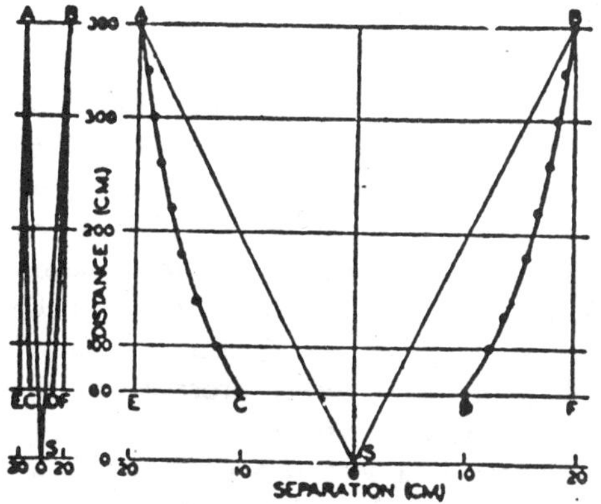

FIG. 16-21. (Boring, 1942, after Hillebrand, 1902.) The alley experiment. *O* looks down a double row of vertical threads and directs *E* who adjusts them so that they appear parallel to *O*. The two rows must actually be made to diverge slightly as they get farther from *O*, or they will seem to converge. Note that the width of the larger drawing is exaggerated by a factor of 10 to bring out the lateral displacement of the threads.

the width of the alley between the rows must increase somewhat as they recede from *O*, but much less than would be demanded to give a constant visual angle.

So much for apparent or phenomenal size. When we turn to judged size, the story is simpler, even when we deal with unknown objects at a great distance. Gibson (1947, 1950a) set up stakes at varied distances from *O* in a field a half-mile long. The stakes varied in height from 15 to 99 in, and *O* had no knowledge of their sizes. His task was to judge the size of the distant (Standard) stake by picking one of a row of graded (Comparison) stakes that matched it. The graded scale-stakes were behind him, so he had to turn around to make his choice; he could not make a direct comparison of the distant and graded stakes. The matches were in very good agreement with the law of size constancy, as the following data on the 71-inch (Standard) stake show:

Distance of Standard (yd)	14	224	784
Height of Comparison (in)	71.9	75.8	75.9
SD, " " " (in)	1.8	7.3	9.8

Four intermediate distances gave comparable results. Even at 784 yards, almost half a mile, when the stake was barely visible, it showed no sign of a shrinkage in judged size; as a matter of fact, it showed a slight tendency in the opposite direction, or overconstancy.

These results show very clearly that one can judge size quite accurately, given adequate clues to the distance Yet it is a very complicated job that the nervous system is doing. Suppose you asked a surveyor to do the job for you. First he would determine a (retinal size) and D (distance), and solve for A (size of Standard). Then he would substitute D_c (distance of Comparison stakes) and solve for a_c (image size of matching Comparison stake). He could then pick the stake from among the others. This sort of reasoning shows that any theory of "unconscious geometry" is silly, if taken literally. But *O*, like an electronic computer, does the equivalent operations in an automatic and immediate fashion. Furthermore, nobody is surprised that *O* can make such judgments, for they seem "natural." It is only when one realizes the complexity of the perceptual processes that he realizes how hard it will be to work out the underlying mechanisms.

Brunswik's experiment. Throughout the discussion we have assumed that *O* acts like an automatic computer in solving for the unknown term in the equation $a = A/D$. But can we get any direct evidence on the process of solution? Brunswik (1944) collected data that cast some light. He and another *O* made independent judgments on a series of 180 objects; in each case they estimated the size (A), distance (D), and projected size (a). The first two estimates were made in meters, which were the linear units most familiar to both *E* and *O*. Projected size was estimated in terms of the size the object would look in a camera, compared to the markings on a meter stick at one meter from the lens. The objects varied from printed letters at a few inches to buildings several miles away.

Brunswik treated his results in several ways. In terms of both average errors and correlations, he showed that the estimates of size and distance were more accurate than were estimates of projected size. At first glance this seems to destroy the equation-solving theory. Remember that visual angle, retinal size, or projected size is the one term of the equation that is stimulus-bound, and hence the keystone of the equation. But Brunswik and his other *O* could give better estimates of the solution than of the most stable term! Size and distance estimates were often inconsistent. This was particularly striking in some specific cases. Thus, the *O* looked at a 10½-meter column at an actual distance of 11 m, with a calculated projective size of .955 m. She estimated its height as 2.9 m; to be consistent with the equation, she should have reported the distance as 3.03 m, but she actually estimated it at 9.

But before we throw the equation overboard, perhaps we should remember what *O* was doing. In the first place, she was making estimates in arbitrary units. There is a big difference between saying that one object is twice as big as another, and actually estimating the height of each object in feet or meters. The same holds for distance. Or, to put it otherwise, we have fairly accurate ideas of familiar sizes and distances, if we think in behavioral or relative terms, but we are not very good at expressing them in feet and inches. Hence, our solutions of the equation relating size to distance are not made in terms of feet and inches, but rather by some more direct processes in the central nervous system.

There is a second way in which attempts to analyze depth perception go astray. When we ask for estimates of size or distance, or especially projective size, we are breaking into a very complex process. The total process is geared to produce behavior that is nicely adjusted to the world of objects. For example, there is a pencil on my desk. I cannot estimate its distance accurately in inches, or even draw a line to represent its distance from my eye. But I *can* look at it, close my eyes, and then pick up the pencil without fumbling. This does not mean that we should sit back in awe at the accuracy of perception; we must analyze the elements which make up this complex process, but we must not lose sight of the fact that such analysis sometimes disrupts the nice interaction among factors. We must always keep in mind the *function* of perception; it guides our behavior accurately in a world of objects.

Several kinds of "size." The reader may be a bit puzzled at the different ways in which the word *size* has been used; perhaps we should review them. First there is *real* or *physical size;* the value we get by laying a yard- or meterstick on the object. Then there is *retinal size* or visual angle, which is size/distance, both in physical units. Next comes *judged size,* which we have used to mean the physical size of a comparison object judged to be equal to the standard; it might also be called behavioral or functional size, for it is based on our reactions to a world of objects. *Apparent* or *phenomenal size* is an introspective affair; it refers to the fact that a man at a great distance may "look" small, although we judge him to be as tall as another man a few feet away. Finally, there is *estimated size,* which is a direct guess in terms of feet or meters. Unfortunately, these distinctions are not always kept clear in discussions; *subjective* or *perceived size* may mean judged, apparent, or estimated size. To add to the confusion, most of these adjectives may also be applied to distance, as *estimated distance, physical distance,* etc. We must be very careful to keep our terms straight.

Judged distance of known objects. In the Holway and Boring (1941) experiments the task was to judge the size of an unknown object in the presence of various depth cues. Ittelson (1951) did essentially the opposite experiment; he obtained depth judgments when the only cue was the size of a known object. All objects were exposed 7½ ft behind a screen. A peephole restricted *O* to monocular vision and prevented movement parallax. Accommodation is not important at this distance. The depth judgments were obtained by setting a target at the apparent distance of the test object; the target was in full binocular vision, with other incidental depth cues present. Among the test objects were three playing cards, one of normal size, one of half size, and one of double size, shown one at a time. *O* had no reason to doubt that they were all of normal size (A). If he judged the distance of a card by the retinal size (a), in accordance with our formula, $a = A/D$ (i.e., $D = A/a$), the half-size card would seem to be at double distance, and the double-size card at half distance. The average results from five *O*s were as follows:

Card	*Predicted D (ft)*	*Obtained D (ft)*
Normal	7.5	7.5
Half-size	15.0	15.0
Double-size	3.8	4.6

The agreement with prediction is as good as we could expect, and confirmatory results were obtained in parallel experiments of the same author. His data afford striking evidence of the part played by known (or assumed) size in depth perception. It is difficult to see how Pratt (1950) can minimize the importance of retinal size of known objects as a depth cue.

Emmert's law. Up to the present, we have been concerned with the size and distance of perceived objects. We saw that the simple equation, $a = A/D$, applies to the geometry of objects and images, and that it also holds for various types of perceived sizes and distances.

This equation has been called Euclid's Law. Taken at its face value, it would seem to say that the further an object is, the smaller it should look (if by "look" we refer to retinal size). But there is one apparent exception to this law. In 1881, Emmert (Boring, 1942) pointed out that an afterimage actually looks bigger if it is projected on a more distant surface. As a matter of fact, the judged size of the image is proportional to the distance; this is Emmert's law. But a little clear thinking will show that Emmert's law is just a special case of the familiar equation.

First let us consider the experiment. Fixate a one-inch square of white paper on a black background, placed 10 inches from the eye. This will establish a black afterimage (p. 396) corresponding in size to the retinal area stimulated. Now project the image onto a white surface, and measure the size of the (black) area. If the projection surface is at the original distance, 10 inches, the image will cover a square inch. If the projection surface is 20, 50, 100, or 1,000 inches away, the image will be 2, 5, 10, or 100 inches in diameter on the background. The point is, of course, that the physiological process aroused by the original fixation has a fixed retinal size (a); the "object" size (A) will vary directly with the perceived distance (D). This problem has been discussed by Boring (1910, 1912), Edwards (1950) and Young (1950, 1951). The situation would seem highly similar to that used by Holway and Boring for size constancy (p. 480).

The moon illusion. Most readers will have noticed that the moon appears much larger when it is low in the sky. It is sometimes stated that this is a simple physical phenomenon, due to the fact that the image of the horizon moon is spread by the scattering or diffusion of its rays by the atmosphere. But it has been shown repeatedly that any such physical effect is trivial and quite inadequate to explain the illusion. It has been recognized since Ptolemy that the effect was somehow dependent on apparent distance (Boring, 1942). Perhaps the most exhaustive experiments on the illusion were done by Boring and his associates (Boring, 1943). They worked on the top of a high building, using both real and artificial moons. In some cases they could move the real moon from the zenith to the horizon, or vice versa, with the aid of mirrors mounted on long supports. Their final conclusion was that the illusion was largely dependent on the direction of the eyes in relation to the head. If *O* lies on his back, the zenith moon looks big, and the horizon moon appears small. The obvious explanation would seem to be that turning the eyes upward tends to give a slight reflex divergence, which would increase the strain to maintain convergence, which would, in turn, serve as a cue to decreased distance. Now if the moon were judged to be nearer at the zenith than at the horizon, it would seem smaller at the zenith, since retinal size is unchanged. The only trouble with this explanation is that *O* usually reports the moon to *look* further away at the zenith, instead of nearer. Perhaps this is another one of the peculiar secondary effects one gets in depth perception, when he taps in at various levels of the perceptual process. (Compare the postage stamp experiment, p. 477.) At any rate, the moon illusion is a fascinating topic.

Shape constancy. We are now prepared to say a little about the perception of form in three dimensions. A square sheet of paper resting on the surface of a desk looks square, even though it is slanted to the line of regard in such a manner that the projection on the retina is certainly not square. In a strictly logical fashion one could explain this rather simply: using depth cues, *O* perceives one edge of the paper as further away from the eye than the other, and automatically makes allowance for this increased distance in judging the absolute sizes of near and far edges.

But this implies that *O* can judge the *slant* or inclination of the surface. The actual experimental evidence is that *O* cannot *estimate* slant very well (Stavrianos, 1945). On the other hand, rectangles and ellipses, viewed with various amounts of slant to the line of regard, can be reproduced rather accurately. Thouless (1931) has demonstrated that there is a fair degree of constancy in such reproductions, in the sense that they are more like the shape of the actual object than of the retinal image. This would seem to be another case, like Brunswik's experiment, in which *O* can report more accurately on an end result of a process than he can on the intermediate steps.

There is one other aspect to the problem of form constancy. We saw in the chapter on Form that there are certain forms which are "good," such as squares and circles, and that certain line drawings will take on depth if they make "better" figures in three than in two dimensions. Whether this is due to a basic law of neural organization or to a greater familiarity with regular objects is hard to say. But it follows from this fact that a trapezoid held at right angles to the line of regard will be seen as a square (i.e., a better figure) in a slanted position, as long as there are no depth cues to deny the implied slant. This actually happens in a dark room. The same principle is also at the basis of the distorted room and other illusions we shall discuss subsequently. But for the present we may point out that the perception of form *versus* slant, like the perception of size *versus* distance, is like the old problem of which comes first, the hen or the egg. Each of the pairs represents a mutual and continued interaction, and the particular member of the pair we emphasize at a given moment depends on our purposes (cf. Gibson, 1950a; 1950b).

PERCEPTION OF OBJECTS

We have repeatedly found that laboratory attempts to evaluate single depth cues ran into difficulty through holding other cues constant. If one wishes to isolate the effects of a single cue, the best course is to set up a situation that *eliminates* all other cues. For example, we can eliminate convergence, movement parallax and binocular disparity by having *O* look through a peephole; if *O* can see only with one stationary eye, these cues just do not exist for him at the moment. But the elimination of cues often calls for considerable ingenuity. Outstanding in this respect is the work of Ames and his associates.

Aniseikonia. Ames was interested in the problem of pictorial representation of depth as early as 1925, but it was not until a peculiar visual anomaly turned up at the Dartmouth Eye Clinic that he really started to develop his systematic views. The visual anomaly was *aniseikonia,* meaning *not-equal images.* If the image in one eye is larger than that in the other, it greatly modifies the disparities among images, resulting in incorrect and confusing depth perception. The disorder can be corrected by *size lenses.* Figure 16-22 shows the effect of such a lens on a normal eye; the aniseikonic eye for which this lens was designed would have the opposite distortion.

The peculiar thing about this disorder is that people who have it still perceive the world normally. Houses and walls appear straight, even though they should be distorted in accordance with the optics of the situation. Thus one with a lens like that in Figure 16-22 *should* see the far right-hand corner of the room pulled away from him, and the left-hand corner fairly near, even though they were actually equidistant (as in Fig. 16-23). But he may not! That is, he may not if the wall is made of plaster or brick, which is usually erected square

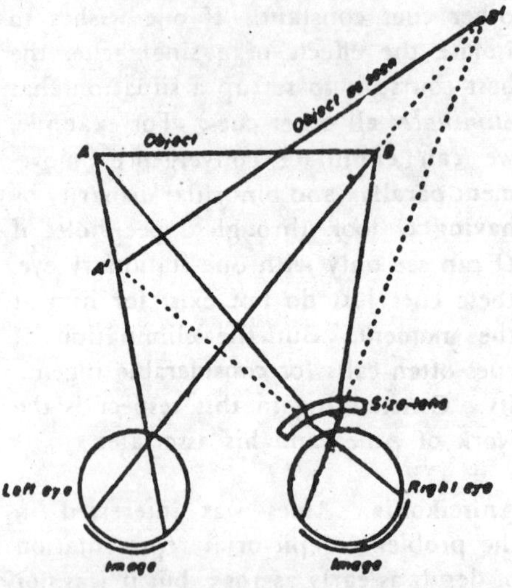

Fig. 16-22. (Bartley, 1950.) Size lenses.

in our culture. But if he is put in a cubicle lined with leaves, the famous *leaf room*, the corners behave as the optical laws predict they should. This makes sense if we realize that there is no reason for *O* to believe that the walls of the leaf room are really squared up. Hence he is free to see them according to the dictates of the unusual binocular disparity. Incidentally, the fact that such a disorder is merely masked by experience with specific objects, rather than basically corrected by a reorganization of space perception, suggests that the mechanism underlying corresponding points is largely native rather than acquired. If a normal *O* wears size lenses for a week, the normal environment no longer looks distorted, but tests like the leaf room show little change in the aniseikonia (Burian, 1943; Ogle, 1950).

When a normal *O* puts on these lenses, he gets the distortion of space in the leaf room, and may get it in other situations. Whether he will get it or not depends on a number of factors, as the nature of the environment and his own stability of object perception (Ames, 1946; Bartley, 1950). Hence, both normal and aniseikonic *O*s should be tested in many situations. One especially good device is the *space eikonometer* (Ogle, 1946). It is essentially a set of strings forming a plane which offers no resistance to the distorting effect of the visual anomaly. The design of these situations and an analysis of the depth cues that they might contain led Ames to build a series of demonstrations. Each of them emphasizes some depth cue; by elimination of other conflicting cues, he has been able to bring out some startling illusions. The impressiveness of the demonstrations is increased because the perception is often quite at variance with the actual object. The illusions have been described in popular magazines as well as in technical books, and recently formed the basis for an inexpensive kit that was widely distributed by Science Service (1952). Perhaps the most complete description is in Ittelson's (1952) manual (cf. Lawrence, 1949; Bartley, 1950; Blake & Ramsey, 1951).

The distorted room. Many of the demonstrations eliminate any possible cues from convergence, disparity, and motion parallax by forcing *O* to look through a peephole. Thus *O* looks through a knothole into a room which appears to be about 10 feet wide, 6 feet deep and 5 feet high. He perceives a couple of perfectly normal windows in the opposite wall. He is then given a blackboard pointer, and told to put his hand through another hole and touch the far right corner of the ceiling with the pointer. Much to his surprise, he falls far short of his aim and cannot even reach the corner. Then he is told to try the far left corner. This time he almost rams the pointer through the corner, which is much closer than it appears. He is finally allowed to look into the room with full normal vision, and a moving head; the room is then obviously skewed. All this will be clear after careful study of Figure 16-23 which

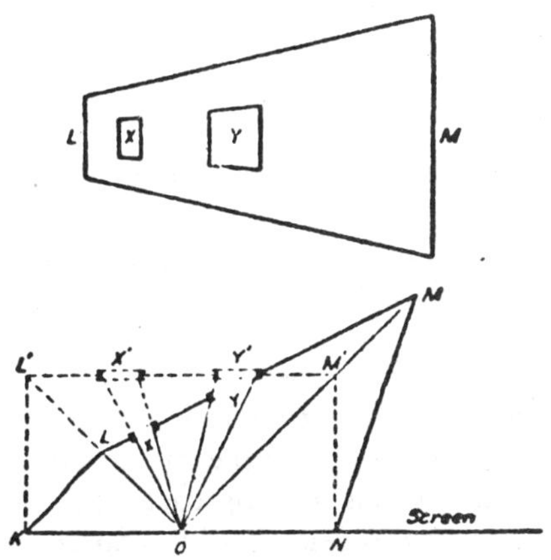

FIG. 16-23. (After Ames, 1946.) Rear wall (upper drawing) and floor plan (lower drawing) of a distorted room. X and Y are windows, while L and M are the left and right ends of the rear wall. The broken lines in the floor plan show a normal rectangular room which would have the same retinal projection. The distorted room was constructed by projecting key lines of sight, as to the windows and corners of a normal room, to the desired distances. The lengths of vertical lines on the rear wall are proportional to their altered distances.

shows the floor and back-wall plan of such a room; the side walls and ceiling would be distorted according to the same projection. It is actually three times as far to the right-hand corner (M) as it is to the left-hand one (L). But remember that *O* has no direct physiological cues to distance, since he is using monocular vision with no possible movement of the eye, and accommodation is an ineffectual cue at such distances. Lacking these cues to D, he must solve the equation $a = A/D$ in terms of a given *a* (retinal image) and an assumed A (reasonable size of a familiar object). Consider the two windows, X and Y. They both subtend the same *a*, and twin windows are usually assumed to be the same size (A). Hence, they appear at the same distance. The same reasoning can be applied to the two vertical sides of one window, or the two corners, L and M. In short, whole families of equations are solved neatly in terms of the familiar rectangular patterns of rooms; hence *O* perceives a rectangular room, as shown by dotted lines on the floor plan. This is only one of a whole group of normal and distorted rooms that would cast the same retinal pattern —or give the same photograph—but *O* sees the most plausible one. In this sense, perception is a bet on the nature of a segment of the real world, and *not* a faithful copy of it. This feature of the Ames demonstrations appeals strongly to those who are interested in the influence of social norms on social perceptions (Cantril, 1947; 1950). It is also suggested as a starting point for a fundamental approach to science (Cantril, Ames, Hastorf, & Ittelson, 1949). On the other hand, this functional view of perception does not seem very new to the experimental psychologist, for it has been familiar since the days of Helmholtz (1866). The thing that *is* interesting to us is that Ames has set up exceedingly clever demonstrations of the effect of some of the familiar depth cues by freeing them from the masking effects of other cues. So let us review a few more of the Ames demonstrations.

Other Ames Demonstrations. 1. *False interposition or covering.* Take two ordinary playing cards, the King and Queen. Mount the K on a rod at 5 feet, and the Q at 10 feet, lined up so that the corner of the K covers part of the Q. View them from a peephole, monocularly; the K will obviously appear nearer than the Q. Now carefully clip out the corner of the Q that was covered by the K, and reverse their positions in depth. Line them up so that the corner of the K just fills the part clipped off the Q. and have *O* look at them through the peephole. He will see a small K *in front of* the Q, instead of a normal-sized K behind the Q, and a corner cut off the latter. This simply means that *O* accepts the most plausible situation, rather than the extremely unusual one you have carefully arranged. This does not mean that *O* thinks it all out in detail; perception is immediate, but it fits the normal world as if it *were* carefully thought out. *O* can report *what*, but not *how*, he perceives.

2. *The trapezoidal window.* *O* stands about 20 feet from an object that looks like a window sash mounted on a vertical rod as an axis. When the rod is rotated slowly, the sash seems to oscillate back and forth through an arc of perhaps 90°. The trick is in the trapezoidal shape of the sash; it is cut from cardboard, shaped like the window on the rear wall of Figure 16-23, and painted to resemble a sash. In other words, the trapezoidal sash has built-in perspective. A little thought shows that the sash will appear slanted even in full-faced view (cf. p. 487) and that it will seem to swing from this slant to the opposite one as it rotates. Of course, the demonstration must be viewed from a fair distance, to eliminate contradictory cues from accommodation, convergence, and other sources, but the illusion is surprisingly strong.

The demonstration may be made even more impressive if objects like a card, ball, or tube are attached to the window. These objects are seen to make full rotations, which makes them appear to pass clear through the "oscillating" sash. Details of construction are given by Ames (1951) and Ittelson (1952). Incidentally, this demonstration is related to the windmill illusion, a case of reversible perspective that has been known for a couple of centuries (Boring, 1942, pp. 270, 305; Miles, 1931a).

3. *The balloons.* There are several other interesting demonstrations, but we shall describe only one more. A pair of partially inflated balloons appear illuminated in an otherwise dark room. *O* views them binocularly at about 20 feet. A simple double bellows is arranged to increase the size of one and simultaneously decrease that of the other. If the size is changed by about 50 percent in a couple of seconds, one balloon seems to approach rapidly as the other recedes. This is a special case of retinal size *versus* object size; an increasing retinal image is normally associated with an approaching object, and vice versa. The size-change cue is more powerful than disparity, especially under conditions of low illumination and poorly defined contour present in this situation.

It is also possible to make the balloons shift relative position by making one brighter and the other dimmer. Just why an increase in brightness makes an object seem to approach is not particularly clear from a functional standpoint—or from any other (cf. p. 463). We need an experiment to determine the precise conditions under which this effect occurs.

The billiard ball experiment. One of the most revealing experiments suggested by these demonstrations was performed by Hastorf (1950). He had *O* set the size of a projected disk of light so that it represented a ping pong ball at the same distance as a specified marker. In a second session *O* made similar settings—"on an object that can be seen as a billiard ball." The actual settings in each case corresponded fairly well to the appropriate retinal size, or visual angle. At the end of the second session *E* set the size of the disk at the average value obtained from *O* during the first (ping pong ball) session, and told him to estimate its distance relative to the marker. The disk was reported as beyond the usual marker. Another group started with "billiard balls," and two more groups set rectangles to represent calling cards or envelopes; the results from all groups were consistent.

Now consider the results in terms of the familiar equation.

In the first session, Hastorf's *O*s were given A (ping pong ball-size) and D (the distance to the specified marker), and were forced to "solve" for *a* (size of retinal image). Regardless of what they thought they were doing, the only variable they could manipulate was the size of the stimulus disk, with the resulting change in the retinal image. Similarly in the first part of the second session they were given a new A (billiard ball) and they responded with a larger setting for *a*. Then, without changing the instructions as to A, they were given a smaller *a*. The only way to keep the equation balanced was to increase D; this is what *O* reported he perceived.

In the Hastorf experiment one of the factors, *a* (retinal size), was under direct stimulus control. A second factor, D (distance of perceived object) was controlled in a very indirect manner; it was related to the distance of another object in the visual field, which in turn was localized by the complex of stimulus and interpretative factors that enter into normal depth perception. The third factor, A (size of perceived object) was determined by a verbal reference to an object of familiar size. Perhaps the most surprising thing about the experiment is that *O* could make settings in such a complicated situation. The key to the explanation rests in the fact that people are so constituted that they perceive *objects localized in space;* they do not see free-floating sensations. In short, they "solve" the equation as best they can. If values for two of the factors, A and D, are given in an unequivocal manner by stimulus and/or experiential factors, *O* can solve for the third factor, *a*, rather easily; lacking precise means of determining A and D, *O* grasps at any clues available, such as instructions or sets. In other words, it is the absence of stronger clues that throws emphasis on the influence of verbal instructions. In fact, many of the Ames demonstrations can be understood most readily in terms of relatively ambiguous stimulus situations, which permit the desired variable to play with full force (cf. p. 487; Ames, 1925).

We emerge from these studies with an important generalization; the less adequately a perception is determined by stimuli, the less stable it will be, and the more subject to subtle factors in *O*. This accounts for such diverse facts as the effect of poverty on judged size of coins (Bruner & Goodman, 1947; Pastore, 1949) and the clinical results with that most ambiguous of all perceptual stimuli, the Rorschach inkblots.

17

EYE MOVEMENTS IN RELATION TO PERCEPTION

As we have seen here and there in previous chapters, one cannot discuss vision without mentioning Eye Movements. It is important that the eye has muscles as well as rods and cones. Some muscles are called *intrinsic*, for they are inside the eyeball. The *ciliary muscle* changes the curvature of the lens, focusing the image sharply on the retina; this was described under *accommodation* (p. 457). The *iris*, or colored portion of the eye, is itself a circular or purse-string type of muscle. It changes the diameter of the pupil as the illumination varies (p. 367).

The movements of the eyeballs themselves are brought about by three pairs of *extrinsic* muscles in each socket. One pair, the *internal* and *external recti*, act like a pair of reins in guiding a horse; they swing the line of regard from right to left. Another pair, the *superior* and *inferior recti*, produce vertical movement in a similar fashion. A third pair, the *inferior* and *superior oblique*, serve to control the rotation of the eyes on the line of regard as an axis. Some actual rotation is required to compensate for head tilt or sideways tipping of the body; thus the eyes can keep an upright view of the visual field.

The obvious function of the four recti is to direct the eye so that light from an object will fall on the *fovea*, the region of best acuity (p. 386). This adjustment is called *fixation*. In some of the lower animals, the eyes work independently. But man possesses binocular vision, which demands that the two images from a given object fall on corresponding points in the two eyes. Binocular vision calls for binocular motor coordination. In the first place, the eyes must make parallel or *conjugate* (= yoked together) movements as they shift fixation to new points, or follow a moving object. In the second place, they must make opposed movements as they change *convergence* to near or far objects. Both types of movement are under visual control in that they may be initiated by objects in the field of view, and also in that their accuracy is checked by the visual results (as double images, inaccurate fixation). But movements are also under the control of impulses from the inner ear, the neck muscles, and the body muscles. Finally, they may be initiated centrally. Try closing both eyes and resting the fingers lightly on the lids. Now imagine looking at an object to the right, and feel the eyes move under the closed lids. Again, imagine shifting fixation back and forth between a near and far object, and feel the convergence movements. A similar experiment with one eye closed and the other open will show that the closed eye shifts appropriately with changing fixation of the open eye. In short, normal eye movements are nicely coordinated in their innervation, whatever the original stimulus for movement. The coordination also extends to the intrinsic muscles; both accommodation and pupil size are associated with shifts of convergence.

Jumps *versus* smooth movements. Even casual watching of someone's eye movements will show that they sometimes occur as fast jumps, and at other times appear as slow sweeps. The former are called *saccadic;* they were discovered by Javal (1878), who observed that the eyes in reading advanced along the line in little jumps (*par saccades*). These movements represent shifts in fixation from object to object. They can be controlled by *O* to a certain extent, in that he can decide when and where to shift his gaze, but it is rare to find an *O* who can control the speed or course of the movement between start and finish. In this way it is like any other jump—a person can decide where he wants to land, but once he "takes off" he has no further control of his trajectory. If he misses his aim, he cannot make corrective movements until he arrives on the ground again.

The relatively slow, sweeping movements have exactly the opposite function; instead of shifting fixation, they serve to maintain fixation on an object that is moving in relation to the head. If the object moves, they are called *pursuit movements;* if the head moves, they are called *compensatory movements.* In either case, their function is to keep the image of the fixated object from moving out of the fovea. To the extent that they achieve their function, the speed and direction of the eye movements are determined by the movement of object or head.

In actual life, these various types of movements occur in endless combination. Certain combinations have special names. Thus, *nystagmus* is a series of alternate sweeps and quick saccadic returns, like those involved in watching telephone poles go past a train window.

This brief description of eye movements has been phrased in terms of external objects, since the function of eye movements is to see objects. But we must emphasize again that eye movements are not completely under visual control. Indeed, they reflect much that is going on in the organism. Since they are often the initial phase in a new adjustment, they are especially valuable as a key to behavior; in competitive sports an opponent often gives away his next move by a shift of the eyes, and many "mind readers" actually read eye movements. For the psychologist they occupy a key position in many topics, not the least of which is perception. It is for this reason that we treat eye movements extensively in this chapter.

METHODS OF OBSERVING AND RECORDING EYE MOVEMENTS

1. Unaided objective observation. Direct observation of *O*'s eye movements is a bit awkward, for *E*'s head gets in the way of what *O* is seeing. Various arrangements of a mirror avoid this difficulty. One way is to place the mirror flat on a table near *O*'s book, have him face the light, and watch his eyes in the mirror from the opposite side of the table (Erdmann & Dodge, 1898). Or, cut a "peephole" in the center of a large page of reading matter, and watch through the peephole. *E* is thus concealed by the paper, and does not distract *O* very much (Miles, 1928b). But such simple observation provides only a rough count or measure of the movements and the intervening fixations of the eyes. Some recording apparatus is needed. A historical review of these methods is given by Carmichael and Dearborn (1947) and important matters of technique are discussed by Wendt & Dodge (1938) and by Wendt (1938). We shall briefly describe most of the methods in the pages that follow.

2. Mechanical registration. The first successful recording apparatus, though soon superseded, deserves mention. It was an adaptation of the standard laboratory method of recording muscular movements on a rotating drum or kymograph While the drum surface is moving steadily from right to left, a writing lever connected to the muscle moves up and down and inscribes a curve on the drum surface (or on paper carried by the drum). The problem of hitching the writing lever to the eyeball was solved by Delabarre (1898) and Huey (1908). A ring of paster of Paris, polished smooth, was applied to the cornea in such a way as not to obstruct the subject's vision. Adhering to the moist surface of the cornea, which was cocainized to prevent pain and winking, the ring was connected by a light rod or thread to the writing lever. This apparatus gave fairly good results which have since been confirmed by more adequate methods.

3. Photographic registration of light reflected from the cornea. A beam of light, thrown from the side and reflected from the smooth surface of the cornea, can be made to record the eye's movement on a steadily moving photographic plate or film (Fig. 17-1). The "bright

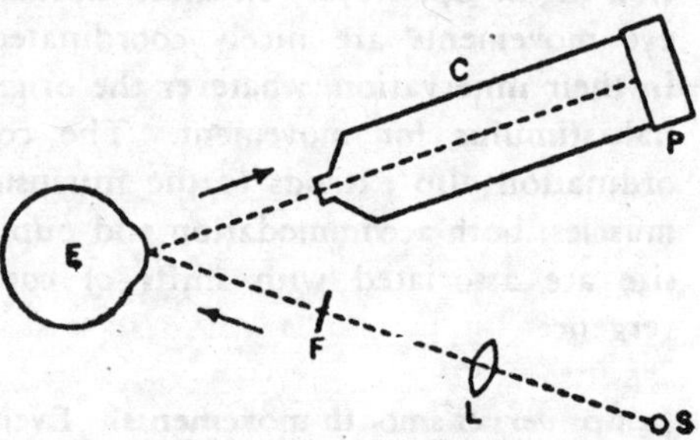

FIG. 17-1. Scheme of the nucleus of the Dodge setup. E is the eye, much exaggerated in size in respect to the rest of the diagram. Light from the source S, as shown by the dotted lines, is reflected from the cornea into the camera. In the ath of the beam are interposed L, a lens which nakes the rays of light parallel, and F, a filter of blue glass which moderates the light shining into the eye without greatly reducing its effect on the photographic plate. C is the bellows of the camera, and P is a special plate holder or film holder, arranged to move the plate or film steadily in a vertical direction while the reflected beam is writing its horizontal movements upon the photosensitive surface. Actually the light and camera are placed much further to the sides than shown here.

spot" on the eye, which is any bright light reflected from the cornea, moves slightly with the eye. It would not move at all if the eyeball were a simple sphere turning about its own center. But the cornea projects forward from the general spherical surface of the eyeball, with the result that, as the eyeball turns, the light strikes the cornea at a changing angle and consequently is reflected in a changing direction. So the reflected beam moves with the eye and can be utilized for recording the eye movement. This method was invented by Dodge about 1900 (see Dodge & Cline, 1901). It has been adapted to various experimental requirements and widely used.

Head movements which would unduly complicate the picture are avoided as far as possible by aid of a head rest or biting board, and in some experiments a separate record of the head movements is obtained along with the eye-movement record. For timing the eye movements and fixations a convenient device consists of a tuning fork or vibrating reed which interrupts the beam of light a certain number of times per second (p. 501, Fig. 17-5).

The Dodge apparatus is properly called a photokymograph because it registers horizontal eye movements upon a vertically moving film. Brief records of considerable value can be obtained even without the moving film by time exposure of a stationary film shielded from all light except the reflected beam from the cornea. In this way records are obtained of the movements in all directions that occur when the eye surveys an object or scene (Stratton, 1902b, 1906; see p. 501). When you "sweep your eyes around a circle," you actually fixate a few points somewhere near the circumference, with intervening saccadic movements, the whole movement being decidedly jerky and angular.

The photokymograph has been elaborated by quite a number of experimenters, as for simultaneous records from both eyes (e.g., by Tinker, 1931), and for simultaneous records of both horizontal and vertical movements of the eyes (e.g., by Jasper & Walker, 1931; and by Clark, 1934). A convenient portable "ophthalmograph" has been developed by the American Optical Company (1937). A few other models will be mentioned under the heading of results

4. Motion pictures of eye movements. At first thought the motion picture camera affords a complete solution of the problem of recording eye movements in all directions. But there are difficulties to overcome. How are you going to use the record? Merely viewing the motion picture will be no better than watching the eyes directly. Judd (1905)

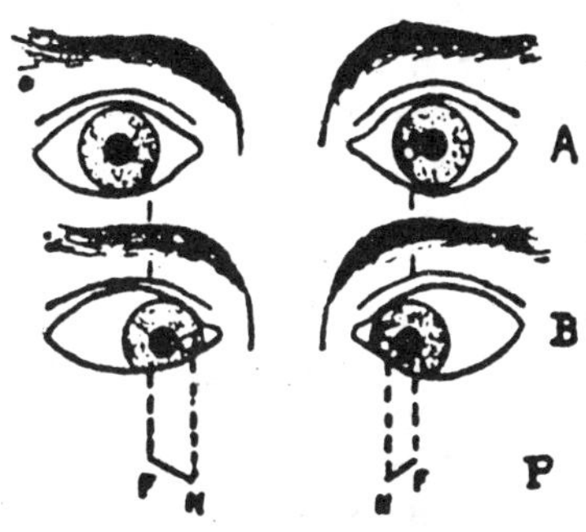

FIG. 17-2. (Judd, 1907.) Method of studying convergence by use of the motion picture camera. The upper pair of eyes is in the parallel position as if looking at a distant object. The lower pair is strongly converged upon a near object lying below the level of the eyes. (The lid movement which accompanies downward eye movement is not represented in this diagram.) On each iris can be seen a spot of China white, and the dotted lines indicate the method of using these spots for plotting the eye movement, F-N between the far and the near object.

found a way to use the picture. He projected each frame separately on a large sheet of paper and marked the position of the eye. He found that a bit of China white, thinly coated with paraffin to make it smooth and durable, could be placed on the cornea without causing any discomfort. It could be so located as to remain in place. It photographed well and provided a definite point to be marked in the projection of each frame. Usually the camera caught the eye during a fixation and the white spot showed the eye's momentary fixation point. When the eye had been caught in motion, the spot showed as a faint streak. Some of the briefest fixations would not be caught at all because the motion picture camera takes a series of exposures separated by blank intervals; and if the rate of the camera is increased, the light thrown on the eye must be disagreeably strong. In spite of all these difficulties some good results have been obtained by this method (Fig. 17-2).

The corneal reflection can be photographed by a motion picture camera, as was done by Brandt (1940, 1945; see above, p. 75) for determining *O*'s fixation points on an advertisement, and by P. R. Wendt (1952) for the same purpose when *O* is viewing a motion picture. Apparently this method is not well adapted for recording the pursuit movements of the eye.

5. An electrical method. Eye movements produce slight electric changes which can be picked up by electrodes attached to the skin near the eyes. If one electrode is attached above and the other below the same eye, upward and downward movements will produce opposite changes of potential which can be picked up, greatly amplified, and then recorded by aid of an oscillograph. If the electrodes are placed near the outer angles of the two eyes, horizontal eye movements are recorded. Both direction and extent of the eye movements are registered.

The potentials in question do not originate in the ocular muscles, as was naturally assumed at first, but are due to the fact that the retina, at the back of the eyeball, is the seat of more active metabolism than the cornea at the front. Consequently, the retina is electrically "negative" in relation to the cornea. With electrodes located above and below an eye, an upward movement of the front of the eye brings the positive pole of the eyeball closer to the upper electrode, the negative pole closer to the lower electrode, and so changes the potential difference between the electrodes in one direction, whereas a downward eye movement will change it in the opposite direction (Mowrer, Ruch & Miller, 1936; Lindsley & Hunter, 1939; Miles, 1939; Hoffman, Wellman & Carmichael, 1939).

This electrical method has some advantages. For one thing, the flexible leads to the electrodes allow the subject some freedom of movement instead of pinning him down to a rigid head rest. Carmichael & Dearborn (1947) found this method well suited for prolonged experiments on fatigue in reading. The subject sat in an isolated room for six hours at a stretch, reading all the time. One pair of electrodes picked up the horizontal eye movements of reading, and another the upward eye movements that occur in blinking. The movements were recorded on an ink-writing polygraph.

The results of this extensive experiment on 20 college and 20 high school students indicated that reading could continue for six hours with very little if any fatigue of the eyes or of reading ability. The speed of reading did not change nor the comprehension of what was read. Eye fixations became slightly less numerous (not necessarily a sign of fatigue), and blinking became definitely more frequent (which may be a sign of fatigue). Perhaps we should not expect much eye fatigue, since the eyes are usually in constant use throughout the waking day. We could expect some fatigue of the ciliary muscle which is constantly in use in close visual work unless moments of relaxation are permitted as they apparently were not in this experiment.

One very important factor in minimizing fatigue effects is interest or motivation. Carmichael & Dearborn kept the reader alert by binding in a few questions on the content at natural breaks in the book; the reader had to attend to his job, or he would not know the answers. Hoffman (1946), not using such quizzes, found a slight loss in efficiency in a half hour; there was a loss in speed under these conditions. The moral for the student is obvious: stop now and then to quiz yourself on what you have read.

6. The afterimage method. It is possible to observe your own eye movements in certain cases. You cannot feel them with any approach to accuracy, but you can sometimes see them directly or indirectly. Helmholtz (1856–66) and other early physiologists made good use of afterimages. By first fixating a small bright light steadily for a while you can obtain a strong, sharp afterimage which moves with the fovea. Where it pauses, there the eyes are fixated, and when it moves from one object to another, or from one word to another in a line of print, it reveals the shifting of fixation. If it wavers or slides, fixation is unsteady. A similar method (Lamansky, 1869) utilizes the brief positive aftersensation that follows momentary stimulation. Let the field of view be dark or very dim except for one small bright light; as you shift your eyes from point to point, every movement leaves a visible streak which traces its course. If the light is intermittent, consisting of 120 flashes per second, the streak is a series of bright dots and each dot represents 1/120 second. Fairly accurate measurements of the speed of some eye movements were obtained by this means before the photographic method was invented. Other subjective methods will be mentioned in connection with the different sorts of eye movement. They still have some value in giving the student first-hand acquaintance with certain phenomena.

FIXATION AND ASSOCIATED EYE MOVEMENTS

The development of photographic methods for recording eye movements in the first decade of the present century opened up a number of diverse fields of research. We can do little more than skim the high spots here; perhaps it will be done most effectively by treating the research under the different types of eye movements involved.

Fixation. As we have already indicated, fixation is neither as precise nor as steady as the name implies. You can demonstrate this fact by fixating a bright point of light or the setting sun (*do not* look at the clear sun, or stare at even the setting sun, for fear of permanent retinal damage). Two successive fixations of such a bright point will usually yield two separate afterimages, indicating that the fixated object was not brought back to exactly the same point each time. Thus, there is a zone or region rather than a point of fixation. Using the motion picture camera, McAllister (1905) abundantly verified the result stated. He found also that the eyes did not remain absolutely motionless even during a single fixation as short as a second. Dodge (1907a) was in general agreement.

For an understanding of visual acuity (p. 384) it is important to know just how much the eye moves during fixation. The methods we have described are not sharp enough to pick up very fine movements (ocular tremors, called *physiological nystagmus*). The best way would be like that used by the physicists in recording galvanometer deflections. A beam of light is thrown on a small mirror, and the reflected beam is recorded on film as the mirror twists slightly with the galvanometer coil. But how can you attach a mirror to the eye? The Delabarre-Huey plaster cup offers a possible lead. Orchansky (1898) tried fastening a mirror to a thin metal cup that fitted on the eyeball. Somewhat similar devices were used by Marx & Trendelenburg (1911) and by Adler & Fliegelman (1934) with fairly good results. But the most adequate method found is to mount a tiny mirror flush with the outer surface of a contact lens (p. 372). As used by Ratliff & Riggs (1950) this method yields photographic records on a continuously moving film.

Typical records are shown in Figure 17·3. Careful examination will detect several types of eye movement during fixation: slow drifts, rapid jerks (sometimes correcting the drifts), and rapid oscillations or tremors. These tremors occur with a frequency of 30–70 cycles per second, and with a median amplitude of 17.5 seconds of arc. The larger tremors are extensive enough to make the image of the fixated point oscillate over several foveal cones. It has sometimes been suggested, as by Marshall & Talbot (1942), that this "scanning" may improve acuity, even as a finger movement over a surface is superior to passive touch. As a check on this theory, Ratliff (1952) tested *O*'s acuity by exposing grids for 75 ms while taking simultaneous records of ocular tremor. He found that poorer acuity was associated with larger drifts and even with larger amounts of the minute tremor. Certainly the eye movements during fixation did not improve acuity, as the scanning theory would predict.

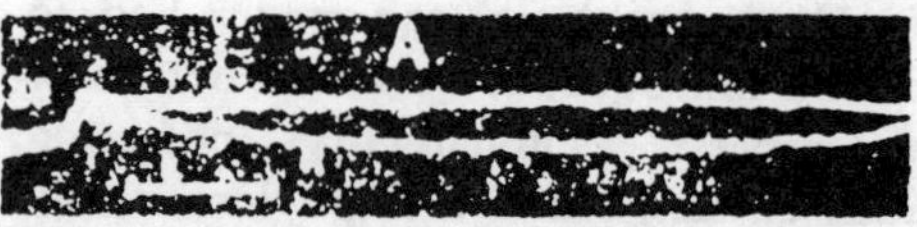

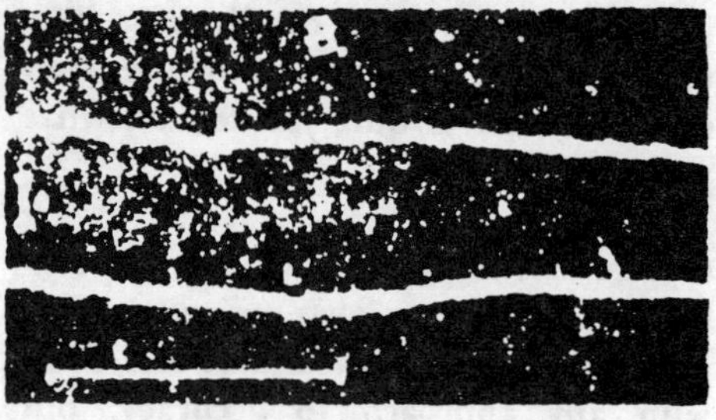

FIG. 17·3. (Riggs & Ratliff, 1951.) Records of eye movements for one subject. The upper record, A, shows one large jerky movement and a slow drift of the right eye (R). The fine tremors are brought out better in B, which is an enlarged section of A. The vertical bar, e, represents 100 seconds of angular rotation of the eye, the horizontal bar, t, is 1/10 seconds long.

But these movements during fixation may have a useful function in longer fixations, for they seem to avoid the effects of rapid local adaptation. This has been demonstrated by a clever modification of the contact-lens method. The beam of light is reflected onto a screen in front of *O*, instead of onto the recording film. In a dark room all *O* can see is the spot of light reflected from the mirror attached to his own eye. When the eye moves, so will the spot, and suitable lenses can be included in the system so that both spot and eye will always move through the same visual angle. In other words, the retinal image remains stationary, despite eye movements. Under these conditions the spot of light fades and disappears within a few seconds, as the stimulated retinal area adapts to the light falling on it (Riggs, Ratliff, Cornsweet & Cornsweet, 1953).

So we can conclude that the small eye movements help us during long fixation, as when we scrutinize an object, even though they cut down acuity for short exposures. The chief remaining problem is how we can account for our ability to see a line of only 0.5 second of visual angle in width, when it is constantly oscillating on the retina. It must be that the central nervous system averages out these oscillations in some way, just as it handles other causes of blur in the retinal image. We have already discussed this general problem in the section on visual acuity (p. 384). (Cf. Galifret, 1951.)

Convergence and relative divergence. By relative divergence is meant the return of the eyes to or toward the parallel position. In distant vision the ocular axes are parallel, in near vision more or less convergent. When a change of fixation occurs from a near to a far object or the reverse, the task imposed on the eyes is more difficult than in the simple conjugate movement, as is clear from the photographic records.

Movements of convergence were photographed by Judd (1907) with the motion picture camera. A sample of his results is shown (Fig. 17-4). There was good evidence that such movements are labored. They take much more time than the conjugate movements and are often interrupted by pauses. The two eyes do not always keep step; one may pause while the other is moving; one may reach its destination and remain there while the other is still feeling around. When the eyes shift their gaze from a far to a near object, the first attempt is likely to leave them imperfectly converged and the object is "seen double." This double vision is corrected by readjusting the direction of one or both eyes.

One cause of the difficulty appears in the records. In passing from a far to a near point the eyes need to turn in opposite directions but they often show first a short movement in the same direction. This easier conjugate movement gets the start of the other and proceeds a short distance before being corrected.

One practical inference is that reading matter should be so held as to minimize the necessity of changes in convergence as the eyes proceed along a line of print. All parts of the *same line* of print should be nearly at the same distance from the eye, so that no change in convergence will be required in reading the line. If a change in convergence is necessary in passing down the page, that is unimportant because the progress of the eyes down a page is slow. Ease of eye movements demands that the page, even though tilted back so as to have the best illumination, should not be tilted to the right or left.

The comparative slowness of movements of convergence and divergence can be observed by a subjective method also, akin to the afterimage method already mentioned. Choose a near and a far object, each of which is distinct and contrasts sharply with a plain background, the near object within a foot or two of the eyes and almost in a direct line with the far object, so that a shift from one object to another requires merely change of convergence. While you look with both eyes at the far object, the near object is seen double; the same happens to the far object when the near object

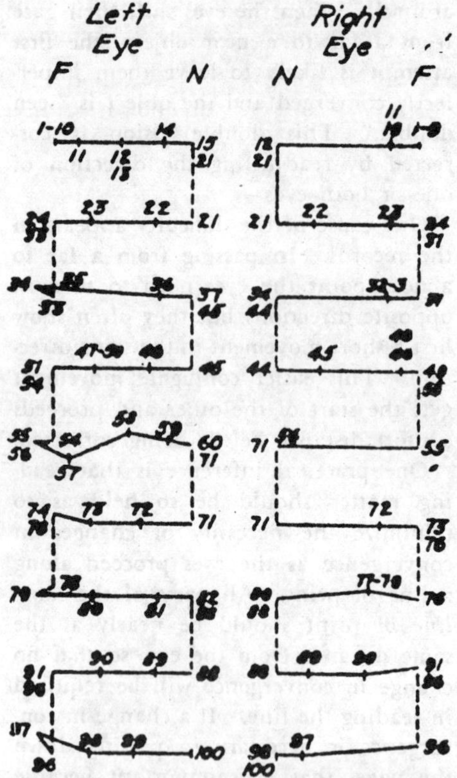

FIG. 17·4. (Judd, 1907.) Movements of convergence and relative divergence. *O*'s eyes were photographed during repeated shifts between a near and a far fixation point, situated directly in front of the nose at distances of 30 and 55 cm. The figure shows the plot obtained from the photographs. The vertical dotted lines indicate the fixation pauses, those under F representing the fixations on the far point and those under N the fixations on the near point. The solid lines, horizontal or nearly so, represent the path of each eye in passing between the near and far fixation points. Both eyes were photographed simultaneously, at the rate of slightly over 10 exposures per second. The numbers written on the record are the successive exposures, and can be taken as time units of approximately 1/10 of a second. The position of each number shows where the spot of China white was found during the successive exposures.

The record starts with the eyes fixating the far point. The left eye remains on this point for the first 10 exposures, moves toward the near point, being caught en route in exposures 12, 13 and 14, and reaches its near fixation by the 15th exposure. It occupied nearly ½ second in this movement of convergence, which was interrupted by a definite pause at the point marked 12 and 13.

The right eye began its first movement of convergence before the left, since exposure 10 caught it on the way, and it reached the goal first (exposure 12 as against 15). Both eyes remained fixated on the near point till exposure 21, when they simultaneously moved to the far point, keeping in perfect step during this movement of (relative) divergence, which occupied about 300 ms. In the next movement of convergence, the left eye made a short conjugate movement along with the right eye (33-34), corrected this and swung into convergence, reaching the near point by exposure 37, nearly 300 ms behind the right eye. Similar behavior occurs further down the record; in fact, with this particular individual, every time the eyes converge, the left eye makes a false start to the left in sympathy with the right eye. Individuals differ in this respect, from habit or because of dominance of one eye or because of lack of perfect balance between the muscles of the two eyeballs.

is fixated. As you shift your gaze from one to the other, the double images merge into one, and the merging may take an appreciable time. The merging is the visual result of the comparatively slow sliding into accurate binocular fixation.

The saccadic movement. This is the simple looking movement, a conjugate movement without complication by change of convergence. It is the reaction of the eyes to a stimulus received in indirect vision, and brings the object into the central area of clear vision. It is the movement used in reading and in surveying any stationary object or scene. There are several remarkable facts about this saccadic movement.

It is the most frequent sort of major eye movement.

It is only very imperfectly felt by the subject. The sensations of movement from the eye muscles and from the eye socket are slight, especially for short movements, and give no reliable indication when the eye is moving and when it is still. *O* cannot count his own saccadic eye movements, and in fact, he usually has an entirely false impression of the behavior of his eyes in reading or in surveying a scene. He imagines himself to be sweeping his eyes by a continuous gradual movement along the line or about the room, whereas all the objective methods show that he is really moving his eyes by jumps with intervening fixations.

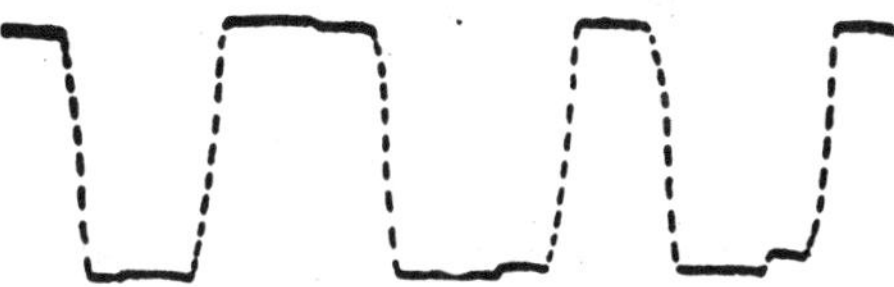

FIG. 17·5. (Dodge & Benedict, 1915.) Long saccadic movements. The eye shifted back and forth between fixation points 40 degrees apart. The light beam was interrupted 100 times per second, and the duration of the movements can be found by counting the dashes. The heavy lines are fixations, during which the separate flashes of the light are too close together on the record to be distinguished. Minute saccadic movements can be seen in many of the fixation periods, and the largest of these little jumps, from the record, covered about 4 degrees and took from 10 to 20 ms. As the original eye movements were horizontal, the figure is best seen from the side. For photographic records of eye movements in reading, see page 505.

It is a coordinated movement of the two eyes. Even if one eye is screened from the page or scene, it still keeps step with the other.

It starts quickly, stops quickly, and makes its journey with little loss of time. A movement over a space of five letters of ordinary print, at a reading distance of a foot, takes 15–20 ms, or about 1/60 sec. The following table from Dodge & Cline (1901) gives the duration of longer movements, their extent being measured by the angle through which the eye swings.[1] The table quotes the average from three subjects.

Extent of movement	*Duration of movement (in ms)*
5°	29
10°	39
15°	48
20°	55
30°	80
40°	100

The longer movements take longer times, though they are more rapid. Individuals differ somewhat: a distance which one covers in 50 ms may take another, 60 ms. For the same individual and the same extent of movement, the time is nearly but not perfectly constant. Almost the same averages were obtained by Tinker (1942) who found significant though not large individual differences. The quickest of his 14 student *O*s took about ⅔ as much time as the slowest to execute a saccadic movement.

FIG. 17·6. (Stratton, 1902b, 1906.) Eye movement in "sweeping the eyes" around a circle. The lines are saccadic movements and the dots fixations. This and similar records by Stratton showed the impossibility of explaining the esthetic pleasure in a seen curve by the supposed smooth sweep of the eyes along the curve.

The speed of the saccadic movement changes somewhat with *O*'s organic condition, being slower in drowsiness or

[1] For movements of twenty degrees or less, along a page held a foot from the eyes, each degree means approximately 1/5 of an inch, so that 5° = 1 inch, 10° = 2 inches, 15° = 3 inches, and 20° = 4 inches (more precisely, 4.23 inches).

under alcohol (Dodge & Benedict, 1915; Miles, 1924, 1929; Miles & Laslett, 1931).

We might expect the reaction time of the saccadic movement to be very short, but it is in fact about the same as that of a hand response to a visual stimulus (p. 16). The saccadic response to a stimulus appearing in indirect vision was found to be 195 ms on the average with a range of individual averages from 125 to 235 ms (Diefendorf & Dodge, 1908).

Vision during eye movements. The function of saccadic movements is to move the eyes from one fixation point to another, and ordinarily objects are not seen during the movements. This fact can be demonstrated in a number of ways. One of the clearest is to set up a couple of screens and three objects arranged as in Figure 17·7. If the

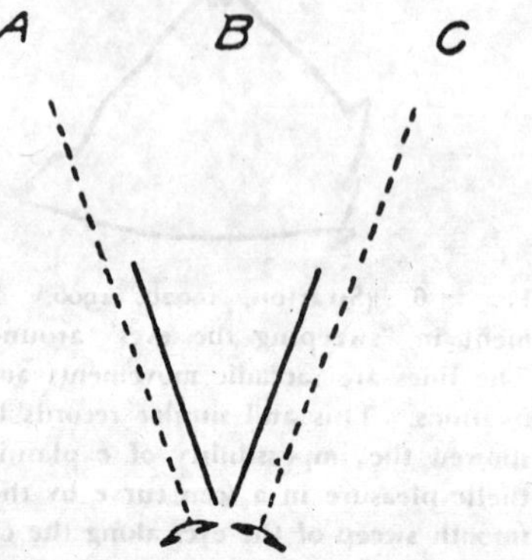

Fig. 17·7. Arrangement of screens for concealing B during fixation of either A or C, but permitting exposure of B during eye movement from A to C.

screens are close enough to the open eye, *O* can see only the single object fixated. Now let him make a saccadic movement from A to C, and report whether or not B is present. He cannot tell, unless he has broken the saccadic movement and fixated B on the way; *E* must watch *O*'s eye carefully to check such unconscious failures to make a single saccadic movement.

When first discovered, this lack of visual perception during saccadic movements was something of a puzzle. Holt (1903) suggested that there was a "central anesthesia" of vision during such movements, but Dodge (1905) and Woodworth (1906b) showed that this was an unnecessary assumption. What happens is clear enough from a functional standpoint. While the eye is jumping from one fixation to another, the whole visual field sweeps across the retina at a rapid rate, and the resulting brief blur is of no value to *O*. Even without any built-in mechanism for blotting out this blur, *O* would soon learn to disregard it. An analogous case is the momentary blackout that occurs during every blink; everyone blinks several times a minute, but it takes special practice to notice the short dark periods. In a similar fashion one can learn to see some of the blurs during saccadic movements. Let there be a bright source of light with a dark background. Fixate some object on its left, and then make a saccadic movement to an object on its right. The light will give a blur or streak, persisting briefly as a positive afterimage. If you try the experiment with a neon light, which flashes 120 times per second on the ordinary alternating current, you will see a dotted or broken line instead of a single blur. These experiments show clearly that one can see during saccadic movements, if there is something with enough contrast to make it stand out from the blurred background.

It is possible to check this point in another way. Set up a rotating disk color mixer, going just fast enough to fuse. Now try making saccadic movements back and forth from points some distance on either side of the disk. You can vary the speed of the saccadic movement by varying the distance between fixation points—the longer, the faster. After some experimentation, you can find conditions such that part of the disk seems to stand still for a flash as the eye passes it. The same sort of experiment can be done with a phonograph turntable. The point is that when the eye is moving at the same speed (in terms of visual angle) as the moving object, the image will be stationary on the retina, yielding clear vision. We shall see later that there are several specific types of eye movements which serve to keep the retinal image stationary in spite of movements of objects in relation to the head; as one would expect, clear vision is maintained during such movements. But during saccadic movements, the only thing one could normally see would be a blur, which certainly is the sort of thing *O* would disregard in the interests of efficient vision of real objects.

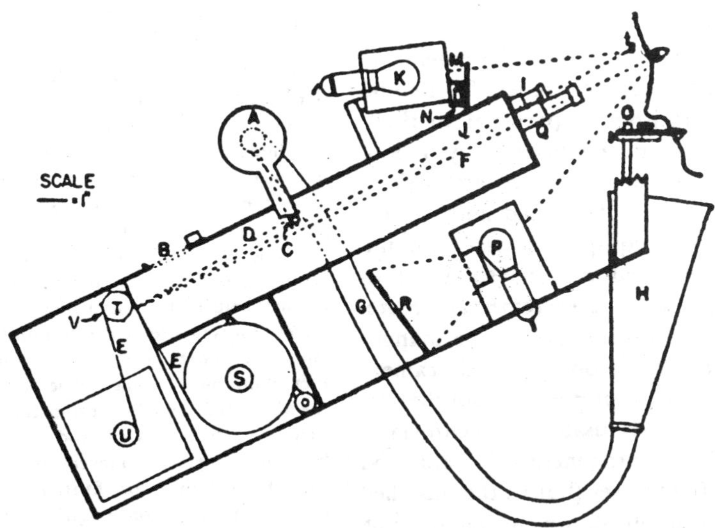

FIG. 17-8. (Tiffin & Fairbanks, 1937.) Setup for recording eye and voice on the same film. While the subject's eyes are directed toward the reading matter, R, a beam of light from the source, P, reflected from his cornea through the lens at Q and along the line FC, strikes the photographic film near T. A motor drive applied at V, draws the film, E, from the spool, S, around T to U. The voice is picked up by the horn, H, and carried through the tube, G, to the oscillograph, A, and the light from this instrument is reflected by a mirror at C to the film beside the eye record. A record of any head movements that occur is provided by a beam of light from the source, K, which is reflected by L, a bead on a spectacle frame worn by the subject, and passes through the lens at I and along the line marked J to the film at T. A time line is provided by a 60-cycle vibrator, N, which interrupts the head-beam at M. B is the focusing window.

The oscillograph, which is the Dorsey phoneloscope, is used here not for obtaining detailed pictures of the voice vibrations but simply for indicating the time when each syllable is spoken (Fig. 17-11). For identification of the syllables, a phonograph record of the subject's oral reading is made simultaneously with the other records.

This apparatus differs from the standard ophthalmograph in the addition of the voice-recording unit and the arrangement for recording head movements. A biting board, O, has been substituted for the more massive head rest. Lens I would normally pick up the right eye, instead of the head bead, L.

EYE MOVEMENTS IN READING

It will be recalled that Javal (1878) observed that the eyes, far from sweeping smoothly across a line of print, executed a series of saccadic movements, fixating at several different points along each line. In the chapter on Attention it is shown that the practiced reader can "take in" several words at a time. Obviously these two facts belong together, and the eye movements in reading should throw light on the reading process and on the operation of eye movements as well. Dodge's corneal reflection method (p. 494) furnished a practical method; since then there have been many investigations aimed at finding general principles, and a host of applied and clinical studies. The equipment has been improved and modified for special purposes. Perhaps the extremes are represented by Tinker's (1931) permanent installation, built on a 70-inch camera barrel, and the neat portable ophthalmograph (Fig. 17-8) usable in a clinician's office. Either instrument will yield good records of both eyes (but in the modified ophthalmograph shown in Figure 17-8 one lens is used to record head movement).

A schematic ophthalmograph record is shown in Figure 17-9, with certain features emphasized. Once the reader is familiar with the phenomena illustrated and explained there, he can find them in actual records. For example, Figure 17-10 includes several records made by Dearborn in 1906. They are monocular, but that is no handicap; for we usually follow the record of only one eye, unless we are interested in checking convergence. With this exception, all of the features shown in the schematic record can be found in several of Dearborn's photographs.

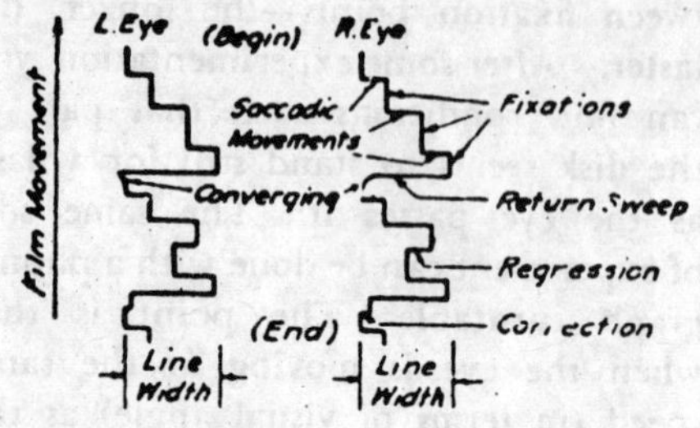

FIG. 17-9. A schematic representation of an eye-movement photograph, such as one would obtain from an ophthalmograph. Since the film moves upward, the record progresses downward. Hence, the length of vertical lines gives the duration of fixations, and that of horizontal lines the extent of lateral eye movements. The width and location of the line of reading matter are indicated below the record for each eye. Starting at the top the record shows four fixations and three saccadic movements in the reading of the first line of print. The two eyes give parallel, conjugate records. But they diverge slightly on the first return sweep and slowly slide back into correct convergence at the beginning of the second line. There is a regressive movement further along on this line. The return sweep for the third line failed to bring the beginning of that line into clear view, and so it was followed by a small corrective movement. The record is cut off after the next fixation. (Actually, the eye movements seldom extend to the very beginning and end of a line of print.)

The average reader shows pretty good coordination of his eyes. They follow the horizontal line pretty well, with little vertical movement. Inaccuracy and loss of convergence in return sweeps are fairly common, but moderate amounts of such anomalies seem to have no clear-cut effect—although bad muscular imbalance, with excessive convergence strain, may be fatiguing (Clark, 1940).

Development of reading skill. Reading is a complex skill, and like all skills, it develops gradually, improving in both

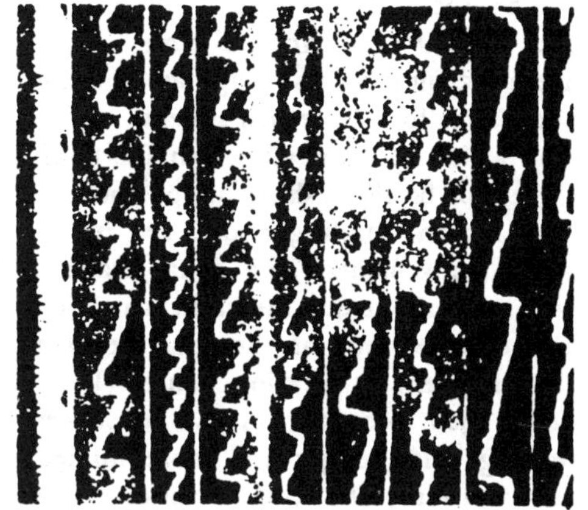

FIG. 17-15. (W. F. Dearborn, 1906.) Photographic records of eye movements in reading. These records are to be read upwards. The short, heavy vertical lines are the fixations. and the lighter oblique lines (almost horizontal) are saccadic movements, the long ones to the left carrying the eye from the end of one line to the beginning of the next, and the little ones to the right carrying it from point to point in the reading of a line. Regressive movements can be seen in most of the records.

The records are from four educated adults, who differed greatly in speed of reading. Each is represented by two records, the first from his reading of material printed in long lines, and the second from his reading of short newspaper lines. In reading newspaper lines, the complete records of the four subjects, when measured, gave the following averages:

Subject	*Fixations per line*	*Average duration of a fixation*
1	3.8	161 ms
2	3.9	216
3	5.5	255
4	5.4	402

precision and in speed. Pencil and paper tests are useful in measuring progress, but eye-movement records are of value in analyzing the details of what is happening. By comparing samples of students at various grade levels (see table below) we see that improvement occurs in three ways. In the first place, there is a steady decrease in the number of fixations per line. This holds true even though the reading material increases in difficulty at each grade. Thus the college student is taking in at least three times as much reading matter per fixation as is the beginning reader. Secondly, the fixations grow shorter as academic level increases; the advanced reader takes in the material faster. Finally, there is a very marked decrease in regressive movements. This means greater regularity in progressing along the lines of print. It is natural to conclude that the ideal reader would have no regressive movements. Actually, a few regressive movements show that the reader is alert to what he is reading, so that he goes back to clear up an obscurity. (Bayle, 1942; Buswell, 1937.) Sometimes the regressive movement should be blamed on the author, rather than on the reader!

Fixations. All the reading is done during the fixational pauses, for there is no clear vision during the intervening saccadic movements. Hence, the number and duration of the fixational pauses have received considerable attention. The number of fixations per line depends on the difficulty of the material as well as the habits of the reader. One of the authors (H.S.) once took eye-movement records of a half dozen visitors who attended an "open house" at the laboratory. Since he agreed to report the results, he kept names and addresses of the *Os*. When the records were developed, he was shocked to see that several showed more fixations per line than the average third-grade student. More careful examination showed surprisingly regular movements, with *no* regressions. A check on the addresses showed that these particular visitors were judges; in legal documents every word is important, and these *Os* had carried over their habit of meticulous reading to the laboratory test. The moral of this tale is that there is no single rate or style of reading that is appropriate to all types of reading material. The good reader is the one who adjusts his speed to the material of the moment. Failure to recognize this rule has led to much faulty advice in remedial reading classes.

The duration of the fixations, as distinguished from their number, is not closely dependent on the difficulty of the material, at least as far as the mode is concerned (Buswell, 1922; Robinson, 1933). Good college freshman will average around 210 ms, while their slower classmates run around 260 ms. (Walker, 1933; Anderson, 1937.) These are considerably longer than the exposure needed for perception of dots or letters; the usual tachistoscopic exposure is about 100 ms, depending on the illumination (p. 93). All of these facts indicate that the number and duration of fixations, and hence the speed of reading, are limited by central, rather than by peripheral factors; that is, *O* moves his eyes only as fast as he can absorb the material.

The saccadic movements themselves take very little of the total time. They average around 22 ms for the short jumps and 40 ms for the return sweeps. If we read a line of print with four fixations, there will be three short jumps and one long return, totaling about 100 ms of actual movement. The four fixations will total about 900 ms, indicating that about 90 percent of the total reading time is spent in fixation pauses (Dearborn, 1906; Schmidt, 1917). In slower reading, with longer and more numerous fixations, the total fixation time may be as high as 95 percent (Tinker, 1936b). In one way, this is a measure of efficiency since it gives the proportion of the total time actually devoted to seeing. As a matter of fact, the perceptual processes undoubtedly go on during the saccadic movements, even though retinal stimulation is not effective with the moving eye. Reading is a continuous process in that the perceptual development of meaning goes on steadily. Perhaps one can think of it as a continuous production process, a machine into which the raw material is tossed by the shovelful. The output will be continuous, as long

EYE MOVEMENTS IN READING, ACCORDING TO SCHOOL GRADE

(*Buswell, 1922*)

A sample of 8–19 children from each grade, of about medium reading ability, had their eyes photographed while reading, and the Mean for each grade is given.

School grade	*Fixations per line of print*	*Mean duration of fixation*	*Regressive movements per line*
I B	18.6	660 ms	5.1
I A	15.5	432	4.0
II	10.7	364	2.3
III	8.9	316	1.8
IV	7.3	268	1.4
V	6.9	252	1.3
VI	7.3	236	1.6
VII	6.8	240	1.5
High School I	7.2	244	1.0
H. S. II	5.8	248	0.7
H. S. III	5.5	224	0.7
H. S. IV	6.4	248	0.7
College	5.9	252	0.5

as there is some raw material in the works. This analogy has another similarity to reading; the rate of input will usually be limited by the rate at which the machine processes the raw material, and not vice versa. In a similar fashion, the eye movements adjust to the rate at which *O* is digesting the sensory input.

The eye-voice span in oral reading. Following our analogy, we can raise the question as to how long it takes *O* to "process" the sensory input. But how can we tell when the process of perceiving is complete? One way is to make *O* read aloud, recording eye movements and speech sounds on the same film. A modification of a standard eye-movement camera that will do this job is shown in Figure 17-8. It is relatively simple to determine when a given word was fixated, when it was uttered, and the length of the delay. A typical record is shown in Figure 17-11.

Buswell (1920) has made fairly extensive studies of the eye-voice span. It varies with the skill of the reader, as the following results indicate.

School grade	*Average eye-voice span in letter-spaces*	
	of three good readers	*of three poor readers*
II	11.0	5.4
VI	11.9	11.2
IX	15.8	11.5
XII	15.9	12.4

There is considerable variation from these average values. In the first place, the oral output goes on at a relatively constant rate, consistent with the proper speed for expressive speech. If *O* hits a difficult spot in the written text, his eye movements slow up, and there may be regressive movements to develop the meaning. Thus, his output tends to catch up with the input, and the eye-voice span drops almost to zero. Once the difficulty is overcome, the eye runs ahead rapidly, until it is again well ahead of the voice. With experienced oral readers the span is as long as eight words, 2 seconds, or a line of print, depending on which unit of measurement one prefers to consider.

This estimate of the "processing time" is based on oral reading in which *O* must develop a word in the context of those

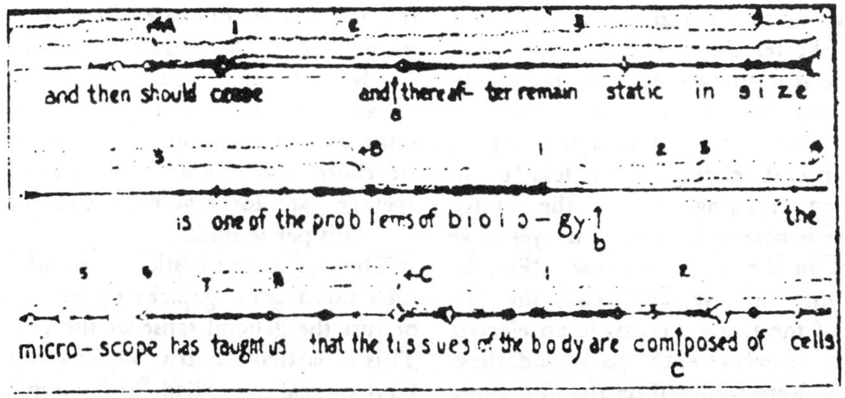

FIG. 17-11. (Tiffin, 1934.) Simultaneous eye-voice record combined with the reading matter. Both eyes are recorded. At A, B, C they swing back to the beginning of a new line; at 1, 2, 3 . . . they move forward along the line. The voice record is just above the printed matter, and the arrows marked a, b, c, show the position of the eyes when the voice has just reached A, B, C. The distances A-a, B-b, C-c show the spatial extent of the eye-voice span at the beginning of the three lines of print. The span is apt to be specially long at the beginning of a line.

that come before and after. The minimum time for perceiving and responding to an isolated word is shorter; reaction time experiments (p. 57) put it at about 4/10 second. But such measurements are misleading when applied to reading, which is a continuous process. The reader does not respond to each word as a new one, just flashed before his eye. He has been prepared for it by earlier words in the sentence, and has seen it in peripheral vision. His response is more than merely shouting the word; he must integrate it into the sentence as a whole. Probably the overlap between visual and vocal processes is our best measure of processing time.

Overlapping processes can be demonstrated in other similar performances such as typing from copy and taking down a telegraphic message from the sounder (pp. 810–813). The ear-hand span in receiving a telegraphic message is specially long because of the amount of organization needed to reduce a series of clicks to a meaningful message. In typing from printed copy, the eye-hand span averages only about 5–6 letter spaces, or about a second. In space it is much shorter than in oral reading, but in time it is about the same—typing being the slower motor process. The number of fixations is much greater in typing than in oral reading, and is least of all in silent reading. When the motor process is necessarily slow, the eyes have to put in the time somehow. (For determining the eye-hand span, the carriage of the typewriter made an electric contact at every tenth space, and these contacts were recorded on the film along with the eye movements; Butsch, 1932.)

Oral *versus* silent reading. The overlap or processing time must not be confused with the speed of reading. As we have indicated, the speed of oral reading is largely set by the demands of speech. The eyes normally go only fast enough to maintain a comfortable lead over the voice. But if *O* reads silently, the limiting effects of speech drop out. For example, Huey (1908) studied the speed with which 20 university students read an interesting novel. The ordinary oral reading ranged from 2.2 to 4.7 words per second; if they tried to speed it up, the oral range shifted to 2.9–6.4. But their ordinary silent rate was between 2.5 and 9.8 words per second. Note that the slower silent readers are little, if any, faster than they were at oral reading. It is possible that these readers were doing what might be called "silent oral reading"—that is, making actual speech movements as they read silently. Many adults have carried over this habit from their early reading lessons; watch people reading, and see how many of them move their lips. This habit acts as a drag on reading rate in two ways. In the first place, it limits reading speed to speech speed. In the second place, it discourages or prevents the integration of material into larger wholes. A skilled reader perceives the words, not singly, but in meaningful phrases. In very rapid reading these units of perception may be quite large. Dearborn (1906) found a professor whose average rate for *Robinson Crusoe* was 11 words per second.

There is some question as to whether such rapid reading picks up all details, or just the general sense of the passage. This is particularly true when we do the kind of reading called "skimming." A person who is thoroughly familiar with a subject can get a pretty good idea of what the author of a new textbook says by glancing at key sentences. It is hard to draw the line between actual reading and such skimming. At the other extreme is the slow and detailed reading of the lawyer (p. 505) or of the student working on an unfamiliar technical subject. We see again that there are as many appropriate rates of reading as there are classes of material and purposes in reading.

Training eye movements. While we are on the subject of individual differences in reading behavior, we might as well say a few words about remedial reading. Considering the importance of reading in school work, one is not surprised that the slow reader has been a challenge to psychologists. With the development of the eye-movement camera, the psychologist had a tool for comparing slow and rapid readers. As one might expect, the slow reader has a relatively large number of fixations and regressive movements per line, and his fixation pauses are long. The obvious remedy was to speed up the eye movements so that they would be smooth and regular. All sorts of methods were tried. The simplest way is to get the pupil to make three regular fixations per line, perhaps in time with a metronome. Another is to use the *Metronoscope*, a gadget which exposes lines of print in successive thirds, forcing *O* to make the desired pattern of eye movements (Taylor, 1937). Dearborn & Anderson (1937) have developed a moving picture film which simulates the reading situation a little better; it has a moving clear region that passes along the line in regular jumps. The eye follows this region, but it has the advantage of some peripheral vision of the rest of the line. There have been a number of careful experiments, with control groups who get no training, all groups being tested before and after the training (or no training) period. There is usually a pronounced gain in the experimental group. But where other control groups have been used, such as a group of children who did motivated library reading while the experimental group practiced with the Metronoscope, *both* groups showed gains (Cason, 1943). The answer seems to be that any method which arouses an interest in greater reading speed will probably work.

Many experts feel that emphasis on training eye movements is tackling the wrong end of the process. As we have indicated above, eye movements are only one link in the chain; the limiting factor is central. Hence, what is necessary is to improve perceptual skills directly and let the eye movements follow (Buswell, 1939).

Does this men that one should forget about eye-movement cameras in the reading clinic? In the first place, it has been shown that the typical short test with a camera like the ophthalmograph yields unreliable results (Imus, Rothney & Bear, 1943; Anderson, 1941; Broom, 1940). This is probably due to the short sample furnished with the instrument, for Tinker (1936c) found that the reliability went up to .80 when samples of 20 to 40 lines were used instead of 5 to 15. In the second place, the eye movement camera encourages too much attention to eye movements instead of a more thorough analysis of the reading skill as a whole. Hence, the camera should be used only by experts with a good psychological training.

This book is not the place to go too deeply into a specialized topic like reading, much less the improvement of reading skills. The student who wishes to study further will find an excellent summary in Tinker's (1946) review. He lists 126 references, mostly from the decade 1935–1944. Many of them were concerned with limited practical problems. The more general problems had already been covered in the widespread exploratory activity that characterized the first quarter of the century as eye-movement cameras became available. Experimental psychologists were intensely interested in such problems as the following:

1. *Does the fixation favor any particular parts of words, or any particular sorts of words?* The answer seems to be that *O* is nearly as likely to fixate a space between words as a letter, to use an extreme example (Fig. 17-12). There is, however, some question as to whether the usual record is accurate enough to locate fixations so precisely.

2. *What part of a line gets the most fixation time?* The answer is that about 30 per cent goes in the first quarter, with the rest evenly divided over the other three quarters. It is possible that the need for corrective movements after the return sweep makes up the excess.

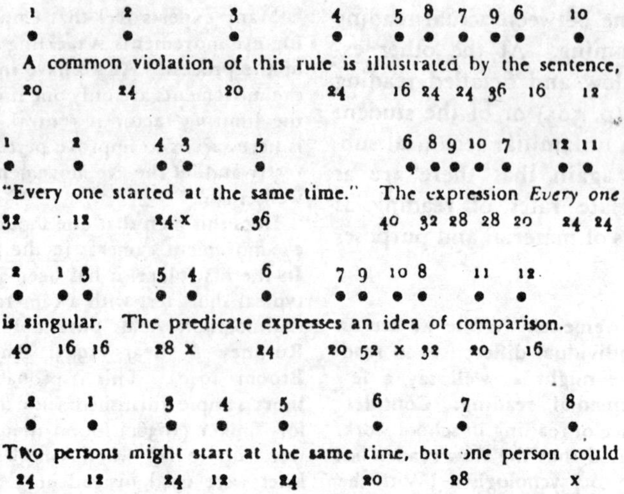

1 2 3 4 5 8 7 9 6 10
A common violation of this rule is illustrated by the sentence,
20 24 20 24 16 24 24 36 16 12

1 2 4 3 5 6 8 9 10 7 12 11
"Every one started at the same time." The expression *Every one*
32 12 24 x 36 40 32 28 28 20 24 24

2 1 3 5 4 6 7 9 10 8 11 12
is singular. The predicate expresses an idea of comparison.
40 16 16 28 x 24 20 52 x 32 20 16

2 1 3 4 5 6 7 8
Two persons might start at the same time, but one person could
24 12 24 12 24 20 28 x

FIG. 17·12. (From Judd & Buswell, 1922.) Fixations in four lines of reading. The dots indicate the location of the fixations. The numbers above the dots give the order of fixations in each line, while the numbers below show the duration of each fixation in hundredths of a sec. Where an x occurs, the duration could not be made out from the record. The reader was a university student. Plots of this type are prepared by projecting the eye-movement photographs onto the original reading material, and noting where each fixation falls. To aid in lining up the image, *O* fixates each of two dots (not shown here) at opposite edges of the reading matter before he starts to read.

5. *How does the eye behave in reading music, foreign languages, mathematical formulas, adding, etc.?* The answers come out about as one who knew the task would anticipate. One interesting point came out from a study of reading Chinese (Shen, 1927). The pattern of eye movements was very different from that used in reading English, as one might expect from the form and direction of Chinese printing. But the reading rate, if scored in terms of content, showed about the same amount of thought taken in per second in both languages. Again we find an emphasis on central, rather than on peripheral limitations.

A more complete discussion of these and related questions will be found in the earlier edition of this text.

PURSUIT MOVEMENTS AND THE PERCEPTION OF MOTION

Up to the present we have been concerned with situations in which the visual object was stationary with respect to *O*. In such cases he sees clearly only during fixation pauses, when the image is stationary on the retina. But what happens when the visual object moves with respect to *O*? The retinal image would be blurred, unless the eyes kept pace with the object. What actually happens is that the eye follows the moving object in a smooth sweep, keeping it neatly fixated on the fovea. Needless to say, *O does* have vision during pursuit movements, but the vision is only sharp for the fixated or pursued object. Put a flat transparent ruler on this page, and slide it back and forth. If you fixate the printed page, seen through the ruler, the page will be clear, but the numbers on the moving ruler will be blurred. Now fixate a number on the ruler; the eyes will execute pursuit movements, the ruler will be clear, but the page will be blurred.

Pursuit movements are pretty accurate

for a small object that you move by hand in this fashion, for the eye movement starts simultaneously with the hand movement; after all, you have been practicing this sort of eye-hand coordination all your life. But it is a different story when the object moves from external forces. If a fixated object starts to move, its image is displaced from the center of vision. There follows a saccadic movement to fixate it again. This merges into a pursuit movement as the object continues to move, but the pursuit movement is apt to be too fast or slow. A corrective saccadic movement is necessary to get the pursuit movement back on the target. If the movement of the object is steady, or even repetitive, like the swinging of a pendulum, the pursuit movements eventually adjust rather nicely to it (Fig. 17-13). Saccadic movements can be superimposed on continuing pursuit movements; for example, you can read a moving page quite adequately, and the movement pattern is clearly the typical reading movement, jump-pause-jump-pause, against a background of regular pursuit.

The speed and direction of an ordinary pursuit movement are determined by the motion of the object. There are two limitations, however. The object may move too slowly or too rapidly for the eye to follow, and it may move too far. How do the eyes behave in watching a procession march up the avenue? They follow one unit until it is uncomfortably far to the left (for example), make a saccadic movement to the right and fixate another unit, and so on. The result is an alternation of pursuit and return saccadic movements—an "optic nystagmus." This same alternation occurs when it is *we* that move past a stationary landscape, as in a train or bus.

Perception of real movement. As we have just noticed, visible movement is perceived when the image of an object remains stationary on the retina of a moving eye. Movement is perceived also

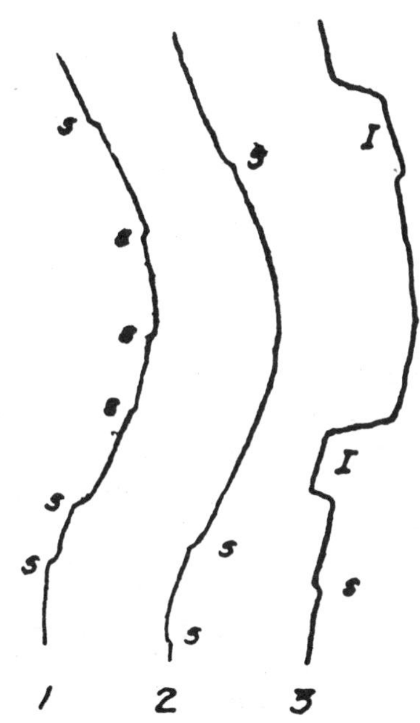

Fig. 17-13. (After Dodge, 1907.) Tracing of photographic record of pursuit movements. The stimulus was a pendulum, followed for several swings. The pendulum was swinging to the right in each of the three records here reproduced. The lines are to be read upward. (1) Starting from a stationary fixation, the eye jumps into a moving fixation which is corrected by several small saccadic movements, s, s, s. (2) After several swings the pursuit movement has become smooth and accurate, with only a few slight saccadic corrections. (3) Disturbance results when the pendulum is hidden for a part of each swing, as at I. With the visual stimulus gone, the eye falls behind and makes a large saccadic movement on the reappearance of the pendulum.

when the eye is stationary while the image moves across the retina. So you must have observed in the ruler experiment a moment ago, for you saw the ruler move even while you held the eyes stationary by fixating the page beneath the moving ruler. This type of perceived movement is at least as common as the type involving pursuit movements; in fact, it is motion along the retina that is the stimulus initiating a pursuit movement. While following an object to the right, you can also see the background streaming to the left. In all these cases there is real stimulus motion to be perceived.

Apparent visual movement. In our day it is a common experience to see motion when no motion is present in the stimulus. On the motion picture screen—or on the television screen—there is no actual motion of the figures. The motion picture camera took a series of snapshots separated by brief intervals of time, and the projector casts these still views and blank intervals on the screen. The motions that you see on the screen are apparent and not real, so far as the picture stimulus is concerned, though they were real in the original scene that was photographed. The fact of apparent visual motion under such conditions became known in 1833 with the invention of the stroboscope, a device for illuminating a moving object with intermittent light. The apparent movement is accordingly also called stroboscopic movement.

The psychological study of this effect, rather desultory for many years, received a great impetus from Wertheimer's paper of 1912. He called it the Phi phenomenon and attached theoretical importance to it as a sensory configuration that had more in it than was present in the series of stimuli. In fact this research of his led to the founding of Gestalt psychology.

Wertheimer simplified the "picture" to the limit and used relatively simple apparatus for showing it. Either a sliding screen or a rotating disk tachistoscope (p. 92) served to present successive views of a line in different positions. He varied the experiment in many ways His results have remained classic, even though subjected to minor revisions and to many additions. He found the duration of the blank interval an important factor in the effect. Let two short vertical lines, 1 cm apart and at reading distance, be exposed one after the other. If the blank interval is 200 ms or more, the appearance corresponds to the reality: two stationary lines seen in succession. If the interval is 30 ms or less, the appearance of succession is entirely lost, and the two lines seem to be simultaneous. When the blank interval lies between the limits mentioned, the appearance is apt to be the motion of a single line from the first position to the second. There are thus two thresholds, one between succession and motion, the other between motion and simultaneity. These thresholds are quite variable and dependent on many factors.

Our familiar scheme, $R = f(S, O)$, is convenient in this situation. R is the observer's perception and report of succession, motion, or simultaneity—as in a three-category psychophysical experiment. The results will be most comprehensible if we consider that the actual fact is succession, so that the most correct report is "succession," the least correct "simultaneity," with "motion" intermediate as a halfway perception of the actual succession. Certain conditions, both S-factors and *O*-factors, make it *difficult to perceive the actual succession.*

The most obvious S-factors were studied by Korte (1915) and his results are sometimes called Korte's laws. He found that the following factors made it difficult to perceive the succession:

Short time interval between the two exposures.
Long space between the two positions.
Low intensity of illumination.

Near the simultaneity-motion threshold, these laws mean that it is more difficult to see apparent motion when the illumination is very low, or when the time gap is very short, or when the space gap is very wide. If the space gap is too wide, you must increase the time gap in order to get apparent movement. This last fact shows up in some data of Corbin (1942). His subjects, from a distance of 10 feet, viewed a line in two successive locations separated by 2–12 inches in a frontal-parallel plane. The farther apart the two locations, the longer the time interval had to be for *O* to see motion. On the average of four *O*s, the simultaneity-motion threshold was as follows:

Separation, inches	2	4	6	8	10	12
Threshold, ms	104	114	129	146	157	173

In this last experiment, as in many others, the two positions of the object are shown repeatedly in alternation, and the oscillatory back-and-forth motion is very striking when it is seen.

Another significant S-factor is degree of similarity or dissimilarity. The more dissimilar the two alternating figures, the more difficult it is to see them as a single figure moving and changing form or color as it moves. If each of the two figures is an arrow pointing to the right, motion is easily seen; but if one arrow points to the right and the other to the left, more time must be allowed and some *O*s will fail to see motion (Orlansky, 1940).

Among *O*-factors there are two at least of importance: practice and set. Many *O*s see no motion on the first few trials and some require many trials before any realistic motion appears (De Silva, 1926; Neuhaus, 1930). Some *O*s waver back and forth between apparent motion and simultaneity, and some show fatigue or adaptation after a long series, seeing motion much less than at the beginning of the experimental session (Gilbert, 1939). Set or attitude has considerable potency; with a critical, analytic attitude *O* may see succession where motion will appear if he "lets himself go" (Stratton, 1911). It would probably be impossible to maintain the critical attitude in viewing a regular motion picture. The simple figures used in the laboratory are much less compelling, though even here the apparent motion is exciting and rewarding—one reason why *O* will let himself go after a while. These central factors must be given some weight in any theory of apparent motion.

Varieties of apparent movement. Just what kind of movement will be reported by *O* depends on the stimulus factors and on central factors such as have been mentioned. He will probably see a simple sliding movement along a straight or curved path (Hall, Earle & Crookes, 1952) when the two stimuli are exactly alike, but a turning movement (clockwise or counterclockwise) when an oblique is followed by a horizontal line. He may see a movement in the third dimension, as when an inverted V is followed by a V right side up and slightly lower in the field. Many varied examples of three-dimensional apparent movement have been published by Steinig (1929), Fernberger (1934), and Orlansky (1940). According to the last author, the more complicated apparent movements serve to fill in a long time interval. Since the stimulus sequence is often a somewhat ambiguous one, *O* will make any one of a number of reasonable responses, quite according to the principle stated by William James (1890, II, 82): "Perception is of definite and probable things." But we must add one word of caution: the apparent movement is a *direct perception*, not an inference. If we expose two dots in the Carmichael tachistoscope (1925), one of which really moves while the other drops out and comes back in another location, *O* will insist that he sees both dots move. When the apparatus is operated slowly enough for him to see what actually happens, he quibbles that he did not really see both dots move, but must have inferred it. Yet from a purely descriptive or phenomenological viewpoint he *did* see both dots move, and the apparent movement was perceived as truly as the real movement (Stratton, 1911; De Silva, 1929). Here as in other kinds of perception—notably depth—a process which appears intellectual and complicated to the scientist who studies it may be quite automatic and direct as far as *O* is concerned. If the reader really grasps this point, he will be well along the road toward an understanding of perception.

Theories of apparent movement. The inference theory—that we actually see only the initial and terminal positions and infer that the object must have moved—was dealt with in the way just indicated by Wertheimer (1912, 1925). He had also some objective evidence: except when the time interval is right, *O* sees the two positions but does not infer any intervening motion. Wertheimer considered two other theories.

The eye-movement theory. Many psychologists like to have something tangible and "peripheral" to appeal to in explaining perception. If the eyes moved across from the initial to the final position, the eye movement might contribute the sensation of motion. Wertheimer ruled out that possibility by showing that two movements *in opposite directions* were seen when two suitable pairs of lines were presented, and Guilford & Helson (1929) on photographing the eyes found no significant relation between the eye movements that occurred and the reports of apparent movement. In viewing a motion picture the eyes as photographed by P. R. Wendt (1952) are engaged most of the time in *fixating* objects, just as in viewing an actual scene.

The brain-field theory. Exner (1875), finding that apparent movement was favored by imperfect accommodation, suggested that the retina was actually stimulated in the region lying between the initial and terminal positions and that a true sensation of movement through this region was thus produced. (Against this theory is the fact that apparent movement occurs even if the first stimulus is applied to one eye and the second to the other. One can readily demonstrate this interocular apparent movement by holding a finger in front of the face and fixating a more distant object. Now close and open the two eyes alternately; the finger will appear to move from side to side, since it stimulates disparate points in the two retinas [p. 459]. If unable to wink the eyes alternately, use a shutter [Langfeld, 1927].) Wertheimer proposed a theory somewhat like Exner's, but with the hypothetical movement of stimulation in the visual cortex instead of in the retina. The cortical excitation aroused by the first stimulus could spread and be attracted toward the region excited by the second stimulus, and the movement of excitation along the cortex could give a sensation of movement, a sort of streak. The more recent work of Köhler and his associates on satiation effects in the visual cortex (p. 424) indicates that there may well be such interacting electrical fields in the cortex. The absence of apparent movement in the first trials and when *O* takes a critical attitude might mean that the streak was not strong enough to be absolutely compelling. But there are some other facts that are difficult to reconcile with Wertheimer's theory.

The stroboscopic effect in a decorticate animal. The pursuit movement of the eyes is aroused only by a moving (or apparently moving) stimulus. K. U. Smith (1940) constructed a spherical surface of white stripes to be seen from inside against a dark background. He placed a guinea pig on a stationary holder inside the sphere with a silk thread attached to the animal's nose and leading to a lever writing on a drum. When the sphere was rotated around the animal, the moving stripes induced pursuit movements of the head (and eyes), alternating with saccadic returns—a typical nystagmus induced by real movement. To get the stimulus conditions for apparent movement, he substituted intermittent flashing light for the steady illumination, each successive flash showing the stripes in a slightly different location. Under these conditions the guinea pig still gave the typical nystagmus. Now the animal's cortex was removed, and after-tests showed the same response as before—nystagmus in response to both continuous and interrupted movement. These results were obtained uniformly in a sufficient number of guinea pigs to justify the conclusion that in this animal the integration of successive "snapshots" into the equivalent of real movement takes place below the cortical level. It may be possible to transpose the Wertheimer theory from the cortex to the lower visual centers.

The space-gap factor in the third dimension. When a line is presented in two alternating positions, these positions lie typically in the same frontal-parallel plane; and the greater their separation, measured in this plane, the greater must be the time interval to secure apparent movement. Corbin's results on this point have been cited on page 513. When this investigator turned or slanted the plane 60° on a vertical axis, and used the same separations as before but now in the oblique plane, the same time thresholds were found as in the frontal-parallel plane, though the retinal separations were only half as great. What counted was the visible separations in space, not the retinal separations and therefore not the separations in the visual area of the cortex. It is hard to reconcile this result with Wertheimer's theory, which seems to imply that the spread of excitation would depend on the actual separations in the cortex (or in a subcortical center).

We seem to be left without any acceptable theory of apparent movement, except perhaps a theory which regards perception as a kind of response to the incoming sensory stimulation and then applies the principle of stimulus generalization (p. 577). If the stimuli received are sufficiently similar to those received from real movement, the perceptual response is likely to be the same. (For further references and discussions, see Koffka, 1931a, b, 1935; Neff, 1936; Graham, 1951.)

Afterimages of seen movement. Besides the apparent movement we have been considering, there are several illusory effects that could be so designated. The swimming of the environment during dizziness is one example, and another is the apparent motion of a solitary bright spot in a dark room; both of these will be considered later in the chapter. Another example is the fascinating "waterfall illusion": after looking at a near-by waterfall for a time, look at the bank and you will see the trees swim upward. Like other visual illusions, this one has a long history

FIG. 17·14. (Sanford, 1898, p. 117.) **A spiral to be rotated for the reverse aftereffect.**

(Boring, 1942). A likely explanation was that the downward pursuit movements established in response to the water persisted when the eyes were turned to the bank. But a similar aftereffect is obtained if you watch a spiral rotating on a color wheel. If the spiral appears to shrink or recede during rotation, it will appear to expand or approach when the rotation is suddenly stopped. Now what sort of eye movements would make an object seem to expand in all directions at once? As a matter of fact, the eye-movement explanation is inadequate even in the case of the waterfall illusion, for you can obtain the same effect after fixating a rock at one side of the fall, with no pursuit movements established. There have been a number of experiments on this illusion (Wohlgemuth, 1911; Hunter, 1914, 1915; Gates, 1934) but no convincing explanations have emerged. Perhaps the visual cortex or part of it becomes adjusted to the continued movement and does not recover instantly from this adjustment when the external movement ceases. For other visual aftereffects see the chapter on Form, page 423.

Apparent visual kinetics. Our question is whether, when we see something move, we seem to see what makes it move. If the apparent motion of an object is due to our own motion in walking or in leaning to one side, we learn to discount the apparent motion and see the object as stationary. When we see the "water falling" or the "smoke rising," our use of these words suggests that they seem to be moving of themselves. We certainly see nothing else making them move. But when we see body A move up against a stationary body B, and B immediately move away in the same direction, it looks as if A set B in motion, as if A imparted motion to B. Even when this action of one body on another is not physically real, the impression is the same: A seems to strike B and give it a push. These statements are based on the extensive experiments of Michotte (1946). As objects he used simply small squares seen through a horizontal slot in a screen (Fig. 17·15). At the beginning of the exposure A and B are a short distance apart and both stationary; then A moves rapidly toward B but stops when it reaches B, and B immediately moves away in the same direction. The observer has a very clear impression of "causation." A acting on

B and propelling it forward. If A moves along with B, instead of stopping when it reaches B, the impression is that A carries B along.

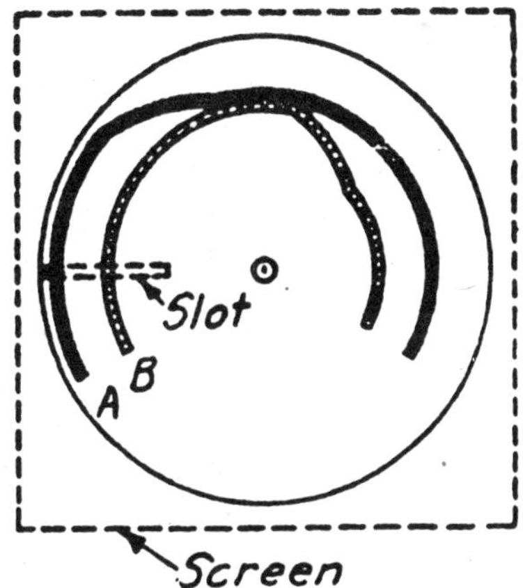

FIG. 17-15. (Michotte, 1946.) Disk for giving kinetic impressions. Through the slot square portions of the stripes A and B are seen, while the disk rotates in the counterclockwise direction behind the screen. As long as stripe A remains at the same distance from the center, the square seen through the slot remains still; but when stripe A approaches the center, the visible part of it approaches B. When A has reached B, A becomes stationary and B begins to move. Stripe B may be drawn on a separate (smaller) disk and its position adjusted so as to vary the time before B starts to move. The stripes are ⅕ in wide, the same as the slot which is 6 in long; O is 5 ft away. A and B are 1.6 in apart at the start, and the speed of the apparent movement is 12 in per second. (In metric units, the stripes and slot are 5 mm wide, the slot is 150 mm long, O's viewing distance is 1.5 m, A and B are 40 mm apart at the outset, and the speed of motion is 300 mm per second.) These measurements were varied. Michotte used also an elaborate two-lantern projection apparatus in some of his numerous variations of the experiment.

Michotte varied the experiment systematically so as to bring out the necessary conditions for the cause-effect impression. The essential S-factors are:

1. There must be two objects. When a single object moves across the field, there is no distinction of cause and effect.

2. The movement of one object must dominate the event, as it does when A moves first.

3. The impact of A on B must be seen in foveal vision; otherwise the two objects are not clearly separate, and the impression is merely that a single object is moving. Fixation on B is best.

4. For the clearest impression of cause and effect, there must be adequate unity or continuity in space, time and direction of motion. Slight discontinuities can be tolerated. A pause of 100 ms or less between A's reaching B and B's starting to move does not wholly destroy the impression of a single action of A upon B. A small space discontinuity, A not quite reaching B, can be tolerated. And the direction of B's movement may deviate somewhat from that of A. When the tolerances are exceeded, the impression received is that of two separate events instead of a single causal process. Michotte rejects any theory that would reduce these visual impressions of causality to a transfer from the motor-kinesthetic sphere. His evidence indicates that the impressions are inherent in the process of seeing a short sequence as a unity of successive stages.

COMPENSATORY EYE MOVEMENTS

When the environment moves, we keep its retinal image fairly stationary through pursuit movements. In the interest of clear vision it is equally important to maintain stable retinal images when the head or body moves in a stationary environment. The movements that do this job are called *compensatory*; they are further subdivided into active and passive compensatory movements, depending on whether they are associated with active movement of the body, or with passive translation (as by a train or rotated chair). Let us consider the active compensatory movements first.

Head-eye coordination. There are really two very different coordinations of the head and the eyes. When fixation is shifting from one object to another, as in *looking to the side,* head and eyes turn in the same direction, and the angular distance between the old and the new fixation point may be covered partly by the head movement and partly by the eyes. When the angular distance is small, as in reading, the head may remain motionless, at least in adults, and leave the eyes to cover the whole distance; but when an object is far around to the side, most of the angle is covered by the head.

Maintaining fixation on a stationary object during active head movements is quite a different coordination. The eyes move counter to the head and maintain the original fixation in spite of the head movement. Thus it is possible and even perfectly easy to continue looking at the same object while moving the head. This is the easiest eye movement to observe: watch your own eyes in a mirror while turning the head from side to side. You would almost suppose the eyes to be merely standing still by inertia, but this cannot be the case. The eyes are not loose in their sockets, not as loose probably as the tongue is in the open mouth; and the tongue does not behave in this compensatory fashion when the head is turned from side to side. (The pursuit movement also can be observed in the mirror: hold the head still and turn the mirror. You thus change the direction in which the eyes must look in order to keep themselves in view; the eyes follow themselves readily if the motion of the mirror is not too fast. The saccadic movement cannot be observed in the mirror, because you cannot keep your eyes directed toward your eyes while shifting them from one object to another.)

This compensatory movement is so much like the pursuit movement that one is tempted to regard them as identical. They look alike in the mirror and they accomplish the same result of maintaining fixation when it would otherwise be lost because of the motion of the object along the retina. Why are they not the same? There is one remarkable difference. The pursuit movement has a long latency, about 200 ms. It takes that time to get the eyes into motion toward a moving object. But if you turn your head while fixating an object of interest, you do not lose your fixation for an instant, since *the compensatory eye movement starts simultaneously with the active head movement.* Moreover the backward eye movement continue to compensate for the progress of the head movement; it maintains steady fixation on the object without any little saccadic movements such as occur during most pursuit movements. In short, the head movement and the compensatory eye movement are coordinated or integrated in a single reaction unit.

These strong claims for the compensatory movement can be checked by observing whether fixation is well maintained during active head movements. Any momentary loss of accurate fixation would be betrayed by a blurring of the object. Read while moving the head—not too violently—and check the statement that no blurring occurs. But the real evidence on this matter comes from photographic records.

Shift of fixation, head movement, and compensatory eye movement often combine into a single pattern. If one looks suddenly to the right, as in localizing a click, the eyes lead in a quick saccadic movement. The heavier and slower head follows, and eventually the trunk may turn, too. The eyes get to the object first and fixate it (with a compensatory backward movement), while the heavier parts continue their turn. Thus the complete act of orientation normally ends with eyes and head central with respect to the body axis; *O* faces the object squarely. Under special conditions we may inhibit the trunk or even the head components, but the whole pattern can still be detected in slight shifts of postural tonus.

Compensation for passive motion. We have already seen that a person looking out from the window of a moving train makes a series of slow sweeps and rapid saccadic refixations. This is the typical pursuit pattern or optic nystagmus. In the same way, if the person sits on a desk chair and is rotated slowly, he will make a similar series of movements as he fixates and follows successive objects in the environment. But now comes a surprising fact: under certain conditions the same pattern of movements occurs when the eyes are closed. Obviously we are not justified in considering them pursuit movements, when they are not under visual control and have nothing to pursue. There must be another mechanism that controls the movements during rotation with closed eyes. Further, it would be reasonable to assume that this mechanism is active also during rotation with eyes open. What is this mechanism?

The nonauditory labyrinth. It will be remembered (p. 326) that the inner ear has a number of passages or tubes above the cochlea. These passages constitute the *nonauditory labyrinth*, or the *vestibular apparatus*. They are filled with endolymph, just as the cochlea is, and are connected to a separate division of the eighth (auditory) nerve. They further resemble the cochlea in that they contain hair cells. Two portions of the vestibular apparatus, the *utricle* and the *saccule*, have gelatinous masses, weighted with *otoliths* (literally, ear stones), attached to the ends of the hair cells. These are nicely adapted to respond to linear acceleration. If the head moves right, left, forward, backward, up or down, the weighted masses will lag behind, bending the hair cells and signaling the change. Note that they respond to acceleration, and not to a steady state of motion. The principle can be illustrated by a familiar example. Suppose you are sitting in a train. When the train starts to move, your own inertia will push you back against the seat, and you will stay that way as long as the speed is increasing; i.e., while the train is undergoing *positive acceleration*. The backward pressure stops as soon as the train attains a steady speed (*zero acceleration*). But when the train slackens its speed (*negative acceleration*) you tend to keep on moving forward. The masses in the utricle and saccule act in very much this same fashion.

From the example, it is easy to see why *gravity* acts like an acceleration downward; it pulls you down in your seat, just as forward positive acceleration pushed you back. But it differs from the acceleration of moving objects, for it is a steady force, always acting on us—and on the utricle and saccule. This is one of the mechanisms which tell us which way is up. What is more important, the mechanism is tied in with the postural system so that we can constantly balance ourselves against the steady pull of gravity. We shall say more of this in a few pages.

The semicircular canals. In addition to the utricle and saccule, there are three tiny ring-shaped tubes in each ear. One of these, the *horizontal* (or lateral) canal, lies in the plane which would pass through the eye and the outer ear opening. The other two semicircular canals, the *superior* and the *posterior*, occupy planes that are at right angles to each other and to the horizontal canal. So the three canals (six, in two ears) can combine to signal any type of rotary acceleration.

Although the canals are small and inaccessible, a long series of careful studies has given us a pretty good idea of how they work (see Wendt, 1951). In each canal there is an *ampulla*, a swelling corresponding to the signet on a signet ring. This contains a group of hair cells whose ends are imbedded in a gelatinous mass, the *cupula*, which pretty well plugs the interior of the canal. If the head is suddenly turned (rotated on its vertical axis) to one side the fluid in the horizontal canals tends to lag, exerting pressure on the cupulae, thus stimulating the attached hair cells and associated nerve fibers. Note that the fluid would soon "catch up" and no longer exert pressure if the head kept rotating at a uniform speed; the stimulation cannot long outlast the positive acceleration. Of course, in ordinary head movements the positive acceleration is promptly followed by a negative one, for the head stops when it has turned the desired distance. This sets up a pressure in the reverse direction.

Now we come to eye movements; the pattern of pressures in the horizontal canals initiates lateral eye movements that are geared to the amount of rotation the head has undergone. We shall examine the details of this response in a moment, but first we must point out that the other two canals combine to take care of the other two possible types of rotation, head-over-heels and pinwheel (i.e., around the side-to-side and front-back axes). We might also add that this description is a bit oversimplified. For one thing, there seems to be a constant background of neural discharge from unstimulated canals so that acceleration acts only to increase or decrease the rate of discharge. A resting discharge is fairly common in sense organs (p. 271) and must be taken into account when we seek a complete physiological description of the processes. But we have already said enough to show how the vestibular senses can signal both active and passive changes in head position and elicit compensatory eye movements.

Compensatory eye movements in head rotation. Most of the interest in compensatory eye movements has been in those which result from rotation. Careful observation will show much that happens, but we need photographic recording to check some of the details of the eye movements.

Place *O* in a chair that can be rotated. Use a sturdy one with arms; an old barber chair is ideal for demonstrations, but you will want a motor-driven one for research. Rotate *O slowly* to the right, about one revolution every 2 seconds for 10 turns, and then stop him. If his eyes are open throughout, a practiced *E* can see how they move, and *O* can report on what he experiences. Bárány (1907) described this widely used method.

1. *Positive acceleration (picking up speed)*

to the right. O's eyes move slowly to the left, keeping an object fixated until it gets uncomfortably far. He then executes a saccadic movement to the right, fixating a new object, pursues it, etc. Insofar as these pursuitlike movements compensate adequately for his rotation, he reports that *he* is rotating in a stationary world. He may also turn the head and upper trunk in the same direction as the slow phase, that is, opposed to the direction of rotation. The head and trunk movements are more pronounced in some animals, notably in birds.

2. *Zero acceleration* (*uniform speed*). Suppose *O*'s chair has picked up full speed in about three turns so he is no longer being accelerated. His canals may well react, through after-discharge, for some time (see p. 18). But after five turns he is approaching a steady state, which will persist until he starts to slow down. The eyes may or may not execute adequate movements, depending on whether the visual world or the semicircular canals dominate his behavior; just what happens here depends on the nature of the stimulus field, and perhaps on individual differences. Both the world and *O* himself may seem to be spinning.

3. *Negative acceleration* (*stopping*). The fluid tends to continue its rotary motion, so pressing the cupulae in the reverse direction; that is, they work just as if *O* were undergoing positive acceleration to the left. Hence, his eyes make slow sweeps to the right, and quick saccadic shifts to the left, just the reverse of those during the start of the rotation. But since *O* is now stationary, the slow movements sweep over the environment, creating an illusion that the world is turning toward the left. Remember that *O* does not see much during the saccadic jumps so that the illusory movement is continuous. He also makes postural adjustments, twisting toward the right, along with the slow phase of the eye movement which is part of the same total adjustment.

Rotation in other planes. Suppose we had rotated *O* head-over-heels, or like a pinwheel, thus stimulating other canals. It is easier to rotate him horizontally but with changed head angle, which amounts to the same thing. Let *O* hold his head on his right shoulder, being careful to "keep his ear down, and nose up," so that a line passed through the ears would be vertical. Now if we rotate him to the right, we stimulate his vertical canals as if he were doing a continuous back somersault. The eye movements are up and down with respect to his head; during positive acceleration, slow phase opposed to rotation, or chinward, and the opposite when rotation is stopped. But remember that his head is sideways; these eye movements are the same with respect to the *environment* as they were in normal horizontal rotation; so his reports are also the same. His postrotation experience and behavior resemble those following normal rotation, too, as long as he keeps his head on his shoulder. But let him lift his head after rotation stops. The postrotation nystagmus persists, with slow phases toward his forehead. As they sweep vertically over the environment, the world seems to fall away in front of him. His postural adjustment is a violent arching backward; in fact, he is apt to get a dangerous fall if there is nothing to restrain him, for he leads with his head rather than with a softer portion of his anatomy.

Of course, we can get the same end results by having *O* hold his head on his left shoulder during rotation to the left. Similarly, it may be seen that reversing only one of the elements, as head on *left* shoulder during right rotation, will reverse the patterns of eye movements and postural adjustments so that *O* will fall forward as soon as he lifts his head after rotation has stopped.

A third type of nystagmus, rotation or spinning movements of the eyeballs, can be produced by holding the head forward or back during rotation. The rotary nystagmus can be observed best in brown-eyed persons, who often have pronounced radial lines in the iris; if *E* holds *O*'s head and looks at the eye after the chair has stopped, the spinning movements are quite clear. When the head is erect, this type of nystagmus makes the world seem to slope off on one side, with *O* throwing himself to the other side.

Once you get the basic principle, you can predict quite well what will happen after any combination of head position and direction of rotation. Errors in prediction usually result from *O's* failure to keep his head in the correct position during rotation; for example, if he points his nose down in addition to holding his head on the right shoulder, two types of nystagmus will be set up, and he will fall diagonally backward. So, if you try this experiment as a parlor game, have a few strong people handy to catch *O* if he dives in an unexpected direction! Do not overdo the amount or speed of rotation, and watch for signs of nausea. Incidentally, the nystagmus (and the distress) can often be stopped promptly by having *O* fixate an object at the end of the slow sweeps. For example, after rotation to the right, *E* can offer his finger as a fixation point, held in the extreme right edge of *O*'s visual field. The fact that saccadic movements are easier to inhibit than are the slow sweeps is often taken to indicate that the saccadic movements are controlled by a higher part of the nervous system. Consistent with this belief is the fact that the fast but not the slow phases can be conditioned (Wendt, 1936b).

Rotation with eyes closed. To what extent are these eye movements the result of vestibular stimulation rather than simple visual pursuit? To check on this question, we may resort to *caloric stimulation*. By irrigating the ear with hot water it is possible to warm one end of the canals, perhaps setting up convection currents (Dohlman, 1925). This procedure gives typical nystagmus, depending to some extent on the head position. Dohlman obtained similar results by alternating air pressures, or by electrical currents.

Dodge developed the most adequate method of settling this question; he recorded horizontal eye movements during rotation with the eyes closed. A small mirror was mounted on a chip of wood which was hinged to a headband. The other end of the chip rested lightly on the closed lid and was moved slightly as the bulging cornea passed under it. The movement of the mirror deflected a beam of light which fell on the slit of a recording camera. The light source and camera were attached to the chair. The method and results were described by Dodge (1921) and by Wendt (1936b, 1938). (See Wendt [1951] for additional references.)

The compensatory eye movements, with eyes closed, are surprisingly adequate. They start with a latency of 50 to 80 ms (Dodge, 1921), to be contrasted with one of 200 ms for visually induced pursuit. With eyes closed, the vestibular-induced eye movements give about 60 percent of complete compensation for the rotation, to be compared with 80 percent obtained when one eye is open, adding visual stimulation. But if the visual world conflicts with vestibular cues, there is mutual inhibition; thus, if *O* sees an environment attached to his chair, rotating with him, compensatory movements are cut to 5 percent, and when the environment rotates in the same direction, but twice as fast as *O*, there is an intermittent shift back and forth between optic and visual nystagmus (Dodge, 1923). So we have clear evidence of two systems of control for rotary nystagmus; visual and vestibular stimulation normally yield consistent patterns of eye movements, keeping the eyes in good relation to the environment during rotation, but the two systems may be thrown into conflict under laboratory conditions.

Short rotations, or even those of 10 turns, such as we described earlier, give a rather complicated picture because the negative acceleration starts before the response to the initial positive acceleration is over (Wendt, 1951). To isolate the effects of a single positive acceleration, we must keep *O* rotating at a uniform rate for some time, with the eyes held closed. The record shows first the ordinary nystagmus geared to the positive acceleration, but outlasting it by half a minute. As this nystagmus dies down, it gives way to a secondary nystagmus in a reverse direction, with the slow phases in the direction of rotation. This inverse nystagmus is weak in several ways; it will be overcome by normal visually induced nystagmus if the eyes are open, and it drops out readily with habituation. As a matter of fact, the normal postrotation nystagmus may also be weakened by habituation, especially if the eyes are open (Dodge, 1923; Mowrer, 1934). There was considerable conflict between psychologists and otologists on this question during World War I, when postrotatory nystagmus was used as a test for the adequacy of the vestibular mechanism in aviators (Dunlap, 1919). Wendt (1951) adduces evidence from experiments with both monkeys and man to show that such habituation represents the results of conflicts between two systems of eye movements, vestibular nystagmus *versus* either visual fixation or wandering due to inattention and relaxation. Habituation makes sense from a functional viewpoint; eye movements are an integral part of the organism's adjustment to a spatial world. So we approach our final topic of the chapter, orientation in space.

ORIENTATION IN SPACE

Gibson (1950a) emphasizes the fact that we perceive a stable visual world, despite the constant changes in our visual field as we move ourselves and our eyes around in space. We have one hint as to how we perform this feat from our study of the compensatory eye movements; for they prevent visible motion in the visual field except when some object is actually moving. There is another factor that we have merely touched on—the continuing effects of gravity. It will be recalled (p. 519) that gravity constantly pulls down the otoliths in the utricle, and it may also have some similar effect on the saccule and semicircular canals. At any rate, this constant tug is an indicator of "which way is up." There are other indicators, such as pressures on the soles of the feet when standing, pull on leg muscles, and especially the weight of the head on the neck muscles. As we might expect, the visual field is also a potent indicator, but we shall say more about that later. The point to be brought out here is that all these indicators feed "information" into the central nervous system, which integrates the information and constantly adjusts the tonus of our various muscles; the result is called *postural tonus*. Without it, we should constantly lose our balance—if we could even get far enough removed from a heap on the ground to have any balance to lose! In terms of the number and fineness of the adjustments involved, the process is fantastically complex, but it works so well that we never notice it until it fails, as when someone opens a door just as we adjust our postural tonus to exert a push against it. Postural tonus is at the same time an adjustment to the spatial world and a background against which we perceive the spatial world. It furnishes a framework for the perception of a stable world. (Much pioneer study of postural tonus is due to Magnus, 1924. There are excellent reviews by Camis, 1930, and by Dusser de Barenne, 1934.)

One way to see the importance of various factors is to observe certain types of deaf people. A defective cochlea is often associated with a defective vestibular apparatus, since both are essentially parts of the same structure. Individuals so afflicted get around fairly normally, for they can orient themselves on visual cues. Even in the dark they may have little trouble, for they still have differential pressures and tugs on the soles of the feet and the various muscles of the body. But place them in the water (with eyes closed) and they are helpless, for the uniform sustaining force of the water gives no adequate differential pressures. It is said that such individuals should avoid swimming, for once the head is under water, shutting off vision, they are as apt to swim down as to the surface. For normal people, floating with eyes closed is an interesting experiment, since it furnishes the only practical way to eliminate all the cues to orientation except those from the vestibule and canals.

The autokinetic phenomenon. Much that we have seen in this chapter shows that the visual field is a very important determiner of orientation. One demonstration of the importance of a visual framework has long been known as the *autokinetic* (self-moving) phenomenon. Put *O* in a perfectly dark room, and then turn on a pinpoint of light. The light may be furnished by a small bulb in a light-tight box, with a small nail hole in one side. In a short time *O* will report that the point of light is moving or drifting. In the complete absence of a visual frame of reference, postural cues are not enough to maintain precise orientation with respect to a single visual stimulus. This phenomenon interested Sherif (1935, 1948), who saw it as an example of the importance of frames of reference in all types of perception, social perceptions included. He showed that suggestion could influence the extent and direction of the illusory movement, and that there were marked individual differences in the responses to such suggestions. This research has become the stock example for illustrating the influence of frames of reference or norms on social perceptions, a topic that bulks large in current social psychology.

If *E* desires to get beyond the sheer descriptive level and *measure* the autokinetic movement, it is a little difficult for obvious technical reasons. One approach is to let *O* try to touch the point of light, as in one of a series of related experiments performed by Sandström (1951). He mounted a piece of circular coordinate paper (actually a perimeter blank) on a wall in a darkroom at about eye level. In this experiment, *O* was allowed to see the chart and to assume a position within comfortable reaching distance. Then the room lights were turned out, leaving only a pinpoint of light at the center of the paper. *O* was asked to stick a map pin into the hole. He usually missed miserably. For 66 *O*s there was a Mean error of 18.8 mm with the right hand, and of 19.7 mm with the left—¾ of an inch. Women were consistently poorer than men, and showed a tendency to hit higher.

Perhaps the failures resulted from inaccuracies of movement rather than of perception. To check this possibility, Sandström gave *O* a pencil to point with, and allowed him to try to find the point of light after a miss. One would expect a fairly direct correction movement to the hole. As a matter of fact, *O* often wandered all over the target sheet, sometimes carefully exploring one area and at other times making large circles around the hole without hitting it. Some *O*s were emotionally disturbed by their inability to find a point of light that they saw so clearly, and they completely lost their orientation, at least with respect to the point of light. Presumably they remained fairly well oriented to gravity, for they did not fall.

Perception of the vertical. A somewhat different reaction happens when the visual world is present but tipped in an unusual fashion. Wertheimer (1912) had *O* look through a tube at a mirror which reflected a room in a tilted position. At first the room appeared tilted, but *O* gradually adapted to the tilt and saw the room as upright—in spite of the fact that his own head was also upright and the retinal image was markedly tilted. Gibson & Mowrer (1938) repeated the experiment and failed to get the effect. The phenomenon in this form is somewhat dependent on subtle conditions of the experiment, such as the cues furnished in the field and the instructions, and perhaps on individual differences among *O*s. Asch & Witkin (1948a) were able to duplicate the Wertheimer results, but they found the mirror a rather limited method for isolating the variables. Hence, they tried some other methods.

The tilted room. Many people are familiar with the tilted room that is a feature of some amusement parks. It is the sort of arrangement you would get if a summer cottage were lifted into a diagonal position by a jack placed under one corner. If you go into such a room, you have a conflict, your visual world *versus* your vestibular and postural mechanisms that respond to gravity. You may stagger a bit, but gravity promptly wins out as far as posture is concerned; it must, or you would fall. However, your visual perception of the vertical is a compromise between that dictated by g (gravity) and that shown by v (visual field). The room looks tilted, but not as much as it actually is. Thus a motionless pendulum will seem to hang at a slant, and water may appear to flow uphill.

Asch & Witkin (1948b) built themselves such a room, so arranged that the amount of tilt of both the room and of *O*'s chair could be varied independently. To measure the perceived vertical, a rod at the rear of the room was adjusted until *O* judged it to be vertical in an absolute sense. There was a significant displacement of the rod toward the direction of the tilt of the room. If *O* were also tilted in his chair, he was much more apt to accept the room as vertical. Perhaps the most surprising thing was the great variability from *O* to *O*. Some clearly depended quite heavily on g factors, while others gave more weight to v. These differences were fairly stable from situation to situation, and seem to be fundamental characteristics of the individual.

In another experiment (Witkin, 1949) *O* was seated in a chair inside a room; both chair and room could be tilted gradually and independently. When the room was tilted, *O* often thought that the chair was tilting in the reverse direction. There was considerable evidence of adaptation to tilting, in that *O* failed to return either the chair or the room to the true vertical when he had a chance to adjust them himself, by turning two cranks. Some *O*s became quite disoriented, to the extent of making inconsistent statements. For example, when the tilt of the room was increased by successive steps of 5 degrees, *O* would report each change, but he would repeatedly insist that the room was still vertical. Others could not decide whether the wall in front of them was a wall or the floor, and even thought they themselves were upside down. As one might have anticipated, some *O*s became ill. This, by the way, indicates that nausea may result from a conflict between visual and postural cues to orientation. The conflict may not be the only cause of nausea (cf. Wendt, 1951), but it would seem to account for at least some cases of motion sickness. In still another experiment, Witkin (1950b) changed the g factor by rotating *O* on a sort of merry-go-round so that centrifugal force would combine with gravity, giving a resultant of forces which would correspond to a body tilt of as much as 33.4 degrees (cf. Gibson & Mowrer, 1938). If a true vertical field were available for visual inspection, there was very little illusion of tipping. But if *O* were in the dark, he set his "vertical" rod at an average value of 24.7 degrees from the vertical. Again there were marked individual differences. These individual differences in the dominance of v or g factors undoubtedly account for some of the discordant results obtained by earlier experimenters. Large groups of *O*s are necessary; Witkin and his associates usually employed about 50 in a single experiment.

Complexity of the visual field is a very important determiner of the dominance of v factors. Least compelling is the pinpoint in the dark, as used in autokinetic movement. Next is a luminous rod (Witkin & Asch, 1948a). A luminous square frame is a little better (Witkin & Asch, 1948b), but is still far inferior to a tilted room seen in full illumination. A field seen in a mirror with vision restricted by a tube is somewhere between these last two situations. The whole picture of orientation is thus complex in detail, but it makes sense.

Posture *versus* perception. However, there is one thing that does not seem to make much sense. In all these experiments we find that *O* may report that *he* is tipped and that the (tipped) *field* is erect, while at the same time he is actually standing erect. As we have seen, the act of standing is an extremely complex process, involving nice adjustment of all the antigravity muscles to the g forces acting on a large number of receptors, both vestibular and kinesthetic. How can *O* be oriented to one vertical as far as posture is concerned, and to another "vertical" for the perception of the visual field? We encounter this type of question also in depth perception (p. 476). The answer would seem to lie in the unusual and complicating factors that are deliberately introduced into these laboratory situations. Normally the visual field, the vestibular apparatus, and all muscular cues are in agreement as to the true vertical. But when they are in conflict, various *O*s react differently. Some show very little effect of the displaced visual field; they base both posture and visual perception on g cues. In other *O*s the v factors are dominant so that they accept the normally vertical and horizontal lines of the visual field at their face value; they perceive the tilted field as vertical, and may even adjust posture to conform. This is especially apt to happen if a correct posture is not important for them, as when they are leaning against a board, or floating in water, or reclining. On the other hand, if they are standing, they are forced to take some account of the g factor, if only from the hard realities of mechanics; otherwise they would fall. It is in these cases that we find the peculiar split between posture and perception that we mentioned at the beginning of this paragraph.

The perception of space. We are now in a position to understand how *O* perceives the location of objects in space.

First there must be a reference point; logically, and in the individual's history this reference point is the body. But a reference point is meaningless unless it is tied into a system of coordinates; these coordinates are furnished by the vestibular and kinesthetic mechanisms. In terms of this system objects are localized with the aid of the spatial aspects of vision and touch; movement is an important element in both. But once a number of objects are localized, the system of coordinates is externalized into "objective" space. Then we complete the circle; the body is also localized in this objective space (Sandström, 1951), and we say it is *oriented* in space. The details of this process include most of the facts we have covered in the last few chapters.

18

LEARNING: INTRODUCTORY SURVEY

The remaining chapters of this book will be concerned with the broad field of Learning and related topics. Everyone knows a lot about learning at a common-sense level, and it is also true that many important scientific results can be reduced to common-sense terms. But the experimental psychologist cannot fruitfully do his work at this level. He has to be more technical. To obtain precise knowledge he sets up limited situations in which he can control the conditions. He breaks up the general field into a number of smaller fields, in some of which he has perhaps not gone far beyond the common-sense level, while in others he has isolated certain significant variables and developed techniques of control. His technical terms reach the greatest precision of meaning when they are given *operational* definitions, i.e., when they are identified by the experimental operations performed and related to the resulting changes in behavior.

In introducing the student to the experimental study of learning we shall follow the same line of advance. First we shall describe the whole field in common-sense terms, and gradually we shall break up the field and utilize technical terms. The present chapter outlines some of the basic problems and methods, selected from the whole field of learning. Later chapters will be devoted to specific subfields or to groups of interrelated experimental problems.

Learning is one of the most active and productive fields of psychological experimentation. The devotion of so many psychologists to this field is justified by the immense practical importance of learning—as in all varieties of education, including psychotherapy considered as a process of reeducation (Dollard & Miller, 1950; Mowrer, 1950). To the psychological theorist the facts of learning, in animals as well as men, present a challenge that cannot be ignored. There are multitudinous facts calling for systematization, and there is the underlying question of the basic mechanism (or mechanisms) of this remarkable and all-important function.

An additional reason for the long-continued vogue of laboratory work on learning is that there is such a wealth of feasible experimentation to be undertaken, such a variety of performances to be learned, such a range of controllable factors to be worked over quantitatively and reduced to orderly "functions"

—or, if you prefer another type of investigation, such a number of sensible hypotheses to be tested. Anyone who wishes to experiment can find something definite to do in this field.

Problem solving, by ideational thinking or otherwise, does not offer the same ready advantages. Definite experimental variables and cleanly testable hypotheses have been hard to find and the whole process seems to be exceedingly variable. Yet problem solving is closely related to learning—or learning to problem solving. Very often a learning process begins with the solution of a problem. The learner must find out what he has to do before he can start to put on speed or build up skill of any sort. The first trial in a maze, for example, is long and variable because it is devoted to exploring the situation and finally discovering the goal. So the learner's task is defined or brought home to him, and on the next trial he begins work on the task. The problem is not fully solved, to be sure, until all the blind alleys are eliminated from the performance, but even after that stage has been reached, much further learning is shown by the increase in speed and smoothness of the run

The learner's *task* consists of a situation and a goal, and we may distinguish two kinds of task, the *problem* and the *lesson*. With a problem to master the learner must explore the situation and find the goal before his task is fully presented. In the case of a lesson, the problem-solving phase is omitted or at least minimized, as we see when the human subject is instructed to memorize this poem or this list of nonsense syllables, to examine these pictures with a view to recognizing them later, or to throw this dart at that target. Can an animal be assigned a "lesson"? If we substitute a short straight runway for the maze, with the entrance at one end and a food box at the other, we minimize the problem-solving phase. Such an experiment is regarded as one in "instrumental conditioning" (p. 546); and in Pavlov's "classical conditioning" experiment the absence of problem solving is still more obvious. When trial-and-error behavior is to be expected, there is a problem; when learning can proceed without trial and error, the task is or has become a lesson. The distinction between a problem and a lesson cannot be regarded as perfectly sharp, since even in memorizing a poem or throwing at a target the learner runs into difficulties that can be surmounted by better technique. Still the distinction has some value in connection with the persistent question whether there are two radically different learning processes. Historically, lessons were first introduced in the human laboratory (Ebbinghaus, 1885), problems in the animal laboratory (Thorndike, 1898).

Granted now that problem solving belongs in this general branch of psychology, why should motivation come in here? Does it not deserve a whole section to itself? Yes, indeed—except that the experimental work on motivation has emerged largely from studies of learning. In order to secure learning the experimenter must provide some incentive, and in order to measure learning he has to hold motivational factors constant. He cannot observe learning directly. What he observes is a performance or series of performances. The performance changes progressively from trial to trial, and this change is the evidence of learning. But the performance will change also with changes in the drive or incentive or state of the organism. Only when these factors are held constant can the change of performance be accepted as a picture and measure of learning. When the performance has reached its apparent limit or "practice level," so that learned ability can be taken as constant, changes of motivational factors can be introduced and the resulting changes in performance utilized in the study of motivation (p. 667). Some of the motivational factors can be brought out most clearly in experiments on animal learning.

It is difficult to formulate a definition of learning that will be broad enough without being too broad. Learning includes much more than intentional memorization and practice. When we find ourselves humming a tune that we have heard, or recognizing a face that we have seen, or falling unintentionally into any habit either desirable or undesirable, we have been learning. Learning is no one specific kind of activity. It is a change that occurs in the organism during many kinds of activity. It shows later as an aftereffect of activity. A later activity is different because of the earlier activity. We are tempted to say that learning is demonstrated whenever a later activity shows some aftereffect of earlier activity. This definition would be so broad as to include the strengthening of a muscle by exercise—as perhaps would be justifiable—but also muscular fatigue which certainly does not belong under learning. We might say that learning produces relatively *permanent* aftereffects, but the "relatively" rather spoils the definition. Some things, like telephone numbers, are learned well enough for immediate use but are soon forgotten. These definitional difficulties, however, do not often disturb the experimenter.

GENERAL SCHEME OF AN EXPERIMENT IN LEARNING

In any experiment on learning, memory, or transfer of training there are three stages. First comes the activity that produces *Learning*, then an *Interval* of time, and finally what may be broadly designated as the stage of *Remembering*, which demonstrates the aftereffect of the learning. The interval between learning and remembering may be long if the experiment is concerned with retention and memory, but very short if it is concerned with learning.

But why need there be any interval at all when learning is being investigated? To answer this question let us ask another: How can learning be demonstrated? If anyone says he has learned a lesson, how can he prove his assertion? He must recite it or give some other evidence of remembering it. The test of learning is remembering. The interval may be kept short so as to minimize forgetting, but there is bound to be an interval between learning and any test or measurement of learning. The interval may have to be slightly prolonged in order to get rid of fatigue and other immediate inhibitory effects of work (Fig. 18-1).

Here the practice went on continuously except for a rest period after 8 minutes of work. But since each minute's work was scored as a unit, the progress of learning was tested, in effect, at one-minute intervals. Undoubtedly there was improvement *within* the first minute so that the level of the minute as a whole was reached somewhere in the middle of that minute. The step up from the first to the second minute,

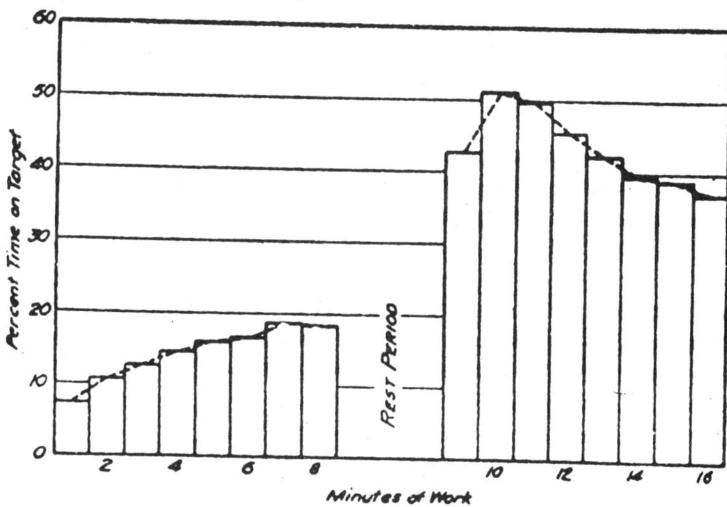

FIG. 18-1. (Data from Ammons, 1947, p. 398, with the three groups combined who worked 8 min before rest and re... 5, 10, or 20 min before resuming work.) Learning curve in rotary pursuit target practice. The apparatus was a Koerth-type pursuit rotor, the target being a smooth brass disk about the size of a 1-cent coin (¾-in diameter), set flush into a 11-in bakelite disk, about 2 in from the edge. The disk rotated horizontally at the rate of 1 revolution per second, so carrying the target rather rapidly in a circular course. The subject "pursued" the target with a flexible hand stylus which could be held in contact with the target but not pressed against it. Recording apparatus showed the time the stylus was on the target, minute by minute. A perfect minute's score would be 100 percent on target, and the practical ceiling after much practice might be up near this limit. But the average score of the 42 women student subjects here was approximately 7 percent in the first minute and increased to 18 percent in 8 min of continuous work without rest. After a rest of 5–20 min, as shown in the figure, the average score jumped to 43 percent and rose quickly to 51 percent but declined gradually during further continuous practice. The experiment was designed to bring out the effects of massed practice and the effects of rest periods.

accordingly, represents the gain from the middle of the first to the middle of the second minute. A line connecting the mid-points of successive minutes thus gives a fair approximation to the learning curve.

This is not a pure learning curve, however, since complicating factors are in evidence. The slight descent (or work decrement) just before the rest period and the continued descent during most of the later work period indicate the presence of what we may be tempted to call fatigue but had better call by the more inclusive term, "inhibitory factors" (pp. 4, 788). And what about the big jump immediately after the rest period? Learning had evidently progressed far enough before the rest to make this higher score possible, but inhibitory factors were largely concealing the true practice effect.

What we have in a learning curve is a series of performances or trials, each trial serving both as a test of what has already been learned and as an opportunity to learn more.

The experimental variables. Since the single datum is to be obtained in a performance, employed as a test of what has been learned and is now remembered, we may revert to our schematic formula, introduced in the first chapter and used in several later chapters:

$$R = f(S, O) \text{ or } R = f(S, A)$$

The R is the subject's performance in the test, the S is his present task, the *O* stands for factors that he brings to the test, and the A stands for antecedent operations by which the experimenter controls the *O*-factors. In a study of learning or memory, S is held constant, i.e., the task is the same in the test as it has been in the preceding learning trials. In a study of transfer the task is an experimental variable, being different in the test from what it has been in the learning trials. Let us assume for the present that S is held constant and that the experimenter has managed to hold constant also the motivational and inhibitory factors so that the test will show how much has been learned and remembered. The test will then show what we may call *learned ability*, which Hull has called "habit strength." Another operationally equivalent term is "memory trace." The question is on what controllable A factors the learned ability depends.

The performance that serves as a test is preceded, we have said, by one or more learning trials and by a time interval since the last learning trial. So the A-factors that affect the test performance are applied directly either to the learning process or to the elapsed interval. The interval can vary in duration and in filling. The length of time between learning and remembering is the variable to use in working out a "curve of forgetting." As to filling, an interval can scarcely be entirely empty of activity, but it may be a period of relaxation or be occupied with activity varying in kind and amount. In an experiment on the causes of forgetting the interval is partly occupied with activity likely to break up the performance that has been learned, for forgetting might be due to such interferences.

The learning variables are extremely numerous. The task itself may vary in kind, in length of lesson, in difficulty of problem. The number of learning trials, the massing or spacing of the trials, the age and organic and emotional state of the learner, the instructions and possible assistance and guidance given him, and still other factors may be systematically varied.

A very important experimental variable in studies of learning is the *immediate sequel* of the response. This sequel may be a reward or a punishment, a successful or an unsuccessful result. One choice in a maze leads into a blind alley, the other choice to the food box. One throw at a target proves to be a hit, another to be a miss. One word spoken in an attempt to recite a poem is correct, another is incorrect. Even the salivary conditioned response in Pavlov's experiment is followed by the reinforcement of food or by the nonreinforcement of no food, at the option of the experimenter who controls not only the situation eliciting the response but also the external result of the response. The positive or negative result obtained on one trial becomes an A-factor in the performance on later trials. This factor can be varied in many ways. A reward can be given on every correct trial or only part of the time; it can be a large or only a small reward; and a negative result can be real punishment or merely absence of reward. Experiments in this field evidently have a bearing on motivation as well as on learning.

The performance which serves as a test of learning or retention must be measured or appraised in some way. In our introductory chapter a list was offered of ways in which a performance can vary quantitatively. These R-variables are available for the measurement of learned ability. They include accuracy, speed and sometimes energy of performance, percent of errors or of correct responses, and resistance to extinction.

Considered as measures of the "learned ability" acquired in the learning process and retained through an interval until the test of remembering, no one of these R-variables is perfect and complete. In Figure 18-2, for example, two measures

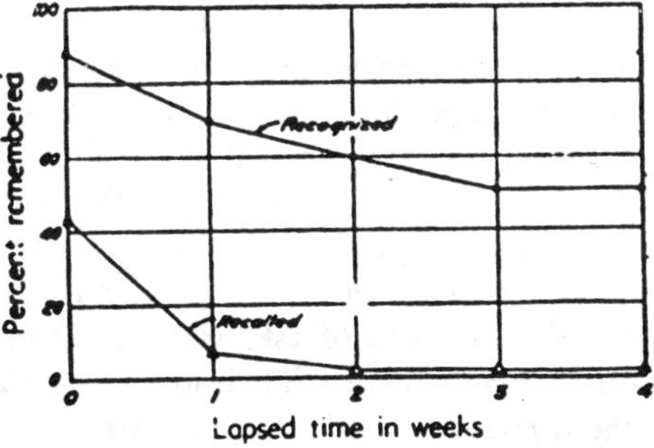

FIG. 18-2. (Data from Burtt & Dobell, 1925.) Retention tested by both recall and recognition. The material consisted of paired commodity and trade-brand names, 100 such pairs being shown to a class by projection lantern, and sets of 20 from the 100 being used for the tests after different intervals. In the recall tests, the commodity names were the stimuli and the brand names were to be given as far as remembered. Following each recall test came a recognition test in which *O* selected from four brand names the one which he believed had been paired with the commodity. The recognition score is much higher than the recall score. Both curves show the negative acceleration (progressive flattening) characteristic of curves of forgetting.

of retention were applied, and the percent of items recognized was much greater than the percent recalled. Similar discrepancies are to be expected whenever two measures of learned ability are compared. Consequently, the "operational" view of learned ability has been forced on the experimenters from the beginning of work in this field. What does learned ability (or habit strength) mean in terms of the operation employed in its measurement? It may mean accuracy of performance, or speed of performance, or resistance to extinction, according to the test employed. Possibly conversion formulas can be worked out for translating one measure into another, but until such a desirable system of close correlations has been achieved, comparable results will have to be obtained by the use of the same measure.

Higher-order R-variables. When we have a series of measured trials, as shown in a learning curve (Fig. 18-3), we have facts at our disposal which go beyond the separate measurements. We can compare the first and last scores and note the *amount of gain*. We can note the slope of the curve which shows the *rate of gain*. In most learning curves the slope is not constant—the curve is not a straight line—but there is a flattening as the learning progresses, i.e., there is *negative acceleration*. We may succeed in fitting an *empirical equation* to the curve and so obtain a compact statement of the course of learning. We may even succeed in fitting a *rational equation* to the data and use it as a test of some hypothesis regarding the learning process. Practice in reaction time yields data that fit a rational equation, as we saw once before (p. 35) and can see again in Figure 18-3. This type of curve and equation will be considered later (p. 665). For the present we shall take note only of the limit or *practice level* observed in many learning curves. The learning starts, not necessarily from an absolute zero, but from a relatively poor score with a certain *room for improvement* or distance to go to the final level.

An important higher-order R-variable is the *number of trials* taken to reach a *criterion*. A criterion is some definite score that must be attained; for example, one perfect recitation of a poem that is being memorized, or five successive errorless runs in a maze, or 80 percent of a minute on target in a pursuit task (p. 531). A task that has been mastered to a certain criterion will usually require further practice after an interval to bring it back to the same criterion, and the number of *relearning* trials will yield a measure of the amount of forgetting.

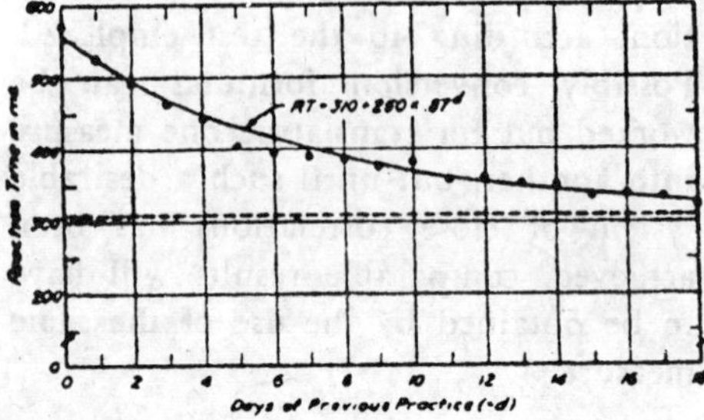

FIG. 18-3. (Data from Franklin & Brozek, 1947, p. 19, with two groups combined that practiced once a day or every second day.) Learning curve for disjunctive reaction time with large body movements. Average data from 12 young men, reacting to three lights. To a green light on their left, the response was to bend down and tap a key on their left; to a red light on the right, to bend down and tap a key on the right; and to a white light directly in front, to bend down and tap both keys. From the run of the data points it seems that the limit or "irreducible minimum" (p. 20) was approximately 310 ms. By the use of semilog paper as explained on page 22 we have fitted a "growth curve" to the data for RT−310, this being the "reducible margin." The fit is not perfect but not too bad. The equation reads that each day's practice reduces the reducible margin to 87 percent of what it was at the start of that day, this statement being correct for the curve and approximately correct for the data as a whole. Learning, according to the equation, is a process of approaching a limit, the gain from a certain amount of practice becoming smaller and smaller and always remaining proportional to the distance still to go—being, in other words, a constant fraction of the distance still to go. The fraction would be constant, that is to say, for the same individual practicing the same task under the same conditions; it might differ for different tasks and different individuals. The "irreducible minimum" here is the same thing as the "practice level," while the "reducible margin" is obviously the same as "room for improvement" or "distance still to go."

Evidently the criterion can be higher or lower. If the task is to learn the names of 12 persons whose photographs are shown, the criterion assigned by *E* may be any 6 correct names, or any 9, or all 12. The higher the criterion, the more trials are needed to reach it. From his record sheet, *E* might even count up the trials taken to reach successive criteria of 1, 2, 3, . . . 11, 12 correct. Instead of asking for the score on each successive trial, *E* might ask for the number of trials taken to reach each successive criterion—just as in a foot race we usually ask how long it takes to run a quarter mile, a half mile, or a mile, rather than how far the runner gets in 1 minute, 2 minutes, or 4 minutes.

Group learning curves. The individual learner's progress from his initial score to his practice level is likely to show irregular ups and downs which would be ironed out in a group average. There are some statistical difficulties here. The distribution of the individual scores on each trial may be quite skewed—a difficulty which can often be avoided by the device of log times or log number of errors (p. 62); or the Median can be computed instead of the Mean. These devices break down in many experiments where the final score is zero errors or 100 percent items correct

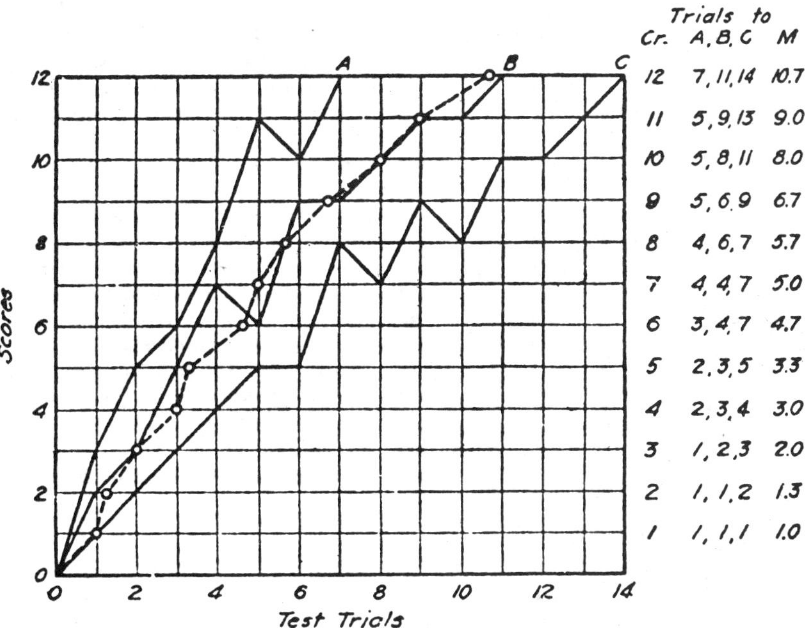

FIG. 18-4. Construction of a Melton average learning curve. The data are supposed to come from a 12-item lesson such as learning the names of 12 photographed persons. Ordinary learning curves for the three learners, A, B and C, are plotted. (The first presentation of the picture-name pairs counts as number zero test trial, so that the score in the first test trial is the score after one presentation.) The question then is, regarding each of the learners, on which test trial he reached or passed each successive criterion. Learner A reached or passed criteria 1, 2, and 3 on his first test trial, criteria 4 and 5 on the second trial, and so on. Reversals are not counted against the learner; A reached criterion 11 on the fifth trial and his loss of a point on the sixth trial is disregarded. The columns at the right show these results for each separate learner and the Mean for the three. For example, the 7-correct criterion was reached or passed after 4, 4, and 7 presentations; and the Mean of 5 is shown on the broken line which gives the average curve for the three learners.

because some individuals reach this criterion in fewer trials than others. The best device for meeting this difficulty was introduced by Melton (1936; Melton & von Lackum, 1941): instead of computing average scores for successive trials, compute average numbers of trials to reach successive criteria (Fig. 18-4). Even so, you will often have to cope with skew distributions.

An older method of averaging learning curves, often employed in studies of animal learning, was first suggested by Vincent (1912) and is called the Vincent curve even though modified in detail (Hilgard, 1938; Munn, 1950, pp. 226–230). The individual's speed of learning is disregarded or equated, the individual curves being all made of the same length along the base line, and the ordinates are then averaged at convenient intervals. In order to give equal weight to every individual, the procedure used in Figure 18-5 can be followed; it asks what percent of each individual's total gain is accomplished in each successive tenth (or sixth, or twentieth) of his learning trials. Such a curve has a limited value in the study of the *shape* of the learning curve, espe-

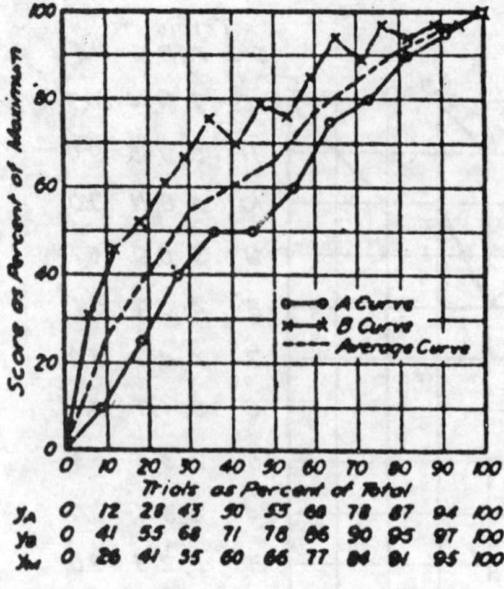

FIG. 18·5. One way of constructing a Vincent curve. The rationale of the process is as follows. Along the base line, the initial trial is numbered zero, and the number of subsequent trials to the attainment of the criterion is called 100 percent, whatever the actual number may be for any learner. Along the ordinate, the initial score is called zero and the final score 100 percent.

In the present example a maze is learned by two suppositious rats, A and B. Rat A starts with 20 errors to be eliminated, each error later eliminated being 5 percent of the total gain to criterion, and he reaches the criterion in 11 trials beyond the zero trial, each trial thus being approximately 9 percent of the total number. Rat B starts with 33 errors, each error eliminated being approximately 3 percent of the total gain, and he reaches the criterion in 17 trials, each trial being approximately 6 percent of the total number. The x and y for each point on the A and B curves are computed as follows:

Subject A					Subject B				
Trial	x	*Errors*	*% errors*	y*	*Trial*	x	*Errors*	*% errors*	y*
0	0	20	100	0	0	0	33	100	0
1	9	18	90	10	1	6	23	69	31
2	18	15	75	25	2	12	18	54	46
3	27	12	60	40	3	18	16	48	52
4	36	10	50	50	4	24	13	39	61
5	45	10	50	50	5	29	11	33	67
6	55	8	40	60	6	35	8	24	76
7	64	5	25	75	7	41	10	30	70
8	73	4	20	80	8	47	7	21	79
9	82	2	10	90	9	53	8	24	76
10	91	1	5	95	10	59	5	15	85
11	100	0	0	100	11	65	2	6	94
					12	71	4	12	88
					13	76	1	3	97
					14	82	2	6	94
					15	88	1	3	97
					16	94	1	3	97
					17	100	0	0	100

*y = 100 − % errors (Subject A)

*y = 100 − % errors (Subject B)

When the A and B curves have been drawn, the base line is divided into ten equal parts, perpendiculars are erected, the ordinates of A and B are measured on each perpendicular, and a point on the Vincent curve is obtained by averaging the A and B ordinates. The linear interpolation required can, of course, be done arithmetically instead of graphically.

cially near its beginning where the moot question is whether there is not a brief period of positive acceleration preceding the commonly observed negative acceleration.

The irregularities of an individual learning curve have to be disregarded or ironed out in some way. The reasonable assumption is that fluctuations occur both up and down from the true curve so that we shall be safe in steering a middle course between the data points.

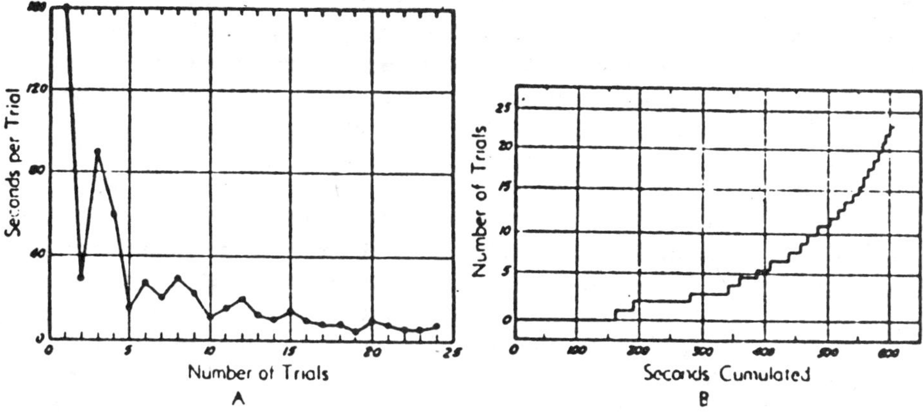

FIG. 18·6. (Data from Thorndike, 1898, p. 15.) Different learning curves from the same data. A cat was given 24 trials in a puzzle box, the time taken in each performance being recorded. When the abscissa shows the number of trials and the ordinate the time occupied by each performance, as in curve A, the general decrease of the time is clear, while the variation from trial to trial also obtrudes itself and complicates the picture. When the performance times are *cumulated* along the abscissa, with each completed performance shown by a short upward step of the curve, as in B, the intertrial variability is unobtrusive and what stands out is the rate of performance, shown by the slope of the curve which approaches a maximum. In spite of their differing appearance, the two curves show exactly the same facts, and every fact that is present in one is present also in the other. The negative acceleration which is characteristic of learning curves shows in A as a flattening of the curve, but in B by gradual approximation to an oblique straight line. If this learning curve had been followed by satiation or extinction, the cumulative curve would have flattened out into a horizontal line. In Skinner's well-known setup (p. 546) the cumulation is made and recorded automatically by the apparatus.

Safer, perhaps, is the device of the moving average. A *cumulative* curve will make the irregularities less conspicuous to the eye and so bring out the regularity that is concealed by the fluctuations (Fig. 18·6B, compared with 6A).

Is there a typical learning curve? There are dozens of different ways in which one may plot learning curves, and an almost infinite variety of shapes that the curves may take. But perhaps it would be helpful to have a generalized curve to bring out some of the features frequently encountered. This curve would have some measure of practice, the independent variable, on the base line: trials, hours of practice, etc. The ordinate would be marked off in some unit of proficiency, the dependent variable: words of typing per minute, hits on a target, or percentage of nonsense syllables correctly anticipated. This gives a rising curve as that in Figure 18·4. We frequently meet reversed curves, in which improvement is shown by a fall in level; this happens when we use number of errors per trial in a maze, or length of time to complete successive units of a task (Fig. 18·6A), but we shall adhere to the more natural rising type of curve in this discussion.

The one feature we are almost certain to find is a gradual leveling off toward the end of the curve. That is, further improvement seems to get harder and harder, as if *O* were approaching some sort of a limit. At one time it was thought that there was a fairly rigid "physiological limit" for a given *O* in a specific task. As we noted previously, there *is* often a mathematical limit that a specific learning curve seems to approach, and one can call it a physiological limit if he wishes. Perhaps a better term is *final practice level*, especially if we play down the word *final*. It is a final practice level or limit only so long as we keep method and motivation constant; every golfer lives in the hope that a new trick will knock a few points off his practice level, and sprinters usually run a lot faster during meets than they do in daily practice. There is no doubt that most learning curves show a period of negative acceleration or decreasing gains as they approach a limiting value; the point is that we should think of the limit as holding good for a specific curve, under specific conditions, rather than as a hard-and-fast, over-all ceiling.

Many curves have a level region long before the final level. These periods of no improvement (or even slight loss) are called *plateaus*. They are very apt to discourage the learner, for he may mistake them for final limits. Perhaps this practical aspect was largely responsible for the extensive attention they received from psychologists during the first three decades of the present century (see Hunter, 1934, and the first edition of this book). It gradually became clear that there was no single explanation for all plateaus, much depending on the specific conditions of each experiment. Often a plateau can be regarded as the practice limit for one way of performing a task; if *O* improves his method of attack, or if *E* increases the incentive, a new learning curve starts up from the old practice level. Or there may be a certain difficult element in the task which blocks progress till mastered. The reader can try out such explanations on the various examples of plateaus he will meet later.

The shape of the beginning portion of the learning curve is less predictable (cf. Hunter, 1934). It often rises at a rapid rate from the very first trial, gradually slowing down, as in Figure 18-1. But some curves show an initial period of positive acceleration, with very little gain for the first few trials. There is a hint of this on the first few trials of Rat A, Figure 18-5. A curve that shows an initial period of positive acceleration, followed by a period of steady gain, and then ends with negative acceleration as the limit is approached, is said to be *sigmoid*. Hull (1934b) points out that such sigmoid curves are frequently obtained in conditioning, where learning starts from true zero. Later (1943) he proposed a theoretical explanation for the sigmoid form. The obvious implication is that if this initial period of positive acceleration is missing in a particular learning experiment, it shows that we have started practice on a task that is already partially learned (Culler & Girden, 1951). For example, the average male student shows a very flat curve for dart throwing; not only does he lack any sign of initial positive acceleration, but also he often seems to start pretty close to his final level. The obvious explanation is that boys have acquired considerable skill in throwing objects long before they start lab. Just the opposite effect of prior experience—a slow start followed by positive acceleration—is likely to occur when the new task conflicts with established habits (Lewis & Shephard, 1951).

The influence of the basic unit. Unfortunately these analyses are based on the assumption that we always have equal-unit scales with which to measure progress in learning. The choice of a satisfactory scale is one of the toughest problems in psychology, as we point out here and there throughout this book. One can get very different curves from the same set of data, depending on what units are used on the ordinate. For example, an acquisition curve for typing can be plotted as *words typed per minute*, which might well yield a sigmoid curve, or as *time needed to type 100 words*, which would yield an inverted curve with a very sharp initial slope. Or consider rifle shooting. If the target is very small, the beginner will probably miss it completely for the first 20 trials, thus staying at zero score, and insuring a period of positive acceleration as he gradually "finds" the target. On the other hand, a very large target might be so easy to hit that *O* would start in with a good score, and rapidly approach the maximum of 100 percent hits.

There are ways of developing scales that have some claim to equality of unit throughout their length, but this is not the place to evaluate them (cf. Hull, Felsinger, Gladstone & Yamaguchi, 1947). In the absence of such scales, any attempt to develop a generalized function to fit *all* learning curves is premature (cf. Woodrow, 1940; Hull, 1943; Hilgard, 1951). But as a purely practical matter, *E* usually adopts some convenient scale that will give usable scores throughout learning; *O* will start well above zero score, but never get beyond the upper end of the scale. To the extent that the resulting curves usually show a period of decreasing gains as *O* approaches his limit, we may say that there *is* a typical learning curve. But the exact form of any particular curve can be understood only in terms of the variables involved in that particular learning situation. In analyzing these variables, the learning curve is an invaluable tool.

PURPOSE AND DESIGN OF LEARNING EXPERIMENTS

We might better say "purposes" and "designing" since the experimenter's interest and hope are not always the same, and he will design his experiment to suit his purpose. We have been emphasizing the type of experiment designed so as to vary some experimental variable quantitatively in the hope of obtaining a graded effect on some response variable. Many important problems cannot be attacked in quite this manner because the experimental variable is an either-or affair and not an affair of more or less. We may wish to discover whether printed material is better remembered than the same material presented to the ear rather than to the eye. We can obtain an answer, to be sure, and we can find how much better one language medium is than the other in this respect. We can quantify our R-variable, but we cannot find any intermediate steps between the ear and the eye. There are many problems that are necessarily of this sort, and there are still others that are best attacked first by the relatively simple either-or type of experiment and only later by the more elaborate quantitative procedure.

The purely exploratory type of experiment should not be despised. Especially in human beings, the variety of tasks that are learned and the variety of abilities, adjustments, and maladjustments that are acquired is so vast that exploration is as much in order as in zoology or geology. Learning is a by-product of other activities rather than a specific activity on its own account. Even though the basic result for learning may always be the same—something like the establishment of an association or of an S—R connection—the matrix of activity and conditions in which this result is produced varies enormously and some conditions are more favorable than others for producing the result. Since the experimentalist treasures the hope that his investigations will be utilized in such applied fields as education and psychotherapy, it behooves him to do some exploring in those directions, and probably in many others.

There are perhaps three types of experiment on learning: the exploratory type, the first-mentioned type symbolized by our familiar $R = f(S, A)$, and the hypothesis-testing type. Some psychologists would place this last one at the top of the scale of merit, and it certainly can be the most exciting. It introduces the sporting spirit into the laboratory, since your hypothesis may either be supported or rejected by the results of your experiment—or, unfortunately, the matter may remain in the realm of doubt, as often happens. You may find that the number of subjects has been too small and that the "null hypothesis" cannot be rejected. You are then tempted to take a stronger negative attitude toward the hypothesis than your data justify. In fact, many experiments ought to be repeated before being published.

Control groups, counterbalanced order of conditions, and factorial design find much use in experiments on learning. They all present statistical problems which deserve careful attention in advance of the collection of data. Some such experimental methods will be found in the later chapters.

Of the following chapters, the first four are based largely, but not entirely, on animal experiments. Human results are cited under Conditioning, Discrimination Learning, Maze Learning, and Motivation. This latter topic will be found closely related to the three preceding. Human learning comes to the fore in the next block of chapters, on Memory, on Transfer and Interference, and on Economy in Learning and Performance. The final chapter, on Problem Solving, considers both animal and human evidence in this important though not well-developed field of psychology.

While a good deal will be said of the prominent theories of learning and retention, and of several less comprehensive theories, this book does not attempt to settle the controversial issues, nor even to present a systematic survey of the theories like that of Hilgard (1948). As the list of chapters shows, the treatment is focused primarily on typical achievements of men and animals so far as these depend on learning, problem solving, and motivation.

19

CONDITIONING

The experimental psychologist is greatly indebted to those few pioneers who found ways of attacking the problems of learning by definite methods—ways of controlling the conditions under which some performance was learned and ways of recording and measuring the changes that occurred in the performance. One of these pioneers was Ebbinghaus (1885) with his methods for the study of memorizing and retention. Another was the Russian physiologist, Pavlov. Other physiologists, to be sure, have contributed greatly to the methodology of psychological problems, such as reaction time and the sensory processes, but scarcely any besides Pavlov have concerned themselves seriously with the problem of learning Most physiologists have been willing to leave that problem to psychology with a somewhat dubious hope that psychology will eventually handle it by scientific methods.

PAVLOV'S CONDITIONAL REFLEX

At the turn of the present century this already eminent Russian physiologist was pursuing his studies of the glandular secretions involved in the digestive processes. In general, he found these secretions law-abiding, in the sense that they followed definite stimuli in a predictable fashion. They were, in short, reflex secretions. But sometimes they varied and seemed capricious. The physiologists were inclined to dismiss such "psychic" secretions as presumably caused by the animal's "thoughts" and "emotions," and so not subject to physiological laws though they might be to psychological laws. Pavlov had little respect for such psychology as he knew about in that early day. He believed that every part of the digestive process must be subject to natural law and accessible by the rigorous objective methods of physiology. After some hesitation he made the momentous decision to devote himself and his laboratory to the investigation of these variable secretory phenomena.

Pavlov and his associates very soon had a measure of success in this novel task. They assured themselves that the "psychic" secretions were elicited by stimuli, just as were the ordinary reflex secretions. But the relationship between stimuli and secretions varied from dog to dog and from time to time in the same dog. For example, the sight of a certain food pan or other piece of apparatus would elicit a strong flow of saliva from one dog, but little or none from another. Pavlov saw that these variations must be due to the past history of each animal and that the stimulus-response connections must have been built up in the dogs' brains. His hope was that experimental study of these acquired reactions would throw light on the nature of brain processes and demonstrate that the cerebral hemispheres no less than the digestive organs belonged squarely in the province of physiology. He held that a stimulus-response connection mediated by the hemispheres was entitled to be called a reflex just as truly as one mediated by subcortical centers, provided only it were shown to be law-abiding.

In 1904 Pavlov first used the Russian term which could best be translated as *conditional reflexes* for these S—R connections that were acquired during the lifetime of the individual animal. They were to be contrasted with the *unconditional reflexes* that were inborn and common to the species. In English, however, as in the translation of his own book (1927), these Russian terms have been rendered as *conditioned* and *unconditioned*, which make less sense and are sometimes confusing. Consider the bell which will be experimentally associated with food; at the outset it is a to-be-conditioned stimulus but not yet a conditioned stimulus, though it is often so called.

The Law of Reinforcement. Perhaps the most compact statement of Pavlov's first law is a paraphrased version of one proposed by Skinner (1938).

The occurrence of an unconditional reflex in temporal contiguity with a conditional reflex increases the strength of the latter.

Unlike the more familiar statements of this law, no attempt is made to define the terms in the basic statement. Hence, we must add some definitions and comments. The unconditional stimulus (Su) is usually strongly attached to the unconditional response (Ru) at the start of the experiment; they constitute the unconditional reflex (UR). The conditional stimulus (Sc) may or may not tend to evoke the conditional response (Rc) before the first reinforcement; that is, the conditional reflex (CR) may exist at zero strength, or it may have some positive value. This conception of a reflex existing at zero strength makes it possible to avoid the usual double statement of the law, which first tells how the CR gets started, and then how it is strengthened.

A few other comments are in order. In the first place, the law of reinforcement is an operational one; it simply describes what *E* does, and what he finds. There is a growing tendency to use reinforcement in a limited explanatory sense, as in Spence's (1951) distinction between reinforcement (effect) and nonreinforcement (contiguity) theories. Readers who are familiar with this more restricted usage must remember that we are employing the term with its traditional and literal meaning.

The usual statements of Pavlov's law imply that Rc and Ru are identical, although Pavlov's own writings show clearly that they are often quite different. We shall have more to say about this later, but here we must point out that our version of the law leaves that question open, i.e., it is a general statement of the law. For the same reason it uses *temporal contiguity;* later we will see that Sc almost always starts before Su, although there may be some overlap in time. Finally, we should point out that some writers, unhappy over Pavlov's broad usage of *reflex*, have tended to substitute the more general term *conditional response* for Sc—Rc. This leads to confusion; so we shall always use *conditional reflex* (*CR*) for the Sc—Rc sequence, reserving *conditional response* (Rc) for the response end of the arc. (Cf. Skinner, 1938.)

The law we have just given, especially in its more usual forms, rarely strikes the reader as very new. Indeed, it was anticipated by the Law of Contiguity, already discussed in the chapter on Association. Perhaps the chief virtue of the law is its objective formulation, which makes possible some experimental investigation of the factors involved.

The Law of Extinction. Pavlov's second law *was* new, and does not seem to have been clearly anticipated by anyone.

If a conditional reflex is elicited without reinforcement by an unconditional reflex, the conditional reflex is weakened or inactivated.

Later history. These two laws were established at the beginning of the century. From then until the time of his death (1936), even during the turbulent days of the Russian Revolution, Pavlov and his associates extended and refined the laws This later work was not readily available to American psychologists until the translation of Pavlov's two books (1927, 1928). But the two basic laws were extremely appealing to the behaviorists, who were looking for objective methods. The decade following Watson's (1916) espousal of the CR saw a widespread use of Pavlov's laws in textbooks ranging from general to abnormal psychology. The treatment was generally quite uncritical, and often omitted Pavlov's law of extinction. During this period there were a few experiments conducted in America, notably by Mateer (1918) on conditioned feeding movements in children, and by Cason (1922a, 1922b) on pupillary and eyelid conditioning. Watson's only study, except for the exploratory work reported in 1916, seems to have been the famous conditioning of fear in little Albert (Watson & Raynor, 1920).

The next decade was one of constantly accelerating research. Liddell started a series of investigations on sheep (1926). Schlosberg's investigation of the human conditional knee jerk appeared in 1928, followed by Upton's use of conditional breathing reactions to determine auditory thresholds of guinea pigs (1929a, b). In 1940, when Hilgard & Marquis wrote their excellent review, *Conditioning and learning*, they listed 973 references, perhaps half of which were in English. Razran's 1937 bibliography listed 1,100 titles, a good share of them in Russian. Unfortunately the Russian work had little influence on American psychologists, for Russian is a difficult language, and there were few who could summarize the material. Bekhterev was reasonably well known outside Russia, largely through the translation of his book into French (1913a) and German (1913b). A contemporary of Pavlov, he worked mostly with the flexion reflex based on shock, using both human and animal *O*s.

A preview of the variables. Since 1940 there has been less exploratory work. The experiments that have been done are designed to test theories and to measure the relations among variables. Although conditioning is popularly used as a synonym for learning, the conditioning situation per se is a very good one for the study of specific variables. Unlike the maze, for example, it permits *E* to maintain control of the stimuli, and thus indirectly of the responses. This recommends the CR situation for the study of theoretical questions, especially those involving accurate measurement. Let us examine the variables that are studied.

Rc, the conditional response, is almost always the dependent variable to be directly measured. A number of different measures of its strength are available: *amplitude* of the response (as height in centimeters or saliva in drops, etc.), *latency* of the response (compare reaction time), *percent frequency* of the trials on which the response occurs, *rate* at which the response occurs, and its *resistance to experimental extinction.* Sometimes one and sometimes another of these measures is more convenient. Unfortunately, they are often not closely correlated (Hilgard & Marquis, 1940; Humphreys, 1943a; Hall & Kobrick, 1952). This difficulty, often encountered elsewhere in psychology, implies that the same measure must be used throughout when exact quantitative comparisons are desired.

Ru, the unconditional response, is often worth measuring in terms of amplitude and latency.

Sc, the conditional stimulus, is an important experimental variable. In the vast majority of CR experiments, it is kept at a constant value. When it is varied in a quality dimension, we have an experiment on generalization and discrimination. For example, a dog conditioned to salivate at a tone of one pitch will also respond with less secretion to other tones spaced along the pitch scale. It is possible that Sc generalization occurs also in the intensity dimension: if the dog is trained to a tone of a certain loudness, he may tend to give weaker responses to tones that are louder or softer. But changes in Sc intensity may have another effect; in general, stronger stimuli elicit stronger responses, and Rc is probably no exception to this rule.

If Sc is held constant, one is enabled to investigate the effect on Rc of several different *O*-variables (or A-variables, p. 532). It is convenient to group these *O*-variables and refer each group to a construct or *intervening variable.* Thus *drive* is an inferred *O*-variable that can be controlled, in the case of the hunger drive, by hours since last feeding. A second major intervening variable is *strength of conditioning,* or strength of the result of conditioning, i.e., the conditional reflex, CR. It is extremely important to distinguish CR strength from Rc strength. The actual response, Rc, can be directly measured from trial to trial. Its strength on a given trial is a function of (1) the strength of Sc on that trial, (2) the momentary strength of drive, and (3) the changes produced in the nervous system by previous trials. It is this last factor that is called CR strength. Hull (1943, 1950, 1951) calls it S—R habit strength and designates it by the symbol $_{S}H_{R}$.

This construct, CR strength, took shape rather late in the history of conditioning. As a matter of fact, it was not very necessary until the advent of instrumental conditioning. In classical conditioning, both drive and Sc were usually held constant so that the strength of Rc faithfully mirrored the progress of conditioning. But now that we have the construct, we find it a handy one.

CR strength depends on what has happened in the previous trials of the conditioning process. The following A-variables are among those relevant:

Number of reinforced trials (Acquisition).

Number of unreinforced trials (Extinction).

Time interval between Sc and Su (Delayed and Trace CR). In instrumental conditioning the interval is Rc—Su.

Strength of drive and of reinforcement

(Su) in *previous* trials. These variables are the main topics in the chapter on Motivation, Su appearing there as "incentive." Both these factors have a strong effect on Rc, i.e., on *performance*, but their effect on CR strength is by no means clear-cut and sure.

Strength of Sc (in previous trials). The strength of Sc on a given trial is likely to affect the strength of Rc on that trial, as we have said. The strength of Sc on previous trials might affect the CR strength left in the organism by those trials. Since confusion on this matter is likely to occur, as it has sometimes in the past, we shall take a look at some experiments that make the distinction clear.

Amplifying an experimental design of Hovland (1937b) and confirming his relevant findings, Grant & Schneider (1949) conditioned four groups of 20 adults to the sequence tone–shock, with the galvanic skin response (or PGR, p. 137) as the response to be attached to the tone (Sc). The groups were trained with different tone intensities. After conditioning, each group was subdivided, one quarter being tested at each tone intensity. The extinction test of CR strength was used. By the statistical technique, analysis of variance, it was possible to separate the effect of tone intensity during conditioning from its effect during the test—in short, to distinguish between its effect on CR strength and its effect on Rc strength. The result was that Rc was stronger, the stronger the tone during the test, whereas CR was practically the same for all the intensities used in the conditioning process. This result may prove to have considerable importance in relation to theories of conditioning. (A loud dinner bell may make you jump up more quickly, but you can learn the connection bell–dinner just as easily with a gentle tinkle. Or can you? Perhaps the extinction test is not sufficient evidence.)

Many of the variables mentioned have been investigated at length, yielding rather pretty curves. Hull even constructed an elaborate formula which included most of these variables, and persistently improved the mathematical statement of the functions involved. Some psychologists (as Hilgard, 1948) feel that we have not yet reached the stage for putting all our eggs in one basket, as it were, and tying ourselves down to such a formula. Before we can write a general equation for the effects of reinforcement, for example, we should know more about the fundamental mechanism of this process. If there are two basically different types of reinforcement, it would be foolish to try to write one equation to cover both. Hence, we shall find it profitable to devote our next section to this topic.

THE NATURE OF REINFORCEMENT

As we have just noted, the distinguishing feature of Pavlov's method was that *E* maintained control of the stimuli and responses; the presentation of Su was not dependent on whether or not the animal made a particular response. The developing CR, tone-salivation, was reinforced by the unconditional reflex, food-salivation, regardless as to whether zero, five, or fifty drops of saliva were given as Rc to the tone. The reinforcement was not considered as a reward or punishment for salivating. But some of the earlier workers in conditioning overlooked this rather obvious point. For example, Watson (1916, 1919) sometimes used an electrified grid from which the animal could remove his foot, thus avoiding the shock; Watson called this a conditioning experiment, but referred to the shock as punishment on one page and as Su on another. Perhaps it would have been better if we had kept the term conditioning for the *classical conditioning* situation, and used other names for experiments in which presentation of Su is contingent upon the correct response (Schlosberg, 1937b). But as it has actually worked out, we call these experiments *instrumental conditioning:* the adjective stresses the major way in which they differ from classical CR.

Types of instrumental conditioning. *Avoidance conditioning.* Watson's experiment is a typical example of this type. A light (Sc) regularly precedes a foreleg shock (Su) by a couple of seconds. If the electrodes are attached to the leg, so that the animal cannot avoid the shock, we have a typical example of classical conditioning. But if the foot rests on a grill so that the shock can be avoided by a prompt foreleg flexion (Rc), we are dealing with avoidance conditioning. This is actually more complicated to analyze than appears at first glance; therefore, we shall reserve further discussion of avoidance conditioning until later (pp. 554–556).

Escape training. Here the animal must learn to make a response that will escape a harmful Su. For example, Mowrer (1940a) put rats in a cage with a gridded floor and gradually increased the electric charge on the grid. The rat made varied responses until he happened to depress a lever that shut off the shock. A minute or so later the shock started to build up again, but this time the rat pressed the lever a bit sooner. Eventually, the slightest shock led to immediate lever-pressing; the rat had learned to escape from the shock. In this simple form we may consider lever-pressing to be Rc, shock to be Su, and the varied running and squealing as Ru. But it does not stay this simple—it soon turns into avoidance conditioning, as the rat responds to the sight of the cage (Sc) by continued lever-pressing.

Operant conditioning. Skinner (1932, 1938) is responsible for simplifying the old problem box (Thorndike, 1898) to such an extent that it could be called a conditioning experiment. The rat is placed in a small box which contains a lever and an automatic food dispenser.

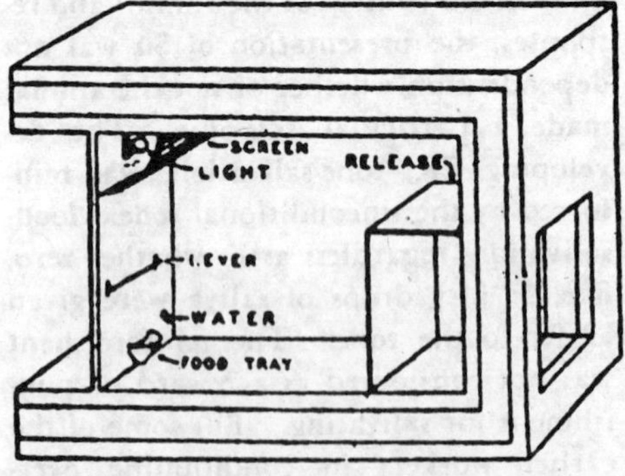

FIG. 19-1. (Skinner, 1938.) Apparatus for operant conditioning.

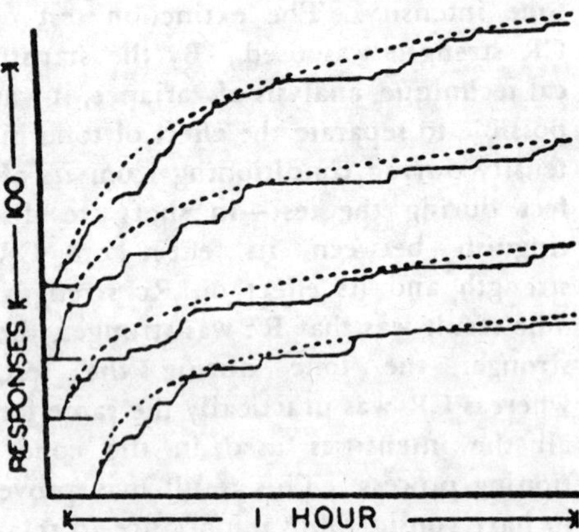

FIG. 19-2. (Skinner, 1938.) A cumulative curve of operant conditioning and extinction.

Pressure on the lever (Rc) causes a small pellet of food (Su) to drop into a dish, and the rat eats the pellet (Ru). The conditional stimulus (Sc) is not readily identifiable—it may be the sight of the lever or its smell. The failure to use a controllable Sc made it impossible to employ the typical measures of strength of CR, as percent frequency or latency, so Skinner used *rate of responding* as his basic measure (Figs. 19-1, 19-2). More recent studies of operant conditioning have often used discrete Sc, thus making available the other measures of strength of conditioning (p. 558).

Comparison of classical and operant conditioning. The importance of operant conditioning is that it brings out clearly a second way of handling reinforcement. Unlike the case in classical conditioning, the food (Su) does not come until Rc has been made. The diagrams in Figure 19-3 may represent the two types; it will be noted that they appear to be quite different. Many attempts have been made to reduce these two diagrams to one, but nobody has succeeded in doing it to everyone's satisfaction. It is possible that there are at least two different types of conditioning, each with its own law of reinforcement. We shall discuss this in more detail in a moment. But first we must point out that both classical and operant conditioning have very many points in common; they both show generalization, extinction, external inhibition, and a number of other similar phenomena. Further, both situations produce a typical sequence:

Sc—Rc—Su—Ru

This sequence is clear in the diagram (Fig. 19-3) for operant conditioning; it is also found in most classical conditioning, in which the optimal interval between Sc and Su is usually long enough to permit the conditional response to anticipate the unconditional stimulus (p. 570).

In spite of the similarities between classical and operant conditioning, the fact remains that each type, or the diagram which represents it, suggests its own theory of reinforcement. Classical conditioning has given rise to what may be called *contiguity theories*, of which there are several varieties. Operant conditioning, by stressing the *effect* of the conditional response in producing the (rewarding) unconditional stimulus, suggests a type of theory like Thorndike's Law of Effect (1898, 1911; p. 550). But many psychologists are not content to have two theories, one for each diagram;

Classical Conditional Reflex

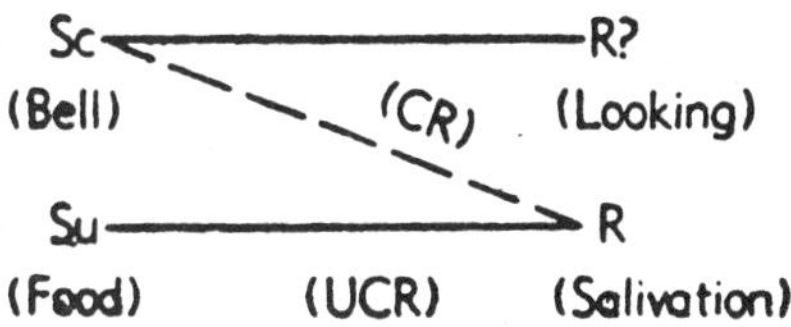

Operant Conditional Reflex

(CR) (UCR)

Sc——Rc ... Su——Ru

(Lever) (Press) (Food) (Eat)

FIG. 19-3. Diagrams of classical and operant conditioning. *Upper:* Pavlovian conditioning. The responses are difficult to label. R? is a pricking up of the ears and turning of the head toward the bell; it usually drops out early in conditioning. Salivation may be either Rc or Ru, depending on whether it is elicited by Sc or Su. *Lower:* Operant conditioning. The conditional stimulus, Sc, is of less importance in this type of conditioning. It serves chiefly to release the response rather than to elicit it. The dotted line indicates that Rc produces Su because of the nature of the apparatus. All other lines designate S—R relationships, that is, reflexes.

they consider it more parsimonious to try to extend one theory to fit both diagrams. Let us examine the two families of theories and see how they fit the various experimental results.

Contiguity theories. Pavlov's law of conditioning (p. 542) is clearly a statement of a contiguity theory, for it makes conditioning dependent on presenting Sc contiguously in time with Su—Ru. But the law is only a first approximation; Pavlov spent much of his life expanding it. There are at least three important points: (1) There must be a temporal order as well as contiguity; Sc must come before Su (see p. 557). (2) Conditioning will go in the direction of the stronger reflex. That is, the first time you pair a buzzer and food you get two responses; the dog turns his head toward the buzzer (an "investigatory reflex") and then salivates when the food comes. After a number of pairings, the weaker investigatory reflex drops out, and the dog salivates in response to the buzz as well as to the food. (3) Rc is not identical with Ru, although the simple statement of the law would lead one to assume that it was. Pavlov stressed the similarity between conditional and unconditional responses because he used the salivary response as his major index, and saliva is saliva, whether it is Rc or Ru. But in his books Pavlov (1927, 1928) frequently pointed out that the dog did many other things in response to Sc, such as approaching the food dish. In fact, Pavlov often used the term *signalizing* for the relationship between Sc and Su; the buzzer was a signal of food-to-come. All of these facts make it apparent that Pavlov thought of conditioning as tying together the central effects of stimuli. We need not go into his neurological theories of brain function here—we must remember that Pavlov, as a physiologist, was primarily interested in conditioning as a method of studying cortical functioning—but it is important to notice that the essential contiguity was one of stimuli, and also that Su was the primary reinforcing agent.

Pavlov's theory of reinforcement is often called a *stimulus-substitution theory*. This is accurate only if we realize that the substitution is not complete. The dog does not start to eat the buzzer in place of the food. A better description is to say that he responds appropriately to the temporal sequence by preparing for the food when the buzzer sounds. An especially good example of this type of preparatory response is found in some observations of Liddell, James & Anderson (1934) on sheep (pp. 576, 676). An animal had been conditioned to flex his foreleg in response to a metronome, using unavoidable shock as Su. Normally the sheep stood in a stock and merely lifted the leg in response to Sc. But if the sheep was lying down on his side when Sc was sounded, he first got up, and then lifted the leg.

Expectancy theory. A broadly conceived stimulus-substitution theory, in which Sc comes to signal shock- (or food-) about-to-come, is almost indistinguishable from Tolman's expectancy theory of learning. This theory has had its greatest application in studies of maze learning, and will be discussed more fully in a later chapter (p. 646). It is a common-sense theory, which essentially states that the animal learns to expect certain sequences of stimulation, and acts appropriately. This theory gives a good description of what happens in a typical classical conditioning experiment. For example, consider Upton's (1929a, b) study on guinea pigs. He repeatedly followed a tone by a shock, and found that the animals soon developed a conditional anticipatory shift in the breathing rhythm. The Rc was a smoothing out and regularizing of breathing, variously described as *flutter* or *the lullaby effect*, and differed strikingly from the sharp intake which was the typical Ru to shock. This effect has been observed consistently in several species by Liddell and his coworkers and also in the cat (Wever, 1930) and rat (Schlosberg, 1934). The shift in breathing rhythm is often the first sign of conditioning, and it suggests that the animal is being alerted for the oncoming shock. In fact, the whole picture of restless and diffuse activity that is so characteristic of early stages of conditioning (cf. p. 576) encourages the onlooker to say, "The animal obviously expects the shock." Perhaps the most serious objection to an expectancy theory is that it smacks of introspecting for the rat—although Tolman (1938) probably should not be accused of such anthropomorphic thinking, for he treats expectancy as an intervening variable, and tries to anchor it on both the stimulus and response side. (Fig. 19-4).

Guthrie's S—R contiguity theory. The preceding theories held that the essential contiguity was between Sc and Su; Guthrie (1935) took Pavlov's law literally and assumed that the contiguity was between Sc and Ru. He holds that all stimuli that are acting at the moment a response is made immediately become associated with that response. If the same stimuli were all present on the next trial, the same response would be made. At first glance this would seem to pre-

Classical Conditioning

	Explore			Consummate.	
Stage 1.	Sc ______	Ro	. . . .	Su ______	Ru
	Bell	Look		Food	Eat
	Prepare			Consummate	
Stage 2.	Sc ______	Rc	. . . .	Su ______	Ru
	Bell	Salivate		Food	Eat

Operant Conditioning

	Explore			Consummate	
Stage 1.	Sc ______	Ro	. . . .	Su ______	Ru
	Lever	Press		Food	Eat
	Prepare			Consummate	
Stage 2.	Sc ______	Rc	. . . .	Su ______	Ru
	Lever	Press		Food	Eat

Fig. 19-4. Similarity of classical and operant conditioning. Stage 1 represents the behavior in the early trials; Stage 2 after conditioning has occurred, i.e., after the original exploratory behavior, Ro, has given way to anticipatory behavior, Rc. The dots here indicate the short time interval between Sc (with its R) and Su. According to this diagram, the only difference between the two types of conditioning is that Rc is the same as Ro in the operant type, but not in the classical type. This difference may not be important; it merely arises from the different exploratory movements aroused by the bell and by the lever—looking and listening in one case, manipulation in the other. The manipulation brings reward, but looking and listening can cease without stopping the food supply. Suppose *E* should give food only when the dog pricked up his ears; this exploratory movement would certainly become the Rc (as in the similar experiment of Grindley, 1932).

dict complete conditioning after a single reinforcement, which obviously rarely happens. Guthrie points out that the usual protracted series of conditioning trials is necessary because the same pattern of stimuli is never present on two successive trials. Although Sc and incidental environmental stimuli are held constant, there are differences in postural and other internal stimuli from trial to trial. But if Su is regularly used to evoke Ru, this response eventually becomes conditioned to all stimuli that occur in the restricted experimental situation; and as more and more of them become yoked to the response, CR gradually becomes stronger. Although it grew out of Pavlov's first law, Guthrie's theory requires some subsidiary assumptions if it is to fit all of the facts observed in the classical conditioning experiment. Especially difficult are the differences between Rc and Ru that are handled so well by the stimulus-substitution contiguity theories. On the other hand, Guthrie's theory does reasonably well in handling many of the facts of operant and other forms of instrumental conditioning. Here he considers the role of reward or punishment to be simply a way of getting the animal out of the stimulus situation, and thus preventing the stimuli from being attached to a different response. For example, as the rat wanders around the Skinner box he is continually attaching new responses to the stimulus situation; scratching, sniffing, stretching, etc. But once he presses the lever food appears, and markedly changes the stimulus situation. This leaves the last response, lever-pressing, the one that stays connected to the sight of the bar, so that the animal will make that response again when he finishes his pellet of food and looks up.

The other contiguity theories do not do so well when they get to instrumental conditioning. Pavlov never really had to face the problem of extending his theory, for he limited himself to a relatively invariant response, salivation. For him, salivation was merely an index of excitation of a cortical area: anything that aroused the food area automatically produced salivation. But when we get to situations in which the animal has to modify its response, then signalizing or anticipation is not enough. In addition to sensory association, it is necessary for us to have a principle to account for response modification, something like the law of effect.

Effect theories. The most widely known of the early versions of this type of theory was Thorndike's Law of Effect. As stated in 1911, it pointed out that "satisfying consequences" (rewards, or escape from punishment) strengthened an S—R connection, while "annoying consequences" (punishment) weakened it. This version of the theory is circular, for the only way we can tell whether or not a given consequence is satisfying is by observing to see whether or not the animal repeats the response that produced the alleged reward. That is, we say an animal likes a food if he comes back for more. Then we say that the animal comes back for more because he likes it! This type of circular argument is not very "satisfying" to psychologists, although it may have practical value; once we have demonstrated that a certain food has reward value for a given animal in one situation, we may use this food as an incentive in many other learning situations (p. 660).

Drive-reduction theory. One attempt to break this circularity is found in Hull's (1943) behavioral theory. He substitutes *drive reduction* for both satisfiers and annoyers. That is, any S—R sequence that is followed by a reduction in strength of a drive will be reinforced. Thus, when the rat sees the lever and presses it, the food which follows reduces the hunger drive, and strengthens the tendency to press the lever the next time it appears. Or when the rat runs through the door from a charged floor, the powerful drive induced by shock is reduced so that the animal is more apt to make a quick exit the next time he is on that floor. The critical reader may say that we have not avoided the circularity of the old argument; drive may sound more objective than satisfiers, but how can you measure it? There are several ways in which drive is the better construct. We shall defer much of the discussion to the chapter on Motivation, but here we may point to two of its advantages. In the first place, drive varies with need, and can be experimentally controlled by depriving the animal of something basic to his system. Thus, we may have a "12-hour hunger drive," and similar control can be exercised over thirst, sex, and others. Secondly, there is a high probability that drives may eventually be identified with specific physiological processes. Some protagonists of the drive-reduction theory, as Spence (1951), are content to forget physiology for the present and let drive stand as a purely psychological construct, but it seems unduly wasteful to discard any help the physiologists can give us in this difficult problem of reinforcement.

As we have just indicated, a simple drive-reduction theory seems to handle reward and escape learning rather well. More careful examination will show certain inadequacies. For example, the drive reduction that results from eating one pellet of food must be essentially nil, for a rat will eat 30 or more of these pellets without showing any signs of satiation. In fact, there is evidence that one or two pellets will act as an appetizer, actually increasing drive. To account for the reinforcing effect of a single pellet, Hull invokes the concept of secondary reinforcement; any stimulus that has been *associated* with drive reduction will itself acquire reinforcing properties. Thus even the click of the pellet dispenser has some "reward" value. But here we find ourselves getting pretty close to signaling and expectancy theories; we have a stimulus acting as a reinforcer without any actual reduction in need.

Another minor difficulty with the theory is that some stimuli seem to have primary reinforcing value even though they do not satisfy a need or decrease a drive. A notable example is the sugar substitute, saccharine, which has no nutritive properties but acts as a reward (cf. pp. 661, 662, 684). It could be said that it acquires secondary reward value because it tastes like sugar, a good drive reducer; but unlike typical secondary rewards, saccharine does not lose its reinforcing power in a long-continued extinction series.

Drive reduction in classical conditioning. We run into additional difficulty when we try to apply the drive-reduction theory to classical conditioning. The difficulty is sometimes glossed over by a loose use of the word reinforcement. For example, Spence (1951) in his recent chapter "Theoretical Interpretations of Learning," repeats Hull's 1942 explanation of Pavlov's salivary conditioning, i.e., "that 'food in the mouth' constitutes a reinforcing state of affairs, very possibly a secondary one, by virtue of the past association of this stimulation with hunger-drive reduction." This explana-

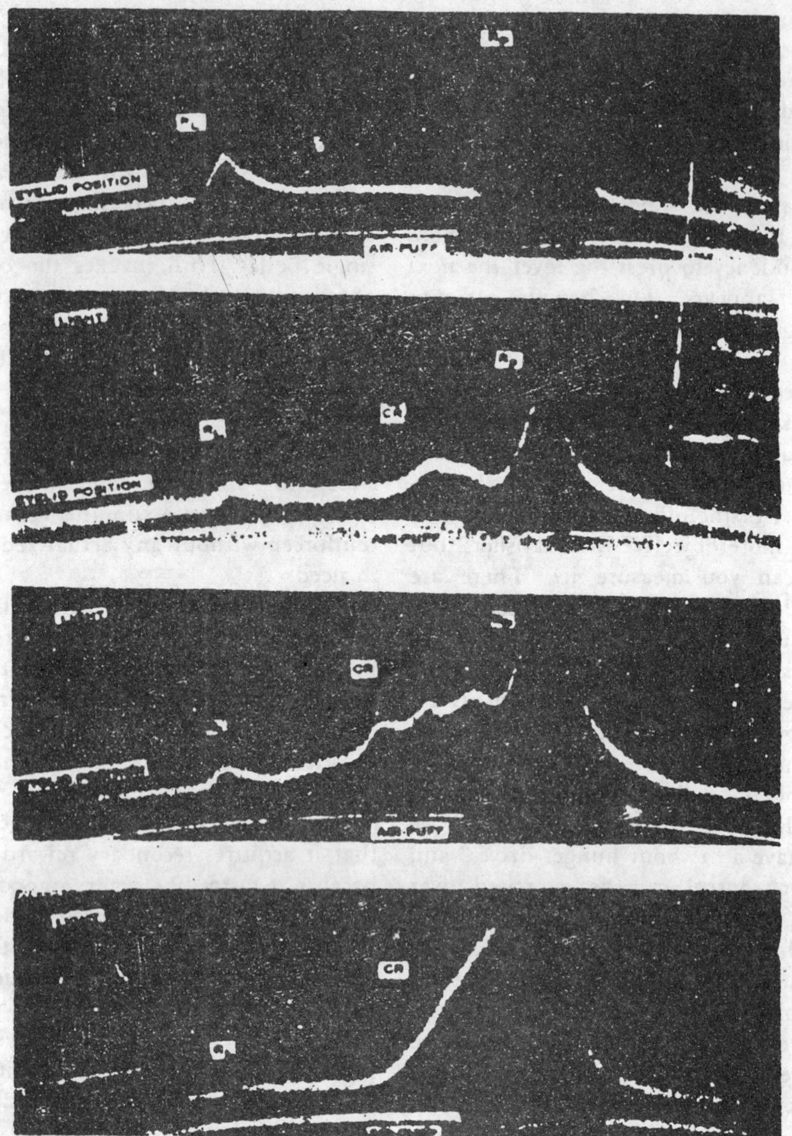

Fig. 19-5. (Hilgard, 1936.) Conditioned eyelid response in a human subject. Sc was the "light," a sudden moderate increase in the illumination of a disk on which *O*'s eyes were fixated; Su, a puff of air against the front of the eye. The light preceded the puff by 400 ms. Time in 1/20 sec (strong vertical lines) and 1/100 sec. The first record shows only the two reflex responses to the stimuli. R_L is a small reflex lid movement elicited by the sudden increase of illumination. If you count the vertical lines between the dark band at the top (shown better in the second record) and the beginning of the R_L response, you find its latency is about 100 ms. In this series (the light being of only moderate intensity) this original reflex shows a tendency to adapt out. R_P, the unconditional reflex (Ru) to the puff of air, is a fairly complete lid closure. Its latency, measured from the break in the "air-puff" signal line, is about 50 ms. The response labeled "CR" is the conditional eyelid response, which we would label Rc (using CR only for the S—R unit; Sc—Rc, the connection established by conditioning). This response first appears in the second record with a latency, measured from "light," of about 550 ms. In the third record it increases in size and complexity, but a shorter latency of about 200 ms. In the bottom record it shows a slight *increase* in latency and merges with Ru. It tends to become a "delayed CR," (see p. 565).

tion might be satisfactory to account for the building up of a salivary CR after it once got started, but at the start of the experiment there is no Sc—Rc connection to be strengthened. For example, the dog responds to a flashing light (Sc) by looking at it, not by salivating. According to this theory, one would expect the investigatory reflex to be strengthened by the drive-reduction incident on feeding so that the dog would learn to look steadily at the light instead of salivating.

On the other hand, the original law of effect has somewhat less difficulty with many types of classical conditioning. Preliminary salivation is rewarded to some extent in that it prepares the mouth for the food powder, increasing the stimulating value of the reward. Or, in the case of Pavlov's defense type of salivary CR (Su is dilute acid in mouth) the saliva decreases the stimulating value of the noxious acid by diluting it. In the unavoidable-shock experiment, another type of classical conditioning (cf. p. 554), the shift in breathing rhythm and the increased muscular tension may make it easier for the animal to "take" the shock. But there are some cases of classical conditioning that do not seem to come under even the broadest formulation of the law of effect. One of them is the psychogalvanic response, which is extremely easy to condition. This Ru, a sharp increase in the electrical conductivity of the skin, is readily evoked by shock as Su. If a light is used as Sc, and is paired with the shock for five trials, it evokes its own increase in conductivity as Rc. We shall say more about this CR situation later in the chapter, for it is a very useful one, but here we shall merely point out that the anticipatory change in electrical conductivity of the skin does not seem to decrease the effectiveness of the shock—hence the decrease is certainly not rewarded.

Another reflex that is widely used in conditioning studies is the eye blink. It is extremely popular, for it has two major advantages: (1) it can be elicited readily in animals as diverse as man, monkey, dog, and rat (cf. Hilgard & Marquis, 1940); and (2) the lid has so little inertia that it gives a very fine record of the time relations of the responses. In a typical experiment, the subject has his head held in a rest, and the shadow of the eyelid falls on a moving photographic surface (see the record from the Dodge pendulum photochronograph, Fig. 19-5). In front of his eyes is a lighted patch; increase in its brightness is the usual Sc. A puff of air to the cornea of the eye serves as Su and results in a brisk wink (Ru). If the light precedes the puff by a half second, there gradually develops an anticipatory wink (Rc). This wink is rewarded in that it keeps the puff of air off the sensitive cornea. It would seem to be a good example of effect learning. But one can get essentially the same conditioning with a different Su, as a loud noise or a mild shock to the cheek; in both of these cases it is hard to see what advantage *O* gets by his anticipatory wink. The net result is that we are inclined to question the applicability of the law of effect to any of the eyelid studies. On the other hand, it is clear that this CR is a "natural" for either a signalizing or expectancy theory. As a matter of fact, it was work on this reflex that led Hilgard and his co-workers to apply the expectancy theory to classical conditioning (see Hilgard and Marquis, 1940, for discussion and references).

Dual theories of reinforcement. The difficulty in applying one theory to both classical and instrumental conditioning has led many to believe that there are actually two mechanisms of reinforcement. Skinner (1935, 1938) drew a strict distinction between classical and operant conditioning; he suggested that the classical conditioning was largely of autonomic responses and followed Pavlov's law, while operant conditioning was typically of skeletal muscle and depended on effect. Schlosberg (1937b) surveyed a large number of conditioning experiments and thought that the distinction was between diffuse preparatory responses (classical conditioning) and more precise and adaptive ones (effect). More recently, Mowrer (1947, 1950), who had earlier been a staunch advocate of a single (effect) theory, swung over to a dual one. He makes a sharper distinction than did the earlier writers between the kinds of responses to which the two theories apply: all autonomic responses follow the Pavlovian principle, while skeletal ones are reinforced through drive reduction. This position is probably a bit extreme, for the autonomic centers are not sharply separated in the central nervous system from those that control skeletal responses (p. 134). Further, many of the diffuse preparatory responses, as increase in muscle tension and bracing for a shock, involve skeletal muscles. Hence, it seems more likely that the distinction is between diffuse anticipatory responses and more precise adaptive ones. To go even further, the diffuse responses that fit Pavlov's law so neatly may represent only the motor discharge resulting from activation of the sensory centers. To put it in another way, the animal anticipates the oncoming Su and responds in a more or less appropriate manner, dependent on inherited reflexes and past learning. But the drive-reduction or effect principle is necessary to account for the selection and stabilization of the precise, adaptive, and successful response. Perhaps we can make the distinction still clearer by using common-sense terms: the animal learns what stimuli are coming through classical conditioning, and then finds what to do about them by instrumental conditioning.

Application of the theories to avoidance conditioning. So far we have been applying the theories to extremely simple situations. As a matter of fact, there is considerable doubt whether there are many pure cases of either classical or instrumental conditioning; most actual experiments probably utilize both types of reinforcement, as we may bring out from the results of E. J. Gibson (1952). She used young goats as subjects, with electrodes on the foreleg to deliver the Su of shock. The connecting wires permitted free movement of the animal about the laboratory room. The Sc was a dimming of the room illumination for 10 seconds before the shock. The kids soon began to respond to this warning signal, but the Rc varied from animal to animal and from trial to trial. Backing off was the most frequent Rc in the early trials, but there were others, such as a stiff, motionless posture, walking forward, side-stepping, rearing up, and flexion of the leg about to be shocked. After about 100 trials this last response became the most frequent, but it never became the exclusive one as long as classical conditioning was used—that is, with unavoidable shock. But if this flexion response was rewarded by termination or omission of the shock it soon became stabilized. Perhaps we are justified in saying that the kid learned the dimming-shock sequence in both classical and instrumental situations, but that only the instrumental situation permitted the animal to learn something constructive to do about the oncoming shock.

Roughly comparable studies have been done on two other species, rats and guinea pigs. Schlosberg (1934, 1936, 1937b) fastened rats in a holder and recorded breathing and foreleg withdrawal in response to shock. The shock was delivered through an electrode attached to the foreleg, so connected that the animals could be conditioned under avoidable or unavoidable shock. Sc (light or buzzer) came on for ½ second, the last third of which was accompanied by shock. The time relations were such that an animal could avoid the (avoidable) shock by an anticipatory Rc, or shorten it by a brisk Ru. The results showed no evidence for effect learning. What little difference there was between the two conditions favored the unavoidable shock. This would be expected from Pavlov's law, for the unavoidable shock was more regular and was never shortened by the rats' response. Consistent with this general result was the fact that the animals rarely developed beyond the diffuse-response stage; the light elicited struggling, shifts in breathing, and squeals, but rarely a precise leg flexion. One animal that did develop a precise flexion conformed even more strikingly to Pavlov's laws. Once the response developed, this rat regularly avoided the shock (when on avoidable shock) by his anticipatory Rc. The result was extinction of the response in a few trials, as Pavlov would have predicted. But then the animal got the shock again on the next few trials, so becoming reconditioned, avoided a few shocks, becoming extinguished again, and so on through several cycles. There was no evidence that avoiding the shock "stamped in" the successful response, as the law of effect would predict.

Avoidance in a free situation. This apparent breakdown of the law of effect, and also the difficulty encountered in the attempt to establish anything beyond a diffuse CR, are probably due to the fact that an animal as low as the rat cannot readily learn precise responses when restrained and shocked. Hunter (1935) found that rats in a circular runway did learn faster with avoidable than with unavoidable shock. An especially interesting series of observations involved guinea pigs in a squirrel-cage gadget (Brogden, Lipman & Culler, 1938). The rotating runway was so arranged that some animals could avoid the shock by running promptly in response to Sc, while others had to take the shock every time. Both arrangements yielded similar learning curves for the first three experimental days; by that time the pigs were making anticipatory runs on about a quarter of the trials. The unavoidable-shock animals never got much "better" than this, but those that could avoid the shock continued to improve and by the eighth day were beating the shock on 100 percent of the trials. Again it looks as if both groups soon learned to expect the shock, while only one group had a possible method of avoiding it; the other group could just as well remain where they were (Culler, 1938).

However, there is another possible interpretation. F. D. Sheffield (1948) repeated the experiment and found that an animal shocked while running on one trial was less likely to run on the next trial. In agreement with Guthrie's theory (p. 550) Sheffield explains that the shock received during a run would break up the running pattern and so lessen the likelihood of running in response to the next presentation of Sc. This disturbance would happen quite frequently in the unavoidable-shock animals, while those that could avoid the shock by running would be spared this disrupting effect of shock on the developing CR. (See also Logan, 1951.)

The drive-reduction theorists also have an explanation for avoidance conditioning. They postulate an acquired drive of fear or anxiety, which is induced by the shock and becomes conditioned to Sc and to the shock chamber. This drive is reduced when the animal successfully gets out of the shock chamber. This theory and the supporting experiments of N. E. Miller will be discussed under the head of Motivation (p. 674).

Summary of reinforcement theories. In order to present the theories fairly, the preceding discussion has leaned rather markedly toward the view that there are two mechanisms of reinforcement and that both operate in varying combinations in perhaps the great majority of conditioning and other learning situations. Each of the two comes under the spotlight in its own type situation. The classical salivary conditioning experiment of Pavlov is well described by the statement that reinforcement occurs whenever the unconditional stimulus follows a conditional *stimulus,* so that the conditioning consists essentially in a yoking together or associating of the cerebral effects of the two stimuli. The operant conditioning experiment of Skinner is better described by the statement that reinforcement occurs when the unconditional stimulus follows a conditional *response* so that its mechanism consists essentially in providing or selecting a response that produces the unconditional stimulus. In both cases we must remember that the unconditional stimulus is only to be defined as one which dependably elicits a response, so that the same circularity, or empiricism, is present here as in Thorndike's attempt to define "effect" (p. 550). Once the CR has been established, we have in both cases the same sequence, Sc—Rc—Su—Ru, and the question is how this behavior sequence is established. What must be established is an adjustment in the organism to the environmental sequence, Sc—Su. Pavlov's dog seems to learn this sequence by merely listening and waiting, while Skinner's rat has to press the bar to make the environmental sequence occur. If we grant in either case that the animal's receptive-perceptual system is capable of registering the environmental sequence, the closely connected effector system will surely follow suit (Woodworth, 1947).

But neither this nor any other attempt to extend either major theory of reinforcement to cover both classical and instrumental conditioning has succeeded in winning general approval. In the period between 1925 and 1935 a much simplified contiguity theory of the Pavlovian type was dominant; Guthrie's present theory, emphasizing S--R association by contiguity, is of this type. The following decade was marked by the increasing ascendancy of a drive-reduction theory. Now, in the early 1950s, there is at least a hint that the pendulum is swinging back again. Until the pendulum stops swinging it might be wise to recognize the possibility of at least two types of reinforcement—Tolman (1945) has suggested that there may be a half dozen fairly distinct types of learning! But if the reader insists on adopting a single general-purpose theory, he may well consult the book by Hilgard (1948) and the chapter by Spence (1951), and not make his choice until he has read these two discussions at least, for each of them approaches the problem from a different theoretical angle.

THE PROBLEM OF EXTINCTION

As we have seen, many psychologists received Pavlov's law of conditioning with considerable enthusiasm. It filled the need for an objective view of the old association by contiguity (p. 44). But the law of extinction, which was entirely new, had a very different reception. Some psychologists ignored it, others doubted it, and still others tried to explain extinction as merely a case of conditioning. The reason is not hard to find; extinction seemed directly opposed to the old law of frequency, renamed the Law of Exercise by Thorndike (1911), which was at the bottom of repetitious classroom drill and of the old adage, "Practice makes perfect." Pavlov pointed out that repetition of the S—R sequence, bell–salivation, actually rendered the connection nonfunctional unless each trial also included reinforcement by food. This did not seem to make sense. But when extinction was repeatedly demonstrated in CRs as diverse as conditional eyelid reflexes in man (Hilgard & Marquis, 1940) and lever-pressing in rats (Skinner, 1938), it became necessary to re-examine the law of exercise. (To be fair to Thorndike we should add that he had always regarded his law of effect as of equal importance with the law of exercise and by 1931 had relegated exercise to a subordinate place. But his system did not include any clear recognition of extinction.)

A very simple experiment will demonstrate what is wrong with the law of exercise (cf. Culler, 1938). Ask a child his name, and assume that he answers correctly. You have now exercised the S—R connection, *name?–Johnnie,* and should have strengthened it. Ask him again, and you do seem to have strengthened it, for he responds with a louder "Johnnie." But try it a few more times in rapid succession. Johnnie will soon stop responding and go off to more interesting activities. Repetition has extinguished a well-established S—R instead of strengthening or even maintaining it.

This little experiment brings out the factor which was omitted from the law of exercise; namely, incentive. There is reason to believe that even a well-learned act will not be performed without some incentive and that a new act will not be learned without some incentive, i.e., without reinforcement of some sort. Unfortunately the actual reinforcement in a specific example of learning is often hard to identify. Further, the reinforcement that maintains the strength of a CR may be different from that used in the original conditioning. For example, Finch & Culler (1934b) first established a conditioned foreleg flexion in a dog by shock applied to the forefoot and then shifted the shock to the thorax. The substitute reinforcement served as punishment for every failure to lift the leg in response to Sc, and thus prevented extinction of the response that had been set up by shock to the foot. They pointed out that substitute reinforcements may account for the puzzling persistence of habits which seem to keep going from sheer inertia.

Very few psychologists would still question the reality of extinction, either as a laboratory phenomenon or as an important everyday fact. But there is less agreement on its explanation, and we may well examine the most debated theories and see how they fit the experimental results.

Forgetting. Is extinction anything else than a case of forgetting? A few facts will show that the two phenomena are quite different. In forgetting there is a lapse of time between the learning and the memory test. Extinction occurs during an actual series of repetitions of Sc—Rc, and even increases with the number of unreinforced trials. Further, it can readily be demonstrated that an extinguished CR is not a forgotten one. Apply Sc again after an intermission, and you witness the phenomenon of "spontaneous recovery."

The Graham-Gagné runway. A surprisingly adequate instrument for demonstrating spontaneous recovery is a simple elevated runway, 36 inches long, with a starting box on one end, and a food box on the other (Fig. 20-3, p. 586). When the starting box door is opened (Sc), the rat runs to the food box and eats. One may take emergence from the food box as a convenient Rc and measure the strength of the CR in terms of *latency*, the time between the opening of the door and the moment the rat gets clearly out of the box. It is usual to plot latency in log seconds. A curve for the acquisition of this operant CR is shown in Figure 19-6; note that the latent times approach a minimum in less than 15 trials. Now continue the experiment with no food in the goal box; latency climbs steadily as extinction develops. When a rat has reached an arbitrary criterion, staying in the starting box for 3 minutes on one trial, the response can be considered extinguished.

Now we can demonstrate *spontaneous recovery*. Close the door and leave the rat in the starting box for a certain interval after the last extinction trial, and then open the door again. He will usually come out, the latency will tell you the strength of his CR, and you can see how much of the extinctive inhibition has worn off. Try different recovery periods on several groups of ani-

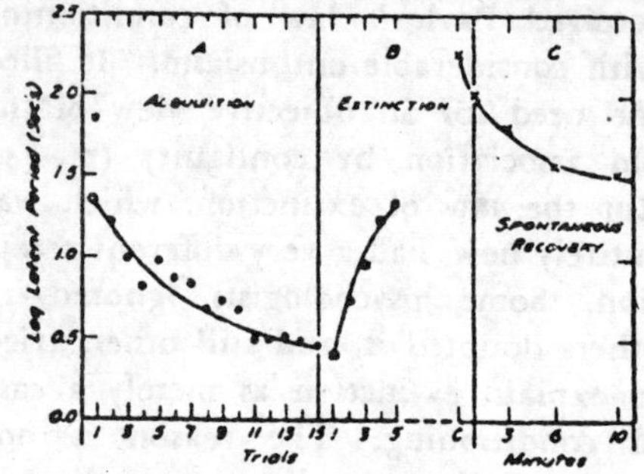

FIG. 19-6. (After Graham & Gagné, 1940.) The acquisition, extinction, and spontaneous recovery of a simple running response. The measure of response strength is the length of time it took the rats to emerge from the starting box onto a runway which had a food box at the other end. These *latent times* were converted into logarithms before averaging, to avoid skewed distributions.

The solid circles represent mean log latencies of 15 successive rewarded trials. The curve is computed from a rational equation. Note that the curve starts from a hollow circle, which is a theoretical origin somewhat below the actual first trial.

Immediately after the last acquisition trial, food was omitted from the goal box; the first five extinction trials only are plotted. Extinction was continued for each rat until its latency reached 180 seconds (log = 2.26), but the whole curve cannot be plotted since some rats took more trials than others.

As soon as the extinction criterion had been reached, the door of the starting box was closed for either 1, 3, 6 or 10 minutes to permit spontaneous recovery. Since there were 20 rats, only five could be assigned to each recovery interval. Even so, the points (shown by X X) are surprisingly regular. Note that extinction was carried "below zero"; the criterion was longer than the original latency. Even 10 minutes of spontaneous recovery is not enough to get the response back to the theoretical zero (hollow circle at the extreme left).

mals. The results are plotted as curve C in Figure 19-6.

This experiment shows clearly that extinction is not to be explained by forgetting, for if the CR were forgotten, it could not recover after an additional lapse of time. Extinction would seem to involve an active process which blocks or neutralizes the CR. When this active process is weakened by the passage of time, the CR is no longer blocked, and is said to have recovered.

Adaptation. If the lecturer suddenly raps the table in the middle of a dry discussion, the students are startled; they look up and some may even jump. But if the rap is repeated every few seconds, it rapidly loses its effectiveness. The students have become "adapted" to the stimulus, we commonly say. Since the example is much like a case of experimental extinction, we are tempted to try to explain extinction in terms of adaptation. As a matter of fact, this type of adaptation shows such formal characteristics of extinction as spontaneous recovery and disinhibition. These parallels have been pointed out by Humphrey (1930, 1933) who found similar adaptation to repeated sudden stimuli in snails and turtles. Such negative adaptation has been demonstrated in the reflex response of the spinal rat to repeated tapping of the tail (Prosser and Hunter, 1936) and in certain abdominal reflexes in man (Lehner, 1941). Apparently there is a widespread tendency for a stimulus to lose its effectiveness on continued unreinforced repetition. But we know less about adaptation in general than we do about experimental extinction in particular so that we gain nothing by using the more general term. Furthermore, the general term has been applied to so many phenomena, ranging from "dark adaptation" to "adaptation to the environment," that its dynamic meaning is extremely vague. This is not to deny that some of the examples of adaptation may shed light on the nature of extinction. It is perfectly possible that negative adaptation of the startle response in the turtle and extinction of the eyelid CR in man may depend on the same processes, but the scientific task is to find out what these processes are rather than to shift names for the phenomenon.

Inhibition. Pavlov himself attributed extinction to a process called inhibition. He postulated two opposed processes in the nerve centers, excitation and inhibition, both being effects of peripheral stimuli. The feeding center was thrown into the state of excitation by food in the mouth and even by the sound of a metronome after conditioning. Hence, the salivary CR. But the conditional stimulus also produced central inhibition which was rather evanescent, dissipating rapidly, but which could build up to a considerable amount in a series of trials. When the omission of reinforcement cut off the major source of excitation, the continued repetition of Sc threw the advantage to inhibition and resulted in extinction of the CR.

Pavlov's rather speculative ideas of what goes on in the brain may be of little importance. Some psychologists go so far as to reject the concept of inhibition, although it seems to be a necessary—and respectable—concept in physiology. Others, such as Miller & Dollard (1941), substitute for inhibition a process akin to fatigue which can accumulate and act as a drive toward resting. Still others, such as Spence (1951) and Hull (1950a, 1951), strip Pavlov's concepts of physiological implications and use them as constructs in a purely behavioral sense. Hull's "reactive inhibition" has behavioral properties like those of Pavlov's "internal inhibition," in that it nullifies excitation, accumulates with repetition of a CR, but dissipates rapidly. It acts as a negative drive and plays an important part in theories of motivation (p. 669).

Interference. The theories mentioned so far are all two-process theories, demanding one process for conditioning and a different kind of process for extinction. The interference theory (Guthrie, 1935; Wendt, 1936a) gets along with a single process. This theory maintains that extinction is merely the learning of a new response to the old conditional stimulus. When pressing the bar ceases to secure a food pellet, the rat begins to vary his response so far as the situation allows (Antonitis, 1951; cf. Stanley, 1952). Undoubtedly interference is often a factor in extinction, but it may not be the whole story.

There are still other possible factors in the extinction of a CR. Razran (1939a) mentions several and confronts them with an array of facts gleaned largely from Russian sources. For the present we may test the interference theory against that of internal or reactive inhibition and try to ascertain which has more predictive potency.

The normal course of extinction. An extinction curve is usually like an acquisition curve drawn backward (as in Fig. 19-6, page 558). This fact does not discriminate between our two theories; for the new and interfering habit should develop according to the typical learning curve, and there is no obvious reason why inhibition should develop in a radically different way. But it might be possible to modify the experimental variables in such a way as to change the extinction curve and to predict the change from one or another theory. One possibility is suggested by the well-known fact of more rapid learning with spaced than with closely massed practice trials (p. 786)—a rule which seems to hold good of conditioning (p. 562). Accordingly, the interference theory would predict that extinction (being the learning of a new response) would be more rapid when the extinction trials were well spaced. The inhibition theory would predict exactly the opposite: each unreinforced trial contributes its portion of inhibition; and the shorter the interval between trials, the more rapidly the undissipated inhibition would accumulate.

The experimental results are not in full agreement but they tend to show more rapid extinction during massed extinction trials. Pavlov so reported (1927, p. 61), and other Russian studies gave similar results (Razran, 1933, 1939a). The conditional eyelid reflex in dogs has shown the same (Hilgard & Marquis, 1935), and so also with the runway operant in rats (Gagne, 1941). In a rather complicated lever-pressing situation, Rohrer (1947) found massed extinction faster when the CR was strong to start with and the hunger drive high. The reverse conditions (few previous reinforcements, low drive) gave a slight but not significant tendency toward faster extinction with spaced extinction trials. For the human eyelid CR, Porter (1939) found no difference between massed and spaced extinction, while Reynolds (1945) got slightly faster massed extinction. There have been several studies on rats in alley-type runways (Porter, 1938; V. F. Sheffield, 1950; Stanley, 1952), mostly showing little difference between massed and spaced extinction. Sheffield's experiment is apparently the only one yielding a clear difference in favor of greater effectiveness for spaced extinction. From a comparable experiment Stanley drew the conclusion that the empty food box induced a state of excitement (frustration) which persisted during a series of massed trials, causing the rat to run faster and show less extinction.

Perhaps we are justified in emphasizing the results from the relatively simple conditioning experiments, since the alley runways are complicated by curtains, food boxes, etc. Even if we take all the cited experiments into consideration, we find three or four clearly favoring greater effectiveness for massed extinction trials, as against one doubtful case on the opposite side of the question. On the whole, the inhibition theory has made a better prediction than the interference theory.

Spontaneous recovery. The fact that an extinguished CR will recover, partially at least, during an intermission was used as an argument against the forgetting theory of extinction. It is evidently consistent with the assumption that internal inhibition dissipates rapidly and so releases the blocked CR. But the interference theory also would predict spontaneous recovery from the known fact that recent learning tends to fade out more rapidly than older learning (Jost's law, p. 730).

Disinhibition. Pavlov recognized a second type of inhibition, which he called "external inhibition." It was produced by any unfamiliar and extraneous stimulus which attracted the animal's attention (elicited the "investigatory reflex," in Pavlov's terms)—we would call it "distraction," and it was evidently a kind of interference. External inhibition made trouble in the laboratory until sound-resisting experimental chambers were provided, for any sudden noise would interfere with the dog's orderly behavior. When a CR was being built up, an external inhibitor would diminish the salivation on the next trial; but if an established CR was being extinguished, the same external inhibitor would increase the next response. Pavlov's interpretation was that external inhibition worked against the process that was dominant at the time. When the dominant process was internal inhibition, this inhibition was itself inhibited. He called this effect "disinhibition." It is not surprising that psychologists who disliked inhibition regarded this suggestion as adding insult to injury. But the fact remains that the phenomena are very easy to demonstrate. Again we can make use of the Graham-Gagné runway. If a slight noise is made just before the entrance door opens (Sc) on a conditioning trial, the latent time of that trial is lengthened, showing that the CR is momentarily weakened. But if the same slight sound is made just before a trial midway in an extinction series, the latency is shortened, indicating disinhibition (Gagné, 1941a).

While psychologists were a bit slow in taking disinhibition seriously, they came around to the use of sound-resistant boxes for conditioning experiments on rats at least. With human subjects the problem is not solved so easily, for a soundproof room is cumbersome, and the isolation may be as disturbing as most extraneous stimuli to which the human subject becomes "adapted" rather quickly. Still it is probable that the professor remains a potent disinhibitor if he wanders around an undergraduate laboratory while extinction is being tried on student subjects.

Now to return to the theories. Obviously inhibition supplies an adequate explanation for disinhibition. But the interference theory has an answer, too. It simply says that a novel stimulus evokes a response conflicting with that other response which was interfering with the original CR. This particular game seems to result in a tie.

We shall meet disinhibition again later in the present chapter. In general, it may occur whenever internal or reactive inhibition is present in significant amounts, as in discrimination and trace conditioning.

Partial extinction during massed learning trials. Internal or reactive inhibition, according to the general definition, should occur even when the CR is reinforced. With a fairly long time allowed between trials for the inhibition to dissipate, the performance could improve rapidly, but with massed trials this would not occur because of the accumulation of inhibition. After a rest the performance could show a great improvement due to the absence of internal inhibition, much as in the learning curve on page 531 and in the phenomenon of reminiscence, page 796. Pavlov had noticed (1927, p. 234) that "inhibition can develop also when the conditioned reflexes are reinforced." Other examples were reported by Hilgard & Marquis (1935) and Hilgard & Campbell (1936) who gave massed reinforcement trials to dogs, monkeys, and men, using the eyelid CR. Half of the trials were given on one day, and the other half 24 hours later. They found that the CR was stronger on the first trial of the second day than it had been on the last trial of the first day. This result is understandable in terms of the accumulation of internal inhibition, which would depress the strength of the CR toward the end of a session of massed trials. The overnight rest would give plenty of time for the inhibition to dissipate and allow the CR to reveal its full strength.

Hovland (1936b) reasoned that inhibition developing during reinforced trials (which he called "inhibition of reinforcement") could account for a puzzling phenomenon sometimes encountered during the process of extinction, when the CR increases during the first few trials before beginning its expected decrease. He conditioned the galvanic skin response to a tone which preceded the Su of shock by only half a second. The human subjects were readily conditioned. The 24 conditioning trials were massed, coming once a minute, and the five extinction trials followed at the same interval and without any break, but one group of subjects had half-hour rests after the eighth and sixteenth conditioning trials. Since these rests would prevent much accumulation of inhibition, the extinction trials should go down from the start—as they did (Fig. 19-7). But Group B, not having had any rests, would begin the extinction series with considerable accumulated inhibition, which would then dissipate rapidly and allow the CR to increase for a few trials.

This inhibition of reinforcement (or during reinforcement) is a factor to bear in mind in the planning of a conditioning experiment. It explains the poor results sometimes obtained. For example, Schlosberg (1934) found that 200 pairings of buzz and shock, massed into a half-hour session, yielded very little conditioning in the white rat. Much better results were obtained in the same length of time if the rat were given only 20 trials. When the experimenter is trying to condition a quick response, like hand flexion, knee jerk, or eyelid closure, he is tempted to mass trials, for he can easily get in a large number of reinforcements by giving trials every 5 or 10 seconds. *Such massing of trials masses inhibition as well, and defeats its own end.*

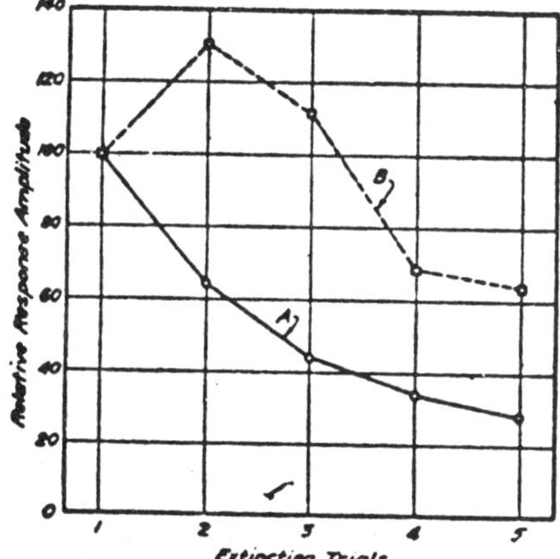

FIG. 19·7. (From Hovland, 1936b.) Extinction curves with and without an initial hump. There were 20 adult human subjects in each group, Group A having half-hour rests twice during the conditioning series which preceded these five extinction trials, and Group B having the 24 trials with no rests. The amplitude of the galvanic response in the first extinction trial of each group is taken as 100 percent, and the relative amplitude of the other trials is shown by the data points.

Slow extinction after intermittent reinforcement. An ultra-simple theory of reinforcement could go as follows: Each time the CR is reinforced, its strength is increased; and each time it occurs without reinforcement, its strength is diminished. Such a theory could be easily put to the test. Instead of giving reinforcement on every trial during the conditioning series, intersperse unreinforced trials, and finally proceed to an extinction series in which every trial goes unreinforced. Extinction should be very rapid, being indeed already partly accomplished by the preceding unreinforced trials.

In the bar-pressing task Skinner (1938) found it possible to maintain a high rate of response by giving reinforcement on only a part of the trials. If the rat, after being conditioned to press the bar and obtain a pellet, presses but obtains no pellet, he is likely to press again and again before giving up; and if after several unrewarded pressings he does obtain another pellet, he keeps up the pressing activity. After such intermittent reinforcement (either "periodic," with a pellet say once a minute; or in "fixed ratio," with a pellet after 50 pressings) an extinction series requires a great number of trials.

Skinner and his associates have been making an extensive investigation of the effects of various schedules of reinforcement on the rate of responding, the results to be published soon in book form. They have been using the pigeon, rather than the rat, and are able to obtain surprisingly high rates of responding with infrequent rewards; for example, with only one reinforcement every 10 minutes, the pigeon may peck 25 times per minute for the whole 10-minute interval (Skinner, 1953b). The response is usually a peck at a button or key—a "natural" response for the pigeon. See Ferster (1953) for details of technique.

Could a similar result be obtained in classical conditioning? Something of the sort could be predicted from the expectancy theory. In an eyelid-conditioning experiment, for example, with light as Sc and puff as Su, reinforcement on every trial would build up an unqualified positive expectancy "Light always followed by puff," and such an expectancy would suffer a sharp setback when reinforcements suddenly ceased at the beginning of an extinction series; expectancy would change and extinction should be rapid. Intermittent reinforcement would build up only a qualified expectancy, "Light sometimes followed by puff," there would be no sharp change at the beginning of the extinction series, and extinction should be delayed and gradual.

Humphreys (1939) tested these predictions, with results shown in Figure 19-8. The interspersed unreinforced trials slowed the acquisition of the CR very slightly, but the frequency level reached in 96 trials was nearly the same after 50 percent and 100 percent of reinforced trials. So the extinction series started from approximately the same level in both groups. But the first three extinction trials produced a sudden drop after 100-percent reinforcement, and no immediate drop at all after 50-percent reinforcement.

The same result—slow or delayed extinction after intermittent reinforcement—was obtained by the same author with the human GSR (Humphreys, 1940), and this "Humphreys effect" has later been verified by other experimenters and in several learning tasks such as the simple runway and T maze with rats. (See a review of pertinent results and theories, Jenkins & Stanley, 1950.)

Here, certainly, was a challenge to the reinforcement theorists, and they mobilized their resources to meet it. They invoked the principle of stimulus generalization (p. 577), and especially the generalization gradient. When the conditional stimulus is somewhat altered, the conditional response becomes less strong and certain. The complete stimulus (or cue) that elicits the conditional response includes more than the Sc applied by the experimenter. It includes persisting aftereffects left behind in the organism from the preceding trial. The puff, shock, food, or other Su received on one trial may leave behind residual stimuli (e.g., bits of food) which are elements in the total cue on the next trial. When every trial is reinforced, these residual elements remain constant during the conditioning series but change abruptly at the start of the extinction series. A sudden response decrement can be predicted. But after intermittent reinforcement the situation will be different. When Su has been omitted on one trial, its aftereffects are absent from the next trial, and if the subject responds to Sc on that trial (and often gets reinforcement), he becomes conditioned to a variable cue which does not change at the outset of the extinction series. Hence, no immediate response decrement can be predicted.

From this general analysis a more

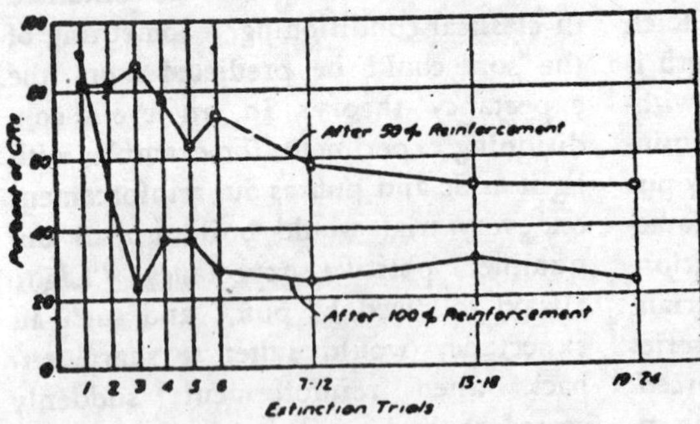

FIG. 19-8. (From Humphreys, 1939a.) Extinction of the conditioned eyelid response after always-given *vs.* intermittent reinforcement. Each group contained 22 students. The Sc—Su sequence was light-puff, with an interval of 400 ms between onset of light and puff. The interval between trials was 30 seconds, with a minute's rest after each 12 trials, and 48 trials on each of two successive days. The 100-percent group got the puff on every trial, the 50-percent group on only half the trials in shuffled arrangement. A third group, given blank trials (rests) in place of the unreinforced trials of the 50-percent group, gave the same results as the 100-percent group.

specific prediction was made by V. F. Sheffield (1949). If the conditioning trials are well spaced so as to allow the aftereffects of one trial to fade out before the following trial, it should make little difference in extinction whether reinforcement has been intermittent or consistent. Rats ran a 4-foot alley from starting box to food box, the total time taken being the response measure. Half of them had closely massed training trials, the other half had 15-minute intervals between trials. Half of each half got food on every trial, the other half only on 50 percent of the trials. Half of each quarter had massed and half spaced extinction trials. So various possible factors were balanced. The result was as predicted: the extinction curves were practically identical after 50-percent and 100-percent reinforcement when the conditioning trials had been well spaced; but 50-percent reinforcement gave the slower extinction when the conditioning trials had been massed.

A hypothesis cannot be proved, though it can perhaps be disproved. But if a hypothesis predicts previously unknown results, it shows some power and deserves some credit. The expectancy hypothesis deserves credit for predicting the Humphreys effect, and the fortified reinforcement hypothesis for predicting the differential effect of massed and spaced learning trials. The latter hypothesis could have predicted the Humphreys effect, and probably expectancy could have predicted the Sheffield results. Both hypotheses attempt to say what goes on in an organism confronted with sudden or gradual shifts from reinforcement to nonreinforcement. Quite possibly the S—R analysis is an analysis of expectancy. At least, it may point the way to experimental study of expectancy which is certainly a genuine factor in human behavior.

Very often a supposedly "crucial experiment" yields results that can be explained by two or more different theories. How then are we to make any progress? The history of science has furnished the answer: as we determine more and more facts and increasingly exact relationships among the facts, some theories reveal their inadequacy and give way to better ones. After all, the ultimate "truth" of a theory is less important to the experimentalist than its value in organizing known results and pointing the way to further experiments.

TIME RELATIONS

Simultaneous, Delayed, and Trace CR. Up to this point we have been concerned chiefly with "simultaneous CRs"—those obtained with Sc and Su given at approximately the same time. For example, a metronome is started, and food follows in a few seconds. It is also possible to establish a CR with a marked time lag between Sc and Su. Thus, if the metronome regularly starts one minute before the food, but overlaps the food in time, we have the "delayed CR." And if we present the metronome for one minute, turn it off for one minute, and then give food we call the result a "trace CR." The latter term conforms to the obvious fact that the subject must be responding to a trace left by Sc (metronome) in the nervous system, since the metronome is no longer sounding when the CR appears. The actual Sc must be some neural trace or reverberation of the metronome.

A delayed CR is harder to set up than a simultaneous one, and a trace CR is still more difficult to establish. To obtain a trace CR, accordingly, you may start with a simultaneous CR, convert it into a delayed CR, and finally into the desired trace CR.

Inhibition of delay. In well-established delayed and trace CRs, the response begins only shortly before Su is scheduled to come. For example, in one experiment Pavlov regularly presented food 180 seconds after the onset of Sc; salivation began about 30 seconds before the food arrived. Why this delay? Pavlov invoked internal inhibition; he assumed that Sc had two effects, arousing excitation in the nerve center and at the same time setting up an inhibitory state which held the excitation in check. As the time for Su approached, the inhibition waned and left excitation free to produce salivation. Needless to say, this explanation has not gone unchallenged by the protagonists of the interference theory of inhibition. Guthrie (1933) suggests that all conditioning is strictly simultaneous. He explains the delay by assuming that Sc initiates a posture or some continuing behavior in the animal. The metronome might make the dog look steadily at the food dish, and internal stimuli produced by this motor response would keep up the same response. These postural adjustments could change gradually during the interval of delay. When the food finally arrives, the resulting response becomes conditioned to the particular response-induced stimuli that are characteristic of the particular delay. Pavlov had actually observed a drowsy posture early in the delay period, succeeded by an alert posture as the time for food approached—perfect evidence, to his way of thinking, of central states of inhibition and excitation. He likened the drowsy posture to hypnosis or sleep; in fact he regarded the latter two states as due to widespread internal inhibition.

Disinhibition of the inhibition of delay. If Pavlov is right, it should be possible to disinhibit this internal inhibition by a sudden new stimulus, and so make the dog salivate long before the end of the delay period. In the example above, with the salivary response occurring regularly about 150 seconds after the metronome started to tick, an extra stimulus of light presented early in this period should cause an immediate secretion of saliva. The prediction was verified, and many similar instances were reported from Pavlov's laboratory. Rodnick showed the same thing in the case of the human psychogalvanic response, and supplied further evidence for the inhibition of delay by demonstrating spontaneous recovery after rest, resulting in a shortened latency of the delayed CR (Rodnick, 1937a, 1937b; Switzer, 1934).

These results are not inconsistent with an interference theory. Such a theory holds that disinhibition is simply interference exerted by the response to the extra stimulus on the postural response which was already interfering with the CR. In short, the extra stimulus breaks up the posture which was bridging the interval of delay. But some additional assumptions are required to explain why the CR happens at all, for it was presumably attached to the posture which is now broken up.

Short-interval time relations. When Pavlov considered time relations, he usually dealt with rather gross units of time, for salivation is a slow process. But the vast majority of American studies have been made on skeletal responses which are more appropriately measured in fractions of a second. Here the classifications proposed by Pavlov cause some trouble. For example, the leg movement of the knee-jerk reflex starts about 50 ms after the hammer hits the patellar tendon. To set up a simultaneous CR, one might try sounding a bell (Sc) at the same time that the hammer strikes the tendon (Su). Such timing yields very poor conditioning; it is much better to sound the bell about ⅓ of a second before the tendon tap (Schlosberg, 1928).

Once the question of optimal time relations was raised in connection with fast CRs, a long chain of investigations followed. One important early study was that of Wolfle (1930, 1932). She used a sound as Sc, a shock to the finger as Su, and the response was hand withdrawal. There were several groups of adult subjects, each with a different Sc—Su interval. For some groups the sound came as much as 3 seconds before the shock, while for others it came as much as 2 seconds *after* the shock. The results are shown in Figure 19-9. As will be seen, a forward interval of from ⅓ to ⅔ seconds was most favorable for conditioning.

Several interesting points are brought out by this study. Why, in the first place, should conditioning be so poor when the sound came a second or more before the shock? The explanation is probably to be sought in voluntary blocking of the hand withdrawal; with so long an interval, the subject could set himself not to pull the hand away until he actually got the shock. We shall discuss this matter of attitudinal control in a later section.

Backward conditioning. Wolfle found only a slight amount of conditioning when the sound came after the shock. Perhaps the surprising fact was that *any* occurred. From a functional point of view it makes no sense for the subject to withdraw his hand in response to a signal that comes after the shock. Pavlov asserted firmly that backward conditioning of the salivary reflex was impracticable, though later he retracted somewhat, admitting that an unstable and temporary backward CR could be obtained under certain conditions (1927, pp. 27, 393). Some American workers reported a slight amount of backward conditioning (Switzer, 1930, with the eyelid CR) while others reported essentially none (Bernstein, 1934, same CR).

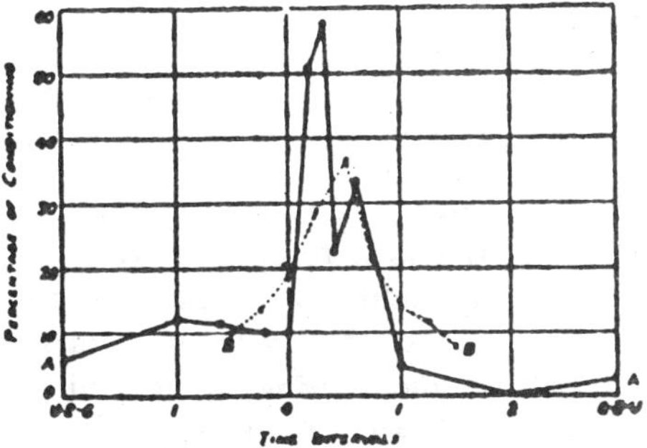

FIG. 19-9. (Wolfle, 1932.) Efficiency of conditioning hand withdrawal as a function of time relations of stimulation. The ordinate represents the percentages of test trials on which a CR was obtained. The base line shows the time relations between Sc and Su. To the right of the zero point, the auditory stimulus came before the shock; but to the left of zero, shock came first. The data represent two separate experiments. The differences between the two curves are probably largely due to chance.

This puzzling situation was much clarified by Spooner & Kellogg (1947) who repeated Wolfle's experiment but also recorded the latencies of the responses (Fig. 19-10). The latency of the normal forward CR was much greater than that of the backward one. The two were somehow radically different.

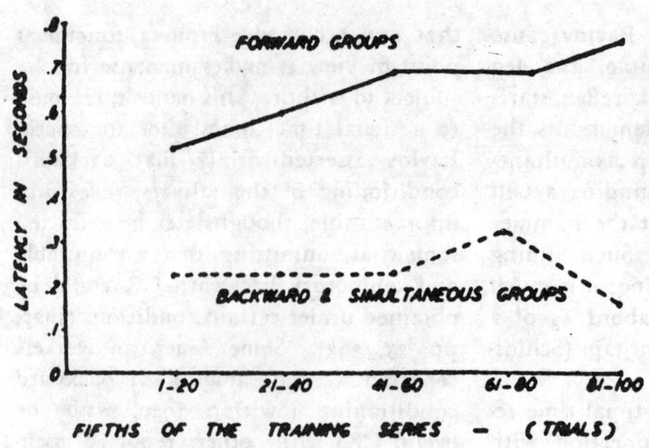

FIG. 19-10. (Spooner & Kellogg, 1947.) Mean latencies obtained in forward and backward conditioning. Six groups of ten college women served as subjects, the buzz (Sc) coming for the different groups before, after or simultaneously with the unavoidable shock (Su). There were 100 well-spaced trials, ⅕ of them being test trials in which the buzz alone was given. The latency of the conditioned response on these test trials was much greater for forward than for backward conditioning; and with forward conditioning the latency increased as the conditioning series progressed, the subject becoming conditioned to the buzz-shock internal of 0.5, 1.0, or 1.5 seconds. It was also found that the forward CR became progressively more frequent, while the backward CR tended more and more to drop out. The simultaneous buzz-shock combination gave essentially the same results as the shock-buzz or backward pairs with time intervals of 0.50 and 0.25 seconds.

Sensitization and pseudoconditioning. It was gradually recognized that any "backward conditioning" that appeared was not true conditioning and did not depend on the pairing of Sc and Su. What took place in the organism was "reflex sensitization." The shock or other noxious stimulus sensitized the appropriate protective reflexes so that any sudden stimulus would call them out. That is, the subject was all ready to pull his hand away, or to close his eyes, and a sudden sound tripped off the hair-trigger response. The tripping stimulus happened to be Sc—any other might have served as well. Reflex sensitization seems to account for any backward conditioning that has been found; and we can conclude that little if any conditioning occurs unless Sc comes a short time before Su.

A convincing example of sensitization is found in an experiment on goldfish by Sears (1934). The Sc was a light, the Su a shock. On testing the light before training he found it to cause the fish to swim excitedly. He adapted out this original response to light and then gave a series of isolated shocks—*not* paired with the light. The shocks "pepped up" the fish so that they again responded to the light, or even to a vibratory stimulus.

Wendt (1930) had encountered a more complicated example of sensitization in his experiment on the conditional knee jerk. He was tapping both patellar tendons at a ⅕-second interval, so that the tap at the left knee served as Sc for a conditional kick of the right leg. Under these conditions he obtained some typical CRs with a latency of 200–300 ms, but also some kicks of the right leg with a definitely shorter latency, 120–180 ms. From clinical literature, and from one of his own subjects, he found evidence of an (unconditional) crossed reflex with about that latency. He concluded that his training procedure tended to sensitize this normally inactive reflex.

Sensitization of a different kind—re

ceptor sensitization—came to light in a series of experiments on eyelid conditioning by Grant and his collaborators. As shown in Figure 19-11, there are two reflex responses to a sudden increase of illumination (here a much greater increase than in the experiment described with Fig. 19-5, p. 552). Both of these reflexes have a shorter latency than the "proper CRs." We can distinguish:

Short-latency reflex, with latency of 50–110 ms;
Medium-latency reflex, with latency of 120–240 ms;
Proper CRs, with latency of 250–450 ms.

The medium-latency or "Beta" responses are scarcely present when the retina is moderately light-adapted, but are numerous when it is dark-adapted. It was customary to count as eyelid CRs all responses with a latency of 120–450 ms; but since the experiments usually involved some progressive dark adaptation, the medium-latency "CRs" were probably unconditional reflexes. Continuing during an extinction series under dark adaptation, the Beta responses mask the extinction effect (Grant & Hake, 1951). (Speculatively, we may suggest that the short-latency reflex is elicited by stimulation of the cones in

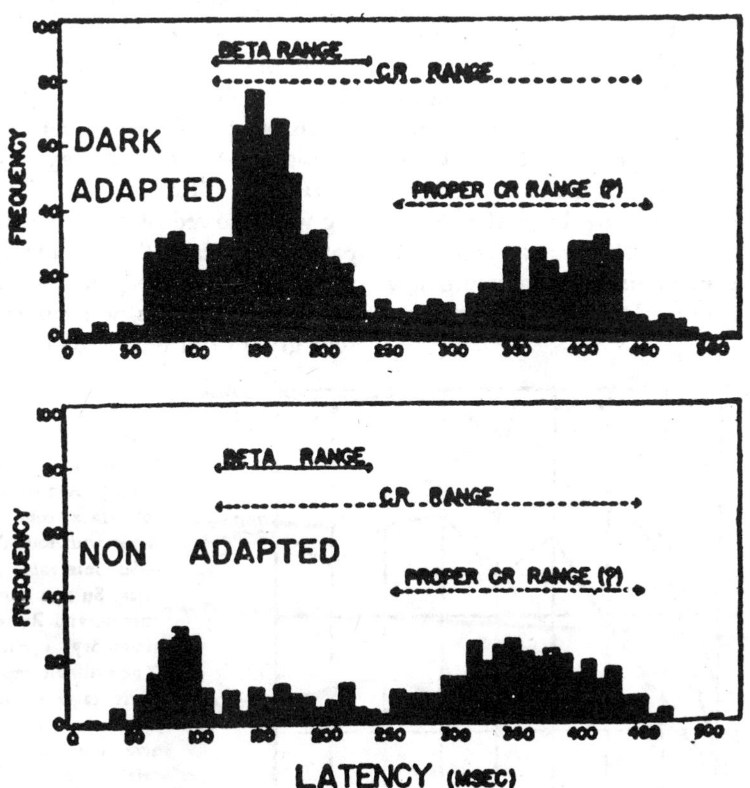

FIG. 19-11. (Grant & Norris, 1947.) Latency distributions of all eyelid responses evoked by a strong light during the course of a conditioning experiment on human subjects. The upper figure represents the results from dark-adapted subjects; the lower one, from light-adapted subjects. The Beta range represents a secondary response to light, often confused with the CR.

the fovea, while the medium-latency reflex is due to the rods outside the fovea, which undergo dark adaptation to a much greater degree than the cones—see pp. 368–370.)

The pseudoconditioning procedure consists in applying Su a number of times without Sc. This mode of sensitization had no demonstrable efficiency, compared with dark adaptation, in the eyelid experiments (Grant, Norris & Boissard, 1947). In other conditioning experiments, however, it has often been found that a strong stimulus may sensitize its natural response so that almost any other stimulus will trip off the same response. The circumspect experimenter will not only try out his Sc in advance, to make sure whether it already elicits the response he wishes to condition. He will at times run a control group by the pseudoconditioning procedure (Harriş, 1941; Wickens & Wickens, 1942). Much of the early work on conditioning may have been affected by different types of sensitization and should be re-examined to make sure how much genuine learning was demonstrated.

Conditioning of the eyeblink as a function of Sc—Su interval. Earlier we saw that the eyelid reflex has very little inertia and so is ideal for the study of temporal relationships among the stimuli and responses involved in conditioning. Hilgard (1936) employed this reflex in his pioneer study of such basic facts as the optimal Sc—Su interval, and the latencies of the various responses: Rc, Ru, and Rl (the original response to Sc, light). As the precise values of these temporal relationships became of theoretical importance, quite a little experimental effort was devoted to more detailed studies.

Reynolds (1945c) paired a click (Sc) with a puff of air to the cornea (Su), and recorded the response with the Dodge Pendulum Photochronograph. He divided his *Os* into groups of 10, each group being assigned to one of the following Sc—Su intervals: 250, 450, 1150, or 2250 ms. The progress of conditioning was followed by counting the anticipatory responses, that is, the CRs that appeared before the puffs. Figure 19-12 presents the acquisition curves for the four groups run under conditions of dis-

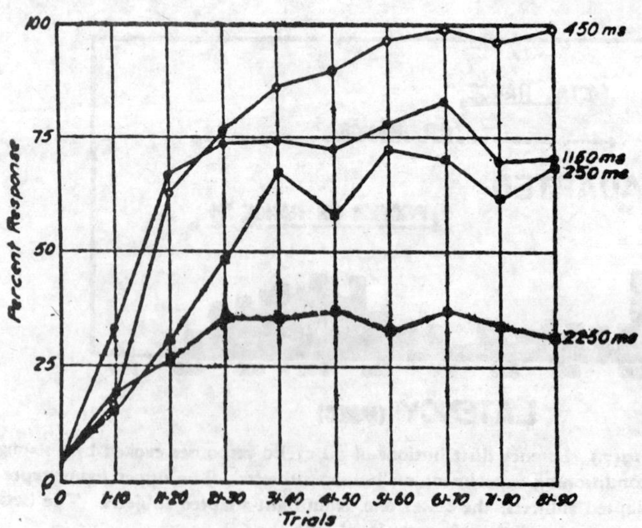

Fig. 19-12. (Reynolds, 1945c.) Acquisition curves for trace conditioned reflexes with four different Sc—Su intervals. Sc was a click, Su was a puff to the cornea, and Rc was the anticipatory eyelid closure. The ordinate represents the percentages of anticipatory closures recorded in successive sets of ten training trials.

tributed practice (there were also some groups run under massed practice, but they do not concern us here). Two things are quite clear: (1) there is no great difference in *rate* of acquisition, for all groups approach their final level in about 40 trials; and (2) there *is* a marked difference in *final level,* with conditioning clearly best in the 450-ms group.

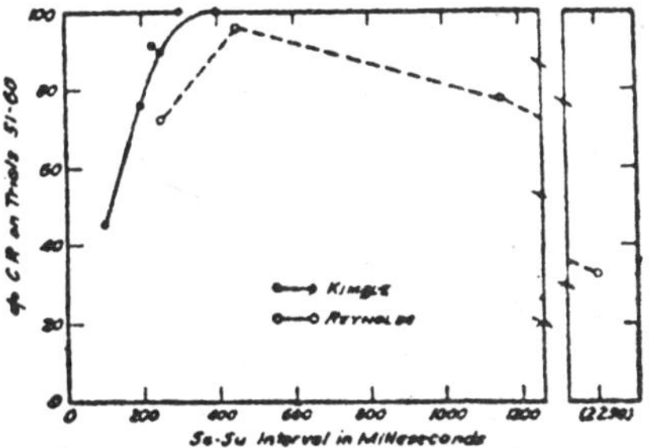

FIG. 19-13. Strength of conditioning as a function of interval of delay. Reynolds' (1945c) data are plotted as open circles, and Kimble's (1947) as solid circles. Although Reynolds used a *trace* CR to a click and Kimble used a *delayed* CR to a light, the data are reasonably comparable. The ordinate shows the percentage of trials on which the CR appeared; Reynolds used anticipatory responses during trials 51–60, but Kimble had to depend on a single test trial for each *O*, inserted somewhere between trials 51 and 60. (See text.) Note that the base line has been broken to get the 2,250 ms interval on the graph.

If we are interested in the final level, we can examine the results more readily in a different graph. The open circles in Figure 19-13 show the level reached on trials 51–60, as a function of interval of delay. If we had a few more points we would probably be able to construct a smooth curve, falling off either side of an optimum around a half second. But the Reynolds data are quite inadequate at the short end of the time continuum. In the first place, there is only one point below 450 ms. Further, dependence on anticipatory CRs is risky at short Sc—Su intervals, for many of the Rcs are undoubtedly obscured by the response to the puff. Kimble (1947) designed an experiment to correct these difficulties. The method was similar to that of Reynolds, except that Kimble (1) used short delay intervals, and (2) inserted test trials in which the puff was omitted. Kimble plotted acquisition curves like Reynolds', using anticipatory CRs, and compared them with curves based on test trials. There was not much difference between the two indices of conditioning for Kimble's 400-ms group, for this delay interval gave plenty of time for the CR to "beat the puff." But for the shorter intervals it was clear that unreinforced test trials gave the better index. Hence the best estimate we can make of the final level of conditioning for each time group is the percentage of *O*s who gave CRs on the last test trial. These percentages are added to Figure 19-13 as solid circles. The curve sketched in probably represents the time function better than do the points, for each point is based on only 10–13 *O*s. Although the 300- and 400-ms groups look alike, that is because they have hit the ceiling of 100 percent; the 400-ms group stood up a little better during an extinction session.

The Reynolds-Kimble data give us the best picture we have to date of the function which relates Sc—Su interval to strength of conditioning. This function is of importance for theory. For example, Hull (1943) holds that it represents the rate of waxing and waning of the "stimulus trace" in the neural centers. If this view is true, the optimal Sc—Su interval would depend on the speed of the receptor system rather than on that of the reflex response. The fast-acting receptor systems of vision, audition and touch should have about the same optimum Sc—Su interval, but the slower-acting senses like smell and taste should have a longer one (p. 16). On the other hand, it should make no difference in the optimum interval whether the CR were based on the fast lid reflex or on the slow PGR. The data on fast reflexes—eyelid, knee jerk, hand withdrawal—were available in at least approximate form when Hilgard & Marquis (1940) emphasized the need for comparable data on a slow reflex. Yet it took over a decade for anyone to get around to this simple job. White & Schlosberg (1952) conditioned PGR to a light, using several groups of human subjects, each group with a different Sc—Su interval. The resulting curve is so much like the Kimble-Reynolds one of Figure 19-13 that close inspection would be required to tell them apart. It seems clear that the time interval between the two stimuli, Sc and Su, is important in classical conditioning, whereas the stimulus-response interval, Su—Ru, as measured at the periphery, is of relatively small importance. We have here another bit of evidence for the stimulus-association or expectancy theory of classical conditioning.

ATTITUDINAL AND "VOLITIONAL" FACTORS

When Watson (1916) adopted the new and objective CR as a foundation for behaviorism, he thought he had gotten rid of the vexatious problem of volition, along with the other difficulties that went with introspection as a basic method. But as so often happens, he did not get rid of the problem by denying its existence. Man has much in common with the other members of the animal kingdom, but he also possesses something that no other animal has—a highly developed language. One does not need to make any metaphysical assumptions about the workings of this mechanism, for one can observe it in action. Every time *E* tells *O* what to do, whether it be to sit in a chair, or to press a key when he sees a light, or to hold his hand on an electrode which will deliver a shock, *E* is determining *O*'s behavior. In most experimental situations the instructions are explicit, and leave little to *O*'s interpretation. But in the typical CR situation they are usually left vague with respect to the responses involved. In the hand withdrawal, for example, *E* is careful *not* to tell *O* to pull the hand away (Rc) in response to the bell (Sc), for then it would simply be a reaction time experiment. Undoubtedly some misguided *Es* have told their *Os* *not* to pull the hand away before the shock (Su) and have hoped to establish a CR strong enough to break through the instructions and all the complex processes that the instructions have set up. If no specific instructions are given, *O* will make some up for himself—he will try to guess what he is supposed to do. He is apt to instruct himself to keep his hand on the electrode unless it should come off in spite of him. He holds it there until the shock forces it off, and may persist in this behavior for hundreds of trials, thinking it would show "weakness" to pull the hand away!

Is the conditional hand withdrawal voluntary? This question was first raised by Hamel (1919) who answered it in the affirmative, basing his conclusion partly on the introspections of his subjects, but chiefly on the latency of the CR. He found CR latency about the same as that of a similar voluntary hand movement, and approximately twice that of the reflex response to the shock. This long latency of the CR has been often verified in other responses. But we cannot argue that two processes have the same mechanism merely on the ground that they take the same amount of time. There can be little question that activity of the cerebral cortex is involved in both the conditional hand withdrawal and the voluntary hand movement of the reaction time experiment; and the same sense-organ and muscle latencies are included in both CR and RT. So there is good reason for expecting similar total latencies, without assuming identical mechanisms.

The question whether or not a given response is voluntary is beset by many complexities, as pointed out by Peak (1933). Unfortunately, she found no simple answer that would work in all cases. Responses that are called voluntary may be distinguished from those called reflex by one or more of the following: (1) descriptive characteristics, as form, latency; (2) their determinants, as stimulus intensity, previous instructions; (3) their functional relationships to the determinants. When you try to apply these determinants to the conditional hand withdrawal, you soon become convinced that this CR is not clearly either voluntary or involuntary. It has the latency typical of voluntary responses, but is not set up by (explicit) instructions. Indeed, the subject often cannot inhibit the CR if he is told to attempt to do so. (See Hilgard & Marquis, 1940, pp. 260–273.) Of one thing we can be certain: the CR is not voluntary in the usual sense of "deliberate." On the contrary, it often functions in direct opposition to the wishes of the subject.

Attitudinal factors in conditioning. From this discussion it is apparent that the attitude of the subject must be a very important factor in human CR experiments. There are several ways to control this factor. The most obvious, perhaps, is to make the subject engage in other activity, as reading while the knee jerk is being conditioned (Schlosberg, 1928). This is a bit like trying to condition a leg flexion in dogs while the animal is eating; it certainly does not give Sc or Su very favorable soil on which to work. Another method is to use subjects in whom the voluntary controls are not operative. This can be done with the hand-withdrawal CR by using children, who presumably have less ability to restrain the hand withdrawal. Osipova (see Razran, 1933) studied the rate of formation of this CR in 327 normal and subnormal school children, aged 7–19. Subnormal children, and those under 14 formed the CR more rapidly than did the older ones. There is a need to study hand withdrawal at earlier ages, when the child is just beginning to acquire language.

The salivary CR. One might think of still another way of controlling the attitudinal factor; use a response that isn't under voluntary control. A large number of such responses come to mind. The eyelid reflex and the knee jerk are partially free from such control, while the psychogalvanic response and salivary secretion seem to be completely involuntary. But peculiarly enough, it is the latter response which has given us some of the best evidence for the effects of attitudes on the formation of the CR.

Perhaps the earliest attempt to study this CR in man was made by Lashley (1916a, b). He developed a suction cup that clung to the inside of the cheek and collected saliva. He soon gave up, after finding that the CR was too unstable—the subject "saw through" the experiment too readily. Krasnagorski, as well as Lenz (Razran, 1933) used a similar method with some success, perhaps because of better control of stimulating conditions. In 1935 Razran reported a new and simple method of recording the salivary response in human subjects. He used small dental cotton rolls placed under the tongue to absorb the saliva. By weighing the rolls before and after they had been in the mouth for one minute, he could readily determine how much saliva had been absorbed. Several subjects could be run at one time, for the rolls were kept in individual waterproof envelopes until *E* had time to weigh them. Of course, the rolls themselves stimulated some flow of saliva so that it was necessary to correct the experimental data by subtracting the "resting" level of secretion.

In his first major study with this method, Razran (1935) used 37 subjects, for a total of over 800 experimental hours. The conditional stimuli were metronome, nonsense syllables, words, and digits; the unconditional stimuli (in decreasing order of effectiveness) were eating pretzels, watching someone eat pretzels, sucking a mint, thinking of steak, or of pretzels. But neither conditioning nor extinction proceeded in a regular fashion. One subject might develop a CR in a few trials, another none, while a third person might actually decrease his resting level of secretion in the presence of Sc. Razran assumed that these differences among subjects were due to their attitudes, which had not been rigidly determined by instructions. So he tried giving subjects positive and negative instructions at different times. For example, if he told them to try to associate the nonsense syllable with eating pretzels, he usually got positive results, but if he told them to *avoid* forming the association, zero or negative conditioning was apt to result. Razran explained his results by assuming that a CR in adult subjects is dependent on two factors: (1) a quantitative physiological factor, depending on the number of repetitions and "linkage strength" of the two stimuli, and (2) a psychological, qualitative, "yes-no" factor. The first factor is the one that operates in animals, and is the one to which the laws of conditioning apply directly. The second factor develops in the child around the age of three to five and obscures the functioning of the first factor. The past experience of *O*, through language symbols, builds up a "choosing and rejecting system." The ultimate explanation of this system may be in terms of principles like those of conditioning, but at the descriptive level it has quite different laws.

Not content with the mere demonstration of the importance of attitudes, Razran (1939) developed a simple technique for controlling them. He presented a series of Sc during a long eating period, having misinformed the subjects as to the purpose of the experiment. For example, he gave 40 flashes of colored lights (Sc) during a 2-minute period of eating pretzels (Su), having told his subjects that he was trying to "find out the effects of eye fatigue on digestion." With this technique, none of many subjects, during several hundred total hours of experimentation, gave any sign of thinking he was expected to secrete saliva in response to Sc. As a result, the data show striking confirmation of Pavlov's main behavioral findings in acquisition, extinction, spontaneous recovery, generalization, etc.

The nature of voluntary control. In considering these results, one is immediately faced with the question as to how attitudes can control a response like salivary secretion, which is involuntary. In its main outlines, the answer is clear; you cannot control salivary secretion directly, but you can do so in an indirect fashion. If you wish to stimulate the flow of saliva, you have but to think of a nice, juicy steak. When you "think" of a steak, you are undoubtedly setting up central processes—and perhaps even peripheral ones, like subvocal speech—that have been associated with steak in the past. These symbolic processes are presumably stimulus-released, like any others—perhaps by verbal stimuli, administered by *E* or by the subject himself. What Razran's subjects were controlling by their attitudes was the formation of associations between Sc (a light, for example) and Su (the salty taste of pretzels).

The attitudinal factor that Razran demonstrated so clearly probably complicates all studies of the CR in man.

Consider the psychogalvanic reflex (GSR)—not only is it involuntary, but most people do not even know they have one! Yet the psychogalvanic CR will often drop out entirely if *E* merely says "O K, no more shocks (Su). I just want to try the light (Sc) a few more times." If the subject really believes *E* and ceases to expect a shock after the light, the response conditioned to the light drops out almost immediately (Cook & Harris, 1937; Mowrer, 1938).

Attitudinal factors in the eyelid CR. Humphreys (1943a) reported the intercorrelations between various measures of the strength of the conditional and unconditional eyelid response during acquisition and extinction. When he subjected these intercorrelations to factor analysis, he found evidence for two factors, like those of Razran. The physiological factor is related to the magnitudes of the response to puff and of the original response to light, and to both acquisition and extinction amplitudes of Rc. The attitudinal factor is related to acquisition and extinction latency, and to extinction frequency.

A statistical analysis like this one starts with experimental results and attempts to trace back their variation to the factors which caused them—in this case, to random variations from subject to subject in physiological and attitudinal factors. In some ways it is more convincing to reverse the process, vary the attitudes, and see what happens. J. Miller (1939) did this. He ran six groups of 20–25 subjects with instructions ranging from (1) "Be sure you do not wink or start to wink before you have felt the puff" to (6) "In case you feel your eyes closing or starting to close, do nothing to prevent it." The inhibitory instructions (1) yielded Rc on 26 percent of the trials, while the facilitatory instructions (6) led to a frequency of 71 percent. Intermediate instructions gave intermediate results. Comparable results were obtained by Hilgard & Humphreys (1938a), and by Norris & Grant (1948).

In the light of all these studies, there can be little doubt that attitude is a very important factor in human conditioning. Does this mean that one can find out little about the basic laws of conditioning by human experiments? If this were true, much that we have written in this chapter might be discarded. For example, the best material on the relationship between length of the delay period (Sc—Su interval) and strength of the CR came from experiments with the human eyelid. Fortunately we have comparative data on this CR from other species. The results on the rat (Hughes & Schlosberg, 1938), the dog (Hilgard & Marquis, 1935), monkeys (Hilgard & Marquis, 1936), and man (Hilgard & Campbell, 1936) show some interspecies differences, but the differences are less striking than the similarities. Apparently a process like conditioning the eyelid must be a deep-seated one, common over a wide range of animals. In man, attitudinal factors may retard the operation of the basic process, but these factors can be controlled well enough by instructions to keep them from obscuring the basic process.

The acquisition of voluntary control. Previously we pointed out that involuntary responses, like salivation and psychogalvanic responses, can be controlled indirectly by arousing symbolic processes that are associated with their stimuli. Hudgins (1933) utilized this method to teach his subjects to contract (or dilate) the pupil on command, or even "at will." He first conditioned the pupillary contraction to the sound of a bell (Sc), using an increase in light as Su. This took 125–225 trials. Then the subject was instructed to squeeze a hand dynamometer and say "Contract" on *E*'s command "Contract." The dynamometer was wired to turn on the bell and light as the hand pressure increased. After another 200 trials it was possible to omit hand response, bell, and light, and still get pupillary contraction in response to *E*'s command "Contract." Eventually it was found that some subjects could produce pupillary contraction by saying "Contract" in a whisper, or even subvocally. Hunter & Hudgins (1934) pointed out that this response was "voluntary" by any reasonable definition of the word. Incidentally, the response showed no evidence of extinction, even though it was elicited repeatedly without reinforcement by the original light (Su).

It is unfortunate that this neat experiment has not been successful in the hands of others. Steckle & Renshaw (1934) and Steckle (1936) failed to obtain Hudgins' results. Hudgins (1935) pointed out some of the inadequacies in their method. As we have emphasized earlier (p. 179) the pupillary response is a difficult one with which to work.

GENERALIZATION AND DISCRIMINATION

A CR in process of establishment usually shows marked spread, or *generalization*, on both the stimulus and response side. For example, Liddell, James & Anderson (1934) conditioned foreleg flexion, based on shock, to the sound of a metronome in sheep. In the early stages of conditioning, almost any sound would trip off the response. Further, the response was diffuse and widespread, rather than concentrated in the foreleg. It was only after considerable conditioning that the sheep developed a precise foreleg flexion as a response fairly specific to the metronome. A great deal of research has been devoted to sensory generalization; let us clear up the relatively neglected response generalization first (p. 676).

Response generalization. The diffuse, widespread response during early stages of conditioning is found in other animals than the sheep. Schlosberg (1934, 1936) reported that the CR based on foreleg shock in the rat consisted of a fairly generalized struggle, speeded breathing, and squeal. As a matter of fact, the rats rarely developed to the stage of a precise lifting of the foreleg. Culler & Mettler (1934) found that dogs start out in a similar fashion, but the response gradually becomes localized to the shocked limb, as in the sheep. It is not always necessary to pass through the first stage of diffuse responses; some dogs limit the response to the shocked leg from the first (Wolf & Kellogg, 1940). The difference probably depends on the level of excitement of the dog. If the dog is frightened, or if the shock is strong, he is thrown into violent activity by the shock, and consequently by its associated stimulus, the buzz (Sc). The cerebral cortex undoubtedly plays a major role in making the responses more precise; a dog whose cortex has been removed never gets beyond the stage of diffuse conditioning (Culler & Mettler, 1934).

It will be noted that these experiments all utilized shock as Su. One is less apt to obtain—or to notice—such response generalization when dealing with other classical CR situations, like the eyelid or salivary, where the response is limited to a single member. But a similar phenomenon probably shows up in various operant situations. As a matter of fact, one of the most notable aspects of trial-and-error learning is the elimination of superfluous responses. Anyone who has watched a rat in a Skinner box has been exasperated by the fact that the rat does everything possible except pressing the lever the first time it is placed in the box. But on later trials, the rat gets down to business promptly, and presses the lever without superfluous activity. Whether or not the same mechanisms are responsible for the early diffuse activity and its elimination in both classical and operant conditioning, the parallels are interesting.

Sensory generalization. Hovland (1937a) introduced a neat way of measuring the amount of sensory generalization as a function of distances within a sense modality. The Sc was a tone, and the unconditional reflex was the GSR. Shock was paired with a tone of 1,937 cycles until a good CR had been established. Then *E* tested for generalization by presenting other tones (1,000, 468, and 153 cycles) spaced by successive steps of 25 j.n.d.'s (just noticeable differences, p. 235) from the original Sc. The height of the generalized GSR could thus be stated as a function of psychologically equal steps along the pitch continuum. The resulting gradient can be seen in the Mean GSR obtained from 20 *Os*:

18.3 mm when the original tone was sounded;
14.9 mm when the tone 25 j.n.d. away was sounded;
13.6 mm when the tone 50 j.n.d. away was sounded;
12.9 mm when the tone 75 j.n.d. away was sounded.

The gradient is far from steep in view of the wide range of pitch tested. There is a suggestion of negative acceleration, since the first step away from the original stimulus gives the largest drop in the GSR.

The experiment was actually more complex than noted above. All four tones were equated for loudness, to avoid any possible influence from this variable. Further, Hovland trained half his subjects on the lowest pitch, rather than the highest, and averaged his results in terms of steps-removed-from-Sc, just in case the higher (or lower) tone happened to be the more effective stimulus.

Since the exact shape of the generalization gradient became an issue of considerable theoretical importance in building theories of discrimination (Spence, 1937, Razran, 1938), Humphreys (1939) decided to test the function within the first 25 j.n.d. step. He chose the upper two of Hovland's frequencies, 1967 and 1,000 cycles, representing a 25 j.n.d. step, and interpolated two more, 1,718 and 1,311, representing 5 and 15 j.n.d. steps, respectively. The obtained generalization gradient seemed negatively accelerated; in fact, most of the drop came in the first step of five j.n.d.'s. This group had been trained with 100-percent reinforcement; what would happen if he used 50-percent reinforcement, which is probably more like what happens in a typical choice or discrimination session? Humphreys tried such a group, and found almost complete generalization, a "flat gradient." Obviously the form of the generalization gradient is dependent on the method of training. It also depends on the steps used in scaling the dimension, as shown by the fact that there was significantly greater generalization to the octave (984 cycles) below the Sc (1,967 cycles) than to a slightly closer frequency (1,000 cycles). This result suggests that if the interval chosen for testing the gradient is a familiar musical interval, there may be differences in the shape of the gradient. In view of these complications, Humphreys urges caution in accepting the negatively accelerated gradient as a final one.

The greater generalization over the octave than to intermediate points is not limited to a musically trained subject; Blackwell and Schlosberg (1943) found it in rats. Apparently it is based on some fundamental neural mechanism. Hence pitch is not a good dimension to use if we wish to find the basic form of generalization gradient. Hovland (1937b) tried the loudness continuum, using steps spaced by 50 j.n.d.'s, and found a very slightly concave gradient. But when the scale was adjusted to sones (p. 239) which constitute a more defensible measure of equal psychological units, his curve shows a slight suggestion of positive acceleration. As we have already indicated, it is necessary to correct the obtained values for the effect of the loudness of the test tones on the amplitude of Rc, before we can measure the strength of the generalized CR. This makes loudness a difficult continuum to use.

Visual generalization. Schlosberg and Solomon (1943, our p. 34) trained rats to jump to a white card in a 2-door Lashley jumping stand, always using a black card as the negative one. The training was so gradual that the rats never jumped to the black card, a procedure which avoided the complications that result from punished wrong responses. After the latency of the response had reached a minimum in the training series, rats were tested with light-gray, mid-gray, and dark-gray cards. These cards had been chosen by human subjects, who picked a mid-gray that appeared halfway between white and black, and then bisected the intervals to obtain the light gray and dark gray. They thus represented equal steps along a psychological continuum for human subjects. The steps seemed to be equal for the rats, too. When these intervals are plotted along a base line, and the log latency of the jump to each card is plotted on the ordinate (Fig. 19-14) a straight-line gradient (unbroken line) appears. Schlosberg and Solomon argue that the primary generalization gradient should be linear, if appropriate units are used for both ordinate and abscissa. The question as to what constitutes proper units is, of course, the major question. But it seems clear that the primary generalization gradient is nothing more than another name for "similarity," and that measures of similarity should be linearly related to each other if they are measuring the same thing.

A distinction must be made between a primary generalization gradient, and the one which may appear if reinforcement or extinction is given at more than one point on the primary continuum which constitutes our base line. The heavy line in Figure 19-14 resulted from regular reinforcement of the white card, when paired with the black—that is, reinforcement at one end of the continuum, and nonreinforcement at the other. It is thus a primary generalization gradient. But after this had been obtained, the rats were given further training, contrasting light gray with dark gray. This differential reinforcement strengthened the response to LG, and weakened that to DG, resulting in an S-shaped gradient when the whole range was considered (no tests were made with DG *vs.* B, for technical reasons). By such differen-

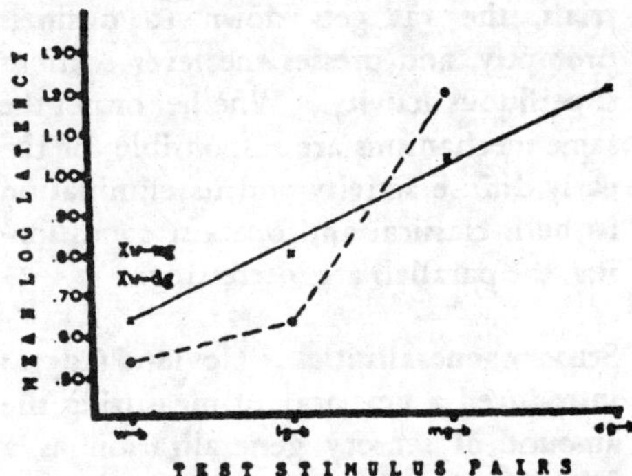

FIG. 19-14. The probable shape of the generalization gradient, in terms of mean log latency. The stimulus pairs (indicated on the base line) were chosen so that light gray, middle gray and dark gray mark off equal-appearing intervals along the white-black continuum. The solid line represents the probable form of the primary generalization gradient since the rats were trained on W—B. The two additional points above W—B represent values for white—dark-gray and white—middle-gray, respectively. The broken line shows the influence of additional training on LG—DG.

tial reinforcement, one can probably erect a large assortment of secondary gradients. You may think of the primary gradient as a slightly flexible strip of metal; if you raise one end (by reinforcement) the strip may or may not sag a bit in the middle. But it can be bent if you push up at some points, and down at others (differential reinforcement).

The upshot of this discussion is that the form of the generalization gradient depends on the units used to measure both base line and ordinate, and on the method of reinforcement and testing. It is certainly rash to conclude that the gradient resembles a negative growth function if the base line is expressed in units of j.n.d.'s, as by Hull (1943, p. 185).

Spatial generalization on the skin. Pavlov explained generalization in terms of a wave-like "irradiation" of excitation, originating at a point in the cortex corresponding to Sc, and spreading to neighboring points. Inhibition showed similar irradiation and served to delimit the spread of excitation when a discrimination was being established. Perhaps the best place to test this theory would be the skin, for it is known that the skin surface is represented on the cerebral cortex in a spatial pattern that resembles a rough and distorted map. Experiments on dogs (Pavlov, 1927, p. 152ff; Anrep, 1923) seemed to bear out this theory, for they found indications of such waves spreading over the skin surface as they tested for generalization. These experiments were seriously criticized by Loucks (1933) on several grounds; perhaps the most serious was the failure to report all the data.

Bass and Hull (1934) carried out an experiment very similar to the Anrep study. They arranged a row of four vibrotactile stimulators spaced at 16-inch intervals along the back and leg of human subjects. The stimulator at one end of the row was paired repeatedly with a shock to the hand, to set up a conditional GSR. *E* then tested the response to each of these stimulators 32 times, continuing to reinforce the original Sc, but not the others. This method of differential reinforcement extinguishes the CR to the generalized stimuli, while maintaining the original CR. The Mean CR was 5.74 to the positive stimulus but progressively less to the generalized stimuli, being 5.63, 4.75, and 3.36, respectively—all measured in mm deflection of the galvanometer. This is a fairly steep gradient, but it must be remembered that the method of differential reinforcement had been used. This experiment does not prove irradiation, the wavelike spreading assumed by Pavlov, for no effort was made to study the temporal characteristics of the development of generalization (Loucks, 1937).

A further test of the irradiation hypothesis was carried out by Grant and Dittmer (1940). In one group of subjects they attached the vibrotactile stimulators 3½–4 inches apart on the back. In the other group, the stimulators were arranged an inch apart from the fingertip to the wrist. Now it is well-established that the cortical areas serving the skin surface of the hand are much more spread out than those serving the back. Hence if irradiation took place over the cortex in a strictly spatial fashion, the generalization gradient should be much sharper for the hand than for the back. But when they measured both gradients, much as Bass and Hull had done, they found that the two gradients were about equally steep. As further evidence against Pavlov's irradiation hypothesis, Grant and Dittmer point out that the Bass & Hull data are not consistent with the way in which leg and back areas are arranged in the cerebral cortex. In short, generalization gradients may be demonstrated, but they are not consistent with Pavlov's view that they reflect distances between corresponding cortical points. Instead, they are more nearly consistent with the subject's idea of where his various skin areas are located in space.

A criticism of the concept of generalization. Generalization gradients play a very important part in many theories of behavior. This is particularly true of Hull's attempt (1943) to write such a theory in quantitative terms. Lashley & Wade (1946) seriously threatened this whole structure when they challenged just about everything that had been written about CR generalization. Hull (1947) replied to Lashley & Wade, but did not come to grips with some of their objections. Some of the Lashley-Wade criticisms are probably well-founded, but the truth probably lies between the two extreme positions. Unfortunately, the truth about stimulus generalization will undoubtedly turn out to be complex. Razran (1949) after reviewing the literature, including a lot of Russian studies as well as the more familiar ones, ends up with the belief that there is much pseudogeneralization (cf. pseudoconditioning, pp. 568–570) but that there is also some true generalization. The latter is a rough affair, following a crude and qualitative gradient with only a few steps.

Semantic generalization. If a response is conditioned to one word, will it generalize to words that are similar? Is the dimension of similarity to be defined in physical terms, or in meaning of the words? One experiment may be described here to illustrate the method. Riess (1946) conditioned the GSR, with a buzzer as Su, to five simple words, scattered in a list of visually presented neutral words. After conditioning, he used new lists; scattered in these lists were homo-

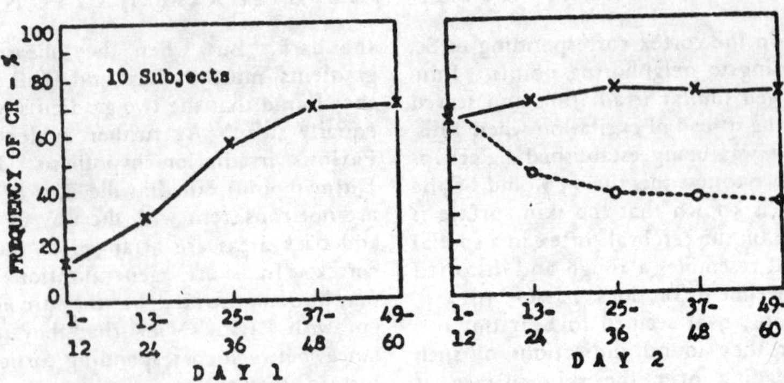

FIG. 19-15. (Hilgard, Campbell & Sears, 1938.) Conditioned responses followed by differentiation.

phones, antonyms, and synonyms of the original Sc. Thus, if the original word combined with the buzzer was WON, the corresponding test words would be *ONE*, LOST, and BEAT. The extent of generalization to these words would be measured by the net gain (postconditioning minus preconditioning) in amplitude of response, compared with the net gain of the words which had been accompanied with the buzzer during conditioning. Riess used four different age groups, and made all of them think they were learning the word lists; he explained the buzzer as a signal, and the GSR apparatus as a method of measuring their sweat reaction to the warm room.

The results show an interesting change with age. The youngest group, mean age 7¾, showed greatest generalization to the homophone, followed by the antonym and the synonym. For the next group, age 10.7, the antonym stood higher than the homophone or the synonym. But with the two oldest groups, 14 and 18½, respectively, the synonym took first place, followed by the antonym and homophone. It would be interesting to compare these results with data on similar groups in the association experiment.

Patterning of conditional stimuli. In an experiment like that of Riess, the subjects are obviously responding to a pattern of stimuli, rather than to the single components that make up the words. One of the early experiments on patterning was done by Humphrey (1928) who showed that a tone which had become Sc for finger withdrawal did not produce the response when presented as part of a melody. In spite of the importance of this problem for behavior theory, there was little further work in America for almost a decade. Then Razran started a program which resulted in seven papers (see Hilgard & Marquis, 1940, for references). He used his salivary conditioning technique, with patterns of form, color, and tone as Sc. He found he could establish a CR to a pattern even though the component parts of the pattern were relatively ineffective. These pattern CRs were more resistant to extinction than simple ones, were retained better, and generalized freely. He made some interesting observations about the relationship between "good" and "poor" patterns as determined by the CR technique—they did not always agree with the Gestalt principles (p. 408).

Discrimination. Discrimination is, in a sense, the reverse of generalization; the less the response to one stimulus generalizes to a similar one, the better the discrimination between the two stimuli. Optimum discrimination is established by differential reinforcement. This process is well illustrated in an experiment by Hilgard, Campbell & Sears (1938). In Figure 19-15 the left-hand graph represents the development of an eyelid CR to a light in one window, always reinforced by a puff of air. On the second day the light might appear in either of two windows; if it came in the old one it was followed by a puff, but if in the new window, there was no reinforcement. The right-hand figure shows how the discrimination developed. Continued reinforcement maintained the response to the original Sc, while failure to reinforce extinguished the generalized CR. This experiment will illustrate the method; to cover the topic of discrimination, we need the entire next chapter.

SUMMARY

The classical CR experiment would seem to be one in which the experimenter maintains control of three major independent variables (Sc, Su, and thus Ru) and studies the resulting changes in the dependent variable (Rc). In instrumental conditioning, *E* generally relinquishes control of Sc, and he makes Su dependent on the appearance of Rc. In avoidance conditioning, the situation is still more complex, for there may well be a combination of the two previous types. We are not certain whether or not the same fundamental mechanism of reinforcement is involved in the various types of conditioning. However, there are a large number of phenomena that show up in all types of conditioning, being relatively independent of the method of reinforcement, the stimuli, and responses employed, or even the animal species used as subject. Prominent among these phenomena are Reinforcement, Extinction, Disinhibition, Generalization, and Discrimination. Measures of Response Strength common to all types are Latency, Amplitude, Frequency of Occurrence, and Resistance to Extinction.

It is possible to write equations for many of these phenomena, expressing the dependent variable, Rc, as a function of the past and present stimulation by Sc and Su. These equations are often written to include intervening (usually *O*-) variables as strength of CR (sometimes written $_{S}H_{R}$), Drive, Stimulus Trace, and even Attitudes. Other intervening variables or constructs may be used, such as Kinesthetic Stimuli, Anxiety, or Expectation. Some of these constructs are open to possible direct observation, while others are not. Until we settle upon a really adequate set of variables, either observed or inferred, the equations we write will merely be descriptive, often under very limited experimental conditions. Until that time the CR experiment will continue to be a fruitful source of hypotheses as well as data. Further, in the chapters on receptive processes (p. 348) we have found the CR method a handy one for determining the sensory capacities of animals.

Some of the early critics of the CR maintained that it was too simple to deserve a place in psychology. The many psychologists who have studied the topic during the last quarter century are more apt to complain that it is too complex for their purpose—the discovery of the basic laws of behavior. Perhaps we must eventually find a still simpler technique, or look for the basic laws in an animal more primitive than the white rat. Physics is sometimes traced back to Galileo's observations of a simple pendulum!

20

DISCRIMINATION LEARNING

One of the standard experiments in animal psychology requires the subject to choose between two doors or two alleys opening out of a small chamber and leading, the one to some reward such as food, the other to no reward and perhaps to punishment. If the positive door or alley were always the one on the right, or always the one on the left, the problem would be easy for the animal, as in a very simple maze. But in the present experiment the positive door or alley, being sometimes on the right and sometimes on the left, is marked with some sign or cue, which the animal must learn to follow to the food pan. The negative door or alley is blank or else marked with some different cue. If the cues are white and black cards affixed to the doors or alley walls, the white being positive and shifted frequently from side to side, the problem is surprisingly difficult for a rat. Many trials may be required to get him to follow the positive cue regularly.

Purpose of the experiment. This experiment was originally designed for testing the senses of animals. Take an animal that has learned to choose the white door or alley regularly, substitute light gray and dark gray for the white and black, and see whether he chooses the light gray or quickly learns to do so. Bring the grays closer and closer together in brightness until you reach the animal's limit of light-dark discrimination. The experiment is obviously one in animal psychophysics. But before it can serve that purpose, the animal must learn to follow the positive cue.

A human subject in the comparable psychophysical experiment is instructed

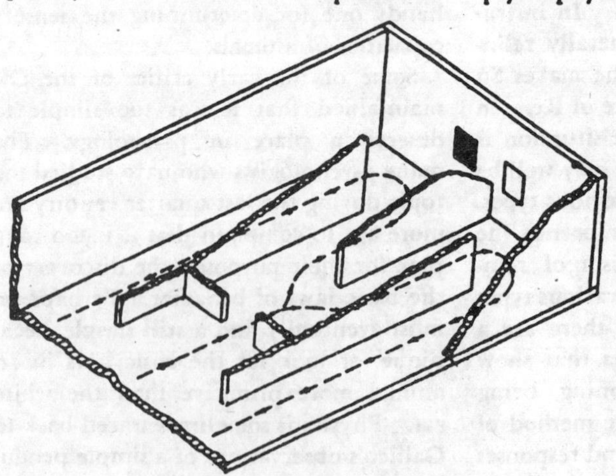

FIG. 20-1. (After Yerkes, 1907; Yerkes & Watson, 1911.) Partial floor plan of an old standard discrimination box. The heavy lines are walls and partitions, the little squares represent the positive and negative cues on the wall, and the broken lines are the alternative routes, one of which leads to food according to the location of the positive cue.

to tell which stimulus is brighter. He knows in advance what he has to look for, while the animal has to find out for himself. It would tax our ingenuity to give an acceptable formula stating exactly what the animal has to learn. We cannot say that a rat has to learn the difference between light and dark, for his behavior in other situations often shows a spontaneous preference for a dark alley as against a bright one. We cannot say that he has to learn the motor act of approaching a desirable object, for he is doing that much of the time in his everyday life. We can say that he has to learn in a particular situation to approach the white and not the black object—or that he has to acquire an "association" between the bright stimulus and the positive response—a formula acceptable to many psychologists and noncommittal on the important question whether or not this association is established by means of a cognitive process such as recognizing the white-marked alley as something good, while the dark alley is "no good." At any rate, the rat's problem in the discrimination box is to find a cue that will lead him regularly to the food box.

Sometimes a rat persists almost indefinitely in a "position habit" such as always taking the left-hand alley. He finds food half the time, which is not a bad average in animal life. He has no reason to assume, we may say, that any cue would lead him to food all the time. It may take many trials to bring the rat to the point of paying any attention (apparently) to the visual cues. The human subject in any comparable experiment is told or soon learns that he can be right all the time. For some such reason the rat suffers a serious handicap here; as compared with a human subject, his inferiority is much more marked in this cue learning than in learning a maze where the food box remains in a fixed place instead of shifting from place to place in arbitrary fashion.

Apparatus problems. Because the discrimination box was used for the study of an animal's sensory capacities, the early experimenters took great pains to control the stimulus variables such as light intensity, while they made little effort to facilitate the animal's learning. Slow learning was regarded as presumably inevitable. The white-black discrimination habit could be established in a reasonable number of trials, say 100–200. But when Lashley (1930) embarked on an extensive study of pattern vision in the rat, calling for discrimination of a square from a circle, or of an upright from an inverted equilateral triangle, the number of trials increased enormously and often without any indication that the rat would ever learn. Lashley tried out a novel setup which gave much quicker learning. This *jumping stand* apparatus in its original form is shown in Figure 20-2. Several improved forms have since been constructed (Lashley, 1938; Tolman, 1939; Finger, 1941; Feldman, 1948; Ehrenfreund, 1948).

In the preliminary training the stand is placed close to an open door with food behind, and the rat walks in. The stand is moved back little by little till the rat begins to jump the gap, and in some experiments the gap is gradually widened to 10 inches (25 cm) or more. The rat is first offered the easy choice between a closed black door and an open door with food beyond. Then a white door is substituted for the open one. With the black and white doors shifted from side to side in random order, the positive response to the white is often established in as few as four to five trials—quite an improvement from the 100 or more necessary in the older apparatus, though a single trial may take longer because of the rat's tendency to hesitate before jumping. He looks before he leaps.

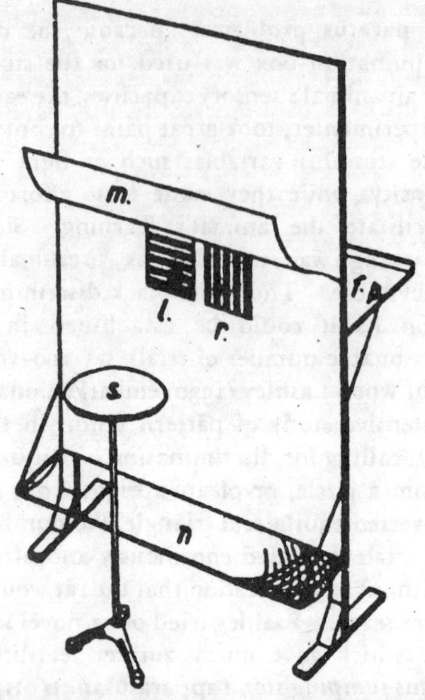

FIG. 20-2. (Lashley, 1930.) Jumping stand apparatus. The rat jumps against one of the doors which show different cues, positive and negative. By jumping against the correct door the rat pushes it open and finds food on the feeding platform just behind. If he jumps against the wrong door, which is locked, he falls into the net and is taken out by *E* and replaced on the jumping stand for another try.

Why does the jumping stand get so much more learning per trial than the older apparatus? No systematic experimental study has been made of this problem, but important differences between the two setups have been pointed out by Munn (1931) and by others. The jumping stand has several probable advantages:

1. Since the rat looks where he is going o land, the cues can be placed where he will look squarely at them. When he hesitates and looks at both doors before jumping, it is still more certain that he gets good reception of the cues.

2. The rat has to direct his response to the object bearing the cue.

3. Reward or punishment is prompt and closely connected with the cue. The rat opens a door and finds food close behind it, or he strikes a locked door and it throws him into the net.

4. The rat comes to take his task seriously as is evident from his hesitant behavior. He becomes alert to possible cues. His primary drives toward food and away from falling awaken a secondary drive toward close examination of the doors.

Along with its advantages the jumping stand has some drawbacks. The preliminary training of a rat to jump against a closed door is time-consuming and not always successful. From a theoretical standpoint it is sometimes desirable to omit punishment so as to have only a single drive in operation. Believing that the main requirement is to insure adequate stimulation from the cues and direct response to one of them, Munn (1931) designed an apparatus such that the animal walked instead of jumped to a door, pushed it open with his nose, and found food close behind. The amount of learning per trial was apparently less than with the jumping stand but much greater than with the older box. The number of trials to reach satisfactory discrimination was about as follows:

	Old box	*Munn*	*Lashley*
Black door *vs.* white door	100–200	80	4–5
Horizontally *vs.* vertically striped door	260	100	27
Upright vs. inverted equilateral triangle on door	600+	70	29

Munn gave a shock for each incorrect response, but this punishment is less direct than the bump and fall in the jumping apparatus.

Another way of insuring close inspection of cues is the pulling-in technique. A monkey, as has long been known (Hobhouse, 1901), quickly learns to pull in a food container placed on the floor beyond reach but attached to an accessible string. If there are two such containers, one smaller than the other but always containing the food, the monkey quickly learns to utilize this size cue, and he can learn to use brightness cues and shape cues (Klüver, 1931, 1933). The rat also can easily be taught to pull in a food container by aid of a string; and if one container is much heavier than the other but contains the food, the rat learns in about 100 trials to choose the heavy container regularly (McCulloch, 1934; McCulloch & Pratt, 1934). Visual cues have perhaps not been tried on the rat with this technique.

Still another simple device for presenting concrete objects as the positive and negative cues has been employed very successfully on monkeys by Harlow (1944). If two small objects such as a pill box and an oil can are placed side by side just within a monkey's reach, with food always concealed under the pill box, he quickly learns to choose the pill box. In a series of such problems with different cue objects the monkey improves to the point of making only one to two errors in each new problem. He learns to look for cues in this experimental situation.

Scoring the responses. We can do more than simply count the errors. Finger (1941) recorded the force of each jump and measured the reaction time or latency with a stop watch. Both force and latency proved to be valuable measures. When a rat had jumped against the wrong door and fallen into the net, his next jump was apt to show greater latency but also greater force. The delay could mean caution in picking a door, and the extra force could be the instinctive effort to overcome resistance.

DISCRIMINATION WITHOUT DIRECT COMPARISON

It has often seemed self-evident that discrimination depends on comparison and that two stimuli must be present at the same time, or nearly so, in order to be compared. Probably this is true when very small differences must be observed, as in the determination of difference thresholds of brightness or pitch (pp. 378, 333). But we know from human psychophysics that the Method of Single Stimuli is perfectly feasible. The subject lifts a single weight and judges it to be heavy, medium, or light, and after becoming acquainted with the range of weights used in the experiment, he makes these "absolute judgments" easily and consistently. We also know from Pavlovian experiments on stimulus generalization and differentiation (p. 580) that it is perfectly feasible, by presenting two stimuli separately, one followed by reinforcement and the other not, to build up a conditioned response to the one and not to the other. Such results have suggested theories of discrimination learning that do not require any comparison of stimuli (Schlosberg & Solomon, 1943, see p. 578). According to a no-comparison theory, a rat on the jumping stand, confronted by two doors bearing different cue stimuli, looks at the doors in turn until he "gets the green light," i.e., until one of the cues exerts a sufficient pull to elicit the jumping response. The pull of a stimulus depends on several factors such as past reinforcements, position habits, and preferences for light or dark places.

Single Stimuli in discrimination learning. Interest in the comparison and no-comparison theories has led several investigators to try the experiment of presenting the positive and negative cues *successively*, one door at a time, always with food hidden only behind the positive cue.

Solomon (1948) used the jumping stand with only one door present at once. A white door was positive; a black door negative with the usual punishment. The latency of the jump was the important measure. After a few falls into the net the rat became cautious; the latency of all his jumps increased for a few trials, after which the correct jumps became quicker while the incorrect ones became slower and tended to drop out altogether. Good discrimination was established in as few as 6–20 trials. Latency was thus shown to be a sensitive index of the progress of learning, and very quick learning seemed to result from the single-door technique.

The runway problem, introduced by Graham & Gagné (1940), has been found suitable for the study of discrimination learning by the single-stimulus procedure. It is a very simple problem, which is much used also in the study of conditioning (p. 558). All the rat has to do, when the door of the starting box is opened, is to come out (with a measurable latency) and proceed over a straight runway into the food box (with a measurable running time). After obtaining the food a few times he begins to cut down his latency and speed up his running. To adapt this apparatus for discrimination, Verplanck (1942) provided alternative runway surfaces, one black and one white, with food boxes to match. White was positive—food in the box; black was negative—no reward there, but no punishment either, except a brief confinement in the empty box. After a preliminary series of eight positives, during which the rat learned to come out quickly

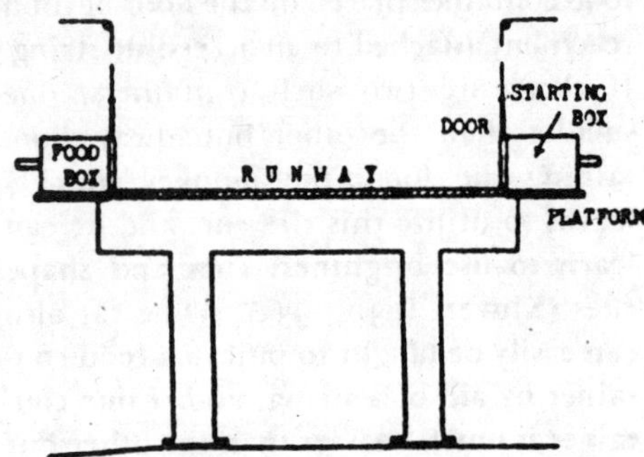

Fig. 20-3. (Graham & Gagné, 1940.) The straight runway used in experiments on conditioning, extinction, and spontaneous recovery, and adapted for discrimination learning. The wooden runway is elevated above its supports and is certainly a one-lane road, being ¾ inch or 1½ inches wide in different experiments. The starting box door is opened by E to start a trial, and the food box door is closed as soon as the rat has entered.

and run rapidly, there followed a series of four-trial cycles, each cycle consisting of three negatives and one positive. What the rat now learned was to run slowly (exploringly) or not at all on black, while increasing his speed on white. In a group of 24 rats, this discrimination was clearly present after four cycles (16 trials) and became more marked in later trials. This experiment was repeated and extended with confirmatory results by Raben (1949), as shown in Figure 20-4.

A much shortened runway was used by Hull (1950b) for one-door discrimination experiments. The distance from the starting-box to the food compartment was only 8 inches. An electric timer measured the time from *E*'s opening of the starting-box door to *O*'s opening of the food compartment door. On this latter door was either a white spot signaling food or a black spot signaling no food in the food compartment. At first, however, these signals were not used, food being present on every trial till the rat had learned to pass rapidly across the runway. When this "latency" had been reduced

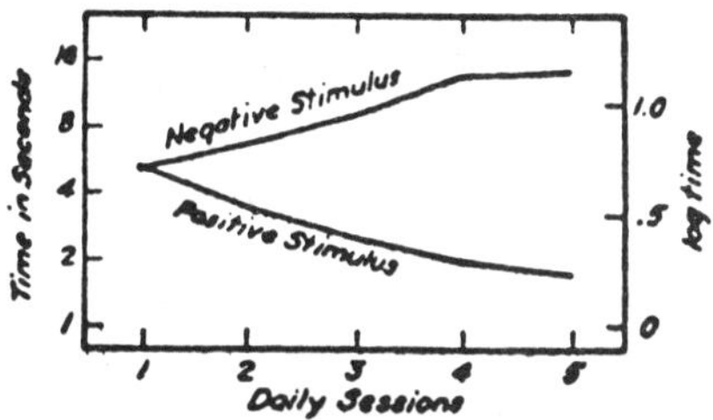

FIG. 20·4. (After Raben, 1949.) Brightness discrimination as shown by running time. When the runway and food box were white, there was food in the box; when they were dark gray, 1/20 as bright as the white, there was no food there. Each day there were five of the "cycles" described in the text. As the curve shows, running time at first was about 5 seconds on either a white or a dark runway, but on succeeding days the run became faster on the white and slower on the dark gray, till finally it took only about 2 seconds on white as against 14 seconds on gray. Smaller brightness differences also were found to be discriminated, but the learning proceeded more slowly and less surely. In these experiments only one cue was present at a time and there was no punishment for errors.

from about 3 seconds to less than ½ second, the signals were introduced with the effect of slowing all the responses somewhat, but only a little in the case of the white or food door, and very much in the case of the black or no-food door. After several days of this differential training the response to the black door was delayed as much as a whole minute, while the response to the white door hovered around ⅔ second.

The bar-pressing problem. No doubt the Skinner box (p. 546) could be utilized for experiments parallel to those already described. For example, there could be two bars, only one of which secured the food pellets. If the same bar were always correct, only place discrimination would be called for, as in a simple T maze (p. 624). But suppose a light were thrown sometimes on one bar and sometimes on the other, the illuminated bar giving food. The experiment would parallel the two-door experiments already considered. To parallel the one-door experiments the box would contain a single bar, sometimes illuminated and sometimes not, with food obtained only when the bar was illuminated. This type of experiment was introduced by Skinner (1938, p. 178) with one difference which may or may not be a factor in speed of learning: the illumination was not thrown on the bar alone but suffused the whole interior of the box. The rat was free to press the bar at any time, the question being how frequently —at what rate—he pressed it under the different experimental conditions. This technique was employed by Frick (1948) in a study of brightness discrimination. Under bright illumination pellets were obtainable by bar pressing, but no pellets were obtainable under weak or medium illumination. After certain difficulties were overcome the results were fairly parallel to those cited from Raben's runway experiment (Figure 20·4).

The Skinner-type box, in which a pigeon pecks at a translucent key or button (p. 563) provides a very effective situation for the study of discrimination. Various images or colors can be projected onto the button and their effects noted on the rate of pecking. For example, by reinforcing pecks only when the button is red, and never when it is green, we may get the bird pecking at

100 times as rapid a rate for red as for green. One advantage of the method is the fact that the discriminative stimulus is directly in front of the pigeon as he pecks. Another useful device is the use of variable-interval reinforcement, which gives a high rate of responding with very few reinforcements (Skinner, 1953b; Ferster, 1953).

From the preceding experiments it certainly appears that the single stimulus procedure is quite favorable for cue learning, perhaps fully as favorable as the simultaneous presence of both positive and negative cues. In a direct attack on this question Grice (1949) conducted parallel experiments with single and paired doors. The cues were white disks standing out from a black wall, one disk being much larger than the other (5 and 8 cm in diameter) so that only an easy discrimination was required. In the middle of each disk was a small door to be pushed open (unless locked) by the rat's nose, a bit of food being found behind the door. The small disk was positive. For one group of rats the two disks stood side by side; for another group only a single disk was present in any trial. As soon as a rat made a choice, a screen was lowered preventing any further response on that trial. How should the progress of discrimination learning be measured? With two doors present, the errors were counted, and the gradual decrease in their number gave a learning curve. With a single door, the response time was measured, and the response to the positive cue became gradually quicker while that to the negative cue became slower. Any relatively slow response to the positive cue or relatively quick response to the negative cue was counted as an error. Errors decreased at about the same rate under both conditions, and learning was fairly complete in about the same number of trials, 25-27 on the average. If, then, learning is equally rapid with and without the opportunity for direct comparison, the conclusion seems to be that comparison plays no essential part in discrimination learning. The response to one cue is established by reinforcement while response to the other cue is extinguished by nonreinforcement. A similar experiment of Norris (1950), however, gave even faster learning with single than with paired stimuli. Should this result be confirmed, we are left with the unexpected task of accounting for the *disadvantage* of having both cues present at once.

Further checks on the comparison and no-comparison theories. If the cues, positive and negative, are really learned separately, certain consequences can be predicted and tested experimentally. For example, in the Grice setup just described, first train the rats to go to the large disk, before presenting the small disk at all; then pair the two disks. Little new learning should be required if the large disk is now positive, but much new learning should be required if the small disk is now positive because the established habit of going to the large disk must be overcome. This result was obtained by Grice (1948b), but not by Lashley & Wade (1946) with the jumping stand, perhaps because of the strong factor of punishment for incorrect jumps. For another example, first present a white and a black door with the white door positive. After choice of the white door is established, present just two white doors, and the tendency should be strong to enter either one of these doors; but present just two black doors, and the tendency should be strong to avoid both of them. This result was obtained by Webb (1950) and interpreted as contrary to any relational theory; for if the preliminary training had established a response to the black-white *relation*, this response could not be carried over to a situation that lacked that relation. A very similar result was reported earlier by Lashley (1942, p. 262): rats first learned to jump to a triangle rather than a circle; being then shown two triangles, they jumped readily to either of them; but being shown two circles, they refused to jump. Lashley interpreted this result as meaning that the rats had learned to respond to a specific cue rather than to a total configuration. But he still held that perception of relations was basic to any discrimination.

WHAT ARE THE EFFECTIVE CUES IN SUCCESSFUL DISCRIMINATION?

We turn now to a problem that has exercised the experimenters in many parts of psychology, the problem of detecting what cues are actually utilized in making any distinctive response. It is a familiar problem in perception. In the visual perception of the third dimension, quite a number of cues are possible, but which ones are actually functional when we see the distance of an object? The direction of a sound is heard, but how? An expert reader reads much too rapidly to spell out the words, and we want to know what data he uses. These are not easy questions to answer, and no more is it a simple task to ferret out the cues that govern the rat's behavior in discrimination learning. Several ingenious methods have been devised for the investigation of this matter in animals, children, and adults.

Equivalent Stimuli. When a certain response has been established to a certain stimulus, what will be the response to a new stimulus substituted for the old one in a situation that is otherwise unchanged? If the response remains the same, the new stimulus can be called "equivalent" to the old. It may not be equivalent in all respects, but it does elicit the same response. A human subject may notice the difference in stimuli while still making the same response. An animal subject, too, may give some sign of noticing the difference, as by a slow and hesitant response to the new stimulus—in which case the new stimulus is behaviorally not fully equivalent to the old, but it may be nearly equivalent in that it elicits the response with the same frequency or probability as the old. Stimulus "equivalence" has been spoken of mostly in connection with discrimination learning.

In a somewhat different context a stimulus is said to be "generalized" if other stimuli can be substituted for it and elicit the same response. The original context here was Pavlov's study of conditioning. The facts can also be included under the general head of "transfer" (p. 733), since what has been learned under certain conditions is carried over or transferred to other stimuli or other conditions.

In introducing his Method of Equivalent Stimuli, Klüver (1931) said that his purpose was to find out "which aspects of the stimulus situation are primarily effective." The experiment consisted of two steps, training and tests. In the training series the animal learned to make the positive response consistently to one of two stimuli. In the subsequent tests, two other stimuli were substituted, the question being whether the animal would make the positive response consistently to either of these new stimuli. The subjects were monkeys; the stimulus objects were two boxes, each box being attached to a string, 5 feet long, by which the monkey could pull the box along the floor to his cage. One box contained food, the other none during the training, but both contained food during the tests. To maintain the learned discrimination intact, the regular training was renewed from time to time during any long series of tests.

We shall cite a few of Klüver's experiments, which he reported briefly in 1932 and more fully in 1933.

1. *Weight discrimination*. The two boxes were alike in visual appearance but differed in weight, the heavier containing the food reward. The monkey was first taught to pull in only one box in any one trial. There followed a long period, 200–450 trials, with only 50-50 success. The monkey then began to "compare" the weights, pulling each box a few inches before making a decision. From this point on learning was rapid. Eventually it was no longer necessary for the monkey to try both weights. If the first one tried was the heavy one, he pulled it in promptly; but if it was the light one, he simply shifted to the other box and pulled it in. He was relying on what we call "absolute judgments" in human weight discrimination. Or, we may say, he recognized the correct box by its "feel." This heavy box weighed 1350 grams at the time when the first "comparisons" were made—the first sign of weight being used as a cue. It was then reduced to 900, to 750, to 600, and finally to 450 grams, the light box being meanwhile kept throughout at 150 grams, but these changes in the heavy weight did not change the monkey's behavior. After this training, *transposition tests* were given; i.e., the stimulus values were shifted so that the old heavy weight was paired with one still heavier, or the old lighter weight with one still lighter. Thus, the 150-gram weight was omitted and the 450-gram weight, to which consistent positive responses had been made, was paired with a much heavier weight. In this test the monkey soon came (though getting food for either choice) to reject the old heavy weight for the new, still heavier one. Similarly, when the heavy weights were omitted and the previously negative 150-gram box was paired with a still lighter one, the monkey soon shifted to a consistent choice of the 150-gram box. Several other weight pairs were tried, with the monkey consistently choosing the heavy weight of each pair except when the difference became too small. Seven monkeys gave essentially these same results.

If we ask the stock "transposition" question, whether these animals were responding on an absolute or relative basis, we have to answer, "Partly the one and partly the other." If we ask what is probably a more significant question, as to what cue the animals learned to follow, the answer is that they learned to take a heavy box. It is better to say "heavy box" rather than "heavier box" because of the tendency to depend on absolute judgments as the learning progressed. How heavy is "heavy"? It depends on the range of weights used, just as it does in a human psychophysical experiment by the Method of Absolute Judgments or Single Stimuli (p. 217).

2. *Size discrimination*. The two boxes, now equal in weight, were provided with rectangular black cardboard fronts, one twice as large in area as the other (15 by 20 and 10 by 15 cm). The larger box contained the food. Learning was somewhat more rapid than in weight discrimination. Comparison took the form of looking alternately at the two box fronts. After this training,

transposition tests were fairly successful, except that, when both rectangles were much larger or much smaller than the original pair, there was no consistent choice. When the original areas were preserved but the shape changed to squares, circles, or hexagons, the larger was chosen consistently. Large size was obviously the positive cue. But it was the large *object*, the large box front, that was the cue, rather than the large visual stimulus, for when the boxes were shown at different distances from the monkey, so that their retinal sizes were equal or even reversed, the same box as before was consistently chosen—an example of "size constancy" (p. 480). This result is reported in Klüver (1933, pp. 162 and 168). Other tests also showed that the monkeys were reacting to object size, not to mere retinal size (1933, pp. 172 ff.).

There were many other indications in the monkeys' behavior of responses to perceived objects rather than to raw stimuli. The most definite evidence for this view is the fact that a monkey's motor behavior is adjusted to the distance, size, and shape of objects. However conscientiously we try to avoid anthropomorphism, we cannot but agree with one of Klüver's final conclusions from his extensive study of monkeys (1933, p. 313):

> Now it is true that the world surrounding us, that is, the world of man, is not a "diffused" something: it is "organized" or "structured." In this world we find "objects," and these objects have definite properties. . . . Let us now turn to the world of monkeys. There is no doubt that many simian actions and reactions are also referable to what we call "objects." The way certain objects are grasped, pushed, torn, thrown, picked up, or reacted to visually shows that the something the monkey is reacting to has not only "thing-character" for us but, it seems, also for the monkey. . . . We are convinced that for the monkey too there exist "objects" with definite properties.

The world of rats has not been so fully studied, though rats certainly appear to respond to objects in spatial relations. Since we know the world of man and to some extent the world of monkeys, we may query why it is important for the psychologist to know the world of rats. The answer is that many fundamental experiments on learning use rats as subjects, so that it is important to know whether the rat is responding to raw stimuli or whether in his case, as in the human and simian cases, the stimuli serve as signs of objects and objective facts with which the rat has to deal in his motor behavior.

Cues in figure discrimination. Just because a rat learns to choose a door marked with a white triangle as against one marked with a white circle, it does not follow that the triangular shape is his positive cue, for the wide white base would be sufficient and the remainder of the figure might be disregarded. Lashley (1938) made an extensive series of experiments by the method of equivalent stimuli, his purpose being to discover the exact cues utilized by the rat in the discrimination of figures. White figures were pasted on two black doors in the jumping apparatus, the whole background being black. The positive cue was on the two doors in random order. When the rat had mastered a problem to the criterion of 20 consecutive correct responses, the tests for equivalent stimuli were begun, with food now obtained by either choice, and with regular training resumed from time to time so as to maintain the learned discrimination intact. The criterion of equivalence was a consistent choice of one of the new figures, even though the latency of response might be increased. "The new figures . . . introduce a disturbing element

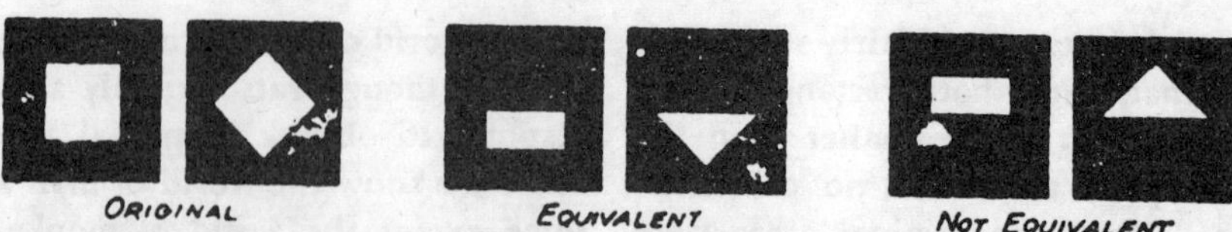

FIG. 20-5 (After Lashley, 1938.) Doors as marked in the jumping apparatus. After rats had learned to jump consistently to the white square as against the diamond, they were tested with the lower halves which proved to be equivalent to the originals, and with the upper halves which were not equivalent.

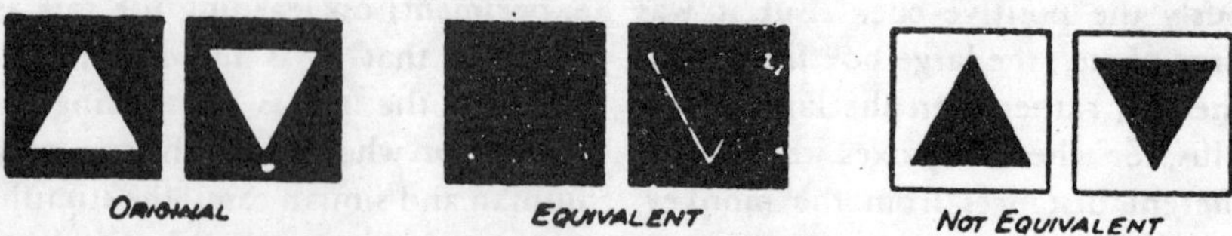

FIG. 20-6. (After Lashley, 1938.) Rats learned in an average of 53 trials to jump to the upright as against the inverted white triangle. They carried over this habit to the white outlines but not to the black-on-white triangles.

The animal hesitates for long periods, turning back and forth from one card to the other. Errors are most often made in the first trials, as if the animal were trying out both figures before settling down to a consistent selection of one" (1938, pp. 128–129).

A few of Lashley's results will be cited. When the two white figures were a square and a diamond, as in Figure 20-5, with the square positive, five rats learned to choose the square consistently. They were then tested with the lower halves of the two figures, and they all consistently chose the lower half of the square. But when tested with the upper halves, all made chance scores. Evidently they had been responding, not to the entire square and diamond, but to the lower parts or even to the black stripe beneath the square.

When the animals had learned to discriminate an upright from an inverted triangle, or a triangle from a cross, white on black, they carried the habit over readily to white outlines of the same figures, or to the same figures in light gray on dark gray, but not to the same in black on white. "In all cases where the brightness relations of figure and ground were reversed complete loss of discrimination has resulted" (p. 143). Mere shape apart from light and dark was not their cue. We ourselves do not recognize a face when light and dark are interchanged in a photographic negative.

The rat learns rather quickly to choose the larger—or the smaller—of two white circles, one twice as large in area as the other. But it is not certain that size rather than amount of light is the cue, and the size and shape of the black background are other possibilities. The equivalence tests indicated that any one of these may be the cue, and that individual rats differ in the cue they pick up from such a configuration.

The *range of stimulus equivalence* differs from one rat to another. If a large number of stimulus pairs are employed in the testing, some rats will accept many of these pairs as equivalent to the pair they have learned, while other rats accept only a few pairs as equivalent. What would be the effect of destroying a portion of the cerebral cortex? Would it increase or decrease the range of equivalent stimuli? We might argue either way according to our conception of cerebral function. Experiments show that the range is *increased,* i.e., the animal is less discriminating when his brain is impaired—a result in line with the fact that discrimination rather than stimulus generalization has to be learned (Maier, 1941; Wapner, 1944).

Two theories of discrimination learning. From his extensive experience with rats learning their cues in the old discrimination box and in the jumping stand apparatus, Lashley reached a very definite impression of the learning process. Summing up his results on discrimination of figures he said (1938, p. 160): "Where the pattern contains many items, the animal solves the problem by disregarding most and reacting to a part-figure." And in a later discussion he formulated the basic postulates of his theory as follows (1942, p. 242):

1. When any complex of stimuli arouses nervous activity, . . . certain elements or components become dominant for reaction while others become ineffective. This constitutes a "set" to react to certain elements.

2. In any trial of a training series, only those components of the stimulating situation which are dominant . . . are associated. Other stimuli which excite the receptors are not associated because the animal is not set to react to them.

An exactly opposed theory was propounded by Spence (1936) and by Hull (1943, 1950b, 1951). Based on Hull's general theory of learning, it can be stated in the following terms:

1. *All stimuli* acting on the receptors at the moment when a successful (reinforced) response is initiated become associated with that response.

2. *Every time* any stimulus is present when a successful response is being initiated, the particular stimulus-response association is strengthened. That is, the building up of an S—R association is a continuous, cumulative process.

This theory also postulates that associations are weakened by nonreinforcement, and that this extinction process is cumulative and applies to every stimulus present when an unsuccessful response is initiated. At any given time, then, the strength of an S—R association depends on the balance of all previous reinforcements and nonreinforcements. As between two possible responses to a given situation, that one will occur which has the greater S—R strength. In ordinary life the picture is complicated by stimulus generalization, but in a well-planned experiment it should be possible to estimate the strength of each alternative association and so to predict which response will occur.

The difference between the two theories may be clarified if we start with the question: "What stimulus is the rat responding *to* when he jumps (or runs) to one of the two doors in a discrimination apparatus?" Hull and Spence answer that he is responding to *all* the stimuli received at the moment. Lashley answers that the rat is apt to focus on *one* stimulus characteristic and respond to that one, disregarding the rest. Suppose the rat makes a lucky choice of the right-hand door which bears a large white circle. According to Hull and Spence, he is responding to its position, color, size, and shape and getting reinforcement for each one of these S—R units; while according to Lashley, the rat is responding at the moment to only one of these "stimuli" and getting reinforcement for that cue alone. If on the contrary this same jump were unsuccessful, all of these S—R units would be weakened, according to Hull and Spence; while, according to Lashley, only the cue that was used would be weakened, other possible cues being unaffected because not in use.

Presolution cues. These opposed theories lend themselves to testing by transfer experiments. One presupposition of the experimenters is that they can distinguish a "presolution period," when the animal is succeeded only by chance, *i.e.*, in about 50 percent of the trials, and the "solution period," when the successes are increasing either suddenly or gradually from the 50-percent to the 100-percent level. Lashley has been disposed to grant that the animal is not responding at all to the correct cue during the presolution period, nor even starting to form the correct association. According to Hull and Spence, the correct association is being formed and strengthened every time from the beginning when a successful response occurs.

"Hypotheses in rats." This challenging expression was used by Krechevsky (1932a, 1932b) to dramatize the fact that the rat's responses during the presolution period are not truly haphazard in frequency but show some consistency and regularity. Just because the responses have only a chance relation to the correct cue, we cannot assume them unrelated to some other cue. The animal may be following a false lead and being pretty consistent about it. What cues is a rat likely to pick up and follow? Position habits and preference for dark places are well-known characteristics of rat behavior in the laboratory. If neither position nor darkness is the correct cue, the question is whether either of these false cues is followed consistently during the presolution period or some part of it. Krechevsky took the day's work, 40 trials, as a unit and considered each individual rat separately. With two doors or alleys to choose from and no position habit in operation, about 50 percent of responses take the right-hand and 50 percent the left-hand door. And to demonstrate a position habit, you must have significantly more than 50 percent on one side. How large a deviation from 50 percent would be accepted as satisfactory evidence of a position habit—or of the consistent use of any cue? Krechevsky adopted the high criterion of $3SD_p$ above 50 percent, where $SD_p = \sqrt{pq/N}$, p and q each being .50, and N in his case being the 40 trials per day. By pure chance the 75-percent level, or 30 out of 40, would be reached only about once in 1,000 such days. By this criterion there was satisfactory evidence for the persistent trying of a false cue before it was given up for some other lead (Figures 20-7, 20-8).

Reversed cues. The existence of a presolution period, where one is demonstrated, offers the experimenter a chance to test the two theories of discrimination learning. For example, in the first four to five days of Figure 20-7, the rat is dominated by the position habit and is making correct responses only incidentally. Since he is making no use of the positive cue he has not yet begun to associate that cue with food, according to Lashley, and consequently it will make no difference to this rat if the cues are reversed from this time on. He has learned nothing and has nothing to unlearn. According to the Hull-Spence theory, he must have already learned a good deal, for the correct response was being made incidentally about half the time, and every time it was made it was reinforced. Consequently if the experimenter should reverse the cues from the fifth day on, the rat would have to unlearn a half-formed association.

The cue-reversal technique was in-

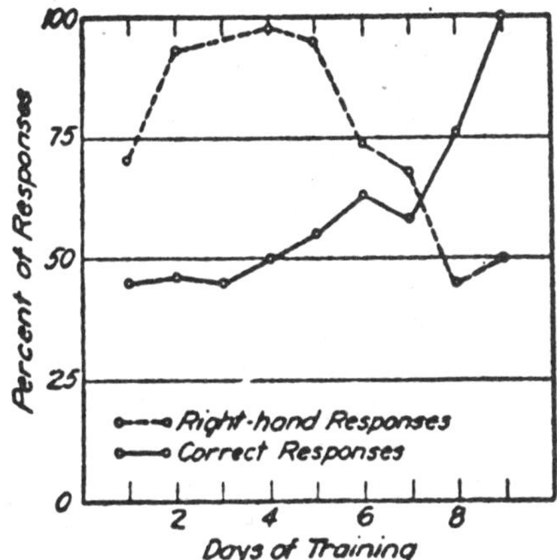

Fig. 20-7. (After Krechevsky, 1932A.) Shift from a position habit to the correct cue. This is the record of an individual rat making 40 responses per day. The positive cue was a hurdle which had to be jumped to enter the alley leading to food, the hurdle being on the right in half the trials and on the left in half. The rat soon developed a position habit, taking the right-hand alley almost every time for several days—the hurdle alley only about 50 percent of the time. Later, the position habit went down to 50 percent and the correct choice went up to 100 percent. Here the presolution period lasted about five days, since there was no clear sign until the sixth day that the correct cue was being used.

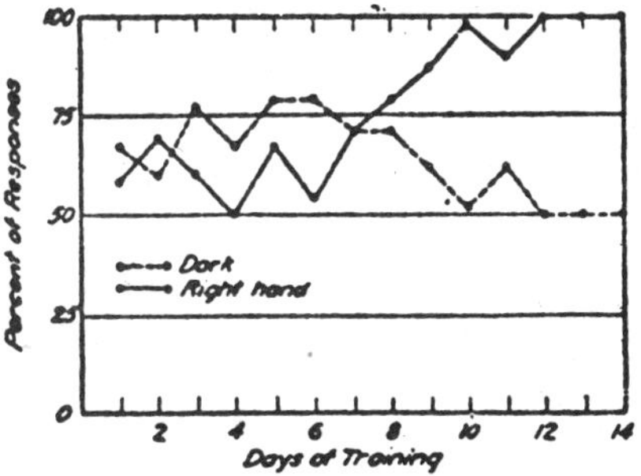

Fig. 20-8. (Data from Krechevsky, 1932B.) Shift from one false cue to another false one. In order to secure a longer presolution period, an insoluble problem was presented: food could not be obtained more than half the time by following any cue consistently. Two likely cues were always present: position and dark *versus* light. Half of the time the right-hand alley was light and the left-hand one dark; half of the time the reverse. This rat showed some initial preference for the dark and also for the right-hand alley. The dark choice increased to a reliable degree of dominance, only to give way later to the right-hand choice which became entirely dominant. (In the rat's favor it should be added that a routine position habit was the most laborsaving way of dealing with the situation—a solution indeed of the insoluble problem. It avoided hesitation and excess effort, while securing all the available positive reinforcement.)

troduced by McCulloch & Pratt (1934) before the Hull-Spence theory was definitely announced. Rats that had learned to pull in a food tray by a string (p. 585) were shown two trays, side by side on the floor before the cage, each attached to a string. One tray weighed three times as much as the other (75 and 25 grams). Food was in the lighter tray at first but later in the heavier tray. This reversal occurred for one group as soon as the individual rat began to improve his score (after 84 trials, median); for another group after only 28 trials, long before the first sign of learning; while for the control group the heavier tray was positive from the start. The trials before reversal we may call false training, and the results showed that the more false training to overcome, the slower the learning. To reach the level of 75-percent correct choices, the number of trials required was approximately:

With no false training	96 trials
With 28 trials of false training	126 trials after reversal
With 84 trials of false training	166 " " "

These results support the Hull-Spence theory, also known as the "continuity theory," the meaning being that the learning process is continuous from the start, without any real break between the presolution and solution periods.

Other experiments employing this technique have reached the same general result, namely that even small amounts of false pretraining impede the main learning process. With rats as subjects the experimenter can make sure of a presolution period by first inducing a position habit. Simply reward the animal several times for the choice of the right-hand door, and while the position habit continues introduce the positive and negative cues for a moderate number of trials; finally reverse the cues and continue until they are well learned. This plan was followed by Spence (1945) with light and dark as the cues and by Ehrenfreund (1948) with an upright and an inverted equilateral triangle as the cues. These two researches from the Iowa laboratory reached parallel results. We shall outline Ehrenfreund's experiment. He shows in the first place that figures to be discriminated should be placed where the rat will naturally look squarely at them. In the jumping apparatus the rat fixates the spot where he is going to land, and the cue figures should therefore be near the bottom of the door. Cue learning is slow if the cues are located high on the door, apparently because the rat must first learn to look there and so secure good pattern vision. In his main experiment, accordingly, Ehrenfreund mounted the white triangles near the base of the black doors.

The first step (after the animals had learned to jump the gap for food) was to induce a position habit, such as the habit of jumping always to the right-hand door. Then the two triangles were introduced, the upright one being positive and appearing equally often on each door, so that in jumping always to the right the rat jumped half the time to the upright triangle and was rewarded, and the other half to the inverted triangle with no reward. There were only 40 trials of this presolution training—not enough in most cases to produce any visible learning of the triangles. Finally, the cues were reversed, the inverted triangle henceforth being positive. The experimental group received the training just described, but the control group during the presolution training received food half the time with the inverted triangle and half the time with the upright triangle. Having thus received reinforcement equally for both triangles, the control group should start its main training with no bias in favor of either cue, while the experimental group should have a bias against the cues as now used. These biases are predicted by Hull and Spence, but according to Lashley both groups should be equally unbiased since they have been following the position habit and paying no attention to the triangles. The results favored Hull and Spence, since the experimental group took an average of 63 trials to master the reversed cues, as against only 37 trials for the control group—a reliable difference.

A similar experiment with similar results was conducted in the Swarthmore laboratory by Ritchie, Ebeling and Roth (1950). In the presolution period one group of rats received false training, another group correct training; and the falsely pretrained group was much retarded in mastering the correct cues.

Modified cues. In his tests of the two theories of discrimination learning, Lashley (1942, p. 258) used a technique somewhat like that of reversed cues. The cues were modified rather than reversed, and the experiment terminated in a test for equivalent stimuli. Instead of a position habit, a habit or set for responding to size was first induced, and then shape was introduced as an incidental cue, so as to see whether shape would acquire cue value. The successive steps in one such experiment are shown in Figure 20-9. The rats first learned to choose a large circle as against a small circle on the two doors of the jumping apparatus. When this choice was well established, a large triangle was substituted for the large circle and was consistently chosen in preference to the small circle. The rats were evidently responding to size. Training was then continued for 200 trials with the large triangle positive and the small circle negative. During this long period, in responding positively to large size, the rats were incidentally choosing the triangle and getting 100-percent reinforcement for so doing. According to Hull and Spence, it would seem, the triangular shape must have acquired positive cue value. Two tests were applied: (1) a triangle and a circle of equal areas were presented, but the rats showed no preference; (2) a large circle and a small triangle were presented, but the rats consistently chose the circle. As far as could be judged by equivalent stimuli, the triangular shape had acquired no cue value, size being still the sole operative cue. Lashley reports: "Several experiments of this general pattern have been carried out with essentially the same result. If the animals are given a set to react to one aspect of a stimulus situation, large amounts of training do not establish association with other aspects, so long as the original set remains effective for reaching the food."

Step 1. Rats learn to choose the large circle when it appears on either door of the jumping apparatus.

Step 2. A large triangle is substituted for the large circle. The rats choose the triangle consistently for 200 trials.

Step 3. Triangle and circle of equal areas being now shown, the rats show no preference.

Step 4. As between a small triangle and a larger circle, the circle is consistently chosen.

FIG. 20-9. (Data from Lashley, 1942, p. 258.) Successive steps in an experiment on size and shape cues.

These two experiments, one favoring the Hull-Spence theory and one the Lashley theory, are after all not directly contradictory to each other. Lashley's tests for equivalent stimuli show that the animals were not actually making any use of the shape cue in spite of all the incidental reinforcement it had received; but some invisible learning may have occurred. Suppose that Step 3 of Figure 20-9 was extended into a learning series, with reinforcement for the triangle or else for the circle: quite possibly the triangle would be learned more quickly than the circle. (Practically this result has been obtained by Bitterman & Coate, 1950.) So Lashley's result does not directly contradict the Hull-Spence theory. On the other hand the reversed-cue experiments do not directly contradict the Lashley theory, except so far as "continuity" is concerned. Lashley's fundamental postulate can be roughly stated in terms of "attention": it is possible for the rat, as it is for the human subject, to attend to a part or aspect of the total stimulus complex—not merely by fixing his eyes there, but also by responding to size rather than shape, or to brightness rather than size, or to some detail that can serve as a target to aim at in jumping. Hull and Spence have said that "all stimuli" present at the right moment become associated with the successful response, but apparently they have not said that all these stimuli become *equally* associated. If some stimuli can become more strongly associated than others present at the same time, a selective factor more or less equivalent to attention must be operating.

Combined and separated cues. Visual cues necessarily have size, shape, color, position, and perhaps other attributes which can be varied and put into different combinations. Let A and B stand for two positive cues, such as white and circle, and let small a and b stand for the corresponding negative cues, black and triangle. So AB is a white circle, a combined positive cue, while ab is a black triangle, the corresponding negative cue. After the subject has learned to choose AB consistently as against ab, he is presented with these alternatives, Ab and aB. Will he choose the white triangle or the black circle? He would have no preference if A and B, now opposed to each other, had been equally associated with the positive response. Usually he shows a strong preference, though the direction of the preference differs with the individual.

This technique has been much used in the delayed reaction experiments, soon to be considered, with one of the variables, say A—a, being the position of the doors or other objects, and the other variable, B—b, often being color; and it is found that position is much more easily learned than color by animals though not always by men. In the discrimination experiments it seems almost certain that the rat notices the location of the doors more readily than the color, size or shape of any signs pasted on the doors. He learns locations and position habits very readily. So do other animals, including the chimpanzee.

The technique just symbolized in letters was employed on chimpanzees by Nissen & Jenkins (1943). The animals learned to choose between two boxes marked with black and white squares, large and small. For "Tom," the positive sign was a small black square, and the negative a large white square. When he had learned to choose the small black square consistently, he was tested with a small white square *versus* a large black square. In 50 such trials, interspersed with many of the regular training trials, he chose the small white square every time. Small size rather than black color was evidently his cue. Some of the other seven chimpanzees were found to choose by color rather than by size, but every one showed a decided preference, 74 percent at least, for either size or color. None of them had associated the two cues equally.

Other recombinations and reductions of cues are possible. The authors just quoted tried some like this, AB *vs.* aB, a small and a large black square, with results similar to those just cited in showing that one of the two combined cues was usually much better learned than the other.

Why one cue should be more easily learned than another, and why individuals should differ in the cue that they learn more easily, are questions that can be answered in terms of "attention value" (p. 74). One stimulus because of its intensity or quality is intrinsically more likely than another to catch attention. And one stimulus or object may be more likely to catch an individual's attention because of his past experience. This last statement, though reasonable enough, would carry more conviction if it could be demonstrated experimentally. An experiment of Lawrence (1950) met this requirement. Two alleys extended side by side straight forward from the entrance. The experiment consisted of three stages: pretraining, training, test. (1) Both alleys were black or else both were white. If they were black, food was in the left-hand alley; but if they were white, it was in the right-hand alley. Black and white were the relevant cues and the rats learned to use them. Meanwhile curtains were present in both alleys half of the time but were irrelevant. (For half of the animals, of course, the curtains were relevant, black and white irrelevant.) In this pretraining the animals learned to "ignore" the irrelevant cues. (2) In the training stage the cues were combined and both relevant; one alley was both black and curtained, the other both white and uncurtained; and the animals learned to take the black-curtained alley whether it was at the left or at the right. This AB—ab stage was mastered very quickly. (3) Finally came the Ab—aB test, one alley being black without curtains, the other white with curtains. The question tested was whether the pretraining, to use certain cues and ignore others, had been transferred to the second stage and so to the test. In the test 27 of the 40 rats did ignore the cues which they had learned to ignore in the first stage. The attention value of the irrelevant cues had been diminished by the pretraining. The author, Lawrence, though well disposed in general toward the Hull-Spence theory, reaches the conclusion that an additional factor must be recognized. It is a perceptual rather than a motor factor, i.e., it operates during the reception of the stimuli rather than during the execution of the overt response. Lashley would probably call it the factor of attention value, but Lawrence prefers to call it the factor of discriminability of stimuli. In learning to respond to the difference between black and white alleys, and to ignore the difference between curtained and uncurtained alleys, the subjects increase the effective difference (discriminability) of the colors and decrease that between curtains and no curtains. It would be premature for us to render a decision between the claims of attention value and discriminability. At least the conclusion seems well established that stimuli present at the moment of a successful response come to be *unequally* associated with the response, because of the operation of a perceptual factor.

"VTE—VICARIOUS TRIAL AND ERROR"

Presumably much could be discovered about the learning process if the subject's responses were carefully examined, instead of merely being tallied as "correct" or "incorrect." A start toward such a more penetrating study is made when we measure the latency of the responses in a discrimination experiment. The *hesitation* that is often observed (pp. 578, 584, 592, 673) may play a part in the subject's labor of finding a dependable cue. In the two-door experiments, hesitation often consists in looking at both doors before jumping to one of them, as Lashley observed (1938) in the course of his tests for equivalent stimuli already considered on page 592. Much earlier (1912) he had observed similar behavior in the old discrimination box and had noticed that a response made after hesitation was likely to be correct. Other early experimenters made similar observations, summarized by Dennis & Russell (1939). The behavior in question has been described as "looking from one door to the other," "alternately facing the two doors," "turning back and forth," or "crouching to jump at one door and then crouching before the other door, before finally jumping."

It was Muenzinger (1938) who gave this behavior the name of vicarious trial and error, abbreviated to VTE. By counting the shifts in each trial before the decisive movement, and by counting the trials that showed some of this behavior, he made VTE into a definite response variable for the experimenter's use. VTE is sensory exploring, i.e., exploring the situation by use of the senses before actually going beyond the choice point.

Shock for correct choices. Muenzinger conducted a long series of experiments on the effect of so-called "punishment" for correct choices instead of for incorrect choices. The rat was offered a choice between a dark and a lighted alley. The light was switched from one alley to the other irregularly in a series of trials, but always it was the lighted alley that led to food. One group of rats got a mild shock from the floor of the dark alley, another group from the floor of the lighted alley, and a third group received no shock in either alley. The setup and results are shown in Figure 20-10.

From the results tabulated under Figure 20-10 we see that the quickest learning occurred when there was shock in the dark alley. When a rat entered that alley he got a shock immediately, the sequence dark–shock was prompt and direct, and the dark–shock association was quickly established. What calls for explanation is the fact that shock in the light alley, on the path to food, was better than no shock. The danger of shock had the effect of increasing VTE at the choice point, and the VTE seemed to be beneficial. Very much the same result was obtained in other experiments with the shock replaced by a gap in the floor or even by glass doors that merely enforced a 5-second delay at the choice point (Muenzinger & Wood, 1935; Muen-

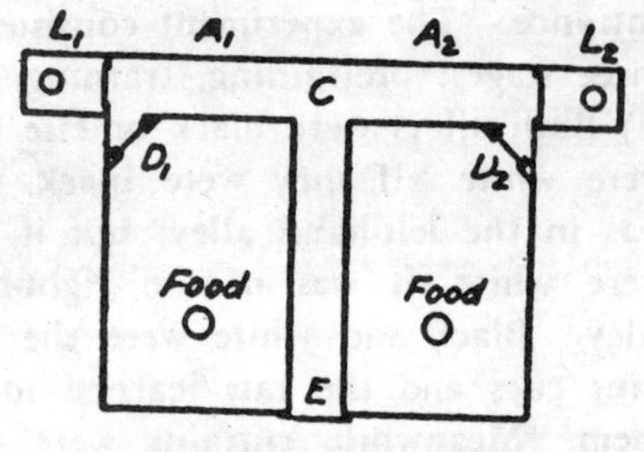

FIG. 20-10. (Muenzinger, 1934a.) A discrimination box modeled after the simple T maze. The rat was placed at E, the entrance, and proceeded to C, the choice point, thence into one of the side alleys, A_1 and A_2, and thence into the adjoining food box if its sliding door was open. If he found this door closed, he would retrace to the choice point, explore the other side alley, find its door open, and obtain food. These doors, D_1 and D_2, could not be seen from the choice point.

Light-dark discrimination was required, with light the positive cue. The 15-watt lamp L_1 illuminated the alley A_1 through a diffusing sheet of ground glass, and similarly the lamp L_2 illuminated the alley A_2. When L_1 was lit the door D_1 was open, the other alley being dark and its door closed. (See Muenzinger & Powloski, 1951, for an improvement of this T discrimination box.)

In some of the experiments hazards were introduced into the side alleys, such as a moderate shock from a floor grid, or a 6-inch gap to be jumped.

Some of the results are tabulated below (from Muenzinger, Bernstone & Richards, 1938):

	Trials to learn	*Dark choices (errors) in first 100 trials*	*VTE in first 100 trials*
No shock	107	23	35
Shock in dark alley	35	11	47
Shock in light alley	45	17	49

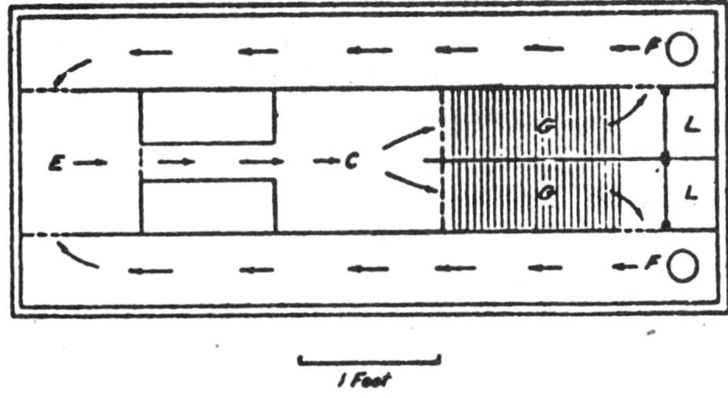

FIG. 20-11. (Wischner, 1947.) A discrimination box with doors to prevent retracing and with floor grids in the approach alleys. The doors are indicated by broken lines, the grids by parallel cross lines. L,L are 40-watt lamps (behind diffusing glass) only one of which is lit on any trial. F,F, are food cups, but only the one next to the lighted lamp contains food on any trial. The rat is placed in E, the entrance compartment, and advances to C, the choice compartment, where he has the choice of a light and a dark alley, G,G. After crossing the grid, which may or may not be charged, he passes through the side door to the food cup and thence back through the side alley into E, where he remains shut in for the 20-30-second interval before the next trial.

This, then, was a light-dark discrimination experiment, with light positive, and with no opportunity for retracing or correction of an error in the same trial. Some results reported by Wischner (1947, 1948, 1950) are tabulated below:

	Trials to learn	*Dark choices in first 100 trials*	*VTE in first 100 trials*
No shock	152	45	7
Shock in dark alley	104	24	21
Shock in light alley	159	55	35

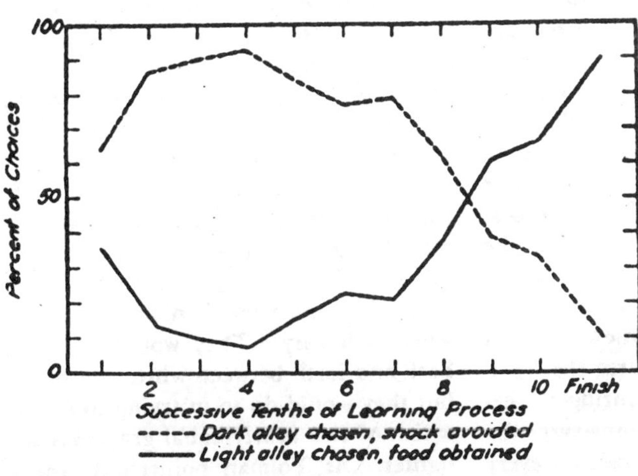

FIG. 20-12. (After Wischner, 1947, p. 278.) The average learning curve of rats in the discrimination box of Figure 20-11, with both food and shock always in the lighted alley. This is a Vincent curve (p. 536) designed to show the general course of learning by a group when the individuals differ considerably in the number of trials required to reach a criterion of mastery. Each individual's curve is divided into tenths along the base line, the percents of dark and light choices are determined for each successive tenth, and the percents of all individuals for the same tenth are averaged. The two curves shown are of course equivalent to each other, but they are both included to bring out the fact that we have here two learning curves. The rats learned first to avoid the shock by taking the dark alley and second to obtain the food by taking the lighted alley. They also learned to minimize the shock. They would "get set before the lighted alley, hop on the grill landing on all four paws, and then hop off, clearing the grill in this fashion with a single contact."

(The last point on each curve lies beyond the limits of the Vincent curve and is added to show that trials were continued until 20 consecutive trials gave only 10 percent of dark choices.)

zinger & Newcomb, 1936; Muenzinger & Fletcher, 1937). The authors' suggestion is that VTE works by prolonging and improving the animal's reception of the important stimuli.

In these experiments the "correction procedure" was followed, i.e., retracing was allowed so that each trial continued until the food was obtained. The noncorrection procedure has yielded somewhat different results, reported under Figure 20-11 (Wischner, 1947).

We need not be disturbed by the discrepancy between the Muenzinger and Wischner experiments in absolute number of trials. Each "trial with correction" continues till the animal reaches the food. If his first choice fails, he corrects it, so in a way having two trials, the second being correct. Each "trial without correction" includes only a single choice, correct or incorrect. But why should shock for correct response make so poor a showing without correction and so good a showing with correction? The reason is pretty clear. When shock is in the lighted alley, with no correction allowed, a rat entering this alley first encounters the shock and later, since he cannot retrace, finds the food. The light quickly becomes a signal of shock, and the rat first learns to avoid the lighted alley, as shown in Figure 20-12. Consequently he does not at first often secure the food reinforcement, and it takes him many trials to form the light-food association. In Muenzinger's experiment with correction, however, the food reinforcement is obtained on every trial and the light-food association can be quickly established. Because of the conflict between the food-seeking and the shock-avoiding tendencies, there is much VTE which apparently assists in the learning.

VTE is usually described as "looking" at both doors or alleys before making the decisive movement, but it is more adequately described as "looking and preparing to move," by crouching to jump, for example. In one experiment (Muenzinger & Gentry, 1931) the cues were auditory: tone *versus* silence. When the tone sounded, there was food in the left-hand alley and shock in the right-hand one; during silence the reverse. VTE was much in evidence and seemed to be helpful. But what good could "looking" do since the visual cues were the same during tone and silence? Well, the important thing for learning is to get a quick sequence of cue, response, reinforcement—for example, a quick sequence of the compound cue, tone plus view of the left-hand alley, followed immediately by jump and food. Such a sequence is well suited to establish an association.

VTE and difficulty of discrimination. Another persistent investigator of VTE has been Tolman. One of his basic observations (1939) was that a rat on the jumping stand exhibited more VTE in learning a white-black discrimination than in learning the more difficult gray-black discrimination. Now human beings in a psychophysical experiment exhibit something much like VTE when discrimination is difficult but not when it is easy. They would not look back and forth between white and black, but they would do so in trying to decide which of two nearly equal grays was the lighter. As Tolman points out (1941), the human subject is told what cue to follow; for example, he is told to point to the lighter gray. The rat has to discover for himself what stimuli are to be followed, and the large white-black difference "catches his eye" sooner than the smaller difference between two grays.

Moreover, the human subject lays aside from the outset any personal preferences he may have for darker shades, or for pointing to the right, or for pointing alternately to right and left. The rat has such preferences to overcome in the course of the experiment, and it is in the process of getting rid of them that VTE is likely to appear. A conflict arises between the existing habit and the incipient tendency to follow the relevant cue. In the individual case shown in Figure 20-13 the VTE clearly helped the animal break away from his position habit.

Carrying this jumping-stand study further, Tolman & Minium (1942) started a group of rats with white-black discrimination, white positive, and continued the experiment for many days after near perfection was attained. The VTE count was high during the period of active learning and then sank to a low level. Now the task was made more difficult by the substitution of light gray for white as the positive stimulus. A few errors crept in and VTE rose for a time and then declined as near-perfect success was regained. Once more the task was made more difficult by the introduction of dark gray as the positive stimulus. Many errors now kept occurring, and VTE rose and remained high. At a gross descriptive level, these rats behaved like human beings in the psychophysical experiment —and in two respects: (1) having learned their "instructions" in the first, white-black, part of the experiment, they showed more VTE when discrimination became more difficult; and (2) when they found errors creeping in, they slowed down and looked more closely at the stimuli. As success is attained, there is a tendency in both rats and men to speed up and become less attentive to the necessary cues; then some errors come in and induce renewed care and effort. Other instances of this sort were observed by Crannell (1942) in a different sort of problem.

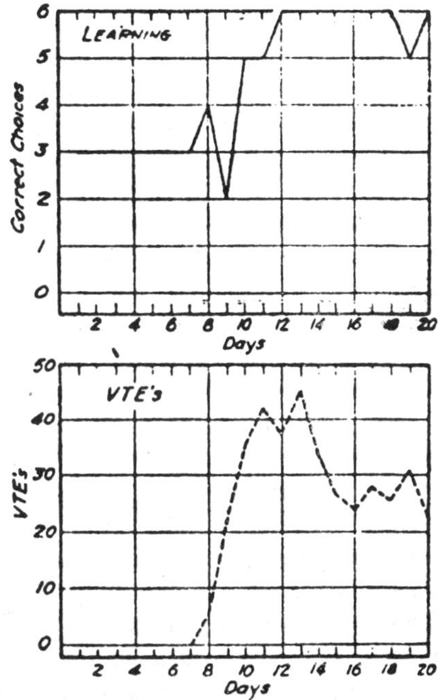

FIG. 20-13. (Tolman, 1939.) Correct choices and VTE counts in the case of a single rat learning a white—black discrimination. White was the positive cue. There were six trials a day on the jumping stand. For the first seven days, this animal jumped to the left-hand door every time, so obtaining the food in exactly half of the trials. So far, there was no hesitation or VTE. But on the third trial of the eighth day, instead of jumping promptly to the left-hand door, which happened to be black, he hesitated, turned to the other (white) door and finally jumped to that door. From that time on he followed the white cue more and more frequently and finally with almost perfect consistency. His VTE count increased during the period of active learning, and declined again when success in obtaining the food had reached the 100-percent level.

VTE has also been observed in maze learning (Jackson, 1943), especially at choice points where the animal has a strong tendency to enter a blind alley. A blind alley that points directly toward the food box creates this sort of difficulty. The tendency to enter the blind alley has to be overcome, and VTE seems to be a factor in overcoming it. This is another example of conflict between an existing tendency and the incipient use of the correct cue. Sometimes it is not so much conflict as uncertainty that gives rise to VTE. When the animal has learned to follow a certain cue consistently, and then a somewhat similar cue is substituted, uncertainty arises and with it hesitation and VTE. We just noticed one example, when a white-black discrimination had been thoroughly learned and then gray was substituted for the white. Lashley reported other examples in his tests for equivalent stimuli (p. 592). If the substituted positive cue is not too different from the old one, it is followed consistently though with hesitation and VTE. If it is too different, the animal lapses into a position habit.

The VTE studies have brought out several points of interest, the most important being perhaps the demonstration of habits and preferences that must be overcome in order to achieve a consistent adaptive response to a novel situation. The subject enters such a situation with pre-existing tendencies that must be overcome, and in the early stages of learning he is apt to pick up false cues that must be brushed aside before the situation is mastered. The learner never starts from scratch but always with a handicap.

THE "DELAYED REACTION"

A form of behavior that is well within human capabilities is suggested by the commands "Ready . . . Go!" At the Ready signal you prepare to perform a certain act but the execution of the act is delayed until you receive the signal to Go. The act may be specified in the Ready signal as when a body of men receives the commands "Forward . . . March," or "To the rear . . . March." The delay may be much longer than a few seconds; it lasts overnight when you put your purse in a certain drawer and know exactly where to find it in the morning. Somehow—whether by aid of words or memory images or by some other symbolic and representative internal process—you are able to remember the location of a perceived object or activate your preparation after an interval of time.

If a similar ability could be demonstrated in subhuman animals, there would be some evidence of rudimentary symbolic processes in them. An experiment for investigating this possibility was designed by Carr and his associates in the Chicago laboratory. It was based on the discrimination experiment, as explained under Figure 20-14, and the first important research on the delayed reaction in animals and young children was performed by Hunter (1913).

The animal receives a stimulus signaling the location of food but is not free to go there until after a delay. The response variable may be the maximum delay that still permits consistently correct responses, or it may be the percent of correct responses after a certain duration of delay; and the animal's behavior during the delay period may throw light on the nature of the "symbolic" process.

The two-stage or indirect method. The experimenter needs to base his delayed-reaction experiment on a well-established discrimination. To approach visible food is a well-established response, and if this response is utilized, a one-stage or direct method is employed. If the discriminative response must first be learned, the method is two-stage or indirect. Both methods were introduced by Hunter, first the two-stage (1913) and later the one-stage (1917). Figure 20-14 gives a dia-

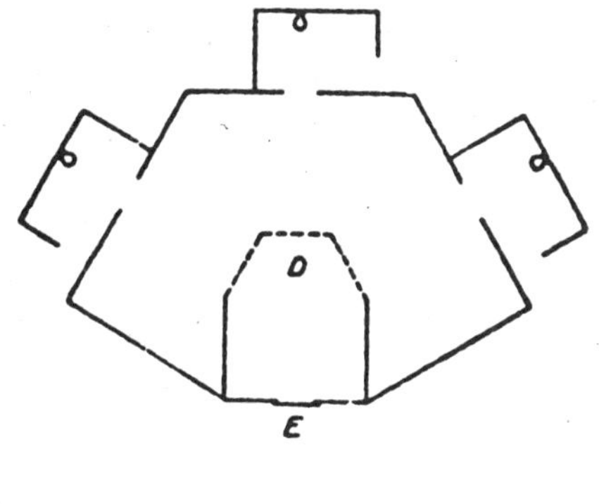

Fig. 20-14. (Hunter, 1913.) Delayed-reaction box. This size was used for rats. The rat was admitted through a door at E to the detention chamber D from which he could look through glass walls (shown here by broken lines) at three open doors, 2½ inches from the glass. Behind each open door is a 3-candlepower bulb. Only one bulb is lighted on any trial. When the experimenter raises the glass barrier, the rat is free to go directly to any one of the three open doors. If he enters the lighted door, he finds himself in a small chamber from which a side door leads around to E where he is given food. If he enters either of the dark chambers, his progress is blocked by the closed side door. The "delay" is introduced by the experimenter, who turns out the signal light before raising the glass barrier. In some of the experiments the detention chamber, now made of wire netting, filled nearly the whole of the large box, so enabling the rat to approach the chosen door more closely and also to move about more freely before the wire barrier was raised. On the whole, the rats did somewhat better, but they still had to stay close to the chosen door in order to complete the correct response after the delay.

gram of the discrimination box used with rats in 1913. The rat had first to learn (by dint usually of 160–300 trials) to obtain food by choosing the lighted door. Delays were then introduced very gradually, the light being turned off while the animal was on his way to the door, then just as he was released by the experimenter's raising the barrier, and then just before he was released. Finally the delay was lengthened until the response broke down, i.e., was not correct in much more than the chance ⅓ of the trials. Most of the rats broke down in less than 2 seconds, but a few held out for 3, 4, or even 10 seconds. They would face toward the lighted door while the light was burning and for a second or two after it went out, but then would lose their aim. This "aim," in the rat's case, was not a steady posture like that of a pointing dog, but a series of attacks on the barrier in the direction of the lighted door. When the rat was released, he went forward as he was momentarily headed, right or wrong. None of Hunter's 13 rats could regain the correct aim consistently after they had lost it. In order to make a correct response after the guiding light had ceased, they had to maintain their bodily orientation. The same was true of his two dogs, but the dogs could maintain their bodily orientation longer, sometimes (but rarely) as long as 5 minutes, by standing, sitting, or lying with the body or at least the head pointed in the right direction. Hunter's four raccoons sometimes showed a different type of behavior. After the signal light went out, they had no need of maintaining a fixed bodily orientation, but could turn from side to side and still go to the correct door when released, provided the delay did not exceed 10–15 seconds.

Young children in a different but fairly comparable setup did not maintain any fixed bodily orientation during the delay, and could still respond correctly after delays of 1–4 minutes and longer. They could attend to other things during the delay and still remember which object had been signaled.

As for the rat, he made a better showing in a similar experiment of Honzik (1931) who however introduced one change: he concealed the three doors behind an opaque screen during the delay period, instead of leaving them visible behind a barrier of glass or wire netting. The rats all succeeded after delays of 7 seconds or more, and they succeeded after running around freely during the delay. An explanation: concealing the doors would prevent any approaches to the wrong doors during the delay, such false responses as would create interfering associations and retroactive inhibition (p. 761).

There was for a time some disposition on the part of many psychologists to question Hunter's finding on raccoons, for it was felt that only by some use of language could a subject remember which door had been lighted after the light had gone out. Children could use verbal means of identification, by saying "middle, right, left." However there was no evidence that the children in Hunter's first experiment used words in this helpful way. They sometimes said, "I know which it is. *This* is the one" (pointing). But it was evidently not the "This" but the pointing that identified the object.

The one-stage or direct method. In Hunter's second experiment (1917), made on a child of 13 months who did not yet talk beyond a few words, the direct or one-stage method was used. The child had already learned to retrieve an object that she saw placed in hiding. Now she was seated with three boxes in an arc in easy reach before her; she watched as a toy was placed in one of the boxes and the lid closed; her eyes were then covered, or she was taken up and turned around, etc.; and finally she was reseated before the boxes and made her choice which was correct in about 80 percent of the trials after a delay of 15 seconds.

Since that time this direct or retrieving method has been extensively used with monkeys and chimpanzees as subjects and with such striking success that no doubt remains of the genuineness of delayed reaction independent of language. A typical one-stage experiment on monkeys was reported by Tinklepaugh in 1928. While the animal was sitting on his customary chair and watching, the experimenter hid a piece of banana under one of two tin cups on the floor. He then took the monkey out of the room for 5 minutes, brought him back to his chair and told him to "go get the food." The monkey unhesitatingly went to the baited cup, lifted it and took the banana. The delay could be much longer than 5 minutes without reaching any precise limit for successful response.

Similar results from the chimpanzee were reported by Yerkes & Yerkes in the same year (1928), with a follow-up study by Tinklepaugh (1932) who demonstrated "multiple delayed reaction" in both monkeys and chimpanzees. Several rooms of the laboratory were made ready by placing on the floor of each room two containers 4-5 feet apart and about 6 feet from a marked spot where the animal was to sit. Brought into the first room and seated at the designated spot, the animal watched the experimenter bait one of the two containers but was not permitted to approach the container. Instead, he was taken into the second room and treated similarly, and so on through the series of rooms. For the test, the animal was then taken again to each room, seated at the same spot and told to "go get the food." In this test the chimpanzees surpassed the monkeys, for while the two monkeys scored 80 percent correct in a series of five rooms, the two chimpanzees scored 90 percent in a series of 10 rooms. Human adults in a similar experiment scored about on a par with the chimpanzees, not making systematic use of linguistic aids such as "right, left, left, right, . . ." According to their introspections, they sometimes used landmarks such as a spot in the floor and often could not tell what cues they were using.

In an interesting variation of the single delayed reaction, Tinklepaugh (1928, 1932), after baiting a container with a banana, secretly substituted a piece of carrot or lettuce, a less preferred food. When the monkey or chimpanzee lifted the container, his behavior indicated surprise and disappointment. He continued to search in the neighborhood for the missing banana. He was set for the particular food as well as for its position.

Delayed reaction to color cues. In striking contrast to this ability of the primates to identify an object by its location is the great difficulty they have in learning to use color as a mark of identification. This contrast was noted by the authors already cited and more definitely by Nissen and his co-workers. The chimpanzee possesses good color sense and can learn without excessive difficulty to use red and green (or black and white) in the discrimination experiment. But if you place before him a red and a green container and bait the red one, and then change their locations while he is not looking, he fails to pick the red one consistently after even a short delay. Only after enormous labor by the experimenter in providing the animal with special training designed to make him more attentive and responsive to the color difference can he be brought to a fair degree of success in delayed reaction to color cues (Nissen, Riesen & Nowlis, 1938; Riesen, 1940; Riesen & Nissen, 1942; Finch, 1942). Human subjects have no difficulty in delayed reaction to color, commonly reporting the use of color names. Chimpanzees or monkeys do not suffer from lack of linguistic aids when locations have to be remembered, probably because spatial relations are so directly "given" in visual perception and so directly followed in motor response.

In a delayed-reaction experiment on children, Miller (1934) pitted color against position by an early use of the Ab—aB technique which we have described on page 598. Two boxes, one red and one yellow, stood a foot apart on the edge of a table before the child, who saw a toy dog placed in one of the boxes. The boxes were then screened for 10 seconds, during which time they were interchanged in position. The screen being removed, the child was told to find the dog. Would he choose by color or by position of the two boxes? The result was very interesting. Children a year old chose mostly by position, but with increasing age color became the dominant cue.

Here again we see that position can be learned and retained without any use of language. With regard to color, we might hastily conclude that the mere ability to use the color names enabled the older children to notice and retain the color cues. But we must remember that human beings do much more with the colors than merely name them. The young child often learns the common color names before using them correctly. He later learns to attend to the colors themselves. In general, discrimination is primarily a matter of perception rather than of motor response. This fact is again brought out in the experiment described under Figure 20-15.

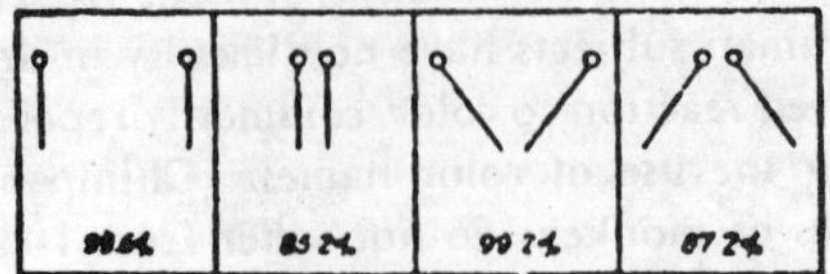

FIG. 20-15. (Data from Nissen, Carpenter & Cowles, 1936.) Delayed reaction in string pulling. Two food cups could be pulled in to the chimpanzee's cage by attached strings. One of the cups was baited with a piece of orange while the animal watched. A screen was then interposed for the delay period which varied from 3 to 120 seconds as the animal became more expert, but was equalized for the four conditions shown in the four sections of the figure. The two cups were either 55 inches or 10 inches apart, and the same was true of the near ends of the strings where the animal pulled them. The percents of correct delayed reactions are shown. When the cups were far apart, practically all the responses were correct, but when the cups were close together, there were many errors. In the first case no harm was done if the response ends of the strings were near together; nor in the second case was it any advantage to separate the response ends of the strings. It was the location of the baited cup, not the prospective response movement, that was retained through the period of delay.

CUE LEARNING BY HUMAN SUBJECTS

If we compare these experiments on discrimination learning with the numerous human experiments on discrimination which go by the name of psychophysics, we can see a good reason for the predominance of animal experiments in the field of discrimination learning. The human subject in a psychophysical experiment is told what cue he has to observe and discriminate. He is instructed in the case of visual stimuli, for example, to compare them in respect to intensity, or extent, or color, or shape; it would be ridiculous to leave it to him to discover the relevant cue if we are seeking to determine his ability in discrimination of intensity. The early psychologists, in trying to extend the psychophysical experiments to animals, were forced to leave it to the animal subject to discover what cue was to be followed, and so what was designed as a psychophysical experiment became an experiment in learning—and quite an important one as we have seen. But if we now desire to carry these animal experiments back to the human laboratory, we find the tasks too easy to yield much information about human learning. Imagine a human adult placed before two boxes, one marked with a triangle and the other with a circle, which are interchanged from trial to trial, and being told, "Choose one of these boxes and I will tell you whether you are right or wrong"! The experimenter would need to be more subtle if he wished to obtain a learning curve or any light on the learning process. The cues would have to be more complex or obscure or conflicting.

In one of the few experiments intended to bring out the process of discrimination learning in human adults, Prentice (1949) took pains to mislead the subjects by offering several false cues that were more obvious than the correct one. It was a "two-door" type of experiment. The subject saw two windows in a screen. One window showed a square, the other a circle. If the square was large, the circle was small, and vice versa; and if the square was white, the circle was black. The subject had two response keys, located under the two windows, one key marked with a square and one with a circle. He was instructed to choose the square or the circle and to signify his choice by pressing the corresponding key. Reward and punishment were provided: a light signal for a correct choice, a buzzer for an incorrect one. In following any of the obvious cues, he would be correct only half the time, since size and shape were irrelevant and all that counted was the location of the white figure. "Press the key on the same side as the white figure" was the solution. Simple enough!—but the setup and instructions were so misleading that 40 percent of the college students who served as subjects failed to reach the solution in 100 massed trials. The experimenter wished to obtain introspective evidence of any "hypotheses" that the subjects were trying out early or late in the learning process. They were asked to report after each trial "why they made the choice they did." False hypotheses were reported in the early trials, and the correct hypothesis or some approximation to it was often reported before the responses became consistently correct.

The reversed-cues technique was tried on one group of subjects. For the first 20 trials (a presumable "presolution period") they were rewarded where they should have been punished, and vice versa; then they were switched without break or comment to the regular rewards and punishments. It took about 20 extra trials to make up for the 20 trials of false training. This result was quantitatively not in agreement with either of the two theories that have been so much debated, those of Lashley and of Hull and Spence (p. 594). For according to Lashley, the presolution period should not count one way or the other, and no extra trials would be required by the group that had the false rewards and punishments. But according to Hull and Spence, the presolution period should be so much to the good for the subjects that received the correct training, and so much to the bad for the others—a difference of 40 trials to be made up. This quantitative reasoning may be open to some debate, and perhaps the most significant new result of this human experiment is contained in the following statement (Prentice, p. 190): "The solution typically appeared as a tentative hypothesis based on summarizing the results of the preceding three or four trials." In other words, the correct hypothesis is decisive, once it emerges; but it emerges as the cumulative effect of reinforcements obtained in a series of lucky successes. Or, in terms of "attention" (p. 74): the question is how the subject ever comes to notice the obscure correct cue, and the answer is that a series of chance successes forces it on his attention. Neither the Lashley nor the Hull-Spence theory, accordingly, can be accepted as adequate, but each has something to contribute. Evidence for this conclusion can be found in other studies, especially in one of Heidbreder (1924) which was reviewed in the first edition of the present book.

The learning of concepts. Experiments on concept formation have followed the general pattern of the discrimination-learning experiments. Behavior governed by concepts requires that the same response shall be made to objects of the same class, but a different response or no response at all to objects not belonging to that class. A relatively simple experiment of this sort was made by Long (1940) on children 3 to 6 years old. A box with two small windows was placed before the child. If he pressed on the correct window, a small bit of candy rolled out to him. Through one window he saw a rubber ball, through the other a rectangular block of wood, and the ball was the positive stimulus. When the child had learned to choose the ball regularly, he was tested for equivalent stimuli (p. 589): spherical objects of various sizes, colors, and materials were paired with various angular objects—and the spheres were consistently chosen. Cylindrical objects substituted for the spheres were usually chosen after a little additional training, and flat cardboard circles were chosen as against flat polygons. When two polygons were presented, the one more nearly circular, i.e., having the larger number of sides, was chosen about 75 percent of the time, except by the youngest children, the three-year-olds. Thus the concept of a sphere or ball, which was no doubt already familiar to these children, was readily adapted to cover other varieties of roundness.

Experiments in naming. For analogous experiments on human adults, the task has been made more difficult by the use of unfamiliar classes of objects, by the requirement that more than two concepts must be formed simultaneously, by the use of nonsense names to be learned for the several concepts, and by other devices. A pioneer experiment was that of Hull (1920).[1] It was modeled after the paired-associates experiment in memory but can also be regarded as a form of the experiment on discrimination learning. Nonsense names were assigned to Chinese characters (Fig. 20-16), and the subject learned to name each character. These characters are compounds of smaller characters known as radicals, and the same radical is embodied in many compound characters. Each of the characters employed by Hull contained one of 12 selected radicals, and all the characters containing the same radical were assigned the same name. The characters were written on separate cards, and the cards were assembled into packs of 12 so that each pack contained all 12 radicals. The procedure was as follows: By aid of a memory apparatus Pack No. 1 was exposed serially and as each character was shown its name was spoken by *E* and repeated by *O*. The second time around,

[1] The older literature on concept formation is more fully covered in the first edition of this book, pp. 800–806.

Word	Concept	Pack I	Pack II	Pack III	Pack IV	Pack V	Pack VI
oo	[illegible]	[illegible]	[illegible]	[illegible]	[illegible]	[illegible]	[illegible]
yer	[illegible]	[illegible]	[illegible]	珍	[illegible]	[illegible]	[illegible]
li	力	[illegible]	動	[illegible]	[illegible]	[illegible]	[illegible]
ta	弓	[illegible]	弧	[illegible]	[illegible]	[illegible]	[illegible]
deg	石	[illegible]	[illegible]	[illegible]	[illegible]	[illegible]	[illegible]
ling	[illegible]	[illegible]	[illegible]	[illegible]	[illegible]	[illegible]	[illegible]

FIG. 20-16. (Hull, 1920.) Six of the radicals used, with their assigned nonsense names, and some characters containing each radical.

O tried to anticipate *E* in pronouncing the names, and the series was repeated until *O* had learned all the names for these 12 characters. Pack No. 2 was now shown, and *O* was told that the same names would be used and that he might try to "guess" the names the first time around. The order of the radicals was different from pack to pack. Six packs were learned and the percent of correct first-trial guesses increased in each successive pack; thus, on the average of 18 subjects:

Pack No.	2	3	4	5	6
Percent correct on first trial	27	38	47	55	56

This increasing ability to identify new representatives of a class was due in part to the subject's effort to discover how the characters called by the same name were alike, i.e., we may say, to his testing of definite hypotheses. The 27-percent correct on the first trial of Pack No. 2 cannot be so explained because *O* had learned Pack No. 1 with no knowledge that a second pack would be presented. It was also true at the end of the experiment that many characters were correctly named although the corresponding classes could not be defined by a sketch of their radicals. This last result has been obtained in other experiments and in ordinary life. Certain objects (or people) appear similar without our being able to specify exactly how they are similar.

Sorting experiments. In a typical sorting experiment several classes of objects are mixed or shuffled and the subject is instructed to classify the objects by sorting them into groups that belong together. It is left to him to discover what classification is appropriate. In one of her numerous experiments on the "attainment of concepts," Heidbreder (1948, p. 202) used a pack of 144 cards, each card with a different drawing on it, and instructed her subjects (18 college women) to sort the pack into 9 piles, "according to a classification which you are to work out for yourself," working as rapidly as possible. The average time taken by the subjects was about 10 minutes. Some of the drawings are reproduced in Figure 20.17. There were three kinds of *things* in the pack, three kinds of nonsense *forms*, and *number groups* of 3, 4, and 6 items. The question was whether the subjects would discover all of these classes by their own efforts. For the subjects as a group the score was 81-percent success in things, 39 percent in forms, and 31 percent in numbers. This result agreed with the result of other experiments by the same author in showing that thing concepts were the most readily attained and used, number concepts the least readily. Thing concepts presumably have the advantage of lying closest to the practical needs of manipulation in ordinary life, while number concepts have the disadvantage of dependence on counting and the use of symbols.

Another form of sorting task, much used as a test for individual differences, presents a collection of objects or drawings which can be classified in several different ways—according to several different systems or principles. After the subject has classified them in one way, he is asked if he can classify them differently. The purpose of the test is to ascertain whether he can shift readily from one basis of classification to another (Weigl, 1941). Goldstein has found that brain-injured patients have great difficulty in making such a shift and has attributed the difficulty to lack of ability for "abstract behavior," i.e., the ability to get away from the concrete situation and regard objects as specimens of a general class (Goldstein & Scheerer, 1941).

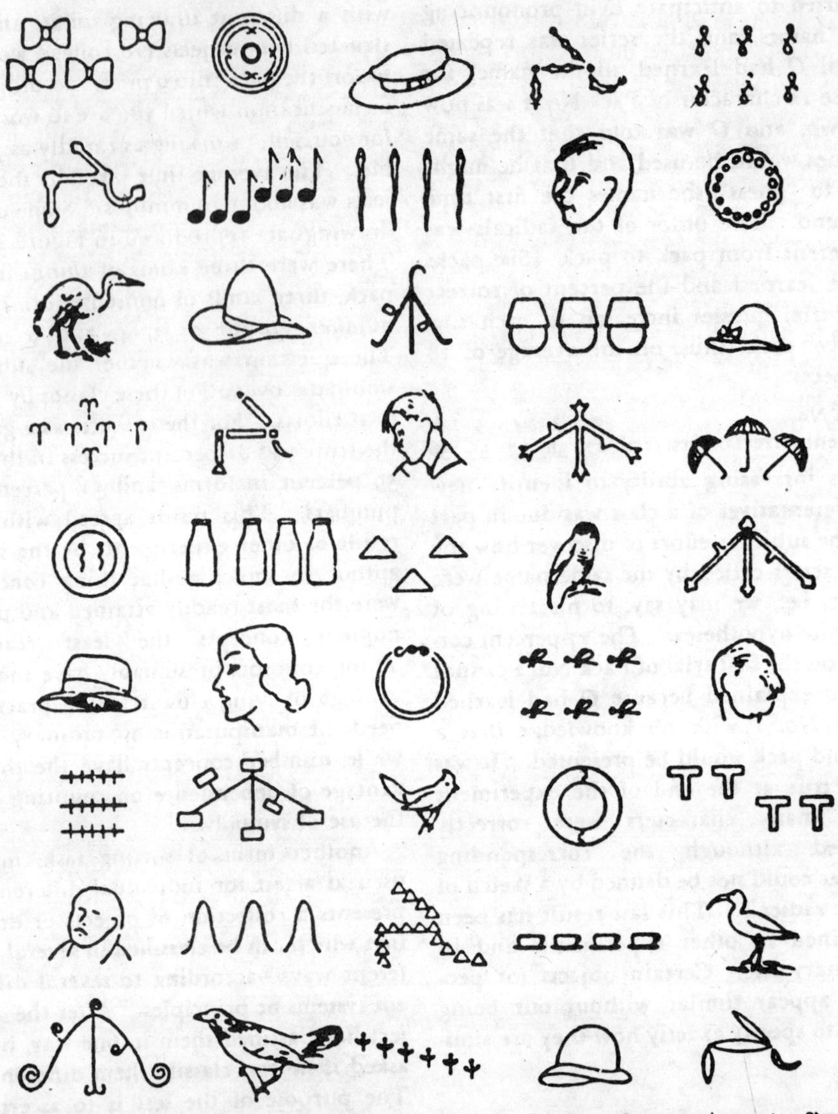

FIG. 20·17. (Heidbreder, 1947, p. 95.) Sample drawings used in a sorting experiment (1948). Each column shows one sample of each of the 9 classes. In all there were 16 specimens of each class, each drawing being on a separate card, and the whole pack of 144 cards being well shuffled.

This kind of task has been utilized by Grant and his co-workers in experiments on shifting cues. There is a pack of 64 cards to be sorted into four labeled compartments, without further instructions except that each throw of a card will be called "right" or "wrong" by the experimenter. The four labels are: a single red triangle; two green stars; three yellow crosses; and four blue circles. So the cards in the pack can be matched with the labels in either color, form, or number. At first *E* arbitrarily calls the cards "right" if they are matched according to *color:* but as soon as 10 consecutive cards are correctly sorted on this basis, he shifts without warning to *form,* then to *number,* and later once more around the list of categories. It took the subjects (96 college students) only three or four trials on the average to discover the first rule, but when the first unheralded shift was made, they required 14 trials to discover what was wrong and find the new rule. The later shifts were more quickly mastered, in 13, 9, and finally in less than 8 trials on the average. The subjects, or some of them, must have learned to expect the shifts. In this experiment, in contrast to Heidbreder's, the number concept was no harder to use than the form, but if anything a little easier, perhaps because the number of items stood out more distinctly (Grant, Jones & Tallantis, 1949).

As we have seen in several instances, experimenters in the field of concept formation are inclined to keep their subjects in the dark as to the nature of the real task, disguising it as a task in sorting or memorizing. Good results can however be obtained by a more straightforward procedure, with the subject informed that different drawings are going to be called by the same name because they are of the same type, and with the experiment continued till the subject gives a fairly adequate definition of each type. One such experiment verified Heidbreder's finding that concepts of things were quickly attained, concepts of numbers slowly—at least by women college students (Wenzel & Flurry, 1948).

For a critical review of many experiments on concept formation, with bibliography, see Vinacke (1951).

21

MAZE LEARNING

The systematic use of animal subjects in the study of learning began about 1900, experiments on the conditional response and on discrimination learning appearing shortly after that date, and experiments with the maze and with the problem box shortly before it. The original interests of the experimenters were in brain physiology or in mental evolution, but the experiments they designed have continued to the present day to be important in the general theory of learning. Evidently we could not do justice to human and animal learning if we left out of account such essential achievements as learning to get about in the environment and to manipulate objects. Thorndike's problem box (1898) called for learning to manipulate a door button or some other object, while Small's maze (1899, 1900) called for learning a fairly complex path. Thorndike's line of study will be considered later (pp. 818 ff.).

Small's study was qualitative rather than quantitative, but for that very reason his careful observations still deserve attention as an introduction to maze learning. He built a 6 × 8-foot reproduction of the famous Hampton Court maze and used it as an instrument of research. It was constructed of wire mesh and placed on a sawdust-covered wooden floor. Some food was placed in the central room of the maze, and two white rats were placed together at the entrance. Working independently they explored back and forth throughout the maze, pausing to dig in the sawdust or bite the wires. The first one reached the food in 15 minutes. They were left in the maze all night, and when tested the next day, they

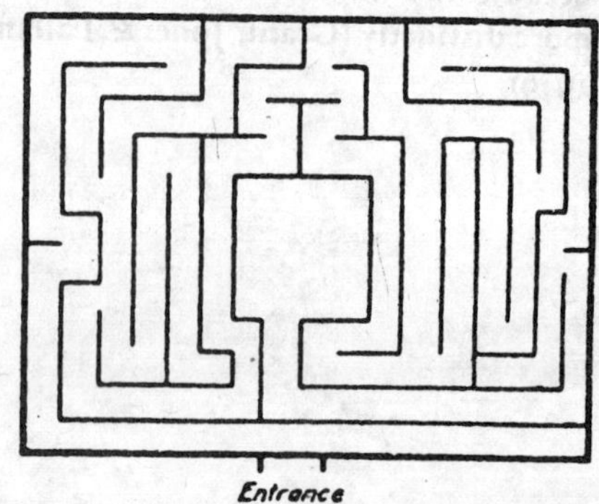

Fig. 21-1. Ground plan of the Hampton Court maze as used by Small and his successors.

covered the distance from entrance to food in 3 minutes. On subsequent trials the time became still shorter and the "errors" (entering a blind alley or retracing the main path) decreased to one or two per trial. In an intermediate stage of the learning they would hesitate near the entrance and then "flash" through to the goal. They would enter a previously explored blind alley slowly and then run out quickly. When not very hungry they would "play by the way, strolling nonchalantly into the blind alleys," but then making a quick dash to the goal box. Even when the run from start to finish was free from errors, it was not a stereotyped motor routine. This maze offered two alternative paths, both leading to the goal but one shorter than the other; the rats came in time to take the shorter route almost exclusively. After the maze had been well learned, the experimenter opened a short cut which the rats quickly adopted. Small's observations led him to the theory that they learned the *place* rather than a sequence of movements. "The central fact in the process seems to be the recognition by the rats of particular parts of the maze."

The fact that the white rat can master a complex maze, and do so fairly quickly, opened up a number of theoretical problems; and in the effort to reach conclusive solutions of these problems psychologists have varied and simplified the maze pattern, standardized the experimental procedure, and quantified the scoring of the animal's performance. These technical improvements will come to light as we proceed.

SENSORY CUES IN MAZE LEARNING

By use of which of the senses did Small's rats find their way through the maze? By smell? Doubtless the odor of food coming diffusely through the wire-mesh walls provided an incentive, but it could not lead the animals along the crooked path. Nor could the animals find the food by following their own previous trails, for in their wanderings they left their scent in the blind alleys as well as along the correct path. Two of the rats became blind during the experiment, and yet learned the maze as quickly as the seeing animals. Small inferred that neither sight nor smell, but most probably touch and kinesthesis provided the essential data for the rat's maze running.

Watson (1907), in repeating and extending these experiments, made a more serious effort to identify the sensory cues. His method was to exclude one sense at a time and determine (a) whether animals that had already learned the maze could still run it without error, and (b) whether previously untrained animals could learn the maze as quickly as the normal animal.

Visual cues he excluded by darkening the room. Animals already trained in the light continued to run the maze correctly in the dark, and untrained animals learned as quickly in darkness as in the light. To make perfectly sure, he blinded some rats by removing their eyeballs, an operation from which rats recover promptly. Blind rats learned the maze as quickly as normal ones, and animals blinded after learning the maze showed only a slight loss in efficiency. The essential cues, it seemed, could not be furnished by the sense of sight.

Other rats were deprived of the sense of smell by an operation which removed the olfactory bulbs, a part of the afferent neural path from the nose to the brain. These anosmic animals learned the maze as readily as normals, or showed no disturbance in running a previously learned maze.

Two rats he made partially deaf by removing from both ears the tympanic membranes and ossicles and then filling the middle-ear cavities with paraffin. These rats learned the maze as quickly as normals.

The cutaneous senses could not be completely eliminated by any feasible operation, but the soles of all the feet were anesthetized in already trained animals without any disturbance of their maze running. Cutting short the vibrissae ("whiskers") made an animal insecure in his movements for a time, but 48 hours later the running of a previously learned maze was perfectly normal; and such animals learned the maze in the normal time. Assuming that any important tactual cues must come from the vibrissae or the soles of the feet, Watson believed that he had pretty well excluded the sense of touch, as well as sight, smell, and hearing.

By the logic of exclusion, therefore, Watson inferred that the essential cues in maze learning and running were furnished by the kinesthetic or muscle sense. Other internal senses, such as the organic and that of the semicircular canals, might play some part; but the external senses were not essential in learning, though undoubtedly employed in exploration.

This conclusion obviously needed to be checked, if possible, by elimination of the kinesthetic sense. Much later Lashley found a way of accomplishing this result in large measure, though not completely (Lashley & Ball, 1929). The afferent neural path from the muscles of the trunk and legs passes up the dorsal columns of the spinal cord and can be transected in the neck region. After general recovery from this operation a rat betrays his loss of kinesthesis by a sprawling gait, dragging his legs, and stepping on the back of the foot instead of the sole. Yet rats that had learned a maze before this operation ran it almost perfectly after the operation, taking more time because of their inefficient gait, but following the correct path without straying into blind alleys. Rats that underwent the operation beforehand learned the maze as easily as normal rats (Ingebritsen, 1932). These facts "argue against the primary importance of kinesthesis in maze learning."

Logically we seem to be driven to the highly improbable conclusion that the essential cues in maze learning are furnished by the semicircular canals or by the stomach and other internal organs. We might continue our detective work by depriving rats of the semicircular canals—an operation that has often been performed in the study of those sense organs—and by cutting the vagus nerves and so depriving an animal of a large share of his organic sensation—another feasible operation. Apparently such experiments have been regarded as superfluous because another conclusion is logically possible, namely, that *no single one of the senses is essential for maze learning.*

Alternative and multiple cues. Usable though not essential cues might be provided by sight, by smell, by touch and kinesthesis, and even by hearing. The animal could use the best cues available, and the normal animal could use a combination of cues from different senses. Once this possibility is recognized we see that Watson's experiment is capable of further development. When he had found that neither blind rats nor anosmic rats were handicapped, he inferred that a blind-anosmic rat would learn the maze as well as a normal rat. This inference has been tested both in walled and in unwalled or open mazes (see below for this distinction). Lindley (1930) used a walled maze with several groups of rats: normal, blind, anosmic, and blind-anosmic. The normal group learned this maze (up to a certain criterion) in a median number of 12 trials, the blind in 14, the anosmic in 27; but for the blind-anosmic group no median could be found, since only 27 percent of this group succeeded in learning the maze. For the open maze we have the extensive data of Honzik (1936) who obtained averages from large groups, 42 or more rats in each group. Their relative learning efficiency is fairly shown by the Mean errors on the twelfth and twenty-fourth trials, as given in the following table:

Mean errors	*on 12th trial*	*on 24th trial*
Normal rats	.1	less than .1
Deaf rats	.2	.1
Anosmic rats	.2	.1
Blind rats	1.5	1.1
Blind-deaf rats	4.2	3.9
Blind-anosmic rats	5.8	5.4
Blind-deaf-anosmic rats	6.2	6.4

As the initial error score on this maze is about 6.5, the blind-deaf-anosmics made practically no progress in 24 trials. The three groups of seeing rats—normal, deaf, and anosmic—differ but little and are reliably superior to any of the blind groups. But to be merely blind is much less of a handicap than to be in addition either deaf or anosmic. The blind rat in the open maze can use either noise cues or odor cues, the latter being better according to the figures, and the difference being statistically reliable. But the blind-deaf-anosmic group, dependent on touch and kinesthesis, were apparently not learning the open maze at all, or only very, very slowly. The author comments as follows: "The conclusion that is forced upon us by the results with blind-deaf-anosmic rats is not that kinesthesis has no function in learning but that an act cannot be learned by kinesthesis alone. It is probable that only after learning on the basis of exteroceptive stimuli has begun can kinesthetic impulses begin to take some part in the perfecting of the habit." Other investigators have expressed similar opinions.

Cues as stimulus variables. In these operative experiments *E* manipulates an *O*-variable, the sensory equipment of the organism. It is possible to study cues also by manipulation of the environment, i.e., of the maze itself and its surroundings. The original mazes, whether constructed of wire mesh or of wood, had walled-in alleys. They allowed the subject no general view of the maze and so excluded one of the chief advantages of vision. They provided abundant tactual cues from the sides of the narrow alleys. Vincent (1912) and Miles (1930) introduced the open or elevated maze, in which the passages are simply wooden strips an inch or two wide, supported from beneath at such a height that the rats will not jump down and far enough apart to prevent their jumping across from one passage to another. There are no side walls to afford useful contacts, but vision is unobstructed.

When walled and open mazes of the same size and pattern are tried on comparable groups of normal rats, the open maze seems to be easier to learn, though the difference is not large or constant. With blind rats, there is a large difference, the open maze being much harder for them. Blind rats are much inferior to normals in the open maze but not in the walled maze. These relations are shown in the following results of Tsang (1934, 1936), the score being the total number of blind alleys entered by the rat in the first 150 trials:

	Walled maze		*Open maze*	
	M	SD_M	M	SD_M
Normal rats	99	14	75	9
Blind rats	108	10	244	18

As an example of the manipulation of visual cues we may cite an experiment of Snygg (1935) who constructed duplicate walled mazes but painted the walls of one maze black throughout, while in the others the blinds were painted white and the through paths black, or the reverse. This visual difference greatly facilitated the learning, cutting trials to learn down from 34 to as few as 7. Even when all the walls are painted alike, the rat can often see a dead end and so avoid the necessity of exploring a blind alley (Robinson & Wever, 1930). It has become a common practice to hang curtains in the alleys so as to prevent this easy discrimination.

Another type of cue-manipulation experiment goes back to Carr's important study of 1917. The principle is this: if an animal is using certain cues in finding his way through a maze, his run will be disturbed by altering these cues. For example, if light from one side of the laboratory room has been utilized as an orienting cue, moving the source of light will disturb the well-learned run. If the disturbance lasts only one or two trials, it may be due to the distraction of novelty, but if much new learning is necessary, the location of the light source was evidently an important cue. A variation of this experiment consists in continually changing certain cues during the learning process and thus retarding the learning if these cues are important. These procedures have been extensively employed by Honzik (1933, 1936) and by Wolfle (1935). Both intramaze and extramaze visual stimuli are found to serve as cues to the normal rat. Very interesting are the olfactory cues that a rat can find in a clean open maze built of wooden strips. If these strips are continually interchanged, normal rats are not much hindered, but blind rats make slow progress in learning. From the blind rat's sniffing at these strips of wood, it seems clear that he can distinguish one alley from another by their odors. Sounds also are utilized in unexpected ways: echoes from the walls, resonance of blind alleys, scratchy noises from different floor boards as the rat races over them, as well as extramaze noises from the street or living cage. Extramaze visual stimuli can be rendered useless by a "house" (Honzik, 1936) or "dome" (Blodgett & McCutchan, 1947) which encloses the maze with a uniform screen. Such surroundings greatly increase the difficulty of some mazes (Walthal, 1948). Another way of destroying some useful extramaze cues is to rotate the maze between trials (Wolfle, 1935).

It seems that the rat will use any cues available to him in the maze. The relative usefulness of any cue depends on the characteristics of the particular maze and of the extramaze environment.

THE MAZE PATTERN AS A FACTOR IN LEARNING

The Hampton Court maze used in the early studies of maze learning (p. 614) was soon felt to be unnecessarily complex and irregular, and many other maze patterns have been designed in the effort to secure a reliable measure of learning ability and in the effort to investigate specific factors in learning (Warden, Jenkins & Warner, 1935, pp. 234–244). For some purposes it is desirable to have all the blind alleys fundamentally alike, as in a T maze where the choice is always between a right and a left turn. The one-unit T maze has been much used (p. 624), and at the other extreme are the multiple T mazes of Stone and others (pp. 619, 639). The Y maze is similar except that the paths diverge at a smaller angle. The U maze is a T maze with an extra corner in each blind alley to conceal the dead end from a subject at the choice point, as in Figure 21-2. This particular pattern can be called semilinear since the correct path extends forward with only slight deviations to the right or left. A completely linear pattern is shown in Figure 21-3; it is practically one-dimensional as contrasted with the out-and-out two-dimensional character of Figure 21-4.

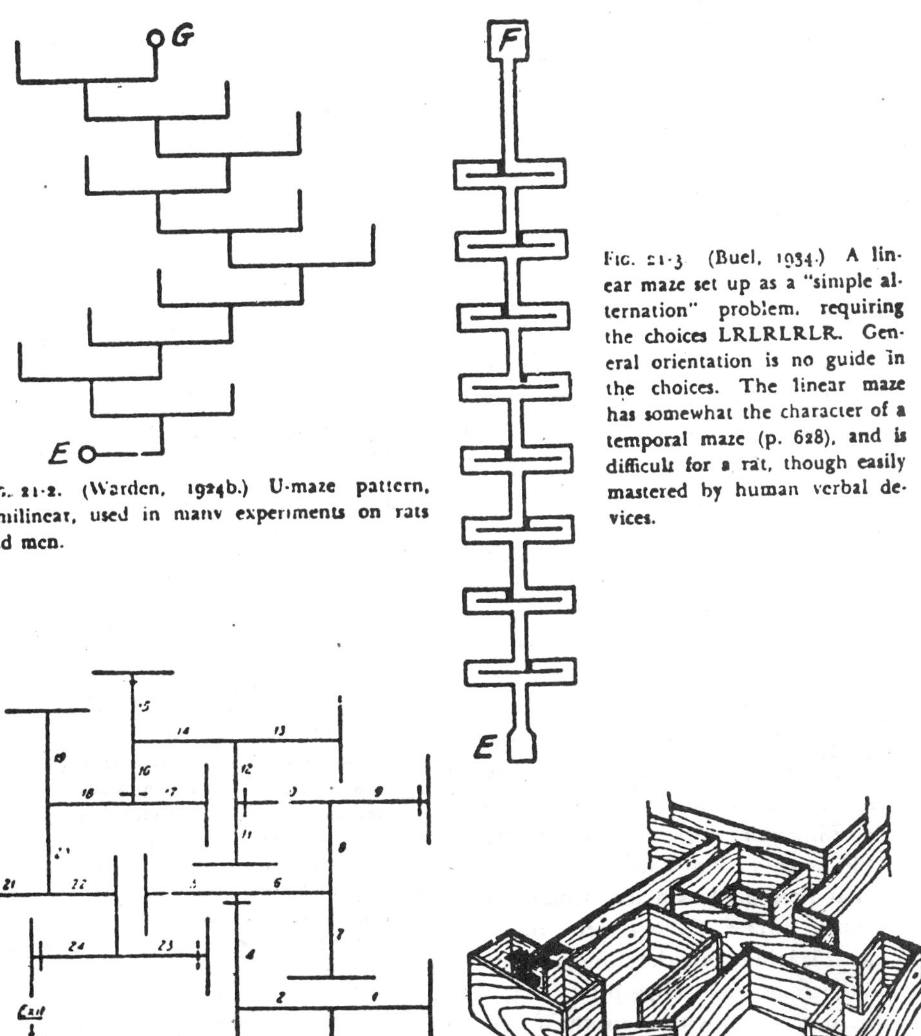

Fig. 21·2. (Warden, 1924b.) U-maze pattern, semilinear, used in many experiments on rats and men.

Fig. 21·3 (Buel, 1934.) A linear maze set up as a "simple alternation" problem, requiring the choices LRLRLRLR. General orientation is no guide in the choices. The linear maze has somewhat the character of a temporal maze (p. 628), and is difficult for a rat, though easily mastered by human verbal devices.

Fig. 21·4. The short cross lines show the location of doors used to limit backtracking. When the animal had passed a door it was closed behind him by *E*. The false doors, indicated by broken cross lines, appeared the same as the true doors but were never locked.

Fig. 21·5. (Stone & Nyswander, 1927.) Detail of construction of the T maze, the plan of the whole maze given in Figure 21·4. The door here shown is at the entrance; the interior doors are not shown. A little of the wire mesh ceiling is shown at the left of the figure.

Such differences in pattern are bound to make a difference in the speed of learning and in the order in which various parts of the same maze are mastered. The most striking pattern effect is the great difficulty of the linear maze as compared with a round-about course (Fig. 21·4). We might expect the opposite since the linear pattern is simpler to the eye. But it is more restricted in cues useful to the learner who has to distinguish one choice point from another so as to respond differently. In a linear maze all the choice points are made exactly alike in intramaze cues, and almost alike in such extramaze cues as the direction of the light. In the roundabout pattern the extramaze stimuli, at any rate, differ from one choice point to another.

A curious fact that shows the importance of the maze pattern has come to light in many studies both in the maze learning of rats and in similar human experiments. When the maze pattern remains the same, the same blind alleys are found to give special difficulty: in an open or an enclosed maze (Miles, 1930); to blind or to seeing rats (Weaver & Stone, 1928; Lindley, 1930); to rewarded or to unrewarded rats, with food present or absent (Tolman & Honzik, 1930); and in the first trials or in later trials, though the correlation here is not so close (Ballachey & Buel, 1934b; Walthal, 1948). In human learning of a given maze pattern, the same blinds are easy or hard whether the pattern is presented as a stylus maze or as a finger maze (Nyswander, 1929); whether it is laid before the subject in one or another position (Higginson, 1937); whether it is traced with the right or left hand (Warden 1924a); and whether it is learned by the verbal, visual, or motor method (Warden, 1924b). The inequality of the blind alleys is reduced by the verbal method, as one would expect, and still the same alleys remain the most difficult (p. 652). When the same maze pattern is learned by both rats and human subjects, the relative difficulty of the alleys is not wholly the same by any means, and yet there is some correspondence (Fig. 21-6).

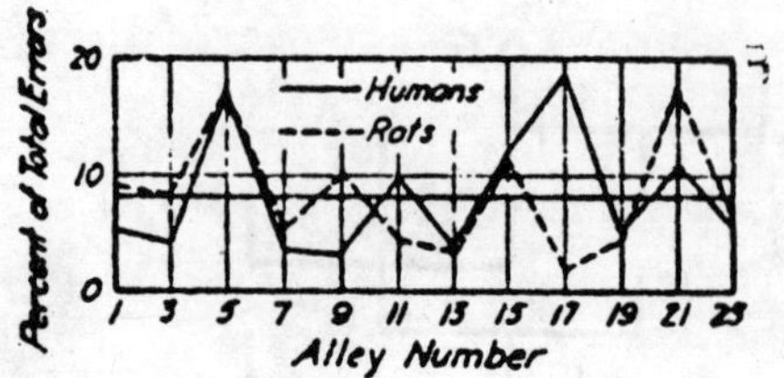

Fig. 21-6. Relative difficulty of the different blind alleys in the Stone 12-unit T maze (Fig. 21-4). Data on rats are from Weaver & Stone (1928), Heron (1930), and Skard (1950)—a total of 170 rats, the different samples being in fair agreement. Data on human subjects are from Husband (1931) and Skard (1950)—a total of 40 humans. The ordinates in the figure show what percent of all the errors (alley entrances) occurred in each alley. If the errors had been equally divided among the 12 blind alleys, each alley would have had 8.3 percent of the total, as indicated by a horizontal line. In fact, alley No. 5 was responsible for twice its share, for rats and humans alike. Alley No. 21 was difficult for both species, but the humans more than the rats resisted the tendency here to anticipate the final turn to the goal. The first two blind alleys, numbered 1 and 3, were soon eliminated by the human subjects, while the rats, as observed by Husband, were inclined to "enter the maze cautiously, nosing around and making slow progress in the first alley or two, then suddenly speed up and dart through the remainder of the pattern accurately." But the only marked difference between the two species is seen at alley No. 17, which was the easiest of all for the rats but the hardest of all for the humans. The forward-going, dodging alternately right and left, tendency of rats protected them from this particular trap, but why it should be so alluring to the human subjects is not clear. The number of human subjects, however, is too small to give reliable percents.

Alternation in maze running. There are several "tendencies," as one may call them—or response probabilities—that show up in maze running in relation to the maze pattern. One is a *tendency to make alternate right and left turns in locomotion*—a tendency to dodge right and left alternately instead of dodging repeatedly to the same side. (It is a valuable asset when you are trying to steer a straight course through a piece of woods!) This tendency was brought to light by Dashiell & Bayroff (1931). In their one-unit maze, No. 1 in Figure 21-7, rats after making the forced right turn at the first corner were likely to make a left turn at

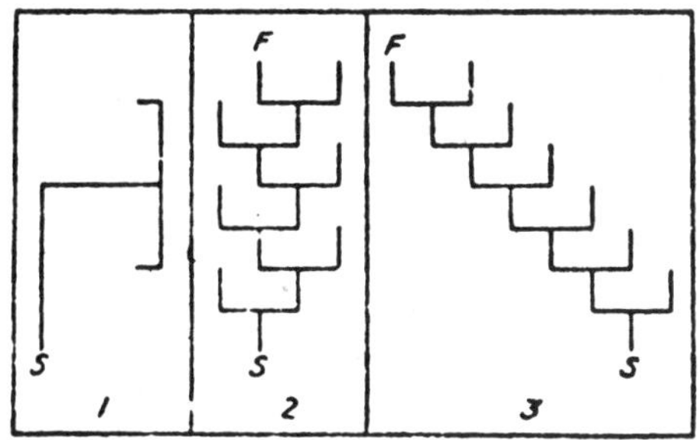

FIG. 21-7. (After Dashiell & Bayroff, 1931.) Maze patterns used in a demonstration of the forward-going tendency.

Pattern 1 was tried on maze-naive animals that had been handled sufficiently to overcome timidity. Of 91 such animals on their first trial, 63 or 69 percent took the left or forward alley at the choice point.

Patterns 2 and 3 were learned by groups of rats, and No. 3 was learned much more rapidly than No. 2. On the average of the first five trials, the blind alleys of No. 2 were entered four times as often as those of No. 3. This difference was obtained in mazes of several sizes of the two patterns.

the choice point following. They did so on the first trial and without any food being present. In U mazes each choice point beyond the first is immediately preceded by a forced turn to the right or left, and the tendency is to choose the reverse turn at the choice point. In maze No. 2 of the same figure, this tendency would predispose the animal to enter all the blind alleys; and this maze was actually found to be very difficult to learn. In maze No. 3 the same tendency leads the animal away from all the blind alleys; and this maze was found to be very easy.

In our Figure 21-2, accordingly, rats would be likely in the early trials—before learning better—to enter the first and second blind alleys, to avoid the third and fourth, to enter the fifth and avoid the sixth, and so on. In a T maze such as our Figure 21-4 there are no forced turns and we cannot say that the rat will reach a choice point immediately after making a certain turn; but we can say that whenever the preceding choice has been correct he will approach the next choice point with a tendency to reverse the turn and so to enter the blind alley or to choose the correct path. We can thus make some predictions as to the relative difficulty of the various blinds in the maze; and these predictions are fairly successful when applied to a large "population." So, in Figure 21-6, p. 620, the curve for rats shows that nearly all the relatively difficult blind alleys are those favored by this tendency to make alternate right and left turns.

The tendency we are considering was originally named the "forward-going tendency" by Dashiell & Bayroff, who carefully distinguished it from any general orientation toward the goal. "Centrifugal swing" was soon suggested as being a more explanatory designation (Schneirla, 1933). If an animal takes a left turn at considerable speed, he is forced to make a wide swing and so approach the right-hand alley at an immediately following choice point. By recording the rat's course in the intervening alley Ballachey & Buel (1934a) found many instances of the predicted behavior. One difficulty with this explanation is that the rat shows the alternating behavior even on the first trial when his locomotion is too slow to generate any strong centrifugal force.

A more comprehensive suggestion is that alternating right and left turns in locomotion are due to Pavlov's "internal inhibition," Hull's "reactive inhibition," which is internal resistance to the immediate repetition of a response. If we assume that the execution of a certain movement generates a (very temporary) inhibition of this sort, we can see how a right turn would throw the advantage to a left turn at a choice point reached a few seconds later.

Another form of alternation in the maze has often been referred to reactive inhibition. This is the *alternation at the same choice point in repeated trials,* a tendency that has been known for many years (Solomon, 1948, pp. 18–26). Place a rat at the entrance to a one-unit T maze; give him a bit of food whichever side he chooses and immediately replace him at the entrance. In over 80 percent of the cases he makes the opposite choice on the second trial, and he does so from the beginning of the experiment (Dennis, 1939; Heathers, 1940). Or, having thoroughly accustomed a rat to finding food in either goal box of the T, remove one arm and give him 10 massed trials to food in the other arm; then replace the arm and immediately give him a choice run—and he will always choose this opposite arm. The tendency to reverse increases with repeated massed runs to the same goal box. It dies out with lapse of time, at first rapidly and then more slowly, being sometimes detectable after as long as 12 hours (Zeaman & House, 1951).

One reason for doubting that this second form of alternation is due to reactive inhibition is that it does not die out much sooner; for other work on reactive inhibition emphasizes its very transient nature. Another reason is that the alternation at a single choice point can be shown to be an alternation, not between ight and left *turns,* but between the two *paths* which open out from the choice point (Montgomery, 1951c, see p. 670).

Both of the mentioned forms of alternation are cut across by another tendency that we have already encountered in discrimination learning (p. 593), the predisposition of individual rats to prefer the right or left side at a choice point, and so to fall into *position habits.*

Evidently the rat does not start from scratch in learning a maze. He starts with some handicaps and some advantages due to his natural tendencies as related to the particular maze pattern. These tendencies appear even on the first trial, before he has located the goal, and many trials and much reinforcement of the correct choices may be necessary to insure an unerring run through the maze.

Goal-dependent tendencies. After the subject has found the goal and been rewarded, new tendencies emerge which depend on the location of the goal in the maze pattern.

Goal gradient. Prompt reward is the most effective reward. There is evidence for this reasonable statement in different fields of learning. If delays are interposed between the successful act and the reward, the longer the delay, the slower the learning. In the maze, the last choice point is closest to the reward and should have an advantage over the choice points farther back along the route. The goal-gradient hypothesis says that, other things being equal, blind alleys will be eliminated in reverse order, beginning with the one closest to the goal (Hull, 1932). As a matter of fact, other things are not equal in most mazes, and the goal gradient seldom appears clearly. It is concealed by the "tendencies" already mentioned and by others still to be considered.

Anticipation. There is an easily demonstrated tendency to make the final turn to the goal prematurely if the maze affords an opportunity for such anticipation. In Figure 21-7, the No. 3 maze which is so easy as it stands can be made very difficult by a mere shift of the food box to the other arm of the final unit. It then calls for five left-hand turns followed by a single turn to the right—an easy task for a subject who can count, but difficult otherwise. A rat, a chimpanzee, or even a heedless human subject is inclined to make the right-hand turn too soon, with the result that the semifinal choice point, instead of being next to the easiest, as it should be according to the goal gradient, becomes the hardest of all (Spragg, 1933, 1934, 1936; Snygg, 1936). Besides the final correct turn, other outstanding turns in such a maze as Figure 21-2 or Figure 21-4 are likely to be anticipated. Anticipation can be explained in part by *stimulus generalization* (similarity of choice points).

Goal pointing. When a maze has been partly learned, the location of the goal has an effect such that alleys leading toward it are more alluring than alleys leading in the opposite direction (Spence & Shipley, 1934). A clean demonstration of this tendency is difficult to achieve because of the interfering tendencies to alternate and anticipate.

General orientation toward the goal. Besides goal pointing there are other indications that a rat after the first few exploratory trials begins to steer in the general direction of the goal. When the direction of the goal is of no help at any of the choice points, as in the linear maze (Fig. 21-3), the maze is difficult to learn; but when the direction of the goal can be of some help, as in Figure 21-4, the maze is relatively easy. The Dashiell checkerboard pattern (Fig. 21-8) offers many equally correct routes from the entrance to the goal, and rats learn very quickly to follow some of these routes. As they vary their route from trial to trial, they cannot be using local cues at the choice points but must be steering in the general direction of the goal.

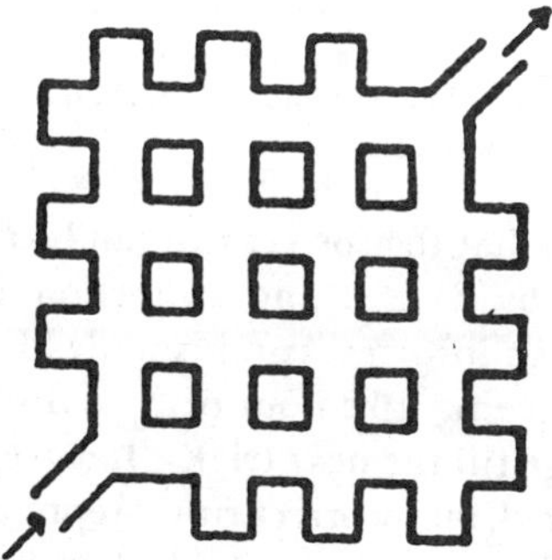

FIG. 21-8. (Dashiell, 1930.) The checkerboard or open-alley maze. The alleys were 4 inches wide. The exit led into a food box. The ceiling light was over the center of the maze where it could not serve as a guide.

FIG. 21-9. (Dashiell, 1930.) An individual rat's first eight runs through the checkerboard maze. In later trials he followed still other routes.

But is it necessary to assume any general orientation toward the goal, any reinforcement of the correct runs, or any learning at all, to account for the rat's behavior in this maze? Great doubt has been expressed, as by Buel & Ballachey (1935). Suppose the rat simply follows his natural tendency to turn alternately right and left. If he turns left at the entrance, his next turn will be to the right, then to the left, and so on. He will infallibly reach the goal without error unless he gets into one of the side pockets. A real difficulty with this explanation can be seen in Figure 21-9. This rat on his first trial did not follow the alternating tendency consistently. He wandered somewhat, though less than most of the other rats tested by Dashiell. Like all the others, however, this rat cut down his wanderings greatly after finding the food box once or twice. He learned something, and in view of the variety of his subsequent routes to the goal, what he learned must have been the location or direction of the food box.

Two outstanding types of route taken by rats in this maze are the L-shaped outside route of this particular animal in trials 5 and

6, and the central zigzag taken in trials 7 and 8. Muhlhan & Stone (1949), using a similar maze, found that the L routes were chosen most in the early trials, but that the zigzag routes became more and more common and dominated after 15–20 trials. The zigzag is no shorter but it *seems* more direct (to a human subject anyway) and it has the advantage of keeping away from the side pockets which often cause trouble.

SOME MATTERS OF TECHNIQUE

Control of conditions. If we were surveying an animal's behavior with particular attention to his ability to find his way, we should probably not select so artificial an environment as the maze. The psychologist has employed the maze for a rather different purpose. He has been investigating the process of learning. Consequently, he has insisted on knowing what cues, intramaze and extramaze, are present and useful to the animal; and the history of these investigations has shown what cues are likely to be useful and should be known to an experimenter and described in his report. He should also know what reinforcements are obtained by the animal. This matter has not been fully worked out. Food in the goal box is a sure incentive to a hungry animal. But, as we shall see later, even reaching an empty goal box and being taken out and placed in the living cage may be sufficient incentive to motivate learning. Success in reaching the goal is sufficient reward for a human subject, and he derives obvious reinforcement even before he reaches the goal when he avoids a treacherous blind alley or reaches a familiar landmark. May not a rat get similar reinforcements while exploring a maze? Reinforcements depend on the state of the animal. Being taken out by the experimenter may be a reward or a punishment according as the animal is accustomed or unaccustomed to being handled.

For quantitative work it is sometimes desirable to impose restrictions on the animal's freedom of movement in a maze. Retracing toward the entrance is a characteristic type of behavior but a nuisance to the experimenter who desires an accurate way of scoring the subject's errors. For this reason one-way doors are often inserted between the successive choice points. Locked doors are used in "forced runs" to the right or left at a choice point.

Correction, noncorrection, and rerun methods. Consider first a maze with a single choice point, like the one-unit T maze that has been much used of late. Let the starting point or entrance be S, and the two food boxes F_1 and F_2, as in Figure 21-10. Let food be present in F_1

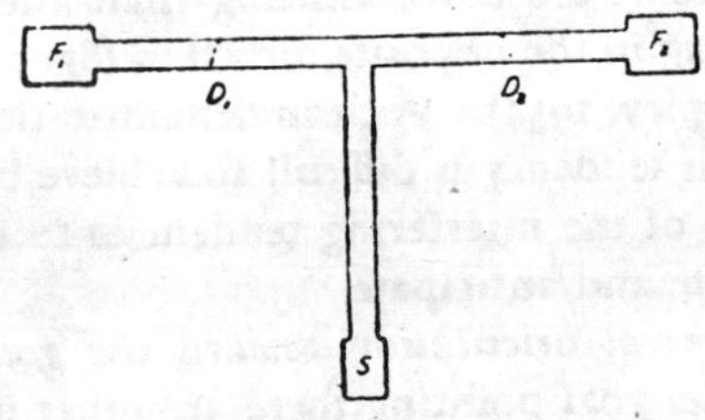

FIG. 21-10. A simple T maze. When the noncorrection method is used, one-way doors at D_1 and D_2 prevent the animal from correcting his first choice. These doors are not used in the correction method.

only, so that the correct run can be represented by SF_1. If no correction is allowed, an incorrect run is simply SF_2, the animal being taken out of F_2 and placed in a cage till the next trial. If correction is allowed, an incorrect run is represented by SF_2F_1 since the animal after finding F_2 empty will eventually arrive at F_1 and obtain some food there.

The reinforcements provided by these two procedures should be carefully considered, as they have been by Hull & Spence (1938), by Kalish (1946), and by Wischner (1947). The last-named experimenter was concerned with discrimination learning, and his results have been cited on pages 601–602. Both methods are alike in rewarding a correct run by a bite of food, but they differ in the effect of an incorrect run. (1) With no correction allowed an incorrect run brings no reward except that of being taken out of the maze, so that reinforcement definitely favors the correct choice and leads to its establishment. (2) With correction allowed an incorrect choice leads to the goal by the indirect route, SF_2F_1. Both choices are thus reinforced by food, but the prompter reinforcement of the correct choice and the extra work involved in the indirect route combine to give the advantage to the correct choice—quite aside from the question of "place learning," to be considered shortly. Either procedure, therefore, may lead rather quickly to the establishment of the correct choice.

But suppose the wrong side has a strong advantage to be overcome. It may be the preferred side because of a well-established position habit, or it may be attractively dark while the correct alley is repellently bright, or there may be a shock in the correct alley. In such cases, with no correction allowed, the animal may go so consistently to the wrong side as never to find the food. Forced runs may be necessary to reveal the presence of food in the other alley; or, after the tendency to go to the wrong side has been sufficiently extinguished by lack of reinforcement, the exploring tendency may take over and lead to the food. Quicker results are obtained by the correction method, though the animal may persist for many trials in following the indirect route, SF_2F_1, to the food.

The rerun method, as it is sometimes called, or try-try-again method, was used by Lashley (1930) in connection with his jumping-stand apparatus for the study of discrimination learning (p. 584). When a rat made a wrong choice and fell into the net, he was picked up by the experimenter and replaced immediately on the stand for another try, and so on, with no change in the stimulus, until the right choice was made. In our T-maze example, an animal going to F_2 is immediately replaced at S, and so on until he makes the correct response, SF_1. This is a noncorrection method but with some differences: (1) the animal is not released from the situation till he has made the correct response; (2) at the minimum interval between successive choices the tendency not to repeat a response (p. 620) has the best chance of counteracting the position habit; (3) the whole continuous series of responses terminating in a correct response and reinforcement is sometimes counted as one trial so that the number of trials required appears remarkably small in comparison with the number required for learning by the other two methods. Accordingly, Muenzinger & Powloski (1951) abandon the counting of "trials" and count instead the number of reinforcements and the total number of false responses.

Scoring the maze performance. Each single trial can be timed, of course, though often that measure is not employed. With a one-unit maze the response can be classed as correct or incorrect, and with a multiple-unit maze the errors can be counted for each trial. The counting of errors is simplified by the use of doors to prevent retracing, and often a rat is allowed to penetrate a blind alley a certain distance, say 4 inches, before an error is scored against him.

For the learning process as a whole, several scores are possible:

1. Number of trials required by the subject to reach a chosen *criterion*, which may be three successive errorless runs, or nine perfect in a sequence of 10 runs, or any other well-defined standard.

2. Total number of errors made before the criterion is reached.

3. Total working time before the criterion is reached.

4. Total time or errors in a specified number of trials counted from the beginning. Here there is no criterion and the learning is usually not complete for all the subjects.

5. Group averages can be computed for any one of the above scores, but care must be exercised in handling the skew distributions that are often obtained.

6. Each subject's learning curve can be plotted from the time or errors in successive trials. For methods of combining individual learning curves, see page 435.

WHAT IS LEARNED IN THE MAZE?

Two questions that have exercised the students of maze learning might be labeled the What and How questions. With a rat as subject, behavior can be examined from trial to trial for evidence on the questions: "What has he learned?" and "How has he learned it?" These questions are related to each other and also to the question of cues, and are not usually kept entirely separate. But in general we may say that the What question has been uppermost in the numerous experiments on motor learning *versus* spatial learning, while the How question dominates in the experiments on the controversial "latent learning." The What question, it would seem, calls simply for an adequate description of the animal's behavior, while the How question calls for some theorizing as to processes going on in the organism.

Behavior in the maze can conceivably be described in two different ways—in two sets of terms which may be called the organismic and the environmental. Usually it is described in environmental terms. The animal is said to enter many blind alleys at first, and to eliminate these blind alleys as learning progresses until finally he takes the shortest route to the goal. But if we limit our description to organismic terms, we say that on the first trial the animal first turns to the right (in the Hampton Court maze, p. 614), advances perhaps 10 slow steps, makes a U-turn, advances 20 slow steps, turns to the right, advances 6 slow steps, and so on; but after several trials he first turns to the left, takes 5 leaps, makes a rapid turn to the right, takes 3 leaps, and so on. Either type of description is possible, but the question is which type gives the more adequate account of the behavioral changes that occur in the process of learning.

Maze running described as a sequence of movements. Watson (1914) regarded a well-learned run through the maze as a chain reflex: "Each movement executed would arouse new contact and kinesthetic impulses which in turn would release the succeeding movements (p. 212). . . . When the useless movements are eliminated the correct movements arise serially without any chaining or linking in any material sense (bonds, connections, etc.) (p. 260)." In these passages Watson was as much interested in explaining how the animal learns as in describing what he learns, but his description is clear enough: the animal eliminates useless movements and finally runs through the maze by a fixed sequence of movements.

Transfer tests. One way of testing this description was suggested by Carr & Watson (1908): after an animal has mastered the maze, change the maze or the conditions and see what the animal carries over by transfer from the previous learning. These experimenters constructed a large maze in which certain alleys could be lengthened or shortened without any change in the necessary turns. Animals trained in the long form until "their reactions had become thoroughly automatic" dashed head on into the ends of some of the shortened alleys, and after being thoroughly trained in the short form, they showed similar disturbances when shifted back to the long form. Their behavior conformed very well to Watson's description.

Another experiment of the transfer type was devised by Macfarlane (1930). A multiple T maze was placed in a tank of water. The water was 8 inches deep, forcing the rats to swim, but a false floor could be inserted, which left the visual appearance of the maze unchanged but required wading instead of swimming—a very different sequence of movements. Six groups of 18 to 20 white rats were used, each group having a certain number of trials with one form of locomotion and being then shifted to the other form by the insertion or removal of the false floor. The table below shows the mean number of errors per rat in the trial just before the shift and in the trial just after the shift.

There was no increase in errors when the shift from one form of locomotion to the other occurred early in training, and only a slight disturbance when it occurred after the maze had been thoroughly learned. When the animals after learning the maze by swimming found solid bottom under their feet for the first time, "they halted, sniffed, stood upright, tested the strength of the wire mesh above them and *then*—traveled down the correct alley. The entire run, for the most part, was made in this hesitant manner." These animals were not carrying over any fixed sequence of movements, but they did carry over something else which enabled them to follow the correct path.

The transfer test has been tried in various forms. Gross disturbances of gait after a cerebellar operation do not prevent a rat from traversing without error a maze learned before the operation (Lashley & McCarthy, 1926). Nor does the three-legged gait forced upon a rat by the amputation of one leg prevent him from running a previously learned maze without errors (Dorcus & Gray, 1932). A mass of such evidence shows that something different from a motor sequence must be learned in the maze.

The temporal maze. Another line of evidence was offered by Hunter (1920). In a spatial maze each choice point has its own location with intra- or extramaze cues distinguishing it from the other choice points. In a temporal maze there is only one choice point, but the animal comes around to it repeatedly and must turn sometimes to the right and sometimes to the left in accordance with a temporal pattern enforced by the experimenter (Fig. 21-11). The simple alternation pattern, RLRL, fits in with the rat's tendency to alternate (p. 620) and

	From swimming to wading		*From wading to swimming*	
	Before	*After*	*Before*	*After*
Shift after 4 trials	7.1	6.3	4.4	3.5
Shift after 12 "	1.3	1.8	1.1	1.4
Shift after 33 "	.2	2.1	.3	1.1

can be learned. But the double alternation pattern, RRLL, conflicts with this tendency to alternate and also with the tendency to anticipate (see below) and seems to be practically insoluble in Hunter's maze. Yet the same motor sequence causes the rat no difficulty in an ordinary spatial maze. In one of his experiments Hunter first ran rats in a spatial maze with 10 choice points, the correct choices being left and right in the order, LLRRLLRRLL, i.e., in continued double alternation. The rats mastered this maze in 5–12 trials. He then shifted them to the temporal maze and required the same sequence of choices. None of the rats carried over the learned sequence or succeeded in mastering the same sequence in the temporal maze. Hunter concluded: "The work on the temporal maze indicates that it is all but impossible to set up a mere temporal sequence of kinesthetic processes with the rat. Running the spatial maze, therefore, must require cues which have space location as well as temporal position. In other words, the rat must recognize in terms of space where he is in the maze."

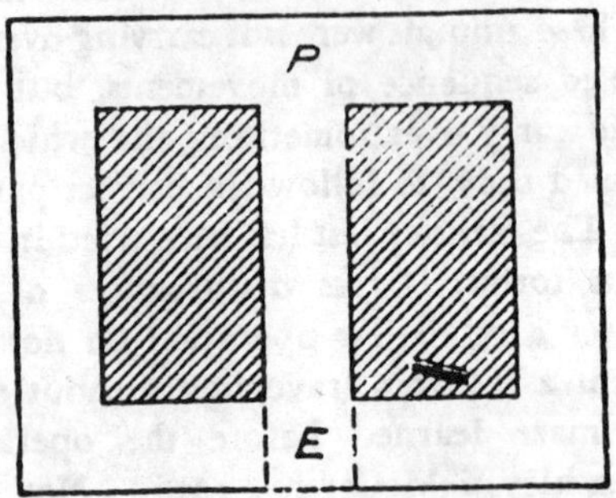

FIG. 21-11. (After Hunter, 1920.) A temporal maze. The correct choice at the point P is sometimes to the left and sometimes to the right, as determined by the experimenter who manipulates the doors indicated by broken lines at E, the entrance (which is also the exit to food placed outside). In simple alternation the correct choices at P are alternately to the left and right. In double alternation there must be, for example, two choices to the left, and then two to the right.

Human adults and not-too-young children have no difficulty with a temporal maze. Put into one with no instructions except to "keep moving," they soon see they have a puzzle to solve and formulate the solution in words and numbers, "Go twice to the right, twice to the left, and so on" (Gellermann, 1931). They are utilizing the symbolic processes of language. They are differentiating the two successive turns to the left by calling them "one" and "two." (Another symbolic process which they could use is like the iambic rhythm of a verse in poetry: -´,-´, emphasizing the second turn to each side and perhaps making a slight pause before shifting to the other side. Even without any such differentiating symbolic response, there could perhaps be an accumulation of stimulus traces, reactive inhibitions and other aftereffects of activity, sufficient to put an animal in a different internal state on his first, second, third, and fourth arrivals at the choice point. Hunter recognized these two possibilities but was inclined to prefer the symbolic process. The rats' failure to master double alternation, therefore, would indicate that symbolic processes were beyond their scope, though within the scope of raccoons (Hunter, 1928), monkeys (Gellermann, 1931), and cats (Karn & Patton, 1939), since these animals mastered double alternation in the temporal maze, though with considerable difficulty. As to rats, however, Hunter and Nagge (1931) found it possible, by carefully planned preliminary training, to bring some of them to the point of a fair performance of double alternation in the temporal maze.

Double alternation in a lever-pressing task is a much easier task for the rat (Schlosberg & Katz, 1943; McGinnies &

Schlosberg, 1945). The lever must be pushed twice to the left and then twice to the right (LLRR) to obtain a pellet of food. Correction was allowed, and the rats were apt to adopt simple alternation, L(R)LR(L)R, or anticipation, L(R)LRR, before settling down to a clear-cut LLRR. The same persistent errors have been observed by others among the investigators mentioned.

The anticipation error shows up clearly in the practice curves obtained by Woodbury (Fig. 21-12). He used a linear maze constructed so as to present the same difficulties as a temporal maze, as nearly as possible. The required sequence may be represented by AABB. The food, then, was located on the B side, and we see from the curves that the rats learned very quickly to choose that side as the last choice point. This B choice spread back to the third choice point, where it was correct, and to the second choice point, where it was incorrect. Meanwhile the A choice at the first choice point was gradually becoming established.

Organismic and environmental space. We have apparently found two examples of pure motor learning, the learning of a sequence of bodily movements without

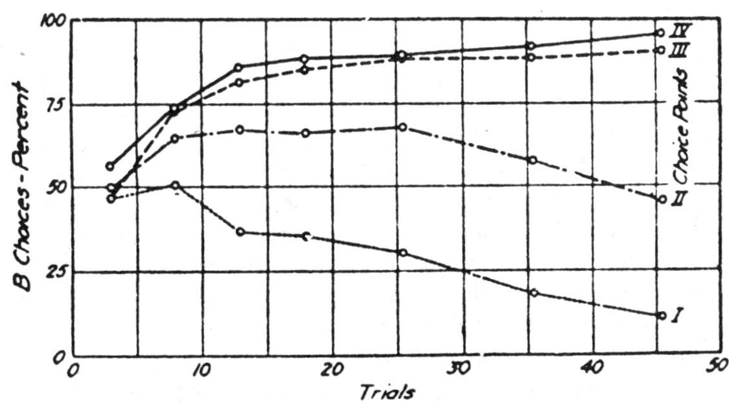

FIG. 21-12. (Data from Woodbury, 1950.) Double-alternation practice in a linear maze. At each choice point there were two doors to choose from. The doors that could be pushed open at the four successive choice points were located RRLL for some rats and LLRR for others, so that the correct pattern in general can be labeled AABB. The B choice, accordingly, was incorrect at choice points I and II, but correct at choice points III and IV. (The "correction method," p. 624, was used, so that errors were promptly corrected by the animal.) Side preferences were ascertained in preliminary trials and balanced out in the group score for 30 rats. Both intra- and extramaze cues were so controlled as to make the four choice points as indistinguishable as possible—except on the basis of their positions or sequence. There were 50 trials, one per day. The data points on the curves show the percent of B choices at each choice point for successive periods of practice, as follows:

Trials 1–5: 150 choices for the group of 30 rats.
" 6–10: 150 " " " " " " "
" 11–15: 150 " " " " " " "
" 16–20: 150 " " " " " " "
" 21–30: 300 " " " " " " "
" 31–40: 300 " " " " " " "
" 41–50: 300 " " " " " " "

The group as a whole had by no means mastered the double-alternation problem, because of the strong tendency to anticipate the B choice at choice point II. But 50 percent of the group had met the criterion of three successive errorless runs.

any reference to the spatial environment. There is the example of human beings learning a sequence of turns by counting them, and there is Carr & Watson's example of rats acquiring an automatic motor habit from long practice. We should notice, however, that neither of these examples is wholly demonstrative. The human subjects in the temporal maze do not necessarily say, "Twice to the right, then twice to the left." They could say equally well, "Twice into *this* alley, then twice into *that* one," so referring to objects in the environment rather than to parts of their own bodies. And the rat turning into what has always been a long alley may start to run a long *distance* rather than a rapid series of leaps. In either case he is in danger of bumping into the end of the alley. Distance is environmental, not organismic.

It is difficult for us to think, observe, or describe in purely organismic terms without any reference to the environment. Organismic space can be analyzed into the three dimensions: right-left, forward-backward, and up-down. The up-down dimension is also (and primarily) environmental, but right-left and forward-backward have no meaning apart from the organism (or some similar object with a front and back). If we find it really necessary to use these terms in describing an animal's learned behavior in a maze, we have to admit that the animal has learned a sequence of right and left turns with intervening advances. On the other hand, if we find it necessary to refer to environmental objects, positions, directions and distances, we have to admit that the animal has acquired certain responses to the spatial environment—that he has in effect learned the characteristics of a particular environment.

When we say that an animal is walking forward or backward, we are speaking in organismic terms, but when we say he is approaching or withdrawing from a certain object or place, we are speaking of movements in environmental space. When we say he turns right or left, our description is organismic, but when we say he is approaching this or that object, it is environmental. The importance of this distinction has been pointed out by Nissen (1950).

One class of approach movements could be regarded as organismic. Positive phototropism, a tendency to turn toward the light and move in that direction, is governed by stimuli from the environment, of course, but scarcely by environmental objects and their spatial relations. When a bit of learned behavior can be described simply as approach to the light, or to the dark, some form of transfer test would be necessary to determine whether any real learning of the environment has occurred. This problem arises in connection with the learning of very simple mazes, as we shall soon see.

Maze learning described as "place learning." The word *place* here can be used in two ways, one more inclusive, the other more restricted. A place in the more inclusive sense is a portion of the environment such as a room, a neighborhood, a town—or such as a maze. It includes objects in certain positions, in certain directions, and at certain distances from each other or from any given point where the subject may be at a given time. A human observer, trying to describe an animal's behavior in a maze, will almost inevitably speak in terms of environmental objects and their spatial relations, but the question is whether such a description is truly necessary and adequate.

In the more restricted sense a place is a position or location, the answer to the question, Where? If a rat has learned where the food is located in a maze, his going to that place can most readily be described in terms of environmental space. Yet it could be described in organismic space, as consisting of turns to the right and left with intervening forward movements. Whether the rat walks to the left or swims to the left, he turns to his left, and the turn could be described in organismic space. Some transfer test or similar check would be needed to make sure whether the organismic description was adequate.

One check is furnished by the Dashiell maze (p. 623). When a rat travels consistently to the corner where the food is located, but by different routes, some with more turns than others, his performance can apparently not be described in terms of organismic space. He seems to be oriented toward a certain spot in the environment.

In organismic terms the goal box is not in any definite location; rather, it is at the end of a definite sequence of forward movements and right and left turns. Now if rats first learn to go for their food from one corner to the opposite corner of a rectangular enclosure, and if part-way partitions are then inserted, the rats negotiate the necessary detours readily. Or, vice versa, if the partitions are present during the original learning and are then removed, seeing rats instantly eliminate the detours and cut straight across the enclosure (Hebb & Williams, 1946). Even blind rats make this readjustment rather easily, guiding themselves by contacts with the partitions and outer walls. Their routes vary somewhat from trial to trial but converge upon the goal (Dennis, 1929). What all these rats carry over from one condition to the other is evidently not a definite sequence of turns; it is, rather, an adjustable route through environmental space toward a definite place.

Let the maze have two goal boxes, one containing food and the other water. A rat learns rather quickly to take the path to food when hungry, and the path to water when thirsty, provided the two boxes are in distinct parts of the maze. The problem is much more difficult, however, if there is only a single goal box which must be approached by one path when food is present and by another path when water is present (Hull, 1933b, Leeper, 1935, Kendler, 1946). In organismic space the problem is the same whether there are two goal boxes or only one, but in environmental space there is a great difference.

In spite of the many scattered observations indicating that rats master the maze by adjusting their behavior to environmental space, rather than to organismic space, it must be admitted that these older observations were made rather incidentally. The experimenters were primarily interested in sensory cues or in problems of motivation. Feeling that a more direct and better controlled attack on the problem of place learning was in order, Tolman and his co-workers devised two new experiments, making use of mazes with a single choice point. One may be called the radiating-path experiment, the other the cross-maze experiment. Other investigators have used the same devices in checking on Tolman's results and conclusions.

The radiating-path or short-cut experiment. This experiment is illustrated by Figure 21-13. The idea is to train the rat to go to a certain location for food, and then to block the previously used path and present a choice of several new paths, the question being whether he will take the direct path to the previous location of the food box. The rat enters the previously used alley from the circular table top. Finding it blocked, he returns to the table and explores around its edge, probably entering some of the

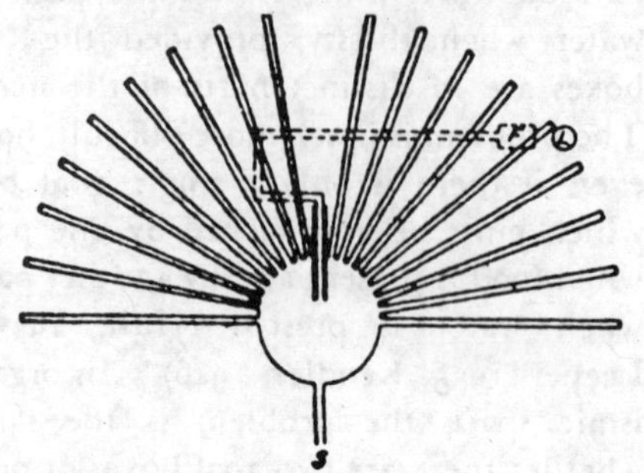

FIG. 21-13. (After Tolman, Ritchie & Kalish, 1946a; Gentry, Brown & Kaplan, 1947.) Radiating-path apparatus. Rats in the pretraining series started at S, advanced to the circular table top (36 inches in diameter), entered the walled alley (heavy lines), and proceeded by the elevated path (dotted lines) to the food box marked F, near the light L. For the test trial, the food box and the dotted-line path were removed, the walled alley was blocked at the far end, and the radiating elevated paths were added. The light was left burning, as before. Some of the experimenters have reduced the number of radiating paths.

new paths a short distance. In the course of a few minutes he may enter one of these paths far enough to justify the experimenter in recording that this path has been chosen. Or the rat may refuse to choose and remain in the circular area till taken out by the experimenter. (This last behavior seems the most appropriate since the rat can doubtless see that the food box is no longer present.) Different paths are chosen by different rats, and the distribution has varied widely from one experiment to another (Tolman, Ritchie & Kalish, 1946a; Gentry, Brown & Kaplan, 1947; Gentry, Brown & Lee, 1948; Ritchie, 1948; Kendler & Gasser, 1948; Kendler & Mencher, 1949). Choices favored by different samples of rats have been: (1) the path leading most directly toward the former location of the food box; (2) the paths closest to the alley originally used; (3) the path leading at right angles toward the side of the room where the food box was previously located; and (4) the path leading similarly toward the opposite side of the room. These differences cannot at present be pinned to known differences in the conditions, and really it is impossible to predict from any theory exactly what the rat should do when he returns to the circular area after finding his previous route blocked.

There may be advantages in a simplified short cut such as the one designed by Wilcoxon & Waters (1948) and shown in Figure 21-14. It is based upon the cross maze soon to be considered. The rats were first trained always to make a left turn (for example) at the choice

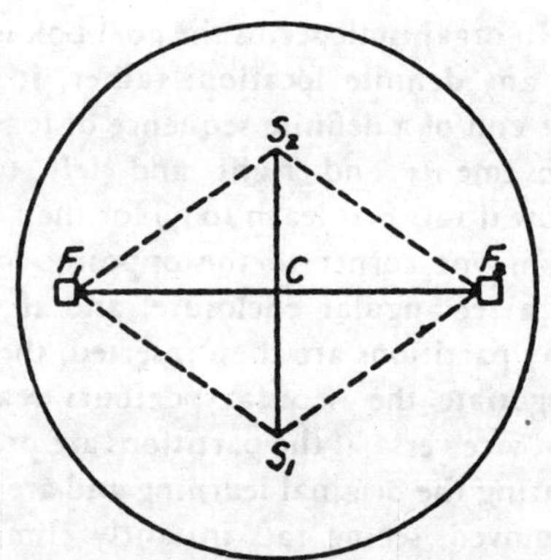

FIG. 21-14. (After Wilcoxon and Waters, 1948.) A cross maze adapted for short-cut experiments. There are two starting boxes, S_1 and S_2, and two food boxes, F_1 and F_2. The solid lines show the only paths present during the learning, the broken lines the only paths present during the short-cut tests. The enclosing circle is a curtain used to eliminate external visual cues.

point, whether approaching it from S_1 or S_2. If started at S_1, they must go to F_1, but if started to S_2, they must go to F_2 in order to find food. Each day they were given four trials in the order $S_1S_2S_2S_1$. When they had reached the criterion of 10 successive correct runs, the trials were continued, but with the old paths (full lines) removed and the short cuts (broken lines) added. Would the animals now go straight from S_1 to F_1, and from S_2 to F_2? No, they showed no consistent tendency, but varied from rat to rat and from trial to trial. Such variability could be predicted from the following causes. (1) They could not carry over to the new situation the choice-point behavior they had learned. (2) They had found food equally in the two food boxes. (3) They would tend to explore the new paths presented at the starting points.

An experiment that has been tried several times uses much more complex mazes. After an animal has learned to run the maze, a short cut is opened that cuts out some of the middle of the maze. Rats explore the short cut and readily pick up the learned route on the far side. The interpretation is not perfectly clear but the facts are certainly important (Honzik, 1933; Wolfle, 1935).

The cross maze or double T maze. There is a single choice point, as in the simple T maze, but this choice point is approached now from one and now from another starting point (Fig. 21-15). The cross maze was introduced by Tolman, Ritchie & Kalish (1946b) for the comparison of what they called place learning and response learning, or, more specifically, *location* learning and *turn* learning. The cross maze lends itself to transfer experiments of two types.

1. Learning is followed by a test under changed conditions. For example, the subject is started at S_1 and finds food at F_1; so he learns to take the route S_1—C—F_1. Then he is started at S_2. What will he carry over to this new situation? Will he carry over the left turn that he has been making at the choice point, or the approach to F_1 that he has also been making? It is a question of organismic *versus* environmental space and of possible conflict between them. An experiment of this sort was tried by Tolman, Ritchie & Kalish (1947a), with

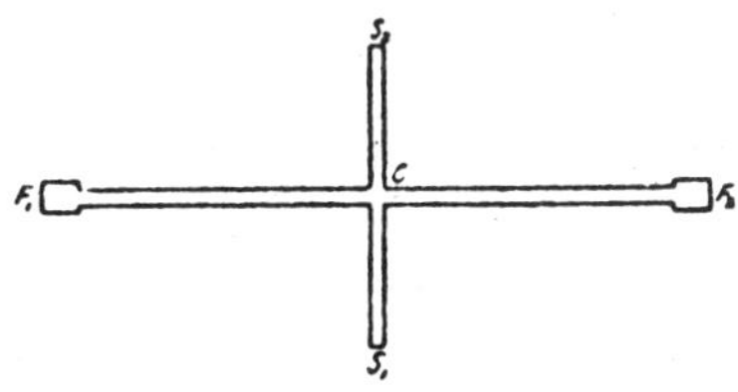

FIG. 21-15. (After Tolman, Ritchie & Kalish, 1946b.) A cross maze, or double T maze. It is an elevated maze, built of wooden strips which are usually 1 or 2 inches wide. Here the short arms from S_1 and S_2 to the choice point C are 2 feet long, and the longer arms from C to F_1 and F_2, the food boxes, are 4 feet long. These dimensions have differed in different experiments. Usually only one of the short arms is present in any one trial. The wooden strips can be interchanged to eliminate possible olfactory cues.

results that indicated conflict, since the animals ran sometimes to F_1 and sometimes to F_2 in the test trials. As a check on this appearance of conflict, another transfer experiment was tried. Only the straight path from F_1 to F_2 was used in the learning trials, the animals being started from F_1 and finding food at F_2. After five trials, the path from S_1 or S_2 was put in place, and the rats with practically no exception ran to F_2 from these new starting points. There was no conflict here, since there had been no practice in making a turn at the choice point. This last, very simple experiment seems to be a perfectly good demonstration of location learning.

2. Two tasks are learned concurrently. The subject is started sometimes from S_1 and sometimes from S_2, with the food always at F_2. If he learns locations, the problem is easy, since he can carry over

to the S_2 trials what he learns in the S_1 trials and vice versa—namely, the constant location of the food. But if he learns turns, the problem is difficult, since the turn that is correct half the time is incorrect the other half. Tolman, Ritchie & Kalish (1946b) found the problem very easy, since their rats reached a high criterion of learning after only 1–8 trials. These rats, therefore, learned the *location* of the food.

In a companion experiment other rats were required to go to F_1 when starting from S_1, but to F_2 when starting from S_2; thus they had always to make a *left turn* at the choice point. The task proved to be very difficult. Only three of the eight rats mastered it, taking 15–22 trials, while the other five fell into a position (or location) habit, going always to the same food box, which was correct half the time, and when locked out there running across to the other food box. The authors concluded that both location learning and turn learning were within the rat's power, with location learning much the easier and probably more natural.

The strong advantage of location learning over turn learning depends, however, on the exact conditions of the experiment, as brought out by later experiments of these same investigators and of others who are inclined to doubt the conclusion just stated. Some conditions that have been found to make a difference are the following.

1. The method employed, whether correction or rerun. Here we may refer back to our discussion of these methods on pp. 624–625. The correction method employed in the experiments just cited operated to the disadvantage of turn learning, as already indicated. For when the location of the food varied, some rats formed the habit of always going to the same location first and then, if necessary, crossing over to the other. But when the food was always in the same location, freedom to correct an initial error was a help rather than a hindrance in learning that location. When this peculiarity of the correction method had been discovered and analyzed (Kalish, 1946), the original experiments were repeated by the rerun method (Tolman, Ritchie & Kalish, 1947b). If a rat made a wrong choice, he was picked up and immediately placed at the same starting point as before, and so on, until he made a correct choice. Thus, only direct runs from the starting point via the choice point to the correct box were reinforced, and the interfering position habits did not get formed. Under these conditions most of the turn-learning group mastered the required constant turn, but the place-learning group still surpassed, as shown by the learning curves in Figure 21-16.

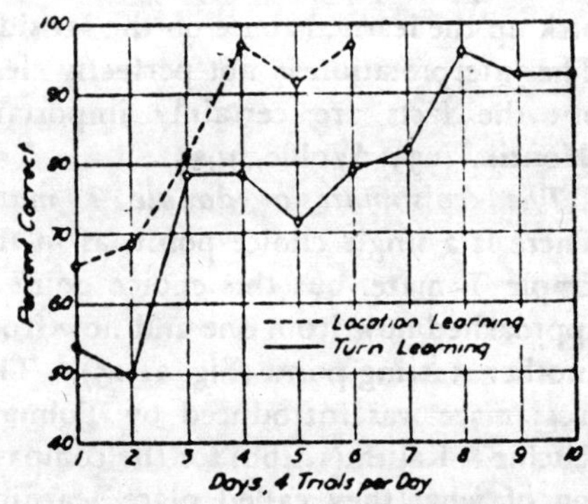

FIG. 21-16. (After Tolman, Ritchie & Kalish, 1947b.) Learning curves for two groups of rats, one group being required to learn a constant location of the food box, the other being required to learn a constant turn at the choice point. There were seven or eight rats in each group, and four trials per day, so that each point on the curves is based on 28 or 32 choices.

The authors, therefore, reaffirmed their previous conclusion: "That, at least for simple maze problems, a fundamental factor in learning is that of locating the goal spatially with respect to the extramaze environment."

2. *Massed vs. spaced learning trials.* To turn always to the same side goes against the tendency to alternate (p. 620), explained by "reactive inhibition," but this inhibition fades out rapidly with the lapse of time. On this basis it was predicted by Thompson & Thompson (1949) that closely massed trials would favor location learning, while trials spaced 15 minutes apart would favor turn learning; and they obtained the predicted result.

3. *Preliminary training.* It is standard procedure to accustom the animals to handling and to the general sort of apparatus used, before the actual beginning of a learning experiment. Suppose, however, that they are first allowed to find food several times in both food boxes of the cross maze, and are then required to go always to one and the same box. Evidently the preliminary training will predispose them to go sometimes to one box and sometimes to the other and so will be a handicap in location learning. But it may be a help in turn learning. This prediction has not been carefully tested, though there is some scattered evidence in its favor.

4. *Cues of location.* There is no such thing as absolute location. An object is located in its surroundings or in relation to another object. In the experiments we are considering, extramaze visual cues of location have usually been provided. The correct food box has been standing near a lighted lamp, for example. If all the rat learns is to go toward the light, there is no genuine spatial learning. In an experiment of Blodgett, McCutchan & Mathews (1949) a simple T maze was so placed that one arm led directly toward a window and the other arm directly away from it. The maze could be placed near the window or 4 feet farther away, without any change in direction. It was easy for rats to learn concurrently to turn to the right—away from the window—in both the near and far placements of the maze. But it was very difficult or impossible for them to learn concurrently to turn right in the near and left in the far placement, though in this arrangement the location of the food was the same throughout. It was easy, in other words, to learn to go away from the window all the time, but not to go away from it half the time and toward it half the time. Other variations of the experiment led to the conclusion that direction was much more easily learned than location.

All these experiments with a single choice point leave us still in doubt whether a rat really learns the location of the food box in the environment, or merely learns to go toward or away from a light—or, it might be in another setup, to or from a buzzer or a hot radiator. There is an experimental difficulty here that has not been overcome. In the more complex mazes, however, with the true path running in various directions, no such "acquired tropism" would lead the animal through to the food box. With respect to human beings, of course, it would be rather absurd even to raise the question whether they can get acquainted with the environment or are limited to organismic space plus some acquired tropisms.

HOW THE MAZE IS LEARNED

A maze presents one or more choice points where there are alternative paths, and typically one path leads into a blind alley while the other leads to a goal box where there is some food or other reward. Taken as a whole the learning process appears to be one of *trial and error*, with the "correct" choices reinforced by relatively prompt reward in the food box, while "errors" are penalized by delay in the blind alleys. The law of effect or reinforcement thus provides a theory of the learning process—a theory worked out in detail by Hull (1932, 1943) and often called a *stimulus-response theory*.

At the outset, however, on his first trial in a maze, the animal has no evidence of food being present. His entrances into blind alleys are not errors but perfectly normal bits of free exploration. Yet it appears from many learning curves that some learning is accomplished even in the first trial. *Learning by exploration* is a fact which might be the best key to the whole learning process. This approach to learning theory seems to be taken by Tolman (1932, 1948), whose proposal is often called a *cognitive theory*.

Without undertaking anything like a thorough comparison and appraisal of these two theories, we shall at least examine some of the experiments designed to reach a decision between them.

That a rat learns something by free exploration is shown by the mere fact that he ceases to explore after a while if he finds no food and no danger present. When first placed alone in a strange maze, he is apt to divide his time between crouching in a corner and trying to escape, but after some exploration these signs of timidity disappear. This emotional adaptation is the first sign of learning. Berlyne (1950), having first familiarized his rats with the interior of a good-sized box, introduced some novel objects, such as three small wooden cubes, and then placed each rat separately in the box. "Each animal remained for some seconds in a state of tense alertness. It then advanced cautiously and, on reaching the stimuli, sniffed at them . . ." for an average time of about 13 seconds, and then settled down in a corner. After being taken out for 10 minutes and then replaced in the box, the rat again examined the cubes but for a few seconds only. In this simple demonstration we have definite evidence of learning by exploration.

Latent learning. As long as the rat is simply wandering about in an empty maze, taking his time and entering freely into blind alleys, the experimenter's customary measures of maze learning—increased speed and progressive elimination of blind alleys—indicate that little is being learned. If anything is learned that would facilitate a rapid and errorless run to the goal, the learning is "latent" or hidden. Now place food in the goal box and see whether any latent learning comes to the surface. Does the rat run for the goal with a speed and correctness that shows acquaintance with the blind alleys and the through route?

There are really two questions involved in the study of latent learning:

1. Is it possible for an animal to have learned more in exploring a situation than shows in his present behavior in that situation?

2. Is it possible for an animal to learn anything in a maze, except by going to the goal and receiving there some reward?

The first question conforms to the literal meaning of "latent learning," but the second is of more real concern to the theorists. There should be no doubt of the reality of latent learning in the literal sense. There are plenty of clear examples:

The early trials in Pavlovian conditioning. The CR does not begin to appear for several or many trials, and yet these trials contribute to its establishment.

The early trials in discrimination learning, according to the "continuity theory" (p. 594).

Performance after extinction of a CR and before spontaneous recovery. The established (learned) CR is temporarily latent.

Any learned performance when motivation is very weak—the kind of thing we recognize in human behavior when we say, "He could do much better if he really tried."

On this last point we may refer to Hull's well-known formula (1943) which represents performance as dependent on the product of habit strength and present drive. If drive is zero, even a strong habit remains latent. A habit learned under weak motivation will not show its full strength unless and until the drive becomes strong. If drive weakens through satiation, performance slackens and habit lapses into a relatively latent state. The important distinction between performance and habit (or learned equipment) was clearly made by Elliott (1928) in connection with maze learning and by Lewin (1917) in connection with the law of association. (See also Leeper, 1935, and Deese, 1950.)

Like every other performance, the performance by which an animal learns a maze must be motivated. The motive, of course, is not that of learning for future use. Learning is a by-product, the drive being hunger in many experiments and the goal being the food in the goal box. As we have said, however, this goal must first be found by exploration. The behavior of animals, and of human children and adults, demonstrates the reality of a basic exploring drive (Harlow, 1953). What is its goal? It may be to check the new environment for anything good or bad, but at any rate it is to find what is there. The goal is reached when the animal finds what is there. In exploration the animal learns what is there rather than any motor performance, for the movements in exploration are variable and die out unless something is found in the maze that awakens some other drive.

We can see how the adherents of a trial-and-error theory would undertake latent learning experiments in the hope of obtaining negative results, while the adherents of learning by exploration would entertain the opposite hope. A comprehensive survey of the experiments on latent learning has been provided by a member of Tolman's group (Thistlethwaite, 1951a).

Restricted exploration. The problem of latent learning was first brought into prominence by the work of Blodgett (1929) who was a member of Tolman's group at the University of California at Berkeley, a group favoring "cognitive" or exploratory learning. Blodgett used a six-unit T maze, provided with gates to prevent retracing, and he ran the rats through from entrance to goal box even in the early trials when the goal box was empty. On the first six trials the experimental group found no food in the goal box, but they were shut in there for 2 minutes and then removed to a special cage (not the home cage) where they were fed only after an hour's delay. This procedure was intended to prevent any association of the goal box with food so that the animals would have no sort of reward for going to the goal box. Beginning with the seventh trial, however, there was food in the goal box. The ideal result for latent learning would be: much entering of blind alleys until food had once been found, and quick elimination of all blind alleys thereafter. Blodgett's results, shown in Figure 21-17, conform quite well to this expectation, though

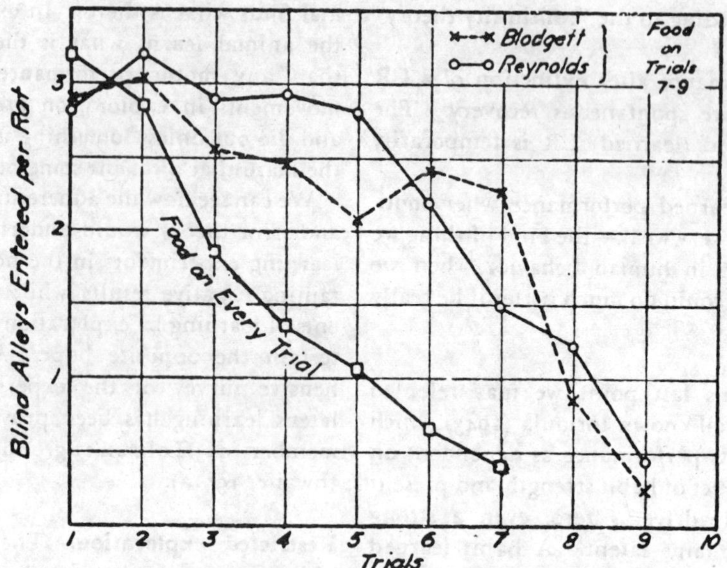

FIG. 21-17. (After Blodgett, 1929, and Reynolds, 1945a.) Maze learning with and without food reward. Both experiments used a six-unit T maze, and the later investigator endeavored to duplicate the conditions employed by the earlier one. The control groups of both investigators gave similar learning curves which are here combined in the curve labeled "Food on every trial." The other two curves show the results obtained when there was no food present in the food box until the seventh trial. Between these two curves there is an obvious discrepancy. On the sixth and seventh trials Blodgett's rats continued to enter many blind alleys (nearly half on the average) but once they had found food in the goal box, they entered comparatively few so that their curve takes a sudden drop: while Reynolds's rats began to avoid the blind alleys on the sixth and seventh trials and simply continued this rapid change after first finding the food, so that their curve does not demonstrate any "latent learning." Both investigators agreed, however, that considerable learning of the maze occurred in the no-food period.

there was some elimination of blind alleys before the introduction of food. The same figure includes the results of Reynolds (1945a), who repeated the experiment with only slight changes. Taken point by point, the two curves do not differ much, but the trends are different, since the Reynolds rats as compared with those of Blodgett entered the blind alleys considerably more in the first five trials, but then began to eliminate them rapidly before finding any food. These two facts may be related: the more exploring in the early trials, the sooner the exploring drive will be satiated, leaving the rats free to go to the goal box and be taken out of the maze. The same experiment has been repeated with slight changes by Meehl & MacCorquodale (1951) with results much like those of Reynolds. Slight differences in the breed and tameness of the rats, in the experimenter's deftness in handling them, and in other experimental conditions, are to be expected and could affect the balance between the exploratory drive and any tendency to go promptly to the goal box. We have to admit a probable conflict between two tendencies: the exploring drive, subject to quick satiation; and some drive toward the goal box. Being taken from the maze and placed in a cage may have been slightly rewarding. And, as Meehl & MacCorquodale suggest, this cage could become a secondary reinforcer as the place where food was obtained, though after an hour's delay.

Tolman & Honzik repeated the Blodgett type of experiment with a complex maze which afforded more opportunity for exploration (Fig. 21-18). There were

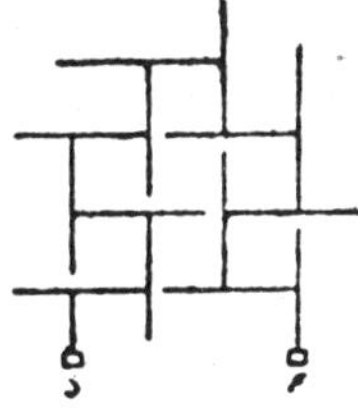

FIG. 21-18. (Tolman & Honzik, 1930.) Diagram of a multiple T maze used in a study of latent learning. S is the entrance, F the goal box. Gates between the successive units were closed behind the rats to prevent retracing. Curtains of black cloth, on each side of every choice point, forced the rats to choose before seeing the far ends of the two alleys. Most of the blind alleys were 15 inches long.

two control groups, one finding food on every trial, the other never finding food in the goal box. One experimental group found food on the first 10 trials, and the other no food on these trials. The conditions for these two groups were then interchanged, and it will be seen from the curves (Fig. 21-19) that the performance levels were approximately interchanged in a very few trials. Comparing the slopes of the "Yes" and "No" groups we are tempted to infer that the animals learned slowly without food reward and much more rapidly with food reward. But have we any right to draw this conclusion? All we have to judge by is performance, which depends on present drive as well as previous learning. How shall we determine whether the "No" group learned more slowly than the "Yes" group? Only by testing both groups under the same drive; and when such a test is made by aid of the "No-Yes" group, its performance indicated that it had learned the maze fully as well without the food reward as the "Yes" group with the reward (p. 667).

In the process of maze learning there are several drives to be considered. At the outset there is the tendency to explore all the alleys, some however being more attractive than others. In proportion as the alleys are sufficiently explored, this tendency becomes satiated, and meanwhile some value becomes attached to the empty goal box from which the animals are removed to a cage. When food has been found in the goal box, the powerful hunger drive works against any further entering of the blind alleys. With regard to the quick increase in blind-alley entrances which occurs when rats that have been finding food in the goal box no longer find any—as shown by the "Yes-No" group in Figure 21-19—this shift in performance is not due to a loss of the

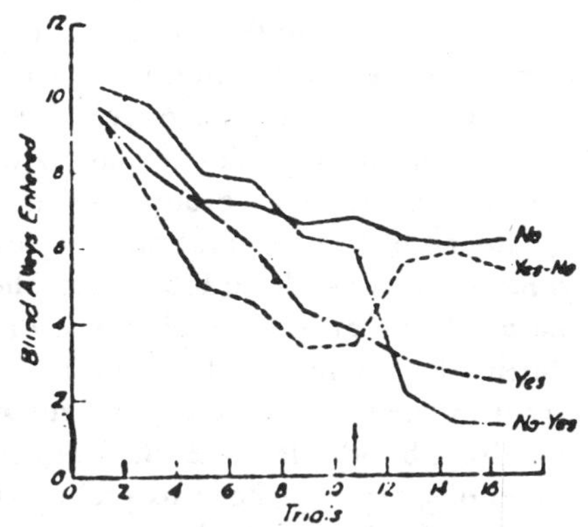

FIG. 21-19. (After Tolman & Honzik, 1930.) Performance of four groups of rats in a 14-unit maze, with and without food in the goal box. One trial per day; 36–41 rats per group. The "Yes" group found food in the goal box on every trial; the "No" group never; the "Yes-No" group on the first 10 trials only; the "No-Yes" group only after the first 10 trials. Each point on these curves (after the first) represents the average of two consecutive trials (2nd and 3rd, 4th and 5th, etc.) The high score at the outset (more than 50 percent of the 14 blind alleys) is due to double or triple entrances of the same blind alley before a rat advanced to the next unit

hunger drive. The rats begin to search the maze for the missing food, as observed by Bruce (1930). He also found (1932, p. 76) that when the food was left in the food box but made inaccessible behind a wire screen, the rats spent much time in the goal box, apparently trying to reach the food, instead of searching so much in the blind alleys.

From all these experiments on "restricted exploration" we can certainly infer that maze learning can be latent in the sense of not showing up in performance. But have the rats learned to go to a specific place, the goal box, with absolutely no reward for so doing? The evidence on this point is not conclusive.

Free exploration. A better view of the effects of exploration might be gained if the animals were allowed to wander freely in the maze before the regular trials began. Lashley (1918) found that 20 minutes of free exploration hastened the subsequent learning of a maze. Haney (1931), working in Tolman's laboratory, gave his experimental group four nights (72 hours) of free exploration in a fairly complex maze, with no food there, their rations being given in their home cages during the daytime. The control group spent the nights in a rectangular runway free from blind alleys. Each group consisted of 30 rats. After this preliminary training, food was placed in the goal box of the maze, and both groups had one trial a day for 18 days. The experimental group started off entering only half as many blind alleys as the controls, and maintained this lead consistently.

In a similar experiment by Buxton (1940) a special effort was made to prevent the goal box from acquiring any reward value during the period of free exploration. The rats were put into the maze and taken out of it at various points. They received food and water only in their home cages during the day, but they spent three nights in the large 12-unit T maze. After this experience each rat was taken from his home cage while hungry and placed directly in the goal box where for the first time he found some food, but he was taken out after a few bites and placed at the maze entrance, the question being whether he could find his way readily back to the food. How many blind alleys would he enter? Only two, on the Median of 48 such rats, while the average was six for rats that had not previously explored this maze. Free exploration certainly can give rats a serviceable acquaintance with a maze.

The single T maze, much used in recent experiments on latent learning, has *two* goal boxes, and the question is whether the rat can learn their distinctive locations by free exploration without distinctive rewards. Seward (1949) made the two goal boxes very different: white *versus* black interior, or rough-floored *versus* smooth-floored. He gave his rats three half-hour periods of free exploration, designed to enable them to locate these two empty boxes in their places in the T. To determine whether they had actually learned their locations, he then gave each rat a few bites of food in one box, and immediately took the rat out and placed him at the entrance. Nearly all the rats (28 out of 32) went directly back to the same box. Other rats—the control group—treated in the same way but without the preliminary exploration of this particular maze showed no such ability to return to the same box, but were just as likely to go to the other one. Had this simple T maze been standing out in a room, these control rats could probably have located the box by reference to extramaze cues; but the maze was entirely surrounded by a one-way screen (cheesecloth with lights inside) so that the location of the boxes had to be learned by exploration of the maze itself.

The same logic underlies an experiment of Tolman & Gleitman (1949). The maze was similar to the one just considered, being a simple T maze with two unlike goal boxes. It had several one-way doors to be pushed open on the way to a goal box. On his first trial a rat worked his way around to one of the goal boxes, where he found two pellets of food. On the second trial he was blocked off from this side but found two pellets in the other goal box. In nine days of this

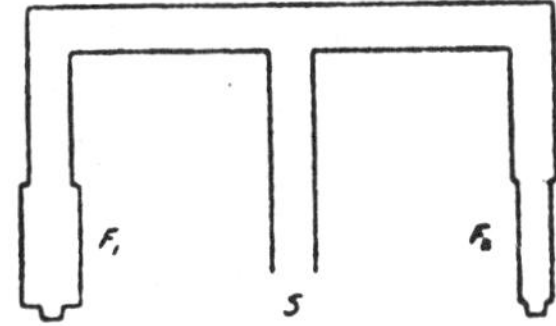

FIG. 21-20. Diagram of modified T maze to illustrate experiments of Seward (1949) and of Tolman & Gleitman (1949). S is the entrance, F_1 and F_2 the two distinctive goal boxes. There were doors to prevent retracing and to block off either arm of the T.

procedure he visited each goal box nine times and obtained equal rewards in both. So much was the period of exploration, and the question was whether the rat had learned the location of the two dissimilar goal boxes. These goal boxes were now detached and taken into another room, where the rat found food in one of them, but received several strong shocks in the other. About half of the 25 rats were shocked in one box, the remainder in the other box. Two hours later, the goal boxes having been restored to their original positions, each rat was given a test trial at the maze, and all but 3 of the 25 turned away from the side of the goal box in which they had been shocked.

Several other excellent experiments, varying in details, have yielded positive results. After free exploration without any distinctive reinforcement in the food box or anywhere else in the maze, the rat is placed for a moment in the food box with food there and is then placed at the entrance, the question being whether he finds his way readily to the food box (MacCorquodale & Meehl, 1951; Deese, 1951; Gilchrist, 1952; Kimball, Kimball & Weaver, 1953; Strain, 1953).

From all these painstaking experiments on free exploration, it is safe to conclude that the rat learns something from such exploration. He learns parts of a maze and their locations—blind alleys, through paths, distinctive end boxes—and what he learns by free exploration is later serviceable in the search for food or the avoidance of danger.

Can a rat learn where food is located except by eating there? That question has not been answered by the experiments cited so far. In free exploration a rat locates parts of a maze such as blind alleys, the through route and the goal box, and this acquaintance with the maze serves him well if he later finds and eats food in the goal box. But can he, like a human being, learn the location of food by merely observing it? To answer this question we shall have to prevent his eating the food that he has found. We might place the food behind a wire screen where he could see and smell it but not reach it. If he were then put back at the entrance, he would probably work his way back to the food—a reasonable prediction from results already cited (especially p. 640). Since the sight and smell of food are doubtless to be counted as "secondary food reinforcement," we could not say he had learned the location of food without some food reinforcement. It would be better to leave the food accessible but to have the rat satiated for food so that his reaction would be to sniff at the food but reject it. Presumably he would get no secondary reinforcement. Such considerations suggested to Spence & Lippitt (1940) a couple of experiments which have proved very intriguing.

Reversed drives. In a simple T or Y maze let one goal box contain food, the other water. A rat that is thirsty but not hungry quickly learns to go to the water box and avoid the food box, but by the device of forced runs he is given plenty of opportunity to observe the location of the food. So much for the training; now for the transfer test. While hungry but no longer thirsty, this rat is placed at the entrance of the maze. Surely he will go to the food which he has so often observed. But no, he continues to go to the same old water box. This result of Spence & Lippitt (1940, 1946) has been essentially confirmed by several other experimenters.

Perhaps these rats had not really noticed the food during the training series when they were food-sated. They had eaten none of it, though they had usually touched and smelled it during the 10 to 15 seconds that they were in the food box. To meet this objection means were adopted making it perfectly sure that the rats' senses were stimulated by the unwanted food. The animals were thirsty but satiated for food during the training series. Water was present in both goal boxes of the T maze, with food also present in one goal box. In Grice's experiment (1948a) the food was spread all over the floor of one goal box so that the rats walked and stood on the food and most of them were observed to sniff it and push it with their noses, though without nibbling it. By the device of forced runs they were made to go to each goal box twice a day for 12 days. On the thirteenth day they were hungry and not thirsty. If they had learned the location of the previously unwanted but now wanted food, they should now go to the food box. But if they had learned only the two locations of the water which they had drunk, about half of them should go to each side. The latter was the observed result, since only 12 of the 23 rats went to the box where the food was located. In a similar experiment by Kendler & Mencher (1948) each goal box was furnished with five little cups set into a small bench, one containing water and the other four containing food in the one goal box but being empty in the other. The water cup was shifted in position from trial to trial so that the rats, being thirsty but not hungry in the training series, had to poke their noses into one or more cups in finding the water. They thus had to distinguish the water from the food, two trials per day for seven days. For the same number of trials they found their water in the foodless box. On the eighth day these rats were tested while hungry and not thirsty, and their first choices were just about 50-50, with 19 rats going to the food box as against 17 to the other box.

Perhaps, then, these rats were much like human beings who notice an inconsequential detail the first time they encounter it but become inattentive to it, "negatively adapted" to it, with frequent repetition. Perhaps the experimenters gave them *too much* opportunity to learn the location of the unwanted food. As a check on this possibility, the last-mentioned experiment was repeated by Kendler & Kanner (1950) with one change—that the food was introduced on only the final 1–2 days of the training series. On the first 5–6 days, one cup in each goal box contained water while all the others were empty, but on the last 1–2 days food was placed in one goal box. Thus the rats might perceive the food without becoming negatively adapted to it. But the test results were the same; the hungry rats divided about 50-50, only 14 out of 31 rats going to the food box. (See, however, Thistlethwaite, 1951b).

Perhaps—for another possibility—strong thirst *inhibits* any attention or responsiveness to unwanted food. A water-seeking rat is too single-minded, we might say, to notice and locate food which he cannot eat at the moment. If he were satiated for both food and water, he might be free of this inhibition. Spence & Lippitt (1940) accordingly designed a companion experiment to the one on reversed drives.

Double-satiation experiments. There is food in one goal box of a simple T maze, and water in the other, but the rat is satiated for both food and water. Without either eating or drinking in the maze, can he learn the different locations of the food and water? Some third drive must probably be active in order to induce him to run the maze time after time. Just being removed promptly from either goal box and returned to his home cage may be sufficient reward (Meehl & MacCorquodale, 1948). Instead of the home cage, a "social cage" containing a few other rats will serve as a sufficient reward (Spence, Bergmann & Lippitt, 1950; Maltzman, 1950). These rewards are obtained by going to either goal box and so will not assist the animal in distinguishing the two boxes. The animals are prone to adopt position habits, preferences for one side of the maze rather than the other, and these preferences have to be balanced or allowed for in the final tests. After an ample series of training trials, some being forced, the rats have been in each goal box equally often, with food in one box and water in the other, but while satiated, for both food and water. Then comes the test of "latent learning": each rat is now made hungry but not thirsty, or thirsty but not hungry, and placed at the entrance to the maze. Will he go to the food box if hungry, to the water box if thirsty? Not, it must be admitted, with any great regularity. Or, at least, in a sample of rats, with position preferences balanced out, will more than the chance 50 percent choose the appropriate goal box? Several samples have been tried by different experimenters and under slightly different conditions, and always more than 50 percent have so chosen. The results have been as follows, in terms of the number of rats choosing correctly on the first test trial:

Spence, Bergmann & Lippitt (1950):	24 out of	39 rats, or	61.5%
Kendler (1947):	7 out of	12 rats, or	58.3%
Maltzman (1950):	17 out of	30 rats, or	56.7%
Meehl & MacCorquodale (1948):	15 out of	24 rats, or	62.5%
MacCorquodale & Meehl (1949):	22 out of	30 rats, or	73.3%
In all	85 out of	135 rats, or	63.0%

Taking each sample by itself we could not reject the "null hypothesis" of mere chance deviation from 50 percent. But with 5 samples giving quite similar percents from similar experiments we are justified in combining the samples, so obtaining a sufficient basis for rejecting the null hypothesis as having a probability of less than 1 percent. That is, we are justified in inferring from these double-satiation experiments that rats can learn the location of food in a maze without actually eating it, or the location of water without actually drinking it. (See also the positive results of Kendler & Levine, 1953.)

Further evidence that rats can learn the location of water without actually drinking (because satiated for water) is provided by a somewhat different experiment of Seward, Levy & Handlon (1950). The rats first learned while thirsty to go to the left-hand goal box of a simple T maze for water, the right-hand box being empty. The water was then shifted to the right-hand box, and one group of these rats, while satiated for water, had six forced trials a day for three days, going to the new water box half the time and to the new empty box half. How much had they learned by visiting the new water box without drinking there? They were now tested while thirsty, and for comparison two control groups were put to the same test, one group having rested since the original learning, and the other group having made the forced runs while thirsty. The first control group thus started from scratch to learn the new location of the water, and the second control group started from a relatively high level, having taken water nine times in the new location. In the five free test trials, the percent going correctly to the new location was as follows for the three groups:

	Trial 1	*Trial 2*	*Trial 3*	*Trial 4*	*Trial 5*
Starting from scratch	19	31	47	78	75
After satiated experience	46	64	73	82	100
After thirsty experience	81	90	95	95	90

Without pretending to say exactly how much the satiated experience had taught the rats, we can see that it had taught them something. They scored somewhere in the middle between the other two groups for the first few trials. Their scores were significantly higher than the scores of the rats that started from scratch, but significantly lower than the scores of the rats that had been thirsty while learning the new location of the water. Actual drinking was not necessary, though it was a great help in the learning.

The results cited from the double-satiation experiments, when compared with the results of the reversed-drive experiments, support the hypothesis that thirst inhibits attention to the location of food—or that the activity of seeking water and drinking it prevents any learning of the location of food. For after the shift from thirst to hunger the rats gave no evidence (only 50:50 choices) of any such learning, while after the shift from double satiation to hunger they did give some positive evidence (63:37 choices). But we are left with the question why these latter rats did not do much better and approach a 100:0 division. There may be other inhibitory factors operating, and some have come to light in other experiments, varying in design, which deserve fuller treatment than we can give them here.

One inhibitory factor is the well-known position preference. When both goal boxes offer equal incentives, or equal lack of incentives, some rats go mostly to the right or to the left, while others show no marked preference. If all these rats are then made hungry instead of thirsty, those with strong position preference will usually make the same choice as before, while those with little preference often shift from the water box to the food box. Position preference thus cuts down the percent of shift (Walker, Knotter & DeValois, 1950).

A similar effect is produced by a regular routine during the training series. Let the right-hand goal box of a T maze contain water, the left-hand box food; and let a rat that is thirsty but not hungry have paired trials, the first trial a free run and the second a forced run to the other box. After a few such pairs, the rat will go regularly first to the right and second to the left; and he is likely to carry over this routine into the test series when he is hungry and no longer thirsty (Littman, 1950).

Another inhibitory factor is suggested by the surprising behavior observed after the shift from thirst to hunger. You would expect the rats to eat greedily when they came upon the food. But no; for the first few trials many of them refuse to eat but struggle to get out of the food box, from which they have been regularly taken out during the training series. Some of them are emotionally disturbed on being kept there longer than the customary few seconds, this disturbance being shown by urination and defecation (Walker, 1948; Littman, 1950). The training series, we may say, has made the maze a drinking place but distinctly *not* an eating place.

We might even argue that it should be impossible for a food-satiated animal to learn the location of food. For if food is something to eat here and now, there is no food when eating is impossible. A food satiated rat will often sniff at the food and then turn away—just as a man with a weak appetite will leave the table declaring that there is nothing there to eat. A man who has eaten his fill may take note of a promising eating place for future reference, and we might expect a rat to carry away a pellet for hoarding. Such behavior has not often been observed in these experiments. Our negative argument, however, goes too far, since *some* learning of the location of food occurs even in food-satiated rats.

Another question may be raised regarding the shift from thirst to hunger motivation (Walker, 1951; Heron, 1949). Can we assume that the internal thirst stimuli are altogether different from the internal hunger stimuli? If they were partly the same, the goal box where thirst motivation was rewarded would also be the place where hunger motivation received some reward so that the animal that had learned to go to this goal box while thirsty might well go to the same place when the internal cues were shifted to hunger. An animal has learned when in a state of want to find what he wants in a certain place. This place has become for him a good place, a want-relieving place. When in a somewhat different state of want he tends to go to the same good place. See also a discussion in the chapter on Motivation (p. 682).

Are the much debated theories really opposed? Most of the authors cited have discussed the theoretical implications of their results, the supposedly opposing theories being those of Hull and of Tolman. Hull is said to espouse a reinforcement[1] or habit-strength theory, Tolman a cognitive theory. Or, Hull has seemed to favor a noncognitive theory, Tolman a nonreinforcement theory. Current discussions express doubt whether the two are really incompatible as positive theories. The animal is confronted by a certain stimulus complex, S. He makes a certain response, R, and there follows a certain result, Rf. The result may be a positive reinforcement, a negative reinforcement, or a neutral effect. The animal goes through the sequence S—R—Rf, and in so going builds up a habit, S—R, or a cognition, S—R—Rf. According to the reinforcement theory, Rf acts to strengthen the habit S—R, but Rf itself is not learned. According to the cognition theory, the whole sequence is learned. As the cognition theory is sometimes stated, you would think that any one sequence would be as readily learned as any other, but there is no reason to make that assumption. Suppose a food satiated rat goes to the left-hand goal box of a T maze and finds food there. According to the Hull theory, he gets no positive reinforcement and so no strengthening of the tendency (habit) to go that way again. According to the Tolman theory, he learns a sequence terminating in something not good to eat (at the time). Such a cognition would lead to avoidance of that place rather than to an approach movement. It seems that both theories might predict the same behavior—at least for the restricted environment of a simple T maze.

If we are interested in the broader question of how animals and human beings acquire their topographical mastery of an environment, we find that both our

[1] Here we follow the custom of recent theorists in using "reinforcement" in the restricted sense of reward or "drive reduction." But see p. 642 for the broader original usage of the term.

opposing theories are provided with accessory postulates of great power for interpreting complex behavior, though not for making any precise predictions. Hull appeals to stimulus generalization, response generalization, and secondary reinforcement. Stimulus generalization means that "similar" stimuli can elicit the same response. Response generalization—if we may use the term as equivalent to Hull's "habit family"—refers to the undoubted fact that the same goal can be reached by more or less different routes, and that when one route has been learned, other near-by routes and slight detours do not need to be separately learned. Secondary reinforcement attaches to landmarks which thus become intermediate goals on the way to the final goal where the drive is consummated. These are all doubtless genuine factors in topographical learning, the only question being whether they do not go beyond motor learning and implicitly assume perception and learning of the objective environment (Hull, 1934a).

Tolman speaks of "expectancies" which are the same as the S—R—Rf sequences already mentioned (p. 637). When such a sequence has been learned, the S is a "sign" that the goal, Rf, will be reached by following the route, R. By mastering such sequences, and also, presumably, by free exploration, an animal builds up a "cognitive map" of a particular environment. He can then utilize the map in finding his way about the environment. The map may be narrow, like a strip road map, or it may embrace objects off to this side and that of a specific route. The word "map" carries an implication that is unnecessary and probably unintended. If you have constructed a map of a region, you can take it away and consult it elsewhere. If you have built up a "memory map" of a route, you can review your trip after reaching home. That is, a memory map would require recall memory. All we need to assume in the rat is recognition memory, available only on ground that has been explored. A trail through the woods, indicated by a series of broken twigs, is an on-the-ground strip map. Anything like the sun on a clear day that enables a hiker to keep his bearings is an element in a broader on-the-ground map. On-the-ground maps are all we need to assume in the rat (Tolman, 1948).

HUMAN MAZE LEARNING

After struggling so long with the problems of maze learning by rats we may query why the maze should be taken over into the human laboratory. Certainly we do not need meticulous experiments to determine whether human beings can utilize visual cues in finding their way about, whether they learn routes through the environment or merely sequences of right and left body turns, or whether in exploring a town while not hungry they are able to learn the location of a promising restaurant. Human beings acquire remarkable ability to find their way about in the environment, but they depend to a large extent on such socially provided aids as well-worn trails, road signs, maps, lighthouses, the mariner's compass, and the radio beam. The maze experiment will throw the human individual on his own unaided resources and may indicate what means he adopts for finding his way. We must not expect too much of it, for the maze is certainly a highly restricted environment that affords only limited scope for the abilities of either rats or men to build up a practical mastery of the spatial environment. Actually, in both the animal and human laboratories, the maze is used mostly as a "lesson," a task to be mastered by a process of learning under controlled conditions. A variety of lessons is desirable in the investigation of learning curves, curves of forgetting, whole and part learning, transfer and interference, incentives and reinforcement, and other problems in learning theory and practical applications. In the present chapter, however, we are concerned specifically with the problems of spatial learning.

Full-size human mazes. A "body maze" for human subjects is apt to be a cumbersome piece of laboratory equipment. Hicks & Carr (1912) constructed an outdoor maze with alleys 2 ft wide bounded by wires strung 2½ ft from the ground. Blindfolded adults and children were run in this maze and compared with normal rats in walled-alley mazes of similar pattern. The average number of trials to learn was about the same for the three groups. The biggest difference was shown on the first trial during which the rats entered the same blind alleys repeatedly, seven times on the average, the human children four times, and the adults only once. The adults were carefully checking off the blind alleys, though unable to retain this knowledge fully from trial to trial. They were told in advance or soon discerned that their job was to avoid blind alleys and find the through route to the exit. Such a set favors slow movements, deliberate choices, and search for useful cues. Being without such an initial set the rats were less inhibited and circumspect.

Perrin (1914) made good use of an outdoor maze in an amusement park. It was approximately circular (dodecagonal), nearly 50 ft in diameter, with alleys 2 ft 4 in wide separated by high walls of wire mesh, and a smooth board floor. From an overhead platform *E.* could observe the blindfolded subjects as they felt their way with both hands. Being highly competent psychologists themselves, they were able to give retrospective reports of their method of solution. "The reports show that without exception the net result from the first trial was a knowledge of the general spatial relations. The relation of exit to entrance, the general course of the true path, was acquired by everybody in the first trial." The total problem then broke up into a number of local problems concerned with difficult parts of the maze. In spite of their correct general orientation the subjects did not acquire any accurate conception of the complicated maze pattern, for the maps which they drew after each trial were distorted in many details. Yet they learned to traverse the maze without errors. We shall have more to say regarding this extensive investigation in a moment.

Another outdoor maze (Batalla, 1943) consisted of 25 cubicles arranged like a horizontal set of pigeonholes. Each cubicle was 3 ft square and separated from its neighbors by wooden walls or cloth curtains 6 ft high. The subject, not blindfolded, on entering a cubicle, found two curtains to choose from, one opening into a blind alley. The maze stood on the ground and the subject's movements were observed from a third-story window of the adjacent building. The subjects were children of three age groups, averaging 3.7, 6.8 and 11.5 years old. The youngest required about 10 trials to reach the criterion of 3 successive correct runs; the intermediate group required about 7 trials; and the oldest required about 5 trials. The youngest group was reliably inferior at this task to the two older groups. About 3 years MA (Mental Age) appeared to be the lower limit of ability to learn this 5-blind-alley maze. After the correct route had been learned, an excellent short cut was opened. No child took it without hesitation, but most of the older children learned to take it after a few trials, while most of the youngest children stuck to the long route trial after trial—a behavior trait for which different explanations could be offered.

The trough maze (Warner Brown, 1932) is a practical piece of indoor apparatus. The passages are boards 1 ft wide laid on the floor, with side walls 3 in high to guide the subject's feet, and with cross-boards in the blind alleys. The tactile-kinesthetic cues picked up by the feet enabled the blindfolded subjects to learn the beginning and end of the maze rather quickly and also to recognize certain intramaze landmarks such as "long straight stretches" and "crooked spots." The maze was learned much more quickly, however, by other subjects who were not blindfolded but wore about the head and shoulders a cardboard screen open only at the top so as to hide the maze but afford a view of the ceiling and the upper part of the windows. Extra-maze cues and orientation in the room were thus shown to be of much help in the early stages of learning. The whole learning process seemed to consist of several stages: (1) general orientation; (2) mastery of the beginning, end, and one or two intervening parts of the maze; (3) enlargement of the mastered parts until they encompassed the whole maze; (4) automatization into a sequence of advances and turns, a pattern in "organismic space" (p. 629).

Hand mazes learned by blindfolded subjects. Besides the outdoor maze already mentioned, Perrin (1914) used a small model of the Hampton Court maze (p. 614). The through path and blind alleys were represented by a complicated slot cut through a thin board. The slot was ½ inch wide, and the whole board measured 16 by 26 inches. Under the board was placed a large sheet of paper resting on a smooth table. The subject followed the slot with a pencil, leaving a record of his wanderings on the paper which was renewed for each new trial. In many similar experiments the subject uses a metal stylus instead of a pencil, and the experimenter records the errors. The subject's cues are tactile and kinesthetic but he is aware of the slot with its straight stretches, corners, branches and dead ends —rather than of sensations in his hand, arm and body. He has the advantage of

FIG. 21-21. (Warner Brown, 1932.) The trough maze for human subjects.

easy orientation with respect to his own body with its right and left, forward and backward directions. He can scarcely lose his bearings altogether as he can when blindfolded in a full size maze. Yet his impressions of angles and distances may be inaccurate, as shown by his attempts to make a drawing of the path he has followed.

Perrin's scientifically trained subjects endeavored to solve the maze problem by planning and reasoning. Some of them tried to build up a visual image of the maze, and some tried to formulate a verbal description of the true path. These intellectual devices were not of much use. The essential thing was to distinguish and identify different parts of the maze and to remember and finally combine these parts.

When his subjects had learned the maze, Perrin tested them, still blindfolded, in a number of ways. He constructed a much smaller maze of the same pattern and found that they traced it with no difficulty and with no errors even on the first trial. He rotated the original maze 90 or 180 degrees and obtained very few errors. He asked them to follow the path backward from goal to entrance and they did so without trouble. He transferred the pencil to their left hands and obtained some errors due mostly to awkwardness. Their success in these tests was surprising in view of the altered tactual-kinesthetic cues and cue patterns. Evidently they knew the maze as an environmental object, and not in terms of "organismic space." It must be admitted, of course, that Perrin's subjects were far from an average sample of the population, being graduate students nearly all of whom distinguished themselves in their later careers. Higginson (1937) and Langhorne (1950) used relatively large groups of college students, who learned a stylus maze and immediately relearned it when it was rotated 90 degrees. They made about ⅓ as many errors in the relearning as in the original learning. Even so, our previous conclusion can stand.

High-relief finger mazes. The stylus-in-a-slot maze is similar to the alley type used with rats; it was the only type available for many years. But Miles (1928a) gave us a human version of the elevated maze, and it has become very popular. It is nothing but a board with a maze pattern slightly raised above the surface so that the subject can follow it with the ball of his index finger (eyes closed, of course). The path may be made by nailing staples in the desired pattern, by sewing and gluing heavy string on a card, or best of all, by making the separate units of stiff wire. If the latter method is used for a multiple U maze (Fig. 21-2) the ends of the units can be bent down, like the points of tacks, and inserted into holes drilled in the baseboard; if extra holes are drilled, the pattern can be changed as easily as the letters on a cafeteria menu. The finger maze is somewhat easier to learn than the stylus maze (Fig. 21-24), for it permits the subject to feel every false path (*cul*, or *cul de sac*). One or the other of these hand mazes is widely used, both in laboratory exercises and in research on a variety of learning problems; they will crop up frequently in the chapters which follow.

Visible mazes for human subjects. If the subject sees the whole maze, his "errors" cannot be counted, since he can explore a blind alley with his eyes while holding his pencil or stylus at the choice point. Porteus (1950), in his well-known maze test for social and practical intelligence, instructs the subject to look ahead and avoid all overt errors. As soon as the

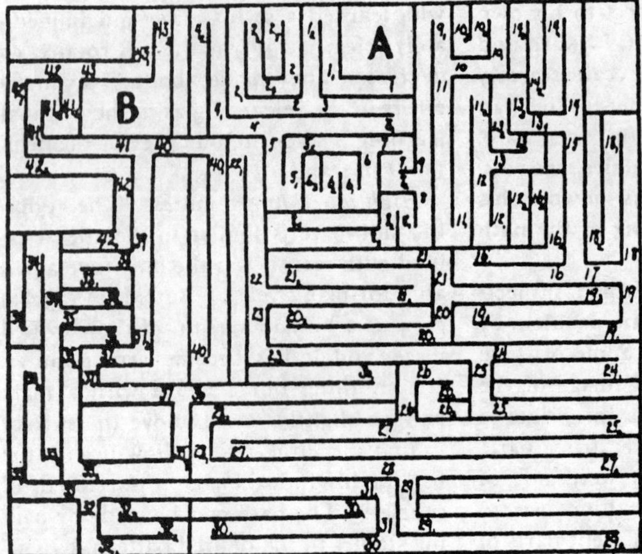

FIG. 21-22. (From Perkins, 1927.) A maze learned by human subjects. The passages in the original were ¾ in wide. The lines were drawn on paper and the maze was laid on a glass-topped table and brightly illuminated from below. The subject sat on a high stool, looking through a tube 1 in in diameter, and moving the tube along the passages in exploring and running the maze. He saw only a small bit of the maze at a time. The experimenter followed the subject's course on a numbered maze (the original had no numbers on it).

subject's pencil enters a blind alley, he is stopped and placed back at the entrance of a duplicate maze. Used in this way the maze is supposed to be a test for "prudence, forethought, mental alertness, and power of sustained attention" as against "impulsiveness, irresolution, suggestibility, nervousness, and excitability."

In other experiments the subject is allowed to see only a small portion of a maze at a time, the idea being to allow him about as much use of vision in a hand maze as he would have in a full-size walled-alley maze. Perkins (1927) used the complex maze shown in Figure 21–22.

The results of Perkins were in general agreement with those obtained from blindfolded human subjects in the full size and stylus mazes. In the first trial the alert subject would get his bearings and learn the general nature of the maze. In the following few trials he would analyze the path into segments to be mastered separately and finally put together—see Figure 21-23. Intermediate goals were found where the true path changed its general direction, and the most difficult blind alleys were either (1) those which pointed toward an intermediate goal or (2) those which anticipated a change in the general direction. The first two and last two blind alleys were quickly eliminated. Another result was that the human subject seldom went just part way into a blind alley; he either explored it to the dead end, or passed by with or without hesitation at the entrance.

Visible paths but invisible stops. Human subjects like to see their work, and a useful device of Carr (1921) makes this possible. The surface of a stylus maze is in full view, but invisible stops are in-

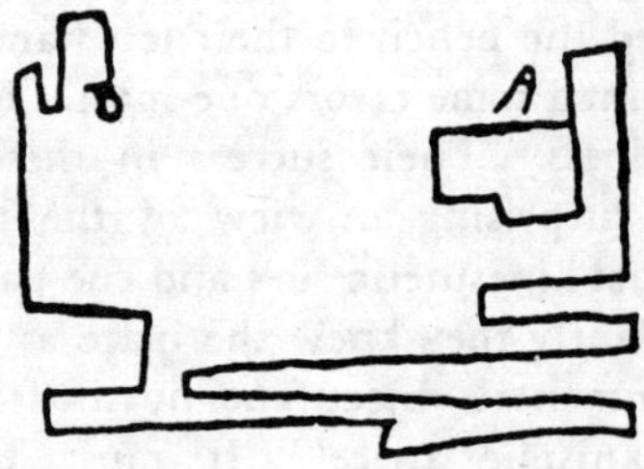

FIG. 21-23. (Perkins, 1927.) One subject's drawing of the maze path after his sixth trial. A = starting point, B = goal.

serted in the bottom of the slot which is expanded to allow room for a metal disk pivoted to the end of the stylus. (Once the stylus is put into the slot at the entrance, it cannot be withdrawn till the goal is reached.) The subject sees the entrance, the goal, and all the paths and intersections, but there is no visible difference between the true path and the blind alleys. He learns in relatively quick time because of two great advantages: he sees the choice points; and when the movement of his stylus is blocked, he can locate that blind alley in the visible maze.

An electrical equivalent of this hidden-stop maze has been used by several investigators. One early example is the "stepping-stone maze" of Barker (1931). The subject sees a board containing a rectangular arrangement of contact points to be touched with his stylus. He is to start at a certain point and advance step by step, forward, right, left, or backward, till he reaches an assigned goal. The metal points which he touches are the ends of screws or bolts which extend through the board and are so wired on the reverse side, in series with a buzzer or other indicator, as to show when he is on and when off the correct path. The current may be utilized also for making a record of errors. Many variations are possible. The pattern may be linear, with two alternatives at each choice point (Brown and Buel, 1940), or with four alternatives (Jones, 1945). Instead of visible contact points, there may be an array of holes with the contacts located underneath, as in a "punch board maze" (Tolman, Hall & Bretnall, 1932). These various forms give the learner the benefit of a visible framework in which he can mentally locate the correct path as he discovers it.

How the maze is learned. A human subject learning an unseen stylus maze is necessarily limited to tactile-kinesthetic cues but is free to utilize them in different ways. Warden (1924b) made a study of the methods adopted by college students. The U maze which they learned (essentially the same as the one marked S in Fig. 21-24) is surprisingly difficult without the aid of vision, and these students required many trials to master it. They were given no advance instructions in efficient ways of learning a maze, but after the learning was completed they were asked to describe their methods. The chief methods fell into three classes: verbal, visual, motor. Probably all the subjects began with "motor learning," simply trying to make the right moves at the right places. The majority found their progress so slow that they sought for some helpful device. Some attempted to build up a visual image of the maze; others resorted to counting and even to an exact formula such as: "One right, three left, two right, one left, two right, one left," though usually the verbal rule adopted was less formal than this. The verbal method was the most, the motor method the least successful, as shown below:

Method	*No. subjects reporting it*	*Trials required to learn*	
		Mean	*Range*
Verbal	25	32	16–62
Visual	18	68	41–101
Motor	17	124	72–195

One trouble with the motor method is that a fixed habit of entering one or more blind alleys may be established and continued without the subject's noticing that anything is wrong. The verbal or counting method alerts the subject to such errors. The visual method seemed to be of little value except when combined with some counting. If the subject actually sees the maze before being blindfolded (Twitmyer, 1931), or if while working he has before him a plan of the invisible maze (Carr, 1921), his progress is greatly facilitated. But when he attempts to build up a visual image of the maze from

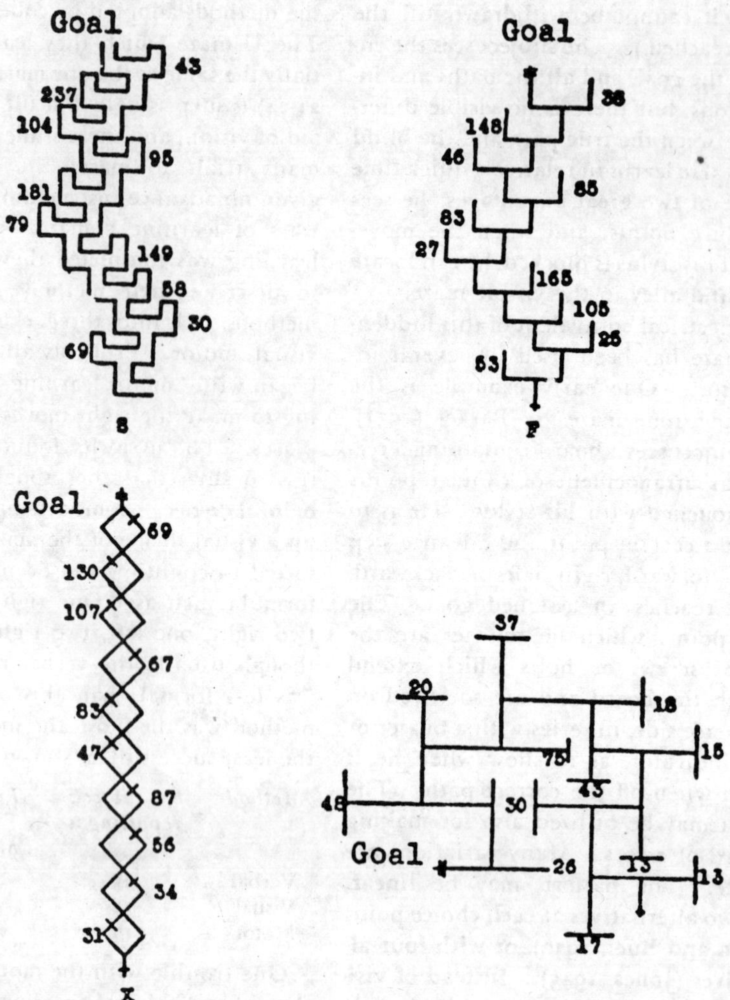

FIG. 21-24. (From Husband, 1931.) A stylus maze, S, and three "high-relief finger mazes"—an invention of Miles (1928a)—learned by comparable adult groups of 20 subjects each. X is a linear maze, S and F are semilinear, and these three are alike in the sequence of correct choices. T has a roughly circular course and is much easier than the others. Another roughly circular stylus maze has been found to be much easier than semilinear mazes such as S (Scott, 1930). The numbers on the patterns give the total count of entrances into each blind alley, by 20 subjects. Study of these numbers reveals the following tendencies: (1) to master the first and last moves quickly; (2) to anticipate the final turn and other changes in the general direction. The T maze is shown to be the easiest by the number of errors. And of the two mazes with the same pattern, S and F, the finger maze is somewhat easier than the stylus maze. The subject while hugging one side of the groove with his stylus may pass an alley on the other side without noticing it; in the finger maze, however, he follows along the wire with his finger and is fully aware of every choice point he encounters. Walsh & Waters (1944) converted this stylus maze (S) into a finger maze by simply having the subject trace the groove with his finger; and they found that a finger group made decidedly fewer errors than a stylus group of subjects.

tactile-kinesthetic data, as in Warden's experiment, he finds it a difficult task.

In a similar experiment by Husband (1931) several different mazes were employed, as shown in Figure 21-24. Few of his subjects reported using a purely visual method. Those who counted the turns learned the three mazes marked S, F, and X much more efficiently than those who depended on motor learning. The linear maze (X) was found to be almost insoluble by pure motor learning; there was so little spatial difference between one choice point and another. Such a maze is much like the temporal maze (p. 628) in requiring the learner to master a bare sequence of right and left turns; but counting greatly simplifies the task. By contrast, the maze marked T, which is the Stone multiple T maze already shown in Figure 21-4, p. 619, has plenty of two-dimensional spatial character, and here the counting method was no better than the motor. Probably this so-called motor learning is really spatial learning, as in animals (p. 630).

If we examine an individual subject's reactions to a single alley, we might expect to find him exploring it to its end on the first trial, penetrating it less deeply on successive trials, then merely hesitating at the entrance and finally running straight past. Something much like this process was observed in rats by Reynolds (1945a). Such gradual elimination of the single alley seems *not* to be characteristic of human learning, as observed by Perkins (1927), by Kellogg & White (1935), and especially by McGeoch & Peters (1933) who made a special study of this matter with blindfolded human subjects learning a stylus U maze, like S in Figure 21-22, and found that over 85 percent of all entrances into the blind alleys were complete penetrations. This striking difference in results may not be a difference between rats and men; it may be due to the different maze patterns employed.

Mental or nonspatial mazes. A maze presents a series of choice points at each of which two or more alternatives are offered. Suppose the alternatives, instead of being two paths, are two letters, one being "correct," the other a "blind alley." A series of such choices can be offered with rules of procedure for enabling the subject to discover sooner or later which are the correct letters. Joseph Peterson (1920, 1922) introduced this sort of "mental maze" and used it effectively in the study of learning theory. (His rules of procedure are stated in the first edition of this book, pp. 153–155, where other more or less similar "mazes" are described.)

Q W E R T Y U I O P
A S D F G H J K L Z

FIG. 21-25. Simplified form of Peterson's mental maze. *E* reads the first vertical pair of letters to *O*, who chooses one of the pair. If *O* makes the wrong choice, *E* repeats the pair until the correct choice is made and then gives the next pair. This is continued until *O* makes one or more errorless "runs." The correct choices are underlined; the maze can be visualized as a linear one (Fig. 21-3; or X in Fig. 21-24).

Maze learning by rats and men. Some obvious differences have come to light in the previous paragraphs. Human subjects have an initial advantage in knowing that there is a goal to be reached, that there are blind alleys to be avoided, and that the same maze is to be traversed trial after trial. They are rewarded (pleased) not only on reaching the goal, but every time they identify and avoid a blind alley or reach an intermediate goal. How much such "secondary reinforcement" rats may obtain has not been thoroughly investigated. Both rats and men learn quickly to avoid the last one or two blind alleys in most mazes, very likely because of the prompt reinforcement at the goal. But human subjects, in contrast to rats, eliminate the first couple of blind alleys quickly. Rats tend to explore the entrance region in trial after trial, as if to identify the situation; human subjects are told or assume that the maze remains the same. If asked why he learns the first part of a maze (or of a list of nonsense syllables, p. 711) so quickly, the human subject is apt to say that his mind is clear at the outset but becomes confused as he advances into the mass of different items. In other words, interference is at a minimum at the beginning and also at the end of the series of responses. But should it not increase to the very end?

Human subjects make good use of their numerical and verbal abilities in certain types of mazes, especially in the linear maze, where they have a great advantage over rats. Mazes that afford more scope for rudimentary spatial ability are easier for both rats and men, and fully as easy for rats as for men. If either rats or men were unable to adjust their behavior readily to the spatial environment, they would have small chance of survival.

The human subject is able to recall the maze path, or some of it, when not actually in the maze. He can draw a map of a maze that he has learned. Usually his map is rough and incomplete in details which he admits he cannot remember without being actually in the maze. That is to say, he can recognize more than he can recall, as in other cases (p. 725). Probably recognition memory is all we need to assume in the rat.

The factors that make one blind alley more attractive or harder to avoid than another were noted on pages 620–624. Zigzagging is perhaps more characteristic of rats, goal-pointing of men, anticipating about equal in both. These tendencies appear early in the learning process and persist in spite of nonreinforcement. First-trial behavior in a hidden-stop linear maze was extensively investigated by Brown & Buel (1940). Individuals differ of course, but certain choices are much more probable than others. At the first choice point, with a right-hand and a left-hand alley to choose from, 60 percent of college students chose the one on the right. Whichever side is found to be correct at the first choice point is likely to be chosen at the second choice point; and more in general, at any choice point the subject is inclined to choose the side that was correct at the just preceding choice point. But when the same side has been correct at two or more successive choice points, he is inclined to choose the other side next. The subject may have no logical basis for these preferences and assumed probabilities, but they show, as was said before with reference to the rat (p. 622), that maze learning does not start from a uniform zero level. It starts from below zero at the difficult choice points and from above zero at the easy points. Reinforcement establishes the easy correct choices quickly and the difficult ones slowly. But maze learning cannot be understood in terms of reinforcement alone; the theorist must take account of the maze pattern and of the tendencies of the organism.

22

MOTIVATION IN LEARNING AND PERFORMANCE

It is recognized in everyday life that a person's performance on a given occasion does not always measure up to his ability. He does not run as fast or shoot as accurately or speak as convincingly as he has on other occasions. He is perhaps not highly motivated, or he may even be overmotivated and so eager to succeed as to lose control of his resources of energy and skill. Both ability and motivation are factors in performance, and if either of them is entirely lacking, the performance does not occur. Ability is like a machine which cannot do its work unless power is applied.

In the laboratory also the importance of these two factors is recognized, as we saw in the experiments on maze learning (pp. 529, 637). When learning—or better, learned ability—is to be measured, motivation must be held constant. Similarly, when motivation is to be measured, learned ability must be held constant. In both cases what we directly measure is performance, but if we hold one factor constant we can use performance to measure the other factor.

FACTORS IN PERFORMANCE

Making use once more of certain symbols introduced in our first chapter, we can say that both motivation and learned ability are "*O*-factors," already present in the organism when a response or performance is to be made, but controlled as far as possible by "A-factors," or antecedent operations of the experimenter. Thus, learned ability, an *O*-factor, depends (in part) on the number of previous trials, an A-factor; and drive, another *O*-factor, can be controlled by the A-factor of hours since last feeding in an animal experiment. For many fundamental experiments on motivation, animals make the best subjects.

Clark Hull (1943, 1950a, 1951) is a major contributor to the analysis of the factors in performance. Learned ability, which he calls habit strength and designates by the letter H, is traced back to several A-variables which do not require consideration here. Motivation also is analyzed into several factors such as drive

(D) and "incentive motivation" (K). When the drive is hunger, D-strength depends on time since last feeding, while K-strength depends on the amount of food given as a reward for a successful response. There is also an inhibitory factor or factor complex (I) which acts in opposition to the positive factors of motivation; it depends on the amount of work or effort involved in the performance and on the time allowed for recovery between trials. Hull endeavors to quantify each *O*-variable by working out a formula for its dependence on an A-variable. For example, he might quantify the hunger factor in a food-getting performance such as bar-pressing. He would vary the time since last feeding while holding constant all other factors in motivation and habit strength, and he would measure some *R*-variable such as the latency of the bar-pressing response. As the time since feeding increased from 1 hour to 24 hours, the response latency might decrease from 60 to 15 seconds (Perin, 1942; Saltzman & Koch, 1948; Kimble, 1951). These data would be fitted by as simple and rational an equation as possible, which would be the desired formula for the potency of the hunger drive. One serious complication is that there are several alternative measures of performance (p. 5), so that it seems necessary to relate each empirical measure to a central ideal measure of performance (which Hull calls "reaction potential"). See, for example, the work of Yamaguchi (1951). We shall not endeavor to check the accuracy of Hull's formulas nor estimate the value of his system as a whole; but we can make good use of some of the motivational factors that he has identified.

It will be convenient to stretch the ordinary meaning of motivation somewhat and make it equivalent to mobilization or activation, so as to cover all *O*-factors not included under the head of ability. A very general factor may be mentioned first.

General level of responsiveness or readiness for activity. The activity cage is a standard piece of equipment in the animal laboratory. There is the squirrel-cage type with its vertical wheel in which the animal can run as much as he will, the number of revolutions of the wheel being recorded by a mechanical counter. And there is the tilting-floor type, which tips slightly in different directions as the animal moves freely about the cage, the number of tips being recorded. With such apparatus many experiments have been made on the amount of "spontaneous activity" and its dependence on such A-variables as the following (Richter, 1927):

The *age* of the animal (including man, according to everyday observation), motor and playful activity tending to decrease after a fairly early age.

Hormones in the blood, secreted by the pituitary, adrenal, thyroid, and sex glands, activity decreasing when one of these glands has been removed.

Drugs, depressant or excitant, or excitant with small and depressant with larger doses.

Fatigue substances, the products of muscular activity, which act much like the last-mentioned class of drugs.

Bodily states of deprivation such as hunger and thirst—a progressive effect (Hall *et al.*, 1953).

Temperature, low external temperature tending to increase activity, low body temperature tending to decrease activity while moderate fever has the opposite tendency.

Illumination, the rat as a nocturnal animal tending to be most active in the dark, while presumably the opposite would hold for the human being.

Emotions, some of which, like anger, frustration and perhaps anxiety, tend to increase motor activity. The energy-releasing function of emotion is treated in another chapter (esp. pp. 133–137).

The animal's movements in an activity cage are only relatively spontaneous. Though the experimenter does not apply specific stimuli at specific moments, and though he may exclude light and mask external sounds by the steady hum of a ventilating fan, the resting animal will be getting pressure and temperature stimuli, and the moving animal will get abundant kinesthetic stimuli as well. The activity level is certainly very low in human sleep, but when a comfortable bed is equipped to serve as an activity cage, changes of posture and other movements are found to occur from time to time (Johnson & Swan, 1930).

Conditions which increase the amount of movement in an activity cage are likely also to increase the amount of activity in other performances. Crossings of the electrified grid of an "obstruction box" (p. 662) to get to the food are more numerous when the rats are living in a cold room than when they are living in a hot room (Moore, 1944). In a conditioning experiment, with differentiation well established between the positive and negative stimuli, the differentiation broke down after the injection of caffein, because the dog began to respond indiscriminately to both stimuli (Pavlov, 1927, pp. 127–128; see also Switzer, 1935). The main difficulty in the discriminative response is to inhibit response to the negative stimulus, and this difficulty is increased when the general level of responsiveness is raised.

DRIVE AND INCENTIVE

Drive and incentive are motivational factors as distinguished from ability. They are related to each other. If we are hungry, food is an incentive, but if we are thirsty and not hungry, water and not food is an incentive. Doubt might be raised whether there are two motivational factors here or only one, but the experimenter sees a difference since, as already said, he controls them by different operations. Drive he varies by time since last feeding, incentive by amount of food. He can hold hunger constant, as well as ability, and still get differences in performance by varying the amount of food reward. There are similar human examples. You would not pay out good money to a restaurant without some motivation. How much you are willing to pay depends on how hungry you are and on how good the food is, i.e., on both drive and incentive, as well as on your financial ability. Both drive and incentive are factors in mobilizing your resources.

Drive and need. The typical animal drives, such as hunger and thirst, are dependent upon organic needs. Food and water are continually being used up in life processes, while waste products are being produced and threatening to accumulate. A need is an organic state of deficiency or excess. Some needs can be corrected by appropriate behavior such as eating and drinking. In the simplest cases a drive is a tendency to behave in a manner that corrects an organic need. Thus need activates drive, and drive activates behavior. But is there any sense in multiplying factors in this way? Why not drop the concept of drive and simply say that behavior is motivated by need?

The difficulty is, there are specific needs that do not give rise to appropriate behavior and there is much behavior that does not arise from any known and present need.

Besides the general need for food there are specific needs for dietary essentials such as protein, vitamins, and certain salts. Some of these specific needs are served by specific drives, i.e., by specific hungers or cravings that can be demonstrated in animal behavior. Feed an animal for a few days on a diet deficient in vitamin B, so creating a great need for this vitamin. Then offer the animal a meal rich in vitamin B and he eats it in preference to a meal lacking the vitamin —or quickly learns to do so (Harris *et al.*, 1933). In this case the specific need activates a specific drive. But similar experiments with vitamins A, D, and G have failed to reveal any corresponding drives, since the animal's choice between two meals is not determined by the presence of the needed vitamin but apparently by the tastes of the foods, a sweet food being preferred to a better but bitter one (Jukes, 1938; Young, 1941, 1948). So there are needs without corresponding drives; the drives without corresponding needs will come to light under the heads of secondary motivation and unorganic motives.

Some organic needs can be made extremely great by the removal of certain endocrine glands. The adrenal cortex supplies a hormone that prevents excessive loss of sodium chloride through the kidney. Removal of the adrenals is rapidly fatal unless the animal has access to some external supply of the salt. Provide the living cage of an adrenalectomized rat with two water bottles, one filled with tap water and the other with a 3-percent salt solution, and you find that he takes this strong salt solution (avoided by a normal rat) in preference to the plain water He thus corrects his salt deficiency and maintains himself in good condition. His choice of the salty water depends on the sense of taste and is lost if the taste nerves are cut (Richter, 1947).

How can an organic need activate a behavioral drive? How can the lack of salt in the blood communicate with the nervous system and arouse appropriate behavior? There are two possible lines of communication: by way of peripheral receptors such as the taste buds of the tongue, and by way of a nerve center affected by the chemical state of the circulating blood. (The respiratory center is tuned by the carbon dioxide of the blood: the more carbon dioxide, the more responsive the center, and the more rapid the breathing; p. 168).

Perhaps, then, salt hunger increases the sensitivity of the taste buds to salt—lowers the stimulus threshold. To test this hypothesis Pfaffman & Bare (1950) applied weak salt solutions to the rat's tongue while picking up and amplifying the action currents from the taste nerves (p. 300). But they obtained the same threshold values from both normal and adrenalectomized rats. The salt preference must be determined by the nerve centers and not by the receptors alone. With plain water in one bottle and salty water in the other, the normal rat shows no preference as long as the salt solution is very weak; he prefers the salt solution if it is moderately strong, but refuses over 2 percent of salt. The adrenalectomized rat prefers even the weakest salt solutions that are above threshold and will drink immense quantities if no stronger solution is available, but he will also accept strong solutions that the normal rat refuses (Young & Chaplin, 1949; Pfaffman & Bare, 1950).

These changes in preference could

scarcely be explained by alterations of peripheral sensitivity. If the sensitivity were decreased, the weakest solutions could not be tasted, and if it were increased, the strong solutions would taste abnormally strong and be surely rejected on the basis of the peripheral factor. Some central mechanism concerned with acceptance or rejection must be affected (tuned) by the salt content of the blood.

The "pangs of hunger" are sensations produced by peristaltic movements of the empty stomach stimulating receptors in the stomach wall. These movements can be recorded by a pneumatic system consisting of a rubber bulb, which the human subject learns to swallow and keep down, connected by a rubber tube up through the gullet and mouth to a recording tambour which writes on a kymograph. Meanwhile the subject records by hand pressure the moments when he feels the pangs, and his hand pressures are found to synchronize with the stomach movements (Cannon, 1934; Wada, 1922). Here we have a clear case of communication from the organic state to the nervous system by way of peripheral receptors. But the hunger drive does not depend altogether on the local sensations. For if the stomach movements are mostly abolished by surgical reduction of the stomach to a tube connecting the gullet with the duodenum (Tsang, 1938)—or if conduction from the stomach receptors to the nervous system is abolished by section of the vagus nerves (Bash, 1939)—the need for food is still met by periodic eating. That the desire for food is something more than hunger pangs was brought out clearly in the important Minnesota experiment on semi-starvation in young adult human subjects (Keys *et al.*, 1950). The organic need for water, similarly, appears to have other means of communicating with the nervous system and obtaining appropriate behavior, besides the localized thirst sensations in the throat (Morgan & Stellar, 1950). In fatigue there are local muscu-

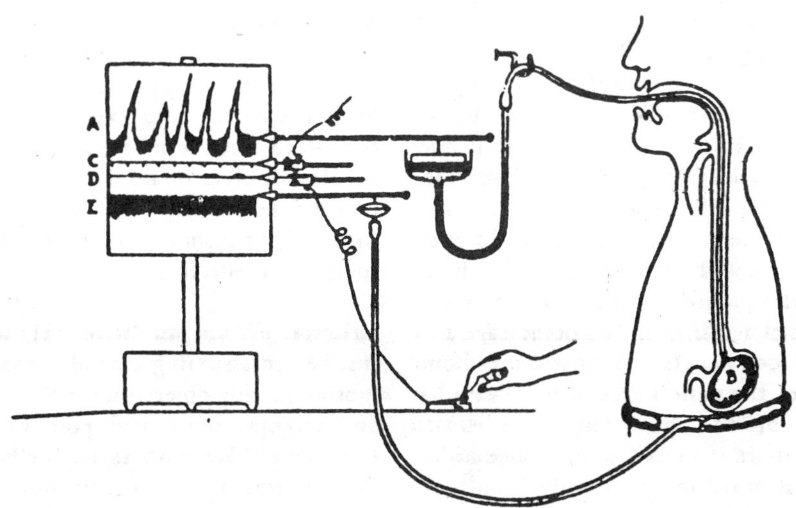

FIG. 22-1. (Cannon, 1934) Setup for registration of stomach movements along with hunger sensations. In the kymograph record, the breathing movements show in both lines A and E, with the much slower stomach contractions also showing in line A. C is a time line in minutes, and D shows the subject's signals recording hunger sensations.

lar pains and also a more general tired feeling which may be due to fatigue products circulating through the brain. Other examples could be cited of organic needs which probably affect brain centers by way of blood chemistry or temperature.

Criteria of a drive. How can we identify and demonstrate a drive? From what has already been said we see that the existence of a need is not sufficient evidence. There must also be appropriate behavior such as that which corrects the need. For example, we know that warm-blooded animals need to maintain an approximately constant body temperature. The autonomic corrective responses of goose flesh and sweating are not always regarded as behavior and therefore are not an ideal demonstration of a behavioral drive. But if the animal seeks shelter from cold or heat, we have evidence of a thermostatic drive.

The food-hoarding drive. If we could credit the squirrel or the hamster with the ability to anticipate future need for food, we could attribute the hoarding of now-unneeded food to the hunger drive. The laboratory rat, anyway, shows no signs of such anticipation but continues to bring food pellets into his home cage even though the experimenter constantly removes them. Since the rat will not ordinarily hoard food except in his home cage, the procedure in a hoarding test is to afford access from the home cage to a bin of food pellets. A rat will take home some of the pellets even if he always has plenty of food there, but he will hoard many more if he is fed only once a day. He will hoard more when the laboratory is cold than when it is warm. However well adapted such behavior is to life in the wild, it does not reveal any actual need (Morgan, 1947), and physiological experiments designed to discover an organic condition behind the hoarding behavior have so far been unsuccessful (Stellar, 1951).

Water hoarding has been observed in thirsty rats. The "pellets" were of absorbent cotton saturated with water. The rat would take a pellet from the bin, carry it home and suck out some water, then run to the bin for another pellet, continuing till he had accumulated many more than he could use at the time (Bindra, 1947). Though a rat will not often hoard pellets of wood, he will hoard food pellets wrapped in aluminum foil, and if half the pellets in the bin are foil-covered, some rats will hoard them in preference to plain food pellets (Licklider & Licklider, 1950). The rat perhaps carries home anything that looks good to him at the moment. At any rate the hoarding drive is closely allied to the homing drive.

Analyzed in terms of need, drive and incentive, some of these investigations vary the incentive—food, water, shiny pellets—for the purpose of defining the incentive. Some of the experiments vary conditions that may affect the drive—feeding schedule and external temperature—and some aim at the discovery of an organic state or need. Even though no need can be identified, we can logically infer a drive from the incentives that are found to be effective.

Criteria of an incentive. If we are justified in assuming that all behavior is motivated, any object that is approached and accepted must have positive incentive value. We wish to go further and discover what property of the object gives it this value. We take note of what our subject does with the object after obtaining it—of the consummation of his performance—as a basis for inferring the nature of the incentive. If a child runs eagerly to obtain an orange but proceeds to roll it on the floor, we infer that a play motive rather than the hunger drive is in operation. We offer substitutes for the original object and so bring out the true nature of the incentive. If the child accepts a ball in place of the orange, that is one thing, but if he accepts a cup of orange juice, that is something else in the way of incentives. (Equivalent incentives remind us of "equivalent stimuli" in the discrimination experiments, p. 589.) We could also observe how persistently the subject approaches and accepts the same incentive, for its incentive value may consist simply in its novelty, appealing to the exploratory drive. Another result we should like to obtain would be some measurement of the relative appeal of different incentives, and so of the relative strength of different drives.

Experimental methods for testing and measuring incentives ask, in effect, whether the subject is willing to *pay for the incentive,* and how much he is willing to pay. He may pay for one incentive by foregoing another—the preference method. He may pay by pain or effort necessary in reaching the incentive—the obstruction method. He may pay by hastening or improving his performance—the learning method. Here we have three distinctive and fruitful types of experiments on motivation (Moss, 1924).

Preference tests for incentive value. The daily intake method, as already mentioned, shows a preference for salt solutions over plain tap water (p. 658). The incentives may be paired and presented simultaneously, or only a single incentive may be offered on any one day. With the latter procedure a preference for water sweetened with saccharine over plain water was demonstrated in rats (Beebe-Center *et al.*, 1948). The solution had to be of moderate strength, neither too weak nor too strong; for with very weak solutions there was no preference, and with very strong solutions the preference went to the unsweetened water. The preference or value curve was of the same shape as found with human beings by verbal report (Fig. 22-2)

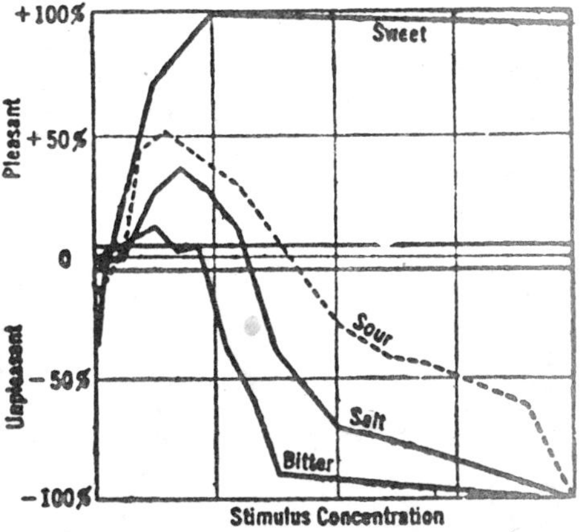

FIG. 22-2. (Data from R. Engel, 1928.) Preponderance of "pleasant" or "unpleasant" judgments as related to the concentration of a sapid solution. The solution, taken into the mouth, was reported as pleasant, neutral, or unpleasant. After each trial 2 minutes were allowed for removing the taste by chewing a little white bread and rinsing the mouth. Graduated solutions of common salt, quinine, tartaric acid, and cane sugar were judged.

The ordinate gives percent "pleasant" minus percent "unpleasant" for seven subjects at each strength of the solutions. The abscissa is proportional to the concentration, the full length of the base line representing a 40-percent sugar solution, a 1.12-percent solution of tartaric acid, a 10-percent salt solution, and a .004-percent solution of quinine sulphate, all by weight. The two horizontal lines just above and below the zero level signal the fact that there is typically a neutral zone between pleasant and unpleasant.

Even the strongest sugar solutions were not unpleasant except to a few individuals when satiated. The other tastes never showed a large preponderance of "pleasant" judgments, but they did show a maximum at relatively weak concentrations.

Verbally expressed preference is an index of incentive value.

A modified form of this single-incentive test for preferences was employed by Weiner & Stellar (1951). They measured the amount drunk from a graduated water tube in a one-hour test period following 15 hours of water deprivation. Sodium chloride was the substance tested. On different days different concentrations of the salt were in the drinking tube. The preference curve, plotted from the amounts drunk, was similar to that shown

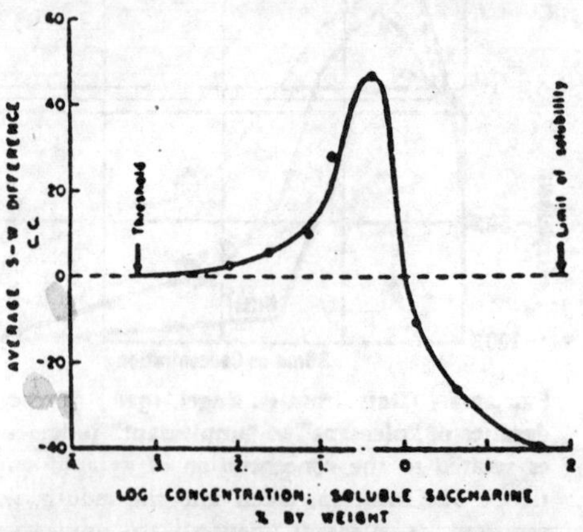

Fig. 22-3. (From Beebe-Center, Black, Hoffman & Wade, 1948.) Preference curve for saccharine solutions as compared with plain water. The preference was measured by a form of the method of Single Stimuli (p. 217). The subjects were 11 rats. In each rat's living cage was a single drinking bottle, filled on some days with plain tap water, on other days with a saccharine solution. The concentration of saccharine varied from day to day from a minimum of less than .01 percent to a maximum of over 40 percent. The data points show how much more (or less) was drunk on saccharine days than on plain water days (S — W).

for saccharine in Figure 22-3, rising from tap water to a maximum and then falling with stronger solutions. The maximum was at slightly under 1 percent of salt in the water. The salt preference appeared even in the first 5 minutes with perfectly unexperienced rats. It is a natural preference, probably with some chemico-physiological basis.

In quite a different sort of preference test (Young, 1947) hungry rats were trained to run from a starting box to a pair of food cups located side by side 15 inches away, take a nibble from one of the cups and return to the starting box. Both cups were lowered out of reach as soon as a single nibble from one cup was taken. Many such trials were given, and the score was the number of times each of the foods was chosen. Dry foods were the incentives: sugar (sucrose), casein, and ground whole wheat. As between sugar and wheat, presented side by side but in alternating positions, about 55 percent of the choices were for sugar as against 45 percent for wheat, a small difference in preference, though reliable because of the many hundreds of choices made by about 30 rats. As between casein and either sugar or wheat the preference was marked, with only 25 percent of the choices favoring casein.

Obstruction tests. A much used piece of apparatus in the animal laboratory is the obstruction box (Fig. 22-4), standardized by Warden and his associates (Jenkins *et al.*, 1926; Warden, 1931). In order to reach the incentive a rat must cross an electrified floor grid. The test procedure, after suitable familiarization, is to put the rat in the entrance compartment, open the door into the connecting passage, let him cross to the incentive and take a nibble of the food (or partake briefly of whatever incentive is being tested), and then pick him up gently and return him to the entrance for another trial. The score is the number of crossings made by the animal in 20 minutes. The more crossings, the higher the indicated incentive value.

The validity of the method as an indi-

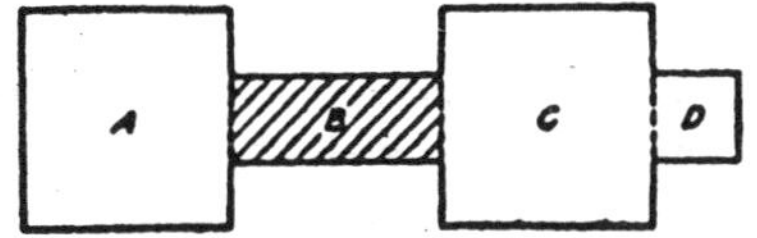

FIG. 22-4. (After Warden, 1931.) Ground plan of an obstruction box. The starting compartment, A, and the main incentive compartment, C, are 10 inches square and 10 inches high, while the connecting passage with floor grid, B, is 10 inches long but only 4 inches wide and high, so that a rat cannot jump the grid and avoid the shock. The incentive is placed in the small compartment, D, which is separated from C by a semitransparent and perforated door. This separation is necessary in experiments on delayed reward or on the sex and maternal drives when the animal incentive must be kept in place. The subject is placed in A, and when the door into B is opened he gets visual and auditory stimuli from the incentive in D. When the subject has crossed B and entered C, the door into D is automatically opened (unless delayed reward is being investigated). A standard procedure is to allow the subject 4 runs without shock and a single run with shock just before the 20-minute test period.

In order to insure fairly uniform shocks in spite of the high and variable resistance of the soles of the feet, an alternating current of high voltage (475) is employed, but with high external resistance (10,000,000 ohms) in the circuit, reducing the shock to .0475 milliamperes. Such shocks, though weak, are usually avoided by the rat unless there is some incentive to be reached.

cator of incentive value and drive strength is shown by such results as the following.

With food as the incentive the number of crossings increases with the time since last feeding, a maximum being reached after about 2 days of deprivation (Warner, 1928).

With a receptive female rat as the incentive, the number of crossings by the male rat increases with the time since the last previous mating, the maximum being reached in about one day (Warner, 1927).

With a male as incentive, the number of crossings of the female rat conforms to her estrous cycle, being much greater in estrum than in diestrum (Warner, 1927).

Its validity being assured, the method can be used for testing the claims of a supposed incentive. In testing for an exploratory drive in rats, the first step is to select as incentives such objects as this animal seems to examine when he encounters them. To demonstrate any incentive value an object must elicit more than the three crossings in 20 minutes that are likely to occur even if the incentive compartment is empty. With an assortment of wooden blocks and shavings, corks, and pieces of rubber and wire mesh in the incentive compartment, an average of six crossings was obtained. The difference is not large nor completely reliable, but the indicated exploratory drive is in line with ordinary laboratory observation (Nissen, 1930).

One more finding of this group of investigators is of special interest (Hamilton, 1929). It concerns the effect of delayed reward. After the hungry rat had crossed the grid and entered the C compartment, a delay was interposed before the door was opened to the small compartment D containing the food incentive. A different group of 20 rats was used for each delay period, with results shown in Figure 22-5. Even a delay of 15 seconds reduced the incentive value considerably, while with a delay of 3 minutes the number of crossings was scarcely greater than when no incentive was offered. The delay could not affect the drive, but it weakened the incentive factor. (Hull posits a separate delay factor, which he calls J, along with the incentive factor K, p. 656.) The delay could also interfere with the learning of the sequence terminating in reward.

Though the electric grid is certainly a very convenient form of obstruction, other forms could be used. Distance to

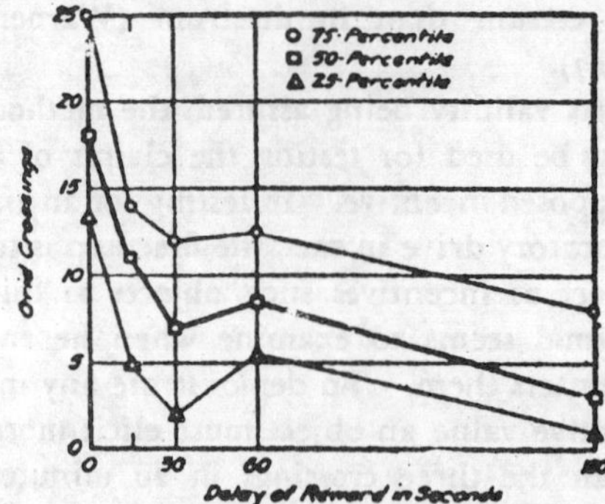

FIG. 22-5. (Data from Hamilton, 1929.) Delayed incentive or reward. After a rat had crossed the electrified floor grid of the obstruction box, he was delayed a certain time before obtaining the food. He was allowed 20 minutes (net, delay time not included) for making as many crossings as he chose.

run or hurdles to climb on the way to an incentive are obvious possibilities. In a chimpanzee experiment by Fletcher (1940) a visible piece of banana could be obtained by pulling in the carriage containing the incentive. The distance to be pulled was 18 feet, which was a constant, but the resistance encountered and the size of the piece of banana were variables. The resistance was provided by a braking device or by a weight that had to be lifted by the movement of the carriage. If the resistance was too great, the animal refused to pull in the carriage, but the larger the incentive the more resistance he would overcome to obtain it.

Learning tests of incentive values. In any learning experiment it is necessary to provide an incentive, and the improvement that occurs from trial to trial is good evidence that the incentive has some value. If we wish to *measure* incentive value or compare the value of different incentives, our problem is more difficult. Consider two ideal learning curves (Fig. 22-6) obtained with all factors constant except that different incentives have been used. The curve that shows greater performance indicates superior incentive, and the two practice levels can serve very well to indicate the difference in incentive value. But we are apt to receive the impression that the higher curve also indicates more rapid learning, so that rate of learning can serve as a second index of incentive value.

How shall we measure the rate of learning? If two curves, as in Figure 22-6, start at the same point and reach their approximate practice levels in the same number of trials, they can be regarded as showing the same rate of learning. They keep pace with each other, reaching the halfway mark in three trials, the three-quarter mark in seven trials, and so on. The practice level differs with the incentive, but the rate of progress toward the practice level in these two curves is the same.

The number of trials required to reach or approximate the practice level is only

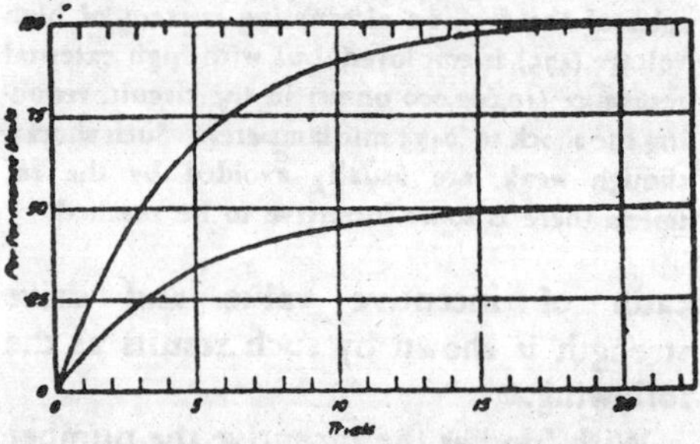

FIG. 22-6. Ideal monophasic learning curves, such as are approximated with simple learning tasks, as in human reaction time (p. 35) or animal runway (p. 558) experiments, when the performance is plotted in terms of speed rather than time, so that the curves rise with improved performance. They show negative acceleration and flatten out into their respective "practice levels." If plotted in terms of time or number of errors the curves would descend, still showing negative acceleration and flattening out into low levels. Theoretically, a practice level is an asymptote which is continually approached but never fully reached. The curves in this figure are drawn from the equation developed in the text.

a rough measure because we cannot tell precisely when that level is adequately reached. And with the negative acceleration characteristic of learning curves, how can we speak of any curve as showing a certain "rate of learning"? Her the growth function, which served us well in ordering the facts of reaction time, may again be what we need. Each trial can be regarded as a push toward the practice level. The pushes are equal so long as motivation is constant, but the resistance to further progress increases as the practice level is approached. Something of that sort can be imagined, but the important assumption is simply this: each trial eliminates the same fraction of the distance still to go to the practice level. In both curves of Figure 22-6, this fraction is 1/5. If we call the original distance to the practice level 1.00, the first trial takes off 1/5, leaving 4/5 or .80 still to go. The next trial takes off 1/5 of this .80, leaving .64; the next trial takes off 1/5 of this .64, leaving .512; and so on. Always, theoretically, there is some remaining distance, and one more trial eliminates 1/5 of it. The fraction removed in one trial differs with different tasks, some being learned more quickly than others. But if our two curves give a true picture, a mere change of incentives does not change the fraction or the rate of learning.

Before testing this hypothesis by actual data, let us reduce our reasoning to an equation. Let the letter F stand for the fraction eliminated in one trial from the distance still to go to the practice level of any simple learning curve. Then we have:

$1 - F$	= the fraction remaining after				1 trial
$(1 - F)^2$ =	"	"	"	"	2 trials
$(1 - F)^3$ =	"	"	"	"	3 trials

and in general

$(1 - F)^n$ =	"	"	"	"	n trials

Therefore, if y stands for the total fraction eliminated in n trials, and $1 - y$ for the fraction remaining, we have

$$1 - y = (1 - F)^n \qquad (1)$$

which is an equation for the pure learning function; and it is a theoretical equation for the simple learning curve if we regard the initial score as zero and the final score as 1.

In any actual learning curve which we wish to test for conformity to this equation, let the initial score (where $n = 0$) be designated as A, and the practice-level as Z, so that $Z - A$ is the total gain from start to finish. Let y be the score on the nth trial, so that $Z - y$ is the remaining distance to the practice level. Then the equation becomes

$$Z - y = (1 - F)^n(Z - A) \qquad (2)$$

or, in logarithmic form,

$$\log (Z - y) = n \log (1 - F) + \log (Z - A) \qquad (3)$$

We can determine Z, the practice level, from the curve. The starting score, A, need not be pinned down to the first trial which is often a doubtful quantity. We can determine A along with $1 - F$ so as to give the best fitting straight line, as was done in Figure 2-6 p. 22. Plot the data on semilog paper, with the values of n on the arithmetical axis and the corresponding values of $Z - y$ as logarithmic ordinates. Fit a straight line to these data points, as well as possible. If the fit is satisfactory, the equation is verified, and the values of $Z - A$ and $1 - F$ can be found from the Y intercept and slope of the straight line.

It should be noted that the practice level in the theoretical equation is an asymptote or mathematical limit which is approached but never reached. Consequently, the equation cannot be used to answer such a question as this: If the practice level is reached in 20 trials, what is the value of F? But it can be used to answer this question: If *half* (or .75 or .90)

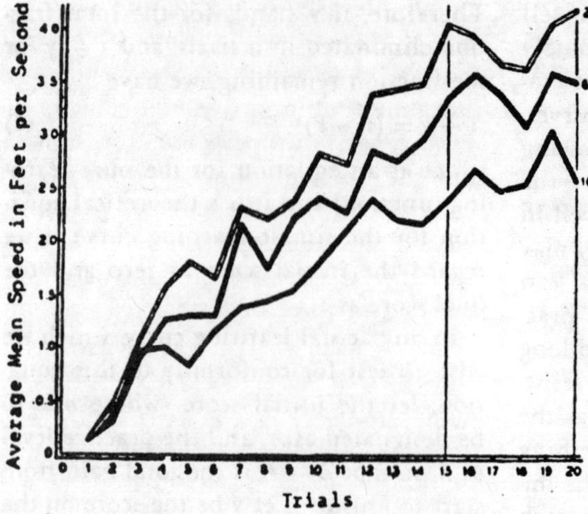

FIG. 22-7. (Crespi, 1942, 1944.) Improvement of performance with different amounts of incentive. The numbers at the right show the amount of incentive in terms of small units of food. There were ten rats in the 16-unit group, seven rats in each of the other groups.

of the distance from A to Z is covered in a certain number of trials, what is the value of F? We obtain the following values. If half the distance from A to Z is covered

in 1 trial, F = .50 — in 5 trials, F = .129
in 2 trials, F = .293 — in 10 trials, F = .067
in 4 trials, F = .159 — in 15 trials, F = .047
in 20 trials, F = .034

Our underlying question in this discussion is whether rate of learning can be used as a measure of incentive value. We need actual data to check the theoretical curves and equations. Now two independent investigations, by Crespi (1942, 1944) and by Zeaman (1949), have found that while our Z, the practice level, depends on the amount of incentive (the greater the incentive, the better the well-learned performance), the rate of learning, F, is the same for different amounts of incentive. In such an experiment all other motivation factors, notably drive (D) and inhibition (I), must be constant so that the incentive factor (K) may come out cleanly. Accordingly these investigators gave their rats only one trial a day, each trial coming after 22-23 hours of food deprivation. The long intertrial interval would minimize the inhibitory factor. Crespi used a 20-foot runway and measured performance by running speed, while Zeaman used a 3-foot runway with latency or starting time as the measure of performance. Crespi found that rate of improvement, as indicated by approach to the practice level, was approximately the same with different amounts of incentive. The three curves in Figure 22-7 level off after approximately the same number of trials. Zeaman found the F fraction to be nearly .30 for all his learning curves (Fig. 22-8); that is, each trial eliminated 30 percent of the distance still to cover toward the limit for any given amount of incentive.

Reynolds (1949, 1950) has obtained the same result in other learning tasks. In a black-white discrimination experiment (1949) with white the positive stimulus, rats reached a criterion of near perfection in the same Mean number of trials, whether the incentive was a very small or a much larger pellet of food. The rate of learning was thus the same for the two incentives. But their performance, as indicated by quickness of choice, was better with the larger incentive. In a simple T maze (1950), rats getting the larger pellet ran faster and made fewer errors, trial by trial, but reached their

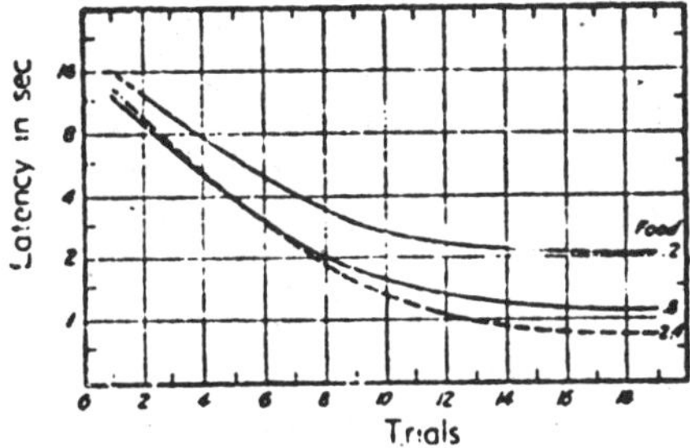

FIG. 22·8. (After Zeaman, 1949.) Smoothed learning curves with different amounts of food incentive. When *E* opened the door from the starting box, the rats at first averaged about 15 sec to get started, but by about the fourteenth trial they reached a level which differed with the amount of incentive in the food box, being 1.9 sec for those rewarded with .2 gm of food, 1.1 sec for those getting .8 gm, and .8 sec for those getting 2.4 gm per trial. Though the ordinate scale in this graph is logarithmic, the curves are not reduced to straight lines because the whole latent times are plotted, not the y — Z times required by equation (3) on page 665. Zeaman's data fitted this equation quite well. His symbols differ from ours but the equation is the same. The three curves reproduced here are a selection from the six curves he obtained with different amounts of incentive, all showing similar characteristics, i.e., different Z levels but the same F value which was approximately .30.

practice levels in about the same number of trials as rats with the smaller incentive.

In Pavlovian conditioning what is the incentive? It can be nothing else than the unconditional stimulus. A puff of air against the cornea is the incentive for the anticipatory partial closing of the eye by the conditioned lid response (p. 552); and the stronger the puff, the greater the incentive to protect the eye by anticipatory closing. Passey (1948) used puffs of four intensities on different groups of college students. From the start the conditioned lid response showed greater amplitude and greater frequency when the stronger puffs were used, but the performance levels in both these respects were reached in about 35 trials, the same for all the groups. Thus the performance level varied with the incentive, while the rate of learning was independent of the amount of incentive—the same result we have seen in the runway, the T maze, and the discrimination experiments.

What will be the effect of a *change* in the amount of incentive after a performance has reached its practice level? Crespi and Zeaman both tried this out. When the incentive was increased in amount, the performance very quickly improved to a new level; and the reverse when the incentive was decreased (Fig. 22·9). These changes in performance were obviously not due to any sudden increase or decrease of ability. They reflected changes in motivation, though drive in the strict sense remained unchanged. They reflected changes in the incentive factor.

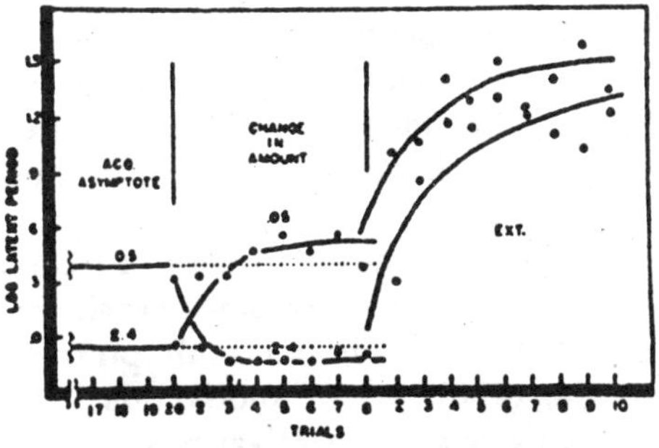

FIG. 22·9. (Zeaman, 1949.) Change of latency produced by change in amount of incentive. One group of eight rats, after receiving the very small reward of .05 gm per trial and reaching a latency level of 2.50 sec, was shifted on the twentieth trial to the much larger reward of 2.4 gm. A similar group was shifted from the large to the small amount of incentive. The two groups quickly traded places in respect to latency. They even showed a sort of contrast effect, as if the small reward seemed extra-small after habituation to the large one, and vice versa. (Crespi obtained the same effect.) Both groups were then subjected to a massed extinction series, the incentive being reduced to zero, and both gave an extinction curve tending toward the original unconditioned latency of something like 15 sec.

Incentives can differ in quality as well as quantity. Foods differ in incentive value, called palatability by Young (1948). Having found, as already stated (p. 662), that rats greatly prefer a nibble of sugar to one of casein, this investigator used his apparatus as a runway with a single food cup containing sugar for one group and casein for another group. The sugar group took much less time to reach the incentive than the casein group. The incentives being then interchanged, the sugar-casein group slowed down while the casein-sugar group put on more speed—a result wholly consistent with that found with changes of quantity.

In one of the experiments on latent learning (p. 639) the same maze was run by two groups of rats, one to food and the other to an empty goal box. The food incentive gave much better performance. But when the incentives were interchanged, it appeared that one group had learned the maze just as quickly as the other. The difference in incentives had affected the performance but not the rate of learning.

The "learning curve" is really a record of successive performances, with each performance dependent on both previous learning and present motivation. To bring into relief the motivational factors, it is important to analyze out the pure learning factor, rate of improvement. The use of the exponential growth function in the analysis of learning curves is due largely to Hull. In 1943 he regarded habit strength as dependent on amount of previous reinforcement and consequently on the quantity of the incentive as well as on the number of reinforcements. So the practice level was included in the measure of habit strength. Crespi (1944, p. 351) made it clear that the practice level did not properly belong in a formula for habit strength. Hull in 1950 and 1951 reaches the same conclusion and his revised formula for habit strength, essentially the same as our equation (1), makes it depend only on the number of reinforced trials and on the factor F.

Our conclusion regarding learning tests for incentive value, then, is that rate of improvement cannot serve the purpose. But the practice level affords an excellent basis for comparing incentive values. We have considered only simple "monophasic" learning curves. It may happen that increased incentive leads to the discovery of a short cut or the development of a "higher unit" (p. 810) and so to a second rise toward a higher practice level.

Resistance to extinction is probably another measure of incentive value. The larger the incentive, the better the performance level and the slower the extinction. Such is Zeaman's (1949) finding in his runway experiment. Resistance to extinction, accordingly, is not a measure of habit strength, a conclusion quite in line with spontaneous recovery. If extinction is due, as Hull says, to accumulated inhibition, this I factor works against K, the incentive factor, not against habit strength; and the greater the K, the more I must accumulate to reduce net motivation to zero.

Another test of incentive value is based on the delayed-reaction experiment (p. 604). The greater the incentive, the longer the possible delay, at least with chimpanzees (Nissen & Elder, 1935).

NEGATIVE DRIVES AND INCENTIVES

By a negative incentive is meant one that is shunned rather than sought, one that an organism moves away from rather than toward, one that we humans, at least, dislike. A shock or any painful stimulus is the typical example, but there are many others: a bitter substance, a nauseous odor, a piercing sound, a bright and flashing light, severe heat or cold. The movements of escape differ with the stimulus and in some cases are clearly instinctive. Thus far, we have only stimulus and response and no use for the concepts of drive and incentive. But if the organism, by use of some learned performance, *escapes* from a noxious stimulus, even partially, or *avoids* it altogether, this performance is motivated and the noxious stimulus acts as an incentive.

The escape or avoidance response to a negative incentive may conflict with the approach to a positive incentive. In the obstruction box (p. 663) food on the far side of the grid is a positive incentive, while the shock in the grid is a negative incentive, and the result depends on the balance of the two forces. A large share of the experimental work on negative incentives is concerned with their role as inhibitors of positive responses.

As usual, we infer drive from incentive, so that we can speak of a drive to avoid or minimize noxious stimuli such as the electric shock.

Varieties of inhibition. An incentive does not have to be noxious in order to be negative in relation to some other incentive. The two may simply be incompatible in that the organism cannot respond positively to both at the same time. One of the foundation stones of Sherrington's great work on the "integrative action of the nervous system" (1906, 1947) was his discovery of *reciprocal inhibition.* Incompatible movements such as turning the eyes to the right and left are so controlled in their nerve centers that with increased activity of one muscle goes decreased activity of its antagonist. The same type of inhibition is observed in human attention and distraction, since in attending to one object you cease attending to another (p. 84).

Pavlov (1927) made much use of the concept of inhibition, as sufficiently shown in the chapter on Conditioning (pp. 5[illegible]–[illegible]65). He distinguished "external" from "internal" inhibition. The interference of one activity with another was external inhibition, while internal inhibition developed in a nerve center through its own activity. Fatigue might be considered an example of internal inhibition, but the examples that Pavlov had in mind were different from fatigue. He was thinking of extinction and of the delayed CR.

Some psychologists have been skeptical of internal inhibition and have sought to explain all the facts by interference. The evidence pro and con has already been discussed (pp. 560–562).

Reactive inhibition. Hull's system (1951) makes use of this factor, regarded as a negative drive, a tendency to avoid immediate repetition of any motor response, especially if the response requires much work or exertion. It is about the same as Pavlov's internal inhibition except that no attempt is made to refer it to a state of the brain. If the same response is repeated with very little time allowed for recovery between trials, reactive inhibition accumulates and weakens the activity, even though the positive motivational factors of drive and incentive are still strong. If drive is weakened by satiation, or incentive by lack of reward, reactive inhibition puts a stop to the activity. Spontaneous recovery from extinction occurs because of the dissipation of the accumulated reactive inhibition; and "reminiscence" after massed learning (p. 796) is attributed to the same cause. The case for reactive inhibition in general has been reviewed by Solomon (1948).

The more work per trial, and the less time between trials, the greater should be the inhibition, according to the theory. These predictions can be checked in relatively simple animal experiments.

In an experiment of Thompson (1944) the work factor was tested in a setup which combined bar-pressing with a one-unit T maze. At the end of each arm of the T was a food pan with a bar to be pressed for a food pellet. One bar required 1½ times as strong a pressure as the other. A group of rats given a choice between 10 and 15 grams of pressure showed no preference, while a group given a choice between 40 and 60 grams showed a very definite preference and learned to get their pellets where less work was required. We can infer that the work has to be considerable in order to act as an effective deterrent.

A similar setup was employed by Montgomery (1951a) in a check on both variables, work per trial and interval between trials. A one-unit Y maze had a food pan and pellet-releasing lever at the end of each arm, the levers being loaded to control the work per pressure. But in this experiment the loads were equal in both arms of the Y. They were different for different groups of rats: 15 grams for one group, 40 grams for another, 90 grams for a third. The factorial design also provided three different intervals between trials: 20, 45, 90 seconds for different subgroups. The performance measure was the time it took the animal to go from the choice point to the lever and press it. The longer this response time at a given stage of practice, the weaker was the indicated net motivation; and, since the positive motivating factors of hunger and amount of food incentive were the same for all groups, any difference in performance could be attributed to the negative factors of work and interval between trials. In 100 learning trials (20 per day) all groups showed great improvement in speed of response, but this performance was better with the smaller loads at every stage of practice. So the work factor came out clearly. As regards the time factor, the rats that were allowed only 20 seconds between trials were consistently slower than the other two groups which were practically equal in performance. We can infer that 45 seconds (or less) is enough rest to permit fairly complete dissipation of reactive inhibition, in this particular performance anyway.

Reactive inhibition versus *exploratory drive.* Evidence in favor of a genuine exploratory drive has been presented on pages 639, 663, and elsewhere. What we have now to consider is a type of behavior that could perhaps be attributed either to this exploring tendency or to reactive inhibition. A good example is the alternation between right and left alleys in repeated trials at the same choice point in a maze (p. 622). When an animal has made a right turn and so developed some reactive inhibition against making that same turn, he would tend to make the left turn on the next trial, provided the muscular work involved was considerable and the elapsed time too short to allow dissipation of the reactive inhibition. As to the time factor, we saw before (p. 622) that alternation at a choice point occurred even when the interval between trials was much longer than in the typical examples of reactive inhibition. As to the work factor, Mowrer & Jones (1943) made the logical prediction that alternation should increase with increase in the work involved in the single response, but they could obtain no such result from their experiment. Montgomery (1951b, c; 1952) has gone into this question most thoroughly. Using the Y maze mentioned in the preceding paragraph he found that a short intertrial interval, such as 20 seconds, favored alternation as would be predicted from reactive inhibition. But the work variable had no effect on the amount of alternation, contrary to prediction from reactive inhibition (and "conditioned inhibition"—Hull, 1951). In a cross maze with two starting points and two goal boxes the rats showed no tendency to make alternate right and left *turns* but did show a definite tendency to go alternately to the two *goal boxes*. Now reactive inhibition would demand alternate turns (no repetition of the same movement), while the exploratory drive demands alternation of places (avoidance of places just explored). Again, when a rat was placed for 10 minutes in a T-shaped runway without any food present, while *E* recorded the parts of the runway successively entered and all the body turns including right and left U turns, there was no tendency to make alternate right and left turns, but there was a definite tendency to enter the three main parts of the T in rotation. In other words, the more recently a rat had explored a certain part, the less likely he was to chose that same part for re-exploration.

Since we are here concerned with negative drives and incentives, we may compare reactive inhibition and the exploring drive in terms of avoidance. Reactive inhibition avoids body movements recently made, while exploration avoids places and things recently explored. Massed repetition of a body movement builds up reactive inhibition, while massed exploration of the same place or thing satiates the tendency to explore that place or thing. Recovery from reactive inhibition proceeds rapidly for the first few seconds and then more and more slowly; the recovery curve for exploration has not been worked out. Muscular work is a direct factor in reactive inhibition but not in exploration.

Reactive inhibition might be called motor satiation; more specifically it is satiation for a particular movement. By contrast we can speak of stimulus satiation when *O* is continuously exposed to the same stimuli (Glanzer, 1953). Recovery from motor satiation will occur during a period of rest from the satiated movement, and recovery from stimulus satiation will occur during a period of absence from the particular stimuli. If a rat after making a left turn at the choice point of a simple T maze is then confined for 10 minutes in the empty end box, his motor satiation should be pretty well gone, leaving him to choose either alley on the next trial, but his stimulus satiation should remain high and make him choose the opposite alley. As 24 out of 25 rats did choose the opposite alley, stimulus satiation proved to be much the better basis for prediction.

Another important characteristic of exploratory behavior has been brought out by Montgomery (1953a). If the exploring drive is a tendency to respond positively to relatively novel external stimuli, a rat that has explored one empty maze for 5 minutes and is immediately transferred to another maze identical in size, shape, and color should do less exploring than if the second maze were different in some respect, if only in color. Simple H mazes were painted inside white, gray, or black, being otherwise alike. As predicted, the less the color difference, the less the exploration in the second maze. The result can evidently not be explained by reactive inhibition.

As to the possible physiology of reactive inhibition, there is not much to be said of a positive nature. The refractory period of nerve and striped muscle is much too brief to account for an inhibition lasting 20 seconds or more. Fatigue is no better as an explanation, for the few repetitions that can generate some reactive inhibition would be apt to produce warming up rather than fatigue. It is, of course, impossible to repeat a movement without an intervening reverse movement (as an extension of the elbow between two flexions), and this reverse movement plays a role in preventing rapid muscular fatigue. Since alternative responses are almost always possible, the tendency to avoid repetition of one movement may be really a tendency to shift to another movement. Shifting tensions in the nerve centers would thus be the basis of reactive inhibition. On this basis it would after all belong under the head of external rather than internal inhibition.

Punishment. We may think of incentives as positive, zero (indifferent), or negative. In exploring a passage in the maze a hungry but not thirsty animal may find food, water, or an electric shock. These outcomes of a response are under the experimenter's control. He must know from other observations of the animal's behavior what will serve as a positive, zero, or negative incentive. If an animal's response to an incentive is escape or avoidance, that incentive is negative and may for convenience be called a punishment.

Punishment for action. In his first formulation of the law of effect in 1898 Thorndike made no mention of punishment, for he had not used any negative incentives in his experiments on cats, dogs, and chicks. He said, in effect, that responses which brought satisfaction were stamped in while those which brought no satisfaction were stamped out. A little later (1911) he substituted "discomfort" or "annoyance" for "no satisfaction," so that his law of effect came to mean that a rewarded S—R was strengthened, but a punished one weakened. Much later (1932a) he subjected the whole problem to a careful re-examination on the basis of new experiments which led him to withdraw the negative half of the law. Punishment, he concluded, did not directly weaken an S—R connection, though it could have indirect effects on learning, as by leading the learner to shift to some other response which might turn out to be rewarded.

To experiment on punishment without immediately following reward, Thorndike utilized the multiple-choice technique. There must be more than two alternatives, since human subjects at least, on finding one of two incorrect, would know that the other was correct. "Implicitly," they would shift to the correct response and get some reinforcement from their knowledge of its correctness. In a typical experiment a list of 200 items was placed before the subject, such as these:

1. *Ahorro*	2. *Apagar*
awful	alienate
thrift	grieve
hatred	annoy
vicious	quench
tumult	effect

The subject, not knowing Spanish, underlined that one of the five English words which he guessed was the best translation. The experimenter told him "Right" for a reward or "Wrong" for punishment and required him to proceed at once to the next item. The list was gone through once a day for several days. The first day's choices were disregarded as being sometimes due to previous knowledge, and a single datum was of this sort: a certain English word was chosen for the first time on a certain trial and was called

"Right" or "Wrong"—Was the same choice repeated on the following trial? Was the tendency to make this choice strengthened by the reward, weakened by the punishment, or was there no effect persisting over the 24-hour interval? If there were no effect carried over the interval, the chance of repetition would be 1 in 5, or 20 percent. With 9 subjects and trials 2-5 to use, the frequencies of repetition were as follows:

Rights: 283/621 times, or 45.6 percent.
Wrongs: 488/2097 times, or 23.3 percent.

The effect of Right was positive and clear; but no negative effect of Wrong was shown. In fact the Wrongs were repeated more rather than less than chance, and the extra 3.3 percent is even reliable because of the large number of cases.

A similar experiment presented items of this sort:

1. *Desition*	2. *Dowlas*
crossing	bowie
situation	fabric
ending	grief
craving	soldier
laziness	howls

The best definition for the unfamiliar English word was to be underlined. There were 400 such items in two lists, with 8 and 9 subjects respectively, and with results as follows:

Of 1,022 Right choices, 633 or 61.9 percent were repeated in the next trial.
Of 2,875 Wrong choices, 737 or 25.6 percent were repeated in the next trial.

Here again the punished responses were repeated with slightly more than chance frequency. As in the case of blind alleys in a maze (p. 620), some false responses are inherently attractive and hard to eliminate.

In a companion experiment on chicks (Thorndike, 1932b) three alleys opened out of the choice compartment, one of them leading to food and the company of other chicks, the other two leading to the punishment of solitary confinement without food for 60 seconds. The abundant data required elaborate treatment but justified the conclusion that punishment exerted very little aftereffect, while reward strongly favored repetition of the rewarded choice.

Seemingly inconsistent with Thorndike's negative conclusion on the effects of punishment are some well-known results from animal experiments on discrimination learning. For example Warden & Aylesworth (1927) trained rats to discriminate between a lighted and an unlighted disk, light being the positive cue, in apparatus much like that shown in Figure 20-1, p. 582. For one group the only incentive was food beyond the lighted disk, while for another group there was also a shock beyond the unlighted one. The reward-only group required 294 trials to reach a certain criterion which the reward-punishment group reached in 56 trials. Here there was no opportunity to shift immediately from the punished response to the rewarded one, since the noncorrection method was employed (p. 624). But what did happen was that the reward-only group ran very rapidly without pausing at the choice point, while the reward-punishment did pause there long enough to obtain good reception of the cues. This effect of punishment has been observed also in the VTE experiments (p. 599). Even though punishment does not "stamp out" a response, then, it can favor learning in two ways: by the prompt shift to an alternative response, and by hesitation at the choice point. If the punishment is too severe, however, the emotional disturbance may greatly interfere with learning.

Perhaps the clearest picture of the uncomplicated effect of punishment is obtained by experiments with the Skinner box. There is practically nothing the rat can do except to press the bar, and during an extinction series there is no reward. Estes (1944) reports such experiments and provides an extensive bibliography of other studies of punishment. First a good rate of bar-pressing is built up by "periodic reinforcement," and then the food pellets are discontinued and a shock is administered from the floor grid whenever the bar is pressed. Ten minutes of severe punishment will reduce the response rate to zero, but on the following day (with no further reward or punishment) bar-pressing will be resumed and continue at a moderate rate for a considerable period of extinction. How long the bar-pressing will continue depends on how firmly this response was established. A well-established response seems to be temporarily suppressed rather than eliminated by punishment.

When a food-getting bar is also a shock-getting bar, the same object (or situation) has both positive and negative incentive values, but the one value does not cancel the other. The negative value can be extinguished by repeated bar-pressings without shock, but the positive value can only be extinguished by repeated pressings without food. In children and other human beings a similar fact is familiar enough though often disregarded: repeated punishment for an act does not deprive that act of its inherent fascination.

Punishment for inaction. What we have been considering is punishment for doing something, but there is also the case of punishment for not doing something. The elementary facts were brought out under the head of escape and avoidance conditioning (p. 546 ff.). Here again we have a conflict. The punishment calls for escape or avoidance, i.e., for quick and vigorous action; on the other side is the natural aversion to superfluous exertion. The subject learns to avoid the shock at the expense of exertion; the exertion decreases in repeated trials till it becomes too weak to avoid the shock; and the cycle may be repeated time and again. Further studies of conflict will be examined later.

Motivation of avoidance. Escape is obviously motivated by the shock or other objectionable stimulus, but avoidance presents a more difficult problem for the psychologist. This problem has obtruded itself in many studies of avoidance conditioning. An experiment of Warner (1932) has been repeated several times with modifications and improvements. A low fence extends across the middle of an elongated box and the rat, placed on one side of the fence, receives a series of shocks from the floor grid. After much jumping about and other agitated behavior the rat gets over to the other side of the fence where he receives no more shocks. Let a buzzer sound for a few seconds before the shocks are turned on: the rat may then become agitated at the sound of the buzzer, but he soon learns to make a smooth, unhurried, neat, efficient jump over the fence in time to avoid the shock. Now shock is a perfectly valid incentive for escape, but what is the incentive for avoidance? Miller (1948, 1951) and Mowrer (1940a; Mowrer & Lamoureaux, 1942) agreed in offering the hypothesis that the buzzer as a warning signal came to arouse the internal state of fear or anxiety. Or, in Miller's experiment (our p. 556), the white compartment where the animal was shocked came to arouse fear. When the animal got out of this compartment or away from the buzzer, the fear abated and by the principle of need reduction the escape movement was reinforced even though no more shocks were received. In a word, then, avoidance is motivated by fear.

In considering whether this hypothesis accounts for all the facts, we must distinguish two phases in avoidance conditioning. In the first stage the animal shows abundant symptoms of fear or some excited state. The rats in Miller's experiment, before learning to open the door from the white to the black compartment, "displayed variable behavior," such as pawing the door, biting the floor grid, running back and forth, crouching, urinating and defecating. In the second phase, however, when the rats had learned to open the door, these signs of fear disappeared. In a somewhat different setup dogs were shocked in the forepaw unless they lifted the paw within 2 seconds after the beginning of a tonal warning signal (Culler, Finch, Girden & Brogden, 1935). Early in the training the shock was likely to arouse agitated behavior with yelping, evacuation, and other "manifestations of fright," and the warning signal aroused some of the same agitation. After a number of trials the localized paw-lifting response began to appear and predominate —a response which was "as unlike the original excited, diffuse behavior as two acts can well be."

Since the behavioral evidence of fear is absent during the second or adaptive phase of avoidance conditioning, we are entitled to ask if there is not some other possible motivation besides a state of fear. We notice that the animal moves from a danger spot to a safe spot, or from a dangerous posture to a safe posture, and query whether safety is not a sufficient positive incentive to maintain the avoidance response and prevent it from being quickly extinguished. To be sure, safety is nothing except in contrast to danger. But once the rat in Miller's experiment has differentiated between the dangerous white compartment and the safe black compartment, he might be motivated to get to the safe place rather than to get away from the dangerous place. So he would avoid the state of fear as well as the actual shock.

In general, when we see an animal or person go from one place to another, say from A to B, we cannot tell from that single fact whether he is running *away from* A or *to* B. We need further data. (1) If we find a negative incentive in A or a positive incentive in B, we can reach a decision. When the animal gets a shock in A and runs to B, we decide that he is running away from A. But when he runs soon enough to avoid the shock, we are left in doubt because there is no actual negative incentive in A when he starts to run. (2) If the animal shows agitated behavior before leaving A, or consummatory behavior such as eating after reaching B, we can reach a decision. But in the present case he shows no such behavior. (3) If in a series of trials the animal runs in various directions from A we can decide that he is running away from A—as in the early trials of the experiments under consideration when the animal's behavior is variable. Or, if he runs to B from various starting points, we can decide that B is his goal and has acquired positive incentive value—a possibility that has apparently not been examined in these avoidance experiments. (4) If the animal speeds up on approaching B, this goal gradient would indicate that B is the goal; but if he leaves A hastily and then slackens his speed, he must be running away from A. This gradient test could best be made on a runway (Brown, 1948). For the present we have only the fact that in a series of successful trials the animal tends to delay his start from A—surely not a symptom of fear.

Partial avoidance. Whatever skepticism may remain as to the positive incentive value of safety to an animal, one thing is sure: fear symptoms disappear as successful ways of dealing with a danger are learned. If a shock cannot be avoided completely, some way of avoiding it partially may be found, as in the experiment of Liddell and his co-workers (Fig. 22-10). These experimenters found the sheep a good subject for conditioning experiments. The animal stands on a table in a loose harness and receives moderate shocks from an electrode attached to one foreleg. A few seconds before each shock a metronome begins to tick. In the early trials the shock arouses violent struggling, and after a few repetitions the animal begins to struggle at the sound of the metronome. With his violent leg and trunk movements go agitated breathing and heartbeat and the psychogalvanic response. As the experiment proceeds, this diffuse CR gives way to one that is localized and precise: at the sound of the metronome the sheep assumes a crouching position and half flexes the leg; when the shock comes, he flexes the leg completely, and then lowers it and visibly relaxes. Though this CR does not wholly avoid the shock, it prepares the animal to "take it." The half-flexed leg is not jerked so violently by the reflex response to the shock. Similar adaptive and unemotional responses to unescapable shock are reported by Brogden, Lipman & Culler (1938, see our p. 555) and by Sheffield (1948).

Frustration. When progress toward a goal is blocked, the barrier, opposition, or interference, while somewhat akin to punishment, is different enough to warrant separate consideration. The typical response to punishment is escape, but to a barrier it is an an attempt to break through. The threat of punishment is apt to arouse fear, but the threat of opposition is apt to arouse the emotional state of anger. In this state the man or animal may make a vicious attack on an inanimate barrier or get into a regular fight with a threatening opponent. A dog seems to regard any unknown intruder of his home grounds as a potential enemy to be promptly attacked. The laboratory rat is likely to attack a strange rat or any rat that has not yet established dominance or accepted submission (Seward, 1945-46).

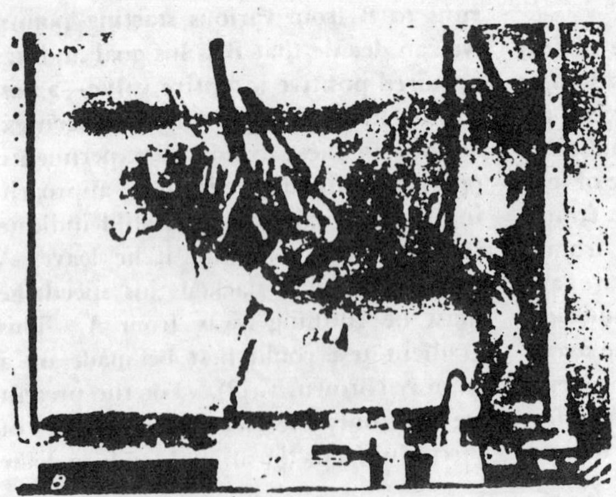

FIG. 22-10. (Liddell, James & Anderson, 1934.) The precise and localized CR to the warning signal preceding a shock to the foreleg. When the shock arrives, the flexion reflex takes over and raises the leg still farther.

A *frustration* can mean any situation that blocks the path to a goal, literally or figuratively; and an *aggression* can be any form of attack or angry response to a situation. A challenging frustration-aggression hypothesis was put forward by a Yale group of investigators (Dollard, Doob, Miller, Mowrer & Sears, 1939). Their thesis: given a frustrating situation, aggressive behavior is the typical response; and, given aggressive behavior, a frustrating situation is the typical cause. They cited a great variety of confirmatory examples and discussed at length the social implications of this thesis. The hypothesis that frustration evokes aggression awakened much interest and was discussed pro and con in the 1941 Symposium on the effects of frustration. Everybody was willing to admit that frustration often led to aggression, but several other possible responses were pointed out even by the Yale group. Sometimes the subject finds a way around the barrier by trial and error or some other problem-solving method; he may be said to defrustrate the situation. Sometimes he simply gives up and perhaps compensates himself by finding some more accessible goal. Sometimes the human subject resorts to fantasy, rationalization, or some other "mechanism" (Sargent, 1948). More experimental work has been done on two other effects of frustration, named regression and fixation.

Regression from a 5-year to a 3-year level of play behavior in nursery-school children was experimentally produced in the play room. Instead of their customary toys the children on a certain day were given some very superior toys and allowed to play with them for a short period but were then frustrated by having these toys taken away and placed out of reach but still in sight behind a wire screen. They still had their customary toys but played in a relatively infantile manner (Barker, Dembo & Lewin, 1941). "Regression" is supposed to be a going back to an earlier stage of development, but since earlier activities are apt to be simpler as well, these two variables are not easily kept separate. If an animal learns first a simple act for obtaining a reward and later a more complex act for obtaining the same reward, and if then the reward is discontinued (extinction series), he is likely to revert to the earlier and simpler act. But if the learning order is reversed, the result is not so clear, though it does show some signs of true regression (Carey, 1951).

A *fixation*, in the sense used by Maier in his experimental studies of frustration (1949), is a stereotyped response or habit which is not broken up by reward and punishment. Maier regards fixation as the typical response to frustration. In his experiments on rats the frustration consisted in an insoluble problem. Using the Lashley jumping stand (p. 584) he offered a choice between two doors marked with black and white circles. The problem of reaching food and avoiding bumps consistently was insoluble because the "correct" door was sometimes marked one way and sometimes the other and was sometimes on the right and sometimes on the left. After many trials most rats adopted a position habit which in some of them was so firmly fixated that they could not learn any better when the problem was made soluble, the reward now being placed always behind the black circle, or always on the side opposite to the individual rat's position habit. The experimenter could wean the rat from the fixation by a form of "guidance," i.e., by opening the door avoided by the rat and gently steering him in that direction. His settled aversion to that door was thus overcome. See Klee (1944) for the most complete experiment of this sort. If the original problem is very difficult but not insoluble, some rats will master it and the others fall into a fixation (Maier & Ellen, 1951). An attempt to adapt the insoluble-problem technique to adult human subjects was not very successful in producing fixation, though it did bring out several other results of frustration—such as aggression, regression, quitting, and resignation (Marquart, 1948). See also Wilensky (1952) for an experimental analysis of the reactions of human subjects to mild frustration.

Conflict of positive and negative motivation. Any positive motive is likely to get into conflict with the negative motive of "reactive inhibition," the tendency to avoid superfluous exertion. The greater the positive incentive, the more exertion is worth while and will be tolerated, as we have already seen (p. 664). Punishment, in a broad sense, can play a similar inhibitory role; only, it is punishment not for doing something nor for failing to do something but simply for being in a situation. Let the situation be a Skinner box, with food to be obtained (periodically) by pressing the bar. In rats well habituated to this procedure, let a tone sound in the midst of the hour's work, and a shock follow when the tone has sounded for 5 minutes (Estes & Skinner, 1941). On the first day there is no great disturbance, but after a number of days the bar-pressing slows down or even ceases altogether while the tone is sounding and resumes speed when the shock has been received. This anxious or apprehensive inhibitory state can be extinguished by prolonging the tone beyond the customary 5 minutes without any shock.

If the subject can do anything toward avoiding the punishment, something quite different from inhibition comes into play. A bright flashing light, for which the white rat has a strong aversion (Keller, 1941), can be conveniently used instead of the electric shock. In an experiment of Tolcott (1948), a Skinner box was equipped with the usual bar for obtaining food pellets and also with a little platform which switched off the light as long as the rat sat on it. After a rat had mastered both of these tricks separately, he was placed in the box while hungry and the light was turned on. The bar and the platform were too far apart for the rat to operate both at the same time. He soon learned to master the situation quite well, however. He would alternate between rapid bar-pressing and long sitting on the platform (Fig. 22-11). In this way he succeeded in obtaining his usual number of pellets in a 15-minute session while still keeping the light off 60 percent of the time. Without the flashing light the rat ate at a moderate rate, indicative of a balance between the degree of hunger and avoidance of surplus exertion. The light created an "emergency," demanding greater activity. The hunger drive was not increased but the avoidance of exertion was decreased.

Analogous results were obtained by Rey (1936) in the course of his extensive study of the guinea pig. Two compartments were separated by a low fence, each compartment having a floor grid. The animals learned to jump from either compartment to the other on receiving a shock or on hearing a buzzer which came on 5 seconds before the shock. After considerable training they adopted the routine of jumping over the fence, turning around and waiting for the next buzz. Then a carrot was placed in one compartment. On finding it the animal started to eat; when the buzzer sounded, he intensified his eating for a while but

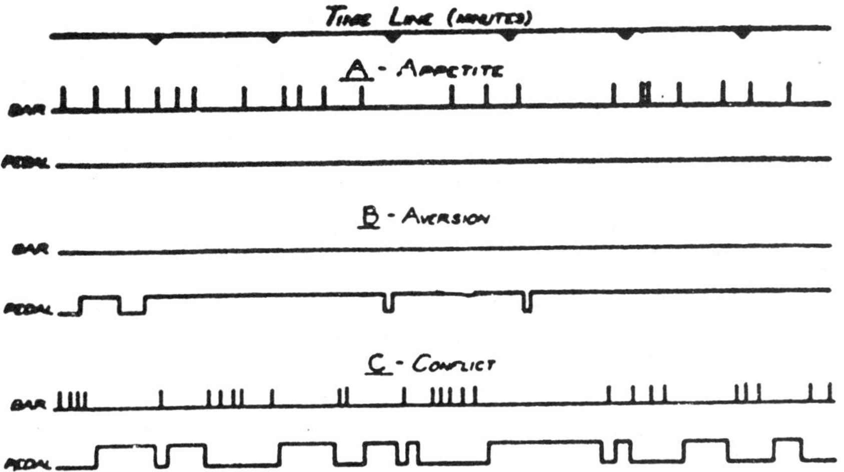

FIG. 22-11. (Tolcott, 1948.) Sample records of food-getting bar responses and light-avoiding pedal responses. Record A was obtained from a hungry rat working in the dark; the bar was pressed at a moderate rate and no response was made to the pedal. Record B was obtained from a food-satiated rat with the light turned on; the bar was not pressed at all, but the pedal was kept down (record line up) most of the time. Record C was obtained from a hungry rat with the light turned on; the rat stayed on the pedal most of the time, but at intervals ran over to the bar and obtained a few pellets.

finally jumped into the other compartment. Similar intensification of positive behavior at the sound of the buzzer occurred when the incentive was a female in the receptive state or another male to fight.

Similarly again (Drew, 1935), rats that had learned to traverse a runway to food were disturbed when a loud bell was introduced into the food box. But they ran faster and ate more rapidly, flattening down their ears as if to minimize the noise.

In distraction experiments (p. 84) the distracting stimulus is the negative incentive, and the human subject often overcomes the distraction by intensifying his work on the appointed task.

SECONDARY INCENTIVES

The experiments belonging here are usually classed under the head of *secondary reinforcement* because they are concerned with learning or extinction. In the present chapter, however, where we use learning and extinction merely as tests for incentives, we can best think of a reinforcer as an incentive. Secondary incentives can be demonstrated by preference or obstruction tests as well as by learning tests. An incentive is called secondary if its incentive value is supposed to depend on association with some primary incentive. The taste of palatable food being a primary incentive, the sight of such food is presumably a secondary incentive. Secondary incentive values are acquired by a process of learning or conditioning.

Time relations in the establishment of a secondary incentive. Hull's well-known statement (1943, 1950a, 1951) is to the effect that any stimulus which occurs consistently "in close conjunction with a reinforcing state of affairs" becomes a secondary reinforcer. In less formal statements, however, he speaks of the secondary reinforcer as closely *preceding* the primary reinforcement, instead of merely being close to it in time. If we scrutinize Miller's comprehensive table (1951, pp. 455-457) of experiments on "learned reward" we find in all the cases a certain sequence of events. First in any trial comes the learned or secondary reward, and then follows the primary reward. A rat in a straight runway enters a white goal box and a moment later eats some food there. After a number of such trials he shows a preference for this white box as against a black one in which he has not been fed, when the two boxes with no food in either of them are placed in the two end positions of a simple U maze (Saltzman, 1949). If food is the goal, the white goal box is a pregoal. Or, we may say, eating the food is the primary goal response, while entering the white goal box is a preliminary goal response. The "secondary" incentive might be called a preliminary incentive.

Similarly, the rat on pressing the bar of a Skinner box first hears the click of the food-delivering mechanism and then gets a pellet of food. The click becomes a secondary incentive, as shown by an extinction series when the delivery of pellets is discontinued; for extinction is slower if the click continues than if it is discontinued along with the pellets (Bugelski, 1938). Modifications of this experiment are designed to test the effect of the time interval between the preliminary signal and the delivery of the pellet. The incentive value of the signal decreases greatly if this interval is lengthened much beyond a second or two (Jenkins, 1950; Bersh, 1951). Either a light or a buzz, if consistently used as a preliminary signal, acquires some incentive value. But if the light is timed to start 1 second *after* the rat has begun to eat his pellet, it acquires no incentive value—perhaps because the rat cannot make any preliminary goal response to the light when he is already eating his pellet (Schoenfeld, Antonitis & Bersh, 1950a; see also the careful analysis of secondary reinforcement in Keller & Schoenfeld, 1950, pp. 231-261).

We shall consider two of these experiments in greater detail. What Jenkins did was: (1) train rats to approach the pan and take a pellet at the sound of the food-delivering mechanism; (2) give a preliminary buzzer signal 1, 3, 9, 27, or 81 seconds before the pellet was delivered and so condition the rats to approach the food pan at the sound of the buzzer; and (3) introduce a bar which, when pressed, sounded the buzzer but gave no food. Exploring this novel object the rats produced the buzz, and the buzz proved to be sufficient incentive to elicit many bar-pressings. However, the buzz gradually lost its incentive value in the absence of the primary food incentive. Meanwhile a control group which did not learn the buzz-food sequence of stage (2) gave only a low rate of bar-pressing in stage (3). As between the experimental groups, the shorter the buzz-food interval in stage (2), the greater the rate of bar-pressing in stage (3). Bersh's experimental design was somewhat different. He used a light instead of a buzz for the preliminary signal and he dispensed with a control group. In stage (1) bar-pressing produced the light but no food, but the rats would press the bar occasionally, giving a measure of the "operant level" (base line). In stage (2) there was no bar present, but only a light-food sequence; when the light had been on a certain number of seconds, a pellet was delivered and the rats learned to go to the pan in response to the light. In stage (3) there was no food, but bar-pressing produced the light, as in stage (1), and the rate of bar-pressing was well above the original operant level, though extinction gradually supervened.

A secondary incentive, regarded as a partial reinforcement, might be expected to reduce the primary drive; or, regarded as a preliminary to the primary incentive, it might be expected to increase the primary drive. Apparently it has neither of these effects (Simon, Wickens, Brown & Pennock, 1951: Miles & Wickens, 1953).

A poker chip or a rubber ball can acquire secondary incentive value by being used as a means of securing food. In a pioneer experiment of Wolfe (1936) chimpanzees were first taught to insert a poker chip in the slot of a food-vending machine which thereupon released a grape into a food pan. They then learned to obtain the chips by lifting a bar in another piece of apparatus, and the incentive value of the chips was demonstrated by an obstruction test: they would lift the bar against considerable resistance in order to obtain a chip. This experiment was carried further by Cowles (1937) who found that the chimpanzees would work for chips till they had accumulated a stock of 10 or 20 which they were then allowed to carry to the food vender and exchange for raisins. The chips could be used as the reward for learning to choose correctly in a discrimination task. In similar though simpler experiments on dogs (Ellson, 1937) and on cats (Smith, 1939), a rubber ball inserted or rolled into an orifice gave immediate access to a bit of food. When this trick had been mastered, the animals went on to learn a method of obtaining the balls. In these experiments the "food token" clearly acquires its secondary incentive value by coming *before* the primary incentive in a regular sequence of events.

The same sequence can be seen when the secondary incentive has a negative value as in Miller's experiment on escape and avoidance (see pages 556, 674). A rat was placed in a white compartment and soon received a shock there. After a few trials the rat manifested fear of the white compartment, or, we may say, the white compartment had acquired negative incentive value. If we think of a primary positive incentive as exerting a pull and of a primary negative incentive as exerting a push, we may regard a secondary incentive as exerting a preliminary pull or push.

Generalization. We use this term in the Pavlovian sense as opposed to *differentiation*, generalization being the primitive state of affairs while differentiation has to be learned (p. 580). The principle of generalization is that different stimuli and different responses may play the same role in behavior. Stimuli that evoke the same response can be called equivalent stimuli, and different responses evoked by the same stimulus can be called equivalent responses (p. 689). Similarly, in our present study we can speak of drive generalization when different drives are equivalent as motivating approach to the same goal object (incentive), and we can speak of incentive generalization when the same drive motivates approach to different goal objects. So we have:

Stimulus generalization: same response to different stimuli;
Response generalization: different responses to same stimulus;
Drive generalization: same incentive appealing to different drives;
Incentive generalization: different incentives appealing to same drive.

As this terminology, though logical enough, may be somewhat confusing, we shall speak of equivalent drives and incentives.

Equivalent drives. Hunger and thirst are equivalent in relation to milk as an incentive, since milk appeals to both these drives. But milk here is a primary incentive. What we wish to know is whether an object which has acquired secondary incentive value to a thirsty animal will have it still when the animal is hungry but not thirsty. A thirsty rat has found water regularly in the left-hand end box of a simple T maze. Later, when he is hungry but no longer thirsty, will he show any inclination to go to this same end box? Yes, a very strong inclination, as we saw in the experiments on latent learning (pp. 642–645). This particular part of the maze, we might say, has become a "good" place, a place where he finds what he wants. When he finds water there but has to go to the other end box for food, the two drives begin to differentiate in relation to this maze (p. 631). One part of the maze (one secondary incentive) comes to appeal to one drive, and another part to another drive.

The experiments belonging under this head are apt to be rather complicated; we shall mention some of the simplest. Teel & Webb (1951) used a one-unit T maze which the rats were first allowed to explore thoroughly. Food was then placed in one end box, nothing in the other, and the hungry rats had two free trials a day, along with two forced trials to insure their entering both boxes equally often. They soon learned to choose the food box in most of their free trials. Meanwhile, on each day while satiated for food and with both end boxes empty, they had one free and one forced trial in the maze—and their free choices were the same in these satiated trials as in the hungry trials. The preference built up in the hungry-reward trials held also for the satiated trials. Presumably they were motivated to be taken out of the maze, as they were equally often from both end boxes, but the balance of "goodness" favored the box where they had always been fed.

In a Skinner box experiment of Estes (1949, Experiment 2), eight thirsty rats learned to press the bar to obtain small drinks of water. Bar-pressing turned on the motor of the water-delivering mechanism, and the sound of the motor slightly preceded the presentation of the little cup of water. Thus, the sound of the motor could become a secondary incentive. An extinction test followed on the next day, with four of the animals now thirsty but not hungry, the other four hungry but not thirsty. For the first few minutes of this test the bar was disconnected from the motor so that bar-pressing produced no sound, but then the connection was made so that bar-pressing produced the motor sound but without any water or food. Both the thirsty and the hungry rats started off with a moderate rate of bar-pressing but soon slowed down when nothing happened. When they began to get the motor sound, they all worked faster for a few minutes but finally gave up in the absence of any primary reward, and the hungry ones gave up sooner than the thirsty ones. The motor sound had some incentive value for both groups; it promised something good. In relation to this secondary incentive the hunger drive was partially but not wholly equivalent to the original thirst drive. The evidence is strengthened by data from other somewhat similar experiments of the same author and also of Webb (1949). The indicated conclusion would probably hold also for the human child who runs to his mother for anything he happens to want. She is the good, well-tested secondary incentive.

Equivalent secondary incentives. The main fact here is not very surprising though its implications are important. Pavlov's dogs after being conditioned to salivate at the sound of a certain tone would salivate also for higher or lower tones. By the same token we can expect a rat to go readily to a white goal box if he has regularly found food in a light gray box. An implication is that differentiation between two boxes will be more difficult, the more alike they are. With food in the left-hand end box of a simple T maze, the hungry rat must learn to differentiate two end boxes which differ in location. If they differ also in color, one being white inside and the other black, differentiation should be more quickly learned. Such is the result of experiments (Denny, 1948; Saltzman, 1950). We can say, as is most customary, that the secondary reinforcement exerted by the color of the positive end box is exerted also in the negative one when both are gray in color, so that both correct and incorrect responses get this secondary reinforcement. Or we can say, if we choose, that the gray color acquires positive incentive value and makes the two end boxes more nearly equal in incentive value than when they differ in color.

Drive generalization and incentive generalization are a pair of very handy conceptual tools for any psychologist who wishes to derive all human motivation from a few basic organic needs. Start with hunger, for example, and let a child become conditioned to gratify this drive at the family table. So the family group acquires secondary incentive value which can be generalized to other social groups even when they are not engaged in eating. Apart from the easygoing plausibility of such explanations, they have a serious difficulty to overcome. Secondary incentive value, so far as we have seen, is extinguished if the primary reward is always withheld. The rat loses interest in the white goal box, the chimpanzee in the poker chips, if these "promises" or "tokens" are never followed by food or some other primary reward.

However, we must distinguish between extinction and satiation—satiation from repetition of a response which obtains the primary incentive, extinction from repetition of a response which fails to obtain it. Or we may say that extinction is the loss of secondary incentive value, while satiation is the loss of primary incentive value. Since satiation and extinction are not always easy to distinguish objectively, the experimentalist is going to have some difficulty in deciding whether human activities are inherently worth while or dependent on external reinforcement.

NONORGANIC PRIMARY DRIVES AND INCENTIVES

A general theory of motivation that is acceptable to many psychologists regards all primary drives as dependent on organic needs. These are homeostatic needs, consisting of a deficiency or excess in the internal economy of the organism —a deficiency of some food substance, for example, or an excess of some waste product. These needs generate tensions in the sensory-neural-muscular system, or external behavior system. When behavior succeeds in reducing a need, behavioral tension also is reduced, and such reduction of a need or tension constitutes the primary reinforcement of the particular behavior. Behavior is thus merely a servant without any primary needs of its own.

Is this not good evolutionary doctrine, putting first things first, the internal organic processes before any sensorimotor relations with the environment? We can scarcely say so with any assurance when we see the amoeba making motor responses to environmental stimuli. In the animal kingdom behavior seems to be just as primitive as digestion. And there is another evolutionary consideration worthy of notice. Survival would be favored if the organism were equipped with native tendencies to make a positive response to certain stimuli and a negative response to others. If sweet substances are usually nutritious and bitter substances usually poisonous, it would be advantageous for the organism to have a chemical sense capable of distinguishing these two classes of substances, and a response system capable of accepting one and rejecting the other. The organism could then make appropriate responses in advance of any actual need reduction.

Native likes and dislikes. Since taste buds in the baby's mouth are stimulated by the milk sugar a little before the milk reaches the stomach and starts to reduce hunger, the argument that our liking for sweet is acquired by conditioning has some plausibility, but not much. Could the baby learn just as readily to like bitter if a little quinine were added to his milk? Ready acceptance of pure sucrose solutions has been demonstrated in many animals, horse, dog, rat, bear, skunk, raccoon, spider, snail, slug, and many species of insects. "I know of no animal which will refuse sucrose solutions" (Frings, 1946).

Saccharine, useful to some people because it is sweet without being nutritious, is useful for the same reason in the study of incentives. We noticed before (p. 661) that rats prefer saccharine-sweetened water to plain water. So it is not too surprising to find them learning to go to that goal box of a one-unit T maze which offers saccharine-sweetened water as against plain water in the other goal box. This preference was not extinguished even after many days and the ingestion of large quantities of the sweetened water. Thus, the sweet substance passed all the tests for a primary incentive, though in this case it did not reduce any organic need (Sheffield & Roby, 1950; see also Carper, 1953).

A companion experiment (Sheffield, Wulff & Backer, 1951) utilized a certain peculiarity of the rat's sex behavior. The male mounts a receptive female and copulates briefly, dismounts for a moment and remounts, as many as a dozen such preliminary acts occurring before ejaculation. This is the rat's instinctive manner of working up to the climax, increasing his drive but getting no physiological need reduction before the final ejaculation. By removing the female after two of these preliminary mountings, the experimenter was able to provide an incentive free of need reduction. The goal box was at the end of a runway, and the female was put into the goal box only after the male had reached it. Speed of running, the dependent variable, increased from trial to trial in a typical learning curve. Secondary reinforcement was ruled out because (1) these young rats had never gone through the complete copulatory sequence and so had had no chance to associate the preliminary stages with the final need reduction, and (2) there was no sign of extinction in 28 trials on the runway. The rat, we may conclude, has a native liking for the preliminary activity and stimulation involved in his sex behavior.

There are certainly other kinds of sensory stimulation that are naturally liked or disliked—accepted or avoided—by animals, as shown by positive and negative phototropism in invertebrates, by the rat's preference for the dark as against a bright light, and by his struggles to escape from a loud high-pitched tone, and even by the stimuli that we know as painful in ourselves and speak of as "noxious" in animals. They are not necessarily injurious; the weak electric shocks which the animal tries to escape are actually doing no damage to his tissues. Pain is a *threat* of injury; by withdrawing from the painful stimulus the organism avoids the injury. These native likes and dislikes have biological utility, but they are not organic needs themselves.

Exploring and manipulating. We have several times offered evidence in favor of an exploratory drive. We now wish to point out that in spite of its obvious biological utility it is not an organic need. It is activated by stimuli from the environment and not by internal processes of the organism. It can qualify as a behavioral drive, distinct from the activity drive. For if exploratory behavior were merely a form of general motor activity, the Y-maze exploration test should get very different results from rats that had been cooped up all day in small living cages, and from rats that had free access all day to an activity wheel. As a matter of fact the exploratory behavior of the two groups was just the same in kind and amount (Montgomery, 1953b).

A manipulatory drive is most clearly manifested in the play of the human child. But even the rat in a Skinner box, before being conditioned to press the bar for food, shows an "operant level" of bar-pressing (Skinner, 1938). In an hour's session his rate of pressing declines irregularly to near zero, with partial recovery before the next daily session. Something like extinction (or satiation) occurs, as it does in the rat's exploration of a maze (Schoenfeld, Antonitis & Bersh, 1950b). Manipulation and exploration are alike in being ways of becoming acquainted with the environment or adjusted to it.

From casual observation of monkeys we should expect them to demonstrate a strong manipulatory drive. The mechanical puzzle shown in Figure 22-12 was employed by Harlow and his associates (1950) in a learning test on four rhesus monkeys. A puzzle was attached to the perch in each animal's living cage and simply left there for the animal to play with, without any food or other extrinsic reward for successful manipulation. These animals had had no previous experience in obtaining rewards for manipulation. Several times a day *E* made the rounds and reset any puzzle

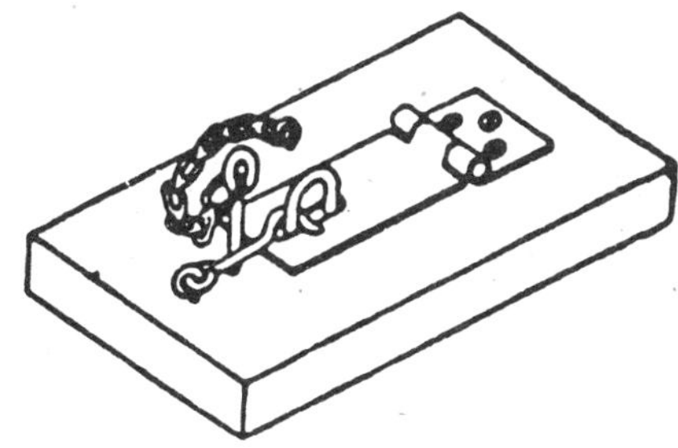

FIG. 22-12. (Harlow, Harlow & Meyer, 1950.) A mechanical puzzle used in a test on monkeys for manipulatory drive. There was no food nor even an empty food hollow in the wood board beneath the iron hasp.

that he found solved (taken apart). After 12 days of this, there were 10 well-spaced test trials with the result that each monkey took the puzzle apart 6, 8, or 9 times, usually in quick time and without any false moves. There was no sign of extinction but every indication that successful manipulation brought its own intrinsic reward. "A manipulation drive, strong and extremely persistent," could reasonably be inferred.

HUMAN DRIVES AND INCENTIVES

The extraordinary variety of human interests presents a developmental problem that seems almost beyond the resources of the experimentalist. With young children as subjects, experiments like those just considered on likes and dislikes and on exploration and manipulation would have a good chance of bringing to light objects (playthings) and activities that have intrinsic incentive value. Woodworth (1918), Allport (1937), and Flugel (1948) have tried to make a case for drives that function autonomously or sustain themselves in the adult even though they may have been acquired as mechanisms (means) for satisfying organic needs. The recent recognition of secondary reinforcement and the motivating power of preliminary goals could be regarded as lending some support to this view, the only question being how long the secondary incentives could resist extinction. Yet, the same line of facts can be used in opposition to the view in question, as by McClelland (1942a) and Rethlingshafer (1943). We shall resist the temptation to pursue this argument on the basis of familiar facts such as the enduring love of many people for music or architecture or mountain scenery.

Motivation of work. Fortunately we do not have to trace every motive to its origin before beginning to find out how incentives operate in human work and achievement. In the laboratory young adult subjects willingly cooperate with the experimenter and are easily motivated to work on a variety of tasks without being bribed by food or even by money, though wages are sometimes useful when much time and regular attendance is required, and a bonus for superior achievement will sometimes enlist extra effort. But there are factors inherent in the task and working conditions that have been revealed by experiment.

Knowledge of results. No doubt the sensory feedback from receptors in the skin and muscles always provides you with some information on the result of any movement. Walking upstairs in the dark you get this sort of information on the important question, when you have reached the top. But often you would welcome the more definite information characteristic of the sense of sight. If you are serving as subject in an ergograph experiment, lifting a 9-pound weight by flexion of the middle finger, doing this once a second under instructions to do your best and keep it up as long as possible, you would like to know how well you are doing. Sensations from the hand are too vague to yield satisfactory information, and you would prefer to see the record of your movements that is being made on the moving paper of a kymograph. In a pioneer study of knowledge of results by Arps (1917, 1920) the kymograph record was sometimes screened from the subject's view and at other times visible to him as he made it. The three subjects found the visible record a great help in holding their attention to the otherwise tedious task and resisting fatigue, and their output of muscular work was from 5 percent to 35 percent greater when the record was visible.

In target practice of various sorts, prompt information on the accuracy of your aim is of obvious value in enabling you to make any necessary corrections. If your hits on the target are too high, you can proceed to aim a little lower. Under certain conditions you can even correct your aim before the target is reached, as illustrated in Figure 22-13 and also in Figure 2-19, p. 41, in the chapter on Reaction Time. For other studies of these corrective adjustments see Woodworth (1899) and Vince (1948b).

A whole series of experiments on target practice with and without knowledge of results has come from the psychological laboratory of Cambridge University, some of them with lines drawn on paper by the subject, others with more elaborate apparatus and more adequate control of conditions (Elwell & Grindley, 1938; MacPherson, Dees & Grindley, 1948, 1949). One task was to draw a series of lines all

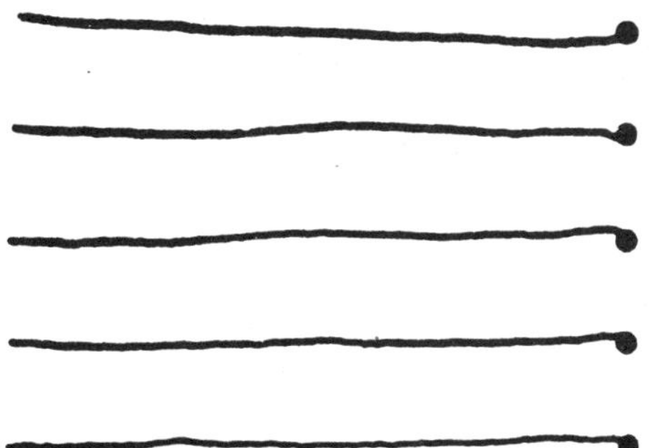

FIG. 22-13. An informal experiment on target practice, showing corrections of the aim as the target is approached. The subject starts from the left, 4–5 inches from the targets, keeps his eye on the target, and tries to reach it by a single movement, fairly rapid yet not too rapid to allow of smooth readjustments. The readjustment can be mostly eliminated by a modified experiment: take aim, then close the eyes while the movement is executed.

of the same length; another, to press a Morse key always for a certain time; a third, to exert a series of equal pressures on a lever. These tasks were like that of throwing darts at a target in that the single attempt could not be corrected (as it could in Fig. 22-13). But, when permitted, the subject could see his errors on the target and try to correct them on the next trial. With this procedure he improved rapidly and reached a level of fair accuracy. But he lost much of this accuracy instantly as soon as the procedure was changed and he could no longer see his results (Fig. 22-14). His interest in the task immediately became less keen, only to revive when knowledge of results was again permitted. It seemed that knowledge of results was a reward, and that lack of this knowledge, like the discontinuance of reinforcement in conditioning experiments, led to extinction. Knowledge of results had a directive or corrective function and it also had incentive value.

In the rotary pursuit task (p. 531), there is of course some knowledge of results, since *O* continually sees his stylus on or off the target. But more definite infor-

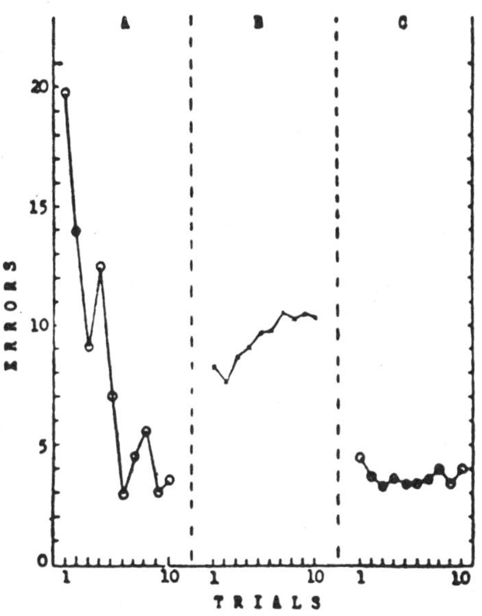

Curve A represents the average errors during the very first run of 10 K trials

Curve B represents the average errors during the whole subsequent 15 N runs

Curve C represents the average errors during the whole subsequent 14 K runs.

O With knowledge of results.

X Without knowledge of results.

FIG. 22-14. (MacPherson, Dees & Grindley, 1948.) Curve of learning and partial extinction in target practice with and without knowledge of results. The task was to hold down a telegraph key for exactly .7 seconds. While the key was closed a condenser was charged, and when the key was released the condenser discharged through a mirror galvanometer, causing a spot of light to come to rest on the "target." The "bull's-eye" was a mark on the target indicating correct duration of the subject's pressure on the key. In the first 10 trials, with Knowledge, he could see the direction and amount of each error, and the curve shows rapid improvement. The next 10 trials, with No knowledge, showed an immediate loss of accuracy. There followed several alternate series of 10 trials with and without knowledge, the subject instantly regaining and losing again the acquired level of accuracy. The curve pools these two kinds of repetitions trial by trial.

mation of his degree of success can be provided by means of an electronic device which immediately sounds a click whenever *O* has remained on target for a certain short time, as half a second. The click undoubtedly has some reward value and serves as an immediate goal. As *O* improves he gets more and more clicks during a 30-second trial. His improvement is definitely more rapid with the click than without it (Reynolds & Adams, 1953).

Definite goals as incentives. A setup that provides knowledge of results can also present definite output standards, and if they are within the subject's reach and acceptable to him, his output will be increased. A pioneer study by Wright (1906) obtained this result, confirmed by a more recent experiment of the same sort by Crawley (1926) who made use of a weight-lifting ergograph fashioned from the familiar gymnasium "chest weight" apparatus. The subject stood with the back of his upper arm supported at shoulder height and lifted the weight by flexion at the elbow, mostly by the biceps muscle. He grasped a handle which was attached to the weight by a cord-and-pulley system, and lifted once every 2 seconds, keeping time with a metronome. Figure 22-15 shows a sample kymograph record made while he was simply "doing his best" without seeing the record. When he watched the record as he made it and was assigned a definite goal—a mark previously made on the kymograph paper showing how long he had gone in his preceding trial—he was motivated to surpass his previous achievement. The results from four young men showed that this extra motivation gave an increased output of about 13 percent when the weight was 15 pounds (about 7 kilos) and similarly with other weights and with leg as well as arm movements. There were practically no exceptions to the rule that "even where the subject swears that he has reached his maximum amount of output . . . the subject will prove himself capable of producing more work" when the incentive is increased. He gets more work from his muscles at the expense of some extra fatigue. We shall have more to say about fatigue and the ergograph in the chapter on "Economy" (pp. 798 ff.).

A similar effect of incentives was noticed in our chapter on Reaction Time (p. 28). When a subject is responding "as quickly as he can," he does not respond as quickly as when he gets immediate information of his time after each trial, nor as quickly as when he gets a shock for any relatively slow response.

The same effect is found in accuracy of perception and judgment. In an experiment on discrimination of length (Hamilton, 1929) the Galton Bar was the appa-

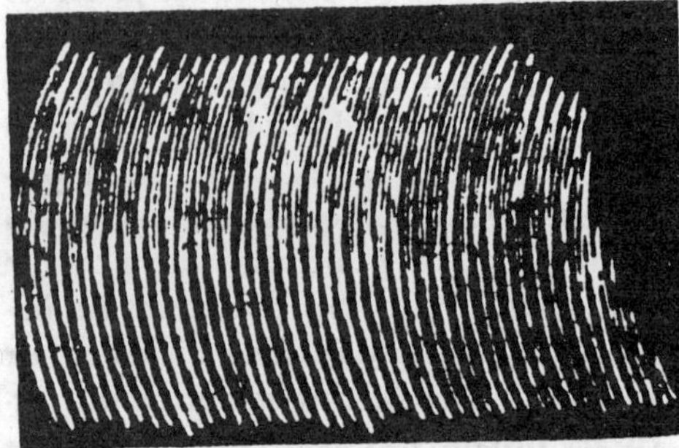

FIG. 22-15. (Crawley, 1926.) A sample ergograph record obtained when the subject was lifting a 15-pound weight once every 2 seconds. After about 35 complete elbow flexions his strength seemed to give out, though it recovered considerably in a 2- or 4-minute rest. The subject did not see this record as it was being made. But on the following day he tried again, this time seeing the kymograph record as he made it, and with a mark at the right on the blank paper showing how far he had gone the day before. With this incentive he could make several additional full strokes. The four subjects were well practiced in lifting the weight before the actual experiment began.

ratus used. The subject attempted to set a marker at the mid-point of a bar 1 meter long. He was allowed a certain leeway which was diminished as he improved with practice. If his setting fell within the margin allowed, he was rewarded by, the ringing of a bell. With this incentive his accuracy improved far beyond the point reached when he simply tried to do his best, time after time, without knowledge of results. In an experiment on the stimulus threshold for a faint light (Holston, 1951) improvement was obtained by means of a "pep talk" and a promise of a bonus for improvement.

An important kind of incentive was utilized by Mace (1931) in an experiment on dart throwing. There were two sizes of target, 5 and 10 inches in diameter, placed 2.5 yards from the subject's position. Five subjects practiced for 4 days, each making 100 throws a day at each target, with average errors as follows, measured in angular deviation of the throw from the bull's-eye:

	Day 1	*Day 2*	*Day 3*	*Day 4*
10-inch target	3.64	3.67	3.69	3.66
5-inch target	3.25	3.20	3.20	3.07

The smaller target was more stimulating, apparently because the subject's intention was to hit "at least within the target," so that he rated his success in distances on the target rather than in angular errors of aim. Probably there is an optimum size of target, or in general an optimum standard, neither too high nor too low, which will arouse the maximum effort.

Information given by a painful stimulus. In one of Pavlov's experiments (1927, p. 29) a strong electric current applied to a dog's skin became an effective signal of meat powder to come. The usual defensive response to a shock dropped out and instead the dog turned toward the food and began to salivate. In the hungry animal food seeking dominated over shock avoidance. If we say that the shock came to "mean" food to the dog, we can see a resemblance between this experiment of Pavlov and a well-known experiment of Tolman, Hall & Bretnall (1932). In their punch-board maze (p. 651) the subject needs information as to whether he has made a correct or incorrect response at each choice point. He may be told "Right" or "Wrong" after each choice, or he may be instructed in advance that a bell will ring after each choice to signify "Right"—or to signify "Wrong" if the instructions so state. Or he may be instructed that a shock will mean "Right"—or that it will mean "Wrong." The shock was made as strong as the individual was willing to take. According to the law of effect, as then understood, this punishment for Wrong should hasten learning, while punishment for Right should retard it. But the results of the experimenters cited, and also of Muenzinger (1934b) and others, show that it makes little difference whether the shock means Right or Wrong. The subject gets equal information in both cases, and his behavior is dominated by the desire to succeed and get through with the task. The experiment has been varied in several ways with results summarized by Jones (1945) whose own experiment was on boys and girls of 13–14 years of age. He used an improved punch-board maze with four alternatives at each choice point and with Right indicated by a disagreeable vibration of the subject's stylus in one condition, but by an agreeable pattern of lights in another. The net result was just about the same under both conditions (Fig. 22-16). The conclusion reached by Jones, as by Muenzinger, is that the subject's motivation to master the maze is altogether dominant

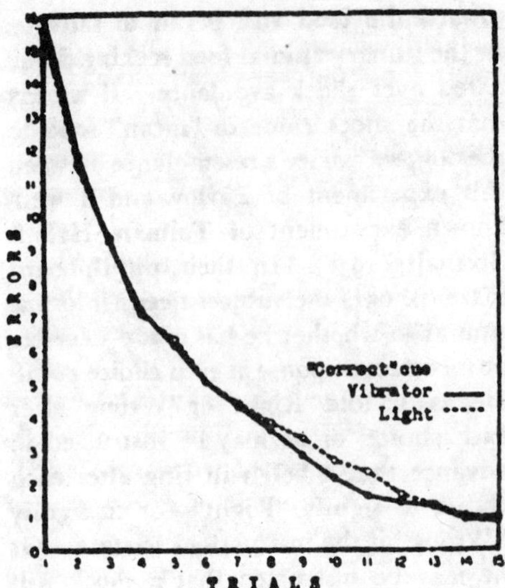

FIG. 22-16. (Jones, 1945.) Learning curves with "Right" indicated by agreeable or by disagreeable stimuli. The disagreeable stimulus was a rapid vibration of the stylus when the subject inserted it into a correct hole; the agreeable stimulus was a pattern of "small red and green luminous points in a miniature Christmas tree" in front of the subject. The subjects were 114 junior high school students. Each subject learned two maze patterns, one with the agreeable and one with the disagreeable signal, the patterns and their time order being balanced in the group as a whole. The two curves do not diverge significantly at any point. It was also found that errors signalled by a disagreeable stimulus were not more quickly eliminated than those indicated by an agreeable signal.

over the immediate pleasantness or unpleasantness of the signals.

In more distinctly social situations, other incentives can be utilized, such as applause, praise or some other form of social recognition—as against blame and loss of "face." People like to participate in group activities and to conform to the beliefs and customs of their friends. Yet competition between individuals or between groups can easily be awakened and made to increase the output of energy. Along these and other lines social psychology is already making great strides in experimental research. The difficulties encountered and special methods adopted are of great interest to the experimentalist, but time and space are lacking here for a thorough examination.

Tendency to complete a task. Some of the most interesting experiments on human motivation have sprung from a certain conception of Kurt Lewin (1935, pp. 60, 180–193, 239–273; 1946, pp. 819–832). The concept is that of a "tense system" generated in a person when he undertakes a task that has a definite goal. The tension is directed toward the goal and will be discharged when the goal is reached. If the performance of a task is interrupted before the goal is reached, tension remains in the system and may lead to the resumption of the performance as soon as circumstances permit; or it may lead to the recall of a recently interrupted task while completed tasks are wiped off the slate and forgotten; or the tension may be relieved by the performance of a similar task.

Resumption of an interrupted performance. An early experimenter in Lewin's Berlin laboratory was Ovsiankina (1928). Her procedure was as follows. A student who has agreed to serve as subject presents himself and is asked without further explanation please to solve a certain puzzle, or to model a dog in clay, or to do some other little task of possible interest but no personal importance to the subject. He quickly becomes absorbed in the task. Without previous warning, however, *E* interrupts by asking him to drop that task and start another. One result comes out at once: the subject tends to resist the interruption and continue what he is doing. He is persuaded to shift to the second task which he is allowed to complete. Then he is left free for a short time without further instructions from *E* who is busy taking notes. The materials of the unfinished first task are still lying on the table, and the subject is apt to resume work on it spontaneously and carry it through to completion. In the course of a two-hour session he is given quite a number of tasks, some being interrupted and others not, with no reasons given. He resumes work very seldom on a task he has completed, but very often on one he has left unfinished. The statistical result: with 28 subjects and a total of 91 interrupted tasks, 72 tasks (79 percent) were resumed. When the interruption appeared to be accidental, the task was always resumed, as it was almost always when the interruption lasted only 2–3 minutes. Some of the subjects, according to their introspective reports, became absorbed in the tasks just as interesting problems, while others regarded them as tests of their own abilities—two motivations which we may call *task interest* and *ego interest*.

Substitute tasks and goals. When one task is interrupted and another substituted, the second may perhaps be a satisfactory substitute for the first and serve to work off the "tension" so that there is no tendency left toward resumption of the first task. Presumably a similar task will serve this purpose while a totally dissimilar second task (which may take the subject out of the laboratory on some errand) will not reduce the tension. The more similar the two tasks, accordingly, the weaker will be the tendency to resume the interrupted task after the second task is completed. This prediction was tested by Lissner (1933). She prepared pairs of very similar tasks, pairs of fairly similar ones, and pairs of very dissimilar ones, and obtained the following results. The interrupted task was resumed:

In 42 percent of the cases when the two tasks were very similar;
In 71 percent of the cases when the two tasks were fairly similar;
In 87 percent of the cases when the two tasks were very dissimilar.

The prediction was verified: the more similar the two tasks, the better satisfied the subject was with the substitute and so the less likely he was to resume the first task. But it was not always possible to judge from the objective task exactly what the subject's goal would be in performing the task. If he started modeling a clay dog and was interrupted and told to model a clay horse, the second task was a satisfactory substitute if his goal was to discover whether he could do such modeling, but not if he had set his heart on producing a good dog—a specific goal for which a horse was no substitute.

A similar experiment was done by Nowlis (1941) in the Yale laboratory where quite a different set of explanatory concepts was in vogue. Still she obtained the same main result, since the interrupted task was most often resumed when the second task was altogether unlike the first. She further devoted especial attention to ego interests. An American college student coming to the psychological laboratory to serve as a subject, and being given a task to perform, is almost sure to regard it as a test of his abilities and hope to do well. At least he would like to have *E* inform him how well he has succeeded. In her main experiment Nowlis used two puzzle tasks, the first being always interrupted and the second always completed. On interrupting the first task she told ⅓ of her 180 subjects that they had done well, and ⅓ that they had done poorly, while the remainder received no comment. Those that received no comment were the most apt to resume this task later, probably because they still hoped to be told how well they had done. Again, when the second task was completed, some subjects were praised, some dispraised, and some left without comment—but it was those praised for the second task who were most apt to resume the first. This last result is not easily explained by either the Yale concepts or the Lewin concepts. We can imagine that the final praise was stimulating and raised the level of motivation and readiness for further activity. (Perhaps this suggestion would be worth trying educationally. When a child is having difficulty with an assigned task and becoming discouraged, shift him to an easier task in which he can succeed and receive merited praise; then see whether he is not encouraged to resume the difficult task.)

Memory for interrupted tasks—the Zeigarnik effect. The most notable experiment from Lewin's Berlin laboratory was done by Zeigarnik (1927). She gave the subject a series of 20 simple, varied tasks, each calling for a few minutes of work. Half of them, scattered through the series, were interrupted (with no opportunity for resumption) and the other half completed. At the end of the series the subject was asked to recall as many as possible of the 20 tasks. On the average about half of them, or a few more, could be recalled. Still on the average, however, 68 percent of the uncompleted (U) tasks were recalled as against only 43 percent of the completed (C) tasks. This predominant recall of the U tasks is the Zeigarnik effect."

Using the ratio U/C as a measure of the effect, we have for Zeigarnik's group of 100 subjects the value, $U/C = 68/43 = 1.60$. Uncompleted tasks were recalled 1.6 times as often as completed tasks. The individual subjects differed considerably, a few giving ratios under 1.00 (recalling more C than U tasks), but the great majority giving ratios over 1.00, some recalling even 3, 4, or 5 times as many of the U as of the C tasks. The Median of these individual ratios was 1.55.

This experiment has been repeated in different laboratories and the Zeigarnik effect has been regularly obtained when the conditions were the same. The conditions required to give the effect have been analyzed by Pachauri (1935–1936) and by Marrow (1938) as well as by Zeigarnik herself. Some relatively technical points are:

1. The tasks that are interrupted for half of the subjects should be completed by the other half—because some tasks may be inherently easier to remember.

2. Each task should have a definite goal so that the subject will know whether he has finished before the interruption. For example, if a task calls for making words out of the letters P-A-I-L-S-T-E, the instructions must specify how many words should be found.

3. The same time, approximately, should be allowed for each task, since tasks are apt to be better recalled if more time has been spent on them.

4. The whole number of tasks should be such that about half of them will be recalled. If they are too few, almost all will be recalled and the Zeigarnik effect will necessarily be lost.

5. The subjects must not know in advance that they are going to be asked to recall the tasks—otherwise they will spoil the effect by taking careful note of every task. On this account the experiment cannot be repeated on the same individuals.

Besides these technical matters there are two factors that have a bearing on the cause of the Zeigarnik effect: the time factor and the motivation factor.

The recall test should follow immediately after the series of tasks. Zeigarnik found that the effect was mostly lost in

24 hours, or even in a quarter of an hour of animated conversation unrelated to the experiment. The "tension" of an interrupted task diffuses away as soon as the subject gets out of the "swing of the experiment."

As to motivation, there are several possible factors. Unsatisfied task-interest would favor recall of a U task. Ego-interest is aroused in individuals who assume they are being tested, but the ego-interest may be either hopeful or fearful. If hopeful, it wishes to resume an unfinished task and so favors recall of such a task; but if fearful, it shrinks from the interrupted task as from a failure and favors forgetting it as soon as possible. If the student subjects suspect that poor test results may be used against their college standing, a reversed Zeigarnik effect may come out strongly (Lewis & Franklin, 1944). Or, at least, the percent of U tasks recalled may be very low when the subjects are worried over their apparent failures (Glixman, 1948, 1949). The individual's "need for achievement" may have a strong influence on the Zeigarnik effect (Atkinson, 1953).

Level of aspiration. You have shot at a target and made a certain score. You are now asked what score you expect, hope, undertake, or aspire to make on the next trial. If you fall short of your prediction, you have a sense of failure; if you equal or surpass it, you have a sense of success even though you do not reach the bull's-eye. If your ego-interest is hopeful you push up your level of aspiration; if it is fearful and defensive, you keep your aspiration down so as to avoid the frustration of failure. The general tendency is to raise your bid after a success and to lower it after a series of failures. Individuals differ and the experiment can perhaps serve as a personality test. A few references: Lewin, Dembo, Festinger & Sears (1944, I, 333–378); Holt (1946); Klugman (1948).

Satiation and cosatiation. Task-interest can be exhausted by massed repetition, as in the experiment of Karsten (1928). She asked the subject, for example, to read a short poem again and again, the only instructions being, "Do this as long as you will. When you do not wish to do it any more you are at liberty to stop." Some subjects had enough after a few repetitions. Others assumed they should continue as long as they could possibly stand it, but they began to show signs of approaching satiation, such as restless movements, slips of the tongue, and anger at the experimenter. When a subject finally gave up, he was immediately given another poem to read, and so on till he refused to read any more poems; then prose passages, etc., till he refused to serve as subject any longer. Rather a terrible experiment, but with some good results: the spread or generalization of satiation, and partial recovery after a day's interval—much as in an extinction series.

Motivation of perception. The process of perceiving, as in seeing an object, is by no means so passive and unmotivated as it usually seems to the perceiver—or as it seems to the behaviorist who thinks it proper to by-pass this process in his study of animal behavior. The Gestalt psychologist is not much better when he speaks of a stimulus as a disturbance and of the perceiving process as a getting rid of the disturbance and restoring internal equilibrium. If that were the goal, the response to a visual stimulus would be to close the eyes. Instead, what we find is a turning of the eyes so as to bring the object into the field of clearest vision, a focusing of the lens for the distance of the object, and convergence of the two eyes so as to secure good stereoscopic vision.

Good reception is the immediate goal of this first part of the perceiving process. The object may be unfamiliar and call for further exploration. The more remote goal may be the finding of food or the escape from danger, but the immediate goal is the establishment and maintenance of good contact with the environment.

Students of motivation have been interested in the relatively remote goals of perception. Will a hungry person be especially likely to see food objects in a complex picture? If the picture is vague and dim, will he even find food objects that are not there? The tachistoscope (p. 92) is a convenient apparatus for experimental work, the test field being dimly illuminated or exposed at first for too short a time to permit a good view of the exposed words or picture (Postman, Bruner & McGinnies, 1948; McClelland & Atkinson, 1948). Similarly, inadequate auditory presentation can be obtained by low "volume" in the presentation of a phonograph record (Skinner's "verbal summator," 1936, 1953a; Vanderplas & Blake, 1949). Instead of the hunger drive, the subject's interests and biases are usually the motivating factors. Familiarity with the words or objects presented may be a disturbing variable, and in general the experiment has to be carefully designed to bring out any significant effects of motivation (Dinsmoor, 1952a). For some positive results and theoretical discussions as well as bibliographies of the field, see a Symposium on perception and personality reported in the *Journal of Personality*, 1949, 18, Nos. 1–2, and reprinted in Bruner & Krech (1950). See also the book by Blake & Ramsey, 1951.

Many of the experiments cited in the last few pages suffer because the independent variables are not well defined. Such terms as "ego-interest" carry meaning at the common-sense level but actually refer to very complicated processes which depend on much of a person's life history. At the present state of research we cannot state the exact requirements of these concepts or constructs. There is a lot of work to be done by the experimentalist who has the courage to tackle these slippery problems—and the skill to arrange the fruitful experiment.

23

MEMORY

A prominent landmark in the century-long history of experimental psychology is a book, *On Memory*, published by Hermann Ebbinghaus in 1885. It is a little book but crammed full of well-designed experiments which opened up an immense new field for scientific psychology. It was in fact the pioneer experimental study in the whole field of learning, retention, and remembering. It was soon followed and has been followed ever since by a great variety of studies in animal learning and the acquisition of human skills. In a broad sense our preceding chapters on Conditioning and on Maze and Discrimination Learning could be included under the general head of Memory. For when a rat has learned the path through a maze to the food box and still follows the correct path after an interval of time, he certainly demonstrates memory for what he has learned. He may not "remember" the original experience of learning the maze, as a human being could, but he does what he previously learned to do; and it would be difficult to frame an adequate definition of memory except in such terms as these, "doing what one has learned to do," though of course in a broad sense of the word "doing."

Before Ebbinghaus there had been much relatively speculative discussion of memory and of the laws of association, but he saw that scientific study should start with the learning process and the establishment of associations. He saw that human learning and retention of verbal material could be studied in the laboratory. Because meaningful words have so many pre-established associations for the human adult, Ebbinghaus simplified and standardized his experiments by the invention of *nonsense syllables*. He also invented certain *memory methods* for controlling the learning and recall of this material. So he introduced a perfectly objective and quantitative approach to the study of human memory. Later workers have followed the same line, extending his methods and using a variety of materials.

Human memory is still a very active field for experimental research. It has yielded a large return in results of both theoretical and practical value. The continued fruitfulness of the field is largely due to its methods, which satisfy even our modern standards for good scientific experiments.

EXPERIMENTAL METHODS FOR THE STUDY OF MEMORY

The stages of memory. It is often stated that there are four stages or phases involved in memory: *impression, reten-*

tion, *recall* (or *reproduction*), and *recognition*. The first three stages correspond roughly to making a recording on a tape recorder, storing it in your file, and then playing it back at a later date—there is no good analogy here for the final stage, recognition. But such analogies must not be taken too seriously, for they neglect the fact that *O* is active, rather than passive. Indeed, the stages themselves are somewhat artificial; for example, during the stage of impression there must obviously be some retention betweeen successive repetitions, and there may be actual attempts to recall the material learned on the previous trial. So we must remember that these names are merely convenient labels for successive parts of an experiment on memory. If we prefer, we may break up the experiment into the learning period, the retaining period, and the testing period. We can see what is happening during the learning period; *O* reads a list over and over. Similarly, we can watch him repeat or recognize the material in the test period. But we can study what happens during the retaining period only indirectly, by finding the difference between *O*'s original and final behavior. That is, if he learned something yesterday, and repeats it today, we can say he has retained it. But what is the *it* which he retained? We do not know, so we call it a *trace*. This construct is convenient, but only if it does not lull us into security by making us think we are *explaining* retention. Nor do we explain *forgetting* by saying that the trace fades with time. Incidentally, the *amount retained* is usually more convenient to measure than is its inverse, the *amount forgotten*, so we shall usually speak of retention rather than of forgetting.

Some of the memory methods are designed to study only one phase, while other methods may be used to investigate the whole sequence. This will be clear as we go over the main methods.

Immediate memory span. This simple method, introduced by Jacobs (1887), furnishes an answer to the question, how large a quantity of a given sort of material can be reproduced perfectly after one presentation. In a typical experiment, *E* has at hand lists of 3–12 digits and instructs *O* as follows: "I will say some numbers; when I have finished, you are to repeat the numbers in the same order." *E* starts with a short list and advances to longer ones, going far enough to reach *O*'s limit. *O* has only one trial with any one list.

DIGIT LISTS FOR MEMORY SPAN

972	641
1406	2730
39418	85943
067285	706294
3516927	1538796
58391204	29081357
764580129	042865129
2164089573	4790386215
45382170369	39428107536
870932614280	541962836702

The score in this experiment is the length of list which *O* can recite perfectly after one hearing. The concept of span, derived from the span of the hand, conveys the idea of width of grasp. How much can be spanned or grasped at once? To guard against favorable and unfavorable accidents, it is best to give the subject more than one list of each length and to go somewhat beyond the point at which he first makes an error. Occasionally he succeeds with a longer list where he has failed with a shorter one. If there were no variability of performance, a single list of each length would be enough and the result would show, for example, that *O* succeeded with all lists up to and including 8 digits and never beyond that point. His span, then, would be 8 digits. Even though the span shows a rather remarkable degree of constancy, there is always some variation and we have to take account of it in our measure. Two inadequate measures are: The longest list which *O always* gets right; and the longest list which he *ever* gets right. A true average span can be obtained by giving, say, three lists of each length and allowing a credit of ⅓ for every perfectly recited list. Suppose *O* gets all the lists correct up to and including 6 digits: we credit him with 6 as a basal value. If above that value he succeeds twice with a 7-digit list, not at all with 8, once with 9, and no further, then his total score is $6 + 3/3 = 7$.

A number of additional refinements may be introduced into the scoring, as adding a half step-interval to each score. Thus, if *O* gets 8 digits correct, but fails on 9, we know his span is at least 8, but not quite 9, so we split the interval and assign him 8½. We faced similar problems in the chapters on Attention and Psychophysics. Indeed, the memory span can be computed much as we calculated the threshold for the Method of Constant Stimuli (Guilford & Dallenbach, 1925).

The method of retained members. In an unstandardized way this method is used in the schoolroom whenever an examination is scored in terms of the number of items correct. As an experimental method it was used by Bolton (1892) and by many successors of whom we list a few contributing to perfect the method: Binet & Henri, 1894; W. G. Smith, 1896; Pohlmann, 1906; Lyon, 1917; Raffel, 1934. The quantity of material presented must exceed the memory span; the quantity reproduced is the score. The length of the presented list needs to be standardized for a given experiment.

This method is convenient and can be used with a variety of material. It is easy to score, if we are satisfied with a simple count of the correctly reproduced items. When two *O*s reproduce correctly the same number of items, but one *O* gives the correct order and the other not, the first *O* clearly shows the greater memory of the presented list; but as soon as we try to devise a scoring system which shall allow partial credits, we find any system arbitrary.

The method of retained members has been applied successfully to memory for the substance of prose passages. It is necessary to choose a passage which can be divided into fairly equal units of meaning (Henderson, 1903).

Connected passage of 100 words, divided into "ideas" or meaning units, for scoring by the method of retained members.

A bear, / climbing over the fence / into a yard / where bees were kept, / began at once / to smash the hives, / and to rob them / of their honey. / But the bees, / to avenge the injury, / attacked him / in a whole swarm together; / and, though they were too weak / to pierce / his rugged hide, / yet, with their little / stings, / they so tormented / his eyes / and nose, / that, unable to endure / the smarting pain, / he tore the skin / off his ears / with his own claws, / and received ample / punishment / for the injury / he did the bees / in breaking / their waxen cells.

Besides the scoring problem, there is another difficulty in the use of this method. It often fails to give a complete measure of the amount retained. It gives the recalled members, rather than the retained members. *O* may be convinced that he is retaining items which he cannot recall at the moment, and his conviction is often verified by a later recall of the missing items (p. 795).

The learning method. The name does not fully characterize the method, which might be called the *learning-time* method. It measures the time (or number of trials) required by *O* to reach a certain standard or criterion of mastery. The criterion may be one perfect recitation of the "lesson," or two out of three, etc. But here we encounter trouble. If *O* does not try to recite until he is sure he has reached the criterion, he may have gone beyond it. Or if he is optimistic, and tries too soon, *E* does not know whether to count the test trial as a learning trial or not. One other trouble with the method is that it penalizes the person who has trouble in mastering one particular item; he may learn 95 percent of the list in six trials, and take an additional six trials for the remaining 5 percent.

The learning method has the advantage of being applicable to a great variety of material which need not be divisible into separate items. It is scored as a whole.

The prompting and anticipation methods (Ebbinghaus, 1902; Robinson & Brown, 1926). These modifications of the learning method serve two purposes: to overcome the uncertainty as to when *O* has learned the list, and to trace the progress of learning. After one or a few presentations of the list, *O* attempts to recite, is quickly prompted whenever he hesitates and corrected whenever he makes an error. The list is gone through in this way time after time until *O* successfully recites it without prompting. This method is particularly satisfactory for use with a memory drum (see below) which exposes the material item by item. if *O* does not anticipate the item before it appears in the window, the machine "prompts" him. The memory drum does most of *E*'s work, leaving him free to tally responses.

Several scores are possible. The total time or number of trials to reach the criterion can be used just as in the regular learning method. A more characteristic score is the number of prompts necessary before *O* reaches the criterion. This score corresponds to one used in maze learning, the number of errors committed before the maze is learned.

This method furnishes a score of errors or prompts, or of items correctly anticipated for each trial and so makes it possible to construct a learning curve for the list as a whole. It is further possible to trace the progress of learning in each separate item in the list. We can tell on which trial a given item was first anticipated and whether it remained in control after once being mastered.

The saving method. *O* has learned a certain lesson which may be a list of nonsense syllables, a poem, a maze, a motor skill. After an interval he is unable to reproduce the lesson. He *relearns* it by the same procedure as before and to the same criterion of mastery, and the time (or number of trials) required for the relearning is compared with that required for the original learning. If there is any retention, some saving will be found. The saving is the difference between the original learning time and the relearning time, and the percent of saving is found by dividing this absolute saving by the original learning time. For time we may substitute number of trials or number of errors or prompts, though these different measures of saving will not ordinarily give the same percentage.

In strictness we should compare the re

learning time, not with the original learning time but with the time it *now* takes to learn an equivalent lesson. This refinement is important when the learning and relearning are carried out under different conditions. For example, if you wish to discover how well material learned by a subject under the influence of alcohol is retained the next day, it will not do simply to compare the learning and relearning time. Instead *O* should learn two equivalent lessons on the second day, a new one and one originally learned under the alcoholic condition. The question is how much of the work required to learn a new list is saved by virtue of the previous learning.

The saving method can be used for other problems than that of retention. How much of the work otherwise required to learn a certain performance is saved by virtue of the fact that *O* has previously learned another performance? This is the problem of transfer (p. 734).

Serial learning *versus* paired associates. In describing the previous methods we have assumed that the material was presented and learned in serial order, like a poem or a list of numbers. But another arrangement is possible, that of *paired associates*. A practical example is the learning of French-English vocabulary, in which the student has to learn to respond with the English word when stimulated with the French one. The order of the pairs is not important; as in drill cards, the pack should be shuffled between trials.

It is unfortunate that this arrangement of materials is usually called the *method* of paired associates, for it is not a method in the same sense that the previous ones were methods. It would be better to speak of *paired-associate learning*, parallel to serial learning. Indeed, almost all of the methods we have described above can be applied to paired associates; there may be one trial or many, and scoring may be by retained members, trials, prompts, or saving. The paired arrangement of materials is particularly useful when we want clear-cut and isolated connections within pairs of items, and is much used in studies of retroactive inhibition (p. 761). It has become increasingly popular in recent years, but goes back to the early days of memory experiments (Calkins, 1894, 1896; Jost, 1897; Müller & Pilzecker, 1900; Thorndike, 1908).

Recognition method. Here we have two radically different sub-methods:

A. *Accuracy of recognition of a single stimulus.* The familiar psychophysical experiment in comparing successive weights or sounds is converted into a memory experiment by lengthening the interval between the two stimuli compared. By this means loss can be demonstrated even in the first half minute after presentation (Wolfe, 1886; Lehmann, 1889; Bentley, 1899; Whipple, 1901, 1902).

B. *Number of items recognized.* For example, 20 pictures are shown one at a time, and then shuffled with 20 other pictures and the whole 40 shown one at a time; in this recognition test *O* responds Yes or No to each picture, meaning by Yes that he recognizes it or judges that it was shown in the first presentation (Binet & Henri, 1894; W. G. Smith, 1905; Strong, 1912, 1913; Achilles, 1920).

The scoring of a recognition test offers some statistical problems. Let us call the stimuli first presented the "old" stimuli and the recognition of any such stimulus a correct recognition. And let us call the stimuli mixed with the old stimuli, in the recognition test, "new" stimuli and a recognition of one of them a false recognition. Then a raw score is simply the number of correct recognitions, and dividing this number by the number of old stimuli gives the percent of correct recognitions. This would be a good measure if *O* never falsely recognized any of the new stimuli, but if he does, he must be penalized somehow. One way is to subtract from the percent of correct recognitions the percent of false recognitions. That gives us the formula:

Score = (percent of old stimuli recognized) — (percent of new stimuli falsely recognized).

If, as is customary but not at all necessary, the number of new stimuli equals the number of old stimuli, this formula reduces to the familiar:

$$\frac{\text{Right} - \text{Wrong}}{\text{N}}$$

where N = the whole number of stimuli in the recognition test, that is, old + new. "Right" = the number of correct responses to *all* stimuli, and "Wrong" similarly. That is, the "Rights" include the Yes responses to old stimuli and the No responses to new stimuli; the "Wrongs" include the No responses to old stimuli and the Yes responses to new stimuli. We could just as well use only the total percent of Rights, which would be 50 percent for chance (meaning no discrimination between the old and the new), and find the reliability of the excess over 50 percent by the regular formula for SD_p, with p taken as .50.

In the recognition test described, an *O* who is guessing has an even chance of getting any stimulus right or wrong, no matter how many new stimuli are mingled with the old. To reduce the chances of being right by guessing, a *multiple-choice* test is used (Baldwin & Shaw, 1895; Zangwill, 1937; Hanawalt, 1937). Each "old" stimulus is shown in a group of new stimuli and *O*'s task is to select the old one. If there are four new stimuli in the group with a single old stimulus, the chances of being right by guessing are only one in five.

The recognition test can be made hard or easy by selecting new stimuli more or less like the old. Recognition is often said to be easier than recall, but its ease or difficulty depends upon the similarity of the new and the old, between which recognition must distinguish.

The reconstruction method (Münsterberg & Bigham, 1894; Gamble, 1909; Smith, 1934). In this interesting method what has to be reproduced is the order or arrangement of the stimuli. The stimuli are first presented in a certain arrangement, then this arrangement is broken up and the stimuli are handed to *O* with instructions to reconstruct the original order. The arrangement may be a simple serial order of the stimuli or it may be a more complex two-dimensional pattern, or even a three-dimensional one. Verbal material can be used, but the method lends itself to the use of colors, shapes and other concrete material.

The score may be a measure of correspondence between the reconstructed and the original arrangement. In case of simple serial order the Spearman formula for correlation by rank differences is an adequate measure. For two- or three-dimensional patterns, a rough score could be obtained, even though an adequate formula might be difficult of derivation. A totally different method of scoring is possible since evidently the trials can be continued until the subject is able to make a perfect reconstruction, the score being the time or number of trials necessary in order to reach a standard of mastery.

Learning during recall. In experiments on retention it is very easy to slip into a methodological error. For example, if you learned a list of syllables to a criterion of one correct repetition, and then tried to recall it after intervals of 5 minutes, 20 minutes, 1 hour, etc., it is unlikely that there would be any sign of progressive forgetting, for each attempt to recall is actually an additional learning trial, a review. The only way to test various retention intervals is to use a separate list, or a matched group of *O*s, for each desired interval. We shall see that this error, in a slightly more subtle form, shows up in some experiments on reminiscence (p. 795).

Even when there is no check on the accuracy of recall, the attempt to reproduce the material strengthens the traces used. But in this case the wrong traces, errors in recall, may also be strengthened. This is one reason that "stories improve with the telling." The same principle causes serious difficulty in the study of changes in memory for perceived figures (p. 776).

MATERIALS USED IN MEMORY EXPERIMENTS

The recognition and reconstruction methods lend themselves to the use of concrete material. The methods that require *O* to *reproduce* what he has learned are limited by *O*'s powers of expression. He cannot be expected to reproduce a picture though he may be asked to make simple drawings. Verbal material is especially easy to express.

For scoring purposes it is convenient to have material consisting of equal units, such as words, two-place numbers, or nonsense syllables. Connected passages can be broken up (for scoring purposes only) into phrases or "ideas" which can at least be counted, though they are not strictly equal units. The learning and saving methods do not require any such division into parts, when the score is the time or number of trials required to master the whole lesson. But the bulk of current research on memory has been done on two types of material, short words and nonsense syllables. The short words are often adjectives, which can vary along many dimensions of meaning (see retroactive inhibition, p. 766). Nonsense syllables deserve a section of their own.

Nonsense syllables. Ebbinghaus (1885) introduced this device not for the purpose of having something difficult to learn but to provide a large quantity of material of fairly uniform difficulty—uniform because entirely lacking in previously established associations *between one item and another*. In preparation for his experiments, he constructed 2,300 nonsense syllables by a mechanical process. Each syllable consisted of a vowel or diphthong with initial and final consonants. Familiar to Germans were 11 vowels and diphthongs, 19 consonants suitable for beginning a word, and 11 suited for an ending, with *ch* and *sch* included as single consonantal sounds. He wrote out all the possible combinations on slips of paper, shuffled them, and drew for each list as many as required, till every syllable had been used, when the slips were reshuffled. Some of these syllables were familiar words, but these were not thrown out; all syllables were taken just as they came. Ebbinghaus was his own *O*, an exceptionally stable and well-trained *O*, and he learned many lists so as to even out inequalities.

Müller & Schumann (1894) introduced greater precision by removing some of these inequalities. They found that alliteration, assonance, or rhyming of neighboring syllables made a soft spot in a list, and that sometimes two adjacent syllables spelled a familiar word and so were easily learned. They secured 12-syllable lists sufficiently uniform to be called "normal" by mechanically following certain rules:

1. No two syllables in the same list shall have the same initial consonant, or the same final consonant, or the same vowel. (They found it possible to use 12 vowels and diphthongs.)

2. The initial consonant of a syllable shall never be identical with the final consonant of the preceding syllable.

3. The list is to be read by *O* in trochaic rhythm, two syllables being regarded as a foot with accent on the first syllable of each foot. The first and last consonants in a foot shall not be identical, though the initial and final consonants of a single syllable may be the same.

4. Though a single syllable may be a familiar word, no two or more adjacent syllables shall constitute a familiar word or phrase. They may suggest a word or phrase but shall not correctly spell a word or phrase.

In English-speaking countries, psychologists have usually assumed that the syllables must not be familiar words and that they must consist of only three letters. These two assumptions, along with the existence of numerous monosyllabic English words, greatly limit the number of available nonsense syllables and make it impossible to follow Müller & Schumann's first rule, since we are limited to six vowels. Nor can we use the simple consonantal sounds which are spelled with two letters, as *ch, sh, th*. Moreover, it has seemed desirable to avoid syllables which, though not correctly spelling familiar words, readily suggest them.

Glaze (1928) attempted to measure the meaningfulness or "association value" of every nonsense syllable consisting of three different letters. Fifteen students were shown one syllable at a time and allowed not over 3 sec. to say whether the syllable conveyed any meaning. Certain syllables, as pil and wom, suggested some meaning to all the 15 *Os*, certain others to 14, others to 12, and so on down. Of the 2,000 syllables tested, 100 suggested no meaning to any one. Glaze's published syllables enable investigators to construct lists of probably equal suggestive value —though Glaze's sample of the population was rather small and narrow. Glaze himself assumed that the best syllables were those of lowest association value, but when he tried memorizing lists of these best syllables he found the task not only difficult but "extremely trying." The syllables most lacking in suggestiveness are uncouth and almost repulsive in appearance. Some of them are scarcely pronounceable, as kyh, quj, xiw. However, they need not be pronounced if the instructions call for oral or written *spelling* of the syllables. Groups of three consonants can be used. These may be found in Hilgard (1951) together with some convenient lists of conventional nonsense syllables, grouped by association value.

Hull (1933a) tried out 320 syllables under conditions of actual learning. *O* memorized a list and also reported immediately any meaning suggested by each syllable as it came. (Lists of 16 syllables, shown at the rate of 2 seconds per syllable, 3 presentations of each list, 20 lists rotated among the 20 student *Os*.) The "association value" averaged about half that of the same syllables in Glaze's experiment, as might be expected since Glaze's *Os* were looking for suggested meanings, while Hull's were learning the sequence of syllables. The correlation between the association values of the same syllables in the two experiments was not high—only .63 when corrected for attenuation–and the correlation between Hull's subgroups of 10 *Os* was only .64, indicating a lot of individual variation in the suggestiveness of a nonsense syllable. Nevertheless the obtained association values of various syllables can be used to build syllable pairs which shall have equal summed association values, and from these pairs to construct lists each of which shall be fairly uniform throughout its extent. Hull (1935) found that in such lists, consisting of alternate higher-value and lower-value syllables, the high-value ones were learned only a little more quickly than the low-value. In learning a list the sequences of syllables probably count for more than the suggestiveness of single syllables. But when several lists of equal difficulty are needed, it is wise to select the syllables from Glaze, Hull or Hilgard so that the mean association value of all lists will be approximately equal. Omit any syllables that duplicate local slang, common brand names, or the initials of new government agencies.

Other nonsense materials. In view of the limitations of three-letter syllables, four-letter syllables have been used by Gamble (1909, 1927) and also (in laboratory classes) by the senior author. The initial or final consonant is double, or the vowel sound is expressed by two letters, or a final silent *e* is used to indicate a "long" preceding vowel, as in *tade*. There are plenty of vowel sounds and diphthongs in English oral speech, and it is possible to construct lists of at least 15 syllables, no two containing the same vowel or diphthong and all readily pronounced; for example,

meev	goje
jish	hool
glet	fape
crad	kise
lerm	roif
sark	twic
thog	bune
chuz	nowk
daux	whab

Over 10,000 four-letter syllables, some of them being English words, can be made in this way (see first edition of this text).

It is also possible to make a large number of nonsense dissyllables, or *paralogs*. A few of the 43,200 dissyllables prepared by the Division of Anthropology and Psychology, National Research Council (Dunlap, 1933) are given below.

babab	gokem	medon	runil
defig	kupod	nigat	tarup
fimur	latuk	polef	zuzuz

Of course we may use groups of digits, but they are very hard to learn. We shall see later that simple geometric drawings, *nonsense figures*, are very useful.

Apparatus. Ebbinghaus (1885) simply spread a list of nonsense syllables before him and read them at a rate of 2/5 seconds per item, keeping time with a metronome or with the ticking of his watch. An early objection to this simple procedure, an objection which has turned out *not* to be very serious, was that the simultaneous presence of several items in the field of view made it possible for associations to be established which otherwise would be impossible, for instance backward associations. Müller & Schumann (1894) avoided this objection and standardized the procedure by pasting the list around a drum which rotated behind a screen and exposed one syllable at a time through a little window in the screen. Some *O*s found it fatiguing to the eyes to read the moving syllables. The drum should move in quick jumps or steps alternating with stationary moments during which the successive items are exposed. Such intermittent motion was provided by Ranschburg's card-changer (1901); by Wirth's memory apparatus (1903), in which a long band carrying the syllables was driven by clockwork and halted from moment to moment by electromagnets timed by a metronome; and also, very conveniently, by Lipmann's memory apparatus (1904, 1908), in which the drum is driven intermittently by a transmission device, the whole apparatus being self-contained and mechanical. These devices have been improved by more recent makers (Fig. 23-1). For work with groups of *O*s a projection memory device is convenient. It can be constructed fairly easily by attaching a geared-down electric motor to a toy motion picture projector, preferably 35 mm.

MEMORIZING

Several challenging facts can be demonstrated with very simple material and procedure, as in a test for digit span.

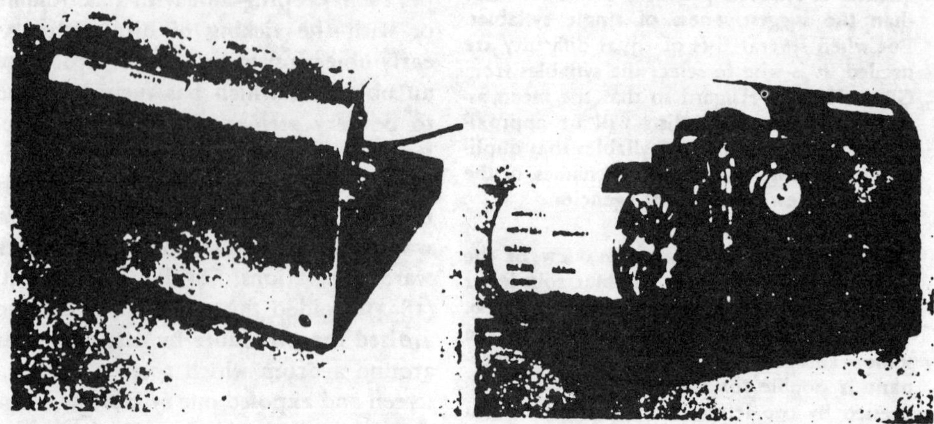

FIG. 23-1. Memory apparatus, design of R. Gerbrands. The Lipmann apparatus so modified as to be driven by a constant speed electric motor instead of by clockwork. The works are concealed from *O* by an aluminum screen; through a window he sees one line of the material at a time. As shown on the right, the paper strip containing the "lesson" is bound around a drum. When the drum is in place on its shaft, the peg on the small wheel engages the cogs of the drum and gives the drum each time a quick push which brings the next line into view. Reduction gear shown above causes the driving wheel to rotate once in 3 seconds, which is the interval between exposures when only one peg is inserted. A more rapid rate can be secured by inserting two or three pegs. The drum in the picture contains a list of paired associates arranged for learning by the prompting method. On seeing the word "umbrella," for example, *O* tries to give its associate before being prompted by the next following exposure.

The fact that the span may run up to 6, 8, or 10 digits indicates some process of synthetic apprehension. The fact that the memory span is limited presents something of an enigma; for if you can recite 6 digits immediately after hearing them, why can you not hold these, take on 6 more and recite the whole 12? If you run over a list of 12 a few times, then you can recite it in its entirety. This effect of repetition is a third fact to be explained; a fourth is the forgetting of the list in a few minutes or hours, and a fifth fact is the possibility of relearning the material with less expenditure of time and effort than was required for the original learning. These fundamental facts have been amplified and quantified in various respects.

Dependence of learning time on quantity of material. The memory span measures the amount of a given material that can be reproduced after a single reading:

2 digits at age of 2½
3 digits at age of 3
4 digits at age of 4½
5 digits at age of 7
6 digits at age of 10 (revised Stanford-Binet scale).

The average for college students without preliminary practice is not over 8. Intensive training of kindergarten children for 78 days increased their average span from 4.4 to 6.4 digits and so brought them up to the 10-year level. After the long vacation in which no further practice occurred, they averaged 4.7, about down to their original level and probably no further above it than could be accounted for by growth (Gates & Taylor, 1925). College students by intensive practice increased their span about 20 percent, the maximum rising from 10 to 14 digits.

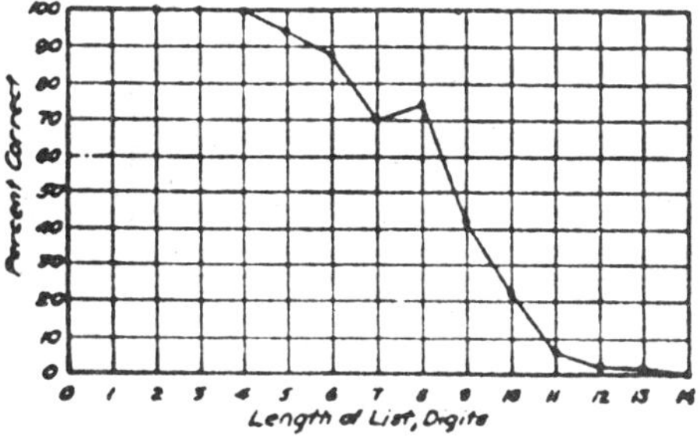

FIG. 23-2. (After Oberly, 1928.) The variable memory span of one individual. After hearing a list of digits read in a monotonous tone at the rate of one digit per second, *O* attempted to write it down. In order to score, his reproduction had to be perfect. In the course of five sessions he tried 50 lists of each length. The graph shows that his reproduction was always perfect with the lists of 2–4 digits and that the percent of perfect responses decreased gradually as the list lengthened. The irregularity in the middle of the curve is probably of no significance. The curve might well be smoothed in that region. Where the curve crosses the 50-percent line we have the indicated Median span, and where it crosses the 25-percent and 75-percent lines we have the Quartiles. The Mean, computed according to the Method of Constant Stimuli (p. 207) is 8.5 digits for this *O*, and the SD is 2.8 digits. The 100 students tested gave individual Means ranging from 6 to 12 or 13 digits, and a general average of 9 digits. It made little difference whether the length of list was increased progressively or whether the various lengths were presented in haphazard order.

Though they were not tested later for permanence of this skill, probably some of it remained, since it depended upon a technique of grouping the digits (Martin & Fernberger, 1929). Figure 23-2 brings out a fact that should not be forgotten, namely that the individual memory span is not a fixed quantity but varies from trial to trial. It varies also with the connectedness of the material, running up to about 15 words for meaningful sentences reproduced verbatim after a single hearing (Mark & Jack, 1952).

Lists exceeding the memory span. If *O* learns a list of 8 digits in one reading (or in 8 seconds), how many readings (or how much time) will it take him to learn a list of 16 digits? This problem cannot be solved by simple proportion, since as a matter of fact when the memory span is exceeded, the time for memorizing takes a sudden jump. If one reading suffices for 8 numbers, three or four may be needed to learn 9. A group of 160 unpracticed college students gave an average digit span of 8, but when more than 8 digits were presented in a list the number reproduced fell on the average to 6. Only 5 percent of the *O*s were able to equal their span when the number presented exceeded the span (Gates, 1916). Digits are rather peculiar materials because there are so few of them and they are so frequently used. When the list consists of disconnected meaningful words, the result is different. Binet & Henri (1894) found with one subject:

5 words presented . . .	5 words reproduced
10 words presented . . .	7 words reproduced
49 words presented . . .	17 words reproduced
100 words presented . . .	25 words reproduced

The absolute number reproduced increases with the number in the list, but the percent decreases. A similar result is obtained by paired associates and also in recognition experiments (Woodworth, 1915b; Strong, 1912).

The total time required to learn a list of items must obviously increase with the length of the list, since more time is taken

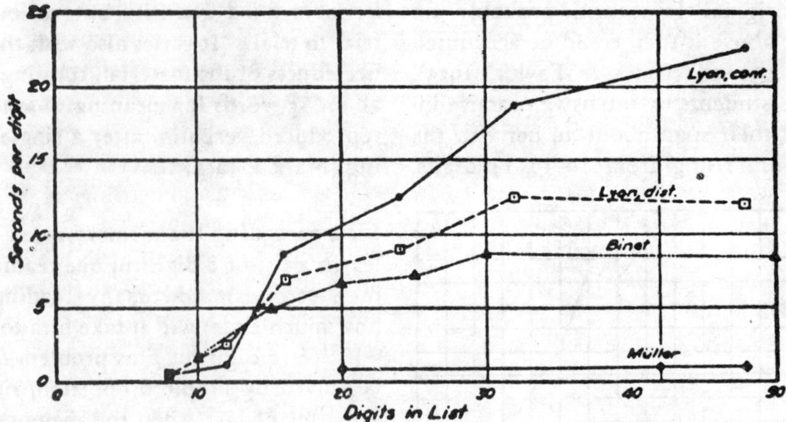

FIG. 23-3. (Data assembled from several sources.) Increase in time-per-item to memorize digit lists of increasing length. Time-per-item seems the best measure of the increasing difficulty of longer lists. The time-per-list can be found from the graph by multiplying the time-per-item by the number of items.

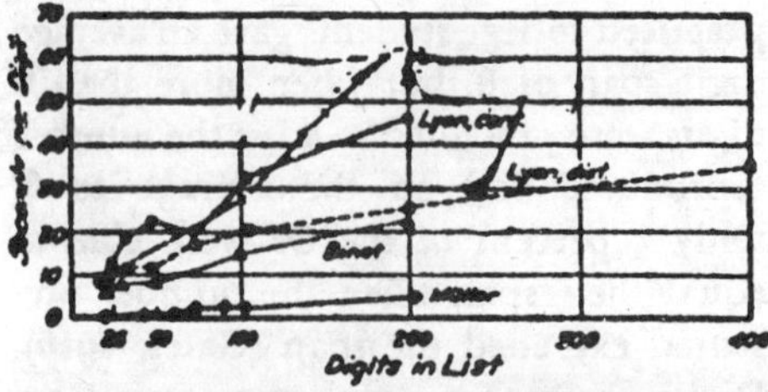

FIG. 23-4. The same as Figure 23-3, on a reduced scale, and covering the whole range of lengths of list. The horizontal scale is more reduced than the vertical with the result that the curves are steeper. This difference of scale needs to be allowed for in comparing the two figures.

The *O*s in these experiments were probably unusually expert in memorizing, only such *O*s having been induced to memorize very long lists. But the general dependence of difficulty on length of list, which shows in these series, would certainly be found with ordinary individuals. The least practiced *O* in this group is the one labeled "Lyon (1)." She was the most expert among 14 students of about twenty years of age selected by Lyon (1917) as presumably good memorizers, and the only one who stuck it out through the list of 200 digits which took her 1 hour 49 minutes to learn. Lyon himself, who was a practiced memorizer, made about the same record as this student in continuous study ("Lyon, cont."). With one reading per day ("Lyon, dist.") his time was considerably less and he was able to memorize a list of 400 digits, which may be more than one could master by continuous study because of fatigue, boredom or lapse of effort. The data taken from Binet (1894) and Müller (1911) were obtained from two "lightning calculators," Binet's subject being a professional, and Müller's a mathematician of remarkable facility with numbers and an extraordinary interest from childhood up in numerical relations. In all these experiments the number lists were presented visually, being laid before *O*, each list as a whole.

for each single reading. The only question is whether the *time-per-item* (or the number of readings) increases with the length of the list. Does more work have to be done on each item when the number of items is large? Such is the fact, as shown in Figures 23-3 and 23-4. Experiments with nonsense syllables, from Ebbinghaus down, have yielded the same general result—increase in learning time-per-item with increase in the number of items in the list, though there are large differences in the absolute times taken by different *O*s. Two practiced *O*s of Henmon (1917) averaged per syllable:

12 sec	when the list contained	10	syllables
20 sec	" " " "	20	"
29 sec	" " " "	30	"

The rate of increase of time-per-item varies in different series, but Thurstone (1930) shows that many series agree approximately with the statement that the time-per-item increases as the square root of the number of items (beyond the memory span).

With *meaningful material*, as prose or poetry, exceptions are encountered in which a long passage is learned in as few readings as a shorter one; but on the whole it is safe to say that the same rule holds here as in the learning of lists of items. The following data are extracted from Lyon (1917) who memorized prose passages, giving them one reading a day:

No. words in passage	*Total time*	*Time per 100 words*
100	9 min.	9 min.
200	24	12
500	65	13
1000	165	16.5
2000	350	17.5
5000	1625	32.5
10000	4200	42
15000	5475	36.5

If we ask why more time-per-item must be devoted to a longer list, the answer is probably to be found in some sort of interference or confusion among the several items; the longer the list, the more items there are to get mixed up, and the longer it takes to get them straightened out. But this common-sense statement is merely preliminary to a search for more fundamental factors. So let us turn directly to a study of the memorizing process.

THE MEMORIZING PROCESS

The most incisive question to be answered by memory experiments is: How? How is the material memorized? An adequate answer would provide both a scientific understanding and a basis for practical rules of efficiency in certain important kinds of learning.

There are several ways of experimenting on this problem. The most obvious way is by introspection. *O* should be able to tell us something of his procedure. We cannot expect introspection to go to the bottom of the dynamic process, yet what it reveals is sometimes important and not open to serious doubt. For example, the adjacent syllables *viz hus* remind *O* of "vicious" and are quickly learned, but after a few repetitions this "association" drops out and the syllable pair stands up of itself. Such reports are common in memory experiments (Reed, 1918; O'Brien, 1921).

For an objective attack on the problem *E* can vary the conditions for learning or for recall. For example, he attempts to prevent the use of "associations" by speeding up the presentation rate to two or three syllables per second. *O* now has no time to find any associations beyond the most obvious ones. Memorizing is somewhat disturbed by the rapid rate; *O* feels under strain and requires more trials to learn but not always more total time. His learning is not completely reduced to the so-called mechanical level (Ogden, 1903; Gamble, 1909, 1916).

G. E. Müller (1911) made a thorough study of the spontaneous associations or aids used by memorizers for facilitating their work. He utilized both introspective reports and a variety of ingenious objective methods. Here are some of the classes of aids found in use:

1. *Familiar items or sequences.* If one nonsense syllable in a list suggests a familiar word, it is quickly learned and stands out as a landmark in the list. If a sequence of digits makes a well-known

date, like 1492, that part of the digit list is a landmark.

2. *Relations and patterns* found in a list transform it from a shapeless mass into something more distinctive. The pattern may be visual, like the contour of the adjacent syllables, *dag yob;* or auditory, like the rhyme of the number groups, 507 and 811. In any list of digits there are sure to be arithmetical relations which catch the eye of an *O* who is interested in numbers and who knows a lot of squares and cubes and prime numbers; he may instantly see 169,324 as a pair of squares and so have something definite to remember.

3. *Interpolated links.* The memorizer is on the alert for any connection that he can impose on the disconnected items given him to learn. He may insert *tall* as a link between *cedar* and *captain,* or *slow* as a link between *simmer* and *tarry.* It is difficult for *E* to put together a list of unrelated words that *O* cannot tie together in some such way.

Such aids in memorizing are naturally regarded with much favor by *O,* but *E* would like to be rid of them. They make the learning task less uniform and introduce variability and unreliability into the quantitative results. Besides, *E* wants to study the formation of new associations, not *O*'s clever utilization of old ones.

Different meanings of association. This word, much used in memory studies, has at least three meanings. When *O* speaks of finding a helpful association in a list of syllables, he is referring to some *meaningful* connection. But the psychological definition of association is much broader; it covers *all* effective connections between one item and another or between stimulus and response. There are however two psychological meanings to be kept apart:

1. *The factual meaning.* Two objects are said to be associated if one reminds you of the other. No theory is involved. If we find as a matter of fact that item A given as a stimulus elicits B as a response, we can say that an association exists between A and B.

2. *The explanatory concept.* The strict association theory regards the A-B connection as something ultimate, not dependent on any perceived relation between A and B, or upon any integral whole embracing A and B. Other theories regard the perceived relation or integral whole as primary and the association as secondary. Some of the experimental results may throw light on this difficult question. Meanwhile we shall try to speak of associations in the purely factual sense.

Serial associations, direct and remote. When a list has been learned to the point of being recited straight through in correct order, what associations have been formed? A chain of direct connections between each item and the next would do the work. But when the list has been only partially learned, the items are recalled with some omissions and displacements of order. Must we not then admit the presence of associations between nonadjacent items? From the (explanatory) law of association by contiguity we could predict some (factual) associations between nonadjacent items, but they should be weaker the less close the contiguity, i.e., the farther apart the items in the list. Ebbinghaus (1885) put this prediction to the test by an ingenious modification of the saving method. His experiment was divided into two-day units. For each such unit he drew from his stock six sets of 16 nonsense syllables, and from each set he prepared two lists of the same syllables in different orders. One of these lists, called the original list, was learned on the first day, and the other, a derived or rearranged list, was learned on the second day so as to show how much saving would result from the previous learning of the same syllables in a different order. The second day's lists were derived from the originals by skipping alternate syllables, by skipping twos, threes, etc., or by reversing the order of the original list. Denote by the numbers 1–16 the syllables in their original order; then the arrangement of certain derived lists was as follows:

Skipping ones:	1	3	5	7	9	11	13	15	2	4	6	8	10	12	14	16
Skipping twos:	1	4	7	10	13	16	2	5	8	11	14	3	6	9	12	15
Skipping threes:	1	5	9	13	2	6	10	14	3	7	11	15	4	8	12	16
Reversed	16	15	14	13	12	11	10	9	8	7	6	5	4	3	2	1

On one day, then, Ebbinghaus learned six original lists and the next day he learned six derived lists. To memorize six original lists required about 21 minutes of concentrated effort. The experiment comprised 17 two-day units for each type of derived list, so that each entry in the following table is the average obtained from $17 \times 6 = 102$ lists of 16 syllables each, memorized first in the original and next day in the derived order, all the work being done by a single *O* who was in excellent practice. (For the reversed order, the number of lists was only 60.) The times are given in seconds per unit of six lists.

	Time for learning original lists	*Time for learning derived lists*	*Time saved in learning derived lists*	*PE of time saved*	*Saving in percent*
Relearning original lists	1266	844	422	15	33.3
Skipping ones	1275	1138	137	16	10.8
Skipping twos	1260	1171	89	18	7.0
Skipping threes	1260	1186	73	13	5.8
Reversed	1249	1094	155	15	12.4
Scrambled lists	1261	1255	6	13	0.5

As indicated by the values of PE (Probable Error), the time saved in learning a systematically derived list is reliably greater than in learning a scrambled list, and reliably less than in relearning the original list. The differences between the several derived lists, in time saved, are not reliably different, though the indication is that the saving diminishes in proportion as more syllables are skipped.

It may seem incredible that there was no saving in learning the scrambled lists. One would expect that mere familiarity with the individual syllables of the original list would facilitate their learning in any order whatever. So it would, undoubtedly, with an *O* just making the acquaintance of nonsense syllables. But we must remember that Ebbinghaus had first prepared and written down his 2,300 nonsense syllables, and that he had used the same syllables repeatedly in the course of his protracted experiments.

These results were taken to mean that there are formed during the original learning of a list of syllables not only the direct serial associations which link each item to its predecessor, but also remote associations linking non-adjacent items, and backward associations; the backward associations being weaker than the forward, and the remote weaker th n the direct. Ebbinghaus summarized his results in these words (as translated by Ruger & Bussenius, 1913):

> With repetition of the syllable series not only are the individual terms associated with their immediate sequents but connections are also established between each term and several of those which follow it. . . . The strength of these connections decreases with the number of the intervening (syllables). . . . Certain connections of the members are . . . actually formed in a reverse as well as in a forward direction. . . . The strength . . . was however considerably less for the reverse connections than for the forward ones.

In spite of the remarkable excellence of this pioneer study, the conclusions of Ebbinghaus go beyond his evidence. He says that "connections are established between *each term* and several of those which follow it." But his results can be explained just as well by supposing that *some* terms, not all, are thus connected. In the derived list obtained by "skipping ones" there would be some saving if only the following remote associations had been formed in learning the original list: 1–3, 5–7, 9–11, 13–15; the other alternate terms need not be associated at all. The method used was global; it measured the saving for the list as a whole and not for the separate parts.

The effect of grouping. Every memorizer from Ebbinghaus down who has had to read or recite a list of nonsense syllables at a rapid rate has inevitably done it in rhythm or at least introduced some accents and pauses. One of the earliest investigations, that of Müller & Schumann (1894), raised the question whether this grouping played any part in the formation of associations. If you read a list of syllables rhythmically, with accents and short pauses as follows,

zut' pam / bip' seg / ron' yad / lus' vob / kij' wof,

each "foot" becomes a sort of unit. If these units play a part in the learning process, we can predict:

1. Stronger associations between the items within a foot than between adjacent items in different feet.
2. Associations between successive feet, each foot being taken as a whole, or between the accented syllables in successive feet.

Müller & Schumann verified these predictions by ingenious modifications of the device of derived lists (more fully described in the first edition of this book, pp. 28–30).

The same results were obtained in a later study of Müller & Pilzecker (1900) by a simpler method. *O* first learned a list of 12 syllables to the point of one correct recitation. After a short pause he was given various single syllables from the list as stimuli with instructions to respond in each case by the first syllable that suggested itself (method of free association, p. 46). If the stimulus was the first member of a foot, *O* was most apt to respond with the second member. But if the second member of a foot was the stimulus, the commonest response was the first member of the same foot, i.e., the preceding rather than the following syllable in the list. The reaction times were consistent with these trends, being shorter for within-foot than for between-foot associations.

When paired associates are being memorized, each pair is necessarily taken as a unit, since *O* is trying to say the second member in response to the presentation of the first member. But with the list of pairs given repeatedly in the same order, there is plenty of "contiguity" between the second member of any pair and the first member of the following pair. If we predict, however, that a test using the second member of a pair as stimulus will frequently elicit the first member of the following pair as response, our prediction will not be verified in the least (Woodworth, 1915a; Reed, 1918; Huang, 1944). The same negative result was clearly shown in extensive experiments by Thorndike (1931, 1932a). He investigated the effects of various types of groupings on the direction of associations. One example makes a dependable lecture demonstration. The class is told to remember what the lecturer is about to say. Then he says,

"John Smith is a psychologist. Henry Jones is an astronomer. Walter Hodge is a biologist."

If the class is now asked to name the psychologist, the majority call out, "John Smith," although this association is both backward and remote, compared to the direct forward one, "Henry Jones." Of course, nobody is greatly surprised at this result, for the sentence structure makes the name and profession belong together. Thorndike calls the principle *belongingness* and points out that it often overrides sheer contiguity as a determiner of association. Contiguity is probably a necessary but not a sufficient condition for the establishment of an association.

Position associations. It is clear that *O* could master a list of items and recite it in perfect order, without learning any sequences at all, if only he succeeded in associating each item firmly with its position in the list. He might number the presented items and associate each item with its number. He might imagine a horizontal row of items, or two rows, one for the first half of the list and another for the last half, and associate each item with its place in the diagram. He might impose a rhythmical pattern on the list, each item having its place in the pattern. At the very least he would probably associate the first item in the list with the initial position and the last item with the final position. He would probably go further than that in a few trials and associate the first few items with their exact positions, and perhaps the last few as well, though we might expect him to work forward from the beginning more than backward from the end. The remaining items would be associated, rather vaguely at first, with the middle of the list. Without making the improbable assumption that *O* would actually learn a list without learning any of the sequences in it, we may at least regard position associations as a likely factor in the learning, and make certain predictions. We can predict that mastery of the list will advance from both ends toward the middle, but more rapidly from the beginning than from the end, so that the part mastered most slowly will not be the exact middle of the list but somewhat nearer the end. In short we can come close to predicting such curves as those of Figure 23-5, which have been familiar since a study of Ebbinghaus in 1902.

Relative difficulty of the beginning, middle and end of a list. Other factors besides position associations have been suggested in explanation of the curves of Figure 23-5. An explanation offered by Lepley (1934), elaborated by Hull (1935), and revised by Hull and his collaborators (1940), is based on condition-

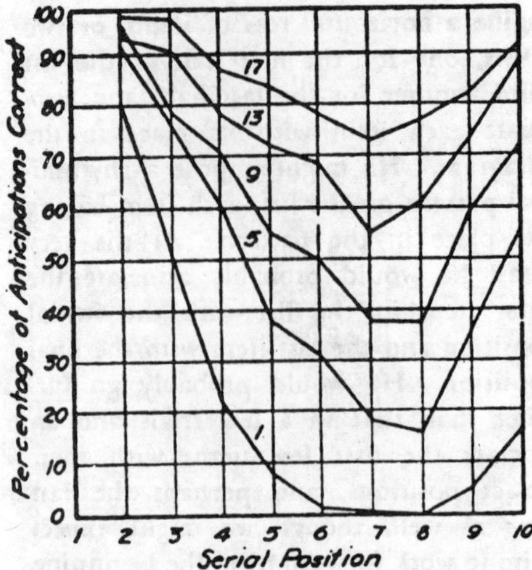

Fig. 23-5. (Robinson & Brown, 1926.) Effect of serial position in memorizing a list of 10 three-place numbers. There were eight lists and 11 *Os*, and each point on the curves gives the percent of successes in the 88 attempts to "anticipate" a number by reciting it before it was shown. The numbers were shown at the rate of one three-place number every 2 sec. The curve marked "1" shows the result after the first presentation of the list, the curve marked "5" shows the successes after 5 presentations, etc. Each three-place number had to be completely reproduced in order to count as a successful anticipation: no partial credits were allowed. By following the curves upward from "1" to "17" one gets an impression of the gradual mastery of the list from both ends inward. The first item in the list was always given as a cue so that the results furnish no score for this position. Other experiments indicate that it would score nearly 100 percent from the first trial.

ing principles. The remote forward associations of Ebbinghaus are assumed, along with opposing inhibitory tendencies akin to Pavlov's "inhibition of delay" (p. 566). This inhibition holds back the delayed CR till the regular time for reinforcement is at hand, and similar inhibitions generated in the process of learning a list are supposed to hold back the saying of a syllable in spite of the remote forward associations. Now if each item in a list has a positive tendency to call out all the later items, and if this positive tendency is balanced by an inhibitory one, the total amount of inhibition should increase from the beginning to the middle of the list and then decrease toward the end.

The greater difficulty of the middle of the list shows up at all stages of learning (Fig. 23-5), and is found in both massed and spaced practice (p. 786) although it is less pronounced in spaced practice (Patten, 1938; Hovland, 1938). This latter finding is consistent with the inhibition theory, since spaced trials allow time for the inhibition to dissipate. However, the beneficial effect of spacing is not confined to the middle of a serial list. McCrary & Hunter (1953) replotted many of the old serial-position curves in terms of *percentages* of total errors by position in the list and found that all the curves then had essentially the same shape. Further, they found the curves very similar for the *relative* distribution of errors along the list in easy and hard serial learning tasks (Fig. 23-6) and with fast *versus* slow learners. It is hard to see how a theory which depends on a single principle like inhibition of delay can explain the similar form of all these curves. McCrary & Hunter concluded that some multiple-factor theory is needed to handle the bow-shaped curve of the serial-position effect.

Generalization and discrimination in memorizing. Another interconnection of the memory and conditioning experiments is by way of Pavlov's *generalization* (which means nondifferentiation, p. 577). As E. J. Gibson pointed out (1940, 1942), "A major necessity of verbal learning is the establishment of *discrimination* among the items to be

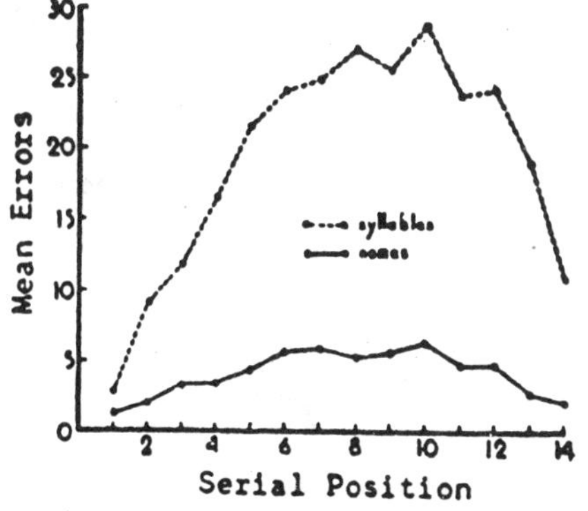

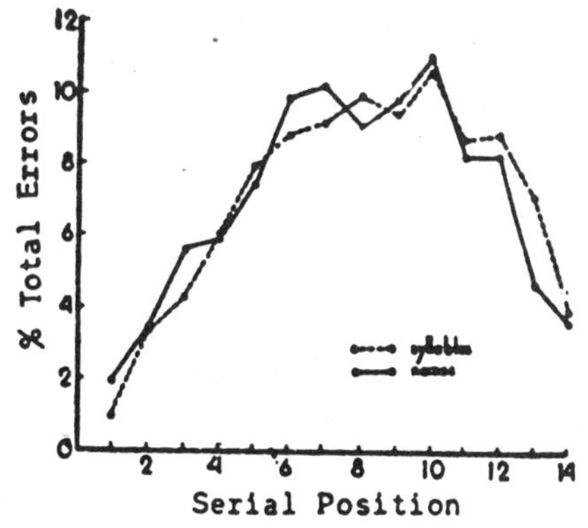

FIG. 23-6. (McCrary & Hunter, 1953.) Serial position effects in lists of 14 nonsense syllables and in (easier) lists of 14 familiar names. The left figure, plotted in terms of the absolute numbers of errors, seems to show a much more marked piling up of errors in the middle of the more difficult list (quite in accordance with the inhibition theory). But when the errors in each serial position are expressed as percentages of the total number of errors for the whole list, the two curves appear identical. (Note that these curves, plotted in errors, are upside down in relation to those of Figure 23-5, which are plotted in terms of correct responses.)

learned," or, "Each item must become unique, discriminable from the others, in order that correct linkages can be formed." At the beginning of the learning process there is much generalization of the nonsense syllables or other strange items. The more similar they are, the more they "generalize" with each other, and the more work has to be done on them to make them unique and capable of definite associations. In her 1942 experiment, this author showed good grounds for relating verbal learning to Pavlov's findings. It was an experiment with paired associates, the stimuli being nonsense figures (a few samples are shown on p. 755 in connection with another experiment of the same author), each figure being paired with a nonsense syllable. In the standard or low-generalization list, the 12 stimulus figures were very dissimilar, but in the high-generalization lists there were only four of the standard figures, the others being variants of these standards. As she predicted, the high-generalization lists were harder to learn than the standard list; they required fully twice as many trials. Early in the learning process, similar figures often got the same response (stimulus generalization), but as the erroneous responses were not reinforced they were eventually extinguished.

The reader may reasonably object that the cards were stacked in favor of the generalization theory by the use of similar stimulus figures. How could the theory apply to ordinary lists of nonsense syllables, so constructed that every item is as different as possible from the others? For one thing, their very lack of meaning is a point of similarity: BAP seems more like ZOT than either is like PIN or TUB. Further, the syllables are similar in the surrounding circumstances; they are presented on the same drum, in the same room, and while *O* is in a uniform posture. The items in the middle of a list are similar in location as compared with those at either end of the list. All these common factors blend the whole list of items, or most of it, into one confused mass in the early stages of learning. But as discrimination among the items is achieved, these same factors tie the list together and contribute to a smooth and unified performance.

Learning, as we see it in the young adults who are the usual subjects in memory experiments, is a very active and varied process—far from a passive reception of stimuli and letting their sequence leave an impression. Yet the basic process of forming a trace and establishing an association may well be "mechanical" and below the level of direct intelligent control. What the intelligent learner can do about it is perhaps to provide a matrix of groupings, meanings, and integrated wholes favorable for the physiological process of establishing traces and connections. Additional light on the higher-level controls may be gained from the learning of visual and other "forms."

As to verbal learning, the first edition of this text considered a number of experiments roughly parallel to those we have discussed, and many more will be found in Hovland (1951) and in McGeoch & Irion (1952). We shall also get further light on the memorizing process from our later chapters on Transfer and Interference and on Economy in Learning and Performance.

The learning of visual forms. It would be a mistake to base our theory of human memory entirely on experiments with verbal material. Much everyday learning is not verbal, as in the obvious case of the young child who recognizes many persons and things before he begins to talk. Shapes and color patterns are learned by some process that is visual rather than verbal.

The most convenient method for experiments here is that of recognition, but a method of reproduction may serve better to bring out the early stages of learning. For an introductory experiment, let the reader examine one of the figures shown here and then close the book and reproduce it with pencil on paper. The differences between the original and the reproduction are due

FIG. 23-7. Three of the many types of figures used in experiments on the learning and retention of visual forms.

partly to incomplete perception, partly to forgetting during the short interval, and partly to the exigencies of drawing. To trace the process of learning a figure, glance at it repeatedly and draw after each glance. To trace the process of forgetting, delay the reproduction for an hour, a day, or a week.

The difficulty of the task can be increased by the use of more complex figures (Fig. 23-8) or by the use of a tachistoscope (p. 92) for very brief exposures.

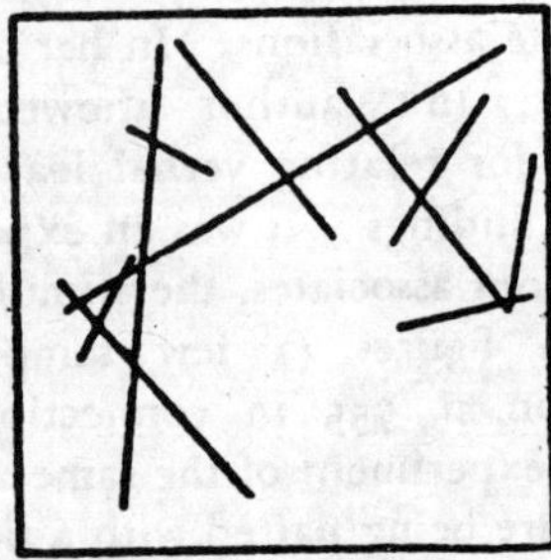

FIG. 23-8. Type of nonsense figure used by Piéron (1920) in experiments on learning and retention. Such a figure was more difficult to learn than a 10-digit list of numbers; it took as long to learn as a 20-digit list. After each 5-second exposure the reproduction was scored for accuracy. The learning curve, and also the curve of forgetting, had approximately the same form with this material as with lists of numbers.

Is the learning of a figure a "photographic" process? We speak of "sense impressions" and of "receiving an impression" of an object, and are likely to conceive the receptive process as analogous to photography—as if in looking at an object we took a picture of it. The memory image would be a revival of this picture. When first attempting to memorize a figure so as to reproduce it from memory, *O* may attempt to establish a visual image of it, but he soon finds that he cannot depend on his image for accurate reproductions. He consequently resorts to a more active type of memorizing in which he analyzes the presented figure (Piéron, 1920).

Exploring the presented figure. Being told that he is to reproduce a figure from memory, *O* is apt to examine it closely for characteristics that he can remember. Two main lines of attack have been described and differently named by different experimenters. Kuhlmann (1906) distinguished a direct and an indirect attack; the direct attack consisted in a critical study of the whole figure, with some details noted and often named; the indirect attack consisted in asking "What is it like?" We might call them (1) *figural analysis* and (2) *reification.* Bartlett (1932) found that a familiar figure was simply named, but an unfamiliar one was regarded either as somewhat like a known object or else as a pattern with a definable plan; in either case there is an "effort after meaning." Granit (1921), too, distinguished two modes of grasping nonsense figures: schematizing the figure, and "association by similarity." Young children used the latter mode almost exclusively; for them a figure must be a "picture of something" and the only question was, "a picture of what?" They found or fancied some resemblance to a thing. The adults were more geometrical; they noted symmetry, rhythm, the repetition of identical parts.

Schema with correction. A nonsense figure, by definition, does not closely resemble any familiar thing nor does it conform exactly to any simple geometric form. If it is likened to a thing, note must be taken also of the way in which it differs from the thing. If it is seen as a geometric form, due account must be taken also of its idiosyncrasy. In either case the process amounts to schematization plus correction. The new = the old with a correction. Such is apparently the general line of attack in assimilating new experience. This type of learning process has been observed by several experimenters who have worked with nonsense figures. Kuhlmann (1906) reported it; the best schema which his *O*s could find for a given figure required some correction. Thus a certain figure was seen as "a square with a nick on the right side." Piéron's *O*s took some of the long lines (see Fig. 23-8) as a frame into which the shorter lines were fitted, but sometimes the schema adopted turned out to be too simple to allow for all the details; the schema then had to be modified. A figure which conforms exactly to a known geometric form or to the outline of a familiar thing is, of course, easy to learn; but so is a figure which fails to conform in an easily definable way, i.e., a figure in which the necessary correction is easy.

Stages in the learning of a figure. An unfamiliar figure becomes known by a process which takes time. Does it become known first in parts which are then combined to make a whole, or is it first known as a whole in which parts are found later? These *a priori* alternatives were set up without due consideration of the reactive character of perception. The unfamiliar figure presents a problem to be solved, and if it is at all difficult we may expect stages of questioning, of trying out and rejecting false leads, and of final satisfaction with some percept. The trial-and-error nature of the process stands out clearly in the pastime of finding the "hidden picture" (see Fig. 23-9).

Fig. 23-9. (Street, 1931.) Type of hidden picture used by Leeper (1935). Some of the figures were easy and some quite difficult. Each figure was first exposed for 20–180 seconds, according to its difficulty, with instructions to identify it as soon as possible. The series was shown a second time with explanation of each. Some weeks later each figure was exposed for only half a second and was practically always (in 97 percent of 930 cases) recognized if it had been "correctly" perceived. The typical process of finding the hidden object "was that the figure would change as an entirety from one pattern to another . . . one unification might appear which was not very satisfactory . . . the figure would next transform itself . . . until finally, perhaps, the correct figure was seen. It is interesting that once an organization had been achieved, however, even when it was considered by a subject as being clearly incorrect, it was found hard to exclude that organization and see something else."

Stages in the process of learning a figure have been studied by the method of repeated exposures. Judd & Cowling (1907) presented a fairly difficult figure in 10-second exposures, with reproduction after each exposure. Some of the *O*s proceeded from part to whole and others from whole to part. Some worked methodically from left to right, first making sure of a few segments and in later exposures adding new segments. Others first got the general outline and then concentrated on parts that were still vague. This latter method seemed at least as efficient as the former.

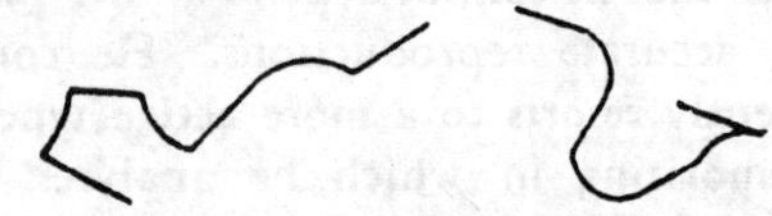

Fig. 23-10. Nonsense figures used by Judd & Cowling (1907).

Fehrer (1935) traced the course of learning from *O*'s reproductions of a figure after successive very brief exposures. Instead of any stereotyped order of events there was a great variety of actual processes. The cases were classified as follows:

Increasing complexity	32 percent
Decreasing complexity	27
Both by turns	25
No change in complexity	16
	100

In the cases of "no change in complexity" the correct number of parts was present even in the first reproduction but some error remained to be corrected. The most general formula for the course of learning a figure, according to Fehrer, distinguishes three stages:

1. An initial state of inaccuracy and instability.
2. A premature, incorrect stabilization.
3. A gradual or sudden elimination of the stable error.

We might say: a questioning stage, a false answer which tends to persist but is finally eradicated and replaced by one that gives satisfaction to the learner.

So we see that *O* does much more than sitting passively and letting the form "impress itself on his memory." He is making an active attempt to organize the material in a satisfactory fashion. The process seems too complex and effortful to be described as an automatic tendency toward equilibrium and "good figure." We shall come back to the memory for forms in connection with the Gestalt and other theories of forgetting (pp. 773-776).

Memory for stories and events. When you read a story or witness a series of happenings, you are learning, as is proved by later remembering, but your learning is more like the learning of a figure than like the learning of a list of nonsense syllables. You have more latitude in making sense out of the material in conformity with your own predilections. Bartlett (1932) was severely critical of the ordinary memory experiments because of their lack of realism in relation to the memory of everyday life. He undertook to make memory experiments more realistic by the use of materials that had some intrinsic interest for the learner. He used figures, pictures, stories, and discussions. He wished to see how *O* would mold and assimilate the material. In one of his stories two young Indians out on the water are met by a war party in canoes who invite them to participate in a raid. One begs off, the other goes and in the fighting is wounded. Brought back home he lives through the night but dies at sunrise. This rather definite story form was readily grasped and well retained, while details dropped out or were changed. The original story made some mention of ghosts, an incidental item as it seemed to the English students who served as *O*s in the experiment. Rightly understood, the story centers around the ghosts and has quite a different plot or meaning from the common-sense outline just given. The true plot was not perceived, and the ghosts tended to drop out of the story. Reading the story *O* *reacts* in his own way, forms his own conception. In reproducing the story he omits, modifies or adds details and so improves the consistency of his story. Usually, however, some striking details remain even if they are not well fitted into the general scheme.

It is often difficult to decide how much of the error in the memory of an event is to be blamed on retention and recall, and how much of it occurred in the original perception. One can easily show (in a simple "testimony" experiment) that people are likely to see things as they expect them to be. For example, if a lecturer usually carries a black brief case to class but one day substitutes a brown one, he can take some demonstration materials out of his brief case after warning the class to watch him carefully, and still most of his students are ready to swear that the brief case was black. A substantial number of more complicated experiments of this general type have been described (Crosland, 1921; Hausen, 1933; Lewis, 1933; Lipmann, 1933). This inaccuracy of observation, especially when the attention is deliberately attracted to the wrong thing, is one of the secrets of the stage magician's success. The disagreement among eyewitnesses of an event is a familiar problem in the courtroom.

But we cannot blame all errors in memory on poor initial impression; the errors often get worse as time goes on. There may be loss of details during retention, but when O tries to reproduce the material, he usually still tells a consistent story. If an item is missing or a bit vague, he fills it in consistently with the whole story as he sees it. We shall have more to say of this in a later section (pp. 774–775), but here we may mention the wartime experiments of Allport & Postman (1947). They deliberately started rumors, and then watched the changes as the rumors spread. Of course, the experiment was complicated in that each person in the chain introduced his own errors of perception and recall, which gave an opportunity for the story to build up rather freely. Allport & Postman stressed the fact that the changes were consistent with the local fears and needs of the storytellers, and this is undoubtedly true of less dramatic studies in memory.

RECALL

In order of time, recall and recognition come after retention, but there is some sense in studying them first because they are used as indications of retention. We can make our study brief for the reason that less is known about these two processes than about the process of learning. The learning process is perhaps more amenable to experimental control. However, there is a modicum of scattered information on recall. Some relevant findings are given under the head of Retroactive Inhibition (p. 761) and in the chapters on Association and Thinking.

In using the term *recall* so broadly as to cover the whole range of activities that are reactivated after being learned, we are not adhering closely to everyday usage. The word *reproduction* would be more pat sometimes and it is often preferred today for the objectively observable kinds of recall (though psychologists used to speak freely of "reproduced ideas").

Under the head of recall, then, may be included all cases in which previously learned reactions are made, and there is a great variety of such cases.

1. Recall of lists, items, facts, material of any sort which has previously been learned and is now intentionally remembered.
2. Execution of any learned act.
3. The calling up of sensory images.
4. Reverie or "free association," without any intention of recalling—"one idea calls up another."
5. Controlled association such as occurs in adding, reading, or conversation. Here the intention is directed toward some other result than the mere recall. In adding, the intention is to find the sum of this column of figures; in reading, to get the meaning of this news item; but the process consists largely in the recall of number combinations and word meanings.
6. Thinking, as in problem solution and the mastery of novel situations. Recall furnishes raw material for thought.

Direct and indirect recall. By "direct" is here meant not necessarily quick, but free from detours and intermediaries. Indirect recall is also called "mediate." Items A and B have been associated, as in a paired-associates experiment, and A is later given as a stimulus with instructions to respond by saying the paired item and then to report the process intervening between stimulus and response, so far as it can be caught by introspection. Sometimes there is nothing to report, but sometimes words, images, thoughts, feelings intervene between stimulus and response; and sometimes these intermediaries obviously lead to the response (p. 65).

Michotte & Portych (1914) presented pairs of related words, as "mathematics—algebra," "epic—hero," "lion—king." A list of 12 pairs was exposed just once, each pair being shown for 4.5 seconds. In the recall test, which came immediately, after a day, or after a week, the first words of the pairs were the stimuli. With the relatively meager amount of learning, direct recall was infrequent: in the immediate test about 1/8 of the correct recalls were reported as being direct; in the later tests, when memory had become indistinct, the instances of direct recall were still fewer.

Among the various intermediaries reported, two classes were of special interest. There was an obviously useful sort, when a meaningful relation, noticed in learning a pair, came up in recalling the correct response word. The recall here followed the same route as had been used in learning the pair. The route did not always lead to the goal; the intermediary might be too general to yield the exact word required. When *O* was stuck, another kind of intermediary often appeared: images and ideas were suggested by the stimulus word though not previously used in learning the pair. Here we see *O* engaged in *searching* for the response word and endeavoring to get some lead from the stimulus word—just as, in trying to recall a name, we look the person over and call up the circumstances in which we met him.

Searching for names is a recall process well deserving of study. William James (1890, I, 251) gave a vivid introspective description:

Suppose we try to recall a forgotten name. The state of our consciousness is peculiar. There is a gap therein, but no mere gap. It is a gap that is intensely active. A sort of wraith of the name is in it, beckoning us in a given direction, making us at moments tingle with a sense of our closeness, and then letting us sink back without the longed-for term. If wrong names are proposed to us, this singularly definite gap acts immediately so as to negate them. They do not fit into its mould. And the gap of one word does not feel like the gap of another. . . . The rhythm of a lost word may be there without a sound to clothe it; or the evanescent sense of something which is the initial vowel or consonant may mock us fitfully, without growing more distinct.

The false names that come up during such a search afford some objective clues to the nature of the process of recall. These false names, especially the first one to come up, show similarity of one kind or another to the true name. Wenzl (1932, 1936) has collected cases and finds the similarity to reside sometimes in the initial sound, sometimes in the rhythm of the whole name (number of syllables, accent), and sometimes in the atmosphere of the name (elegant, aristocratic, commonplace, gloomy, foreign). Wenzl suggests a law of recall: the process of recalling a name starts with general characteristics of the name and advances toward the specific. Woodworth from another collection of cases reaches a similar conclusion. A few examples will show various ways in which the name first recalled resembles the name sought.

Name first recalled	*Correct name*
Rogers	Richards
Schniermann	Spranger
Picquard	Lapicque
Casenaugh	Ranelagh
Walliston	Warburton
Stevens	Stowell
Cheshire	Cheddar
Ferguson	Gallagher
Hirschberg	Fishberg
Cobb	Todd

Name first recalled	*Correct name*
corduroy	gabardine
aspasia	azalea
sycamore	sassafras
Philena	Ophelia
Council Bluffs	Cedar Rapids

You get the right *kind* of name—right in some respect—before you get the right name. Often, of course, the right name comes directly.

Speed of recall. Recall time, a form of reaction time, is the interval between the recalling stimulus and the motor response (usually verbal). It can be measured in a paired-associates experiment, roughly by a stopwatch and more accurately by a chronoscope with a voice key to pick up *O*'s reaction (p. 12). It is variable, the promptest recalls taking about half a second and the slow ones reaching several seconds or an indefinite time. The speed of recall depends greatly on *recency*. In the experiment of Michotte & Portych (1914) the average time for correct responses was as follows:

Immediately after learning	1.5 sec
One day after learning	2.4
One week later	3.0

Müller & Pilzecker (1900) used nonsense syllables. One list was read over many times but not tested for 24 hours, while another list, read only a few times, was tested immediately. The older, better learned lesson gave fully as many correct recalls but they were slow in comparison with the responses from the recent lesson. Old-established responses, unless recently reviewed, come slowly; newly formed associations are quick. Reading and conversation depend for their ease on quick-acting temporary associations which are useful in the given context.

Condition of readiness. A name is "on the tip of your tongue," yet it does not emerge—it is for the moment below the "threshold of recall." It is partially aroused, subexcited, as is shown by the peculiar feeling of nearness and by the fact that a little extra push in the right direction will give complete recall. If A and B have been associated, and some time later A is presented without recalling B, it nevertheless makes B easy to recall or relearn. It puts B into a condition of readiness, the reality of which has been shown in a variety of experiments (Ebbinghaus, 1885; Müller & Schumann, 1894; Müller & Pilzecker, 1900; Ohms, 1910; H. W. Meyer, 1914). We will cite only the experiment of Ohms. Nonsense words were studied and later tested by paired associates. When a word failed of recall, it was spoken to *O* through a poor telephone, or visually exposed for only a small fraction of a second. The auditory or visual presentation was not good enough to enable *O* to understand nonsense words, but he could often understand one when the stimulus for its recall had just been given. If a name is "on the tip of your tongue" and someone pronounces it indistinctly to you, that extra push may be enough to bring the name up above the threshold of recall. The response is in such a condition of readiness that it can be evoked by an otherwise inadequate stimulus (cf. p. 694).

Memory images. An outstanding characteristic of modern experimental psychology is its emphasis on objective experiments. The field of memory is no exception to this rule. As we have just seen, this reliance on objectivity misses some aspects of the act of recalling. One such aspect is the presence of images.

For many people, recalling a person means seeing him "in the mind's eye." It is also possible to have auditory imagery, as in recalling the opening bars of a musical selection. Introspectively, these images seem to be a very important part of the whole process. For example, in the memory-span experiment (p. 696) *O* may visualize the row of digits, and read them off out loud from the visual image. But imagery is such a fluid thing that it is very difficult to study. A number of methods have been used.

1. *The questionary.* Galton (1880) asked many people to recall the breakfast table as it was that morning, and to report whether the objects were well defined, the brightness comparable to the original scene, the colors distinct and natural. This pioneer study brought out some surprises, such as the fact that scholars and scientists were often devoid of such images. Galton was followed by some later investigators who concluded that each individual was strong in a particular type of imagery, as visual, auditory, motor, etc. But a very careful study by Betts (1909), with an expanded form of Galton's questionary, got pretty convincing evidence that the individual who was good in one form of imagery tended to be good in other forms, too.

2. *Association method.* This involves tallying the number of association words (p. 46) that seem to belong to each sense modality. Or *O* is given 5 minutes for mentioning objects having characteristic colors, and another 5 minutes for objects having characteristic sounds.

3. *Analysis of style.* If an author uses many words that describe sounds or sounding objects, he is supposed to be an *audile.* Similarly, much description of scenes would make him a *visile.*

4. *Learning by eye or ear.* Does *O* learn more easily by reading or by listening? The memory span may be used as a test for imagery, on the assumption that a person who has strong visual imagery will recall digits presented visually better than those given orally. One of us (H.S.) has had fair success in laboratory classes with this method; the person who has a better visual than auditory span is apt to prefer reading to lectures. But now and then someone is a glaring exception, as the girl who had excellent visual imagery, but did better on the auditory span. The reason for this paradox turned out to be simple; she visualized the digits as she heard them, but the visually presented digits obliterated her images (digits were presented *seriatim* for both modalities).

5. *Method of distraction.* While *O* is learning a list, he is subjected to distractions in various sense modalities. In theory, a noise should bother people who are using auditory imagery, and holding the tongue between the teeth should distract those who use motor imagery (p. 84).

6. *Spelling.* The person with good visual imagery should have little trouble spelling words backwards. But according to Fernald (1912) visual images of the letters do not "stay put" well enough to be of much use.

7. *The letter square.* Much the same reasoning applies here. *O* learns a square of 9, 16, or 25 letters or digits, reading by rows. Then he is asked to recall them by columns.

8. *Description of a picture.* Visual imagery should permit the most complete descriptions, but the results showed that *O* could do very well in the test by naming the objects as he examined the picture and then remembering only the names (Fernald, 1912).

Angell (1910) and Fernald (1912) tried

out most of these objective tests for imagery and found that they had only low validity. They did not correlate well with *O*'s direct reports of his images, and the direct report was obviously the only sure criterion of the presence of images. Work continued on the topic for some years (F. C. Davis, 1932; Bowers, 1932) but has been inactive recently because of the lack of adequate experimental methods.

Eidetic images. Some individuals, after examining a picture and then being asked to project their image of it on a gray screen, behave as if they were still actually seeing the picture and can describe it in great detail. Such an "eidetic" image is sometimes regarded as a special kind of image, almost photographic. Jaensch (1920) was largely responsible for attracting attention to this phenomenon. It is fairly common in children but rare in adults. It may be related to personality traits. But we know little about the actual nature of the eidetic image, despite a large number of studies; good summaries will be found in Allport (1924) and Klüver (1926, 1928, 1932). At present we cannot tell how the eidetic child establishes his image or whether it is qualitatively different from the ordinary strong visual imagery of many people.

RECOGNITION

As the topic of recall can be broadened to cover association and imagery, so recognition can be made to include the perception of objects. An object is "recognized" as an individual thing or person; it is "perceived" as an object of a certain class. In both cases use is made of past experience, though there may be no conscious reference to the past.

The recognitive processes differ functionally from those of recall in that recognition starts with the object given whereas recall has to find the object. In recall, A is given as a stimulus and some other object, B, is recalled. In recognition, A is given and the same A is recognized. It would seem that recognition is the simpler process. If so, recognition is not to be explained in terms of recall.

Recall and recognition often go together. A fact is recalled and known to be a fact from one's past. It may be dated and located in one's past, more or less definitely, as when you recall a scene and know when and where you saw it. There is no such definite recognition when you recall a bit of the multiplication table. Unconscious plagiarism affords striking examples of recall without recognition.

Ease or difficulty of recognition. Often a face or a name which cannot be recalled is recognized promptly when presented. In a sense, then, recognition is easier than recall. After a list of words or other items has been presented, a recall test, by the method of retained members, gets back a certain number of items. If now all the items are presented, mixed with "new" ones, some of the old items that were not recalled are recognized. An experiment by a similar method was conducted by Achilles (1920) who, however, used different lists of items for the recall and recognition tests and avoided the objection that attempted recall, by placing items in "readiness," would give an undue advantage to the following recognition. A list of 25 items was placed before *O*, and he was allowed 50 seconds in which to study them. He was then asked at once to write down all the items he could recall, or else he was shown a list of 50 items including the 25 "old" ones mixed with 25 new ones and asked to write "Yes" or "No" before each item according as he judged it old or new. There were lists of nonsense syllables, of disconnected words, and of proverbs. The recall and recognition scores, the latter penalized for errors (p. 700), were as follows (averages from 96 *O*s):

	Percentile scores		
	Syllables	*Words*	*Proverbs*
Recall score	12	39	22
Recognition score	42	65	67

The recognition scores here greatly exceed the recall scores. But the advantage of recognition depends partly on the exact form of the tests. A recognition test may be made very difficult by using new items that closely resemble the old.

Recognition according to degree of similarity. In an experiment of Lehmann (1888–89) a gray color was produced by mixing white and black in equal proportions on the color wheel (180° of each). After thirty seconds either that same gray or one some degrees whiter was presented to be judged same or different. Results:

	Amount of difference between grays					
	60°	45°	35°	20°	12°	8°
Net recognition score	87%	90%	70%	63%	20%	17%

As the old and the new became very much alike discrimination failed and the recognition score approached zero.

In G. H. Seward's experiment (1928) 30 fancy papers of varied design and color were shown, with 2-second exposure for each and blank intervals of 4 seconds. When the series was finished, *O* occupied himself for 10 minutes with a vocabulary test and was then given the recognition test, which included 10 of the original fancy papers, 10 rather similar papers, 10 slightly similar, and 10 very different designs. As each specimen was shown, *O* judged whether it had been present in the original series and reacted positively or negatively by pressing one of two telegraph keys, so that his reaction time could be taken. He also rated the confidence of each judgment. Each *O*'s confidence ratings and reaction times were transmuted into a relative scale in which 100 represented his maximum quickness or confidence of response. There were 108 *O*s, students, and each column in the table summarizes 1,080 judgments. All the trends shown in the following table are statistically reliable.

Reading down the first column of figures we find that the response to an identical specimen is positive recognition in 71 percent of cases, negative in

	Stimuli			
	Identical	*Similar*	*Slightly Similar*	*Dissimilar*
Positive responses				
Frequency	71	54	27	8
Confidence	63	57	43	26
Quickness	51	46	38	38
Negative responses				
Frequency	29	46	73	92
Confidence	48	50	60	71
Quickness	37	36	46	56

29 percent. The positive recognitions have an average confidence of 63 (on the 0 to 100 scale) and an average quickness of 51 (on a similar scale). The negative response, nonrecognition of the identical stimulus, is less confident and slower.

As you go from left to right in the table, the positive response becomes less correct and the negative response more correct. Frequency, confidence, and quickness follow these changes in correctness, though without wholly keeping pace. If we compare the two sets of perfectly correct responses, positive to identical stimuli and negative to dissimilar stimuli, we see that the latter has the advantage on all counts. The "No" response to a wholly different stimulus, though negative in form, is definite and emphatic in meaning. The impression of newness or not-belonging is fully as distinct as the impression of familiarity.

These results could easily be rephrased in terms of "generalization" (p. 576). Would that change make them more scientific?

RETENTION

As we have said before, retention can be studied only indirectly; the difference between what *O* could do at the end of the learning period and what he can do on a test after the period of no practice gives us the amount retained. As a test for retention we may use any one of several different measures, as relearning, retained members, recognition, or reconstruction (p. 700). But each of these measures gives a different score. This was pointed out and illustrated in Chapter 18 (p. 533), but it might be well to clinch the point by describing the experiment of Luh (1922). He had his *O*s learn lists of nonsense syllables, and measured retention by various methods. The results are shown in Figure 23-11. Recognition is clearly the most sensitive measure of small amounts of retention, and relearning is quite good after the sharp initial drop. There are really two measures of direct recall: written reproduction, and number of syllables anticipated on the first relearning trial. It is

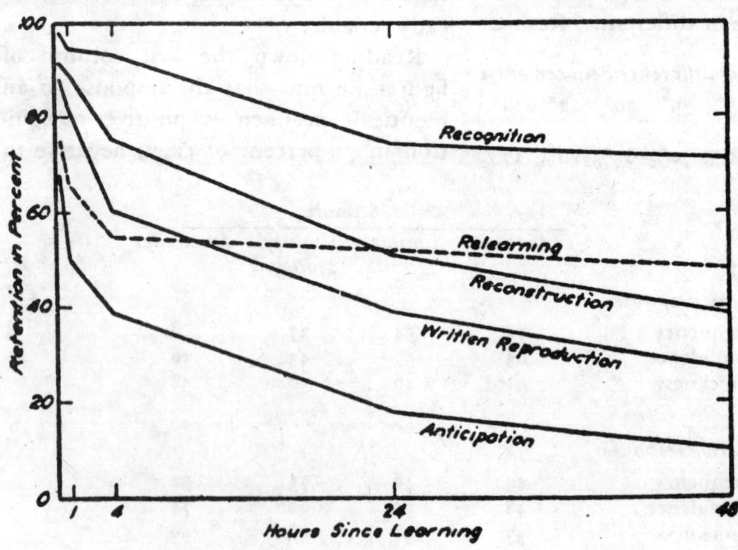

Fig. 23-11. (Luh, 1922.) Retention curves for nonsense syllables measured by five different methods. See text.

typical that recall gives low retention scores. But notice that all five curves have roughly the same form; this means that we can take any one of them as a description of the retention period, provided we are careful to specify our method of measuring retention when we describe an experiment. For suppose E_1 reported 70 percent retention after 2 days, while E_2 found only 10 percent after an equal interval; we might suppose E_2 had a group of morons for *O*s until we found that E_1 used recognition, while E_2 used anticipation as his test of retention.

The curve of forgetting. Among the various experiments included by Ebbinghaus in his pioneer work on memory (1885) the one most often cited is his quantitative study of the loss of retention with the lapse of time. Having before him several theories of the cause of forgetting, he thought none of them very good, and believed that the best program for an experimentalist was to leave the theories aside for the time being and build up a knowledge of the facts which any theory must explain. His specific problem took this form (translation by Ruger & Bussenius, 1913): "If syllable series of a definite kind are learned by heart and then left to themselves, how will the process of forgetting go on when left merely to the influence of time or the daily events of life which fill it?" His procedure was to learn lists of nonsense syllables, lay them aside for a certain interval, relearn them and note the saving in time or number of readings, due to the partial retention of the effects of the first learning. In the course of this investigation he learned over 1,200 lists each containing 13 nonsense syllables. A learning session lasted 18–20 min during which time he learned eight such lists. He took the first list and read it through and through at a steady rate of one syllable every ⅖ sec till it could be recited twice without hesitation and with a consciousness of being correct. After a pause of 15 sec another list was studied and so on till the eight lists had been learned. The total time to learn these eight lists was the original learning time for this unit of work. After a certain lapse of time this same set of lists was relearned to the same criterion. Even after a lapse of 31 days the relearning of a set of eight lists always showed some saving as compared with the original learning. If 1010 sec were required for the original learning of the eight lists, and 31 days later 803 sec were required to relearn them, the saving was 207 sec = 20.5 percent of the original time.

Learning efficiency may differ at different hours of the day and Ebbinghaus found that it did so in his case. It took him 12 percent longer to memorize a list at 6–8 p.m. than at 10–11 a.m. When therefore he wished to determine the loss of retention after 8–9 hours, the original learning came in the favorable time of the day and the relearning in the unfavorable. A deduction of 12 percent of the relearning time was therefore made before computing the saving.

Different lists were learned for each interval. It would not do at all to relearn the same lists after 8 hours, then after 24 hours, and again after 2 days. This procedure gives a practice curve, not a curve of forgetting, for every time the same list is relearned it is more strongly impressed. After several relearnings it can be retained without appreciable loss over a considerable period.

The results of Ebbinghaus are shown in Figures 23-12 and 23-13. There was

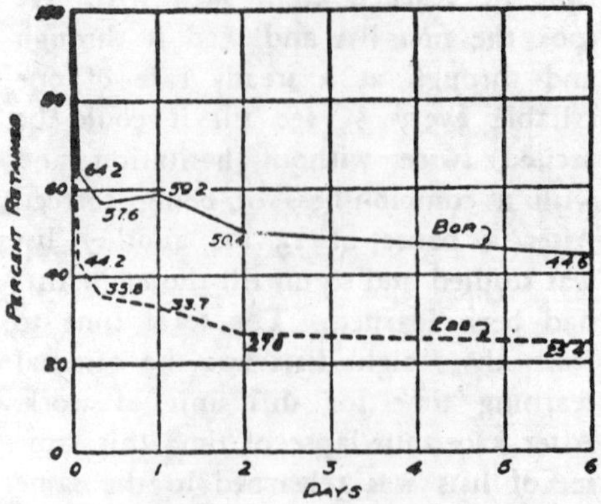

FIG. 23·12. (Data from Ebbinghaus, 1885 and Boreas, 1930.) Curve of retention of lists of nonsense syllables, as determined by the saving method. The Ebbinghaus curve is from one *O* about 40 years old, who learned and relearned over 1200 13-syllable lists. The Boreas curve gives the average for 20 students, each learning one 15-syllable list for each interval. Continuation of these curves is included in Figure 23·15.

The Ebbinghaus data are more fully given below.

Interval	*No. experiments*	*Range of saving %*	*Mean saving %*	PE_M
½ hr	12	45–64	58.2	1
1 "	16	34–54	44.2	1
8–9 "	12	28–48	35.8	1
24 "	26	15–46	33.7	1.2
2 days	26	12–46	27.8	1.4
6 "	26	3–10	25.4	1.3
31 "	45	7–44	21.1	0.8

never any doubt that the work of Ebbinghaus was very thorough and accurate, and the objection that it represented the retention curve of only one individual has now been met by the results of several studies which have all yielded results conforming to the general type of the Ebbinghaus curve. Even the work of Strong (1913) carried out by the recognition method gives essentially the same curve. Its main characteristic is a rapid fall immediately after learning and a gradual flattening out as the interval is prolonged. Forgetting

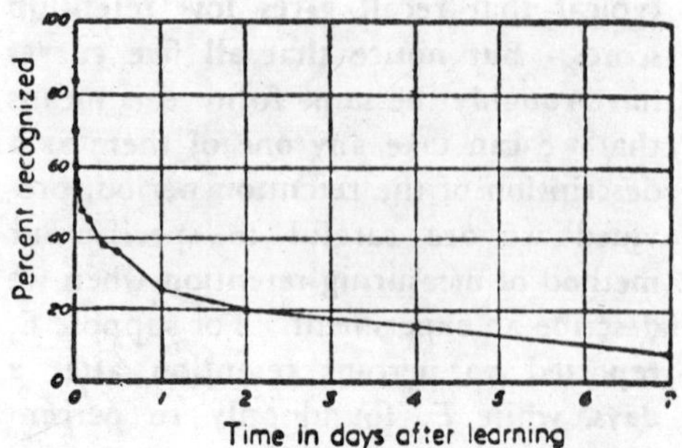

FIG. 23·13. (Data from Strong, 1913.) Curve of retention as determined by the recognition method. The material consisted of "all the common ordinary words," not over three syllables in length, found in the Standard Dictionary. Lists of 20 words were presented visually and were read aloud by *O* "slowly enough to grasp the meaning, but fast enough not to form associations between them." At the bottom of each list was a short problem in arithmetic to be solved mentally as soon as the list had been read, so as to prevent any immediate rehearsal of the words. In the recognition test the 20 words were mixed with 20 others, and *O* designated those which he was sure were in the original list. The score here plotted is that of these confident recognitions, with penalty for new words falsely recognized. Only one list of words was studied at a time, and the recognition test on each list was given before any other list was learned. There were five *O*s and 15 lists in all for each interval between learning and test.

becomes more and more gradual as time advances.

In some of the curves retention is plotted against the logarithm of time. The long and short intervals can thus be got into the same graph without crowding the short ones—that is the practical advantage. Besides, retention declines approximately in proportion to the log of time, and the graph shows to the eye how closely the data conform to this logarithmic law of forgetting. To conform perfectly the data points must lie on a straight line.

If we take the simplest logarithmic

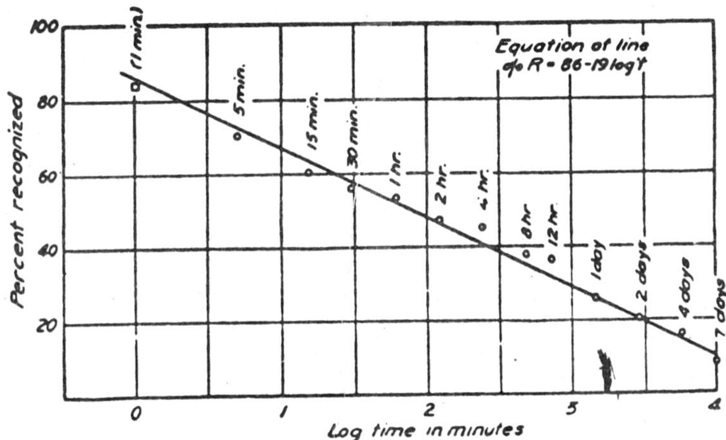

FIG. 23-14. Same data as Figure 23-13, with scores plotted against the logarithm of time. The straight line, drawn in simply by the eye, is a fairly good fit, and the inference is that the retention decreased just about in step with the logarithm of time—or that forgetting (loss of retention) increased as the log of time.

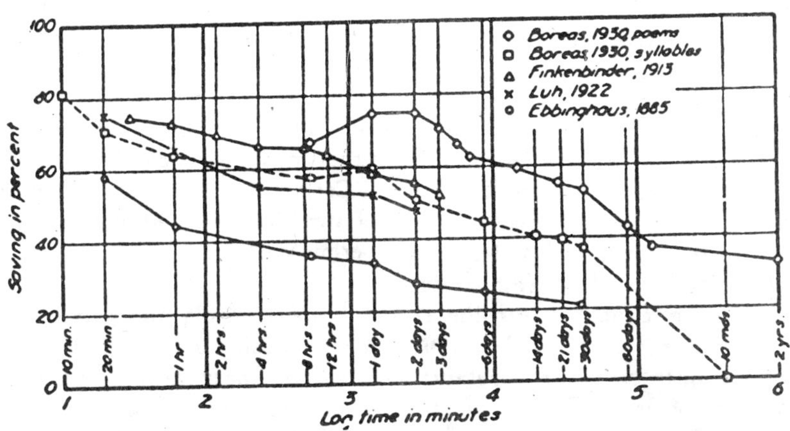

FIG. 23-15. Several retention curves plotted on a logarithmic abscissa. A straight line would fit any of them fairly well, aside from a dip at 8 hours when no correction has been made for diurnal variation, and aside from the drop at 10 months which suggests an eventual complete loss of barely learned nonsense material. The lessons were syllable lists except for the uppermost curve, which was obtained from 20 students whose high retention of poetry may be due in part to voluntary or involuntary rehearsal during the interval between learning and retention test.

equation between retention (R) and time interval (t), namely,

$$R = A - B \log t$$

we have the two constants, A and B, to be determined for each curve. We can determine their values by the method of least squares (or roughly by the eye, aided by a thread stretched through and between the data points, plotted on a logarithmic abscissa) so as to fit the points as closely as a straight line can be made to do. When $t = 1$, $\log t = 0$, and the constant A is thus found to have the corresponding value of R. Thus, if time is measured in minutes, A is the percent of saving at the end of 1 minute; it is the ordinate of the fitted straight line at t = 1. To get the value of B we note the value of R for some other value of t. Thus if t = 10 time units, log t = 1, and B = A — R; i.e., B is the loss in retention from 1 minute to 10 minutes. If we were counting our lapsed time in hours instead of minutes, A would be the retention after 1 hour and B the loss from 1 to 10 hours. The equation says simply that the retention after lapsed time t equals the retention after 1 minute (or hour) minus log t times the loss occurring between 1 and 10 minutes (or hours).[1] These "parameters," A and B, have no special significance, since they are not deduced from any theory as to the process of forgetting (see the discussion of similar problems, pp. 20, 558, 664; see also H. M. Johnson, 1932).

A convenient A-parameter is the amount retained for 24 hours, because this amount is usually measured directly and because the conditions of learning and relearning are then comparable without any correction for learning efficiency at different times of day. Different experimenters have obtained quite a range of values for the percent of retention after 24 hours:

	Percent
Strong, words recognized	26
Krueger, words recalled	27
Ebbinghaus, syllables, saving	34
Luh, syllables, saving	52
Finkenbinder, syllables, saving	58
Boreas, syllables, saving	59
Boreas, poems, saving	75
Radosavljevich (1907), poems, saving	80

[1] Some of the curves of retention plotted against log t seem to differ significantly from a straight line. Ebbinghaus preferred for his curve, not the linear logarithmic equation given above but one allowing for some curvature in the plot against log t, namely:

$$\text{Percent of retention} = \frac{100\,k}{(\log t)^c + k}$$

With k = 1.84 and c = 1.25, this equation gave a good fit to his data; but the parameters, once more, have no special rational significance.

FACTORS AFFECTING THE SPEED OF FORGETTING

It is reasonable to assume that the differences in speed of forgetting depend on two general factors: the initial strength of the trace (degree of learning, depth of impression), and the strength of the factors operating to annul the trace. Besides the individual differences to be expected in both these respects, there will be differences dependent on the conditions of learning and retention. The divergent results can sometimes be attributed to different ways in which the experiments were conducted.

Certain factors in the initial strength of the trace have been worked out experimentally.

1. Underlearning and overlearning. A lesson is said to be underlearned when it has not been brought up to the criterion of one perfect recitation, and overlearned when studied further after the criterion has been met. The additional study must be carried on with the same close attention as before; mere inattentive reading of the lesson does not count as overlearning. When this requirement is met, an overlearned lesson is better retained than one barely learned, and, in general, retention is roughly proportional to the amount of the original learning (Ebbinghaus, 1885; Krueger, 1929). The result cannot be depended on unless *O* is well trained (Luh, 1922; Cuff, 1927).

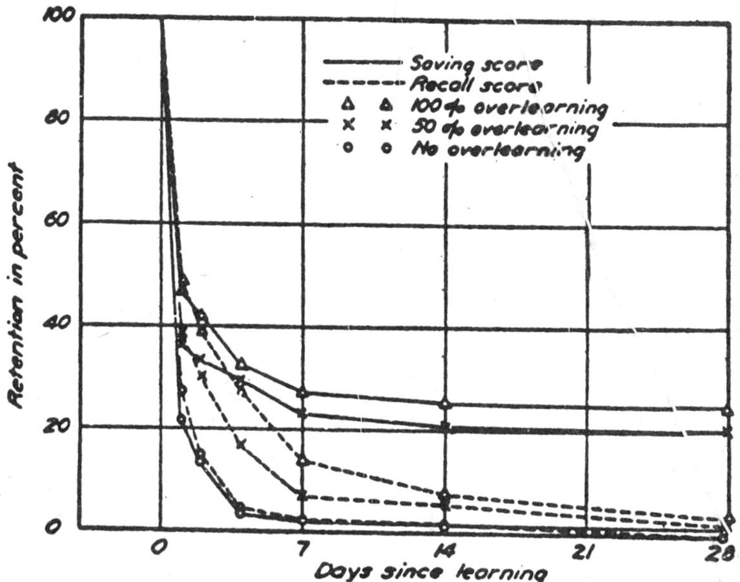

FIG. 23-16. (Data from Krueger, 1929.) Retention after overlearning. Lists of 12 monosyllabic words, all nouns, were presented on a rotating drum at the rate of 2 seconds per word. After four or five presentations, on the average, *O* anticipated all the words in a list. The number of presentations needed in each case to reach this criterion was noted, and in some cases learning stopped there, but in other cases additional presentations were given till the total number was 50 or 100 percent greater than the number needed to reach the criterion. After an interval of 1 day or more, *O* relearned the list to the same criterion, and two retention scores were obtained: the regular saving score and the "recall score" which was the number of correct anticipations on the first relearning trial. Separate groups of 20 students relearned after the different intervals. Errors due to inequality of the word lists were avoided by using the same lists for each interval and by rotating the lists among the members of each group. The averages plotted have high reliability. On the graph the label "100% overlearning" means that the number of additional presentations was equal to the number required to meet the criterion.

2. Distributed and repeated learning. It makes a difference whether the readings given a list or stanza or (probably) any lesson are massed in one continuous series or spaced out and spread over several sittings. The lesson can usually be learned in fewer spaced than massed readings (p. 786), and retention is definitely better after spaced readings. Such is the general outcome of a variety of experiments, the first being again one of Ebbinghaus (1885), who learned and relearned on successive days lists of nonsense syllables and stanzas of Byron's *Don Juan*—always to the point of one perfect recitation—and found that the necessary number of readings decreased from day to day, i.e., that the lesson was progressively better retained, as shown below (and in Fig. 23-17):

Day No.	*1*	*2*	*3*	*4*	*5*	*6*
12-syllable list	16.5	11	7.5	5	3	2.5
80-syllable stanza	7.8	3.8	1.8	.5	0	0

The stanzas, though much longer than the lists, were learned more quickly and better retained—so much better that after the fourth day they needed no more study.

This is one of the most practical results of memory experiments: Material that one wishes to retain for a long period needs to be studied and restudied. The result seems reasonable, but carefully scrutinized it contains a puzzle. On each successive day *O* learns to the same standard of one correct recitation. At the end of each day, he has reached the same degree of mastery. Why then should not forgetting proceed at the same rate? We are forced to conclude that *the trace becomes stronger and*

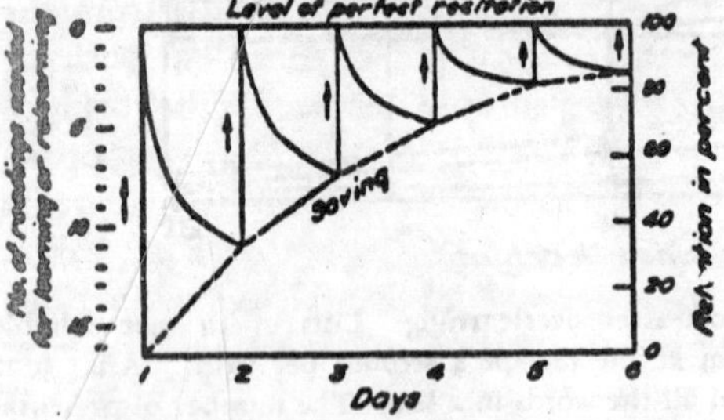

Fig. 23·17. (Data from Ebbinghaus, 1885.) Forgetting is made slower and slower by repeated learning of the same lesson. The "lesson" in this case was a list of 12 nonsense syllables, or, rather, a set of nine such lists learned in immediate succession in a sitting of about 15 minutes, and relearned day after day, always to the point of one correct recitation. The number of trials to learn (relearn) decreased day by day; the saving increased; retention was better and better. The arrows indicate the daily learning by which mastery was pushed up to the recitation level. The descending curves show the probable course of forgetting during each successive period of 24 hours. The data are the average results from learning and relearning 63 lists.

stronger with each relearning. What is the same at the end of each day's learning is not the trace but the immediate recitability or recallability of the lesson, and recall obviously depends not alone upon the trace but also upon the momentary condition of readiness. Readiness depends very much on *recency* of impression.

The results of this work of Ebbinghaus and of similar experiments of his own were formulated by Jost (1897) in the following law: *If two associations are now of equal strength but of different ages, the older one will lose strength more slowly with the further passage of time.*

What Jost means by strength of associations is the same as availability or reproducibility of a lesson. Since availability is demonstrated by recall at the moment of testing we may speak of it as recall value and reformulate the law as follows: If two associations (or lessons) of different ages have equal recall value at present, the older one has more retention value and will be retained better for the future. Retention value is the same as strength of the trace.

This law of Jost's can even be deduced from the general shape of a retention curve. As a lesson becomes old it reaches a flatter part of the curve and its further decline will be slow. Therefore, a young lesson momentarily at the same retention level as an old one is on a steeper part of the curve and doomed to decline more rapidly.

Jost really announced two laws and the one not yet stated usually goes by the name of Jost's law: *If two associations are of equal strength and different ages, further study has greater value for the older one.* This law while consistent with the retention curve could probably not be deduced from it. He set up this law first as a hypothesis to account for the advantage of spaced over massed learning, after finding that this advantage could not be due to fatigue or loss of attention in the massed learning. In scouting around for other possible factors, Jost got the idea that an old association might profit more than a new one from repetition or exercise. To test the hypothesis lists of 12 nonsense syllables were used. An "old" list was one which had been read 20–30 times on the preceding day and which now gave a recall score of 9 percent (average of two *Os*, tested by paired associates, the odd-numbered syllables being the stimuli). A "new" list had been read 4–6 times and was tested only a minute afterward, giving a recall score of 40 percent. So the dice were loaded against the hypothesis, and yet old lessons were more quickly mastered than new ones. For the twc *Os* the averages were:

Old lists, recall score 9 percent, mastered in 10 readings
New lists, recall score 40 percent, mastered in 14 readings

Jost's data are rather meager for founding a "law," but more recent experiments could be cited in corroboration, particularly the results of A. C. Youtz (1941).

All these findings on distribution of learning and on the relations of retention, recall, and relearning fit together very nicely and undoubtedly embody some fundamental law even though that law has not yet been formulated in any adequate way. There is reason to believe that the law adumbrated by all these results is fundamental in the physiology of learning. Much the same relations can be traced in the response of the muscle to exercise and rest.

3. Effect of length of lesson upon retention. Experimenters are agreed that when longer and shorter lessons are learned to the same criterion of one correct recitation (or of 2 correct recitations) subsequent retention is better for the longer lesson. Ebbinghaus's original result has been practically duplicated by later experimenters. He learned lists of different lengths and relearned them after 24 hours, with a saving as follows:

Syllables	*Original learning*	*Saving*
12	17 readings	35 percent
24	45	49
36	56	58

At first thought it is surprising that the harder lesson is better retained, but the mystery clears when we notice that the harder lesson required longer study. The stronger retention results from the greater study and is consistent with results previously discussed. To bring a long lesson up to the point of correct recitation more overlearning of parts is necessary. There is also another factor, where the savings method is used; a long list takes a disproportionately long time to learn, so there is more chance to save time in relearning (Hovland, 1951). With words as paired associates Woodworth (1915b) found longer lessons better retained even if not read any more times. A short lesson can be learned without special effort, but when a keen individual is confronted with a long lesson he is stimulated to organize the material and bind the items together by relations and meanings. The strong structure thus developed is more durable than the relatively loose structure which suffices for immediate reproduction of a short list (cf. Sand, 1939).

4. Retention of different kinds of material. It is not universally true that the lesson which requires more reading is better retained. Meaningful material though quickly learned is better retained than nonsense material. Instances of this are shown in the table on page 728 and in the Boreas curves in Figure 23-15.

Motor skill such as in typewriting has been found to be retained with little loss over long periods. We have to remember that such a performance is enormously overlearned in comparison with the syllable lists used in the laboratory.

But overlearning is not the whole story, for Leavitt & Schlosberg (1944) found much better retention for the pursuit rotor task than for nonsense syllables, even though the amount of practice was carefully equated. They suggested several possible differences in the tasks that might explain the results. One possibility was that the pursuit rotor performance was more organized than the nonsense syllable learning. Van Dusen & Schlosberg (1948) tested this possibility by comparing retention of a verbal and a motor task that both had the same type of organization, that of paired associates. There was no significant difference between retention for verbal and "motor" habits at any retention interval. Incidentally, the better organization of meaningful material may be one reason why it is retained better than nonsense syllables. And how shall we explain the excellent retention of the CR (Hilgard & Humphreys, 1938b)?

5. Vividness. Vivid impressions are better retained than "run of the mine" impressions. This common observation deserves mention if only to offset our (experimentally justified) emphasis on frequency and recency. In ordinary life it is difficult to make perfectly sure of the effect of vividness, because the vivid impression perseverates and is reviewed and so acquires frequency in addition to its original vividness. But we can fairly attribute some of the good retention of meaningful material to its vividness in comparison with nonsense material. Several experimenters (Calkins, 1894, 1896; Jersild, 1929) have demonstrated that a vivid item in a list is favored in immediate recall, and Van Buskirk (1932) demonstrated the same for later recall and relearning. His *O*s learned two 9-syllable lists: in the first list all the syllables were in uniform letters, black on white; in the second list one syllable, occupying the least favored position in the list (as indicated by the results with the first list), was in large red letters on a green background. This syllable was quickly learned; it was recalled by a large number of *O*s in a test one week or two weeks later and, when not at once recalled, was quickly relearned (cf. Köhler & von Restorff, 1935).

24

TRANSFER AND INTERFERENCE

In accordance with the fundamental principle of experimental investigation which requires control of conditions, an experiment on learning or remembering is so designed as to keep the whole situation in view—i.e., in *E*'s view, not necessarily in *O*'s view—with all important factors known, and the whole experiment isolated as far as possible from the daily life of the participants. The experimentalist is sometimes chided for this isolationism, which he can defend as the only way of gaining definite knowledge of the factors in behavior. But he can expand the scope of his experiments somewhat, by bringing into view *two* learning processes and seeing how they interact. Something learned in one task may be carried over ("transferred") to another task, and this transfer may facilitate the learning of the second task, or conceivably have an inhibitory effect and interfere with the second learning. And the mastery of the second task may help or hinder the subsequent performance of the first task. There are many possible varieties of interaction between different learning processes.

Transfer and Interference are evidently matters of great practical importance in all kinds of education. The child's education is supposed to prepare him for adult living, but the schoolroom situation is not the same as the situations he will encounter in life, nor are the specific tasks mastered in school identical with those encountered in adult occupations. So it is a question how far the adult is going to benefit from the knowledge, skills, and attitudes acquired in school. A similar practical question is how much of the aviator's training can be profitably administered on the ground before he undertakes to pilot an actual plane up in the air. Even Freud's transference, which at first seems to belong in an entirely different realm from the psychologist's transfer, has to do with emotional attitudes acquired by the child toward his parents but later transferred to other persons. In general, if we profit from past experience, it must be by transfer from earlier tasks and situations to later ones that are somewhat different; and if we fail to profit from past experience, it must be because of the limitations of transfer.

Scientific interest in transfer and interference. Two entirely separate brain mechanisms or operating systems of the organism could not be affected by mutual transfer or interference. Let the organism learn task A and afterwards attack task B, and do better on B because of the previous mastery of A. We infer that the A and B systems have something in common. What they have in common, if discovered, will tell us something about these operating systems. A system can conceivably be very broad in scope or relatively narrow and specific. A "faculty" was regarded as so broad as to cover all the operations of memory, for example, or of observation, or of esthetic appreciation. A faculty was supposed to be strengthened by exercise on any sort of material and so prepared for use on other materials. In its educational application this theory held that memory, trained in the learning of poems or vocabularies, would be prepared for the memory work of law or business, and that reasoning power, exercised in geometry, would be prepared for use in science or public affairs. The pioneer experimental opponent of this theory was Thorndike (1903) who held that transfer was possible only so far as "identical elements" of performance could be carried over from one task to another. Many subsequent experiments were concerned with these opposed theories.

Less controversial though still in the realm of scientific theory is the frequent use of the "transfer test" in various studies of learning. In the maze experiments there are several examples. Rats mastered a maze while wading in shallow water and continued to follow the correct path when the water was deepened so that they had to swim (p. 627). This transfer test bore on the question of *what is learned* in a maze. Similar transfer tests were used in the study of place learning and latent learning (pp. 633, 642). Other examples are found under the head of discrimination learning. A monkey or rat has learned to obtain food by using a certain cue; now the cue is modified to see how far the new cue is "equivalent" to the old one; and sometimes the nature of the animal's cue is found to be very different from what the human observer would suppose (pp. 589–592). Even the conditioning experiments on stimulus generalization and the generalization gradient (p. 577) can be regarded as experiments on transfer, for *O* first learns to respond to a specific conditioned stimulus and is then tested with more-or-less similar stimuli. So some light is thrown on the brain mechanism that operates in conditioning. In motivation the demonstration of secondary reinforcement makes use of a transfer test; a rat finds food repeatedly in a white goal box at the end of a straight runway and will then master a maze where the same box, now empty, is the only incentive (p. 680). Even a straight extinction series is in a way a transfer test which shows that Pavlov's dog, for example, did not really learn to salivate at the mere sound of a buzzer, but did learn to respond to a buzzer that was regularly followed by food. In general, we may say, a transfer test is used to throw light on the question of what has been learned.

Transfer and transfer effect. In experiments such as have just been reviewed it is often easy to see exactly what responses have been carried over from the first task to the second. In human instances of transfer of training it is sometimes not at all easy to see what elements of skill, knowledge, understanding or emotional adjustment have been carried over, though a pronounced transfer effect is demonstrated. The distinction between the two terms is not always observed, but logically *transfer* means the carrying over of an act or way of acting from one performance to another, whereas *transfer effect* means the effect of this transfer upon the learning or execution of the second performance. The transfer effect may be positive or negative, beneficial or detrimental. The "reversed-cues" experiments (p. 594) provide an example of negative transfer effect. A habit of speedy work carried over from a well-learned task to a new one may impede the learning of the latter—a clear case of positive transfer with a negative transfer effect. To call this a case of "negative transfer" may do no harm, but there are true examples of negative transfer, as when a young man on being released from the army, far from carrying over to civilian life the military habits of promptness and neatness, rebels against them and flies to the other extreme.

DESIGN OF TRANSFER EXPERIMENTS

Two general methods have been used, the first being more obvious to experimenters in the human laboratory and the second to those in the animal laboratory, though both were first used on human subjects.

The fore- and after-test method. This method was the first in use (Volkmann, 1858) and has been much employed in human experiments. Let two tasks be labeled A and B. The subjects are practiced in task A, and before and after this practice they are tested in task B. The question is whether B shows an improvement (or possibly a deterioration) from fore-test to after-test, and whether this improvement can be attributed to the intervening practice.

There may be improvement not attributable to transfer. Task B has received a certain amount of practice in the fore-test, and we must expect some resulting improvement in the after-test. This practice effect may be very large, since improvement is often quite rapid in the first few trials of a new task. A *control group* is needed, to take the fore-test and after-test like the practice group but without the intervening practice. Subtracting the gain of the control group from that of the practice group we obtain the *net gain* attributable to transfer. See Plan 1, below.

It is necessary to match the practice

Plan 1

Practice group: Fore-test in B ..... Practice in A .... After-test in B.
Control group: Fore-test in B .... After-test in B.

Plan 2

Practice on A ...... After-test on B; A and B being equated tasks.

Plan 3

A Single group learns A ...... learns B; A and B being equated tasks.

Plan 4

Transfer group learns A ..... learns B.
Control group .... learns B; the two groups being equated.

Plan 5

Group I learns A .... learns B.
Group II learns B .... learns A; the A and B data being pooled.

and control groups for initial ability in task B, as can be done by making the division into groups on the basis of the fore-test results. We must be justified in assuming equal gains for the two groups, except for the effect of transfer. But we know that *Os* who make a low initial score are likely to show a large gain. If we should use a control group scoring far above or below the practice group in the fore-test, our computed "net gain" would be too large or too small, respectively.

Instead of matched groups, we can sometimes use matched tasks, equated by previous standardization. We can then dispense with the control group and also with the fore-test, as shown in Plan 2. Here, because of the equality of tasks, the first trial on A is equivalent to a fore-test of B, so far as test scores are concerned. The matched tasks are usually very similar: two mazes, two substitution tests, two card-sorting tasks, etc.

The successive-practice method. The method of fore-test and after-test has the disadvantage of looking for transfer at only one stage in the process of mastering the test performance. This performance, which we call B, has been slightly practiced in the fore-test but is still in an early stage of mastery at the time of the after-test when the transfer from A is examined. There are obvious objections to limiting the study of transfer to this single stage. In order to afford a full opportunity for transfer from one performance to another, we therefore expand the after-test into a practice series on B.

The general plan of a successive-practice experiment is to have the same subjects learn first A and then B. If we know that A and B are equally difficult, we need only ask whether B, coming second, is learned more easily than A. To depend on equated tasks would however unduly limit the scope of transfer study. The scope becomes indefinitely wide if we use a matched control group, which simply learns task B, while the transfer group has previous practice with task A. We compare the learning of B after A with the learning of B "from scratch." The tasks A and B can be as dissimilar as we like, provided our groups are equated. Still another plan is to practice one group on A followed by B, and the other group on B followed by A, and pool the groups for first learning and for second learning. Neither tasks nor groups need be strictly equated in this procedure. To the two plans listed under fore- and after-test we add three involving successive practice. See Plans 3, 4, 5.

The matching of groups sometimes necessitates a fore-test, and sometimes is accomplished in other ways, as by the method of "co-twin control," used by Gesell & Thompson (1929). It is often necessary to take account of working conditions so as to have such factors as warm-up and work decrement, as well as forgetting, equal for the different groups (Irion & Gustafson, 1952; Kimble, 1952). Improvement in task B may be due to transfer of motivation rather than to any transfer of learned ability acquired in the practice of task A (Henry, 1951; Fairclough, 1952).

Measures of the transfer effect. We should be able not only to demonstrate the existence of a transfer effect, but also to measure its amount in a given case so as to compare it quantitatively in different cases. We should be able to state its amount in a scale of percents extending from 0 to 100. Zero transfer effect must mean that the preliminary training (A) is of no help at all in the learning of the final task (B). What should 100-percent transfer effect mean? It can best mean that the preliminary training is so helpful that no additional practice is necessary for full mastery of the final task.

A control group or direct-practice group can provide the required zero and 100-percent values, by learning the final task from scratch to the final level. Its initial score fixes the zero mark and its practice level fixes the 100-percent mark. A transfer group (T), fairly matched with the control group (C), has certain preliminary training or experience and then tackles the final task. Suppose the T group in its first trial (or first few trials) on the final task makes a score halfway from the zero to the 100-percent mark: the transfer effect thus measures 50 percent. In general the formula reads,

$$\text{Percent transfer effect} = \frac{\text{T score} - \text{initial C score}}{\text{final C score} - \text{initial C score}} \times 100$$

This method, though without a formula, was extensively used by Cook (1933, 1934b). The formula was provided by Gagné, Foster & Crowley (1948), though they write in the denominator "total possible score" instead of our "final C score." The total or maximum possible score can be stated in advance for some tasks such as a list of syllables or of paired associates to be memorized or a maze to be run with zero errors. But in many cases the maximum can be determined only by experiment; it is the practice level, as for example in the study of Gagné & Foster (1949).

Another good measure of the transfer effect is based on the saving method so much employed in the study of retention (p. 698). How much work on the final task is saved by the preliminary training? A control group learns the final task from scratch to near the practice level in a certain number of trials. The transfer group, after its preliminary training, takes up the final task and learns it up to the same practice level. If the C group requires 20 trials while the T group requires only 12 trials on the final task, the transfer effect amounts to a saving of 8 trials out of 20, or 40 percent.

The saving method can be extended by the use of successive criteria (p. 534). Count the trials required to reach each criterion by the C group and also by the T group, and compute the percent of saving at each level, so tracing the transfer effect throughout the whole learning process.

Transfer measurement in relation to the theoretical learning curve. The equation which we used in the chapter on Motivation (pp. 664–667) may prove useful in the analysis and measurement of transfer. Take this form of the equation:

$$Z - y = (1 - F)^n(Z - A)$$

Here Z is the practice level which the learner approaches; A is the level or score from which he starts, so that Z — A is the "room for improvement," the distance to go from start to finish; F is the rate of improvement, the fraction of the remaining distance covered in any one trial; and y is the score on the nth trial. Here we have three parameters, A, Z, and F, which might be affected by transfer from previous learning. The initial score, A, might be raised because some part of the present maze, for example, was identical with a part of a previously mastered maze; certain blind alleys would be avoided from the start, and the distance to go, Z — A, would be less though the rate of improvement was unchanged. Or F, the rate of improvement, might be increased because of a general facility acquired in running previous mazes. Even Z, the practice level, might be raised by the incentive factor, i.e., because of past experience of finding a good reward in other mazes —or lowered by satiation with the incentive used. The learning curve of a transfer group could differ in any of these ways from that of a control group, and the difference could throw light on the nature of the transfer in a particular case (Fig. 24-1).

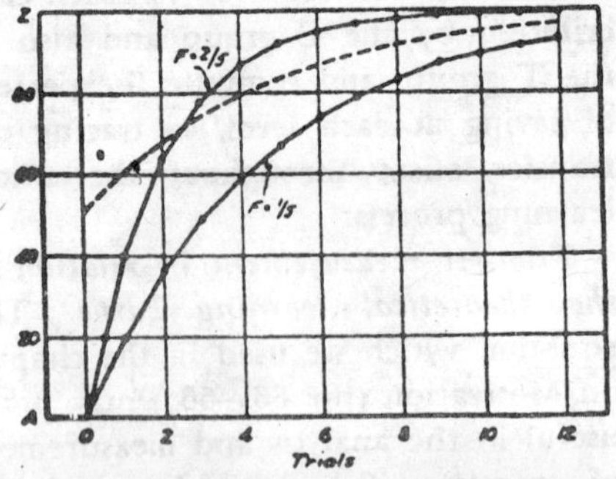

Fig. 24-1. Possible transfer effects on the learning curve. The curve labeled F = 1/5 represents the progress of a control group. The one labeled F = 2/5 supposes the rate of learning to be doubled by transfer from some preliminary training; it starts from the same base line but rises twice as fast toward the same final level. The broken line supposes the distance still to go to the final level to be cut in half by preliminary training, though F is still 1/5 as in the control group. By computation from the theoretical equation we find that the broken curve should save 3.1 trials in reaching each successive level or criterion, while the F = 2/5 curve should reach each level in 44 percent of the number of trials required by the control group.

CROSS EDUCATION, THE TRANSFER OF SKILL FROM ONE BODILY MEMBER TO ANOTHER

It is worth noting that the scientific study of transfer began with our old friends, the psychophysicists. E. H. Weber, the author of Weber's law, had observed that some children trained to write with the right hand were able without further training to produce very good mirror-writing with the left hand. Weber himself possessed a knack which is useful to a biological lecturer in sketching on the blackboard the outline of a bilaterally symmetrical animal —the knack of drawing with both hands simultaneously, the left hand producing a mirror-image of what is drawn by the right hand. Weber did not publish these observations at the time but later communicated them to Fechner who published them in 1858 along with similar observations of his own.

Transfer of perceptual skill. This paper of Fechner on the bilateral transfer of motor skill was appended to a longer paper by A. W. Volkmann, his brother-in-law, who had collaborated with him in some prolonged experiments on the tactual discrimination of two points from one, i.e., on the two-point threshold (p. 293). Volkmann had noted three rather remarkable phenomena: (1) a very marked increase in sensitivity (decrease of the two-point threshold) in the practiced skin area; (2) an almost equal improvement in the corresponding area of the other hand or arm; and (3) the rapid disappearance of this acquired sensitivity in a few days of disuse. The transfer was not general but was confined to areas adjacent or symmetrical to the area receiving the practice. There was good transfer from the tip to the base of the same finger (volar side) and from one finger to another, but not from finger to forearm. Volkmann inferred from the transfer effects that the change due to practice was in the brain and not in the skin.

Dresslar (1894) obtained the same sort of results when the practiced area was on the forearm; the two-point threshold went down enormously on the practiced area and on the bilaterally symmetrical area, but not in other areas. The two adult *O*s reported that the points *felt* very different, after practice, in the area that had been practiced and in other areas. From other work on the two-point threshold (Messenger, 1903; Boring, 1920) the improvement is quite understandable. At distances so small that the two points of the test instrument are not definitely felt as two there is still a little sensory difference which *O* can learn to interpret correctly. The slight cues of one and two must differ greatly in differently structured regions of the skin, but they may be almost identical in bilaterally symmetrical regions.

Bilateral transfer of motor skills. From many experiments it appears clear that skill acquired in a particular task by practice with one hand can often be carried over to the other hand or even to the foot—often but not in every case.

Ball tossing showed transfer from the right hand to the left in five of Swift's six subjects (1903). Measured in terms of saving, the transfer effect was large, amounting to about ⅔ of the work which would otherwise have been required from the left hand. The most obvious factor in the transfer effect was the carrying over of efficient methods of handling the balls, of throwing them so as to avoid collisions, and of recovering control after a poor throw.

Somewhat similar to ball-tossing, though simpler, is the game utilized by Munn (1932) in a transfer experiment with practice and control groups of 50 students each. Both groups took a fore-test of 50 trials with the left hand; the transfer group then made 500 trials with the right hand in the course of an hour, the control group resting for this length of time, and finally both groups took the after-test of 50 trials with the left hand. (The experiment was conducted as an individual, not a group experiment.) The right-hand gain of the transfer group was considerable, from a score of 73 points in the first 50 to a score of 108 points in the last 50 trials. This group scored 50 points with the left hand before and 78 points after the right-hand practice, whereas the gain of the control group was only from 48 to 57 points. The lower an individual's initial score, the larger on the whole was his gain, but the positive transfer effect showed in all parts of the distribution, as shown in this breakdown:

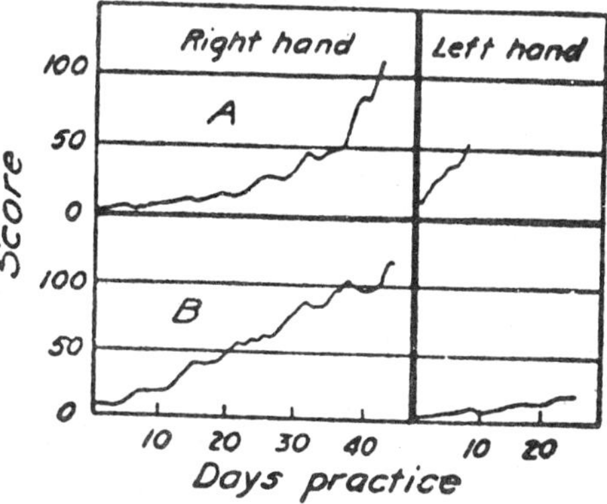

FIG. 24-2. (Swift, 1903.) Transfer from right to left hand in ball tossing. Successive practice method. Two balls were to be kept in the air by tossing them alternately. A trial ended when *O* failed to catch a ball, and the score for the trial was the number of catches. Ten trials a day. The curves give smoothed averages. When the right hand had attained an average score of 100, the left hand began its practice. A and B were right-handed subjects. A shows a positive transfer effect, since his left hand improved much more rapidly than the right; but B's curve shows no sign of transfer, perhaps because, though quite skillful, he was not analytical in his work.

	Initial left-hand score				
	20 or less	21–40	41–60	61–80	81–100
Gain of T group	45	40	23	21	15
Gain of C grou	14	9	14	6	−4

According to the spontaneous comments of Munn's subjects, what was learned and carried over from the right to the left hand consisted largely of points of technique.

In Cook's extensive study of cross education (1933, 1934b, 1935) one major purpose was to test the following hypothesis: transfer from one performing member to another will be greatest in the case of symmetrical members (hand to hand or foot to foot), next greatest in the case of same-sided members (between right hand and foot or between left hand and foot), and least in the case of the diagonal members. This thesis was confirmed in mirror tracing and also in blindfold following of the irregular path shown in Figure 24·3. Some of the results are presented

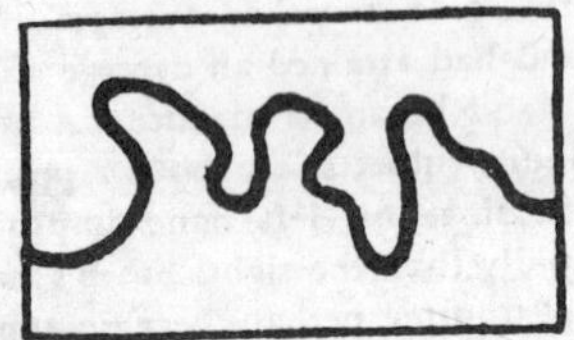

FIG. 24·3. Diagram of stylus "maze" used by Cook (1934b). The heavy line shows the course of a groove, ¼ in wide and 48 in long. The groove flared out beneath so as to accommodate a washer attached to the lower end of the stylus. The washer held the stylus in the groove, while leaving it free to move along the groove. The stylus rod was attached to a handle or, for use with the foot, to the under side of a sandal. Vision of the maze was excluded by a screen. *O* was informed that the path extended in general from left to right and that it was winding but had no blind alleys. He was to try for speed.

in Figure 24·4. In this experiment Cook hoped to avoid such obvious "identical elements" as the visual cues which are essential in ball tossing or mirror tracing and which are the same whether the right or left hand is doing the work —or such as the verbalized rule often found helpful by human subjects for keeping out of blind alleys (p. 651)— or even such as emotional adjustment to the whole laboratory situation. Still there were some "identical elements" left. The path remained objectively the same and in the same position, so that when *O* had become acquainted with the pattern he could make good use of it whatever member was following the pattern. He learned also how to manage the stylus so as to avoid blocking his own movement by excessive pressure against either side of the groove. These factors would account for some transfer, but they would not explain why transfer was greatest to the symmetrical members and least to the diagonal ones. Factors of a more physiological sort would demand consideration.

As pointed out by Milisen & Van Riper (1939), movements of the right and left hands are not bilaterally symmetrical unless they are mirror images of each other. If the right hand moves to the right and the left hand simultaneously to the left, these movements are symmetrical and easily combined. If the right hand moves clockwise around a circle, the left hand must move counterclockwise in order to take full advantage of bilateral symmetry. These authors found most transfer from one hand to the other when the required movements were symmetrical. In their experiment *O* moved a stylus as rapidly as possible around a slot shaped somewhat like a clover leaf. In the fore-

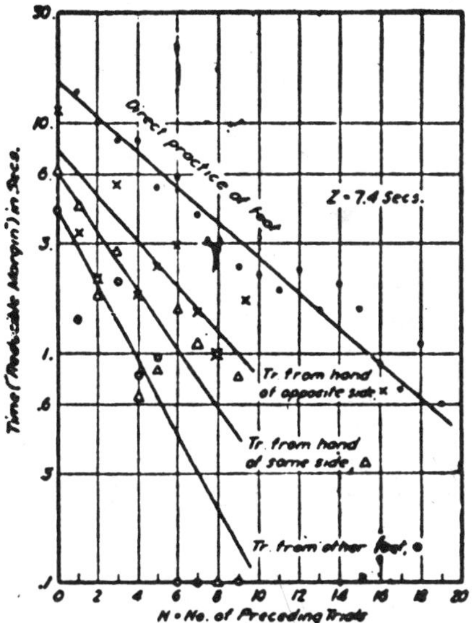

FIG. 24·4. (Data from Cook, 1934b.) Practice curves for a foot following an unseen groove with a stylus. The course of the groove is shown in Figure 24·3. We have plotted the data by aid of the equation on page 737, using semilog paper. The line marked "direct practice of foot" gives the Means for 60 students who learned the task "from scratch" to an approximate practice level, half of them using the right foot and half the left foot. Each of the other lines gives the means of 20 students who practiced with the foot after 20 trials with the other foot, or after practice with the hand on the same side, or with the hand on the opposite side. Since the lines are merely fitted "by the eye" to the data points, we cannot be too sure of the exact slopes or of the exact y-intercepts (where $n = 0$). Taking the lines as they stand we can infer (1) that all the transfer groups started off better than the group that started from scratch, (2) that they improved more rapidly, and (3) that the transfer effect was greatest from the symmetrical member and least from the diagonal member. Cook's data for transfer to the hands are less regular but do show positive transfer effects which are least from the diagonal member, and about equal from the symmetrical and from the same-side member. This method of computing transfer effects does at least make a serious effort to utilize all the data.

and after-tests his left-hand speed was measured in both directions, clockwise and counterclockwise. In between he practiced with the right hand in one direction, clockwise for half of the group and counterclockwise for the other half. The after-test showed for the whole group some transfer gain of the left hand in both directions, but reliably greater gain in the direction opposite to that of the right-hand practice. This result, the authors say, cannot possibly be explained by "common elements" of technique and knowledge of the objective pattern. Bilaterally symmetrical coordinations of muscular movement must play a part.

Transfer in mirror tracing. Tracing a star-shaped figure with a pencil or stylus, when the figure cannot be seen directly but only in a mirror, is a familiar laboratory experiment which yields a large practice effect. Usually the figure to be traced lies on the table with the mirror standing vertically beyond the figure. In this position the mirror reverses the forward and backward directions while leaving right and left unchanged. A right-left line calls for the usual eye-hand coordination, a front-back line must be reversed in the tracing, and an oblique line must be reversed as regards its front-back component but left unchanged as regards its right-left component. The beginner has surprising difficulty with this task but he improves rapidly.

This experiment, introduced by Starch (1910a), is a favorite in transfer studies and a positive transfer effect from one hand to the other is usually found. Ewert (1926) found some of the older claims excessive because of their failure to allow for the practice afforded by the fore-test. His own experiments still showed a net gain from transfer when a control group was introduced as a corrective. Cook (1933), attaching the tracing stylus to a sandal, found considerable transfer from hand to foot and from foot to hand.

Not exactly mirror tracing, but mirror aiming, was tried out in a transfer experiment by Bray (1928). Instead of tracing a star, *O* hit at a target with a pencil held in the hand or strapped to the foot. The target was a vertical line on a frontal-parallel sheet of paper straight in front of *O*'s hand or foot, concealed by a screen from direct vision but visible in a mirror. The mirror stood at the side and reversed right and left. *O* was required to keep time with a metronome and make 36 hits per minute. In trying to correct his aim between hits, he fell victim to the mirror reversal, but improvement occurred, and there were substantial transfer effects both from hand to hand and from hand to foot (Fig. 24-5).

Retrospective reports by Bray's subjects, along with his own observations on their behavior, cast some light on the question of what is transferred from hand to foot or from foot to hand.

1. Some method was found for allowing for the mirror effect. Most commonly *O* learned to disregard the visual appearance except for taking note of an error and to rely on kinesthesis in correcting his aim. Another method was to make a reverse correction; if the hit appeared too far to the left, the aim was still farther to the left. Still another was to take the frame of the mirror as the guide and to aim closer to the frame or farther from it.

2. *O* learned to avoid the impulsive

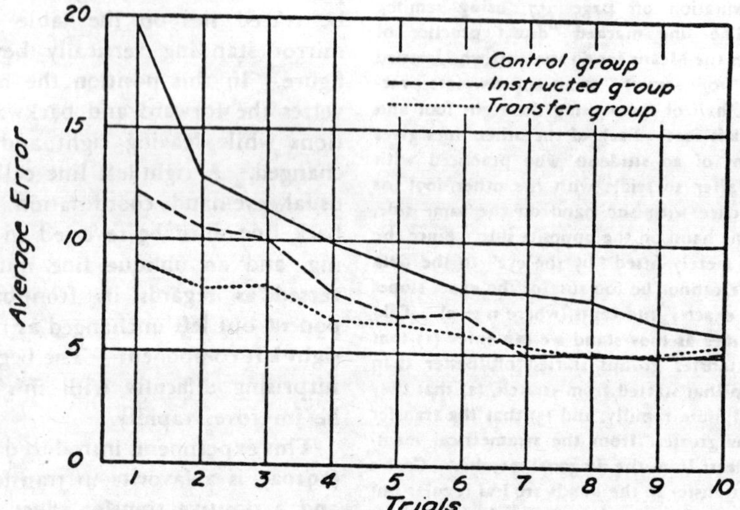

FIG. 24-5. (From Bray, 1928.) Foot mirror-aiming practice, with and without transfer from hand practice. A "trial" consisted of 10 successive hits at the target. The control group of 24 students used the foot without previous hand practice in hitting at the mirror-target; the transfer group of 37 students had at least 10 trials with the hand before starting foot practice; the instructed group of 17 students had no preliminary practice but were familiarized with the apparatus and the mirror effect by visual demonstration along with information on an efficient way of correcting errors and overcoming the mirror effect. Such instruction, as the curves show, was of appreciable help in the foot performance, but transfer from hand practice was still more helpful.

overcorrection which was a disturbing factor in the early trials.

3. *O* lost the nervousness and self-consciousness which were common at the start. "After a few trials the nervous attitude disappeared and was replaced by an air of confidence. Usually, but not always, the confident attitude was carried over to practice with the other limb."

Neurology of bilateral transfer. It seems almost certain that the locus of any practice effect is the cerebral hemispheres and that practice leaves behind some change in the neural structure or condition. In case of bilateral transfer, the operating mechanisms have in part a different cerebral localization, since the right side of the body is connected most directly with the left hemisphere, and the left with the right. Lashley (1924) cauterized the right precentral gyre, i.e., the motor area for the left side of the body, in a monkey, leaving the right hand the preferred hand for fine work. The animal in this state learned to open three latch boxes, manipulating the latches with the right hand and using the left arm only as a prop. In a second operation the motor area for the right hand was destroyed, leaving the right hand weak and stiff and the left, now partially recovered, the preferred hand. Tested with the same latch boxes the animal in the first few trials tried to use the right hand, as he had learned to do, but shifted to the left hand with very little further practice. Evidently neither motor area could have been the locus of the neural change produced by the practice. From Lashley's description of the animal's behavior, it is clear that acquaintance with the boxes as objects was retained. After the second operation the monkey attacked the latches in the right way but was weak and awkward with his right hand and simply substituted the more convenient member. In the original learning he had probably developed no new motor coordinations but had merely adapted old movements to the characteristics of the latches and boxes which he learned by vision combined with manipulation. The locus of such learning, from all we know of the brain, may extend widely over the cortex, into the premotor, parietal and occipital regions. Transfer shows that either hand is available for the use of the same high-level cerebral mechanism.

MEMORY TRAINING

It is rather curious that, while positive results on bilateral transfer have awakened surprise, such results have been expected when the broader question of transfer was broached and the relatively negative results sometimes announced have been received with skepticism. The belief in "formal discipline" seems deeply ingrained. Belief in the efficacy of memory training, certainly a widespread belief, was emphatically called in question by William James. In his view *retentiveness* was a physiological trait which varied with the individual constitution, with age, and with the condition of health, but was not susceptible to training. He endeavored to put his hypothesis to test by some experiments (1890, I, p. 666) which were the first experiments on transfer, aside from those on cross education. His subjects first measured their speed of learning the verses of one poet, then trained themselves at length in memorizing those of another poet, and finally came back to the first poet and determined whether they could memorize his poems more quickly than before. The results showed little transfer effect, and such improvement as did appear was attributed to better methods of *memorizing* rather than to any improvement in retentiveness.

Rapid improvement in memorizing a particular kind of material. James did not state how much his *O*s gained in the practice series itself, but from other experiments in learning the poems of a single author it is certain that great improvement can occur. Ebert & Meumann (1905) conducted a practice experiment in the memorizing of nonsense syllables and found great improvement, which consisted largely in better technique. The learners tried out various devices to assist in the memorizing, abandoned those which were found useless and kept the good ones. They found rhythmic grouping a help. They learned to avoid farfetched "associations." They discovered, to their own surprise, that they were capable of memorizing lists of nonsense syllables, and gained confidence and interest in the work. They eliminated worry, strain and the useless muscular tensions which occur in performing an unfamiliar and difficult task. They became "adapted" to the experimenter and to the laboratory conditions.

Practice in memorizing lists of nonsense syllables, or stanzas of Spenser's *Faerie Queene*, or any other specific kind of lesson, enables the learner to memorize that kind of lesson with greatly increased ease and speed. Shall we call this gain a transfer effect or simply a practice effect? It can be called a transfer effect, since the specific associations established differ from one list or stanza to another. It is transfer within a narrow range, and the interesting question is whether a more general memorizing ability is developed by practice with one kind of lesson and carried over to other kinds.

Meager transfer from one kind of memory lesson to other kinds. In the famous study just mentioned Ebert & Meumann were interested in broad transfer effects. Before and after the practice in learning nonsense syllables they had their *O*s memorize lists of letters, numbers, disconnected words, vocabularies, prose passages, poems, and meaningless visual figures. The aftertests often showed some improvement over the fore-tests, and the authors concluded that a broad transfer effect was demonstrated. The lack of any control group was a serious defect in their experiment, as Dearborn (1909) proved by repeating the experiment *without the practice series*, and obtaining pretty much the same gains from fore-test to after-test. The fore-tests had provided enough specific practice with the various test materials to produce considerable improvement even without any "spread" of the ability acquired in the practice series. Reed (1917) repeated Ebert & Meumann's entire experiment on a practice group of eight students, with a control group of five students, and obtained only small net transfer gains, along with losses, in spite of large gains in the nonsense-syllable practice series. There was certainly no sign of a broad spread of the acquired memorizing ability.

One difficulty with these broad transfer experiments is that of obtaining a control group matched with the transfer group in *all* the varied fore-tests. An experiment of Sleight (1911) was adequate in this respect and is perhaps all the better for having been done on young subjects (84 school girls, average

age 12 years, 8 months). On the basis of fore-test results in ten various memory tasks, four equated groups were formed. Three groups practiced memorizing either poetry, or the substance of prose passages, or tables of measures and similar quantitative facts. A control group took the fore-, mid- and after-tests but occupied themselves with arithmetic or other school work while the other groups were engaged in memory practice. The test materials were carefully prepared and rotated so as to avoid errors due to unequal tests.

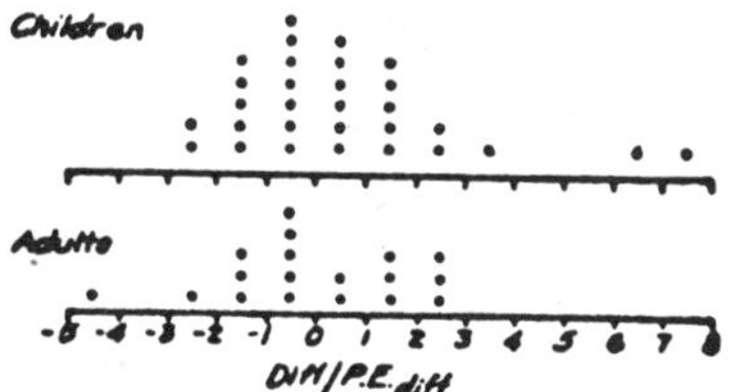

FIG. 24-6. (Data from Sleight, 1911.) Distribution of net group gains and losses in the final tests after memory practice. Children: 3 practice groups and 10 tests, yielding 30 net gains or losses which are here expressed as multiples of their respective PE_{diff}. By chance about half of these differences would lie between ± 1 PE_{diff}. Actually 13 of the 30 differences lie between these limits. The distribution could result from zero transfer effect and chance variation, except for the two large gains which are mentioned in the text. The second distribution is from Sleight's similar experiment on adults and shows one clear negative effect and an apparent surplus of small positive effects.

Sleight's results showed no general improvement in memory resulting from the practice. Net gains and losses of the practice groups were equally numerous, and very few of them were statistically significant. The two groups which practiced memorizing poetry and tables of measures showed significant positive transfer effects in the memorizing of nonsense syllable lists, apparently due to the device of using rhythm. In a similar though less extensive experiment on adult subjects, Sleight found one significant transfer effect but a negative one: after practice in learning the substance of prose passages the adult *Os* showed a net loss in memorizing relatively meaningless material, which they reported to be quite distasteful after the more interesting work of the practice period. Aside from these few instances, the net gains and losses were small and show a chance distribution (Fig. 24-6).

Training in efficient methods of memorizing. One who is trying his best to learn a certain kind of material picks up techniques suited to that material. If generalized, these techniques might be useful with other materials, but the learner is too busy with his specific task to attempt any generalization. So his techniques remain untransferable, but an instructor might make them more transferable. This possibility was tested by Woodrow (1927). He divided a class of students into three groups. The control did only the fore- and after-tests. The uninstructed practice group devoted a total of 3 hours (in 8 periods spread over 4 weeks) to memorizing poems and nonsense syllables. The instructed group divided the same total time between instruction in "proper methods of memorizing" and exercises in memorizing poems and syllables. The fore- and after-tests included memory span for lists of consonants, Turkish English vocabularies, dates of events, poems and prose passages verbatim, and the substance of information items.

In the after-tests the practice group was only about equal to the control, but the instructed group definitely surpassed both the other groups in every test. "In short, the experiment shows that in a case where one kind of training—undirected drill—produces amounts of transference which are sometimes positive and sometimes negative, but always small, another kind of training with the same drill material may result in a transference, the effects of which are uniformly large and positive."

What were these "proper methods of memorizing" in which training was given? Woodrow gives the following list.

1. Learning by wholes.
2. Use of active self-testing.
3. Use of grouping and rhythm.
4. Attention to meaning and use of images and symbols to embody meaning.
5. Mental alertness and concentration.
6. Confidence in one's ability to memorize.
7. In certain cases, as in learning nonsense syllables, the use of secondary associations.

TRAINING IN OBSERVATION

Can you train a person to be a good general observer by giving him intensive practice in some particular task that calls for quick or accurate observation? Thorndike & Woodworth (1901) put this question to the test as part of an attack on the whole doctrine of formal discipline. In one experiment the practice consisted in estimating rectangular areas of 10–100 sq. cm. After each estimate *O* was informed of the true area and thus his improvement was assured. Before and after this special training he was tested in estimating the areas of other rectangles and also of triangles and various shapes. Similar experiments gave practice in the estimation of lengths and weights. The general result was that improvement from fore-test to after-test though often shown was undependable and seldom as great as the improvement in the practiced task. The transfer effects obtained were due, as far as the authors could discover, to specific methods, ideas and useful habits that were carried over from the practice series to the after-test. For example, one *O* tended to overestimate the small areas presented in the practice series. Discovering this error he corrected his estimates and carried over the correction to the larger areas of the test series which he was therefore likely to underestimate. There was sometimes a transfer of emotional adjustment. One person who was timid and overcautious in the fore-test gained confidence during the long practice series and carried over this confidence to the after-test.

The same authors made much use of cancelation test material which affords plenty of opportunity for practice in certain discriminations with transfer tests on other discriminations. (See Martin's later experiment below.) The results were similar to those just stated, and the conclusion seemed logical, though it aroused considerable dissent at the time: "There is no inner necessity for improvement of one function to improve others closely similar to it, due to a subtle transfer of practice. . . . Improvement in them seems due to definite factors." These authors sometimes spoke of these definite factors as common elements or identical elements, and Thorndike said later (1903, 1913), "A change in one function alters any other only in so far as the two functions have as factors identical elements."

As between the theories of formal discipline and of identical elements, psychological discussion has usually favored the latter, since it seems inevitable that there must be something common to two performances if training in one has any effect on the other (H. E. O. James, 1930; Katona, 1940, p. 114).

Not all psychologists like the phrase, "identical elements," which suggests an atomistic approach. Probably "common factors" would be more generally acceptable. The theory can serve as a guidepost, pointing toward something definite and concrete as the cause of any transfer effect, as against anything akin to formal discipline.

In a critical review of numerous experiments, some of them quite recent, on training in perception, E. J. Gibson (1953) shows that the problem of transfer is part of the more general problem, how perceptual improvement is possible.

A cancelation experiment in transfer. Of the many experiments on transfer that have used this sort of material, perhaps the most thorough is that of Martin (1915). His subjects were boys 11–13 years of age, 36 in the practice group and 40 in the control group. All the boys were first assembled and given an initial test series, consisting of two 1-minute trials in several cancelation tasks. The practice group and the control group were nearly equal in this initial test, the practice group being slightly superior. The practice group then worked 40 minutes a day for 16 days on a single task, the canceling of words containing both *a* and *t* in English prose from a book of no special interest to these boys. Improvement was marked. At the beginning of practice the average number of words canceled was 10.26 per minute; at the end of practice the average had risen to 26.65 words per minute. The errors consisted mostly in omitting words that should have been canceled. Accuracy was therefore measured by dividing the number of words canceled by the number that should have been canceled in the reading matter covered by the subject. So measured the accuracy of the practice group in its special task was 79 percent at the start and increased gradually to 96 percent at the finish. When the practice was completed, the boys of both groups were reassembled and put through the same tests as at the outset. The gain from fore-test to after-test of the control group was deducted from that of the practice group, and the remainder was taken as the net gain or transfer effect. The transfer effects shown in the table are to be compared with the direct-practice gain of 16.39 words per minute in speed, and of 17 percent in accuracy.

To be canceled	*Gain in speed*	*P.E.*	*Gain in accuracy*	*P.E.*
a-t words in Spanish prose	6.44 words	0.38	1%	1.92
a and t in a mixed letter series	4.91 letters	1.25	6%	1.30
A in a mixed letter series	3.99 A's	1.39	− 1%	0.62
B in a mixed letter series	1.13 B's	0.93	− 3%	1.06
Number groups containing both 4 and 7	1.08 groups	0.83	− 7%	1.13
e-s words in Spanish prose	0.02 words	0.36	−16%	2.11
e and s in a mixed letters series	—3.89 letters	1.78	− 3%	0.75

What these boys learned in their long and intensive practice in canceling English a-t words included: (1) facility in finding a and t; (2) knowledge of English words containing or not containing, both of these letters; (3) a habit of rapid work in cancelation. Of these transferable factors, the first would help in the first three tests in the table, and the first and second might interfere with the execution of the last two tests—as the results indicate. The speed habit could be and apparently was carried over into all of the after-tests with bad results on accuracy. This type of negative transfer effect is probably rather general. When one is adjusted for a rapid tempo one does not readily slow down —say at the entrance to a village after the open road.

TRANSFER IN MAZE LEARNING

Maze running is so open and observable a form of behavior, in either human or animal subjects, that it affords a good opportunity for the study of *what* is learned—as we have seen, page 626—and for the study of what is transferred from one learning process to another. The method usually employed is that of successive practice. First one maze is learned and then another. Both positive and negative transfer effects can be demonstrated in this way and sometimes the helpful or harmful behavior carried over from one maze to another can be brought clearly to light.

The study of transfer in maze learning began with Webb (1917), who used rats and human subjects. The latter learned stylus mazes of the same patterns as the enclosed mazes learned by the rats. Some patterns were designed to give a negative transfer effect (an alley which was blind in one maze was a part of the true path in the other, etc.). The expected negative effect was not obtained except in certain parts of a maze; the maze as a whole always showed a positive effect. Transfer was fully as good in the rats as in the human subjects. Hunter (1922) using other mazes confirmed Webb's finding that the transfer effect from one maze to another was usually positive.

The work of Webb was repeated with different mazes in the same laboratory (University of Chicago, under Carr) by Wiltbank (1919). Five mazes were used, each group of rats learning the five in a different order and finally relearning the one with which it had started. The transfer effect was positive throughout. Combining all the groups we have the percents saved in each successive maze as compared with the maze learned first:

	Maze No. 2	*No. 3*	*No. 4*	*No. 5*	*Relearning No. 1*
Saving in trials	42	41	54	52	71
" " errors	70	79	82	82	94
" " time	83	87	91	90	92

On the whole, the positive transfer effect is cumulative up to and including the fourth maze learned, and the relearning of the original maze shows some retention of the original learning in spite of the other mazes learned in the interim. The justification for this last statement is the sharp increase in the last column in trials and errors saved. The investigator himself was dubious regarding both of the conclusions we have just drawn because he found many exceptions; but on the whole the conclusions seem warranted by the data.

Cumulative transfer has at any rate been demonstrated in subsequent experiments. Bunch (1944) found that students' interest was maintained when a series of different settings of the punchboard maze (p. 651) was presented for mastery, either all in one session or one maze per day. With the one-per-day arrangement the saving was as follows in successive mazes compared with learning from scratch:

	Maze No. 2	*No. 3*	*No. 4*	*No. 5*
Saving in trials	30	38	50	56
" " errors	43	51	61	69

If a stylus maze, after being learned in one position, is then presented in a

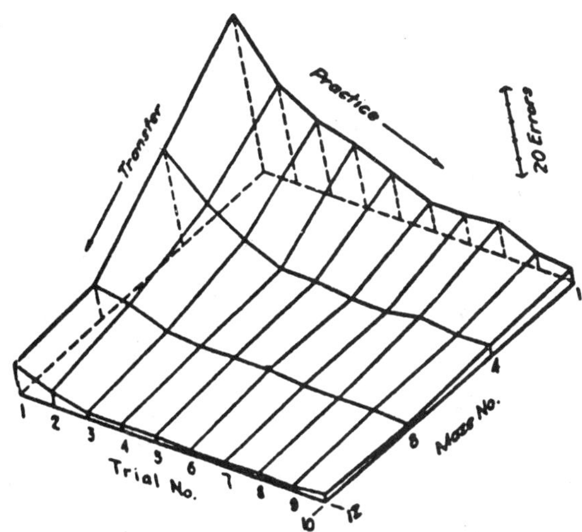

FIG. 24-7. (After Marx, 1944, p. 16.) Cumulative positive transfer effect. Rats, 25 in number, had 10 trials on one maze the first day, 10 trials on another maze the second day, and so on for 12 days. The mazes were all of similar structure, being pieces of the multiple T maze shown in our Figure 21-4, p. 619, some to be run in the forward and some in the reverse direction. Possible inequalities in difficulty were ironed out by a counterbalanced order of mazes for the group as a whole. The figure shows the Mean number of errors on each trial for the first maze, the fourth, the eighth, and the twelfth. The "running" of these rats was actually swimming, since the mazes were flooded with water. The author's analysis showed that improvement continued throughout the whole series of 12 mazes, though with typical negative acceleration.

This tridimensional plot shows the practice curves for the separate mazes by the lines that slope down to the right, and the improvement from maze to maze by the lines that slope down to the left. These transfer lines show the improvement in the first trial on successive mazes, in the second trial, and so on. The whole surface descends but flattens out in both directions.

new position, considerable new learning is necessary but less than in the first position. If it is presented successively in four positions, each differing by 90° from the one before, the improvement is progressive, the transfer effect cumulative (Higginson, 1938; Langhorne, 1948).

As part of a larger experiment Marx (1944) put a group of rats through a series of 12 rather similar water mazes and found improvement to continue throughout the series, though the gains from maze to maze became smaller as the series advanced (Fig. 24-7).

These experiments on cumulative transfer provide what we may call a normal transfer-learning curve, i.e., a normal curve of acquisition of transferable skill, knowledge, and adjustment. The curve is "normal" because the successive tasks are similar in kind and equal in difficulty (the tasks being given in counterbalanced order). This curve, like the usual learning curve, is negatively accelerated, the gain from successive tasks becoming smaller and smaller. To obtain a regular curve of this sort we need uniform tasks. A parallel case is afforded by practice in memorizing lists of nonsense syllables, the lists being similar in make-up and matched in difficulty. The negatively accelerated practice curve so obtained can well be called a transfer-learning curve (p. 744).

There must be a transfer-forgetting curve as well as a transfer-learning curve, but the curve need not have the same shape as the usual curve of forgetting which calls for the relearning of the same task as has been learned before, whereas the transfer-forgetting curve calls for the learning of a new task, usually one that is similar to a previously learned task. This problem was investigated by Bunch (1941) with results such as are shown in Figure 24-8. The transfer effect was much more persistent than the retention of a particular maze. After 120 days the two effects were practically equal. After 30 days, as the figure shows, the rats that had learned the test maze had a great advantage over the rats that had merely had some practice in a similar maze; but at 120 days the advantage was gone. The details of the particular maze were forgotten, and what was retained was merely what could be carried over from a similar maze. Human maze studies by Husband (1947) led to about the same conclusion.

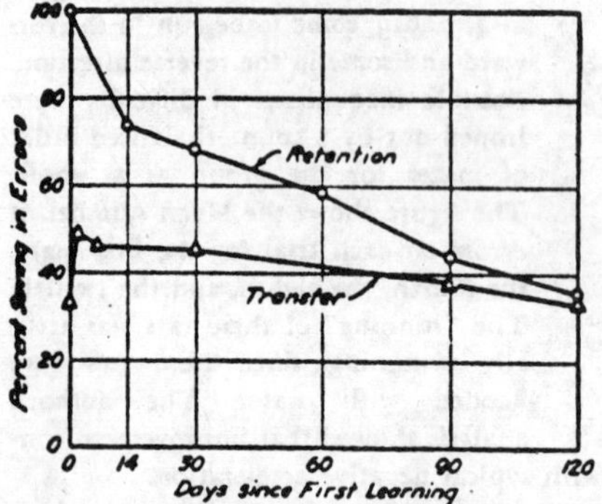

FIG. 24-8. (Bunch, 1941.) Transfer compared with retention after lapses of time since original learning. The final task for the rats was to escape by swimming from a 14-unit T maze flooded with water. The "first learning" for the retention groups was the learning of that same maze to the same criterion (three consecutive errorless trials). Thus the retention curve is the standard curve of retention (or of forgetting) with the saving measured in terms of errors. For the transfer groups the "first learning" was similar, except that the maze was shorter (five units) and different in details and that only three trials were given. The retention percent and the transfer percent were both based on the Mean score of a large control group which learned the 14-unit maze from scratch in 20.4 trials, making 203 errors in the process and requiring 1252 seconds to do the job. Retention and transfer curves for trials and time saved are similar to those reproduced here for errors saved. Massed trials were used in each learning series. Each point on the curves shows the score of a different group of rats.

These and other results obtained in Bunch's laboratory led him to formulate (1939, 1941) an important distinction between two classes of factors in transfer. We may call them broad and narrow factors. The broad class includes adaptation and emotional adjustment to laboratory apparatus and test situations, along with techniques and ways of attacking mazes or, for another example, ways of attacking lists of nonsense syllables. Such factors can be developed in one maze or list as readily as in another. Some of these factors are of course broader, more widely applicable, than others, but they all differ from the strictly narrow factors such as a particular maze pattern or of the content of a particular list of syllables. In the process of learning a particular task both kinds of factors come into play and receive reinforcement. But the broad factors are better retained than the narrow ones, as indicated by the curves of Figure 24-8. A narrow factor such as the habit of making a left turn at the first choice point would be subject to much nonreinforcement and extinction, but a broad factor such as not being afraid of *E*, or such as expecting some reward for work, would stand up in a variety of laboratory situations and be maintained.

The reality of certain broad transfer factors has long been evident in the laboratory. When a rat without preliminary experience is placed at the entrance of a maze, he crouches in a corner or tries to escape over the walls, and so makes slow progress in learning the maze. His fear can usually be overcome by a few short sessions of handling by *E*, with food given in the maze or similar piece of apparatus. Even a problem box is similar enough; a rat that has found food in a box and learned to operate its mechanism shows a marked positive transfer effect when subsequently placed in a maze (Jackson, 1932). He is rid of his fear and also provided with a positive incentive for activity.

A fairly broad technique acquired in maze running is one that enables a rat to avoid blind alleys or waste little time in exploring them. Wiltbank (1919) found his individual rats differing considerably in this respect, some of them becoming so clever as to run a new maze without entering any blind alleys. Since the alleys in Wiltbank's mazes were all straight and fairly short, the technique may have consisted in visual discrimination of a dead end from an open corner. In the mazes used by Marx (1944) the blind alleys were T-shaped like those in our Figure 21-4, p. 619, so that the rat had to penetrate the alley deeply before bringing the dead end into view; but experience in a series of such mazes, Marx found, enabled the rat more and more to avoid exploring the far ends of the alleys. Dashiell also (1920) found rats acquiring a transferable ability to detect a blind alley without exploring it to the end. In many types of problem situations, probably, experience enables the learner to pick up cues that are widely applicable as guides for approach or avoidance.

We have been reporting instances of successful transfer from one task to another and should add that maze experiments sometimes fail to yield transfer effects even when positive effects would be expected because the first and second maze patterns have much in common (Huang & Chang, 1935; Jones & Batalla, 1944). The new task seems to dominate as a whole and prevent analysis and the utilization of "narrow" abilities acquired in the mastery of a preceding task. Specific choices that have been successful in the first task may have to be reversed in the second task, as in a simple T maze, the rats having first learned to go to the left for food and then being required to go to the right. Positive transfer of the old habit gives a negative transfer effect in the learning of the new habit. This negative effect is not too difficult for the rats to overcome, but in a somewhat more complex situation the transfer may make it impossible for rats to shift consistently to the new habit (Carmichael, 1938, 1951).

TRANSFER IN TERMS OF STIMULUS AND RESPONSE

Instead of investigating the transfer of "abilities"—whether broad or narrow in scope—the psychologist may well become more analytical and consider specific stimulus-response units. So reasoned Poffenberger (1915). Such units, built up to great strength in the mastery of one task, may be helpful in a second task or may be useless and even disturbing. The transfer effect may be positive, zero, or negative. To bring to light negative or zero effects, *E* must rule out general adaptation to the laboratory situation, apparatus, and test materials, since such adaptation will certainly yield a large positive transfer effect. Poffenberger accordingly selected subjects who were already familiar with laboratory conditions and test materials. He used tasks of the paired-associates type, consisting therefore of stimulus-response units. In several days of practice, for example, the transfer group responded 100 times to a list of 50 adjectives by saying the opposite of each. In the fore- and after-tests this group and a control group responded to the same list of adjectives by giving an appropriate noun for each. So, the stimulus word *broad* called for the response *narrow* in the practice series but for a response such as *street* or *shoe* in the fore- and after-tests. The transfer group had to inhibit its well-established responses in order to respond correctly in the after-test. The results showed the predicted negative transfer effect, since the transfer group made no gain from fore-test to after-test whereas the control group gained 20 per cent in speed. In other experiments a predicted positive or zero effect was obtained. Poffenberger's conclusions were, essentially, that the transfer effect from the learning of one task to the performance of a second task should be:

1. Positive, when the same stimuli call for the same responses in both tasks;
2. Negative, when the same stimuli call for different responses in the two tasks;
3. Zero, when both stimuli and responses are different in the two tasks.

In letter symbols:

1. S_1—R_1 followed by S_1—R_1 should give a positive transfer effect;
2. S_1—R_1 followed by S_1—R_2 should give a negative transfer effect;
3. S_1—R_1 followed by S_2—R_2 should give a zero transfer effect.

A fourth possibility, not examined at that time, is that the two tasks call for the same responses though not to the same stimuli. For example, let the first task call for the opposites of these stimulus words:

Slow, Poor, Few, Near, Good, Strong, Cheap

and let the second task call for synonyms of these stimulus words:

Rapid, Wealthy, Numerous, Distant, Wicked, Feeble, Costly

What transfer effect would you predict? Wylie (1919) considered this fourth case and predicted a positive transfer effect. He argued that the effect should be positive when the second task demands the same responses as the first task even though the stimuli are different. In letter symbols:

4. S_1—R_1 followed by S_2—R_1 should give a positive transfer effect.

Wylie tested his hypothesis by the successive practice method with rats as subjects. His apparatus (Fig. 24-9) com-

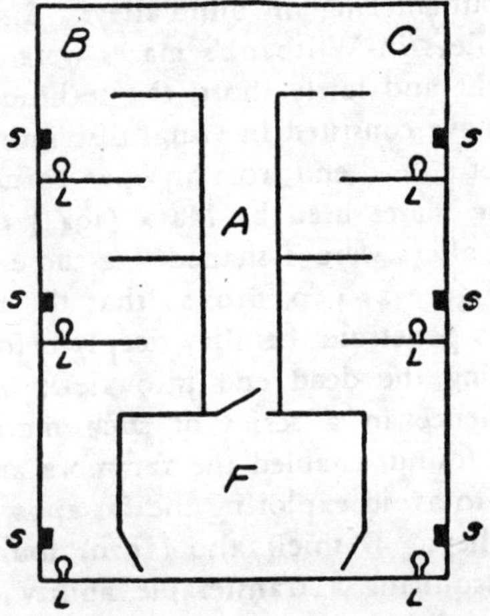

FIG. 24-9. Diagram of apparatus used by Wylie (1919). F, food box in which the rat gets a preliminary nibble, being then thrust out into the alley, A, from which he finds his way back to the food box by one of the side alleys, B and C. S,S,... small sounders emitting clicks when the rat has entered the "wrong" alley; L,L,.. small lights for similar use. Grids in the floor of the side alleys deliver shocks for the same purpose.

prised a food box and an adjacent main alley from which two side alleys led back to the food box. His procedure was first to motivate the rat by giving him a nibble of food in the food box, then to push him out into the main alley and let him find his way back by one of the side alleys. When the rat entered one of the side alleys, *E* sometimes lighted up that alley as a signal that the door from that alley into the food box was closed and the door from the other side alley open. Sometimes *E* did not give the signal but left the door open from the alley which the rat had entered. The rat learned in a long series of trials to enter an alley, whisk around quickly if the light came on, otherwise continue. The learned response to the light was, then, to turn and run to the other alley and so to the food box. When this response had been learned with light as the stimulus, *E* substituted a sound for the light, or with another group a shock for the light. Still other groups first learned to respond to sound or shock and were shifted to another stimulus. The group learning first to respond to a given stimulus served as a control for the groups shifted to that stimulus after learning the correct response to another stimulus. The trials required for learning the response were as follows:

	Trials
Response to sound signal:	
original learning	526
after learning same response to light	152
after learning same response shock	313
Response to light signal:	
original learning	199
after learning same response to sound	150
after learning same response to shock	146
Response to shock signal:	
original learning	191
after learning same response to light	158
after learning same response to sound	124

The transfer was obviously not immediate and automatic. Much new learning was necessary every time the signals were changed. But the new learning was facilitated by carry-over of the differential responses to signal and no-signal. Case 4 seems, therefore, to yield a positive transfer effect, as Wylie had predicted.

A compact confirmation of the main findings of Poffenberger and of Wylie is afforded by an experiment of Bruce (1933). His *Os* first learned a list of nonsense-syllable pairs and then learned a second list which might (1) consist of entirely different syllables, (2) preserve the original response syllables but with new stimulus syllables, or (3) preserve the original stimulus syllables but with new response syllables. A sample of Bruce's results is tabulated here:

	Original pair	*Changed pair*	*Saving percent*
(1)	xal-pom	cam-lup	16
(2)	lan-qip	fis-qip	37
(3)	req-kiv	req-zam	− 9

The 16 percent saved by these previously untrained *Os* in learning a second list of entirely new syllables is the usual transfer of adaptation and memorizing technique. The second line of the table shows an additional positive transfer effect when the old responses are attached to new stimuli. The third line, which is to be compared with the first, shows a negative transfer effect when a new response has to be attached to an old stimulus.

This last case, symbolized by S_1—R_1 followed by S_1—R_2, is rather undependable as a demonstration of negative transfer effect. Inexperienced *Os* are likely to show improvement due to the general factors of adjustment and technique; and well-practiced *Os* may be able to push aside the first task and tackle the second as if it were wholly new. To obtain a striking negative transfer effect, as was argued by Gagné, Baker & Foster (1950), the second task should present the same stimuli as the first task and call for the same responses, but with all partners changed. If the S—R pairs of the first task are represented by A-a, B-b, and C-c, those of the second task might be A-c, B-a, and C-b. This prediction was verified by Porter & Duncan (1953) with lists of 12 pairs of adjectives.

When a list had been learned to a criterion of one errorless trial, the response words were interchanged and the list learned again, but more slowly than before and with many more errors. (It is an interesting experiment to try on yourself. After a few trials of the second list you can give both response words for a given stimulus word but you do not know as yet which of the two is correct in the present list.)

The similarity factor in transfer. We have been speaking as if stimuli and responses also, were either "the same" or "different." Evidently S_1 and S_2 can be more or less different; they can be almost identical or extremely unlike. And this can be said also of R_1 and R_2. A thoroughgoing analysis of transfer in S—R terms must take account of degrees of similarity. The underlying question throughout is whether S—R units established in the first task will facilitate or impede the learning of the second task. When the two tasks present identical stimuli and demand identical responses, we can certainly predict maximum facilitation. (We simply have a single learning process, considered as divided into two successive parts.) When the second task presents new stimuli but demands the old responses, the results just examined show some facilitation but not the maximum amount. Now if the new stimuli differ only slightly from the old, the facilitation should be greater than if they differ very much. There should be a gradient of positive transfer effect corresponding to the similarity gradient of the stimuli symbolized by S_1 and S_2. Other gradients as well can be predicted from a diagram of our four major cases (Fig. 24-10).

Pioneer experiments on the transfer of a response from one stimulus to others

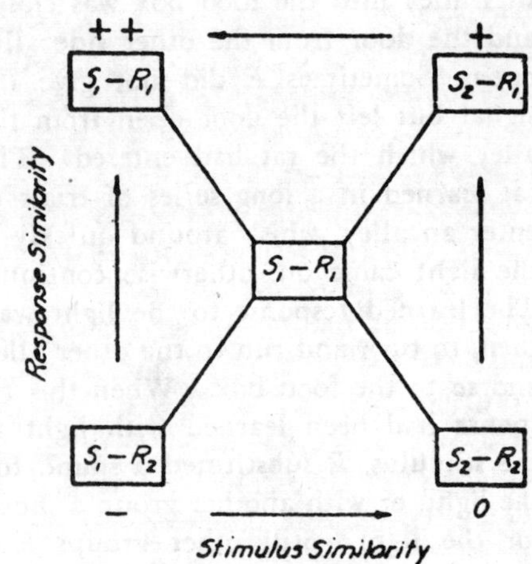

FIG. 24-10. Transfer gradients as predicted from stimulus-response relationships. The first task (from which the transfer stems) is represented by the S_1-R_1 in the center, and the second task (affected by transfer) lies anywhere around the periphery, the four main cases being represented by the corner blocks. As we have already said, the transfer effect from S_1—R_1 to S_1—R_1 is strongly positive, and from S_1—R_1 to S_2—R_1 less strongly positive, so that a gradient of increasing positive transfer should extend through the intermediate region along the top of the diagram, as indicated by the arrow. The other arrows, too, indicate the directions of increasing positive transfer effect (or of decreasing negative effect along the bottom of the diagram). So the upward-pointing arrow at the left means that when the stimuli of the second task are the same as those of the first task, while the respective responses range from very different (R_2) towards identity (R_1), the transfer effect should shift gradually from negative toward strongly positive.

The same diagram can be used for predicting retroactive facilitation or inhibition, conceived as a double or back-action transfer effect. First S_1—R_1 is learned, next (say) S_1—R_2, and finally S_1—R_1 again. Evidently the second task should exert the same negative effect on the first that the first exerts on the second, and we should have retroactive inhibition. If, however, the second task is S_2—R_1, we can predict some retroactive facilitation; and if the second task is S_2—R_2, the retroactive as well as the first transfer effect should be zero. We shall return to this diagram several times. See Osgood (1949) for a similar analysis.

of graded similarity were made by Yum (1931). He prepared sets of nonsense figures, each set consisting of a Standard and four variants which were arranged in order of similarity on the basis of rankings by a group of judges. Each Standard as stimulus (S_1) was paired with a short word as response (R_1) and a list of 15 such pairs was memorized. The following day 15 figures were presented and *O* was asked to recall the associated words, but only three of these figures were Standards, the others falling into four degrees of similarity. With 26 students as subjects, the percent of recall, i.e., of the original R_1 responses, came out as follows:

New stimulus, compared to Standard	*Percent of recall*
Identical	85
Very similar	66
Less similar	49
Still less similar	45
Least similar	36

The steps of the similarity scale were probably not equal, but the response gradient corresponded in general with the similarity of the stimuli.

The scaling of similarity. Before you can demonstrate any relation between similarity and transfer you must have some independent estimate of similarity. You may pool the ranks or ratings obtained from a group of judges, or even use the halving technique or some other refined scaling method (p. 238). Or, you may reason, the more similar two stimuli, the more likely they are to be confused and get the same response. Accordingly, you may try out your proposed stimuli in an experiment like that of Yum, just described, and use the resulting percents as a scale of behavioral similarity or stimulus equivalence (p. 589). This way of securing a similarity scale was followed by E. J. Gibson (1941) in preparation for a series of studies on transfer and interference. Instead of speaking of a similarity scale she spoke of a "generalization" gradient, using this term in the Pavlovian sense (p. 577). If a variant nonsense figure got the response word assigned to the correspond-

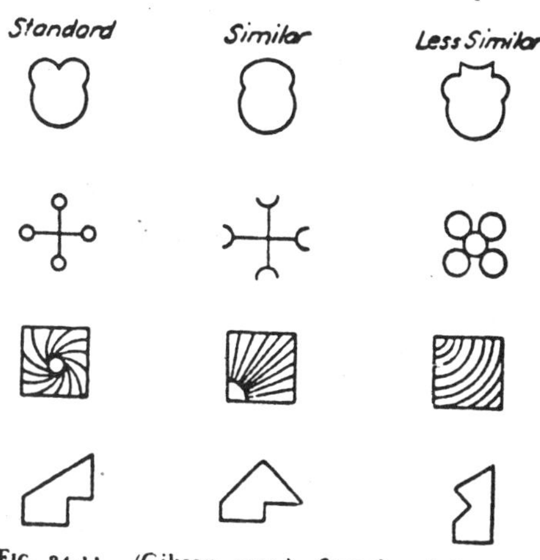

FIG. 24-11. (Gibson, 1941.) Samples of the nonsense figures used in experiments by Gibson and by Hamilton (1943) in studies of transfer and retroaction. Each Standard was given a nonsense name and the subjects had five trials for learning the pairs. On the following day, figures were presented with instructions to recall their names as far as possible, but for any one group of subjects only three or four of 12 Standards were shown, the other stimuli being figures from the similar and dissimilar classes. The percents show how often the original name was given in response to figures presented the second day. Standard, 85 percent; Similar, 41 percent; Less Similar, 10 percent.

ing Standard from 60 percent of her *Os*, Gibson used this percent as expressing the degree of confusion or generalization between these two figures.[1]

[1] This meaning of "generalization" is very different from the usual meaning which is often encountered in the literature of transfer, as when the meager transfer value of special training is attributed to the learner's failure to "generalize" from the special task to the broader application of the acquired ability. Generalization in this ordinary sense is an achievement, but in the Pavlovian sense it is no achievement but a primitive

The procedure of Yum and of Gibson for obtaining a scale of stimulus equivalence or generalization is only fairly satisfactory. It is not as objective or purely behavioral as it seems, because *O* is not instructed what to do when he sees that a presented figure is similar to one of the Standards but not exactly the same. Shall he say the name of the Standard or remain silent? The typical instructions of a recognition experiment seem more adequate. There, *O* is instructed to say "Yes" if he believes the presented figure has been shown before; otherwise, "No"; and a scale of stimulus equivalence can be worked out on this basis (p. 723).

Transfer as related to stimulus similarity. From what has already been said and from our diagram on p. 754, opposite transfer effects are to be expected from stimulus variation according as the second task demands the same responses as the first, or definitely different ones. If the responses remain the same, there should be a positive transfer effect and it should be greater the more the stimuli of the second task resemble those of the first task (upper part of the diagram). If the responses are changed, however, the expected transfer effect is negative or zero and more and more negative with increasing similarity of the new to the old stimuli (lower part of the diagram). Of course, the negative effect may be masked by the transfer of emotional adaptation and improved learning technique, but the gradients should be as predicted.

Pertinent data on stimulus similarity

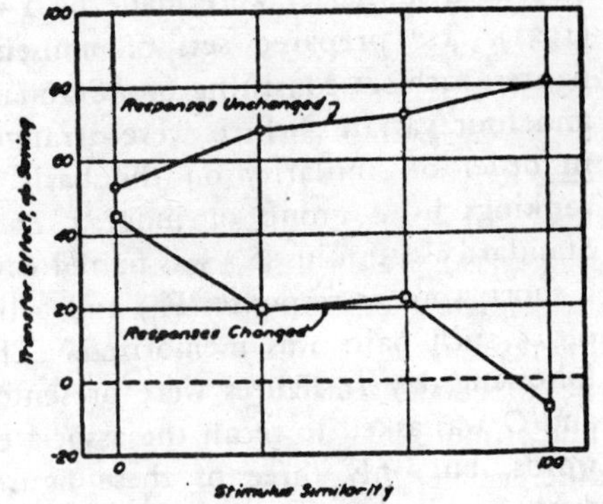

Fig. 24-12. (Data from Gibson, 1941, p. 108; Hamilton, 1943, p. 367.) Stimulus similarity as a factor in transfer. The stimuli were nonsense figures paired with response syllables. First a list of 12 such pairs was learned (to a criterion of eight correct), with the Standard figures as the stimuli. After a few minutes of rest, a second list was learned to the same criterion, the stimuli for different groups of *O*s being of different degrees of similarity to the Standards, as follows: identical, very similar, less similar, dissimilar. In Hamilton's experiment the response syllables were the same in both lists, but in Gibson's new syllables were used in the second list. So, with the S—R units of the first list represented by S_1—R_1, those of the second list were S_2—R_1 in the Hamilton experiment, but S_2—R_2 in that of Gibson. The S_2—R_1 results are shown by the upper curve, the S_2—R_2 results by the lower one. The larger differences and trends are statistically reliable.

Remembering that transfer from S_1—R_1 to S_2—R_2 is theoretically zero as far as the S—R relationships are the effective factors (Fig. 24-10), we can speculatively regard the positive transfer shown in most of the lower curve as due to the more general factors of emotional adaptation and improved learning technique, such as would be quite powerful in the inexperienced but keen college women who served as subjects in these experiments. The same general factors would be equally strong in both experiments. Consequently, we could locate the zero level of S—R transfer about where the two curves lie close together at the left. With increasing stimulus similarity, then, the curve for changed responses moves down from this speculative zero level, while the curve for unchanged responses moves up.

state of behavior, the only achievement being to advance out of this stage by aid of differential reinforcement. Pavlovian generalization might be called nondifferentiation or perhaps primitive generalization.

are contained in the twin experiments of Gibson (1941) and Hamilton (1943) who employed paired associates with nonsense figures as the stimuli. The results (Fig. 24-12) agree fairly well with our predictions. These authors predicted the results in terms of generalization and differentiation of stimuli, according to the important analysis of Gibson (1940). The stimuli of the second list must be differentiated from those of the first list if the responses are to be different; and the greater the similarity the more work of differentiation must be done. But if the same responses are called for by the similar stimuli, the work of differentiation is unnecessary and primitive generalization will help rather than hinder the learning of the second list.

Transfer in relation to response similarity. Task 1 and task 2 must now present the same stimuli but call for different responses, and the new responses of task 2 must be more or less similar to the old ones of task 1. As symbolized by the left half of Figure 24-10, task 1 will consist of a list of $S_1—R_1$ units, task 2 of a list of $S_1—R_2$ units, and R_2 will range from dissimilarity to identity with R_1. The predicted transfer effect will range from negative to strongly positive. The graded responses needed in such an experiment can be words of more or less similar meaning, as explained under Figure 24-13. The results show the predicted gradient, though the transfer effect was positive throughout instead of being negative when the new response words were definitely unlike the old ones. A clear negative effect is hard to obtain in such experiments, probably for the reason suggested in the legend of the preceding Figure.

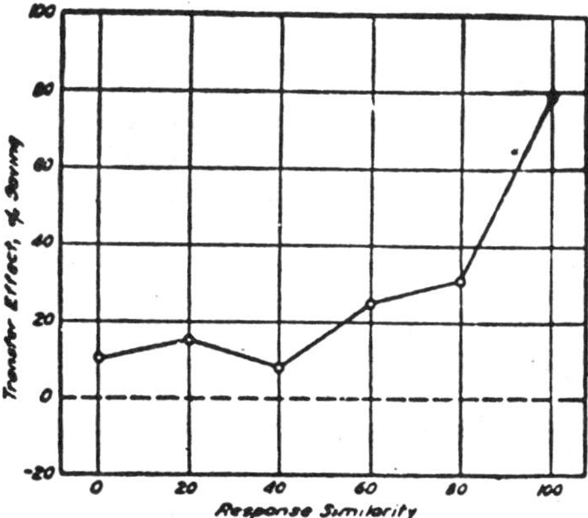

FIG. 24-13. (Data from Morgan & Underwood, 1950.) Response similarity as a factor in transfer. An experiment with paired adjectives, the stimulus and response adjectives of a pair being unrelated in meaning. When a first list of 12 pairs had been learned to a criterion of seven correct, a second list was presented having the same stimulus adjectives but new response adjectives, these new responses differing more or less in meaning from the old ones, according to a similarity scale previously worked out by Haagen (1949). The scale numbers we have used on the base line are only approximate. Here are some sample items from different lists, arranged in order of increasing similarity:

Original pair	*Substitute pair*
noiseless—sincere	noiseless—latent
gorgeous—agile	gorgeous—tripping
jellied—sullen	jellied—downcast
ingrown—angry	ingrown—enraged
willing—dirty	willing—unclean
unseen—equal	unseen—equal

The second list was learned to the same criterion as the first, with a saving in trials to learn. (The saving shown for the identical list is only approximate.) There were 24 *Os*, each one serving in all the conditions, with rotation designed to iron out individual differences, practice effects, and possible inequalities in the difficulty of the various lists.

Transfer of cue differentiation. Our discussion of "transfer in relation to stimulus and response" up to this point suffers from certain limitations. We have considered S—R as a unitary whole, and we have considered only single S—R units. Besides the establishment of an association or "bond" between S and R, there might be some learning of S by itself and of R by itself, and such learning might be transferable. And when a task consists of a *list* of S—R units (paired associates), there might be some confusion or "intralist generalization" impeding the attachment of each response to its particular stimulus.

First a reminder of what has previously been said of response readiness (p. 28), warm-up (p. 148), and especially sensitization in conditioning experiments (p. 568). A response that has been sensitized can be elicited by stimuli never before associated with it. Accordingly, when certain responses have been active in task 1 they are easily elicited in task 2 though the stimuli are new, as in our case of S_2—R_1 transfer. There must be many acquired skills, both manual and verbal, which are readily activated in novel situations. On the perceptual side, too, stimuli and objects which have become familiar in one situation may facilitate learning when they are encountered in another situation, as lists of nonsense syllables are more easily learned if the individual syllables are first made familiar to the learner (Hovland & Kurtz, 1952).

When a task presents two or more stimuli and demands a different response to each one, an important part of the learner's job is that of distinguishing or differentiating the stimuli. If they are very similar, careful attention is necessary in order to attach each stimulus to its proper response. Even if the stimuli are not similar, their different significance as *cues* may be difficult to learn. Our question is whether the cue differentiation acquired in one task can be carried over to another task and yield a positive transfer effect. In an experimental test of this question care must be taken to have the motor responses of the two tasks quite different so that the transfer effect can be attributed to stimulus differentiation alone. We shall cite a few experiments.

Rats first learned to obtain food by pressing the bar of a Skinner box, the bar being inserted into the box at the start of each trial. In the next stage of the experiment a buzzer sounded just before the insertion of the bar as a signal that no food would be obtained. With buzzer, no food; without buzzer, food. In a long series of trials the rats learned not to press the bar when the buzzer sounded. They were now introduced to the runway task and learned to run to the food box when the door of the starting box was opened. Finally, the buzzer was again sounded as a signal of no food in the food box. No immediate transfer was observed but the rats did learn not to run to the food box in fewer trials than they had needed in the Skinner box. There was a saving of 50 percent, indicating a considerable transfer of the cue learning (F. K. Graham, 1943). We should add that half of the rats learned the runway first and the bar-pressing second, with the same result. (See relevant material under Discrimination Learning, pp. 594–599.

In an experiment on groups of college students by Gagné & Baker (1950) the stimulus was a light which was either red or green and located either near the top or near the bottom of a vertical display panel. There were thus four stimuli and each of them was assigned a response letter (as S for upper green, J for lower red). The apparatus exposed the light for 2 seconds and then the response letter, and *O* tried to say the letter before it was exposed. The lights were exposed in random order till *O* had had eight trials for each. After this preliminary training, manual responses were substituted for the letters. On the table were four toggle switches, Nos. 1 and 2 on *O*'s left and Nos. 1 and 2 on his right, a switch on the left to be pressed for an upper light and a switch on the right for a lower light, No. 1 for red and No. 2 for green. *O* held his finger on a central button till a light appeared and then reacted as quickly as possible, his time to reach the correct switch being measured and his errors counted. So the motor responses of this second task were altogether different from those of the first task, though the stimuli were the same. The question was whether *O*'s preliminary practice in using these stimuli as cues for verbal responses would facilitate his using them as cues for manual responses. The transfer group of 32 *O*s, as compared with a control group of the same size, had an initial advantage of about 10 percent in speed and 50 percent in errors, and maintained a lead for 60 trials. According to our diagram on p. 754, such changing of responses to the original stimuli should give a negative transfer effect, but in the present case the original verbal response would not interfere in the least with the manual response. *O* could say or "think" the letter as he pressed the switch and might even use the well-learned verbal response as an aid in directing the manual response, as in the somewhat similar experiment of Rossman & Goss (1951).

Although the preliminary training in these experiments may be said to result in "differentiation of the stimuli," the human subjects certainly needed no special training to enable them to distinguish red from green or the upper from the lower location on the display panel, and the rats needed no special training in distinguishing a buzz from silence. What the subjects learned, we may better say, was to use these stimuli as cues for action. They had to attend to the different stimuli instead of becoming negatively adapted to them. Tasks that demand close attention to the relevant stimuli are the best for purposes of preliminary training (Gibbs, 1951).

"Learning how to learn." Extensive research by Harlow (1949) and his many co-workers has shown that the rhesus monkey, and the young human child as well, given experience in mastering a series of discrimination tasks, learn not only how to perform each separate task, but also how to attack similar tasks efficiently. They acquire a transferable technique of picking up the relevant cues. In one class of tasks, described under Figure 24-14, two objects serve as cues in the single task, and it may take the monkey many trials to select the positive object consistently in spite of its varying position. The next task presents two other objects so that the learning must start afresh. But gradually, in a long series of such tasks, the learning becomes more rapid, until finally the first trial on each task is usually sufficient to establish the positive cue for that task, as is shown by the score of correct responses on the second trial of each new task, which was:

50 percent in the first few tasks;
70 percent after 25 tasks had been mastered;
80 percent " 100 " " " " ;
88 percent " 200 " " " " ;
95 percent " 300 " " " " .

Analysis of the factors in this improvement (Harlow, 1950) showed that the monkey learned to use the object as his cue, ignoring its position, and that he learned to abandon his initial preference

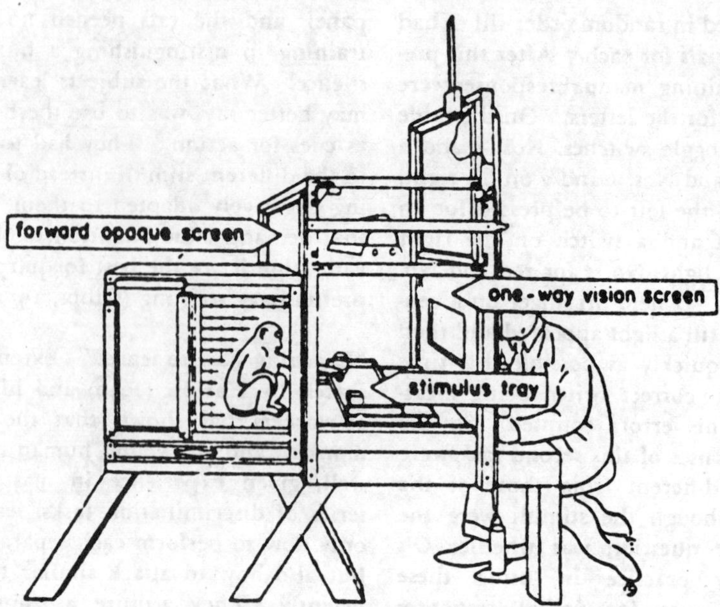

FIG. 24·14. (Harlow, 1949.) The Wisconsin University apparatus for presenting discrimination problems to monkeys. The stimulus tray can be pushed within the monkey's reach and pulled back as soon as he has made a choice. On the tray are two food wells covered with the positive and negative cue objects which are interchanged in quasi-random order. Food is placed in the well under the positive cue and then the "forward opaque screen" is raised giving the monkey access to the stimulus tray. His response is to uncover one of the wells and take the food if his choice has been correct. The cues are small objects of great variety, hundreds of them, so that each new problem can present two novel cues quite different from each other. Unintentional cues from *E* are prevented by the one-way vision screen. The monkeys are well tamed in advance.

or hunch as soon as it was proved incorrect. He may even have learned a bit of social psychology, namely, the lawful and dependable character of human behavior in the laboratory. Yet when *E* proceeded to reverse the cues in the middle of a task, *O* quickly learned to notice the change and readjust his choice. In an experiment of Riopelle (1953) monkeys already experienced in discrimination tasks were given a regular schedule of six tasks daily, the last one being the same as one of the earlier ones of the day but with cues reversed. The interest now was in the first trial of this reversed task. Would the monkey respond as he had learned to do earlier in the day? Certainly, at first, but after many days he learned to approach this task as a new problem, with the first trial purely exploratory, like the first trial with new cue objects. He learned not to carry over specific responses to certain cues but to attack each task as new and independent though of the familiar sort. This type of prolonged transfer experiment has been tried on chimpanzees, and also on young children, with similar results (Hayes, Thompson & Hayes, 1953).

In human skills cues are important for the control and guidance of the necessary movements. Many stimuli are received during the progress of manipulation—visual, auditory, tactile and kinesthetic—some of them being superfluous or even misleading, and others essential for a smooth and accurate operation. The beginner in such a task as assembling a gadget from its parts may be left to his own devices and merely urged to do his best and try for speed. Or, in more leisurely work, he may receive expert instruction on the cues to be observed and similar essentials of good workmanship, along with practical exercises on these matters. Transfer from such preliminary training is much better than from unguided practice (Cox, 1933).

RETROACTION

Just as transfer denotes a forward action of a first learning process upon a second, so retroaction, according to its name, must denote a back action of the second process upon the first. And the effect of retroaction, like that of transfer, can conceivably be either positive or negative. If negative, it would be retroactive inhibition, or retroactive interference.

The two learning processes of which we speak are not simultaneous and cannot literally act on each other. Not the previous learning process but what was learned and is still retained can play a part in the present activity. We can make use here of the construct of *ability*. We are concerned with two specific learned abilities, the previously acquired ability to perform task A and the now-being-acquired ability to perform task B. Ability A may have a positive or negative transfer effect upon the acquisition of ability B, and the retroaction question is whether ability A is being increased or decreased by the new learning ("Ability" seems a good-enough term for our purpose, though doubtless open to some objections. We could speak of a specific skill, technique, know-how or can-do. Hull found nothing better than "habit" though this word, too, carries certain undesired connotations in ordinary speech.)

Measurement of retroaction. What we would really like to measure is the amount of ability A as affected by the subsequent acquisition of ability B. Since we cannot observe an ability directly we have our subjects perform the first task again and relearn it if necessary. The basic paradigm of a retroaction experiment is accordingly:

Learn A . . . Learn B . . . Relearn A.

We must allow for some unavoidable forgetting of A in the interval occupied by the learning of B; a control or straight-retention group must learn and relearn A with no interpolated learning of B, the interval being filled with some interesting occupation believed to have no retroactive effect upon ability A. While we are about it, we may as well provide for an experiment on the "proaction" which may occur when the learning of A is preceded, instead of followed, by the learning of B. Three groups will be sufficient:

Control or Retention Group	Learns A	Rests	Relearns A
Retroaction Group	Learns A	Learns B	Relearns A
Proaction Group	Learns B	Learns A	Relearns A

Evidently there are several variables to be worked over: the time intervals, the degree of learning of A and B, the similarity of A and B, etc.

The first trial or the first few trials of the relearning can be used as a recall test of A, and this test often shows more retroaction or proaction than the complete relearning series.

The customary measure takes the retention score as 100 percent and determines what proportion of this amount is lost (or gained) by the retroaction (or proaction) group. Thus:

$$\text{Retroaction in percent} = \frac{\text{Retention score} - \text{Retroaction score}}{\text{Retention score}} \times 100$$

Retroaction in relation to transfer. The relearning of the first task after the learning of the second or interpolated task affords an opportunity for transfer. There can be transfer from B to A as well as from A to B, and our diagram in Figure 24-10, p. 754, can be used to predict the transfer effect. It ought to be the same from B to A as it was from A to B, since the B-to-A relation in each major case and in the intermediate or similarity cases is the same as the A-to-B relation. Let us consider the major cases in enough detail to bring out the expected back-transfer.

In the limiting "++" case with the two tasks identical, the S—R units being S_1—R_1 throughout, it is no rash prediction to say that both transfer effects will be positive—though the back-transfer effect will be small if the original learning has been pushed to a high level.

In the case which calls for original learning of S_1—R_1, followed by interpolated learning of S_2—R_2 and then by relearning of S_1—R_1, the transfer effect should be zero in both directions, so far as the S—R relations are concerned, though the factors of emotional adjustment and general technique might yield progressive improvement, a retroactive facilitation.

When the responses remain the same while the stimuli are changed (S_1—R_1 followed by S_2—R_1 and finally by S_1—R_1 again) the increasing familiarity and readiness of the responses should make for retroactive facilitation.

In the most interesting case of all, where the stimuli remain the same but the responses change and then change back (S_1—R_1 followed by S_1—R_2 and then by S_1—R_1 again) we can predict from the diagram a double negative transfer effect, which is *retroactive inhibition*.

As to the intermediate cases along the top and bottom of our diagram, the experiments of Gibson (1941) and Hamilton (1943) resulted in gradients parallel to those of Figure 24-12, p. 756. With increasing stimulus similarity of the original and interpolated lists, there was increasing retroactive facilitation provided the responses remained unchanged throughout, but increasing retroactive inhibition when the interpolated list called for new responses.

The locus of retroaction. There are two learning processes during which retroaction might occur. It might occur during the learning of the interpolated task B, or during the relearning of A, the original task. The problem of locus is especially important in regard to retroactive inhibition. We want to know whether the acquisition of ability B involves a decrease of ability A (when the two performances conflict with each other). In learning B do you *unlearn* A? Granted that the existing S_1—R_1 habits impede the formation of the new S_1—R_2 habits, does it necessarily follow that the S_1—R_1 habits are destroyed or even weakened? (When you have learned to read "$2 \times 85 = 170$" in French, have you lost or impaired your ability to read it in English?) In the standard recall and relearning test for retroaction, ability A may make a poor showing because of competition from ability B, rather than because of any weakness of its own. Here is a challenge for the experimentalist; he needs new methods which will show whether the S_1—R_1 units are being weakened as the S_1—R_2 units are being established.

Intrusions. In the process of relearning task A (say a serial list of nonsense syllables), especially during the first few trials, responses often occur that have been learned in task B (a similar list). They are R_2 responses intruding when only R_1 responses are correct. Suppressed intrusions also are reported which *O* has checked in the nick of time and replaced by the correct R_1 responses. Both the suppressed and the overt ones impede the relearning of task A and hold down the relearning scores. They reveal retroactive inhibition in action and show that its locus is the relearning process, partly at least. Competition of A and B responses can be regarded as the cause of retroactive inhibition—the major cause at least. It was so regarded by J. A. McGeoch (1942) in his masterly analysis of this and other problems in the field of human learning; and the same conclusion is supported in the second edition of the same work by McGeoch & Irion (1952).

But intrusions occur also in the learning of the interpolated task B. These are R_1 responses from task A which are now in process of being replaced by the R_2 responses of task B. When such false responses are made and found wrong, or when *O* checks them in time, they are on the way to extinction through nonreinforcement. So task A is being "unlearned" as task B is learned, and this unlearning is responsible for some retroactive inhibition. The locus of retroaction, therefore, is partly in the interpolated learning as well as partly in the relearning (Melton & Irwin, 1940; Melton & von Lackum, 1941).

Shall we say, then, that ability A is destroyed or impaired as the conflicting ability B is established, i.e., that the original S_1—R_1 bonds are broken as the new S_1—R_2 bonds are formed? The old responses have been extinguished, but we know that extinguished responses are capable of spontaneous recovery. Perhaps we should think of ability A as laid aside rather than destroyed, or as temporarily deactivated rather than permanently weakened.

Repeated alternation of conflicting tasks. A convenient motor task for the study of interference makes use of a pack of cards and two sets of pigeonholes, the cards being sorted differently into the two sets. Maximum negative transfer effect can be expected because the two tasks present the same stimuli and call for the same responses but with all partners changed from one task to the other. The results of such an experiment (Fig. 24·15) show marked retroactive inhibition. They also show that the inhibitory effect is transitory and that what we have called ability A is not really destroyed or diminished by interpolated work on task B. Recovery of the previous level of ability after practice of a conflicting task is sometimes complete after a day's intermission, but more often a few relearning trials are necessary before the previous level is attained.

Extensive studies of this general sort have been made by Lewis and his collaborators on several varieties of per-

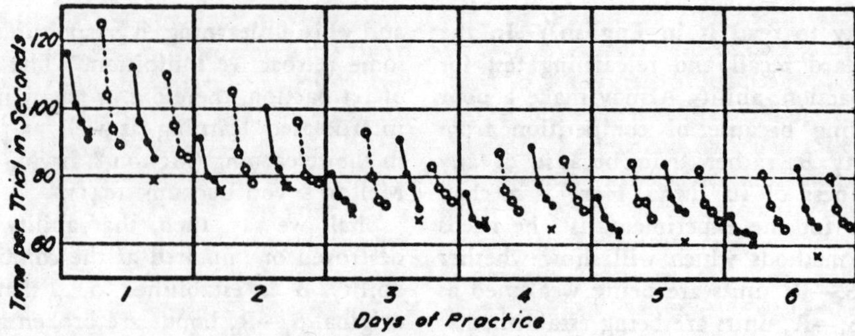

FIG. 24·15. (Data from A. J. Culler, 1912.) Continued improvement in spite of retroactive inhibition in card sorting. A pack of 80 "flinch" cards, eight of a kind, was sorted into ten pigeonholes, and there were two sets of pigeonholes calling for entirely different arrangements of the cards. The retroaction group of 14 young adults shifted from the A to the B arrangement and back again after four trials, with a total of 16 trials a day. The control group of eight young adults sorted eight times daily in the A arrangement only. Between trials there was a half-minute rest. The black dots show the Mean scores of the retroaction group in the A arrangement, the hollow dots the same for the B arrangement, and the crosses show the fourth and eighth daily scores of the control group, for comparison with the fourth and eighth A trials of the retroaction group. Analysis of the graph yields the following results:

As to retroactive inhibition:

1. It is demonstrated by the jump from the fourth to the fifth black dot of each day; also by the corresponding jump of the white dots. The A scores are made poorer by the interpolation of the B task, and the B scores likewise by the interpolation of the A task.

2. It disappears almost completely overnight. Compare the last black dot of each day with the first one of the following day.

As to continued improvement in spite of the retroactive inhibition:

1. It appears in the general trend of the whole graph.

2. It appears most decisively in the fourth black dot of each day. That score is the least affected by retroaction and the most affected by practice alone. If this fourth black dot is compared with the adjacent cross, the two scores are seen to be almost identical day by day.

3. The retroaction group, accordingly, gains as much from its eight daily A trials as the control group gains from *its* eight daily trials. Retroaction inflicts no permanent loss on the A ability.

ceptual-motor skill. The two-hand coordinator, a pursuit task with irregular motion of the target and dual control required to stay on target, was used by Lewis, Smith & McAllister (1952) and by McAllister (1952). Task A was practiced to a certain criterion of time on target. Task B, requiring reversed movements of the control levers, was then practiced to a certain criterion. Finally, task B was relearned. Some relearning was necessary to regain the original criterion; recovery was not wholly "spontaneous." But the amount of necessary relearning was comparatively small. It was less, the lower the original criterion on task A, and also the lower the criterion reached in task B. These findings both make sense. The less skill you have gained in task A, the less you have to lose through retroactive inhibition, and the less relearning you require to regain your previous level. Also, the less thoroughly you master task A, the less conflict you have to overcome in relearning task A. Yet, there are some indications in these motor experiments and in verbal learning as well that two incompatible tasks, both learned very thoroughly, may inter-tere very little when *O* shifts back and forth from one to the other.

The reversed-cue experiment (p. 594) can be expanded into an experiment on retroaction. When the cues are reversed in a discrimination box or in a simple T maze, rats of course carry over the habit that has been formed and show a negative transfer effect in the first few trials, but in the course of time they acquire the reverse habit. Then the cues are re-reversed and the original habit is relearned. With repetition of such shifts the relearning becomes progressively quicker. Both habits increase in strength but interfere less with each other (North, 1950; Gatling, 1952).

A broader view of retroaction. Incompatible tasks, composed of conflicting S—R units, are not unknown in daily life, by any means, but the student or any learner is often concerned with a looser sort of retroaction. He has two lessons to learn and his question is whether learning the second is going to drive the first one "out of his mind." Would it prevent forgetting if he rested for a while between lessons? Usually you think of rest as a means of "freshening up" for the task ahead, but the retroaction question is whether the rest may not allow time for the first-learned lesson to "soak in" and so be better retained in the future. The two lessons are probably not so incompatible that you have to unlearn the first in order to learn the second, but there might be some less direct retroactive effect.

Different theories of retroactive inhibition. We have been speaking in terms of a transfer theory. In our examples task A has consisted of S_1—R_1 units and task B of S_1—R_2 units. In the process of learning task B, the S_1—R_1 units intrude and are extinguished, and in the process of relearning task A, the S_1—R_2 units intrude and impede the re-establishment of the original S_1—R_1 units. Retroaction appears as a back-and-forth transfer, and retroactive inhibition as a double negative transfer effect. This transfer theory is widely accepted though admittedly unable to account quantitatively for the observed effects. It goes back to DeCamp (1915) and Webb (1917).

The original discovery of retroactive inhibition and the first theory for it were the work of Müller & Pilzecker (1900). They had their subjects learn a list of nonsense syllables with a recall test after 6 minutes which were spent either in comparative rest or in strenuous mental activity. The recall score was much better after the rest. They proposed a "soaking-in" or consolidation theory. They had the fact of *perseveration* to utilize. A just seen face, a just heard tune, a just read phrase, or a just learned series of nonsense syllables is likely to "come up" spontaneously. This fact indicates some degree of continued activity following the intense activity of learning. The specific brain processes may remain active and further strengthen the associations used. A few minutes of relaxation will allow the associations to consolidate, whereas strenuous mental activity will check the perseverating activity and put a stop to consolidation.

The consolidation theory would be of great practical importance if it could be demonstrated. The transfer theory certainly accounts for some of the facts but does not necessarily exclude consolidation. The pertinent experimental variables are no doubt the strenuousness of task B, its timing, and its similarity to task A. The variable of strenuousness is difficult for *E* to manipulate. The other two have been tried out in some worth-while experiments.

Similarity of tasks. We have already considered the specific effects of stimulus similarity and response similarity. When a list of items is learned in serial order, each item is a response to the one before it and a stimulus for the one after it. If two lists are composed of similar items, there will be a combination of effects with a net result, according to Osgood's (1949) analysis, of retroactive inhibition. Certainly it is a clear result of many experiments that similarity of tasks A and B is an important condition of retroactive inhibition. If task A presents a list of 4-place numbers, the maximum inhibition is obtained with task B also a list of 4-place numbers. If task A is a certain pattern of five chessmen on the board, the maximum inhibition is obtained when task B is another such pattern to be memorized (Robinson, 1920: Skaggs, 1925). The amount of retroactive inhibition increases with the degree of intertask similarity, as illustrated by some results of McGeoch & McDonald (1931). Their task A was a list of adjectives to be memorized, and their task B was a list of items which were either very unlike the adjectives or more or less like them. These interpolated tasks were learned by different groups of *O*s who scored as follows in the recall and relearning of task A:

Interpolated activity	*Percent recalled*	*Trials to relearn*
Reading jokes	45	5.17
Learning:		
3-place numbers	37	5.08
nonsense syllables	26	7.17
unrelated adjectives	22	6.67
antonyms of originals	18	7.00
synonyms of originals	12	9.08

Greater retroactive inhibition is indicated by lower percent recalled and by more trials taken to relearn the original list.

The intertask similarity which favors retroactive inhibition may lie in the *materials* or in the *operations.* When learning pairs of consonants is the original activity, canceling consonants is similar in material, while learning number pairs is a similar operation. Either kind of similarity will produce retroactive inhibition, and the greatest effect is obtained when the two tasks are similar in both respects (Gibson & Gibson, 1934). When both tasks present long lists of adjectives for study, the items from one list to be later recalled but those from the other list to be recognized, there is less retroactive inhibition than when both tasks call for recall or both for recognition. *O* gets set differently for the two tasks (Jenkins & Postman, 1949). When one list of syllables is presented to the eye and the other list to the ear, retroactive inhibition is less than when both lists are presented the same way (Nagge, 1935). When, with rats as subjects, the drive is shifted from hunger in task A to thirst in task B and back to hunger for the relearning of task A, the retroactive inhibition is less than when the drive remains the same throughout (Wickens, Hall & Reid, 1949). Apparently any condition which tends to make each task a segregated whole tends also to eliminate retroactive inhibition. For this reason, probably, it is difficult to obtain any inhibitory effect between two meaningful prose passages. It is possible to falsify a person's memory of a story if a picture follows which ostensibly illustrates the story but only partially agrees with the story (Davis & Sinha, 1950a, b). Such conditions favor confusion rather than segregation of the two tasks or experiences.

Timing of the two tasks. The question of greatest theoretical and practical importance is whether retroactive inhibition can be minimized by a short rest immediately after the first task has been learned. "Consolidation" would be disturbed if task B followed task A immediately, but would probably not be disturbed if a few minutes of rest intervened. On the other hand, the negative transfer effect should be independent of the lapse of time, at least if task B, consisting of S_1—R_2 units, necessitates the "unlearning" of task A. It is hard to make any firm predictions if task B is merely similar to task A. What are the facts of the matter? It is impossible to say, in view of conflicting results obtained both by the older and by the more recent experimenters (Maeda, 1951; Isahara, 1951; Archer & Underwood, 1951; McGeoch & Irion, 1952).

THEORIES OF RETENTION (OR OF FORGETTING)

As "time marches on," forgetting also marches with it, but one feels that time is not a force that does anything. Something that goes on in time must be the cause of forgetting. We know that suitably spaced reviews will prevent forgetting and that *disuse,* the absence of reviewing, is a necessary condition for forgetting, so that the "law of disuse" has empirical and practical validity. But mere disuse, like empty time, is a negative concept and it tells us nothing about the cause or causes that operate to prevent the lifelong retention of everything that has ever been learned.

It must be something going on in the organism that produces forgetting. Two sorts of organic processes are continually going on. One, which deals with the environment, we may call behavior in a broad sense. The other maintains the life and health of the organism itself, serving its needs in growth, repair, and recovery from fatigue and injury; we may call it maintenance. Forgetting might belong in the sphere of behavior or in that of maintenance. In the behavior sphere, disuse of one performance means that other performances have crowded it out of action, old habits being displaced by new habits, and old experiences erased from memory by the continual inrush of new experiences. There could be a competition for survival between what has already been learned and what is still to be learned. There can be competition also in the sphere of maintenance. When a muscle is frequently exercised, it makes demands on the blood stream and obtains nourishment which maintains and even improves its condition; but when it is long inactive, it cannot compete with the demands of other organs and therefore undergoes some measure of "atrophy from disuse." Maintenance of the nervous system is less well understood, though some pertinent facts are known, such as the urgent need of the brain for an uninterrupted supply of arterial blood. When the neural mechanism of a certain performance remains inactive for a long time, that mechanism quite possibly loses its prime physicochemical condition and becomes less "available," less ready for action, even if its fine details are not altogether obliterated. Experimental psychologists are understandably less impressed by this physiological possibility than by any opportunity they may see for working at the behavioral level on causes of forgetting. But they should not wholly ignore the physiological organism.

The retroaction theory of forgetting. Psychologists have been especially impressed by the facts of retroactive inhibition because in these experiments they were able to produce a little forgetting, and sometimes a lot of it, by the device of interpolated learning. Whether task A was unlearned in the process of learning task B, or whether both tasks were retained and came into competition in a subsequent attempt to perform task A, in either case the learning of task B was a known and controllable cause of the forgetting of task A. McGeoch (1942) from a survey of the experimental evidence concluded that interference provided the best theory of forgetting, for the present at least, and his view has been acceptable to many psychologists. As applied to forgetting in general, however, we must admit the unfortunate existence of certain weak links in the chain of evidence.

1. The only really clean-cut examples of direct interference are obtained when task B calls for new responses to the original stimuli of task A (or to similar stimuli), i.e., when $S_1—R_1$ units are first learned, and $S_1—R_2$ units afterward. But some retroactive inhibition occurs when the two tasks are merely similar without direct interference. There is a weak link here.

2. Between the retroactive inhibition of the laboratory and the forgetting of ordinary life there is a weak link because of the similarity factor. The two laboratory tasks must be similar in order to yield any retroactive inhibition, but the miscellaneous activities of the day are not similar to a lesson which is learned and partly forgotten by the end of the day.

3. Even admitting some slight similarity between any normal activity and any other, we still have the peculiar shape of the curve of forgetting to explain. Why should interference work rapidly at first and then more and more slowly? A gradual, straight-line descent would seem more probable. And why should a meaningful sentence be forgotten more slowly than a list of nonsense syllables, the list being certainly less similar to ordinary daily activities than the sentence?

The effect of sleep immediately after learning. According to the retroaction theory, there should be no forgetting at all during a period of complete inactivity, and very little during sleep. When Jenkins & Dallenbach (1924) put this prediction to an experimental test they obtained evidence for the theory. Sleep following learning as promptly as possible favored retention considerably. Their two student *Os* memorized lists of 10 nonsense syllables to the criterion of one perfect recitation and were tested later by the method of retained members. The intervals between learning and test were spent either in daytime activities or in sleep. The average percent recalled after the different intervals came out as follows:

	1 hour	*2 hours*	*4 hours*	*8 hours*
Awake	46	31	22	9
Asleep	70	54	55	56

According to the percents there was some forgetting during the first two hours (partly spent in going to sleep) but none at all during the following 6 hours of sleep. Jenkins & Dallenbach drew a challenging conclusion: "Forgetting is not so much a matter of the decay of old impressions and associations as it is a matter of the interference, inhibition, or obliteration of the old by the new."

This pioneer experiment was followed up by van Ormer (1932) who used the saving method and made the necessary corrections for learning efficiency at different hours of the day. Syllable lists were first learned either in the morning or just at bedtime and relearned after intervals of waking or of sleep. The saving was definitely greater after sleep, especially with the 8-hour interval (Fig. 24·16). This author accordingly agrees that forgetting, being slower in sleep, must result not from mere lapse of time or "atrophy through disuse," but from "obliteration of the learned material by the waking activity."

According to this view, daytime activity obliterates traces which have already been established. A possible alternative is that sleep immediately after learning favors the "consolidation" of the trace, while activity at that time interferes with this process. Heine (1914, p. 225) designed her experiment with this second alternative in mind. Lists of syllables were memorized either just at bedtime or 2–3 hours earlier, and relearned at the same hour the next day. The three *Os* who followed this schedule gave the following average percents of saving after 24 hours:

	Learned early in the evening	*Learned just before retiring*
Subject L	34 percent	44 percent
" C	36	49
" W	35	42
Average	35	45

Other *Os*, too, learning morning and night, showed better retention of the lists learned just before retiring. We cannot conclude simply that forgetting is slow during sleep, for in this experi-

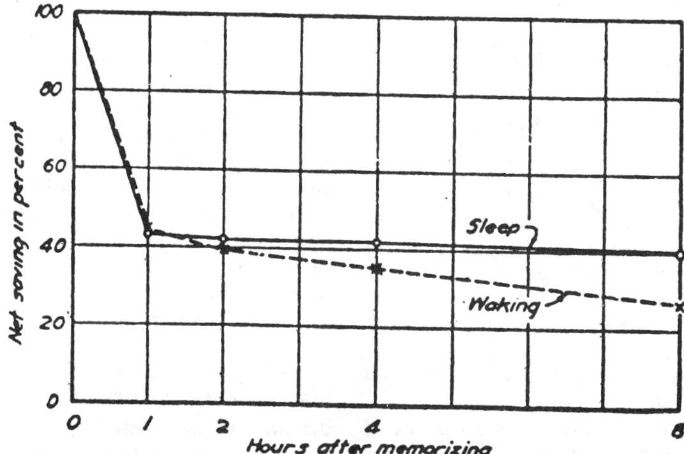

FIG. 24·16. (After van Ormer, 1932.) Effect of sleep immediately after memorizing. Two adult, well-practiced *Os* learned lists of 12 nonsense syllables to the point of one correct recitation, three lists per sitting, and relearned these lists after 1, 2, 4 or 8 hours spent either in sleep or in the daily activities of a (graduate) student. The lists were learned either at 9:30 a.m., or at 11:30 p.m. It took more readings to memorize a new list at 11:30 p.m. than at 9:30 a.m., 11 and 16 percent more for the two *Os*. Similarly, the memorizing efficiency was determined for each of the relearning hours and corrections have been made reducing all hours to the 9:30 a.m. standard. After all corrections have been made there still remains a difference in favor of sleep, and the difference is statistically reliable in the case of the 8-hour interval. Each data point represents the average of 2 × 8 × 3 = 48 lists learned and relearned.

ment the two conditions were alike in the amounts of sleep and activity intervening between learning and the retention test. It was *sleep just after learning* that was shown to be beneficial.

These experiments do not answer all the questions a student would ask from the practical point of view. They do not show whether a lesson learned just before sleep will be well retained for a long time or just overnight. For all we know, the next day's activities would soon cut down the amount retained. The student has to take accourt of his learning efficiency at different times of the day; if it is at a low level in the evening, the advantage of sleep immediately afterward would be lost. And these experiments with nonsense syllables have no direct bearing on the retention of meaningful, well-structured material. Newman (1939) found, with college women as subjects, that the gist of a short story was as well reproduced after 8 waking hours as after 8 hours of sleep, though the inessential items in the story dropped out much more in the daytime.

Experiments on retention during human sleep cannot be wholly adequate because the subjects do not go to sleep instantly after the learning. The cockroach makes a better subject for these experiments, as discovered by Minami & Dallenbach (1946). If given a chance to enter a narrow tube lined with soft material, he creeps in and remains for hours in an inactive sleeplike state. In the experiment the insect first learned to keep out of the darkened end of a bright alley. He got an electric shock whenever he entered the dark end, and it took him on the average about 15–18 shocks to acquire the avoidance habit. He was then immediately "put to sleep" or else placed in a round cage where he was moderately active. In either case he was replaced in the alley after a certain interval of time and tested for retention by the relearning method. The results, in terms of trials and shocks saved in relearning, are shown in Figure 24-17. The number of cases was sufficient to make all the differences between the two conditions highly reliable.

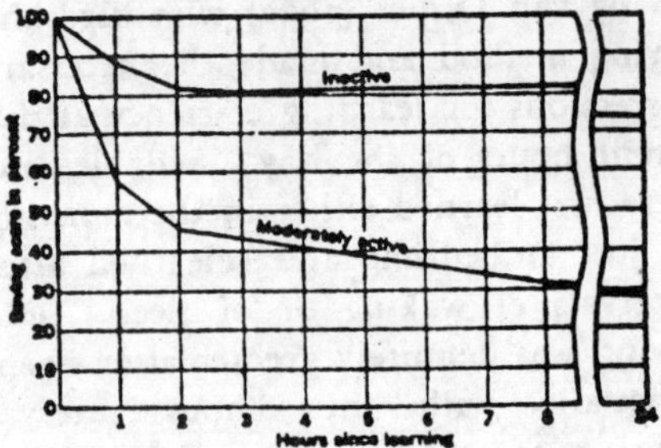

FIG. 24-17. (Minami & Dallenbach, 1946.) Retention favored by inactivity after learning.

Check experiments showed that learning ability was approximately the same after sleep and after moderate activity. A period of extreme activity in a treadmill just before learning greatly diminished the learning ability, and just after learning it greatly diminished subsequent retention of the learned performance.

But there can be forgetting not traceable to intervening activity. At least in goldfish. A bunch of them learned an underwater maze at the moderate temperature of 22° C. and relearned it the next day at the same temperature. Matched groups of them were kept during the interval in cool water (16°) or in warm water (28°). The cool-water group showed the better retention in spite of much greater activity during the interval (French, 1942). The author inferred that there must be a forgetting process independent of retroactive inhibition, dependent on temperature, and better described as "fading" than as interference.

Maintenance factors in retention. The distinction between habit and performance—between a learned ability and the activation of the ability—was important in the study of motivation (p. 664). It is almost the same as the distinction between retention and remembering ("remembering" as a comprehensive term for recall, reproduction, recognition, or any performance of a learned act). What is retained consists of abilities habits, connections, traces; but performance depends also on motivation, and it depends on physical condition. It depends on adequate blood supply to the brain, without which there is a fainting fit and no performance at all. There is a temporary loss of what has been learned, but as this loss is only temporary it is obviously not a loss of retention. Everyone will admit that physiological maintenance is essential for "remembering"—and also for learning—but there is some doubt as to whether maintenance plays any important part in retention proper, i.e., in the consolidation and preservation of memory traces. As to preservation, the main question is whether a disused system of traces will be maintained in functional condition or lose out in intraorganic competition—an elusive problem for the experimental psychologist. As to consolidation, he has found some worthwhile jobs to be done.

Retrograde amnesia after cerebral shock. A young man doing a little mountain climbing with friends falls on his head, being knocked unconscious for a moment and left in a dazed state for a couple of hours. We could not expect him to remember what happened during the dazed state, but the curious and psychologically significant fact is that his memory for the 15 minutes preceding the accident was blank and permanently so. (A personal experience of R. S. W.) Such a "retrograde" amnesia produced by a severe blow on the head has been found present in hundreds of cases observed by physicians (Russell & Nathan, 1946). A memory gap covering at least the few seconds or minutes before an accident seems to be the regular thing when a person is rendered unconscious by a blow on the head. It is the regular thing when a patient is thrown into a brief convulsion by the passage of a current through the head in electric shock therapy, and material memorized just before a shock cannot be recalled a few hours later when the patient has recovered from the daze, though some of it may be recognized (Zubin, 1948). The retrograde memory gap can be explained as due to lack of time for "consolidation of the traces" before the brain is thrown into a subnormal physicochemical condition by the convulsion or by a blow on the head.

Similar convulsions can be produced in rats by a momentary passage of carefully graduated current through the head, the two electrodes being clipped to the external ears. Such animal experiments are likely to throw some light on the reasons why electric shock therapy is beneficial to certain classes of psychotic patients. Of the many experiments that have been performed, we shall consider only a very few that throw some light on retrograde amnesia or the failure of retention for what has been learned shortly before a convulsion. There is a difficulty here since the learning of a maze or discrimination may require many trials, often spaced over several days. Much of the learning has occurred so long before the shock as to be relatively immune to the shock effect. This difficulty can be circumvented by the administration of a shock soon after each trial, since retention of what has been learned in each trial is necessary for any progress from trial to trial. Such was the procedure of Duncan (1949). There were two compartments connected by a little door—a dark compartment with a grid in the floor, and a "safe" but bright compartment. A rat would naturally prefer the dark compartment, but 10 seconds after being placed there he received a shock to the feet. In a series of trials, one trial per day, he learned to go to the light compartment soon enough to avoid the shock. A control group acquired this avoidance response in a few trials, and the cerebral-shock groups learned just as quickly if the shock was administered an hour or more after each trial. But groups receiving the cerebral shock 15 minutes or less after each trial learned more slowly, and the sooner the shock was administered after each trial (20 sec, 40 sec, 60 sec, 4 min, 15 min), the slower was the learning. At the 20-second interval there was practically no progressive improvement. A control experiment showed that fear of the cerebral shock was not a major factor; shocks administered to the hind legs instead of to the head generated much more fear but very little disturbance of the learning process. The author concluded that consolidation in this case must be complete in less than an hour, but not in 15 minutes after a learning trial.

An experiment of Hunt & Brady (1951) was concerned with the effect of electroshock on the retention of an emotional inhibition of motor activity. Sometimes the apparent loss of retention has been regarded as merely the result of motor sluggishness and inefficiency such as is often observed after electroshock treatment; and this experiment provides a check on that possibility. Rats first learned to obtain food by pressing the bar of a Skinner box. Then, in the midst of a bar-pressing session, a clicker began to sound with a floor shock at the end of 3 minutes of clicking. A few such sessions established the reaction of "freezing" to the floor, with inhibition of bar pressing and usually with defecation, a sign of "anxiety." Now came a series of cerebral shocks, 3 a day for 7 days, followed by two days of rest and then by return to the Skinner box. The bar-pressing habit was well retained, but the clicking noise now left the rats undisturbed. They did not "freeze" but continued their bar pressing. The inhibitory emotional response was not permanently lost, however, for it was present in rats tested 30 days after the cerebral shock treatment (Brady, 1951). Though the shock treatment did not follow the learning immediately (as in Duncan's experiment), it was ineffective if delayed for as much as 30 days after the emotional conditioning. A long rest period after the conditioning seemed to allow for consolidation of the emotional response (Brady, 1952).

There are other pertinent facts. In spite of the loss of a habit established shortly before a cerebral shock, a rat is capable of learning a new habit and retaining it well (Duncan; Hunt & Brady). An easy task (water maze) learned before electroshock treatment is well retained afterward, though the retention of a similar but difficult task is much impaired (Russell, 1949). If the difficult task is considerably overlearned, however, post-shock retention is much less impaired (Braun & Albee, 1952). If the rat gets the cerebral current while under ether anesthesia, the general motor convulsion does not appear and the retrograde amnesia also is absent—a result which suggests that the loss of retention is not due directly to the passage of current through the brain but perhaps to poor cerebral circulation resulting from the convulsion (Porter & Stone, 1947; Hunt, Jernberg & Lawlor, 1953). In fact, anoxia produced by compression of the rat's chest, so that he could not breathe for about a minute, had the same effect as electroshock on the retention of a recently learned habit (Hayes, 1953). There is undoubtedly much still to be discovered regarding the physiology of the electroconvulsive shock. As to the causes of forgetting we can say that the traces of what has been well learned are not obliterated though the habits and memories may be suspended and made temporarily unavailable by the cerebral "insult"; but that anything learned or experienced just before the shock may be irretrievably lost because its traces were not sufficiently established.

A Gestalt theory of forgetting. All this talk about loss of "habits" and "S—R units" is likely to seem far removed from the realities of everyday remembering and forgetting. What habit has been lost when you "can't remember who told you this story"? Or what S—R units are working when you recall the shape color of any object? The Gestalt ychologists have approached the study memory from the side of perception. To them it is incredible that the memory trace of an object should consist merely of unorganized bonds. It must have a dynamic unity like that of the sense impression of the same object. The sense impression is not a passive, photographic affair, but is molded by the observer's interests and fundamentally by his tendency to perceive the object as a whole. The perception of the whole dominates the perception of the parts and makes them conform as far as possible to the configuration of the whole. If the whole figure appears circular, slight irregularities are overlooked. Such forcing of the parts to conform to the whole is of course not a voluntary act of the observer; it is not a high-level mental process but inherent in the very process of sense perception.

The stimulus complex received from a present object is quite powerful; it resists the unifying force of perception. The irregularities cannot be wholly overlooked. The memory trace of the object is less powerful, and consequently the object will be remembered as more unitary, better configured, than it was first perceived. So far, the Gestalt theory could go along with either of the theories we have sketched. The memory trace might naturally fade out from biological causes or it might be washed out by retroactive inhibition. In either case it would become weak and unresisting. To Koffka (1935, pp. 493–506) it seemed reasonable to go a step further and postulate something describable as continued subconscious activity of a memory trace, with the whole continually exerting its unifying pressure on the parts, and the parts conforming better and better to the general form of the whole.

From this theory certain predictions could be made: (1) a figure as remembered should be a "better figure" than it appeared when originally seen—more symmetrical, freer from irregularities and gaps, and in short more unified; (2) it should become better and better with the lapse of time; (3) it should never be truly forgotten though it might merge with other remembered figures and no longer be identifiable with its original perception.

As evidence for his theory, Koffka had the results on memory for figures obtained in his laboratory by Wulf (1922). Some time after a figure had been shown —usually a somewhat irregular or unsymmetrical one, not definitely representative of any familiar object—*O* was requested to draw it from memory. Usually the reproduced figure differed more or less from the original, and the changes were classified by Wulf under the heads of regularization ("leveling"), accentuation of some part or characteristic ("sharpening"), and assimilation to some familiar shape or object ("normalization"). Only the first class was strictly according to prediction, but the other classes could be explained. Object assimilation, which is very frequent (J. J. Gibson, 1929; W. Brown, 1935), is likely to occur when the original figure reminds *O* of some object; in trying later to remember the figure he will remember the object and probably draw something that deviates from the original in the direction of the object. So the trace of the figure has merged with the trace of the object. Accentuation or exaggeration of a part or characteristic seems directly contrary to the theoretical prediction, but it is likely to occur when *O* has taken particular note of some feature of the original. This feature behaves like a subwhole with some organizing power of its own. With these alternatives all acceptable, any crucial test of the theory seems impossible. Later experimenters have found it difficult to classify all the reproductions under Wulf's three heads, and they have found a large percent of the reproductions substantially correct, at least when no great lapse of time has intervened since the original presentation—a finding which seems in direct contradiction with the theory, for the theory predicts a systematic change in the memory of any irregular or unsymmetrical nonsense figure. Statistically, there is a tendency toward increased symmetry rather than the reverse (Fehrer, 1935), and Allport (1930) found this tendency strong in 350 school children of 10–13 years of age. He exposed two figures, one bilaterally symmetrical and the other somewhat asymmetrical, and found that the asymmetry was lost in a large percent of delayed reproductions, while the symmetrical figure showed no tendency to become asymmetrical.

Relevant results of older studies. Wulf and Koffka were by no means the pioneers in the study of memory for figures, though their theory of forgetting certainly stimulated interest in this line of work and led to many later experiments. Older exploratory studies had yielded results quite similar to those of the more recent experiments. So Philippe (1897), who presented the figure not to the eye but to the hand for examination but had it reproduced by a drawing made with the eyes open, classified the memory errors or changes under three main heads:

1. Detail is lost or becomes vague and confused.
2. New detail is substituted.
3. Most frequently, the reproduction approaches the typical form of some object—object assimilation.

Kuhlmann (1906) after visual presentation found that a large share of the errors of reproduction could be brought under two heads:

1. Object assimilation.
2. Regularization of several kinds such as making lines exactly equal, horizontal, vertical, symmetrical, etc., that were only approximately so in the stimulus figure.

In attempts to reproduce a story from memory somewhat similar changes have been observed, as by Henderson (1903) who mentioned omission of superfluous and incongruous details and modification of details so as to conform to the general plot and meaning of the story.

Methodological pitfalls. In the study of retention we wish to come as close as possible to the memory trace. The method of reproduction is very convenient if the lesson to be retained is a figure or a story. But when *O* is trying to reproduce a figure or story, especially after a long interval, he does not depend on memory alone. He cannot remember all the details and perhaps not all the essentials. The trace is inadequate. As Bartlett (1932) concluded from his extensive studies of memory, what O really does in attempting to reproduce a story is to *construct* a story. He has probably retained the general form and atmosphere of the original and some of the details, but he draws on his general stock of ideas and interests so as to round out a consistent story. The reproduction corresponds only roughly to the existing memory trace of the original story. Kuhlmann (1906) said about the same of the reproduction of a figure. It "can never be described even half correctly by calling it reproduction. It is rather a construction, not a reconstruction, a construction of a certain result that is accepted in place of the original, and far from a reconstruction of a past perception." In short, the memory trace of a specific figure is only one of several factors in the attempted reproduction. One factor is obviously O's skill in drawing. Often he cannot get down on paper exactly what he wishes to show. If his memory of a figure is vague, he scarcely knows how to represent that vagueness and feels obliged to draw a definite figure which he knows must differ from the original. He would feel it rather absurd to put in irregularities of which he cannot be sure. So his attempted reproduction will tend toward regularity. If it is more regular than the original, we cannot tell whether the trace has become more regular or merely less definite.

Results obtained by reproduction of figures need at least to be checked by some other method. Recognition is free from some of the complications of reproduction and may come closer to the traces. The multiple-choice form of recognition test was introduced for the purpose by Zangwill (1937) and by Hanawalt (1937), with some later modifications by Goldmeier (1941) and by Hebb & Foord (1945). It calls for a good deal of advance preparation on E's part. Each of the original figures must be presented in a collection of more or less similar figures, so that O may select the one that seems to him most like the original. If the original is an outline circle with a 20° gap, the test should offer a choice of circles with gaps ranging by small steps from near zero to 50° or 60° so as to provide for both closure and the opposite (Hebb & Foord, 1945). If the original is a somewhat unsymmetrical nonsense figure, the test should offer similar figures including a symmetrical one and others of various degrees of asymmetry, such as have been drawn by different Os in attempting to reproduce the original. An O who is given such a test after attempting to reproduce the original will often show by his selection that his memory trace is still approximately correct in spite of the error in his reproduction (Hanawalt, 1937).

A method that demands much less preliminary labor is adapted from the psychophysical method of Constant Stimuli (Irwin & Seidenfeld, 1937). A circle with a small gap may be shown and after an interval shown again (the same figure but with a suggestion that the gap is a little different), and O is asked to judge whether the gap is wider or narrower than in the original. If he says it is wider than before, his trace seems to have changed in the direction of closure. Many Os would say "Equal" if allowed, but with only the plus and minus categories to choose from the distribution of a large group does not deviate far from a 50–50 chance (Hanawalt, 1952).

Are the changes in a remembered figure progressive with elapsed time? It is clearly essential to the theory proposed by Wulf and Koffka that the memory trace of a figure must change progressively in the direction of a good, stable figure, i.e., in the direction of a gradual yielding to the internal stresses of its dynamic structure. This implication of the theory is fully admitted, and even emphasized, by these authors. Here, it would seem, we can obtain the best evidence for or against the theory. The older results were regarded by Gestalt adherents as quite favorable to the theory. But these results were vitiated by an error of method which was pointed out by Hanawalt (1937). The old method was to have the same *Os* reproduce a figure first after a short interval and then after longer and longer intervals. "Once the *O* has reproduced the figure, his second reproduction is quite likely to be influenced more by the first reproduction than by the original impression." If his first reproduction of the circle has made the gap smaller than the original, his trace will be modified in that direction, affording a good chance for the second reproduction to deviate further in the same direction. If the original figure has reminded him of a certain object, his first reproduction is likely to show some object assimilation and modify the trace accordingly, so that the second reproduction will show still more of the same effect. If we wish to trace the curve of forgetting, or the natural progress of a trace toward "better figure," we must leave the trace undisturbed as far as possible. We must not strengthen it by continued use nor allow it to be distorted by imperfect reproductions. We cannot hope to follow the course of a single trace in a single individual. We have to work statistically, using *different groups* of *Os* for reproduction at different intervals. The same precaution is necessary if we are using the recognition method or the psychophysical method of Irwin & Seidenfeld.

Hanawalt demonstrated the seriousness of this methodological error by running two parallel experiments; in one experiment he had the same *Os* reproduce the figures at the desired intervals, but in the other he had a fresh group of *Os* for each interval. Forgetting of a whole figure or of its shape and number of parts was much more common at the longer intervals (4 and 8 weeks) when no previous reproductions had been made. Without these reviews the traces evidently became less and less adequate *but there was little sign of a progressive change in any definite direction* (Fig. 24-18). This author's results, as also those of the relatively simple recognition experiment of Hebb & Foord (1945), appear to justify rejection of the theory we have been considering. Really, the more weight we attach to Gestalt factors in perception, and so in the formation of a trace, the less reason we have to assume any continued operation of these same factors during a period of undisturbed retention.

A psychoanalytic theory of forgetting. Freud and his adherents sometimes spoke as if they believed all forgetting to be motivated forgetting and due to a wish to forget. Practically, they meant only that events associated with a sense of guilt or shame were thus forgotten, and that this forgetting was not a loss of retention but an inhibition of recall, the inhibition being removable by psychoanalytic treatment. It might appear impossible to duplicate these conditions in the laboratory. But *E* can manipulate such variables as feeling of failure, ego deflation, and anxiety at the prospect of further threat to the ego. If

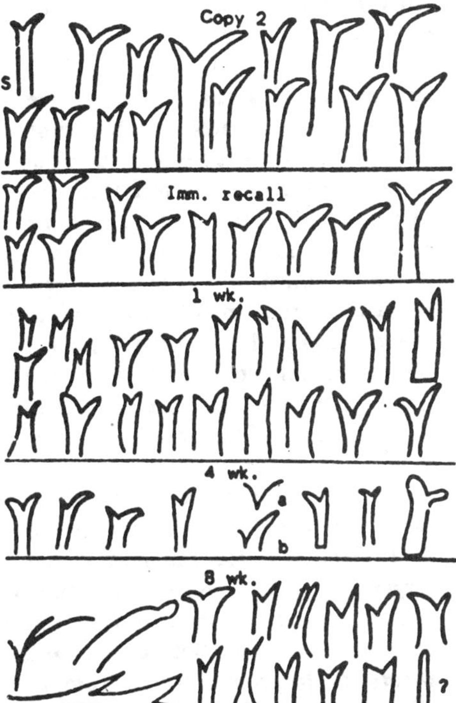

FIG. 24-18. (Hanawalt, 1937.) Drawings from copy and from memory. The original is marked S. The first collection gives sample drawings by different Os while the original was before them. After copying the figure twice, each O reproduced the figure once only, separate groups attempting reproduction after the different intervals stated: immediately, after 1 week, after 2 weeks, or after 8 weeks. The first three Os in the 8-week group reported that the figure reminded them, respectively, of a "figure branched like a tree," of a "tree bud," and of a "tree stem." Another O said it "resembled an M." The reproductions are not selected but include all that were made from memory of this figure.

The "copy" from the visible original serves a double purpose. It furnishes a starting point from which to estimate the memory changes, and it shows that changes often attributed to memory errors are present in the processes of perception and drawing.

E is able to play his part convincingly and lie with good conscience, he can aggravate *O*'s ego deflation by pretended anger or sorrow at *O*'s apparent stupidity. Later in the experiment, *E* can reinflate *O*'s ego by telling the truth about the experiment, allowing him to succeed where he previously "failed," and even praising him for a brilliant performance. The Zeigarnik interrupted-task experiment (p. 692) and the level-of-aspiration experiment (p. 693) have been utilized for the purpose, as well as other methods that have been reviewed by Sears (1943, 1944) and by Zeller (1950a).

A full-fledged experiment on repression can follow the scheme of a retroaction experiment (p. 761) but with two steps added. A certain lesson is first learned. In an immediately following task *O* "fails" and is made to feel very inferior. He is then retested on the first lesson and found (let us say) to have forgotten it partially. Now the interpolated task is resumed and *O* is allowed to "succeed" and regain his self-confidence. Finally, his memory for the original lesson is tested again; he is found (if all goes well) to remember it better than he did in the intermediate test. Schematically:

1. Learn A.
2. Practice B with failure and ego deflation.
3. Test for forgetting of A (repression).
4. More practice on B with success and ego reinflation.
5. Test for recovery of A (repression removed).

Of course there must be a control group which goes through the same stages but with encouragement instead of discouragement in task B. We should note that nothing is done to interfere directly with the memory of task A or to make *O* feel himself inferior in that task. But the two tasks are closely associated in time and place, and the theory of repression calls for forgetting of the circumstances surrounding an act for which *O* has been made to feel ashamed or guilty.

The experimental design just outlined was offered by Zeller (1950a) and used by him (1950b) with some minor refinements in an experiment on college students. His task A consisted of nonsense syllables and his task B (in which *O*'s ego was manipulated) was the "Knox cube test" for immediate memory. He obtained the predicted evidences of repression and de-repression, though he admitted that other interpretations were possible. One difficulty is to distinguish forgetting of what was learned *before* a humiliating experience from poor learning (or relearning) efficiency immediately *after* the experience. In an experiment of simpler design (ABA instead of ABABA) a temporary slump in memorizing ability after humiliation was demonstrated by Sears (1937). Even the apparent repression in ordinary life of the circumstances of a shameful act may be due to poor learning, the humiliated individual tending to withdraw into himself and become temporarily unobservant of the surroundings.

Summary. This chapter has covered a wide range of material. But running through all of it has been the question of what happens to the traces that are left by a given bit of learning. Do they help or hinder future learning? Are the traces modified by later learning? It seems clear that there is interaction between traces and new learning, and that the interaction works both ways, modifying both the trace and the new learning. The net effect of this interaction may be a help or a hindrance, depending on the number of common elements in the two tasks, and how they are set up in S—R terms. These facts suggest that all forgetting is due to the interference exerted by new learning on the traces of earlier learning, but this *retroactive theory of forgetting* is not completely adequate, for there is evidence that metabolic activities play some part in forgetting. Finally, we must be constantly on guard against attributing anything to the retention period that may have happened during learning or recall.

25

ECONOMY IN LEARNING AND PERFORMANCE

From the laws and theory of learning it should be possible to deduce practical suggestions for students and others who have much learning to do and whose work depends on acquired skills or on memory of any kind. Quite a number of practical hints on techniques of memorizing and on conditions favorable to retention could be gleaned from the preceding chapters.

Learning theory, in a broad sense, would urge the importance of "reinforcement." The human learner does not have to be rewarded with food or the satisfaction of any organic need. If he undertakes to accomplish some result and succeeds, that is reinforcement enough. But he should have "knowledge of results," tangible evidence of reaching the goal; and if the goal is distant, some evidence of progress and of reaching an intermediate goal will help him master the long route.

Less prominent in current learning theory, but equally striking in the experimental work on memory, is the advantage of meaningful over rote learning. A connected passage is much more quickly memorized than the same amount of nonsense material. This principle may perhaps be reducible to a form of reinforcement, but at any rate it offers suggestions for economy of learning.

A third general consideration has to do with timing. The phenomena of reactive inhibition and satiation suggest that it must be wasteful of time and effort to go over the same ground repeatedly without any pauses for recovery.

General theory, then, would predict certain rules for economy of learning, or at least certain probable hypotheses to be tried out in the laboratory and in such practical situations as the schoolroom. As a matter of history, however, the outstanding hypotheses in this field were not deduced from general theory but cropped up in the concrete experience of the laboratory.

RECITATION AS AN AID IN LEARNING

In memorizing any sort of material which you can reproduce—a list of nonsense syllables, a poem or prose passage, a piano piece, a drawing—you can proceed by repeated reading, listening or looking, or you can attempt to "recite" or reproduce the material when it is partly learned. You can recite to yourself, feeling free to resume reading, etc., as soon as you are stuck. No doubt alert students have used this method ever since the days of Homer and the Homeridae. Experimental work on the method began about the time of Witasek (1907) who found that recitation could profitably be attempted long before the complete lesson was mastered. This and several other early experiments were reviewed by Gates (1917); practically all of them showed an advantage of recitation over continued rereading of a lesson. Gates himself attempted to discover how early in the learning process recitation could profitably begin. His carefully designed experiment equalized such potentially disturbing factors as practice, lesson difficulty, and individual differences. (Since there were five experimental conditions, there were five squads of subjects and five lessons; by a prearranged schedule the squads and the lessons, and also the practice stages, were rotated so as to come out the same for all the conditions.) The total time allowed for study of a lesson was held constant, e.g., at 9 minutes, but this time was divided differently in the five conditions, as shown in the table above. Each *O* was handed his lesson on a mimeographed sheet and instructed to read straight through and repeat until he got the signal to recite, after which he looked away from the sheet and went through and through by memory as far as possible, consulting the sheet freely. There were two types of lesson: a list of 16 nonsense syllables, and a set of five short but detailed biographies. Immediately after the study period and again some hours later a recall test was given. The Mean percents recalled by 40 eighth-grade school children were as follows (each Mean being followed by its PE_M):

	Nonsense syllables		*Biographies*	
	First test	*Second test*	*First test*	*Second test*
All the time spent in reading	35 ± 1.3	15 ± 0.9	35 ± 1.2	16 ± 0.6
1/5 of time spent in reciting	50 ± 1.4	26 ± 1.6	37 ± 1.5	19 ± 0.8
2/5 of time spent in reciting	54 ± 1.4	28 ± 1.2	41 ± 1.2	25 ± 0.8
3/5 of time spent in reciting	57 ± 1.4	37 ± 1.4	42 ± 1.2	26 ± 0.9
4/5 of time spent in reciting	74 ± 1.8	48 ± 1.8	42 ± 0.8	26 ± 0.8

Similar results were obtained from children as young as 9 years of age. Three facts stand out: (1) The best learning was obtained when a large share of the time was devoted to recitation. (2) The advantage was still present in the test given several hours after the learning, so that recitation favors retention as well as learning efficiency. (3) The advantage of the required recitation was less marked in the meaningful material than in the nonsense syllables, probably because something very much like recitation or anticipation occurs anyway when the learner rereads connected material. Even with a list of nonsense syllables the attentive learner is likely to do some anticipation when he is supposed to be merely reading (Skaggs, Grossman, Krueger & Krueger, 1930).

With adult students as subjects Gates found that the best time to start recitations was about as follows:

After 2 minutes (4–6 readings) with 20 nonsense syllables;

After 3–5 minutes (3–6 readings) with 26 lines of a poem.

The optimal time varies with the individual as well as with the lesson. Time can be lost either in premature attempts to recite or in continued (often inattentive) reading when one is ready to recite.

The results have been confirmed in a variety of later studies. One form of recitation consists of a multiple-choice test immediately after the reading of a 600-word informative article; such an immediate test greatly improves the retention of the material (Spitzer, 1939).

An experiment along the same line but with quite a different setup is reported by Hovland, Lumsdaine & Sheffield (1949). Recruits at a reception center were shown a movie or film strip designed to teach them the "phonetic alphabet" which is used in army signals. (Instead of saying "A-B-D" say "Able-Baker-Dog.") The film strip showed the letters with their "phonetic" equivalents. After the first five letters came a review frame, a similar frame was interpolated after each few letters, and at the end of the alphabet were two reviews of all the letters. Finally, came a test, the letters being shown separately and the equivalents given by the men as far as possible. Many groups of recruits went through this experiment. For half of the groups the review frames showed the letters followed by question marks ("A-?" and "B-?"), and the group was told to call out the equivalents. For the other groups such "audience participation" was not requested, but the equivalents were shown along with the letters. The participating (reciting) groups scored higher than the nonparticipating.

A second experimental variable was introduced: half of the groups were warned in advance to prepare for a test, while the other half were not informed of the coming test. When the test scores for the four conditions are arranged in a square the averages are as follows:

	Recited	
Forewarned	*No*	*Yes*
No	17.2 letters	21.9 letters
Yes	21.2 "	22.5 "

The difference between the No-No group and the others is large and reliable; the other differences are small. Either reciting or preparing for a test hastens the learning and improves the score. The two factors, as the authors suggest, may operate in the same way, for the men who are expecting a test will take an active attitude and do some reciting.

If we ask how recitation can facilitate learning, we obtain several possible answers:

1. Recitation is a direct preparation for the test. In reciting *O* performs the acts that will be required later.

2. Recitation of partly learned material serves as a check—gives knowledge of results so far accomplished. It serves as a reinforcement of what has already been learned. There is a challenge here to the learning theorist, however, since much is learned without recitation or before any recitation is possible. The theorist must eventually show how reinforcement can occur in the mere reading of a lesson.

3. Knowing that he will soon be trying to recite, the learner is stimulated to organize the material, or to notice how it is organized. A certain student in a history class found the lectures very interesting but was frustrated by missing a good deal while taking notes. He determined to take no notes during the lecture, but to outline the lecture mentally as it went along and write it up later the same day. This was strenuous work but it succeeded admirably. The pianist or other musical performer has a serious job of memorization on his hands. In this job a preliminary analy-

sis of the musical structure of the piece has been shown to be a definite help (Rubin-Rabson, 1937).

WHOLE *VERSUS* PART LEARNING

Would it be more economical to memorize a poem or speech as a whole or part by part? By the whole or global method you read the poem through and through until it is mastered. By the part or piecemeal method you divide it into parts and memorize the parts before trying to recite the whole. From general principles we scarcely know what to predict, because different principles predict different results. On the one hand, the whole is more meaningful than the parts; if it is well organized, each part has its place in the structure of the whole but may make little sense when isolated. So meaning and organization favor the whole method. On the other hand, you must probably read the whole through several or many times before you seem to be making any progress in memorizing. To recite the whole is a distant goal; to memorize a part is a quickly attainable goal and affords some satisfaction and encouragement. So the principle of reinforcement favors part learning.

School practice leans toward the part method; "One thing at a time and that done well." Actors and musicians are known in some instances to prefer the global method. The question was put to a laboratory test by Lottie Steffens (1900). She first observed the spontaneous procedure of a number of educated adults and found all of them using mixed methods but with much part study when a nine-line stanza was to be memorized. She then made extensive experiments with five adults and two children, requiring some stanzas and nonsense-syllable lists to be learned piecemeal and others globally. The global method took less time. This was true of every *O* and of both the stanzas and the syllable lists. The advantage of the global method ranged from 2 percent to 26 percent and averaged about 12 percent. The advantage was not always present at first; some practice with the unaccustomed global method was usually necessary before *O* could use it successfully.

Whole and part memorization of serial verbal material. Experiments similar to those of Steffens have often given similar results. A critical review by G. O. McGeoch (1931b) indicated that the whole method had advantages, though some patience, intelligence, and practice were necessary for tackling a long lesson as a whole. Pechstein (1918) tried a "progressive part" method which he believed superior to both the strict whole and the strict part methods. When the parts are first learned separately, much additional study may be necessary to put them together. In the progressive part method you learn Part I, then Part II, then put these two together; now learn Part III, and put I, II and III together; and so on. Reed (1924) agreed that this method was the best for a large share of college students, in the memorization of short poems. G. O. McGeoch (1931a) gave the three methods a thorough trial on average and very bright children of 9–10 years. She prepared booklets in which were typed poems of 12 lines, one line per page for the strict part method (but with the entire poem on the last page), 4 lines per page for the progressive part method, and all 12 lines on the same page for the whole method. The material on each page was to be read through and through in the time allotted which totaled 6 minutes in all cases. At the end of the 6 minutes the children wrote all they could remember. Each of the children studied a poem by each method, the order being balanced within the groups. The bright group reproduced much more than the average group, but the scores were practically the same for every method. The whole method was unfamiliar to the children.

The same lack of any over-all advantage for either whole or part learning of poems was found by Jonckheere (1939) who took special pains to have each part of 2–3 lines make sense by itself.

The whole and part methods of study were compared at a practical level by Hoskins (1936). His material consisted of speeches (intercollegiate debates) on political and economic problems, combined into lessons of 1,500 to 15,000 words. The subjects were 360 college women in groups equated for intelligence and reading scores. Each lesson was studied by two groups, one group reading each paragraph three times before passing to the next, the other group reading the whole lesson through three times. In a second round, with comparable lessons, the whole and part groups were interchanged. The number of readings, but not the study time, was controlled. A few hours after the study period, and again two weeks later, a test was given with true-false and multiple-choice items on the facts and a written statement of *O*'s understanding of the arguments. Analysis of the data revealed no consistent advantage for either the whole or the part method. The test scores for comparable groups were almost identical right through, for both facts and comprehension and for all lengths of lesson.

Whole and part learning of mazes. A maze, like a poem, is a serial affair, to be "recited" as a whole when completely learned. The whole method of learning should have the same advantages and disadvantages in both cases. Pechstein (1917) designed a maze that could be divided into four parts to be learned separately and then put together. This piecemeal method, according to his results on both rats and men, was more economical than global learning of the entire maze. But here, too, different experiments have yielded contradictory results. Hanawalt (1931, 1934), also using both rats and human subjects, found the whole method distinctly better. After the parts were separately mastered much additional learning was required to put the parts together. With the human *O*s, working on a large maze visible only a bit at once (p. 650), 37 percent of the time was spent in learning the four separate parts of the maze, and 63 percent in combining the parts into a complete run.

On this last point, that considerable additional learning is required to put the learned parts of a maze or poem together into the whole, there is no contradiction between the various experimenters. The parts as learned separately do not fit together into the whole. Some *unlearning* of the parts is necessary. A rat that has mastered the first part of a maze separately has learned to find food and eat at the end of this part, and when he finds no food there he shows frustration and may retrace his steps instead of going forward. The end of the first part is no longer the goal, and the beginning of the second part is no longer the entrance. He has to pick up new cues to start him right in the second part. Something of the same kind occurs in the memorizing of a poem. The parts are no longer quite the same when they begin to play their roles in the whole.

Another important consideration was brought out by T. W. Cook (1936, 1937) in his experiments on human *O*s with mazes of different lengths. No decisive general advantage was found for either whole or part learning. Much depends on the length of the maze and of the separate parts. If a part is too small, *O* wastes his time going through it repeatedly, but if the whole is too long, he forgets landmarks that he has observed along the route before he reaches them again on the next trial. For each *O* there is probably an optimal size of learning unit, though this optimal unit may increase with practice in learning mazes or any special material. The individual may need to do some experimenting on his own account in order to discover his own optimal learning unit. Left to his own choice, he will often use the part method when the whole would serve him better, or the reverse (Jensen & Lemaire, 1937).

Whole and part learning of nonserial material. It was because the maze must eventually be run as a whole, or the poem recited as a whole, that the whole method seemed logically to be the best. Now many important memory tasks do not call for the building up of a unified whole. In paired associates (p. 699) only the separate pairs have to be learned, not their sequence. A vocabulary, for example, need not be learned as an ordered list. It can of course be studied "as a whole," i.e., read through and through from beginning to end, or it can be studied in parts, a few words at a time. Strangely enough, it is just here that the whole method has most uniformly been found superior (Brown, 1924; McGeoch, 1931a; Davis & Meenes, 1932). We shall cite the vocabulary experiment of Seibert (1932). She presented lists of English-French equivalents, to be learned so as to give the French in response to the English word. Each list of 12 pairs was presented six times, either as a whole or in smaller study units. The learning was done at the beginning of a class period, and the first test came at the end of the period. The average scores of 44 students, in percent of a perfect score, were as follows:

Study unit	*1 pair*	*4 pairs*	*6 pairs*	*12 pairs*
Percent remembered				
After 50 minutes	35	39	44	49
After 2 days	31	33	34	47

The SD of a difference here is about 4.5 percent, so that the 12-pair or whole method was reliably better than the 1-pair and 4-pair methods.

Card sorting is an example of paired associates; each kind of card is to be thrown into a certain pigeonhole and must be associated with its place in a square, say, of nine pigeonholes. First practice with three kinds of cards, next with a second three, then with the remaining three, before tackling the complete pack; that is the part method. Or start and continue with the entire pack; this whole method is somewhat more economical (Crafts, 1929). The reason may be that the spatial arrangement of the pigeonholes confers a degree of unity on the whole task. To get rid of this total pattern the same author in 1930 shifted to a substitution task. There is a key of 12 letters, each letter being paired with a number which is to be substituted for it on a sheet of many letters. The advantage of the whole method was diminished but not wholly lost. The less chance for a well-patterned performance, the smaller the advantage of the whole method of learning. But there is some residual advantage which may be due to better spacing of the repetitions of an act in the whole method. The repetitions may be too closely massed in time when a small block of paired associates, or a small part of a maze or poem, is gone over and over in quick succession. You cannot say "Sunday—Dimanche" or "The curfew tolls the knell of parting day" several times in a row with full attention to the meaning—as you can when you come back to the same act after an interval. This factor of massing and spacing will be taken up presently.

When the total task calls for four different responses to four different stimuli, preliminary practice on two of these responses (considerable of this preliminary practice, 30–50 trials) will diminish the amount of final practice on the total task. Yet the whole amount of practice, preliminary and final taken together, is greater than when the total task is practiced from the start (Gagné & Foster, 1949).

Whole and part learning of simultaneous coordinations. When both hands take part in a performance, it may be possible to practice each hand separately before the two are combined, and the question is whether this sort of part learning is desirable. A few experiments have attacked such problems with results that favor sometimes the part and sometimes the whole method.

Piano practice offers a good opportunity for work on this problem, since the parts to be played by the right and left hands can be practiced separately at first or both together from the start. In an experiment of R. W. Brown (1933) an experienced pianist learned three new pieces by the hands-together method and three equally difficult pieces by a hands separate method, though in the latter a two-handed trial was frequently interpolated, so that the separate parts were put together progressively. The tempo, controlled by a metronome, was very slow at first and increased by degrees up to the standard for each selection. Early progress was about equal by both methods, but at the higher speeds the hands-separate trials were of little value, and the hands-together method proved to be more economical of time and of course more agreeable musically. Music students differ, however, some finding the part method better (O'Brien, 1943).

A two-handed "finger exercise" was devised by Koch (1923) to be played on two typewriters which recorded the responses. The metronome called for 140 strokes per minute, and the criterion was reached when the exercise was played six times without error. The group of 45 *O*s which practiced both hands together found the task very difficult and confusing at the start because the fingers of the two hands had to be variously combined. The group which practiced each hand separately to the criterion before putting the hands together had a decided advantage in the long run. Of course, there was no musical or other value to be gained by the two-handed performance, except the satisfaction of accomplishing what you set out to do.

A two-handed task quite different from piano playing was studied by Beeby (1930). There were two outline metal squares side by side on a table, squares about 14 cm on a side, made of strips 1 cm wide. With a stylus in each hand, and his eyes closed, *O* tried to follow the two strips simultaneously in the counterclockwise direction, without breaking the contact of stylus and metal strip.

One adult group practiced from the start with both hands together, while a second group had preliminary practice with the separate hands. This latter group had an initial advantage in tackling the two-handed task but soon lost this advantage and at the end of 40 two-handed trials was inferior to the group which had only the two-handed practice, so that the time spent in one-handed practice proved to be entirely wasted. The whole method was definitely superior for this particular performance. There seems to be a dearth of similar studies. Of course, many two-handed performances, as with a bat, an ax, or a broom, cannot very well be split up into one-handed parts.

The net result of all the experimental studies of whole and part learning is something like this: the parts are easier to learn and the learner is often happier and better adjusted to the task if *O* begins with the parts. But he finds that putting the learned parts together requires much additional work. In the end he may have saved time and energy by commencing with the parts—or he may not—much depending on the size of the total "lesson" and on his technique and patience. In a practical situation there is something to be said for the flexible plan of starting with the whole but watching for difficult spots that may call for special attention.

MASSED *VERSUS* SPACED (OR "DISTRIBUTED") LEARNING

Many lessons are too long to be mastered in a single reading or repetition so that the practical question arises whether the repetitions should come without any intermission or whether some time should elapse between each trial and the next. What has theory to suggest? There are two well-known factors to be considered, and two others that may have some importance.

1. *Forgetting.* If the time between trials is so long that everything learned is forgotten and has to be relearned from scratch, the procedure is obviously lacking in economy. Even partial forgetting demands some relearning, some surplus work that could be avoided, so it would seem, by closely massed trials.

2. *Recovery.* Closely massed trials are likely to produce fatigue, boredom, work decrement, "reactive inhibition" (p. 669)—or whatever it is best called—and performance will slump unless recess periods are provided.

The curve of forgetting of barely or partially learned material (p. 729) drops rapidly at first and gradually flattens out. Recovery from moderate work decrement is probably rapid at first, then flattens out, and becomes almost complete in a relatively short time. The two factors taken together suggest that short pauses between trials will prove the most economical. For exact prediction we should know the rates of forgetting and recovery, both of which are likely to differ with the kind of "lesson" that is being learned. Besides, there are two other factors to be brought into the equation.

3. *Warm-up and loss of warm-up.* Usually you do not "get into the swing" of a certain task until you have worked at it for a while, and after a long rest you may have to warm up again before doing your best. Loss of warm-up, like forgetting, suggests that recess periods should not be too long.

4. *Beneficial forgetting.* There are two ways in which some forgetting may help toward mastery and permanent retention.

a. *Escape from interfering responses.*

The "remote associations" formed in the first readings of a list of nonsense syllables (p. 708)—or of a speech or poem—interfere with mastery of the complete ordered series or passage. They lead to false anticipatory responses when you try to recite what you have read. But they are likely to be weaker than the direct associations and to be forgotten more quickly, so that the learner is free from them after an intermission. In practicing an act of skill the beginner may make awkward and inefficient movements and repeat them time after time in massed trials but get away from them when he makes a fresh start after a rest.

b. *Non-dependence on primary (or immediate) memory.* If you look up a telephone number, as "Plaza 4-6315," you can repeat it easily a moment later because it falls within your primary memory span (p. 696). If you wished to retain it for later use, you would gain very little by saying it over and over without pause, still depending on primary memory rather than on any durable associations. To recite it after a lapse of five minutes is not so easy, but if you succeed, you are using and reinforcing these more durable associations.

Forgetting between trials is shown by a slump in performance, an apparent loss of skill or ability, as in Figure 25·1. You would expect some forgetting in this sort of task—holding down a key for exactly $\frac{7}{10}$ of a second. Similar examples of forgetting could easily be found in psychophysical experiments, if the Standard weight or pitch or brightness had to be remembered over any long interval. In spite of the forgetting, some improvement from day to day can be seen in the figure; more of the acquired ability is retained than shows in the first trial of the day. The distinction between learning and performance, which we found important in experiments on motivation (p. 664), is equally important in the study of massing and spacing.

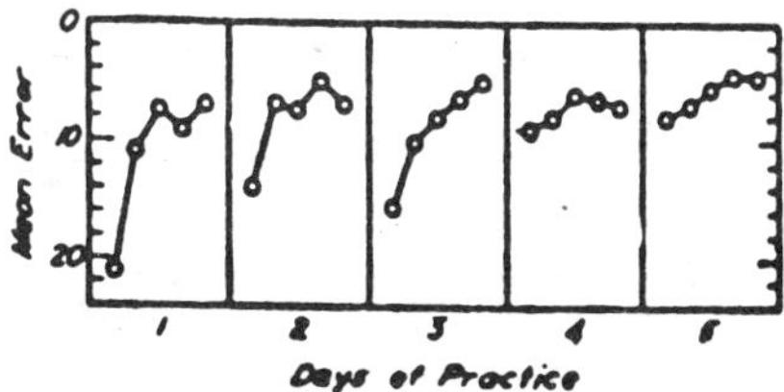

FIG. 25·1. (Macpherson, Dees & Grindley, 1949.) Learning to depress a Morse key for a duration of .7 seconds. By an arrangement of condenser and galvanometer, *O*'s approach to the "bull's-eye" was shown after each attempt; i.e., the practice was with prompt "knowledge of results." The 10 daily trials were at 12-second intervals and each data point shows the Mean error for 10 *O*s, two successive trials by each *O*. The loss at the beginning of days belongs under the head of forgetting. The error reported is in arbitrary units measured on the galvanometer scale. The figure is so drawn as to make a rise mean improvement (cf. p. 687).

Overnight forgetting in a very different task is shown in Figure 25·2, especially by the spaced group of learners. Here "forgetting" may be loss of warm-up or adjustment to the peculiar requirements of the task. But this figure brings out also an overnight *gain of the massed group* in the first few days of practice, along with a loss during the massed trials of the day. The overnight gain shows recovery from a temporary work decrement. Apparent loss during a series of massed trials with apparent gain during rest periods is characteristic of tasks which call for motor learning—better, for perceptual-motor learning since the tasks call for accurate as well as rapid work. A striking example was shown in an earlier chapter (p. 531).

Since we admit that our "learning curves" are really successive-performance curves, we recognize also that the gains

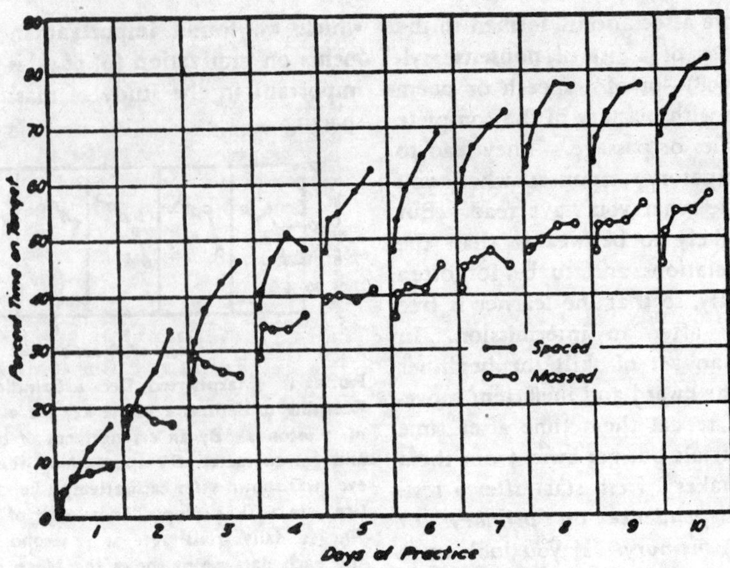

FIG. 25-2. (After Kimble & Shatel, 1952.) Massed and spaced practice on a pursuit rotor which turned at the rate of 78 revolutions per minute. Two groups, 10 college students in each, had trials 30 seconds long, 15 trials a day for 10 days. The massed group had only a 5–10 seconds rest between trials, the spaced group 65–70 seconds. Our curves here are *smoothed* within each day except for the first, second and last trials of the day which are shown separately so as to bring out (1) the warm-up jump from the first to the second trial of each day's work; (2) the common decline of the massed group following the warm-up; (3) the overnight recovery from this decline; and (4) the overnight loss after a day of rising scores. In spite of the complications introduced into the curves by warm-up and work decrement, the general course ot learning can be seen. The second trial of each day is freest from these complications. The massed group, by this criterion, begins to fall behind in learned ability after two days, and the spaced group is definitely headed for a higher level, so long as the conditions remain the same. From other experiments there is evidence that the two groups might exchange levels if the conditions were interchanged for a couple of days.

and losses shown in the curves are not always changes in amount learned, in ability, knowledge, or what Hull called habit strength and designated by the symbol $_{S}H_{R}$. We shall drop the subscripts and use the letter H alone to refer to any learned ability of any kind. When we say that performance must be distinguished from "learning," we mean it must be distinguished from the "learned" (and retained). Work decrement during massed practice is not a loss of H, nor is the subsequent recovery a gain of H. Even the overnight forgetting is not mostly a loss of H, as we see from the fact that only a little relearning may be necessary to restore performance to its previous level (Fig. 25-1). Learned ability is even increasing during the massed trials that show a decline in performance, the increase being demonstrated by the gain after a rest.

The work decrement often seen in massed trials, since it is not a loss of H, can be laid to the accumulation of inhibitions, which we may designate by the letter I, again following Hull, though here again we are departing from his restricted definition. He defined "reactive inhibition" as affecting a specific movement that had just been made, but in the motor skill experiments a considerable variety of movements is made, no one being immediately repeated. (See also our previous discussion of exploratory activity, p. 670.)

Conditioned inhibition. As a logical deduction from his conditioning principles, Hull postulated (1943, 1951) that something which we might call "conditioned resting" must occur. During continuous work the accumulating *reactive* inhibition becomes a drive toward rest. When a rest occurs, this drive is "reduced" by dissipation of the reactive inhibition. Now let some signal (conditioned stimulus) precede the rest. The response of resting, or at least of getting ready to rest, will become conditioned to the signal and be reinforced by the following reduction of the drive toward rest. The signal may be external, like the (very effective) warning bell that sounds shortly before the closing bell of a lecture. Or the signal may be a feeling of fatigue or boredom; the habit can easily be formed of obtaining momentary relief by obeying such an internal signal. Like other conditioned responses, but unlike reactive inhibition, this inhibitory factor would not dissipate during rest but would persist and produce a permanent work decrement.

This concept of conditioned inhibition should be useful in a theory of massed and spaced practice. So it would seem, but serious difficulties have been pointed out by Underwood (1953). The experimenter needs to know much more than he does now on how to produce conditioned inhibition and on how to identify and measure the resulting work decrement. To produce it he must manipulate his work and rest periods so as to build up the need for rest and also reduce the need repeatedly. Spaced trials would seem the ideal arrangement—say half-minute work periods with intervening half-minute rests—but little work decrement is demonstrable after such a series. Perfectly massed practice ought not to develop much conditioned inhibition because of the absence of rests—unless we can agree with Kimble (1949a, b) that massed practice makes little involuntary rests unavoidable in the midst of the work. If so, a 10-minute rest period after 8 minutes of massed work, printing inverted letters, should remove the accumulated reactive inhibition but leave the conditioned inhibition intact, so that the rate of work after this rest should exceed the rate of a continuing massed group but fall short of the rate of a parallel spaced group. It does so, but very likely because the spaced group, having accomplished more in the same time, has actually learned more (Wasserman, 1951). If massed practice really leaves behind it a permanent work decrement, impairing all future work on the same task, the practical implications are very serious.

The motor skills experiments, of which a great number have been made, amply demonstrate the value of spacing rather than massing, so far at least as performance is concerned. Several specific questions remain to be answered: as to how long the rest periods should be; as to whether learning, as well as temporary performance, is favored by spacing; and as to whether spacing is always advantageous or only in certain kinds of tasks. Finally the interesting phenomenon of "reminiscence" is closely related to massed and spaced learning.

Optimal length of rest pauses. Printing the letters of the alphabet upside down, with emphasis on speed, is a convenient task for obtaining abundant data in a class experiment. From Figure 25-3 it appears that the optimum intertrial rest pause for this learning task is about 45 seconds; at least longer rests were no better when the work periods were 1 minute long. Presumably with longer work periods longer rests would be necessary to allow the additional inhibition to dissipate. In a pursuit task with an oscillating target (Travis 1937) and 5-minute work periods, 20-minute rests gave the most rapid improvement, 5-minute rests next, and rests of 2 days much less rapid. In a maze experiment with rats (Warden, 1923) a 12-hour interval came out better than either 6 or 24 hours. The optimum interval probably differs with the kind of task as well as with the length of the work period.

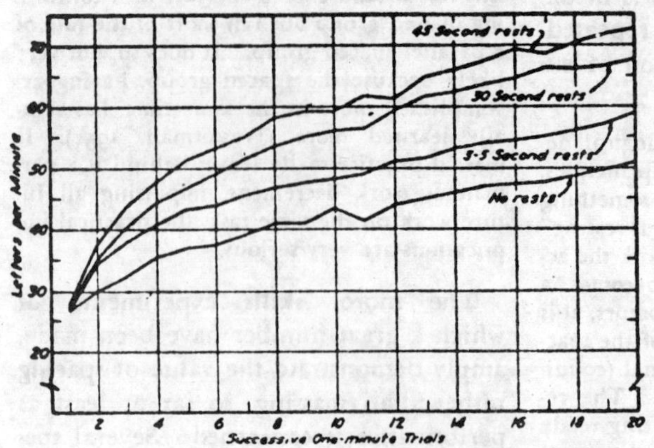

FIG. 25-3. (Data from Kientzle, 1946.) The optimum intertrial rest for a particular learning task. The task was to print the capital letters upside down, from right to left in each line so that if the page were inverted, the letters would appear right side up and in alphabetical order. Time was called at the end of each minute's work and a rest was given before the next trial except in the case of the massed group. The lowest curve shows the successive Mean scores of the 91 students in the massed group. There were 115 students who had either 3 or 5 seconds per rest period, 56 who had 30 seconds, 42 who had 45 seconds. There were still other groups. With 10 or 15 seconds of rest the curves fell in due order between the curve for 3-5 seconds and that for 30 seconds, but with rests of more than 45 seconds (up to seven days) there was no further gain. In rotary pursuit practice, with work periods of 22 seconds, rest periods of 1-2 minutes were better than either shorter or longer ones (Ammons, 1950).

For the present, in the absence of universally applicable laws, each practical situation will require its own specific investigation to determine the optimal work and rest periods.

The bald question of massing *versus* spacing is almost sure to yield misleading answers in some cases. Spacing may be too wide, and therefore inferior to massing, even though a short pause between trials is decidedly advantageous (Riley, 1952). Yet an interval of a day or longer has been found superior to massed trials in memorizing a list of nonsense syllables or of numbers (Ebbinghaus, 1885; Piéron, 1913; Perkins, 1914) or in learning the substance of a prose passage (English, Welborn & Killian, 1934).

In experiments that have shown an advantage for massing over spacing, the spacing has been wide, usually a day or more between trials, so leaving the possibility open that rest intervals of a minute or two would have been the best arrangement. But we can say this at least: the *disadvantage of wide spacing* is greater for some learning tasks than for others. There seem to be two kinds of task that suffer especially from wide spacing.

1. *Short lessons.* Lyon (1917) needed less time to memorize a list of only 12 digits in continuous readings than in one reading per day. With longer lists the advantage shifted to one daily reading and became very great when the lists were extremely long (100-200 digits). Similarly with mazes of different lengths: rats learn a short one in fewer massed than widely spaced trials, but a long one in fewer trials, one per day, than massed (Pechstein, 1921; S. A. Cook, 1928). The important factor here is probably *forgetting* which would be slight in a few quick repetitions of a short lesson but considerable when the trials were a day apart. On the other hand, the I factor would be important in massed repetitions of a long lesson.

2. *Lessons that demand much exploration to discover the correct responses.* A "spider maze" designed by T. W. Cook (1944) has six blind alleys at each

choice point. His human subjects learned it much more quickly in massed trials than with one trial per day. He got the same result with a "mental maze" which offered six choices at each choice point. (*O* had to discover by trial and error which of the numbers, 1–6, was correct at each point.) He predicted this result from a consideration of the serious consequences of forgetting in such a task; over a 24-hour interval *O* would often forget the correct choices and have to discover them again. Similar results have been obtained by Garrett (1940) and by Ericksen (1942).

An advantage for massed trials has been predicted on another basis. In exploratory activity there is a tendency to avoid immediate repetition of the same choice at a choice point (p. 622). Hence massing should favor complete exploration and avoidance of stereotyped errors. In short, massing should favor variability of attack on a problem. This prediction is logical only if the trials are "noncorrection" (p. 624), for with correction allowed the varied attack occurs in the single trial, whether massed or spaced. In everyday experience, continuous work on a difficult problem often has an effect just the opposite of variability of attack; we find ourselves in a monotonous rut from which we escape only by taking a recess from that particular problem (p. 838). It appears that both massing and wide spacing should give varied attack on a difficult problem —massing because of the I factor, spacing because of the factor of "beneficial forgetting."

Massing may impair performance but not learning. A surprising result in the chapter on Motivation (p. 667) was the quick shift of performance upward with increase of incentive, and downward with its decrease. The practice curves seemed to show much more rapid learning with the larger incentive, but the test of changed incentives indicated that the rate of learning was the same. Something of the same kind might hold of massed and spaced learning: the massed performance would be held down by the I factor and still learning might proceed as rapidly as in spaced learning. Give the massed group a few intertrial rests and its performance might improve so promptly as to demonstrate more previous learning, more H, than had appeared on the surface during the massed practice. Discontinue the rests of the spaced group and its performance might decline to a level appropriate for continuous work. Such results are shown in Figure 25-4, though the performance shifts are not great enough to prove that the two groups had been learning equally fast.

There are other ways of tackling the very important question whether massed practice is after all unfavorable for *learning* as distinguished from the temporary *performance* level. A good way is to give two groups of *O*s equal time for practice, one group with and the other without short interpolated rests, and then to test them after a comparatively long interval, say 24 hours. The test conditions must of course be the same for both groups. These requirements are met by the first trial of each day's work in Figure 25-2, page 788. During each day's work the massed group lags far behind the spaced group because of the inhibition that accumulates during continuous work, but at the start (first and second trials) of the next day, when I has dissipated, the massed group is seen not to be so far behind after all. Still it is considerably behind; massed learning, according to

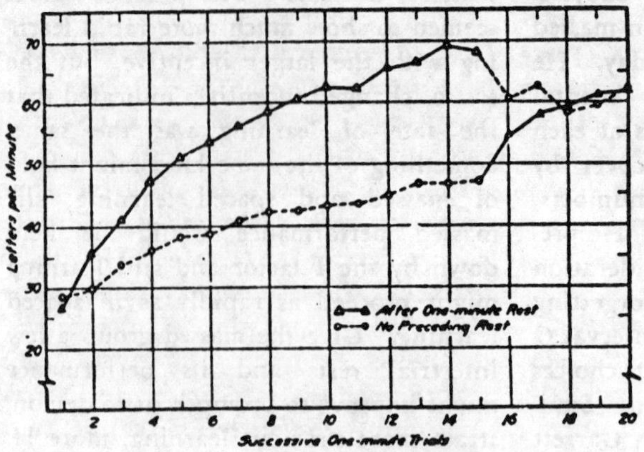

Fig. 25-4. (Data from Kientzle, 1949.) Performance changed by shift from massed to spaced trials or the reverse. The task was the same as described under Figure 25-3. One group of 81 students worked with 1-minute rests between trials, but the rests were discontinued beginning after Trial 15 and the performance promptly slackened. Another group (N = 92) worked for 15 minutes without pause and quickly improved when 1-minute rests were then introduced. With a few more trials the two groups might have interchanged performance levels. At least the massed group had learned more than showed in their performance before rest.

this test, is slower than spaced though not so slow as the performance curves would suggest. Very similar results were obtained by Adams (1952), though his curves show the massed group gaining on the spaced group and almost equaling it at the start of the fifth day's work. These studies both used the pursuit rotor. In an experiment in code learning (Fig. 25-5) the spaced group kept well ahead of the massed group throughout the single session of practice, but in a retention test two weeks later the massed group was found to be only slightly inferior.

Interpolate a single rest period at any time during a half hour of continuous work (target pursuit) and you get an immediate improvement, putting the rested group far ahead of the control group which is working along without any rest. The advantage is not fully maintained but at the end of the half hour the once-rested group is still somewhat ahead of the control group (Norris, 1953). It appears that the rest has enabled the learner to master the task more thoroughly

The rate of learning can be estimated from the number of trials required to reach (or closely approximate) the practice level or asymptote of the learning curve. As in the chapter on Motivation (pp. 664–667), we judge the learning rate to be the same in two curves if the practice levels are reached in the same number of trials, or, more adequately, if the F fraction is the same. The four curves in Figure 25-3 may be approaching different practice levels at the same rate—or they may be approaching the same practice level at different rates, the massed curve more slowly than the others. The practice would have to be carried further in order to make a decision possible. The same is true of the human eyelid conditioning curves obtained by Spence & Norris (1950) with different intertrial intervals: the shorter the interval, the lower the asymptote (in terms of CR frequency), but the different levels are approximately reached in the same number of trials. The curves shown for rotor pursuit learning by Adams (1952) look more as if the massed group were approaching the same practice level as the spaced group, but at a slower rate. The evidence from this line of attack is still indecisive.

When the learning is carried *to a cri-*

terion, such as one perfect recitation of a list of 12 nonsense syllables, a larger number of trials is needed if they are closely massed than if 2-minute pauses intervene between successive trials. From this fact alone we cannot infer that the massed learning has been slower than the spaced; the massed learners may have had to master the list more thoroughly in order to recite it while carrying the load of accumulated inhibition. If so, as pointed out by Hovland (1940a), a retention test 24 hours later, when the I has dissipated, should give a higher recall score for the massed group. But the opposite was the case; the spaced group gave the higher retention score. By this test, then, less is actually learned in a massed trial than in one preceded by a short rest.

The logical conclusion from the various tests of learning in massed and spaced trials seems to be as follows. The inhibitions that accumulate in massed trials depress performance and give an exaggerated impression of poor learning. But spacing possesses a positive advantage over and above its relative freedom from the I factor. The numerous investigators working on this problem at the present time would certainly not agree on an explanation. But we may call attention to a neglected factor, mentioned on page 787 with the label, "Nondependence on primary memory." When time elapses between trials, the learner is forced to utilize associations that are not perfectly fresh and ready—to notice cues that he would slur over in immediate repetition. These cues and associations should be used and reinforced now because they will be needed in later remembering. Jost's laws (p. 730) can be explained in the same way.

The advantage of spacing is sufficiently general, even though not universal, to serve as a practical guide when a lesson is being learned for future use. If we resort to massed study because we wish

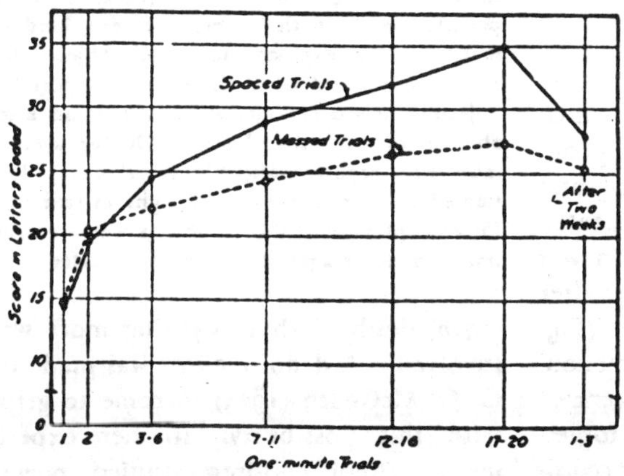

FIG. 25·5. (Data from Epstein, 1949.) Practice in code substitution with and without rests between trials. Each minute a paragraph was to be coded by substituting g for t for b, etc., the code remaining the same but a different paragraph being presented on successive pages of the 20-page test booklet. When *E* called time at the end of each minute, *O* turned the page and proceeded at once with the next page in massed practice, but found a blank page in spaced practice which he turned after a minute's rest. Groups of 37–40 college students. The spaced group gained in output much more rapidly than the massed group In the massed trials of the retention test the spaced group had a small initial lead ($t = 2.30$), which maintained for many additional trials—a fair inference being that the spaced group had learned little more in the original 20 trials though not nearly so much more as would be suggested by the output curves. Almost identical curves had been obtained in the same performance by Gentry (1940) who however did not give a retention test. The results are consistent with the hypothesis that learning is almost as rapid with massed as with spaced trials, though output lags in massed trials because of accumulated inhibitions.

to accomplish as much as possible in a single sitting, we can reasonably hope for considerable recovery after rest from the inhibitory effects of massing. Massed learning is more efficient than it appears at the time. Even so, short pauses for relaxation between intensive study periods will usually be worth while. In this connection a finding of Hovland (1938, 1949) and of Underwood & Viterna (1951) deserves consideration. They found that increased time per item during the presentation of a list was much more helpful to the learner than a pause between repetitions of the list. In learning a vocabulary of 15 items, for example, you might allow 2 seconds per item with a pause of 30 seconds between repetitions of the list, or you might allow 4 seconds per item with no pause between repetitions. Either way you would go through the list once per minute, but you would probably save several minutes by the second procedure, which favors careful attention to the important cues.

REMINISCENCE

Ballard in 1913 made a discovery which was certainly curious and might prove important in the theory of learning and remembering. He found in repeated tests that a partially learned poem was not so well recalled immediately after the learning as a day or two later (Fig. 25-6). As a name for this phenomenon, he adopted the old word "reminiscence," newly defined as the opposite of forgetting. The curve of forgetting, accordingly, started with a rise in some cases instead of the usually pictured rapid fall.

Is reminiscence due simply to rehearsal? Ballard was well aware of this possibility. He found in fact that many of the children had reviewed what they could remember of the poem in the interval between the immediate and the later test. He did not believe the reminiscence wholly due to such rehearsal, nor did Nicolai (1922), but Williams

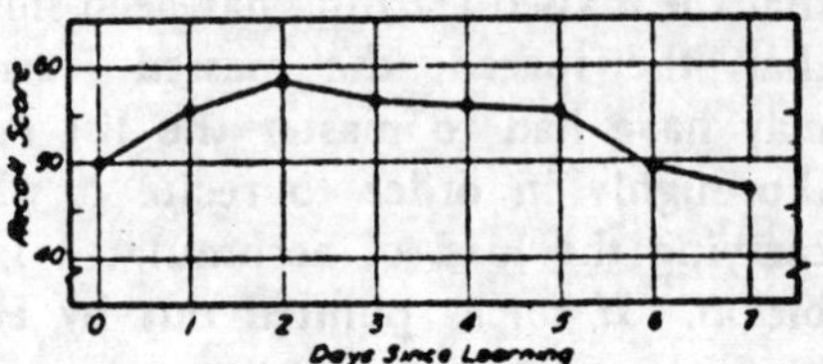

FIG. 25-6. (Data from Ballard, 1913.) Reminiscence. The recall scores are relative, the Mean immediately after learning being taken as 50 points. Ballard's extensive experiments were made on London school children of about 12 years of age, accustomed to memorize poems as a regular school exercise. The poem that gave these particular results was very interesting to the children; a less interesting one gave less reminiscence. Young adults showed only a little reminiscence, while 6-year-olds showed even more than the 12-year-olds. In a repetition of this experiment on many Chicago school children Williams (1926) found some reminiscence in the younger groups (average age, 9.7 years) but not in the older groups. Nicolai (1922) obtained positive results with a very different kind of material. He exposed 10 small objects for 10–15 seconds and asked the child to report the objects immediately afterward and again after an hour of other school work. On the average more were reported after the hour's delay than immediately; in one group of eight 12-year-olds, for example, 7.2 of the 10 objects were recalled immediately as against 8.4 one hour later.

(1926) doubted that anything more was involved. A definite effort was made by G. O. McGeoch (1935) to come to grips with this possibility. In her experiments school children studied poems for 5 minutes with recall tests immediately and again 24 hours later. After the tests were all completed, the children were asked whether they had remembered any parts of the poems during the interval and were told that such reviewing was quite in order. Some reviewing was reported by 84 percent of the younger children (Grades 3–4) and by 70 percent of the older group (Grades 9–11). But, strangely enough, those who denied reviewing showed as much reminiscence as those who reported it. McGeoch concluded that rehearsal was not the whole explanation.

It is easy to see how rehearsal could prevent a subsequent test score from falling, but how could it raise the score? It could only strengthen the memory of the lines of a poem (or other items) that were rehearsed. If an item that had been recalled in the immediate test was rehearsed a little later, that item would be strengthened. But how could an item be strengthened that was *not* recalled in the first test? It must have emerged during the rehearsal. That in itself would be reminiscence! (English & Edwards, 1941.) So reminiscence remains unexplained, and some factor besides rehearsal must be sought.

Oscillation of recall. A probable explanation was suggested by Warner Brown (1923). When a poem or list of nonsense syllables has been studied but not completely learned, some items may be recalled at one moment, missed on the next trial, and recalled again later. Such "oscillation at the threshold of recall," as Hull called it much later (Hull *et al*, 1940; Hull, 1951), had been a familiar phenomenon since the early days of memory experimentation. In successive tests of the same lesson, accordingly, items not recalled in the first test have a chance of emerging in the second. Brown gave a large class of students 5 minutes in which to write the names of the 48 United States from memory; he then lectured for half an hour on quite a different subject, and finally gave the class 5 minutes again for recalling the names of the states. Here are the average results per student:

States recalled in first test	36.41
Same states recalled also in second test	34.37
Additional states per student recalled in second test	5.29
Total score in second test	39.66

The average student forgot two states in the second test that he had remembered in the first, but remembered five in the second test that he had forgotten in the first. He was not likely to forget an item that he had recently remembered, and he had a chance of remembering some that he had missed at first. So he increased his total score and showed the reminiscence effect.

A related factor was pointed out by Raffel (1934): when *O* has been trying to recall a collection of items and has got some of them, he has stirred up the whole nest of associations and brought other items closer to the threshold of recall—brought them into a "state of readiness" (p. 720). If you try to recall a poem from long ago and get only a few snatches of it, other bits are likely to emerge a little later, until the whole poem may be reconstructed from memory.

Measurement of reminiscence. The direct evidence of reminiscence after study of ordinary memory material such as a list of items is the emergence of items in a second test that were not recalled in a first test. Such item reminiscence has often been verified. In order to derive a measure of reminiscence from the total recall scores in early and later tests, we must have a base line from which to measure. If the original learning terminates after a fixed *number of trials*, the score on the last trial only shows what has been learned on the preceding trials;

the immediately following trial (or test) will normally show improvement which is not reminiscence but simply additional learning (Bunch, 1938). But if the original learning terminates when each *O* reaches a certain *criterion*, as 8 items correct out of a list of 12, an immediately following test will normally show a loss, because the criterion has been reached at a momentary peak of the oscillation (Melton, 1936). In spite of the decrease in total score, reminiscence could be present as shown by the emergence of additional items. These difficulties can be circumvented by the use of matched groups, both groups to be treated alike in the original learning but one group to be tested immediately (or soon) afterward and the other group only after a longer interval (Gray, 1940; Buxton, 1943; Ward, 1937). Of course, this method of matched groups does not reveal item reminiscence; for that purpose, the same individuals must take both the earlier and the later test.

Short-time reminiscence. It may not have been clear to the reader what reminiscence has to do with economy in learning and particularly with massing and spacing. The early students of reminiscence were not concerned with the economy problem, but they were almost necessarily using massed learning —5 minutes for study of a short poem, for example. Reminiscence indicated that massed learning accomplished more than showed immediately afterward. But if there was reminiscence after the lapse of a day or more, something of the sort might appear after a few minutes or even half a minute. This result was obtained by Ward (1937) and regarded as an example of reminiscence which he defined as "an increase in function during a period of time in which there is no overt practice on the learned activity." (We might better say, "improved performance after a period of no overt practice.") This definition was accepted by Hovland (1938) and by many other experimenters, though with some doubt whether a reminiscence that died out in 20 minutes could be the same as the one that gained from a 1-day to a 2-day lapse of time (Figs. 25-6 and 25-7).

At any rate, clean-cut experiments can be conducted with lists of syllables or disconnected words to be memorized by the anticipation method. A control or base-line group is tested as soon as possible and an experimental group after 2 minutes or some other short rest period. Since rehearsal during the rest period would complicate the quantitative results this period is filled with color naming or some other activity that presumably prevents rehearsal without introducing retroactive inhibition (p. 766). An *O* who knows he is to be tested in a few moments is likely to see through this device of *E* and do some rehearsing after all, which may or may not improve his score (Withey, Buxton & Elkin, 1949; Rohrer, 1949; Archer, 1953).

Instead of asking how recall can *improve* with the lapse of time we may look for inhibitory factors that keep the recall score *down* immediately after massed learning. Two such factors have been suggested, corresponding to Pavlov's external and internal inhibition (pp. 559, 561), that is, respectively, to interfering associations and reactive inhibition or work decrement (p. 669). When you have partly learned a list of words or syllables and become moderately familiar with them, you are likely to say them at the wrong time, mostly too early in the series. But these false response tendencies, not being rein-

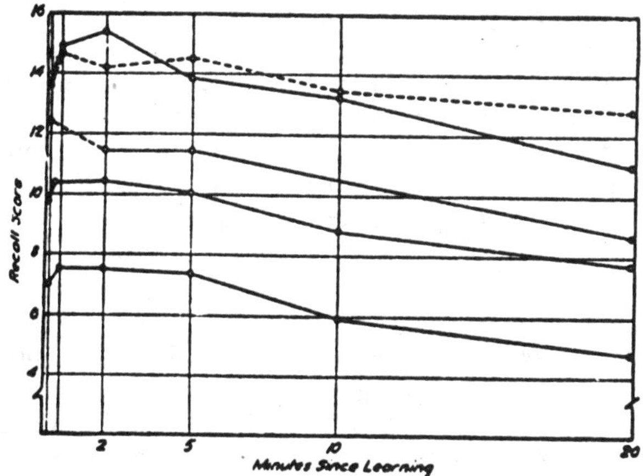

FIG. 25-7. Quick reminiscence. A list of nonsense syllables or of adjectives was presented over and over on a memory drum or film strip at the rate of 2 seconds per item, with 6 seconds between repetitions, till each *O* met a certain criterion, and a recall test was given after one or another of these intervals: 6 seconds, 30 seconds, 2 minutes, 5 minutes, 20 minutes. There was only one recall test for each list. From below upward in the figure the experiments were as follows:

Ward (1937): lists of 12 syllables learned to criterion of 7 syllables correctly anticipated.
Ward (1937): lists of 12 syllables learned to criterion of 12 syllables correctly anticipated.
Melton & Stone (1942): lists of 16 adjectives learned to criterion of 12 correctly anticipated. Here there was no recall test after 30 seconds; also there was no quantitative reminiscence.
Buxton (1949), broken line: lists of 16 adjectives learned to criterion of 16 correctly anticipated.
Buxton (1949), solid line: lists of 16 syllables learned to criterion of 16 correctly anticipated.

forced, should be forgotten more quickly than the correct responses which have been reinforced; and this "differential forgetting" would raise the score of correct responses after an interval of rest (J. A. McGeoch, 1942). This interference factor was stressed by Hovland (1939, 1951) though with recognition also of reactive inhibition (Hovland & Kurtz, 1951).

A serious objection to differential forgetting was raised by McClelland (1942b) on the basis of a novel type of memory experiment. A pair of adjectives being exposed, *O* had to choose one of them. If he chose the "right" one, a bell sounded. There were 20 such pairs, presented at the rate of 2.5 seconds per pair, with a 6-second pause between repetitions of the list. The order of pairs differed from each repetition to the next. When the criterion of 15 right choices was reached, one group of *O*s continued learning without intermission, and a matched group had 2 minutes of rest before continuing. Rest was of considerable benefit. Here any forgetting that occurred would decrease the right choices (which had been partially learned), not the wrong choices (which represented original preferences of some sort). Therefore, differential forgetting during the rest interval would presumably favor the wrong choices rather than the right ones. At any rate reactive inhibition was a more likely cause of the poor learning without rest because of the hectic activity called for, by the rapid tempo. When the time per pair was doubled during the learning, the 2-minute rest period was of no benefit, and there was no sign of reminiscence.

Work decrement, accumulated inhibition as *O* struggles with material that is hard to differentiate and organize, seems at present the main factor in short-time reminiscence, and the reminiscence is a sign that performance during the continuous work does not reveal the full extent of what has been learned. It must be admitted, however, that this short-time reminiscence in *verbal learn-*

ing is a rather slight effect, varying from experiment to experiment, and often absent. It has been studied under a variety of conditions, but the experimenters are not yet able to state exactly under what conditions it will show itself.

When we turn to *motor learning*, we find a very different state of affairs. Reminiscence, defined as improved performance after a short rest, is a large effect and very dependable. We have already seen several good examples of it (pp. 531 and 788). The large reminiscence effect in target pursuit and other examples of motor learning represents recovery from a large work decrement. The large work decrement is probably due to the strictly continuous nature of the work and perhaps also to some actual muscular fatigue, general as well as local. Where muscular fatigue is the main factor in work decrement, as with well-practiced *O*s in an ergograph experiment (p. 803), the recovery after rest may restore the performance to its original level, not more than that. But where learning is progressing during the continuous work, as in the two figures just cited, reminiscence is clearly more than recovery, for the performance after rest shoots up to a higher level than was present even at the beginning of the previous practice. Reminiscence is an important phenomenon, as we have said before, because it demonstrates that more than shows at the moment is being learned during massed practice.

No single theory can explain all types of reminiscence. The reason for this is clear if we look at our original definition of reminiscence (p. 794). Put simply, reminiscence is a preliminary hump in the curve of forgetting, a short period of improvement in performance during a period of no practice, when we would expect a drop. In some cases this hump is an artifact, due to the fact that the first retention trial is compared with the last learning trial, rather than with an immediate postlearning trial of a control group. In other cases, reminiscence is undoubtedly due to uncounted and informal practice during the retention period. But the most interesting cases of reminiscence are those in which the early part of the retention period permits the dissipation of fatigue, tension, and other decremental factors that had depressed performance at the end of the learning period; there is a gain in performance after rest, despite a possible loss in habit strength (forgetting).

WORK AND FATIGUE

The reader has undoubtedly noticed the similarity between fatigue, as the term is popularly used, and reactive inhibition. As a matter of fact, Hull (1943) treated reactive inhibition as a negative drive state, corresponding to the need for rest (see chapter on Motivation, and also Kimble, 1949a). This definition might apply equally well to fatigue. Perhaps the main difference between the two terms is the more limited meaning of reactive inhibition, which grew out of fairly specific experiments in conditioning and learning; fatigue is an extremely broad term, with half a dozen different meanings. But a vast amount of research, both theoretical and applied, has been done under the name of fatigue, and we should at least take a quick glance over the field.

Muscular fatigue. A few pages back we used this phrase to describe one possible basis of the large work decrement found in massed practice on certain motor tasks. We were referring to the decreased capacity of a muscle that follows continued or repeated contraction. This is, of course, the classic meaning of fatigue—or if not classic, at least the meaning that dominated psychological and physiological thinking during the early part of the present century. The simplest example of this type of fatigue can be demonstrated in the *nerve-muscle preparation*, a muscle and attached motor nerve dissected out of the hind leg of a frog, and kept moist in physiological saline solution. If the nerve is stimulated, the muscle will twitch, and it is easy to record the strength of contraction with appropriate equipment. If we stimulate the nerve by 50 small electric shocks per second the twitches will summate into a smooth contraction. But if we continue stimulation for 10 seconds, the height of the contraction will gradually fall, and will eventually drop to zero; the muscle is completely fatigued. After a brief rest from stimulation the muscle will recover some of its contractility, but may still show after-effects from the first fatigue period.

A complete understanding of this simple experiment would require a thorough knowledge of the processes involved in muscular contraction, a subject which is not too thoroughly worked out yet by the physiologists. But in a loose way, we can say that the muscle *expends energy*. The process uses up fuel (e.g., glycogen), which may be thought of as the stored-up energy, but it also uses oxygen and produces waste products like carbon dioxide and lactic acid. Fatigue may result from a deficiency in either fuel or oxygen, or from an accumulation of waste products. The fuel deficiencies are usually temporary ones, occurring in the small immediately available supplies; even in the excised nerve-muscle preparation there are large reserves from which the local reserves can be replenished, and in the intact organism there are elaborate systems of reserves. The oxygen reserves are less adequate at all levels, and even relatively small amounts of waste products will block the contractile process if they are allowed to accumulate. In the small excised frog muscle, oxygen and wastes are readily interchanged with the saline solution in which the muscle is immersed, but in the intact organism the muscles are highly dependent on the circulatory system for this interchange.

Equilibration. Fatigue results when a muscle uses up fuel or oxygen faster than it can be replaced, or accumulates waste products faster than they can be cleared away. It is like the state of bankruptcy which results from spending beyond one's income. This analogy makes it clear why a muscle like the heart can keep on contracting for decades without signs of fatigue; the rate of energy expenditure is kept in pace with income. There are many other examples in which muscles similarly maintain an adequate bank balance over long periods. A healthy man may walk steadily for hours without much fatigue, once he has developed muscles and blood supply that can handle the work output as it occurs without running a deficit. Nerves are singularly resistant to fatigue, for the nerve impulse uses only minute (but measurable) amounts of energy, and there are relatively large reserves within the fibers. But one can demonstrate a kind of fatigue in the nerve by stimulating at a rate of perhaps 100 times per second, so that each impulse travels in the relative refractory phase of its predecessor. There will still be 100 impulses per second, but each will be smaller than the normal impulse; the nerve fiber balances its budget by cutting down expenditures so that they just balance income (see pp. 268–270). This so-called *equilibration* is a very handy concept to remember. Something quite parallel can be observed even in the laborer who automatically adopts a rate of digging that he can maintain for the expected work period; almost any book on applied psychology will tell you that the hourly work output is higher on an eight-hour day than on a ten-hour day. In other words, it is probably only in laboratory experiments, athletic events, and rare emergencies that either a muscle or the whole organism reaches the end-point of fatigue that might be called exhaustion. On the contrary, it is usually very difficult to find objective behavioral evidence of fatigue after a day of work, as we shall see later.

The ergograph. The nerve-muscle preparation is very instructive, but as psychologists we would like to study work in the intact human being. The nearest thing we can find to the nerve-muscle preparation is the movement of a single member. For example, we can arrange a hand rest that immobilizes all but the middle finger and make *O* pull weight repeatedly by bending this ger. Of course, there will be a writing point and moving drum to record the pulls. Such apparatus is called an *ergograph*. Figure 25-8 shows the most famous, developed by Mosso (1890) and widely used. In addition to the writing point, there is often a cumulative recording tape that gives the total distance the weight has been lifted. The amount of work done in a given period is the weight times the total distance, usually expressed in metric units (kilogrammeters). Equally useful is the shape of the curve obtained by recording the series of pulls on a slow-moving writing surface; the resulting *ergograms* or *work curves* are illustrated in Figure 25-9. (See also p. 688, in the chapter on Motivation).

The Mosso ergograph is somewhat cumbersome in actual use. For one thing, it is rather difficult to fasten the unused fingers and the hand securely enough so that *O* cannot move them, or even pull a bit with his whole arm when the finger gives out. Further, immobilizing the unused fingers prevents normal coordinated movement of the free finger; Ash (1914) found that the middle finger would recover from its "exhaustion" as soon as the other fingers were released from the restraining clamps. It is probably more satisfactory to use a gadget with a pistol grip to grasp and a trigger to pull repeatedly, or a thong and finger rest that can be pulled together by a pinching movement of thumb and finger. If a spring is substituted for the weights, and a pen for the older smoked drum, the whole apparatus can be mounted on a light board that will slip across the table if *O* tries to substitute an arm movement for the finger. Other ergographs have been made for other parts of the body, as the bicycle ergograph for the legs, and a modification of the gymnasium "chest weights" for the arm (Yochelson, 1930).

The locus of "muscular" fatigue. It seems obvious that muscular fatigue must occur in the muscles, but actually this is true only in a limited sense. The

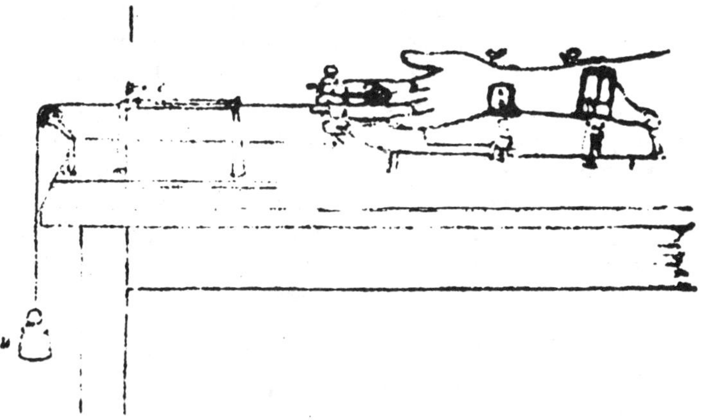

FIG. 25-8. (From Howell, 1900.) The Mosso ergograph. Note the hand rest, which is designed to limit movement to the middle finger. The wire running from the middle finger to the weight is attached to a carriage on tracks; the pointer sticking up from this carriage records the strokes on a kymograph drum (not shown).

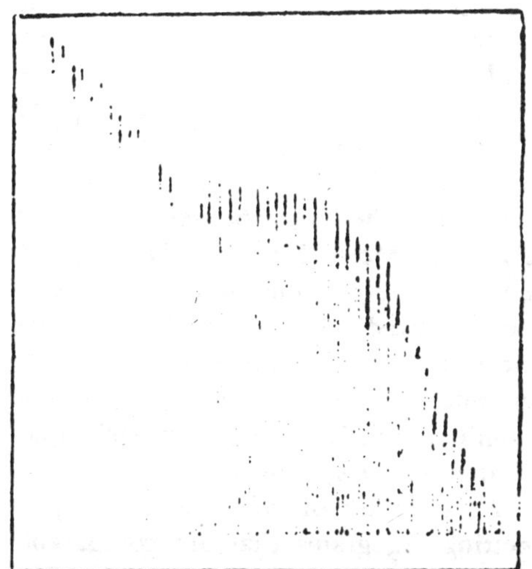

FIG. 25-9. Sample ergogram. The rather abrupt drop from extensive lifts to zero lifts often occurs with the weight ergograph.

early experiments seemed to indicate that the fatigue breakdown occurred considerably higher up in the nervous system. Let us go back to the nerve-muscle preparation. After the muscle has stopped responding to stimulation of its nerve, it is possible to get a fair contraction by applying the electrodes directly to the muscle. It is also possible to demonstrate that the nerve is still functioning. Hence failure must have occurred at the junction of nerve and muscle; whether it was the fatigue of the fine nerve branches, or of a special junctional tissue, or a slowing down of the muscle which mistuned it in relation to the nerve impulse (Fulton, 1926) need not concern us here. Similarly, it can easily be shown that the finger muscle is quite capable of lifting the weight after *O* is quite sure he cannot move it a bit. As early as 1890, Mosso found that an "exhausted" finger could be made to respond by electric stimulation (through the skin) of either the muscle or its motor nerve. The implication is that the fatigue has occurred higher up in the nervous system. But this need not mean that some connections in the higher centers have failed through metabolic changes. More probable is the view that the response is inhibited by sensory impulses arising in the muscle itself. Thorndike suggested something like this in 1914 when he pointed out that work falls off because it becomes unbearable. Anyone who has worked on an ergograph—or in any situation which produces marked fatigue—knows that "it hurts" to keep on going after a certain stage (Woodworth, 1903). It is true, as Robinson (1934) pointed out, that the painful stage gives way to numbness if *O* persists in pulling up the weight, but inhibitory impulses may still be flowing from the muscle to lower centers. As a matter of fact, there is some physiological evidence for such reflex inhibition (Matthews, 1933; Seyffarth, 1940). The inhibitory impulses are probably stimulated by chemical changes in the muscles during fatigue—perhaps by accumulation of waste products, for the impulses increase when the muscle is forced to contract with impaired circulation. So muscular fatigue in the intact organism turns out to be due, not to any passive failure of the muscle or of its controlling neural paths, but to an active feedback which protects the muscle from overwork. This general principle applies even to "mental" fatigue; indeed, Thorndike was thinking of things like computation when he first proposed his theory.

The form of the work curve. The ergograms all start out with strong strokes, and end up with weak ones or failure to lift the weight at all. But within these limits there are all sorts of variations. There may be a small rise in the early part of the curve, our familiar *warming up*. Or there may be a slight rise at the end, called *end spurt*, especially if *O* knows he is about to reach the end of the work period. A *beginning spurt* shows as a few strong strokes at first, followed by a rapid fall as *O* finds he has started with a bit too much enthusiasm to maintain. *Practice effects* are undesirable in work curves. A large amount of research has been devoted to finding out the conditions under which these various phenomena occur (Robinson, 1934; Bills, 1948); rate and type of work, instructions, and incentives all play a part. But one of the most important variables, the personality of *O*, is harder to tie down. Individual differences between *O*s were noted by Mosso himself. The individuality of ergograms has undoubtedly been noticed by most people who have worked with them, but has usually been considered an unfortunate variable to be eliminated in favor of general principles (but cf. Yochelson, 1930).

As a matter of fact, the difficulty of getting ergograms that are comparable from time to time and from *O* to *O* is a severe limitation on the method, and may be responsible for the decreased use of the ergograph in recent years. One *O* may start with a large initial spurt, and then show a rapid fall, quitting at the first discomfort, whereas another may start with a moderate level, but maintain this level over a long period—in fact, some *O*s seem to approach a stage of equilibration, continuing to pull the weight until stopped by a blister from the finger strap, rather than "fatigue." One of the writers (H.S.) has amused himself in undergraduate laboratories by trying to predict the form of a student's ergogram; occasional striking correspondence between work habits on the ergograph and in his studies suggests that the method might be the basis of a personality test

Length of work and rest periods. In spite of all the variables that complicate the picture, work output does show a decrement from beginning to end of the ergogram. As we saw above, this decrement seems to be caused by inhibitory impulses initiated by accumulation of fatigue products in the arm or finger muscles. A period of inactivity permits the circulation to remove this accumulation. It follows that recovery from fatigue will be slower in large muscle groups and after strong and continued exertion. Manzer (1927) studied this question, using six tasks which ranged in massiveness from the finger ergograph to a modified rowing machine that used most of the body. The *Os* were well practiced, and worked smoothly in time with a metronome. The basic method was to have *O* work on a given task until he could no longer make a contraction. Then there was a rest period of 5, 10 or 20 minutes, followed by another work period on the same task. Recovery was calculated by comparing the output during the second period with that of the first period, expressing the results in percent. The over-all results are shown in Figure 25-10 which suggests a smooth, negatively accelerated curve, approaching complete recovery somewhat beyond 20 minutes. But this smooth curve is somewhat misleading, for it combines all tasks and all *Os*, ironing out a lot of variability. There were even some indications that a short rest period is better than a long one.

Manzer found that he could get fairly stable curves by running two *Os* through repeated cycles of work and rest. These curves showed very little work accomplished in the last quarter of each work period, suggesting that continuing work during fatigue is wasteful. From this follows the recommendation that is frequently made in books on industrial psychology and efficiency; insert a rest period whenever the work curve starts to show a marked decrement, thus avoiding fatigue, and maintaining an optimal output. The extreme example of this practice is seen in the experiment of Maggiora (1890) who found that finger contractions could be continued indefinitely if separated by 10-second pauses, but that it took rests of 2 hours for recovery between work periods in which the response was carried to exhaustion. Manzer figured that he could have gotten 14 times as much work out of his *Os* if he had followed Maggiora's radical spacing! Incidentally, it is fairly obvious that such spacing simply permits a balancing of the budget by decreasing energy expenditure to match income, to use the analogy we gave under the section on equilibration.

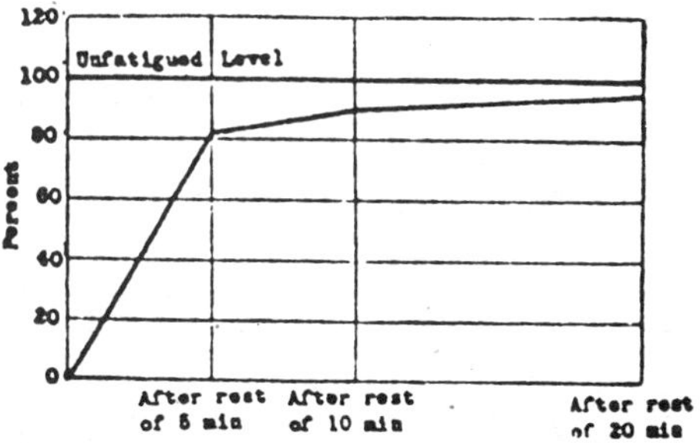

FIG. 25-10. (Manzer, 1927.) Recovery from fatigue after various rest periods. The total amount of work done after rests of 5, 10, or 15 minutes is expressed as a percentage of that done during the pre-rest fatiguing period. The figure is based on averages of ergograms from several different muscle groups, ranging from the finger ergograph to rowing. See text.

Mental work. Up to the present we have been discussing work that involved the repeated contraction of specific muscles, permitting rather gross local changes that would be expected to produce work decrement or fatigue. Now let us jump to the other extreme, mental work. It is true that we need not consider mental work to consist of nerve impulses running in closed circuits in the brain, for there is evidence that some muscles are involved in thinking. Perhaps we should call it *sedentary* rather than mental work (Ryan,

1947). But as Robinson (1934) has pointed out, the responses involved in thinking are small and varied, and scarcely of the type that should lead to fatigue. So there comes up the question as to whether or not there is any fatigue in thinking.

The best-known experiment in this field is that of Arai (1912), who multiplied four-place by four-place numbers "in her head" for 11 hours running, with surprising lack of decrement. Her work output did drop to about 50 percent of its original value in the first 6 hours, but it dropped no further in the next 5 hours. Although it is unlikely that many could reproduce Arai's performance (cf. Painter, 1916), there are many curves for mental work that show little decrement. For example, Figure 25-11

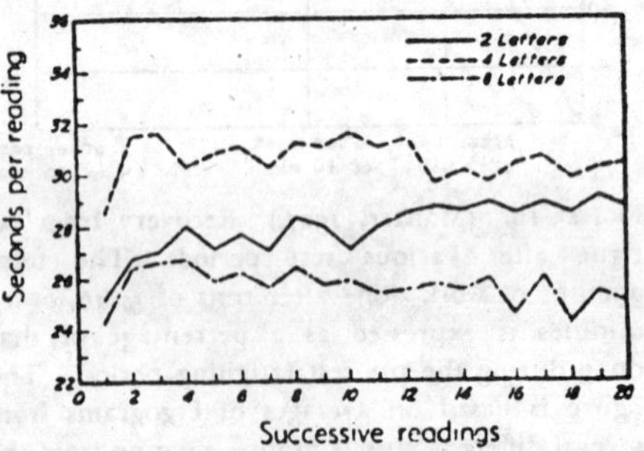

FIG. 25-11. (Robinson & Bills, 1926.) Work curves for reading cards containing 100 letters. The three lines correspond to cards made up of 2, 4, and 8 different letters, respectively.

gives the results of an experiment by Robinson & Bills (1926) in which 18 practiced *O*s read cards, each of which contained 100 letters. One set of cards contained only two *different* letters (abbaaaba . . . .), a second set had four (abcddcaba . . . .), and the third set had eight letters. Except for a beginning spurt on trial one, the three curves are fairly horizontal through trial 2-20. Although the average curves show no clear indication of loss in speed, individual curves from this type of work often show evidence of fatigue in the form of momentary blocks: short periods in which *O* does not respond in the usual rhythm (p. 81). These blocks are much more frequent in homogeneous than in varied work. Hence, Robinson (1934) emphasized the importance of homogeneity of task as one of the major factors in producing work decrement.

But to come back to over-all performance curves; Thorndike (1914; 1917), Hollingworth (1914b), and Poffenberger (1927, 1928, 1942) have all reported little decrement—or even a gain—during long periods of mental work. A typical set of results is shown in Figure 25-12, in which the heavy lines represent the changing work output. Note that there was a gain in efficiency on the intelligence test (probably a practice effect), no change on two others, and a clear loss only on addition. These results are consistent with Robinson's hypothesis we just mentioned, for addition is the most homogeneous, and the intelligence test the most varied of the tasks. But all four tasks show one change in common, a gradual increase in what might be called "that tired feeling," which is shown by the dashed line, based on subjective estimates made regularly by the workers. The discrepancy between the work output and subjective reports has been found in many other studies, and has led to much discussion. One group, of which Poffenberger was an early and outstanding example, holds that *O* maintains his output at the cost of greater effort, and expends more energy in doing the same amount of work. Unfortunately, neither Poffenberger nor anyone else seems to have adequately demonstrated the increased energy consumption. The other extreme is represented

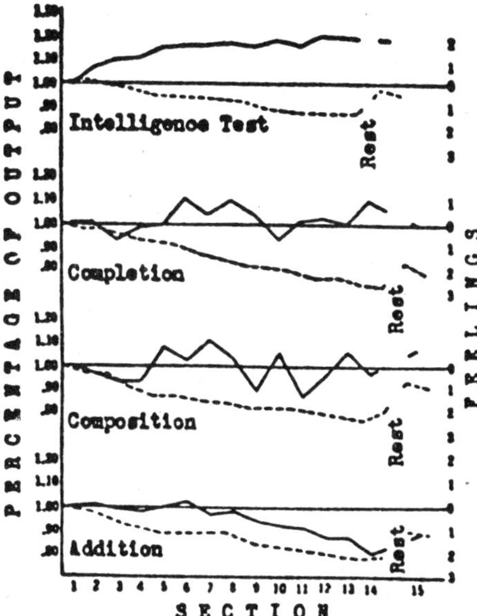

FIG. 25-12. (Poffenberger, 1942.) Relation between output and feeling of fatigue in four forms of mental work. The solid lines represent output in four different tasks: taking an intelligence test, completing sentences, judging compositions, and addition. The work periods were scored in units of about 20 minutes each, so that each curve represents about 5½ hours of work. The broken lines show the feeling of fatigue as rated by *O* at the end of each work period on a scale ranging from (1) Extremely good to (7) Extremely tired. All curves are plotted to show change from the original level, rather than absolute values.

by Bartley & Chute (1947), who stress the subjective reports, and even define fatigue as the experience of feeling tired. They emphasize the importance of conflict in producing fatigue, as so defined, and use phrases like "an over-all state—of the person as a whole," and "one form of an attempt to escape or retreat from a situation." Since fatigue for them is neither impairment nor a simple function of impairment, the divergence of Poffenberger's curves causes Bartley & Chute no trouble.

Perhaps we should not be too much disturbed by Bartley & Chute's peculiar use of the word fatigue, for many psychologists have given up the term as too vague and all-inclusive (Muscio, 1921)—and the word is barely present in the index of the recent edition of Howell's *Physiology* (Fulton, 1950). If reinterpreted, Bartley & Chute's distinction between the general tired feeling and work efficiency may be valid, at least for tasks that do not demand maintained muscular work. The tired feeling may well reflect actual changes in the muscles involved in maintaining the sitting posture incident to the work, and may have little relation to the actual work done. The lack of decrement in the work output may be another example of equilibration.

Other work situations. We have emphasized two extreme ends of a continuum; but between the concentrated muscular work of the ergograph and the "mental" work of taking an intelligence test there range a multitude of tasks that are much more common in daily life, as well as in industry. We shall not discuss them, except to point out that they show most of the phenomena we have described above. Bills' *Psychology of Efficiency* (1943) and Ryan's *Work and Effort* (1947) summarize much of the research on these tasks, particularly in relation to industrial work. Many of the earlier applied treatments of this subject fell into the error of generalizing too freely from ergograms. For example, a widely used illustration of daily work curves is that reproduced in Figure 25-13. Warm-up and work decrement show clearly. But these "typical" curves were based on fairly heavy muscular work, and may be contrasted with those of Figure 25-14, based on lighter work.

In recent years there has been an increasing tendency to recognize the importance of variables other than simple fatigue. The outstanding example of this tendency is found in the Western Electric studies (Roethlisberger & Dickson, 1939). In an effort to determine the effect of working conditions, as illumination and rest periods, they set up a small group of workers in a separate room. This group steadily improved its output, no matter how conditions were changed. It soon became obvious that the significant variable was *morale;* the workers took pride in their status as a team receiving special attention. Although morale and other motivational factors are of great importance in determining work output in practical situations (as they are in the ergograph), there is danger that the pendulum will swing too far so that industrial psychologists will forget the lower-level variables inherent in the organism.

Changes in quality of work. In addition to changes in amount of work done per unit time, there may be other changes. As early as 1927 Weinland showed that the *variability* of stroke am-

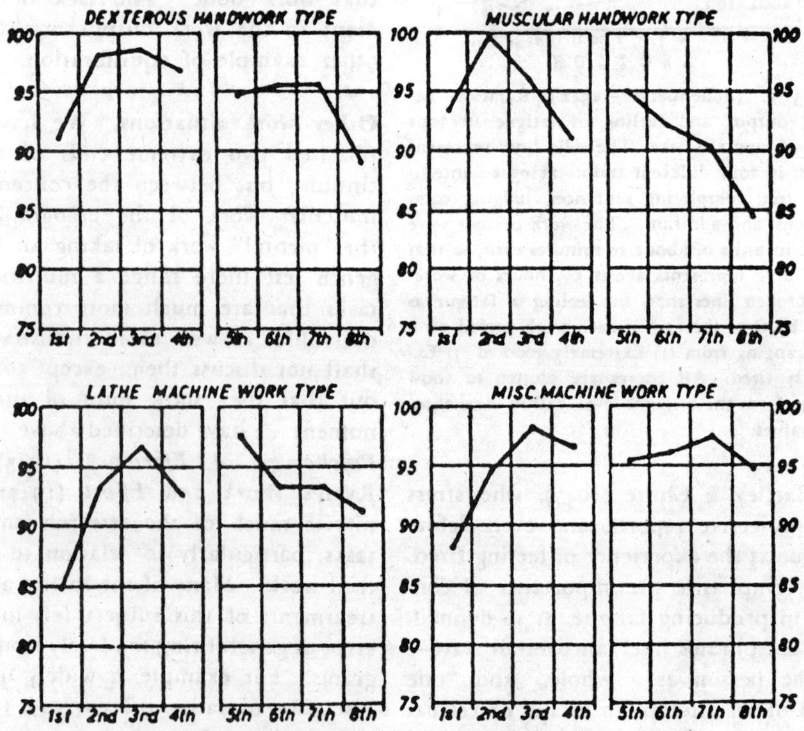

FIG. 25-13. (Goldmark, Hopkins, Florence & Lee, 1920). Composite hourly performance curves for two metalworking plants. The ordinate takes 100 as the highest attainable output. Note that performance falls off markedly in the hour before lunch, and again in the last hour, regardless of the length of the working day.

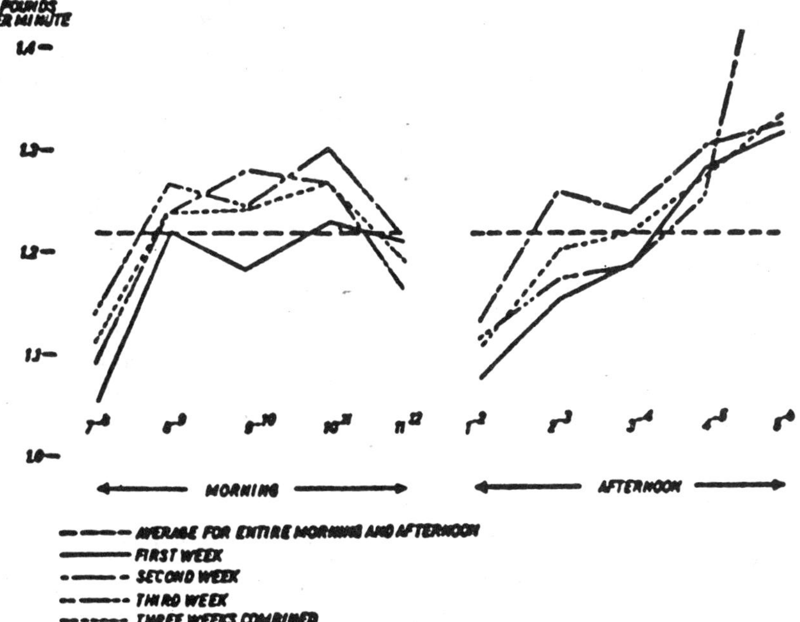

FIG. 25-14. (Link, 1919.) Hourly performance curves on successive weeks of visual inspection of cartridge shells. Note that there is an end-spurt in the afternoon, instead of the drop found in heavier work (Fig. 25-13).

plitude increased steadily throughout the ergogram. Sometimes the variability will increase markedly when there is no decrement in mean performance (see Chapanis, Garner & Morgan, 1949).

The fact that quality of work may give a very sensitive index of fatigue is nicely illustrated by a series of experiments by Bartlett and his associates. Their basic point is that methods like those designed for muscular work are unsatisfactory when applied to highly skilled performances, such as those demanded of an aviator or bombardier. So they set up a complex panel full of instruments and controls, and had *O* work for two hours at making adjustments appropriate to constantly changing dial readings and signals. The most striking change as fatigue built up was an increasing "indifference zone" in the dial readings; it seemed that *O* lowered his standards so that he would let a dial pointer drift further off the correct position before he corrected it. *O* did not realize that he was doing this, but thought he was actually improving. The deterioration was found only when the task was kept complicated, and it did not occur with continued work on a single dial. Other indications of fatigue in the complicated task were a loss of accurate timing of elements, and a general tendency to lose the "wholeness" of the task, so that *O* responded to the elements in isolation (Bartlett, 1943). The general approach seems fruitful in studying many factors that enter into efficiency, as the changes incident to increasing age (Welford, 1951).

Generalized fatigue. So far we have been concerned with what might be called specific fatigue, the changes in per formance of a given task which result from continued work on that task. But there are both theoretical and practical reasons for asking how much this fatigue generalizes to other tasks. On the theoretical side, it may tell us something about the nature of fatigue. Is all fatigue local, so that the effects of one task will show up on another only if they involve common elements (Robinson, 1934)? Or do fatigue products spread through the whole system, cutting the efficiency of all behavior? On the practical side, it is often difficult to get a measure of efficiency directly from the fatiguing task, as automobile driving; in such cases, can we assess the amount of fatigue by a battery of tests after the work?

In general, the research in this field has been quite unsatisfactory. We shall describe one experiment to illustrate the method. Ryan & Warner (1936) ran six *O*s through a total of about 240 days, alternating between days on which they drove 300 miles, and control days on which there was only an hour of driving. A battery of tests was administered every morning and evening. The loss between morning and evening tests on the control days served as a reference base for the loss on driving days. All of the tests showed losses as a result of driving. Percentage-wise, the losses were greatest in error scores on color-naming and on a *long* hand-steadiness test. Mental addition and postural sway lost about 10 percent. There were only slight losses in time scores for color-naming, visual efficiency, and a short test of hand-steadiness. One physiological test was included, the time it took a red streak to disappear after the skin had been scratched; this test also showed a fatigue effect.

This study was unusually successful in finding evidences of fatigue by the test method. It was well designed, but notice that it was necessary to use many experimental sessions on each *O* to overcome variability. Hence there were only six *O*s, which may not be a representative sample of the population. And remember that the fatiguing task was hard, for driving 300 miles in 1936 was more than a light afternoon drive! These considerations, and the relatively small changes that were obtained, indicate that the test battery method is not practical for measuring the fatigue produced by ordinary activities. In fact, the frequent failure to find decrement by test batteries was one of the reasons why Bartley and Chute preferred to define fatigue in subjective terms.

Why do test batteries rarely show fatigue? One obvious answer to this question is that most tasks produce a lot less fatigue than we expect them to produce. This was clear even in the work-curve method, where we saw that *O* usually adjusts his output to a rate which he can maintain over the assigned period. Most of the decrements were found when *O* was forced to maintain a rate set by *E*, as in the ergograph, or in Bartlett's simulated cockpit. One of the objections to the production line in industry is that the worker cannot set his own pace. This is particularly hard on older workers (Welford, 1951).

A second answer to our question is in terms of motivation. The *O* may compensate for decreased capacity to work by increased effort. For example, he can produce a spurt of work at the end of the ergogram if *E* encourages him. Similarly, students seem to work for long hours without too much loss of efficiency when an exam is approaching. According to this line of reasoning, the failure of short tests to pick up fatigue would be attributed to a person's ability to spurt, or to exert extra effort for a brief time. Note that the longer and harder of the two hand-steadiness tests was the more effective in the driving experiment described above.

In an effort to put this answer to an experimental test, many attempts have been made to obtain some objective measure of increased effort. Since we devoted several pages (175-179) to this general topic earlier, we shall simply remind the reader that Ryan, Cottrell and Bitterman (1951) concluded that electrical potentials from the muscles furnished a measure of the effort required to overcome glare in a visual task.

The role of tension in learning and performance. A rereading of the earlier pages on muscular tension (174 ff.) will suggest many relations with the material covered in the present chapter. For example, it is an interesting exercise to see how the form of the learning curve on the pursuit rotor under partially distributed practice (Fig. 25-2) could be explained in terms of changing patterns of both generalized and local muscular tensions. Ammons (1947a, 1947b, 1950) has constructed a miniature system which predicts the effect of changing distributions of work and rest on this task. He uses three formal constructs: *warm-up, temporary work decrement*, and *permanent work decrement*. Kimble (1949a, 1949b, 1949c) has made a roughly similar analysis of curves from printing the alphabet backward (p. 790), as well as from motor tasks (Kimble & Horenstein, 1948; Kimble & Bilodeau, 1949). He identifies the two work decrements as *reactive inhibition* and *conditioned inhibition*, respectively. It is perfectly possible that both of the work decrements might be due to build-up of excess tensions that interfere with the performance of the task. Remember that one uses much more than the eye and hand in keeping the contact on the moving target of the pursuit rotor; the task is performed against a very complex postural pattern of contractions in all the muscles of the body. The early stages of learning a difficult task typically show much excess postural tension, which would build up during a trial, thus accounting for temporary work decrement. A rest would permit a drop in these tensions, improving performance at the start of the next trial, but massed practice would favor the continued build-up of tensions. Permanent work decrement would be explained in terms of an habitual excess tension resulting from continued massed trials. We presented a possible relationship between warm-up and tension in an earlier discussion (p. 148).

This is not the place to develop a complete theory, even for the pursuit rotor, nor to summarize the existing evidence for such a theory. Our purpose is merely to suggest that the study of the level and distribution of muscular tensions has much to contribute to an understanding of learning and performance, as well as to the more obvious topics of emotion and motivation.

EFFICIENT ACQUISITION OF A SKILL

During World War II there was a great need to select and train men rapidly in a large number of rather difficult skills. In addition to the usual skills of everyday life, there were new tasks, as flying and navigating planes, spinning knobs to keep optical and radar sights (and ultimately, guns) on the target, and a host of others. Psychologists were very busy developing and administering selection and training programs. Needless to say, they applied the general principles that will be found throughout this text, and especially in this chapter. Some of the broad outlines of this work will be found in Chapanis, Garner & Morgan (1949). Bray (1948) has reported the research done for the various services by a large group of psychologists in civilian status, and the Army Air Force has brought out

19 monographs (Flanagan *et al*, 1947–48). Other summaries appeared in the *Psychological Bulletin*, and the detailed reports are widely scattered in official publications. Much of the research was directed toward practical problems, and done under the press of wartime demands, but there may well be a lot of fundamental scientific knowledge buried in this extensive literature. The problem is to pick out the findings which are of general and permanent significance from those which are of merely limited and temporary value. But for our present purpose we shall select one practical skill and see what the psychologist had to offer. Our choice will be the learning to receive International Morse Code, a skill for which there was an almost insatiable demand during a war which depended so heavily on radio communications.

Pioneer studies of learning code. In 1897 and 1899 Bryan & Harter reported some studies of the progress made by students training to become professional telegraphers. The curves for receiving code are among the earliest learning curves, and they are probably the best known curves in the psychological literature. In fact, they have long been standard for demonstrating plateaus. Both students in the original study made steady progress until they had *almost* achieved the minimal acceptable rate for receiving signals, and then they leveled off for a period of several weeks of no further progress. Eventually the curve started upward again, and continued well beyond the minimum criterion. Bryan and Harter explained these plateaus in terms of hierarchies or levels of habits. The beginner first learns to receive letters, to hear the sound pattern *dit dah* (.–) and say *A*, or *dit dit dit* (. . .) as meaning *S*, etc. Gradually he learns to combine these elements into larger groups, and hears them as words, rather than as single letters. Eventually he gets the knack of "lagging behind" the incoming signals, to allow the development of larger meanings, just as the practiced oral reader lets his voice lag a half line or so behind his eye (p. 507). Bryan and Harter thought that a plateau occurred when the student reached the maximum speed permitted by a low-level habit and had not yet developed proficiency in the habit at the next level of complexity.

To check this hypothesis, they tested another student with disconnected letters, disconnected words, and connected discourse. As can be seen in Figure 25-15, the plateau showed up only in the curve for connected discourse—or perhaps we should say that all three curves leveled off below the main line rate, and only the curve for connected discourse started up again. This was taken as confirmation for their hypothesis, and the whole affair seemed so neat that it was widely reported in textbooks. Further, a roughly comparable account was worked out for typing (Book, 1908), and teaching methods were developed to avoid difficult shifts from one habit level to a higher one.

It was recognized that the plateau was not universal in learning curves. Bryan and Harter found none in the *sending* of telegraphic messages. (For other early evidence on the conditions tending to produce a plateau, see the first edition of this book, pp. 165–169). As to the receiving of telegraphic messages, the status of the plateau was undisturbed until 1943, when Taylor (1943b) published a review covering a considerable number of studies that had not been generally known by American psychologists. Tay-

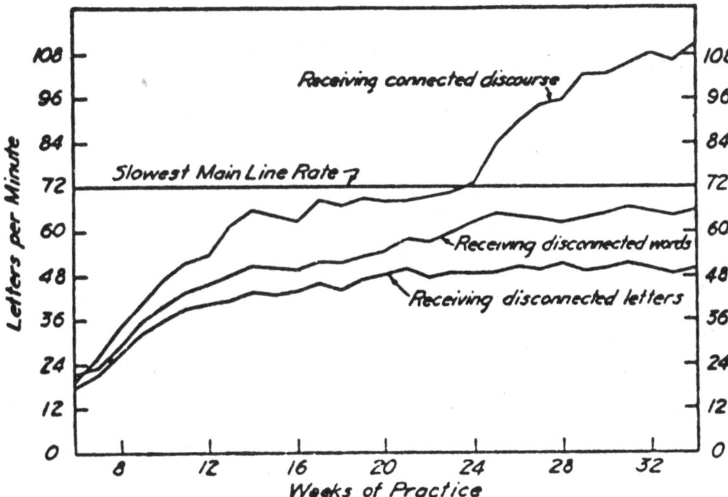

Fig. 25-15. (From Bryan & Harter, 1899.) Learning curves of a student who had begun the study about 6 weeks before the first of the weekly tests. The three curves show progress in *receiving:* bottom curve, disconnected letters; middle curve, disconnected words; top curve, connected discourse.

lor's review cast doubt on the plateau and even on the habit hierarchy. By coincidence, a month after Taylor's review there appeared an experimental study by Reed & Zinszer (1943) who found long plateaus quite exceptional in the records of 43 highly motivated college students who had taken a wartime semester course in telegraphy. Other recent studies also indicate that the plateau is not a necessity in this learning process (Windle, 1952). It should be noted that these many wartime students of telegraphy did not reach the level of rapid meaningful messages. Their duty was to receive the alphabetic characters rapidly and accurately, since the messages they were to receive were coded in a double sense.

An efficient method for teaching code. As mobilization for the war got under way, many colleges introduced courses that would prepare students for military duties. Code classes were an obvious bet, and many psychologists jumped at the opportunity to do research on this traditional topic. The most extensive of these studies was probably that of Keller and his associates, which eventually established a method which was adopted for general use by the War Department (Bray, 1948).

Keller described his method in 1943. It combined several principles that have already been mentioned in these chapters. It was a modification of the method of paired associates, which involves regular reinforcement. The students were given work sheets like that shown in Figure 25-16. A signal was sounded, and the student was given three seconds to print the corresponding letter in the first space. At the end of three seconds, the instructor announced the correct letter. The student left the space beneath his original response blank if he had been correct, but entered the right letter in the box if he had been wrong or had not responded. Then the next signal came, etc. The first block of the figure illustrates these possibilities; the first signal was S (. . .), but was called O (—— —— ——). The second signal, A, was called correctly. The student made no response to the third signal, 2, and miscalled the next two.

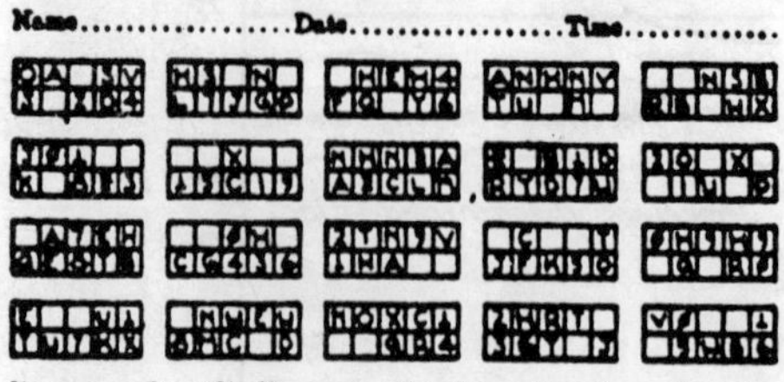

FIG. 25-16. (Keller, 1943.) Practice sheet for the code-voice method. See text for explanation.

This "code-voice" method had other advantages in addition to the prompt reinforcement of each response. The form of the work sheets made it easy to tally scores and plot learning curves—and we know that knowledge of results is a powerful incentive. As originally used, it employed all 36 symbols (26 letters, 10 digits) from the outset, thus qualifying as a "whole" method (p. 782). One other general principle was applied, in that the temporal pattern of sounds for each letter was kept the same as it would have been in full-speed telegraphy; that is, each letter was sent at normal speed, even though there were long intervals between the letters.

Keller found that his students made a very high rate of progress, compared to available reports of regular code schools using the older methods. But other college experimenters (Reed & Zinszer, 1943; Taylor, 1943a) also commented on the superior learning rate of their students. In fact, Taylor had independently tested three features of the Keller method (prompt reinforcement, whole method, and standard-speed presentation of signals) using a single feature on each of three experimental groups. No one of his experimental groups was superior to his control group. So we could not be sure that Keller's method was really superior to the conventional ones; perhaps his students were highly motivated, or superior to start with, or possibly it was the distributed practice made necessary by the conventional 50-minute class period that made his students learn quickly. But these were war times, and there was no immediate opportunity to isolate single variables. The method seemed effective, so it was tested at an army camp, and found to be more effective than the standard method in use at the time.

The later studies of the method were covered by research reports that are not generally available in university libraries. A short summary and a few references will be found in Bray (1948), and a more complete treatment in Windle (1952). We shall mention only one other highlight, the advantage of distributed practice. Students spent 8 weeks at code school. Normally, they practiced code for 7 hours a day for the first 5 weeks, and devoted the last 3 weeks to other topics. Keller thought such massed practice might be wasteful, so he tried spreading out the code instruction over the whole 8 weeks, devoting 4 hours daily to code, and the rest to other topics. It turned out that the 4-hour group was as good as the usual 7-hour group at the end of 5 weeks, despite the shorter hours of practice. Of course they still had 3 more weeks to practice code, for they had been taking up their other topics along with the code; they ended up markedly superior to the massed group. Incidentally, it seemed to be the number of hours per day that counts; breaking up the 4-hour period into 4 single hours per day didn't give further improvement.

Other phases of code learning. Of course, students had to learn to transmit as well as to receive, and there were some studies on this problem—although sending got less attention, for it seems to be the easier thing to learn. Selection of promising candidates was another important problem, for there are great individual differences in the ability to learn code. Much effort was devoted to the development of code aptitude tests, but that subject is beyond the scope of this book; again we will refer the interested reader to Bray (1948) and Windle (1952). But we will say a few words about one other problem, that of the confusion between signals, for it is fundamentally a question of generalization and discrimination, topics we have previously discussed in other contexts.

Errors in receiving can be of two types, a failure to identify the letter at all, or a mistaken identification. These two types of errors may ultimately be due to the same mechanism, an interference between responses attached to two similar stimuli. Thus F (. . – .) is apt to be confused with L (. – . .). Several of the early reports were concerned with the analysis of these errors (Spragg, 1943; Keller & Taubman, 1943; Keller & Schoenfeld, 1944), and there was general agreement on which were the serious ones. There was less agreement on how to overcome the confusions and we still cannot be sure whether it is better to group similar characters or to use a whole method in learning the alphabet.

Fortunately, most of the errors drop out after about 10 hours of practice, but one type of error persists, called the *dotting error* (Keller & Schoenfeld, 1944; Keller, 1953). It is due to the underestimation of dots, and is particularly serious within three groups of characters; a given signal in the list below is apt to be heard as the one just below it.

6 is –	*5* is	*4* is . . . . –
B is – . . .	*H* is	*V* is . . . –
D is – . .	*S* is . . .	*U* is . . –

This type of errors is so persistent that it might be wise to drop those students who show them excessively at early stages of training (Keller & Schoenfeld, 1944). Or the code itself might be improved by substituting new signals for the middle character of each group (B, H and V). This change would meet with a lot of resistence from those who already know the present code, but as Keller (1953) points out, International Morse Code eventually displaced the older and somewhat different American Morse Code.

In summary, we can see that when psychologists tackled the problem of training telegraphers, they applied their general principles and methods to the selection of personnel, the course of training, and even to the basic task itself. Roughly the same story could be told for a number of other skills, although the research was probably most extensive in the case of code—or perhaps the reports are just more readily available in this field. From a scientific standpoint, one major weakness of much of the war research was a failure to use control groups to prove the effectiveness of some of the recommended practices. Indications of this tendency can be seen in the account we have given of the work on code. But this wasn't the leisurely research of the laboratory; the services wanted answers in a hurry, and they got pretty good ones from the wartime research of the psychologists!

26

PROBLEM SOLVING: THINKING

If the experimentalist could show us how to think clearly, and how to solve our problems successfully and expeditiously, his social contribution would be very great. It would be very great if he could do as well in this field as he has already done and is likely to do in the related field of learning. So far, he has found the field of problem solution comparatively difficult to cultivate. Yet the beginnings he has made, the experiments he has devised, and the results he has achieved are well worth attention. We should find plenty to discuss if we allowed ourselves to stray far from the laboratory and evaluate the many theoretical and practical suggestions made by logicians and others interested in the achievements and failures of the human intellect. We shall not even present the work of our closer colleagues, the factor analysts, in their attempt to identify and measure the primary abilities that work together in reasoning and creative thinking (Spearman, 1927; Thurstone, 1938; Stephenson, 1947; Guilford *et al*, 1951, 1952). Eventually experimenters may find use for the "factors" in designing transfer experiments that will show ways of improving a student's reasoning ability.

Preliminary definition of terms might be a time-consuming process but we shall cut it short. A problem, we may say, exists when *O*'s activity has a goal but no clear or well-learned route to the goal He has to explore and find a route. When he has found a route, he has achieved a solution though not necessarily the best solution. In a maze, for example, he may take several trials before eliminating all excess motion. "Thinking" is more difficult to define satisfactorily, but we may say that it occurs when *O*'s explorations go beyond the immediately given situation and utilize memories and previously formed concepts. If his car stalls and refuses to start, he thinks of various possible causes and of ways to check on them. A problem may be presented verbally, leaving it to *O* to imagine the situation and find the solution wholly by thinking. Even when the whole situation is laid out before his eyes, he may examine it thoughtfully and perhaps reveal some of his thoughts by talking to himself.

Two main types of experiment. Since the solution of a problem occupies considerable time, one obvious job for the experimenter is to discover what goes on during this time. If we call the problem the stimulus and the solution the response, *E*'s job is to trace the process intervening between S and R. This is the type of experiment suggested by the formula, S—*O*—R (pp. 2–3). Another type of experiment is suggested by the formula, R = f(S, A). Here *E* introduces definite experimental variables and observes their effects on *O*'s response, i.e., on the success and form of *O*'s attempted solution. The experimental variable may be an S-factor, a systematic variation of the problem; or it may be an A-factor, a variation in the antecedent conditions such as previous learning in a transfer experiment. In other fields of psychology, as perception, learning, and motivation, the R = f(S, A) experiments have been very fruitful; we need more of them in the study of problem solving (Heidbreder, 1948b). Historically, more interest and controversy have centered on the other type of experiment which we shall consider first.

PROCESS-TRACING EXPERIMENTS

A person who is thinking may sit quietly, perhaps with his eyes closed, and nevertheless come through after a while with a pat answer to a question. In spite of the apparent absence of either sensory or motor activity, something has been going on in his head, or in his organism anyway, and this something has been a very effective activity and sometimes an intense activity since he may tell you he has been "thinking hard." This internal activity might be akin to sense perception or to muscular action. It might be indicated by *O*'s reportable memory images of objects and events or by *E*'s instrumental records of slight muscular contractions. Here was a challenge to the early experimenters. Could they obtain satisfactory evidence of imagery or of muscular activity occurring and apparently playing an essential part in the process of thinking?

The introspective "thought experiment." Shortly after 1900 several investigators in different laboratories devised a form of experiment which was certainly straightforward and obvious enough. They asked *O* to solve some simple problem and then recount his conscious experience from the moment when the problem was given till the solution was reached. He was instructed to *describe* his experience, not to explain it. His function was to provide the raw data which *E* would subsequently analyze and interpret. Experimental technique consisted mostly in putting *O* at his ease, in understanding his reports, and in selecting problems which would elicit genuine thought and still be solved quickly so that *O* could make his retrospective report while the experience was fresh in memory. The time *O* took to reach a solution could be measured with a stop watch or chronoscope.

On one main point the results obtained in different laboratories were in excellent agreement. All *O*s reported thinking of what we may call *objects* in a broad sense, including things, persons, events, and states of affairs. In short, their reports were like those you get if you ask a person to report what he sees in an actual scene or happening. Some objects thought about may be imaginary, and some may be rather abstract as when one thinks of "the dog" as a kind of animal or of the relative importance of heredity and environment in making people different.

But when the *O*s were asked what *mental images* they had of these objects, their reports showed much disagreement, as we should expect from the great individual differences found in the study of imagery (p. 721). Some reported visual images, some auditory, some kinesthetic, some verbal. Some reported vivid images, some mostly vague and scrappy ones. Some insisted that at the moment of a clear flash of thought they had no true images at all but only an awareness of some relationship or other "object" in our broad sense. Many psychologists would not accept testimony of this kind which they said must be due to imperfect introspection. So arose the "imageless-thought" controversy which raged for some years and ended in a stalemate. A much fuller account of it can be found in the first edition of this book, pages 784–789, and in the books by Titchener (1909) and Humphrey (1951).

The disagreement about images should not be allowed to obscure the agreement on thought of objects. In the latter respect the results of the old thought experiment are perfectly predictable. There is an obvious kinship between thought and sense perception. With your eyes open you see objects, and with them closed you think of objects.

Muscular movements in thinking. Watson (1914) drew a different conclusion from the imageless-thought controversy, which seemed to him to discredit the introspective method and to clear the decks for a motor theory of thinking. He proposed to regard the thought process as consisting of slight muscular movements, especially (but not exclusively) speech movements. Thinking would thus be "subvocal talking," for the most part, and the best record of a thought process would be obtained by applying sensitive recording instruments to the speech organs. Early records obtained from tambour or lever systems applied to the tongue gave rather baffling results, since slight speech movements occurred during some but not all silent speech and since the pattern of a whispered phrase was not duplicated by the pattern of the same phrase when merely "thought." But these recording systems were not sensitive or quick acting enough to catch the rapid succession of actual speech movements—and silent speech is still more rapid (Max, 1934).

Action currents led off from a muscle, amplified and recorded by means of a rapid galvanometer, are a much more sensitive indicator of slight motor activity. There are difficulties to be overcome: currents leak in from neighboring muscles, and the muscle being investigated may be in a state of continued but variable tension. *O* lies down and is trained to relax. Then he is given such tasks as silent recitation of a familiar poem or mental addition and multiplication. Action currents sometimes appear in the tongue and lips—sometimes elsewhere. If he is asked to imagine an arm movement, action currents appear in the arm muscles; if he imagines a visible object, they appear in the eye region (Jacobson, 1932; Shaw, 1940; Aserinsky & Kleitman, 1953).

The speech muscles of deaf persons who talk with their fingers are located in the forearm, where they are readily tapped by electrodes applied to the skin (Max, 1937). Easy linguistic tasks such as reading a news item are usually performed without any participation of the forearm muscles, but the harder task of memorizing the item usually brings in the action currents, though without any visible finger movements. Easy addition or multiplication usually shows no currents, but harder examples usually show some. The more intelligent and better-educated subjects show little forearm activity whereas others show much more. Any deaf *O* shows more forearm activity if he begins to fear his arithmetic is going wrong. The last fact, taken alone, would suggest that all these forearm action currents represent diffuse muscular tension rather than speech movements. But control experiments on hearing *O*s showed comparatively little forearm involvement in the solution of the problems (p. 178).

However, diffuse muscular tension can certainly occur during work on a difficult problem. In some experiments of Davis (1937, 1938), with action currents from the forearm and neck led off through high amplification to an electron oscillograph, *O* first had 5 minutes to get relaxed and then began to memorize a difficult poetic passage from Browning, or to multiply a 3-place by a 2-place number "in his head." There was a large increase of the action currents during work on the task, with gradual recovery during the subsequent rest. Individuals differed considerably, and those who were more successful in performing the tasks showed on the whole *less* increase of muscle currents during the work. With continued practice on a type of problem went a decrease in the muscle currents. Therefore, the muscle currents were an index, not of the efficiency of the mental work, but of its laboriousness or of the difficulty experienced. We remember that the sympathetic division of the autonomic is active during mental work and especially when difficulty is encountered (p. 156; Sears, 1933). The increased muscular tension and the PGR probably both indicate a mobilization of *O*'s forces, but whether the extra energy helps solve the problem is not so certain. There is some evidence from stabilimeter experiments (Grinsted, 1941) that *O* is apt to become almost motionless (though perhaps tense) while thinking effectively and to start moving more freely when finished with a bit of thinking—just as you may stand stock-still for a moment when an interesting thought occurs to you during a walk.

As to speech *movements*, the evidence for their always being present during thinking is not convincing. Much more convincing is introspective evidence of some sort of internal speech which in some persons is certainly auditory rather than motor—and we must remember that speech is an auditory affair as well as a form of motor behavior. (The child understands words that he hears before he can say them himself.) However, some active thinking apparently occurs without *any* sort of internal speech. So, in the imageless-thought experiments there were many reports to this effect: "An illuminating thought occurred to me like a flash but entirely without any words at first." Hadamard (1949) quotes Einstein as testifying that he thinks, mathematically, in signs and images and not in words. Hadamard says the same of himself and agrees also with Galton who found it difficult to translate his thoughts into words—a difficulty which many of us certainly experience at times. Meyers (1948) found that dysphasic patients, in spite of their severe loss of speech due to cerebral lesions, were not significantly inferior to normals in the solution of nonverbal problems of the multiple-choice type introduced by Yerkes (1921).

Trial and error in problem solution. We are still asking what goes on between S and R, between the presentation of a problem and the attainment of a solution. Our preceding search for sensory images or for speech movements has called for minute, almost microscopic examination of the process, but we may perhaps learn more from a broader view of the whole course of events. Is it a straight advance from S to R, or does it involve a searching hither and thither for promising leads? If the route to the goal were perfectly clear from the start, there would be no problem to solve. Given a genuine problem, there must be some exploratory activity, more or less in amount, higher or lower in intellectual level.

The much used phrase, *trial and error*, ought logically to mean the same as exploration or searching for a goal. It ought not to carry any derogatory shade of meaning, but often it is so used and means that the problem solver is not doing as well as he could, not planning ahead and utilizing all the available information. As a purely descriptive term, without any disparaging implications, it applies very well to problem solving at any level. In the history of psychology the term goes back to Alexander Bain (1855, 1864, 1870). He used it in his analysis of the "constructive intellect." An inventor or artist needs, according to Bain, a command of the material to be used, a "feeling of the end to be served," and the ability to judge when that end has been satisfactorily attained. The inventive process is one of "groping and experiment." "In all difficult operations for purposes or ends, the rule of trial and error is the grand and final resort." Similarly, Pillsbury (1910) described reasoning as a process of ideational trial and error.

The term was introduced into animal psychology by Lloyd Morgan (1894) to describe the process by which his dog learned such tricks as opening a gate by raising the latch with his muzzle, or carrying a knobbed cane by seizing it near the center of gravity. It was a gradual process of many trials and seemed not to involve any clear perception of cause and effect.

Puzzle box problems. Lloyd Morgan's lead was quickly followed by Thorndike (1898). He devised a number of problem boxes with doors to be opened by turning a door button, pressing a lever, or pulling a string attached to the outside bolt. As subjects, he used mostly young cats. His generalized description of their behavior went as follows:

> The behavior of all but Nos. 11 and 13 was practically the same. When put into the box the cat would show evident signs of discomfort and of an impulse to escape from confinement. It tries to squeeze through any opening; it claws or bites at the bars or wire; it thrusts its paws out through any opening and claws at everything it reaches; it continues its efforts when it strikes anything loose and shaky; it may claw at things within the box. . . . For eight or ten minutes it will claw and bite and squeeze incessantly. With 13, an old cat (18 months), and 11, an uncommonly sluggish cat, the behavior was different. They did not struggle vigorously or continually. . . . In either case . . . the impulse to struggle . . . is likely to succeed in letting the cat out of the box. The cat that is clawing all over the box in her impulsive struggle will probably claw the string or loop or button so as to open the door. And gradually all the other non-successful impulses will be stamped out and the particular impulse leading to the successful act will be stamped in. . . .
>
> Vigor, abundance of movements, was observed to make differences between individuals. . . . It works by shortening the first times, the times when the cat still does the act largely by accident. . . . Attention, often correlated with lack of vigor, makes a cat form an association quicker after he gets started. No. 13 shows this somewhat. The absence of a fury of activity let him be more conscious of what he did do.

Because the animal's mastery of the problem was gradual rather than sudden, Thorndike inferred that there was no "seeing through the situation," for if the animal had achieved insight after a while, the trial and error would naturally have come to an abrupt end, and the individual learning curve would have shown a sudden drop in time per trial—which was only rarely the case. (One of Thorndike's curves is shown in Fig. 18-6, p. 537.)

It is reasonably clear from Thorndike's condensed description, and still clearer from the detailed protocols of Adams (1929) who repeated some of the same experiments, that trial-and-error behavior in cats consists, not of miscellaneous *movements* unrelated to the environment, but of manipulatory responses to various *objects*. Moreover the animal's activity soon becomes limited to the objects near the door and food. These statements hold good of rats as well (Lashley, 1935, pp. 31–35) and emphatically of monkeys as we have already seen (p. 591).

Even after a cat has pretty well mastered a puzzle box, her movements vary from trial to trial, though her activity is concentrated in a certain region and on a certain latch, string, etc. But if the box is so arranged that the cat always approaches the critical object from the same direction, considerable stereotypy is observed (Guthrie & Horton, 1946). In a Skinner box provided with a long bar, the rat comes to press the bar more and more at the same point as long as the supply of food pellets continues. In an extinction series his responses scatter widely only to become stereotyped again with the resumption of reinforcements (Antonitis, 1951). Perhaps we can fairly summarize these results by saying that the animal first learns to manipulate certain objects, and then gradually settles down into fixed movement patterns.

Nonpuzzle problems. A puzzle box, like a maze, is a blind situation for an animal. It does not lie open for inspection at the outset and for that reason trial-and-error behavior is inevitable. If problems could be designed that were entirely aboveboard, with no essential object concealed, perhaps the animal would see the means-end relations and not find any trial and error necessary. So reasoned Hobhouse (1901) and he devised a number of problems which have been much used in later studies of insight and trial and error, such as:

1. String pulling. The lure is attached to a string; by pulling, the animal secures the reward.
2. String discrimination. The lure is attached to one of 2–3 strings; the animal sees the lure attached. The question is whether he will pull the right string.
3. Reaching-stick or poker, used to pull in an object which lies beyond the reach of the unaided paw.
4. Two sticks. The animal is provided with a short stick to use in reaching a longer stick with which in turn he can reach the lure.
5. Obstacle. A box or other obstacle is placed in the animal's way, the question being whether he will remove the box.
6. Tube and rod. The lure is placed inside the tube, and can be pushed or pulled out with the rod.
7. Footstool. A stool or box must be moved underneath the lure in order to reach the latter.

Hobhouse tried these problems on cats, dogs, otters, elephants, a monkey, and a chimpanzee. Some of the animals learned the tricks but not without trial and error. The difficulty, he found, was to get the animal to attend to the important object. For example, a cat saw a bit of meat placed upon a card and the card laid on a shelf with an attached string hanging down to the floor. The cat appeared not to notice the string at first, but when it finally caught her eye she responded promptly and appropriately. With more than a single string present, even a monkey does not always observe closely enough to see which string is attached to the reward (Fig. 26-1).

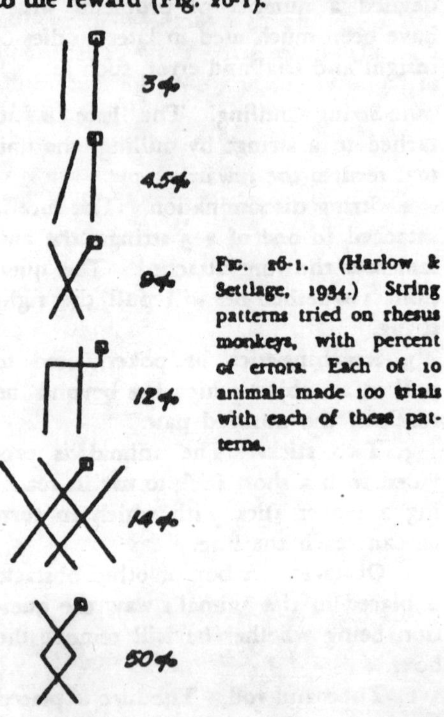

FIG. 26-1. (Harlow & Settlage, 1934.) String patterns tried on rhesus monkeys, with percent of errors. Each of 10 animals made 100 trials with each of these patterns.

Trial-and-error manipulation sometimes necessary. In his celebrated studies of chimpanzee intelligence Köhler (1917, 1924) objected strongly to problems of the puzzle-box type. He insisted that all the essential conditions of a problem must lie open to the animal's inspection if insight were to be shown and trial-and-error behavior avoided. He accordingly used problems similar to those of Hobhouse. Yet his chimpanzees did not ordinarily solve the problems by mere inspection. They were more deliberate than a cat or monkey is likely to be but still were inclined to act without first examining the situation fully. They would try some approach to the goal which was doomed to failure, as a human observer could easily see. For example, in a form of the footstool problem, a banana was suspended from the ceiling of a room which had smooth, unscalable walls, and a box was present but not under the lure. All the animals made repeated attempts to reach the lure by jumping, but Sultan, by all tests the most intelligent of the group, soon ceased jumping, paced up and down, suddenly stood still in front of the box, moved it quickly toward the lure, mounted and jumped from it, securing the banana. The single-box problem having been mastered, two boxes were provided and the banana was hung higher. Sultan placed one box under the lure and measured the distance with his eyes, but did not mount. After a while he fetched the other box but instead of placing it on top laid it beside the first, held it up in the air toward the lure, etc., etc. This day's trial ended in complete failure. After several further trials with help from *E*, Sultan began to place one box on the other, but only after much blind experimenting did he succeed in placing the upper one flat and stably on the lower. In another experiment a loop at the end of a rope was hung over a hook on the wall, but instead of lifting the loop off the hook the chimpanzees engaged in a variety of tugging and thrashing movements. Another surprising example is given in Figure 26-2. Such behavior is not as stupid as it seems, for weight, stability, friction, elasticity, and many similar properties of things cannot be seen but have to be learned by manipulation in the first place.

The three-dimensional shape of an object is another characteristic that often cannot be discovered by mere inspection without manipulation. Three-dimensional movements are specially difficult to perceive or imagine accurately. That is the reason why the mechanical puzzles, so popular from time to time, are hard to solve and comprehend. Ruger (1910), who used such puzzles

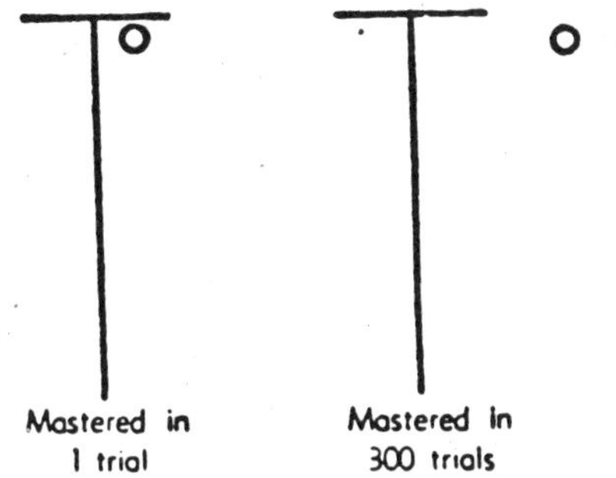

FIG. 26-2. (Kellogg & Kellogg, 1933.) Scheme of the hoe experiment. In a comparative study of the early development of a human child and a baby chimpanzee, the hoe problem was first presented when the child was 15 months old and the chimpanzee somewhat younger but at about the same stage of development. A piece of apple lay on the floor behind a wire screen which did not quite reach the floor but left a space for the hoe. Both subjects succeeded at once in the simplest problem, when the hoe had only to be pulled. But when the apple was placed somewhat to the side, the response still consisted in a straight pull. Both subjects behaved in this way, and mastery was achieved only after a long practice series.

in his intensive study of problem solving by human adults, asked his subjects to examine a puzzle carefully and try to solve it without any manipulation, but they were never able to reach a complete solution by this procedure which most of them found very irksome. After *O* had solved a puzzle "in principle," he still had a long way to go before he could manipulate it skilfully, and in the process of acquiring skill he encountered subordinate problems which he could not see from the outset but only after he had become well acquainted with the puzzle by actual manipulation. We have here several reasons for the prevalence and practical inevitability of trial and error (see Fig. 26-3).

The testing of hypotheses as a form of trial and error. In the experiments of Duncker (1935, 1945) educated adults were given arithmetical and geometrical problems to solve, and also simple physical problems. For example, when a steel ball falls upon a steel plate, the impact momentarily flattens the ball which regains its shape in the rebound. How could you show that the ball is actually flattened? In solving any such problem—or any problem—you have to analyze what is given and what is required. You have to work from both ends until you can bridge the gap between them. In considering what is given you are likely to overlook some of the requirements, and in considering what is required you are likely to forget exactly what is given. So you come up with solutions which are imperfect. Each such solution, as also the satisfactory one that ends your search, can be called a hypothesis, and the process of solving a problem consists largely in the generation and testing of hypotheses. Exactly how your hypotheses are generated you cannot say; it is a difficult question left without any complete answer by Duncker and also by Claparède (1934), whose study is somewhat similar to Duncker's though with different types of problems presented. Both investigators agree that past experience and previously formed concepts are reactivated by the difficulties of the present task.

In Heidbreder's (1924) extensive experiments on problem solution, *O*'s task was to discover the rules of a game by trial and error. Her outstanding result

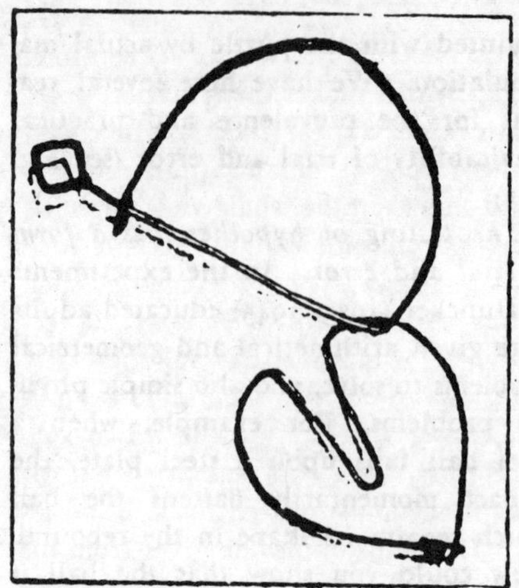

FIG. 26-3. The "Heart and Bow" puzzle, used by Ruger (1910). The problem is to separate the heart from the bow. One subject's record is as follows:

Trial No.	Time of solution	O's report
1	351.0 sec	"I have no idea in the world how I did it. I remember moving the loop of the heart about the end of the bar, and the two pieces suddenly came apart. I think I can do it sooner next time, not because I know just how to do it, but I remember the parts of the puzzle which I brought together in the first success."
2	256.4	"Do not yet know what movements to make."
3	155.0	"Success was still largely chance; did not anticipate except that I knew there was a certain part of the puzzle to work at. Hold the heart in the right hand and the bow in the left. Move the loop of the heart through the end of the bow. Can't describe the other movements; the rest is chance. Think I will get it next time."
4	27.0	
5	33.0	
6	50.0	
7	49.6	
8	28.0	
9	13.6	
10	13.7	
11	6.0	"It is easier to run the loop of the heart *under* the end of the bar. Had done this before but just realized its importance."
12	9.5	
13	8.0	"Noticed that when the bow is in a vertical position the bar on the upper side should be in a horizontal position. Pass the loop underneath, and with a sort of twist pass the end of the bar through the loop of the heart."
14	5.0	"Went through as anticipated. Feel that I understand solving the puzzle."
15	3.6	
16	4.8	
17	3.6	

was the existence of *spectator behavior*. The more common *participant behavior* consists in trying out hypotheses. In spectator behavior *O* has no hypothesis to test; all his guesses have been proved erroneous, and he can only make random responses and watch for some new hypothesis to emerge, as it often does after a while. Spectator behavior may perhaps afford an answer to the question of how hypotheses arise. The receptive attitude may be just what is necessary to allow some hitherto unnoticed aspect of the situation to take effect.

Unnecessary trial and error. Sometimes a distinction is drawn between stupid and intelligent errors, or between wild hypotheses and those that are fairly sensible even though inadequate. The difference is only one of degree. In struggling with a difficult construction puzzle, *O* makes many false moves but they all lie "well within the range of the plausible . . . the subject responds only to those elements of the situation which he has perceived to have some significance" (Morgan, 1934). Another investigator who reached this conclusion on the basis of extensive experiments was Kubo (1933).

Yet there are many false leads which might be rejected instantly, and "trial and error" often refers to errors of this sort. Székely (1947) presented this problem: "Here are 32 matchsticks in blocks of 4 which are arranged in a square,

4	4	4
4		4
4	4	4

The task is to take away 4 sticks and rearrange the remainder so that there shall be 12 sticks in each side of the square." One *O* took away the 4 at one corner, but then replaced them and removed the 4 at another corner. He took the first step without considering what the second step would be. Another *O* also followed the maxim of "one step at a time" and progressed as far as this arrangement,

5	3	4
2		2
4	3	5

He could advance no further since he was unwilling to disturb the two horizontal sides which already met the requirements. A third *O* got a better start by reasoning that all the sides should be treated alike; and a fourth did still better by starting with the query, "How can there be 4 sides of 12 sticks each and only 28 sticks in all?" Even he had to do some minor trial and error "in his head" before reaching the full solution.

Wertheimer (1945), in his important study of productive thinking, insisted that trial and error could and should be avoided altogether once all the necessary data were at hand. What is necessary, according to his Gestalt principles, is to take an open-minded receptive view of the whole problem, always keeping the whole before you and examining the parts only as parts of the whole. Therefore, the gap which makes the situation problematical will appear and then be closed by the forces of organization. He admitted that even the whole view might be wrongly centered and that "recentering" might be necessary, but he regarded such shifting of the point of view as too reasonable to be classified as trial and error. It is trial and error in the nonderogatory sense, however, if any leads which suggested themselves and were tried out (or thought through) proved to be blind alleys. In the examples he gives from his own thinking, such false leads were present, as they probably always are with difficult problems. With simpler problems (like those in Fig. 26-4, p. 826) instances are found of fairly direct though gradual approach to the solution.

We cannot despise trial-and-error behavior as mere waste motion unworthy of intelligent human beings. It serves to eliminate leads which promise well but prove to be blind alleys. It supplies information that cannot be obtained by pure inspection of the situation. It makes the materials familiar to the person who has to deal with them. At the very least it affords an outlet for the impulsive tendency to be doing something and prevents the thinker from going to sleep or otherwise going out of the field (Biber *et al*, 1942). A playful attitude is sometimes more productive than a rigid determination to advance along a certain line which may be a false lead.

Insight in problem solution. Evidently trial and error would not lead to a solution unless there were some way of checking on the errors. Success or failure, reinforcement or nonreinforcement, provides a check. But the question is whether *perception* of the sequence of events plays any part—whether *O* perceives in one case what blocked his progress and in another case what helped him toward the goal. As we have seen, Thorndike (1898) inferred from the *gradual* process of learning that no perception of the means-end relations occurred in his cats. Working with chimpanzees, Yerkes (1916) found evidence for insight in the many *sudden* transitions from trial-and-error behavior to the correct response. Other evidence was found in the good *retention* of the correct response, once it had been made, and in its *transfer* to somewhat modified situations. The same three criteria of insight in animals were used by Köhler (1917, 1924). They had previously been used by Ruger (1910) in his study of problem solving in human adults who also gave clear verbal indications of insight such as the exclamation, "Oh, I see now," with a report of what they had seen. Human insight, far from being an all-or-none affair, varies in degree, the lowest degree being what Ruger called "locus analysis." Just as a cat soon learns to work at the door of a puzzle box, a human subject may notice the mere place or part of a puzzle where success has occurred. This insight is *hindsight* when it first occurs but functions as *foresight* on the next trial and eliminates much superfluous trial and error. Insight often advances by stages, as in the report under Figure 26-3. Another example is cited from Gottschaldt's (1933) experiments on children. An 8-year-old boy was supplied with 60 long, slender blocks and asked to build a tower which should reach to the ceiling.

Starting with great confidence, he first lays the blocks flat but finds that there are not nearly enough of them to reach when laid thus. He clears away the first structure and tries a single pillar of the blocks, end to end, but this construction is too unstable to be carried high. He now pauses as if in thought and begins again with "arches" consisting of two uprights and a cross piece, repeating the arch vertically. Finding this structure unstable, he places blocks at the side to brace it, and also sets up a second arch on the floor parallel to the first. Then, apparently without seeing ahead, he lays two connecting blocks across from one arch to the other and at this moment seems to see how the problem can be solved. He proceeds in each successive story to set up two parallel arches tying them together by two cross pieces. This first attempt however collapses, but he does not change his method except to use more accuracy in placing the blocks.

Stages and degrees of insight. Working in the laboratory of Köhler and Wertheimer at Berlin, Duncker (1935) found that the solution of a complex problem proceeded by steps, one partial insight after another. Insight of the lower degree was shown when *O* saw that he could apply a previously learned rule to a new problem, but for insight of the higher degree *O* must see the reason for the rule. Wertheimer (1945) in his last book did not cite this extensive work of Duncker and apparently regarded Duncker's lower degree of insight as no insight at all. For true insight, according to Wertheimer, one must lay aside rules and formulas and examine the concrete situation for itself. Past experience could play a role in present insight only so far as the past experience was insightful. Yet when you have once seen why the sum of the angles of a triangle equals two right angles, you do not need to remember the reason every time you see how to apply this principle to a new problem in geometry. And when the child "sees" how to turn on the light by pressing the wall switch, can we deny that he has a flash of insight? No insight gets to the bottom of either physical or psychological processes.

The role of past experience in present insight. Various experiments afford many instances of insightful use of previously learned rules and principles. A special study of this question was made by Durkin (1937). Her material consisted of flat construction puzzles, which proved to have several advantages in the study of problem solving. Everything was in sight; there were no hidden properties requiring to be learned by manipulation. The pieces were easy to identify so that "thinking aloud" and "retracing the solution" were comparatively easy. And an objective record could be made by sketches or photographs of the state of affairs at critical stages in the process. The five small squares were given separately and after each had been solved once, the pieces from all were presented in a mixed assemblage with instructions to construct a Greek cross from all the pieces. Some *O*s were given this last problem without the previous experience in constructing the small squares.

The protocol of one *O* who solved the large cross after experience with the small squares affords a vivid instance of the "flash" experience (Fig. 26-4). This moment of insight or sudden reorganization was clearly dependent on the use of knowledge acquired in solving the small squares. More than that, the "flash" amounted to a realization that this knowledge could be now put to use. Such sudden reorganization did not appear in the protocols of *O*s who were given the large cross without previous experience with the small squares, though some of these *O*s solved the large cross by a process which the author called "gradual analysis" in which relevant relationships were discovered one after another.

Another example of insight dependent on previous experience is given by Birch (1945b). Young chimpanzees with no previous experience in playing with sticks failed completely when first given the reaching-stick problem, but solved it instantly after a few days of opportunity to play with sticks in other ways than reaching.

PROBLEM SOLUTION AS RELATED TO TRANSFER

In the studies so far considered in this chapter the experimenter has been examining the process of problem solution without attempting to facilitate or impede the process by any definite experimental factors. Another type of experiment is possible. *E* can introduce difficulties; he can present a problem in such a way as to confuse *O* or suggest a false lead; or he can give *O* preliminary training or mistraining and thus make a given problem easy or difficult. A systematic study of sources of difficulty is well worth while, and in fact a good deal has already been done along this line. We can tie the various experiments to our formula, R = f(S, A), the experimental variable belonging under the head of S or of A. An S-variable is present in the problem as presented, an A-variable in antecedent conditions such as preliminary training, instruction, or motivation. The R-variable is some index of *O*'s degree of success or failure in attempting to solve the problem. His solution may be more or less adequate, and his way of attacking the problem may be more or less efficient. The experiments now to be considered are here classified more or less appropriately under the heads of Transfer, Set, and Information given and utilized. The general question is whether *E* cannot introduce controls which will make a problem predictably easy or difficult to solve.

Positive and negative transfer effects. Though we have spoken as if the previ-

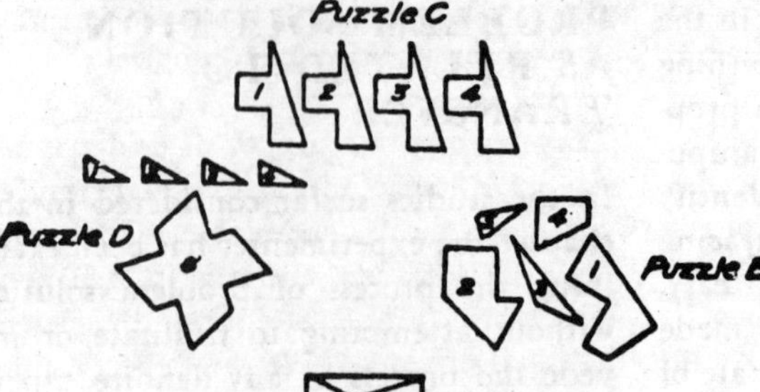

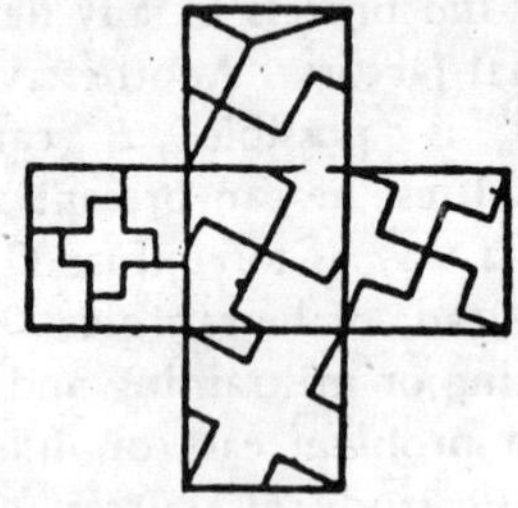

FIG. 26·4. (Durkin, 1937.) · Flat construction puzzles. Puzzle A required a square to be constructed from the pieces 1, 2, 3, 4; and so with the other lettered puzzles. The total cross was to be made of all the pieces presented in disarrangement. The protocol of one solution of the large cross, by an *O* who had previously solved the five small squares, is presented below.

Moves	*O's Remarks*
1. Looks over whole board. Eyes move rapidly. Fingers many pieces, particularly D_5 (observation).	1. Seems to be all the pieces I've used before ————I wonder if all really here. (Recall, not in relation to present goal.)
2. Picks up D_5.	2. Logical to start with big cross (D_5) (implied Analysis)
3. Fingers B_5.	3. Maybe the little cross will complicate the thing. (Analysis)
4. Places D_5 at bottom center so it looks like a cross and would not make a square.	4. No ready solution but will start with this (D_5).
5. Piles them up in assorted order.	5. Get all similar pieces together so if one works all will.
6. Looks around at all pieces and fingers the little cross.	6. Maybe with little cross as center ——— This has to be much broader than these arms at center. (Analysis)
7. Fingers B_4.	7. Maybe this little cross ought to be started out as a square, because so many pieces need a big center. (Analysis)
8. Picks up B_1—stops, hesitates, and is very quiet a moment ————	8. (Raised his voice and said excitedly) This is a good one, the real solution finally hits me. Make five squares and this can be the center.
9. Makes the five squares with only one error and puts them together to form the Greek cross.	

ously considered experiments did not introduce any experimental factors, in one respect they did, since they sometimes presented a series of problems and noted transfer effects. Thorndike (1898) noticed that experience with one puzzle box sometimes facilitated the solution of another one. A cat that had learned to pull a loop hanging in one part of the box readily mastered a similar or even a dissimilar loop hanging in another part. A little later, Kinnaman (1902) made a systematic study of transfer in the rhesus monkey. There were boxes to be entered for food, each box being fastened by a different device. Experience greatly increased the monkey's directness of attack upon these fastenings. In the early problems he would putter around the outside of the box and attack the edges and corners, but later he concentrated his efforts upon the fastenings.

In Ruger's (1910) experiments on human puzzle solving there were many instances of *negative* transfer effect. Let two puzzles have the same fundamental principle but differ in details and demand somewhat different manipulation. By attempting to carry over the same manipulation from one puzzle to the other *O* gets into difficulty and may be worse off than if he had never learned the first puzzle.

A good example of this difficulty is afforded by the "pyramid puzzle" (also called the "Chinese tower") which has been found useful by several experimenters, especially by Seashore (1938). The game can be played with five coins of different sizes. Mark three locations, A, B, and C, in a triangular arrangement on a sheet of paper. Pile the coins conically, with the smallest on top, at location A. The game is to get the coins into the same conical pile at location C. You may use location B as necessary, but you must move only one coin at a time and never place a larger coin above a smaller one. If you tackle five coins to start with, you will probably find the problem difficult. If you start with only two coins in the pile and advance step by step to the larger piles, you are likely to encounter the negative transfer effect just mentioned. But it is possible to discern a principle, or rule of action, that will guide you smoothly through the whole series of problems

Transfer of principles or of understanding. We found once before that transfer was much more dependable if the training consisted not entirely in drill but largely in careful attention to efficient methods of work. We can expect a similar result in problem solution: the better a principle has been understood in one problem, the more likely it is to be utilized in another problem (Bartlett, 1951).

"Trouble shooting." One important kind of practical problem is that of locating the cause of the trouble when a machine or operation goes wrong. A guiding principle of general applicability to such problems is simply this: "Analyze the situation and the symptoms of trouble so as not to overlook any likely cause." This admonition may be emphasized in a lecture, but it strikes home most effectively if given in direct connection with a baffling problem (Marks, 1951; Fattu & Mech, 1953).

Intelligence tests. Selz (1935) found it possible to raise the scores of retarded children 11–13 years old, not by direct coaching but by getting the children to criticize each others' errors. This training was limited to a completion test (a story with words left out). A child would write his completed sentence on the board and the other children would point out the errors and argue the case if the child was inclined to defend his work. The first sentence of the story read, "On a hot summer day I sat on the bank of the Rhine, in the cool . . . . of a tree." One child inserted "sunshine," responding vaguely to the general atmosphere of the occasion. Other children promptly pointed out what we may call the lack of precision in this response and the desirability of checking on one's response by reading the story right through. Only a couple of hours were devoted to this exercise, but the children evidently began to see the need for both precision and taking account of the whole, for in an after-test they showed considerable improvement, as compared with a matched control group, not only in sentence completion but also in analogies and number-series continuation.

A principle of physics. At quite a different intellectual level, two groups of students received some instruction on the moment of inertia, one group having a formal lecture on the subject and the other group an object lesson in which they tried to predict the behavior of a torsion pendulum and found that their prediction was in error. A few days later they were given a problem of this sort: Two spheres are the same in size and exterior appearance, and also in weight, one however being a solid ball of light metal and the other a hollow shell of heavy metal. Could you tell them apart by rolling them? Transfer was much better from the object lesson than from the formal lecture (Székely, 1950).

Match-stick geometrical problems. Transfer of principles was considered from the Gestalt point of view by Katona (1940). *O*'s task was to increase or decrease the number of squares by relocating a certain number of sticks, as in Figure 26·5. Two kinds of principles were suggested, one arithmetical, the other geometrical or configurational. The one might be introduced by such elementary tasks as these: to construct two squares with seven sticks, to construct three squares with ten sticks, and then to take away two sticks from the ten and leave

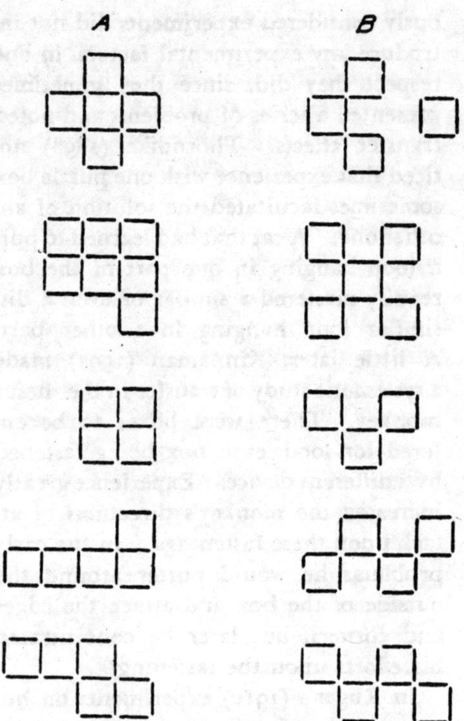

Fig. 26·5. (Selected from Katona, 1940, p. 79.) Match-stick problems. Each A figure can be changed into the paired B figure, or vice versa, with only three sticks moved (with only two sticks moved in the bottom pair). Katona showed an A figure alone (or sometimes a B figure alone) with instructions such as these: "Here are five equal squares. The task is to make four similar squares out of the five by changing the position of three sides." For suggesting the "arithmetical" principle, he could show the first A figure and point out that it was composed of 16 sticks, just enough for four squares if no stick were allowed to have the double function of serving as a side of two squares. This suggestion was given only once. For suggesting the "configurational" principle, the uppermost A figure was shown first as composed of five paper squares, one of them being then moved away; next the same figure was made of match sticks so that when one square of them was moved away there were only four squares. It was apparently left to *O* to discover that one side of this square could be left in position so that only three sticks had to be moved. The two principles were of course suggested to different groups of subjects, not both to the same group.

two squares. One stick can function as a side of two adjacent squares. To get the maximum number of squares from a given number of sticks, accordingly, make the squares adjacent; and to decrease the number of squares prevent them from being adjacent. Katona presented this arithmetical principle more abstractly, though with an example. The configurational principle calls attention to the whole pattern which may be compact or loose, the loose patterns having some open spaces, either corner holes or side holes. To decrease the number of squares, open up holes; to increase it, close the holes. Katona did not present this principle verbally but showed examples designed to lead *O* to see the figures in this way. He found that the configurational principle gave somewhat better transfer than the arithmetical, when new problems of the same sort were given, though both were better than repetitious drill intended to lead *O* to memorize the particular moves necessary in one or two of the problems.

Probably the best teaching method would combine the arithmetical and the configurational suggestions, as was done by Reid (1951) in presenting a famous matchstick problem: To construct four triangles out of six sticks, each side of the triangles to be the length of one stick. Of 35 college students, 10 solved the problem without any help. Then an arithmetical suggestion was given: With only six sticks available for four triangles, each stick must be a side of two triangles. Eight *O*s solved the problem without further aid. Finally, geometrical suggestions were given to the effect that the arrangement must be compact and that triangles lying to this side and that must somehow be brought together so that the triangles can become adjacent and every stick form a common side of two triangles. With these aids 10 additional *O*s succeeded, leaving seven who were still unsuccessful. The great difficulty of this problem is due to *O*'s implicit assumption that all the triangles will lie in one plane, flat on the table. We shall have more to say of fixed assumptions soon, under the head of "set."

Educational experiments. It appears from the preceding experiments that problem-solving ability is partly a matter of principles, procedures, and techniques that can be taught and learned and then applied to new problems within a given field—though how widely the transfer may spread is not clear. The schools should be able to accomplish something in this direction within fields of much importance to the student at the time and in later life. Probably many school experiments have attempted to find dependable means of accomplishing this result. One or two such experiments may be cited. Salisbury (1934), using matched groups in each of several school grades, gave courses of carefully prepared lessons in *outlining* general reading matter and obtained from the experimental groups a positive transfer effect in certain school subjects, and in reading comprehension and reasoning ability. Such improvement was present in the seventh school grade and more markedly in the high school. Brembeck (1949), using matched groups of college students, gave courses in argumentation with fore- and after-tests in critical thinking, and obtained a positive transfer effect. R. L. Thorndike (1950) showed a number of ways in which the school could teach the principles and techniques of problem solving; he emphasized perseverance, flexibility, willingness to suspend judgment till the evidence is in, a critical attitude toward sources of information, and a habit of checking the conclusions reached. But no single school subject is certain to inculcate these principles. Thus Wesman (1945) repeated some older experiments of E. L. Thorndike, but with much better data, on the important question whether growth of intelligence during the high school years depended on the school subjects taken; but he, like Thorndike, was unable to demonstrate any clear advantage of one school subject over another. Much depends, probably, on how a subject is taught and on how it is studied.

SET AS A FACTOR IN PROBLEM SOLVING

The reality of the "set" factor as a preparatory adjustment for performing a task has been shown in reaction time (p. 28), controlled association (p. 57), the judgment of lifted weights (p. 227), and perhaps elsewhere in the preceding chapters. Often set is visible as a posture of readiness, like that of the runner poised for a quick start. Where no particular posture is externally observable, the behaviorists are able to avoid any mentalistic implications by speaking of a hypothetical internal posture of muscular tensions. We know set, however, chiefly from its facilitative and inhibitory effects on behavior; it facilitates responses for which *O* is prepared and tends to inhibit any competing responses. As an intervening variable it is tied to these effects on the output side, while on the input side it is tied to *E*'s instructions, to signals such as conditioned stimuli, or to the obvious requirements of the situation with which *O* is confronted. In some kinds of experiment it is a dependable A-variable.

In a pioneer discussion of Einstellung, the German term for set, von Kries (1895) gave many examples: set for the context which determines the meaning of an otherwise ambiguous word, set for the "signature" in music which determines whether a black or a white key on the piano is struck in response to a certain note in the printed score, set for the state of a game which determines the next move, and orientation in the existing spatial or social situation.

Unfortunately the word *set* in some of its many uses suggests fixity and inflexibility, implications which are by no means intended in the standard psychological usage. A ready posture gives way to the actual performance and is not reinstated until the same act is to be performed again. We need a better word but none has been introduced. "Adjustment" would sometimes serve the purpose but it carries other meanings in psychology. "Readiness" carries the right meaning but is awkward to use.

Advantages of set, i.e., of being prepared. The positive value of a set is due to its facilitation of appropriate responses and inhibition of inappropriate; its disadvantages appear when it does the reverse because it is not adequately oriented to the given situation or to the goal (Johnson, 1944b; Harlow, 1951). Some experiments bring out the advantages and some the disadvantages, but the dynamic reality of set is shown in either case.

Set in controlled association. One of the most successful early attempts to submit thinking to experimental study was the work of Watt (1905). His method was mostly introspective though he made some use of associative reaction times. He used word stimuli and assigned such tasks as these: whole—part or part—whole, subordinate or supraordinate concept. His procedure was first to assign a task and after a short foreperiod to expose a stimulus word. When *O* had responded he was asked to give a retrospective account of his experience. The retrospective reports showed the foreperiod to be occupied as follows when the task was relatively new and unfamiliar. O made the task clear to himself in a verbal, visual or kinesthetic form. He defined the relation, or found an example, or imagined a diagram or gesture symbolizing the relation. When the stimulus word arrived, the reaction followed sometimes automatically, sometimes after an interval of waiting or searching, sometimes after false reactions had been suppressed. Only in this last case did the definite consciousness of the task emerge again during the main period; usually it was confined to the foreperiod.

When the same task had continued for a series of stimulus words, the conscious awareness of the task faded out even from the foreperiod and was reduced to a mere feeling of readiness. The preparation lost its specificity as a conscious state, but not as an adjustment, for it still insured correct responses. With practice the set became at once less conscious and more efficient.

Watt's main result was the efficiency of the task-set or preparation, along with the fact that this preparation was completed during the foreperiod. It worked by *selecting in advance*. It did not select during the main period from among several responses called up by the stimulus word, but it limited the field of response in advance of the stimulus word so that only responses conforming to the task were ordinarily called up.

This experiment of Watt was repeated and amplified by May (1917) who varied the conditions in several ways and made more use of the objective results. He constructed apparatus for presenting both the task and the stimulus word visually and for varying the length of the foreperiod at either *E*'s or *O*'s option. When O had control, he exposed the task word and then the stimulus word as soon as he felt ready. With practice his foreperiod became shorter; he needed less time to get set for the task. When E controlled the length of the foreperiod, varying it from zero to half a second, O's reaction time was shorter the longer the foreperiod, i.e., the more complete his preparation.

The effect of practice to level down the conscious process of preparation was well illustrated by the reports of one O who started with a complete outfit of motor schemes or adjustments, one for each of the task relations. These adjustments felt definitely muscular at first, but "gradually lost their bodily or muscular aspect and became, as he termed it, 'more neural.' Later this neural process seemed to him to fade out" into mere spatial diagrams, which in turn faded into attitudes of readiness and finally gave way to an entirely automatic process. "We have here a descending series of processes with the length of the foreperiod getting shorter as the series descends."

The introspective reports of getting ready and of being ready have some validity since they check with the objectively measured durations of the foreperiod and of the reaction time. These experiments yield three kinds of evidence for the reality of set: O's awareness of preparing and of preparedness, the time records and practice effects, and the correctness of the responses.

Direction in problem solving. What Maier (1930) called "direction" is an important kind of set. O is likely to assume that the goal lies in a certain direction, literally or figuratively. If his assumption is false, he must somehow change his direction before he can solve the problem. One of Maier's problems (Fig. 26-6) called for the construction of

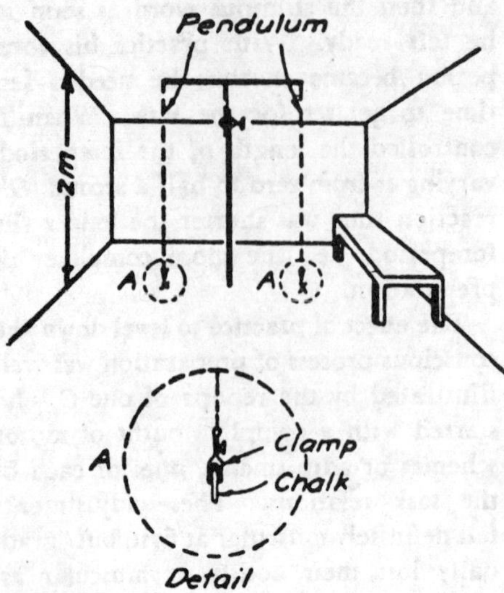

FIG. 26-6. (Maier, 1930.) The pendulum problem, solved.

two pendulums, suspended so that in swinging they would leave marks on the floor at certain places. The available materials were wooden strips, clamps, wires, crayons, and a heavy table which was not to be moved, besides the walls and low ceiling of the room. Without some assistance the problem was extremely difficult for college students. The subordinate problems or "parts" were explained by *E:* (a) he showed how to make a plumb line out of a clamp attached to a wire; (b) he showed how to make a long strip by clamping two short ones together; (c) he showed how to wedge a double strip horizontally across the open door. If these three devices were properly combined, the whole problem would be solved, but the students all assumed that the table or walls would have to be used, without thinking of the ceiling unless their attention was called to it by *E's* remarking that the problem would be easy if only there were some nails in the ceiling. Given this direction plus the "parts," a fair share of the students reached the approved solution shown in Figure 26-6, but practically no one succeeded fully without the organizing factor of direction.

When this experiment was repeated by Weaver & Madden (1949) the results were different to this extent, that some *Os* found the adequate direction for themselves without having it suggested by *E.* Their solutions took the form shown at the left under D in Figure 26-7, which is certainly just as good as the approved one shown beside it, if not a little better because easier to set up. Subjects given no help at all produced almost nothing, but the others accomplished something though many of their structures were too unstable to permit free swinging of the pendulums or too short to mark the floor at the prescribed points. Once started in a certain direction and seeing some hope of success, they seemed unwilling to scrap what they had begun and make a fresh start.

Disadvantages of set. It is possible to devise problems that are sure to be misleading. They either make *O* start out in a wrong direction, or they induce him to persist in a line of attack that is right at the start but needs to be changed later.

Reverse detours. Any problem, as Köhler once said, calls for a detour of some sort, for if the path to the goal were perfectly clear and direct, there would be no problem. But some detours are especially difficult. To start out at 180° from the goal direction "goes against the grain." In apes and monkeys this difficulty is brought out by the "stick detour" problem. After the simple reaching-stick problem is mastered, the lure is placed in a box or drawer which is open at the top and at the far end, but closed at the near end and sides, so that the lure must first be pushed away from the animal—a detour of 180°. Köhler found

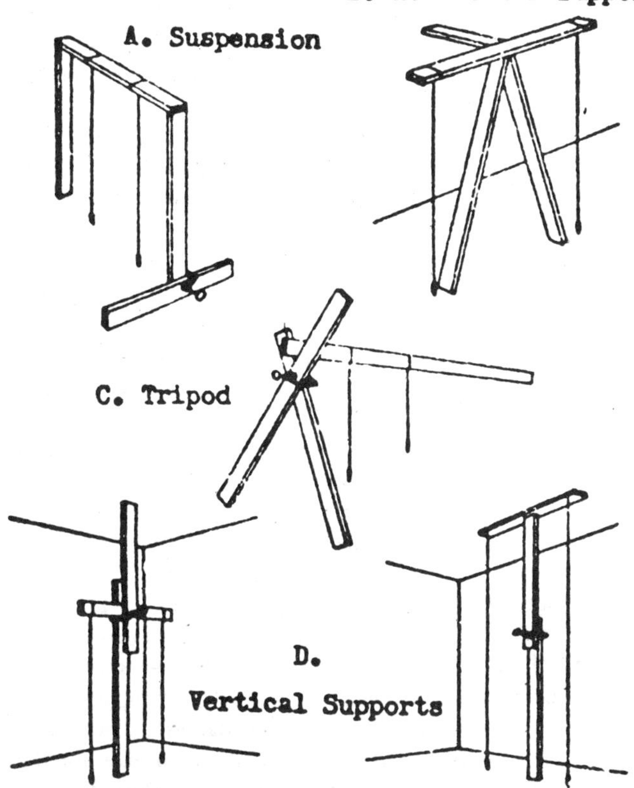

FIG. 26-7. (Weaver & Madden, 1949.) Four lines of attack on the two-pendulum problem. The A structures, in spite of the clamped-on floor piece, were unstable because of the varied lengths of the available strips. The B structures were intended to achieve some stability by leaning against the wall. The tripod or C structures were more stable but too short horizontally. Only the two types of D structures achieved stability by a jointed strip wedged between floor and ceiling and successfully met all the requirements. The A, C and D plans were about equally frequent.

this a difficult problem for chimpanzees, as did Guillaume & Meyerson (1930). Their most intelligent animal tried every other possibility first: moving the drawer, poking the banana over one side of the drawer, which meant a 90° instead of a 180° detour, spearing the fruit with the stick, or smashing it and getting a taste from the stick. The "correct" solution occurred at first partly by accident, when some other line of attack brought the banana close to the open end of the drawer; then it was pushed out and around. The process of gaining mastery was gradual. This problem was apparently beyond the ability of a very clever Cebus monkey (Klüver, 1937).

In one of Gottschaldt's (1933) experiments on young children, a short stick is present in the child's play pen, and outside are two sticks, a long and a medium one; but only the long one will reach to the lure beyond. The normal 6-year-old will disregard the superfluous medium stick but use his short one to pull in the long one and then use the long one to secure the reward. He does not do so well if the lure is *almost* within reach of his short stick. When a problem can almost be solved by an easy method the adoption of a more difficult method encounters unusual obstacles; the resistance to the detour is too great, the "vector" toward the lure too strong (Lewin, 1935.

p. 83). A similar obstacle to first-class work on a problem is created by excessive eagerness to obtain the reward, as in Birch's (1945a) experiments on chimpanzees under different degrees of hunger.

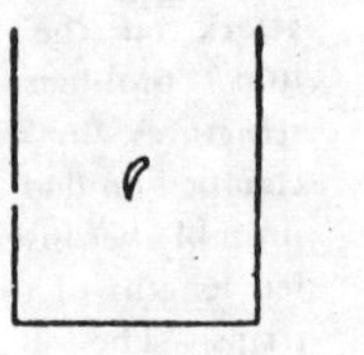

Fig. 26-8. Drawer detour problem. A fine-meshed wire netting prevents the animal from reaching directly into the drawer from inside his cage. He has a stick with which the banana can be pushed out of the far end of the drawer and then pulled within reach at the side.

There are various "trick puzzles," as the human adult is apt to consider them, which call for a sort of reverse detour, a back-and-forth movement inconsistent with one's natural expectation of a straightforward progress toward the goal—as in these examples:

A Captain with 50 men comes to the edge of a river and finds the only boat to be one in which two children are playing but which is so small that it will hold only one man and not even a child in addition. How does the Captain manage to get all his men ferried across?

Another trick puzzle:

How can you bring up from the river exactly 6 quarts of water when you have only a 4-quart and a 9-quart pail to measure with?

Yet another:

A man stopping at a hotel ran out of money and would have no more for 23 days. The landlord would not trust him, but as he had a heavy gold chain of 23 links, the landlord agreed to accept one link in payment on each successive day and to restore the chain on the receipt of the money. Problem, how many links does the owner have to cut in order to fulfill his engagement? The answer is 2 links.

Detouring is offensive to the natural man (or rat) who likes to follow his nose, to look at the goal and go where he is looking. What he must learn, and does learn in a more or less generalized way, is the utility of detours.

"Functional fixity." This term of Duncker's (1935, 1945) refers to a disadvantage of set which, by contrast with the preceding one, depends on learning and transfer or interference. An object that has one customary function is not easily seem to be suitable for a quite different function. A hairbrush is not easily seen as a possible trowel. Remember the negative transfer from $S_1—R_1$ to $S_1—R_2$ (p. 752). Duncker showed how this factor interfered with mathematical thinking as well as with the solution of simple mechanical problems. We shall cite one of his simpler experiments as repeated by Adamson (1952). The problem is to mount three small candles in burning position on the surface of a vertical wall or screen. Lying scattered on a table is a miscellaneous assortment of objects, none of them suitable for the purpose except three pasteboard boxes of different sizes, one of which contains candles, another matches, and the third thumbtacks. If the boxes are emptied and tacked to the wall, the candles can be mounted on them by the use of a little of their own melted wax. But the boxes, as presented, are serving the function of containers, and *O* has to deprive them of this function before using them as candleholders. For a control group, however, the boxes are empty to start with so that their function as containers is less obtrusive. Within a time limit of 20 minutes, 24 out of 28 in the control group of college students solved the problem, as against only 12 out of 29 in the experimental group—a reliable difference.

A differently designed experiment of Birch & Rabinowitz (1951) made use of one of Maier's problems. Two strings are hanging from the ceiling to the floor, and *O*'s task is to tie them together; but they are so far apart that he cannot reach the second while holding the first. The solution is to convert one of them into a swinging pendulum by the use of some heavy object as a bob. In this particular experiment two heavy objects were at hand, one being an electric switch and the other a relay. The students who served as subjects were not very familiar with these objects but became acquainted with one or the other of them in a preliminary wiring job. Most of the *Os* needed a suggested "direction" before thinking of a pendulum, but after *E* had "accidentally" swung one string by brushing against it, all quickly solved the problem. The point is that 17 out of 19 of them used for the pendulum bob the object which they had *not* used as an electrical device. The distinctly electrical object did not fit into their set for a weight.

Simple examples of "functional fixity" are afforded by puzzle pictures or by disarranged sentences like this one: "Till midnight no in there was at the money."

Compound tasks and sets. The runner on the mark is set not only for a quick start but also for an immediate shift to top speed if the race is short or to moderate speed if it is long. At the entrance of a visible maze (p. 649) the human learner is set not only for the first move but also for looking ahead and avoiding the blind alleys. A maze or detour problem used on 12-year-old children by Koyanagi (1953) called for the rolling of a ball by aid of a stick along some sloping passages. Near the goal there was a hole into which the ball would surely drop unless *O* was ready in advance to cover the hole with a suitable tool that lay conveniently to hand. Only the bright children acquired the complete behavior pattern quickly; the children of subaverage intelligence maneuvered the ball happily through most of the maze only to fall into the trap at the end, as if their one-stage set interfered with the acquisition of the complete two-stage set.

Jersild (1927) made a special study of rapid shifting back and forth between two tasks, as between giving opposites and subtracting 3, with stimulus lists like the following:

Give opposites	*Subtract 3*	*Alternately give opposite and Subtract 3*
last	64	expensive
talkative	72	41
dangerous	47	timid
gay	80	59
broad	49	stale
past	35	26
secret	43	shaky
sharp	56	38
innocent	62	stormy
masculine	35	50
useful	44	thrifty
shallow	51	93

College students far from being disturbed, rather preferred the alternating to the more monotonous work, and actually worked faster in the combined tasks, provided the tasks and stimuli were *dissimilar.* (There was a loss of speed in shifting between adding 3 and subtracting 3, or between giving opposites of adjectives and opposites of verbs.) Jersild's main result is the demonstrated existence of sets of higher order in which *O* is prepared for two or more types of response.

Instead of prescribing the shifts to be made, as in the preceding experiment, Schroder & Rotter (1952) gave *O* an opportunity to *learn* to shift. The task called for classifying certain cards according to the design or color on them, and if the basis of classification was changed frequently, *O* learned to be ready for a change and to shift his line of attack quickly.

The "blinding" effect of a too persistent set. When the task calls for the same kind of response to each stimulus in a list or series, the task set persists throughout the list and enables *O* to advance rapidly and smoothly through the series. A list may consist of anagrams, groups of disarranged letters, each group to be formed into a single word. The normal procedure of educated adults in solving an anagram is thus described by Sargent (1940): "All subjects typically used a 'whole approach' for the first few seconds; then, if an 'immediate reorganization' did not occur, they turned to a 'part approach' which was characterized by trial-and-error manipulation of letters." The procedure is far from stereotyped and the general anagram-set is simply directed toward finding a word in each group of letters, but the set can be given a more specific direction. Rees & Israel (1935) presented groups of five letters so arranged that every one could be solved by the same rule: Take the given letters in the order 34521. So *lecam* became *camel*. Nothing was said of any such rule, and the student *O*s for the most part never formulated it, but they soon became conditioned to the uniform sequence and advanced rapidly down the list. In a list of 30 items, the first 15 were soluble only by the rule, but the last 15 had other possible solutions also, as *pache* may be either *cheap* or *peach*. The question was whether the set would persist and blind *O* to the alternative solutions. The result was definitely positive; the rule was followed right through the list and only a very few of the alternative solutions were produced. (With or without modifications this experiment is a favorite in laboratory courses; the paper cited gives lists of anagrams.)

The set we have just been considering is a readiness for a certain procedure, i.e., for taking the given letters in a certain order. A set can be induced also for a certain class of solution words, such as names of plants and flowers. After a long series of this kind, *O* is apt to carry over the set to a test series of anagrams which can be solved either in the same way or otherwise. This result of Rees & Israel was later confirmed by Maltzman & Morrisett (1953). The set for a certain order of letters is naturally more effective, since it guides *O*'s procedure from the start.

This inhibitory or "blinding" effect of set was regarded as a very serious disadvantage by Luchins (1942). He found the water-measuring puzzle well suited for dramatic demonstrations of the effect. *O* was asked to solve a number of "numerical problems" calling for the measurement of definite quantities of water by means of certain measuring jars as specified for each problem:

Problem	*Jars regarded as given*			*Required*
No.	*A*	*B*	*C*	*Amount*
1	29	3		20 quarts
2	21	127	3	100 "
3	14	163	25	99 "
4	18	43	10	5 "
5	9	42	6	21 "
6	20	59	4	31 "
7	23	49	3	20 "
8	15	39	3	18 "
9	28	76	3	25 "
10	18	48	4	22 "
11	14	36	8	6 "

The introductory two-jar problem was explained after *O* had worked on it a few minutes: "Fill the 29-quart jar and pour from it 3 quarts 3 times; 29 — 3 — 3 — 3 = 20." The second problem was then presented and explained after 3 minutes of work. This and all the following problems except No. 9 are soluble by the formula, B — A — 2C, that is to say by the imaginary procedure of first filling the largest jar and then pouring off the A jarful once and the C jarful twice. But all the problems after the sixth are soluble more simply without any use of the largest jar. The question was whether *O* would become so set for the three-jar procedure as to be blind to the opportunity to use a more direct two-jar procedure. The results showed that *O* did become so set in the majority of cases all the way from the grade school to the level of graduate students. Control groups given only the initial two-jar problem followed by Nos. 7–11 usually continued to use the two-jar procedure, but groups that learned to use the three-jar procedure where it was necessary usually persisted in it throughout the list, overlooking the simpler possibilities. The author attempted in various ways to protect his subjects from this deplorable blindness, but without much success.

Perhaps the blindness was not so deplorable after all. The problems as presented were certainly unrealistic (imagine yourself trying to pour water out of a 127-quart jar), but even when *E* introduced a little realism by letting the numbers stand for cubic centimeters instead of quarts, and by providing appropriate small containers and water for actual manipulation, still *O* was most likely to concentrate on the arithmetic rather than on the concrete situation and to follow the three-jar procedure (Luchins & Luchins, 1950). The students often persisted in the three-jar procedure because they wished to show how, given the big jar full, they could withdraw just enough water to leave the required amount. The children were apt to regard the experiment as merely another school exercise in which they should learn and apply a rule for solving a certain type of arithmetical problems. Perhaps indeed, as urged by Wertheimer (1945), school children are too much trained to follow authoritarian rules blindly.

The Luchins-type experiment has been utilized in later investigations of learning theory and of personality traits. Youtz (1948) found that increasing the number of problems solved successfully by one procedure—increasing the number of reinforcements of this procedure—also increased its resistance to extinction when the later problems demanded a second procedure. Massed trials favor the establishment of a fixed procedure, according to the results of Kendler, Greenberg & Richman (1952), who also improved the setup by using beans instead of water, with actual containers labeled in cubic inches. Rokeach (1950) used the individual's persistence in a fixed procedure as an index of "rigidity"; and Guetzkow (1951) distinguished the individual's set-strength from his ability to overcome a set and make a fresh attack on a problem.

The overcoming of a particular set. Quite apart from the persistence of a set from one little problem to another in a series is the matter of fixed assumptions which often hamper the solution of a single difficult problem. Such an assumption is like a long, complicated blind alley in a maze which you explore almost indefinitely, back and forth, without ever becoming sure it is a blind alley. Ruger (1910, see above p. 821) in his work with puzzles gave particular attention to this source of difficulty. He found some *Os* excessively stubborn in adhering to one line of attack in spite of continued failure. He found two ways of combating this *O*-factor. (1) He asked *O* to formulate the assumption underlying his attempts to solve the puzzle and then to consider what alternative assumptions were possible. In some instances *O* thus became aware for the first time of the successful line of attack. This technique put a stop to fruitless repetition and proved to be "a very valuable means of furthering efficiency in the solution of the problem." (2) When *O* was floundering about and making no progress, *E* asked him to lay the puzzle aside for a while. "In some cases the puzzle was solved almost immediately on coming back to it later in the day. The particular set of consciousness had been broken up by this change and new points of view were possible. There were a number of rather striking cases of a similar sort on first awaking in the morning."

Here we have two promising leads for experimental work on problem solution —leads which have not been followed up to any great extent in the laboratory. But we have a large mass of testimony from creative thinkers to the effect that laying aside a baffling problem for a while is often the only way to reach a satisfactory solution. We shall cite a little of this evidence in the following section.

"Incubation"—laying aside a problem as a step toward solution. The word *incubation* may serve as a useful catchword though it implies a theory which we do not accept, preferring as we do a theory suggested by the immediately preceding quotation from Ruger. Laying aside a problem is a means of getting rid of a false set or "direction" and so giving the true direction a chance to emerge.

Helmholtz, a brilliant inventor and discoverer in several scientific fields, including psychology as well as physiology and physics, took occasion at a dinner in honor of his seventieth birthday to report something of his methods of work on original problems (1896).

> I must say that those fields of work have become ever more agreeable to me in which one need not depend on lucky accidents and "happy thoughts." But as I have found myself pretty often in the uncomfortable position of having to wait for happy thoughts, the experience I have gained on the question, when and where they came to me, may perhaps be useful to others. . . . So far as my experience goes, they never came to a fatigued brain and never at the writing desk. It was always necessary, first of all, that I should have turned my problem over on all sides to such an extent that I had all its angles and complexities "in my head" and could run through them freely without writing. To bring the matter to that point is usually impossible without long preliminary labor. Then, after the fatigue resulting from this labor had passed away, there must come an hour of complete physical freshness and quiet well-being, before the good ideas arrived. Often they were there in the morning when I awoke, just according to Goethe's oft-cited verses, and as Gauss also once noted. But they liked specially to make their appearance while I was taking an easy walk over wooded hills in sunny weather. The smallest amount of alcohol seemed to frighten them away.

So far as Helmholtz offers a theory, it is based on fatigue and the recovery from fatigue. The intensive preparatory work is an essential part of the story. An earlier psychologist (Carpenter, 1876) offered the theory of "unconscious cerebration" occurring during the interval of rest. He had gathered many instances from inventors, artists, and poets of their laying a problem aside and finding that after sleep or recreation just what they wanted "came into their heads," and he agreed with Oliver Wendell Holmes and other thinkers that the brain must have been working on the problem while conscious attention was otherwise occupied.

The theory of unconscious work was revived by the great mathematician Poincaré (1908) who had noticed in his own case that it was often safe to lay a problem aside and wait for the solution to emerge later. Fruitful unconscious work, however, must be "first preceded and then followed by a period of conscious work. These sudden inspirations are never produced . . . except after some days of voluntary efforts which appeared absolutely fruitless. . . . The second period of conscious work . . . is necessary to work out the results of the inspiration . . . to verify them."

Following up Helmholtz and Poincaré, Graham Wallas (1926) distinguished "four stages of creative thought" which he named preparation, incubation, illumination, verification. In many cases, he admitted, the stages might overlap in time.

Data from inventors and scientists. The abundant testimony collected by Rossman (1931) and by Meinecke (1934) from inventors, and by Platt & Baker (1931) from chemists, shows that the "four stages" are matters of first-hand experience to many original thinkers. They make it a rule to assemble all available information and work intensively for a quick solution; and sometimes they succeed in this first effort. But often they have to give up for the time and wait for the saving idea to emerge. Sometimes it comes during discussion of the problem with other people, but sometimes at an odd moment when one is relaxed and not concerned at all with the problem, as while walking or riding, or while dressing, gardening, golfing, fishing, attending a concert or church service, daydreaming, or lying in bed before going to sleep or after awaking.

Most of the inventors seemed to adopt the easy hypothesis of unconscious work as the explanation of the illumination. One chemist who had considered the psychology of the matter more deeply, presents a different hypothesis along with some fresh facts:

> The two factors that seem to be involved are first, so thorough a study of the problem and of the data that your mind is quite completely saturated with the subject. Then, second, a period of intermission or rest, and an apparent solution or proper method of attack comes to your mind when you are not formally working on the problem and have no papers in front of you. . . . I remember one morning I took my bath, shaved, took another bath, and in reaching out for a dry towel suddenly became aware that this was my second bath and that my mind had been deeply concentrated on a problem for half an hour. . . . I give this as an example . . . because it gives a clear picture of what is going on. The mind is fresh; it is so full of the problem that there is no need to refer to anything and it is in deep concentration. . . . With a rested mind soaked full of data on a problem, and in deep concentration, I would expect a man to solve a problem if he ever can solve it.

These numerous observations appear well deserving of acceptance so far as concerns the necessity for intensive work on a problem followed by laying the problem aside. The last quotation raises an important question regarding the "flash" of illumination. If the flash is the climax of a short period of very intense thought, there is no need for the hypothesis of unconscious work during the incubation period.

Data from poets and artists. In an inquiry among living lyric poets, 55 of them, Patrick (1935) found the four-stage creative process to be typical; and she found the same in a similar inquiry among 50 pictorial artists (1937). Although a minority are accustomed to write a poem on the spur of the moment —or to sketch a picture of what they happen to see before them—72 percent of the poets and 76 percent of the artists report a stage of incubation. Two examples:

> I saw the moon coming out of a cloud, which reminded me of a white owl. I car

ried that idea around several days before I finally wrote a poem on it.

I often carry an idea around for several weeks before I make a picture, though sometimes longer. I got ideas last summer to do now. The ideas recur from time to time while I am occupied with other things.

Though Patrick accepts the four stages as a valid outline of the creative process, she adds the important point that the problem is not entirely absent from conscious thought during the stage of incubation. *"The incubated idea or mood recurs from time to time* during the incubation period. When the idea recurs, there is a chance of some work being done upon it." The work done on the problem during incubation is however not seriously directed toward the main goal. "As soon as the mood or idea becomes definitely related to a specific goal, we have the third stage of illumination or inspiration."

This author went on to see whether the four stages could be found in miniature in an experimental situation. She had surprising success in obtaining a lyric or picture produced under the experimenter's eye, with oral expression of thoughts occurring during the process. As a stimulus for the lyric, the picture of a mountain landscape was used; a poem was laid before the artists. The subject was requested to obtain any suggestion he pleased from the stimulus material, and to take as much time as he pleased in his composition. On the average, and with much variation, about 20 minutes were used.

That the poets and artists were not hampered by the experimental conditions appeared from their testimony and from the excellence of their products, some of which were later published.

The three overt stages, preparation, illumination, and revision, were easily identified in the protocols. At first manifold impressions and memories occurred, but usually nothing was committed to paper. After a time a decision emerged, and figures were rapidly blocked out or a few lines of a poem roughly formulated. Though the three overt stages overlapped in time, on the whole they came in the usual order. The suggestions tended to come early, the first sketch or draft in the middle, and the revisions near the end. The presence of incubation was indicated "if an idea occurred early in the report, recurred one or more times, and at last appeared as the chief topic" of the poem or picture. By this criterion incubation was surely present in 64 percent of the poets and 84 percent of the artists.

In a similar experiment (Eindhoven & Vinacke, 1952; Vinacke, 1952) artists were asked to produce in the laboratory a publishable picture illustrative of a given poem. Their behavior was observed by *E* and recorded in 5-minute periods. There was so much overlapping of preparation, illumination, and verification (or critical revision) as to lead the investigators to the conclusion that the "stages" would better be called "processes." No distinct stage of incubation was demonstrated.

It is of course difficult in a single laboratory session to check on the statement that complete laying aside of a difficult problem can be an important step toward eventual solution.

Theories of incubation. The obvious theory—unconscious work, whether conceived as mental or as cerebral—should be left as a residual hypothesis for adoption only if other, more testable hypotheses break down (Skinner, 1953a). Several other hypotheses have been suggested in what precedes.

Since the problem does *consciously re-*

cur from time to time during the period of incubation, though without effortful work done upon it, partial solutions may be obtained.

If the illumination comes in a period, short or long, of *intense concentration* on the problem, the assumption of previous unconscious work is gratuitous.

The *freshness* or lack of brain fatigue which seems to be necessary for illumination may furnish a sufficient explanation.

The parallel but simpler case of the recall of a name, after futile attempts followed by dropping the matter, suggests that an essential factor in illumination is the *absence of interferences* which block progress during the preliminary stage. When the thinker makes a false start, he slides insensibly into a groove and may not be able to escape at the moment. He falls into certain assumptions which restrict his sector of exploratory activity, and as long as he continues actively at work, he does not escape from these assumptions, as he often does on coming back to the problem after giving it a rest. Several of the inventors noted a fact which favors this interpretation: the happy idea, when it came, amazed them by its simplicity. They had assumed a more complicated solution to be necessary. According to this line of evidence, the incubation period simply allows time for an erroneous set to die out and leave the thinker free to take a fresh look at his problem.

REASONING AS THE UTILIZATION OF INFORMATION

The solution of a problem usually calls for the utilization of given information as well as for the assembling of enough information to justify a conclusion. The problem-solver may fail to gather adequate information, but even if he has all the necessary information at hand, he may fail to put the data together—to structure it—in such a way as to reveal the interrelations of the various items and justify a conclusion. He may not see how to sift the wheat from the chaff—the useful from the superfluous and misleading information—put before him in a detective story. He may lose track of information already obtained and ask unnecessary questions, as in the game of Twenty Questions (Taylor & Faust, 1952). Sitting on a jury, he may be swayed this way and that by the evidence for and against the suspect (Weld & Danzig, 1940).

Given certain limited information, the would-be deductive reasoner may go wrong in either of two ways. He may not utilize all the given information, or he may draw a conclusion that goes beyond what he is given. The experimenter can manipulate the given information, making it his experimental variable, his S-factor, and setting traps for the unwary reasoner so as to show up the difficulties in reasoning.

Failure to utilize information. A novel form of task designed to elicit reasoning of an informal sort consisted of a short story that led up toward a climax but was left for *O* to finish (Bartlett, 1939). The experiment was tried on English subjects of different educational levels and also on some Eskimos. In all the groups it was found that few individuals utilized all the information impartially. The climax was commonly determined either by certain details or by some social convention of the social group.

For quantitative studies of reasoning it is desirable to know exactly how much information *O* has at his disposal and how completely he utilizes it. This point was made by Whitfield (1951), who presented a matching problem: eight objects were to be placed in a series of eight locations, the correct arrangement to be discovered by trial and error, with information after each trial as to which objects were correctly placed. It was a "rational learning" problem, the same as if the numerals from 1 to 8 were to be assigned in some unknown order to the letters from A to H. Suppose that after the first trial *O* is told he has correctly numbered the letter D but no others. His task on the next trial is to number D as before and to avoid repeating errors by numbering all the other letters differently. Most of the *O*s adopted some system, as by keeping the erroneous numbers in the same cyclical order and advancing them one step on each successive trial. So they utilized all the positive and negative information available, since one arrangement was as probable as any other except for the numbers already fixed.

Logical elimination. A number of gold coins of the same denomination are alike in appearance but some one of them is known to be counterfeit and therefore lighter than the others. Given only a simple balance *O* is required to find the counterfeit with certainty but in the smallest possible number of weighings (Simmel, 1953). It soon becomes clear that the same number of coins must be placed in each pan of the balance, and *O* is apt to place half of any even number of coins on each side. But in so doing he often fails to extract all the information possible from the single weighing. Logically, the balance has three pans, as can be seen in the fundamental case of three coins. Place one coin on each side of the balance; if they are equal, the third coin must be the counterfeit. On this basis you can show that two weighings will be sufficient for any number up through 9, three weighings for any number up through 27, and four weighings for any number up through 81 coins.

A much simpler logical problem was tried on young children by Welch & Long (1943). A girl is said to have been made sick by some one of the foods, A, B, C. When she eats A and B together she becomes sick, when she eats B and C she is not sick, when she eats A and C she is sick. Which food makes her sick? (Some of this information is redundant.) This problem was much too difficult for normal children at the Mental Age of 5½ years and fairly difficult even for those two years older.

In his extensive studies of mental growth, Burt (1919, 1921) made good use of certain logical puzzles of an informal sort. He presented all the necessary information and asked the child to draw the conclusion, as in the examples:

7-year level	All wall-flowers have four petals: this flower has three petals. Is this a wall-flower?
10-year level	There are four roads here: I have come from the south and want to go to Melton: The road at the right leads somewhere else: Straight ahead it leads only to a farm. In which direction is Melton—North, South, East, or West?

Each item was typed on a separate card and laid before *O*, who was asked for his reasons after he had responded. Comparison of easy with difficult items revealed some of the factors of difficulty. The formal logical structure made little difference. Much more important were the kind and quantity of the data presented. As to kind, the data must be within the range of the child's knowledge, or he will not reason about them correctly. As to quantity, some maturity was needed for handling a large mass of data.

Another difficulty comes out clearly in the linear type of syllogism, and is essentially a difficulty in lining up the three terms. An example:

> Three boys are sitting in a row: Harry is to the left of Willie: George is to the left of Harry. Which boy is in the middle?

This item was passed by 50 percent of the [illegible] year-olds. If the two premises are simply transposed, the item is passed by [illegible] percent of the same age group. A similar difficulty appears in the following item:

> Edith is fairer than Olive: but she is darker than Lily. Who is darker, Olive or Lily?

In this form it was passed by 46 percent of the 8-year group, but the percent went up to 72 when a slight verbal change was made:

> Lily is fairer than Edith: Edith is fairer than Olive. Who is the fairest, Lily or Olive?

The children who succeeded with the first form reported that they had to turn the first premise around before seeing the answer. Much older subjects experience difficulty when the same relation is expressed by two opposite words. This sort of syllogism is easily clarified by the use of a straight line as a diagram. Introspective studies of syllogistic reasoning by Störring (1908) and his pupils revealed several ways in which adult subjects tried to cope with these and other difficulties.

Conclusions which go beyond the given information. Much erroneous reasoning consists in drawing conclusions from certain given information which are not implied in that information. Sometimes the errors are due to the reasoner's failure to see exactly what the given information amounts to; he tacitly assumes that he has more information than he really has. At other times his errors are due to his prejudices and preferences; he is influenced in his thinking by factors which are not included in the given information. We shall begin with the first source of errors.

The fascinating science of logic, though it is by no means a psychology of the reasoning process, is useful to the experimenter because it provides a check on the validity of conclusions. It analyzes the given information into definite propositions or "premises" and shows what can validly be inferred from just those premises.

A proposition consists of two terms connected by the copula, as in the statement, "The sky is blue," and a negative proposition contains the word "not" or some equivalent. Also, a quantifying word such as "all" or "some" may modify the subject term. "Some" here means "at least some" and does not imply "not all." From the statement that "All X is Y" you can infer that "Some X is Y."

A proposition, then, may be affirmative or negative, and it may be an all-statement or a some-statement. There are thus four types of propositions, commonly designated by letter symbols:

A—All X is Y—universal affirmative—*all yes* proposition
E—No X is Y—universal negative—*all no* proposition
I—Some X is Y—particular affirmative—*some-yes* proposition
O—Some X is not Y—particular negative—*some-no* proposition

Conversion of a single proposition. We are familiar with the warning that the converse of a true proposition is not necessarily true. Logical analysis shows when a converse is valid and when invalid. To convert a proposition is to interchange the subject and predicate. The converted proposition is not valid, i.e., not implied in the original proposition, except in certain cases. The converse of an E proposition is necessarily valid: if no X is Y, obviously no Y can be X. The converse of an I proposition is necessarily valid. But an A proposition cannot be converted without changing *all* to *some;* and an O proposition cannot be converted at all. From "Some X is not Y" we cannot tell whether all, some, or none of Y is X. But Eidens (1929) found that highly educated persons, not trained in the science of logic, were willing to accept the simple converse of all four propositions. Such errors are due to the verbal form of the propositions and are not committed when the information is given in diagrams.

Euler's circles. Back in the eighteenth century, the great Swiss mathematician, Euler, was conducting a correspondence course in logic, his pupil being a German princess. In the hope of removing some of the obscurities of the subject, he invented a set of diagrams which have proved a great help to successive generations of students. The diagrams are based on the relations of inclusion and exclusion. All the X's are supposed to be included in one circle, all the Y's in another circle. If the X circle is included in the Y circle we see that all X is Y and, conversely, *some* Y is X. If the X and Y circles are entirely separate, no X is Y and, conversely, no Y is X.

Classes X and Y coincide — X=Y

Class X is included in class Y — Y, X

Class Y is included in class X — X, Y

Classes X and Y overlap — X, Y

Classes X and Y are mutually exclusive — X, Y

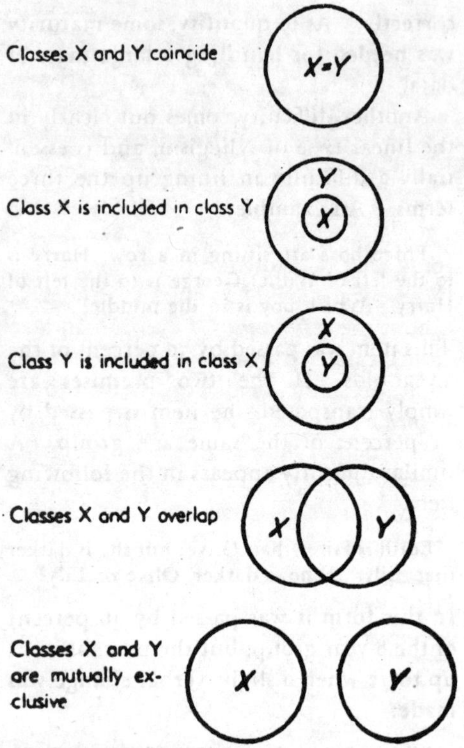

Fig. 26-9. Euler's diagrams, with equivalent verbal statements. These propositions can be simply converted. If X = Y, then Y = X. If X excludes Y, then Y excludes X. If X overlaps Y, then Y overlaps X. If X is included in Y, then Y includes X; and if X includes Y, then Y is included in X.

So long as we stick to the diagrams, we have no difficulty with conversion. But when we attempt to translate the ordinary propositions into diagrams, we find our information often insufficient. There is no ambiguity in the E proposition, which means the same as the last diagram. But A can mean either of the first two diagrams, I can mean any one of diagrams 2–4, and O can mean any one of diagrams 3–5. To express the meaning of the overlapping diagram in ordinary propositions, we should need three: Some X is Y, Some X is not Y, Some Y is not X.

The errors committed in drawing inferences are largely due to the ambiguity of the standard propositions of logic. These propositions are however such as are used in ordinary speech. This ambiguity of common speech, as compared with the clarity of the diagrams, seems in itself a cogent argument against the theory that thinking is essentially silent speech. Often we have to get away from speech in order to think clearly.

In order to diagram a syllogism we need three circles. If we add the proposition, Class Z is included in class Y, we see that the relation of X and Z is clear in case of diagrams 1, 3 and 5, but ambiguous in the other two cases. If we know only that X and Z are both included in Y, we can make no further statement about the relations of X and Z. In many other cases the diagrams clarify relations that are obscure in ordinary propositions.

Syllogisms as problems in reasoning. A syllogism consists of two premises and a conclusion. Each of these propositions contains two terms, but the whole syllogism contains only three terms, since the "middle term," present in both premises, is not present in the conclusion. The middle term serves as a bridge or link between the other two. The first premise links one of the other terms with the middle term, the second premise links the remaining term with the middle term, and then the middle term is eliminated, leaving only the two other terms linked in the conclusion. But this elimination does not stand the test of logic except under certain conditions. Consider the following syllogism, with M standing for the middle term:

All X is M;
All Y is M;
Therefore, all X is Y.

It is very likely to be accepted in this symbolic form. If you substitute "Eskimo" for X, "Africans" for Y, "dark-haired" for M, and of course "are" for "is," you see that the conclusion is false. If you replace "Eskimo" by "Hottentots," the conclusion is true. But it is just as invalid or fallacious in one case as in the other. The symbolic statements have the advantage of freedom from truth or falsity (which are irrelevant in logic), while the concrete statements can take the place of diagrams and bring out the relations clearly.

Wilkins (1928) in an experiment on 81 college men presented logically identical syllogisms with letter terms and with word terms, in order to see whether the more abstract or the more concrete material was handled more correctly. She prepared her material in the form of a paper and pencil test. On opening his test booklet, *O* was confronted with a series of problems like the following:

> All good ballet dancers have many years of training; some of the dancers in this musical comedy have many years of training; therefore
>
> a. some of the dancers in this musical comedy are good ballet dancers.
>
> b. all good ballet dancers are in this musical comedy.
>
> c. some of the dancers in this musical comedy are not good ballet dancers.
>
> Or, the same thing in symbols:
>
> All a's are b's; some c's are b's; therefore
>
> a. some c's are a's.
> b. all a's are c's.
> c. some c's are not a's.
>
> The instructions were "to put a plus sign before every conclusion which you are sure follows necessarily from the given statements . . . a minus sign before every conclusion that does not necessarily follow from the given statements. If no conclusion can be drawn from the given statements, put a minus sign before each of the conclusions following."

The main result was the greater difficulty of the syllogisms presented in letter terms. The average score was 76 percent correct for the letter terms, 84 percent for the syllogisms expressed in familiar words. The difference is statistically reliable, though not very great. A score of 50 percent correct in this test was no better than chance.

Why should college students accept so many invalid conclusions? A large share of the errors can be laid to the ambiguity of the word *some*. In logic, it means *at least some*, while in ordinary usage it often carries the implication, *not all*. It would ordinarily be rather misleading to say that "Some soldiers were killed" if the truth were that all were killed. Following the ordinary usage, many students believed they could infer from "Some X is Y" that therefore "Some X is not Y." But careful study of the results revealed another source of error.

The "atmosphere effect." Woodworth & Sells (1935) proposed the hypothesis that the global impression or "atmosphere" of the premises was an important factor in erroneous reasoning. "An affirmative atmosphere in the premises makes it easy to accept an affirmative conclusion, etc." The atmosphere of a single premise makes it easy to accept the converse, as Eidens had found (p. 810). When the premises are alike, being both A propositions, or both E, or both I, or both O, the atmosphere corresponds. When the premises differ, the atmosphere is mixed, and supplementary hypotheses are required to predict the effect on the reasoner. The following hypotheses seemed reasonable:

1. A negative premise creates a negative atmosphere, even when the other premise is affirmative.
2. A particular ("some") premise creates a *some* atmosphere, even when the other premise is universal.

The atmosphere hypothesis, with these supplementary hypotheses, was subjected to a rigid test by Sells (1936). His test material appeared as follows:

1. AT PT I AF If all x's are y's;
   And if all z's are x's:
   Then all z's are y's.

2. AT PT I AF If no x's are y's;
   And if all z's are y's;
   Then some z's are x's.

Each conclusion was to be checked (see the letters at the left) as "absolutely true," "probably true," "indeterminate," or "absolutely false." Abundant time was allowed. To avoid cluttering up the results with errors due to misinterpretation of "some," the meaning attached to the term in logic was carefully explained in advance. The subjects were 65 educated adults, not trained in formal logic. (Familiarity with the rules of logic would enable you to reject many conclusions instantly. Many of those presented violate the rule that no valid conclusion can be drawn from two negative premises.)

There were 180 items like the above, of which only 52 were valid syllogisms. The 128 invalid items included two examples of every possible combination of the propositions, A, E, I, and O. The table on page 847 shows the percent of invalid conclusions accepted.

Since these conclusions were all invalid, their acceptance depended on nonlogical factors. The data are fully in accord with the hypothesis that the atmosphere effect, or global impression, is a potent factor. Invalid conclusions are more often accepted if favored by atmosphere.

The atmosphere effect can be demonstrated with other forms of the test besides the one used by Sells which asks the subject to pass judgment on a stated conclusion. He may be given a blank conclusion to fill in, such as

No M is X;
No Y is M;
Therefore, ... Y is X.

Or he may be offered a choice of five alternative conclusions, A, E, I, O, and "None of the conclusions seem to follow

Premises presented	*Conclusion favored by atmosphere*	*Invalid conclusion presented*			
		A	*E*	*I*	*O*
AA	A	58	14	63	17
EE	E	21	38	25	34
II	I	27	9	72	38
OO	O	14	16	38	52
AE	E	11	51	13	63
EA	E	8	64	12	69
AI	I	33	4	70	32
IA	I	36	15	75	36
AO	O	15	26	42	76
OA	O	13	33	28	75
EI	O	8	40	22	62
IE	O	11	42	22	63
EO	O	13	29	29	44
OE	O	15	31	24	48
IO	O	12	19	31	64
OI	O	11	23	33	71

logically." Using this last farm, Morgan & Morton (1944) obtained a strong atmosphere effect from a large group of college students. They also confirmed Wilkins' finding that the reasoning was somewhat more logical when meaningful words were substituted for the bare letter terms.

The atmosphere effect is not confined to syllogisms. In speaking or writing you are likely to make the verb agree with the singular or plural atmosphere of the subject phrase instead of with the grammatical subject, as in the following examples:

> The laboratory equipment in these situations were in many instances essentially the same as those used before.
>
> Is trial and error blind or not?

How does atmosphere operate? Presumably one quickly becomes set for the global impression of the given information and responds accordingly. Accurate reasoning demands an analysis of what is given, with careful attention to the interrelations of the bits of information, and a reduction of the whole to a consistent pattern.

The intrusion of extraneous knowledge, belief or emotional bias. It is obviously desirable to derive your conclusion entirely from the premises even when the logical conclusion is palpably false or unacceptable. How otherwise could a scientist deduce and test the consequences of a proposed hypothesis? But we are not always so logical. In any thorough attempt to demonstrate and measure the effect of prejudice or other emotional factors the psychologist has to allow for the atmosphere effect and also for the blunting effect of purely symbolic premises. He cannot simply compare the conclusion accepted by *O* with what is logically valid; he must compare the conclusion possibly warped by prejudice with the conclusion when meaningful but unemotional terms are used. Morgan & Morton (1944) based their "emotional" syllogisms on the hopes and fears of wartime. Using their multiple-choice form of test (already mentioned) they determined the percents of choices conforming to logic, to atmosphere, and to war interests, with a residual percent due to unknown causes. These percents came out as follows:

	Logic	*Atmosphere*	*Bias*	*Unknown*
Letter terms	27	44	—	29
Neutral words	33	46	—	21
War interests	20	26	36	18

The bias effect was quite strong here, often overriding the atmosphere effect, though it should be said that the syllogisms were rather difficult—the information given rather complicated.

Gorden (1953) found a considerably smaller effect of bias for or against Russia in a group of college students who were strongly motivated to be logical in choosing their conclusions. The syllogisms presented were invalid but an atmosphere "often" or "to a great degree," so that of uncertainty was introduced into the premises by qualifying words such as the moderate I and O conclusions appeared safe to most subjects. The conclusions chosen were dominated by atmosphere in the great majority of cases, but bias was shown in a considerable number. Other studies of bias in syllogistic reasoning have been made by several experimenters, as by Janis & Frick (1943), by Lefford (1946), and by Thistlethwaite (1950). They have used a variety of setups and statistical treatments but have found the bias effect present in more or less strength. With all the factors involved in the ordinary man's attempts to reason from verbal information—logic, atmosphere, bias, and reading ability or understanding of oral statements—any complete measurement of the factors is a difficult task. The experimentalists are making progress, however, not only at this point but throughout the field of problem solution.

Looking back now over the whole chapter we cannot fail to see that problem-solving behavior is predictable in several important respects. It is variable and exploratory, to be sure, and yet laws have been discovered that have considerable practical value. Those psychologists who have labored in this field need not feel apologetic. On the contrary they are justified in urging younger laborers to come out and join them in a field which promises well for the future.

Bibliographical Index of Authors

ABBREVIATIONS

In the following list of journal abbreviations our principal deviations from the American Psychological Association standards are the omission of punctuation marks and the use of capital *Ps* for the noun *Psychology* and a small *ps* for the adjective *psychological* and foreign equivalents. Thus considerable additional space was available for the text. The page numbers appearing within brackets are references to text citations.

AAF	Army Air Forces
Abh	Abhandlungen
Abnor	Abnormal
Abt	Abteilung
Acad	Academy
Acoust	Acoustical
Akad	Akademie
Allg	Allgemein
Amer	American
Anat	Anatomy, anatomical, anatomisch
Ang	Angewandt
Ann	Annales, annali, annals, année, annuaire, annual
Appl	Applied
Arb	Arbeiten
Arch	Archiv, archives, archivio
Ass	Association
Beh	Behavior, behaviour
Beih	Beihefte
Ber	Berichte
Biol	Biological, biologique, biologisch
Br	British
Bull	Bulletin
Cell	Cellular, cellule
Centralbt	Centralblatt
Chem	Chemical, chemistry
Clin	Clinical
Coll	College
Comp	Comparative
Cong	Congress
Cont	Contributions
C R	Comptes rendus
Devel	Development
Dis	Disease
Educ	Education, educational
Eng	Engineering
Ergbd	Ergänzungsband
Exp	Experimental
Fac	Facultad
Fed	Federal
Forsch	Forschung
Genet	Genetic
Genl	General
Ges	Gesamte, gesellschaft
Handbh	Handbuch
Handbk	Handbook
Hlth	Health
Indust	Industrial

Insan	Insanity	*Proc*	Proceedings
Inst	Institute, institution	*Ps*	Psychological, psychologie, psychology
Internatl	International	*Psbiol*	Psychobiology
J	Journal	*Pstech*	Psychotechnische
Jap	Japanese	*Psychiat*	Psychiatrie, psychiatry
K	Königliche	*Psychol*	Psychologist
Kon	Kongress	*Publ*	Publication, publisher
Lab	Laboratory	*Q*	Quarterly
Laryng	Laryngologisch, laryngology	*R*	Royal
Mag	Magazine	*Rec*	Record
Med	Medical, medicine	*Ref*	Reference
Mem	Memoir, memorial	*Rept*	Report
Ment	Mental	*Res*	Research
Mikro	Mikroskopische	*Rev*	Review, revista, revue
Mon	Monthly	*Rhino*	Rhinology
Monat	Monatsschrift	*Sch*	School
Monatb	Monatsblätter	*Sci*	Science, scientific
Monogr	Monograph	*Sem*	Seminary
Nat	Natural, nature, naturel	*Sinnesorg*	Sinnesorgange
Natl	National	*Sinnesphys*	Sinnesphysiologie
Nerl	Nerlandaises	*Sitzber*	Sitzungsberichte
Nerv	Nervous	*Skand*	Skandiavisch
Nervenkr	Nervenkrankheiten	*So*	South, southern
Neu	Neurological, neurologisch, neurology	*Soc*	Social, société, society
		St	Studies, study
Neurophys	Neurophysiological, neurophysiology	*Suppl*	Supplement
		Teach	Teachers
Norm	Normal	*Tec*	Technical, technic
Ophth	Ophthalmology	*Trans*	Transactions, translated translator
Opt	Optical		
Optom	Optometry	*U*	University
Oto	Otolaryngology	*Unif*	Unified
Otol	Otology	*Univ*	University publisher
Päd	Pädagogisch	*US*	United States
Path	Pathological, pathology	*Wiss*	Wissenschaft, wissenlich
Ped	Pedagogical, pedagogy, pediatrics		
		Wschr	Wochenschrift
Per	Personality	*Yrbk*	Yearbook
Pflüg	Pflügers	*Z*	Zeitschrift
Philos	Philosophy	*Zool*	Zoology
Phys	Physiological, physiologie, physiology	*#*	Number
Preuss	Preussisch		

INDEX

rate of mental association. *J educ Ps* 8, 97-102. [60]

Anderson, O. D. *See* Liddell, H. S. 1934.

Andrews, H. L. *See* Jasper, H. H. 1936.

Angell, J. R. 1910. Report of the committee of the American Psychological Association on the standardizing of procedure in experimental tests. *Ps Monogr* # 53, 61-107. [721]

Anrep, G. V. 1923. The irradiation of conditioned reflexes. *Proc Roy Soc B* 94, 404-426. [579]

Ansbacher, H. 1937. Perception of number as affected by the monetary value of the objects. *Arch Ps N.Y.* #215. [429]

Antonitis, J. J. 1951. Response variability in the white rat during conditioning, extinction, and reconditioning. *J exp Ps* 42, 273-281. [560, 819]

—— *See also* Schoenfeld, W. N. 1950a, b.

Antonovitch, S. *See* Golla, F. L. 1929.

Arai, T. 1912. Mental fatigue. *Teach Coll Cont Educ* #54. [804]

Archer, E. J. 1953. Retention of serial nonsense syllables as a function of rest-interval responding rate and meaningfulness. *J exp Ps* 45, 245-252. [796]

——, Underwood, B. J. 1951. Retroactive inhibition of verbal associations as a multiple function of temporal point of interpolation and degree of interpolated learning. *J exp Ps* 42, 283-290. [767]

Armington, J. C. 1952. A component of the human electroretinogram associated with red color vision. *J opt Soc Amer* 42, 393-401. [373]

Army Air Forces. 1947-1948. *Aviation psychology progress research reports.* #1-19. Washington 25, D.C., Government Printing Office.

Arnheim, R. 1928. Experimentell-psychologische Untersuchungen zum Ausdrucksproblem. Untersuchungen zur Lehre von der Gestalt. IV. *Ps Forsch* 11, 2-132. [116]

Arps, G. F. 1917. A preliminary report on 'work with knowledge versus work without knowledge of results.' *Ps Rev* 24, 449-455. [686]

—— 1920. Work without knowledge of results versus work with knowledge of results. *Ps Monogr* #125. [686]

d'Arsonval, A. 1888. Remarques à propos de la production d'électricité chez l'homme. *C R Soc Biol Mem* 40, 142-144. [138]

Asch, S. E., Witkin, H. A. 1948a. Studies in space orientation. I. Perception of the upright with displaced visual fields. *J exp Ps* 38, 325-337. [525]

——, —— 1948b. Studies in space orientation. II. Perception of the upright with displaced visual fields and with body tilted. *J exp Ps* 38, 455-477. [525]

—— *See also* Witkin, H. A. 1948a, b.

Aschaffenburg, G. 1895. Experimentelle Studien über Associationen. *Ps Arb* 1, 209-299. [59, 65]

—— 1897. Experimentelle Studien über Associationen. II theil. *Ps Arb* 2, 1-83. [54]

Aserinsky, E., Kleitman, N. 1953. Regularly occurring periods of eye motility, and concomitant phenomena during sleep. *Science* 118, 273-274. [816]

Ash, I. 1914. Fatigue and its effect upon control. *Arch Ps N.Y.* #31. [800]

Atkinson, J. W. 1953. The achievement motive and recall of interrupted and completed tasks. *J exp Ps* 46, 381-390. [693]

—— *See also* McClelland, D. C. 1948.

Atkinson, R. C., Ammons, R. B. 1952. Experiential factors in visual form perception. II. Latency as a function of repetition. *J exp Ps* 43, 173-178. [406]

Auerbach, F. *See* Kries, J. V. 1877.

Ax, A. F. 1951. The physiological differentiation of fear and anger in humans. *Amer Psychol* 6, 271. [179, 183]

Aylesworth, M. *See* Warden, C. J. 1927.

B

Backer, R. *See* Sheffield, F. D. 1951.

Bagchi, B. K., Greenwald, D. U. 1937. Electrodermal changes during certain types of attention. *J genl Ps* 17, 235-248. [156]

Bain, A. 1855, 1864. *The senses and the intellect.* Lond., Parker. [818]

—— 1870. *Mental science, a compendium of psychology, and the history of philosophy.* N. Y., Appleton. [818]

Baker, B. A. *See* Platt, W. 1931.

Baker, K. E. *See* Gagné, R. M. 1950; Graham, C. H. 1948.

Baker, K. H. 1937. Pre-experimental set in distraction experiments. *J genl Ps* 16, 471-478. [87]

—— *See* Tinker, M. A. 1938.

Baker, L. M., Eliott, D. N. 1948. Controlled and free association-times with identical stimulus- and response-words. *Amer J Ps* 61, 535-539. [61]

Baldwin, J. M., Shaw, W. J. 1895. Memory for square-size. *Ps Rev* 2, 236-239, 259-273. [700]

Bales, J. F., Follansbee, G. L. 1935. The aftereffect of the perception of curved lines. *J exp Ps* 18, 499-503. [423]

Ball, J. *See* Lashley, K. S. 1929.

Ballachey, E. L., Buel, J. 1934a. Centrifugal swing as a determinant of choice-point behavior in the maze running of the white rat. *J comp Ps* 17, 201-223. [621]

——, —— 1934b. Food orientation as a factor determining the distribution of errors in the maze running of the rat. *J genet Ps* 45, 358-370. [620]

—— *See also* Buel, J. 1935.

Ballard, P. B. 1913. Oblivescence and reminiscence. *Br J Ps Monogr* #2. [794]

Banister, H. 1926a. Three experiments on the localization of tones. *Br J Ps* 16, 265-292. [356]

—— 1926b. A suggestion towards a new hypothesis regarding the localization of sound. *Br J Ps* 17, 142-153. [355]

Bappert, J. 1923. Neue Untersuchungen zum Problem des Verhältnisses von Akkommodation und Konvergenz zur Wahrnehmung der Tiefe. *Z Ps* 90, 167-203. [476, 477]

Bárány, R. 1907. *Physiologie und Pathologie des Bogengang-apparates beim Menschen.* Vienna, Deuticke. [520]

Barclay, W. D. *See* Bousfield, W. A. 1950.

Barcroft, J., Florey, H. 1929. The effects of exercise on the vascular conditions in the spleen and the colon. *J Phys* 68, 181-189. [169]

Bard, P. 1934. Emotion. I. The neuro-humoral basis of emotional reactions. *Handbk genl exp Ps* 264-311. C. Murchison, ed. Worcester, Clark Univ Press. [108]

Bare, J. K. *See* Pfaffmann, C. 1950.

Barker, R. G. 1931. The stepping-stone maze: a directly visible space-problem apparatus. *J Genl Ps* 5, 280-285. [651]

——, Dembo, T., Lewin, K. 1941. Frustration and regression: an experiment with young children. *U Iowa St Child Welfare* 18, #1. [677]

Barlow, J. *See* Henderson, M. T. 1945.

Bartlett, F. C. 1932. *Remembering: an experimental and social study.* Lond., Cambridge Univ Press. [715, 717, 774]

—— 1939. Thinking. *Centenaire de Th. Ribot,* 281-285. Agen, Imprimerie Moderne. [841]

—— 1943. Fatigue following highly skilled work. *Proc Roy Soc B* 131, 247-257. [807]

—— 1950. Incentives. *Br J Ps* 41, 122-128.

—— 1951. *The mind at work and play.* Lond., Allen. [827]

Bartlett, N. R. *See* Graham, C. H. 1939, 1940.

Bartlett, R. J. 1927. Does the psychogalvanic phenomenon indicate emotion? *Br J Ps* 18, 30-50. [157]

Bartley, S. H. 1934. Relation of intensity and duration of brief retinal stimulation by light to the electrical responses of the optic cortex of the rabbit. *Amer J Phys* 108, 397-408. [19]

—— 1935. The comparative distribution of light in the stimulus and on the retina. *J comp Ps* 19, 149-154. [376]

—— 1939. Some factors in brightness discrimination. *Ps Rev* 46, 337-358. [27]

—— 1941. *Vision, a study of its basis.* N. Y., Van Nostrand. [371]

—— 1950. *Beginning experimental psychology.* N. Y., McGraw-Hill. [488]

—— 1951. The psychophysiology of vision. *Handbk exp Ps* 921-984. S. S. Stevens, ed. N. Y., Wiley. [371, 382, 385, 389]

——, Chute, E. 1947. *Fatigue and impairment in man.* N. Y., McGraw-Hill. [175, 805]

—— *See also* Fry, G. A. 1935.

Bash, K. W. 1939. An investigation into a possible organic basis for the hunger drive. Contribution to a theory of the hunger drive. *J comp Ps* 28, 109-160. [659]

Bass, M. J., Hull, C. L. 1934. Irradiation of a tactile conditioned reflex in man. *J comp Ps* 17, 47-65. [34, 579]

Batalla, M. *See* Jones, H. E. 1944.

Batalla, M. B. 1943. The maze behavior of children as an example of summative learning. *J genet Ps* 63, 199-211. [647]

Baxter, B. 1942. A study of reaction time using factorial design. *J exp Ps* 31, 430-437. [40]

——, Travis, R. C. 1938. The reaction time to vestibular stimuli. *J exp Ps* 22, 277-282. [18]

Bayle, E. 1942. The nature and causes of regressive movements in reading. *J exp Educ* 11, 16-36. [505]

Bayley, N. 1928. A study of fear by means of the psychogalvanic technique. *Ps Monogr* # 176. [155]

Bayroff, A. G. *See* Dashiell, J. F. 1931.

Bazett, H. C., McGlone, B., Brocklehurst, R. J. 1930. The temperatures in the tissues which accompany temperature sensations. *J Phys* 69, 88-112. [281]

Bear, R. M. *See* Imus, H. A. 1938.

Beck, L. H. 1950. Osmics: olfaction. *Medical physics* Vol. 2, 658-664. O. Glasser, ed. Chic., Year Book Publishers. [321]

——, Miles, W. R. 1947. Some theoretical and experimental relationships between infrared absorption and olfaction. *Science* 106, 511. [321]

Beebe-Center, J. G. 1949. Standards for use of the gust scale. *J Ps* 28, 411-419. [243, 302]

——, Black, P., Hoffman, A. C., Wade, M. 1948. Relative per diem consumption as a measure of preference in the rat. *J comp phys Ps* 41, 239-251. [661, 662]

——, Waddell, D. 1948. A general psychological scale of taste. *J Ps* 26, 517-524. [243, 244]

—— *See also* Berg, R. L. 1941.

Beeby, C. E. 1930. An experimental investigation into the simultaneous constituents in an act of skill. *Br J Ps* 20, 336-353. [785]

Beitel, R. J., Jr. 1934. Spatial summation of subliminal stimuli in the retina of the human eye. *J genl Ps* 10, 311-327. [375]

Békésy, G. v. 1930. Sur la Theorie de l'Audition. *Ann ps,* 31, 63-96. [221]

—— 1950. Microphonics produced by touching the cochlear partition with a vibrating electrode. *J acoust Soc Amer* 23, 29-35. [328]

——, Rosenblith, W. A. 1948. The early history of hearing—observations and theories. *J acoust Soc Amer* 20, 727-784. [323]

Bekhterev, V. M. 1913a. *La psychologie objective.* Paris, Alcan. [543]

—— 1913b. *Objektive Psychologie; oder, Psychoreflexologie, die Lehre von den Assoziationsreflexen.* Leip., Teubner. [543]

Bell, Ch. 1806, 1844. *Essays on the anatomy of expression in painting.* Lond., Longmans, Green. [111]

Bellis, C. J. 1932–1933. Reaction time and chronological age. *Soc exp Biol Med Proc* 30, 801-803. [36]

Bender, M. B. *See* Weinstein, E. A. [illegible]

Bender, W. R. G. 1933. The effect of pain and emotional stimuli and alcohol on pupillary reflex activity. *Ps Monogr* #198. [179]

Benedict, F. G. *See* Dodge, R. 1915.

Bentley, M. 1899. The memory image and its

qualitative fidelity. *Amer J Ps* 11, 1-48. [699]

Benussi, V. 1904. Zur Psychologie der Gestalterfassens. Meinong, A., *Untersuch Gegenstandstheorie* 303-448. [421]

—— 1912. Stroboskopische Scheinbewegungen und geometrischoptische Gestalttäuschungen. *Arch ges Ps* 24, 31-62. [421, 422]

—— 1914a. Die atmungssymptome der Lüge. *Arch ges Ps* 31, 244-273. [186]

—— 1914b. Gesetze der inadäquaten Gestaltauffassung. *Arch ges Ps* 32, 396-419. [421]

Berg, R. L., Beebe-Center, J. G. 1941. Cardiac startle in man. *J exp Ps* 28, 262-279. [164, 182]

Berger, G. O. 1886. Über den Einfluss der Reizstärke auf die Dauer einfacher psychischer Vorgänge mit besonderer Rücksicht auf Lichtreize. *Philos St* 3, 38-93. [24]

Berger, H. 1929. Über das Electrenkephalogramm des Menschen. *Arch Psychiat Nervenkr* 87, 528-570. [180]

Bergmann, G. *See* Spence, K. W. 1950.

Berkeley, G. 1709. *An essay towards a new theory of vision.* Dublin, Jeremy Pepyat. Reprint. 1922. N. Y., Dutton. [465]

Berlyne, D. E. 1950. Novelty and curiosity as determinants of exploratory behavior. *Br J Ps* 41, 68-80. [636]

Bernstein, A. L. 1934. Temporal factors in the formation of conditioned eyelid reactions in human subjects. *J genl Ps* 10, 173-197. [567]

Bernstone, A. H. *See* Muenzinger, K. F. 1938.

Berrien, F. K. 1939. Finger oscillations as indices of emotion. I. Preliminary validation. II. Further validation and use in detecting deception. *J exp Ps* 24, 485-498, 609-620. [180]

Berry, J. H. *See* Worchel, P. 1952.

Berry, R. N. 1948. Quantitative relations among vernier, real depth and stereoscopic depth acuities. *J exp Ps* 38, 708-721. [473, 474]

——, Riggs, L. A., Duncan, C. P. 1950. The relation of vernier and depth discrimination to field brightness. *J exp Ps* 40, 349-354. [472]

—— *See also* Riggs, L. A. 1949.

Berry, W. 1927. Color sequences in the afterimage of white light. *Amer J Ps* 38, 584-596. [396]

Bersh, P. J. 1951. The influence of two variables upon the establishment of a secondary reinforcer for operant responses. *J exp Ps* 41, 62-73. [680]

—— *See also* Schoenfeld, W. N. 1950a, b.

Berthold, F., Jr. *See* Karwoski, T. F. 1945.

Betts, G. H. 1909. *The distribution and functions of mental imagery.* N. Y., Teachers Coll, Columbia Univ. [721]

Biber, B., Murphy, L. B., Woodcock, L. P., Black, I. S. 1942. *Child life in school, a study of a seven-year-old group.* N. Y., Dutton. (Esp. pp. 298-344.) [823]

Biddulph, R. *See* Shower, E. G. 1931.

Biervliet, J. J. van. 1894. Ueber den Einfluss der Geschwindigkeit des Pulses auf die Zeitdauer der Reactionszeit bei Schalleindrücken. *Philos St* 10, 160-167. [38]

—— 1895. Ueber den Einfluss der Geschwindigkeit des Pulses auf die Zeitdauer der Reactionszeit bei Licht- und Tasteindrücken. *Philos St* 11, 125-134.

Bigham, J. *See* Münsterberg, H. 1894.

Billings, M. L. 1914. The duration of attention. *Ps Rev* 21, 121-135. [77]

Bills, A. G. 1927. The influence of muscular tension on the efficiency of mental work. *Amer J Ps* 38, 227-251. [89, 175]

—— 1931. Blocking: a new principle of mental fatigue. *Amer J Ps* 43, 230-245. [82]

—— 1935a. Some causal factors in mental blocking. *J exp Ps* 18, 172-185. [82]

—— 1935b. Fatigue, oscillation, and blocks. *J exp Ps* 18, 562-573. [82]

—— 1937. Blocking in mental fatigue and anoxemia compared. *J exp Ps* 20, 437-452. [82]

—— 1943. *The psychology of efficiency.* N. Y., Harper. [805]

—— 1948. Studying motor functions and efficiency. *Methods of Psychology* 459-497. T. G. Andrews, ed. N. Y., Wiley. [802]

——, Stauffacher, J. C. 1937. The influence of voluntarily induced tension on rational problem solving. *J Ps* 4, 261-271. [176]

—— *See also* Robinson, E. S. 1926.

Bilodeau, E. A. *See* Kimble, G. A. 1949.

Bindra, D. 1947. Water-hoarding in rats. *J comp phys Ps* 40, 149-156. [660]

—— *See also* Licklider, J. C. R. 1948.

Binet, A. 1890. La concurrence des états psychologiques. *Rev philos* 29, 138-155. [88]

—— 1894. *Psychologie des grands calculateurs et joueurs d'échecs.* Paris, Hachette. [706]

——, Henri, V. 1894. La mémoire des mots. *Ann Ps* 1, 1-23. [697, 699, 705]

Birch, H. G. 1945a. The role of motivational factors in insightful problem-solving. *J comp Ps* 38, 295-317. [834]

—— 1945b. The relation of previous experience to insightful problem-solving. *J comp Ps* 38, 367-383. [825]

——, Rabinowitz, H. S. 1951. The negative effect of previous experience on productive thinking. *J exp Ps* 41, 121-125. [835]

Birmingham, H. P. *See* Taylor, F. V. 1949.

Bishop, G. H. 1944. The peripheral unit for pain. *J Neurophys* 7, 71-80. [281]

—— 1946. Neural mechanisms of cutaneous sense. *Phys Rev* 26, 77-102. [281, 282]

Bitterman, M. E. 1944. Fatigue defined as reduced efficiency. *Amer J Ps* 57, 569-573. [180]

—— 1945. Heart rate and frequency of blinking as indices of visual efficiency. *P exp Ps* 35, 279-292. [180]

——, Coate, W. B. 1950. Some new experiments on the nature of discrimination learning in the rat. *J comp phys Ps* 43, 198-210. [597]

—— *See also* Ryan, T. A. 1950.

Black, I. S. *See* Biber, B. 1942.

—— 1945. *The psychology of seeing.* N. Y., Philosophical Library. [75, 496]
Braun, H. W., Albee, G. W. 1952. The relation between retention after electroshock convulsions and degree of learning in the rat. *J comp phys Ps* 45, 14-17. [772]
Bray, C. W. 1928. Transfer of learning. *J exp Ps* 11, 443-467. [742]
—— 1948. *Psychology and military proficiency.* Princeton, Princeton Univ Press. [809, 811, 812, 813]
—— *See also* Wever, E. G. 1930a, b, c, d; 1938; 1940a, b.
Breese, B. B. 1899. On inhibition. *Ps Monogr* #11. [399]
—— 1909. Binocular rivalry. *Ps Rev* 16, 410-415. [399]
Brembeck, W. L. 1949. The effects of a course in argumentation on critical thinking ability. *Speech Monogr* 16, 177-189. [829]
Bressler, J. 1933. Judgments in absolute units as a psychophysical method. *Arch Ps N.Y.* #152. [213, 217]
Bretnall, E. P. *See* Tolman, E. C. 1932.
Brewer, E. D. *See* Elsberg, C. A. 1935.
Brewster, D. 1856. *The stereoscope, its history, theory and construction.* Lond., Murray. [467]
Bridges, K. M. B. 1932. Emotional development in early infancy. *Child Devel* 3, 324-341. [110]
Brigham, C. C. 1932. *A study of error,* N. Y., Coll Entrance Exam Bd. [118]
Brink, F., Jr. 1951. Excitation and conduction in the neuron. Synaptic mechanisms. *Handbk exp Ps* 50-93, 94-120. S. S. Stevens, ed. N. Y., Wiley. [271]
Brocklehurst, R. J. *See* Bazett, H. C. 1930.
Brodhun, E. *See* König, A. 1888.
Brody, E. B. 1941. The influence of age, hypophysectomy, throidectomy, and thyroxin injection on simple reaction time in the rat. *J genl Phys* 24, 433-436. [36]
Brogden, W. J., Lipman, E. A., Culler, E. 1938. The role of incentive in conditioning and extinction. *Amer J Ps* 51, 109-117. [555, 676]
—— *See also* Culler, E. 1935; Gregg, L. W. 1950; Kloehn, N. W. 1948.
Broom, M. E. 1940. The reliability of the reading graph yielded by the ophthalmograph. *Sch & Soc* 52, 205-208. [509]
Brown, C. H., Van Gelder, D. 1938. Emotional reactions before examinations. I. Physiological changes. *J Ps* 5, 1-9. [166]
Brown, J. S. 1948. Gradients of approach and avoidance responses and their relation to level of motivation *J comp phys Ps* 41, 450-465. [675]
——, Slater-Hammel, A. T. 1949. Discrete movements in the horizontal plane as a function of their length and direction. *J exp Ps* 39, 84-95. [40]
Brown, M. A. *See* Robinson, E. S. 1926.
Brown, R. H. 1937. The bright visibility curve of the rabbit. *J genl Ps* 17, 323-338. [370]
—— *See also* Graham, C. H. 1939.
Brown, R. W. 1933. The relation between two methods of learning piano music. *J exp Ps* 16, 435-441. [785]
Brown, T. 1820. *Lectures on the philosophy of the human mind.* 4 vols. Edin., Tait. [43, 48]
Brown, U. *See* Simon, C. W. 1951.
Brown, W. L. *See* Gentry, G. 1947. 1948.
Brown, Warner. 1910. The judgment of difference. *Calif U Publ Ps* 1, 1-71. [216]
—— 1914. The judgment of very weak sensory stimuli. *Calif U Publ Ps* 1, 199-269. [216]
—— 1923. To what extent is memory measured by a single recall? *J exp Ps* 6, 377-382. [795]
—— 1924. Whole and part methods in learning. *J educ Ps* 15, 229-233. [784]
—— 1932. Auditory and visual cues in maze learning; spatial integrations in a human maze. *Calif U Publ Ps* 5, 115-134. [648]
—— 1935. Growth of 'memory images.' *Amer J Ps* 47, 90-102. [774]
——, Buel, J. 1940. Response tendencies and maze patterns as determiners of choice in a maze. *J comp Ps* 29, 337-399. [651, 654]
Brozek, J. *See* Franklin, J. C. 1947; Keys, A. 1950.
Bruce, R. H. 1930. The effect of removal of reward on the maze performance of rats. *Calif U Publ Ps* 4, 203-214. [640]
—— 1932. The effect of removal of reward on the maze performance of rats. *Calif U Publ Ps* 6, 65-82. [640]
Bruce, R. W. 1933. Conditions of transfer of training. *J exp Ps* 16, 343-361. [753]
Bruner, J. S., Goodman, C. C. 1947. Value and need as organizing factors in perception. *J abnor soc Ps* 42, 33-44. [491]
——, Krech, D. eds. 1950. *Perception and personality, a symposium.* Durham, Duke Univ Press. [694]
—— *See also* Postman, L. 1948.
Brunswik, E. 1929. Zur Entwicklung der Albedowahrnehmung. *Z Ps* 109, 40-115. [429, 435, 436]
—— 1933. Untersuchungen über Wahrnehmungsgegenstände. I. Die Zugänglichkeit von Gegenständen für die Wahrnehmung und deren quantitative Bestimmung. *Arch ges Ps* 88, 377-418. [429]
—— 1934. *Wahrnehmung und Gegenstandswelt.* Leip., Deuticke. [429]
—— 1944. Distal focussing of perception: Size-constancy in a representative sample of situations. *Ps Monogr* #254. [484]
—— 1947. *Systematic and representative design of psychological experiments.* Berkeley, Univ Calif Press. [6]
Bryan, W. L., Harter, N. 1897. Studies in the physiology and psychology of telegraphic language. *Ps Rev* 4, 27-53. [810]
——, —— 1899. Studies on the telegraphic language. *Ps Rev* 6, 345-375. [810]
Bryant, S. *See* Cattell, J. McK. 1889.
Buchanan, A. R. 1948. *Functional neuro-anatomy.* Phila., Lea & Febiger. [135]

Buel, J. 1934. The linear maze. I. "Choice-point expectancy," "correctness," and the goal gradient. *J comp Ps* 17, 185-199. [619]

——, Ballachey, E. L. 1935. Limiting factors in the effect of the reward upon this distribution of errors in mazes. *Ps Rev* 42, 28-42. [623]

—— *See also* Ballachey, E. L. 1934a, b; Brown, Warner, 1940.

Bugelski, R. 1938. Extinction with and without sub-goal reinforcement. *J comp Ps* 26, 121-134. [680]

Bühler, K. 1913. *Die Gestaltwahrnehmungen*. Stuttgart, Spemann. [416]

—— 1922. *Handbuch der Psychologie*. Jena, Fischer. [432]

Bujas, Z. 1937. La mesure de la sensibilité différentielle dans le domaine gustatif. *Acta Inst Ps Univ Zagreb* 2, 1-18. [302]

Bunch, C. C. 1929. Age variations in auditory acuity. *Arch Oto* 9, 625-636. [347]

Bunch, M. E. 1938. The measurement of reminiscence. *Ps Rev* 45, 525-531. [796]

—— 1939. Transfer of training in the mastery of an antagonistic habit after varying intervals of time. *J comp Ps* 28, 189-200. [750]

—— 1941. A comparison of retention and transfer of training from similar material after relatively long intervals of time. *J comp Ps* 32, 217-231. [749, 750]

—— 1944. Cumulative transfer of training under different temporal conditions. *J comp Ps* 37, 265-272. [748]

Burian, H. M. 1943. Influence of prolonged wearing of meridional size lenses on spatial localization. *Arch Ophth* 30, 645-666. [488]

Burkamp, W. 1923. Versuche über das Farbenwiedererkennen der Fische. *Z Sinnesphys* 55, 133-170. [437]

Burnett, N. C., Dallenbach, K. M. 1928. Heat intensity. *Amer J Ps* 40, 484-494. [283]

Burns, M., Dallenbach, K. M. 1933. The adaptation of cutaneous pain. *Amer J Ps* 45, 111-117. [286]

Burt, C. 1919. The development of reasoning in school children. *J exp Ped* 5, 68-77, 121-127. [842]

—— 1921. *Mental and scholastic tests*. Lond., King. [842]

Burtt, H. E. 1921. The inspiration-expiration ratios during truth and falsehood. *J exp Ps* 4, 1-23. [187]

—— 1948. *Applied psychology*. N. Y., Prentice-Hall. [75]

——, Dobell, E. M. 1925. The curve of forgetting for advertising material. *J appl Ps* 9, 5-21. [533]

Burzlaff, W. 1931. Methodologische Beiträge zum Problem der Farbenkonstanz. *Z Ps* 119, 177-235. [433, 434]

Bussenius, C. E. *See* Ruger, H. 1913.

Buswell, G. T. 1920. An experimental study of the eye-voice span in reading. *Suppl Educ Monogr* #17. [507]

—— 1922. Fundamental reading habits: a study of their development. *Suppl Educ Monogr* #21. [506]

—— 1935. *How people look at pictures*. Chic., Univ Chicago Press. [77]

—— 1937. How adults read. *Suppl Educ Monogr* #45. [505]

—— 1939. Remedial reading at the college and adult levels. *Suppl Educ Monogr* #50. [509]

—— *See also* Judd, G. H. 1922.

Butsch, R. L. C. 1932. Eye movements and the eye-hand span in typewriting. *J educ Ps* 23, 104-121. [508]

Buxton, C. E. 1940. Latent learning and the goal gradient hypothesis. *Cont ps Theory* 2, #6. [640]

—— 1943. The status of research in reminiscence. *Ps Bull* 40, 313-340. [796]

—— 1949. Repetition of two basic experiments on reminiscence in serial verbal learning. *J exp Ps* 39, 676-682. [797]

—— *See also* Withey, S. 1949.

Buzby, D. E. 1924. The interpretation of facial expressions. *Amer J Ps* 35, 602-604. [114, 115]

C

Cairnes, W. B. *See* Jastrow, J. 1891-1892.

Calkins, M. W. 1894. Association. *Ps Rev* 1, 476-483. [699, 732]

—— 1896. Association: an essay analytic and experimental. *Ps Monogr* #2. [699, 732]

Cameron, A. T. 1947. The taste sense and the relative sweetness of sugars and other sweet substances. *Sci Rept Series* #9, 1-72. [303]

Camis, M. 1930. *The physiology of the vestibular apparatus*. Trans. R. S. Creed. Oxford, Clarendon. [523]

Campbell, A. A. *See* Hilgard, E. R. 1936, 1937, 1938.

Cannon, W. B. 1915, 1929. *Bodily changes in pain, hunger, fear and rage*. N. Y., Appleton [109, 179]

—— 1932. *The wisdom of the body*. N. Y., Norton. [170]

—— 1934. Hunger and thirst. *Handbk genl exp Ps* 247-263. C. Murchison, ed. Worcester, Clark Univ Press. [659]

Cantril, H. 1947. *Understanding man's social behavior*. Princeton, Office Public Opinion Research. [489]

—— 1950. *The "why" of man's experience*. N. Y., Macmillan. [489]

——, Ames, A., Jr., Hastorf, A. H., Ittelson, W. H. 1949. Psychology and scientific research. *Science* 110, 461-464, 491-497, 517-522. [489]

——, Hunt, W. A. 1932. Emotional effects produced by the injection of adrenalin. *Amer J Ps* 44, 300-307. [136]

Carey, J. P. 1951. Reinstatement of previously learned responses under conditions of extinction: a study of 'regression.' *Amer Psychol* 6, 284. [677]

Carmichael, L. 1925. A device for the demonstra-

——, McCleary, R. A. 1953. Interposition as a cue for the perception of relative distance. *J genl Ps* 48, 113-132. [462]

Chaplin, J. P. *See* Young, P. T. 1949.

Chappell, M. N. 1929. Blood pressure changes in deception. *Arch Ps N.Y.* #105. [188]

—— 1931. A comparison of blood-pressure methods. *J genet Ps* 39, 398-403. [190]

Chase, A. M. *See* Hecht, S. 1936.

Cheatham, P. G., White, C. T. 1952. Temporal numerosity. I. Perceived number as a function of flash number and rate. *J exp Ps* 44, 447-451. [100]

Chocholle, R. 1943. Relation de la latence d'une sensation auditive différentielle avec l'amplitude d'une variation brusque de fréquence . . . d'intensité. *Bull biol* 137, 643-644, 751-752. [27, 261]

—— 1945. Variation des temps de réaction auditifs en fonction de l'intensité à diverses fréquences. *Ann ps* 41-42, 65-124. [19, 20, 38]

Chow, K. L. *See* Lashley, K. S. 1951.

Christensen, P. R. *See* Guilford, J. P. 1951, 1952.

Churcher, B. G. 1935. A loudness scale for industrial noise measurement. *J acoust Soc Amer* 6, 216-226. [238, 334]

Chute, E. *See* Bartley, S. H. 1947.

Claparède, E. 1924. Pourquoi baille-t-on? *Intermed des educateurs.* [157]

—— 1925. Les temps de réaction et la psychologie appliquée. *Arch de Ps* 19, 277-284. [36]

—— 1931. *L'education fonctionnelle.* Neuchâtel, Delachaux. [157]

—— 1934. La genese de l'hypothèse. *Arch de Ps* 24, 1-154. [821]

Clark, B. 1934. A camera for simultaneous record of horizontal and vertical movements of both eyes. *Amer J Ps* 46, 325-326. [495]

—— 1940. Binocular anomalies and reading ability. *Amer J Opth* 23, 885-891. [504]

Clay, J. *See* Harris, L. J. 1933.

Cline, T. S. *See* Dodge, R. 1901.

Coate, W. B. *See* Bitterman, M. E. 1950.

Cobb, P. W. 1934. The dependence of flicker on the dark-light ratio of the stimulus cycle. *J opt Soc Amer* 24, 107-113. [382]

Coffin, J. I. *See* Shipley, W. C. 1945.

Cohen, B. H. *See* Bousfield, W. A. 1952.

Cohen, J., Ogdon, D. P. 1949. Taste blindness to phenyl-thio-carbamide and related compounds. *Ps Bull* 46, 490-498. [301]

Cohn, J. 1894. Experimentelle Untersuchungen über die Gefühlsbetonung der Farben, Helligkeiten, und ihrer Combinationen. *Philos St* 10, 562-603. [253]

Cole, L. E. 1929. The localization of tactual space: a study of average and constant errors under different types of localization. *Genet Ps Monogr* 5, 339-450. [294]

Coleman, J. C. 1949. Facial expressions of emotions. *Ps Monogr* # 296. [120]

Conklin, E. S. 1927. *Principles of abnormal psychology.* N. Y., Holt. [69]

Conklin, J. I. 1951. Three factors affecting the general level of electrical skin-resistance. *Amer J Ps* 64, 78-86. [140]

Conrad, H. S., Harris, D. 1931. The free association method and the measurement of adult intelligence. *Calif U Publ Ps* 5, 1-45. [53]

Cook, C. *See* Graham, C. H. 1937.

Cook, S. A. 1928. The effect of various temporal arrangements of practice on the mastery of an animal maze of moderate complexity. *Arch Ps N.Y.* #98. [790]

Cook, S. W., Harris, R. E. 1937. The verbal conditioning of the galvanic skin reflex. *J exp Ps* 21, 202-210. [575]

Cook, T. W. 1933. Studies in cross education. I. Mirror tracing the star-shaped maze. *J exp Ps* 16, 144-160. [737, 740, 742]

—— 1934a. Binocular and monocular relations in foveal dark adaptation. *Ps Monogr* #202. [369]

—— 1934b. Studies in cross education. III. Kinaesthetic learning of an irregular pattern. *J exp Ps* 17, 749-762. [737, 740]

—— 1935. Studies in cross education. IV. Permanence of transfer. *J exp Ps* 18, 255-266. [740]

—— 1936. Factors in whole and part learning a visually perceived maze. *J genet Ps* 49, 3-32. [784]

—— 1937. Whole versus part learning the spider maze. *J exp Ps* 20, 477-494. [784]

—— 1944. Factors in massed and distributed practice. *J exp Ps* 34, 325-334. [790]

Coombs, C. H. 1938. Adaptation of the galvanic response to auditory stimuli. *J exp Ps* 22, 244-268. [151]

—— *See also* Shock, N. W. 1937.

Cooper, S. F. 1928. The effect of brightness in the range of attention experiments. *Amer J Ps* 40, 254-274. [95]

Coppée, G. E. *See* Kemp, E. H. 1937.

Corbin, H. H. 1942. The perception of grouping and apparent movement in visual depth. *Arch Ps N.Y.* #273. [513]

Cordes, G. 1901. Experimentelle Untersuchungen über Associationen. *Philos St* 17, 30-77. [65]

Cornsweet, J. C. *See* Riggs, L. A. 1953.

Cornsweet, T. N. *See* Riggs, L. A. 1953.

Cottrell, C. L. *See* Ryan, T. A. 1950.

Cotzin, M., Dallenbach, K. M. 1950. 'Facial vision': the role of pitch and loudness in the perception of obstacles by the blind. *Amer J Ps* 63, 485-515. [361]

—— *See also* Supa, M. 1944.

Courts, F. A. 1939. Relations between experimentally induced muscular tension and memorization. *J exp Ps* 25, 235-256. [176]

—— 1942. Relations between muscular tension and performance. *Ps Bull* 39, 347-367. [175, 176].

Cowles, J. T. 1937. Food-tokens as incentives for learning by chimpanzees. *Comp Ps Monogr* #71. [681]

—— *See also* Nissen, H. W. 1936.
Cowling, D. J. *See* Judd, C. H. 1907.
Cox, G. M. *See* Gaskill, H. V. 1941.
Cox, J. W. 1933. Some experiments on formal training in the acquisition of skill. *Br J Ps* 24, 67-87. [761]
Crafts, L. W. 1929. Whole and part methods with non-serial reactions. *Amer J Ps* 41, 543-563. [784]
—— 1930. Whole and part methods with unrelated reactions. *Amer J Ps* 42, 591-601. [784]
Craik, K. J. W. 1939. The effect of adaptation upon visual acuity. *Br J Ps* 29, 252-266. [386]
Cramer, T. 1923. Über die Beziehung des Zwischenmediums zu den Transformations- und Kontrasterscheinungen. *Z Sinnesphys* 54, 215-242. [443]
Crane, H. W. 1915. A study in association reaction and reaction time. *Ps Monogr* #80. [60, 61, 64, 66]
Crannell, C. W. 1942. The choice point behavior of rats in a multiple path elimination problem. *J Ps* 13, 201-222. [603]
Crawley, S. L. 1926. An experimental investigation of recovery from work. *Arch Ps N.Y.* #85. [688]
Crespi, L. P. 1942. Quantitative variation of incentive and performance in the white rat. *Amer J Ps* 55, 467-517. [666]
—— 1944. Amount of reinforcement and level of performance. *Ps Rev* 51, 341-357. [666, 668]
Crews, A. *See* Henderson, M. T. 1945.
Critchley, Mc.D. 1939. *The language of gesture.* N. Y., Longmans, Green. [121]
Crocker, E. C. 1945. *Flavor.* N. Y., McGraw-Hill. [310]
——, Dillon, F. N. 1949. Odor directory. *Amer Perfum* 53, 297-301, 396-400. [310]
——, Henderson, L. F. 1927. Analysis and classification of odors. *Amer Perfum* 22, 325-327, 356. [310]
Crookes, T. C. *See* Hall, K. R. L. 1952.
Crosland, H. R. 1921. A qualitative analysis of the process of forgetting. *Ps Monogr* #130. [717]
—— 1929. The psychological methods of word-association and reaction-time as tests of deception. *Oregon U Publ Ps* #1. [53, 66]
Crowe, S. J., Guild, S. R., Polvogt, L. M. 1934. Observations on the pathology of high-tone deafness. *Bull Johns Hopkins Hosp* 54, 315-379. [348]
Crowley, M. E. *See* Gagné, R. M. 1948.
Crown, S. 1947. A controlled association test as a measure of neuroticism. *J Per* 16, 198-208. [70]
Cruikshank, R. M. 1941. The development of visual size constancy in early infancy. *J genet Ps* 58, 327-351. [438]
Cuff, N. B. 1927. The relation of overlearning to retention. *George Peabody Cont Educ* #43. [728]
Culler, A. J. 1912. Interference and adaptability. *Arch Ps N.Y.* #24. [764]
Culler, E. 1926a. Thermal discrimination and Weber's law. *Arch Ps N.Y.* #81. [291]
—— 1926b. Studies in psychometric theory. *Ps Monogr* #163. [215]
—— 1938. Recent advances in some concepts of conditioning. *Ps Rev* 45, 134-153. [555, 557]
——, Finch, G., Girden, E., Brogden, W. 1935. Measurements of acuity by the conditioned-response technique. *J genl Ps* 12, 223-227. [675]
——, Girden, E. 1951. The learning curve in relation to other psychometric functions. *Amer J Ps* 64, 327-349. [538]
——, Mettler, F. A. 1934. Conditioned behavior in the decorticate dog. *J comp Ps* 18, 291-303. [576]
—— *See also* Brogden, W. J. 1938; Finch, G. 1934a, b.
Cummings, S. B. 1938. The effect of local anesthesia on tactile and vibratory thresholds. *J exp Ps* 23, 321-338. [280]
Cureton, E. E. *See* Wicker, W. 1953.

D

Dallenbach, K. M. 1923a. Some new apparatus. *Amer J Ps* 34, 90-95. [74]
—— 1923b. Position *vs.* intensity as a determinant of clearness. *Amer J Ps* 34, 282-286. [74]
—— 1927. The temperature spots and end-organs. *Amer J Ps* 39, 402-427. [275-277]
—— 1939. Pain: history and present status. *Amer J Ps* 52, 331-347. [285]
—— *See also* Ammons, C. H. 1953; Burnett, N. C. 1928; Burns, M. 1933; Cotzin, M. 1950; Ferrall, S. C. 1930; Foster, D. 1950; Glanville, A. D. 1929; Guilford, J. P. 1925; Jenkins, J. G. 1924; Levine, H. A. 1936; Lowenstein, E. 1930; Minami, H. 1946; Neff, W. S. 1936; Stone, L. J. 1936; Supa, M. 1944; Worchel, P. 1947.
Dambach, K. 1929. Die Mehrfacharbeit und ihre typologische Bedeutung. *Z Ps Ergbd* #14. (Doktor-dissertation, Tübingen.) [89]
Danzig, E. R. *See* Weld, H. P. 1940.
Darrow, C. W. 1927. Sensory, secretory and electrical changes in the skin following bodily excitation. *J exp Ps* 10, 197-226. [142]
—— 1934. Quantitative records of cutaneous secretory reactions. *J genl Ps* 11, 445-448. [140, 142]
—— 1935. Emotion as relative functional decortication: the role of conflict. *Ps Rev* 42, 566-578. [109]
—— 1936. The galvanic skin reflex (sweating) and blood-pressure as preparatory and facilitative functions. *Ps Bull* 33, 73-94. [142, 143]
—— 1937a. The equation of the galvanic skin reflex curve. I. The dynamics of reaction in relation to excitation-background. *J genl Ps* 16, 285-309. [140]
—— 1937b. Neural mechanisms controlling the palmar galvanic skin reflex and palmar sweating. *Arch Neu Psychiat* 37, 641-663. [143]
—— 1946. The electroencephalogram and psychophysiological regulation of the brain. *Amer J Psychiat* 102, 791-798. [181]

——, Heath, L. L. 1932. Reaction tendencies relating to personality. *St in dynamics behavior* 59-261. K. S. Lashley, ed. Chic., Univ Chicago Press. [147, 152]
——, Jost, H., Solomon, A. P., Mergener, J. C. 1942. Autonomic indications of excitatory and homeostatic effects in the electroencephalogram. *J Ps* 14, 115-130. [182]
—— *See also* Freeman, G. L. 1935.
Darwin, C. 1872. *Expression of the emotions in man and animals.* Lond., Murray. [112]
Dashiell, J. F. 1920. Some transfer factors in maze learning by the white rat. *Psbiol* 2, 329-350. [751]
—— 1930. Direction orientation in maze running by the white rat. *Comp Ps Monogr* #32. [623]
—— 1937. Affective value-distances as a determinant of esthetic judgment-times. *Amer J Ps* 50, 57-67. [33, 264]
——, Bayroff, A. G. 1931. A forward-going tendency in maze running. *J comp Ps* 12, 77-94. [621]
Davies, H. M. *See* Trotter, W. 1909.
Davis, A. J., Meenes, M. 1932. Factors determining the relative efficacy of the whole and part methods of learning. *J exp Ps* 15, 716-727. [784]
Davis, D. R., Sinha, D. 1950a. The effect of one experience upon the recall of another. *Q J exp Ps* 2, 43-52. [766]
——, —— 1950b. The influence of an interpolated experience upon recognition. *Q J exp Ps* 2, 132-137. [766]
Davis, F. C. 1932. The functional significance of imagery differences. *J exp Ps* 15, 630-661. [722]
Davis, H., ed. 1947. *Hearing and deafness.* N. Y., Murray Hill. [326]
—— *See also* Galambos, R. 1943, 1944, 1948; Saul, L. J. 1932; Stevens, S. S. 1935, 1936, 1938.
Davis, R. C. 1930. Factors affecting the galvanic reflex. *Arch Ps N.Y.* #115. [149, 150]
—— 1934. Modification of the galvanic reflex by daily repetition of a stimulus. *J exp Ps* 17, 504-535. [146, 147]
—— 1937. The relation of certain muscle action potentials to "mental work." *Indiana U Publ Sci Ser* #5. [817]
—— 1938. The relation of muscle action potentials to difficulty and frustration. *J exp Ps* 23, 141-158. [817]
—— 1940. Set and muscular tension. *Indiana U Publ Sci Ser* #10. [30]
—— 1942. Methods of measuring muscular tension. *Ps Bull* 39, 329-346. [175]
—— 1948. Motor effects of strong auditory stimuli. *J exp Ps* 38, 257-275. [184]
—— 1952. The stimulus trace in effectors and its relation to judgment responses. *J exp Ps* 44, 377-390. [228]
——, Kantor, J. R. 1935. Skin resistance during hypnotic states. *J genl Ps* 13, 62-81. [146]
—— *See also* Payne, B. 1940.
Dawson, E. H., Harris, B. L. 1951. Sensory methods for measuring differences in food quality. U.S.D.A. Infor Bull, #34. [233]
Dearborn, W. F. 1906. The psychology of reading. *Arch Philos Ps Sci Meth* #4. [504, 505, 506, 508]
—— 1909. The general effects of special practice in memory. *Ps Bull* 6, 44. [744]
——, Anderson, I. H. 1937. A new method for teaching phrasing and for increasing the size of reading fixations. *Ps Rec* 1, 459-475. [509]
—— *See also* Carmichael, L. 1947.
DeCamp, J. E. 1915. A study of retroactive inhibition. *Ps Monogr* #84. [765]
Dees, V. *See* MacPherson, S. J. 1948, 1949.
Deese, J. 1950. A quantitative derivation of latent learning. *Ps Rev* 57, 291-294. [637]
—— 1951. The extinction of a discrimination without performance of the choice response. *J comp phys Ps* 44, 362-366. [641]
—— 1952 *The psychology of learning.* N. Y., McGraw-Hill.
Deitrick, J. E. *See* Hanlon, L. W. 1949.
Delabarre, E. B. 1898. A method of recording eye-movements. *Amer J Ps* 9, 572-574. [494]
Dembo, T. *See* Barker, R. G. 1941; Lewin, K. 1944.
Dempsey, E. W. 1951. Homeostasis. *Handbk exp Ps* 209-235. S. S. Stevens, ed. N. Y., Wiley. [110, 180]
Dennis, W. 1929. The sensory control of the white rat in the maze habit. *J genet Ps* 36, 59-90. [631]
—— 1939. Spontaneous alternation in rats as an indicator of the persistence of stimulus effects. *J comp Ps* 28, 305-312. [622]
——, Russell, R. W. 1939. Comments on recent studies of *VTE*. *J genet Ps* 54, 217-221. [599]
Denny, M. R. 1948. The effect of using differential end boxes in a simple T-maze learning situation. *J exp Ps* 38, 245-249. [683]
De Silva, H. R. 1926. An experimental investigation of the determinants of apparent visual movement. *Amer J Ps* 37, 469-501. [513]
——, 1929. An analysis of the visual perception of movement. *Br J Ps* 19, 268-305. [514]
—— 1938. The human element in stopping a car. *Brake Service* 8, 9-12. [42]
De Valois, R. L. *See* Walker, E. L. 1950.
Dickson, W. J. *See* Roethlisberger, F. J. 1939.
Diefendorf, A. R., Dodge, R. 1908. An experimental study of the ocular reactions of the insane from photographic records. *Brain* 31, 451-489. [502]
Dieterici, C. *See* König, A. 1893.
Dillon, F. N. *See* Crocker, E. C. 1949.
Dimmick, F. L. 1933. The dependence of auditory experience upon wave amplitude. *Amer J Ps* 45, 463-470. [337]
Dinsmoor, J. A. 1952a. The effect of hunger on discriminated responding. *J abnor soc Ps* 47, 67-72. [694]
—— 1952b. A discrimination based on punishment. *Q J exp Ps* 4, 27-45. [691]
Dittmer, D. G. *See* Grant, D. A. 1940.
Dobell, E. M. *See* Burtt, H. E. 1925.

lung: Der persönlichen Gleichung zweiter Theil. *Pflüg Arch ges Phys* 11, 403-432. [514]

F

Fairbanks, G., Hoaglin, L. W. 1941. An experimental study of the durational characteristics of the voice during expression of emotion. *Speech Monogr* 8, 85-90. [123]

——, Pronovost, W. 1939. An experimental study of the pitch characteristics of the voice during expression of emotions. *Speech Monogr* 6, 87-104. [123]

—— *See also* Tiffen, J. 1937.

Fairclough, R. H., Jr. 1952. Transfer of motivated improvement in speed of reaction and movement. *Res Q Amer Ass Hlth* 23, 20-27. [736]

Farmer, E., Chambers, E. G. 1925. Concerning the use of psychogalvanic reflex in psychological experiments. *Br J Ps* 15, 237-254. [144, 150]

Farnum, E. C. *See* Seashore, C. E. 1908.

Fattu, N. A., Mech, E. V. 1953. The effect of set on performance in a "trouble shooting" situation. *J appl Ps* 37, 214-217. [827]

Faust, W. L. *See* Taylor, 1952.

Fechner, G. T. 1858. Beobachtungen welche zu beweisen scheinen dass durch die Uebung der Glieder der einen Seite die der andern zugleich mit geübt werden. *Ber Sächs Ges Wiss Leipzig Math-Phys Cl* 10, 70-76. [738]

—— 1860. *Elemente der Psychophysik*. Leip., Breitkopf & Härtel. [192, 226, 235]

—— 1876. *Vorschule der Aesthetik. Theil 1 & 2.* Leip., Breitkopf & Härtel. [252]

Fehrer, E. V. 1935. An investigation of the learning of visually perceived forms. *Amer J Ps* 47, 187-221. [716, 774]

—— *See also* Helson, H. 1932.

Feiverson, P. *See* Kleitman, N. 1938.

Feldman, R. S. 1948. An automatically controlled Lashley discrimination mechanism. *Amer J Ps* 61, 414-419. [583]

Feleky, A. 1914. The expression of the emotions. *Ps Rev* 21. 33-41. [116]

—— 1916. The influence of emotions on respiration. *J exp Ps* 1, 218-241. [173, 187]

—— 1922. *Feelings and emotions*. N. Y., Pioneer Press. [116, 118, 126]

Felsinger, J. M. *See* Gladstone, A. I. 1947; Hull, C. L.. 1947.

Fendrick, P. 1937. The influence of music distraction upon reading efficiency. *J educ Ps* 31, 264-271. [87]

Féré, C. 1888. Note sur les modifications de la résistance électrique sous l'influence des excitations sensorielles et des émotions. *C R Soc Biol Mem* 40, 217-219. [138]

Fernald, M. R. 1912. The diagnosis of mental imagery. *Ps Monogr* #58. [721]

Fernberger, S. W. 1919. An introspective analysis of the process of comparing. *Ps Monogr* #117. [226]

—— 1921. A preliminary study of the range of visual apprehension. *Amer J Ps* 32, 121-133. [92, 94]

—— 1928. False suggestion and the Piderit model. *Amer J Ps* 40, 562-568. [114, 115]

—— 1930. The use of equality judgments in psychophysical procedures. *Ps Rev* 37, 107-112. [216]

—— 1931a. Instructions and the psychophysical limen. *Amer J Ps* 43, 361-376. [214]

—— 1931b. On absolute and relative judgments in lifted weight experiments. *Amer J Ps* 43, 560-578. [217, 230]

—— 1934. New phenomena of apparent visual movement. *Amer J Ps* 46, 309-314. [513]

—— 1948. The figural after-effect in the third dimension of visual space. *Amer J Ps* 61, 291-293. [425]

—— *See also* Martin, P. R. 1929.

Ferrall, S. C., Dallenbach, K. M. 1930. The analysis and synthesis of burning heat. *Amer J Ps* 42, 72-82. [283]

Ferree, C. E. 1906. An experimental examination of the phenomena usually attributed to fluctuation of attention. *Amer J Ps* 17, 81-120. [79, 80]

—— 1913. The fluctuation of liminal visual stimuli of point area. *Amer J Ps* 24, 378-409. [79, 80]

Ferster, C. B. 1953. The use of the free operant in the analysis of behavior. *Ps Bull* 50, 263-274. [588]

Fessard, A. 1926. Les temps de réaction et leur variabilité, étude statistique. *Ann Ps* 27, 215-224. [37]

Festinger, L. *See* Lewin, K. 1944.

Fieandt, K. v. 1938. *Über Sehen von Tiefenbildern bei wechselnder Beleuchtungsrichtung.* Helsinki, Ps Inst, Univ Helsinki. [463]

Finch, G. 1942. Delayed matching-from-sample and non-spatial delayed response in chimpanzees. *J comp Ps* 34, 315ff. [607]

——, Culler, E. 1934a. Effects of protracted exposure to a loud tone. *Science* 80, 41-42. [348]

——, —— 1934b. Higher order conditioning with constant motivation. *Amer J Ps* 46, 596-602. [557]

—— *See also* Culler, E. 1935.

Findley, A. E. 1924. Further studies of Henning's system of olfactory qualities. *Amer J Ps* 35, 436-445. [308]

Finesinger, J. E. *See* Verzeano, M. 1949.

Finger, F. W. 1941. Quantitative studies of "conflict." I. Variations in latency and strength of the rat's response in a discrimination-jumping situation. *J comp Ps* 31, 97-127. [583, 585]

——, Spelt, D. K. 1947. The illustration of the horizontal-vertical illusion. *J exp Ps* 37, 243-250. [419]

Finkenbinder, E. O. 1913. The curve of forgetting. *Amer J Ps* 24, 8-32. [728]

Fishback, J. *See* Köhler, W. 1950.

Fisher, R. A. 1949. *The design of experiments.* 5th ed. Lond., Oliver. [2]

Fite, W. *See* Angell, J. R. 1901.

Fitts, P. M., Simon, C. W. 1949. Effect of horizontal vs vertical stimulus-separation on performance in a dual-pursuit task. *Amer Psychol* 4, 304-305. [89]

Flanagan, John C. *Aviation psychology progress research report.* #1. *See* Army Air Forces. 1947.

Fletcher, D. F. *See* Young, C. W. 1948.

Fletcher, F. M. 1940. Effects of quantitative variation of food-incentive on the performance of physical work by chimpanzees. *Comp Ps Monogr* 16, #82. [664]

—— *See also* Muenzinger, K. F. 1937.

Fletcher, H. 1929. *Speech and hearing*, N. Y., Van Nostrand. [339, 340, 344]

—— 1934. Loudness, pitch, and the timbre of musical tones and their relation to the intensity, the frequency, and the overtone structure. *J acoust Soc Amer* 6, 59-69. [339]

—— 1953. *Speech and hearing in communication.* N. Y., Van Nostrand. [328]

——, Munson, W. A. 1933. Loudness, its definition, measurement, and calculation. *J acoust Soc Amer* 5, 82-108. [334, 335]

Fliegelman, M. *See* Adler, F. A. 1934.

Florey, H. *See* Barcroft, J. 1929. Drury, A. N. 1929.

Florey, M. E. *See* Drury, A. N. 1929.

Flugel, J. C. 1948. L'Appétit vient en mangeant: some reflexions on the self-sustaining tendencies. *Br J Ps* 38, 171-190. [686]

Flurry, C. *See* Wenzel, B. M. 1948.

Flynn, B. M. 1943. Pitch discrimination. The form of the psychometric function and simple reaction time to liminal differences. *Arch Ps N.Y.* #280. [221, 263]

Foley, J. P., Jr. 1935. The effect of context upon perceptual differentiation. *Arch Ps N.Y.* #184. [414]

——, MacMillan, Z. L. 1943. Mediated generalization and the interpretation of verbal behavior. V. 'Free association' as related to differences in professional training. *J exp Ps* 33, 299-310. [70]

Folgmann, E. E. E. 1933. An experimental study of composer-preferences of four outstanding symphony orchestras. *J exp Ps* 16, 709-724. [255, 256]

Follansbee, G. L. *See* Bales, J. F. 1935.

Foord, E. N. *See* Hebb, D. O. 1945.

Forbes, A. *See* Wells, F. L. 1911.

Forbes, G. 1945. The effect of certain variables on visual and auditory reaction times. *J exp Ps* 35, 153-162. [40]

Forbes, T. W. 1939. A method for analysis of the effectiveness of highway signs. *J appl Ps* 23, 669-684. [74]

——, Landis, C. 1935. The limiting A.C. frequency for the exhibition of the galvanic skin ('psychogalvanic') response. *J genl Ps* 13, 188-193. [139]

—— *See also* Landis, C. 1933.

Ford, A. 1929. Attention-automatization: an investigation of the transitional nature of mind. *Amer J Ps* 41, 1-32. [86]

Fossler, H. R. 1930. Disturbances in breathing during stuttering. *Ps Monogr* #181. [171, 172]

Foster, D., Scofield, E. H., Dallenbach, K. M. 1950. An olfactorium. *Amer J Ps* 63, 431-440. [312]

Foster, H. *See* Gagné, R. M. 1948, 1949, 1950.

Fox, B. H. 1951. Figural after-effects: "satiation" and adaptation. *J exp Ps* 42, 317-326. [425]

Franklin, J. C., Brozek, J. 1947. The relation between distribution of practice and learning efficiency in psychomotor performance. *J exp Ps* 37, 16-24. [534]

Franklin, M. *See* Lewis, H. B. 1944.

Freeman, F. N. 1916. *Experimental education.* Bost., Houghton Mifflin. [95]

Freeman, G. L. 1934. *Introduction to physiological pyschology.* N. Y., Ronald. [89]

—— 1939. Changes in tension-pattern and total energy expenditure during adaptation to 'distracting' stimuli. *Amer J Ps* 52, 354-360. [87]

—— 1940. The relationship between performance level and bodily activity level. *J exp Ps* 26, 602-608. [177]

—— 1948a. *Physiological psychology.* N. Y., Van Nostrand. [175]

—— 1948b. *The energetics of human behavior.* Ithaca, Cornell Univ Press. [175]

——, Darrow, C. W. 1935. Insensible perspiration and the galvanic skin reflex. *Amer J Phys* 111, 55-63. [144]

——, Pathman, J. H. 1942. The relation of overt muscular discharge to physiological recovery from experimentally induced displacement. *J exp Ps* 30, 161-174. [182]

Freiberg, A. D. 1937a. 'Fluctuations of attention' with weak tactual stimuli: a study in perceiving. *Amer J Ps* 49, 23-36. [79]

—— 1937b. 'Fluctuation of attention' with weak auditory stimuli: A study in perceiving. *Amer J Ps* 49, 173-197. [81]

French, J. W. 1942. The effect of temperature on the retention of a maze habit in fish. *J exp Ps* 31, 79-87. [770]

French, N. R., Steinberg, J. C. 1947. Factors governing the intelligibility of speech sounds. *J acoust Soc Amer* 19, 90-119. [342]

—— *See also* Steinberg, J. C. 1946.

Frey, M. *See* von Frey, M.

Frick, F. C. 1948. An analysis of an operant discrimination. *J Ps* 26, 93-123. [587]

—— *See also* Janis, I. L. 1943.

Frings, H. 1947. Biological backgrounds of the "sweet tooth." *Turtox News* 24, 133-134. [684]

Froeberg, S. 1907. The relation between magnitude of the stimulus and the time of the reaction. *Arch Ps N.Y.* #8. [25]

Frois-Wittmann, J. 1930 The judgment of facial expression. *J exp Ps* 13, 113-151. [116, 117, 118, 120]

Fry, G. A., Bartley, S. H. 1935. The effect of one border in the visual field upon the threshold of another. *Amer J Phys* 112, 414-421. [376, 413]

——, Robertson, V. M. 1935. The physiological basis of the periodic merging of area into background. *Amer J Ps* 47, 644-655. [81]

Fulcher, J. S. 1942. "Voluntary" facial expressions in blind and seeing children. *Arch Ps N.Y.* #272. [131]

Fullerton, G. S., Cattell, J. McK. 1892. On the perception of small differences. *Philos Series* #2. Phila., Univ Pennsylvania Press. [212, 221, 223, 228, 251]

Fulton, J. F. 1926. *Muscular contraction and the control of movement.* Balt., Williams & Wilkins. [801]

——, ed. 1950. *Howell's textbook of physiology.* 16th ed. Phila., Saunders. [801, 805]

G

Gage, F. H. 1934 An experimental investigation of the measurability of auditory sensation. *Proc R Soc B* 116, 103-122. [240]

—— *See also* Shaxby, J. H. 1932

Gagné, R. M. 1941a. External inhibition and disinhibition in a conditioned operant response. *J exp Ps* 29, 104-116. [561]

—— 1941b. The effect of spacing of trials on the acquisition and extinction of a conditioned operant response. *J exp Ps* 29, 201-216. [560]

——, Baker, K. E. 1950. Stimulus pre-differentiation as a factor in transfer of training. *J exp Ps* 40, 439-451. [758]

——, ——, Foster, H. 1950. On the relation between similarity and transfer of training in the learning of discriminative motor tasks. *Ps Rev* 57, 67-79. [753]

——, Foster, H. 1949. Transfer of training from practice on components in a motor skill. *J exp Ps* 39, 47-68. [737, 785]

——, ——, Crowley, M. E. 1948. The measurement of transfer of training. *Ps Bull* 45, 97-130. [737]

—— *See also* Graham, C. H. 1940.

Galambos, R. 1943. Flight in the dark: a study of bats. *Sci Mon* 56, 155-162. [359]

——, Davis, H. 1943. The response of single auditory nerve fibers to acoustic stimulation. *J Neurophys* 6, 39-57. [328]

——, —— 1944. Inhibition of activity in single auditory nerve fibers by acoustic stimulation. *J Neurophys* 7, 287-303. [328, 345]

——, —— 1948. Action potentials from single auditory nerve fibers? *Science* 108, 513. [328]

——, Griffin, D. R. 1942. Obstacle avoidance by flying bats: the cries of bats. *J exp Zool* 89, 475-490. [328]

—— *See also* Griffin, D. R. 1941; Morgan, C. T. 1951.

Galifret, Y. 1950–1951. Les mouvements oculaires pendant la fixation et l'acuité visuelle. *Ann Ps* 49, 389-391. [499]

Galli, A. 1934. Percezione totalizzatrice della forma attraverso alla fovea centrale nella luce crepuscolare. *Arch ital Ps* 12, 137-240. [406]

——, Hochheimer, W. 1934. Beobachtungen an Nachzeichnungen mehrdeutiger Feldkonturen. *Z Ps* 132, 304-334. [412]

——, Zama, A. 1931. Untersuchungen über die Wahrnehmung ebener geometrischer Figuren, die ganz oder teilweise von anderen geometrischen Figuren verdeckt sind. *Z Ps* 123, 308-348. [415]

Galloway, A. *See* Wallach, H. 1946.

Galton, F. 1879–1880. Psychometric experiments. *Brain* 2, 149-162. [44, 721]

—— 1883. *Inquiries into human faculty and its development.* Lond., Macmillan. [251]

Gamble, E. A. McC. 1898. The applicability of Weber's law to smell. *Amer J Ps* 10, 82-142. [315]

—— 1909. A study of memorising various materials by the reconstruction method. *Ps Monogr* #43. [700, 703, 707]

—— 1916. Rate of repetition and tenacity of impression. *Ps Monogr* #96, 103-151. [707]

—— 1927. A study of three variables in memorizing. *Amer J Ps* 39, 223-234. [703]

Garner, W. R. 1952a. Some statistical aspects of half-loudness judgments. *J acoust Soc Amer* 24, 153-157. [240]

—— 1952b. An equal discriminability scale for loudness judgments. *J exp Ps* 43, 232-238. [240]

—— *See also* Chapanis, A. 1949; Miller, G. A. 1944; Morgan, C. T. 1951; Saltzman, I. J. 1948.

Garrett, H. E. 1940. Variability in learning under massed and spaced practice. *J exp Ps* 26, 547-567. [791]

—— 1951. *Great experiments in psychology.* 3d ed. N. Y. Appleton-Century-Crofts.

—— 1953. *Statistics in psychology and education.* N. Y., Longmans, Green. [259]

Gaskill, H. V., Cox, G. M. 1941. Patterns in emotional reactions. II. Heart rate and blood pressure. *J genl Ps* 24, 409-421. [181]

Gasser, W. P. *See* Kendler, H. H. 1948.

Gates, A. I. 1916. The mnemonic span for visual and auditory digits. *J exp Ps* 1, 393-403. [705]

—— 1917. Recitation as a factor in memorizing. *Arch Ps N.Y.* #40. [780]

—— 1947. *The improvement of reading.* 3d ed. N. Y., Macmillan. [103]

——, Taylor, G. A. 1925. An experimental study of the nature of improvement resulting from practice in a mental function. *J educ Ps* 16, 583-592. [705]

Gates, G. S. 1923. An experimental study of the growth of social perception. *J educ Ps* 14, 449-461. [118]

Gates, L. W. 1934. The after-effect of visually observed movement. *Amer J Ps* 46, 34-46. [516]

Gatling, F. 1952. The effect of repeated stimulus reversals on learning in the rat. *J comp phys Ps* 45, 347-351. [765]

Gault, R. H. 1927. "Hearing" through the sense organs of touch and vibration. *J Franklin Inst* 204, 329-358. [296]

—— 1936. Recent developments in vibro-tactile research. *J Franklin Inst* 221, 703-719. [296]

Gelb, A. 1929 Die "Farbenkonstanz" der Seh-

dinge. *Handbh norm path Phys* 12 (1), 591-678. [429, 441]
—— 1932. Die Erscheinungen des simultanen Kontrastes und der Eindruck der Feldbeleuchtung. *Z Ps* 127, 42-59. [450]
Geldard, F. A. 1940. The perception of mechanical vibration. I. History of a controversy. II. The response of pressure receptors. III. The frequency function. IV. Is there a separate "vibratory sense"? *J genl Ps* 22, 243-308. [295, 296]
—— 1950. Somesthesis and the chemical senses. *Ann Rev Ps* 1, 71-86. [285]
—— 1953. *The human senses.* N. Y., Wiley.
——, Gilmer, B. von H. 1934. A method for investigating the sensitivity of the skin to mechanical vibration. *J genl Ps* 11, 301-310. [295]
——, Weitz, J. 1948. Unpublished. [295]
Gellermann, L. W. 1931. The double alternation problem. I. The behavior of monkeys in a double alternation temporal maze. II. The behavior of children and human adults in a double alternation temporal maze. III. The behavior of monkeys in a double alternation box-apparatus. *J genet Ps* 39, 50-72, 197-226, 359-392. [628]
Gentry, E. *See* Muenzinger, K. R. 1931.
Gentry, G., Brown, W. L., Kaplan, S. J. 1947. An experimental analysis of the spatial location hypothesis in learning. *J comp phys Ps* 40, 309-322. [632]
——, ——, Lee, H. 1948. Spatial location in the learning of a multiple-T maze. *J comp phys Ps* 41, 312-318. [632]
Gentry, J. R. 1940. Immediate effects of interpolated rest periods on learning performance. *Teach Coll Cont Educ* #799. [793]
Gerbrands, R. *See* Haggard, E. A. 1947.
Gertz, E. 1921. Psychophysische Untersuchungen über die Adaptation im Gebiet der Temperatursinne und über ihren Einfluss auf die Reiz- und Unterschiedsschwellen. *Z Sinnesphys* 52, 1-51, 105-156. [289, 290]
Gesell, A., Thompson, H. 1929. Learning and growth in identical infant twins. *Genet Ps Monogr* 6, 1-124. [736]
Gibbs, C. B. 1951. Transfer of training and skill assumptions in tracking tasks. *Q J exp Ps* 3, 99-110. [759]
Gibson, E. J. 1939. Sensory generalization with voluntary reactions. *J exp Ps* 24, 237-253. [39]
—— 1940. A systematic application of the concepts of generalization and differentiation to verbal learning. *Ps Rev* 47, 196-229. [712, 757]
—— 1941. Retroactive inhibition as a function of degree of generalization between tasks. *J exp Ps* 28, 93-115. [755-756, 757, 762]
—— 1942. Intra-list generalization as a factor in verbal learning. *J exp Ps* 30, 185-200. [712]
—— 1952. The role of shock in reinforcement. *J comp phys Ps* 45, 18-30. [554]
—— 1953. Improvement in perceptual judgments as a function of controlled practice or training. *Ps Bull* 50, 401-431. [747]
——, Gibson, J. J. 1934. Retention and the interpolated task. *Amer J Ps* 46, 603-610. [766]
Gibson, J. J. 1929. The reproduction of visually perceived forms. *J exp Ps* 12, 1-39. [774]
—— 1933. Adaptation, after-effect, and contrast in the perception of curved lines. *J exp Ps* 16, 1-31. [423]
—— 1937a. Adaptation, after-effect, and contrast in the perception of tilted lines. II. Simultaneous contrast and the areal restriction of the after-effect. *J exp Ps* 20, 553-569. [424]
—— 1937b. Adaptation with negative after-effect. *Ps Rev* 44, 222-244. [424]
—— 1950a. *The perception of the visual world.* Bost., Houghton Mifflin. [362, 464, 469, 480, 483, 487, 523]
—— 1950b. The perception of visual surfaces. *Amer J Ps* 63, 367-384. [487]
——, Mowrer, O. H. 1938. Determinants of the perceived vertical and horizontal. *Ps Rev* 45, 300-323. [525, 526]
——, Radner, M. 1937. Adaptation, after-effect and contrast in the perception of tilted lines. I. Quantitative studies. *J exp Ps* 20, 453-467. [424]
—— *See also* Gibson, E. J. 1934.
Gilbert, G. M. 1939. Dynamic psychophysics and the Phi phenomenon. *Arch Ps N.Y.* #237. [513]
Gilbert, J. A. 1894. Researches on the mental and physical development of school-children. *Yale St Ps* 2, 40-100. [36]
Gilchrist, J. C. 1952. Characteristics of latent and reinforcement learning as a function of time. *J comp phys Ps* 45, 198-203. [641]
—— *See also* Wenger, M. A. 1948.
Gilinsky, A. S. 1951. Perceived size and distance in visual space. *Ps Rev* 58, 460-482. [482]
Gill, M. *See* Rapaport, D. 1946.
Gilliland, A. R. *See* Eckstrand, G. 1948.
Gilmer, B. von H. *See* Geldard, F. A. 1934.
Gilroy, F. J. *See* Hanlon, L. W. 1949
Girden, E. 1940. The role of the auditory area of the cortex. *Amer J Ps* 53, 371-383. [358]
—— *See also* Culler, E. 1935, 1951.
Gladstone, A. I., Yamaguchi, H. G., Hull, C. L., Felsinger, J. M. 1947. Some functional relationships of reaction potential ($_sE_r$) and related phenomena. *J exp Ps* 37, 510-526. [262]
—— *See also* Hull, C. L. 1947.
Glanville, A. D., Dallenbach, K. M. 1929. The range of attention. *Amer J Ps* 41, 207-236. [94, 100]
Glanzer, M. 1953. The role of stimulus satiation in spontaneous alternation. *J exp Ps* 45, 387-393. [671]
Glass, L. *See* Hansen, R. 1936.
Glaze, J. A. 1928. The association value of nonsense syllables. *J genet Ps* 35, 255-269. [702]
Gleitman, H. *See* Tolman, E. C. 1949.
Glen, J. S. 1940. Ocular movements in reversibility of perspective. *J genl Ps* 23, 243-281. [77]
Glixman, A. F. 1948. An analysis of the use of the interruption-technique in experimental studies of "repression." *Ps Bull* 45, 491-506. [693]

—— 1949. Recall of completed and incompleted activities under varying degrees of stress. *J exp Ps* 39, 281-295. [693]
Godlove, I. H. *See* Munsell, A. E. D. 1933.
Goldfarb, W. 1941. An investigation of reaction time in older adults and its relationship to certain observed mental test patterns. *Teach Coll Cont Educ* #831. [36]
Goldman, A. *See* von Frey, M. 1915.
Goldmark, M. D., Hopkins, P. S., Florence, L., Lee, F. S. 1920. Studies in industrial physiology. Fatigue in relation to working capacity. *Publ Hlth Bull* #106. [806]
Goldmeier, E. 1941. Progressive changes in memory traces. *Amer J Ps* 54, 490-503. [775]
Goldschmidt, E. F. *See* Boas, E. P. 1932.
Goldstein, K., Scheerer, M. 1941. Abstract and concrete behavior: an experimental study with special tests. *Ps Monogr* #239. [611]
Golla, F. L., Antonovitch, S. 1929. The respiratory rhythm in its relation to the mechanisms of thought. *Brain* 52, 491-509. [169]
Goodell, H. *See* Hardy, J. D. 1951.
Goodenough, F. L. 1932. Expression of the emotions in a blind-deaf child. *J abnor soc Ps* 27, 328-333. [130]
—— 1935. The development of the reactive process from early childhood to maturity. *J exp Ps* 18, 431-450. [36]
—— 1942. The use of free association in the objective measurement of personality. *Studies in personality* 87-103. Q. McNemar, M. A. Merrill, eds. N. Y., McGraw-Hill. [70]
—— 1946. Semantic choice and personality structure. *Science* 104, 451-456. [70]
Goodfellow, L. D. 1933. The sensitivity of the finger-tips to vibrations at various frequency levels. *J Franklin Inst* 216, 387-392. [295]
Goodman, C. C. *See* Bruner, J. S. 1947.
Gordon, E. I. *See* Griffitts, C. H. 1924.
Gorden, R. L. 1953. The effect of attitude toward Russia on logical reasoning. *J soc Ps* 37, 103-111. [848]
Goss, A. E. *See* Rossman, I. L. 1951.
Gottschaldt, K. 1926. I. Über den Einfluss der Erfahrung auf die Wahrnehmung von Figuren. *Ps Forsch* 8, 261-317. [414, 415]
—— 1929. II. Über den Einfluss der Erfahrung auf die Wahrnehmung von Figuren. *Ps Forsch* 12, 1-87. [411, 415]
—— 1933. Der Aufbau des kindlichen Handelns. *Z ang Ps, Beih* #68. [824, 833]
Gould, J., Morgan, C. T. 1942. Auditory sensitivity in the rat. *J comp Ps* 34, 321-329. [328]
Graham, C. H. 1930. An investigation of binocular summation. 1. The fovea. *J genl Ps* 3, 494-510. [399]
—— 1934a. Psychophysics and behavior. *J genl Ps* 10, 299-310.
—— 1934b. Vision. III. Some neural correlations. *Handbk genl exp Ps* 829-879. C. Murchison, ed. Worcester, Clark Univ Press. [372, 375, 382]
—— 1951. Visual perception. *Handbk exp Ps* 868-920. S. S. Stevens, ed. N. Y., Wiley. [471, 515]
——, Baker, K. E., Hecht, M., Lloyd, V. V. 1948. Factors influencing thresholds for monocular movement parallax. *J exp Ps* 38, 205-223. [474]
——, Bartlett, N. R. 1939. The relation of size of stimulus and intensity in the human eye. II. Intensity thresholds for red and violet light. *J exp Ps* 24, 574-587. [375]
——, —— 1940. The relation of size of stimulus and intensity in the human eye. III. The influence of area on foveal intensity discrimination. *J exp Ps* 27, 149-159. [375, 379]
——, Brown, R. H., Mote, F. A., Jr. 1939. The relation of size of stimulus and intensity in the human eye. I. Intensity thresholds for white light. *J exp Ps* 24, 555-573. [375]
——, Cook, C. 1937. Visual acuity as a function of intensity and exposure-time. *Amer J Ps* 49, 654-661. [384, 386]
——, Gagné, R. M. 1940. The acquisition, extinction, and spontaneous recovery of a conditioned operant response. *J exp Ps* 26, 251-280. [558, 586]
——, Granit, R. 1931. Comparative studies on the peripheral and central retina. VI. Inhibition, summation, and synchronization of impulses in the retina. *Amer J Ps* 98, 664-673. [375]
——, Kemp, E. H. 1938. Brightness discrimination as a function of the duration of the increment in intensity. *J genl Phys* 21, 635-650. [378, 379]
——, Margaria, R. 1935. Area and the intensity-time relation in the peripheral retina. *Amer J Phys* 113, 299-305. [373, 374, 379]
——, Riggs, L. A., Mueller, C. G., Solomon, R. L. 1949. Precision of stereoscopic settings as influenced by distance of target from a fiducial line. *J Ps* 27, 203-207. [472]
—— *See also* Hsia, Y. 1951; Riggs, L. A. 1947.
Graham, F. K. 1943. Conditioned inhibition and conditioned excitation in transfer of discrimination. *J exp Ps* 33, 351-368. [758]
Granit, R. 1921. A study on the perception of form. *Br J Ps* 12, 223-247. [715]
—— 1930. Comparative studies on the peripheral and central retina. *Amer J Phys* 94, 41-50. [381]
—— 1933. The components of the retinal action potentials in mammals and their relation to the discharge of the optic nerve. *J Phys* 77, 207-239. [372]
—— 1945. Color receptors of the mammalian retina. *J Neurophys* 8, 195-210. [372, 389]
—— 1947. *Sensory mechanisms of the retina.* Lond., Oxford Univ Press. [389]
——, Harper, P. 1930. Comparative studies on the peripheral and central retina. II. Synaptic reactions in the eye. *Amer J Phys* 95, 211-228. [381]
—— *See also* Graham, C. H. 1931.
Grannis, U. B., Walker, W. W. 1936. The effect on tactual localization of movement during stimulation. *J exp Ps* 19, 417-428. [294]
Grant, D. A., Dittmer, D. G. 1940. A tactile gen-

eralization gradient for a pseudo-conditioned response. *J exp Ps* 26, 404-412. [579]
——, Hake, H. W. 1951. Dark adaptation and the Humphreys random reinforcement phenomenon in human eyelid conditioning. *J exp Ps* 42, 417-423. [569]
——, Jones, O. R., Tallantis, B. 1949. The relative difficulty of the number, form, and color concepts of a Weigl-type problem. *J exp Ps* 39, 552-557. [613]
——, Norris, E. B. 1947. Eyelid conditioning as influenced by the presence of sensitized Beta-responses. *J exp Ps* 37, 423-433. [569]
——, ——, Boissard, S. 1947. Dark adaptation and the pseudo-conditioned eyelid response. *J exp Ps* 37, 434-439. [570]
——, Schneider, D. E. 1949. Intensity of the conditioned stimulus and strength of conditioning. II. The conditioned galvanic skin response to an auditory stimulus. *J exp Ps* 39, 35-40. [545]
—— *See also* Norris, E. B. 1948.
Grant, V. W. 1942. Accommodation and convergence in visual space perception. *J exp Ps* 31, 89-104. [478]
Gray, A. A. 1900. On a modification of the Helmholtz theory of hearing. *J Anat Phys Lond* 34, 324-350. [328]
Gray, S. 1940. The influence of methodology upon the measurement of reminiscence. *J exp Ps* 27, 37-44. [796]
Gray, W. L. *See* Dorcus, R. M. 1932.
Green, H. C. *See* Potter, R. K. 1947.
Green, R. F. *See* Guilford, J. P. 1951.
Greenberg, A. *See* Kendler, H. H. 1952.
Greenwald, D. U. *See* Bagchi, B. K. 1937.
Gregg, L. W., Brogden, W. J. 1950. The relation between reaction time and the duration of the auditory stimulus. *J comp phys Ps* 43, 389-395. [25]
Grether, W. F. 1938. Pseudo-conditioning without paired stimulation encountered in attempted backward conditioning. *J comp Ps* 25, 91-96.
Grice, G. R. 1948a. An experimental test of the expectation theory of learning. *J comp phys Ps* 41, 137-143. [642]
—— 1948b. The acquisition of a visual discrimination habit following response to a single stimulus. *J exp Ps* 38, 633-642. [588]
—— 1949. Visual discrimination learning with simultaneous and successive presentation of stimuli. *J comp phys Ps* 42, 365-373. [588]
Griffin, D. R. 1944. Echolocation by blind men, bats and radar. *Science* 100, 589-590. [359]
—— 1950. Measurements of the ultrasonic cries of bats. *J acoust Soc Amer* 22, 247-255. [359]
——, Galambos, R. 1941. The sensory basis of obstacle avoidance by flying bats. *J exp Zool* 86, 481-506. [359]
—— *See also* Galambos, R. 1942.
Griffitts, C. H., Gordon, E. I. 1924. The relation between the Traube-Hering and attention rhythms. *J exp Ps* 7, 117-134. [81]
Grindley, G. C. 1932. The formation of a simple habit in guinea-pigs. *Br J Ps* 23, 127-147. [549]
—— *See also* Elwell, J. L. 1938; MacPherson, S. J. 1948, 1949.
Grings, W. *See* Trueblood, H. 1950.
Grinsted, A. D. 1941. Bodily movement as related to problem solving. *J exp Ps* 29, 370-379. [817]
Grossart, F. 1921. Das tachistoskopische Verlesen unter besonderer Berücksichtigung des Einflusses von Gefühlen und der Frage des objektiven und subjektiven Typus. *Arch ges Ps* 41, 121-200. [68]
Grossman, S. *See* Skaggs, E. B. 1930.
Guetzkow, H. 1951. An analysis of the operation of set in problem-solving behavior. *J genl Ps* 45, 219-244. [837]
Guild, S. R. *See* Crowe, S. J. 1934.
Guilford, J. P. 1927. 'Fluctuations of attention' with weak visual stimuli. *Amer J Ps* 38, 534-583. [80, [illegible]]
—— 1928. The method of paired comparisons as a psychometric method. *Ps Rev* 35, 494-506. [254]
—— 1929. An experiment in learning to read facial expressions. *J abnor soc Ps* 24, 191-202. [117]
—— 1932. A generalized psychophysical law. *Ps Rev* 39, 73-85. [224]
—— 1936. *Psychometric methods*. N. Y., McGraw-Hill. [201, 207, 252, 254]
——, Dallenbach, K. M. 1925. The determination of memory span by the method of constant stimuli. *Amer J Ps* 36, 621-628. [697]
——, Green, R. F., Christensen, P. R. 1951. A factor-analytic study of reasoning abilities. II. Administration of tests and analysis of results. *U So Calif Rept Ps Lab* #3. [814]
——, Helson, H. 1929. Eye-movements and the phi-phenomenon. *Amer J Ps* 41, 595-606. [314]
——, Park, D. G. 1931. The effect of interpolated weights upon comparative judgments. *Amer J Ps* 43, 589-599. [229]
——, Wilson, R. C., Christensen, P. R. 1952. A factor-analytic study of creative thinking. II. Administration of tests and analysis of results. *U So Calif Rept Ps Lab* #8. [814]
—— *See also* Hackman, R. B. 1936.
Guillaume, P., Meyerson, I. 1930. Recherches sur l'usage de l'instrument chez les singes: I. Le problème du détour. *J de Ps* 27, 177-236. [833]
Guillot, M. 1948a. Sur quelques caractères des phénomènes d'anosmie partielle. *C R Séances Soc Biol* 142, 161-162. [317]
—— 1948b. Anosmies partielles et odeurs fondamentales. *C R Acad Sci* 226, 1307-1309. [317]
Gullette, R. *See* Landis, C. 1925.
Günther, H. *See* Hahn, H. 1933.
Gustafson, L. M. *See* Irion, A. L. 1952.
Guthrie, E. R. 1933. Association as a function of time interval. *Psy Rev* 40, 355-367. [566]
—— 1935, 1952. *The psychology of learning*. N. Y., Harper. [550, 560]
——, Horton, G. P. 1946. *Cats in a puzzle box*. N. Y., Rinehart. [819]

H

Haagen, C. H. 1949. Synonymity, vividness, familiarity, and association value ratings of 400 pairs of common adjectives. *J Ps* 27, 453-463. [757]

Hackman, R. B., Guilford, J. P. 1936. A study of the 'visual fixation' method of measuring attention value. *J appl Ps* 20, 44-59. [75]

Hadamard, J. 1949. *An essay on the psychology of invention in the mathematical field*. Princeton, Princeton Univ Press. [817]

Hadley, J. M. 1941. Some relationships between electrical signs of central and peripheral activity. II. During 'mental work.' *J exp Ps* 28, 53-62. [182]

Hadsell, K. C. *See* Shipley, W. C. 1945.

Haggard, E. A. 1945. Experimental studies in affective processes. II. On the quantification and evaluation of "measured" changes in skin resistance. *J exp Ps* 35, 46-56. [140]

—— 1949. On the application of analysis of variance to GSR data. I. The selection of an appropriate measure. II. Some effects of the use of inappropriate measures. *J exp Ps* 39, 378-392, 861-867. [140]

——, Gerbrands, R. 1947. An apparatus for the measurement of continuous changes in palmar skin resistance. *J exp Ps* 37, 92-98. [139]

Hahn, H. 1930. Die Psycho-physischen Konstanten und Variablen des Temperatursinnes. *Z Sinnesphys* 60, 198-232. [290]

—— 1934. Die Adaptation des Geschmackssinnes. *Z Sinnesphys* 65, 105-145. [303]

—— 1942. Tiempo de reaccion visual y sus variaciones por el factor altura. *Anales Fac Ciencias Med Lima* 25, 101-115. [38]

——, Günther, H. 1933. Über die Reize und die Reizbedingungen des Geschmackssinnes. *Pflüg Arch ges Phys* 231, 48-67. [302]

——, Kuckulies, G., Taeger, H. 1938. Eine systematische Untersuchung der Geschmacksschwellen. *Z Sinnesphys* 67, 259-306. [299]

Haig, C. *See* Hecht, S. 1936.

Hake, H. W. *See* Grant, D. A. 1951.

Hall, C. S. *See* Tolman, E. C. 1932.

Hall, J. *See* Wickens, D. D. 1949.

Hall, J. F., Kobrick, J. L. 1952. The relationships among three measures of response strength. *J comp phys Ps* 45, 280-282. [544]

——, Smith, K., Schnitzer, S. B., Hanford, P. V. 1953. Elevation of activity level in the rat following transition from ad libitum to restricted feeding. *J comp phys Ps* 46, 429-433. [656]

Hall, K. R. L., Earle, A. E., Crookes, T. G. 1952. A pendulum phenomenon in the visual perception of apparent movement. *Q J exp Ps* 4, 109-120. [513]

Halverson, H. M. 1922a. The role of intensity in auditory wave phase. *Ps Monogr* #140. [356]

—— 1922b. Binaural localization of tones as dependent upon differences of phase and intensity. *Amer J Ps* 33, 178-212. [356]

—— 1924. Tonal volume as a function of intensity. *Amer J Ps* 35, 360-367. [337]

Hamburger, F., Jr. *See* Dorcus, M. R. 1938.

Hamel, I. A. 1919. A study and analysis of the conditioned reflex. *Ps Monogr* #118. [572]

Hamilton, E. L. 1929. The effect of delayed incentive on the hunger drive in the white rat. *Genet Ps Monogr* 5, 137-166. Reprinted: C. J. Warden, 1931. [663, 664]

Hamilton, F. M. 1907. The perceptual factors in reading. *Arch Ps N.Y.* #9. [103]

Hamilton, H. C. 1929. The effect of incentives on accuracy of discrimination. *Arch Ps N.Y.* #103. [688]

Hamilton, R. J. 1943. Retroactive facilitation as a function of degree of generalization between tasks. *J exp Ps* 32, 363-376. [755, 756, 757, 762]

Hamilton, Sir Wm. 1859. *Lectures on metaphysics and logic*. V.1, lect. xiv. Edin., Blackwood. [90]

Hammer, E. R. 1949. Temporal factors in figural after-effects. *Amer J Ps* 62, 337-354. [425]

Hanawalt, E. M. 1931. Whole and part methods in trial and error learning. *Comp Ps Monogr* #35. [783]

—— 1934. Whole and part methods in trial and error learning: human maze learning. *J. exp Ps* 17, 691-708. [783]

Hanawalt, N. G. 1937. Memory trace for figures in recall and recognition. *Arch Ps N.Y.* #216. [700, 775, 776, 777]

—— 1942. The rôle of the upper and lower parts of the face as a basis for judging facial expressions. I. In painting and sculpture. *J genl Ps* 27, 331-346. [120]

—— 1944. The rôle of the upper and the lower parts of the face as a basis for judging facial expressions. II. In posed expressions and "candid camera" pictures. *J genl Ps* 31, 23-36. [120]

—— 1952. The method of comparison applied to the problem of memory change. *J exp Ps* 43, 37-42. [775]

Handbook of human engineering data. 1949-1953. 2d ed. rev. Medford 55. Mass. Tufts Coll Bookstore. [180, 221, 473]

Handlon, J. H., Jr. *See* Seward, J. P. 1950.

Hanes, R. M. 1949a. A scale of subjective brightness. *J exp Ps* 39, 438-452. [244, 245, 261]

—— 1949b. The construction of subjective brightness scales from fractionation data: a validation. *J exp Ps* 39, 719-728. [244, 261]

Haney, G. W. 1931. The effect of familiarity on maze performance of albino rats. *Calif U Publ Ps* 4, 319-333. [640]

Hanford, P. V. *See* Hall, J. F. 1953.

Hanlon, L. W., Romaine, M., Gilroy, F. J., Deitrick, J. E. 1949. Lithium chloride as a substitute for sodium chloride in the diet. *J Amer med Ass* 139, 688-692. [301]

Hansen, R., Glass, L. 1936. Über den Geruchssinn in der Schwangerschaft. *Klin Wschr* 15, 891-894. [317]

Hardy, J. D., Goodell, H., Wolff, H. G. 1951. The influence of skin temperature upon the pain threshold as evoked by thermal radiation. *Science* 114, 149-150. [293]

—, Oppel, T. W. 1937. Studies in temperature sensation. III. The sensitivity of the body to heat and the spatial summation of the end organ responses. *J clin Invest* 16, 533-540. [285]

Hargreaves, F. J. *See* Harris, L. J. 1933.

Harlow, H. F. 1944. Studies in discrimination learning by monkeys. *J genl Ps* 30, 3-21. [585]

— 1949. The formation of learning sets. *Ps Rev* 56, 51-65. [759, 760]

— 1950. Analysis of discrimination learning by monkeys. *J exp Ps* 40, 26-39. [759]

— 1951. Thinking. *Theoretical foundations of psychology* 452-505. H. Helson, ed. N. Y., Van Nostrand. [830]

— 1953. Mice, monkeys, men, and motives. *Ps Rev* 60, 23-32. [637]

—, Harlow, M. K., Meyer, D. R. 1950. Learning motivated by a manipulation drive. *J exp Ps* 40, 228-234. [685]

—, Settlage, P. H. 1934. Comparative behavior of primates. VII. Capacity of monkeys to solve patterned string tests. *J comp Ps* 18, 423-435. [820]

Harlow, M. K. *See* Harlow, H. F. 1950.

Harmon, F. L. 1933. The effects of noise upon certain psychological and physiological processes. *Arch Ps N.Y.* #147. [87]

Harper, P. *See* Granit, R. 1930.

Harper, R. S., Boring, E. G. 1948. Cues. *Amer J Ps* 61, 119-123. [268]

—, Stevens, S. S. 1948. A psychological scale of weight and a formula for its derivation. *Amer J Ps* 61, 343-351. [242]

Harriman, A. E. *See* Ross, S. 1949.

Harris, B. L. *See* Dawson, E. H. 1951.

Harris, D. *See* Conrad, H. S. 1931.

Harris, J. D. 1941. Forward conditioning, backward conditioning, pseudo-conditioning, and adaptation to the conditioned stimulus. *J exp Ps* 28, 491-502. [570]

— 1948. *Some relations between vision and audition.* (Prog Rept #1, Project NM 000-009). New London, Conn. Naval Med Res Dept.

— 1952. Pitch discrimination. *J acoust Soc Amer* 24, 750-755. [222]

—, Rawnsley, A. I., Kelsey, P. 1951. Studies in short-duration auditory fatigue. I. Frequency differences as a function of intensity. *J exp Ps* 42, 430-436. [336]

— *See also* Rawnsley, A. I. 1952.

Harris, L. J., Clay, J., Hargreaves, F. J., Ward, A. 1933. Appetite and choice of diet. The ability of the vitamin B deficient rat to discriminate between diets containing and lacking the vitamin. *Proc R Soc B* 113, 161-190. [638]

Harris, R. F. *See* Cook, S. W. 1937.

Harter, N. *See* Bryan, W. L. 1897, 1899.

Hartline, H. K. 1934. Intensity and duration in the excitation of single photoreceptor units. *J cell comp Phys* 5, 229-247. [374]

— 1938. The response of single optic nerve fibers of the vertebrate eye to illumination of the retina. *Amer J Phys* 121, 400-415. [27]

Hastorf, A. H. 1950. The influence of suggestion on the relationship between stimulus size and perceived distance. *J Ps* 29, 195-217. [491]

— *See also* Cantril, H. 1949.

Hauer, P. 1926. Die Kaltempfindlichkeit der Genitalien. *Z Biol* 85, 265-274. [279]

Hausen, L. 1933. Das inhaltliche Gedächtnis. *Arch ges Ps* 88, 635-683. [717]

Haycraft, J. B. 1889. The objective cause of sensation. Part III. The sense of smell. *Brain* 11, 166-178. [319, 320]

Hayes, C. *See* Hayes, K. J. 1953.

Hayes, K. J. 1953. Anoxic and convulsive amnesia in rats. *J comp phys Ps* 46, 216-217. [773]

—, Thompson, R., Hayes, C. 1953. Discrimination learning set in chimpanzees. *J comp phys Ps* 46, 99-104. [760]

Hayes, S. P. 1935. Facial vision or the sense of obstacles. *Perkins Publ* 12, 1-45. [360]

— 1941. *Contributions to a psychology of blindness.* N. Y., Amer Foundation for the Blind. [360]

Hazzard, F. W. 1930. A descriptive account of odors. *J exp Ps* 13, 297-331. [309]

Head, H., Rivers, W. H. R., *et al.* 1920. *Studies in neurology.* 1, 55-65, 225-339. 2, 810-832. Lond., Frowde. [281]

Heath, L. L. *See* Darrow, C. W. 1932.

Heathers, G. L. 1940. The avoidance of repetition of a maze reaction in the rat as a function of the time interval between trials. *J Ps* 10, 359-380. [622]

Hebb, D. O. 1946. Emotion in man and animal: An analysis of the intuitive processes of recognition. *Ps Rev* 53, 88-106. [123, 124]

— 1949. *The organization of behavior.* N. Y., Wiley. [110, 403, 411, 426]

—, Foord, E. N. 1945. Errors of visual recognition and the nature of the trace. *J exp Ps* 35, 335-348. [775, 776]

—, Williams, K. 1946. A method of rating animal intelligence. *J genl Ps* 34, 59-65. [631]

Hecht, M. *See* Graham, C. H. 1948.

Hecht, S. 1921. The nature of foveal dark adaptation. *J genl Phys* 4, 113-139. [369, 370]

— 1928. On the binocular fusion of colors and its relation to theories of color vision. *Proc Natl Acad Sci* 14, 237-241. [401]

— 1934. Vision. II. The nature of the photoreceptor process. *Handbk genl exp Ps* 704-828. C. Murchison, ed. Worcester, Clark Univ Press. [366, 370, 371, 381, 385]

— 1944. Energy and vision. *Amer Scient* 32 159-177. [377]

—, Chase, A. M., Shlaer, S., Haig, C. 1936. The regeneration of visual purple in solution. *Science* 84, 331-333. [371]

—, Hsia, Yun. 1945. Dark adaptation following light adaptation to red and white lights. *J opt Soc Amer* 35, 261-267. [370]

—, Mandelbaum, J. 1938. Rod-cone dark adap

tation and vitamin A. *Science* 88, 219-221. [371]
——, Mintz, E. U. 1939. The visibility of single lines at various illuminations and the retinal basis of visual resolution. *J genl Phys* 22, 593-612. [384, 385]
——, Shlaer, S., Pirenne, M. H. 1942. Energy, quanta, and vision. *J genl Phys* 25, 819-840. [371, 377]
Heidbreder, E. 1924. An experimental study of thinking. *Arch Ps N.Y.* #73. [609, 821]
—— 1947. The attainment of concepts. III. The process. *J Ps* 24, 93-138. [612]
—— 1948a. The attainment of concepts. VI. Exploratory experiments on conceptualization at perceptual levels. *J Ps* 26, 193-216. [611]
—— 1948b. Studying human thinking. *Methods of psychology* 96-123. T. E. Andrews. ed. N. Y., Wiley. [815]
Heider, G. M. 1932. New studies in transparency, form, and color. *Ps Forsch* 17, 13-55. [452]
Heine, R. 1914. Über Wiedererkennen und rückwirkende Hemmung. *Z Ps* 68, 161-236. [769]
Heineman, C. *See* Schlosberg, H. 1950.
Heiser, F. 1932. Stimulus temperature and thermal sensation. *Arch Ps N.Y.* #138. [276]
Helmholtz, H. v. 1850. Über die Methoden, kleinste Zeittheile zu messen, und ihre Anwendung für physiologische Zwecke. Trans. On the methods of measuring very small portions of time, and their application to physiological processes. *Philos Mag* 1853, 2. 4, 6, 313-325. [10]
—— 1856–1866. *Handbuch der physiologischen Optik*. Trans. J. P. C. Southall, 1924–1925. 3 Vols. Rochester, N. Y., Opt Soc of Amer. [383, 389, 428, 461, 470, 489, 497]
—— 1863 & 1865. 1912. *Die Lehre von den Tonempfindungen als physiologische Grundlage für die Theorie der Musik*. Braunschweig, F. Wieweg. *On the sensations of tone*. N. Y., Longmans, Green. [327, 339, 340, 344]
—— 1896. Vorträge und Reden. Vol 1. Braunschweig, Vieweg. [838]
Helmick, J. S. *See* Seashore, R. H. 1941.
Helson, H. 1938. Fundamental problems in color vision. The principle governing changes in hue, saturation, and lightness of non-selective samples in chromatic illumination. *J exp Ps* 23, 439-476. [448]
—— 1947. Adaptation-level as frame of reference for prediction of psychophysical data. *Amer J Ps* 60, 1-29. [231, 233]
—— 1948. Adaptation-level as a basis for a quantitative theory of frames of reference. *Ps Rev* 55, 297-313. [149]
——, Fehrer, E. V. 1932. The rôle of form in perception. *Amer J Ps* 44, 79-102. [407]
——, Jeffers, V. B. 1940. Fundamental problems in color vision. II. Hue, lightness, and saturation of selective samples in chromatic illumination. *J exp Ps* 26, 1-27. [448]
—— *See also* Guilford, J. P. 1929; Michels, W. C. 1949; Shaad, D. J. 1931.
Henderson, E. N. 1903. Memory for connected trains of thought. *Ps Monogr* #23. [697, 774]
Henderson, L. F. *See* Crocker, E. C. 1927.
Henderson, M. T., Crews, A., Barlow, J. 1945. A study of the effect of music distraction on reading efficiency. *J appl Ps* 29, 313-317. [87]
Henmon, V. A. C. 1906. The time of perception as a measure of differences in sensations. *Arch Philos Ps sci Meth N.Y.* #8. [33, 262]
—— 1917. The relation between learning and retention and amount to be learned. *J exp Ps* 2, 476-484. [706]
Henneman, R. H. 1935. A photometric study of the perception of object color. *Arch Ps N.Y.* #179. [444, 446]
Henning, H. 1915–1916. Der Geruch. I, II, III, IV. *Z Ps* 73, 161-257; 74, 305-434; 75, 177-230; 76, 1-127. [305, 306]
—— 1924. *Der Geruch*. Leip., Barth. [305, 306, 308, 311, 320]
—— 1927. Psychologische Studien am Geschmacksinn. *Handbh biol Arbeitsmeth* 6 A. [300]
Henri, V. *See* Binet, A. 1894.
Henry, F. M. 1951. Increase in speed of movement by motivation and by transfer of motivated improvement. *Res Q Amer Ass Hlth* 22, 219-228. [736]
Henschel, A. *See* Keys, A. 1950.
Hering, E. 1861–1864. *Beiträge zur Physiologie* Leip., Engelmann. [459]
—— 1874. Zur Lehre vom Lichtsinn. *Wein Akad Wiss Sitzbr* 69 (3), 85-104. [389, 429, 449]
—— 1876. Zur Lehre von der Beziehung zwischen Leib und Seele. I. Über Fechner's psychophysisches Gesetz. *Wien Akad Wiss Sitzbr* 72 (3), 310-348. [429, 449]
—— 1877. Grundzüge einer Theorie des Temperatursinns. *Wien Akad Wiss Sitzbr* 75 (3), 101-135. [288]
—— 1879. Der Raumsinn und die Bewegungen des Auges. *Handbh Phys* 3, 343-601. L. Hermann, ed. Leip., Vogel. [429]
—— 1907, 1920. *Grundzüge der Lehre vom Lichtsinn*. 1st ed, Leip., Engelmann; 2d ed, Berlin, Springer. [389, 429, 432]
Hermanides, J. 1909. *Over de constanten der in der olfaktometrie gebruikelijke negen standaardgeuren*. Thesis. Utrecht. [315]
Hermann, L. 1890. Phonophotographische Untersuchungen. *Pflüg Arch ges Phys* 47, 44-53. [340]
Heron, W. T. 1930. The test-retest reliability of rat learning scores from the multiple T-maze. *J genet Ps* 38, 101-113. [620]
—— 1949. Internal stimuli and learning. *J comp phys Ps* 42, 486-492. [645]
Herrmann, J. 1926. Gesamterlebnisse bei Gerüchen. *Neue ps St* 1, 473-506. [309]
Hess, E. H. 1950. Development of the chick's response to light and shade cues of depth. *J comp Phys Ps* 43, 112-122. [463]
Heymans, G. 1896. Quantitative Untersuchungen über das "optische Paradoxon". *Z Ps* 9, 221-255. [419, 420, 422]
—— 1897. Quantitative Untersuchungen über die

Zöllnersche und die Loebsche Täuschung. *Z Ps* 14, 101-139. [419]

Heyninx, A. 1919. *Essai d'olfactique physiologique.* Thèse, Bruxelles. [320]

Hicks, V. C., Carr, H. 1912. Human reactions in a maze. *J Animal Beh* 2, 98-125. [647]

Higginson, G. D. 1937. Maze learning with knowledge of pattern similarity. *J exp Ps* 20, 223-243. [620, 649]

—— 1938. A comparative study of maze learning with and without knowledge of pattern similarity. *J genl Ps* 18, 63-78. [749]

Hilgard, E. R. 1936. The nature of the conditioned response. I. The case for and against stimulus substitution. *Ps Rev* 43, 366-385. [552, 570]

—— 1938. A summary and evaluation of alternative procedures for the construction of Vincent curves. *Ps Bull* 35, 282-297. [535]

—— 1948. *Theories of learning.* N. Y., Appleton-Century-Crofts. [46, 540, 545, 556]

—— 1951. Methods and procedures in the study of learning. *Handbk exp Ps* 517-567. S. S. Stevens, ed. N. Y., Wiley. [539, 702]

——, Campbell, A. A. 1936. The course of acquisition and retention of conditioned eyelid responses in man. *J exp Ps* 19, 227-247. [562, 575]

——, ——, Sears, W. N. 1937. Conditioned discrimination: the development of discrimination with and without verbal report. *Amer J Ps* 49, 564-580. [580]

——, ——, —— 1938. Conditioned discrimination: the effect of knowledge of stimulus-relationships. *Amer J Ps* 51, 498-506. [579, 580]

——, Humphreys, L. G. 1938a. The effect of supporting and antagonistic voluntary instructions on conditioned discrimination. *J exp Ps* 22, 291-304. [575]

——, —— 1938b. The retention of conditioned discrimination in man. *J genl Ps* 19, 111-125. [732]

——, Marquis, D. G. 1935. Acquisition, extinction, and retention of conditioned lid responses to light in dogs. *J comp Ps* 19, 29-58. [543, 560, 562, 575]

——, —— 1936. Conditioned eyelid responses in monkeys, with a comparison of dog, monkey, and man. *Ps Monogr* #212. [575]

——, —— 1940. *Conditioning and learning.* N. Y., Appleton-Century-Crofts. [544, 553, 557, 571, 573, 581]

Hillebrand, F. 1894. Das Verhältnis von Accommodation und Konvergenz zur Tiefenlokalisation. *Z Ps* 7, 97-151. [475]

—— 1902. Theorie der scheinbaren Grösse bei binocularem Sehen. *Wien Denkschr Akad Wiss (Math. Nat. Kl.)* 72, 255-307. [483]

Hillegas, M. B. 1912. A scale for the measurement of quality in English composition by young people. *Teach Coll Rec* 13, 4, 5-55. [260]

Hirsch, A. 1861-1864. Expériences chronoscopiques sur la vitesse des différentes sensations et de la transmission nerveuse. *Soc Sci natl Bull* 6, 100-114. [10, 16]

Hirsch, M. J., Horowitz, M., Weymouth, F. W. 1948. Distance discrimination. III. Effect of rod width on threshold. *Arch Ophth* 39, 325-332. [471]

Hoagland, H. *See* Adrian, E. D. 1931; Cattell, J. McK. 1931.

Hoaglin, L. W. *See* Fairbanks, G. 1941.

Hobhouse, L. T. 1901. *Mind in evolution.* N. Y., Macmillan. [585, 819]

Hochheimer, W. *See* Galli, A. 1934.

Hoffman, A. C. 1946. Eye-movements during prolonged reading. *J exp Ps* 36, 95-118. [497]

——, Wellman, B., Carmichael, L. 1939. A quantitative comparison of electrical and photographic techniques of eye-movement recording. *J exp Ps* 24, 40-53. [496]

—— *See also* Beebe-Center, J. G. 1948.

Hoffmann, J. 1927. Experimentell-psychologische Untersuchungen über Leseleistungen von Schulkindern. *Arch ges Ps* 58, 325-388. [102]

Hoisington, L. B. *See* Wells, E. F. 1931.

Hollingworth, H. L. 1909. The inaccuracy of movement. *Arch Ps N.Y.* #13. [230]

—— 1910. The central tendency of judgment. *J Philos Ps sci Meth* 7, 461-469. [230]

—— 1911a. Judgments of the comic. *Ps Rev* 18, 132-156. [257]

—— 1911b. Judgments of persuasiveness. *Ps Rev* 18, 234-256. [257]

—— 1912. The influence of caffein on mental and motor efficiency. *Arch Ps N.Y.* #22. [38]

—— 1914a. Professor Cattell's studies by the method of relative position. *Arch Ps N.Y.* #30. [257]

—— 1914b. Variations in efficiency during the working day. *Ps Rev* 21, 473-491. [804]

—— 1939. Perceptual fluctuation as a fatigue index. *J exp Ps* 24, 511-519. [77]

Holm, K. G. 1903. Die Dauer der Temperaturempfindung bei constanter Reiztemperatur. *Arch Phys Skand* 14, 242-258. [289]

Holston, R. P. 1951. Some effects of motivation on visual discrimination. *Amer Psychol* 6, 318. [689]

Holt, E. B. 1903. Eye-movement and central anaesthesia. I. The problem of anaesthesia during eye-movement. *Ps Monogr* #17. [502]

—— 1931. *Animal drive and the learning process.* N. Y., Holt. [178]

Holway, A. H., Boring, E. G. 1941. Determinants of apparent visual size with distance variant. *Amer J Ps* 54, 21-37. [480, 481, 485]

——, Hurvich, L. M. 1937. Differential gustatory sensitivity to salt. *Amer J Ps* 49, 37-48. [302]

—— *See also* Zigler, M. J. 1935.

Honzik, C. H. 1931. Delayed reaction in rats. *Calif U Publ Ps* 4, 307-318. [606]

—— 1933. Maze learning in rats in the absence of specific intra- and extra-maze stimuli. *Calif U Publ Ps* 6, 99-144. [628, 633]

—— 1936. The sensory basis of maze learning in rats. *Comp Ps Monogr* #64. [616, 618]
—— *See also* Tolman, E. C. 1930.
Hopkins, P. S. *See* Goldmark, M. D. 1920.
Horenstein, B. R. *See* Kimble, G. A. 1948.
Hornbostel, E. M. v. 1923. Beobachtungen über ein- und zweiohriges Hören. *Ps Forsch* 4, 64-114. [359]
——, Wertheimer, M. 1920. Über die Wahrnehmung der Schallrichtung. *Akad Wiss Berlin. Preuss Sitzber*, 388-396. [355]
Horowitz, M. *See* Hirsch, M. J. 1948.
Horton, G. P. 1934. The effect of intense and prolonged acoustical stimulation on the auditory sensitivity of guinea pigs. *J comp Ps* 18, 408-417. [348]
—— 1935. An experimental study of stimulation deafness in guinea pigs. *Ann Otol Rhino Laryng* 44, 252-259. [348]
—— *See also* Guthrie, E. R. 1946.
Hoskins, A. B. 1936. The effectiveness of the part and the whole methods of study. *George Peabody Cont Educ* #189. [783]
House, B. J. *See* Zeaman, D. 1951.
Hovey, H. B. 1928. Effects of general distraction on the higher thought processes. *Amer J Ps* 40, 585-591. [84]
Hovland, C. I. 1936a. The influence of adaptation illumination upon visual reaction time. *J genl Ps* 14, 346-359. [25]
—— 1936b. "Inhibition of reinforcement" and phenomena of experimental extinction. *Proc Natl Acad Sci* 22, 430-433. [562, 563]
—— 1937a. The generalization of conditioned responses. I. The sensory generalization of conditioned responses with varying frequencies of tone. *J genl Ps* 17, 125-148. [577]
—— 1937b. The generalization of conditioned responses. II. The sensory generalization of conditioned responses with varying intensities of tone. *J genet Ps* 51, 279-291. [545, 577]
—— 1938. Experimental studies in rote-learning theory. III. Distribution of practice with varying speeds of syllable presentation. *J exp Ps* 23, 172-190. [712, 794, 796]
—— 1939. Experimental studies in rote-learning theory. V. Comparison of distribution of practice in serial and paired-associate learning. *J exp Ps* 25, 622-633. [797]
—— 1940. Experimental studies in rote-learning theory. VI. Comparison of retention following learning to same criterion by massed and distributed practice. *J exp Ps* 26, 568-587. [793]
—— 1949. Experimental studies in rote-learning theory. VIII. Distributed practice of paired-associates with varying rates of presentation. *J exp Ps* 39, 714-718. [794]
—— 1951. Human learning and retention. *Handbk exp Ps* 613-689. S. S. Stevens, ed. N. Y. Wiley. [714, 731, 797]
——, Kurtz, K. H. 1951. Experimental studies in rote-learning theory. IX. Influence of work-decrement factors on verbal learning. *J exp Ps* 42, 265-272. [797]
——, —— 1952. Experimental studies in rote-learning theory. X. Pre-learning syllable familiarization and the length-difficulty relationship. *J exp Ps* 44, 31-39. [758]
——, Lumsdaine, A. A., Sheffield, F. D. 1949. *Experiments on mass communication*. Princeton, Princeton Univ Press. [781]
——, Riesen, A. H. 1940. Magnitude of galvanic and vasomotor response as a function of stimulus intensity. *J genl Ps* 23, 103-121. [150, 182]
—— *See also* Hull, C. L. 1940.
Howard, H. J. 1919. A test for the judgment of distance. *Amer J Ophth* 2, 656-675. [470]
Howes, D. H., Solomon, R. L. 1950. A note on McGinnies' "Emotionality and Perceptual Defense." *Ps Rev* 57, 229-234. [158]
—— *See also* Solomon, R. L. 1951.
Hsia, Y. 1943. Whiteness constancy as a function of difference in illumination. *Arch Ps N.Y.* #284. [441, 449]
——, Graham, C. H. 1951. Spectral sensitivity of the cones in the dark adapted human eye. *Proc Natl Acad Sci* 38, 80-85. [389]
—— *See also* Hecht, S. 1945.
Huang, I. 1944. Experimental studies on the role of repetition, organization, and the intention to learn in rote memory. *J genl Ps* 31, 213-217. [711]
——, Chang, C. 1935. Identical elements and transfer of maze learning. *Chung Hwa educ Rev* 23, 55-65. (*See Ps Abst* 1936, 10. #4944.) [751]
Hubbard, L. M. 1924. Complex signs in diagnostic free association. *J exp Ps* 7, 342-357. [69]
Hudgins, C. V. 1933. Conditioning and the voluntary control of the pupillary light reflex. *J genl Ps* 8, 3-51. [575]
—— 1935. Steckle and Renshaw on the conditioned iridic reflex: a discussion. *J genl Ps* 12, 208-214. [576]
—— *See also* Hunter, W. S. 1934.
Huey, E. B. 1908. *The psychology and pedagogy of reading*. N. Y., Macmillan. [494, 508]
Hughes, B., Schlosberg, H. 1938. Conditioning in the white rat. IV. The conditioned lid reflex. *J exp Ps* 23, 641-650. [575]
Hughes, J. W. 1940. The upper frequency limit for the binaural localization of a pure tone by phase difference. *Proc R Soc B* 128, 293-305. [356]
Hugony, A. 1935. Über dis Empfindung von Schwingungen mittels des Tastsinnes. *Z Biol* 96, 548-553. [295]
Hulin, W. S. 1935. The effect on tactual localization of movement during stimulation. *J exp Ps* 18, 97-105. [291]
——, Katz, D. 1935. The Frois-Wittmann pictures of facial expression. *J exp Ps* 18, 482-498. [116, 118]

Hull, C. L. 1920. Quantitative aspects of the evolution of concepts. *Ps Monogr* #123. [610]

—— 1932. The goal gradient hypothesis and maze learning. *Ps Rev* 39, 25-43. [622, 636]

—— 1933a. The meaningfulness of 320 selected nonsense syllables. *Amer J Ps* 45, 730-734. [702]

—— 1933b. Differential habituation to internal stimuli in the albino rat. *J comp Ps* 16, 255-273. [631]

—— 1934a. The concept of the habit-family hierarchy and maze learning. *Ps Rev* 41, 33-52, 134-152. [646]

—— 1934b. The factor of the conditioned reflex. *Handbk genl exp Ps* 382-455. C. Murchison, ed. Worcester, Clark Univ Press. [538]

—— 1935. The conflicting psychologies of learning—a way out. *Ps Rev* 42, 491-516. [702, 711]

—— 1942. Conditioning: outline of a systematic theory of learning. *Natl Soc St Educ 41 Yrbk* 61-95. [37, 553]

—— 1943. *Principles of behavior*. N. Y., Appleton-Century. [4, 538, 539, 544, 551, 571, 578, 579, 593, 636, 637, 655, 668, 678, 789, 798]

—— 1947. The problem of primary stimulus generalization. *Ps Rev* 54, 120-134. [580]

—— 1949. Stimulus intensity dynamism (*V*) and stimulus generalization. *Ps Rev* 56, 67-76. [24, 48, 261]

—— 1950a. Behavior postulates and corollaries—1949. *Ps Rev* 57, 173-180. [544, 559, 655, 679]

—— 1950b. Simple qualitative discrimination learning. *Ps Rev* 57, 303-313. [544, 586, 593]

—— 1951. *Essentials of behavior*. New Haven, Yale Univ Press. [4, 48, 544, 559, 593, 655, 669, 671, 679, 789, 795]

——, Felsinger, J. M., Gladstone, A. I., Yamaguchi, H. G. 1947. A proposed quantification of habit strength. *Ps Rev* 54, 237-254. [539]

——, Hovland, C. I., et al. 1940. *Mathematico-deductive theory of rote learning*. New Haven, Yale Univ Press. [711, 795]

——, Lugoff, L. S. 1921. Complex signs in diagnostic free association. *J exp Ps* 4, 111-136. [69]

——, Spence, K. W. 1938. "Correction" vs. "non-correction" method of trial and error learning in rats. *J comp Ps* 25, 127-145. [625]

—— *See also* Bass, M. J. 1934; Gladstone, A. I. 1947.

Hummel, E. 1926. Die Veränderung des Systemes der Temperaturempfindungen durch die Adaptation. *Arch ges Ps* 57, 305-394. [292]

Humphrey, G. 1928. The effect of sequences of indifferent stimuli on a reaction of the conditioned response type. *J abnor soc Ps* 22, 194-212. [580]

—— 1930. Extinction and negative adaptation. *Ps Rev* 37, 361-363. [559]

—— 1933. *The nature of learning in its relation to the living system*. Lond., Paul. [illegible]

—— 1951. *Thinking: an introduction to its experimental psychology*. Lond., Methuen. [816]

Humphreys, L. G. 1939a. The effect of random alternation of reinforcement on the acquisition and extinction of conditioned eyelid reactions. *J exp Ps* 25, 141-158. [564]

—— 1939b. Acquisition and extinction of verbal expectations in a situation analogous to conditioning. *J exp Ps*, 25, 294-301.

—— 1939c. Generalization as a function of the method of reinforcement. *J exp Ps* 25, 361-372. [577]

—— 1940. Extinction of conditioned psychogalvanic responses following two conditions of reinforcement. *J exp Ps* 27, 71-75. [564]

—— 1943a. Measures of strength of conditioned eyelid responses. *J genl Ps* 29, 101-111. [544, 575]

—— *See also* Hilgard, E. R. 1938a, b.

Hunt, H. F., Brady, J. V. 1951. Some effects of electro-convulsive shock on a conditioned emotional response ("anxiety"). *J comp phys Ps* 44, 88-98. [772]

——, Jernberg, P., Lawlor, W. G. 1953. The effect of electroconvulsive shock on a conditioned emotional response: the effect of electroconvulsive shock under ether anesthesia. *J comp phys Ps* 46, 64-68. [772]

Hunt, J. McV., ed. 1944. *Personality and the behavior disorders*. 2 vols. N. Y., Ronald. [70]

Hunt, W. A. 1941. Anchoring effects in judgment. *Amer J Ps* 54, 395-403. [250]

——, Volkmann, J. 1937. The anchoring of an affective scale. *Amer J Ps* 49, 88-92. [280]

—— *See also* Cantril, H. 1932; Landis, C. 1935, 1939.

Hunter, T. A. *See* Travis, L. E. 1931.

Hunter, W. S. 1913. The delayed reaction in animals and children. *Beh Monogr* #6. [604]

—— 1914. The after-effect of visual motion. *Ps Rev* 21, 245-277. [516]

—— 1915. Retinal factors in visual after-movement. *Ps Rev* 22, 479-489. [516]

—— 1917. Delayed reaction in a child. *Ps Rev* 24, 74-87. [606]

—— 1920. The temporal maze and kinaesthetic sensory processes in the white rat. *Psbiol* 2, 1-17. [627, 628]

—— 1922. Habit interference in the white rat and in human subjects. *J comp Ps* 2, 29-[illegible] [748]

—— 1928. The behavior of raccoons in a double alternation temporal maze. *J genet Ps* 35, 37[illegible]-388. [628]

—— 1934. Experimental studies of learning. *Handbk genl exp Ps* 497-570. C. Murchison, ed. Worcester, Clark Univ Press. [538]

—— 1935. Conditioning and extinction in the rat. *Br J Ps* 26, 135-148. [555]

—— 1942. Visually controlled learning as a function of time and intensity of stimulation. *J exp Ps* 31, 423-429. [97]

——, Hudgins, C. V. 1934. Voluntary activity from the standpoint of behaviorism. *J genl Ps* [illegible] 198-201. [576]

——, Nagge, J.W. 1931. The white rat and [illegible]

double alternation temporal maze. *J genet Ps* 39, 303-319. [628]

——, Sigler, M. 1940. The span of visual discrimination as a function of time and intensity of stimulation. *J exp Ps.*26, 160-179. [95 f, 376]

—— *See also* Lindsley, D. B. 1939; McCrary, J. W. 1953; Prosser, C. L. 1936.

Hurvich, L. M., Jameson, D. 1951. The binocular fusion of yellow in relation to color theories. *Science* 114, 199-202. [363, 401]

—— *See also* Holway, A. H. 1937.

Husband, R. W. 1931. Comparative behavior on different types of mazes. *J genl Ps* 5, 234-244. [620, 652, 653]

—— 1947. Positive transfer as a factor in memory. *Proc Iowa Acad Sci* 54, 235-238. [750]

I

Imus, H. A., Rothney, J. W. M., Bear, R. M. 1943. Photography of eye movements. *Amer J Optom* 20, 231-247. [509]

Inbau, F. E. 1942, 1948. *Lie detection and criminal interrogation.* Balt., Williams & Wilkins. [186, 190]

Ingebritsen, O. C. 1932. Maze learning after lesion in the cervical cord. *J comp Ps* 14, 279-294. [616]

Inglis, E. *See* Willey, C. F. 1937.

Ipsen, G. 1926a. Über Gestaltaufassung. Erörterung des Sanderschen Parallelogramms. *Neu. ps St* 1, 167-278. [230, 419, 420]

Irion, A. L., Gustafson, L. M. 1952. "Reminiscence" in bilateral transfer. *J exp Ps* 43, 321-323. [736]

—— *See also* McGeoch, J. A. 1952.

Irwin, F. W., Seidenfeld, M. A. 1937. The application of the method of comparison to the problem of memory change. *J exp Ps* 21, 363-381. [775, 776]

Irwin, J. M. *See* Melton, A. W. 1940.

Ishihara, S. 1920. *Series of plates designed as tests for color blindness.* Tokyo. Chic., C. S. Stoelting. [395]

Isihara, I. 1951. The process of retroactive inhibition in retention. *Jap J Ps* 21 (3/4), 18-23. [767]

Israel, H. C. *See* Rees, H. J. 1935.

Ittelson, W. H. 1951. Size as a cue to distance; static localization. *Amer J Ps* 64, 54-67. [485]

—— 1952. *The Ames demonstrations in perception.* Princeton, Princeton Univ Press. [488, 490]

——, Ames, A., Jr. 1950. Accommodation, convergence, and their relation to apparent distance. *J Ps* 30, 43-62. [478]

—— *See also* Cantril, H. 1949.

J

Jack, O. *See* Marks, M. R. 1952.

Jackson, L. L. 1943. VTE on an elevated maze. *J comp Ps* 36, 99-107. [603]

Jackson, T. A. 1932. General factors in transfer of training in the white rat. *Genet Ps Monog* 11, 1-59. [751]

Jacobs, J. 1887. Experiments on "prehension." *Mind* 12, 75-79. [696]

Jacobson, E. 1932. The electrophysiology of mental activities. *Amer J Ps* 44, 677-694. [178, 816]

—— 1938. *Progressive relaxation.* Chic., Univ Chicago Press. [173, 178]

—— 1939. The neurovoltmeter. *Amer J Ps* 52, 620-624. [177]

—— 1940. An integrating voltmeter for the study of nerve and muscle potentials. *Rev sci Instr* 11, 415-418. [177]

—— 1951. Muscular tension and the estimation of effort. *Amer J Ps* 64, 112-117. [177, 178]

Jaensch, E. R. 1920. Zur Methodik experimenteller Untersuchungen an optischen Anschauungsbildern. *Z Ps* 85, 37-82. [722]

James, H. E. O. 1930. The transfer of training. *Br J Ps* 20, 322-332. [746]

James, W. 1884. What is an emotion? *Mind* 9, 188-205. [107]

—— 1890. *Principles of psychology.* 2 vols. N. Y., Holt. [107, 514, 719, 743]

James, W. T. *See* Liddell, H. S. 1934.

Jameson, D. *See* Hurvich, L. M. 1951.

Janis, I. L., Frick, F. 1943. The relationship between attitudes toward conclusions and errors in judging logical validity of syllogisms. *J exp Ps* 33, 73-77. [848]

Jasper, H. H., Andrews, H. L. 1936. Human brain rhythms. I. Recording techniques and preliminary results. *J genl Ps* 14, 98-126. [13]

——, Walker, R. Y. 1931. The Iowa eye-movement camera. *Science* 74, 291-294. [495]

Jastrow, J., Cairnes, W. B. 1891–1892. The interference of mental processes—a preliminary survey. *Amer J Ps* 4, 219-223. [88]

Javal, L. E. 1878. Essai sur la Physiologie de la Lecture. *Ann D'Oculistique* 82, 242-253. [493, 504]

Jeffers, V. B. *See* Helson, H. 1940.

Jeffress, L. A. 1928. Galvanic phenomena of the skin. *J exp Ps* 11, 130-144. [138]

—— 1940. The pitch of complex tones. *Amer J Ps* 53, 240-250, [339]

Jenkins, J. G., Dallenbach, K. M. 1924. Oblivescence during sleep and waking. *Amer J Ps* 35, 605-612. [768]

Jenkins, T. N. 1926. Facilitation and inhibition. *Arch Ps N.Y.* #86. [15, 27, 39]

——, Warner, L. H., Warden, C. J. 1926. Standard apparatus for the study of animal motivation. *J comp Ps* 6, 361-382. Reprinted: C. J. Warden, 1931. [662]

—— *See also* Warden, C. J. 1935.

Jenkins, W. L. 1937. Adaptation in isolated cold spots. *Amer J Ps* 49, 1-22. [292]

——. 1938a. Studies in thermal sensitivity. 3. Adaptation with a series of small annular stimulators. 4. Minor contributions. 5. The reactions of untrained subjects to simultaneous warm ⊥ cold stimulation. 6. The reactions of untrained subjects to simultaneous warm + cold + electric shock. *J exp Ps* 22, 164-177, 178-185, 451-461, 564-572. [292]

—— 1938b, c. Studies in thermal sensitivity. 7. Further synthetic evidence against the Alrutz theory. 8. Analytic evidence against the Alrutz theory. *J exp Ps* 23, 411-416, 417-422. [283]

—— 1939. Nafe's vascular theory and the preponderance of evidence. *Amer J Ps* 52, 462-465. [293]

—— 1940. Studies in thermal sensitivity. 14. Part-whole relations in seriatim warm-mapping. *J exp Ps* 27, 76-80. [284, 285]

—— 1941. Studies in thermal sensitivity. 16. Further evidence on the effects of stimulus temperature. *J exp Ps* 29, 413-419. [284]

—— 1951. Somesthesis. *Handbk exp Ps* 1172-1190. S. S. Stevens, ed. N. Y., Wiley. [285, 293]

Jenkins, W. O. 1950. A temporal gradient of derived reinforcement. *Amer J Ps* 63, 237-243. [680]

——, Postman, L. 1949. An experimental analysis of set in rote learning. Retroactive inhibition as a function of changing set. *J exp Ps* 39, 69-72. [766]

——, Stanley, J. C., Jr. 1950. Partial reinforcement: a review and critique. *Ps Bull* 47, 193-234. [564]

—— *See also* Nissen, H. W. 1943.

Jensen, E. M., Reese, E. P., Reese, T. W. 1950. The subitizing and counting of visually presented fields of dots. *J Ps* 30, 363-392. [99]

Jensen, M. B., Lemaire, A. 1937. Ten experiments on whole and part learning. *J educ Ps* 28, 37-54. [784]

Jernberg, P. *See* Hunt, H. F. 1953.

Jerome, E. A. 1942. Olfactory thresholds measured in terms of stimulus pressure and volume. *Arch Ps N.Y.* #274. [314]

——, Proshansky, H. 1950. Factors in the assay and use of guidance devices. *Blindness: modern approaches to the unseen environment* 462-494. P. A. Zahl, ed. Princeton, Princeton Univ Press. [361]

Jersild, A. T. 1927. Mental set and shift. *Arch Ps N.Y.* #89. [835]

—— 1929. Primacy, recency, frequency, vividness. *J exp Ps* 12, 58-70. [732]

Jevons, W. S. 1871. The power of numerical discrimination. *Nature* 3, 281-282. [90, 92]

Johannsen, D. E. 1930. A quantitative study of binocular color vision. *J genl Ps* 4, 282-308. [401]

Johanson, A. M. 1922. The influence of incentive and punishment upon reaction-time. *Arch Ps N.Y.* #54. [28]

Johnson, D. M. 1939. Confidence and speed in the two-category judgment. *Arch Ps N.Y.* #241. [262, 263]

—— 1944a. Generalization of a scale of values by the averaging of practice effects. *J exp Ps* 34, 425-436. [231, 248]

—— 1944b. A modern account of problem solving. *Ps Bull* 41, 201-229. [830]

Johnson, E. P. 1949. The electrical response of the human retina during dark-adaptation. *J exp Ps* 39, 597-609. [373]

—— *See also* Riggs, L. A. 1949.

Johnson, H. M. 1932. Some follies of 'emancipated' psychology. *Ps Rev* 39, 293-323. [728]

——, Swan, T. H. 1930. Sleep. *Ps Bull* 27. [657]

Jonckheere, T. 1939. Le Procédé fragmentaire et le Procédé global dans la technique de la mémorisation. *Centenaire de Th. Ribot* 403-413. Paris, Imprimerie Moderne. [783]

Jones, F. N. 1940. The chronaxy of cold and warmth. *Amer J Ps* 53, 216-228. [282]

——, Jones, M. H. 1941. The chronaxy of pain. *Amer J Ps* 54, 240-242. [282]

—— *See also* Jones, M. H. 1952.

Jones, F. P., Kennedy, J. L. 1951. An electromyographic technique for recording the startle pattern. *J Ps* 32, 63-68. [174, 184, 185]

Jones, H. E. 1928. Conditioned psychogalvanic responses in infants. *Ps Bull* 25, 183-184. [152]

—— 1930a. The galvanic skin reflex in infancy. *Child Devel* 1, 106-110. [144, 152]

—— 1930b. The retention of conditioned emotional reactions in infancy. *J genet Ps* 37, 485-498. [152]

—— 1937. Reaction-time and motor development. *Amer J Ps* 50, 181-194. [36]

—— 1939. Principles and methods of the adolescent growth study. Procedures of the adolescent growth study. *J consult Ps* 3, 157-159, 177-180. [165]

—— 1943. *Development in adolescence.* N. Y., Appleton-Century. [165]

—— 1945. Trial and error learning with differential cues. *J exp Ps* 35, 31-45. [689, 690]

——, Batalla, M. 1944. Transfer in children's maze learning. *J educ Ps* 35, 474-483. [751]

——, Wechsler, D. 1928. Galvanometric technique in studies of association. *Amer J Ps* 40, 607-612. [151, 153]

Jones, H. M. *See* Mowrer, O. H. 1943.

Jones, M. H., Jones, F. N. 1952. The critical frequency of taste. *Science* 115, 355-356. [300]

—— *See also* Jones, F. N. 1941.

Jones, O. R. *See* Grant, D. A. 1949.

Jost, A. 1897. Die Assoziationsfestigkeit in ihrer Abhängigkeit von der Verteilung der Wiederholungen. *Z Ps* 14, 436-472. [561, 699, 730]

Jost, H. *See* Darrow, C. W. 1942.

Judd, C. H. 1897. Some facts of binocular vision. *Ps Rev* 4, 374-389. [477]

—— 1899. A study of geometrical illusions. *Ps Rev* 6, 241-261. [419, 420]

—— 1902. Practice and its effects on the perception of illusions. *Ps Rev* 9, 27-39. [419, 422]

—— 1905. Movement and consciousness. *Ps Monogr* #29. [419, 420, 422, 495]

—— 1907. Photographic records of convergence and divergence. *Ps Monogr* #34. [495, 499, 500]

——, Buswell, G. T. 1922. Silent reading: a

study of various types. *Suppl Educ Monogr* #23. [510]

——, Cowling, D. J. 1907. Studies in perceptual development. *Ps Monogr* #34. [716]

Judd, D. B. 1951. Basic correlates of the visual stimulus. *Handbk exp Ps* 811-867. S. S. Stevens, ed. N. Y., Wiley. [365, 367, 388, 389]

—— *See also* Newhall, S. M. 1943.

Jukes, C. L. 1938. Selection of diet in chicks as influenced by vitamins and other factors. *J comp Ps* 26, 135-156. [658]

Jung, C. G. 1919. *Studies in word-association.* N. Y., Moffat. [54, 59, 60, 67, 68, 69]

——, Riklin, F. 1904. Diagnostische Assoziationstudien. *J Ps Neu* 3, 193-215. [67]

—— *See also* Peterson, F. 1907.

K

Kaempffert, W. 1952. *Science in review.* N. Y. *Times*, Oct. 5, P E. 9. [469]

Kalish, D. 1946. The non-correction method and the delayed response problem of Blodgett and McCutchan. *J comp Ps* 39, 91-108. [625, 634]

—— *See also* Tolman, E. C. 1946a, b; 1947a, b.

Kanner, J. H. *See* Kendler, H. H. 1950.

Kanner, L. 1931. Judging emotions from facial expressions. *Ps Monogr* #186. [107, 118, 126]

Kantor, J. R. *See* Davis, R. C. 1935.

Kaplan, S. J. *See* Gentry, G. 1947.

Karbe, M. *See* Strughold, H. 1925.

Kardos, L. 1929. Die "Konstanz" phänomenaler Dingmomente. *Beitr Problemgeschichte Ps* (Bühler Festschr) 1-77. Jena, Fischer. [432]

—— 1934. Ding und Schatten. *Z Ps Ergbd* #23. [442]

Karn, H. W., Patton, R. A. 1939. The transfer of double alternation behavior acquired in a temporal maze. *J comp Ps* 28, 55-61. [628]

Karslake, J. S. 1940. The Purdue eye-camera. A practical apparatus for studying the attention value of advertisements. *J appl Ps* 24, 417-440. [75]

Karsten, A. 1928. Psychische Sättigung. *Ps Forsch* 10, 142-254. [693]

Karwoski, T. F., Berthold, F., Jr. 1945. Psychological studies in semantics. II. Reliability of the free association tests. *J soc Ps* 22, 87-102. [53, 70]

——, Schachter, J. 1948. Psychological studies in semantics. III. Reaction times for similarity and difference. *J soc Ps* 28, 103-120. [53]

Katona, G. 1929. Zur Analyse der Helligkeitskonstanz. *Ps Forsch* 12, 94-126. [439, 446]

—— 1940. *Organizing and memorizing: Studies in the psychology of learning and teaching.* N. Y., Columbia Univ Press. [746, 828]

Katz, A. *See* Schlosberg, H. 1943.

Katz, D. 1911. Die Erscheinungsweisen der Farben und ihre Beeinflussung durch die individuelle Erfahrung. *Z Ps Ergbd* #7. [429, 430]

—— 1925. Der Aufbau des Tastwelt. *Z Ps Ergbd* #11. [294]

—— 1930. *Der Aufbau der Farbwelt.* 2d ed. Leip., Barth. Trans R. B. Macleod & C. W. Fox, *The world of colour.* Lond., Paul, 1935. [429, 430, 439, 444, 446]

Katz, Daniel. *See* Hulin, W. S. 1935.

Katz, S. H. *See* Allison, V. C. 1919.

Katzell, R. A. 1948. Relations between the activity of muscles during preparatory set and subsequent overt performance. *J Ps* 26, 407-436. [30]

Kaufman, E. L., Lord, M. W., Reese, T. W., Volkmann, J. 1949. The discrimination of visual number. *Amer J Ps* 62, 498-525. [99]

Keller, F. S. 1941. Light-aversion in the white rat. *Ps Rec* 4, 235-250. [678]

—— 1943. Studies in international Morse code. I. A new method of teaching code reception. *J appl Ps* 27, 407-415. [811, 812]

—— 1953. Stimulus discrimination and Morse code learning. *N.Y. Acad Sci Trans* Series 2, 15, 195-203. [813]

——, Schoenfeld, W. N. 1944. Studies in international Morse code. III. The efficiency of the code as related to errors made during learning. *J appl Ps* 28, 254-266. [813]

——, —— 1950. *Principles of psychology.* N. Y., Appleton-Century-Crofts. [680]

——, Taubman, R. E. 1943. Studies in international Morse code. II. Errors made in code reception. *J appl Ps* 27, 504-509. [813]

Kelley, C. M. *See* Wells, F. L. 1922.

Kelley, T. L. 1913. The association experiment: individual differences and correlations. *Ps Rev* 20, 479-504. [53]

Kellogg, L. A. *See* Kellogg, W. N. 1933.

Kellogg, W. N. 1929. An experimental comparison of psychophysical methods. *Arch Ps N.Y.* #106. [200]

—— 1930. An experimental evaluation of equality judgments in psychophysics. *Arch Ps N.Y.* #112. [216]

——, Kellogg, L. A. 1933. *The ape and the child.* N. Y., McGraw-Hill. [821]

——, White, R. E. 1935. A maze test of Dunlap's theory of learning. *J comp Ps* 19, 119-148. [653]

—— *See also* Spooner, A. 1947; Wolf, I. S. 1940.

Kelsey, P. *See* Harris, J. D. 1951.

Kemp, E. H. 1935. A critical review of experiments on the problem of stimulation deafness. *Ps Bull* 32, 325-342. [348]

—— 1936. An experimental investigation of the problem of stimulation deafness. *J exp Ps* 19, 159-171. [348]

——, Coppée, G. E., Robinson, E. H. 1937. Electric responses of the brain stem to unilateral auditory stimulation. *Amer J Phys* 120, 304-322. [19]

—— *See also* Graham, C. H. 1938.

Kendall, W. E. *See* Seashore, R. H. 1941.

Kendler, H. H. 1946. The influence of simultaneous hunger and thirst drives upon the learning of two opposed spatial responses of the white rat. *J exp Ps* 36, 212-220. [631]

—— 1947. A comparison of learning under motivated and satiated conditions in the white rat *J exp Ps* 37, 545-549. [643]

——, Gasser, W. P. 1948. Variables in spatial learning. I. Number of reinforcements during training. *J comp physiol Ps* 41, 178-187. [632]

——, Greenberg, A., Richman, H. 1952. The influence of massed and distributed practice on the development of mental set. *J exp Ps* 43, 21-25. [837]

——, Kanner, J. H. 1950. A further test of the ability of rats to learn the location of food when motivated by thirst. *J exp Ps* 40, 762-765. [642]

——, Levine, S. 1953. A more sensitive test of irrelevant-incentive learning under conditions of satiation. *J comp phys Ps* 46, 271-273. [643]

——, Mencher, H. C. 1948. The ability of rats to learn the location of food when motivated by thirst—an experimental reply to Leeper. *J exp Ps* 38, 82-88. [642]

——, —— 1949. Variables in spatial learning. II. Degree of motivation during training and test trials. *J comp phys Ps* 42, 493-501. [632, 648]

Kennedy, J. L., Travis, R. C. 1947. Prediction of speed of performance by muscle action potentials. *Science* 106, 410-411. [178]

——, —— 1948. Prediction and control of alertness. II. Continuous tracking. *J comp phys Ps* 41, 203-210. [31, 178]

—— *See also* Travis, R. C. 1947, 1949.

Kent, G. H., Rosanoff, A. J. 1910. A study of association in insanity. *Amer J Insan* 67, 37-96, 317-390. [50, 54, 56, 61]

Keys, A., Brozek, J., Henschel, A., Mickelson, O., Taylor, H. L. 1950. *The biology of human starvation*. 2 vols. Minneapolis, Univ Minnesota Press. [659]

Kientzle, M. J. 1946. Properties of learning curves under varied distribution of practice. *J exp Ps* 36, 187-211. [790]

—— 1949. Ability patterns under distributed practice. *J exp Ps* 39, 532-537. [782]

Kiesow, F. 1894. Ueber die Wirkung des Cocain und der Gymnemasäure auf die Schleimhaut der Zunge und des Mundraums. *Philos St* 9, 510-527. [279]

—— 1895. Untersuchungen über Temperaturempfindungen. *Philos St* 11, 135-145. [282]

—— 1903. Ein Beitrag zur Frage nach den Reaktionszeiten der Geschmacksempfindungen. *Z Ps* 33, 453-461. [17]

Killian, C. D. *See* English, H. B. 1934.

Kimball, L. T. *See* Kimball, R. C. 1953.

Kimball, R. C., Kimball, L. T., Weaver, H. E. 1953. Latent learning as a function of the number of differential cues. *J comp phys Ps* 46, 274-280. [641]

Kimble, G. A. 1947. Conditioning as a function of the time between conditioned and unconditioned stimuli. *J exp Ps* 37, 1-15. [571]

—— 1949a. An experimental test of a two-factor theory of inhibition. *J exp Ps* 39, 15-23. [789, 798, 809]

—— 1949b. A further analysis of the variables in cyclical motor learning. *J exp Ps* 39, 332-337. [789, 809]

—— 1949c. Performance and reminiscence in motor learning as a function of the degree of distribution of practice. *J exp Ps* 39, 500-510. [809]

—— 1951. Behavior strength as a function of the intensity of the hunger drive. *J exp Ps* 41, 341-348. [656]

—— 1952. Transfer of work inhibition in motor learning. *J exp Ps* 43, 391-392. [736]

——, Bilodeau, E. A. 1949. Work and rest as variables in cyclical motor learning. *J exp Ps* 39, 150-157. [809]

——, Horenstein, B. R. 1948. Reminiscence in motor learning as a function of length of interpolated rest. *J exp Ps* 38, 239-244. [809]

——, Shatel, R. B. 1952. The relationship between two kinds of inhibition and the amount of practice. *J exp Ps* 44, 355-359. [788]

Kinder, E. F. *See* Syz, H. C. 1928.

Kinnaman, A. J. 1902. Mental life of two MACACUS RHESUS monkeys in captivity. *Amer J Ps* 13, 98-148, 173-218. [827]

Klee, J. B. 1944. The relation of frustration and motivation in the production of abnormal fixations in the rat. *Ps Monogr* #257. [677]

Kleitman, N. 1939. *Sleep and wakefulness*. Chic., Chicago Univ Press. [164, 174]

—— 1950. The sleep-wakefulness cycle. *Problems of consciousness*. 15-61. H. A. Abramson. N. Y., Macy Jr. Foundation. [146, 174, 179]

——, Ramsaroop, A. 1948. Periodicity in body temperature and heart rate. *Endocrinology* 43, 1-20. [146, 179]

——, Titelbaum, S., Feiveson, P. 1938. The effect of body temperature on reaction time. *Amer J Phys* 121, 495-501. [37]

—— *See also* Aserinsky, E. 1953.

Klemm, O. 1919. Untersuchungen über die Lokalisation von Schallreizen. Über den Anteil des beidohrigen Hörens. *Arch ges Ps* 38, 71-114. [354]

—— 1920. Untersuchungen über die Lokalisation von Schallreizen. Über den Einfluss des binauralen Zeitunterschiedes auf die Lokalisation. *Arch ges Ps* 40, 117-146. [354, 355]

Klineberg, O. 1938. Emotional expression in Chinese literature. *J abnor soc Ps* 33, 517-520. [120, 132]

—— 1940, 1954. *Social Psychology*. N. Y., Holt.

Kloehn, N. W., Brogden, W. J. 1948. The alkaline taste. *Amer J Ps* 61, 90-93. [299]

Klugman, S. F. 1948. Emotional stability and level of aspiration. *J genl Ps* 38, 101-118. [693]

Klute, J. *See* Evans, R. M. 1944.

Klüver, H. 1926. An experimental study of the eidetic type. *Genet Ps Monogr* 1, 71-230. [722]

—— 1928. Studies on the eidetic type and on eidetic imagery. *Ps Bull* 25, 69-104. [722]

—— 1931. The equivalence of stimuli in the

behavior of monkeys. *J genet Ps* 39, 3-27. [585, 589]
—— 1932. Eidetic phenomena. *Ps Bull* 29, 181-203. [722]
—— 1933. *Behavior mechanisms in monkeys.* Chic., Chicago Univ Press. [585, 590, 591]
—— 1937. Re-examination of implement-using behavior in a cebus monkey after an interval of three years. *Acta ps* 2, 347-397. [833]
Knotter, M. C. *See* Walker, E. L. 1950.
Knower, F. H. 1941. Analysis of some experimental variations of simulated vocal expressions of the emotions. *J soc Ps* 14, 369-372. [123]
—— *See also* Dusenbury, D. 1938, 1939.
Knudsen, V. O. 1928. "Hearing" with the sense of touch. *J genl Ps* 1, 320-352. [295]
Kobayashi, T., Matsui, M. 1938. [On the condition of reaction time. II.] *Rept 6th Cong Jap Ps Ass* 90-94. [29]
Kobrick, J. L. *See* Hall, J. F. 1952.
Koch, H. L. 1923. A neglected phase of the part-whole problem. *J exp Ps* 6, 366-376. [785]
Koch, S. *See* Saltzman, I. 1948.
Koester, T. 1945. Time error and sensitivity in pitch and loudness discrimination as a function of time interval and stimulus level. *Arch Ps N.Y.* #297. [219]
—— Schoenfeld, W. N. 1945. Modified methods of constant and single stimuli in pitch discrimination. *Amer J Ps* 58, 540-544. [219]
——, —— 1947. Some comparative data on differential pitch sensitivity under quantal and non-quantal conditions. *J genl Ps* 36, 107-112. [221]
Koffka, K. 1912. *Zur Analyse der Vorstellungen und ihrer Gesetze.* Leip., Quelle. [47]
—— 1931a. Die Wahrnehmung von Bewegung. *Handbh norm pathol Phys* 12 (2), 1166-1214. Berlin, Springer. [515]
—— 1931b. Psychologie der optischen Wahrnehmung. *Handbh norm pathol Phys* 12 (2), 1215-1271. Berlin, Springer. [515]
—— 1932. Some remarks on the theory of colour constancy. *Ps Forsch* 16, 329-354. [450]
—— 1935. *Principles of Gestalt psychology.* N. Y., Harcourt, Brace. [444, 450, 481, 515, 773, 774]
Köhler, W. 1909. Akustische Untersuchungen. *Z Ps* 54, 241-289. [341]
—— 1917, 1924. *Intelligenzprüfungen an Menschenaffen.* Berlin, Springer. Trans. *The mentality of apes.* Lond., Kegan, Paul. [820, 824]
—— 1923. Zur Theorie des Sukzessivvergleichs und der Zeitfehler. *Ps Forsch* 4, 115-175. [226, 227]
—— 1938. *The place of value in a world of facts.* N. Y., Liveright. [424]
—— 1940. *Dynamics in psychology.* N. Y., Liveright. [424]
—— 1941. On the nature of associations. *Proc Amer philos Soc* 84, 489-502. [773]
—— Emery, D. A. 1947. Figural after-effects in the third dimension of visual space. *Amer J Ps* 60, 159-201. [425]
——, Fishback, J. 1950. The destruction of the Müller-Lyer illusion in repeated trials. 1. 2. *J exp Ps* 40, 267-281, 398-410. [425, 426]
——, von Restorff, H. 1935. Analyse von Vorgängen im Spurenfeld. II. Zur Theorie der Reproduktion. *Ps Forsch* 21, 56-112. [732]
——, Wallach H. 1944. Figural after-effects: an investigation of visual processes. *Proc Amer Philos Soc* 88, 269-357. [424, 452]
Kohlrausch, A. 1931. Tagessehen, Dämmersehen, Adaptation. *Handbh norm pathol Phys* 12 (2), 1499-1594. Berlin, Springer. [367, 369, 394]
Komuro, K. 1921. Le minimum perceptible de l'odorat dans une enceinte absolument inodore. *Arch néerl Phys* 6, 20-24. [310, 312]
König, A. 1897. Die Anhängigkeit der Sehschärfe von den Beleuchtungsintensität. *K Akad Wiss Berlin Sitzber* 559-575. [385]
——, Brodhun, E. 1888. Experimentelle Untersuchungen über die psychophysische Fundamentalformel in Bezug auf den Gesichtssinn. *K Akad Wiss Berlin Sitzber* 917-931. [224, 378]
——, Dieterici, C. 1892. Die Grundempfindungen in normalen und anomalen Farbensystemen und ihre Intensitätsverteilung im Spektrum. *Z Ps* 4, 241-347. [394]
Kopera, A. 1931. Untersuchungen über die Unterschiedsempfindlichkeit im Bereiche des Geschmacksinns. *Arch ges Ps* 82, 273-307. [302]
Kopfermann, H. 1930. Psychologische Untersuchungen über die wirkung zweidimensionaler Darstellungen körperlicher Gebilde. *Ps Forsch* 13, 293-364. [410, 411]
Kopp, G. A. *See* Potter, R. K. 1947.
Korte, A. 1915. Kinematoskopische Untersuchungen. *Z Ps* 72, 193-296. [512]
Korte, W. 1923. Über die Gestaltauffassung im indirekten Sehen. *Z Ps* 93, 17-82. [104]
Koyanagi, K. 1953. An experimental study on relations between the intellectual cognition and the intellectual activity in children. *Tohoku ps Folia* 13, 100-113. [835]
Kraepelin, E. 1883. Ueber die Einwirkung einiger medicamentöser Stoffe auf die Dauer einfacher psychischer Vorgänge. *Philos St* 1, 417-462, 573-608. [38]
—— 1892. *Über die Beeinflussung einfacher psychischer Vorgänge durch einige Arzneimittel.* Jena, Fischer. [54]
Krech, D. *See* Bruner, J. S. 1950
Krechevsky, I. 1932a. "Hypotheses" versus "chance" in the pre-solution period in sensory discrimination-learning. *Calif U Publ Ps* 6, 27-44. [594, 595]
—— 1932b. The genesis of "hypotheses" in rats. *Calif U Publ Ps* 6, 45-64. [594, 595]
Kreezer, G. 1938. The neurological level of the factors underlying time-errors. *Amer J Ps* 51, 18-45. [228]
Kries, J.v. 1895. Über die Natur gewisser mit den

psychischen Vorgängen verknüpfter Gehirnzustände. *Z Ps* 8, 1-33. [830]

—— 1897. Über die absolute Empfindlichkeit der verschiedenen Netzhautteile im dunkeladaptierten Auge. *Z Ps* 15, 327-351. [367]

—— 1929. Zur Theorie des Tages- und Dämmerungssehens. *Handbh norm pathol Phys* 12 (1), 679-713. Berlin, Springer. [365]

——, Auerbach, F. 1877. Die Zeitdauer einfachster psychischer Vorgänge. *Arch Anat Phys Abt* 297-378. [53]

——, Nagel, W. A. 1900. Weitere Mittheilungen über die functionelle Sonderstellung des Netzhautcentrums. *Z Ps* 23, 161-186. [367]

Krueger, L. *See* Skaggs, E. B. 1930.

Krueger, W. *See* Skaggs, E. B. 1930.

Krueger, W. C. F. 1929. The effect of overlearning on retention. *J exp Ps* 12, 71-78. [728, 729]

Kubis, J. F. *See* Staudt, V. 1948; Welch, L. 1947.

Kuckulies, G. *See* Hahn, H. 1938.

Kubo, Y. 1933. An experimental study of "insight." *Jap J appl Ps* 2, 82-113. [823]

Kuhlmann, F. 1906. On the analysis of the memory consciousness. *Ps Rev* 13, 316-348. [715, 774]

Kurath, H. 1921. *The semantic sources of the words for the emotions in Sanskrit, Greek, Latin and the Germanic languages.* Menasha, Wis., Banta. [107]

Kurtz, K. H. *See* Hovland, C. I. 1951, 1952.

Kwalwasser, J. 1926. The vibrato. *Ps Monogr* #167. [123]

L

Lacey, O. L. 1947. An analysis of the appropriate unit for use in the measurement of level of galvanic skin resistance. *J exp Ps* 37, 449-457. [140]

——, Siegel, P. S. 1948. An improved potentiometric circuit for measuring the galvanic skin response. *Amer J Ps* 61, 272-274. [139]

——, —— 1949. An analysis of the unit of measurement of the galvanic skin response. *J exp Ps* 39, 122-127. [140, 141]

—— *See also* Duffy, E. 1946.

Lackum, W. J. v. *See* Melton, A. W. 1941.

Ladd-Franklin, C. 1929. *Colour and colour theories.* N. Y., Harcourt, Brace. [363, 366, 389, 396]

Ladd, G. T., Woodworth, R. S. 1911. *Physiological psychology.* N. Y., Scribner's. [294, 418]

Lahy, B. 1939. Étude statistique de l'autonomie des temps de reprise par rapport aux temps de réaction. *Ann ps* 40, 193-198. [41]

Lamansky, S. 1869. Bestimmung der Winkelgeschwindigkeit der Blickbewegung, respective Augenbewegung. *Pflüg Arch ges Phys* 2, 418-422. [497]

Lamoreaux, R. R. *See* Mowrer, O. H. 1942.

Landgren, S. *See* Anderson, B. 1950.

Landis, C. 1924. Studies of emotional reactions. II. General behavior and facial expression. *J comp Ps* 4, 447-509. [120, 130]

—— 1925. Changes in blood pressure during sleep as determined by the Erlanger method. *Amer J Phys* 73, 551-555. [163]

—— 1926. Studies of emotional reactions. V. Severe emotional upset. *J comp Ps* 6, 221-242. [166]

—— 1953. An annotated bibliography of flicker fusion phenomena, 1740–1952. Univ Michigan, Ann Arbor. [382]

——, Forbes, T. W. 1933. An investigation of methods of measurement of the electrical phenomena of the skin. *Psychiat Q* 7, 107-114. [144]

——, Gullette, R. 1925. Studies of emotional reactions. III. Systolic blood pressure and inspiration-expiration ratios. *J comp Ps* 5, 221-253. [166, 187]

——, Hunt, W. A. 1935. The conscious correlates of the galvanic skin response. *J exp Ps* 18, 505-529. [156]

——, —— 1939. *The startle pattern.* N. Y., Farrar. [184]

Landis, C. *See* Forbes, T. W. 1935.

Lane, C. E. *See* Wegel, R. L. 1924.

Lange, C. G. 1885, 1922. *Om Sindsbevægelser et psyko. fysiolog. studie.* Lund, Jac. *The emotions.* Balt., Williams & Wilkins. [107]

Lange, L. 1888. Neue Experimente über den Vorgang der einfachen Reaction auf Sinnesreizen. *Philos St* 4, 479-510. [32]

Langfeld, H. S. 1918. The judgment of emotion by facial expression. *J abnor soc Ps* 13, 172-184. [116]

—— 1927. Apparent visual movement with a stationary stimulus. *Amer J Ps* 39, 343-355. [514]

—— 1931. A response interpretation of consciousness. *Ps Rev* 38, 87-108. [178]

—— *See also* Boring, E. G. 1939, 1948.

Langhorne, M. C. 1948. The effects of maze rotation on learning. *J genl Ps* 38, 191-205. [740]

—— 1950. The influence of the temporal order of the interpolation of maze rotation on retroactive inhibition. *J genl Ps* 43, 283-294. [649]

Langworthy, O. R., Richter, C. P. 1930. The influence of efferent cerebral pathways upon the sympathetic nervous system. *Brain* 53, 178-193. [143]

Lanier, L. H. 1934. The interrelations of speed of reaction measurements. *J exp Ps* 17, 371-399. [40]

—— 1941a. An experimental study of "affective conflict." *J Ps* 11, 199-217. [155]

—— 1941b. Incidental memory for words differing in affective value. *J Ps* 11, 219-228. [155]

——, Carney, H. M., Wilson, W. D. 1935. Cutaneous innervation: an experimental study. *Arch Neu Psychiat* 34, 1-60. [281]

Larsen, M. J. *See* Lewis, D. 1937.

Larson, J. A. 1923. The cardio-pneumo-psychogram in deception. *J exp Ps* 6, 420-454. [190]

—— 1932. *Lying and its detection.* Chic., Chicago Univ Press. [190]

Lashley, K. S. 1912. Visual discrimination of size and form in the albino rat. *J animal Beh* 2, 310-331. [599]

—— 1916a. The human salivary reflex and its use in psychology. *Ps Rev* 23, 446-464. [573]

—— 1916b. Reflex secretion of the human parotid gland. *J exp Ps* 1, 461-493. [573]

—— 1918. A simple maze: with data on the relation of the distribution of practice to the rate of learning. *Psychobiol* 1, 353-367. [640]

—— 1924. Studies of cerebral function in learning. V. The retention of motor habits after destruction of the so-called motor areas in primates. *Arch Neu Psychiat* 12, 249-276. [743]

—— 1930. The mechanism of vision. I. A method for rapid analysis of pattern vision in the rat. *J genet Ps* 37, 453-460. [583, 584, 625]

—— 1935. Studies of cerebral function in learning. XI. The behavior of the rat in latch box situations. *Comp Ps Monogr* #52. [819]

—— 1938. The mechanism of vision. XV. Preliminary studies of the rat's capacity for detail vision. *J genl Ps* 18, 123-193. [583, 592, 593, 599]

—— 1942. An examination of the "continuity theory" as applied to discriminative learning. *J genl Ps* 26, 241-265. [589, 593, 596, 597]

——, Ball, J. 1929. Spinal conduction and kinaesthetic sensitivity in the maze habit. *J comp Ps* 9, 71-105. [616]

——, Chow, K. L., Semmes, J. 1951. An examination of the electrical field theory of cerebral integration. *Ps Rev* 58, 123-136. [426]

——, McCarthy, D. A. 1926. The survival of the maze habit after cerebellar injuries. *J comp Ps* 6, 423-432. [627]

——, Wade, M. 1946. The Pavlovian theory of generalization. *Ps Rev* 53, 72-87. [579, 580, 588]

Laslett, H. R. *See* Miles, W. R. 1931.

Lauder, B. A. *See* Patterson, P. M. 1948.

Lauenstein, O. 1933. Ansatz zu einer physiologischen Theorie des Vergleichs und der Zeitfehler. *Ps Forsch* 17, 130-177. [228, 229]

Lawlor, W. G. *See* Hunt, H. F. 1953.

Lawrence, D. H. 1950. Acquired distinctiveness of cues. II. Selective association in a constant stimulus situation. *J exp Ps* 40, 175-188. [598]

Lawrence, M. 1919. *Studies in human behavior*. Princeton, Princeton Univ Press. [488]

—— *See also* Wever, E. G. 1940a, b.

Lazarus, R. S., McCleary, R. A. 1951. Autonomic discrimination without awareness: a study of subception. *Ps Rev* 58, 113-122. [158]

Leavitt, H. J., Schlosberg, H. 1944. The retention of verbal and of motor skills. *J exp Ps* 34, 404-417. [732]

Lee, H. *See* Gentry, G. 1948.

Leeper, R. 1935. The role of motivation in learning. A study of the phenomenon of differential motivation control of the utilization of habits. *J genet Ps* 46, 3-40. [631, 637, 716]

Leeper, R. W. 1948. A motivational theory of emotion to replace "emotion as disorganized response." *Ps Rev* 55, 5-21. [110]

Lefford, A. 1946. The influence of emotional subject matter on logical reasoning. *J genl Ps* 34, 127-151. [848]

Lehmann, A. 1888-1889. Ueber Wiedererkennen. *Philos St* 5, 96-156. [699]

Lehner, G. F. J. 1941. A study of the extinction of unconditioned reflexes. *J exp Ps* 29, 435-456. [559]

Le Magnen, J. 1942–1943. Étude d'une méthode d'analyse qualitative de l'olfaction. *Ann Ps* 43-44, 249-264. [314]

—— 1944–1945. Étude des facteurs dynamiques de l'excitation olfactive. *Ann Ps* 45-46, 77-89. [314]

—— 1948a. Analyse d'odeurs complexes et homologues par fatigue. *C R Acad Sci Paris* 226, 753-754. [317]

—— 1948b. Un cas de sensibilité olfactive se présentant comme un caractère secondaire féminin. *C R Acad Sci Paris* 226, 694-695. [317]

Lemaire, A. *See* Jensen, M. B. 1937.

Lemmon, V. W. 1927. The relation of reaction time to measures of intelligence, memory and learning. *Arch Ps N.Y.* #94. [33f, 40]

Lenk, E. 1926. Über die Optische Auffassung Geometrisch-Regelmässiger Gestalten. *Neue Ps St* 1, 573-612. [417]

Leonardo da Vinci. 1585. *Trattato della Pittura*. Napoli. (ed used: 1733.) German Trans. 1882 V. 2. *Das Buch von der Malerei*. Wien. 1882. (*Quellenschriften für Kunstgeschichte*. Bd. 15-18.) [464]

Lepley, W. M. 1934. Serial reactions considered as conditioned reactions. *Ps Monogr* #205. [711]

Leventhal, T. *See* Witkin, H. A. 1952.

Levine, H. A., Dallenbach, K. M. 1936. Adaptation of cold spots under continuous and intermittent stimulation. *Amer J Ps* 48, 490-497. [292]

Levine, S. *See* Kendler, H. H. 1953.

Levy, I. *See* Elsberg, C. A. 1935.

Levy, N. *See* Seward, J. P. 1950.

Lewin, K. 1917. Die psychische Tätigkeit bei der Hemmung von Willensvorgängen und das Grundgesetz der Assoziation. *Z Ps* 77, 212-247. [637]

—— 1935. *A dynamic theory of personality, selected papers*. N. Y., McGraw-Hill. [690, 833]

—— 1946. Behavior and development as a function of the total situation. *Manual Child Ps* 819-832. L. Carmichael, ed. N. Y., Wiley. [690]

——, Dembo, T., Festinger, L., Sears, P. S. 1944. Level of aspiration. *Handbk pers & beh disorders* 333-378. J. McV. Hunt, ed. N. Y., Ronald. [693]

—— *See also* Barker, R. G. 1941.

Lewis, D., Larsen, M. J. 1937. The cancellation, reinforcement and measurement of subjective tones. *Proc Natl Acad Sci* 23, 415-421. [343]

——, Shephard, A. H. 1951. Prior learning as a factor in shaping performance curves. *Proc Nat Acad Sci* 37, 124-131. [538]

——, Smith, P. N., McAllister, D. E. 1952. Retroactive facilitation and interference in performance on the modified two-hand coordinator. *J exp Ps* 44, 44-50. [764]

Lewis, D. R. 1948. Psychological scales of taste. *J Ps* 26, 437-446. [243]

Lewis, E. C. 1908. The effect of practice on the perception of the Müller-Lyer illusion. *Br J Ps* 2, 294-306. [423]

Lewis, F. H. 1933. Note on the doctrine of memory-trace. *Ps Rev* 40, 90-96. [717]

Lewis, H. B., Franklin, M. 1944. An experimental study of the role of the ego in work. II. The significance of task-orientation in work. *J exp Ps* 34, 195-215. [693]

Lewis, T. 1942. *Pain.* N. Y., Macmillan. [281]

Lichten, W., Lurie, S. 1950. A new technique for the study of perceived size. *Amer J Ps* 63, 281-282. [481]

Lickley, J. D. 1919. *The nervous system.* N. Y., Longmans, Green. [326]

Licklider, J. C. R. 1951. Basic correlates of the auditory stimulus. *Handbk exp Ps* 985-1039. S. S. Stevens, ed. N. Y., Wiley.

——, Bindra, D., Pollack, I. 1948. The intelligibility of rectangular speech-waves. *Amer J Ps* 61, 1-20. [341]

——, Miller, G. A. 1951. The perception of speech. *Handbk exp Ps* 1040-1074. S. S. Stevens, ed. N. Y., Wiley. [342]

—— *See also* Licklider, L. C. 1950.

Licklider, L. C., Licklider, J. C. R. 1950. Observations on the hoarding behavior of rats. *J comp phys Ps*, 43, 129-134. [660]

Liddell, H. S. 1926. A laboratory for the study of conditioned motor reflexes. *Amer J Ps* 37, 418-419. [543]

——, James, W. T., Anderson, O. D. 1934. The comparative physiology of the conditioned motor reflex, based on experiments with the pig, dog, sheep, goat, and rabbit. *Comp Ps Monogr* #51. [548, 549, 576, 676]

Lindley, S. B. 1930. The maze-learning ability of anosmic and blind anosmic rats. *J genet Ps* 37, 245-267. [616, 620]

Lindquist, E. F. 1940. *Statistical analysis in educational research.* Bost., Houghton Mifflin.

Lindsley, D. B. 1950. Emotions and the electroencephalogram. Reymert, M. L., *Feelings and emotions: The Mooseheart symposium,* 238-246. N. Y., McGraw-Hill. [181]

—— 1951. Emotion. *Handbk exp Ps* 473-516. S. S. Stevens, ed. N. Y., Wiley. [108, 109, 135, 136, 143, 162, 179, 180, 185]

——, Hunter, W. S. 1939. A note on polarity potentials from the human eye. *Proc nat Acad Sci* 25, 180-183. [496]

Link, H. C. 1919. A practical study of industrial fatigue. *J indust Hygiene* 1, 233-237. [807]

Linnæus, C. 1752. Odores Medicamentorum. *Amoenitates Academicae.* 1756, 3, 183-201. [305]

Lipman, E. A. *See* Brogden, W. J. 1938.

Lipmann, O. 1904. Der Einfluss der einzelnen Wiederholungen auf verschieden starke und verschieden alte Assoziationen. *Z Ps* 35, 195-233. [703]

—— 1908. Ein neuer Expositions Apparat mit rückweiser Rotation für Gedächtnis- und Lernversuche. *Z Ps* 49, 270-277. [703]

—— 1933. Methoden der Aussagepsychologie. *Handbh bio Arbeitsmeth* 6, Teil C, II 2, 967-1056. [717]

Lippitt, R. *See* Spence, K. W. 1940, 1946, 1950.

Lipps, T. 1897. *Raumaesthetik und geometrisch-optische Täuschungen.* Leip., Barth. [419]

Lissner, K. 1933. Die Entspannung von Bedürfnissen durch Ersatzhandlungen. *Ps Forsch* 18, 218-250. [691]

List of 43,200 dissyllable words and paralogs. 1933. Mimeograph copy. Washington, D. C. Natl Res Council. [703]

Littman, R. A. 1950. Latent learning in a T-maze after two degrees of training. *J comp phys Ps* 43, 135-147. [644, 645]

Lloyd, V. V. *See* Graham, C. H. 1948; Mueller, C. G. 1948.

Locke, J. 1700. *An essay concerning humane understanding.* In 4 bks. 4th ed. Lond., Awnsham & John Churchil. [43]

Locke, N. M. 1935. Color constancy in the rhesus monkey and in man. *Arch Ps N.Y.* #193. [437]

Logan, F. A. 1951. A comparison of avoidance and nonavoidance eyelid conditioning. *J exp Ps* 42, 390-393. [556]

Long, L. 1937. A study of the effect of preceding stimuli upon the judgment of auditory intensities. *Arch Ps N.Y.*, #209. [217, 230, 231]

—— 1940. Conceptual relationships in children: the concept of roundness. *J genet Ps* 57, 289-315. [609]

—— *See also* Welch, L. 1943.

Lord, M. W. *See* Kaufman, E. L. 1949.

Loucks, R. B. 1933. An appraisal of Pavlov's systematization of behavior from the experimental standpoint. *J comp Ps* 15, 1-47. [579]

—— 1937. Reflexology and the psychobiological approach. *Ps Rev* 44, 320-338. [579]

Lowell, F. *See* Woodrow, H. 1916.

Lowenstein, E., Dallenbach, K. M. 1930. The critical temperatures for heat and for burning heat. *Amer J Ps* 42, 423-429. [283]

Lu, T. W. *See* Wang, C. H. 1929.

Luchins, A. S. 1942. Mechanization in problem solving: the effect of Einstellung. *Ps Monogr* 54, #248. [836]

——, Luchins, E. H. 1950. New experimental attempts at preventing mechanization in problem solving. *J genl Ps* 42, 279-297. [837]

Luchins, E. H. *See* Luchins, A. S. 1950.

Luckiesh, M. 1922. *Visual illusions.* N. Y., Van Nostrand. [418]

Lugoff, L. S. *See* Hull, C. L. 1921.

Luh, C. W. 1922. The conditions of retention. *Ps Monogr* #142. [724, 728]

Lumsdaine, A. A. *See* Hovland, C. I. 1949.

Lund, F. H. 1927. The role of practice in speed of association. *J exp Ps* 10, 424-433. [57]

Luria, A. R. 1932. *The nature of human conflicts.* N. Y., Liveright. [36, 166, 189]

Lurie, M. H. *See* Stevens, S. S. 1935.

Lurie, S. *See* Lichten, W. 1950.

Lyon, D. O. 1917. *Memory and the learning process.* Balt., Warwick & York. [697, 707, 790]

M

McAllister, D. E. *See* Lewis, D. 1952.

McCarthy, D. A. *See* Lashley, K. S. 1926.

McCleary, R. A. 1950. The nature of the galvanic skin response. *Ps Bull* 47, 97-113. [143]

—— *See* Chapanis, A. 1953; Lazarus, R. S. 1951.

McClelland, D. C. 1942a. Functional autonomy of motives as an extinction phenomenon. *Ps Rev* 49, 272-283. [686]

—— 1942b. Studies in serial verbal discrimination learning. I. Reminiscence with two speeds of pair presentation. *J exp Ps* 31, 44-56. [797]

——, Atkinson, J. W. 1948. The projective expression of needs. I. *J Ps* 25, 205-222. [694]

MacCorquodale, K., Meehl, P.E. 1949. "Cognitive" learning in the absence of competition of incentives. *J comp phys Ps* 42, 383-390. [643]

——, —— 1951. On the elimination of cul entries without obvious reinforcement. *J comp phys Ps* 44, 367-371. [641]

—— *See also* Meehl, P. E. 1948, 1951.

McCrary, J. W., Hunter, W. S. 1953. Serial position curves in verbal learning. *Science* 117, 131-134. [712, 713]

McCulloch, T. L. 1934. Performance preferentials of the white rat in force-resisting and spatial dimensions. *J comp Ps* 18, 85-111. [585]

——, Pratt, J. G. 1934. A study of the pre-solution period in weight discrimination by white rats. *J comp Ps* 18, 271-290. [585, 595]

McCurdy, H G. 1950. Consciousness and the galvanometer. *Ps Rev* 57, 322-327. [154]

McCutchan, K. *See* Blodgett, H. C. 1947, 1949.

MacDonald, M. K. 1922. An experimental study of Henning's system of olfactory qualities. *Amer J Ps* 33, 535-553. [306, 308, 320]

McDonald, W. T. *See* McGeoch, J. A. 1931.

Mace, C. A. 1931. The influence of indirect incentives upon the accuracy of skilled movements. *Br J Ps* 22, 101-114. [689]

McFarland, R. A. 1937. Psycho-physiological studies at high altitudes in the Andes. IV. Sensory and circulatory responses of the Andean residents at 17,500 feet. *J comp Ps* 24, 189-220. [38]

Macfarlane, D. A. 1930. The role of kinesthesis in maze learning. *Calif U Publ Ps* 4, 277-305. [627]

McGarvey, H. R. 1943. Anchoring effects in the absolute judgment of verbal materials. *Arch Ps N.Y.* #281. [249, 250, 251]

McGehee, W. 1937. The free-word association of elementary school children. *J genet Ps* 50, 441-455. [60]

—— 1938. The free word association of elementary school children. II. Verbal responses. *J genet Ps* 52, 361-374. [60]

McGeoch, G. O. 1931a. The intelligence quotient as a factor in the whole-part problem. *J exp Ps* 14, 333-358. [782, 784]

—— 1931b. Whole-part problem. *Ps Bull* 28, 713-739. [782]

—— 1935. The conditions of reminiscence. *Amer J Ps* 47, 65-89. [794]

McGeoch, J. A. 1942. *The psychology of human learning.* N. Y., Longmans, Green. [763, 768, 797]

——, Irion, A. L. 1952. *The psychology of human learning.* 2d ed. N. Y., Longmans, Green. [714, 763, 767]

——, McDonald, W. T. 1931. Meaningful relation and retroactive inhibition. *Amer J Ps* 43, 579-588. [766]

——, Peters, H. N. 1933. An all-or-none characteristic in the elimination of errors during the learning of a stylus maze. *J exp Ps* 16, 504-523. [653]

McGinnies, E. 1949. Emotionality and perceptual defense. *Ps Rev* 56, 244-251. [105, 158]

—— 1950. Discussion of Howes' and Solomon's note on "Emotionality and Perceptual Defense." *Ps Rev* 57, 235-240. [158]

——, Schlosberg, H. 1945. The effects of electroshock convulsions on double alternation lever-pressing in the white rat. *J exp Ps* 35, 361-373. [629]

—— *See also* Postman, L. 1948.

McGlone, B. *See* Bazett, H. C. 1930.

Mach, E. 1914. *The analysis of sensations.* Trans. 5th ed. by S. Waterlow. Chic., Open Court. [412]

MacLeod, R. B. 1932. An experimental investigation of brightness constancy. *Arch Ps N.Y.* #135. [443, 449]

—— 1940. Brightness-constancy in unrecognized shadows. *J exp Ps* 27, 1-22. [416]

MacLeod, S. 1952. A construction and attempted validation of sensory sweetness scales. *J exp Ps* 44, 316-323. [244, 302, 303]

MacMillan, Z. L. *See* Foley, J. P., Jr. 1943.

MacPherson, S. J., Dees, V., Grindley, G. C. 1948. The effect of knowledge of results on learning and performance. II. Some characteristics of very simple skills. *Q J exp Ps* 1, 68-78. [686, 687]

——, ——, —— 1949. The effect of knowledge of results on learning and performance. III. The influence of the time interval between trials. *Q J exp Ps* 1, 167-174. [787]

Madden, E. H. *See* Weaver, H. E. 1949.

Maeda, Y. 1951. Zur experimentellen Untersuchung über Faktoren der Reproduktionshemmung. I. Über Hemmungswirkungen auf die Reproduktion. *Jap J Ps* 21, (3-4), 1-17. [767]

Mager, A. 1920. Die Enge des Bewusstseins. *St Ps Philos* (Münchener) #5. [90]

Maggiora, A. 1890. Les lois de la fatigue étudiées dans les muscles de l'homme. II. *Arch ital Biol* 13, 187-241. [803]

Magnus, R. 1924. *Körperstellung.* Berlin, Springer. [174, 523]

Maier, N. R. F. 1930. Reasoning in humans. I. On direction. *J comp Ps* 10, 115-143. [831, 832]

—— 1937. Reasoning in rats and human beings. *Ps Rev* 44, 365-378.

—— 1941. The effect of cortical injury on equivalence reactions in rats. *J comp Ps* 32, 165-190. [593]

—— 1949. *Frustration: the study of behavior without a goal.* N. Y., McGraw-Hill. [677]

——, Ellen, P. 1951. The effects of lactose in the diet on frustration-susceptibility in rats. *J comp phys Ps* 44, 551-556. [678]

Major, D. R. 1895. On the affective tone of simple sense-impressions. *Amer J Ps* 7, 57-77. [251]

Malamud, D. I. 1946. Value of the Maller Controlled Association Test as a screening device. *J Ps* 21, 37-43. [70]

Maller, J. B. 1936. *A controlled association test.* N. Y., Author. [70]

Malmo, R. B., Shagass, M. S. 1949. Physiologic study of symptom mechanisms in psychiatric patients under stress. *Psychosom Med* 11, 25-29. [182]

Maltzman, I. 1950. An experimental study of learning under an irrelevant need. *J exp Ps* 40, 788-793. [643]

——, Morrisett, L., Jr. 1953. Effects of task instructions on solution of different classes of anagrams. *J exp Ps* 45, 351-354. [836]

Mandelbaum, J. *See* Hecht, S. 1938.

Manzer, C. W. 1927. An experimental investigation of rest pauses. *Arch Ps N.Y.* #90. [803]

Marbe, K. 1893. Die Schwankungen der Gesichtsempfindungen. *Philos St* 8, 615-637. [79]

—— *See also* Thumb, A. 1901.

Margaria, R. *See* Graham, C. H. 1935.

Marks, M. R. 1951. Problem solving as a function of the situation. *J exp Ps* 41, 74-80. [827]

—— Jack, O. 1952. Verbal context and memory span for meaningful material. *Amer J Ps* 65, 298-300. [705]

Marquart, D. I. 1948. The pattern of punishment and its relation to abnormal fixation in adult human subjects. *J genl Ps* 39, 107-144. [678]

Marquis, D. G. *See* Hilgard, E. R. 1935, 1936, 1940.

Marrow, A. J. 1938. Goal tensions and recall. *J genl Ps* 19, 3-35; 37-64. [692]

Marshall, W. H., Talbot, S. A. 1942. Recent evidence for neural mechanisms in vision leading to a general theory of sensory acuity. *Biol Symposia* 7, 117-164. [198]

——, ——, Ades, H. W. 1943. Cortical response of the anesthetized cat to gross photic and electrical afferent stimulation. *J Neurophys* 6, 1-15. [19]

Marston, W. M. 1917. Systolic blood pressure symptoms of deception. *J exp Ps* 2, 117-163. [188]

—— 1923. Sex characteristics of systolic blood pressure behavior. *J exp Ps* 6, 387-419. [188]

—— 1938. *The lie detector test.* N. Y., R. E. Smith. [186]

Martin, L. J., Müller, G. E. 1899. *Zur Analyse der Unterschiedsempfindlichkeit.* Leip., Barth. [217]

Martin, M. A. 1915. The transfer effects of practice in cancellation tests. *Arch Ps N.Y.* #32. [747]

Martin, P. R., Fernberger, S. W. 1929. Improvement in memory span. *Amer J Ps* 41, 91-94. [705]

Marx, E., Trendelenburg, W. 1911. Über die Genauigkeit der Einstellung des Auges beim Fixieren. *Z Sinnesphys* 45, 87-102. [498]

Marx, M. H. 1944. The effects of cumulative training upon retroactive inhibition and transfer. *Comp Ps Monogr* #94. [749, 751]

Mateer, F. 1918. *Child behavior.* Bost., Badger. [543]

Mathews, R. *See* Blodgett, H. C. 1949.

Matsui, M. *See* Kobayashi, T. 1938.

Matthews, B. H. C. 1933. Nerve endings in mammalian muscle. *J Phys* 78, 1-53. [802]

Max, L. W. 1934. An experimental study of the motor theory of consciousness. I. Critique of earlier studies. *J genl Ps* 11, 112-125. [178, 816]

—— 1935. An experimental study of the motor theory of consciousness. III. Action-current responses in deaf-mutes during sleep. . . . *J comp Ps* 19, 469-486. [178]

—— 1937. Experimental study of the motor theory of consciousness. IV. Action-current responses of the deaf during awakening, kinesthetic imagery and abstract thinking. *J comp Ps* 24, 301-344. [178, 816]

May, M. A. 1917. The mechanism of controlled association. *Arch Ps N.Y.* #39. [57, 61, 831]

Mayer, A., Orth, J. 1901. Zur qualitativen Untersuchung der Association. *Z Ps* 26, 1-13. [65]

M'Dowall, R. J. S. 1933. The physiology of the psycho-galvanic reflex. *Q J exp Phys* 23, 277-285. [142]

Mech, E. V. *See* Fattu, N. A. 1953.

Meehl, P. E., MacCorquodale, K. 1948. A further study of latent learning in the T-maze. *J comp phys Ps* 41, 372-396. [643]

——, —— 1951. A failure to find the Blodgett effect, and some secondary observations on drive conditioning. *J comp phys Ps* 44, 178-183. [638]

—— *See also* MacCorquodale, K. 1949, 1951.

Meenes, M. *See* Davis, A. J. 1932.

Meinecke, G. 1934. Einige technische Konstruktionsaufgaben und deren Lösungsmethoden. *Arch ges Ps* 92, 249-254. [839]

Melton, A. W. 1936. The end-spurt in memorization curves as an artifact of the averaging of individual curves. *Ps Monogr* #212. [535, 796]

——, Irwin, J. M. 1940. The influence of degree of interpolated learning on retroactive inhibition and the overt transfer of specific responses. *Amer J Ps* 53, 173-203. [763]

——, von Lackum, W. J. 1941. Retroactive and proactive inhibition in retention: evidence for a two-factor theory of retroactive inhibition. *Amer J Ps* 54, 157-173. [535, 763]

——, Stone, G. R. 1942. The retention of serial lists of adjectives over short time intervals with varying rates of presentation. *J exp Ps* 30, 295-310. [797]

Mencher, H. C. *See* Kendler, H. H. 1948. 1949.

Menzerath, P. 1908. Die Bedeutung der sprachlichen Geläufigkeit oder der formalen sprachlichen Beziehung für die Reproduktion. *Z Ps* 48, 1-95. [59, 60, 62, 65]

Mergener, J. C. *See* Darrow, C. W. 1942.

Merkel, J. 1885. Die zeitlichen Verhältnisse der Willensthätigkeit. *Philos St* 2, 73-127. [32]

Merry, G. N. 1922. Voice inflection in speech. *Ps Monogr* #140. [122]

Messenger, J. F. 1903. Perception of number through touch. *Ps Monogr* #17. [739]

Metfessel, M. F. 1928. What is the voice vibrato? *Ps Monogr* #178. [122]

Mettler, F. A. 1948. *Neuroanatomy*. St. Louis, Mosby. [135]

—— *See also* Culler, E. 1934.

Metzger, W. 1930. Optische Unterschungengen am Ganzfeld. II. Zur Phänomenologie des homogenen Ganzfelds. *Ps Forsch* 13, 6-29. [406]

Meumann, E. *See* Ebert, E. 1905.

Meyer, D. R. *See* Harlow, H. F. 1950.

Meyer, H. W. 1914. Bereitschaft und Wiedererkennen. *Z Ps* 70, 161-211. [720]

Meyer, M. F. 1950. *How we hear, how tones make music*. Bost., Branford. [328]

Meyers, R. 1948. Relation of "thinking" and language: an experimental approach, using dysphasic patients. *Arch Neu Psychiat*, Chic., 60, 119-139. [817]

Meyerson, I. *See* Guillaume, P. 1930.

Michels, W. C., Helson, H. 1949. A reformulation of the Fechner law in terms of adaptation-level applied to rating-scale data. *Amer J Ps* 62, 355-368. [237, 251]

Michotte, A. 1946. *La perception de la causalité*. Louvain, Institut Supérieur de Philosophie. [516, 517]

——, Portych, Th. 1914. Deuxième étude sur la mémoire logique. La reproduction après des intervalles temporels de différentes longueurs. *Études ps* 1, 237-264. [719,720]

Mickelson, O. *See* Keys, A. 1950.

Miles, C. C. *See* Terman, L. M. 1936.

Miles, R. C., Wickens, D. D. 1953. Effect of a secondary reinforcer on the primary hunger drive. *J comp phys Ps* 46, 77-79. [681]

Miles, W. R. 1924. Alcohol and human efficiency. *Carnegie Instit Publ* #333. Washington, D. C. [502]

—— 1928a. The high relief finger maze for human learning. *J genl Ps* 1, 3-14. [649, 652]

—— 1928b. The peep-hole method for observing eye movements in reading. *J genl Ps* 1, 373-374. [494]

—— 1929. Horizontal eye movements at the onset of sleep. *Ps Rev* 36, 122-141. [502]

—— 1930. The comparative learning of rats on elevated and alley mazes of the same pattern. *J comp Ps* 10, 237-261. [617, 620]

—— 1931a. Movement interpretations of the silhouette of a revolving fan. *Amer J Ps* 43, 392-405. [490]

—— 1931b. Studies in physical exertion. II. Individual and group reaction time in football charging. *Res Q Amer Physical Educ Ass* 2, #3. [42]

—— 1939. The steady potential of the human eye in subjects with unilateral enucleation. *Proc natl Acad Sci* 25, 128-137. [496]

—— 1942. Psychological aspects of ageing. *Problems of ageing* 756-784. E. V. Crowdry, ed. Balt., Williams & Wilkins. [36]

—— 1943. Red goggles for producing dark adaptation. *Fed Proc* 2, 109-115. [370]

——, Laslett, H. R. 1931. Eye movement and visual fixation during profound sleepiness. *Ps Rev* 38, 1-13. [502]

—— *See also* Beck, L. H. 1947.

Milisen, R., Van Riper, C. 1939. Differential transfer of training in a rotary activity. *J exp Ps* 24, 640-646. [740]

Miller, D. C. 1922. *The science of musical sounds*. N. Y., Macmillan. [340]

Miller, G. A. 1951. *Language and communication*. N. Y., McGraw-Hill. [342]

——, Garner, W. R. 1944. Effect of random presentation on the psychometric function. Implications for a quantal theory of discrimination. *Amer J Ps* 57, 451-467. [221]

—— *See also* Licklider, J. C. R. 1951.

Miller, J. 1939. *The effect of facilitatory and inhibitory attitudes on eyelid conditioning*. Ph.D. Yale Univ [575]

Miller, N. E. 1934. The perception of children. A genetic study employing the critical choice delayed reaction. *J genet Ps* 44, 321-339. [607]

—— 1948. Studies of fear as an acquirable drive. I. Fear as motivation and fear-reduction as reinforcement in the learning of new responses. *J exp Ps* 38, 89-101. [674]

—— 1951. Learnable drives and rewards. *Handbk exp Ps* 435-472. S. S. Stevens, ed. N. Y., Wiley. [680]

——, Dollard, J. 1941. *Social learning and imitation*. New Haven, Yale Univ Press. [559]

—— *See also* Dollard, J. 1939, 1950; Mowrer, O. H. 1936.

Minami, H., Dallenbach, K. M. 1946. The effect of activity upon learning and retention in the cockroach. *Amer J Ps* 59, 1-58. [770]

Minium, E. *See* Tolman, E. C. 1942.

Minturn, A. L., Reese, T. W. 1951. The effect of differential reinforcement on the discrimination of visual number. *J Ps* 31, 201-231. [99]

Mintz, E. U. *See* Hecht, S. 1939.

Misbach, L. E. 1932. Effect of pitch of tone-stimuli upon resistance and cardio-vascular phenomena. *J exp Ps* 15, 167-183. [149]

Mistschenko, M. N. 1933. Über die mimisch

Gesichtsmotorik der Blinden. *Folia Neuropath Estonia* 13, 24-43. [130]
Misiak, H. 1947. Age and sex differences in critical flicker frequency. *J exp Ps* 37, 318-332. [382]
—— 1951. The decrease of critical flicker frequency with age. *Science* 113, 551-552. [382]
Moede, W. 1933. Zeitstudien auf dem Kraftwagen. *Indust Psychotech* 10, 165-172. [42]
Moldenhauer, W. 1883. Über die einfache Reactionsdauer einer Geruchsempfindung. *Philos St* 1, 606-614. [17]
Moncrieff, R. W. 1944. *The chemical senses.* N. Y., Wiley. [298, 304, 319]
Montgomery, K. C. 1951a. An experimental investigation of reactive inhibition and conditioned inhibition. *J exp Ps* 41, 39-51. [670]
—— 1951b. "Spontaneous alternation" as a function of time between trials and amount of work. *J exp Ps* 42, 82-93. [670]
—— 1951c. The relation between exploratory behavior and spontaneous alternation in the white rat. *J comp phys Ps* 44, 582-589. [622, 670]
—— 1952. A test of two explanations of spontaneous alternation. *J comp phys Ps* 45, 287-293. [670]
—— 1953a. Exploratory behavior as a function of "similarity" of stimulus situations. *J comp phys Ps* 46, 129-133. [671]
—— 1953b. The effect of activity deprivation upon exploratory behavior. *J comp phys Ps* 46, 438-441. [685]
Moore, K. 1944. Controlled temperatures and preliminary measures of motivation of the white rat. *J exp Ps* 34, 516-524. [657]
Moore, M. G. 1930. Gestalt vs. experience. *Amer J Ps* 42, 453-455. [415]
Morgan, C. 1934. Characteristics of problem-solving behavior of adults. *Iowa Univ St Educ* 9, #5. [823]
Morgan, C. Lloyd. 1894. *An introduction to comparative psychology.* Lond., Scott. [818]
Morgan, C. T. 1942. *Physiological psychology.* N. Y., McGraw-Hill. [238]
—— 1947. The hoarding instinct. *Ps Rev* 54, 335-341. [660]
——, Garner, W. R., Galambos, R. 1951. Pitch and intensity. *J acoust Soc Amer* 23, 658-663. [335]
——, Stellar, E. 1950. *Physiological psychology.* 2d ed. N. Y., McGraw-Hill. [110, 162, 659]
—— *See also* Chapanis, A. 1949; Gould, J. 1942; Stevens, S. S. 1941.
Morgan, J. J. B. 1916. The overcoming of distraction and other resistances. *Arch Ps N.Y.* #35. [85]
——, Morton, J. T. 1944. The distortion of syllogistic reasoning produced by personal convictions. *J soc Ps* 20, 39-59. [847]
Morgan, M. I., Ojemann, R. H. 1942. A study of the Luria method. *J appl Ps* 26, 168-179. [189]
Morgan, R. L., Underwood, B. J. 1950. Proactive inhibition as a function of response similarity. *J exp Ps* 40, 592-603. [757]
Morisett, L. Jr. *See* Maltzman, I. 1953.
Morton, J. T. *See* Morgan, J. J. B. 1944.
Moss, F. A. 1924. Study of animal drives. *J exp Ps* 7, 165-185. [661]
Mosso, A. 1890. Les lois de la fatigue étudiées dans les muscles de l'homme. *Arch ital Biol* 13, 123-186. [800, 802]
—— 1892, 1904, 1915. *Die Ermüdung.* Leip., Hirzel. *Fatigue.* N. Y., Putnam. [800, 802]
Mote, F. A. *See* Graham, C. H. 1939; Riggs, L. A. 1947.
Mowrer, O. H. 1934. The modification of vestibular nystagmus by means of repeated elicitation. *Comp Ps Monogr* #45. [523]
—— 1938. Preparatory set (expectancy)—a determinant in motivation and learning. *Ps Rev* 45, 62-91. [575]
—— 1940a. Anxiety-reduction and learning. *J exp Ps* 27, 497-516. [546, 674]
—— 1941. Preparatory set (expectancy)—further evidence of its 'central' locus. *J exp Ps* 28, 116-133. [106]
—— 1947. On the dual nature of learning—A re-interpretation of "conditioning" and "problem-solving." *Harvard educ Rev* 17, 102-148. *See also Learning theory and personality dynamics.* 1950. [554]
—— 1950. *Learning theory and personality dynamics.* N. Y., Ronald. [528, 554]
——, Jones, H. M. 1943. Extinction and behavior variability as functions of effortfulness of task. *J exp Ps* 33, 369-386. [670]
——, Lamoreaux, R. R. 1942. Avoidance conditioning and signal duration. A study of secondary motivation and reward. *Ps Monogr* #247. [674]
——, Ruch, T. C., Miller, N. E. 1936. The corneo-retinal potential difference as the basis of the galvanometric method of recording eye movements. *Amer J Phys* 114, 423-428. [496]
—— *See also* Dollard, J. 1939; Gibson, J. J. 1938.
Mueller, C. G. 1951. Frequency of seeing functions for intensity discrimination at various levels of adapting intensity. *J genl Phys* 34, 463-474. [210]
——, Lloyd, V. V. 1948. Stereoscopic acuity for various levels of illumination. *Proc Natl Acad Sci* 34, 223-227. [472]
—— *See also* Graham, C. H. 1949; Riggs, L. A. 1947.
Muenzinger, K. F. 1934a. Motivation in learning. I. Electric shock for correct response in the visual discrimination habit. *J comp Ps* 17, 267-277. [600]
—— 1934b. Motivation in learning. II. The function of electric shock for right and wrong responses in human subjects. *J exp Ps* 17, 439-448. [689]
—— 1938. Vicarious trial and error at a point of choice. I. A general survey of its relation to learning efficiency. *J genet Ps* 53, 75-86. [600]

——, Bernstone, A. H., Richards, L. 1938. Motivation in learning. VIII. Equivalent amounts of electric shock for right and wrong responses in a visual discrimination habit. *J comp Ps* 26, 177-186. [600]

——, Fletcher, F. M. 1937. Motivation in learning. VII. The effect of an enforced delay at the point of choice in the visual discrimination habit. *J comp Ps* 23, 383-392. [602]

——, Gentry, E. 1931. Tone discrimination in white rats. *J comp Ps* 12, 195-205. [602]

——, Newcomb, H. 1936. Motivation in learning. V. The relative effectiveness of jumping a gap and crossing an electric grid in a visual discrimination habit. *J comp Ps* 21, 95-104. [602]

——, Powloski, R. F. 1951. Motivation in learning. X. Comparison of electric shock for correct turns in a corrective and a non-corrective situation. *J exp Ps* 42, 118-124. [625]

——, Wood, A. 1935. Motivation in learning. IV. The function of punishment as determined by its temporal relation to the act of choice in the visual discrimination habit. *J comp Ps* 20, 95-106. [600]

Muhlhan, G. J., Stone, C. P. 1949. Effects of electroconvulsive shocks on rat behavior in a Dashiell-type of water maze. *J comp phys Ps* 42, 17-26. [624]

Müller, G. E. 1904. *Die Gesichtspunkte und die Tatsachen der psychophysischen Methodik.* Wiesbaden, Bergmann. [207]

—— 1911. Zur Analyse der Gedächtnistätigkeit und des Vorstellungsverlaufes. *Z Ps Ergbd* #5. [707]

——, Pilzecker, A. 1900. Experimentelle Beiträge zur Lehre vom Gedächtniss. *Z Ps Ergbd #1.* [699, 710, 720, 765]

——, Schumann, F. 1889. Ueber die psychologischen Grundlagen der Vergleichung gehobener Gewichte. *Pflüg Arch ges Phys* 45, 37. [227]

——, —— 1894. Experimentelle Beiträge zur Untersuchung des Gedächtnisses. *Z Ps* 6, 81-190, 257-339. [701, 703, 710, 720]

—— *See also* Martin, L. J. 1899.

Munn, N. L. 1931. An apparatus for testing visual discrimination in animals. *J genet Ps* 39, 342-358. [584]

—— 1932. Bilateral transfer of learning. *J exp Ps* 15, 343-353. [739]

—— 1940. The effect of the knowledge of the situation upon judgment of emotion from facial expressions. *J abnor soc Ps* 35, 324-328. [121, 126, 130]

—— 1946, 1951. *Psychology.* Bost., Houghton Mifflin. [362, 365, 387, 395]

—— 1950. *Handbook of psychological research on the rat.* Bost., Houghton Mifflin. [535]

Münnich, K. 1940. Die Reaktionsleistung in Abhängigkeit von der Körperlage. *Indust Psychotech* 17, 49-83. [38]

Munsell, A. E. D., Sloan, L. L., Godlove, I. H. 1933. Neutral scale values. I. Munsell neutral value scale. *J opt soc Amer* 23, 394-411. [238, 251]

Munsell, A. H. 1915. *Atlas of the Munsell color system.* Maldin, Mass., Wadsworth, Howland. [380, 388]

Munson, W. A. 1947. The growth of auditory sensation. *J acoust Soc Amer* 19, 584-591. [335]

—— *See also* Fletcher, H. 1933.

Münsterberg, H., Bigham, J. 1894. Memory. *Ps Rev* 1, 34-38, 453-461. [700]

Murchison, C. ed. 1934. *Handbk genl exp Ps* Worcester, Clark Univ Press.

Murphy, G. 1917. An experimental study of literary vs. scientific types. *Amer J Ps* 28, 238-262. [59]

—— 1921. A comparison of manic-depressive and dementia praecox cases by the free-association method. *Amer J Insan* 77, 545-558. [53]

—— 1923. Types of word-association in dementia praecox, manic-depressives, and normal persons. *Amer J Psychiat* 2, 539-571. [52]

—— 1949. *Historical introduction to modern psychology.* 2d ed. N. Y., Harcourt, Brace. [237]

Murphy, L. B. *See* Biber, B. 1942.

Musatti, C. L. 1931. Forma e assimilazione. *Arch ital Ps* 9, 61-156. [409]

Muscio, B. 1921. Is a fatigue test possible? *Br J Ps* 12, 31-46. [805]

N

Nafe, J. P. 1934. The pressure, pain, and temperature senses. *Handbk genl exp Ps* 1037-1087. C. Murchison, ed. Worcester, Clark Univ Press. [293]

——, Wagoner, K. S. 1936. The experiences of warmth, cold, and heat. *J Ps* 2, 421-431. [293]

——, —— 1941. The nature of pressure adaptation. *J genl Ps* 25, 323-351. [287]

Nagel, W. A. *See* Kries, J. v. 1900.

Nagge, J. W. 1935. An experimental test of the theory of associative interference. *J exp Ps* 18, 663-682. [766]

—— *See also* Hunter, W. S. 1931.

Nathan, P. W. *See* Russell, W. R. 1946.

Nathanson, L. M. *See* Wagman, I. H. 1942.

Needham, J. G. 1934a. The time-error in comparison-judgments. *Ps Bull* 31, 229-243. [226]

—— 1934b. The time error as a function of continued experimentation. *Amer J Ps* 46, 558-567. [227, 228]

Neff, W. D. 1947. The effects of partial section of the auditory nerve. *J comp Phys Ps* 40, 203-215. [349]

—— *See also* Shuknecht, H. F. 1951; Wever, E. G. 1947.

Neff, W. S. 1936. A critical investigation of the visual apprehension of movement. *Amer J Ps* 48, 1-42. [515]

——, Dallenbach, K. M 1936. The chronaxy of pressure and pain. *Amer J Ps* 48, 632-637. [282]

Nelson, L. *See* Sidis, B. 1910.

Neuhaus, W. 1930. Experimentelle Untersuchung

der Scheinbewegung. *Arch ges Ps* 75, 315-458. [513]

Neumann, E. 1950. *A study of palmar skin resistance.* Thesis. Ph.D. Brown Univ. [145]

Newcomb, H. *See* Muenzinger, K. F. 1936.

Newhall, S. M. 1923. Effects of attention on the intensity of cutaneous pressure and on visual brightness. *Arch Ps N.Y.* #61. [227]

—— 1950. A method of evaluating the spacing of visual scales. *Amer J Ps* 63, 221-228. [250, 261]

——, Nickerson, D., Judd, D. B. 1943. Final report of the OSA. Subcommittee on the Spacing of the Munsell Colors. *J opt Soc Amer* 33, 385-418. [430]

Newman, E. B. 1939. Forgetting of meaningful material during sleep and waking. *Amer J Ps* 52, 65-71. [770]

—— 1948. Hearing. *Foundations of Ps* 313-350. E. G. Boring, H. S. Langfeld, & H. P. Weld, eds. N. Y., Wiley. [330]

—— 1950. Hearing. *Ann Rev Ps* 1, 49-70. [330]

——, Volkmann, J., Stevens, S. S. 1937. On the method of bisection and its relation to a loudness scale. *Amer J Ps* 49, 134-137. [240]

—— *See also* Stevens, S. S. 1934; 1936a, b; 1937; Wallach, H. 1949.

Newton, Sir I. 1704. *Opticks.* Lond., S. Smith. [362]

Nickerson, D. *See* Newhall, S. M. 1943.

Nicolai, F. 1922. Experimentelle Untersuchungen über das Haften von Gesichtseindrücken und dessen zeitlichen Verlauf. *Arch ges Ps* 42, 132-149. [794]

Nie, L. W. *See* Boyd, D. A., Jr. 1949.

Nissen, A. E. 1928. *Influence of emotions upon systolic blood-pressure.* Thesis. M.A. Columbia Univ (unpublished). [164]

Nissen, H. W. 1930. A study of exploratory behavior in the white rat by means of the obstruction method. *J genet Ps* 37, 361-376. Reprinted in C. J. Warden, 1931. [663]

—— 1950. Description of the learned response in discrimination behavior. *Ps Rev* 57, 121-131. [630]

——, Carpenter, C. R., Cowles, J. T. 1936. Stimulus—versus response—differentiation in delayed reactions of chimpanzees. *J genet Ps* 48, 112-136. [608]

——, Elder, J. H. 1935. The influence of amount of incentive on delayed response performances of chimpanzees. *J genet Ps* 47, 49-72. [668]

——, Jenkins, W. O. 1943. Reduction and rivalry of cues in the discrimination behavior of chimpanzees. *J comp Ps* 35, 85-95. [598]

——, Riesen, A. H., Nowlis, V. 1938. Delayed response and discrimination learning by chimpanzees. *J comp Ps* 26, 361-386. [607]

—— *See also* Riesen, A. H. 1942.

Nixon, H. K. 1924. Attention and interest in advertising. *Arch Ps N.Y.* #72. [75]

—— 1926. *An investigation of attention to advertisements.* N. Y., Columbia Univ Press. [75]

Norris, E. B. 1950. Discrimination learning with paired and single stimulus presentation. *Amer Psychol* 5, 257. [588]

—— 1953. Performance of a motor task as a function of interpolation of varying lengths of rest at different points in acquisition. *J exp Ps* 45, 260-264. [792]

——, Grant, D. A. 1948. Eyelid conditioning as affected by verbally induced inhibitory set and counter reinforcement. *Amer J Ps* 61, 37-49. [575]

—— *See also* Grant, D. A. 1947; Shipley, W. C. 1946; Spence, K. W. 1950.

North, A. J. 1950. Improvement in successive discrimination reversals. *J comp phys Ps* 43, 442-460. [765]

Nowlis, H. H. 1941. The influence of success and failure on the resumption of an interrupted task. *J exp Ps* 28, 304-325. [691]

Nowlis, V. *See* Nissen, H. W. 1938.

Nutting, P. G. 1908. The luminous equivalent of radiation. *Bull Bur Standards* 5, 261-308. [224]

Nyswander, D. B. 1929. A comparison of the high relief finger maze and the stylus maze. *J genl Ps* 2, 273-289. [620]

—— *See also* Stone, C. P. 1927.

O

Oberly, H. S. 1924. The range for visual attention, cognition and apprehension. *Amer J Ps* 35, 332-352. [94, 95]

—— 1928. A comparison of the spans of 'attention' and memory. *Amer J Ps* 40, 295-302. [705]

O'Brien, C. C. 1943. Part and whole methods in the memorization of music. *J educ Ps* 34, 552-560. [785]

O'Brien, F. J. 1921. A qualitative investigation on the effect of mode of presentation upon the process of learning. *Amer J Ps* 32, 249-283. [707]

O'Connor, J. 1928. *Born that way.* Balt., Williams & Wilkins. [51]

—— 1934. *Psychometrics.* Cambridge, Harvard Univ Press. [53]

Ogden, R. M. 1903. Untersuchungen über den Einfluss der Geschwindigkeit des Lesens auf das Erlernen und Behalten von sinnlosen und sinnvollen Stoffen. *Arch ges Ps* 2, 93-189. [707]

Ogdon, D. P. *See* Cohen, J. 1949.

Ogle, K. N. 1946. Theory of the space-eikonometer. *J opt Soc Amer* 36, 20-32. [488]

—— 1950. *Researches in binocular vision.* Phila., Saunders. [461, 488]

Ohma, S. 1922. La classification des odeurs aromatiques en sous-classes. *Arch néerl Phys* 6, 567-590. [310, 316]

Ohms, H. 1910. Untersuchung unterwertiger Assoziationen mittels des Worterkennungsvorganges. *Z Ps* 56, 1-84. [720]

Ojemann, R. H. *See* Morgan, M. I. 1942.

Olsson, L. *See* Anderson, B. 1950.

Oppel, T. W. *See* Hardy, J. D. 1937.

Orchansky, J. 1898. Eine Methode die Augenbewegungen direkt zu untersuchen (Ophthalmographie). *Zbl Phys* 12, 785. [498]

Orlansky, J. 1940. The effect of similarity and difference in form on apparent visual movement. *Arch Ps N.Y.* #246. [518]

Orth, J. *See* Mayer, A. 1901.

Osgood, C. E. 1949. The similarity paradox in human learning. *Ps Rev* 56, 132-143. [754, 766]

Ovsiankina, M. 1928. Die Wiederaufnahme unterbrochener Handlungen. *Ps Forsch* 11, 302. [690]

P

Pacaud, S. 1942. Contribution a l'étude des mouvements volontaires. *Ann Ps* 40, 152-170. [40]

Pace, E. A. 1902. Fluctuations of attention and after-images. *Philos St* 20, 232-245. [79, 80]

Pachauri, A. R. 1935. A study of Gestalt problems in completed and interrupted tasks. *Br J Ps* 25, 365-380, 447-457. [692]

—— 1936. A study of Gestalt problems in completed and interrupted tasks. *Br J Ps* 27, 170-180. [692]

Painter, W. S. 1916. Efficiency in mental multiplication under extreme fatigue. *J educ Ps* 7, 25-30. [804]

Pan, J. G. *See* Wang, C. H. 1929.

Panum, P. L. 1858. Physiologische Untersuchungen über das Sehen mit zwei Augen. Kiel, Schwers. [468]

Park, D. G. *See* Guilford, J. P. 1931.

Parker, G. H. 1922. *Smell, taste, and allied senses in the vertebrates.* Phila., Lippincott. [297]

Parsons, J. H. 1924. *An introduction to the study of colour vision.* 2d ed. Cambridge, Univ Press. [396]

Paschal, F. C. 1941. The trend in theories of attention. *Ps Rev* 48, 383-403. [106]

Passey, G. E. 1948. The influence of intensity of unconditioned stimulus upon acquisition of a conditioned response. *J exp Ps* 38, 420-428. [667]

Passy, J. 1892. Note sur les minimums perceptibles de quelques odeurs. *C R Soc Biol* 44, 84-88. [320]

—— 1893. L'odeur dans la série grasse. *C R Soc Biol* 45, 479-481. [319]

Pastore, N. 1949. Need as a determinant of perception. *J Ps* 28, 457-475. [491]

Paterson, D. G., Tinker, M. A. 1929. Studies of typographical factors influencing speed of reading. *J appl Ps* 13, 120-130. [103]

——, —— 1947. The effect of typography upon the perceptual span in reading. *Amer J Ps* 60, 388-396. [103]

Pathman, J. H. *See* Freeman, G. L. 1942.

Patrick, C. 1935. Creative thought in poets. *Arch Ps N.Y.* #178. [839]

—— 1937. Creative thought in artists. *J Ps* 4, 35-73. [839]

Patten, E. F. 1938. The influence of distribution of repetitions on certain rote learning phenomena. *J Ps* 5, 359-374. [712]

Patterson, E. 1930. A qualitative and quantitative study of the emotion of surprise. *Ps Monogr* #181. [155]

Patterson, P. M., Lauder, B. A. 1948. The incidence and probable inheritance of "smell blindness." *J Hered* 39, 295-297. [318]

Pattle, R. E., Weddell, G. 1948. Observations on electrical stimulation of pain fibers in an exposed human sensory nerve. *J Neurophys* 11, 93-98. [285]

Patton, R. A. *See* Karn, H. W. 1939.

Paulhan, F. 1887. La Simultanéité des Actes Psychiques. *Rev Scient* 39, 684-689. [88]

Pauli, R. 1924. Der Umfang und die Enge des Bewusstseins. *Z Biol* 81, 93-112. [90]

Pavlov, I. P. 1927. *Conditioned reflexes.* Trans. G. V. Anrep. N. Y., Oxford Univ Press. [542, 543, 548, 560, 562, 567, 579, 657, 669, 689]

—— 1928. *Lectures on conditioned reflexes.* Trans. W. H. Gantt. N. Y., International. [543, 548]

Payne, B., Davis, R. C. 1940. The role of muscular tension in the comparison of lifted weights. *J exp Ps* 27, 227-242. [227]

Peak, H. 1933. An evaluation of the concepts of reflex and voluntary action. *Ps Rev* 40, 71-89. [572]

Pearce, C. H. *See* Willey, C. F. 1937.

Pechstein, L. A. 1917. Whole vs. part methods in motor learning. *Ps Monogr* #99. [783]

—— 1918. Whole vs. part methods in learning nonsensical syllables. *J educ Ps* 9, 379-387. [782]

—— 1921. Massed vs. distributed effort in learning. *J educ Ps* 12, 92-97. [790]

Peckham, R. H. 1936. Eye-movements during 'retinal rivalry.' *Amer J Ps* 48, 43-63. [400]

Pendleton, C. R. 1928. The cold receptor. *Amer J Ps* 40, 353-371. [277, 279]

Pennock, L. *See* Simon, C. W. 1951.

Perin, C. T. 1942. Behavior potentiality as a joint function of the amount of training and the degree of hunger at the time of extinction. *J exp Ps* 30, 93-113. [656]

Perkins, N. L. 1914. The value of distributed repetitions in rote learning. *Br J Ps* 7, 253-261. [790]

—— 1927. Human reactions in a maze of fixed orientation. *Comp Ps Monogr* #21. [650, 653]

Perlman, H. B. *See* Shuknecht, H. F. 1951.

Perrin, F. A. C. 1914. An experimental and introspective study of the human learning process in the maze. *Ps Monogr* #70. [647, 648]

Peskin, J. C. 1942. The regeneration of visual purple in the living animal. *J genl Phys* 26, 27-47. [371]

Peters, H. N. *See* McGeoch, J. A. 1933.

Peterson, F., Jung, C. G. 1907. Psychophysical investigations with the galvanometer and pneumograph in normal and insane individuals. *Brain* 30, 153-218. [153]

Peterson, J. 1920. The backward elimination of errors in mental maze learning. *J exp Ps* 3, 257-280. [653]

—— 1922. Learning when frequency and recency

factors are negative. *J exp Ps* 5, 270-300. [653]
Pfaffmann, C. 1935. An experimental comparison of the method of single stimuli and the method of constant stimuli in gustation. *Amer J Ps* 47, 470-476. [217, 219]
—— 1941. Gustatory afferent impulses. *J cell comp Phys* 17, 243-258. [300]
—— 1951. Taste and smell. *Handbk exp Ps* 1143-1171. S. S. Stevens, ed. N. Y., Wiley. [298, 304, 312, 313, 321]
——, Bare, J. K. 1950. Gustatory nerve discharges in normal and adrenalectomized rats. *J comp phys Ps* 43, 320-324. [658]
——, Schlosberg, H. 1953. An analysis of sensory methods for testing flavor. *Contract Research Project*. 7-84-15-007. *File* P-1102. *Rept*. 7. Brown Univ. [298]
Philip, B. R. 1934. Reaction time in children. *Amer J Ps* 46, 379-396. [34]
Philippe, J. 1897. Sur les transformations de nos images mentales. *Rev philos* 43, 481-493. [774]
Philpott, S. J. F. 1932. Fluctuations in human output. *Br J Ps Monogr* #17. [83]
Physiological mechanisms in animal behavior. 1950. *Symposia Society for Experimental Biology* #4. N. Y., Academic Press. [R]
Piderit, T. 1859. *Mimik und Physiognomik*. Detmold, Meyers. 4th ed., 1925. [112]
Pierce, A. H. 1901. *Studies in auditory and visual space perception*. N. Y., Longmans, Green. [350, 357]
Piéron, H. 1913. Recherches expérimentales sur les phénomènes de memoire. *Ann Ps* 19, 91-193. [790]
—— 1919. De la loi de variation des temps de latence en fonctions des intensités excitatrices par les sensations auditives. *C R Soc Biol* 82, 1116-1118. [21]
—— 1920. Researches comparatives sur la mémoire des formes et celle des chiffres. *Ann Ps* 21, 119-148. [714, 715]
—— 1928. Technique de laboratoire et appareils. *Ann Ps* 27, 234-241. [15]
—— 1929. De la summation spatiale des impressions lumineuses au niveau de la fovea. *Ann Ps* 30, 87-105. [375]
—— 1937. Recherches sur la latence de perception des accroissements de luminosité. *Ann Ps* 37, 1-16. [263 f]
—— 1952. *The sensations*. New Haven, Yale Univ Press.
Pikler, J. 1928. Grund und Figur bei schwacher Beleuchtung. *Z Ps* 106, 316-326. [406]
Pillsbury, W. B. 1897. A study in apperception. *Amer J Ps* 8, 315-393. [102]
—— 1910. *The psychology of reasoning*. N. Y., Appleton. [818]
Pilzecker, A. *See* Müller, G. E. 1900.
Piper, H. 1903. Über Dunkeladaptation. *Z Ps* 31, 161-214. [369]
Pirenne, M. H. 1943. Binocular and uniocular threshold of vision. *Nature Lond* 152, 698. [398]
—— 1945. On the variation of visual acuity with light intensity. *Proc Cambridge philos Soc* 42, 78-82. [385]
—— 1948. *Vision and the eye*. Lond., Chapman & Hall. [365, 373, 377, 385]
—— *See also* Hecht, S. 1942.
Platt, W., Baker, B. A. 1931. The relation of the scientific "hunch" to research. *J chem Educ* 8, 1969-2002. [839]
Poffenberger, A. T. 1912. Reaction time to retinal stimulation with special reference to the time lost in conduction through nerve centers. *Arch Ps N.Y.* #23. [17, 25]
—— 1915. The influence of improvement in one simple mental process upon other related processes. *J educ Ps* 6, 459-474. [751]
—— 1927. The effects of continuous mental work. *Amer J Ps* 39, 283-296. [804]
—— 1928. The effects of continuous work upon output and feelings. *J appl Ps* 12, 459-467. [804]
—— 1942. *Principles of applied psychology*. N. Y., Appleton-Century. [87, 804, 805]
Pohlmann, A. 1906. *Experimentelle Beiträge zur Lehre vom Gedächtnis*. Doctor's dissertation. Göttingen Univ. [697]
Poincaré, H. 1908. *Science et méthode*. Paris, Flammarion. [838]
Pollack, I. *See* Licklider, J. C. R. 1948.
Polvogt, L. M. *See* Crowe, S. J. 1934.
Polyak, S. L. 1941. *The retina*. Chic., Univ Chicago Press. [365, 384]
Porter, J. M., Jr. 1938a. Adaptation of the galvanic skin response. *J exp Ps* 23, 553-557. [151]
—— 1938b. Extinction of an acquired response as a function of the interval between successive non-rewarded trials. *J comp Ps* 26, 261-270. [560]
—— 1939. Experimental extinction as a function of the interval between successive non-reinforced elicitations. *J genl Ps* 20, 109-134. [560]
Porter, L. W., Duncan, C. P. 1953. Negative transfer in verbal learning. *J exp Ps* 46, 61-64. [753]
Porter, P. B., Stone, C. P. 1947. Electro-convulsive shock in rats under ether anesthesia. *J comp phys Ps* 40, 441-456. [772]
Porteus, S. D. 1950. *The Porteus maze test and intelligence*. Palo Alto, Calif. Pacific Books. [649]
Portych, Th *See* Michotte, A. 1914.
Postman, L. 1946. The time-error in auditory perception. *Amer J Ps* 59, 193-219. [227, 228]
——, Bruner, J. S., McGinnies, E. 1948. Personal values as selective factors in perception. *J abnor soc Ps* 43, 142-154. [104, 691]
—— *See also* Allport, G. W. 1947; Jenkins, W. O. 1949.
Potter, R. K., Kopp, G. A., Green, H. C. 1947. *Visible speech*. N. Y., Nostrand. [340]
Powell, V. E. *See* Silverman, J. J. 1944.
Powloski, R. F. *See* Muenzinger, K. F. 1951.
Pratt, C. C. 1933a. The time-error in psychophysical judgments. *Amer J Ps* 45, 292-297. [229]
—— 1933b. Time-error in the method of single stimuli. *J exp Ps* 16, 798-814. [230]

—— 1950. The role of past experience in visual perception. *J Ps* 30, 85-107. [485]
Pratt, J. G. *See* McCulloch, T. L. 1934.
Prentice, W. C. H. 1948. New observations of 'binocular yellow.' *J exp Ps* 38, 284-288. [401]
—— 1949. Continuity in human learning. *J exp Ps* 39, 187-194. [608, 609]
Preston, M. G. 1936. Contrast effects and the psychophysical judgments. *Amer J Ps* 48, 389-402. [228]
Prideaux, E. 1920. The psychogalvanic reflex, a review. *Brain* 43, 50-73. [156]
Priest, I. G. 1920. Note on the relation between frequencies of complementary hues. *J Opt Soc Amer* 4, 402-404. [392]
Pronovost, W. *See* Fairbanks, G. 1939.
Proshansky, H. *See* Jerome, E. A. 1950.
Prosser, C. L., Hunter, W. S. 1936. The extinction of startle responses and spinal reflexes in the white rat. *Amer J Phys* 117, 609-618. [559]

R

Rabinowitz, H. S. *See* Birch, H. G. 1951.
Radner, M. *See* Gibson, J. J. 1937.
Radosavljevich, P. R. 1907. Das Behalten und Vergessen bei Kindern und Erwachsenen nach experimentellen Untersuchungen. *Päd Monogr* #1. [728]
Raffel, G. 1934. The effect of recall on forgetting. *J exp Ps* 17, 828-838. [697, 795]
—— 1936. Recovery of sensitivity to prick and touch after pressure block, with a note on the sensitivity of hair spots. *J genl Ps* 15, 13-21. [281]
Ramsaroop, A. *See* Kleitman, N. 1948.
Ramsey, G. V. *See* Blake, R. R. 1951.
Ranschburg, P. 1901. Apparat und Methode zur Untersuchung des optischen Gedächtnisses für medizinische und pädagogisch-psychologische Zwecke. *Monatsschr Psychiat Neu* 10, 321-333. [703]
Rapaport, D., Gill, M., Schafer, R. 1946. *Diagnostic psychological testing.* 2 vols. Chic., Year Book Publishers. [70]
Ratliff, F. 1952. The role of physiological nystagmus in monocular acuity. *J exp Ps* 43, 163-172. [498]
——, Riggs, L. A. 1950. Involuntary motions of the eye during monocular fixation. *J exp Ps* 40, 687-701. [498]
—— *See also* Riggs, L. A. 1951, 1953.
Ratoosh, P. 1949. On interposition as a cue for the perception of distance. *Proc Natl Acad Sci* 35, 257-259. [462]
Rawnsley, A. I., Harris, J. D. 1952. Studies in short-duration auditory fatigue. II. Recovery time. *J exp Ps* 43, 138-142. [336]
—— *See also* Harris, J. D. 1951.
Rayner, R. *See* Watson, J. B. 1920.
Razran, G. H. S. 1933. Conditioned responses in animals other than dogs. *Ps Bull* 30, 261-324. [560, 573]
—— 1935. Conditioned responses: an experimental study and a theoretical analysis. *Arch Ps N.Y.* #191. [573]
—— 1937. Conditioned reflexes: a classified bibliography. *Ps Bull* 34, 191-256. [543]
—— 1938. Transposition of relational responses and generalization of conditioned responses. *Ps Rev* 45, 532-538. [577]
—— 1939a. The nature of the extinctive process. *Ps Rev* 46, 264-297. [560]
—— 1939b. Studies in configural conditioning. II. The effect of subjects' attitudes and task-sets upon configural conditioning. *J exp Ps* 24, 95-105. [574]
—— 1949. Stimulus generalization of conditioned responses. *Ps Bull* 46, 337-365. [580]
Reed, H. B. 1917. A repetition of Ebert and Meumann's practice experiment in memory. *J exp Ps* 2, 315-346. [744]
—— 1918. Associative aids. I. Their relation to learning, retention, and other associations. II. Their relation to practice and the transfer of training. III. Their relation to the theory of thought and to methodology in psychology. *Ps Rev* 25, 128-155, 257-285, 378-401. [707, 711]
—— 1924. Part and whole methods of learning. *J educ Ps* 15, 107-115, 592-595. [782]
——, Zinszer, H. A. 1943. The occurrence of plateaus in telegraphy. *J exp Ps* 33, 130-135. [811, 812]
Rees, H. J., Israel, H. C. 1935. An investigation of the establishment and operation of mental sets. *Ps Monogr* 46, #210. [836]
Reese, E. P. *See* Jensen, E. M. 1950.
Reese, T. W. 1943. The application of the theory of physical measurement to the measurement of psychological magnitudes, with three experimental examples. *Ps Monogr* #251. [245]
—— *See also* Jensen, E. M. 1950; Kaufman, E. L. 1949; Minturn, A. L. 1951.
Reeves, P. 1918. Rate of pupillary dilation and contraction. *Ps Rev* 25, 330-340. [368]
Rehwoldt, F. 1911. Über respiratorische Affektsymptome. Mit Atlas von 25 Tafeln. *Ps St* 7, 141-195. [170, 173]
Reid, J. W. 1951. An experimental study of "analysis of the goal" in problem-solving. *J genl Ps* 44, 51-69. [829]
Reid, L. S. *See* Wickens, D. D. 1949.
Renshaw, S. 1945. The visual perception and reproduction of forms by tachistoscopic methods. *J Ps* 20, 217-232. [103]
—— *See also* Steckle, L. G. 1934.
Rethlingshafer, D. 1943. Experimental evidence for functional autonomy of motives. *Ps Rev* 50, 397-407. [686]
Rey, A. 1936. Les conduites conditionnées du cobaye. *Arch de Ps* 25, 217-312. [678]
Reynolds, B. 1945a. A repetition of the Blodgett experiment on 'latent learning.' *J exp Ps* 35, 504-516. [638, 653]
—— 1945b. Extinction of trace conditioned responses as a function of the spacing of trials

during the acquisition and extinction series. *J exp Ps* 35, 81-95. [560]
—— 1945c. The acquisition of a trace conditioned response as a function of the magnitude of the stimulus trace. *J exp Ps* 35, 15-30. [570, 571]
—— 1949. The acquisition of a black-white discrimination habit under two levels of reinforcement. *J exp Ps* 39, 760-769. [666]
—— 1950. Acquisition of a simple spatial discrimination as a function of the amount of reinforcement. *J exp Ps* 40, 152-160. [666]
——, Adams, J. A. 1953. Motor performance as a function of click reinforcement. *J exp Ps* 45, 315-320. [688]
—— *See also* Adams, J. A. 1952.
Ribot, Th. 1939. *Centenaire de Th. Ribot*. Agen. Imprimerie Moderne.
Rich, G. J. 1916. A preliminary study of tonal volume. *J exp Ps* 1, 13-22. [336]
—— 1919. A study of tonal attributes. *Amer J Ps* 30, 121-164. [336, 337, 341]
Richards, L. *See* Muenzinger, K. F. 1938.
Richards, W. J. 1951. The effect of alternating views of the test object on vernier and stereoscopic acuities. *J exp Ps* 42, 376-383. [201]
Richman, H. *See* Kendler, H. H. 1952.
Richter, C. P. 1924. The sweat glands studied by the electrical resistance method. *Amer J Phys* 68, 147. [143]
—— 1926. The significance of changes in the electrical resistance of the body during sleep. *Proc Natl Acad Sci* 12, 214-222. [143, 144]
—— 1927. Animal behavior and internal drives. *Q Rev Biol* 2, 307-343. [656]
—— 1929a. Physiological factors involved in the electrical resistance of the skin. *Amer J Phys* 88, 596-615. [142]
—— 1929b. Pathological sleep and similar conditions studied by electrical skin resistance method. *Arch Neu Psychiat* 21, 363-375. [143]
—— 1931. Sleep produced by hypnotics studied by the electrical skin resistance method. *J Pharm exp Therap* 42, 471-486. [143]
—— 1942. Self-regulatory functions. *Harvey Lectures* Ser 38, 63-103.
—— 1947. Biology of drives. *J comp phys Ps* 40, 129-134. [658]
——, Woodruff, B. G. 1942. Facial patterns of electrical skin resistance; their relation to sleep, external temperature, hair distribution, sensory dermatomes and skin disease. *Johns Hopkins Hosp Bull* 70, 442-459. [144]
——, ——, Eaton, B. C. 1943. Hand and foot patterns of low electrical skin resistance. Their anatomical and neurological significance. *J Neurophys* 6, 417-424. [144]
—— *See also* Langworthy, O. R. 1930; Wang, C. H. 1928.
Ricker-Ovsiankina, M. A. *See* Ovsiankina, M.
Riedel, C. 1937. Über die Abhängigkeit optischer Kontraste von Gestaltbedingungen. *Neue ps St* 10, 1-44. [451]
Riesen, A. H. 1940. Delayed reward in discrimination learning by chimpanzees. *Comp Ps Monogr* #77. [607]
——, Nissen, H. W. 1942. Non-spatial delayed response by the matching technique. *J comp Ps* 34, 307-313. [607]
—— *See also* Hovland, C. I. 1940; Nissen, H. W. 1938.
Riess, B. F. 1946. Genetic changes in semantic conditioning. *J exp Ps* 36, 143-152. [580]
Riesz, R. R. 1928. Differential intensity sensitivity of the ear for pure tones. *Physical Rev* 31, 867-875. [223, 334]
Riggs, L. A. 1937. Dark adaptation in the frog eye as determined by the electrical response of the retina. *J cell comp Phys* 9, 491-510. [372]
—— 1941. Continuous and reproducible records of the electrical activity of the human retina. *Proc Soc exp Biol Med* 48, 204-207. [372]
——, Berry, R. N., Wayner, M. 1949. A comparison of electrical and psychophysical determinations of the spectral sensitivity of the human eye. *J opt Soc Amer* 39, 427-436. [372]
——, Johnson, E. P. 1949. Electrical responses of the human retina. *J exp Ps* 39, 415-424. [373]
——, Mueller, C. G., Graham, C. H., Mote, F. A. 1947. Photographic measurements of atmospheric "boil." *J opt Soc Amer* 37, 415-420. [467]
——, Ratliff, F. 1951. Visual acuity and the normal tremor of the eyes. *Science* 114, 17-18. [498]
——, ——, Cornsweet, J. C., Cornsweet, T. N. 1953. The disappearance of steadily fixated visual test objects. *J opt Soc Amer* 43, 495-501. [499]
—— *See also* Berry, R. M. 1950; Graham, C. H. 1949; Ratliff, F. 1950.
Rikimaru, J. 1937. Taste deficiency for P.T.C., with special reference to its hereditary nature. *Jap J Ps* 12, 33-54. [301]
Riklin, F. *See* Jung, C. G. 1904.
Riley, D. A. 1952. Rote learning as a function of distribution of practice and the complexity of the situation. *J exp Ps* 43, 88-95. [790]
Riopelle, A. J. 1953. Transfer suppression and learning sets. *J comp phys Ps* 46, 108-114. [760]
Ritchie, B. F. 1948. Studies in spatial learning. VI. Place orientation and direction orientation. *J exp Ps* 38, 659-669. [632]
——, Ebeling, E., Roth, W. 1950. Evidence for continuity in the discrimination of vertical and horizontal patterns. *J comp phys Ps* 43, 168-180. [596]
—— *See also* Tolman, E. C. 1946a, b; 1947a, b.
Rivers, W. H. R. *See* Head, H. 1920.
Roberts, M. L. *See* Shipley, W. C. 1946.
Roberts, S. O. *See* Carmichael, L. 1937.
Roberts, W. H. 1932. A two-dimensional analysis of the discrimination of differences in the frequency of vibrations by means of the sense of touch. *J Franklin Inst* 213, 283-311. [295]
Robertson, V. M. *See* Fry, G. A. 1935.
Robinson, E. H. *See* Kemp, E. H. 1937.
Robinson, E. S. 1920. Some factors determining

the degree of retroactive inhibition. *Ps Monogr* #128. [766]

—— 1932. *Association theory today*. N. Y., Century. [46]

—— 1934. Work of the integrated organism. *Handbk genl exp Ps* 571-650. C. Murchison. ed. Worcester, Clark Univ Press. [802, 804, 808]

——, Bills, A. G. 1926. Two factors in the work decrement. *J exp Ps* 9, 415-443. [804]

——, Brown, M. A. 1926. Effect of serial position on memorization. *Am J Ps* 37, 538-552. [698, 712]

Robinson, E. W., Wever, E. G. 1930. Visual distance discrimination in the rat. *Calif U Publ Ps* 4, 233-239. [618]

Robinson, F. P. 1933. The role of eye movements in reading with an evaluation of the techniques for their improvement. *Iowa St U Aims Prog Res* #39. [506]

Robinson, G. A. *See* Smith, K. R. 1951.

Roby, T. B. *See* Sheffield, F. D. 1950.

Rodnick, E. H. 1937a. Characteristics of delayed and trace conditioned responses. *J exp Ps* 20, 409-425. [566]

—— 1937b. Does the interval of delay of conditioned responses possess inhibitory properties. *J exp Ps* 20, 507-527. [566]

——, Shakow, D. 1940. Set in the schizophrenic as measured by a composite reaction time index. *Amer J Psychiat* 97, 214-225. [37]

Roethlisberger, F. J., Dickson, W. J. 1939. *Management and the worker*. Cambridge. Harvard Univ Press. [806]

Rogers, S. 1941. The anchoring of absolute judgments. *Arch Ps N.Y.* #261. [217, 231, 243, 249]

Rohrer, J. H. 1947. Experimental extinction as a function of the distribution of extinction trials and response strength. *J exp Ps* 37, 473-493. [560]

—— 1949. Factors influencing the occurrence of reminiscence: Attempted formal rehearsal during the interpolated period. *J exp Ps* 39, 484-491. [796]

Rokeach, M. 1950. The effect of perception time upon rigidity and concreteness of thinking. *J exp Ps* 40, 206-216. [837]

Romaine, M. *See* Hanlon, L. W. 1949.

Rosanoff, A. J. *See* Kent, G. H. 1910.

Rosenblith, W. A. *See* Békésy, G. v. 1948.

Rosenzweig, M. R. *See* Wallach, H. 1949.

Ross, S., Harriman, A. E. 1949. A preliminary study of the Crocker-Henderson odor-classification system. *Amer J Ps* 62, 399-404. [310]

Rossman, I. L., Goss, A. E. 1951. The acquired distinctiveness of cues: The role of discriminative verbal responses in facilitating the acquisition of discriminative motor responses. *J exp Ps* 42, 173-182. [759]

Rossman, J. 1931. *The psychology of the inventor*. Washington, D.C., Inventors Publ. [839]

Roth, W. *See* Ritchie, B. F. 1950.

Rothney, J. W. M. *See* Imus, H. A. 1938.

Rotter, J. B. *See* Schroder, H. M. 1952.

Rubin, E. 1915. *Synsoplevede Figurer*. Copen., Gyldendalska. [403, 411]

—— 1921. *Visuell wahrgenommene Figuren*. Copen., Gyldendalska. [403, 411]

Rubin-Rabson, G. 1937. The influence of analytical pre-study in memorizing piano music. *Arch Ps N.Y.* #220. [782]

Ruch, T. C. 1946. The nervous system. *Howell's textbk phys* 305-366, 385-400, 408-438, 463-545. J. F. Fulton. ed. Phila., Saunders. [238]

—— 1951. Sensory mechanisms. *Handbk exp Ps* 121-153. S. S. Stevens, ed. N. Y., Wiley. [270]

—— *See also* Mowrer, O. H. 1936.

Ruckmick, C. A. 1921. A preliminary study of the emotions. *Ps Monogr* #136. [116, 118, 126]

—— 1928. *The mental life*. N. Y., Longmans, Green. [116]

—— 1938. The truth about lie detection. *J appl Ps* 22, 50-58. [186]

Rudolph, H. 1903. *Der Ausdruck der Gemütsbewegungen des Menschen*. Text and over-size atlas. Dresden, Kuehtmann. [116]

Rudolph, H. J. 1947. *Attention and interest factors in advertising*. N. Y., Funk & Wagnalls. [75]

Ruediger, W. C. 1907. The field of distinct vision. *Arch Ps N.Y.* #5. [103, 105]

Ruger, H. 1910. The psychology of efficiency. *Arch Ps N.Y.* #15. [821, 822, 827, 837]

——, Bussenius, C. E. 1913. *Memory*. N. Y., Teachers College. Columbia Univ. [710, 725]

Rupp, H. 1923. Über optische Analyse. *Ps Forsch* 4, 262-300. [409]

Russell, R. W. 1949. Effects of electroshock convulsions on learning and retention in rats as functions of difficulty of the task. *J comp phys Ps* 42, 137-142. [772]

—— *See also* Dennis, W. 1939.

Russell, W. R., Nathan, P. W. 1946. Traumatic amnesia. *Brain* 69, 280-300. [771]

Rutherford, W. 1886. A new theory of hearing. *J anat Phys Lond* 21, 166-168. [328]

Ryan, A. H., Warner, M. 1936. The effect of automobile driving on the reactions of the driver. *Amer J Ps* 48, 403-421. [808]

Ryan, T. A. 1947. *Work and effort. The psychology of production*. N. Y., Ronald. [175, 803, 805]

——, Cottrell, C. L., Bitterman, M. E. 1950, 1951. Muscular tension as an index of effort. *Amer J Ps* 63, 317-341; 64, 117-124. [178, 809]

S

Sackman, H. 1949. *A combination method of reaction time and correct responses as a measure of learning*. Thesis M. A. (unpublished) Columbia Univ. [42]

Saidullah, A. 1927. Experimentelle Untersuchungen über den Geschmacksinn. *Arch ges Ps* 60, 457-484. [302]

Salisbury, R. 1934. A study of the transfer effects of training in logical organization. *J educ Res* 28, 241-251. [829]

Salmon, T. N. *See* Blakeslee, A. F. 1935.

Saltzman, I., Koch, S. 1948. The effect of low intensities of hunger on the behavior mediated by a habit of maximum strength. *J exp Ps* 38, 347-370. [656]

Saltzman, I. J. 1949. Maze learning in the absence of primary reinforcement: a study of secondary reinforcement. *J comp phys Ps* 42, 161-173. [680]

—— 1950. Generalization of secondary reinforcement. *J exp Ps* 40, 189-193. [683]

——, Garner, W. R. 1948. Reaction time as a measure of span of attention. *J Ps* 25, 227-241. [41, 97, 99]

Sand, M. C. 1939. The effect of length of list upon retroactive inhibition when degree of learning is controlled. *Arch Ps N.Y.* #238. [731]

Sander, F. 1926. Optische Täuschungen und Psychologie. *Neue Ps St* 1, 161-166. [420]

Sandström, C. I. 1951. *Orientation in the present space.* Stockholm, Almgvist & Wicksell. [524, 527]

Sanford, E. C. 1888–1889. Personal equation. *Amer J Ps* 2, 1-38, 271-298, 403-430. [10]

—— 1898. *A course in experimental psychology.* Bost., Heath. [418, 516]

Sargent, S. S. 1940. Thinking processes at rious levels of difficulty. *Arch Ps N.Y.* #249. [836]

—— 1948. Reaction to frustration—a critique and hypothesis. *Ps Rev* 55, 108-114. [677]

Saul, L. J., Davis, H. 1932. Action currents in the central nervous system. I. Action currents of the auditory tract. *Arch Neu Psychiat* 28, 1104-1116. [330]

Schachter, J. *See* Karwoski, T. F. 1948.

Schafer, R. *See* Rapaport, D. 1946.

Scheerer, M. *See* Goldstein, K. 1941.

Schellenberg, P. E. 1930. *A group free association test for college students.* Ph.D. Thesis Univ Minnesota. (Unpublished) [51, 56]

Schiff, E., Dougan, C. Welch, L. 1949. The conditioned PGR and the EEG as indicators of anxiety. *J Abnor Soc Ps* 44, 549-552. [152]

Schilling, W. 1921. The effect of caffein and acetanalid on simple reaction time. *Ps Rev* 28, 72-79. [38]

Schlosberg, H. 1928. A study of the conditioned patellar reflex. *J exp Ps* 11, 468-494. [543, 567, 573]

—— 1934. Conditioned responses in the white rat. *J genet Ps* 45, 303-335. [549, 555, 562]

—— 1936. II. Conditioned responses based upon shock to the foreleg. *J genet Ps* 49, 107-138. [555]

—— 1937a. Reaction time apparatus. *J genet Ps* 50, 47-61. [14]

—— 1937b. The relationship between success and the laws of conditioning. *Ps Rev* 44, 379-394. [546, 554, 555]

—— 1941a. A scale for judgment of facial expressions. *J exp Ps* 29, 497-510. [124, 125, 127]

—— 1941b. Stereoscopic depth from single pictures. *Amer J Ps* 54, 601-605. [469, 480]

—— 1947. A laboratory period in the first course in psychology. *Amer Psychol* 2, 384-387. [13]

—— 1948. A probability formulation of the Hunter-Sigler effect. *J exp Ps* 38, 155-167. [36, 376]

—— 1950. A note on depth perception, size constancy, and related topics. *Ps Rev* 57, 314-317. [462]

—— 1952. The description of facial expressions in terms of two dimensions. *J exp Ps* 44, 229-237. [125, 126, 127, 128]

——, Heineman, C. 1950. The relationship between two measures of response strength. *J exp Ps* 40, 235-247. [47, 61, 64]

——, Katz, A. 1943. Double alternation lever-pressing in the white rat. *Amer J Ps* 56, 274-282. [628]

——, Solomon, R. L. 1943. Latency of response in a choice discrimination. *J exp Ps* 33, 22-39, 361-372. [578, 585]

——, Stanley, W. C. 1953. A simple test of the normality of twenty-four distributions of electrical skin conductance. *Science* 117, 35-37. [140]

—— *See also* Blackwell, H. R. 1943; Casperson, R. C. 1950; Hughes, B. 1938; Leavitt, H. J. 1941; McGinnies, E. 1945; Pfaffmann, C. 1953; Stanley, W. C. 1953. Van Dusen, F. 1948; White, C. T. 1952.

Schmidt, W. A. 1917. An experimental study in the psychology of reading. *Suppl Educ Monogr* #2. [506]

Schneider, C. 1932. Untersuchungen über die Unterschiedsempfindlichkeit verschieden gegliederter optischer Gestalten. *Neue ps St* 4, 85-159. [417]

Schneider, D. E. *See* Grant, D. A. 1949.

Schneirla, T. C. 1933. Some comparative psychology. *J comp Ps* 16, 307-315. [621]

Schnitzer, S. B. *See* Hall, J. F. 1953.

Schoen, M. 1922. An experimental study of the pitch factor in artistic singing. *Ps Monogr* #140. [122]

Schoenfeld, W. N., Antonitis, J. J., Bersh, P. J. 1950a. A preliminary study of training conditions necessary for secondary reinforcement. *J exp Ps* 40, 40-45. [680]

——, ——, —— 1950b. Unconditioned response rate of the white rat in a bar-pressing apparatus. *J comp phys Ps* 43, 41-48. [685]

—— *See also* Keller, F. S. 1944, 1950; Koester, T. 1945, 1947.

Schorn, M. 1928. Experimentelle Untersuchungen über die Mehrfachhandlung. *Z Ps* 108, 195-221. [90]

Schriever, H. 1926. Ueber den Warmeschmerz. *Z Biol* 85, 67-84. [280]

——, Strughold, H. 1926. Ueber die der Nasen- und Rachenschleimhaut eigentümlichen Empfindungsqualitäten. *Z Biol* 84, 193-206. [279]

Schriever, W. 1925. Experimentelle Studien über stereoskopisches Sehen. *Z Ps* 96, 113-170. [463]

Schroder, H. M., Rotter, J. B. 1952. Rigidity as learned behavior. *J exp Ps* 44, 141-150. [835]

Schultze, M. 1866. Zur Anatomie und Physiologie der Retina. *Arch mikro Anat* 2, 175-286. [366]

Schulze, R. 1906. *Die Mimik der Kinder beim*

künstlerischen Geniessen. Leip., Voigtländer. [130]
—— 1912. *Experimental psychology and pedagogy*, Lond., Allen. [130]
Schumann, F. 1898. Zur Psychologie der Zeitanschauung. *Z Ps* 17, 106-148. [226]
—— 1902. Beiträge zur Analyse der Gesichtwahrnehmungen. *Z Ps* 30, 241-291, 321-339. [226]
—— 1904. Einige Beobachtungen über die Zusammenfassung von Gesichtseindrücken zu Einheiten. *Ps St* (Schumann) 1, 1-32. [409, 413]
—— 1921–1922. Das Erkennungsurteil. *Z Ps* 88, 205-224. [102]
—— *See also* Müller, G. E. 1889, 1894.
Science Service, Inc. 1952. Optical illusions unit. *Things of science, No. 144*. 1719 N St., N.W., Washington 6, D.C. [488]
Scofield, E. H. *See* Foster, D. 1950.
Scott, J. C. 1930. Systolic blood-pressure fluctuations with sex, anger and fear. *J comp Ps* 10, 97-114. [166, 167]
Scott, T. C. 1930. The retention and recognition of patterns in maze learning. *J exp Ps* 13, 164-207. [652]
Searle, L. V., Taylor, F. V. 1948. Studies of tracking behavior. I. Rate and time characteristics of simple corrective movements. *J exp Ps* 38, 615-631. [41]
Sears, P. S. *See* Lewin, K. 1944.
Sears, Richard. 1933. Psychogalvanic responses in arithmetical work. *Arch Ps N.Y.* #155. [151, 157, 817]
Sears, Robert R. 1934. Effect of optic lobe ablation on the visuo-motor behavior of goldfish. *J comp Ps* 17, 233-265. [568]
—— 1937. Initiation of the repression sequence by experienced failure. *J exp Ps* 20, 570-580. [778]
—— 1943. Survey of objective studies of psychoanalytic concepts. *Soc Sci Res Council Bull* #51. [777]
—— 1944. Experimental analysis of psychoanalytic phenomena. *Personality and the behavior disorders*. 306-332. J. McK. Hunt, ed. N. Y., Ronald. [777]
—— *See also* Dollard, J. 1939.
Sears, W. N. *See* Hilgard, E. R. 1937.
Seashore, C. E., Carter, E. A., Farnum, E. C., Sies, R. W. 1908. The effect of practice on normal illusions. *Ps Monogr* #38. [423]
Seashore, R. H. 1938. The pyramid puzzle, a useful device in studying thought. *Amer J Ps* 51, 549-557. [827]
——, Starmann, R., Kendall, W. E., Helmick, J. S. 1941. Group factors in simple and discriminative reaction times. *J exp Ps* 29, 346-349. [40]
—— *See also* Seashore, S. H. 1941.
Seashore, S. H., Seashore, R. H. 1941. Individual differences in simple auditory reaction times of hands, feet and jaws. *J exp Ps* 29, 342-345. [40]
Sedgewick, G. H. W. *See* Bousfield, W. A. 1944. 1952.
Seibert, L. C. 1932. A series of experiments on the learning of French vocabulary. *Johns Hopkins U St Educ* #18. [784]
Seidenfeld, M. A. *See* Irwin, F. W. 1937.
Seifert, F. 1917. Zur Psychologie der Abstraktion und Gestaltauffassung. *Z Ps* 78, 55-144. [414]
Sells, S. B. 1936. The atmosphere effect: an experimental study of reasoning. *Arch Ps N.Y.* #200. [846]
—— *See also* Woodworth, R. S. 1935.
Selz, O. 1935. Versuche zur Hebung des Intelligenzniveaus. *Z Ps* 134, 236-302. [827]
Semmes, J. *See* Lashley, K. S. 1951.
Senden, M. v. 1932. *Raum- und Gestaltauffassung bei operierten Blindgeborenen vor und nach der Operation*. Leip., Barth. [403]
Senders, V. L. 1948. The physiological basis of visual acuity. *Ps Bull* 45, 465-490. [385]
Settlage, P. H. *See* Harlow, H. F. 1934.
Setzepfand, W. 1935. Zur Frequenzabhängigkeit der Vibrationsempfindung des Menschen. *Z Biol* 96, 236-240. [295]
Seward, G. H. 1928. Recognition time as a measure of confidence. *Arch Ps N.Y.* #99. [723]
—— *See also* Seward, J. P. 1934.
Seward, J. P. 1945. Aggressive behavior in the rat. I-III. *J comp Ps* 38, 175-197, 213-238. [676]
—— 1946. Aggressive behavior in the rat. IV. Submission as determined by conditioning, extinction, and disuse. *J comp Ps* 39, 51-76. [676]
—— 1949. An experimental analysis of latent learning. *J exp Ps* 39, 177-186. [640]
——, Levy, N., Handlon, J. H., Jr. 1950. Incidental learning in the rat. *J comp phys Ps* 43, 240-251. [644]
——, Seward, G. H. 1934. The effect of repetition on reaction to electric shock. *Arch Ps N.Y.* #168. [150]
Seyffarth, H. 1940. The behaviour of motor-units in voluntary contraction. *Norske Videnskaps-Akad Oslo. Nat-Naturv Kl Skrifte* #4. [802]
Shaad, D. J., Helson, H. 1931. Group presentation in the method of constant stimuli as a time-saving device. *Amer J Ps* 43, 422-433. [218]
Shagass, M. S. *See* Malmo, R. B. 1949.
Shakow, D. *See* Rodnick, E. H. 1940.
Shatel, R. B. *See* Kimble, G. A. 1952.
Shaw, W. A. 1940. The relation of muscular action potentials to imaginal weight lifting. *Arch Ps N.Y.* #247. [816]
Shaw, W. J. *See* Baldwin, J. M. 1895.
Shaxby, J. H., Gage, F. H. 1932. The localization of sounds in the median plane. *Med Res Council Special Rept Series* #166. Lond. [356]
Sheehan, M. R. 1938. A study of individual consistency in phenomenal constancy. *Arch Ps N.Y.* #222. [438]
Sheffield, F. D. 1948. Avoidance training and the contiguity principle. *J comp phys Ps* 41, 165-177. [555, 676]
——, Roby, T. B. 1950. Reward value of a non-nutritive sweet taste. *J comp phys Ps* 43, 471-481. [684]
——, Wulff, J. J., Backer, R. 1951. Reward value

of copulation without sex drive reduction. *J comp phys Ps* 44, 3-8. [684]
—— *See also* Hovland, C. I. 1949.
Sheffield, V. F. 1949. Extinction as a function of partial reinforcement and distribution of practice. *J exp Ps* 39, 511-526. [565]
—— 1950. Resistance to extinction as a function of the distribution of extinction trials. *J exp Ps* 40, 305-313. [560]
Sheldon, W. H. 1940. *The varieties of human physique*. N. Y., Harper. [37]
Shen, E. 1927. An analysis of eye movements in the reading of Chinese. *J exp Ps* 10, 158-183. [510]
Shepard, J. F. 1906. Organic changes and feeling. *Amer J Ps* 17, 522-584. [163, 164]
—— 1914. *The circulation and sleep, with Atlas*. N. Y., Macmillan. [163]
Shephard, A. H. *See* Lewis, D. 1951.
Sherif, M. 1935. A study of some social factors in perception. *Arch Ps N.Y.*, #187. [524]
—— 1948. *An outline of social psychology*. N. Y., Harper. [524]
Sherman, M. 1927. The differentiation of emotional responses in infants. I. Judgments of emotional responses from motion picture views and from actual observation. II. The ability of observers to judge emotional characteristics of the crying infants, and of the voice of an adult. *J comp Ps* 7, 265-284, 335-351. [120, 121, 130]
—— 1928. The differentiation of emotional responses in infants. III. A proposed theory of the development of emotional responses in infants. *J comp Ps* 8, 385-394. [121]
Sherrington, C. S. 1897. On reciprocal action in the retina as studied by means of some rotating discs. *J Phys* 21, 33-54. [450]
—— 1906, 1948. *The integrative action of the nervous system*. New Haven, Yale Univ Press. [173, 400, 669]
Shipley, W. C., Coffin, J. I., Hadsell, K. C. 1945. Affective distance and other factors determining reaction time in judgments of color preference. *J exp Ps* 35, 206-215. [33, 264]
——, Norris, E. D., Roberts, M. L. 1946. The effect of changed polarity of set on decision time of affective judgments. *J exp Ps* 36, 237-243. [33]
—— *See also* Spence, K. W. 1934.
Shlaer, S. *See* Hecht, S. 1936, 1942.
Shock, N. W. 1944. Physiological changes in adolescence. *Natl Soc St Educ 43 Yrbk* 56-79. [164, 165]
——, Coombs, C. H. 1937. Changes in skin resistance and affective tone. *Amer J Ps* 49, 611-620. [154]
Shower, E. G., Biddulph, R. 1931. Differential pitch sensitivity of the ear. *J acoust Soc Amer* 3, 275-287. [222, 333]
Shuknecht, H. F. 1950. A clinical study of auditory damage following blows to the head. *Ann Otol Rhino Laryng* 59, 331-358. [349]
——, Neff, W. D., Perlman, H. B. 1951. An experimental study of auditory damage following blows to the head. *Ann Otol Rhino Laryng* 60, 273-289. [349]
Sidis, B., Nelson, L. 1910. The nature and causation of the galvanic phenomenon. I. The nature of the galvanic phenomenon. *Ps Rev* 17, 98-146. [141]
Siegel, P. S. *See* Lacey, O. L. 1948, 1949.
Sies, R. W. *See* Seashore, C. E. 1908.
Sigler, M. *See* Hunter, W. S. 1940.
Siipola, E. M. 1941. The relation of transfer to similarity of habit-structure. *J exp Ps* 28, 233-261.
Silverman, J. J., Powell, V. E. 1944. Studies on palmar sweating. I. A technique for the study of palmar sweating. *Amer J med Sci* 208, 297-305. [142]
Simmel, M. L. 1953. The coin problem: a study in thinking. *Amer J Ps* 66, 229-241. [842]
Simon, C. W., Wickens, D. D., Brown, U., Pennock, L. 1951. Effect of the secondary reinforcing agents on the primary thirst drive. *J comp phys Ps* 44, 67-70. [681]
—— *See also* Fitts, P. M. 1949.
Sinden, R. H. 1923. Studies based on the spectral complementaries. *J opt Soc Amer* 7, 1123-1153. [392]
Sinha, D. *See* Davis D. R. 1950a, b.
Sisk, T. K. 1926. The interrelations of speed in simple and complex responses. *George Peabody Cont Educ* #23. [40]
Sisson, E. D. 1935. Eye-movements and the Schröder stair-figure. *Amer J Ps* 47, 309-311. [421]
Sivian, L. J., White, S. D. 1933. On minimum audible sound fields. *J acoust Soc Amer* 4, 288-321. [325, 353]
Skaggs, E. B. 1925. Further studies in retroactive inhibition. *Ps Monogr* #161. [766]
—— 1930. Studies in attention and emotion. *J comp Ps* 10, 375-419. [171]
——, Grossman, S., Krueger, L., Krueger, W. 1930. Further studies of the reading-recitation process in learning. *Arch Ps N.Y.* #114. [780]
Skard, Ø. 1950. A comparison of human and animal learning in the Stone multiple T-maze. *Acta ps* 7, 89-109. [620]
Skinner, B. F. 1932. On the rate of formation of a conditioned reflex. *J genl Ps* 7, 274-285. [546]
—— 1935. Two types of conditioned reflex and a pseudo-type. *J genl Ps* 12, 66-77. [554]
—— 1936. The verbal summator and a method for the study of latent speech. *J Ps* 2, 71-107. [694]
—— 1938. *The behavior of organisms*. N. Y., Appleton-Century. [542, 543, 546, 554, 557, 563, 587, 685]
—— 1953a. *Science and human behavior*. N. Y., Macmillan. [694]
—— 1953b. Some contributions of an experimental analysis of behavior to psychology as a whole. *Amer Psychol* 8, 69-78. [563, 588]
—— *See also* Estes, W. K. 1941.
Skramlik, E. v. 1925. Über die Lokalisation der

Empfindungen bei den niederen Sinnen. *Z Sinnesphys* 56, 69-140. [309, 311, 319]
—— 1926. Die Physiologie des Geruchs- und Geschmackssinnes. *Handbh Phys niederen Sinne Bd. 1.* Leip., Thieme. [300]
—— 1937. Psychophysiologie der Tastsinne. *Arch ges Ps Ergbd* #4. [275, 294]
Slater-Hammel, A. T. *See* Brown, J. S. 1949.
Slaughter, J. W. 1901. The fluctuations of the attention in some of their psychological relations. *Amer J Ps* 12, 313-334. [79]
Sleight, W. G. 1911. Memory and formal training. *Br J Ps* 4, 386-457. [741, 745]
Sloan, L. L. *See* Munsell, A. E. D. 1933.
Small, W. S. 1899–1900. An experimental study of the mental processes of the rat. *Amer J Ps* 11, 133-164. [614]
—— 1900–1901. Experimental study of the mental processes of the rat. II. *Amer J Ps* 12, 206-239. [614]
Smith, H. C., Boyarsky, S. 1943. The relationship between physique and simple reaction time. *Character & Pers* 12, 46-53. [37]
Smith, K. *See* Hall, J. F. 1953.
Smith, K. R. 1948. The satiational theory of the figural after-effect. *Amer J Ps* 61, 282-286. [426]
—— 1951. Intermittent loud noise and mental performance. *Science* 114, 132-133. [85]
Smith, K. U. 1940. The neural centers concerned in the mediation of apparent movement vision. *J exp Ps* 26, 443-466. [515]
Smith, M. D. 1934. The reproduction of colour patterns. *Br J Ps* 25, 63-76. [700]
Smith, M. F. 1939. The establishment and extinction of the token-reward habit in the cat. *J genl Ps* 20, 475-486. [681]
Smith, P. N. *See* Lewis, D. 1952.
Smith, W. G. 1896. The place of repetition in memory. *Ps Rev* 3, 21-31. [697]
—— 1904–1905. A comparison of some mental and physical tests in their application to epileptic and to normal subjects. *Br J Ps* 1, 240-260. [699]
Smith, Whately. 1922. *The measurement of emotion.* Lond., Paul. [54, 153]
Snedecor, G. W. 1946. *Statistical methods applied to experiments in agriculture and biology.* 4th ed. Ames, Ia., Collegiate Press.
Snygg, D. 1935. The relative difficulty of mechanically equivalent tasks. II. Animal learning. *J genet Ps* 47, 321-336. [617]
—— 1936. Mazes in which rats take the longer path to food. *J Ps* 1, 153-166. [623]
Solomon, A. P. *See* Darrow, C. W. 1942.
Solomon, R. L. 1943. Latency of response as a measure of learning in a 'single-door' discrimination. *Amer J Ps* 56, 422-432. [586]
—— 1948. The influence of work on behavior. *Ps Bull* 45, 1-40. [622, 670]
——, Howes, D. H. 1951. Word frequency, personal values, and visual duration thresholds. *Ps Rev* 58, 256-270.
—— *See also* Graham, C. H. 1949; Howes, D. H. 1950; Schlosberg, H. 1943.
Spearman, C. 1904. The proof and measurement of association between two things. *Amer J Ps* 15, 72-101. [257]
—— 1908. Method of 'right and wrong cases' (constant stimuli) without Gauss' formulae. *Brit J Ps* 2, 227-242. [207, 209]
—— 1927. *The abilities of man, their nature and measurement.* N. Y., Macmillan. [814]
Speich, R. 1927. Reproduktion und psychische Aktivität. *Arch ges Ps* 59, 225-338. [88]
Spelt, D. K. *See* Finger, F. W. 1947.
Spence, K. W. 1936. The nature of discrimination learning in animals. *Ps Rev* 43, 427-449. [593]
—— 1937. The differential response in animals to stimuli varying within a single dimension. *Ps Rev* 44, 430-444. [577]
—— 1945. An experimental test of the continuity and non-continuity theories of discrimination learning. *J exp Ps* 35, 253-266. [596]
—— 1951. Theoretical interpretations of learning. *Handbk exp Ps* 690-729. S. S. Stevens, ed. N. Y., Wiley. [542, 551, 553, 556, 559]
——, Bergmann, G., Lippitt, R. 1950. A study of simple learning under irrelevant motivational-reward conditions. *J exp Ps* 40, 539-551. [643]
——, Lippitt, R. 1940. "Latent" learning of a simple maze problem with relevant needs satiated. *Ps Bull* 37, 429. [642, 643]
——, —— 1946. An experimental test of the sign-Gestalt theory of trial-and-error learning. *J exp PS* 36, 491-502. [642]
——, Norris, E. B. 1950. Eyelid conditioning as a function of the inter-trial interval. *J exp Ps* 40, 716-720. [792]
——, Shipley, W. C. 1934. The factors determining the difficulty of blind alleys in maze learning by the white rat. *J comp Ps* 17, 423-436. [623]
—— *See also* Hull, C. L. 1938.
Spitzer, H. F. 1939. Studies in retention. *J educ Ps* 30, 641-656. [781]
Spooner, A., Kellogg, W. N. 1947. The backward conditioning curve. *Amer J Ps* 60, 321-334. [567, 588]
Spragg, S. D. S. 1933. Anticipation as a factor in maze errors. *J comp Ps* 15, 313-329. [623]
—— 1934. Anticipatory responses in the maze. *J comp Ps* 18, 51-73. [623]
—— 1936. Anticipatory responses in serial learning by the chimpanzee. *Comp Ps Monogr* #62. [623]
—— 1943. The relative difficulty of the Morse code alphabet characters learned by the whole method. *J exp Ps* 33, 108-114. [813]
Stanley, J. C., Jr. *See* Jenkins, W. O. 1950.
Stanley, W. C. 1952. Extinction as a function of the spacing of extinction trials. *J exp Ps* 43, 249-260. [560]
——, Schlosberg, H. 1953. The psychophysiological effects of tea. *J Ps* 36, 435-448. [148]
—— *See also* Schlosberg, H. 1953.

Starch, D. 1908. Perimetry of the localization of sound. *Ps Monogr* #38. [350, 357]
—— 1910a. A demonstration of the trial and error method of learning. *Ps Bull* 7, 20-23. [741]
—— 1910b. Mental processes and concomitant galvanometric changes. *Ps Rev* 17, 19-36. [158]
Starmann, R. *See* Seashore, R. H. 1941.
Staudt, V., Kubis, J. F. 1948. The psychogalvanic response (GPR) and its relation to changes in tension and relaxation. *J Ps* 25, 443-453. [157]
Stauffacher, J. C. 1937. The effect of induced muscular tension upon various phases of the learning process. *J exp Ps* 21, 26-46. [176]
—— *See also* Bills, A. G. 1937.
Stavrianos, B. K. 1945. The relation of shape perception to explicit judgments of inclination. *Arch Ps N.Y.* #296. [487]
Steckle, L. C. 1936. Two additional attempts to condition the pupillary reflex. *J genl Ps* 15, 369-377. [576]
——, Renshaw, S. 1934. An investigation of the conditioned iridic reflex. *J genl Ps* 11, 3-23. [576]
Steffens, Lottie. 1900. Experimentelle Beiträge zur Lehre vom ökonomischen Lernen. *Z Ps* 22, 321-382, 465. [782]
Steinberg, J. C. 1934. Application of sound measuring instruments to the study of phonetic problems. *J acoust Soc Amer* 6, 16-24. [340]
——, French, N. R. 1946. The portrayal of visible speech. *J acoust Soc Amer* 18, 4-18. [340]
—— *See also* French, N. R. 1947.
Steinig, K. 1929. Untersuchungen über die Wahrnehmung der Bewegung durch das Auge. IV. *Z Ps* 109, 291-336. [513]
Steinman, A. 1944. Reaction time to change, compared with other psychophysical methods. *Arch PS N.Y.* #292. [27, 38, 263]
——, Veniar, S. 1944. Simple reaction time to change as a substitute for the disjunctive reaction. *J exp Ps* 34, 152-158. [263]
Stellar, E. 1951. The effects of experimental alterations of metabolism on the hoarding behavior of the rat. *J comp phys Ps* 44, 290-299. [660]
—— *See also* Morgan, C. T. 1950.
Stephenson, W. 1947. 'Objective' processes in perceiving and thinking. *Miscellanea psychologica Albert Michotte*, 225-236. Paris, Libraire Philos. [814]
Sterzinger, O. 1924. Zur Prüfung und Untersuchung der abstrakten Aufmerksamkeit. *Z ang Ps* 23, 121-161. [82]
—— 1928. Über die sog. Verteilung der Aufmerksamkeit. *Z ang Ps* 29, 177-196. [88]
Stevens, S. S. 1934a. The volume and intensity of tones. *Amer J Ps* 46, 397-408. [337]
—— 1934b. The attributes of tones. *Proc Natl Acad Sci* 20, 457-459. [337]
—— 1934c. Tonal density. *J exp Ps* 17, 585-592. [337]
—— 1935. The relation of pitch to intensity. *J acoust Soc Amer* 6, 150-154. [335]
—— 1936. A scale for the measurement of a psychological magnitude: loudness. *Ps Rev* 43, 405-416. [238, 239]
—— 1939. On the problem of scales for the measurement of psychological magnitudes. *J unif Sci* 9, 94-99. [98, 228]
—— 1942. Rectilinear rectification applied to voltage integration. *Electronics* 15, 40-41. [178]
—— 1946. On the theory of scales of measurement. *Science* 103, 677-680.
—— (ed). 1951a. *Handbook of experimental psychology*. N. Y., Wiley.
—— 1951b. Mathematics, measurement, and psychophysics. *Handbk exp Ps* 1-49. S. S. Stevens, ed. N. Y., Wiley. [141]
——, Davis, H. 1936. Psychophysiological acoustics: pitch and loudness. *J acoust Soc Amer* 8, 1-13. [329]
——, —— 1938. *Hearing; its psychology and physiology*. N. Y., Wiley. [325, 329, 330, 334]
——, ——, Lurie, M. H. 1935. The localization of pitch perception on the basilar membrane. *J genl Ps* 13, 297-315. [334, 349]
——, Morgan, C. T., Volkmann, J. 1941. Theory of the neural quantum in the discrimination of loudness and pitch. *Amer J Ps* 54, 315-335. [221]
——, Newman, E. B. 1934. The localization of pure tones. *Proc Natl Acad Sci* 20, 593-596. [357]
——, —— 1936a. The localization of actual sources of sound. *Amer J Ps* 48, 297-306. [357]
——, —— 1936b. On the nature of aural harmonics. *Proc Natl Acad Sci* 22, 668-672. [344]
——, Volkmann, J. 1940. The relation of pitch to frequency, a revised scale. *Amer J Ps* 53, 329-353. [241]
——, ——, Newman, E. B. 1937. A scale for the measurement of the psychological magnitude pitch. *J acoust Soc Amer* 8, 185-190. [240, 241, 247]
—— *See also* Boring, E. G. 1936; Harper, R. S. 1948; Newman, E. B. 1937.
Stone, C. P., Nyswander, D. B. 1927. The reliability of rat learning scores from the multiple-T maze as determined by four different methods. *J genet Ps* 34, 497-524. [619]
—— *See also* Muhlhan, G. J. 1949; Porter, P. B. 1947; Weaver, H. E. 1928.
Stone, G. R. *See* Melton, A. W. 1942.
Stone, L. J., Dallenbach, K. M. 1936. The adaptation of areal pain. *Amer J Ps* 48, 117-125. [286]
Storlie, A. *See* Telford, C. W. 1946.
Störring, G. 1906. Experimentelle Beiträge zur Lehre vom Gefühl. *Arch ges Ps* 6, 316-356. [172]
—— 1908. Experimentelle Untersuchungen über einfache Schlussprozesse. *Arch ges Ps* 11, 1-127. [843]
Strain, E. R. 1953. Establishment of an avoidance gradient under latent-learning conditions. *J exp Ps* 46, 391-399. [641]
Strassburger, R. C. 1950. Resistance to extinction of a conditioned operant as related to drive

level at reinforcement. *J exp Ps* 40, 473-487.

Stratton, G. M. 1902a. The method of serial groups. *Ps Rev* 9, 444-447. [199]

—— 1902b. Eye-movements and the aesthetics of visual form. *Philos St* 20, 336-359. [495]

—— 1906. Symmetry, linear illusions, and the movements of the eye. *Ps Rev* 13, 82-96. [495]

—— 1911. The psychology of change: how is the perception of movement related to that of succession? *Ps Rev* 18, 262-293. [513, 514]

Straub, W. 1938. Psychische Alkoholwirkung und Blutalkoholgehalt. *Z Arbeitsps* 11, 127-130. [38]

Street, R. F. 1931. *A Gestalt completion test.* N. Y., Teachers Coll, Columbia Univ. [716]

Strong, E. K. 1911. The relative merit of advertisements. *Arch Ps N.Y.* #17. [257]

—— 1912. The effect of length of series upon recognition memory. *Ps Rev* 19, 447-462. [699, 705]

—— 1913. The effect of time-interval upon recognition memory. *Ps Rev* 20, 339-372. [699, 726]

Strong, O. S., Elwyn, A. 1943. *Human neuroanatomy.* Balt., Williams & Wilkins. [135]

Strughold, H. 1926. Das Verhalten der Horn- und Bindehaut des menschlichen Auges gegen Wärmereize. *Z Biol* 84, 311-320. [278]

——, Karbe, M. 1925. Vitale Färbung des Auges und experimentelle Untersuchung der gefärbten Nervenelemente. *Z Biol* 83, 297-308. [279]

—— *See also* Schriever, H. 1926.

Stumpf, K. 1883. *Tonpsychologie.* Vol. 1. Leip., Hirzel. [240]

Summers, W. G. 1939. Science can get the confession. *Fordham Law Rev* 8, 334-354. [186]

Sumner, F. B. 1898. A statistical study of belief. *Ps Rev* 5, 616-631. [257]

Supa, M., Cotzin, M., Dallenbach, K. M. 1944. "Facial vision": the perception of obstacles by the blind. *Amer J Ps* 57, 133-183. [360]

Suter, J. 1912. Die Beziehungen zwischen Aufmerksamkeit und Atmung. *Arch ges Ps* 25, 78-150. [171, 173]

Sutherland, J. 1946. The relationship between perceptual span and rate of reading. *J educ Ps* 37, 373-380. [103]

Swan, T. H. *See* Johnson, H. M. 1930.

Swenson, H. A. 1932. The relative influence of accommodation and convergence in the judgment of distance. *J genl Ps* 7, 360-380. [478]

Swift, E. J. 1903. Studies in the psychology and physiology of learning. *Amer J Ps* 14, 201-251. [739]

Switzer, S. A. 1930. Backward conditioning of the lid reflex. *J exp Ps* 13, 76-97. [567]

—— 1933. Disinhibition of the conditioned galvanic skin response. *J genl Ps* 9, 77-100. [152]

—— 1934. Anticipatory and inhibitory characteristics of delayed conditioned reactions. *J exp Ps* 17, 603-620. [566]

—— 1935. The effect of caffeine on experimental extinction of conditioned reactions. *J genl Ps* 12, 78-94. [657]

Symposium: *Food acceptance methodology.* 1954. Washington, D.C. Natl Research Council. [233]

Symposium on effects of frustration. 1941. N. E. Miller, R. R. Sears, S. Rosenzweig, G. Bateson, D. Levy, G. W. Hartmann. *Ps Rev* 48, 337-366. [677]

Symposium on perception and personality. 1949. *J pers* 18, #1-2. Reprinted, J. S. Bruner, D. Krech. 1950. [694]

Syz, H. C. 1926a. Psycho-galvanic studies on sixty-four medical students. *Br J Ps* 17, 54-69. [153]

—— 1926b. Observations on the unreliability of subjective reports of emotional reactions. *Br J Ps* 17, 119-126. [153]

——, Kinder, E. F. 1928. Electrical skin resistance in normal and in psychotic subjects. *Arch Neu Psychiat* 19, 1026-1035. [147]

Székely, L. 1947. Zur Psychologie des inneren Verhaltens beim Lernen, Denken und Erfahren. *Theoria* 13, 157-182. [823]

—— 1950. Productive processes in learning and thinking. *Acta ps* 7, 388-407. [828]

T

Taeger, H. *See* Hahn, H. 1938.

Talbot, S. A. *See* Marshall, W. H. 1942. 1943.

Tallantis, B. *See* Grant, D. A. 1949.

Tarchanoff, J. 1890. Ueber die galvanischen Erscheinungen in der Haut des Menschen bei Reizungen der Sinnesorgane und bei verschiedennen Formen der psychischen Thätigkeit. *Pflüg Arch ges Phys* 46, 46-55. [138]

Taubman, R. E. 1950. Studies in judged number. I. The judgment of auditory number. II. The judgment of visual number. *J genl Ps* 43, 167-194, 195-219. [100, 101]

—— *See also* Keller, F. S. 1943.

Taves, E. H. 1941. Two mechanisms for the perception of visual numerousness. *Arch Ps N.Y.* #265. [98, 245]

Taylor, D. W. 1943a. The learning of radiotelegraphic code. *Amer J Ps* 56, 319-353. [812]

—— 1943b. Learning telegraphic code. *Ps Bull* 40, 461-487. [810]

——, Faust, W. L. 1952. Twenty questions: efficiency in problem solving as a function of size of group. *J exp Ps* 44, 360-368. [841]

Taylor, E. A. 1937. *Controlled reading.* Chic., Chicago Univ Press. [509]

Taylor, F. V., Birmingham, H. P. 1948. Studies of tracking behavior. II. The acceleration pattern of quick manual corrective responses. *J exp Ps* 38, 783-795. [40]

—— *See also* Searle, V. 1948.

Taylor, G. A. *See* Gates, A. I. 1925.

Taylor, H. L. *See* Keys, A. 1950.

Taylor, R. W. 1901. The effect of certain stimuli upon the attention wave. *Amer J Ps* 12, 335-345. [79]

Teel, K. S., Webb, W. B. 1951. Response evocation on satiated trials in the T-maze. *J exp Ps* 41, 148-152. [682]

Telford, C. W. 1931. The refractory phase of

voluntary and associative responses. *J exp Ps* 14, 1-38. [29]
——, Storlie, A. 1946. The relation of respiration and reflex winking rates to muscular tension during motor learning. *J exp Ps* 36, 512-517. [182]
Terman, L. M., Miles, C. C. 1936. *Sex and personality*. N. Y., McGraw-Hill. [70]
Thelin, E., Altman, E. R. 1929. Identification of monocular functions. *J exp Ps* 12, 79-87. [398]
Thiéry, A. 1895. Ueber geometrisch-optische Täuschungen. *Philos St* 11, 307-370. [419]
Thistlethwaite, D. 1950. Attitude and structure as factors in the distortion of reasoning. *J abnor soc Ps* 45, 442-458. [848]
—— 1951a, 1952. A critical review of latent learning and related experiments. *Ps Bull* 48, 97-129; 49, 61-71. [637]
—— 1951b. An experimental test of a reinforcement test of latent learning. *J comp phys Ps* 44, 431-441. [643]
Thomas, Garth J. 1949. Equal-volume judgments of tones. *Amer J Ps* 62, 182-201. [338]
Thompson, H. *See* Gesell, A. 1929.
Thompson, J. 1941. Development of facial expression of emotion in blind and seeing children. *Arch Ps N.Y.* #264. [131]
Thompson, J. P. *See* Thompson, M. E. 1949.
Thompson, M. E. 1944. Learning as a function of the absolute and relative amounts of work. *J exp Ps* 34, 506-515. [670]
——, Thompson, J. P. 1949. Reactive inhibition as a factor in maze learning. II. The role of reactive inhibition in studies of place learning versus response learning. *J exp Ps* 39, 883-891. [635]
Thompson, R. *See* Hayes, K. J. 1953.
Thorndike, E. L. 1898. Animal intelligence; an experimental study of the associative processes in animals. *Ps Monogr* #8. [529, 537, 546, 547, 550, 614, 672, 818, 824, 827]
—— 1903. *Educational psychology*. N. Y., Lemcke & Buechner. [734, 746]
—— 1904. *An introduction to the theory of mental and social measurements*. N. Y., Science Press. [257]
—— 1908. Memory for paired associates. *Ps Rev* 15, 122-138. [699]
—— 1910. Handwriting. *Teachers Coll Rec* 11, (2) 1-81. [260]
—— 1911. *Animal intelligence, experimental studies*. N. Y., Macmillan. [547, 557, 672]
—— 1913. *Educational psychology*. Vol. II. *The psychology of learning*. N. Y., Teachers Coll, Columbia Univ. [746]
—— 1914. *Educational psychology*. Vol. III. *Mental work and fatigue and individual differences and their causes*. N. Y., Teachers Coll, Columbia Univ. [804]
—— 1917. The curve of work and the curve of satisfyingness. *J appl Ps* 1, 265-267. [804]
—— 1931. *Human learning*. N. Y., Century. [711]
—— 1932a. *The fundamentals of learning*. N. Y., Teachers Coll, Columbia Univ. [672, 711]
—— 1932b. Reward and punishment in animal learning. *Comp Ps Monogr* #39. [673]
——, Woodworth, R. S. 1901. The influence of improvement in one mental function upon the efficiency of other functions. *Ps Rev* 8, 247-261, 384-395, 553-564. Reprinted: R. S. Woodworth, 1939; H. E. Garrett, 1951. [746]
Thorndike, R. L. 1950. How children learn the principles and techniques of problem-solving. *Natl Soc St Educ 49 Yrbk* Pt 1, 196-216. Chic. [829]
Thorne, F. C. 1934. The psychophysical measurement of the temporal course of visual sensitivity. *Arch Ps N.Y.* #170. [199]
Thouless, R. H. 1930. The technique of experimentation on the psycho-galvanic reflex phenomenon and the phenomenon of Tarchanoff I & II. *Br J Ps* 20, 219-240, 309-321. [142]
—— 1931. Phenomenal regression to the "real" object. I & II. *Br J Ps* 21, 339-359; 22, 1-30. [142, 429, 451]
Thumb, A., Marbe, K. 1901. *Experimentelle Untersuchungen über die psychologischen Grundlagen der sprachlichen Analogiebildung*. Leip., Engelmann. [50, 61, 62]
Thunberg, T. 1901. Untersuchungen über die relative Tiefenlage der kälte-, wärme-, und schmerzpercipirenden Nervenenden in der Haut und über das Verhältniss der Kältenervenenden gegenüber Wärmereizen. *Arch Phys Skand* 11, 382-435. [283, 290]
Thurlow, W. R. 1943a. Studies in auditory theory. 1. Binaural interaction and the perception of pitch. 2. The distribution of distortion in the inner ear. *J exp Ps* 32, 17-36, 344-350.
Thurstone, L. L. 1927a. A law of comparative judgment. *Ps Rev* 34, 273-286. [254, 261]
—— 1927b. The method of paired comparisons for social values. *J abnor soc Ps* 21, 384-400. [254]
—— 1928a. An experimental study of nationality preferences. *J genl Ps* 1, 405-425. [254]
—— 1928b. The phi-gamma hypothesis. *J exp Ps* 11, 293-305. [221]
—— 1930. The learning function. *J genl Ps* 3, 469-493. [707]
—— 1938. Primary mental abilities. *Psychometr Monogr* #1. [814]
—— 1948. Psychophysical methods. *Methods of psychology* 124-157. T. G. Andrews, ed. N. Y., Wiley. [254]
Tiffen, J. 1931. Some aspects of the psychophysics of the vibrato. *Ps Monogr* #187. [122]
—— 1934. Simultaneous records of eye movements and the voice in oral reading. *Science* 80, 430-431. [507]
——, Fairbanks, G. 1937. An eye-voice camera for clinical and research studies. *Ps Monogr* #215. [503]
——, Westhafer, F. L. 1940. The relation between reaction time and temporal location of the

stimulus on the tremor cycle. *J exp Ps* 27, 318-324. [37]
Tigerstedt, C. 1926. Der Blutdruck des Menschen bei psychischer Exzitation. *Arch Phys Skand* 48, 138-146. [165]
Tinker, M. A. 1931. Apparatus for recording eye-movements. *Amer J Ps* 43, 115-118. [495, 504]
—— 1936a. Eye movement, perception, and legibility in reading. *Ps Bull* 33, 275-290.
—— 1936b. Time taken by eye movements in reading. *J genet Ps* 48, 468-471. [506]
—— 1936c. Reliability and validity of eye-movement measures of reading. *J exp Ps* 19, 732-746. [509]
—— 1942. Individual and sex differences in speed of saccadic eye movements. *Studies in personality* 271-280. Q. McNemar, M. A. Merrill, eds. N. Y., McGraw-Hill. [501]
—— 1946. The study of eye movements in reading. *Ps Bull* 43, 93-120. [509]
—— 1947. Illumination standards for effective and easy seeing. *Ps Bull* 44, 435-450. [180]
——, Baker, K. H. 1938. *Introduction to methods in experimental psychology*. N. Y., Appleton-Century. [51]
—— *See also* Paterson, D. G. 1929, 1947.
Tinklepaugh, O. L. 1928. An experimental study of representative factors in monkeys. *J comp Ps* 8, 197-236. [606, 607]
—— 1932. Multiple delayed reaction with chimpanzees and monkeys. *J comp Ps* 13, 207-243. [606, 607]
Titchener, E. B. 1901. *Experimental psychology. Qualitative*. N. Y., Macmillan. [2, 246]
—— 1905. *Experimental psychology. Quantitative*. N. Y., Macmillan. [2, 12, 197, 246, 247]
—— 1909. *Lectures on the experimental psychology of the thought-processes*. N. Y., Macmillan. [107, 293, 816]
—— 1910. *A textbook of psychology*. N. Y., Macmillan.
—— 1916. A note on the compensation of odors. *Amer J Ps* 27, 435-436. [311]
—— *See also* Boring, E. G. 1923.
Titelbaum, S. *See* Kleitman, N. 1938.
Todd, J. W. 1912. Reaction to multiple stimuli. *Arch Ps N.Y.* #25. [26]
Tolcott, M. A. 1948. Conflict. A study of some interactions between appetite and aversion in the white rat. *Genet Ps Monogr* 38, 83-142. [646, 678, 679]
Tolman, E. C. 1932, 1949. *Purposive behavior in animals and men*. N. Y., Appleton-Century-Crofts. [636]
—— 1938. The determiners of behavior at a choice point. *Ps Rev* 45, 1-41. Reprinted: E. C. Tolman, 1951. [550]
—— 1939 Prediction of vicarious trial and error by means of the schematic sowbug. *Ps Rev* 46, 318-336. Reprinted: E. C. Tolman, 1951. [583, 602, 603]
—— 1941. Discrimination vs. learning and the schematic sowbug. *Ps Rev* 48, 367-382. [602]
—— 1945. A stimulus-expectancy need-cathexis psychology. *Science* 101, 160-166. Reprinted: E. C. Tolman. 1951. [556]
—— 1948. Cognitive maps in rats and men. *Ps rev* 1948, 55, 189-208. Reprinted: E. C. Tolman. 1951. [636]
—— 1951. *Collected papers in psychology*. Berkeley, Univ Calif Press.
——, Gleitman, H. 1949. Studies in learning and motivation. I. Equal reinforcements in both end-boxes, followed by shock in one end-box. *J exp Ps* 39, 810-819. [641]
——, Hall, C. S. Bretnall, E. P. 1932. A disproof of the law of effect and a substitution of the laws of emphasis, motivation and disruption. *J exp Ps* 15, 601-614. [651, 689]
——, Honzik, C. H. 1930. Degrees of hunger, reward and non-reward, and maze learning in rats. *Calif U Publ Ps* 4, 241-275. [620, 639]
——, Minium, E. 1942. VTE in rats. Overlearning and difficulty of discrimination. *J comp Ps* 34, 301-306. [603]
——, Ritchie, B. F., Kalish, D. 1946a. Studies in spatial learning. I. Orientation and the short-cut. *J exp Ps* 36, 13-24. [632]
——, ——, —— 1946b. Studies in spatial learning. II. Place learning versus response learning. *J exp Ps* 36, 221-229. [633, 634]
——, ——, —— 1947a. Studies in spatial learning. IV. The transfer of place learning to other starting paths. *J exp Ps* 37, 39-47. [633]
——, ——, —— 1947b. Studies in spatial learning. V. Response learning vs. place learning by the non-correction method. *J exp Ps* 37, 285-292. [634]
Tower, S. S. 1943. Pain; definition and properties of the unit for sensory reception. *Res Publ Ass Ner ment Dis* 23, 16-43. [272]
Trautscholdt, M. 1883. Experimentelle Untersuchungen über die Association der Vorstellungen. *Philos St* 1, 213-250. [45]
Travis, L. E., Hunter, T. A. 1931. Tremor frequencies. *J genl Ps* 5, 255-260. [180]
Travis, R. C. 1937. The effect of the length of the rest period on motor learning. *J Ps* 3, 189-194. [789]
—— 1948. Measurement of accommodation and convergence time as part of a complex visual adjustment. *J exp Ps* 38, 395-403. [42]
——, Kennedy, J. L. 1947. Prediction and automatic control of alertness. I. Control of lookout alertness. *J comp phys Ps* 40, 457-461. [31, 178]
——, —— 1949. Prediction and control of alertness. III. Calibration of the alertness indicator and further results. *J comp phys Ps* 42, 45-57. [31, 178]
—— *See also* Baxter, B. 1938; Kennedy, J. L. 1947, 1948.
Trendelenburg, W. *See* Marx, E. 1911.
Tresselt, M. E. 1947. The influence of amount of practice upon the formation of a scale of judgment *J exp Ps* 37, 251-260. [229]

—— 1948. The effect of the experiences of contrasted groups upon the formation of a new scale of judgment. *J soc Ps* 27, 209-216. [230]
Trimble, O. C. 1928. Some temporal aspects of sound localization. *Ps Monogr* #176. [355]
Troland, L. T. 1929-1932. *The principles of psychophysiology*. 3 Vols. N. Y., Van Nostrand. [244, 380, 393]
Trotter, W., Davies, H. M. 1909. Experimental studies in the innervation of the skin. *J Physiol Lond.* 38, 134-246. [281]
Trovillo, P. V. *See* Wicker, W. 1953.
Trueblood, H., Grings, W. 1950. A DC amplifier for GSR and low-frequency potential measurement. *J Ps* 30, 401-403. [139]
Truman, S. R., Wever, E. G. 1928. The judgment of pitch as a function of the series. *Calif U Publ Ps* 3, 215-223. [230]
Tsang, T.-C. 1934. The functions of the visual areas of the cerebral cortex of the rat in the learning and retention of the maze. I. *Comp Ps Monogr* #50. [617]
—— 1936. The functions of the visual areas of the cerebral cortex of the rat in the learning and retention of the maze. II. *Comp Ps Monogr* #57. [617]
Tsang, Y. 1938. Hunger motivation in gastrectomized rats. *J comp Ps* 26, 1-17. [659]
Tschermak-Seysenegg, A. v. 1939. Über Parallaktoskopie. *Pflüg Arch ges Phys* 241, 455-469. [474]
—— 1942, 1952. *Einführung in die physiologische Optik*. München, Bergmann. Trans: *Introduction to physiological optics*. Springfield, Ill., Thomas.
Tudor-Hart, B. 1928. Studies in transparancy, form and color. *Ps Forsch* 10, 255-298. [440]
Tufts, F. L. 1907. Spectrophotometry of normal and color-blind eyes. *Physical Rev* 25, 433-452. [382, 394]
Tufts College. 1949. *See Handbook of human engineering data*. 1949–1953.
Turnbull, W. W. 1944. Pitch discrimination as a function of tonal duration. *J exp Ps* 34, 302-316. [336]
Tussing, L. 1941. Perceptual fluctuations of illusions as a possible physical fatigue index. *J exp Ps* 29, 85-88. [77]
Twitmyer, E. M. 1931. Visual guidance in motor learning. *Amer J Ps* 43, 165-187. [651]

U

Underwood, B. J. 1949. *Experimental psychology, an introduction*. N. Y., Appleton-Century-Crofts. [2]
—— 1953. Learning. *Ann Rev Ps* 4, 31-58. [789]
——, Viterna, R. O. 1951. Studies of distributed practice. IV. The effect of similarity and rate of presentation in verbal discrimination learning. *J exp Ps* 42, 296-299. [794]
—— *See also* Archer, E. J. 1951; Morgan, R. L. 1950.
Upton, M. 1929a. The auditory sensitivity of guinea pigs. *Amer J Ps* 41, 412-421. [543, 548]
—— 1929b. Functional disturbances of hearing in guinea pigs after long exposure to an intense tone. *J genl Ps* 2, 397-412. [348, 543, 548]
Urban, F. M. 1909. Die psychophysischen Massmethoden als Grundlagen empirischer Messungen. *Arch ges Ps* 15, 261-355. [207]
—— 1912. Hilfstabellen für die Konstanzmethode. *Arch ges Ps* 24, 236-243. [207]
Urbantschitsch, V. 1875. Ueber eine Eigenthümlichkeit der Schallempfindungen geringster Intensität. *Centralbl med Wissensch*, 13, #37, 625-629. [78, 79]

V

Van Buskirk, W. L. 1932. An experimental study of vividness in learning and retention. *J exp Ps* 15, 563-573. [732]
Vanderplas, J. M., Blake, R. R. 1949. Selective sensitization in auditory perception. *J Pers* 18, 252-266. Reprinted: J. S. Bruner, D. Krech. 1950. [694]
Van Dusen, F., Schlosberg, H. 1948. Further study of the retention of verbal and motor skills. *J exp Ps* 38, 526-534. [732]
Van Gelder, D. *See* Brown, C. H. 1938.
van Ormer, E. B. 1932. Retention after intervals of sleep and of waking. *Arch Ps, N.Y.* #137. [769]
Van Riper, C. *See* Milisen, R. 1939.
Veniar, S. *See* Steinman, A. 1944.
Vernon, M. D. 1934. The perception of inclined lines. *Br J Ps* 25, 186-196. [424]
—— 1937. *Visual perception*. N. Y., Macmillan. [464, 480]
Vernon, P. E. 1934–1935. Auditory perception. I. & II. *Br J Ps* 25, 123-139, 265-283. [407]
—— *See also* Allport, G. W. 1931.
Verplanck, W. S. 1942. The development of discrimination in a simple motor habit. *J exp Ps* 31, 441-464. [586]
Verzeano, M., Finesinger, J. E. 1949. An automatic analyzer for the study of speech in interaction and in free association. *Science* 110, 45-46. [47]
Vinacke, W. E. 1951. The investigation of concept formation. *Ps Bull* 48, 1-31. [613]
—— 1952. *The psychology of thinking*. N. Y., McGraw-Hill. [840]
—— *See also* Eindhoven, J. E. 1952.
Vince, M. A. 1948a. The intermittency of control movements and the psychological refractory period. *Br J Ps* 38, 149-157. [41]
—— 1948b. Corrective movements in a pursuit task. *Q J exp Ps* 1, 85-103. [686]
Vincent, S. B. 1912. The function of the vibrissae in the behavior of the white rat. *Beh Monogr* #5. [535, 617]
Viterna, R. O. *See* Underwood, B. J. 1951.
Volkmann, A. W. 1858. Über den Einfluss der Übung auf das Erkennen räumlicher Distanzen. *Ber Sächs Ges Wiss Leipzig Math-Phys Cl* 10, 38-69. [735, 738]

Volkmann, J. 1932. The method of single stimuli. *Amer J Ps* 44, 808-809. [217]
— *See also* Hunt, W. A. 1937; Kaufman, E. L. 1949; Newman, E. B. 1937; Stevens, S. S. 1937, 1940, 1941.
von Frey, M. 1894. Beiträge zur Physiologie des Schmerzsinns. *Ber Sächs Ges Wiss Leipzig Math-Phys Cl* 46, 185-196, 283-296. [274, 282]
— 1895. Beiträge zur Sinnesphysiologie des Haut. *Ber Sächs Ges Wiss Leipzig Math-Phys Cl* 47, 166-184. [278, 279, 282]
—, Goldman, A. 1915. Der zeitliche Verlauf der Einstellung bei den Druckempfindungen. *Z Biol* 65, 183-202. [286]
Von Hornbostel. *See* Hornbostel, E. M, v.
Von Kries. *See* Kries, J. v.
von Restorff, H. *See* Köhler, W. 1935.
Von Skramlik. *See* Skramlik, E. v.
Von Szeliski, V. 1924. Relation between the quantity perceived and the time of perception. *J exp Ps* 7, 135-147. [97]
Vörckel, H. 1922. Reaktionszeit bei willkürlicher Kontraktion und Erschlaffung der Beuger und Strecker des Vorderarms. *Z Biol* 75, 79-90. [19]

W

Wada, T. 1922. An experimental study of hunger in its relation to activity. *Arch Ps N.Y.* #47. [659]
Waddell, D. *See* Beebe-Center, J. G. 1948.
Wade, M. *See* Beebe-Center, J. G. 1948; Lashley, K. S. 1946.
Wagman, I. H., Nathanson, L. M. 1942. Influence of intensity of white light upon pupil diameter of the human and of the rabbit. *Proc Soc exp Biol Med* 49, 466-470. [368]
Wagner, A. H. 1930. An experimental study in control of the vocal vibrato. *Ps Monogr* #181. [123]
Wagner, J. 1918. Experimentelle Beiträge zur Psychologie des Lesens. *Z Ps* 80, 1-75. [103]
Wagoner, K. S. *See* Nafe, J. P. 1936, 1941.
Wald, G. 1942. Visual systems and the vitamins A. *Biol Symposia* 7, 43-71. [371]
— 1945. Human vision and the spectrum. *Science* 101, 653-658. [367]
— 1950. Eye and camera. *Sci Amer* 183 (2), 32-41. [365, 371]
Walker, E. L. 1948. Drive specificity and learning. *J exp Ps* 38, 39-49. [645]
— 1951. Drive specificity and learning. Demonstration of a response tendency acquired under a strong irrelevant drive. *J comp phys Ps* 44, 596-603. [645]
—, Knotter, M. C., DeValois, R. L. 1950. Drive specificity and learning. The acquisition of a spatial response to food under conditions of water deprivation and food satiation. *J exp Ps* 40, 161-168. [644]
Walker, R. Y. 1933. The eye-movements of good readers. *Ps Monogr* #199. [506]
— *See also* Jasper, H. H. 1931.
Walker, W. W. *See* Grannis, U. B. 1936.
Wallach, H. 1938. Über die Wahrnehmung der Schallrichtung. *Ps Forsch* 22, 238-266. [358]
— 1940. The role of head movements and vestibular and visual cues in sound localization. *J exp Ps* 27, 339-368. [358]
— 1948. Brightness constancy and the nature of achromatic colors. *J exp Ps* 38, 310-324. [445]
—, Galloway, A. 1946. The constancy of colored objects in colored illumination. *J exp Ps* 36, 119-126. [451]
—, Newman, E. B., Rosenzweig, M. R. 1949. The precedence effect in sound localization. *Amer J Ps* 62, 315-336. [355, 358]
— *See also* Köhler, W. 1944.
Wallas, G. 1926. *The art of thought*. N. Y., Harcourt, Brace. [839]
Waller, A. D. 1919. Concerning emotive phenomena. I. Periodic variations of conductance of the palm of the human hand. II. The influence of drugs upon the electrical conductivity of the palm of the hand. *R Soc Lond Proc B* 91, 17-31, 32-43. [146]
Walsh, B. L., Waters, R. H. 1944. Finger versus stylus learning of the same maze. *J genl Ps* 31, 283-286. [652]
Walshe, F. M. R. 1942. The anatomy and physiology of cutaneous sensibility: a critical review. *Brain* 65, 48-112. [280]
Walthall, W. J., Jr. 1948. The influence of different maze surroundings on learning. *J comp phys Ps* 41, 438-449. [618, 620]
Wang, C. H., Pan, J. G., Lu, T. W. 1929. The galvanic skin reflex in normal, thalamic, decerebrated and spinal cats under anaesthesia. *Chinese J Phys* 3, 109-122. [149]
—, Richter, C. P. 1928. Action currents from the pad of the cat's foot produced by stimulation of the tuber cinereum. *Chinese J Phys* 2, 279-283. [143]
Wapner, S. 1944. The differential effects of cortical injury and retesting on equivalence reactions in the rat. *Ps Monogr* #262. [593]
— *See also* Witkin, H. A. 1952.
Warburton, F. A. 1943. Influence of short rest pauses on fluctuations of attention. *Br J Ps* 33, 162-171. [83]
Ward, A. *See* Harris, L. J. 1933.
Ward, L. B. 1937. Reminiscence and rote learning. *Ps Monogr* #220. [796, 797]
Warden, C. J. 1923. The distribution of practice in animal learning. *Comp Ps Monogr* #3. [789]
— 1924a. Primacy and recency as factors in cul-de-sac elimination in a stylus maze. *J exp Ps* 7, 98-116. [620]
— 1924b. The relative economy of various modes of attack in the mastery of a stylus maze. *J exp Ps* 7, 243-275. [619, 620, 651]
— 1931. *Animal motivation: experimental studies on the albino rat*. N. Y., Columbia Univ Press.
—, Aylesworth, M. 1927. The relative value of reward and punishment in the formation of a

visual discrimination habit in the white rat. *J comp Ps* 7, 117-127. [673]
——, Jenkins, T. N., Warner, L. H. 1935. *Comparative psychology: Vol. I. Principles and methods*. N. Y., Ronald. [618]
—— *See also* Jenkins, T. N. 1926.
Warner, L. H. 1927. A study of sex behavior in the white rat by means of the obstruction method. *Comp Ps Monogr* #22. Reprinted: C. J. Warden. 1931. [663]
—— 1928. A study of hunger behavior in the white rat by means of the obstruction method. *J comp Ps* 8, 273-299. Reprinted C. J. Warden. 1931. [662, 663]
—— 1932. The association span of the white rat. *J genet Ps* 41, 57-90. [674]
—— *See also* Jenkins, T. N. 1926; Warden, C. J. 1935.
Warner, M. *See* Ryan, A. H. 1936.
Warren, H. C. 1897. The reaction time of counting. *Ps Rev* 4, 569-591. [97]
—— 1921. *A history of the association psychology*. N. Y., Scribner's. [43]
——, Carmichael, L. 1930. *Elements of human psychology*. Bost., Houghton Mifflin. [299]
Warwick, R. T. T. *See* Allison, A. C. 1949.
Wasserman, H. N. 1951. The effect of motivation and amount of pre-rest practice upon inhibitory potential in motor learning. *J exp Ps* 42, 162-172. [789]
Waters, R. H. *See* Walsh, B. L. 1944; Wilcoxon, H. C. 1948.
Watson, J. B. 1907. Kinesthetic and organic sensations: their role in the reactions of the white rat to the maze. *Ps Monogr* #33. [615]
—— 1914. *Behavior, an introduction to comparative psychology*. N. Y., Holt. [626, 816]
—— 1916. The place of the conditioned-reflex in psychology. *Ps Rev* 13, 89-117. [193, 543, 545, 572]
—— 1919. *Psychology from the standpoint of a behaviorist*. Phil., Lippincott. [545]
—— Rayner, R. 1920. Conditional emotional reactions. *J exp Ps* 3, 1-14. [543]
—— *See also* Carr, H. 1908; Yerkes, R. M. 1911.
Watt, H. J. 1905. Experimentelle Beiträge zu einer Theorie des Denkens. *Arch ges Ps* 4, 289-436. [29, 57, 830]
Wayner, M. *See* Riggs, L. A. 1949.
Weaver, H. B. 1942. A study of discrimination serial actions: manual response to color. *J exp Ps* 31, 177-201. [83]
Weaver, H. E., Madden, E. H. 1949. "Direction" in problem solving. *J Ps* 27, 331-345. [832, 833]
——, Stone, C. P. 1928. The relative ability of blind and normal rats in maze learning. *J genet Ps* 35, 157-177. [620]
—— *See also* Kimball, R. C. 1950.
Webb, L. W. 1917. Transfer of training and retroaction, a comparative study. *Ps Monogr* #104. [748, 765]
Webb, W. B. 1948. A motivational theory of emotions. *Ps Rev* 55, 329-335. [110]
—— 1949. The motivational aspect of an irrelevant drive in the behavior of the white rat. *J exp Ps* 39, 1-14. [682]
—— 1950. A test of "relational" vs. "specific stimulus" learning in discrimination problems. *J comp phys Ps* 43, 70-72. [588]
—— *See also* Teel, K. S. 1951.
Weber, C. O. 1942. Effects of practice on the perceptual span for letters. *J genl Ps* 26, 347-351. [103]
Weber, E. H. 1834. *De pulsu, resorptione, auditu et tactu*. Leip., Koehler. *See also Annotationes Anatomicae et Physiologicae*. 1851. Vol. 1. 1-175. [194, 738]
—— 1846. Tastsinn und Gemeingefühl. *Handwörterbh Phys Wagner* 3 (2), 481-588. [288]
Wechsler, D. 1925. The measurement of emotional reaction. *Arch Ps N.Y.* #76. [146, 153, 156]
—— *See also* Jones, H. E. 1928.
Weddell, G. 1941. The pattern of cutaneous innervation in relation to cutaneous sensibility. *J Anat Lond* 75, 346-367. [280]
—— *See also* Pattle, R. E. 1948.
Wegel, R. L. 1932. Physical data and physiology of excitation of the auditory nerve. *Ann Otol Rhino Laryng* 41, 740-779. [332]
——, Lane, C. E. 1924. The auditory masking of one pure tone by another and its probable relation to the dynamics of the inner ear. *Physical Rev* 23, 266-285. [345]
Weigl, E. 1941. On the psychology of so-called processes of abstraction. *J abnor soc Ps* 36, 3-33. [611]
Weinberg, M. *See* Allen, F. 1925.
Weiner, I. H., Stellar, E. 1951. Salt preference of the rat determined by a single-stimulus method. *J comp physiol Ps* 44, 394-401. [662]
Weinland, J. D. 1927. Variability of performance in the curve of work. *Arch Ps N.Y.* #87. [806]
Weinstein, E. A., Bender, M. B. 1943. Integrated facial patterns elicited by stimulation of the brain stem. *Arch Neu Psychiat* 50, 34-42. [130]
Weitz, J. 1939. Vibratory sensitivity as effected by local anesthesia. *J exp Ps* 25, 48-64. [296]
Welborn, E. L. *See* English, H. B. 1934.
Welch, L., Kubis, J. F. 1947. Conditioned PGR (psychogalvanic response) in states of pathological anxiety. *J nerv ment Dis* 105, 372-381. [152]
——, Long, L. 1943. Comparison of the reasoning ability of two age groups. *J genet Ps* 62, 63-76. [842]
—— *See also* Schiff, E. 1949.
Weld, H. P., Danzig, E. R. 1940. A study of the way in which a verdict is reached by a jury. *Amer J Ps* 53, 518-536. [841]
—— *See also* Boring, E. G. 1939, 1948.
Welford, A. T. 1951. *Skill and age, an experimental approach*. Lond., Oxford Univ Press. [807, 808]
Wellman, B. *See* Hoffman, A. C. 1939.
Wells, E. F., Hoisington, L. B. 1931. Pain adapta-

tion. A contribution to the Von-Frey-Goldscheider controversy. *J genl Ps*, 5, 352-367. [285]

Wells, F. L. 1907. A statistical study of literary merit. *Arch Ps N.Y.* #7. [257]

—— 1911a. Practice effects in free association. *Amer J Ps* 22, 1-13. [54, 59, 68]

—— 1911b. Some properties of the free association time. *Ps Rev* 18, 1-23.

—— 1927. *Mental tests in clinical practice*. Yonkers, N.Y., World Book. [68, 69]

——, Forbes, A. 1911. On certain electrical processes in the human body and their relations to emotional reactions. *Arch Ps N.Y.* #16. [153]

——, Kelley, C. M. 1922. The simple reaction in psychosis. *Amer J Psychiat* 2, 53-59. [37]

—— *See also* Woodworth, R. S. 1911.

Wells, G. R. 1913. The influence of stimulus-duration on reaction time. *Ps Monogr* #66. [25]

—— *See also* Dunlap, K. 1910.

Wendt, G. R. 1930. An analytic study of the conditioned knee jerk. *Arch Ps N.Y.* #123. [568]

—— 1936a. An interpretation of inhibition of conditioned reflexes as competition between reaction systems. *Ps Rev* 43, 258-281. [560]

—— 1936b. The form of the vestibular eye-movement response in man. *Ps Monogr* #212. [522]

—— 1938. Methods of recording action. *Arch Ps N.Y.* #228. [15, 522]

—— 1951. Vestibular functions. *Handbk exp Ps* 1191-1223. S. S. Stevens, ed. N. Y., Wiley. [520, 522, 523, 526]

——, Dodge, R. 1938. Practical directions for stimulating and for photographically recording eye-movements of animals. *J comp Ps* 25, 9-49. [494]

Wendt, P. R. 1952. Development of an eye camera for use with motion pictures. *Ps Monogr* 66, #339. [496, 514]

Wenger, M. A. 1941. The measurement of individual differences in autonomic balance. *Psychosom Med* 3, 427-434. [182]

—— 1942. The stability of measurement of autonomic balance. *Psychosom Med* 4, 94-95. [182]

—— 1943. An attempt to appraise individual differences in level of muscular tension. *J exp Ps* 32, 213-225. [182]

—— 1948. Studies of autonomic balance in Army Air Forces personnel. *Comp Ps Monogr* #101. [182]

——, Ellington, M. 1943. The measurement of autonomic balance in children: Method and normative data. *Psychosom Med* 5, 241-253. [179]

——, Gilchrist, J. C. 1948. A comparison of two indices of palmar sweating. *J exp Ps* 38, 757-761. [142]

Wenzel, B. M. 1948. Techniques in olfactometry: a critical review of the last one hundred years. *Ps Bull* 45, 231-247.

—— 1949. Differential sensitivity in olfaction. *J exp Ps* 39, 129-143. [314, 315]

——, Flurry, C. 1948. The sequential order of concept attainment. *J exp Ps* 38, 547-557. [613]

Wenzl, A. 1932. Empirische und theoretische Beiträge zur Erinnerungsarbeit bei erschwerter Wortfindung. *Arch ges Ps* 85, 181-218. [719]

—— 1936. Empirische und theoretische Beiträge zur Erinnerungsarbeit bei erschwerter Wortfindung. *Arch ges Ps* 97, 294-318. [719]

Werner, H. 1935. Studies on contour. I. Qualitative analyses. *Amer J Ps* 47, 40-64. [413]

—— 1937. Dynamics in binocular depth perception. *Ps Monogr* #218. [468]

—— 1938. Binocular depth contrast and the conditions of the binocular field. *Amer J Ps* 51, 489-497. [474]

Wertheimer, M. 1905. Experimentelle Untersuchungen zur Tatbestandsdiagnostik. *Arch ges Ps* 6, 59-131. [66]

—— 1912. Experimentelle Studien über das Sehen von Bewegung. *Z Ps* 61, 161-265. [512, 514, 525]

—— 1923. Untersuchungen zue Lehre von der Gestalt II. *Ps Forsch* 4, 301-350. [408]

—— 1925. *Drei Abhandlungen zur Gestalttheorie*. Erlangen, Philosophischen Akademie. [514]

—— 1945. *Productive thinking*. N. Y., Harper. [823, 824, 837]

—— *See also* Hornbostel, E. M. v. 1920.

Wesman, A. 1945. A study of transfer of training from high school subjects to intelligence. *Teachers Coll* C. U. *Contr Educ* #909. [830]

Wessel, N. Y. *See* Carmichael, L. 1937.

Westhafer, F. L. *See* Tiffin, J. 1940.

Westphal, E. 1911. Über Haupt- und Nebenaufgaben bei Reaktionsversuchen. *Arch ges Ps* 21, 219-434. [90]

Wever, E. G. 1927. Figure and ground in the visual perception of form. *Amer J Ps* 38, 194-226. [407]

—— 1930. The upper limit of hearing in the cat. *J comp Ps* 10, 221-233. [549]

—— 1949. *Theory of hearing*. N. Y., Wiley. [296, 323, 324, 329, 330, 332, 334, 336]

——, Bray, C. W. 1930a. Auditory nerve impulses. *Science* 71, 215. [328]

——, —— 1930b. Action currents in the auditory nerve in response to acoustical stimulation. *Proc Natl Acad Sci* 16, 344-350. [328]

——, —— 1930c. Present possibilities for auditory theory. *Ps Rev* 37, 365-380. [328]

——, —— 1930d. The nature of acoustic response: the relation between sound frequency and frequency of impulses in the auditory nerve. *J exp Ps* 13, 373-387. [328]

——, —— 1938. Distortion in the ear as shown by the electrical responses of the cochlea. *J acoust Soc Amer* 9, 227-233. [344]

——, ——, Lawrence, M. 1940a. Locus of distortion in the ear. *J acoust Soc Amer* 11, 427-433. [345]

——, ——, —— 1940b. The origin of combination tones. *J exp Ps* 27, 217-226. [345]

——, Lawrence, M. 1954. *Physiological acoustics*. Princeton, Princeton Univ Press. [345]

——, Neff, W. D. 1947. A further study of the effects of partial section of the auditory nerve. *J comp phys Ps* 40, 217-226. [349]

——, Zener, K. E. 1928. The method of absolute judgment in psychophysics. *Ps Rev* 35, 466-493. [217, 229, 230]

—— *See also* Robinson, E. W. 1930; Truman, S. R. 1928.

Weymouth, F. W. *See* Hirsch, M. J. 1948.

Wheatstone, C. 1838. On some remarkable, and hitherto unobserved phenomena of binocular vision. Part 1. *Lond R Soc Philos Trans* 371-394. [465]

—— 1852. On some remarkable, and hitherto unobserved phenomena of binocular vision. Part 2. *Philos Mag* series 4(3) 504-523. [477]

Whipple, G. M. 1901, 1902. The analytical study of the memory image and the process of judgment in the discrimination of clangs and tones. *Amer J Ps* 12, 409-457, 13, 219-268. [226, 699]

—— 1914-15. *Manual of mental and physical tests.* 2d ed. Pt. I. II. Balt., Warwick & York. [93, 180]

White, C. T., Schlosberg, H. 1952. Degree of conditioning of the GSR as a function of the period of delay. *J exp Ps* 43, 357-362. [571]

—— *See also* Cheatman, P. G. 1952.

White, R. E. *See* Kellogg, W. N. 1935.

White, S. D. *See* Sivian, L. J. 1933.

Whitfield, J. W. 1951. An experiment in problem solving. *Q J exp Ps* 3, 184-197. [842]

Wickens, C. D. *See* Wickens, D. D. 1942.

Wickens, D. D., Hall, J., Reid, L.S. 1949. Associative and retroactive inhibition as a function of the drive stimulus. *J comp phys Ps* 42, 398-403. [766]

——, Wickens, C. D. 1942. Some factors related to pseudo-conditioning. *J exp Ps* 31, 518-526. [570]

—— *See also* Miles, R. C. 1953; Simon, C. W. 1951.

Wicker, W., Cureton, E. E., Trovillo, P. V. 1953 The polygraphic truth test. A symposium. *Tenn Law Rev* 22, 1-64. [191]

Wiersma, E. 1901. Untersuchungen über die sogenannten Aufmerksamkeitsschwankungen. *Z Ps* 26, 168-200. [79]

Wilcoxon, H. C., Waters, R. H. 1948. Spatial orientation in the white rat. *J exp Ps* 38, 412. [632]

Wilensky, H. 1952. The performance of schizophrenic and normal individuals following frustration. *Ps Monogr* #344. [678]

Wilkins, M. C. 1928. The effect of changed material on ability to do formal syllogistic reasoning. *Arch Ps N.Y.* #102. [845]

Willey, C. F., Inglis, E., Pearce, C. H. 1937. Reversal of auditory localization. *J exp Ps* 20, 114-130. [350]

Williams, K. *See* Hebb, D. O. 1946.

Williams, O. 1926. A study of the phenomenon of reminiscence. *J exp Ps* 9, 368-387. [794]

Willmer, E. N. 1946. *Retinal structure and colour vision.* Cambridge, Univ Press. [396]

Wilson, R. C. *See* Guilford, J. P. 1952.

Wilson, W. D. *See* Lanier, L. H. 1935.

Wiltbank, R. T. 1919. Transfer of training in white rats upon various series of mazes. *Beh Monogr* #17 [748, 751]

Windle, C. D. 1952. *Studies in radiotelegraphy.* Thesis Ph.D. Columbia Univ. (Microfilm Univ. Micro., Ann Arbor, Mich.) [811, 812, 813]

Wirth, W. 1903. Ein neuer Apparat für Gedächtnissversuche, mit sprungweise fortschreitender Exposition ruhender Gesichtsobjecte. *Philos St* 18, 701-714. [703]

—— 1927. Die Reaktionszeiten: Beitrag zur psychophysischen Systematik. *Handbh norm pathol Phys* 10, 525-599. Berlin, Springer. [32]

Wischner, G. J. 1947. The effect of punishment on discrimination learning in a non-correction situation. *J exp Ps* 37, 271-284. [601, 602, 625]

—— 1948. A reply to Dr. Muenzinger on the effect of punishment on discrimination learning in a non-correction situation. *J exp Ps* 38, 203-204. [601]

—— 1950. VTE and efficiency of discrimination learning involving shock for correct choice. *Amer Psychol* 5, 252-253. [601]

Witasek, S. 1907. Über lesen und Rezitieren in ihren Beziehungen zum Gedächtnis. *Z Ps* 44, 161-185, 246-282. [780]

Withey, S., Buxton, C. E., Elkin, A. 1949. Control of rest interval activities in experiments on reminiscence in serial verbal learning. *J exp Ps* 39, 173-176. [796]

Witkin, H. A. 1949. Perception of body position and of the position of the visual field. *Ps Monogr* #302. [525]

—— 1950a. Individual differences in ease of perception of embedded figures. *J Per* 19, 1-15. [416]

—— 1950b. Perception of the upright when the direction of the force acting upon the body is changed. *J exp Ps* 40, 93-106. [526]

——, Asch, S. E. 1948a. Studies in space orientation. III. Perception of the upright in the absence of a visual field. *J exp Ps* 38, 603-614. [526]

——, —— 1948b. Studies in space orientation. IV. Further experiments on perception of the upright with displaced visual fields. *J exp Ps* 38, 762-782. [526]

——, Wapner, S., Leventhal, T. 1952. Sound localization with conflicting visual and auditory cues. *J exp Ps* 43, 58-67. [358]

—— *See also* Asch, S. E. 1948a, b.

Wittenborn, J. R. 1943. Factorial equations for tests of attention. *Psychomet* 8, 19-35. [83]

Wittmann, J. 1925. Beiträge zur Analyse des Hörens bei dichotischer Reizaufnahme. *Arch ges Ps* 51, 21-122. [355]

Wohlgemuth, A. 1911. On the after-effect of seen movement. *Br J Ps Monogr* #1. [516]

Wolf, I. S., Kellogg, W. N. 1940. Changes in general behavior during flexion conditioning and

their importance for the learning process. *Amer J Ps* 53, 384-396. [576]
Wolf, S., Wolff, H. G. 1942. Evidence on the genesis of peptic ulcers in man. *J Amer med Assoc* 120, 670-675. [168, 183]
——, —— 1943. *Human gastric function*. N. Y., Oxford Univ Press. [183]
Wolf, S. G. *See* Wolff, H. G. 1949.
Wolfe, H. K. 1886. Untersuchungen über das Tongedachtniss. *Philos St* 3, 534-571. [699]
Wolfe, J. B. 1936. Effectiveness of token-rewards for chimpanzees. *Comp Ps Monogr* #60. [681]
Wolff, H. G. 1948. *Headache and other head pains*. N. Y., Oxford Univ Press. [183]
——, Wolf, S. G. 1949. *Pain*. 2d ed. Springfield, Ill., Thomas. [286]
—— *See also* Hardy, J. D. 1951; Wolf, S. 1942 1943.
Wolfle, D. L. 1935. The effect of continuous interchange of alley sections on the maze behavior of rats. *J comp Ps* 19, 91-106. [618, 633]
Wolfle, H. M. 1930. Time factors in conditioning finger-withdrawal. *J genl Ps* 4, 372-378. [567]
—— 1932. Conditioning as a function of the interval between the conditioned and the original stimulus. *J genl Ps* 7, 80-103. [567]
Wood, A. *See* Muenzinger, K. F. 1935.
Woodburne, L. S. 1934. The effect of a constant visual angle upon the binocular discrimination of depth differences. *Amer J Ps* 46, 273-286. [471]
—— 1950. Double, triple, and quadruple repetition in the white rat. *J comp phys Ps* 43, 490-502. [629]
Woodcock, L. P. *See* Biber, B. 1942.
Woodrow, H. 1914. The measurement of attention. *Ps Monogr* #76. [29, 30]
—— 1915. Reactions to the cessation of stimuli and their nervous mechanism. *Ps Rev* 22, 423-452. [26]
—— 1927. The effect of type of training upon transference. *J educ Ps* 18, 159-172. [745]
—— 1933. Weight-discrimination with a varying standard. *Amer J Ps* 45, 391-416. [230]
—— 1938. The effect of pattern upon simultaneous letter-span. *Amer J Ps* 51, 83-96. [103, 104]
—— 1940. Interrelations of measures of learning. *J Ps* 10, 49-73. [539]
——, Lowell, F. 1916. Children's association frequency tables. *Ps Monogr* #97. [51]
Woodruff, B. G. *See* Richter, C. P. 1942.
Woodworth, R. S. 1899. The accuracy of voluntary movement. *Ps Monogr* #13. [686]
—— 1903. *Le mouvement*. Paris, Doin. [802]
—— 1906b. Vision and localization during eye movements. *Ps Bull* 3, 68-70. [502]
—— 1914. Professor Cattell's psychophysical contributions. *Arch Ps N.Y.* #30. [224]
—— 1915a. A revision of imageless thought. *Ps Rev* 22, 1-27. Reprinted: R. S. Woodworth. 1939. [711]
—— 1915b. The influence of retention of conditions favoring quickness of learning. *J Philos* 12, 246. [705, 731]
—— 1918. *Dynamic psychology*. N. Y., Columbia Univ Press. [686]
—— 1938. *Experimental psychology*. N. Y., Holt. [118, 141, 201, 207, 258, 259, 397]
—— 1939. *Psychological Issues. Selected papers*. N. Y., Columbia Univ Press.
—— 1947. Reinforcement of perception. *Amer J Ps* 60, 119-124. [556]
——, Sells, S. B. 1935. An atmosphere effect in formal syllogistic reasoning. *J exp Ps* 18, 451-460. [846]
——, Wells, F. L. 1911. Association tests. *Ps Monogr* #57. [82]
—— *See also* Ladd, G. T. 1911; Thorndike, E. L. 1901.
Worchel, P., Berry, J. H. 1952. The perception of obstacles by the deaf. *J exp Ps* 43, 187-194. [360]
——, Dallenbach, K. M. 1947. "Facial vision": perception of obstacles by the deaf-blind. *Amer J Ps* 60, 502-553. [360]
—— *See also* Ammons, C. H. 1953.
Wreschner, A. 1907–1909. Die Reproduktion und Assoziation von Vorstellungen. *Z Ps Ergbd* #3. [54, 59, 60, 61]
Wright, N. *See* Young, C. W. 1948.
Wright, W. D. 1934. The measurement and analysis of colour adaptation phenomena. *Proc R Soc B* 115, 49-87. [369]
—— 1947. *Researches on normal and defective colour vision*. St. Louis, C. V. Mosby. [396]
Wright, W. R. 1906. Some effects of incentives on work and fatigue. *Ps Rev* 13, 23-34. [688]
Wulf, F. 1922. Über die Veränderung von Vorstellungen (Gedächtnis und Gestalt). *Ps Forsch* 1, 333-373. Trans. W. D. Ellis. 1939. 136-148. [773, 774]
Wulff, J. J. *See* Sheffield, F. D. 1951.
Wundt, W. 1862. *Beiträge zur Theorie der Sinneswahrnehmung*. Leip., C. F. Winter'sche. [475]
—— 1874, 1911. *Grundzüge der physiologischen Psychologie*. Leip., Engelmann. [432]
—— 1883. Über psychologische Methoden. *Philos St* 1, 1-38. [10]
—— 1896. *Grundriss der Psychologie*. Leip., Engelman. Trans. C. H. Judd. [107]
—— 1911. *Grundzüge der physiologischen Psychologie*. 6th ed. Vol. 3. Leip., Engelmann. [432]
Wylie, H. H. 1919. An experimental study of transfer of response in the white rat. *Beh Monogr* #16. [752]

Y

Yamaguchi, H. G. 1951. Superthreshold reaction potential ($S^E R$) as a function of experimental extinction. *J exp Ps* 41, 391-400. [656]
—— *See also* Gladstone, A. I. 1947; Hull, C. L. 1947.
Yamane, K. 1935. Untersuchungen über taktil-motorische Figurwahrnehmung. *Jap J Ps* 10, 327-390. [416]
Yerkes, D. N. *See* Yerkes, R. M. 1928.

Yerkes, R. M. 1907. *The dancing mouse.* N. Y., Macmillan. [582]

—— 1916. The mental life of monkeys and apes, a study of ideational behavior. *Beh Monogr* #12. [824]

—— 1921. A new method of studying the ideational behavior of mentally defective and deranged as compared with normal individuals. *J comp Ps* 1, 369-394. [817]

——, Watson, J. B. 1911. Methods of studying vision in animals. *Beh Monogr* #2. [582]

——, Yerkes, D. N. 1928. Concerning memory in the chimpanzee. *J comp Ps* 8, 237-271. [606]

Yochelson, S. 1930. *Effects of rest-pauses on work decrement.* Ph.D. Thesis. Yale Univ. [800, 802]

Young, C. W., Fletcher, D. F., Wright, N. 1948. On olfaction and infra-red radiation theories. *Science* 108, 411-412. [321]

Young, F. A. 1950. Boring's interpretation of Emmert's law. *Amer J Ps* 63, 277-280. [486]

—— 1951. Concerning Emmert's law. *Amer J Ps* 64, 124-128. [486]

Young, P. T. 1928. Auditory localization with acoustical transposition of the ears. *J exp Ps* 11, 399-429. [350]

—— 1941. The experimental analysis of appetite. *Ps Bull* 38, 129-164. [658]

—— 1947. Studies of food preference, appetite and dietary habit. VII. Palatability in relation to learning and performance. *J comp phys Ps* 40, 37-72. [662]

—— 1948. Studies of food preferences, appetite and dietary habit. VIII. Food-seeking drives, palatability and the law of effect. *J comp phys Ps* 41, 269-300. [658]

—— 1949. Emotion as disorganized response—a reply to Professor Leeper. *Ps Rev* 56, 184-191. [110]

——, Chaplin, J. P. 1949. Studies of food preference, appetite, and dietary habit. X. Preferences of adrenalectomized rats for salt solutions of different concentrations. *Comp Ps Monogr* #5. [658]

Youtz, A. C. 1941. An experimental evaluation of Jost's laws. *Ps Monogr* #238. [731]

Youtz, R. P. 1948. The relation between number of confirmations of one hypothesis and the speed of accepting a new and incompatible hypothesis. *Amer Psychol* 3, 248-249. [837]

Yum, K. S. 1931. An experimental test of the law of assimilation. *J exp Ps* 14, 68-82. [755]

Z

Zama, A. *See* Galli, A. 1931.

Zangwill, O. L. 1937. An investigation of the relationship between the processes of reproducing and recognizing simple figures, with special reference to Koffka's trace theory. *Br J Ps* 27, 250-276. [700, 775]

Zartman, E. N., Cason, H. 1934. The influence of an increase in muscular tension on mental efficiency. *J exp Ps* 17, 671-679. [89]

Zeaman, D. 1949. Response latency as a function of the amount of reinforcement. *J exp Ps* 39, 466-483. [666, 667, 668]

——, House, B. J. 1951. The growth and decay of reactive inhibition as measured by alternation behavior. *J exp Ps* 41, 177-186. [622]

Zegers, R. T. 1948. Monocular movement parallax thresholds as functions of field size, field position, and speed of stimulus movement. *J Ps* 26, 477-498. [474]

Zeigarnik, B. 1927. Über das Behalten von erledigten und unerledigten Handlungen. *Ps Forsch* 9, 1-85. [692, 777]

Zeller, A. F. 1950a. An experimental analogue of repression. I. Historical summary. *Ps Bull* 47, 39-51. [777, 778]

—— 1950b. An experimental analogue of repression. II. The effect of individual failure and success on memory measured by relearning. *J exp Ps* 40, 411-422. [778]

Zener, K. E. *See* Wever, E. G. 1928.

Ziehen, Th. 1898–1900. *Die Ideenassoziation des Kindes.* Berlin, Reuther. (*Saml Abh Geb Päd Ps Phy* 1, #6; 3, #4.) [54, 63]

Zigler, M. J. 1920. An experimental study of visual form. *Amer J Ps* 31, 273-300. [412]

—— 1932. Pressure adaptation-time: a function of intensity and extensity. *Amer J Ps* 44, 709-720. [287]

—— 1935. The experimental relation of the two-point limen to the error of localization. *J genl Ps* 13, 316-332. [294]

——, Holway, A. H. 1935. Differential sensitivity as determined by amount of olfactory substance. *J genl Ps* 12, 372-382. [315]

Zimmer, A. 1913. Die Ursachen der Inversionen mehrdeutiger stereometrischer Konturenzeichnungen. *Z Sinnesphys* 47, 106-158. [420]

Zinszer, H. A. *See* Reed, H. B. 1943.

Zotterman, Y. *See* Anderson, B. 1950.

Zubin, J. 1948. Memory functioning in patients treated with electric shock therapy. *J Per* 17, 33-41. [771]

Zwaardemaker, H. 1895. *Die Physiologie des Geruchs.* Leip., Engelmann. [305, 311, 316]

—— 1922. Odeur et chimisme. *Arch néerl Phys* 6, 336-354. [319, 320]

—— 1925. *L'odorat.* Paris, Doin. [305]

Subject Index

An asterisk, *, is a suggestion to "See" or "See also."

B

E

I

N